SEX MATTERS

THE SEXUALITY AND SOCIETY READER

FOURTH EDITION

SEX MATTERS

THE SEXUALITY AND SOCIETY READER

FOURTH EDITION

MINDY STOMBLER

DAWN M. BAUNACH

WENDY SIMONDS

ELROI J. WINDSOR

ELISABETH O. BURGESS

W. W. NORTON & COMPANY

New York · London

W. W. Norton & Company has been independent since its founding in 1923, when William Warder Norton and Mary D. Herter Norton first published lectures delivered at the People's Institute, the adult education division of New York City's Cooper Union. The Nortons soon expanded their program beyond the Institute, publishing books by celebrated academics from America and abroad. By midcentury, the two major pillars of Norton's publishing program—trade books and college texts—were firmly established. In the 1950s, the Norton family transferred control of the company to its employees, and today—with a staff of four hundred and a comparable number of trade, college, and professional titles published each year—W. W. Norton & Company stands as the largest and oldest publishing house owned wholly by its employees.

Editor: Karl Bakeman
Associate Editor: Nicole Sawa
Managing Editor, College: Marian Johnson
Project Editor: Linda Feldman
Media Editor: Eileen Connell
Media Associate Editor: Laura Musich
Media Editorial Assistant: Cara Folkman
Editorial Assistant: Lindsey Thomas
Marketing Manager, Sociology: Julia Hall
Production Manager: Vanessa Nuttry
Photo Editor: Evan Luberger
Permissions Manager: Megan Jackson
Text Design: Lissi Sigillo
Art Director: Hope Miller Goodell
Composition: Jouve North America
Manufacturing: LSC Communications

Photo credits: p. 1, Fe Delos-Santos, University of Connecticut; p. 51, Elaine Harley; p. 112, Ericka McConnell; p. 186, Courtesy of Ritch C. Savin-Williams; p. 258, Courtesy of Leonore Tiefer; p. 341, Courtesy of Indiana University; p. 441, Steven Epstein; p. 491, Photo courtesy of David Mejias; p. 579, Courtesy of Lynn Chancer; p. 649, Courtesy of Jacqueline Boles

Copyright © 2014 by W. W. Norton & Company, Inc.

This book was previously published by Pearson Education, Inc.

Library of Congress Cataloging-in-Publication Data.
Sex matters : the sexuality and society reader / [edited by] Mindy Stombler, Dawn M. Baunach, Wendy Simonds, Elroi J. Windsor, Elisabeth O. Burgess. — Fourth edition.
    pages cm
Includes bibliographical references and index.
    ISBN 978-0-393-93586-8 (pbk. : alk. paper)   1. Sex—Social aspects.   2. Sex—Social aspects—United States.   3. Sex in popular culture—United States.   4. Sex customs—United States.
    I. Stombler, Mindy.
HQ16.S46 2014
306.70973—dc23

                                                                                                      2013038009

W. W. Norton & Company, Inc., 500 Fifth Avenue, New York, NY 10110-0017
wwnorton.com

W. W. Norton & Company Ltd., Castle House, 75/76 Wells Street, London W1T 3QT

    4 5 6 7 8 9 0

In loving memory of Chet Meeks (1973–2008).

Here's hoping the afterlife is full of sinful pleasures.

If not, please come back.

Actually, just come back.

CONTENTS

PREFACE

We live in a sex-saturated society. We hear of sex drive, sex toys, sex machines, sex slaves, sex scandals, sex gods, sex crimes, and sexaholics. Sex permeates every aspect of our lives from advertising to politics to our relationships with others. Yet we rarely consider the historical, legal, and sociocultural contexts of sexuality. Many people take the current state of sexual attitudes and practices in our society for granted, as if they are natural and thus unchangeable. Understanding contemporary sexual matters requires considering how sexuality varies across time and place and how it is modeled, molded, and even manipulated by those around us. Consider, for instance, the influence of social contexts as you read the following scenarios:

- Imagine that you've chosen to have sex for the first time. How do you know what to do? How do you plan on pleasing your partner? Yourself? Do you turn for guidance to books or magazines, pornographic videos, or the wall of the public bathroom? What makes you excited? Nervous? Will you practice safe sex?
- Imagine that you and your partner do things together that you've never heard about before but make you feel transported, ecstatic, or orgasmic. Or imagine you feel nothing much during your encounters or that you feel disgusted or that you're not even sure if you have "had sex." Imagine that you want to stop but your partner won't. What would you do? Whom would you tell?
- Imagine that you and your partner are the same sex. Would you feel comfortable showing affection in public? Can you imagine a cultural context in which you wouldn't have

to worry about others' reactions? Can you imagine how dating someone of the same sex might be beneficial to you?
- Imagine that an evening of partying ends in an unplanned "one night stand." You or your partner become pregnant. Would you see the pregnancy as something to celebrate? To ignore? To hide? To terminate? Would your family and friends share your feelings? Would their reaction be the same if you were 15 or you were 45? What if your partner were much older or younger than you? Or of a different race, ethnicity, or religion?
- Imagine that you've made a careful decision to refrain from sexual activity. Which circumstances might compel such a decision? Would it be hard to maintain your resolve? Or imagine, by contrast, that you've sought out as much sexual activity as you can find. Either way, who would support your decision to be celibate or sexually adventurous? Who might challenge it? How would these responses be different, depending on your age, gender, or social status?

SEXUALITY AND SOCIETY

If you vary the time, place, or cultural setting of the scenarios, you'll find that your feelings, the decisions you would make, and the reactions of those around you will probably change. These variations occur because the social norms governing sexual behavior are continually in flux. Other social factors, such as your religious beliefs, level of education, economic status, ethnicity, gender, and age, influence sexual activity and its meaning. All of what follows are influenced by society: what counts as a sex act, how often we have sex, what is considered erotic, where we have sex, the age when we begin having sex, with whom we have sex, what we do when we are having sex, how often we desire sex, our reasons for having or avoiding sex, whether we pay others or get paid for sex, and whether we coerce our sexual partners. Although often characterized as a purely biological and often uncontrollable phenomenon, sex is, in fact, social. The readings we have selected portray sex as a social issue influenced by culture, politics, economics, media, education, medicine, law, family, and friends.

SEX MATTERS

Our title reflects the content of the book in two ways. First, we have included research articles and essays on a variety of sexual matters. Second, the title supports our assertion that sex, and the study of sexuality, *matters*. There is much to learn about sexuality. Despite the prevalence of sexual matters in public life and the media, as well as its private significance, scholars researching sexuality have difficulty getting institutional and financial support. Funding agencies, politicians, and many academics do not take sexuality seriously.

Yet the study of sexuality is burgeoning, as evidenced by the proliferation of courses on sexuality in colleges and universities throughout the United States. This book applies social theory and methods to the study of sexuality. The Spotlight on Research feature, which profiles the work of sex researchers, enhances the empirical focus in each chapter. Each of these interviews echoes the fact that sex really does matter.

THEMES OF THIS BOOK

This book is designed to promote sex-positivity and to provide an opportunity for students to reflect on the ways that contexts affect sexual meanings. We believe that consensual sex, in all its forms, regardless of actors, can be beneficial. We have selected pieces that historicize and thus challenge the cultural stigmatization and marginalization of some sexualities and the valorization of others. To us, part of sex positivity means, for example, promoting the pursuit of sexual pleasure and not centering sex education around danger and disease. To be sex-positive is to recognize that sex can be enriching and to affirm that sex matters.

Each of our chapters highlights the dual themes of social construction and social control. In other words, society—composed of social institutions and the individuals within them—constructs our understanding of sexuality and influences our behaviors, attitudes, and sexual identities. The readings illustrate that some social institutions and some members of society have more power to control and define a society's sexual agenda than others. At the same time, social control is usually met with social resistance, and we offer readings that feature examples of successful individual and cultural resistance to societal expectations and oppression.

Chapter 1, "Categorizing Sex," explores how society constructs and socially controls sexual categories. We challenge readers to question what should count as having sex, a topic with wide-ranging legal and health implications. Readings on intersex and transgender sexualities encourage us to consider the viability of our current categories of "male" and "female," and "man" and "woman," what it takes to change one's sex, and who controls sex assignment and reassignment. Other readings question current methods of categorizing sexual orientation and sexual identity. What does it mean to be straight, gay, lesbian, or bisexual? Is sexual identity a matter of behavior, erotic attraction, or self-definition? What role does community play in the construction of our sexual identities? Although existing categories can be helpful for understanding commonalities, they also collapse a wide variety of experiences and feelings into inflexible and essentialized divisions. As the readings show, sexual categories vary across societies, cultures, and time.

Chapter 2, "Investigating Sexuality," presents historical and contemporary sex research and theory and considers ethical, political, and methodological issues involved in conducting sex research. The readings introduce the unique challenges and rewards of conducting sex research. The association of sex with privacy creates a level of anxiety and reluctance among would-be research participants that is unmatched in other areas of research. For example, the cultural unwillingness to see adolescents as sexual beings discourages parents from allowing minors to participate in sex research, yet adolescents report benefitting from participating in sex research. Differing religious teachings on sexuality add to the controversial nature of sex research. The protest efforts of fundamentalist religious groups have successfully limited governmental support of art, health, and research programs that involve sexuality. Furthermore, because sexuality has historically been viewed as too trivial to merit social research, funding agencies are reluctant to support sex research. Yet researchers who rise to the challenge offer unique insights on sexual attitudes, behaviors, and identities.

Chapter 3, "Representing Sex," presents a variety of interpretations of the ways that U.S. culture depicts sexualities and sexual activities. For example, media (books, songs, magazines, videos, internet imagery, etc.) both reflect and create ideas about sexuality. Cultural representations of sexuality affect viewers or readers in a variety of ways by telling powerful stories about appropriate sexual activity and what happens to individuals who deviate from cultural expectations. Cultural representations tell us about who we are, where we've been, and where we're going. The critical perspectives presented in the readings demonstrate the varieties of possible interpretations of various representations.

Chapter 4, "Learning about Sex," examines the messages about sexuality people receive and how they engage with the meanings of these messages. Youth (ranging from young children to older teenagers) confront a variety of sex information—and misinformation—that informs their sexual attitudes and behaviors. The readings in this chapter explore the different messages youth encounter in media, school, and family contexts. Across cultures, youth are taught rather differently about sex based on assumptions about their capacities to act as autonomous sexual beings. As active consumers of messages, youth make sense of sexuality meanings in ways that vary across gender, race, class, and sexual identity. And as lifelong learners, sex education is not just for youth.

Chapter 5, "Sexual Bodies," addresses how we eroticize bodies, body parts, and bodily functions and explores how notions of the erotic can encourage us to manipulate our bodies. Societal discourse both celebrates and stigmatizes the body and its functions. What is sexy about a person's body? Most people can come up with distinct body types or features that are appealing or unappealing to them. Yet ideas about what is sexy and what is not are culturally constructed. For example, some people use surgery to craft "sexier" bodies, whereas others' life-saving surgeries challenge norms about bodily function and sexuality. Cultural constructions of the sexual body also function as a form of social control—shaping how we feel about our own bodies, framing our interactions with others, and even forcing us to manipulate our bodies, both voluntarily and involuntarily, to meet cultural expectations. The articles in this chapter explore many traditional ideas about sexuality that emphasize the gendered and racialized nature of sexual bodies.

Chapter 6, "Sexual Practices," examines how people behave sexually. As you read the articles in this section, think about how social norms, laws, religion, families, friends, and partners influence our sexuality and shape our behavior. Also, think about the tremendous diversity in sexual practices reflected in these articles. Although how we enact our sexuality varies immensely, these readings demonstrate what can happen when we vary from expected and accepted ways of acting sexually. Finally, these articles also remind us that the ways we enact sexual behaviors profoundly impact social relationships across the life course.

Chapter 7, "Sexual Disease," illustrates how society treats sexually transmitted infections (STIs)—commonly called sexually transmitted diseases (STDs)—quite differently from other communicable diseases. STIs are the only major group of diseases categorized by their method of transmission, rather than by their symptoms or the parts of the body they affect. People infected with STIs are stigmatized, creating a shield of secrecy in which some people deny to themselves that they have an STI, fail to tell their partners, and avoid seeking treatment. The stigma and perceptions of risk surrounding STIs affect the resources that the government and medical agencies opt to dedicate to fight them. For example, when AIDS was first discovered, it was seen as a "gay" or "African" disease and received little attention. In spite of intense efforts by gay activists, AIDS was considered a national emergency only when it began infecting white, middle-class heterosexual Americans. Regardless of the manageability of sexually transmitted infections, fears associated with them continue to be a powerful tool in the control of sexuality.

Chapter 8, "Social Control of Sexuality," illustrates how sexuality is managed and directed by forces both internal and external to individuals. Whereas much research on sexuality emphasizes individual responsibility, in this section we explore the structural factors that influence sexual attitudes and behav-

iors. Social institutions such as family, law, and medicine control sexual behavior through systems of rewards and punishments. Interpersonal interactions further constrain sexual choices through means such as harassment and labeling. This chapter explores how the mechanisms of social control are often turned against certain groups and how the social control of sexuality is a powerful weapon of oppression. Some selections highlight how social control is a two-way street, with the forces of control and resistance in constant conflict.

Although people like to think of sex as an intimate—and ideally pleasant—activity, it can be used as a weapon of violence and control to humiliate, degrade, and hurt. The readings in Chapter 9, "Sexual Violence," illustrate the complexities of defining rape and rape victimization. They deal with various types of sexual assault, rape of sex workers, date or acquaintance rape, the rape of men, rape on campus, and rape during war. The articles presented in this section also illustrate the diversity of sexual violence and the historical and sociocultural context for the rape myths that support this violence. Although women are the primary targets of sexual violence, no group is exempt. Sexual violence cuts across all social categories. This chapter also questions assumptions about what counts as sexual violence when consent is not clearly defined and when pain and degradation are part of sexual fantasies and play. The articles presented here contain graphic and sometimes upsetting or shocking information; it is our hope that readers will not simply be overwhelmed, but will learn how sexual violence is prevalent in our culture as a form of social control and how it is "structured" into our society in a myriad of ways. With knowledge, we can work more effectively for change.

Chapter 10, "Commercial Sex," explores the commodification of sexuality. Despite numerous laws regulating the sale of sexual services, commercial sex continues to be both a profitable business and a source of abuse. We address the tensions between the freedom to express sexuality through commercial avenues and the exploitation and control of sexuality through its sale. The readings examine who profits financially from the sex industry, who works in the sex industry, and who consumes its products.

ACKNOWLEDGMENTS

Revising this book for the fourth edition was a challenge and a treat. We would like to thank our editor, Karl Bakeman, for unbridled enthusiasm, support, and reassuring hand-holding during our transition, as well as Nicole Sawa, associate editor, and Linda Feldman, project editor, whose eagle-eyed attention to detail and efficiency buoyed our confidence that the fourth edition would be the best yet. Other wonderful Norton team members included Megan Jackson, permissions manager; Vanessa Nuttry, production manager; Lindsey Thomas, editorial assistant; Hope Miller Goodell, associate design director; Julia Hall, marketing manager; Laura Musich, media associate editor; Evan Luberger, assistant photo editor; Lynne Cannon Menges, copyeditor; Beth Rosato, proofreader; and Heather Laskey, indexer. The W. W. Norton staff has worked incredibly hard to publish this edition in record time with white glove service. We love a publisher that works hard and plays hard (and we enjoy being included in both)!

We also extend our thanks to the following reviewers, who helped us shape the book: Mark Hardt, Montana State University Billings; Janice McCabe, Florida State University; Carla A. Pfeffer, Purdue University North Central; Jill White, University of Wisconsin, Green Bay; and Chris Wienke, Southern Illinois University.

We are grateful to the researchers and scholars who took time out of their busy schedules to be interviewed for the Spotlight on Research features. Their dedication to the field of sex research, their humor in the face of monetary and political challenges, and their willingness to share personal experiences make us optimistic about the future of sex research. We want to thank the authors who wrote original pieces for the fourth edition. Their contributions make the book bigger and better (not that size matters . . .).

We edited this book in an incredibly supportive environment. Our colleagues in the department of sociology at Georgia State University provided unequivocal support for "Team Sex." The department, and particularly chair Donald Reitzes, provided a great deal of practical support by providing graduate student assistance and expense money. We received crucial assistance from Kelsey Schwarz, Marik Xavier-Brier, Lanier Basenberg, Eryn Grucza Viscarra, Lesley Reid at Georgia State University, and Ana-Alicia Farrar and Alicia Hagin at Salem College. We appreciate the contributions of Megan Tesene, Amanda Jungels, and Beth Cavalier to compile this book's wonderful instructor's manual as well. Special thanks to Mandy Swygart-Hobaugh, librarian extraordinaire, who assisted with our obscure search requests. Thanks to Anne Tamar-Mattis, executive director of Advocates for Informed Choice (AIC) for insights on legal rights of intersexuals, and Sarah Creighton for providing updated information on clinical practices. We also appreciate the expertise of CDC medical officer, Mona Saraiya, who helped us better understand the ways the HPV vaccination campaign is addressing both boys and girls.

Thanks to our families and friends for their encouragement and support. In particular, Mindy would like to thank her son, Moey Rojas, for the scintillating conversations about sex (the noncoital sex talk was especially interesting); her parents, Lynne and Milton Stombler; and her partner, Nate Steiner (they don't come any more loving, supportive, and mensch-like). Dawn thanks Jeff Mullis and their four cats. Wendy thanks Jake and Ben Simonds-Malamud; Gregg Rice; and Bumble,

Hinky, and Puff Simonds for their sweetness. Elroi thanks Aly, Avie, and Izzy Windsor for being a fantastic family. Elisabeth appreciates the support of Leila Burgess-Kattoula, Ehsan Kattoula, and the rest of her family and friends.

This book would not have been possible without our dedicated and discerning undergraduate students, graduate students, and writing consultants. We appreciate them for letting us know their favorite readings, for fearlessly voicing their opinions, and for asking tough questions.

This project is truly an example of collaborative feminist work. With Mindy Stombler as the team's "dominatrix," and the constant mutual support among all team members, creating this book often felt more like fun than work. We hope you have as much fun reading this book as we had putting it together.

ABOUT THE CONTRIBUTORS

THE EDITORS

Mindy Stombler, Ph.D., is a senior lecturer of sociology at Georgia State University. Her past research has focused on the production of sexual collective identities. For example, she explored how men in gay fraternities negotiated their dual identities of being gay and being Greek and how they reproduced hegemonic masculinity. Her current research focuses on power relations and oral sex as well as a variety of pedagogical issues.

Dawn M. Baunach, Ph.D., is an associate professor of sociology at Georgia State University. Her research interests include sexuality and gender inequalities, statistics and methodologies, social demography, and the sociology of food. She is currently studying various sexual attitudes and behaviors, including same-sex marriage, sexual prejudices, sexual disclosure, and bullying.

Wendy Simonds, Ph.D., is a professor of sociology at Georgia State University. She is the author of *Abortion at Work: Ideology and Practice in a Feminist Clinic, Women and Self-Help Culture: Reading between the Lines,* coauthor with Barbara Katz Rothman of *Centuries of Solace: Expressions of Maternal Grief in Popular Literature,* and coauthor with Barbara Katz Rothman and Bari Meltzer Norman of *Laboring On: Birth in Transition in the U.S.* She is currently doing research on more life and death issues, all too vaguely defined at present to describe here.

Elroi J. Windsor, Ph.D., is an assistant professor of sociology at Salem College in Winston-Salem, North Carolina. Windsor's teaching and research interests include gender, sexuality, health, and embodiment. Most recently, Windsor researched the disparate regulation of transgender and cisgender consumers of surgical body modification, finding that despite similar embodied experiences, having a cisgender gender status determined respondents' abilities to pursue surgery autonomously and with institutional support.

Elisabeth O. Burgess, Ph.D., is the director of the Gerontology Institute and an associate professor of gerontology and sociology at Georgia State University. Her research interests focus on changes in intimate relations over the life course, including involuntary celibacy, sexuality and aging, and intergenerational relationships. In addition, Dr. Burgess writes on theories of aging and attitudes toward older adults.

THE AUTHORS

Katie Acosta is an assistant professor of sociology at Georgia State University.

Philippe Adam is a senior research fellow at the National Centre in HIV Social Research at the University of New South Wales in Sydney, Australia.

John Archer is a professor and the research coordinator in the School of Psychology at the University of Central Lancashire in Preston, Lancashire of the United Kingdom.

Elizabeth A. Armstrong is an associate professor of sociology and organizational studies at the University of Michigan in Ann Arbor.

Alison Bain is an associate professor of geography at York University in Ontario, Canada.

Christina Barmon is a doctoral student in the department of sociology at Georgia State University.

Mark J. Bartkiewicz is a research assistant at the Gay, Lesbian and Straight Education Network.

Alexis A. Bender is a postdoctoral research fellow at the U.S. Army Public Health Command's Behavioral and Social Health Outcomes Program at Aberdeen Proving Ground, Maryland.

Elizabeth Bernstein is an associate professor of women's studies and sociology at Barnard College, Columbia University in New York City.

Madelyn J. Boesen is a research associate at the Gay, Lesbian and Straight Education Network.

Heather D. Boonstra is a senior public policy associate in the Guttmacher Institute's Washington, D.C. office.

Allan M. Brandt is the Amalie Moses Kass Professor of the History of Medicine and the dean of the Graduate School of Arts and Sciences at Harvard University in Cambridge, Massachusetts.

Virginia Braun is an associate professor in the school of psychology at the University of Auckland in Aotearoa/New Zealand.

Barbara G. Brents is a professor of sociology at the University of Nevada, Las Vegas.

K. L. Broad is an associate professor at the University of Florida in Gainesville. She holds joint appointments in the departments of sociology, criminology, and law and in the center for women's studies and gender research.

Marni A. Brown is an assistant professor of sociology at Georgia Gwinnett College in Lawrenceville, Georgia.

Vern L. Bullough was, before his death, a distinguished scholar and professor emeritus in the history department at California State University in Northside.

Mark Carrigan is a social theorist and doctoral candidate in the department of sociology at the University of Warwick in the United Kingdom.

Elizabeth Cavalier is an assistant professor of sociology at Georgia Gwinnett College in Lawrenceville, Georgia.

Greta Christina is the editor of *Paying for It: A Guide to Sex Workers for Their Clients* and is the author of *Why Are You Atheists So Angry? 99 Things That Piss Off the Godless*. She has written and edited several other books and has contributed to numerous magazines, newspapers, and anthologies. She blogs at freethoughtblogs .com/greta.

Cary Gabriel Costello is an associate professor of sociology and coordinator of LGBT studies at the University of Wisconsin in Milwaukee.

Richard A. Crosby is the DDI Endowed Professor and chair in the department of health behavior at the University of Kentucky in Lexington.

Robert Darby (www.historyofcircumcision .net) is an independent scholar, cultural historian, and freelance writer. He is the author of *A Surgical Temptation: The Demonization of the Foreskin and the Rise of Circumcision in Britain* and, most recently, an edited volume of George Drysdale's polemic on Victorian sexual mores, *Elements of Social Science: Physical, Sexual and Natural Religion*. He lives in Canberra, Australia.

Christina M. Dardis is a doctoral student in the department of psychology at Ohio University in Athens.

Michelle Davies is a senior lecturer in the School of Psychology at the University of Central Lancashire in Preston, Lancashire of the United Kingdom.

Clive M. Davis is a professor emeritus of psychology at Syracuse University in New York.

Georgiann Davis is an assistant professor of sociology at Southern Illinois University in Edwardsville.

John de Wit is the director of the National Centre in HIV Social Research at the University of New South Wales in Sydney, Australia.

Elizabeth M. Diaz is a senior research associate at the Gay, Lesbian and Straight Education Network.

Denise Donnelly is an associate professor emeritus of sociology at Georgia State University.

Katie M. Edwards is an assistant professor of psychology at the University of New Hampshire in Durham.

Loree Erickson is a community organizer and porn star academic at York University in Toronto, Canada.

Jeffrey Escoffier is the director of the Health Media and Marketing group at the New York City Department of Health. He writes on sexuality, gay history and politics, and social theory, and has taught history and politics of sexuality at the Universities of California at Berkeley and Davis, Rutgers University, and the New School University. He is the author of *Bigger Than Life: The History of Gay Porn Cinema from Beefcake to Hardcore* and the editor of *Sexual Revolution*.

Breanne Fahs is an associate professor of women and gender studies at Arizona State University.

Amy M. Fasula is a behavioral scientist at the Centers for Disease Control and Prevention.

Elizabeth Fee is the chief historian at the U.S. National Library of Medicine, part of the National Institutes of Health, in Bethesda, Maryland.

Michelle Fine is a Distinguished Professor of psychology at the City University of New York.

Stacey May Fowles is a writer and magazine professional living in Toronto, Canada.

Katherine Frank is a scholar in residence in the department of sociology at American University and an adjunct faculty member of the College of the Atlantic in Bar Harbor, Maine.

Jesus Maria Garcia-Calleja is an infectious disease epidemiologist in the department of HIV/AIDS of the World Health Organization in Geneva, Switzerland.

Ina May Gaskin is the executive director of the Farm Midwifery Center in Summertown, Tennessee.

Nicola Gavey is an associate professor of psychology at the University of Auckland in New Zealand.

Christine A. Gidycz is a professor and the director of clinical training in the department of psychology at Ohio University in Athens.

Judith Gordon was, before her death, a nursery school teacher and journalist.

Sol Gordon is a professor emeritus of child and family studies at Syracuse University in New York and former director of the university's Institute for Family Research and Education.

Stacy Gorman is doctoral student in the department of sociology at Georgia State University.

Cynthia A. Graham is a senior lecturer in health psychology at the University of Southhampton in the United Kingdom and a research fellow with The Kinsey Institute for Research in Sex, Gender, and Reproduction and The Rural Center for AIDS/STD Prevention at Indiana University in Bloomington.

Mary L. Gray is an associate professor in the department of communication and culture with adjunct appointments in American studies, anthropology, and gender studies at Indiana University in Bloomington. She is also a senior researcher at Microsoft Research New England.

Gary Greenberg is a freelance writer and practicing psychotherapist in Connecticut. He is the author of *The Noble Lie: When Scientists Give the Right Answers for the Wrong Reasons* and *Manufacturing Depression: The Secret History of a Modern Disease*.

Emily A. Greytak is a senior research associate at the Gay, Lesbian and Straight Education Network.

Laura Hamilton is an assistant professor of sociology at the University of California in Merced.

Corie J. Hammers is an assistant professor of women's, gender, and sexuality studies at Macalester College in Saint Paul, Minnesota.

Chong-suk Han is an assistant professor of sociology at Middlebury College in Vermont.

Brandon J. Hill is a research associate at The Kinsey Institute for Research in Sex, Gender, and Reproduction and a graduate student in the department of gender studies at Indiana University in Bloomington.

Jan Hoffman is a journalist with the *New York Times*.

Amanda M. Jungels is a postdoctoral research fellow at the U.S. Army Public Health Command's Behavioral and Social Health Outcomes Program at Aberdeen Proving Ground, Maryland.

Patty Kelly is a visiting assistant professor at Haverford College in Philadelphia, Pennsylvania.

Michael Kimmel is professor of sociology at the State University of New York at Stony Brook.

Lindsay King-Miller is a teacher and freelance writer based in Colorado.

Kathryn (Hausbeck) Korgan is an associate professor of sociology and senior associate dean of the graduate college at the University of Nevada, Las Vegas.

Joseph G. Kosciw is the senior director of research and strategic initiatives at the Gay, Lesbian and Straight Education Network.

Lisette Kuyper works as a researcher at the Netherlands Institute for Social Research with the emancipation, youth, and family research group.

Meghan Davidson Ladly is a journalist with the *New York Times*.

Jill Lepore is the David Woods Kemper '41 Professor of American History at Harvard University in Cambridge, Massachusetts.

Meika Loe is an associate professor of sociology and director of women's studies at Colgate University in Hamilton, New York.

Zakiya Luna is a UC President's Postdoctoral Fellow at the University of California, Berkeley. She is affiliated with the School of Law and departments of gender and women's studies and sociology.

Lenore Manderson is a professor of medical anthropology in the school of psychology and psychiatry (faculty of medicine) and school of political and social inquiry (faculty of arts) at Monash University in Australia.

Layli (Phillips) Maparyan is the Katherine Stone Kaufmann '67 Executive Director of the Wellesley Centers for Women and professor of Africana studies at Wellesley College in Massachusetts.

Sara I. McClelland is an assistant professor of psychology and women's studies at the University of Michigan in Ann Arbor.

Naomi B. McCormick was a distinguished teaching professor of psychology at the State University of New York in Plattsburgh, a fellow with the American Psychological Association, and a fellow and past-president of the Society for the Scientific Study of Sexuality.

PJ McGann is a lecturer of sociology at the University of Michigan in Ann Arbor.

Glenn J. Meaney is a lecturer of psychology and sexuality, marriage, and family studies at Saint Jerome's University at the University of Waterloo in Ontario, Canada.

Chet Meeks was, before his death, an assistant professor of sociology at Georgia State University.

Robin R. Milhausen is an associate professor of family relations and human sexuality at the University of Guelph in Ontario, Canada.

Chris Miller was a student at Saint Olaf College in Northfield, Minnesota.

Kim S. Miller is a senior advisor for youth prevention at the Centers for Disease Control and Prevention.

Lisa Jean Moore is a professor of sociology and women's studies at Purchase College of the State University of New York in Purchase.

Jeffery S. Mullis is a senior lecturer of sociology at Emory University in Atlanta, Georgia.

Adina Nack is a professor of sociology at California Lutheran University in Thousand Oaks.

Joane Nagel is a university distinguished professor of sociology at the University of Kansas in Lawrence.

Catherine Jean Nash is an associate professor of geography at Brock University in Ontario, Canada.

Amy Palder is a teaching fellow in sociology and the director of Institutional Research and Effectiveness at Oglethorpe University in Atlanta, Georgia.

Neal A. Palmer is a senior research associate at the Gay, Lesbian and Straight Education Network.

Stephanie Pappas is a senior writer for LiveScience.com.

Madison Park is a health writer and producer for CNN.

Scott Poulson-Bryant is a novelist, founding editor of *Vibe* magazine, and a doctoral candidate in American studies at Harvard University in Cambridge, Massachusetts.

Nicole Reynolds is an associate professor of English and women's and gender studies at Ohio University in Athens.

Leila J. Rupp is a professor of feminist studies at the University of California, Santa Barbara.

Maura Ryan is a lecturer of sociology at Georgia State University.

B. J. Rye is an associate professor of psychology and sexuality, marriage, and family studies at St. Jerome's University at the University of Waterloo in Ontario, Canada.

Stephanie A. Sanders is a professor of gender studies and associate director of The Kinsey Institute for Research in Sex, Gender, and Reproduction at Indiana University in Bloomington.

Teela Sanders is a reader in sociology at the University of Leeds in the United Kingdom.

Carmine Sarracino is a professor of English at Elizabethtown College in Pennsylvania.

Amy T. Schalet is an assistant professor in sociology at the University of Massachusetts at Amherst.

George P. Schmid is an epidemiologist in the department of HIV/AIDS of the World Health Organization in Geneva, Switzerland.

James Scott is an assistant professor of mathematics and statistics at Colby College in Waterville, Maine.

Kevin M. Scott is an associate professor of English at Albany State University in Georgia.

Emily Segar was a student at Saint Olaf College in Northfield, Minnesota.

Nadia Shapkina is an assistant professor of sociology at Kansas State University in Manhattan.

Elisabeth Sheff is one of a handful of global experts on polyamory, an educational consultant, and expert witness serving sexual and gender minorities.

Tobin Siebers is the V. L. Parrington Collegiate Professor of Literary and Cultural Criticism at the University of Michigan in Ann Arbor.

Adam Sonfield is a senior public policy associate at Guttmacher Institute's Washington, D.C. office.

Monica Southworth was a student at Saint Olaf College in Northfield, Minnesota.

Diana Spechler is an author of novels, including *Who by Fire* and *Skinny*, and has written for the *New York Times, GQ, Esquire, Wall Street Journal, Salon,* and *Slate,* among others.

Amy C. Steinbugler is an assistant professor of sociology at Dickinson College in Carlisle, Pennsylvania. The reading comes from a larger book project, *Beyond Loving: Intimate Race-work in Lesbian, Gay, and Straight Interracial Relationships.*

Evelina Sterling is a doctoral student in the department of sociology at Georgia State University.

Carla E. Stokes is a women's health and teen expert, health educator, and founder of Helping Our Teen Girls in Real Life Situations, Inc (HOTGIRLS).

Brian Sweeney is an assistant professor of sociology and anthropology at LIU Post in Brookville, New York.

Ann Swidler is a professor of sociology at the University of California, Berkeley.

Mattilda Bernstein Sycamore (www.mattildabernsteinsycamore.com) is most recently the author of *The End of San Francisco* and the editor of *Why Are Faggots So Afraid of Faggots?: Flaming Challenges to Masculinity, Objectification, and the Desire to Conform.*

Iddo Tavory is an assistant professor of sociology at the New School for Social Research in New York City.

Verta Taylor is a professor of sociology at the University of California, Santa Barbara.

Megan M. Tesene is a doctoral student in the department of sociology at Georgia State University.

Harper Jean Tobin is the director of policy at the National Center for Transgender Equality.

David Tonyan was a student at Saint Olaf College in Northfield, Minnesota.

Jessica A. Turchik is a psychology postdoctoral fellow at the National Center for PTSD, VA Palo Alto Health Care System and the department of psychiatry and behavioral sciences at Stanford University School of Medicine.

Jocelyn Wacloff was a student at Saint Olaf College in Northfield, Minnesota.

Lisa Wade is an associate professor of sociology at Occidental College in Los Angeles, California and is the founder and principle writer of the blog *Sociological Images.*

Jayne Walker is a former research student in the School of Psychology at the University of Central Lancashire in Preston, Lancashire of the United Kingdom.

Donna Walton is a certified cognitive behavioral therapist, motivational speaker, and founder of LEGGTalk, Inc.

Jane Ward is an associate professor of women's studies at the University of California in Riverside.

Margot Weiss is an assistant professor of American studies and anthropology at Wesleyan University in Middletown, Connecticut.

Jeffrey Wiener is a researcher at the Centers for Disease Control and Prevention.

Brian G. Williams is an epidemiologist with the World Health Organization in Geneva, Switzerland.

Liesbeth Woertman is a professor of psychology at the University Utrecht in the Netherlands.

Marik Xavier-Brier is a doctoral student in the department of sociology at Georgia State University.

William L. Yarber is a professor in the applied health science department, professor of gender studies, senior director of the Rural Center for AIDS/STD Prevention, and senior research fellow at The Kinsey Institute for Research in Sex, Gender, and Reproduction at Indiana University in Bloomington.

1

CATEGORIZING SEX

AN INTERVIEW WITH

MARYSOL ASENCIO

Marysol Asencio, M.P.H., Dr.P.H., is a professor at the University of Connecticut with a joint appointment in Human Development and Family Studies and El Instituto: The Institute of Latina/o, Caribbean, and Latin American Studies. Dr. Asencio focuses on the intersections of Latina/o sexualities and sexual health with gender, race/racialization, socioeconomic status, and migration. Dr. Asencio has authored, edited, and co-edited a number of books and special issues of journals on Latina/os and their sexualities in addition to peer-reviewed articles, chapters, and other publications. Her edited volume, Latina/o Sexualities: Probing Powers, Passions, Practices, and Policies *(Rutgers University Press, 2010), emerges from her Ford Foundation-funded project mapping the state of sexuality research on Latina/os.*

What led you to begin studying sexuality?

I entered graduate school with a research interest in women's reproductive health issues, which at the time ironically rarely dealt with issues of sexuality. It was mostly focused on family planning, contraceptive use, and maternal-child issues. However, this was also shortly after the medical community had identified AIDS when it was briefly referred to as GRID (Gay-Related Immune-Deficiency). It was a time when the lack of understanding of sexuality, as well as the biases about sexuality and certain racial/ethnic and sexual minorities, was exposed in a dramatic and deadly manner. The quickly advancing epidemic affected me personally as well, with the loss of several friends and colleagues. It was a frightening and frustrating time. It not only influenced me to enter sex research but it also awakened me to the need for community-based research and social justice advocacy for marginalized populations in order to promote evidenced-based health and social policy.

How do people react when you tell them you study sexuality?

Over the course of my career, I have gotten the impression that for some colleagues who do not do this type of research, sex research is not viewed as serious or important. This is a big concern in terms of having an academic career in sexuality research. Will you be hired because the work is seen as being in the margins of a particular discipline or in academia as a whole? When you tell the average person that you teach human sexuality, there is usually some laughter and a perception that it is a course that provides sexual entertainment rather than a forum for serious, rigorous, and challenging research and scholarship.

What ethical dilemmas have you faced as you've studied sexuality? Could you tell us about a particularly thorny dilemma and how you solved it?

I was working on a research project on gay men and prostate health with a couple of colleagues. Given that at the time there were no published studies on gay men with prostate cancer, we decided to conduct focus groups with diverse populations of gay men (racial/ethnic and socioeconomic) to see what concerns they had around prostate screening, diagnosis, treatment and its after-effects (many of them being sexual in nature). We used standard procedures that were established for recruiting men into the study, including a $40 stipend for participation. Towards the end of the study, we were trying to move away from middle-class participants and outreach to poorer marginalized, and in some cases homeless, gay men. What resulted was that our outreach efforts yielded potential participants who seemed as if they were claiming to be "gay" or "transgendered women" in order to receive the stipend. It is difficult to determine if someone was "gay" or "transgender" since we depend on reported self-identity.[1] If we accepted their assertions that they were gay men or transgendered women when there were signs that they may not be, we would bias our results. Also, given that they said they "matched" the criteria, there was very little rationale for turning them away other than none of the researchers believing this was the case based on other arguably unreliable cues. There was no way to know for sure.

We addressed this ethical dilemma[2] by providing every participant with the stipend and then reiterating the fact that although they consented to participate, they could leave at any time without having to give back the stipend. We hoped that those who were questionable in terms of meeting the study criteria would not feel they needed to participate. We went from around 22 people who showed up for the focus group to seven who remained. All the participants we had serious questions about left. It cost us some funds, but we had few options given our approved human subjects protocol and the volatility of the situation. This incident allowed us to consider ways to minimize this problem in future studies. However, it also demonstrates that the use and/or amount of stipends for research participation as well as the self-identification of sexual orientation and gender can in some cases become problematic depending on the particular research population and research needs.

What do you think is most challenging about studying sexuality?

While I think the field as a whole has become more accepted, the research is still "suspect." It is assumed to be potentially harmful until proven not harmful, in particular when dealing with the sexuality of those under the age of 18. There are significant barriers to getting detailed sexual histories of participants; discussing sexual acts; and attending locations that are designated as sexual such as strip clubs, brothels, etc. Sex research often depends on non-sex researchers (Institutional Review Boards [IRBs], funders, and communities) who may view this type of research as different from other forms of research or who believe that we ought not to ask about sex or that it is a voyeuristic enterprise.

Why is sex research important?

Sexuality is central to understanding a great deal about humanity and society. As someone who researches Latina/os and sexuality, I was once asked why I "waste" my time as a researcher on sexuality when I could be studying more important issues for the Latina/o community, such as poverty and racism. First of all, studying sexuality involves understanding all its intersections and connections with issues such as poverty and racism. Second, if you look at political debates in this country, sexuality plays a major role (e.g., contraception, abortion, same-sex marriage, teen pregnancy, etc.). Moreover, the outcomes of those debates many times affect racial/ethnic and sexual minorities and low-income individuals and families in ways that disadvantage or minimize their experiences. Therefore, sex research furthers our understanding of power, marginalization, and other social issues.

Of the projects you've done over the course of your academic career, which was most interesting and why?

My first large independent qualitative research on adolescent sexuality was most interesting because I was still learning about sexuality research. It was eye opening. I remember when I asked one of my female respondents about the first time she had sexual intercourse, she went on to explain how she was raped as a child by an uncle and she wanted to make it clear to me that she saw herself as a "virgin" and would like me to characterize her as such. She had still not had, at the age of 18, "consensual" first sexual intercourse. It was very important to her sense of dignity and control of her sexuality to be seen as a virgin. She also told me that what she did not like about questionnaires that asked her "if she had ever had sexual intercourse," was that they did not reflect her experience or her wish "not" to be characterized as a "sexually active" teen or not a "virgin." I learned a great deal about the meanings attached to sexuality from those adolescents and I am very grateful that they shared their lives with me.

If you could teach people one thing about sexuality, what would it be?

I would say that sexuality is not just about identity and behaviors; it is a portal to understand society and issues of power.

Is there anything else you'd like to add?

One thing that I would like to add is that I hope as the field continues to grow it will attract researchers from many different backgrounds and experiences. I believe, as with any subject matter, that the more diverse the researchers are, in terms of demographic backgrounds and life experiences, the more opportunity there is for various perspectives and insights to be brought into our understanding of sex and sexuality.

NOTES

1. It is important to note that many transgendered women do maintain their prostate even if they have had hormonal and surgical alterations to their bodies.

2. For a full account see Descartes, Lara, Marysol Asencio and Thomas O. Blank. 2011. Paying Project Participants: Dilemmas in Research With Poor, Marginalized Populations. *Advances in social work* 12(2): 218–225.

ARE WE HAVING SEX NOW OR WHAT?

GRETA CHRISTINA

When I first started having sex with other people, I used to like to count them. I wanted to keep track of how many there had been. It was a source of some kind of pride, or identity anyway, to know how many people I'd had sex with in my lifetime. So, in my mind, Len was number one, Chris was number two, that slimy awful little heavy metal barbiturate addict whose name I can't remember was number three, Alan was number four, and so on. It got to the point where, when I'd start having sex with a new person for the first time, when he first entered my body (I was only having sex with men at the time), what would flash through my head wouldn't be "Oh, baby, baby you feel so good inside me," or "What the hell am I doing with this creep," or "This is boring, I wonder what's on TV." What flashed through my head was "Seven!"

Doing this had some interesting results. I'd look for patterns in the numbers. I had a theory for a while that every fourth lover turned out to be really great in bed, and would ponder what the cosmic significance of the phenomenon might be. Sometimes I'd try to determine what kind of person I was by how many people I'd had sex with. At eighteen, I'd had sex with ten different people. Did that make me normal, repressed, a total slut, a free-spirited bohemian, or what? Not that I compared my numbers with anyone else's—I didn't. It was my own exclusive structure, a game I played in the privacy of my own head.

Then the numbers started getting a little larger, as numbers tend to do, and keeping track became more difficult. I'd remember that the last one was *seventeen* and so this one must be *eighteen*, but then I'd start having doubts about whether I'd been keeping score accurately or not. I'd lie awake at night thinking to myself well, there was Brad, and there was that guy on my birthday, and there was David and . . . no, wait, I forgot that guy I got drunk with at the social my first week at college . . . so that's seven, eight, nine . . . and by two in the morning I'd finally have it figured out. But there was always a nagging suspicion that maybe I'd missed someone, some dreadful tacky little scumball that I was trying to forget about having invited inside my body. And as much as I maybe wanted to forget about the sleazy little scumball, I wanted more to get that number right.

It kept getting harder, though. I began to question what counted as sex and what didn't. There was that time with Gene, for instance. I was pissed off at my boyfriend, David, for cheating on me. It was a major crisis, and Gene and I were friends and he'd been trying to get at me for weeks and I hadn't exactly been discouraging him. I went to see him that night to gripe about David. He was very sympathetic of course, and he gave me a backrub, and we talked and touched and confided and hugged, and then we started kissing, and then we snuggled up a little closer, and then we started fondling each other, you know, and then all heck broke loose, and we rolled around on the bed groping and rubbing and grabbing and smooching and pushing and pressing and squeezing. He never did actually get it in. He wanted to, and I wanted to too, but I had this thing about being faithful to my boyfriend, so I kept saying, "No, you can't do that, Yes, that feels so good, No, wait that's too much. Yes, yes, don't stop. No, stop that's enough." We never even got our clothes off. Jesus Christ, though, it was some night. One of the best, really. But for a long time I didn't count it as one of the times I'd had sex. He never got inside, so it didn't count.

Later, months and years later, when I lay awake putting my list together, I'd start to wonder: Why doesn't Gene count? Does he not count because he never got inside? Or does he not count because I had to preserve my moral edge over David, my status as the patient, ever-faithful, cheated-on, martyred girlfriend, and if what I did with Gene counts then I don't get to feel wounded and superior?

Years later, I did end up fucking Gene and I felt a profound relief because, at last, he definitely had a number, and I knew for sure that he did in fact count.

Then I started having sex with women, and, boy, howdy, did *that* ever shoot holes in the system. I'd always made my list of sex partners by defining sex as penile-vaginal intercourse—you know, screwing. It's a pretty simple distinction, a straightforward binary system. Did it go in or didn't it? Yes or no? One or zero? On or off? Granted, it's a pretty arbitrary definition, but it's the customary one, with an ancient and respected tradition behind it, and when I was just screwing men, there was no compelling reason to question it.

But with women, well, first of all there's no penis, so right from the start the tracking system is defective. And then, there are so many ways women can have sex with each other, touching and licking and grinding and fingering and fisting—with dildoes or vibrators or vegetables or whatever happens to be lying around the house, or with nothing at all except human

bodies. Of course, that's true for sex between women and men as well. But between women, no one method has a centuries-old tradition of being the one that counts. Even when we do fuck each other there's no dick, so you don't get that feeling of This Is What's Important, We Are Now Having Sex, objectively speaking, and all that other stuff is just foreplay or afterplay. So when I started having sex with women the binary system had to go, in favor of a more inclusive definition.

Which meant, of course, that my list of how many people I'd had sex with was completely trashed. In order to maintain it I would have had to go back and reconstruct the whole thing and include all those people I'd necked with and gone down on and dry-humped and played touchy-feely games with. Even the question of who filled the all-important Number One slot, something I'd never had any doubts about before, would have to be re-evaluated.

By this time I'd kind of lost interest in the list anyway. Reconstructing it would be more trouble than it was worth. But the crucial question remained: What counts as having sex with someone?

It was important for me to know. You have to know what qualifies as sex because when you have sex with someone your relationship changes. Right? *Right?* It's not that sex itself has to change things all that much. But knowing you've had sex, being conscious of a sexual connection, standing around making polite conversation with someone while thinking to yourself, "I've had sex with this person," that's what changes things. Or so I believed. And if having sex with a friend can confuse or change the friendship, think how bizarre things can get when you're not sure whether you've had sex with them or not.

The problem was, as I kept doing more kinds of sexual things, the line between *sex* and *not-sex* kept getting more hazy and indistinct. As I brought more into my sexual experience, things were showing up on the dividing line demanding my attention. It wasn't just that the territory I labeled *sex* was expanding. The line itself had swollen, dilated, been transformed into a vast gray region. It had become less like a border and more like a demilitarized zone.

Which is a strange place to live. Not a bad place, just strange. It's like juggling, or watch-making, or playing the piano—anything that demands complete concentrated awareness and attention. It feels like cognitive disso-nance, only pleasant. It feels like waking up from a compelling and realistic bad dream. It feels like the way you feel when you realize that everything you know is wrong, and a bloody good thing too, because it was painful and stu-pid and it really screwed you up.

But, for me, living in a question naturally leads to searching for an answer. I can't simply shrug, throw up my hands, and say, "Damned if I know." I have to explore the unknown fron-tiers, even if I don't bring back any secret trea-sure. So even if it's incomplete or provisional, I do want to find some sort of definition of what is and isn't sex.

I know when I'm *feeling* sexual. I'm feeling sexual if my pussy's wet, my nipples are hard, my palms are clammy, my brain is fogged, my skin is tingly and super-sensitive, my butt mus-cles clench, my heartbeat speeds up, I have an orgasm (that's the real giveaway), and so on. But feeling sexual with someone isn't the same as having sex with them. Good Lord, if I called it sex every time I was attracted to someone who returned the favor I'd be even more bewildered than I am now. Even *being* sexual with someone isn't the same as *having* sex with them. I've danced and flirted with too many people, given and received too many sexy, would-be-seductive backrubs, to believe otherwise.

I have friends who say, if you thought of it as sex when you were doing it, then it was. That's an interesting idea. It's certainly helped me construct a coherent sexual history without being a revisionist swine: redefining my past according to current definitions. But it really just begs the question. It's fine to say that sex is whatever I think it is; but then what do I think it *is*? What if, when I was doing it, I was *wonder-ing* whether it counted?

Perhaps having sex with someone is the conscious, consenting, mutually acknowl-edged pursuit of shared sexual pleasure. Not a bad definition. If you are turning each other on and you say so and you keep doing it, then it's sex. It's broad enough to encompass a lot of sexual behavior beyond genital contact/orgasm; it's distinct enough *not* to include every instance of sexual awareness or arousal; and it contains the elements I feel are vital—acknowledgment, consent, reciprocity, and the pursuit of pleasure. But what about the situ-ation where one person consents to sex with-out really enjoying it? Lots of people (myself included) have had sexual interactions that we didn't find satisfying or didn't really want and, unless they were actually forced on us against our will, I think most of us would still classify them as sex.

Maybe if *both* of you (or all of you) think of it as sex, then it's sex whether you're having fun or not. That clears up the problem of sex that's consented to but not wished-for or enjoyed. Unfortunately, it begs the question again, only worse: now you have to mesh different people's vague and inarticulate notions of what is and isn't sex and find the place where they overlap. Too messy.

How about sex as the conscious, con-senting, mutually acknowledged pursuit of sexual pleasure of *at least one* of the people involved. That's better. It has all the key com-ponents, and it includes the situation where one person is doing it for a reason other than sexual pleasure—status, reassurance, money, the satisfaction and pleasure of someone they love, etc. But what if *neither* of you is enjoying it, if you're both doing it because you think the other one wants to? Ugh.

I'm having trouble here. Even the conventional standby—sex equals intercourse—has a serious flaw: it includes rape, which is something I emphatically refuse to accept. As far as I'm concerned, if there's no consent, it ain't sex. But I feel that's about the only place in this whole quagmire where I have a grip. The longer I think about the subject, the more questions I come up with. At what point in an encounter does it *become* sexual? If an interaction that begins nonsexually turns into sex, was it sex all along? What about sex with someone who's asleep? Can you have a situation where one person is having sex and the other isn't? It seems that no matter what definition I come up with, I can think of some real-life experience that calls it into question.

For instance, a couple of years ago I attended (well, hosted) an all-girl sex party. Out of the twelve other women there, there were only a few with whom I got seriously physically nasty. The rest I kissed or hugged or talked dirty with or just smiled at, or watched while they did seriously physically nasty things with each other. If we'd been alone, I'd probably say that what I'd done with most of the women there didn't count as having sex. But the experience, which was hot and sweet and silly and very, very special, had been created by all of us, and although I only really got down with a few, I felt that I'd been sexual with all of the women there. Now, when I meet one of the women from that party, I always ask myself: Have we had sex?

For instance, when I was first experimenting with sadomasochism, I got together with a really hot woman. We were negotiating about what we were going to do, what would and wouldn't be okay, and she said she wasn't sure she wanted to have sex. Now we'd been explicitly planning all kinds of fun and games—spanking, bondage, obedience—which I strongly identified as sexual activity. In her mind, though, *sex* meant direct genital contact, and she didn't necessarily want to do that with me. Playing with her turned out to be a tremendously erotic experience, arousing and stimulating and almost unbearably satisfying. But we spent the whole evening without even touching each other's genitals. And the fact that our definitions were so different made me wonder: Was it sex?

For instance, I worked for a few months as a nude dancer at a peep show. In case you've never been to a peep show, it works like this: the customer goes into a tiny, dingy black box, kind of like a phone booth, puts in quarters, and a metal plate goes up; the customer looks through a window at a little room/stage where naked women are dancing. One time, a guy came into one of the booths and started watching me and masturbating. I came over and squatted in front of him and started masturbating too, and we grinned at each other and watched each other and masturbated, and we both had a fabulous time. (I couldn't believe I was being paid to masturbate—tough job, but somebody has to do it . . .). After he left I thought to myself: Did we just have sex? I mean, if it had been someone I knew, and if there had been no glass and no quarters, there'd be no question in my mind. Sitting two feet apart from someone, watching each other masturbate? Yup, I'd call that sex all right. But this was different, because it was a stranger, and because of the glass and the quarters. Was it sex?

I still don't have an answer.

Diversity in Conceptualizing Having "Had Sex"

Stephanie A. Sanders, Brandon J. Hill, William L. Yarber, Cynthia A. Graham, Richard A. Crosby, and Robin R. Milhausen

INTRODUCTION

Understanding the significance of the word "sex" has implications for biomedical research, sexuality education, and clinical practice. When hypotheses involving sex are tested, a misclassification bias inevitably occurs.[1,2]

METHODS
Data Collection and Sample Characteristics

The Centre for Survey Research at Indiana University conducted a telephone survey of Indiana residents using random-digit-dialling. Of the eligible contacts, 39% ($n = 504$) completed interviews. Of these, 486 (96.4%; 204 males, 282 females) provided valid answers to "had sex" questions; this group constituted the current sample. Age ranged from 18 to 96 years, with men (mean age 46.50 years) significantly younger than women (mean age 50.6 . . .). The majority (91.3%) identified themselves as white.

Measures

In addition to demographic questions, the following stem question was asked after an introduction indicating we were assessing attitudes and not behavioural history: "Would you say you 'had sex' with someone if the most intimate behavior you engaged in was. . . ." The 14 specific behavioural items and their abbreviations are listed in the table on the following page. Valid responses were "yes" or "no". [MG = manual-genital; OG = oral-genital; PAI = penile-anal intercourse; PVI = penile-vaginal intercourse]

DISCUSSION

In this representative sample of adult residents in one state in the USA, there was no universal agreement as to what behaviours constituted having "had sex". These findings highlight the diversity of opinions regarding which behaviours constitute having "had sex". The large majority believed that PVI was having "had sex", but one in five answered "no" to PAI, three in ten answered "no" to OG and more than half answered "no" for MG. Overall, men and women answered similarly.

Given the diversity of opinions about what constitutes having "had sex", it is likely that people across gender and age groups may answer questions about how many partners they "had sex" with or how many times they "had sex" using varying criteria. They may think of different behaviours when researchers or practitioners use this phrase. Thus, the results provide empirical evidence supporting the need to use behaviour-specific terminology in sexual history taking, sex research, sexual health promotion, and sex education. . . .

ACKNOWLEDGEMENTS

This research was supported by the Rural Center for AIDS/STD Prevention and The Kinsey Institute for Research in Sex, Gender and Reproduction at Indiana University, Bloomington.

Percentage and 95% confidence intervals of the sample (n = 486) answering "yes" for each behaviour

WORDING OF ITEM: WOULD YOU SAY YOU "HAD SEX" WITH SOMEONE IF THE MOST INTIMATE BEHAVIOR YOU ENGAGED IN WAS . . .	ABBREVIATION	% RESPONDENTS ANSWERING "YES" (95% CI)
You touched, fondled or manually stimulated a partner's genitals?	MG-performed	44.9 (40.5–49.3)
A partner touched, fondled, or manually stimulated your genitals?	MG-received	48.1 (43.7–52.5)
You had oral (mouth) contact with a partner's genitals?	OG-performed	71.0 (67.0–75.0)
A partner had oral (mouth) contact with your genitals?	OG-received	72.9 (69.0–76.9)
Penile-vaginal intercourse?	PVI	94.8 (92.9–96.7)
Penile-vaginal intercourse with no ejaculation; that is, the man did not "come"?	PVI-no ejaculation	89.1 (86.3–91.9)
Penile-vaginal intercourse with no female orgasm; that is, the woman did not "come"?	PVI-no female orgasm	92.7 (90.4–95.0)
Penile-vaginal intercourse, but very brief?	PVI-very brief	94.4 (92.3–96.5)
Penile-vaginal intercourse with a condom?	PVI-condom	93.3 (91.0–95.6)
Penile-anal intercourse?	PAI	80.8 (77.3–84.3)
Penile-anal intercourse with no male ejaculation; that is, the man did not "come"?	PAI-no ejaculation	79.5 (75.9–83.1)
Penile-anal intercourse with no female orgasm; that is, the woman did not "come"?	PAI-no female orgasm	81.1 (77.6–84.6)
Penile-anal intercourse, but very brief?	PAI-very brief	81.8 (78.4–85.2)
Penile-anal intercourse with a condom?	PAI-condom	82.0 (78.6–85.4)

Source: Stephanie A. Sanders, Brandon J. Hill, William L. Yarber, Cynthia A. Graham, Richard A. Crosby, Robin R. Milhausen: "Misclassification bias: diversity in conceptualisations about having 'had sex'," *Sexual Health* 7(1): 31–34. http://www.publish.csiro.au/nid/164/paper/SH09068 .htm. © CSIRO 2010. Reprinted by permission of CSIRO Publishing.

NOTES

1. Crosby RA, DiClemente RJ, Holtgrave DR, Wingood GM. 2002. Design, measurement, and analytic considerations for testing hypotheses relative to condom effectiveness against non-viral STIs. *Sex Transm Infect* 78: 228–31. doi: 10.1136/sti. 78.4.228.

2. Sanders, SA, Reinisch, JM. 1999. Would you say you "had sex" if . . . ? *JAMA* 281: 275–7. doi:10.1001/jama.281.3.275

"BRINGING INTERSEXY BACK"? INTERSEXUALS AND SEXUAL SATISFACTION

GEORGIANN DAVIS

INTRODUCTION

From as early as a prenatal ultrasound image, genitalia are classified into a sex binary—males have penises and females have vaginas. However, for decades now, scholars have argued that this troubling two-sex model is socially constructed through processes that begin in the medical profession (e.g., Dreger, 1998a; Fausto-Sterling, 1993; Karkazis, 2008; Kessler, 1990; Preves, 2003). One of the very best examples of both the problem with the two-sex model and evidence that it is socially constructed is intersexuality,[1] conditions where one is born with "ambiguous genitalia, sexual organs, or sex chromosomes" that deviate from the "norm" (Preves, 2003, 2). According to the Intersex Society of North America, over twenty different intersex conditions have been identified by the medical profession (Consortium, 2006).

One example of intersexed bodies occurs among people with androgen insensitivity syndrome (AIS). Individuals with AIS have XY sex chromosomes yet are unable to, during gestation and beyond, partially (PAIS) or completely (CAIS) metabolize androgens, an umbrella term for male sex hormones, most notably testosterone. Individuals with PAIS are usually diagnosed at birth because it results in ambiguous external genitalia (usually a larger clitoris that resembles a small penis) with either internal or external testes. Individuals with CAIS also have XY sex chromosomes, but unlike those with PAIS, they do not have ambiguous external genitalia. Instead, they commonly have what appears to be a "nor-mal" looking vagina and internal undescended testes. Since the genital ambiguity of CAIS lies internally rather than externally, it generally is not diagnosed until adolescence when females are expected to begin menstruation. Rather than accept intersexuality as a naturally occurring disruption of the two-sex model,[2] the medical profession surgically removes or modifies intersex genitalia to fit into the sex binary, providing evidence that sex is a socially constructed phenomenon (Fausto-Sterling, 1993, 24; see also Dreger, 1998a, b; Fausto-Sterling, 2000a, b; Karkazis, 2008; Kessler, 1998, 1990; Preves, 2003, 2000).

Background

Intersexuality makes the two-sex model that organizes our bodies visible, and it also challenges any form of sex categorization. Although some scholars have argued that we should organize bodies into multiple sex categories, going beyond the two we currently recognize (e.g., Fausto-Sterling, 1993), plural sex categorization is neither truly possible nor entirely logical (Kessler, 1998). To categorize bodies by sex, regardless of the number of sex categories made available, is a difficult task because "few, if any, physical characteristics are exclusive to one sex" (Karkazis, 2008, 22–23). For example, testosterone is not found exclusively in male bodies; nor is estrogen. Instead of attempting to sex-categorize intersex bodies by biological markers, medical professionals need to shift their focus to "sexual variability," embracing the diverse appearance of genitals without requiring categorization (Kessler, 1998).

A BRIEF HISTORY OF INTERSEX GENITAL SURGERY

Rather than accept intersexuality as a challenge to the sex binary and evidence of naturally occurring sexual variability, the medical profession has historically approached it as an abnormality that can be surgically corrected. In the twentieth century, technological advancements provided the medical profession at large with the tools to surgically "shoehorn" individuals who deviated from the sex binary system to fit into a male or female body (Fausto-Sterling, 1993, 24; see also Dreger, 1998a, b; Fausto-Sterling, 2000a, b; Karkazis, 2008; Kessler, 1998, 1990; Preves, 2003, 2000). Doctors assumed that surgery would reduce the stigma and shame associated with not comfortably fitting into the narrow sex, gender, and sexuality categorization system (Dreger, 1998a; Fausto-Sterling, 2000a, 1996; Kessler, 1998, 1990; Preves, 2003, 2002). However, in many cases, intersex genital surgery isn't medically necessary. For example, although intersexuals were often told that they were at a high risk for developing gonadal cancer (e.g., Preves, 2003), there is minimal evidence to support this claim. The presumed strong correlation between intersexuality and cancerous germ cell tumors is not consistently predicted (see Cools et al., 2006).

The surgical modification of genitalia impacts all aspects of intersexuals' lives, especially sexual pleasure, by disrupting genital sensation (Karkazis, 2008; Preves, 2003). Genital surgeries leave many intersexuals feeling mutilated, unable to achieve sexual satisfaction, and in some instances, incontinent (Preves, 2003). A recent study documented that almost half of all intersexuals who underwent genital surgery were dissatisfied with surgical outcomes (Köhler et al., 2012). While such evidence raises awareness of intersexuals' sexual dissatisfaction, it also situates the problem narrowly onto scalpels and the medical providers who

use them. Some medical professionals who are experts on intersexuality have themselves advocated for the end of intersex genital surgeries (Köhler et al., 2011; Lee et al., 2006).

Given that intersexuality is usually diagnosed when one is a minor, it is up to the individual's parent(s) to grant surgical consent. It might seem unusual for any parent to authorize a medical provider to perform a surgery that in many cases is cosmetic, medically unnecessary, or purely preventative (see Cools et al., 2006). However, parents of intersexual children, like many in our society, are uninformed about sexual variability and consequently follow medical recommendations without hesitation. For this reason, the validity of parental consent has been questioned (Dreger, 1998b).

Feminist critiques of intersex genital surgery (e.g., Dreger, 1998b; Fausto-Sterling, 1993; Kessler, 1998) helped adult intersexuals organize collectively together in the 1990s (Karkazis, 2008; Preves, 2003). The goal of the intersex rights movement was simple: to end the surgical modification of intersex genitalia (e.g., Karkazis, 2008; Preves, 2003). Since the surgeries are usually performed on minor children who do not have a legal voice of their own, intersex activists accused medical professionals of performing nonconsensual female genital cutting, which is an illegal practice in the United States among non-intersexed females (Chase, 2002).

FROM "INTERSEX" TO "DISORDERS OF SEX DEVELOPMENT"

By the year 2000, after a decade of protests by adult intersex activists, the American Academy of Pediatrics issued a consensus statement on the medical management of intersex conditions. The document had a number of recommendations including that intersex infants "should be referred to as "your baby" or "your child"—not "it," "he," or "she," (Committee, 2000, 138). However, surgery was still an option. The guidelines advised doctors to inform parents that their baby's "abnormal appearance can be corrected and the child raised as a boy or a girl as appropriate" (Committee, 2000, 138). The guidelines also stated that a number of factors should be considered when determining which "gender assignment" should be recommended for a given intersex child. Most notably, these factors included "fertility potential" and "capacity for normal sexual function" (Committee, 2000, 141).

Many medical professionals hold cissexist and heteronormative ideologies, which are especially problematic in the case of the medical management of intersexuality, because these ideologies are relied on during gender assignment and imposed on intersexuals and their bodies. Cissexism is the belief that gender is authentic only when it is neatly aligned with sex (Serano, 2007), and heteronormativity is "the suite of cultural, legal, and institutional practices that maintain normative assumptions that there are two and only two genders, that gender reflects biological sex, and that only sexual attraction between these 'opposite' genders is natural or acceptable" (Schilt and Westbrook, 2009, 441; see also Kitzinger, 2005). For example, an intersexual's gender assignment is recommended based on capacity for "normal [hetero]sexual function" and "fertility potential" (Committee, 2000, 141). Only women can become pregnant in the eyes of most medical professionals, and thus, many seem to think that all bodies capable of pregnancy must then be "female." The guidelines suggested that "[a]ll female infants virilized because of [congenital adrenal hyperplasia, or CAH] or maternal androgens are potentially fertile and should therefore be raised as girls" (Committee, 2000, 141). And assessments of prospects for "normal" sexual function presume heterosexual partnering, which exemplifies a heteronormative ideology. Because those born with CAH, a type of intersexuality, are capable of pregnancy despite having

a large clitoris that resembles a small penis, medical professionals will only define them as female.[3] They ignore the possibility that this person might desire to penetrate using their phallus, so to them, surgery is only logical. In other words, medical professionals fail to see any possibilities beyond gender- and sexual-normative bodies when they make their gender and medical intervention recommendations.

In 2006, the American Academy of Pediatrics revised their policy regarding the treatment of intersexual infants due to "progress in diagnosis, surgical techniques, understanding psychosocial issues, and recognizing and accepting the place of patient advocacy" (Lee et al., 2006, 488). They offered new recommendations in this policy revision, including avoiding unnecessary surgical intervention. The consensus statement notes:

Because orgasmic function and erectile sensation may be disturbed by clitoral surgery, the surgical procedure should be anatomically based to preserve erectile function and the innervation of the clitoris. Emphasis is on functional outcome rather than a strictly cosmetic appearance. It is generally felt that surgery that is performed for cosmetic reasons in the first year of life relieves parental distress and improves attachment between the child and the parents; the systematic evidence for this belief is lacking. (Lee et al., 2006, 491)

The guidelines also recommend a nomenclature shift away from "intersex" and "sex reversal" terminology in favor of new "disorders of sex development (DSD)" language (Lee, 2006, 488).

Only five years after the consensus statement was published, current evidence suggests that intersexuality has become an outdated term in the medical profession (Davis, 2011). Medical terminology is a concern because history has shown us that there are implications to naming and defining conditions as disorders (e.g., Brown, 2007, 1995, 1990; Conrad, 2007; Cooksey and Brown, 1998). Consider, for example, attention deficit hyperactivity disorder (ADHD). In the 1990s, Conrad (2007) argues that ADHD diagnosis expanded to include adults that weren't previously diagnosed in ways that had lasting implications on how individuals, after diagnosis, understood and explained their behaviors.

Given what is known about the medicalization process, is it possible that the sexual struggles intersexuals experience are not only due to genital surgery? If surgery was the only cause of sexual dissatisfaction, there would be significant differences in sexual satisfaction between those who were surgically modified and those who were not. Yet, empirical studies do not support such expectations (Köhler et al., 2012; van der Zwan et al., in press). In a study of intersexuals that included those who had genital surgeries and those who did not, sexual dissatisfaction was still alarmingly high. Regardless of surgical history, 37.5 percent of intersexuals reported dissatisfaction with their sex life and 44.2 percent reported sexual anxieties. The majority of intersexuals (68.2%) reported that their sexual dissatisfaction was the result of their "abnormality" (Köhler et al., 2012). In a different study, similar results were obtained, with 41 percent of intersex women reporting sexual distress, irrespective of surgical status (van der Zwan et al., in press). Would ending genital surgeries solve the dissatisfaction experienced by intersexuals? Is it possible that the sexual dissatisfaction reported by intersexuals is situated in a larger medicalization process and not just in the operating room? What can we learn from intersexuals who report more positive sexual experiences?

Methods

Relying on extensive qualitative data including over 300 hours of informal observations in the public meeting spaces of intersex organizational meetings and 65 in-depth interviews with intersexuals, intersex activists, parents of intersex children, and medical professionals who are experts on such conditions, I studied how intersexuality is understood, contested, and experienced by those in the community. Most data were collected from October of 2008 to August of 2010. A few additional interviews took place in April 2011. As a feminist with an intersex condition, I collected the data from an informed standpoint.

Informants were initially recruited from four organizations: the Intersex Society of North America (ISNA), Accord Alliance, the Androgen Insensitivity Syndrome Support Group-USA[4] (AISSG-USA), and Organisation Intersex International (OII). Participants were targeted from these four organizations because, based on my initial assessment of their websites, each organization appeared to be involved in the intersex rights movement in different ways. For instance, ISNA and OII are activist organizations, while AISSG-USA is a support group, and Accord Alliance is an organization that seeks to distribute educational resources to medical professionals. I also employed snowball sampling by asking initial informants to name others who might share different views from their own (Biernacki and Waldorf, 1981).

Findings

Regardless of surgical history, all of the intersexuals I interviewed reported experiencing sexual struggles at some point in their lives. Everyone was also critical of surgical interventions when conducted on minor children who weren't capable of or legally allowed to refuse consent for medical treatment. The intersex rights movement was formed in the 1990s, united by this critique (e.g., Chase, 2002; Preves, 2003). However, intersexuality remains medicalized, most recently with the disorder of sex development (DSD) terminology (Davis, 2011). Support for the new DSD terminology was mixed[5] among the 37[6] individuals with intersex/DSD conditions whom I interviewed.

While it is outside the scope of this reading to adequately explain *why* individuals with such conditions embraced the DSD nomenclature while others rejected it, the decision can briefly be explained as resulting from DSD proponents desiring to work alongside medical professionals in a medical context with medical terms to promote social change. Here, I focus specifically on *how* the terminology—which is situated in a larger medicalization process—is connected to sexual dis/satisfaction rather than focus on *why* individuals chose the terminology that they did.

I begin my analysis establishing that intersexuals who were surgically modified commonly reported emotional and physical struggles because of their genital surgery. I next highlight the differences between those who embrace the new DSD terminology that upholds the two-sex model and those who reject it. I then describe the sexual struggles that surfaced, regardless of sexual history, for many intersexuals who sought sexual pleasure. I end by reporting three different responses to sexual struggles that involved avoiding intimacy, seeking heterosexual encounters, or rejecting medicalization and the *disorder* of sex development terminology that pathologizes bodies.

THE CONSEQUENCES OF INTERSEX GENITAL SURGERY

Consistent with previous research (e.g., Karkazis, 2008; Preves, 2003), of the 37 intersexuals I interviewed, 33 underwent genital surgery as children, leaving them emotionally and physically scarred (89%). The emotional consequences of surgery resulted from individuals being lied to by their parents and doctors who attempted to keep their diagnoses a secret (see also Karkazis, 2008; Preves, 2003). For example, Ana shared:

When I was 12 . . . I was told [by my parents and doctors] that my ovaries had not formed correctly

and that there was a risk of cancer and that they needed to be removed. And I had lots of examinations including of my genitals, but I was never made aware [prior to surgery] that anything was going to be taken away [from down] there. So it was a big shock to me [when I woke up after surgery]. And I really had some work to do when I was eventually ready to do it . . . from the trauma that I had from waking up from my surgery to realize that what was between my legs was gone.

Prior to the 2000 medical consensus statement that advised against such deception, intersexuals like Ana were often lied to about their diagnosis because doctors were concerned that the intersex diagnosis might disrupt a child's gender identity formation. While this deception is far less common today, possibly reducing the emotional consequences of surgery, intersex genital surgeries continue (see Davis, 2011).

Intersex genital surgeries are also problematic because they can result in physical consequences. Pidgeon[7] shared, "my clitoris is gone . . . My vagina looks really fucked up . . . There's some scar tissue there and . . . penetration hurts." Only four of the 37 intersexuals interviewed were not surgically modified (11%). Given the physical consequences of surgery, it wasn't a surprise that only one of the four unaltered intersexuals interviewed desired surgical modification. Although Pidgeon indicated she would ultimately support any intersexual adult who chose to have genital surgery, she still would passionately advise against it:

[N]ever let them touch you in terms of surgery. That's number one. If they ask about surgery or ask your opinion, don't do that. Don't do surgery, no matter what they say. . . . You'll love your body somehow, some way, and you don't need surgery to love your body and love yourself. . . . If you fuck with your body, you can never change that. But if you don't fuck with your body, you can change your acceptance of your body.

Given that intersex genital surgeries result in a loss of sexual pleasure, the question that arises is why do they continue? Many medical professionals claim intersex genital surgeries promote health by minimizing cancer risks, despite only minimal evidence for such claims (see Cools et al., 2006). Another more plausible explanation for why intersex genital surgeries continue has to do with the two-sex binary model that medical professionals, like many throughout society, believe should neatly map onto gender and sexual binaries (Davis, 2011). For instance, Donna was told by her doctor, "you can go to college . . . have sex with any boy you want to." She also shared that "he pushed [her] to be feminine, he pushed [her] to be heterosexual, [and] he pushed [her] to give in to boys." Pidgeon had a similar experience. When she was 10 or 11 in the 1990s, a doctor asked her:

Wouldn't you like to have normal sex with your husband when you're older? We can just fix [your vagina], we can make it a little bit bigger for you. It's just a little snip incision, and [your vagina] will just be a little bit bigger. And then you can feel like normal women and have normal sex.

Intersexuals like Donna and Pidgeon were pressured by medical professionals to undergo surgery in order to fit into the sex binary. Surgically constructed as females, doctors assumed Donna and Pidgeon would adopt a feminine identity and partner with men. However, as I show in the sections that follow, the sex binary model isn't enforced exclusively through surgery. Even those who were able to avoid surgical intervention reported emotional and physical insecurities at some point in their lives, which suggests that the sex binary is connected to a much broader medicalization process beyond surgery.

SEXUAL IDENTITIES AND MEDICAL TERMINOLOGY

Medical professionals frame intersex normalcy (especially after genital surgery) as something one can achieve by romantically partnering with someone of the "opposite" gender. This might, in part, explain why most of the intersexuals I interviewed identified as "straight" or "heterosexual" (32%). However, almost as many intersexuals identified as lesbian, gay, or homosexual (30%). Fewer intersexuals identified themselves as bisexual (11%), queer (11%), or asexual (8%), and several others (8%) either refused to identify themselves, reported that their sexuality was "complicated," or noted that they were "unsure."

DSD is medical terminology that upholds the two-sex system, while intersex language is an identity characteristic that challenges its existence. Given that medical professionals favor DSD terminology because it maintains ideologies that sex, gender, and sexuality are all neatly biologically correlated (Davis, 2011), it makes sense that those who preferred the DSD nomenclature were also more likely to claim a "straight" or "heterosexual" sexuality and actively sought, or maintained, a romantic relationship with an individual of the "opposite" gender. More specifically, among the 32 percent of individuals with an intersex/DSD condition who identified as straight or heterosexual, 75 percent preferred the DSD nomenclature over intersex terminology. When I asked Vanessa what terminology she preferred, she shared, "disorder of sex development . . . I'm pretty comfortable with that . . . intersex [terminology] rubs me the wrong way." Although Hannah wasn't as critical of intersex terminology as was Vanessa, she still preferred DSD language: "I like 'DSD' . . . because if you say 'DSD' [sex is] kind of camouflaged. When you say 'intersex,' it has the word 'sex' right in it and it's like, 'what?' It's kind of a red flag for people."

On the other hand, those who preferred intersex terminology over the DSD nomenclature more often than not identified as "lesbian," "gay," "bisexual," "asexual," or "queer." To be exact, just over 86 percent of those who identified as LGBA or Q preferred intersex terminology while the others either welcomed DSD language (9%) or reported being indifferent about the terminology (5%). They were usually not concerned with fitting into a sex binary that medical professionals believed could neatly be mapped onto gender and sexuality binaries; instead, they typically rejected it. Kimberly shared, "I love the term 'intersex.' For me, it really truly describes me. I am somewhere in between. I believe there's a continuum; it's not a dichotomy." While most who favorably viewed intersex terminology were in same-gender relationships, not all were. Several were, in fact, living in one gender, usually as women, while partnered with a person of the "opposite" gender, usually men. For example, Leigh, a woman who identified as queer, was in a long-term committed relationship with a man. Jeanne, a woman who identified as bisexual, was also involved with a man. Similarly, Chris, a man who identified as asexual, was also partnered with an individual of the "opposite" gender before her untimely death. By rejecting the DSD nomenclature, some intersexuals are able to avoid the medical profession's attempt to force their bodies into sex, gender, and sexuality categories assumed to be neatly biologically correlated.

IN SEARCH OF SEXUAL SATISFACTION

Regardless of surgical history and position on DSD terminology, all of the intersexuals I interviewed indicated some form of sexual anxiety about their "abnormal" bodies. Aimee, who has had surgery, expressed that even the very thought of a romantic relationship resulted in a "crippling effect of fear." Mariela, who also has had surgery, commented, "I'm worried about falling in love and when to disclose. . . . What if . . . he decides he doesn't want to be with me anymore?" Stevie, who had

surgery as a young child, explained how the silencing of her experience affected her ability to relate to others:

So not only was I wounded physically through surgery . . . which I still am dealing with and may surgically revise at some point. . . . I was wounded by the mantling of my very existence being something that should not be discussed . . . the whole notion of connecting with other people especially in intimate relationships.

The few individuals who were not surgically modified offer evidence that the sexual struggles common to intersexuality are not exclusively due to surgery. Kimberly, who has not had surgery, shared, "In relationships I have had, it's always really bothered me that I feel I have to disclose that I'm intersex before I get physically intimate with anybody because it's not like I could fake being normal. . . . I've always resented that." Caitlyn, who also has not had surgery, echoed this sentiment: "Being in sexual relationships with people, that was really hard. I didn't have a positive relationship with my sexuality when I wasn't being honest with the people I was sleeping with." As I describe in the following section, these sexual struggles are dealt with in different ways.

RESPONDING TO SEXUAL STRUGGLES

Intersexuals in this study often employed one of three strategies to handle their sexual struggles: 1) avoid sexual intimacy; 2) seek out heterosexual encounters; or 3) reject medicalization. Intersexuals were not confined to a particular given strategy, although most chose one and never shifted from it.

The first strategy involved avoiding sexual intimacy, and is perhaps the most disheartening. Emily explained, "I don't do intimacy very well. . . . Somewhere around 30 [years old] or so I decided to screw it. I might just not even bother anymore. . . . I'll just be single. . . . That's worked out better." Marilyn, a 50-year-old woman, expressed something similar: "I still haven't had sex. . . . I haven't had a date in the last 20 years. Not a single date." Aimee also avoided intimacy, which even her therapist could not help her overcome. Aimee reported her therapist would say, "I don't really know how to help you with this, other than to tell you: you need to just get out there and get some experience and get over it." Avoiding sexual intimacy was a reliable response to sexual struggles because it offered intersexuals the ability to escape their fears of abnormality. However, this strategy was limited because it leaves the sexual struggles avoided rather than confronted.

The second strategy of dealing with the sexual struggles associated with intersexuality centered on heterosexual encounters that served to validate one's assigned sex (presumed to be neatly biologically correlated with gender and sexuality). This strategy was encouraged by medical professionals who, (as described earlier) urge intersexuals to romantically partner with individuals of the "opposite" gender. In the eyes of medical professionals, heterosexuality is the desired outcome of medical intervention. Individuals with intersex conditions often worry that they are "freaks" or "abnormal" because of their atypical sex anatomies. One way to overcome these feelings was to engage in sexual encounters with the "opposite" gender. Tara said, "I slept with a decent amount of guys that I . . . don't think I should have, but I think it was the whole fact that I wanted to feel like a . . . a woman." Leigh had a similar experience: "When I was a young adult . . . like 16 through . . . 20, I went through this period where I was trying to prove to myself that I was feminine and I just engaged in some risky sexual behaviors [with men]. I think that really interfered with my

life, and left some lasting marks." Jenna also looked to heterosexual encounters to normalize her body and feel appropriately gendered. She shared:

I still have issues with the fact that I have AIS. . . . It's not a debilitating sort of thing . . . but . . . I think about it frequently. . . . I don't feel like I'm less of a woman or anything . . . but one thing I have noticed about me like sexually is that . . . I have something to prove. . . . I'm like . . . I'm a woman, damn it! . . . And I'm going to take care of business and . . . you're gonna be like: . . . "That's the best I ever had!" . . . . It's like on some sort of subconscious level . . . I want to prove that I'm a woman and I can take care of this man's needs.

When I asked Jenna to elaborate, she provided an example:

Let's say that your orgasm is a 100 on a scale of 0 to 100 . . . for me having my partner reach climax which obviously with a dude it's ridiculously easy . . . but having my partner climax is 95 out of 100. . . . It doesn't make me . . . but the satisfaction I get from that . . . is almost as much as me orgasm-ing . . . cause I'm like: FUCK YEAH! I DID THAT!!! THIS XY!! BA BAM! I'm not joking that's how I am! . . . I'm like THAT'S WHAT I'M TALKING ABOUT!

Tara, Leigh, and Jenna all sought out heterosexual activity in order to normalize their intersex conditions. By engaging in heterosexual activity, they were able to feel, in Leigh's words, "feminine."

The third strategy involved rejecting medicalization by holding onto intersex as an identity characteristic in the face of the new DSD nomenclature. Caitlin described what the term "intersex" meant to her: "I feel very emotionally connected to that word because it really did change my life for the better. So kind of moving away from that word does definitely bring up some emotional response of like no! [Intersex] really empowered me." Those who chose to employ this third strategy reached liberation without relying on others, something they wished everyone with intersex conditions could experience. Consequently, they were critical of those who supported DSD terminology. Millarca explained:

These girls [who favor DSD] are in relationships because they're trying to be normal. They don't want to be different, but they are different and they can't accept that. We're different. You're different, and I'm different. That's where the turmoil lies . . . in trying to be something you're not. If you can accept who you are, like I have, like other people have, what other people say don't mean shit. You're not trying to switch into some other box where you know damn well you can't fit into.

The first step in this strategy's process of overcoming sexual struggles involved embracing intersexuality while rejecting the search for normalcy.

Although Millarca was critical of those "trying to be normal," she was also sympathetic. She hoped they would eventually come around. Many of those who hold onto intersex terminology spoke of sexual satisfaction as a process that began with information about the condition. Irene shared, "I grew up being heterosexual, and . . . I think I evolved as I found out my condition. I felt more in touch with both sides of how I feel and so I feel I'm somewhere in between." Leigh, who earlier in her life had used the strategy of seeking out heterosexual encounters to minimize feelings of abnormality (the second strategy), decided in her twenties to embrace her intersexuality and reject the two-sex model. Although she remained interested in men, she now identifies as queer. This strategy reduced the sexual struggles she experienced as a teenager. Similarly, as a teenager, Ana adopted the first strategy of avoiding intimacy by burying "any hint of sexuality at all." Now, as a partnered woman in her late thirties, she embraces her sexuality, and a more fluid one at that. She revealed, "I probably could have gone either way. But I probably decided at one point that women are for me and I'll put my energy there and I won't

think about it anymore." Kimberly had a similar experience:

Growing up, and dealing with being intersexed and ashamed and the secrecy, I was very asexual. I simply didn't allow myself to have an orientation. I didn't allow myself to be attracted to anybody. Now I can be, and I'm really enjoying it. I think [my female partner's right], I never wore dresses before because I never felt I could pull them off. Now I feel like I can. I've got enough ego to really enjoy the body [*laughing*].

Rejecting the medicalization of intersexuality by rejecting the language of "disorder" resulted in a very real form of liberation that was often enforced by supportive friendship networks. Leigh expressed: "My friends have been incredibly supportive and really love me for this. One of my friends actually made me a t-shirt for my birthday one year that said, 'She's bringing intersexy back.'"

CONCLUSION

The sexual struggles associated with intersexuality need to be understood as part of a broader medicalization process and not just in relation to surgical history. The danger of focusing exclusively on surgery is that it reduces the medicalization process to the operating room. Intersex genital surgery poses real problems for intersexuals, but it is not the only piece in the medicalization puzzle. While sexual struggles are common to people's experience of intersexuality, some intersexuals minimized them by enacting one or more of three strategies: avoiding intimacy; seeking out heterosexual encounters; or rejecting medicalization by "bringing intersexy back." If we accept that sex is something that everyone should be able to experience if they so desire, the first strategy seems to fall short. Many intersexuals who adopt this strategy do not voluntarily *choose* it. Instead, they feel it is the only option, given their sexual insecurities. The second strategy is also inadequate in that it involves engaging in heterosexual encounters not for one's own sexual pleasure, but for validation that one is appropriately gendered. Rather than eliminate insecurities, this strategy tended to create new ones. The third strategy seems to be the most liberatory. By rejecting the medicalization of intersexuality, and the pathologizing *disorder* of sex development terminology that goes along with it, intersexuals can begin to overcome their sexual anxieties in the search for sexual pleasure. Kimberly says it best:

There is a lot of freedom in living outside the rules. If you can make that switch into seeing the freedom, it's really fabulous. . . . You get to really, truly, have an authentic experience that's all your own, and you start seeing how being "normal" is so limiting.

REFERENCES

Biernacki, Patrick, and Dan Waldorf. 1981. "Snowball Sampling: Problems and Techniques of Chain Referral Sampling." *Sociological Methodology* 10:141–163.

Blackless, Melanie, Anthony Charuvastra, Amanda Derryck, Anne Fausto-Sterling, Karl Lauzanne, and Ellen Lee. 2000. "How Sexually Dimorphic Are We? Review and Synthesis." *American Journal of Human Biology* 12:151–166.

Brown, Phil. 2007. *Toxic Exposures: Contested Illnesses and the Environmental Health Movement*. New York: Columbia University Press.

———1995. Naming and framing: The social construction of diagnosis and illness. *Journal of Health and Social Behavior*, 35: 34–52.

———1990. "The Name Game: Towards a Sociology of Diagnosis." *The Journal of Mind and Behavior* 11(3/4): 385–406.

Chase, Cheryl. 2002. " 'Cultural Practice' or 'Reconstructive Surgery'? U.S. Genital Cutting, the Intersex Movement, and Medical Double Standards." Pp. 126-151 in Stanlie M. James and Claire C. Robertson. (Eds.) *Genital Cutting and Transnational Sisterhood: Disputing U.S. Polemics*. Chicago: University of Illinois Press.

Committee on Genetics: Section on Endocrinology and Section on Urology. 2000. "Evaluation of the newborn with developmental anomalies of the external genitalia." *Pediatrics* 106:138–142.

Conrad, Peter. 2007. *The Medicalization of Society: On the Transformation of Society*. Baltimore, MD: Johns Hopkins University Press.

Consortium on the Management of Disorders of Sex Development. 2006. "Clinical Guidelines for the Management of Disorders of Sex Development in Childhood." Retrieved January 13, 2012: www .accordalliance.org/dsd-guidelines.html.

Cooksey, Elizabeth. C., and Brown, Phil. 1998. "Spinning on its Axes: DSM and the Social Construction of Psychiatric Diagnosis." *International Journal of Health Services* 28(3):525–554.

Cools, Martine, Stenvert L. S. Drop, Katja P. Wolffenbuttel, J. Wolter Oosterhuis, and Leendert H. J. Looijenga. 2006. "Germ Cell Tumors in the Intersex Gonad: Old Paths, New Directions, Moving Frontiers." *Endocrine Reviews*. 27(5):468–484.

Davis, Georgiann. 2011. " 'DSD is a Perfectly Fine Term' ": Reasserting Medical Authority Through a Shift in Intersex Terminology. In McGann, PJ, and Hutson, D.J. (Eds.), *Sociology of Diagnosis* (155–182). United Kingdom: Emerald.

Dreger, Alice Domurat. 1998a. *Hermaphrodites and the Medical Intervention of Sex*. Cambridge, MA: Harvard University Press.

———1998b. "Ambiguous Sex—or Ambivalent Medicine? Ethical Issues in the Treatment of Intersexuality." *Hastings Center Report* 28(3):24–35.

Fausto-Sterling, Anne. 2000a. *Sexing the Body: Gender Politics and the Construction of Sexuality*. New York, NY: Basic Books.

———2000b. "The Five Sexes, Revisited." *The Sciences* 40(4):18–23.

———1996. "How to Build a Man." In *Science and Homosexualities*, ed. Vernon A. Rosario, 219–225. New York: Routledge.

———1993. "The Five Sexes: Why Male and Female Are Not Enough." *The Sciences* 33(2):20–25.

Karkazis, Katrina. 2008. *Fixing Sex: Intersex, Medical Authority, and Lived Experience*. Durham, NC: Duke University Press.

Kessler, Suzanne J. 1998. *Lessons from the Intersexed*. New Brunswick, NJ: Rutgers University Press.

———1990. "The Medical Construction of Gender: Case Management of Intersexed Infants." *Signs* 16(1):3–26.

Kitzinger, Celia. 2005. "Heteronormativity in Action: Reproducing the Heterosexual Nuclear Family in After-hours Medical Calls." *Social Problems* 52(4): 477–98.

Köhler, Birgit, Eva Kleinemeier, Anke Lux, Olaf Hiort, Annette Gruters, Ute Thyen, and the DSD Network Working Group. 2012. "Satisfaction with Genital Surgery and Sexual Life of Adults with XY Disorders of Sex Development: Results from the German Clinical Evaluation Study." *Journal of Clinical Endocrinology & Metabolism*. 97(2): 577–588.

Lee, Peter. A., Houk, Christopher. P., S. Faisal Ahmed, and Ieuan A. Hughes. 2006. "Consensus Statement on Management of Intersex Disorders." *Pediatrics* 118(2):488–500.

Preves, Sharon E. 2003. *Intersex and Identity: The Contested Self*. New Brunswick, NJ: Rutgers University Press.

———2002. "Sexing the Intersexed: An Analysis of Sociocultural Responses to Intersexuality." *Signs* 27(2)523–556.

———2000. "Negotiating the Constraints of Gender Binarism: Intersexuals Challenge Gender Categorization." *Current Sociology* 48(3):27–50.

Schilt, Kristen, and Laurel Westbrook. 2009. "Doing Gender, Doing Heteronormativity: 'Gender Normals,' Transgender People, and the Social Maintenance of Heterosexuality." *Gender & Society* 23(4):440–464.

Serano, Julia. 2007. *Whipping Girl: A Transsexual Woman on Sexism and the Scapegoating of Femininity*. Emeryville, CA: Seal Press.

van der Zwan, Yvonne G., Nina Callens, Stenvert Drop, Martine Cools, Catharina Beerendonk, Katja P. Wolffenbuttel, and Arianne Dessens. In press. "Do surgical interventions influence psychosexual and cosmetic outcomes in women with Disorders of Sex Development?" *ISRN Endocrinology*.

NOTES

1. I use the language of "intersex" and "intersexuality" throughout this paper as opposed to "disorders of sex development" for three reasons. First, due to the greater visibility such words have had in academic publications over the newer terminology "disorders of sex development," I felt it was necessary to continue to reach a broader audience. Second, recent publications in the medical sciences have, for the most part, abandoned "intersex" language despite the fact that not all individuals with such conditions prefer "disorders of sex development" terminology. Third, and the main reason for my choice in terminology, as an individual with an intersex condition, I prefer intersex language over DSD nomenclature.

2. Although we don't have any reliable estimates that capture the frequency of intersexuality in the population, attempts at estimating the intersexed population have been made. Blackless et al. (2000), for example, have estimated that intersexuality appears in 1 in 100 births. However, Fausto-Sterling (2000a) offers a different estimate that ranges from 1 in 1,000 to 1 in 2,000. These different estimates warrant skepticism of any attempts to estimate the prevalence of intersexuality.

3. It should be noted infertile heterosexuals are still understood as appropriately gendered.

4. Androgen Insensitivity Syndrome Support Group-USA was recently renamed AIS-DSD Support Group for Women and Families.

5. Since the numbers of individuals who supported DSD terminology and those who were against it were similar, I find it misleading to use majority and minority terminology in this context.

6. One intersexed individual out of the 37 noted here is a medical professional with an intersex condition.

7. Participant has indicated preference for this spelling of the chosen pseudonym. In an earlier publication, the pseudonym was spelled "Pigeon" (see Davis, 2011).

THE PERILS AND PLEASURES OF SEX FOR TRANS PEOPLE

HARPER JEAN TOBIN

In the popular imagination, people who cross gender boundaries are rarely seen as happy, healthy people in satisfying sexual relationships. We are typically slotted into stereotypes such as asexual confidante, freaky fetish object, lonely tragic hero(ine), or conniving deceiver. Think of films like *The Crying Game, Boys Don't Cry, All About My Mother, Transamerica* or even *Hedwig and the Angry Inch*. In reality, transgender people are as sexually diverse as anyone else, just as we are diverse in race, class, gender, age, and geography. In recent surveys, one-quarter to one-third of trans people identified themselves as gay or lesbian (transgender men who love men and transgender women who love women), and another one-quarter to one-third identified as heterosexual. A similar number of transgender people identified as bisexual, and the rest identified as "queer" or something else.[1] Fifty percent of transgender people are partnered or married according to a recent national survey,[2] and many others are single and happily sexually active. Transgender people practice monogamy, polyamory, abstinence, recreational sex, kinky sex, and conventional sex. We have the same range of desires for intimacy, power, vulnerability, security, intense sensations, orgasms, creativity, playfulness, and more. And we face the same sexual challenges: inhibition, difficulty communicating effectively, difficulty getting aroused or reaching orgasm, sexual trauma, and anxieties about our performance and our bodies. This essay explores how these desires and challenges are impacted by having an identity, a life experience, and in many cases a body, that does not conform to cultural expectations about gender.

WHO ARE TRANS PEOPLE?

Every person has a *gender identity*—an internal sense of self that we are aware of from a young age, which usually corresponds to the gender we are assigned at birth. You've probably most often encountered the word *transgender* in reference to people who are assigned one gender at birth but who strongly identify and eventually go through a *gender transition* to live their daily lives as members of the "opposite" gender. Such a person may be a transgender woman (such as myself) who was assigned male at birth but lives and identifies as a woman, or a transgender man, who was assigned female at birth but lives and identifies as a man. When used in this way, the term *transgender* is roughly synonymous with the older term *transsexual*.

But "transgender" can also refer to a wide variety of people whose identities and self-expressions vary from gender norms. *Transgender* (used interchangeably in this essay with the abbreviated "*trans*") can encompass identities that don't fit the narrative of male-to-female or female-to-male transition. Many people identify as *genderqueer*, meaning that they identify and express themselves in ways that mix or defy categories of male and female, but which feel simply authentic to them. Genderqueer individuals "describe their gender identity as being a combination of female and male; as neither female nor male but as a different gender altogether; or as somewhere 'in between' female and male."[3] Some genderqueer folks prefer to use gender-neutral pronouns such as *ze* and *hir*.

Whether we identify as male, female, genderqueer, or something else, trans people often reshape our bodies to better reflect our internal sense of self. This can involve daily steps such as binding one's chest to present a flatter appearance, as well as more permanent steps such as hormone therapy or surgery. A common misconception is that gender transition equals genital reconstruction surgery. While genital reconstruction is essential for some people, genitals are not the end-all and be-all of gender. Some of us have arrived at this truth because we accept that the bodily changes we might want are out of reach, for financial or medical reasons. Some of us, taking into account the limitations of current surgical techniques and the stress, pain, and risk of complications that accompany any major surgery, have simply not felt the need to take every possible medical step. According to national survey data, only about 20 percent of transsexual women have had some sort of genital surgery, and only about 5 percent of transsexual men have. While "top" surgery to achieve a flatter chest is the most common gender surgery for trans men, not all of them have that either.[4]

That means that most (though not all) trans people have bodies that, to varying degrees, differ from the norm. A trans woman like myself may have breasts that are curvy or completely flat. She may still have the genitals she was born with, their size and function perhaps altered by estrogen and testosterone blockers. She may call that part of her body her *clit*, her *cock*, her *ladystick*, her *girldick*, her *strapless* (as opposed to strap-on), or any other term, or she may prefer not to refer to it explicitly. These variations in language reflect the basic fact that every person's genitals develop from the same fetal anatomical structures; the penis and clitoris, labia and scrotum, are basically the same body parts to begin with. A trans man may have a surgically flattened chest or a fleshier one that has not been surgically altered, which he may or may not bind, may

or may not refer to as *breasts*, and may or may not like to have touched. He may have a hormonally and perhaps also surgically enhanced phallus, smaller than most *cisgender* (i.e., non-transgender) men's phalluses, but much larger than a cisgender woman's clitoris. And he may have an orifice he refers to as a *pussy*, a *front hole*, a *manhole*, or any other terms, or he may prefer not to talk about that body part in such explicit ways.

Being trans can present some dating challenges. If you are genderqueer, it can be uncomfortable to explain to a potential date that you aren't the girl or boy they think you look like. If you've transitioned to living as a gender different from the one you were assigned at birth, there is no perfect moment on a date to tell someone that certain things about your body or your history aren't what they might expect. Coming out as trans to a potential partner carries risks: encountering reactions of shock and disdain; being rejected by way of mockery and humiliation; being reduced to a freaky fetish object; and possibly even experiencing a violent reaction. Dating or hooking up with a trans or genderqueer person can inspire insecurities for some people about their own identities. Jakob Hero, a gay trans man, relates the dilemma this can present when one is the catalyst for such anxieties: "From my first interactions with gay men I have had to hold, comfort, and reassure them while they go through total crises about my body. For the first few years after transition I was very open to them and to their struggles [regarding my body and gender history], but eventually it took its toll."[5] I've heard a lot of stories like that—about lovers, dates, tricks, gay and straight, men and women, freaking out that they're attracted to someone with an unexpected identity or body part. But as the statistics previously cited would suggest, many trans folks of all sexualities are happy and successful in their romantic partnerships and dating adventures, such as Bryn Kelly, a trans woman who wrote in an essay about her boyfriend:

I love how I can drag his ass to trans [events] and he is totally nonplussed. I love how he can be the only non-trans person in a room and not think there's anything all that unusual. . . . I know that some people who know about my trans history might have a few questions about his sexuality but one thing I love about him is how he really has no problems with it. When I ask him, "Are you ever worried that people might think you're gay?" He says, "Nah. Besides, there's nothing wrong with being gay."[6]

NAVIGATING BODIES AND IDENTITIES

Once trans people connect with a sexual partner—for a night or a lifetime—we have to figure out what to do together, and that is my main subject here. Many of us, trans and cisgender, struggle with cultural ideals about male and female bodies and beauty that our own bodies and gender expressions may not match—worrying whether your body is thin enough, pretty enough, hairless enough, normal enough, ad nauseam, can be a real obstacle to intimacy. Many of us have sometimes felt that, as S. Bear Bergman writes, "There's no part of me able to trust that this complicated body with all its speed bumps and dead ends will remain a viable route once someone is seriously considering setting off on it, when all the limitations are so visible."[7]

Trans people frequently experience a gap between our innate sense of identity and the meanings inscribed on specific parts of our bodies. Our culture assigns gendered names and meanings to body parts. *This body part*, says our culture, *is a penis—it is a male part, and it makes you a man. And this*, it says, *is a vulva—it is a female part, and it makes you a woman.*[8] The disconnect many people feel between their gender identity and these cultural definitions assigned to body parts has been crudely described as

being *trapped in the wrong body*. For some trans people, this disconnect manifests as discomfort or ambivalence about certain parts of our bodies. The prospect of letting other people see and touch certain parts of our bodies, and receiving and giving pleasure through them, can be frightening. Sometimes we fear that particular sexual activities would contradict our deepest sense of self, or even invalidate it.

For some of us, our anxiety is not so much about our own relationship with our bodies, as about whether another person will see, understand, and accept our bodies, our identities, and our desires. Sometimes we fear that seeing and interacting with our bodies will cause our lovers, our health care providers, or others in our lives to doubt or reject our identities—and, perhaps, to either reject us or reduce us to a sexual fetish. Or, we fear that others will desire us, or will truly see us as we see ourselves, only so long as our own desires don't include sexual activities that they might deem inconsistent with our identities. We might have been told in the past that our identities or desires are not valid, and we may have struggled not to internalize those messages. We may struggle to find a language to communicate to our partners how we see our bodies and our desires in a way that honors who we are.

We all have the right to sexual pleasure, regardless of our gender identity, our anatomy, or the steps we have or have not taken to outwardly affirm that identity. Even if we expect to make (further) changes to our bodies to make them better reflect our identity at some point in the future, we shouldn't have to wait that long to have a sexual relationship, or just a sexual fling. We deserve to have intimacy and pleasure with the bodies we have, right here, right now. To do that, we have to ask ourselves questions that anyone might ask, such as: *What is it that I value or need sexually? Physical closeness? Emotional intimacy? The opportunity to be vulnerable, or to experience my partner's vulnerability? The opportunity to take or to surrender con-*

trol? To have or to give a partner orgasms? To feel affirmed as a man, a woman, masculine, feminine, beautiful, strong, dominant, submissive, boy, girl, or something else?

To those questions trans people must add an understanding of what stands between us and our desires. *What is it about sex, or the prospect of sex, that is uncomfortable for me in the body I have?* It may be engaging in particular acts that we tend to think of as male or female, masculine or feminine. It may be being unable to engage in particular physical acts we long for. For some, it is having a partner see, touch, talk about, or think about certain parts of their body. Or, it may be seeing, touching, talking, or thinking about certain parts of one's own body, certain ways of being touched that feel better or worse, more discordant or "just right." The answers are different for every trans person. Together with our partners, we figure out how to move away from the feelings and associations that make good sex difficult, and toward being our truest and most satisfied sexual selves. That means not only identifying sexual acts that do and don't work for us, but also finding ways to approach and contextualize specific acts so that they feel right for us.

Some trans people prefer to focus their sexual energy on their partner's body instead of their own. Driving one's partner wild can, for many, be the most exciting and satisfying part of sex. Butch queer activist Koja Adeyoha—who prefers to mix gendered pronouns—spoke at a recent sexuality conference about identifying as a *stone butch*, which s/he explained means that "I limit access to myself sexually and emotionally . . . and I express my desire through other people." Bastien said that s/he used to struggle with this and experience it as "a really pathologized identity for me," feeling that somehow s/he ought to want and be comfortable with his body being the center of sexual attention. But, s/he reflected, s/he and her partner ultimately realized that "this can

just be a hot thing that we embrace." Wanting to control or limit how we are sexually viewed or touched doesn't have to be viewed as a hang-up to get over. On the contrary, embracing the kinds of sex that work for you, and clearly identifying and letting go of the kinds that don't, can be incredibly freeing.

For some of us, it's not so much about whether or not our bodies are touched and stimulated, but *how*. Certain kinds of touch can feel affirming and others discordant. A man may like to have his chest stroked and his nipples played with, but dislike having his chest cupped or squeezed like a woman's breasts. A trans woman may not like to have her genitals directly touched by a partner, but may get off from grinding against a lover's body, wearing a strap-on dildo, or stimulating herself while being anally penetrated. A genderqueer person might enjoy receiving oral sex, but dislike having hir genitals licked in a way ze associates with going down on a woman. Instead, ze may want hir partner to wrap her lips around hir *dicklet* (hir term for the body part that cisgender women call the clitoris) and suck it, more in the manner we associate with a blowjob.

Talking about the acts we're sharing with our partners in a way that reflects our own conception of our bodies and identities can also be essential to feeling connected to our identities. A friend of mine, a gay trans man, relates struggling in one of his past relationships to navigate sex acts he physically enjoyed in a way that allowed him to feel affirmed in his male identity. Notice the ways he reimagines and renames his sexual body in this struggle:

[O]ne of the many reasons why it didn't work was totally different assumptions we came to sex with. I rarely [fucked my partner], because there wasn't room for the communication and logistics required for me to strap-on without completely derailing the sex for him. . . . After I got naked with him (which was after we'd had what I consider sex many times), we almost exclusively had coitus. Coitus is easy, [but challenged my ability to feel seen as a gay man because] gay men didn't have coitus. But all the same, I love [coitus], and I love it best when my partner tells me how good it feels to have my cock in his vagina, even though the physical reality is the opposite [i.e., that my partner is penetrating me]. That kind of mental play and flexibility requires imagination and talking dirty to show everyone else how you're imagining things[.][9]

The "mental play and flexibility" and dirty talk my friend describes can make all the difference in bridging the apparent gap between body and identity—and between ambivalent sex and good sex. It can allow him to collaborate with his partner to feel confident and sexy putting on a strap-on cock, rather than to feel that his lack of typical male genitals was highlighted by the need to pause to put on a harness. Similarly, it can allow him to feel seen and affirmed in his maleness while enjoying being penetrated in a body part associated with femaleness.

For some trans folks, less common sexual practices such as BDSM (short for bondage/discipline, dominance/submission, and sadomasochism) can provide spaces of erotic empowerment—a space in which top and bottom, dominant and submissive, or other erotic roles can be much more salient than gender. In BDSM communities explicit and detailed sexual negotiation, including discussing specific language in an encounter, is also more normalized, which can make hooking up with someone new a less intimidating prospect. Moreover, BDSM practices can involve intense erotic experiences that aren't focused on genital sex, such as flogging, spanking, or temporary piercing—providing intense physical excitement and release without genitals or orgasms even being involved.

A trans woman in a BDSM relationship with another woman shared the following:

My girlfriend is also my submissive. I love making her suck my cock—and that is the way we talk about it. I'm embarrassed by my body in so many ways. I

usually don't like being seen naked or talking about my genitals explicitly—but when we are playing, it's different. When I am in control of her, whatever I desire is okay and she is eager to give it to me. Penetrating her with my body, any part of my body, makes sense.[10]

Erotic role-play can also provide, for some, a space to enact scenarios that allow us to explore or affirm our identities. Genderqueer and mixed-race writer A.P. Andre, for example, writes about experimenting with gender roles during sex as a key part of "trying to figure out what genders I am or might be and also figure out my personal relationship to black masculinity. That's been, at times, a scary process for me. So, when we're having sex and I'm able to use the space to play with the male parts of my identity and to play with being a boy, it feels very safe for me. I really appreciate that, because I feel like it's not a very safe world for the expression of black masculinity in any body. But in bed, in a sexual context [with partners I trust], I can go there with myself and see what it means to be masculine—well, I'm not a very masculine boy!—but see what it means to be a very femme-y boy, and have it celebrated and eroticized."[11]

We all have the right to define our identities, and to choose and define the meanings of our sexual practices, rather than having them assigned based on any cultural script. Queer communities have effectively modeled and affirmed myriad combinations of masculinity/femininity, male/female, active/passive and penetrating/receiving. Plenty of cisgender women enjoy penetrating their partners, and plenty of cisgender men love being penetrated. This is demonstrated by many heterosexual couples who enjoy strap-on "pegging" (i.e., a woman penetrating her male partner with a strap-on dildo). From these increasingly commonplace insights it also follows that if (for example) you identify as a man, no one can tell you that any part of your body, or anything you choose to do with it, is not male. In this way, trans and genderqueer people strive to claim ownership of our bodies, resisting dominant cultural scripts, and refusing to acknowledge any incongruity or reason for shame in our bodies or our desires— a fine aspiration for anyone and everyone.

HOW TO HAVE SEX WITH A (TRANS) PERSON

In hir essay, "Made Real," Sassafras Lowrey observes that for trans and genderqueer people, sex can be a minefield, riddled with dangers— the danger of feeling divorced from our bodies, of being misperceived, and of being unable to realize our true desires. "Our minds," Lowrey writes, are "so indoctrinated by narrow definitions of sex, we come to think it's an act which can never include us." At the same time, ze observes, sex can affirm who we are, make us feel whole and at home in ourselves. To be seen and to connect with someone as just who you truly are—a sweet boy, a strong woman, a beautiful gender-fluid person—can heal and strengthen. "Sex," Lowrey writes, "gave me my body back."[12]

As previously noted, sex can be complicated for everyone, and trans and genderqueer people are not so different from cisgender people in that regard. We all would benefit from more and better communication with our partners about the kinds of sex we want to have. For that reason, this essay concludes with some specific suggestions for sexual communication that may be particularly salient if one's partner is trans, but which are applicable to—and would probably make for better sex with—anyone.

First, *avoid relying on assumptions about your partner*. Try not to assume what a person's identity is, what their body is like, what words they like to use for it, or what they like to do with it. These assumptions can limit your ability to truly see and connect with each other. Second, *ask where and how your partner wants to be touched*. This is more effective—and more fun—than trial and error. They may be able to tell you exactly what works and doesn't for them—or they may be in the process of figuring that out, in which case your asking helps give them permission to be unsure and to explore and figure it out with you. Third, *ask what words they use for their body parts*. The right words can be huge turn-ons and the wrong ones huge turn-offs, and which is which is different for everyone. Just ask, "What do you call this part of you?"—then you can talk dirty with confidence. Again, your partner may still be figuring out what works for them, and you can help them do that by being flexible and open to trying different terms and seeing how each one feels for them. Fourth, *communicate your own desires*. It takes (at least) two to connect, and while what you have in mind may not be the same, you won't know if you don't express it. Fifth, *respect your partner's boundaries*. This is the basic obligation we owe all our sexual partners. We all have different boundaries, and they may fluctuate. Respecting them makes hot, connected sex possible. Finally, and critically, *make space for creativity*. The ways people can connect sexually are virtually unlimited, and they aren't—or don't need to be—determined or limited by our identities. It may take negotiation and practice to discover the places where your partner's desires and boundaries can match up with your own. Although our sexual needs and desires are infinitely varied, the fundamentals of good sex are similar for everyone. For trans people—and indeed for everyone—sex can and should be a safe place where we can connect with, explore, and affirm ourselves and one another.

NOTES

1. JM Grant, LA Mottet, J Tanis, et al. 2011. *Injustice at Every Turn: A Report of the National Transgender Discrimination Survey*, 29. Washington, DC: National Center for Transgender Equality and National Gay and Lesbian Task Force; Genny Beemyn and Susan Rankin. 2011. *The Lives of Transgender People*, 33–34. New York, NY: Columbia University Press.

2. JM Grant, LA Mottet, J Tanis, et al. 2011. *Injustice at Every Turn: A Report of the National Transgender Discrimination Survey*, 29. Washington, DC: National Center for Transgender Equality and National Gay and Lesbian Task Force.

3. Genny Beemyn and Susan Rankin. 2011. *The Lives of Transgender People*, 147. New York, NY: Columbia University Press.

4. JM Grant, LA Mottet, J Tanis, et al. 2011. *Injustice at Every Turn: A Report of the National Transgender Discrimination Survey*, 79. Washington, DC: National Center for Transgender Equality and National Gay and Lesbian Task Force.

5. Jakob Hero, "Out of the Darkness." 2011. In Morty Diamond (ed.). *Trans/love: Radical Sex, Love & Relationships Beyond the Gender Binary*, 26, 27–28. San Francisco: Manic D. Press.

6. Brynn Kelly, "Fifty Reasons I Love My Man," 2011. In Morty Diamond (ed.). *Trans/love: Radical Sex, Love & Relationships Beyond the Gender Binary*, 60, 62–63. San Francisco: Manic D. Press.

7. S. Bear Bergman, "Gay Men, Queer Men, and Me." 2009. In *The Nearest Exit May Be Behind You: Essays*, 164, 168 Vancouver: Arsenal Pulp Press.

8. On the social construction of gendered bodies, see generally Suzanne J Kessler and Wendy McKenna. 1978. *Gender: An Ethnomethodological Approach* (University of Chicago Press); Anne Fausto-Sterling, *Sexing the Body: Gender Politics and the Construction of Sexuality*. 2000. (New York, NY: Basic Books). The Australian Family Court succinctly summarized the issue when it concluded, after a review of current medical science, that "[a]ttributing some kind of primacy to [a particular] aspect of the person [in determining a person's gender] is not a medical conclusion. It is a social or legal one." *Kevin v. Att'y Gen.* (Re Kevin), (2001) 165 Fam. L.R. 404, 463 (Austl.).

9. Personal communication, October 2009.

10. Personal communication, October 2009.

11. A.P. Andre and Luis Gutierrez-Mock, "In Our Skin." 2010. In Kate Bornstein and S. Bear Bergman (eds.). *Gender Outlaws: The Next Generation*, 157, 159 Berkeley, CA: Seal Press.

12. Sassafras Lowrey, "Made Real." 2011. In Morty Diamond (ed.). *Trans/love: Radical Sex, Love & Relationships Beyond the Gender Binary*, 96, 96–97. San Francisco: Manic D. Press.

STRAIGHT DUDE SEEKS SAME: MAPPING THE RELATIONSHIP BETWEEN SEXUAL IDENTITIES, PRACTICES, AND CULTURES

JANE WARD

In January of 2005, I discovered the following personal ad in the Casual Encounters section of Craigslist Los Angeles, an online community bulletin board:

Let's Stroke It Together NOW! All (Str8) Guys to Str8 Porn, Hot:
I have done this now about 20 times and it never fails to amaze me how hot it can get. Nothing gay here at all, just two guys, watching hot porn, stroking until just before the point of no return and stopping. It hits the ceiling when we finally pop. Something about two guys stroking it together touches most guys and they feel comfortable after about 3 minutes, then it's heaven. Testosterone city!

When I read this ad for the first time, I was at a meeting with queer feminist colleagues, all of whom, including myself, marveled at the suggestion that the ad was anything but gay. At best, we imagined that this man was sexually repressed; at worst, we imagined his life "in the closet" and the pain caused by so much internalized homophobia. Yet as we scanned through three days of Craigslist postings, we discovered dozens of similar ads in which straight men were soliciting sex with other men.

The ads point to the complex and often seemingly contradictory relationship between sexual identities, sexual practices, and sexual cultures. Is there really "nothing gay here at all"? What are the social and political stakes of arguing that there is or isn't something gay about sex between straight-identified men? And why were my friends and I (as queer) so invested in owning a cultural space that is so decidedly intent on identifying with heterosexuality?

Metro-sexuality discourses and television shows such as *Queer Eye for the Straight Guy* have inundated us with knowledge about the pairing of heterosexual sex and ostensibly queer culture (Miller 2005). However, sociological knowledge about how same-sex sexuality lives and flourishes within "heterosexual culture" has generally been limited to the study of total institutions, such as prisons and the military, in which heterosexual sex is presumably unavailable (Kaplan, 2003, Schifter, 1999). In response to these questions and the lack of sociological research that engages them, I decided to conduct a small pilot study of the "STR8 dude" community on Craigslist in order to explore a different side of queer heterosexuality—gay sex for the straight guys, or what I call "dude sex." Research assistants and I collected and coded 118 Craigslist ads in which straight-identified men solicited sex with other men.[1] The findings of the study point not only to the ways in which heterosexuality is constructed and authenticated among men who have sex with men, but also to the limitations of current sociological analyses of these kinds of sexual relationships. Despite the temptation to view the men who post on Craigslist as closeted or to invoke other ideas about repressed homosexuality, I emphasize here the theoretical and political importance of reading their ads as they wish them to be read—as one among myriad manifestations of *heterosexuality*.

Like Blackness in the nineteenth century, homosexuality is often implicitly subject to a one-drop rule, in which any same-sex sexual experience muddies the waters of heterosexuality at best, and marks one as either an open or repressed homosexual, at worst. Even to the extent that we allow for the identity "bisexual," this identity is also frequently suspect as a form of repressed homosexuality (Hutchins and Ka'ahumanu, 1991). On the one hand, the one-drop system maintains heterosexual privileges by policing the boundaries of heterosexuality and homosexuality and ensuring that the smallest indiscretion can become cause for harassment, isolation, or violence. Even those carefully prescribed social contexts in which we allow heterosexuals to engage in queer transgression, presumably without being severely stigmatized (e.g., adolescent boys "experimenting," college women making out at parties for male onlookers) are accompanied by shame and self-doubt that can only be assuaged by disclaimers about developmental theories or drunkenness. On the other hand, to "own" all same-sex sexuality as queer terrain has also been a useful political strategy for the lesbian and gay movement, and one that has been supported by scholarship on sexuality. From Kinsey's (1948) sexual identity scale to Adrienne Rich's (1980) lesbian continuum, many theorists of sexual identity have asserted that almost *everyone* engages in some form of same-sex desire and practice, and that variation is largely a matter of degree or quantity. Continuum models of sexual identity lay the groundwork for resisting the gay/straight binary, yet do so by illustrating that many people who call themselves "straight" might actually be closer to the gay end of the continuum. In the end, it appears we are all invested, for different reasons, in calling as many people and behaviors "gay" as possible, a practice that leaves the gay/straight binary intact.

As Eve Sedgwick explains in *Epistemology of the Closet* (1992), the notion of "the closet" implies a real or essential "gay self" that is waiting to be revealed. It implies some truth of sexuality that exists outside of the social pro-cess of its naming and confession. Similarly, continuum models of sexuality tend to rank people as more or less gay or straight based on the quantity of their same-sex desires and practices, overlooking the social context in which sexuality is given form and shape. Are straight women who "get it on" when they get drunk at parties "more gay" than lesbian couples I know who, for many reasons, rarely ever have sex anymore? Are the straight dudes on Craigslist "more gay" than a man who comes out in his late 50s and spends several years finding a sexual partner? According to social constructionist theory, it is difficult to answer these questions because homosexuality and heterosexuality do not refer to essential aspects of the self or some quantifiable set of sexual practices, but to the culturally and historically specific language used to explain and regulate sexuality (Almaguer, 1993, Blackwood and Wieringa, 1999, Fausto-Sterling, 2000, Foucault, 1978, Seabrook, 1999). In other words, gay and straight are what we decide they are, and how we make these decisions varies across time and place.

GAY SEX VERSUS DUDE SEX

The erotic culture of dude sex highlights the ways that "gay" and "straight" cannot be reduced to sexual practice, especially in a time when the queer eye (aesthetic tastes, fashion, and the ability to make a fine risotto) is marketed for mass consumption. In contrast with the logic that gay and straight are opposite ends of a behavioral and gender-based binary, the STR8 dudes who post on Craigslist view "gay" as a *chosen* identity that is not particularly linked to *who* is having sex, or *what* sexual acts are involved. Instead, being gay is about *how* sex is done. Among STR8 dudes, "gay" is a *cultural* phenomenon with which one can identify or disidentify, a form of gender expression, and a community affiliation—*not* a description of one's sexual practice. In a clever turn, STR8 dudes on Craigslist assert that it is willingness to consume queer culture that makes others queer—and conversely, it is commitment to the symbols of heterosexual masculinity that keeps them straight. The following ads, representative of dozens of others, illustrate how STR8 dudes authenticate their heterosexuality while soliciting sex with other men.

STR8 for STR8 Dudes:
I'm STR8 looking to mess around with another STR8 dude from time to time. Discreet and looking for more than one time hook-time hookups so if you respond, have the balls to follow through with this ad and meet up.

STR8 Bud Smoke-n-Stroke (420):
Any other hot straight dudes wanna smoke out, kick back and jack off to some hot porn? Like to kick it with another bro and work out a load together? . . . We'll just be jacking only—no making out, no touching, no anal bullshit. And smoking out!!!

STR8 Drunk Dude Looking to Get Off:
Hi there. Looking to lay back, have some beers, etc. and watch some STR8 porn this evening. I'm 5.10, brown hair, brown eyes white dude.

Authentic heterosexuality is established in part by demonstrating one's disinterest in presumably gay activities ("anal bullshit"), as well as one's interest in hyper-masculine activities. STR8 dudes are often drunk or stoned, they watch heterosexual porn, and they maintain a clear emotional boundary between them that draws upon the model of adolescent friendship, or the presumably harmless, "proto-sexual" circle jerk.[2] Reference to "being buddies" and "having the balls" to have sex with another dude also helps to reframe dude sex as a kind of sex that bolsters, rather than threatens, the heterosexual masculinity of the participants. Only those who are "man enough" will want dude sex or be able to handle it. Yet what is perhaps the most important evidence of heterosexuality provided by STR8 dudes in their posts, and at the heart of STR8 dudes' culture of desire, is

the discursive presence (and yet literal absence) of women in their sexual encounters. Unlike in similar websites for gay men, women are a central part of STR8 dudes' erotic discourse. In some cases, women are referenced as acceptable or preferable but unavailable sex partners, reinforcing that dude sex is an insignificant substitute for "real" sex:

Laid back STR8 guy seeks same for j/o [jerk off] buddy: Easygoing STR8 Caucasian male seeks same—looking for a buddy to stroke with who enjoys STR8 porn and sex with women but who is cool and open minded. I'm not gay but do like to show off and have done some bi stuff in the past. Interested in jerk off only. I'm in shape and attractive, and this is no big deal to me. Don't have girlfriend right now and wanted to get off today so hit me back if interested.

In an alarming number of other cases, violence against women is advertised as a central part of the sexual encounter. STR8 dudes explain that while masturbating together, they will talk about women's bodies and imagine sex with women. The desire to act out the gang rape of a woman is also common, although not always explicit, such as in the following ad:

Whackin Off to Porn:
STR8 porn. Gang bang. STR8, bi-curious masculine white guy lookin for a masculine guy. Get into stroking bone with a bud, talkin' bout pussy and bangin' the bitch.

While the phrases "gang bang" and "bangin' the bitch" are used in this ad, it is unclear who the object of the gang bang will be. In most ads, heterosexual porn and *talk* about women's bodies serves the function of incorporating the objectification of women into dude sex. In a few ads, however, such as the following, women were represented by blow-up dolls that dudes would have sex with in lieu of an available woman.

Any Straight/Bi Guys Want to Help Me Fuck My Blow-up Doll???
Come on guys . . . we can't always pick up the chick we want to bone right??? So let's get together and fuck the

hell out of my hot blow-up doll. Her mouth, her pussy, and her ass all feel GREAT. Just be cool, uninhibited, horny, and ready to fuck this bitch. It's all good here. . . .

In some cases, women are invited to observe dude sex, yet even in these cases, it is the sex between the two STR8 dudes that is the event. While women are present in the encounter, they reinforce the heterosexuality of the men involved, even as their role is clearly voyeuristic and ancillary:

Wanna Bang a STR8 Dude in Front of His Girl: This is a fantasy of mine, and hey it's new years, why not? I'd like to bang a STR8 guy in the ass in front of his chick. I'd even bang a STR8 dude 1 on 1 if you want. I'm not into guys that sound/act like chicks. I'm really not into guys, I just think it's kinky/hot to do this.

The link between dude sex and the gang rape of women suggests that we may read dude sex as a sexualized form of (heterosexual) male bonding that is facilitated by misogyny and violence against women. Gang rapes, not typically viewed as homosexual sex, nonetheless involve men cheering on and witnessing the orgasms of other men. Like in the Craigslist ads, women's bodies are the objects of violence, while the expression of agentic sexuality occurs among and between the men involved. This pattern suggests that dude sex is a sexual and often violent expression of heterosexual masculinity and heterosexual culture, quite distinct from gay male culture in which misogyny typically manifests as the invisibility, rather than the objectification, of women (Ward, 2000). Marilyn Frye (1983), in her analysis of drag queens, argues "What gay male affectation of femininity seems to be is a serious sport in which men may exercise their power and control over the feminine, much as in other sports. . . . But the mastery of the feminine is not feminine. It is masculine." Similarly, we might consider that while dude sex makes use of and masters homosexual sex, this deployment of homosexual sex in the service of heterosexuality is not homosexuality. It

is heterosexuality, or, to be more accurate, it is heterosexual culture. Indeed, there may be "nothing gay here at all."

GAY MEN PRETENDING TO BE STRAIGHT?

In her recent book *Black Sexual Politics* (2004), Patricia Hill Collins examines the subculture of men on the DL (down low)—Black men who have sex with men but don't identify as gay or bisexual and are typically married or have girlfriends. Benoit Denizet-Lewis, the journalist who first wrote about the down low phenomenon in the *New York Times Magazine*, describes the DL as a reaction to the (white) racialization of gay male culture. Denizet-Lewis (in Collins, 2004, p. 173) explains: "Rejecting a gay culture that they perceive as white and effeminate, many Black men have settled on a new identity, with its own vocabulary and customs and its own name: Down Low. There have always been men—Black and white—who have had secret sexual lives with men. But the creation of an organized, underground subculture made up of Black men who otherwise live straight lives is a phenomenon of the last decade." Men on the DL also meet in specialized websites and chat rooms, and like the STR8 dudes on Craigslist, they neither identify as gay nor wish to participate in gay male culture. While Denizet-Lewis suggests that the DL culture is a response to a racial system in which homosexuality is perceived as a "white thing" and Black masculinity is linked to fatherhood, it's important to note the existence of other Black identities, such as "same-gender loving," that simultaneously take pride in same-gender relationships *and* Blackness by rejecting the centrality of whiteness in gay culture.[3] In other words, being on the DL is not the only way to have sex with men while asserting one's Blackness; instead, it reflects a particular desire to participate in Black hyper-masculinity, relationships with women, and heterosexual culture.

Yet Patricia Hill Collins consistently reads men on the DL as closeted and gay, referring to them as "a new subculture of gay men" and arguing that, "for men on the DL, masculinity that is so intertwined with hyper-heterosexuality renders an openly gay identity impossible" (p. 207). While I agree with Collins' contention that the DL identity reflects a particularly complex positionality informed by race, gender, and sexual desire, I want to complicate the suggestion that men on the DL are closeted gay men who cannot come out because they are constrained by homophobia and racism. Such arguments obscure the processes through which Black men *do* assert nonheterosexual identities even in the face of homophobia and racism, as well as obscure the authentic pleasure that DL men take in heterosexual culture, heterosexual identity, and relationships with women.

Recent analyses of men on the DL reflect the temptation to invoke the closet as a means of understanding all same-sex sexuality that is not willing to call itself "gay" (see also King, 2004). In part this is due to the ideology of the contemporary lesbian and gay rights movement, in which many queers themselves assert basic rights based on the premise that sexual identity is biologically determined and just waiting to be discovered, revealed, outed. Seduced by this logic myself, my first reaction to the STR8 dudes' ads was to perceive the men who wrote them as closeted gay men, and my second reaction was to perceive them as "real" gay men pretending to be straight in order to satisfy a fetish for "real" straight men. After hearing from many gay male friends about their desire to seduce straight men, I became attentive to the possibility that the Casual Encounters section of Craigslist might be a place in which gay men seduce one another by posing as straight. While the vast majority of the ads gave no indication of familiarity with gay culture, and generally expressed disdain for it, some posts seemed to hold the tell-tale signs of "undercover" gay men, such as the following:

Do You Like Stroking Your Dick with Another STR8 Guy? I Got STR8 Porn!:
Looking to host in West LA, laid back, chill watchin extremely hot porn, all kinds. Pullin' out your cock when you get your woody, start playing with it more, take off your clothes and watch porn jackin all the way, watchin your buddy or buddies get horned up and on fire. The testosterone is in the air, you see him rapidly jerkin and stopping, you do the same thing, for however long it feels good. Looking at him stroke is hot for you, the same for him. Finally you can't hold back, he can't either, he shoots right before you and seeing his dick surt [sic] all that cum makes your orgasm all the more intense. THE RULES ARE THERE ARE NO RULES!!! GAY GUYS THIS IS PROBABLY NOT YOUR CUP OF TEA, no clones, baseball capped generic guys here, real guys, real passion, real woodies.

While the long and indulgent description of the sex itself is somewhat distinct from the other more minimalist and emotionless ads, what brought my attention to this post was the reference to "clones," "cup of tea," and "real passion." The latter are simply language choices that seemed out of sync with the macho tenor of the other ads, however the reference to "clones"—a queer insider term popular in the 1970s to describe straight-acting gay men—suggests an intimate familiarity with gay male culture. Ironically, the very expression of desire for "real" straight men (and not straight-acting gay men) is what casts suspicion on the authentic heterosexuality of this STR8 dude. In other words, what is suspicious in this ad is neither the sex it describes, nor the meaning it attributes to the sexual encounter. Instead it is the cultural reference to queer worlds of knowledge that makes me think that, indeed, there is "something gay" in this particular ad!

CONCLUSIONS: THE SIGNIFICANCE OF CULTURE

Academic discussion regarding the social construction of sexual identities often revolves around whether we might privilege sexual practice as the unit of analysis, or whether scholars of sexuality are better served by focusing our attention on the meanings and identities that social actors assign to sexual practices. In the Casual Encounters section of Craigslist, neither sex itself nor the self-identifications of the men who post there are useful guides for delineating the boundaries of queer and non-queer, or establishing political alliances with queer stakeholders. From a queer perspective, to de-queer the sex described on Craigslist is to give up the epistemological pleasure of self-righteous knowing, owning, outing, and naming. In the face of homophobia and heterosexism, the self-righteous pleasure of honing one's "gaydar" is one of few queer luxuries. Yet this study suggests that de-queering various forms of same-sex sexuality may be a quicker route to queer liberation than one that builds solidarity around sex acts. Instead, shared *culture*—including aesthetic preferences, a sense of collective identity, and participation in a community of resistance—may better help us determine whom we "own" as queer scholars and activists. While I am not inclined to want to swell the ranks of heterosexuals or argue that fewer people engage in same-sex desire than we think, this study does point to the theoretical and political usefulness of disowning or "sending back home" (to heterosexual culture) the STR8 dudes who have the "balls" to have sex with one another.

Such a project accomplishes three important interventions. First, this analysis invites us to give name to new identities and practices that aren't predicated on the idea of essential, hidden gayness, and that demonstrate the multiplicity and richness of queer as well as heterosexual sexual expressions. Building upon Sedgwick's call to transcend theories of the closet, which privilege and reify sexual practices, we may then map same-sex sexuality across identities, cultures, and space.

Second, what are straight and gay if not sexual practices? I suggest we view these distinctions as primarily sociocultural categories, or cultural spheres that people choose to inhabit in large part because they experience a cultural fit. Some men like to have sex with men in the bathrooms of gay bars after dancing to techno music, others like to have sex with men while watching straight porn and talking about bitches. Because the only thing these experiences have in common are sex acts between men, we might view heterosexuality, then, as a system of erotic relations and a cultural experience that appeals to people who choose to be straight. Conversely, we might view queerness as a system of erotic relations and a cultural experience that appeals to people who choose to be queer.

Lastly, where is the power in this analysis and what does this mean for the queer movement? In social movement context, redefining queer and non-queer as cultural affiliations implies that queer "rights" serve to protect not everyone who engages in same-sex sexuality, but all those who are excluded from, and alienated by, hegemonic STR8 culture—gender freaks, all kids in gay-straight alliances, all people who are or are willing to be part of this thing we call "gay." Such an approach refuses biological determinism, the essentialism of the closet, and distinctions between "us" and "them" rooted in the gay/straight binary. But perhaps more importantly, if it's not same-sex sexual practices that bind us, we must examine and take responsibility for the cultural spheres that we produce. Queer culture becomes not simply the outgrowth of resistance to oppression—although it certainly is this—but an available repertoire of aesthetic distinctions, personal preferences, and comforts we call home: dyke haircuts, techno music, drag shows, queer jokes, leather, and so on. To view queerness as constitutive of these pleasures, as opposed to some agreed upon set of rights linked to sexual practices, will keep queerness intact regardless of movement gains or losses.

NOTES

The research described in this article was supported by an Investigator Development grant to the author from the Wayne F. Placek Fund of the American Psychological Foundation.

1. This pilot study was approved by the Internal Review Board at the University of California, Riverside. Research assistants and I collected and coded 118 ads, which represented all of the ads placed during a nine-day period (from January 6 through January 15, 2005) in which straight-identified men solicited sex with other men. We collected and coded ads until we determined that we had coded enough ads to identify the primary and recurring discursive methods used by STR8 dudes on Craigslist to construct and authenticate their heterosexuality.

2. While many ads focus on masturbation, 65% of ads coded in this study expressed desire for, or openness to, oral or anal sex.

3. Same-gender loving is a concept created by and for black men and women in same-gender relationships. The term has been embraced as one that rejects the white origins of the identities "gay" and "lesbian," and focuses more on the practice and culture of "loving" people of the same gender. See www.fobrothers.com, "a reference-based online community for the same-gender loving black man."

REFERENCES

Almaguer, Tomás. 1993. "Chicano Men. A Cartography of Homosexual Identity and Behavior." In Abelove, Barale and Halperin (eds.) *The Lesbian and Gay Studies Reader.* New York: Routledge.

Blackwood, Evelyn and Saskia Wieringa. 1999. *Female Desires and Transgender Practices across Cultures.* New York: Columbia University Press.

Collins, Patricia Hill. 2004. *Black Sexual Politics: African Americans, Gender, and the New Racism.* New York: Routledge.

Fausto-Sterling, Anne. 2000. In *Sexing the Body: Gender Politics and the Construction of Sexuality.* New York: Basic Books.

Foucault, Michel. 1978. *The History of Sexuality: An Introduction.* New York: Vintage Books.

Frye, Marilyn. 1983. "Lesbian Feminism and Gay Rights." In *The Politics of Reality: Essays in Feminist Theory.* New York: Crossing Press.

Hutchins, Loraine and Lani Ka'ahumanu (eds.). 1991. *Bi Any Other Name: Bisexual People Speak Out.* New York: Alyson Publications.

Kaplan, Danny. 2003. *Brothers and Others in Arms: The Making of Love and War in Israeli Combat Units.* New York: Harrington Park Press.

King, J. L. 2004. *On the Down Low: A Journey Into the Lives of "Straight" Black Men Who Sleep With Men.* New York: Broadway.

Miller, Toby. 2005. "A Metrosexual Eye on Queer Guy." *GLQ: A Journal of Lesbian and Gay Studies.* Volume 11, Number 1, pp. 112–117.

Rich, Adrienne. 1980. "Compulsory Heterosexuality and Lesbian Existence." *Signs: Journal of Women in Culture and Society.* Volume 5, Number 4, pp. 631–660.

Schifter, Jacobo. 1999. *Macho Love: Sex Behind Bars in Central America.* New York: Harrington Park Press.

Seabrook, Jeremy. 1999. *Love in a Different Climate: Men Who Have Sex With Men in India.* New York: Verso.

Sedgwick, Eve Kosofsky. 1992. *Epistemology of the Closet.* Berkeley: University of California Press.

Ward, Jane. 2000. "Queer Sexism: Rethinking Gay Men and Masculinity." In Peter Nardi (ed.) *Gay Masculinities.* Thousand Oaks, CA: Sage Publications.

GAY BY CHOICE? THE SCIENCE OF SEXUAL IDENTITY

GARY GREENBERG

When he leaves his tidy apartment in an oceanside city somewhere in America, Aaron turns on the radio to a light rock station. "For the cat," he explains, "so she won't get lonely." He's short and balding and dressed mostly in black, and right before I turn on the recorder, he asks me for the dozenth time to guarantee that I won't reveal his name or anything else that might identify him. "I don't want to be a target for gay activists," he says as we head out into the misty day. "Harassment like that I just don't need."

Aaron sets a much brisker pace down the boardwalk than you would expect of a doughy 51-year-old, and once convinced I'll respect his anonymity, he turns out to be voluble. Over the crash of the waves, he spares no details as he describes how much he hated the fact that he was gay, how the last thing in the world he wanted to do was act on his desire to have sex with another man. "I'm going to be perfectly blatant about it," he says. "I'm not going to have anal intercourse or give or receive any BJs either, okay?" He managed to maintain his celibacy through college and into adulthood. But when, in the late 1980s, he found himself so "insanely jealous" of his roommate's girlfriend that he had to move out, he knew the time had come to do something. One of the few people who knew that Aaron was gay showed him an article in *Newsweek* about a group offering "reparative therapy"—psychological treatment for people who want to become "ex-gay."

"It turns out that I didn't have the faintest idea what love was," he says. That's not all he didn't know. He also didn't know that his same-sex attraction, far from being inborn and inescapable, was a thirst for the love that he had not received from his father, a cold and distant man prone to angry outbursts, coupled with a fear of women kindled by his intrusive and overbearing mother, all of which added up to a man who wanted to have sex with other men just so he could get some male attention. He didn't understand any of this, he tells me, until he found a reparative therapist whom he consulted by phone for nearly 10 years, attended weekend workshops, and learned how to "be a man."

Aaron interrupts himself to eye a woman in shorts jogging by. "Sometimes there are very good-looking women at this boardwalk," he says. "Especially when they're not bundled up." He remembers when he started noticing women's bodies, a few years into his therapy. "The first thing I noticed was their legs. The curve of their legs." He's dated women, had sex with them even, although "I was pretty awkward," he says. "It just didn't work." Aaron has a theory about this: "I never used my body in a sexual way. I think the men who actually act it out have a greater success in terms of being sexual with women than the men who didn't act it out." Not surprisingly, he's never had a long-term relationship, and he's pessimistic about his prospects. "I can't make that jump from having this attraction to doing something about it." But, he adds, it's wrong to think "if you don't make it with women, then you haven't changed." The important thing is that "now I like myself. I'm not emotionally shut down. I'm

From "Gay by Choice? The Science of Sexual Identity" by Gary Greenberg, *Mother Jones*, August 27, 2007. © 2007, Foundation for National Progress/Mother Jones. Reprinted courtesy of *Mother Jones*.

comfortable in my own body. I don't have to be drawn to men anymore. I'm content at this point to lead an asexual life, which is what I've done for most of my life anyway." He adds, "I'm a very detached person."

It's raining a little now. We stop walking so I can tuck the microphone under the flap of Aaron's shirt pocket, and I feel him recoil as I fiddle with his button. I'm remembering his little cubicle of an apartment, its unlived-in feel, and thinking that he may be the sort of guy who just doesn't like anyone getting too close, but it's also possible that therapy has taught him to submerge his desire so deep that he's lost his motive for intimacy.

That's the usual interpretation of reparative therapy—that to the extent that it does anything, it leads people to repress rather than change their natural inclinations, that its claims to change sexual orientation are an outright fraud perpetrated by the religious right on people who have internalized the homophobia of American society, personalized the political in such a way as to reject their own sexuality and stunt their love lives. But Aaron scoffs at these notions, insisting that his wish to go straight had nothing to do with right-wing religion or politics—he's a nonobservant Jew and a lifelong Democrat who volunteered for George McGovern, has a career in public service, and thinks George Bush is a war criminal. It wasn't a matter of ignorance—he has an advanced degree-and it *really* wasn't a psychopathological thing—he rejects the idea that he's ever suffered from internalized homophobia. He just didn't want to be gay, and, like millions of Americans dissatisfied with their lives, he sought professional help and reinvented himself.

Self-reconstruction is what people in my profession (I am a practicing psychotherapist) specialize in, but when it comes to someone like Aaron, most of us draw the line. All the major psychotherapy guilds have barred their members from researching or practicing repar-

ative therapy on the grounds that it is inherently unethical to treat something that is not a disease, that it contributes to oppression by pathologizing homosexuality, and that it is dangerous to patients whose self-esteem can only suffer when they try to change something about themselves that they can't (and shouldn't have to) change. Aaron knows this, of course, which is why he's at great pains to prove he's not pulling a Ted Haggard. For if he's not a poseur, then he is a walking challenge to the political and scientific consensus that has emerged over the last century and a half: that sexual orientation is inborn and immutable, that efforts to change it are bound to fail, and that discrimination against gay people is therefore unjust.

But as crucial as this consensus has been to the struggle for gay rights, it may not be as sound as some might wish. While scientists have found intriguing biological differences between gay and straight people, the evidence so far stops well short of proving that we are born with a sexual orientation that we will have for life. Even more important, some research shows that sexual orientation is more fluid than we have come to think, that people, especially women, can and do move across customary sexual orientation boundaries, that there are ex-straights as well as ex-gays. Much of this research has stayed below the radar of the culture warriors, but reparative therapists are hoping to use it to enter the scientific mainstream and advocate for what they call the right of self-determination in matters of sexual orientation. If they are successful, gay activists may soon find themselves scrambling to make sense of a new scientific and political landscape.

In 1838, a 20-year-old Hungarian killed himself and left a suicide note for Karl Benkert, a 14-year-old bookseller's apprentice in Budapest whom he had befriended. In it he explained that he had been cleaned out by a blackmailer who was now threatening to expose his homosexuality, and that he couldn't face either the shame or the potential legal trouble that would follow. Benkert, who eventually became a writer, moved to Vienna, and changed his name to Karoly Maria Kertbeny, later said that the tragedy left him with "an instinctive drive to take issue with every injustice." And in 1869, a particularly resonant injustice occurred: A penal code proposed for Prussia included an anti-sodomy law much like the one that had given his friend's extortionist his leverage. Kertbeny published a pamphlet in protest, writing that the state's attempt to control consensual sex between men was a violation of the fundamental rights of man. Nature, he argued, had divided the human race into four sexual types: "monosexuals," who masturbated, "heterogenits," who had sex with animals, "heterosexuals," who coupled with the opposite sex, and "homosexuals," who preferred people of the same sex. Kertbeny couldn't have known that of all his literary output, these latter two words would be his only lasting legacy. But while homosexual conduct had occurred throughout history, the idea that it reflected fundamental differences between people, that gay people were a sexual subspecies, was a new one.

Kertbeny wasn't alone in creating a sexual taxonomy. Another anti-sodomy-law opponent, lawyer Karl Heinrich Ulrichs, proposed that homosexual men, or "Uranians," as he called them (and he openly considered himself a Uranian, while Kertbeny was coy about his preferences), were actually a third sex, their attraction to other men a manifestation of the female soul residing in their male bodies. Whatever the theoretical differences between Ulrichs and Kertbeny, they agreed on one crucial point: that sexual behavior was the expression of an *identity* into which we were born, a natural variation of the human. In keeping with the post-Enlightenment notion that we are morally culpable only for what we are free to choose, homosexuals were not to be condemned or restricted by the state. Indeed, this was Kert-

beny and Ulrichs' purpose: Sexual orientation, as we have come to call this biological essence, was invented in order to secure freedom for gay people.

But replacing morality with biology, and the scrutiny of church and state with the observations of science, invited a different kind of condemnation. By the end of the nineteenth century, homosexuality was increasingly the province of psychiatrists like Magnus Hirschfeld, a gay Jewish Berliner. Hirschfeld was an outspoken opponent of anti-sodomy laws and championed tolerance of gay people, but he also believed that homosexuality was a pathological state, a congenital deformity of the brain that may have been the result of a parental "degeneracy" that nature intended to eliminate by making the defective population unlikely to reproduce. Even Sigmund Freud, who thought people were "polymorphously perverse" by nature and urged tolerance for homosexuality, believed heterosexuality was essential to maturity and psychological health.

Freud was pessimistic that homosexuality could be treated, but doctors abhor an illness without a cure, and the twentieth century saw therapists inflict the best of modern psychiatric practice on gay people, which included, in addition to interminable psychoanalysis and unproven medications, treatments that used electric shock to associate pain with same-sex attraction. These therapies were largely unsuccessful, and, particularly after the Stonewall riots of 1969—the clash between police and gays that initiated the modern gay rights movement—patients and psychiatrists alike started questioning whether homosexuality should be considered a mental illness at all. Gay activists, some of them psychiatrists, disrupted the annual meeting of the American Psychiatric Association for three years in a row, until in 1973 a deal was brokered. The APA would delete homosexuality from its *Diagnostic and Statistical Manual of Mental Disorders*

(DSM) immediately, and furthermore it would add a new disease: sexual orientation disorder, in which a patient can't accept his or her sexual identity. The culprit in SOD was an oppressive society, and the cure for SOD was to help the gay patient overcome oppression and accept who he or she really was. (SOD has since been removed from the DSM.)

The APA cited various scientific papers in making its decision, but many members were convinced that the move was a dangerous corruption of science by politics. "If groups of people march and raise enough hell, they can change anything in time," one psychiatrist worried. "Will schizophrenia be next?" And their impression was confirmed when the final decision was made not in a laboratory but at the ballot box, where the membership voted by a six-point margin to authorize the APA to delete the diagnosis of homosexuality. It may be the first time in history that a disease was eliminated by the stroke of a pen. It was certainly the first time that psychiatrists determined that the cause of a mental illness was an intolerant society. And it was a crucial moment for gay people, at once getting the psychiatrists out of their bedrooms and giving the weight of science to Kertbeny and Ulrichs' claim that homosexuality was an identity, like race or national origin, that deserved protection.

Three decades later, at least one group is still raising hell about the deletion: the National Association for the Research and Therapy of Homosexuality (NARTH), an organization founded by Charles Socarides, a psychiatrist who led the opposition to the 1973 APA vote . . .

But the men of NARTH (nearly all the 75 attendees are white men) aren't spewing nearly as much hellfire and brimstone as I expected. They do seem to hug a lot—many reparative therapists are ex-gay themselves, and, someone explains, part of being ex-gay is learning to be same-sex affectionate without

being same-sex sexual—and maybe some of those hugs last a little too long, but it's mostly like every other convention: bad coffee, worse Danish, dry-as-dust lectures . . .

Some gay rights lawyers point out that whatever biology's role in sexual orientation, it should not be legally paramount. The Supreme Court has ruled that the immutability of a group's identifying characteristics is one of the criteria that entitle it to heightened protection from discrimination (and some cases establishing gay rights were decided in part on those grounds), but, according to Suzanne Goldberg, director of the Sexuality and Gender Law Clinic at Columbia Law School, there's a far more fundamental reason for courts to protect gay people. "Sexual orientation does not bear on a person's ability to contribute to society," she notes. "We don't need the science to make that point." Jon Davidson, legal director of Lambda Legal, agrees, adding that if courts are going to ask about immutability, they shouldn't focus on biology. Instead they should focus on how sexual orientation is so deeply woven into a person's identity that it is inseparable from who they are. In this respect, Davidson says, sexual orientation is like another core aspect of identity that is clearly not biological in origin: religion. "It doesn't matter whether you were born that way, it came later, or you chose," he says. "We don't think it's okay to discriminate against people based on their religion. We think people have a right to believe whatever they want. So why do we think that about religion and not about who we love?"

[Sean] Cahill [former director of the National Gay and Lesbian Task Force Policy Institute]—who says he doesn't think he was born gay—points out that even if it is crucial for public support, essentialism has a dark side: the remedicalization of homosexuality, this time as a biological condition that can be treated. Michael Bailey, a Northwestern University psychologist who has conducted some of the key studies of the genetics of sexual orientation, infuriated the gay and lesbian community with a paper arguing that, should prenatal markers of homosexuality be identified, parents ought to have the right to abort potentially gay fetuses. "It's reminiscent of eugenicist theories," Cahill tells me. "If it's seen as an undesirable trait, it could lead in some creepy directions." These could include not only abortion, but also gene therapy or modulating uterine hormone levels to prevent the birth of a gay child.

Psychology professor Lisa Diamond may have the best reason of all for activists to shy away from arguing that homosexuality is inborn and immutable: It's not exactly true. She doesn't dispute the findings that show a biological role in sexual orientation, but she thinks far too much is made of them. "The notion that if something is biological, it is fixed—no biologist on the planet would make that sort of assumption," she told me from her office at the University of Utah. Not only that, she says, but the research—which is conducted almost exclusively on men—hinges on a very narrow definition of sexual orientation: "It's what makes your dick go up. I think most women would disagree with that definition," she says, not only because it obviously excludes them, but because sexual orientation is much more complex than observable aspects of sexuality. "An erection is an erection," she says, "but we have almost no information about what is actually going on in terms of the subjective experience of desire." . . .

Diamond cautions that it's important not to confuse plasticity—the capacity for sexual orientation to change—with choice—the ability to change it at will. "Trying to change your attractions doesn't work very well, but you can change the structure of your social life, and that might lead to changes in the feelings you experience." This is a time-honored way of handling unwanted sexual feelings, she points out. "Jane Austen made a career out of this: People

fall in love with a person of the wrong social class. What do you do? You get yourself out of those situations." . . .

Which isn't all that different from what they say at NARTH—that people like Aaron who hate the gay lifestyle and don't want to be gay should leave the gay bars, do regular guy things with men, and put themselves in the company of women for romance. And indeed the NARTHites know all about Diamond's work. "We know that straight people become gays and lesbians," NARTH's outgoing president Joseph Nicolosi told the group gathered in Orlando. "So it seems totally reasonable that some gay and lesbian people would become straight. The issue is whether therapy changes sexual orientation. People grow and change as a result of life experiences, especially personal relationships. Why then can't the experience of therapy and the relationship with the therapist also effect change?" Diamond calls this interpretation a "misuse" of her research— "the fluidity I've observed does not mean that reparative therapy works"—but what is really being misused, she says, is science. "We live in a culture where people disagree vehemently about whether or not sexual minorities deserve equal rights," she told me. "People cling to this idea that science can provide the answers, and I don't think it can. I think in some ways it's dangerous for the lesbian and gay community to use biology as a proxy for that debate." . . .

NARTH is perfectly positioned to exploit [Americans' confusion about sexuality] by arguing that sexual orientation can be influenced by environmental conditions, and that certain courses are less healthy than others. That's how NARTHites justify their opposition to extending marriage and adoption rights to gay people: not because they abhor homosexuality, but because a gay-friendly world is one in which it is hard for gay people to recognize that they are suffering from a medical illness.

Of course, in deploying medical language to serve its strategic interests, NARTH is only following the lead of Kertbeny and Hirschfeld, the original gay activists, and their modern counterparts who, despite minimizing the importance of biology, resort to scientific rhetoric when it suits their purposes. "People can't try to shut down a part of who they are," says Sean Cahill. "I don't think it's healthy for people to change how their body and mind and heart work."

But medicine, which is what we rely on to tell us what is "healthy," will always seek to change the way people's bodies and minds and hearts work; yesterday's immutable state of nature is tomorrow's disease to be cured. Medical science can only take its cues from the society whose curiosities it satisfies and whose confusions it investigates. It can never do the heavy political lifting required to tell us whether one way of living our lives is better than another. This is exactly why Kertbeny originated the notion of a biologically based sexual orientation, and, to the extent that society is more tolerant of homosexuality now than it was 150 years ago, that idea has been a success. But the ex-gay movement may be the signal that this invention has begun to outlive its usefulness, that sexuality, profoundly mysterious and irrational, will not be contained by our categories, that it is time to find reasons other than medical science to insist that people ought to be able to love whom they love.

Queer by Choice, Not by Chance: Against Being "Born This Way"

By Lindsay King-Miller

I am a queer woman planning to get married next year in a state where my marriage will not be legally recognized. It will probably not surprise you to learn that, sometimes, being gay is not easy. Coming out to your family is nerve-wracking, people yell slurs and threats when you hold hands on the street, and most lesbian movies are just terrible. With all those drawbacks, those of us who spend our lives with a partner of the same sex must really have no choice in the matter—or so goes the prevailing wisdom of the gay rights movement. It's not our decision; it's genetic; we can't help to whom we're attracted. If it were up to us, wouldn't we turn our backs on all the abuse and discrimination and get nice and legally married without a second thought?

Well, no. Not all of us anyway. Some of us have figured out that, despite being underrepresented in Western culture at almost every level, despite facing homophobia and transphobia and gender policing and the disapproval of our families, being gay can actually be fantastic.

In direct opposition to both the mainstream gay movement and Lady Gaga, I would like to state for the record that I was not born this way. I have dated both men and women in the past, and when I've been with men, I never had to lie back and think of Megan Fox. I still notice attractive men on the street and on television. If I were terrified of the stigma associated with homosexuality, it would have been easy enough to date men exclusively and stay in the closet my whole life.

Obviously, no one sits down and makes a rational decision about who to fall in love with, but I get frustrated with the veiled condescension of straight people who believe that queers "can't help it," and thus should be treated with tolerance and pity. To say "I was born this way" is to apologize for the person I am and for whom I love. It's like saying I would be different if I could. I wouldn't. . . .

. . . So why would I want to be any other way?

The answer, of course, is that I wouldn't—and, more importantly, that it shouldn't matter.

The "born this way" argument is frequently used in defense of gay rights, but whether or not I deserve the same rights as straight people has nothing to do with whether I chose to be the way I am. I deserve equal rights because I'm an equal. I'm a human being sharing my life with the person I love. The life I have now is not something I ended up with because I had no other options. Make no mistake—it's a life I chose.

Source: "Queer by Choice, Not by Chance: Against 'Being Born This Way'," *The Atlantic*, September 12, 2011. Reprinted by permission of the author.

STRAIGHT GIRLS KISSING

LEILA J. RUPP AND VERTA TAYLOR

The phenomenon of presumably straight girls kissing and making out with other girls at college parties and at bars is everywhere in contemporary popular culture, from Katy Perry's hit song, "I Kissed a Girl," to a Tyra Banks online poll on attitudes toward girls who kiss girls in bars, to AskMen.com's "Top 10: Chick Kissing Scenes." Why *do* girls who aren't lesbians kiss girls? Some think it's just another example of "girls gone wild," seeking to attract the boys who watch. Others, such as psychologist Lisa Diamond, point to women's "sexual fluidity," suggesting that the behavior could be part of how women shape their sexual identities, even using a heterosexual social scene as a way to transition to a bisexual or lesbian identity.

These speculations touch on a number of issues in the sociology of sexuality. The fact that young women on college campuses are engaging in new kinds of sexual behaviors brings home the fundamental concept of the social construction of sexuality—that whom we desire, what kinds of sexual acts we engage in, and how we identify sexually is profoundly shaped by the societies in which we live. Furthermore, boys enjoying the sight of girls making out recalls the feminist notion of the "male gaze," calling attention to the power embodied in men as viewers and women as the viewed. The sexual fluidity that is potentially embodied in women's intimate interactions in public reminds us that sexuality is gendered and that sexual desire, sexual behavior, and sexual identity do not always match. That is, men do not, at least in contemporary American culture, experience the same kind of fluidity. Although they may identify as straight *and* have sex with other men, they certainly don't make out at parties for the pleasure of women.

The hookup culture on college campuses, as depicted in "Hooking Up: Sex in Guyland" in Chapter 8, facilitates casual sexual interactions (ranging from kissing and making out to oral sex and intercourse) between students who meet at parties or bars. Our campus is no exception. The University of California, Santa Barbara, has a long-standing reputation as a party school (much to the administration's relief, it's declining in those rankings). In a student population of twenty thousand, more than half of the students are female and slightly under half are students of color, primarily Chicano/Latino and Asian American. About a third are first-generation college students. Out of over two thousand female UC Santa Barbara students who responded to sociologist Paula England's online College and Social Life Survey on hooking-up practices on campus, just under one percent identified as homosexual, three percent as bisexual, and nearly two percent as "not sure."

National data on same-sex sexuality shows that far fewer people identify as lesbian or gay than are sexually attracted to the same sex or have engaged in same-sex sexual behavior. Sociologist Edward Laumann and his colleagues, in the National Health and Social Life Survey, found that less than two percent of women identified as lesbian or bisexual, but over eight percent had experienced same-sex desire or engaged in lesbian sex. The opposite is true for

From "Straight Girls Kissing" by Leila J. Rupp and Verta Taylor, in *Contexts*, August 2010, Vol. 9, No. 3 pp. 28–32. Copyright © 2010, American Sociological Association. Reprinted by permission of SAGE Publications.

men, who are more likely to have had sex with a man than to report finding men attractive. Across time and cultures (and, as sociologist Jane Ward has pointed out, even in the present among white straight-identified men), sex with other men, as long as a man plays the insertive role in a sexual encounter, can bolster, rather than undermine, heterosexuality. Does the same work for women?

The reigning assumption about girls kissing girls in the party scene is that they do it to attract the attention of men. But the concept of sexual fluidity and the lack of fit among desire, behavior, and identity suggest that there may be more going on than meets the male gaze. A series of formal and informal interviews with diverse female college students at our university, conducted by undergraduates as part of a class assignment, supports the sociological scholarship on the complexity of women's sexuality.

THE COLLEGE PARTY SCENE

What is most distinctive about UC Santa Barbara is the adjacent community of Isla Vista, a densely populated area made up of two-thirds students and one-third primarily poor and working-class Mexican American families. House parties, fraternity and sorority parties, dance parties (often with, as one woman student put it, "some sort of slutty theme to them"), and random parties open to anyone who stops by flourish on the weekends. Women students describe Isla Vista as "unrealistic to the rest of the world . . . It's a little wild," "very promiscuous, a lot of experimenting and going crazy," and "like a sovereign nation . . . a space where people feel really comfortable to let down their guards and to kind of let loose." Alcohol flows freely, drugs are available, women sport skimpy clothing, and students engage in a lot of hooking up. One sorority member described parties as featuring "a lot of, you know, sexual dance. And some people, you know, like pretty much are fucking on the dance floor even though they're

really not. I feel like they just take it above and beyond." Another student thinks "women have a little bit more freedom here." But despite the unreality of life in Isla Vista, there's no reason to think life here is fundamentally different than on other large campuses.

At Isla Vista parties, the practice of presumably heterosexual women kissing and making out with other women is widespread. As one student reported, "It's just normal for most people now, friends make out with each other." The student newspaper sex columnist began her column in October 2008, "I kissed a girl and liked it," recommending "if you're a girl who hasn't quite warmed up to a little experimentation with one of your own, then I suggest you grab a gal and get to it." She posed the "burning question on every male spectator's mind . . . Is it real or is it for show?" As it turns out, students offered three different explanations of why students do this: to get attention from men, to experiment with same-sex activity, and out of same-sex desire.

GETTING ATTENTION

Girls kissing other girls can be a turn-on for men in our culture, as the girls who engage in it well know. A student told us, "It's usually for display for guys who are usually surrounding them and like cheering them on. And it seems to be done in order to like, you know, for the guys, not like for their own pleasure or desire, but to like, I don't know, entertain the guys." Alcohol is usually involved: "It's usually brought on by, I don't know, like shots or drinking, or people kind of saying something to like cheer it on or whatever. And it's usually done in order to turn guys on or to seek male attention in some way." One student who admits to giving her friend what she calls "love pecks" and engaging in some "booby grabbing" says "I think it's mainly for attention definitely. It's usually girls that are super drunk that are trying to get attention from guys or are just really just having fun like when my roommate and I did it at our date party . . . It is alcohol and for show. Not experimentation at all." Another student, who has had her friends kiss her, insists that "they do that for attention . . . kind of like a circle forms around them . . . egging them on or taking pictures." One woman admitted that she puckered up for the attention, but when asked if it had anything to do with experimentation, added "maybe with some people. I think for me it was a little bit, yeah."

EXPERIMENTATION

Other women agree that experimentation is part of the story. One student who identifies as straight says "I have kissed girls on multiple occasions." One night she and a friend were "hammered, walking down the street, and we're getting really friendly and just started making out and taking pictures," which they then posted on Facebook. "And then the last time, this is a little bit more personal, but was when I actually had a threesome. Which was at a party and obviously didn't happen during the party." She mentions "bisexual tendencies" as an explanation, in addition to getting attention: "I would actually call it maybe more like experimentation." Another student, who calls herself straight but "bi-curious," says girls do it for attention, but also, "It's a good time for them, something they may not have the courage to express themselves otherwise, if they're in a room alone, it makes them more comfortable with it because other people are receiving pleasure from them." She told us about being drunk at a theme party ("Alice in Fuckland"): "And me and 'Maria' just started going at it in the kitchen. And this dude, he whispers in my ear, 'Everyone's watching. People can see you.' But me and 'Maria' just like to kiss. I don't think it was like really a spectacle thing, like we weren't teasing anybody. We just like to make out. So we might be an exception to the rule," she giggled.

In another interview, a student described a friend as liking "boys and girls when she's drunk . . . But when she's sober she's starting to like girls." And another student who called herself "technically" bisexual explained that she hates that term because in Isla Vista "it basically means that you make out with girls at parties." Before her first relationship with a woman, she never thought about bisexuality: "The closest I ever came to thinking that was, hey, I'd probably make out with a girl if I was drinking." These stories make clear that experimentation in the heterosexual context of the hookup culture and college party scene provides a safe space for some women to explore non-heterosexual possibilities.

SAME-SEX DESIRE

Some women go beyond just liking to make out and admit to same-sex desire as the motivating factor. One student who defined her sexuality as liking sex with men but feeling "attracted more towards girls than guys" described her coming out process as realizing, "I really like girls and I really like kissing girls." Said another student, "I've always considered myself straight, but since I've been living here I've had several sexual experiences with women. So I guess I would consider myself, like, bisexual at this point." She at first identified as "one of those girls" who makes out at parties, but then admitted that she also had sexual experiences with women in private. At this point she shifted her identification to bisexual: "I may have fallen into that trap of like kissing a girl to impress a guy, but I can't really recollect doing that on purpose. It was more of just my own desire to be with, like to try that with a woman." Another bisexual woman who sometimes makes out with one of her girlfriends in public thinks other women might "only do it in a public setting because they're afraid of that side of their sexuality, because they were told to be heterosexual you know . . . So if they make out, it's only for the show of it, even though they may like it they can't admit that they do."

The ability to kiss and make out with girls in public without having to declare a lesbian or bisexual identity makes it possible for women with same-sex desires to be part of the regular college party scene, and the act of making out in public has the potential to lead to more extensive sexual activity in private. One student described falling in love with her best friend in middle school, but being "too chicken shit to make the first move" because "I never know if they are queer or not." Her first sexual relationship with a bisexual woman included the woman's boyfriend as well. In this way, the fact that some women have their first same-sex sexual encounter in a threesome with a man is an extension of the safe heterosexual space for exploring same-sex desire.

HETEROFLEXIBILITY

Obviously, in at least some cases, more is going on here than drunken women making out for the pleasure of men. Sexual fluidity is certainly relevant; in Lisa Diamond's ten-year study of young women who originally identified as lesbian or bisexual, she found a great deal of movement in sexual desire, intimate relationships, and sexual identities. The women moved in all directions, from lesbian to bisexual and heterosexual, bisexual to lesbian and heterosexual, and, notably, from all identities to "unlabeled." From a psychological perspective, Diamond argues for the importance of both biology and culture in shaping women as sexually fluid, with a greater capacity for attractions to both female and male partners than men. Certainly the women who identify as heterosexual but [are] into kissing other women fit her notion of sexual fluidity. Said one straight-identified student, "It's not like they're way different from anyone else. They're just making out."

Mostly, though, students didn't think that making out had any impact on one's identity as heterosexual: "And yeah, I imagine a lot of the girls that you know just casually make out with their girlfriends would consider themselves straight. I consider myself straight." Said another, "I would still think they're straight girls. Unless I saw some, like level of like emotional and like attraction there." A bisexual student, though, thought "they're definitely bi-curious at the least . . . I think that a woman who actually does it for enjoyment and like knows that she likes that and that she desires it again, I would say would be more leaning towards bisexual."

EVERYBODY BUT LESBIANS

So, although girls who kiss girls are not "different from anyone else," if they have an emotional reaction or really enjoy it or want to do it again, then they've apparently crossed the line of heterosexuality. Diamond found that lesbians in her study who had been exclusively attracted to and involved with other women were the only group that didn't report changes in their sexual identities. Sociologist Arlene Stein, in her study of lesbian feminist communities in the 1980s, also painted a picture of boundary struggles around the identity "lesbian." Women who developed relationships with men but continued to identify as lesbians were called "ex-lesbians" or "fakers" by those who considered themselves "real lesbians." And while straight college students today can make out with women and call themselves "bi-curious" without challenge to their heterosexual identity, the same kind of flexibility does not extend to lesbians. A straight, bi-curious woman explained that she didn't think "the lesbian community would accept me right off because I like guys too much, you know." And she didn't think she had "enough sexual experience with . . . women to be considered bisexual." Another student, who described herself as "a free flowing spirit" and has had multiple relationships with straight-identified women, rejected the label "lesbian" because "I like girls" but "guys are still totally attractive to me." She stated that "to be a lesbian meant . . . you'd have to commit yourself to it one hundred percent. Like you'd have to be in it sexually, you'd have to be in it emotionally. And I think if you were you wouldn't have that attraction for men . . . if you were a lesbian."

In contrast to "heteroflexibility," a term much in use by young women, students hold a much more rigid, if unarticulated, notion of lesbian identity. "It's just like It's okay because we're both drunk and we're friends. It's not like we identify as lesbian in any way. . . ." One woman who has kissed her roommate is sure that she can tell the difference between straight women and lesbians: "I haven't ever seen like an actual like lesbian couple enjoying themselves." Another commented "I mean, it's one thing if you are, if you do identify as gay and that you're expressing something." A bisexual woman is less sure, at first stating that eighty percent of the making out at parties is for men, then hesitating because "that totally excludes the queer community and my own viewing of like women who absolutely love other women, and they show that openly so, I think that it could be either context." At that point she changed the percentage to fifty percent: "Cause I guess I never know if a woman is like preferably into women or if it's more of a social game." A bisexual woman described kissing her girlfriend at a party "and some guy came up and poured beer on us and said something like 'stop kissing her you bitch,'" suggesting that any sign that women are kissing for their own pleasure puts them over the line. She went on to add that "we've gotten plenty of guys staring at us though, when we kiss or

whatever, [and] they think that we're doing it for them, or we want them to join or whatever. It gets pretty old."

So there is a lot of leeway for women's same-sex behavior with a straight identity. But it is different than for straight men, who experience their same-sex interactions in a more private space, away from the gaze of women. Straight women can be "barsexual" or "bi-curious" or "mostly straight," but too much physical attraction or emotional investment crosses over the line of heterosexuality. What this suggests is that heterosexual women's options for physical intimacy are expanding, although such activity has little salience for identity, partner choice, or political allegiances. But the line between lesbian and non-lesbian, whether bisexual or straight, remains firmly intact.

RECOMMENDED RESOURCES

Lisa M. Diamond. 2009. *Sexual Fluidity: Understanding Women's Love and Desire.* (Harvard University Press). A longitudinal study of women's shifting sexual behaviors and identities in the contemporary United States.

Laura Hamilton. 2007. "Trading on Heterosexuality: College Women's Gender Strategies and Homophobia." *Gender & Society*, 21:145–72. Looks at the sexual constructions adopted by college-aged women.

Arlene Stein. 1997. *Sex and Sensibility: Stories of a Lesbian Generation.* (University of California Press). A sociological study of American lesbian feminist communities in the 1980s.

Elisabeth Morgan Thompson and Elizabeth M. Morgan. 2008. " 'Mostly Straight' Young Women: Variations in Sexual Behavior and Identity Development." *Developmental Psychology*, 44/1:15–21. A psychological study of U.S. college students' shifting sexual behaviors and identities.

Jane Ward. 2008. "Dude-Sex: White Masculinities and 'Authentic' Heterosexuality Among Dudes Who Have Sex With Dudes." *Sexualities*, 11:414–434. A sociological study that complicates the concept of "men who have sex with men."

Bisexuality and Bi Identity

PJ McGann

"Sexuality" conceals significant complexity. Even when limited to basic components, sexuality is an amalgamation of what we do, what we wish we could do, what we think about doing, how we see ourselves, and how others see us.[1] Which of these components is (or should be) most important when defining "sexuality" is socially and individually variable. Social groups also "package" the basic components of sexuality—behavior, desire, and identity—in different ways. Thus, different cultures, different historical moments, even subcultures within a larger society sometimes have different "sexualities." Contemporary forms of desire are defined by the sexual anatomy of the partners; hence, homo, hetero, and bi. As recently as the 1930s, though, sexualities were defined by gender expression. Thus, traditionally masculine men who had sex with effeminate males were considered "normal" men, but their "Fairy" partners were seen as "third-sexers" (Chauncey, 1994). Although the categories of sexuality are social creations, we don't usually experience them that way. Sexualities seem natural. We take for granted that there are sexual "types" of people, and presume that sexual behavior, desire, and identity "line up"—that what we *do* and what we *think* "match" who we *are*, and that who we are corresponds to our society's sexual categories.

Identity, though, is a complex thing. *Individual* identity is who we are to ourselves; *social* identity is who we are to others. These facets of identity don't always align; sometimes this is intentional (as when someone is "in the closet"), sometimes not (as when we think somebody's sexuality is one thing, but it is something else). Either way, sexual identity is built on a culture's sexual categories and is dependent on others for recognition. Identity, then, isn't just something individuals "have." It is instead a process that emerges from dynamic interplay with the social world. Consider how we "know" someone's sexual identity. Even if they don't tell us directly, individuals "announce" identity through appearance, gestures, and acts. For such announcements to work, others must know how to interpret the signs (a wedding ring, for instance), know which sexuality they point to, and accept the signs as legitimate indicators of the person's sexuality. However, the prevalence, persistence, and visibility of the hetero–homo binary underpins belief that most people are "really" straight or gay/lesbian. Such "monosexism" fuels anti-bisexual stereotypes and skepticism of the reality of bisexuality, leaving bi identity in a precarious position (James, 1996; Rust, 1993, 2002).[2]

Contemporary bisexual *identity*—a sense of self based on attraction to more than one gender—is linked to the emergence of bisexual politics in the early to mid 1970s. Bisexual behavior existed before then, of course, as did bisexuality as a category of sexuality, but people didn't necessarily think of themselves as "bi" (Savin-Williams, 2005; Weinberg et al., 1994). Even when they did, "bi" often wasn't an identity recognized by others (Rust, 2000, 2002; Storr, 1999; Udis-Kessler, 1996). This changed when a newly visible bisexuality[3] converged with countercultural ideals of sexual and gender experimentation, leading to the creation of local bisexual groups. The first were mostly male, and by 1978 there were only four such groups in the nation. Things changed significantly in the 1980s, as women—many of whom had previously identified as lesbian—founded bi networks in cities such as Minneapolis, Chicago, New York, and Boston. By the mid 1980s explicitly political organizations had formed, ultimately leading to regional, national, and international conferences. By the early 1990s there were college courses and several books on bisexuality, as well as a national bisexual organization. After initial resistance, in 1993 lesbian and gay organizations formally recognized bisexuality (Hutchins, 1996; Rust, 2000, 2002; Udis-Kessler, 1996). As "bisexuality" became socially visible and more positively defined it became possible not only to act bisexually, but to *be* a bisexual.

Visibility and recognition created a base for bi identity, but even today, bisexuality is still not necessarily valued. Stereotypes of bisexuals as immature, deceitful, and promiscuous persist. The gendered nature of the images means female and male bisexuals face different attitudes. For example, both gays and lesbians have criticized bisexuals for a presumed unwillingness to "fully" come out. But gay men have historically been more tolerant of bisexual behavior than have lesbians, a discrepancy rooted in critique of male control of female sexuality and the politicization of lesbianism (Echols, 1989; Rust, 1995; Stein, 1992; Udis-Kessler, 1996).

In contrast to the suspicion and, at times, hostility, female bisexuals have faced from some lesbians, straight society sometimes celebrates female bi behavior. Indeed, some forms are deeply eroticized. But even ostensibly positive "hot bi babe" stereotypes—more liberated, more daring, with a large if not insatiable sexual appetite—constrain, given how easily such images facilitate objectification (Sheff, 2005). What's more, in a context of gender inequality, female bisexuality is consumed for male plea-sure, yet dismissed as not "really" sex. This situation may provide cover for "hetero-flexible" sexual exploration but the hyper-visibility may undermine bi identity (however unintentionally). In contrast, male bi behavior is less visible but more roundly denounced in the dominant culture. Concerns about the "Down Low" phenomenon demonize African American and Latino men as dishonest and scorn them as sources of contaminating disease, attitudes which reflect racial inequality and historic fear of Black male sexuality (see "Deconstructing Down Low Discourse" in Chapter 8). There may be less overt hostility directed at the private sex of white "str8 dudes," but the clandestine nature of it and Down Low sexuality alike suggests homophobia and underscores the threat male same-sex activity may pose to heterosexuality and masculinity (see "Straight Dude Seeks Same" in this chapter).

The depiction of male bisexual activity as the deceitful selfishness of closeted gays, and the "embrace" of female bisexuality are two sides of the same monosexist coin. Despite bisexual activism, many insist that everyone is "really" either gay or straight. The rigidity of the hetero-homo binary leaves little room for the both/and of bisexuality. Confusion and disagreement as to what bisexuality is—attraction to *both* genders? attraction *regardless* of gender?—compounds the instability, yet underscores the social nature of identity. The "in between-ness" of bisexuality provokes debate. As discussion proceeds, new categories emerge—queer, fluid, pan- and omni-sexual—giving individuals new ways to make sense of their sexual experience in terms (potentially) intelligible to others.

NOTES

1. A more complete consideration of sexuality would include things such as emotional connection, capacity, preference, lifestyle, group membership, community involvement, political commitment, and so on.

2. The complexity of heterosexual identity is often overlooked—not because heterosexuality is inherently more stable or natural, but because it is the default, taken-for-granted form of sexuality woven into (and thus supported by) nearly every other social institution.

3. The visibility was linked to the high profile coming out of pop icons such as David Bowie, Elton John, and Kate Millet; films such as *Cabaret* (1972) and *The Rocky Horror Picture Show* (1975); and stories about "bisexual chic" in *Time* and *Newsweek* (1974).

REFERENCES

Armstrong, Elizabeth. 1995. "Traitors to the Cause? Understanding the Lesbian/Gay 'Bisexuality Debates.'" In Naomi Tucker (ed.) *Bisexual Politics: Theories, Queries, and Visions.* Binghamton, NY: Haworth.

Chauncey, George. 1994. *Gay New York: Gender, Urban Culture, and the Gay Male World, 1890–1940.* New York: Basic Books.

Echols, Alice. 1989. *Daring to be Bad: Radical Feminism in America, 1967–1975.* Minneapolis: University of Minnesota.

Hutchins, Loraine. 1996. "Bisexuality: Politics and Community." In Beth A. Firestein (ed.) *Bisexuality: The Psychology and Politics of an Invisible Minority.* Thousand Oaks, CA: Sage.

James, Christopher. 1996. "Denying Complexity: The Dismissal and Appropriation of Bisexuality in Queer, Lesbian, and Gay Theory." In Brett Beemyn and Mickey Eliason (eds.) *Queer Studies: A Lesbian, Gay, Bisexual, and Transgender Anthology.* New York: NYU.

Rust, Paula C. Rodriguez. 1993. " 'Coming Out' in the Age of Social Constructionism: Sexual Identity Formation Among Lesbian and Bisexual Women." *Gender & Society.* 71: 50–77.

———1995. *Bisexuality and the Challenge to Lesbian Politics.* New York: NYU.

———2000. "Popular Images and the Growth of Bisexual Community and Visibility." In *Bisexuality in the United States: A Social Science Reader.* New York: Columbia University.

———2002. "Bisexuality: The State of the Union." *Annual Review of Sex Research.* 13: 31—68.

Savin-Williams, Ritch C. 2005. *The New Gay Teenager.* Cambridge, MA: Harvard University.

Sheff, Elisabeth. 2005. "Polyamorous women, sexual subjectivity, and power." *Journal of Contemporary Ethnography.* 34, 3: 251—283.

Stein, Arlene. 1992. "Sisters and Queers: the Decentering of Lesbian Feminism." *Socialist Review.* 22, 1: 33–55.

Storr, Merl. 1999. "Editor's Introduction." In *Bisexuality: A Critical Reader.* London: Routledge.

Udis-Kessler, Amanda. 1996. "Identity/Politics: Historical Sources of the Bisexual Movement." In Brett Beemyn and Mickey Eliason (eds.) *Queer Studies: A Lesbian, Gay, Bisexual, and Transgender Anthology.* New York: NYU.

Weinberg, Martin S., Colin J. Williams, and Douglas W. Pryor. 1994. *Dual Attraction: Understanding Bisexuality.* New York, NY: Oxford University Press.

2

INVESTIGATING SEXUALITY

AN INTERVIEW WITH

MIGNON R. MOORE

Mignon R. Moore, Ph.D., is Associate Professor of Sociology and African American Studies at UCLA. She is the recipient of several honors including an early Faculty Career Award from the Woodrow Wilson Foundation and a national award from the Human Rights Campaign for her professional work and outreach with LGBT communities of color. Her 2011 book Invisible Families: Gay Identities, Relationships and Motherhood among Black Women *(University of California Press) examines how lesbian women of color form and raise families and experience their gay identities while retaining connections to their racial/ethnic communities. She also holds a grant from the National Institutes of Health for her study examining the social histories, current health outcomes, and sources of social support for older African American sexual minorities. A related project examines the relationships Black LGBT people have with their racial and religious communities, and the characteristics of LGBT protest in racial community contexts.*

What led you to begin studying sexuality?

I became interested in studying various aspects of sexuality, particularly as they relate to African American women, in part because of the existing negative stereotypes in society and in the literature regarding Black women and their processes of family formation. Much of the research on this population lacks an in-depth analysis of the choices Black women and girls make around their bodies, their relationships, and more generally their lives. My dissertation examined the predictors of early sexual debut and pregnancy among African American adolescents in high-poverty neighborhoods. Rather than compare them to their White, middle-class peers as other work had done, I looked at the risk and protective factors within these social contexts that were associated with more positive outcomes for these young women.

I began studying lesbian, gay, and bisexual women in 2003. After meeting and getting to know a working-class Black lesbian couple, I realized that the literature in LGBT studies, family studies, and even in African American studies provided almost no information about the family experiences of Black gay women. I wrote *Invisible Families: Gay Identities, Relationships and Motherhood among Black Women* as a corrective to these literatures, and as a way to increase the visibility of working-class and middle-class gay women of color.

How do people react when you tell them you study sexuality?

These days, people usually show great interest in the type of work I do and the methods I use for uncovering and studying LGBT populations. However, when I first started my book project, the country was not talking as openly about gay sexuality. This was before many of the political debates on legalizing same-sex marriage had really begun to permeate the discourse of regular, everyday people. At earlier stages in my career I was hesitant to let people know that the focus of my research was Black gay women. I feared I would be marginalized in the scholarly community, or that my work would be ignored and seen as insignificant. However, I knew that there were important sociological understandings that would come from this work, and that it was necessary to be brave and to take the lead in helping several areas of study move forward.

What ethical dilemmas have you faced as you've studied sexuality? Could you tell us about a particularly thorny dilemma and how you solved it?

When writing my book *Invisible Families*, I had to decide how much to reveal about my own sexuality. I knew that readers would want to know whether I am gay and how that might have influenced my research, both in the data collection and in the way I portray the families in the study. I knew that once it was written in the book that I am a gay woman, it would stand forever and anyone who read the book would know. I grew up in a conservative Christian denomination and knew that some of the parishioners in my family's church might read the book. I worried that my parents would be uncomfortable with their friends knowing about my sexuality. Nevertheless I decided to be upfront about my sexuality in the book because I did not want fear of knowledge to be present in the work or in my own personal life. Thus far, my parents have only had positive things to say about my work. They are proud of my accomplishments.

What do you think is most challenging about studying sexuality?

One of the most challenging things about studying sexuality is that it elicits such strong feelings from so many groups! Sexuality is something that is difficult for people to talk about, particularly those who deem themselves "respectable." Several studies have shown, for example, that even many physicians are uncomfortable talking about sexuality with their patients. It is an area of scholarship that has not always received serious consideration in the field of sociology, so as a sociologist studying lesbian families I have had to show connections between sexuality and other areas of the discipline that are more easily accepted, such as family and gender.

Why is sex research important?

The study of sexuality in society is important because it gives us a window into an important aspect of human behavior. Studying the sexuality of different groups adds to our understandings of how social groups operate. I focus on the ways context influences how individuals in groups understand their own sexuality.

Of the projects you've done over the course of your academic career, which was most interesting and why?

Completing my book *Invisible Families* was one of the most challenging and rewarding feats of my career because it required me to forge new ground in several fields of study. In the book I challenge several assumptions in the feminist literature, I show a new applicability to the intersectionality paradigm, and I make visible the multi-faceted lives of a stigmatized population. Ultimately I want people to know that social contexts, including race, ethnicity, gender, region, social class, and religiosity—all influence how individuals enact a sexuality.

ALFRED KINSEY AND THE KINSEY REPORT

VERN L. BULLOUGH

The more I study the development of modern sexuality, the more I believe in the importance and significance of Alfred Kinsey. Although his research was on Americans, it came to be a worldwide source of information about human sexuality and set standards for sex research everywhere. In America and much of the world, his work was a decisive factor in changing attitudes toward sex. Within the field of sexuality, he reoriented the field, moving it away from the medical model and medical dominance, to one encompassing a variety of disciplines and approaches. In short, his work has proved revolutionary.

To understand what Kinsey wrought, one must look at the field of sexuality when Kinsey began his studies. One must also look briefly at Kinsey as an individual to understand his accomplishments.

SEX RESEARCH, 1890–1940

The modern study of sexuality began in the nineteenth century, and these early studies were dominated by physicians. It was assumed that since physicians were the experts on body functions, they should be the experts regarding sexual activities. In a sense, this was a divergence from the past, when sexuality had been regarded almost entirely as a moral issue. And although there were still moral issues involved, physicians were also judged as qualified to speak on these issues as well. Although few physicians had any specialized knowledge on most sexual topics, except perhaps for sexually transmitted diseases, this did not prevent them from speaking with authority on most aspects of human sexuality.

Havelock Ellis, one of the dominant figures in promoting sexual knowledge in the first third of the twentieth century, said that he sought a medical degree primarily because it was the only profession in which he could safely study sex. Inevitably, most of the so-called experts were physicians. Equal in influence to Ellis was Magnus Hirschfeld, another physician. Both Ellis and Hirschfeld compiled what could be called sexual histories, as Kinsey later compiled. Ellis, however, acquired almost all of his histories from correspondence of volunteers and, as far as I know, never interviewed anyone. Hirschfeld, later in his career, compiled many case histories based on interviews, but early on he depended mainly on historical data and personal knowledge. Unfortunately, Hirschfeld used only a small portion of his data in his published books, and before he could complete a comprehensive study of sexuality, his files were destroyed by the Nazis (Bullough, 1994).

Although some of the data physicians reported about sex [were] was gathered from their own practices, these [data] were usually interpreted in terms of traditional views and were supplemented by historical materials or reports of anthropologists [in order] to increase their authenticity. Simply put, most physicians writing about sex were influenced more by the zeitgeist of the time rather than by any specialized base of knowledge. A few early physician investigators, such as the American obstetrician

From "Alfred Kinsey and the Kinsey Report: Historical Overview and Lasting Contributions" by Vern L. Bullough, *Journal of Sex Research*, Vol. 35, Issue 2, 1998, pp. 127–131. Copyright © 1998 Routledge, reprinted by permission of the publisher (Taylor & Francis Ltd, http://www.tandf.co.uk/journals).

Robert Latou Dickinson (Dickinson and Beam, 1931, 1934), had over 1,000 case studies, but most had only a handful. As the twentieth century progressed, the ordinary physician probably was regarded as the easiest available authority on sex, but most of the medical writings on sexual topics came from psychiatrists, particularly those who were psychoanalytically trained (Bullough, 1997). Unfortunately, even the most comprehensive sex studies undertaken by psychiatrists, such as that of George Henry, were flawed by the assumptions of the investigators interpreting data. For example, they assumed that homosexuals were ill. Moreover, whether the answers to their questions were valid for determining differences with heterosexuals is uncertain, as there was a lack of any comparative study of heterosexuals (Henry, 1941).

Still, assumptions about medical expertise remained. When the Committee for Research in the Problems in Sex (CRPS), the Rockefeller-funded grant-giving body operating under the umbrella of the National Research Council, began to explore the possibilities of carrying out surveys of sexual behavior, they first sought out physicians. For example, Adolf Meyer of Johns Hopkins University was commissioned to complete a study of attitudes of medical students, but failed to complete his work. The only social scientists funded in the first 20 years of the CRPS were psychologists, although anthropological consultants and members of other fields provided occasional input. Lewis Terman, for example, was given funds to carry out studies on attitudes toward sex and marriage. Though his and similar studies were valuable, they depended on questionnaires rather than interviews to gather their data (Terman, Buttenweiser, Ferguson, Johnson, and Wilson, 1938), and the sexual part of their studies was secondary to other interests. Even though one of the major reasons the CRPS had been created

in 1921 was to complete such general studies, the committee members were either unwilling or unable to find a person to carry out this kind of study. I suspect that the first factor was more important than the second: There is considerable evidence to indicate that the committee members were uncomfortable with studies on actual sexual behavior and much preferred to fund what might be called bench (i.e., laboratory-based) scientists to social scientists. I should add that this attitude was not shared by the Rockefeller Foundation or John D. Rockefeller, Jr.: both funded other survey projects dealing with sex, including that of Katherine Bement Davis (1929).

Funding for research projects when Kinsey began his work operated much more according to an old-boy network than it does today. There was little advertisement of fund availability and individuals were invited to apply, had to be nominated to apply, or had to have a connection. Certain universities and individuals dominated the disbursement of the money available. To an observer [today] examining most of the research grants given for sex research, the relationships look almost incestuous.

Unfortunately for the committee, sex activity could not be studied exclusively in the laboratory or even in the field by observing animals or gathering historical data. There had been nongrant-supported popular studies of sex, but their samples were not representative and the questionnaires were poorly designed. Moreover, in keeping with its reliance on academia, the committee seemed reluctant to give its imprimatur to individuals conducting such studies. What was needed was a person willing to blaze new trails, dispassionately examining sex without the preconceived notions of most of the physicians then involved in writing about sex. The qualified individual or individuals needed an academic connection, preferably one with an established reputation for scientific studies.

KINSEY COMES ON THE SCENE

It was in this setting that Kinsey entered the scene. He was the right person at the right time; that is, a significant amount of money was available for sex research and there was an interest within the CRPS for some general kind of survey of American sex behavior. Who was Kinsey?

In terms of overall qualification, Kinsey's best asset was that he was a bench scientist, a biologist with a Ph.D. from Harvard, and an internationally known expert on gall wasps. But he was also a broad-based scientist. Unlike most research scientists today, who often are part of a team, researchers in the 1930s in the United States were self-dedicated and carried a major teaching load. Kinsey, for example, simultaneously taught general biology, published two editions of a popular introductory general biology text, two editions of a workbook, and a general text on methods in biology, and carried out major research. His entry into sex seems to have been serendipitous, taking place after he had completed his studies on gall wasps. Professors at the University of Indiana had discussed the possibility of an introductory cross-discipline course on marriage, then a topic beginning to receive some attention in academic circles. Kinsey was not only involved in such discussions but took the lead. In 1938, he was invited to coordinate and direct the new course on marriage and family. As a sign of the time, the course was taught by an all-male faculty from a variety of disciplines, including law, economics, sociology, philosophy, medicine, and biology.

Before the appearance of courses on marriage and family, the academic discussion of human sexuality had been confined to lectures in the hygiene-type courses that had been established on many campuses in the second decade of the twentieth century, largely through the efforts of the American Social Hygiene Association. The approach to sex of these hygiene classes was quite different from that of the marriage and family courses, as they generally emphasized the dangers of sexually transmitted diseases and masturbation. In a sense, these hygiene-type courses were conceived to preserve sexual purity, whereas the sexual portions of marriage and family courses provided information, following the outlines of the better sex manuals of the time.

Kinsey went even further in his discussion of sexuality than the sex-positive marriage manuals, and soon clashed with Thurman Rice, a bacteriology professor who had written extensively on sex, primarily from the point of view of eugenics. For many years, Rice had delivered the sex lectures in the required hygiene course, where the males were separated from the females when he gave his lectures. Kinsey deliberately had not included Rice in his recruited faculty, which probably furthered Rice's antagonism. Rice was typical of an earlier generation of sex educators in that he considered moral education an essential part of sex education. He believed and taught that masturbation was harmful, condemned premarital intercourse, and was fearful that Kinsey's course on marriage was a perversion of academic standards. For example, he charged Kinsey with asking some of the women students about the length of their clitorises. To show that his accusations were based on more than gossip, Rice demanded the names of students in Kinsey's class so that he could verify such classroom voyeurism. Rice opposed Kinsey's questioning of students because he believed that sexual behavior could not and should not be analyzed by scientific methods because it was a moral topic, not a scientific one. Rice's perspective thus was perhaps typical of the hygiene approach to sex.

Kinsey had probably been doing at least some of the things that Rice mentioned because he had approached sex as a taxonomist—as one interested in classifying and describing—as a dispassionate scientist and not as a reformer or politician. In a sense, he was a political innocent. He believed that science could speak for itself, and he criticized his faculty colleagues who took any kind of political stand. He refused to join organizations that he felt had any kind of political agenda, including the Society for the Scientific Study of Sexuality (SSSS) in its early years.

There is, however, much more to Kinsey's interest in sex than the dispassionate scientist. In his personal life, he was not inhibited about body functions. Even before starting his course on marriage, he had sought information about the sex life of his students. His openness about sex (see Jones, 1997: 1997a) was what Rice objected to.

It might well be that when Kinsey began teaching the sex course, he was undergoing a kind of midlife crisis, feeling that he had come to know all he wanted to know about gall wasps and needing to explore new fields. Sex to him represented an unexplored new field where comparatively little was known, and where there was much information to be gleaned. He began his study as he had that of gall wasps: finding out what was known and, in the process, building up a personal library of serious books on sex (hardly any of these had found their way into university libraries) and reading extensively. He also sought first-hand information by questioning his students about topics such as their age at first premarital intercourse, frequency of sexual activity, and number of partners.

All this gave fodder to Rice and his allies, including a number of parents who, perhaps at Rice's urging, complained about the specific sexual data given in the course and particularly about questions that Kinsey asked of his students. The president of the university, Herman Wells, a personal friend of Kinsey who had appointed him coordinator of the course, counseled him and gave him two options: to continue to teach the course and give up some of his probing of student lives, or to devote more time to his sex research and not teach the course. Because Kinsey had already begun to extend his interviews off campus, the answer was perhaps inevitable. Although Kinsey continued to teach courses in biology, his load was reduced, and much of his life came to be devoted to sex research.

Because Kinsey was already well connected to the scientific establishment, his initial efforts to study sex received encouragement from the CRPS. He received an exploratory grant from them in 1941, during which time he would be evaluated as to suitability for a larger grant. George W. Corner, a physician member and later the chair of the CRPS, visited Kinsey as one of the grant investigators to determine whether Kinsey deserved further funding. He was tremendously impressed and reported that Kinsey was the most intense scientist he had ever met. He added that Kinsey could talk about little besides his research. According to Corner (1981), Kinsey was an ideal person for a grant to study sex:

He was a full professor, married with adolescent children. While carrying on his teaching duties in the zoology department he worked every available hour, day and night, traveling anywhere that people would give him interviews. He was training a couple of young men in his method of interviewing. Dr. Yerkes and I submitted separately to his technique. I was astonished at his skill in eliciting the most intimate details of the subject's sexual history. Introducing his queries gradually, he managed to convey an assurance of complete confidentiality by recording the answers on special sheets printed with a grid on which he set down the information gained, by unintelligible signs, explaining that the code had never been written down and only his two colleagues could read it. His questions included subtle tricks to detect deliberate misinformation. (p. 268)

Important to the continuation of the grant was the support of the university administration and its president, which Kinsey received despite sniping by some fellow faculty members such as Rice and others who regarded Kinsey's interest in sex with suspicion. As Corner's reference to Kinsey's family indicates, the committee wanted to make certain that the researcher had no special agenda except, perhaps, to establish some guides to better marriages. Kinsey satisfied them on this account and was well aware that any indication otherwise might endanger his grant. Thus, his own sex life remained a closed book, only to be opened by later generations of scholars (Jones, 1997). The CRPS came to be so committed to Kinsey that by the 1946–1947 academic year, he was receiving half of the committee's total budget.

Before the interviews stopped with Kinsey's death, about 18,000 individuals had been interviewed, 8,000 by Kinsey himself. Kinsey strongly believed that people would not always tell the truth when questioned about their sexual activities and that the only way to deal with this was through personal interviews in which the contradictions could be explored. He did not believe that self-administered questionnaires produced accurate responses: He regarded them as encouraging dishonest answers. He also recognized that respondents might lie even in a personal interview, but he provided a variety of checks to detect this and believed his checks were successful. Subjects were usually told that there were some contradictions in their answers and were asked to explain them. If they refused to do so, the interview was terminated and the information not used. Kinsey was also aware of potential bias of the interviewer. He sought to overcome this bias by occasionally having two people conduct the interviews at different times and by relying mainly on four interviewers, including himself, to conduct the study. If there was a bias, it came to be a shared one. The questions, however, were so wide-ranging that this too would limit much of the potential for slanting the data in any one direction. Following taxonomic principles, he wanted to gather data from as many

subjects as possible, and he hoped initially to conduct 20,000 interviews and later to conduct 80,000 more. He did not live to achieve this. Before he died, the funding sources had dried up for such research, and other methods based on statistical sampling grew more popular.

WHAT KINSEY DID

Kinsey's major accomplishment was to challenge most of the assumptions about sexual activity in the United States. In so doing, he aroused great antagonism among many who opposed making sexual issues a matter of public discussion and debate. One reason for the antagonism is that he brought to public notice many sexual practices that previously had not been publicly discussed. Although Kinsey prided himself as an objective scientist, it was his very attempt to establish a taxonomy of sexual behaviors—treating all activities as more or less within the range of human behavior—that got him into trouble. Karl Menninger, for example, said that "Kinsey's compulsion to force human sexual behavior into a zoological frame of reference leads him to repudiate or neglect human psychology, and to see normality as that which is natural in the sense that it is what is practiced by animals" (quoted in Pomeroy, 1972, p. 367).

Most sex researchers today accept the fact that total objectivity in our field is probably impossible. Some of Kinsey's difficulty resulted from his belief that he could be totally objective. He did not realize that the way he organized his data sometimes could challenge his objectivity, even though the organization seemed logical. For example, Kinsey developed a seven-point bipolar scale, which was one of the standard methods of organizing data in social science research at that time. He did not trust people's self-classification as homosexual or heterosexual. Therefore, he decided that regardless of how they might have classified themselves, the only objective indicator that he could use was to define sex in terms of outlet—namely, what activity resulted in orgasms.

In most seven-point scales, the extremes are represented by 0 and 6 (or by 1 and 7, depending upon the number with which the scale starts). Most people tend to respond using the middle of the scale. When one rates heterosexual orgasm as 0 and homosexual orgasm 6, a logical decision in terms of taxonomy, he in effect weights the scale by seeming to imply that exclusive heterosexuality is one extreme and exclusive homosexuality the other. Although his data demonstrated that far more people were identified as exclusively heterosexual than as any other category, his scale also implied that homosexuality was just another form of sexual activity, something that I think Kinsey believed was true. For his time and place this was revolutionary. His discussion of homosexuality and its prevalence resulted in the most serious attacks upon him and his data (Kinsey, Pomeroy, and Martin, 1948).

Kinsey was a trailblazer, openly and willingly challenging many basic societal beliefs. It was not only his dispassionate discussion of homosexuality that roused controversy, but also his tendency to raise questions that society at that time preferred to ignore. In his book on males, for example, he questioned the assumption that extramarital intercourse always undermined the stability of marriage and held that the full story was more complex than the most highly publicized cases led one to assume. He seemed to feel that the most appropriate extramarital affair, from the standpoint of preserving a marriage, was an alliance in which neither party became overly involved emotionally. Concerned over the reaction to this, however, he became somewhat more cautious in the book on females. He conceded that extramarital affairs probably contributed to divorces in more ways and to a "greater extent than the subjects themselves realized" (Kinsey, Pomeroy, Martin, and Gebhard, 1953, p. 31).

Kinsey was interested in many different sexual behaviors, including that between genera-

tions (i.e., adults with children or minors). One of his more criticized sections in recent years is the table based on data he gathered from pedophiles. He is accused of not turning these people over to authorities, although one of the major informants was already serving time in jail for his sexual activities when interviewed. Kinsey gathered his data wherever he could find it, but he also reported on the source of his data. His own retrospective data tended to show that many individuals who experienced intergenerational sex as children were not seriously harmed by it, another statement that got him into trouble.

Kinsey is also criticized for his statistical sampling. Although his critics (even before his studies were published) attempted to get him to validate his data with a random sample of individuals, he refused on the grounds that not all of those included in the random sample would answer the questions put to them and that, therefore, the random sample would be biased. It is quite clear that Kinsey's sample is not random and that it overrepresents some segments of the population, including students and residents of Indiana. Part of the criticism, however, is also due to the use and misuse of the Kinsey data without his qualifications. This is particularly true of his data on same-sex relationships, which are broken down by age and other variables and therefore allowed others to choose the number or percentage of the sample they wanted to use in their own reports.

Another assumption of American society that Kinsey also challenged was the asexuality of women. This proved the issue of greatest controversy in his book on females. A total of 40% of the females he studied had experienced orgasm within the first months of marriage, 67% by the first six months, and 75% by the end of the first year. Twenty-five percent of his sample had experienced orgasm by age of 15, more than 50% by the age of 20, and 64% before marriage. On the other hand, he also reported cases in which women failed to reach orgasm after 20 years of marriage. In spite of the controversies over his data on orgasms, it helped move the issue of female sexuality on to the agenda of the growing women's movement of the late 1960s and the 1970s, and to encourage further studies of female sexuality.

In light of the challenges against him, Kinsey ignored in his writings what might be called sexual adventurers, paying almost no attention to swinging, group sex, and alternate lifestyles such as sadism, masochism, transvestism, voyeurism, and exhibitionism. He justified this neglect by arguing that such practices were statistically insignificant. It is more likely that Kinsey was either not interested in them or not interested in exploring them. He was also not particularly interested in pregnancy or sexually transmitted diseases. However, he demystified discussion of sex insofar as that was possible. Sex, to him, was just another aspect of human behavior, albeit an important part. He made Americans and the world at large aware of just how big a part human sexuality played in the life cycle of the individual and how widespread many kinds of sexual activities were.

Kinsey was determined to make the study of sex a science, a subject that could be studied in colleges much the same way that animal reproduction was, with succeeding generations of researchers adding to the knowledge base. He succeeded, at least in the long run. He had a vision of the kind of studies that still needed to be done, some of which were later done by his successors at Indiana and elsewhere, but he himself died before he could do them and the funds dried up.

Another of his significant contributions was to establish a library and to gather sources about sexuality from all over the world. He blazed a trail for future sex researchers: The library he established at Indiana University served as an example that helped many of us to persuade other university libraries to collect works from this field. Although there are now several impressive collections of this kind in the country, Kinsey's collection is still tremendously important.

In sum, Kinsey was the major factor in changing attitudes about sex in the twentieth century. His limitations and his personal foibles are appropriately overshadowed by his courage to go where others had not gone before. In spite of the vicious attacks upon him during his last few years of life, and the continuing attacks today, his data continue to be cited and used (and misused). He changed the nature of sexual studies, forced a reexamination of public attitudes toward sex, challenged the medical and psychiatric establishment to reassess its own views, influenced both the feminist movement and the gay and lesbian movement, and built a library and an institution devoted to sex research. His reputation continues to grow, and he has become one of the legends of the twentieth century. . . .

REFERENCES

Bullough, V. L. 1994. *Science in the bedroom: A history of sex research*. New York: Basic Books.

Bullough, V. L. 1997. American physicians and sex research. *Journal of the History of Medicine*, 57, 236–253.

Corner, G. W. 1981. *The seven ages of a medical scientist*. Philadelphia: University of Pennsylvania Press.

Davis, K. B. 1929. *Factors in the sex life of twenty-two hundred women*. New York: Harper.

Dickinson, R. L., and Beam, L. 1931. *A thousand marriages*. Baltimore: Williams and Wilkins.

Dickinson, R. L., and Beam, L. 1934. *The single woman*. Baltimore: Williams and Wilkins.

Henry, G. 1941. *Sex variants: a study of homosexual patterns* (2 vols.). New York: Hoeber.

Jones, J. H. 1997, August 2 and September 1. Annals of sexology: Dr. Yes. *New Yorker*, pp. 99–113.

Jones, J. H. 1997a. *Kinsey: A Public/Private Life*. New York: Norton.

Kinsey, A., Pomeroy, W., and Martin, C. 1948. *Sexual behavior in the human male*. Philadelphia: Saunders.

Kinsey, A., Pomeroy, W., Martin, C., and Gebhard, P. 1953. *Sexual behavior in the human female*. Philadelphia: Saunders.

Pomeroy, W. B. 1972. *Dr. Kinsey and the Institute for Sex Research*. New York: Harper and Row.

Terman, L., Buttenweiser, P., Ferguson. L., Johnson, W. B., and Wilson, D. P. 1938. *Psychological factors in marital happiness*. New York: McGraw-Hill.

LARGE SCALE SEX: METHODS, CHALLENGES, AND FINDINGS OF NATIONALLY REPRESENTATIVE SEX RESEARCH

AMANDA M. JUNGELS AND STACY GORMAN

"We know gossip about the sex lives of famous people . . . what we don't know—and what is of immensely greater importance—is what the rest of us ordinary folks have been doing between the sheets."[1]

Have you ever wondered how old the average American is when they lose their virginity? Or how many sexual partners they have in a lifetime? Since Alfred Kinsey completed his revolutionary sex research in the 1950s, sex researchers have been struggling to answer these questions (and many more) about Americans' sexual practices. While Kinsey's research was large scale (collecting the sexual histories of more than 18,000 Americans), his sample was not representative of the general population; at the time, Kinsey did not believe that it was possible to collect data on sexual practices successfully from a random sample of Americans (Kinsey Institute 2011; Michael, Gagnon, Laumann, and Kolata 1994). Since the 1950s, few researchers have taken on the challenge of conducting large-scale representative studies on the sexual practices of Americans, "perhaps because it was considered too dull, trivial, and self-evident to deserve attention" (Laumann, Gagnon, Michael and Michaels 1994a:37). Yet Americans still wanted information about sexual practices, despite the lack of reliable information that was available. So they turned to less-than-reliable data gathered by mainstream publications like *Cosmopolitan*, *Redbook*, and *Playboy* (Laumann et al., 1994a; Michael et al., 1994). Unfortunately, magazine surveys are fraught with many problems; a major one is that their samples are usually drawn from a small portion of the magazine's own readers. Thus, their samples are not representative of the general American population (i.e., *Redbook* readers are mostly affluent married White women); in addition, those who volunteer to participate in such surveys may be very different from those who do not (Michael et al., 1994). So, when we want to know information about Americans' sexual behavior— to answer these questions about the "average American," or Americans in general—a nationally representative sample is necessary.

Nationally representative research is useful in a number of ways, but foremost is the fact that it is the only kind of research that allows us to generalize to the overall population. Representative samples use probability sampling techniques, which means that everyone in the population has an equal and known chance of being selected to participate. But how does one randomly select a set of Americans in a way that ensures that everyone has an equal chance of participating? There is no "list" of Americans that one could randomly select from; even a semi-complete list (from each state's Department of Motor Vehicles, for example) would exclude some people (those who cannot afford to own a car, cannot drive, or who use public transportation might be excluded from such a list).

There are a variety of ways to do it, but many researchers use multi-stage area probability sampling. Two of the studies reviewed in this reading used this form of sampling—the National Health and Social Life Survey, conducted in the early 1990s, and the National

Survey of Family Growth, which has been conducted every few years since the 1970s. Both of these studies began their sampling by using Primary Sampling Units (PSUs), which are large geographic areas (including major metropolitan areas or several counties grouped together). The researchers randomly selected a set of PSUs; within these larger areas, they selected smaller areas that are analogous to neighborhoods (called "segments"). After randomly selecting segments, they listed all addresses within each segment. Not every address in a given neighborhood is a residential address—there are vacant lots, empty houses, and businesses. To address this issue, researchers would often dispatch an assistant who traveled the neighborhood and confirmed which addresses were residences. After this information had been confirmed, the researchers randomly selected addresses to include, and then randomly selected someone from the household to participate.

While nationally representative surveys are an important part of understanding the lives of the general population, there are many challenges to conducting such large-scale research. The greatest of these challenges—whether the research is about sexual behavior or not—is ensuring that the sample reflects the demographic characteristics of the population and that no groups are left out of the sample. For example, while researchers acknowledge that sampling "households" is an acceptable method of drawing a national sample, around 3 percent of the population in this country do not live in households and will be excluded (those in institutional settings such as college students in dorms, individuals in prisons or jails, seniors in assisted living facilities, homeless people, etc.) (Laumann et al., 1994a). A related challenge is that members of racial and ethnic minority groups are often underrepresented in national samples. To combat this pattern, most nationally representative surveys "oversample" minor-

ity groups to ensure that they are represented in final samples in high enough numbers for analysis. Sexual minorities (particularly salient to sex researchers) such as gay men and lesbians are not as "easily identifiable" as members of racial and ethnic minority groups, making it challenging to oversample them (Michael et al., 1994:29). A final challenge of large-scale research is that it describes "general" experiences and patterns; these patterns do not always coincide with an individual's specific experience. Large-scale representative studies offer us a "snapshot" of the American population at the time the research is conducted (Michael et al., 1994).

But selecting a representative sample is not the only challenge that researchers have to face. In addition to practical design challenges, researchers also must contend with the cost of implementing such large surveys. Outside of government agencies, there are few organizations with the resources to fund large projects, and receiving government funding is fraught with complications and problems (see "Challenges of Funding Sex Research" later in this chapter). Two of the studies reviewed in this reading had major funding challenges—the National Health and Social Life Survey lost its government funding in the 1990s, and the National Survey of Sexual Health and Behavior used exclusively private funding because of the lack of available government funding (Reece, Herbernick, Schick, Sanders, Dodge, and Fortenberry, 2010a). The government funds the National Survey of Family Growth, but it does not focus exclusively on sexual practices or attitudes.

We present findings below for all three of these nationally representative surveys, as well as discuss their challenges, strengths, and limitations. Ideally, comparisons would be made across studies to look for changes across time in the sexual behaviors of the participants; however, this is difficult because of major differences across the studies themselves. The methods used and questions asked are not the same across all three studies, and there are even differences in the specific focuses and goals of the researchers. For these reasons, we highlight what we consider to be major findings which might be new or different in comparison to other studies, or that challenge mainstream perceptions of the "average American's" sexual experiences.

NATIONAL HEALTH AND SOCIAL LIFE SURVEY (1994)

The National Health and Social Life Survey (NHSLS) began in 1987 as a government-funded effort to better understand Americans' sexual practices, largely in response to the developing HIV/AIDS crisis (Laumann, Michael, and Gagnon 1994b). Besides Kinsey's results, scholars had very little information about Americans' sexual behaviors. What was missing was how sexual behaviors had changed in the intervening years and how sexual behaviors and attitudes would impact sexually transmitted infection rates (Laumann et al., 1994a).

Designing and implementing the study was complicated by the fact that the researchers from the University of Chicago and the government officials who were spearheading the project seemed to have different goals (Michael et al., 1994). The researchers wanted to include broad questions about sexual behavior, but government officials wanted a strict focus on sexually transmitted infections (STIs) and HIV/AIDS. The researchers wanted to include broad questions about a wide variety of issues connected to sexuality, arguing that so little was known about American sexual practices that they would not assume to know what factors were relevant; government officials argued that some topics (including masturbation) had nothing to do with the transmission of STIs and thus should be excluded from the research (Michael

et al., 1994). Given that government approval (and funding) was necessary to conduct the research, the research team relented and narrowed their field of study to specific health and HIV/AIDS-related questions (Michael et al., 1994).

After the research team had refined the survey and research design, they awaited approval from several government agencies that were involved with the funding of the project. During this review process, the magazine *Science* ran a story about the project, illustrated with a picture from the film *Bob and Carol and Ted and Alice*—a film about two couples that partner-swap (Laumann et al., 1994b). Several conservative members of Congress honed in on the article and photo and began attacking the research. Representative William Dannemeyer argued that the research was "a plot by homosexuals to legitimate the normality of gay and lesbian lifestyles . . . and the project staff had an anti-family agenda" (Laumann et al., 1994b:35). Dannemeyer also deliberately sensationalized the content of the study by reading questions from the survey out of context on the floor of Congress and to the press (Laumann et al., 1994b). Defending the scientific merits of the study was left to the few in Congress and government who supported the project because the research team was under a government gag order (Laumann et al., 1994b). In 1991, after several years of debate and deadlock, the House of Representatives removed all funding for the project (Laumann et al., 1994b). The research team eventually received private funding from several organizations (although the amount was significantly reduced) and, "freed of political constraints," was able to conduct much broader research; unfortunately the reduction in funding meant dramatically reducing the scale of the project (Michael et al., 1994:28).

The NHSLS used the multi-stage sampling technique that was outlined earlier, and researchers collected data through in-depth ninety-minute interviews (Laumann et al., 1994a, Michael et al., 1994). The researchers used some of the time their survey was being investigated by Congress to do pre-tests of the survey. Important findings from these pre-tests guided the full-scale national study; for example, they learned that terms like "vaginal," "anal," "heterosexual," and "homosexual" were not well understood by the general public—but they could not use slang terms for fear of offending or confusing respondents (Michael et al., 1994). Instead, questions were constructed to include a definition. For instance, questions about anal sex would explain that this refers to a penis entering the rectum or butt. They also investigated by whom their respondents would be most comfortable being interviewed. Using focus groups with people of different ages, races, and socioeconomic backgrounds, they learned that almost everyone (regardless of age, race, and gender) agreed that they would be most comfortable with middle-aged White women (Michael et al., 1994). Despite concerns about getting people to participate in sex research, almost 80 percent of those contacted to participate were successfully interviewed (Laumann et al., 1994a; Michael et al., 1994). Overall, the NHSLS included a representative sample of 3,432 respondents (Laumann et al., 1994a; Michael et al., 1994).

FINDINGS OF THE NATIONAL HEALTH AND SOCIAL LIFE SURVEY[2]

The researchers behind the NHSLS approached their task from a distinctly sociological perspective, acknowledging that "an individual's social environment affects sexual behavior" (Laumann et al., 1994a:4). Any number of social factors, including age, race, socioeconomic status, and gender affect an individual's sexual behavior, the meanings they associate with sex, and even what they believe "counts" as sex. The NHSLS attempted to describe the relationships between an individual's social position and their sexual practices and attitudes by looking at patterns that developed between them (Laumann et al., 1994a).

Sexual Behaviors and Number of Sexual Partners

Popular media often tell us that the average American has a varied and exciting sex life, including high numbers of sex partners and very frequent sex; the NHSLS suggests that these representations are inaccurate. According to the NHSLS, the vast majority of Americans tended to be monogamous, had either zero or one partners per year, and had fewer than four sexual partners after age 18. In terms of gender differences, men had sex earlier in life and reported more sexual partners over their lifetimes than women.

Sexual Orientation

One of the most innovative parts of the NHSLS was how the researchers measured sexual orientation. Many Americans believe that same-sex sexual behavior, identity, and desire are intrinsically linked. Guided by a sociological perspective, the researchers measured these concepts separately. While there was, of course, some overlap between desire, behavior, and identity (for example, most individuals who self-identified as gay or lesbian also reported same-sex desire and behaviors), there were significant numbers of participants who reported either same-sex desire without corresponding behavior or same-sex behavior without corresponding self-identification. Further reinforcing the idea that desire, behavior, and self-identity are conceptually different is the fact that ten percent of men reported either same-sex attraction, desire, or identity but less than three percent of men indicated all three; similarly, eight percent of women reported some form of same-sex sexuality (either desire, behavior, or self-identity) but less than 2 percent of women reported all three (Erickson and Steffen 1999).

Forced Sex

One of the results that Laumann and his colleagues found most shocking were the rates of forced and coerced sex among the respondents. The researchers found that almost 22 percent of women reported that they had been forced by a man to do something sexual that they did not want to do; almost all (over 95%) reported that they knew the person that forced them. Interestingly, less than three percent of men reported that they had forced a woman to do something sexual they did not want to do. One of the explanations that Laumann and his colleagues offered for this gap was a difference in sexual scripts; men, they argued, are encouraged to "negotiate" for sex with women, and women are encouraged through traditional gender roles to resist sex. The resultant conflict creates "not a gender gap, but a gender chasm" between men and women's understanding of forced sex (Michael et al., 1994:221).

LIMITATIONS OF THE NATIONAL HEALTH AND SOCIAL LIFE SURVEY

Because it used an area probability sample, the NHSLS excluded those individuals who did not live in a household. The limited availability of funding forced the researchers to limit the sample size, which resulted in some minority groups (gays and lesbians, for example, and some racial/ethnic groups) being inadequately represented. In addition, the sample age range had to be limited to those between the ages of 18–59 (Michael et al., 1994).

Despite the care with which the interview questions were created, the wording of some of the questions has been criticized. For example, one of the major findings of the NHSLS was that women had less sexual experience than men, and reported being less interested in every type of sexual activity compared to men (Erickson and Steffen 1999; Michael et al.,

1994). To understand what kinds of activities people found appealing, respondents were asked to rate a wide variety of sexual activities, ranging from oral sex and anal stimulation to group sex and sex with a stranger. Some critics have argued that what was excluded from this list are "activities that women's sexual scripts define as pleasurable, such as kissing and mutual masturbation . . . the authors, like many male researchers before them, described a world in which men owned desire and initiated sexual activity and women chose whether to respond" (Erickson and Steffen 1999:215).

CONTINUOUS NATIONAL SURVEY OF FAMILY GROWTH (2006–2010)

The National Survey of Family Growth (NSFG) was originally created in 1971 by the Centers for Disease Control and Prevention. Over time, the NSFG has changed dramatically, but the goal of the study—to interview a nationally representative sample of Americans about pregnancy, marriage, and contraceptive use through in-person interviews—has remained the same (Groves, Mosher, Lepkowski, and Kirgis, 2009). Since 1973, data have been gathered every several years using the area probability technique. Each time a cycle was completed, major changes were made. When it was first conducted in 1973, for example, only women who had been or were married were included because it was deemed "too sensitive" to ask women who had never been married about pregnancy and marriage (Martinez, Copen and Abma 2011). Over the years, many modifications have been made: young people, never-married women, and adult men were added to the sample, and changes in technology have allowed researchers to use laptops and interviewing software to encourage participants to answer honestly about sensitive topics and questions (Groves et al., 2009; Martinez et al., 2011).

By the time the sixth cycle of the NSFG was completed in 2002, American society had changed dramatically. It was becoming prohibitively expensive to continue using the same data collection methods (including recruiting participants) because Americans were less willing to participate in large-scale research (Groves et al., 2009). To address these changes, the NSFG underwent a major methodological and design change in 2006. Rather than doing data collection in one 12-month cycle, the researchers decided to collect data continuously throughout the year by using a rotating sample of PSUs (Groves et al., 2009). Collecting data continuously saved the researchers money by allowing them to employ a smaller number of highly skilled interviewers. It also meant researchers could release results more often. More than three-quarters of those contacted participated in the 2006–2010 cycles of the NSFG. Interviewers conducted 22,682 face-to-face interviews with men and women between the ages of 15–44 over that four-year period (Martinez et al., 2011).

FINDINGS OF THE 2006–2008 NATIONAL SURVEY OF FAMILY GROWTH[3]
Sexual Behaviors and Number of Sexual Partners

The findings across the most recent cycles of the NSFG have remained remarkably consistent. The median number of lifetime sexual partners has remained essentially the same since 2002 (3.2 for women and 5.1 for men). Some behaviors are quite common among adults; for example, almost all adult women (98%) and adult men (97%) have engaged in vaginal intercourse. Oral sex is also quite common among adults. The vast majority of those aged 20–24 have engaged in heterosexual oral sex (70% of men and 85% of women). Regard-

TABLE 8.1   Rates of Giving/Receiving Oral Sex Among Adults Aged 20–24, by Race and Gender

	GAVE	RECEIVED
White		
Men	73.9%	77.1%
Women	77%	80.3%
African American		
Men	59.8%	78.6%
Women	66%	81%
Hispanic		
Men	70.6%	84.2%
Women	69.4%	67.8%

less of race, rates of giving and receiving oral sex are very similar across genders; in general, those who have given have also received. These numbers change, though, when comparing young adults (aged 20–24) of different races and genders (see Table 8.1). African American women were less likely than White or Hispanic women to report *giving* oral sex; similarly, African American men were much less likely than Hispanic or White men to report *giving* oral sex. Interestingly, these proportions change when considering the numbers of young adults that report *receiving* oral sex. In this case, Hispanic women were much less likely to report receiving oral sex; African American women and White women reported nearly equal rates of receiving. Among men, Hispanic men were the most likely to report receiving oral sex, with African American men and White men reporting slightly lower rates.

SEXUAL IDENTITY

Like the National Health and Social Life Survey from the 1990s, the NSFG assessed sexual orientation in a variety of ways and found differing levels of same-sex activities depending on how they were measured; they also found large gender differences in the reporting of same-sex sexual experiences. For example, in the 2008 NSFG, approximately one percent of women and two percent of men self-identified as homosexual and approximately four percent of women and one percent of men self-identified as bisexual. Those numbers are significantly lower than the percentage of women (12.5%) and men (5.2%) that reported they had "any same-sex sexual experiences." The ability to compare findings across time is one of the major strengths of the NSFG, especially since there is "considerable fluidity in the development and expression of sexual behavior and orientation over time" (Gartrell, Bos, and Goldberg 2011:3). For example, comparing the data for adolescent girls across the cycles shows that since 2002, the percentage of girls who had sex with boys had dropped significantly while the percentage of girls reporting same-sex contact doubled (from 5% to 10%) (Gartrell et al., 2011). The adolescent girls in the most recent cycles were also older the first time they had sexual contact with boys when compared with girls in the earlier cycles, and were less likely than the earlier cohorts to have experienced a pregnancy (Gartell et al., 2011).

LIMITATIONS OF THE NATIONAL SURVEY OF FAMILY GROWTH

Like the National Health and Social Life Survey, the NSFG excludes those who do not live in a household. In addition, because the original focus of the NSFG was fertility and marriage, it only includes people who are in their reproductive years. While it is beneficial to have teens included in the study, the baby boomer generation is rapidly aging out of their reproductive years—excluding a large portion of the population from participating in the NSFG.

One concern with the NSFG is how the survey measures same-sex sexual behaviors. The most recent cycle of the NSFG uses very broad criteria to measure women's same-sex behavior (assessing oral sex and "sexual experiences" with other women), but very specific measures when measuring the same-sex practices of men (whether they had performed or received oral or anal sex with another man). This could lead to larger numbers of women being classified as having same-sex sexual behavior. The difference in wording might also reflect traditional understandings of gender and sexuality, namely, that sexual acts can be quantified as events that involve genital penetration alone.

NATIONAL SURVEY OF SEXUAL HEALTH AND BEHAVIOR (2010)

By the early 2000s, sexual norms and attitudes in the United States had shifted again. Doctors were frequently prescribing Viagra and other medications to help with sexual dysfunction, allowing older adults to engage in sexual practices later in the life course; attitudes about same-sex practices were liberalizing; sex education in schools continued on an abstinence-only path; and access to the Internet and social networking sites was now widespread (Reece, Herbenick, Schick, Sanders, Dodge and Fortenberry 2010a). Clearly, more research was needed to understand how these changes in American society were affecting our sexual lives, especially with regard to adults who were past middle age. In 2007, researchers at the Center of Sexual Health Promotion at Indiana University partnered with Church and Dwight Co., Inc. (the makers of Trojan condoms) to conduct a nationally representative study about sexual behavior (Herbenick, Reece, Schick, Sanders, Dodge, and Fortenberry, 2010a).

The National Survey of Sexual Health and Behavior was designed with the intention of assessing how individuals "make health-related decisions once they decide to become sexually active" (Reece et al., 2010a:245). Unlike the earlier large-scale studies that used face-to-face interviews, the NSSHB relied on an Internet-based survey—the first of its kind. The researchers partnered with a private company to create a representative sample that was then used to conduct research via the Internet (Herbenick et al., 2010a). The probability sample they created used both phone numbers and addresses, allowing those individuals who only used cell phones to be included. Respondents were initially contacted through mailings and phone calls; once they agreed to participate they either accessed the Internet on their own to complete the survey or they were provided a computer and Internet access by the research company (Herbenick et al., 2010a). In total, there were 5,865 participants in the NSSHB (Herbenick et al., 2010a).

FINDINGS FROM THE NATIONAL SURVEY OF SEXUAL HEALTH AND BEHAVIOR[4]
Sexual Behaviors over the Life Course

One of the major strengths of the NSSHB is the broad age range of the respondents, which allowed the researchers to better understand the "developmental trajectory of sexual expression" (Herbenick et al., 2010:261a). The NSSHB demonstrated how the behaviors individuals engaged in changed over the life course. For example, masturbation was more common than partnered sexual activities for men under the age of 24 and over the age of 50. Vaginal intercourse, too, was quite common—it was the most common sexual activity for men and women between the ages of 25 and 49, but became less frequent among women beginning at age 30. Oral sex and anal sex "appear to be well established aspects of a contemporary sexual repertoire" (Herbenick et al., 2010a:259);

40 percent of respondents had engaged in anal sex during their lifetime (an increase since the NHSLS in 1994). Despite cultural fears of rampant sexual activity among young people, teen sex was episodic and "safer" than anticipated. Less than one-third of teens had partnered sex in the past year; when partnered sex does occur, ". . . condom use appears to have become a normative behavior for many adolescents" (Fortenberry, Schick, Herbenick, Sanders, Dodge, and Reece 2010:314).

Sexual Behaviors at Last Sexual Encounter

Some of the most interesting findings from the NSSHB concerned what types of behaviors people engaged in when they last had sex. The researchers investigated where individuals had sex, with whom they had sex (i.e., a relationship partner, a friend/acquaintance, etc.), any sexual difficulties that occurred, whether they had an orgasm, and how pleasurable they rated the encounter (Herbenick et al., 2010c). While vaginal intercourse was most common, participants reported more than 41 combinations of sexual activities (including giving and receiving oral sex, anal sex, and partnered masturbation) (Herbenick et al., 2010c). Both men and women reported that they were more likely to have an orgasm if they engaged in a variety of behaviors; women in particular reported higher rates of orgasm if vaginal intercourse was paired with other behaviors (Herbenick et al., 2010c). Despite both genders reporting high rates of pleasure at their last encounter, men tended to overestimate how often their female partner had an orgasm. The vast majority of men (85%) reported their partner had an orgasm, compared to the 64 percent of women who said they did. This gap is too large to be explained by same-sex couples included in the study; while there may be a variety of explanations for this, more research is needed to explore the inconsistency (Herbenick et al., 2010c).

Who individuals had sex with also appeared to affect both their evaluations of their last encounter and the rates that they orgasmed, but the effects were different for men and women. Men reported that they experienced greater arousal, pleasure, and fewer problems when their last encounter was with a relationship partner than when it was with someone with whom they were not in a relationship. The researchers concluded that this difference might occur because as men age and experience sexual difficulty, being comfortable with and receiving patience from a partner is important (Herbenick et al., 2010c). Women, on the other hand, reported more sexual difficulties when their last encounter was with a relationship partner than not. This finding challenges the common notion that for women, love and emotional connection are necessary in order to be sexually satisfied. Though the majority of those who participated in the NSSHB were in a relationship, a significant number of men (30%) and women (18%) of all ages reported that their last sexual encounter was with a "friend" or "new acquaintance," indicating that the "friends with benefits" phenomenon is not limited to young adults (Herbenick et al., 2010c).

LIMITATIONS OF THE NATIONAL SURVEY OF SEXUAL HEALTH AND BEHAVIOR

Like the other nationally representative studies already described, the NSSHB relied on household-level data, which excludes institutionalized individuals. And although the NSSHB features a broader age range than other large-scale sex surveys, it is not representative of older adults, who may be more likely than adults of younger ages to be in an institutional setting (i.e., hospitalized or in an assisted living facility). Older adults might also be less comfortable using computers and the Internet. Like the other studies reviewed in

this reading, the NSSHB did not oversample some minority groups (in particular, those with same-sex behaviors) (Herbenick et al., 2010a). Because the NSSHB was significantly more public health and life course focused than the previous studies, the questions were structured much differently; this makes it very difficult to compare results across time (from, for example, the NHSLS). The use of the Internet was both a strength and a weakness; while the Internet might create the feeling of increased confidentiality when reporting stigmatized behaviors, it was unclear whether this held true for all ages. Also, it was unclear whether individuals who could not read or were not comfortable using a computer would have been as likely to participate (Reece et al., 2010a).

Although the NSSHB collected detailed information about sexuality across age groups, what it lacks is contextual data. One of the benefits of in-person interviewing is that it allows the researcher to build rapport with the participant, promoting disclosure and offering insight into individuals' sexual experiences. Previous studies allowed for analysis of sexual experiences taking into consideration individuals' life experience and social demographics (like age, race, and class), something that the NSSHB cannot offer (Reece et al., 2010a). The NSSHB is less sociological than the National Health and Social Life Survey; while health information is certainly important and valuable, it is equally important to understand the sociological context of sexual behaviors, including how our social groups and culture shape our understanding of sex and our sexual practices.

CONCLUSION

Using probability sampling methods and conducting representative research is an important way for us to understand the sexual behaviors of large portions of Americans. Though these methods are complex and come with a host of challenges (including inadequate funding, limited government support, and the shortcomings of the methods themselves), the studies outlined in this article show the value of large-scale research on sexual behaviors. Research conducted by mainstream publications, such as *Cosmopolitan* and *Playboy*, are inadequate and often misleading, giving a false impression of what is "normal" under the guise of "research." Readers must be critical of these studies, analyzing the research design and sampling methodology to fully understand how the research was conducted and whether it is valid. In addition to large-scale sexual surveys, many qualitative and in-depth studies have been done on small populations. Although these studies are not generalizable to the larger population, they do contribute a nuanced understanding of sexual practices, attitudes, and identities that are sometimes lost in large-scale representative research. If we want to continue to answer questions about the "average American" and what their sexual lives are like, the government and the general public must support both quantitative and qualitative research projects.

NOTES

1. Erickson and Steffen 1999:207.

2. All results from Laumann et al., 1994a (unless otherwise noted).

3. All data are from Chandra, Mosher, Copen and Sionean 2011 (unless otherwise noted).

4. All data from Herbenick, Reece, Schick, Sanders, Dodge and Fortenberry, 2010a (unless otherwise noted).

REFERENCES

Chandra, Anjani, William D. Mosher, Casey Copen, and Catlainn Sionean. 2011. "Sexual Behavior, Sexual Attraction and Sexual Identity in the United States: Data from the 2006–2008 National Survey of Family Growth." National Center for Health Statistics, *National Health Statistics Reports*, Number 36.

Erickson, Julia A., with Sally A. Steffen. 1999. *Kiss and Tell: Surveying Sex in the Twentieth Century*. Cambridge, MA: Harvard University Press.

Fortenberry, J. Dennis, Vanessa Schick, Debby Herbenick, Stephanie Sanders, Brian Dodge, and Michael Reece. 2010. "Sexual Behaviors and Condom Use at Last Vaginal Intercourse: A National Sample of Adolescents Ages 14 to 17 Years." *Journal of Sexual Medicine*, 7:5, 305–314.

Gartrell, Nanette K., Henny M.W. Bos, and Naomi G. Goldberg. 2011. "New Trends in Same-Sex Sexual Contact for American Adolescents?" *Archives of Sexual Behavior*, 40:6, 1–3.

Groves, Robert M., William D. Mosher, James M. Lepkowski, and Nicole G. Kirgis. 2009. "Planning and Development of the Continuous National Survey of Family Growth." National Center for Health Statistics, *Vital Health Statistics*, 1:48.

Herbenick, Debby, Michael Reece, Vanessa Schick, Stephanie Sanders, Brian Dodge, and J. Dennis Fortenberry. 2010a. "Sexual Behavior in the United States: Results from a National Probability Sample of Men and Women Ages 14–94." *Journal of Sexual Medicine*, 7:5, 255–265.

———. 2010b. "Sexual Behaviors, Relationships, and Perceived Status Among Adult Women in the United States: Results from a Probability Sample." *Journal of Sexual Medicine*, 7:5, 277–290.

———. 2010c. "Event-Level Analysis of the Sexual Characteristics and Composition Among Adults Ages 18–59: Results from a National Probability Sample." *Journal of Sexual Medicine*, 7:5, 346–361.

"Alfred Kinsey's 1948 and 1953 Studies." Retrieved from http://www.kinseyinstitute.org/research/ak-data.html on December 8, 2011.

Laumann Edward O., John H. Gagnon, Robert T. Michael, and Stuart Michaels. 1994a. *The Social Organization of Sexuality: Sexual Practices in the United States*. Chicago: University of Chicago Press.

Laumann, Edward O., Robert T. Michael, and John H. Gagnon. 1994b. "A Political History of the National Sex Survey of Adults." *Family Planning Perspectives*, 26:1, 34–38.

Martinez, Gladys, Casey E. Copen, and Joyce C. Abma. 2011. "Teenagers in the United States: Sexual Activity, Conceptive Use and Childbearing, 2006–2010." National Survey of Family Growth, National Center for Health Statistics. *Vital Health Statistics*, 23:31.

Michael, Robert T., John H. Gagnon, Edward O. Laumann, and Gina Kolata. 1994. *Sex in America: A Definitive Survey*. Boston: Little Brown and Co.

Reece, Michael, Debby Herbenick, Vanessa Schick, Stephanie Sanders, Brian Dodge, and J. Dennis Fortenberry. 2010a. "Guest Editorial: Background and Considerations on the National Survey of Sexual Health and Behavior (NSSHB) from the Investigators." *Journal of Sexual Medicine*, 7:5, 243–245.

——— 2010b. "Sexual Behaviors, Relationships, and Perceived Health Status Among Adult Women in the United States: Results from a Probability Sample." *Journal of Sexual Medicine*, 7:5, 291–304.

Doing It Differently: Women's and Men's Estimates of Their Number of Lifetime Sexual Partners

Mindy Stombler and Dawn M. Baunach

A recent national survey of sexual practices found that men report having more sexual partners than women over the course of their lifetimes (Smith et al., 2011). Theoretically, heterosexual men's and women's estimates should be the same, because for each new female partner a man adds to his "lifetime account," a woman adds a new male partner to her "lifetime account." The discrepancy between women's and men's estimates remains even when researchers define *sexual partners* very specifically and account for possible sampling problems (such as undersampling female sex workers). What explains the gender gap in claims people make about numbers of sexual partners?

One possibility is that women and men misrepresent their number of lifetime sexual partners to others. Our society tends to hold a double standard regarding the sexual behavior of women and men. Men who have a great deal of sexual experience generally are not subject to shame (and in some circles their behavior is lauded), whereas women with "too many" lifetime partners are stigmatized. Attempts to give interviewers the socially approved response (called *social desirability bias*) may lead women to intentionally underreport their numbers or men to inflate theirs.

Another possibility is that people misrepresent their behaviors to themselves. If women discount partners for whom they feel little affection, such partners could slip from memory, thereby erroneously lowering their reported lifetime account. Women and men also rely on different estimation strategies. Women tend to enumerate (actually count), whereas men tend to give rough estimates (Brown and Sinclair, 1999; Weiderman, 1997). Weiderman (1997) notes a clear tendency for men reporting larger numbers of lifetime sexual partners to choose numbers that end in 0 or 5. Men prefer "round" numbers rather than exact counts.

The number of sexual partners that women and men report does become more similar when researchers shorten the time frame for estimation to the past year or the past five years (see the table below), indicating that both men and women estimate more accurately over a shorter period of time. In addition, the cultural meaning that we attach to our accumulated lifetime number of sexual partners carries more weight than, say, the number of partners we might have in a year. Taking the double standard into account, we can understand why it might be in women's best interest to carefully consider their number of lifetime sexual partners and in men's best interest to round up.

	MEAN NUMBER OF SEXUAL PARTNERS		
	Women (n = 1,153)	Men (n = 891)	Difference Men - Women
Last Five Years	1.64	2.10	0.46
Last Year	0.96	1.28	0.32

Source: General Social Survey, 2010.

REFERENCES

Brown, Norman R., and Robert C. Sinclair. 1999. "Estimating number of lifetime sexual partners: Men and women do it differently." *The Journal of Sex Research*, 36: 3, 292–297.

Smith, Tom W., Peter Marsden, Michael Hout, and Jibum Kim. 2011. *General Social Surveys, 1972–2010* [machine readable data file] / Principal Investigator, Tom W. Smith; Co-Principal Investigator, Peter V. Marsden; Co-Principal Investigator, Michael Hout; Sponsored by National Science Foundation. Chicago, IL: National Opinion Research Center [producers]; Storrs, CT: The Roper Center for Public Opinion Research, University of Connecticut [distributor].

Weiderman, Michael. 1997. "The truth must be in here somewhere: Examining the gender discrepancy in self-reported lifetime number of partners." *The Journal of Sex Research*, 34: 4, 375–386.

RACISM AND RESEARCH: THE CASE OF THE TUSKEGEE SYPHILIS STUDY

ALLAN M. BRANDT

In 1932 the U.S. Public Health Service (USPHS) initiated an experiment in Macon County, Alabama, to determine the natural course of untreated, latent syphilis in black males. The test comprised 400 syphilitic men, as well as 200 uninfected men who served as controls. The first published report of the study appeared in 1936 with subsequent papers issued every four to six years, through the 1960s. When penicillin became widely available by the early 1950s as the preferred treatment for syphilis, the men did not receive therapy. In fact on several occasions, the USPHS actually sought to prevent treatment. Moreover, a committee at the federally operated Center for Disease Control decided in 1969 that the study should be continued. Only in 1972, when accounts of the study first appeared in the national press, did the Department of Health, Education, and Welfare halt the experiment. At that time seventy-four of the test subjects were still alive; at least twenty-eight, but perhaps more than 100, had died directly from advanced syphilitic lesions.[1] In August 1972, HEW appointed an investigatory panel which issued a report the following year. The panel found the study to have been "ethically unjustified," and argued that penicillin should have been provided to the men.[2]

This article attempts to place the Tuskegee Study in a historical context and to assess its ethical implications. Despite the media attention which the study received, the HEW *Final Report,* and the criticism expressed by several professional organizations, the experiment has been largely misunderstood. The most basic questions of *how* the study was undertaken in the first place and *why* it continued for forty years were never addressed by the HEW investigation. Moreover, the panel misconstrued the nature of the experiment, failing to consult important documents available at the National Archives which bear significantly on its ethical assessment. Only by examining the specific ways in which values are engaged in scientific research can the study be understood.

RACISM AND MEDICAL OPINION

A brief review of the prevailing scientific thought regarding race and heredity in the early twentieth century is fundamental for an understanding of the Tuskegee Study. By the turn of the century, Darwinism had provided a new rationale for American racism.[3] Essentially primitive peoples, it was argued, could not be assimilated into a complex, white civilization. Scientists speculated that in the struggle for survival the Negro in America was doomed. Particularly prone to disease, vice, and crime, black Americans could not be helped by education or philanthropy. Social [Darwinists] analyzed census data to predict the virtual extinction of the Negro in the twentieth century, for they believed the Negro race in America was in the throes of a degenerative evolutionary process.[4]

From "Racism and Research: The Case of the Tuskegee Syphilis Study" by Allan Brandt, *Hastings Center Report*, Vol. 8, No. 6, 1978, pp. 21–29. © 1978 The Hastings Center. Reprinted by permission of John Wiley and Sons, Inc.

The medical profession supported these findings of late nineteenth- and early twentieth-century anthropologists, ethnologists, and biologists. Physicians studying the effects of emancipation on health concluded almost universally that freedom had caused the mental, moral, and physical deterioration of the black population.[5] They substantiated this argument by citing examples in the comparative anatomy of the black and white races. As Dr. W. T. English wrote: "A careful inspection reveals the body of the negro a mass of minor defects and imperfections from the crown of the head to the soles of the feet. . . ."[6] Cranial structures, wide nasal apertures, receding chins, projecting jaws, all typed the Negro as the lowest species in the Darwinian hierarchy.[7]

Interest in racial differences centered on the sexual nature of blacks. The Negro, doctors explained, possessed an excessive sexual desire, which threatened the very foundations of white society. As one physician noted in the *Journal of the American Medical Association*, "The negro springs from a southern race, and as such his sexual appetite is strong; all of his environments stimulate this appetite, and as a general rule his emotional type of religion certainly does not decrease it."[8] Doctors reported a complete lack of morality on the part of blacks:

Virtue in the negro race is like angels' visits—few and far between. In a practice of sixteen years I have never examined a virgin negro over fourteen years of age.[9]

A particularly ominous feature of this overzealous sexuality, doctors argued, was the black males' desire for white women. "A perversion from which most races are exempt," wrote Dr. English, "prompts the negro's inclination towards white women, whereas other races incline towards females of their own."[10] Though English estimated the "gray matter of the negro brain" to be at least a thousand years behind that of the white races, his genital organs were overdeveloped. As Dr. William Lee Howard noted:

The attacks on defenseless white women are evidences of racial instincts that are about as amenable to ethical culture as is the inherent odor of the race. . . . When education will reduce the size of the negro's penis as well as bring about the sensitiveness of the terminal fibers which exist in the Caucasian, then will it also be able to prevent the African's birth-right to sexual madness and excess.[11]

One southern medical journal proposed "Castration Instead of Lynching," as retribution for black sexual crimes. "An impressive trial by a ghost-like kuklux klan [sic] and a 'ghost' physician or surgeon to perform the operation would make it an event the 'patient' would never forget," noted the editorial.[12]

According to these physicians, lust and immorality, unstable families, and reversion to barbaric tendencies made blacks especially prone to venereal diseases. One doctor estimated that over 50 percent of all Negroes over the age of twenty-five were syphilitic.[13] Virtually free of disease as slaves, they were now overwhelmed by it, according to informed medical opinion. Moreover, doctors believed that treatment for venereal disease among blacks was impossible, particularly because in its latent stage the symptoms of syphilis become quiescent. As Dr. Thomas W. Murrell wrote:

They come for treatment at the beginning and at the end. When there are visible manifestations or when harried by pain, they readily come, for as a race they are not averse to physic; but tell them not, though they look well and feel well, that they are still diseased. Here ignorance rates science a fool. . . .[14]

Even the best educated black, according to Murrell, could not be convinced to seek treatment for syphilis.[15] Venereal disease, according to some doctors, threatened the future of the race. The medical profession attributed the low birth rate among blacks to the high prevalence of venereal disease which caused stillbirths and miscarriages. Moreover, the high rates of syphilis were thought to lead to increased insanity and crime. One doctor writing at the turn of the century estimated that the number of insane Negroes had increased thirteen-fold since the end of the Civil War.[16] Dr. Murrell's conclusion echoed the most informed anthropological and ethnological data:

So the scourge sweeps among them. Those that are treated are only half cured, and the effort to assimilate a complex civilization driving their diseased minds until the results are criminal records. Perhaps here, in conjunction with tuberculosis, will be the end of the negro problem. Disease will accomplish what man cannot do.[17]

This particular configuration of ideas formed the core of medical opinion concerning blacks, sex, and disease in the early twentieth century. Doctors generally discounted socioeconomic explanations of the state of black health, arguing that better medical care could not alter the evolutionary scheme.[18] These assumptions provide the backdrop for examining the Tuskegee Syphilis Study.

THE ORIGINS OF THE EXPERIMENT

In 1929, under a grant from the Julius Rosenwald Fund, the USPHS conducted studies in the rural South to determine the prevalence of syphilis among blacks and explore possibilities for mass treatment. The USPHS found Macon County, Alabama, in which the town of Tuskegee is located, to have the highest syphilis rate of the six counties surveyed. The Rosenwald Study concluded that mass treatment could be successfully implemented among rural blacks.[19] Although it is doubtful that the necessary funds would have been allocated even in the best economic conditions, after the economy collapsed in 1929, the findings were ignored. It is, however, ironic that the Tuskegee Study came to be based on findings of the Rosenwald Study that demonstrated the possibilities of mass treatment.

Three years later, in 1932, Dr. Taliaferro Clark, Chief of the USPHS Venereal Disease Division and author of the Rosenwald Study report, decided that conditions in Macon County merited renewed attention. Clark believed the high prevalence of syphilis offered an "unusual opportunity" for observation. From its inception, the USPHS regarded the Tuskegee Study as a classic "study in nature,"* rather than an experiment.[20] As long as syphilis was so prevalent in Macon and most of the blacks went untreated throughout life, it seemed only natural to Clark that it would be valuable to observe the consequences. He described it as a "ready-made situation."[21] Surgeon General H. S. Cumming wrote to R. R. Moton, Director of the Tuskegee Institute:

The recent syphilis control demonstration carried out in Macon County, with the financial assistance of the Julius Rosenwald Fund, revealed the presence of an unusually high rate in this county and, what is more remarkable, the fact that 99 per cent of this group was entirely without previous treatment. This combination, together with the expected cooperation of your hospital, offers an unparalleled opportunity for carrying on this piece of scientific research which probably cannot be duplicated anywhere else in the world.[22]

Although no formal protocol appears to have been written, several letters of Clark and Cumming suggest what the USPHS hoped to find. Clark indicated that it would be important to see how disease affected the daily lives of the men:

The results of these studies of case records suggest the desirability of making a further study of the effect of untreated syphilis on the human economy among people now living and engaged in their daily pursuits.[23]

It also seems that the USPHS believed the experiment might demonstrate that antisyphilitic treatment was unnecessary. As Cumming noted: "It is expected the results of this study may have a marked bearing on the treatment, or conversely the non-necessity of treatment, of cases of latent syphilis."[24] . . .

SELECTING THE SUBJECTS

Clark sent Dr. Raymond Vonderlehr to Tuskegee in September 1932 to assemble a sample of men with latent syphilis for the experiment. The basic design of the study called for the selection of syphilitic black males between the ages of twenty-five and sixty, a thorough physical examination including x-rays, and finally, a spinal tap to determine the incidence of neurosyphilis.[25] They had no intention of providing any treatment for the infected men.[26] The USPHS originally scheduled the whole experiment to last six months; it seemed to be both a simple and inexpensive project.

The task of collecting the sample, however, proved to be more difficult than the USPHS had supposed. Vonderlehr canvassed the largely illiterate, poverty-stricken population of sharecroppers and tenant farmers in search of test subjects. If his circulars requested only men over twenty-five to attend his clinics, none would appear, suspecting he was conducting draft physicals. Therefore, he was forced to test large numbers of women and men who did not fit the experiment's specifications. This involved considerable expense since the USPHS had promised the Macon County Board of Health that it would treat those who were infected, but not included in the study.[27] Clark wrote to Vonderlehr about the situation: "It never once occurred to me that we would be called upon to treat a large part of the county as return for the privilege of making this study. . . . I am anxious to keep the expenditures for treatment down to the lowest possible point because it is the one item of expenditure in connection with the study most difficult to defend despite our knowledge of the need therefor."[28] Vonderlehr responded: "If we could find from 100 to 200 cases . . . we would not have to do another Wassermann on useless individuals. . . ."[29]

Significantly, the attempt to develop the sample contradicted the prediction the USPHS had made initially regarding the prevalence of the disease in Macon County. Overall rates of syphilis fell well below expectations; as opposed to the USPHS projection of 35 percent, 20 percent of those tested were actually diseased.[30] Moreover, those who had sought and received previous treatment far exceeded the expectations of the USPHS. Clark noted in a letter to Vonderlehr:

I find your report of March 6th quite interesting but regret the necessity for Wassermanning [sic] . . . such a large number of individuals in order to uncover this relatively limited number of untreated cases.[31]

Further difficulties arose in enlisting the subjects to participate in the experiment, to be "Wassermanned," and to return for a subsequent series of examinations. Vonderlehr found that only the offer of treatment elicited the cooperation of the men. They were told they were ill and were promised free care. Offered therapy, they became willing subjects.[32] The USPHS did not tell the men that they were participants in an experiment; on the contrary, the subjects believed they were being treated for "bad blood"—the rural South's colloquialism for syphilis. They thought they were participating in a public health demonstration similar to the one that had been conducted by the Julius Rosenwald Fund in Tuskegee several years earlier. In the end, the men were so eager for medical care that the number of defaulters in the experiment proved to be insignificant.[33]

To preserve the subjects' interest, Vonderlehr gave most of the men mercurial ointment, a noneffective drug, while some of the younger men apparently received inadequate dosages of neoarsphenamine.[34] This required Vonderlehr to write frequently to Clark requesting supplies. He feared the experiment would fail if the men were not offered treatment. . . .

The readiness of the test subjects to participate of course contradicted the notion that blacks would not seek or continue therapy.

The final procedure of the experiment was to be a spinal tap to test for evidence of neuro-syphilis. The USPHS presented this purely diagnostic exam, which often entails considerable pain and complications, to the men as a "special treatment." Clark explained to Moore:

We have not yet commenced the spinal punctures. This operation will be deferred to the last in order not to unduly disturb our field work by any adverse reports by the patients subjected to spinal puncture because of some disagreeable sensations following this procedure. These negroes are very ignorant and easily influenced by things that would be of minor significance in a more intelligent group.[35]

The letter to the subjects announcing the spinal tap read:

Some time ago you were given a thorough examination and since that time we hope you have gotten a great deal of treatment for bad blood. You will now be given your last chance to get a second examination. This examination is a very special one and after it is finished you will be given a special treatment if it is believed you are in a condition to stand it. . . .

REMEMBER THIS IS YOUR LAST CHANCE FOR SPECIAL FREE TREATMENT. BE SURE TO MEET THE NURSE.[36]

The HEW investigation did not uncover this crucial fact: the men participated in the study under the guise of treatment.

Despite the fact that their assumption regarding prevalence and black attitudes toward treatment had proved wrong, the USPHS decided in the summer of 1933 to continue the study. Once again, it seemed only "natural" to pursue the research since the sample already existed, and with a depressed economy, the cost of treatment appeared prohibitive—although there is no indication it was ever considered. Vonderlehr first suggested extending the study in letters to Clark and Wenger:

At the end of this project we shall have a considerable number of cases presenting various complications of syphilis, who have received only mercury and may still be consid-

ered untreated in the modern sense of therapy. Should these cases be followed over a period of from five to ten years many interesting facts could be learned regarding the course and complications of untreated syphilis.[37]

"As I see it," responded Wenger, "we have no further interest in these patients until they die."[38] Apparently, the physicians engaged in the experiment believed that only autopsies could scientifically confirm the findings of the study. . . .

Bringing the men to autopsy required the USPHS to devise a further series of deceptions and inducements. Wenger warned Vonderlehr that the men must not realize that they would be autopsied:

There is one danger in the latter plan and that is if the colored population become aware that accepting free hospital care means a post-mortem, every darkey will leave Macon County and it will hurt [Dr. Eugene] Dibble's hospital.[39]

The USPHS offered several inducements to maintain contact and to procure the continued cooperation of the men. Eunice Rivers, a black nurse, was hired to follow their health and to secure approval for autopsies. She gave the men non-effective medicines—"spring tonic" and aspirin—as well as transportation and hot meals on the days of their examinations.[40] More important, Nurse Rivers provided continuity to the project over the entire forty-year period. By supplying "medicinals," the USPHS was able to continue to deceive the participants, who believed that they were receiving therapy from the government doctors. Deceit was integral to the study. When the test subjects complained about spinal taps one doctor wrote:

They simply do not like spinal punctures. A few of those who were tapped are enthusiastic over the results but to most, the suggestion causes violent shaking of the head; others claim they were robbed of their procreative powers (regardless of the fact that I claim it stimulates them).[41]

Letters to the subjects announcing an impending USPHS visit to Tuskegee explained: "[The doctor] wants to make a special examination to find out how you have been feeling and whether the treatment has improved your health."[42] In fact, after the first six months of the study, the USPHS had furnished no treatment whatsoever.

Finally, because it proved difficult to persuade the men to come to the hospital when they became severely ill, the USPHS promised to cover their burial expenses. The Milbank Memorial Fund provided approximately $50 per man for this purpose beginning in 1935. This was a particularly strong inducement as funeral rites constituted an important component of the cultural life of rural blacks.[43] One report of the study concluded. "Without this suasion it would, we believe, have been impossible to secure the cooperation of the group and their families."[44]

Reports of the study's findings, which appeared regularly in the medical press beginning in 1936, consistently cited the ravages of untreated syphilis. The first paper, read at the 1936 American Medical Association annual meeting, found "that syphilis in this period [latency] tends to greatly increase the frequency of manifestations of cardiovascular disease."[45] Only 16 percent of the subjects gave no sign of morbidity as opposed to 61 percent of the controls. Ten years later, a report noted coldly, "The fact that nearly twice as large a proportion of the syphilitic individuals as of the control group has died is a very striking one." Life expectancy, concluded the doctors, is reduced by about 20 percent.[46]

A 1955 article found that slightly more than 30 percent of the test group autopsied had died *directly* from advanced syphilitic lesions of either the cardiovascular or the central nervous system.[47] Another published account stated, "Review of those still living reveals that an appreciable number have late complications of syphilis which probably will result, for some at least, in contributing materially to the ultimate cause of death."[48] In 1950, Dr. Wenger had concluded, "We now know, where we could only surmise before, that we have contributed to their ailments and shortened their lives."[49] As black physician Vernal Cave, a member of the HEW panel, later wrote, "They proved a point, then proved a point, then proved a point."[50]

During the forty years of the experiment the USPHS had sought on several occasions to ensure that the subjects did not receive treatment from other sources. To this end, Vonderlehr met with groups of local black doctors in 1934, to ask their cooperation in not treating the men. Lists of subjects were distributed to Macon County physicians along with letters requesting them to refer these men back to the USPHS if they sought care.[51] The USPHS warned the Alabama Health Department not to treat the test subjects when they took a mobile VD unit into Tuskegee in the early 1940s.[52] In 1941, the Army drafted several subjects and told them to begin antisyphilitic treatment immediately. The USPHS supplied the draft board with a list of 256 names they desired to have excluded from treatment, and the board complied.[53]

In spite of these efforts, by the early 1950s many of the men had secured some treatment on their own. By 1952, almost 30 percent of the test subjects had received some penicillin, although only 7.5 percent had received what could be considered adequate doses.[54] Vonderlehr wrote to one of the participating physicians, "I hope that the availability of antibiotics has not interfered too much with this project."[55] A report published in 1955 considered whether the treatment that some of the men had obtained had "defeated" the study. The article attempted to explain the relatively low exposure to penicillin in an age of antibiotics, suggesting as a reason: "the stoicism of these men as a group; they still regard hospitals and medicines with suspicion and prefer an occasional dose of time-honored herbs or tonics to modern drugs."[56] The authors failed to note that the men believed they already were under the care of the government doctors and thus saw no need to seek treatment elsewhere. Any treatment which the men might have received, concluded the report, had been insufficient to compromise the experiment.

When the USPHS evaluated the status of the study in the 1960s they continued to rationalize the racial aspects of the experiment. For example, the minutes of a 1965 meeting at the Center for Disease Control recorded:

Racial issue was mentioned briefly. Will not affect the study. Any questions can be handled by saying these people were at the point that therapy would no longer help them. They are getting better medical care than they would under any other circumstances.[57]

A group of physicians met again at the CDC in 1969 to decide whether or not to terminate the study. Although one doctor argued that the study should be stopped and the men treated, the consensus was to continue. Dr. J. Lawton Smith remarked, "You will never have another study like this; take advantage of it."[58] A memo prepared by Dr. James B. Lucas, Assistant Chief of the Venereal Disease Branch, stated: "Nothing learned will prevent, find, or cure a single case of infectious syphilis or bring us closer to our basic mission of controlling venereal disease in the United States."[59] He concluded, however, that the study should be continued "along its present lines." When the first accounts of the experiment appeared in the national press in July 1972, data were still being collected and autopsies performed.[60]

THE HEW FINAL REPORT

HEW finally formed the Tuskegee Syphilis Study Ad Hoc Advisory Panel on August 28, 1972, in response to criticism that the press descriptions of the experiment had triggered. The panel, composed of nine members, five of them black, concentrated on two issues. First,

was the study justified in 1932 and had the men given their informed consent? Second, should penicillin have been provided when it became available in the early 1950s? The panel was also charged with determining if the study should be terminated and assessing current policies regarding experimentation with human subjects.[61] The group issued their report in June 1973.

By focusing on the issues of penicillin therapy and informed consent, the *Final Report* and the investigation betrayed a basic misunderstanding of the experiment's purposes and design. The HEW report implied that the failure to provide penicillin constituted the study's major ethical misjudgment; implicit was the assumption that no adequate therapy existed prior to penicillin. Nonetheless medical authorities firmly believed in the efficacy of arsenotherapy for treating syphilis at the time of the experiment's inception in 1932. The panel further failed to recognize that the entire study had been predicated on nontreatment. Provision of effective medication would have violated the rationale of the experiment—to study the natural course of the disease until death. On several occasions, in fact, the USPHS had prevented the men from receiving proper treatment. Indeed, there is no evidence that the USPHS ever considered providing penicillin.

The other focus of the *Final Report*—informed consent—also served to obscure the historical facts of the experiment. In light of the deceptions and exploitations which the experiment perpetrated, it is an understatement to declare, as the *Report* did, that the experiment was "ethically unjustified," because it failed to obtain informed consent from the subjects. The *Final Report's* statement, "Submitting voluntarily is not informed consent," indicated that the panel believed that the men had volunteered *for the experiment.*[62] The records in the National Archives make clear that the men did not submit voluntarily to an experiment; they were told and they believed that they were getting free treatment from expert government doctors for a serious disease. The failure of the HEW *Final Report* to expose this critical fact that the USPHS lied to the subjects—calls into question the thoroughness and credibility of their investigation.

Failure to place the study in a historical context also made it impossible for the investigation to deal with the essentially racist nature of the experiment. The panel treated the study as an aberration, well-intentioned but misguided.[63] Moreover, concern that the *Final Report* might be viewed as a critique of human experimentation in general seems to have severely limited the scope of the inquiry. The *Final Report* is quick to remind the reader on two occasions: "The position of the Panel must not be construed to be a general repudiation of scientific research with human subjects."[64] The *Report* assures us that a better designed experiment could have been justified:

It is possible that a scientific study in 1932 of untreated syphilis, properly conceived with a clear protocol and conducted with suitable subjects who fully understood the implications of their involvement, might have been justified in the pre-penicillin era. This is especially true when one considers the uncertain nature of the results of treatment of late latent syphilis and the highly toxic nature of therapeutic agents then available.[65]

This statement is questionable in view of the proven dangers of untreated syphilis known in 1932.

Since the publication of the HEW *Final Report,* a defense of the Tuskegee Study has emerged. These arguments, most clearly articulated by Dr. R. H. Kampmeier in the *Southern Medical Journal,* center on the limited knowledge of effective therapy for latent syphilis when the experiment began. Kampmeier argues that by 1950, penicillin would have been of no value for these men.[66] Others have suggested that the

men were fortunate to have been spared the highly toxic treatments of the earlier period.[67] Moreover, even these contemporary defenses assume that the men never would have been treated anyway. As Dr. Charles Barnett of Stanford University wrote in 1974, "The lack of treatment was not contrived by the USPHS but was an established fact of which they proposed to take advantage."[68] Several doctors who participated in the study continued to justify the experiment. Dr. J. R. Heller, who on one occasion had referred to the test subjects as the "Ethiopian population," told reporters in 1972:

I don't see why they should be shocked or horrified. There was no racial side to this. It just happened to be in a black community. I feel this was a perfectly straightforward study, perfectly ethical, with controls. Part of our mission as physicians is to find out what happens to individuals with disease and without disease.[69]

These apologies, as well as the HEW *Final Report,* ignore many of the essential ethical issues which the study poses, The Tuskegee Study reveals the persistence of beliefs within the medical profession about the nature of blacks, sex, and disease—beliefs that had tragic repercussions long after their alleged "scientific" bases were known to be incorrect. Most strikingly, the entire health of a community was jeopardized by leaving a communicable disease untreated.[70] There can be little doubt that the Tuskegee researchers regarded their subjects as less than human.[71] As a result, the ethical canons of experimenting on human subjects were completely disregarded.

The study also raises significant questions about professional self-regulation and scientific bureaucracy. Once the USPHS decided to extend the experiment in the summer of 1933, it was unlikely that the test would be halted short of the men's deaths. The experiment was widely reported for forty years without evoking any significant protest within the medical community. Nor did any bureaucratic mechanism exist within the government for the periodic reassessment of the Tuskegee experiment's ethics and scientific value. The USPHS sent physicians to Tuskegee every several years to check on the study's progress, but never subjected the morality or usefulness of the experiment to serious scrutiny. Only the press accounts of 1972 finally punctured the continued rationalizations of the USPHS and brought the study to an end. Even the HEW investigation was compromised by fear that it would be considered a threat to future human experimentation.

In retrospect the Tuskegee Study revealed more about the pathology of racism than it did about the pathology of syphilis; more about the nature of scientific inquiry than the nature of the disease process. The injustice committed by the experiment went well beyond the facts outlined in the press and the HEW *Final Report*. The degree of deception and damages have been seriously underestimated. As this history of the study suggests, the notion that science is a value-free discipline must be rejected. The need for greater vigilance in assessing the specific ways in which social values and attitudes affect professional behavior is clearly indicated.

NOTE

* In 1865, Claude Bernard, the famous French physiologist, outlined the distinction between a "study in nature" and experimentation. A study in nature required simple observation, an essentially passive act, while experimentation demanded intervention which altered the original condition. The Tuskegee Study was thus clearly not a study in nature. The very act of diagnosis altered the original conditions. "It is on this very possibility of acting or not acting on a body," wrote Bernard, "that the distinction will exclusively rest between sciences called sciences of observation and sciences called experimental."

EDITOR'S NOTE

On May 16, 1997, President Bill Clinton apologized to the participants in the Tuskegee Study. He acknowledged that the U.S. government had done "something that was wrong—deeply, profoundly, and morally wrong."

REFERENCES

1. The best general accounts of the study are "The 40-Year Death Watch." *Medical World News* (August 18, 1972), pp. 15–17; and Dolores Katz, "Why 430 Blacks with Syphilis Went Uncured for 40 Years," Detroit *Free Press* (November 5, 1972). The mortality figure is based on a published report of the study which appeared in 1955. See Jesse J. Peters, James H. Peers, Sidney Olansky, John C. Cutler, and Geraldine Gleeson, "Untreated Syphilis in the Male Negro: Pathologic Findings in Syphilitic and Nonsyphilitic Patients," *Journal of Chronic Diseases* 1 (February 1955), 127–48. The article estimated that 30.4 percent of the untreated men would die from syphilitic lesions.

2. *Final Report* of the Tuskegee Syphilis Study Ad Hoc Advisory Panel, Department of Health, Education, and Welfare (Washington, D.C.: GPO, 1973). (Hereafter, HEW *Final Report*).

3. See George M. Frederickson, *The Black Image in the White Mind* (New York: Harper and Row, 1971), pp. 228–55. Also, John H. Haller, *Outcasts From Evolution* (Urbana, Ill.: University of Illinois Press, 1971), pp. 40–68.

4. Frederickson, pp. 247–49.

5. "Deterioration of the American Negro," *Atlanta Journal-Record of Medicine* 5 (July 1903), 287–88. See also J. A. Rodgers, "The Effect of Freedom upon the Psychological Development of the Negro," *Proceedings* of the American Medico-Psychological Association 7 (1900), 88–99. "From the most healthy race in the country forty years ago," concluded Dr. Henry McHatton, "he is today the most diseased." "The Sexual Status of the Negro—Past and Present," *American Journal of Dermatology and Genito-Urinary Diseases* 10 (January 1906), 7–9.

6. W. T. English, "The Negro Problem from the Physician's Point of View," *Atlanta Journal-Record of Medicine* 5 (October 1903), 461. See also, "Racial Anatomical Peculliarities," *New York Medical Journal* 63 (April 1896), 500–01.

7. "Racial Anatomical Peculiarities," p. 501. Also, Charles S. Bacon, "The Race Problem," *Medicine* (Detroit) 9 (May 1903), 338–43.

8. H. H. Hazen, "Syphilis in the American Negro," *Journal of the American Medical Association* 63 (August 8, 1914), 463. For deeper background into the historical relationship of racism and sexuality see Winthrop D. Jordan, *White Over Black* (Chapel Hill: University of North Carolina Press, 1968: Pelican Books, 1969), pp. 32–40.

9. Daniel David Quillian, "Racial Peculiarities: A Cause of the Prevalence of Syphilis in Negroes," *American Journal of Dermatology and Genito-Urinary Diseases* 10 (July 1906), p. 277.

10. English, p. 463.

11. William Lee Howard, "The Negro as a Distinct Ethnic Factor in Civilization," *Medicine* (Detroit)

9 (June 1903), 424. See also, Thomas W. Murrell, "Syphilis in the American Negro," *Journal of the American Medical Association* 54 (March 12, 1910), 848.

12. "Castration Instead of Lynching," *Atlanta Journal-Record of Medicine* 8 (October 1906), 457. The editorial added: "The badge of disgrace and emasculation might be branded upon the face or forehead, as a warning, in the form of an 'R,' emblematic of the crime for which this punishment was and will be inflicted."

13. Searle Harris, "The Future of the Negro from the Standpoint of the Southern Physician," *Alabama Medical Journal* 14 (January 1902), 62. Other articles on the prevalence of venereal disease among blacks are: H. L. McNeil, "Syphilis in the Southern Negro," *Journal of the American Medical Association* 67 (September 1916), 1001–04; Ernest Philip Boas, "The Relative Prevalence of Syphilis Among Negroes and Whites," *Social Hygiene* 1 (September 1915), 610–16. Doctors went to considerable trouble to distinguish the morbidity and mortality of various diseases among blacks and whites. See, for example, Marion M. Torchia, "Tuberculosis Among American Negroes: Medical Research on a Racial Disease, 1830–1950," *Journal of the History of Medicine and Allied Sciences* 32 (July 1977), 252–79.

14. Thomas W. Murrell, "Syphilia in the Negro: Its Bearing on the Race Problem," *American Journal of Dermatology and Genito-Urinary Diseases* 10 (August 1906), 307.

15. "Even among the educated, only a very few will carry out the most elementary instructions as to personal hygiene. One thing you cannot do, and that is to convince the negro that he has a disease that he cannot see or feel. This is due to lack of concentration rather than lack of faith; even if he does believe, he does not care; a child of fancy, the sensations of the passing hour are his only guides to the future." Murrell, "Syphilis in the American Negro," p. 847.

16. "Deterioration of the American Negro," *Atlanta Journal-Record of Medicine* 5 (July 1903), 288.

17. Murrell, "Syphilis in the Negro; Its Bearing on the Race Problem," p. 307.

18. "The anatomical and physiological conditions of the African must be understood, his place in the anthropological scale realized, and his biological basis accepted as being unchangeable by man, before we shall be able to govern his natural uncontrollable sexual passions." See, "As Ye Sow That Shall Ye Also Reap," *Atlanta Journal-Record of Medicine* 1 (June 1899), 266.

19. Talliaferro Clark, *The Control of Syphilis in Southern Rural Areas* (Chicago: Julius Rosenwald Fund, 1932), 53–58. Approximately 35 percent of the inhabitants of Macon County who were examined were found to be syphilitic.

20. See Claude Bernard, *An Introduction to the Study of Experimental Medicine* (New York: Dover, 1865, 1957), pp. 5–26.

21. Taliaferro Clark to M. M. Davis, October 29, 1932. Records of the USPHS Venereal Disease Division, Record Group 90, Box 239, National Archives, Washington National Record Center, Suitland, Maryland. (Hereafter, NA-WNRC). Materials in this collection which relate to the early history of the study were apparently never consulted by the HEW investigation. Included are letters, reports, and memoranda written by the physicians engaged in the study.

22. H. S. Cumming to R. R. Moton, September 20, 1932, NA-WNRC.

23. Clark to Davis, October 29, 1932, NA-WNRC.

24. Cumming to Moton, September 20, 1932, NA-WNRC.

25. Clark Memorandum, September 26, 1932, NA-WNRC. See also, Clark to Davis, October 29, 1932, NA-WNRC.

26. As Clark wrote: "You will observe that our plan has nothing to do with treatment. It is purely a diagnostic procedure carried out to determine what has happened to the syphilitic Negro who has had no treatment." Clark to Paul A. O'Leary, September 27, 1932, NA-WNRC.

27. D. G. Gill to O. C. Wenger, October 10, 1932, NA-WNRC.

28. Clark to Vonderlehr, January 25, 1933, NA-WNRC.

29. Vonderlehr to Clark, February 28, 1933, NA-WNRC.

30. Vonderlehr to Clark, November 2, 1932, NA-WNRC. Also, Vonderlehr to Clark, February 6, 1933, NA-WNRC.

31. Clark to Vonderlehr, March 9, 1933, NA-WNRC.

32. Vonderlehr later explained: "The reason treatment was given to many of these men was twofold: First, when the study was started in the fall of 1932, no plans had been made for its continuation and a few of the patients were treated before we fully realized the need for continuing the project on a permanent basis. Second it was difficult to hold the interest of the group of Negroes in Macon County unless some treatment was given. "Vonderlehr to Austin V. Diebert, December 5, 1938. Tuskegee Syphilis Study Ad Hoc Advisory Panel Papers, Box 1, National Library of Medicine, Bethesda, Maryland. (Hereafter, TSS-NLM). This collection contains the materials assembled by the HEW investigation in 1972.

33. Vonderlehr to Clark, February 6, 1933, NA-WNRC.

34. H. S. Cumming to J. N. Baker, August 5, 1933, NA-WNRC.

35. Clark to Moore, March 25, 1933, NA-WNRC.

36. Macon County Health Department, "Letter to Subjects," n.d., NA-WNRC.

37. Vonderlehr to Clark, April 8, 1933, NA-WNRC. See also, Vonderlehr to Wenger, July 18, 1933, NA-WNRC.

38. Wenger to Vonderlehr, July 21, 1933, NA-WNRC. The italics are Wenger's.

39. Wenger to Vonderlehr, July 21, 1933, NA-WNRC.

40. Eunice Rivers, Stanely Schuman, Lloyd Simpson, Sidney Olansky, "Twenty-Years of Followup Experience In a Long-Range Medical Study," *Public Health Reports* 68 (April 1953), 391–95. In this article Nurse Rivers explains her role in the

experiment. She wrote: "Because of the low educational status of the majority of the patients, it was impossible to appeal to them from a purely scientific approach. Therefore, various methods were used to maintain their interest, Free medicines, burial assistance of insurance (the project being referred to as 'Miss Rivers' Lodge'), free hot meals on the days of examination, transportation to and from the hospital, and an opportunity to stop in town on the return trip to shop or visit with their friends on the streets all helped. In spite of these attractions, there were some who refused their examinations because they were not sick and did not see that they were being beneifited." (p. 393).

41. Austin V. Diebert to Raymond Vonderlehr, March 20, 1939, TSS-NLM, Box 1.

42. Murray Smith to Subjects, (1938), TSS-NLM, Box 1. See also, Sidney Olansky to John C. Cutler, November 6, 1951, TSS-NLM, Box 2.

43. The USPHS originally requested that the Julius Rosenwald Fund meet this expense. See Cumming to Davis, October 4, 1934, NA-WNRC. This money was usually divided between the undertaker, pathologist, and hospital. Lloyd Isaacs to Raymond Vonderlehr, April 23, 1940, TSS-NLM, Box 1.

44. Stanley H. Schuman, Sidney Olansky, Eunice Rivers, C. A. Smith, Dorothy S. Rambo, "Untreated Syphilis in the Male Negro: Background and Current Status of Patients in the Tuskegee Study," *Journal of Chronic Diseases* 2 (November 1955), 555.

45. R. A. Vonderlehr and Taliaferro Clark, "Untreated Syphilis in the Male Negro," *Venereal Disease Information* 17 (September 1936), 262.

46. J. R. Heller and P. T. Bruyere, "Untreated Syphilis in the Male Negro: II. Mortality During 12 Years of Observation," *Venereal Disease Information* 27 (February 1946), 34–38.

47. Jesse J. Peters, James H. Peers, Sidney Olansky, John C. Cutler, and Geraldine Gleeson, "Untreated Syphilis in the Male Negro: Pathologic Findings in Syphilitic and Non-Syphilitic Patients," *Journal of Chronic Diseases* 1 (February 1955), 127–48.

48. Sidney Olansky, Standley H. Schuman, Jesse J. Peters, C. A. Smith, and Dorothy S. Rambo, "Untreated Syphilis in the Male Negro, X. Twenty Years of Clinical Observation of Untreated Syphilitic and Presumably Nonsyphilitic Groups," *Journal of Chronic Diseases* 4 (August 1956), 184.

49. O. C. Wenger, "Untreated Syphilis in Male Negro," unpublished typescript, 1950, p. 3. Tuskegee Files, Center for Disease Control, Atlanta, Georgia. (Hereafter TF-CDC).

50. Vernal G. Cave, "Proper Uses and Abuses of the Health Care Delivery System for Minorities with Special Reference to the Tuskegee Syphilis Study," *Journal of the National Medical Association* 67 (January 1975), 83.

51. See for example, Vonderlehr to B. W. Booth, April 18, 1934; Vonderlehr to E. R. Lett, November 20, 1933, NA-WNRC.

52. Transcript of Proceedings—Tuskegee Syphilis Ad Hoc Advisory Panel," February 23, 1973, unpublished typescript, TSS-NLM, Box 1.

53. Raymond Vonderlehr to Murray Smith, April 30, 1942; and Smith to Vonderlehr, June 8, 1942, TSS-NLM, Box 1.

54. Stanley H. Schuman, Sidney Olansky, Eunice Rivers, C. A. Smith, and Dorothy S. Rambo, "Untreated Syphilis in the Male Negro: Background and Current Status of Patients in the Tuskegee Study," *Journal of Chronic Diseases* 2 (November 1955), 550–53.

55. Raymond Vonderlehr to Stanley H. Schuman, February 5, 1952. TSS-NLM, Box 2.

56. Schuman et al., p. 550.

57. "Minutes, April 5, 1965" unpublished typescript, TSS-NLM, Box 1.

58. Tuskegee Ad Hoc Committee meeting—Minutes, February 6, 1969," TF-CDC.

59. James B. Lucas to William J. Brown, September 10, 1970, TF-CDC.

60. Elizabeth M. Kennebrew to Arnold C. Schroeter, February 24, 1971, TSS-NLM, Box 1.

61. See *Medical Tribune* (September 13, 1972), pp. 1, 20; and Report on HEW's Tuskegee Report," *Medical World News* (September 14, 1973), pp. 57–58.

62. HEW *Final Report*, p. 7.

63. The notable exception is Jay Katz's eloquent "Reservations About the Panel Report on Charge 1," HEW *Final Report*, pp. 14–15.

64. HEW *Final Report*, pp. 8, 12.

65. Hew *Final Report*, pp. 8, 12.

66. See R. H. Kampmeier, "The Tuskegee Study of Untreated Syphilis," *Southern Medical Journal* 65 (October 1972), 1247–51; and "Final Report on the Tuskegee Syphilis Study,'" *Southern Medical Journal* 67 (November 1974), 1349–53.

67. Leonard J. Goldwater, "The Tuskegee Study in Historical Perspective," unpublished typescript, TSS-NLM; see also "Treponemes and Tuskegee," *Lancet* (June 23, 1973), p. 1438; and Louis Lasagna, *The VD Epidemic* (Philadelphia: Temple University Press, 1975), pp. 64–66.

68. Quoted in "Debate Revives on the PHS Study," *Medical World News* (April 19, 1974), p. 37.

69. Heller to Vonderlehr, November 28, 1933, NA-WNRC; quoted in *Medical Tribune* (August 23, 1972), p. 14.

70. Although it is now known that syphilis is rarely infectious after its early phase, at the time of the study's inception latent syphilis was thought to be communicable.

The fact that members of the control group were placed in the test group when they became syphilitic proves that at least some infectious men were denied treatment.

71. When the subjects are drawn from minority groups, especially those with which the researcher cannot identify, basic human rights may be compromised. Hans Jonas has clearly explicated the problem in his "Philosophical Reflections on Experimentation," *Daedalus* 98 (Spring 1969), 234–37. As Jonas writes: "If the properties we adduced as the particular qualifications of the members of the scientific fraternity itself are taken as general criteria of selection, then one should look for additional subjects where a maximum of identification, understanding, and spontaneity can be expected—that is, among the most highly motivated, the most highly educated, and the least 'captive' members of the community."

Doing More Good than Harm? The Effects of Participation in Sex Research on Young People in the Netherlands

Lisette Kuyper, John de Wit, Philippe Adam, and Liesbeth Woertman

INTRODUCTION

. . . Ethical guidelines for research with human participants stress the importance of minimizing potential harm for participants while maximizing the anticipated benefits (American Psychological Association, 2002; National Institutes of Health, 1979; World Medical Association, 2008). Institutional Review Boards (IRBs) determine whether the potential risks for participants are justified and if potential harm is outweighed by the anticipated benefits of the study.

IRBs' and researchers' decisions regarding social or psychological research proposals and protocols seem, due to a lack of sufficient empirical data, mostly based on worst-case scenarios, assumptions, and anecdotes (DePrince and Freyd, 2004; Gunsalus et al., 2007; Newman and Kaloupek, 2004; Oakes, 2002; Rosenbaum and Langhinrichsen-Rohling, 2006; Rosnow, Rotheram-Borus, Ceci, Blank, and Koocher, 1993; Wagener et al., 2004; Walker, Newman, Koss, and Bernstein, 1997). . . .

. . . In the absence of empirical data regarding the effects of participation in sex research on young people, research regarding adolescents and sexuality might be an area in which judgments based on political, cultural, religious or emotional grounds can easily influence the decision of IRBs and researchers. These actors may be hesitant, both with respect to including adolescents who can be seen as a vulnerable population (Flicker and Guta, 2008) as well as in asking questions on sexual topics, which are commonly considered as private and sensitive (Lee and Renzetti, 1990). . . .

THE CURRENT STUDY

. . . Persisting high rates of sexually transmitted infection (STI) (Gavin et al., 2009), sexual victimization and perpetration (Barter, McCarry, Berredge, and Evans, 2009; Gavin et al., 2009; Young, Grey, and Boyd, 2009), and adolescent pregnancies (Gavin et al., 2009; Organisation of Economic Co-Operation and Development, 2008; Singh and Darroch, 2000) among young people warrant and require further research on their sexual health. It seems therefore important to examine empirically the effects of participation in sex research on young people. . . .

The current study examined the effects of asking questions about various sexual topics in a large-scale sexuality study in a diverse sample of Dutch adolescents. The research questions guiding the current study were: (1) What are the levels of distress, need for help, and positive feelings resulting from participation in a self-report questionnaire study on sexuality; (2) Do negative and positive effects differ between various sociodemographic subgroups with regard to gender, age, educational level, ethnicity, religiosity, and sexual orientation; (3) Do negative and positive effects differ between participants who have experience with different forms of sexual victimization (e.g., verbal manipulation, situational abuse and sexual violence) and adolescents who have no such experiences; and (4) Do negative and positive effects differ between participants who have experience with sexual risk behaviors (e.g., a high number of sexual partners, sexual experience with casual partners) and participants who have no such experiences?

METHOD
Participants

The sample consisted of 889 sexually experienced young people in The Netherlands. More females (74.0%) than males (26.0%) participated. The participants were between 14 and 26 years old ($M = 18.70$, $SD = 2.52$), and were roughly equally distributed among different educational levels (48.6% lower educational level, 51.4% higher educational level). Young people from non-Western ethnic backgrounds made up 11.4 percent of the sample. The majority (67.5%) of the participants did not consider religion of personal importance. Almost one fifth (18.8%) of the sample reported sexual experience with a same-sex partner.

Procedure

This study was part of a survey of the sexual behaviors and experiences of adolescents and young adults in The Netherlands. . . .

Random sampling was not undertaken, as the study sought to include only sexually active young people 15–25 years old. . . .

Three different online questionnaires were completed by the participants. . . .

RESULTS

Prevalence of Experienced Effects of Participation in the Study ($N = 889$)

	% (TOTALLY) AGREE
Distress	
The questions gave me bad thoughts about things that happened to me	16.5
The questions made me sad	7.8
The questions made me feel down	16.5
(Totally) agree with at least one distress item	26.7
Need for help	
I felt a need for help due to the questions	2.4
I went looking for help due to the questions	1.9
(Totally) agree with at least one need for help item	3.5
Positive feelings	
I liked it that I was able to give my opinion	75.9
I found it a relief to share my experiences	28.7
I think it is important that surveys like these are carried out	89.2
I think it is important that young people can speak up about their opinions on sexuality	93.1
(Totally) agree with at least one positive feeling item	96.5

DISCUSSION

. . . Overall, the negative effects of participation in this study appeared to be limited, while the benefits of participation seemed substantial. On an individual level, the balance between "avoiding harm" and "doing good" seemed to be disrupted for only a small fraction of the participants. . . .

. . . Despite the limitations and remaining questions, the current study showed that young people were not severely distressed by participating in sex research, and actually gained benefits from it. This helps to caution researchers and IRBs in being overly protective and overly sensitive towards sex research among young people, and overemphasizing their vulnerability. An overly sensitive attitude might even send the wrong message of considering young people incompetent to join sex research and undermine their agency. As Widom and Czaja (2005) point out, the ethical principle of respect even demands that vulnerable groups like young people have the right to join research projects, and ethical principles warn against the exclusion of specific groups from the benefits that scientific research has to offer. Ultimately, young people might also experience negative effects (e.g., not feeling like being heard or being represented, and no development in scientific knowledge on their sexual health) from *not* participating in sex research.

ACKNOWLEDGMENTS

The data used in the current study were collected as part of a study on sexual coercion among young people, which was funded by ZonMw (The Netherlands Organisation for Health Research and Development) (Grant number 124260002). We would like to thank Mirre Hubers of ZonMw for reminding us of the importance of addressing the effects of research participation of young people.

REFERENCES

American Psychological Association. 2002. *Ethical principles of psychologist and APA report and code of conduct.* Retrieved from http://www.apa.org/ethics/code/code.pdf.

Barter, C., McCarry, M., Berridge, D., and Evans, K. 2009. *Partner exploitation and violence in teenage intimate relationships.* Retrieved from http://www.nspcc.org.uk/Inform/research/findings/partner_exploitation_and_violence_report_wdf70129.pdf.

DePrince, A. P., and Freyd, J. J. 2004. Costs and benefits of being asked about trauma history. *Journal of Trauma Practice, 3,* 23–35.

Flicker, S., and Guta, A. 2008. Ethical approaches to adolescent participation in sexual health research. *Journal of Adolescence, 42,* 3–10.

Gavin, L., MacKay, A. P., Brown, K., Harrier, S., Ventura, S. J., Kann, L., . . . Ryan, G. 2009. *Sexual and reproductive health of persons aged 10–24 years, United States, 2002–2007.* Retrieved from http://www.cdc.gov/mmwr/PDF/ss/ss5806.pdf.

Gunsalus, C. K., Bruner, E. M., Burbules, N.C., Dash, L., Finkin, M., Goldberg, J. P., et al. 2007. The Illinois White Paper: Improving the system for protecting human subjects: Counteracting IRB "Mission Creep". *Qualitative Inquiry, 13,* 617–649.

Lee, R. M., and Renzetti, C. M. 1990. The problems of researching sensitive topics: An overview and introduction. *American Behavioral Scientist, 33,* 510–528.

National Institutes of Health. 1979. *The Belmont report. Ethical principles and guidelines for the protection of human subjects of research.* Retrieved from http://ohsr.od.nih.gov/guidelines/belmont.html.

Newman, E., and Kaloupek, D. G. 2004. The risks and benefits of participating in trauma-focused research studies. *Journal of Traumatic Stress, 17,* 383–394.

Oakes, J. M. 2002. Risks and wrongs in social science research. An evaluator's guide to the IBR. *Evaluation Review, 26,* 443–479.

Organisation of Economic Co-Operation and Development. 2008. *Share of birth outside marriage and teenage births.* Retrieved from http://www.occd.org.proxy.library.uu.nl/dataoecd/38/6/40278615.pdf.

Rosenbaum, A., and Langhinrichsen-Rohling, J. 2006. Meta-research on violence and victims: The impact of data collection methods on findings and participants. *Violence and Victims, 21,* 404–409.

Rosnow, R. L., Rotheram-Borus, M. J., Ceci, S. J., Blank, P. D., and Koocher, G. P. 1993. The institutional review board as a mirror of scientific and ethical standards. *American Psychologist, 48,* 821–826.

Singh, S., and Darroch, J. E. 2000. Adolescent pregnancy and childbearing: Levels and trends in developed countries. *Family Planning Perspectives, 32,* 14–23.

Wagener, D. K., Sporer, A. K., Simmerling, M., Flome, J. L., An, C., and Curry, S. J. 2004. Human participants' challenges in youth-focused research: Perspectives and practices of IBR administrators. *Ethics and Behavior, 14,* 335–349.

Walker, E. A., Newman, E., Koss, M., and Bemstein, D. 1997. Does the study of victimization revictimize the victims? *General Hospital Psychiatry, 19,* 403–410.

Widom, C. S., and Czaja, S. J. 2005. Reactions to research participation in vulnerable subgroups. *Accountability in Research, 12,* 115–138.

World Medical Association. 2008. *Declaration of Helsinki. Ethical principles for medical research involving human subjects.* Retrieved from http://www.wma.net /en/30publications/10policies/b3/17c.pdf.

Young, A. M., Grey, M., and Boyd, C. J. 2009. Adolescents' experiences of sexual assault by peers: Prevalence and nature of victimization occuring within and outside of school. *Journal of Youth and Adolescence, 38,* 1072–1083.

SEXUALITY AND SOCIAL THEORIZING

DENISE DONNELLY, ELISABETH O. BURGESS, AND WENDY SIMONDS[1]

INTRODUCTION

Many of us don't think of sexuality and theorizing as two things that go together, but theories can be very useful in helping us understand sexuality. Theories are simply ways of viewing and organizing the world and of making sense of what happens. Sociologists use theories to understand, explain, predict, question, or change social behaviors and trends. Theories about sex vary dramatically across time and place, and reflect the social and moral thinking of the day.

In addition to helping us understand the history and context of sexuality, theories also provide explanations for sexual attitudes and behavior: why there are differences in how people think about sex or how people behave sexually, how societal norms and laws regarding sex arise and are enforced, and how and why change takes place. Sexuality is important in most of our lives, yet many people don't understand it, are uncomfortable talking about it, and don't know where to go to get their questions answered. Sexuality theories can provide explanations and answers, but no one theory is appropriate for addressing all questions and concerns about sexuality. Thus, we are especially interested in the ways in which sociological theories help us understand the social construction and social control of sexuality.[2]

We'll begin by reviewing what some early thinkers (called sexologists) had to say about sexuality. Then, we'll examine the utility of sociological theory for studying sex, and end with some current theories, questions, and challenges. As you'll see, theories about sexuality are constantly offered, challenged, revised, and rejected. Throughout the reading, we'll be asking "What relevance does theory have for helping us understand the social construction and control of sexuality?"

LAYING THE GROUNDWORK: THE SEXOLOGISTS

We're probably all familiar with Sigmund Freud, sometimes called "The Father of Modern Psychoanalysis," who felt that sexuality was a driving force in human behavior (Freud, [1938] 1995), but there were other important early thinkers as well. For example, at the end of the nineteenth century (prior to most of Freud's work), Richard von Krafft-Ebing ([1871] 1965) cataloged types of sexual deviance, and later on, Havelock Ellis (1942) pondered the differences between normal and abnormal sexuality and appealed for tolerance of a wide array of sexual behaviors.[3]

Freud, the most theoretical of the early sexologists, based his observations on the people he treated, who were mainly wealthy Victorians. Freud believed that sex was a basic drive that motivated most people, and that sexuality was formed early in life. He theorized that, as toddlers, young boys fell in love with their mothers (the "Oedipus complex") and that young girls fell in love with their fathers (the "Electra complex"). He suggested that each wanted the same-sex parent out of the way. He introduced the terms "penis envy" and "castration anxiety," arguing that young girls envied boys' penises, and that young boys were anxious about keeping theirs, for they feared that their fathers would castrate them to win the rivalry over their mothers. According to Freud, in order to resolve these issues and become healthy heterosexual adults, children had to learn to identify with their same-sex parents. Freud also made many controversial statements about women's sexuality, including his supposition that women have two types of orgasms (clitoral and vaginal), with the vaginal being superior, and that recollections of sexual abuse are simply the fantasies of neurotic young women who fantasize about their fathers and crave excitement in their lives.[4]

Some of the ideas of Freud and his contemporaries may seem very outdated by today's standards, but these sexologists still influence the ways in which scholars think about sexuality and the ways therapists treat sexual problems. The work of these early sexologists resisted the social control of sexuality by challenging state and religious definitions of normal and abnormal sexual practices and contributed to the social construction of sexuality by openly discussing sexual variability, the origins of homosexuality, and the relation of women to sexuality. While their perspectives may lack the social and historical sophistication of later theories, their ideas have persisted through the years.

In the United States during the mid-twentieth century, the study of sexuality shifted from theorizing to research. Using models drawn from the biomedical sciences, researchers such as Alfred Kinsey (Kinsey, Pomeroy, and Martin, 1948; Kinsey, Pomeroy, Martin, and Gebhard, 1953) and William Masters and Virginia Johnson (1966; 1970), provided an empirical base for testing the ideas and theories of earlier scholars. Although they were primarily researchers, their findings have influenced the ways in which Americans think about sexuality today.[5]

THE CONTRIBUTIONS OF TWENTIETH-CENTURY SEX RESEARCHERS TO SEXUAL THEORIZING

Alfred Kinsey is probably the best known of the twentieth-century sex researchers. His curiosity about human sexuality led him and his team to survey 12,000 Americans and to write *Sexual Behavior in the Human Male* (1948) and *Sexual Behavior in the Human Female* (1953). His books created a huge controversy and were even banned in some areas. This negative publicity increased the visibility of his work, exposing his ideas on sexuality to hundreds of thousands of average Americans. He challenged the conservative ways in which sexuality was constructed by documenting the range of sexual practices among Americans and discussing numerous taboo topics including female orgasm, masturbation, and homosexuality. Moreover, Kinsey argued that "normal and abnormal" and "good and bad" were labels created to control sexuality. He illustrated the wide diversity in sexual expression in the United States and noted the discrepancies between public standards for sex and private expressions of sexuality. The research of Kinsey and his peers raised questions about the theories of Freud and the early sexologists, and laid the groundwork for more recent theories such as postmodernism and queer theory, which we discuss later.[6]

From the mid-sixties to the mid-eighties, Masters and Johnson (1966; 1970) further challenged social constructions of sexuality by observing volunteers engaging in masturbation and coitus in their labs, while hooked up to monitors. Although their samples were not representative, their data and theories on human sexual response are still used by clinicians today.[7] For example, they demonstrated that the clitoris is the seat of the orgasm (in direct contradiction to Freud's earlier theorizing) and documented similarities and differences in male and female sexual response. Masters and Johnson also argued that couples' sexual problems were not caused by neuroses or disorders, but instead resulted from poor communication, marital conflict, or a lack of information. Their findings greatly influence the ways in which both scholars and the general public think about and theorize sexuality today by questioning prior theories and providing an empirical basis for many of our later theories.

SOCIOLOGICAL THEORIES AND SEXUALITY

Our discussion of theorizing about sexuality will focus on differences between "traditional" sociological theories and those—such as feminism and postmodernism—that emerged in reaction to these perspectives. Traditional sociological theories include structural functionalism, conflict theory, symbolic interactionism, and exchange theory. Although most classical sociological theory (written in late nineteenth and early twentieth centuries) did not explicitly address issues of sexuality, those who wrote on the subject usually did so within the context of marriage, emphasizing the social control of intimate relations. For instance, Marx ([1888] 1978) and Durkheim ([1897] 1979) analyzed the regulatory practices of marriage, while Max Weber called sexual love "the greatest irrational force of life" ([1915] 1958: 343). Weber saw religious forces as seeking to diminish love's power through regulation—again, referring to marriage. Other lesser-known theorists of this era, such as Marianne Weber, Charlotte Perkins Gilman, and Anna Julia Cooper, examined marriage as a gendered form of social control over sexuality.

Structural-functionalism, or systems theory,[8] strongly influenced social thought and policy in the post–World War II years. According to structural functionalists, society was organized into parts (or structures), each of which had a specific function to fill. When each was performing its function, the system would run smoothly. In families, for example, men were supposed to be wage earners and administrators, while women were supposed to be housewives, mothers, and caretakers. The structural functionalists argued that things worked best when each person knew her or his role and stuck to it (Parsons and Bales, 1955). Regarding sexuality, they argued that men were "naturally" the aggressors, and were always ready and willing to have sex, while women were "naturally" more reticent and submissive, and had to be coaxed into sexual situations. Men continually pushed the boundaries, while women constantly enforced them. Women had "pure" natures, while men were more experienced sexually, and expected to be "worldly." According to structural functionalism, the system functioned best only when heterosexuals married, had children together, and raised them in two-parent families. From this traditional perspective, sociologists viewed homosexuals and others who did not fit into the nuclear family model as "dysfunctional" or "deviant." Examples include Albert J. Reiss's writing on street hustlers (1961), and Laud Humphreys's ethnographic exploration of sex in public restrooms (1970).

Structural-functionalism and deviance theories dominated sociology and influenced the social construction and control of sexuality into the 1970s. Social movements—for civil rights, sexual rights, women's rights, and gay/lesbian rights—led to questioning of the status quo, and eventually raised questions that led to theoretical change. What about men who weren't sexually aggressive or promiscuous, and women who were? Were they really "dysfunctional" as the theory suggested, or were they simply part of a normal range of behaviors (as Kinsey's analysis indicated)? Was the system really running smoothly, or was it simply supporting the largely white, male, middle-class status quo? Where did single mothers, people of color, gays and lesbians, and those who enjoyed nonmarital sex fit in? Because of these questions, sociological theorizing about sexuality took several turns.

Conflict theorists (Buss and Malamuth, 1996; Eisenstein, 1978) argued that the systems surrounding marriage, family, and sexuality were not running smoothly at all, and that the norms of the day were oppressive to many people. Anyone who fell outside a very narrow range of behaviors was penalized and often ostracized as well. At best, these nonconformists were considered deviants, and punished with social stigma. At worst, they were arrested, jailed, institutionalized, or even killed because of their sexuality. In many states, this social control extended to laws against having sex with someone of the same sex, someone of a different racial or ethnic group, or someone to whom you were not married (D'Emilio and Freedman, 1997).

Conflict theorists also asked questions about sexual rights and freedoms and examined how arrangements of the day (such as marriage) were benefiting some people (men), while hurting others (women) (Eisenstein, 1978). They questioned the status quo and pushed for social change, arguing that as long as sexual practices were conducted between consenting adults, they shouldn't be considered dysfunctional, abnormal, or illegal; and that current sexual arrangements were in need of examination and, potentially, elimination. Contemporary applications of conflict theory are also evident in global and political economy approaches to sexuality (Altman, 2001) that examine "how economic and political transformations have shaped sexual experiences, identities, politics, and desires" (Gamson and Moon, 2004: 56).

While conflict theorists challenged norms, systems, and stability, they often neglected any examination of the interpersonal level. Indeed, not all people wanted to be "freed" from conformity and stability, and some stayed in sexual relationships because of love and commitment, despite elements of institutional oppression (Simmel, 1964). And while the conflict theorists explained change very well, they sometimes lacked explanations for stability. On the whole, conflict theories did a better job of explaining structural and systematic sexual oppression than they did of explaining individual behaviors. In contrast, symbolic-interaction and exchange theories—which we review next—emphasized the individual level of analysis.

Symbolic interaction theorists were less concerned with social structures and institutions, and more concerned with how individuals interacted sexually (Plummer, 2003). These theorists examined the meanings attached to sexual behaviors and how behavior changes based on interactions with others (Goffman, 1959). Symbolic interaction helps explain the social construction of sexuality—why people interpret others as they do, why misunderstandings occur, and how individuals form opinions about themselves as sexual beings. However, because the symbolic interaction theorists focus on microlevel interactions (between dyads or small groups), they tend to underestimate the role of social institutions and structures in controlling sexual behavior.

One theory that emerged from the symbolic interactionist perspective was social constructionist theory (Berger and Luckmann, 1966). Proponents of this perspective argued that through interaction, individuals create shared meanings that are reinforced by norms, laws, and social institutions. Social construction theory helps us understand why people label some components of sexuality "right" and others "wrong," and why there is so much pressure to conform to sexual norms (Plummer, 2003).

Another direction taken by symbolic interaction theory was sexual scripting theory (Gagnon and Simon, 1973; 1987). These theories, based on an acting analogy (Goffman, 1959), suggest that humans have scripts for sexual behavior that tell us who to be attracted to, how to behave sexually, and even how to feel about our sexual experiences. Sexual scripts exist on the social level, the interpersonal level, and the individual level. Cultural scripts are contained in the broader norms of a society and define what is legal or illegal, permissible or not permissible. Interpersonal scripts tell us how to act with partners and how to respond to certain situations, while individual (or intrapsychic) scripts influence how we view ourselves and evaluate our sexuality.

Taking a slightly different perspective, exchange theorists argued that sexuality was in many ways a transaction or trade. Unlike the structural functionalists who focused on maintaining stability, the exchange theorists posited that relationships are only stable so long as people feel they are getting a fair deal (Thibault and Kelly, 1967). If the balance tilts too far in their partner's favor, they may withhold sex, have an affair, begin using pornography, or even withdraw from the relationship entirely in an attempt to tip the balance of power back in their own favor (Donnelly and Burgess, 2006). One early exchange theorist was Waller (1938), who suggested that in a heterosexual relationship, women exchange their looks, youth, and sexuality for a man's status, money, and security. The couple bargain with each other—and the one who has the least interest in continuing the relationship has the upper hand. Much popular wisdom contained in "self-help" books (such as Robin Norwood's 1990 book, *Women Who Love Too Much*) is still based on these notions.

Critics of exchange theory point out that like conflict theory, it strips the role of love, emotion, and sacrifice from understanding romantic and sexual relationships. Exchange theorists assume that individuals act in rational, utilitarian ways (attempting to maximize rewards and minimize costs), and that they are always motivated by self-interest. Moreover, they assume that value can be attached to all aspects of a relationship, and that people actually measure the quantity and quality of sexual interactions. A final critique of this theory is that, like symbolic interaction, it pays little attention to the larger social context in which exchanges take place.

In sum, traditional sociological theories tended not to place sexuality at the center of their theorizing, but rather addressed sexuality within the context of families, couples, relationships, and deviance. While these theories may help us understand the social control and construction of sexuality, they tend to describe, rather than question, existing social arrangements. Challenges to these ways of thinking about sex often came from other disciplines and from countries outside the United States.

CHALLENGES AND ALTERNATIVES TO TRADITIONAL SOCIOLOGICAL THEORIZING

With the emerging sexual freedom of the 1970s, sexual research and theorizing became less taboo. Although it was still marginal to most of mainstream sociology, some theorists began to place sexuality at the center of their inquiries. These new perspectives challenged sociologists' silence with regard to issues of sex and sexuality and pushed the boundaries of traditional social sciences. Although they posed a wide variety of questions, we focus on those asked by three groups: feminists, postmodernists, and queer theorists. These theorists draw on ideas and explanations from a variety of disciplines across the humanities and social sciences. While it is impossible to address all the contributions of these three theoretical perspectives, we will introduce a few of the key themes for understanding the social construction and control of sexuality. First, we'll examine the challenges posed by feminist theories.

By feminist theory, we mean a variety of (often competing) perspectives, or feminisms.[9] At the heart of these perspectives is the idea that patriarchal (male-run) societies are oppressive to women, and that women must have both freedom and choice if they are to contribute to society and become fully participatory adults.

Feminists identify "the personal as political," meaning that the troubles women face as a result of sexism are not simply individual private issues (such as an abusive male partner), but rather part of a larger public problem (domestic violence) best solved through political change (Weedon, 1999). Three key contributions of feminist theory include feminist discussions of the gendered nature of sexuality; heterosexuality as a form of social control; and the notion of intersectionality.

First, feminists question the ways in which sexuality has been constructed, and note that these constructions favor men in a variety of ways. At the intersection of gender and sexuality, for example, they point out that men control women's sexuality by defining it in masculine and heterosexual terms (Rich, 1980). All women are presumed to be heterosexual, men are presumed to be the initiators of sex, and the sex act itself is defined in terms of male performance (Tiefer, 1995). Traditionally, "sex" meant that a man inserted his penis into a woman's vagina, and other forms of sexuality were seen as "not quite sex." When the man ejaculated, "sex" was over. Moreover, feminists questioned the usefulness of the very categories we use for sex and gender, illustrating that gender itself is a social construction and that using biological essentialist arguments[10] about "women's natural place" is also a means of social control (Elshtain, 1981; Epstein, 1988).

Feminist theory about sexual violence, such as rape and sexual harassment, explored how violence is a tool of social control by men, and pointed out that restrictions on abortion, birth control, and sexual expression were oppressive to women and denied them choice (Brownmiller, 1976; Kelly, 1988; Russell, 1998). Some feminists (Dworkin, 1987; 1989; MacKinnon, 1989) theorized that because of the power differentials between men and women, all heterosexual sex had an element of force behind it. They saw heterosexual sex and rape as existing on a continuum, with the common element being male control of female sexuality. In contrast, a coalition of sex-positive feminist theorists campaigned for the recognition of women's agency in sexuality, and began to organize groups such as dancers and prostitutes into professional unions and organizations (see Nagle, 1997).

A second strand of theory emerged from the work of lesbian feminists who theorized that the institution of heterosexuality and restrictive notions about "normal" sexuality limit what counts as sexual. Adrienne Rich (1980) argued that heterosexuality is central to patriarchy and, thus, not a choice but rather a form of social control of women. Moreover, she theorized that there is not a clear distinction between lesbians and heterosexual women but instead argued women's experiences can be understood on a lesbian continuum. This continuum describes the range of women's experiences with other women, including identifying with them, bonding with them, and sharing sexual experiences.

As feminism promised to give "voice" to women, many asked "whose voice?" For example, Gayle S. Rubin (1984) argued that feminist theories of sex must account for the oppression of all sexual minorities, not just women. She posited that the state and other social institutions reinforce an erotic hierarchy that defines "normal" sexual behavior, emphasizing heterosexual, marital, monogamous, vanilla sex,[11] and demonizing other sexual practices. Not always popular with mainstream feminists, these theories drew on many of the same ideas as postmodern and queer theories that we discuss later.

Marginalized groups of women, such as women of color, poor women, women with little or no formal education, and women from non-Western nations, argued that the majority of feminist theorizing ignored their standpoints and assumed that white middle class women's experiences represented everyone (hooks, 1981; 1984; Lorde, 1984; Moraga and Anzaldúa, 1983;

Mohanty, Russo, and Torres, 1991). For example, African American feminist theorists (sometimes called "womanists") argued that while white women may suffer because of their gender status, the color of their skin gives them privilege to be protected sexually and depicted as virginal or pure. In contrast, black women have been seen as sexually accessible and their history has been one of rape and exploitation by both white and black men (Davis, 1983; Hill Collins, 2004; hooks, 1984; Wyatt, 1997).

Initially, critics of white feminist thought focused primarily on racial differences, arguing that the standpoint of African American women was ignored in feminist theorizing, but eventually sociologists such as Patricia Hill Collins (1991; 2004) pointed out that intersectionality—the ways in which a *variety* of statuses and characteristics intersect—needed to be taken into account when thinking about female sexuality. Intersectionality theory contended that not only does one's race affect the ways sexuality is experienced and perceived, but so does one's class, age, ability, sexual orientation, and nation. Essentially, there can be no single perspective on black women's sexuality, poor women's sexuality, or the sexuality of women in non-Western nations.

While feminists critiqued the gender order, postmodernists questioned the usefulness of grand theories to explain the social world and wondered whether it was meaningful to search for universal, all-encompassing truths about society.[12] They argued that there was no "right" way of seeing or describing the world, and that no two people shared the same reality. They posited that ideas about right and wrong and good and bad had no inherent meanings, but were simply social constructions that had emerged from modern society. They questioned the concept of modernity itself, and wondered if modern society, with its emphasis on science, positivism, and progress, was really beneficial to humanity.

Moreover, the postmodernists recommended that we not take the social order at face value, but instead work to deconstruct existing structures (such as language, law, or sexuality) by examining their various components (such as history, discourse, and interaction). In contrast to earlier theorists, postmodernists emphasized that the power to control and construct sexuality does not lie with one central entity (such as government), but is constantly negotiated by a variety of ways of talking or thinking about a topic, coming from a variety of groups (such as religion, activist movements, or the legal system).

Applying these ideas to sexuality, postmodern theorists argued that sexuality has been produced in socially and culturally specific ways. Michel Foucault (1978) examined the construction of sexuality by analyzing a variety of discourses and sexual practices. In the *History of Sexuality,* he rejected "the repressive hypothesis" that blamed the Victorians for the shame and guilt that people in many Western societies felt about sexuality, and instead examined the influence of the scientific discourse on these constructions of sexuality. He rejected the dominant belief that modern industrial societies, such as the Victorians, "ushered in an age of increased sexual repression" (49). Rather, he argued that multiple sources of power (for instance, religion, medicine, education, law) dominated our understandings of sexuality and sought to manipulate sexual attitudes and practices according to their own (often very profitable) agendas. He went on to say that scientific disciplines, such as psychology and medicine, control sexualities, but while they inform us, they also dominate us. Individuals internalize the norms set by scientists, and monitor their own behavior in an effort to conform to the scientific constructions of sexuality.

Postmodern perspectives have appealed to a wide variety of scholars, and some feminist postmodernists felt that feminism and postmodernism could be complementary. For example, both groups questioned concepts such as objectivity, universality, and reason, claiming that what is considered objective in a given culture at a particular time in history reflects the interests of those in power. Moreover, both feminists and postmodernists have worked to avoid the tendency to construct theories based on the experiences of privileged groups of women (Flax, 1990; Nicholson, 1990).

Although the deconstruction of modern ideas about sexuality is a useful theoretical exercise, critics maintain that it is more of an intellectual exercise than an explanatory framework. They note that while postmodernism critiques and deconstructs modernity and objectivity, it suggests no alternatives and provides no agenda for social change. While postmodern perspectives have gained some acceptance in sociology (Mirchandani, 2005), the larger contribution of this perspective has likely been its influence on queer theory.

Drawing on the energy of the gay and AIDS movements of the 1980s and the academic perspectives of postmodernism, feminism, and gay and lesbian studies, queer theorists (Seidman, 1996; Stein and Plummer, 1996; Sullivan, 2003) challenged the identities seen as normative and natural in our culture, insisting they were instead, "arbitrary, unstable, and exclusionary" (Seidman, 1996: 11).[13] For example, queer theorists argued that sexuality is structured as a "binary opposition" (meaning that our culture has constructed heterosexuality and homosexuality as opposites), with heterosexuality given the label of good and homosexuality the label of bad or immoral. These labels are then used for social control, as evidenced by the passage of laws against same-sex marriage and adoption. Additionally, focusing on some identities and not others silences or excludes the other experiences. Part of the queer theorists' project is to continually question and deconstruct current beliefs about sexual, gender, and sex iden-

tities. By questioning binary social categories such as male or female, masculine or feminine, and heterosexual or homosexual, queer theorists demonstrate how these sexual categories and identities are actually fluid and not necessarily natural. Rather, they argue that current categorizations of sexuality, gender, and sex are tied to power, and that some institutions and groups have more power to define what is sexually acceptable than others do. Queer theorists believe transsexuals, the intersexed, and those immersed in drag culture are boundary crossers, challenging rigid categories of sex, gender, and sexual identity (c.f. Butler, 1990; Currah, 2001).

When they speak of "queering" sexuality, queer theorists are not talking about making everyone gay or lesbian. Instead, they are questioning (or "queering") existing sexual arrangements that privilege heterosexual, coupled, monogamous adults. This queering reveals the biases our ideas are constructed on, and demonstrates how certain groups benefit from current constructions of sexual identities. In general, queer theorists argue that it is important to separate the sexual behaviors that people participate in from the moral judgments of those with power in a society.

For all its contributions to sexuality theory, queer theory does not appeal to everyone and some scholars question its usefulness for sociological inquiry. For instance, Namaste (1996) and Green (2002) question the explanatory power of queer theory and argue that their focus on the abstract ignores the social realities of real sexual beings. Furthermore, Gamson and Moon (2004) debate the value of queer theory for addressing traditional sociological problems such as systems of oppression, and suggest that contributions of social theories, such as intersectionality and political economy, are more useful for sociological research.

Feminists, postmodernists, and queer theorists challenge the boundaries on which much of sexual theorizing takes place, while also building on some aspects of earlier theories and ideas. The common thread among the theories presented in this section is that current arrangements are socially constructed and must be questioned. They posit that old ideas about sexuality may not be useful or relevant, and indeed act as a form of social control—silencing, excluding, and even harming groups of people.

As you might imagine, these theories are confusing to many students, and aren't necessarily that popular with "mainstream" society. Most people take existing structures (institutions, norms, and conventions) surrounding sexuality at face value, and rarely think to question (or deconstruct) them. People assume that existing patterns of behavior exist because that is what works best for society, and that to go against these rules, beliefs, and norms would be to invite chaos. Even when people violate these widely held prohibitions, such as the ones against premarital sex or adultery, they often still feel that as a whole, these rules benefit society. Moreover, these norms are upheld and enforced by social institutions such as religion, family, education, the legal system, and the economy. To question them feels—and may well be—dangerous.

CAN THEORY HELP US UNDERSTAND SEXUALITY?

So, back to our original question—can social theories help us understand sexuality? We think so. Although each of the theories presented here is based on a different assumption and operates at a different level, they all provide us with ways of understanding the sexual behavior of individuals and groups, the development of social norms, and the underpinnings of social policies regarding sexuality. These theories invite us to ask interesting questions and to push the boundaries of our knowledge. The most liberatory theories, in our view, are the ones that reject notions of normalcy, resist moralizing, and question biological or essentialistic views of sexual behavior. Rather than providing answers, such theories delight in muddying the waters and raising new questions. Will we ever have a theory that explains all aspects of sexuality? Probably not. But by theorizing about sex, we broaden our understandings of ourselves and of the world around us. And, it very well may be that the most interesting parts of sexuality are in the questions, not in the answers!

NOTES

1. The authors would like to thank Mindy Stombler and Dawn M. Baunach, who were integral in defining the structure and content of this article and providing valuable perspectives on theory and sexuality and essential editorial advice. In addition, we acknowledge the assistance of Elisabeth Sheff, Elroi Windsor, Elizabeth Cavalier, Amy Palder, Robert Adelman, and Chet Meeks, who read earlier versions of this article and participated in numerous theoretical debates on sexuality.

2. By social construction we mean the process by which people create ideas, meanings, categories, and values through interaction. Social control refers to a system of rewards and punishments intended to control or influence others' behavior.

3. The field of sexology and the scientific study of sexuality emerged in the late nineteenth century. Sigmund Freud, Richard von Krafft-Ebing, and were integral to the development of sex research and our understanding of sexuality. These scholars in the late nineteenth and early twentieth centuries were trained in the medical profession and, thus, approached issues of sexuality using a medical model. The ideas of these early sex researchers contributed to our theoretical understanding of sexuality in more ways than we can discuss in this essay. For more on the history of sex research see Bullough (1995), and for classic writings of this era see Bland and Doan (1998) and Barreca (1995).

4. The latter was a revision to his earlier theory. Initially, he believed that sexual abuse was real, but because of his colleagues' disbelief, Freud revised his theory and marked his patient's recollections of child sexual abuse down to "fantasy."

5. For more on Kinsey, see Reading 7 in this book. For additional information on sex research during the twentieth century see Ericksen (1999) and Bullough (1995).

6. During the first half of the twentieth century several other researchers conducted sex surveys of specific populations, including Katherine Bement Davis's

research on female sexuality (1929) and Evelyn Hooker's work on male sexuality (1956; 1957; 1958), and expanded our understanding of sexual variation and the social construction of sexual deviance.

7. Teifer (1995) provides a thorough critique of Masters and Johnson's sample and their findings about the human sexual response cycle.

8. For many scholars, the distinction between these theories is the level of analysis. Structural-functionalism addresses the structural or societal level of analysis and systems theory explores the microlevel issues of families and individuals.

9. Additionally, the term *feminism* covers theory, belief systems, and political action. Many times it is difficult to distinguish among them because the boundaries between academic perspectives and practices are not always clear.

10. Biological essentialism argues that women are naturally different from men because of their ability to become mothers, and that these differences mean that women are better suited to certain roles and men to others.

11. *Vanilla sex* refers to standard heterosexual practices, and excludes such variations as sadomasochism (BDSM), fetish, and kink.

12. The ideas of postmodernism and poststructuralism are intertwined and trace their roots to French philosophers such as Foucault (1978) and Lyotard (1984). As with feminism, there are many variations and conflicting perspectives on these theories. In this article we are focusing on postmodernism.

13. Like the feminists and postmodernists, queer theorists do not always agree or even acknowledge the same texts. In addition to Foucault, discussed previously, Judith Butler (1990; 1993) and Eve [Sedgwick] (1990) produced works widely acknowledged to be central to queer theory. In this article we emphasize sociological interpretations of queer theory.

REFERENCES

Altman, Dennis. 2001. *Global Sex*. Chicago: University of Chicago Press.

Barreca, Regina, ed. 1995. *Desire and Imagination: Classic Essays in Sexuality*. New York: Meridian.

Berger, Peter L., and Thomas Luckmann. 1966. *The Social Construction of Reality*. New York: Doubleday.

Bland, Lucy, and Laura Doan, ed. 1998. *Sexuality Uncensored: The Documents of Sexual Science*. Chicago: University of Chicago Press.

Brownmiller, Susan. 1976. *Against Our Will: Men, Women, and Rape*. New York: Bantam Books.

Bullough, Vern. 1995. *Science in the Bedroom: A History of Sex Research*. New York: Basic Books.

Buss, David M., and Neil Malamuth. 1996. *Sex, Power, Conflict: Evolutionary and Feminist Perspectives*. London: Oxford University Press.

Butler, Judith. 1990. *Gender Trouble: Feminism and the Subversion of Identity*. New York: Routledge.

Butler, Judith. 1993. *Bodies that Matter: On the Discursive Limits of "Sex."* New York: Routledge.

Currah, Paisley. 2001. "Queer Theory, Lesbian and Gay Rights, and Transsexual Marriages." In *Sexual Identities, Queer Politics* (pp. 178–199), edited by Mark Blasius. Princeton, NJ: Princeton University Press.

Davis, Angela Y. 1983. *Women, Race, and Class*. New York: Vintage Books.

Davis, Katherine Bement. 1929. *Factors in the Sex Life of Twenty-Two Hundred Women*. New York: Harper.

D'Emilio, John D., and Estelle B. Freedman. 1997. *Intimate Matters, Second Edition*. Chicago: University of Chicago Press.

Donnelly, Denise, and Elisabeth O. Burgess. 2006. Involuntary Celibacy in Long-Term Heterosexual Relationships. Unpublished Manuscript.

Durkheim, Emile. [1897] 1979. *Suicide: A Study in Sociology*. New York: Free Press.

Dworkin, Andrea. 1987. *Intercourse*. New York: Free Press.

Dworkin, Andrea. 1989. *Pornography: Men Possessing Women*. New York: Dutton.

Eisenstein, Zillah. 1978. "Developing a Theory of Capitalist Patriarchy and Socialist Feminism." *Capitalist Patriarchy and the Case for Socialist Feminism*, by Zillah Eisenstein. New York: Monthly Review Press.

Ellis, Havelock. 1942. *Studies in the Psychology of Sex, Volumes 1 and 2*. New York: Random House.

Elshtain, Jean Bethke. 1981. *Public Man, Private Woman*. Princeton, NJ: Princeton University Press.

Epstein, Cynthia Fuchs. 1988. *Deceptive Distinctions: Sex, Gender, and the Social Order*. New Haven, CT: Yale University Press and Russell Sage Foundation.

Ericksen, Julia A. 1999. *Kiss and Tell: Surveying Sex in the Twentieth Century*. Cambridge, MA: Harvard University Press.

Flax, Jane. 1990. "Postmodern and Gender Relations in Feminist Theory." In *Feminism/Postmodernism* (pp. 39–63), edited by Linda J. Nicholson. New York: Routledge.

Foucault, Michel. 1978. *The History of Sexuality: An Introduction, Volume 1*. New York: Vintage Books.

Freud, Sigmund. [1938] 1995. *The Basic Writings of Sigmund Freud*. Translated by A. A. Brill. New York: Modern Library.

Gagnon, John H., and William Simon. 1973. *Sexual Conduct: The Social Sources of Human Sexuality*. Chicago: Aldine.

Gagnon, John H., and William Simon. 1987. "The Sexual Scripting of Oral Genital Contacts." *Archives of Sexual Behavior* 16:1–25.

Gamson, Joshua, and Dawne Moon. 2004. "The Sociology of Sexualities: Queer and Beyond." *Annual Review of Sociology* 30:47–64.

Goffman, Erving. 1959. *The Presentation of Self in Everyday Life*. New York: Anchor.

Green, Adam Isaiah. 2002. "Gay but not Queer: Toward a Post-Queer Study of Sexuality." *Theory and Society* 31:521–545.

Hill Collins, Patricia. 1991. *Black Feminist Thought: Knowledge, Consciousness, and the Politics of Empowerment*. New York: Routledge.

Hill Collins, Patricia. 2004. *Black Sexual Politics: African Americans, Gender, and the New Racism*. New York: Routledge.

Hooker, Evelyn. 1956. "A Preliminary Analysis of Group Behavior of Homosexuals." *Journal of Psychology* 42: 217–225.

Hooker, Evelyn. 1957. "The Adjustment of the Male Overt Homosexual." *Journal of Projective Techniques* 21:18–31.

Hooker, Evelyn. 1958. "Male Homosexuality in the Rorschach." *Journal of Projective Techniques* 23:278–281.

hooks, bell. 1981. *Ain't I a Woman: Black Women and Feminism*. Boston: South End Press.

hooks, bell. 1984. *Feminist Theory: From Margin to Center*. Boston: South End Press.

Humphreys, Laud. 1970. *Tearoom Trade: Impersonal Sex in Public Places*. Chicago: Aldine.

Kelly, Liz. 1988. *Surviving Sexual Violence*. Boston: Cambridge University Press.

Kinsey, Alfred C., Wardell B. Pomeroy, and Clyde E. Martin. 1948. *Sexual Behavior and the Human Male*. Philadelphia: Saunders.

Kinsey, Alfred C., Wardell B. Pomeroy, Clyde E. Martin, and Paul H. Gebhard. 1953. *Sexual Behavior and the Human Female*. Philadelphia: Saunders.

Krafft-Ebing, Richard von. [1871] 1965. *Psychopathia Sexualis: A Medico-Forensic Study*. Translated by Harry E. Wedeck. New York: Putnam.

Lacan, Jacques. [1972–1973] 1998. *On Feminine Sexuality: The Limits of Love and Knowledge*. Translated by Bruce Fink. New York: Norton.

Lyotard, Jacques. [1979] 1984. *The Postmodern Condition: A Report on Knowledge*. Translated by G. Bennington and B. Massumi. Minneapolis: University of Minnesota Press.

Lorde, Audre. 1984. *Sister Outsider: Essays and Speeches*. Trumansburg, NY: Crossing Press.

MacKinnon, Catherine A. 1989. *Toward a Feminist Theory of the State*. Cambridge, MA: Harvard University Press.

Marx, Karl. [1888] 1978. "Manifesto of the Communist Party." In *The Marx-Engels Reader, Second Edition* (pp. 469–500), edited by Robert C. Tucker. New York: W. W. Norton.

Masters, William H., and Virginia Johnson. 1966. *Human Sexual Response*. Boston: Little, Brown.

Masters, William H., and Virginia Johnson. 1970. *Human Sexual Inadequacy*. Boston: Little, Brown.

Mirchandani, Rekha. 2005. "Postmodernism and Sociology: From Epistemological to Empirical." *Sociological Theory* 23:86–115.

Mohanty, Chandra Talpade, Ann Russo, and Lourdes Torres. 1991. *Third World Women and the Politics of Feminism*. Bloomington: Indiana University Press.

Moraga, Cheríe, and Gloria Anzaldúa. 1983. *This Bridge Called My Back: Writings by Radical Women of Color*. New York: Kitchen Table/Women of Color Press.

Nagle, Jill, ed. 1997. *Whores and Other Feminists*. London: Routledge.

Namaste, Ki. 1996. "'Tragic Misreadings': Queer Theory's Erasure of Transgender Subjectivity." In *Queer Studies: A Lesbian, Gay, Bisexual, and Transgender Anthology* (pp. 183–203), edited by Brett Beemyn and Mickey Eliason. New York: New York University Press.

Nicholson, Linda J., ed. 1990. *Feminism/Postmodernism*. New York: Routledge.

Norwood, Robin. 1990. *Women Who Love Too Much*. New York: Pocket Books.

Parsons, Talcott, and Robert F. Bales. 1955. *Family, Socialization and the Interaction Process*. Glencoe, IL: Free Press.

Plummer, Ken. 2003. "Queers, Bodies, and Postmodern Sexualities: A Note on Revisiting the 'sexual' in Symbolic Interaction." *Qualitative Sociology* 26:515–530.

Reiss, Albert J., Jr. 1961. "The Social Integration of Queers and Peers." *Social Problems* 9:102–120.

Rich, Adrienne. 1980. "Compulsory Heterosexuality and Lesbian Existence." *Signs: Journal of Women in Culture and Society* 5:631–660.

Rubin, Gayle S. 1984. "Thinking Sex: Notes for a Radical Theory of the Politics of Sexuality." In *Pleasure and Danger: Exploring Female Sexuality* (pp. 267–319), edited by Carole S. Vance. New York: Routledge.

Russell, Diana. 1998. *Dangerous Relationships: Pornography, Misogyny, and Rape*. Thousand Oaks, CA: Sage.

Sedgwick, Eve. 1990. *Epistemology of the Closet*. Berkeley: University of California Press.

Seidman, Steven, ed. 1996. *Queer Theory/Sociology*. Malden, MA: Blackwell Publishers.

Simmel, Georg. 1964. *Conflict and the Web of Group Affiliations*. New York: Free Press.

Stein, Arlene, and Ken Plummer. 1996. "'I Can't Even Think Straight': 'Queer' Theory and the Missing Sexual Revolution in Sociology." In *Queer Theory/Sociology* (pp. 129–144), edited by Steven Seidman. Oxford, UK: Blackwell.

Sullivan, Nikki. 2003. *A Critical Introduction to Queer Theory*. New York: New York University Press.

Thibaut, J., and H. Kelley. 1967. *The Social Psychology of Groups*. New York: John Wiley and Sons.

Tiefer, Leonore. 1995. *Sex Is Not a Natural Act and Other Essays*. Boulder, CO: Westview Press.

Waller, Willard Walter. 1938. *The Family: A Dynamic Interpretation*. New York: Dryden.

Weber, Max. [1915] 1958. "Religious Rejections of the World and Their Directions." In *From Max Weber: Essays in Sociology* (pp. 323–362), edited by H. H. Gerth and C. Wright Mills. New York: Oxford University Press.

Weedon, Chris. 1999. *Feminism, Theory, and the Politics of Difference*. Oxford, UK: Blackwell.

Wyatt, Gail Elizabeth. 1997. *Stolen Women: Reclaiming Our Sexuality, Taking Back Our Lives*. New York: John Wiley and Sons.

SEXING UP THE SUBJECT: METHODOLOGICAL NUANCES IN RESEARCHING THE FEMALE SEX INDUSTRY

TEELA SANDERS

Despite the interdisciplinary accounts of the sex industry, apart from some reflective revelations (for instance by Hart, 1998; Hubbard, 1999a; Maher, 2000; Melrose, 2002; O'Connell Davidson, 1998; O'Neill, 1996; Sharpe, 2000; Shaver, 2005) researchers have been reluctant to report on the methodological demands of this topic. These pieces of work highlight the importance of reflexivity in the researcher process—a research account that is aware that the researcher is of the world being studied and therefore should be included in the process of analysis. . . . This article explores the methodological challenges that question existing procedural boundaries and push the parameters of the qualitative method as the subject becomes increasingly sexual. Drawing on my own ethnography in the indoor prostitution markets (see Sanders, 2005a), this article reflects mostly on research into female adult consensual prostitution but will refer to other aspects of the non-contact sexual services such as pornography and erotic dancing.

STUMBLING AT THE FIRST HURDLE: ETHICS COMMITTEES

Much of what has been written about the ethics of fieldwork and the sex industry focuses on what happens in the field. Yet increasingly, one of the first stumbling blocks for the researcher (especially students) is gaining approval for the project from the internal institution's ethics committee. With these regulatory bodies becoming an increasing part of funding applications and university bureaucracies, having a vague plan and heading into the field is becoming less of an option. Anecdotally it can be said that ethics committees have treated the sex industry as a problematic area of inquiry, which can sometimes result in projects failing at this initial stage. An example from Mattely (1997) demonstrates how funding research into prostitution continues to be stifled by stigma and excluded by research councils. This section teases out three familiar areas of suspicion that are charged at those wanting to research sex work: the methods employed, the setting of the fieldwork and concerns for the reputation of the institution.

Methodological concerns are often raised at ethics committees when the method of inquiry is based on an ethnographic style that places informality at the heart of the data collection. Invariably this method requires lengthy periods of observation, interviews that can take the form of informal conversations and other methods that are unorthodox in the minds of positivist thinkers. As a result committees can query the validity of the methods, whether enough information will be collected and the quality of the data. For instance, in situations where interviews cannot be taped, data collection relies on fieldnotes and memory, which raises questions about how information can be accurately recorded. In addition, as Shaver (2005) documents, researchers in

From "Sexing Up the Subject: Methodological Nuances in Researching the Female Sex Industry" by Teela Sanders, *Sexualities*, Vol. 9, No. 4, 2006, pp. 449–468. © 2006, SAGE Publications. Reprinted by Permission of SAGE Publications.

the sex industry are constantly struggling with the unknown size and boundaries of the population, leading to queries of sample representation. Covert methods have also been adopted in sex work research highlighting the difficulties of informing all parties that are being observed, often for the sake of access and at the request of sex workers and managers. Ethics committees are usually hostile to covert methods as they can appear unethical and potentially dangerous for the researcher. Stereotypes and misunderstandings about the research setting exacerbate these generic concerns about the methods often employed when studying the sex work field.

The setting, whether it is a "red light district", crack house or illegal brothel, is often the focus of concern raised by ethics committees. Is this the correct environment for research to be conducted, or for a student to be initiated into the research culture? Questions of danger always arise because of stereotypes that link prostitution to criminality, especially drug-related crimes. Associations between HIV, drug-injecting sex workers, vicious and violent male pimps and the sex work setting all surface with the prospects of researching the sex industry. Fuelled by assumptions about the type of people who organize and work in the sex industry, as well as the men that buy sex, the researcher is expected to take extra precautions when assessing participants and fieldsites. In addition, the routines that the researcher will be expected to engage in usually entail long hours in fairly unknown or secluded locations, often late at night, and sometimes alone.

The danger that the researcher is exposed to is a central concern of officials, but this can sometimes be a disguise for more pressing anxieties about the reputation of the institution. As a postgraduate student my own research (which was originally based on an internet survey of the sex work community) was scrutinized by the senior officials in the university before it was vetoed as an unacceptable area of inquiry and methodological design (see Sanders, 2005b). Behind this decision was apprehension related to preserving the reputation of the university and concerns about media headlines that linked students to the seedy underworld environment in the name of completing a doctorate. . . .

However, there are solutions to these ethical trials. The plethora of successful work in this field, using both ethnographic and more mainstream methods, is a testament to the appropriateness of the sex industry as a fieldsite. The general literature that explains the limitations of informed consent in all circumstances and the acceptability of covert inquiry within an ethical framework that prioritizes the anonymity of those being studied, can be used to demonstrate the feasibility of the design. There are few horror stories reported (this does not mean that researchers have not experienced some difficult and vulnerable situations), and good quality accounts of ethnography explain the basic rules of engagement such as finding a gatekeeper that acts as a protector (Hart, 1998: 55; O'Connell Davidson and Layder, 1994). Therefore, it can be demonstrated that despite common conceptions, there are regulators (health workers, sauna owners, police, key informants) in the sex industry that researchers can align themselves with in order to stay out of trouble and learn the local scene.

In addition, researchers in this field can rely on the professional codes of practice promoted by the subject discipline that set out procedures, obligations and expectations of the research process (for example the British Sociological Association produces guidelines for its members). Often universities have their own codes of etiquette, which can include safety procedures when researchers are working alone or at night for instance. Basic safety checks such as never meeting people alone in private, always in a public place, letting a third party know of your whereabouts and checking in after the session has ended, are assurances that go a long way to maintaining safety (see Shaver, 2005: 302 for a thorough account of safety procedures for sex work researchers). The potential dangers and strong stereotypes associated with the sex industry are issues that researchers have to confront before the project gets off the ground. Although this means that research designs are perhaps over scrutinized and charged with queries that expect more insight from the novice researcher, this encourages the researcher to be reflective even at this initial stage. Thinking ahead to foreseeable problems, having a set of plan "B's" if the initial methods fail, and taking time out of the field-work to reassess are good practice in an intense and volatile environment.

ACCESS AND ACCEPTANCE INTO THE SEX INDUSTRY

For the researcher, the legal status of prostitution and the actual environment are the key considerations when planning the access route.

Prostitution is often located outside a legitimate legal framework or even where the sex industry is legitimate, there are always issues of stigma and deviancy to consider. The different environments that facilitate street and off street prostitution offer some peculiarities (for a lengthy discussion see Shaver, 2005). On the street, the environment is vulnerable, as women mainly work at night, in deserted and unlit industrial areas, in an economy that can be linked to other forms of acquisitive crime. Indoors, although not usually characterized by the violence and vulnerabilities of the street scene, the premises of illegal brothels may be well known but getting a foot in the door is a difficult prospect—especially if the researcher

is a woman. Owners, managers and workers are suspicious of unknown inquirers, and women who enter the building are normally looking for work (i.e. competition) or are spying for the opposition. Rarely has it been reported that a researcher has introduced herself or himself to sex workers without a third party mediating the initial introductions.

To side-step these closed environments researchers use various gatekeepers to overcome initial hostilities. Some access routes have been outside the sex work environment. For example the criminal justice system (prisons, bail hostels, courts, probation service and so on) or sexual health and welfare services have traditionally been a successful introduction route to women and men involved in prostitution. Specific sex work outreach projects (see Cooper et al., 2001) have been the most prolific gatekeepers, as their established and trusted ties with street workers and indoor establishments provide researchers with the opportunity to prove their credibility. Hubbard (1999b: 233) explains four principles that must be demonstrated to outreach projects and sex workers to achieve success in the negotiation phase. First, the investigator must establish how the research will produce knowledge to help reduce stigma surrounding prostitution; second, that the researcher has an insight into the reality of prostitution and the circumstances in which sex is sold; third, a recognition that prostitution is a legitimate form of work; and fourth, a belief that health and safety risks should be minimized for sex workers. However, as Melrose (2002: 340) documents, securing access through sexual health projects is not straightforward. This route can be met with refusal because of concerns that the research will demand too much time from the project, disagreement with the premise of the research or the worry that their clients are "over-researched" or exploited. . . .

ACCESSING PRIVATE AND THE PUBLIC LIVES

Once access to sex establishments or sex workers has been achieved, researchers then negotiate whether the research will be conducted in either the working environment or in the private lives and spaces of the sex workers. Despite the difficulties of the prostitution environment, research is often conducted in the working spaces of the commercial sex exchange. By striking "research bargains" and "exchanges" that involve giving out condoms, sterile needle equipment and hot drinks on the street, researchers have been able to observe successfully how the street markets operate. . . . A combination of methods (usually a mixed approach that includes observations and interviews) appears to be a successful recipe for data collection. . . .

Entering the private worlds of women who are involved in activities that are largely disapproved of presented additional ethical issues. On the few occasions I was permitted into the private worlds of participants I would often be asked to collude with the secrecy stories that sex workers had constructed to hide their money-making activities. I would have to pretend I was a colleague from the office, or an acquaintance whilst I chatted to a participant's husband, or was invited to stay for tea with the children. An example of the role-playing that I describe in the next section shows how it is an essential tool in the field.

MAKING SENSE OF THE SEXUAL FIELD

When actually doing research in the sex industry where the exchange of sexual services, bodily functions and flesh-to-flesh contact is the everyday trade, the reality of research cannot avoid these characteristics. Although there are similarities with other illicit economies, the setting of the sex industry is unique because the combination of studying sex and money in a illegal arena affects how the research is executed, the dilemmas for the researcher and the immediacy of making decisions in the "sexual" field. For those who are unaware, a typical sauna or brothel can be characterized by televisions showing hardcore pornography, pornographic magazines, sex toys, domination equipment, a menu of sexual services on offer, an explicit photographic gallery of the women who are available and other sex paraphernalia. This environment can be distasteful at best but is often violently shocking and disturbing.

The sexual subtext of the environment is impossible to escape as participants are in their work clothes (which usually consists of very little), buying into the fantasies that tempt customers to part with their cash (see Sanders, 2005c). The physical sexual environment is not the only sexualized element to the fieldwork setting. Men are constantly wandering into the premises and engaging in a set of negotiations with the receptionist (maid) and then (often in private) with the sex worker. Men linger in the communal lounge while they wait for a worker to finish her current client, idling the time away by flicking through a pornographic magazine or watching graphic images on the screen, before they are called to the shower room and finally the specifically chosen bedroom, until, 30 minutes later they come out the other side, £60 lighter. This routinization of the sexual negotiation is a process with which the observer becomes familiar (and perhaps desensitized) and after several sessions of data collection, the process of negotiating sexual services becomes part of the momentum of the fieldwork. . . .

My own experiences of being in the sexual field of the sauna and brothel involved two other methodological nuances that at the time became routinized yet had an intrinsic effect on the way in which information was collected, my role in this foreign arena, and establishing rapport with participants. First, as my role in the sauna was overt to the sex workers but, at the request of the managers, the clients were unaware of my researcher status and I was often propositioned by interested customers. Men would assume I was another worker or a new member of the team and would make propositions and innuendo that had to be managed. Initially flustered, embarrassed and uncomfortable, I soon adopted strategies to deflect their requests: I would either pretend I was "fully booked", a friend of a worker or a sexual health professional, switching between these roles depending on how confident I felt at the time and the amount of back up I had from those around me. Ultimately, role-playing became a necessity in the field, especially where a delicate "research bargain" existed that required keeping my researcher status anonymous to one party while others were aware of the investigation.

Second, the majority of the fieldwork in the indoor sex work venues was conducted amongst women who were semi-naked for most of the time. For instance, my interviews with Beryl, a 39-year-old mother of four who had worked in a range of sex markets for 20 years, took place in the 30-minute slot she allocated each day as her "preparation time" before she welcomed her first customer. In this time Beryl was showering, shaving, applying make-up, styling her hair, putting on lingerie and at the same time answering my questions. It became natural to see women naked as they changed from one outfit to another, were flitting between bathroom and bedroom or needed a hand squeezing into a particular costume. These situations were non-sexualized and non-erotic as the women conducted their behaviour in a professional matter-of-fact manner, relegating luxurious lingerie or kinky outfits to the function of a work uniform. Participants approached their work and ultimately the display of their bodies in an entirely pragmatic, de-sexualized and business-like manner with no sense of shame, embarrass-

ment or vulnerability. Explaining their trade as a combination of physical, sexual and emotional labour, the role of the body and their sexuality was afforded different meanings in the context of a money-making economic exchange.

WHAT IS PARTICIPANT OBSERVATION IN THE SEX INDUSTRY?

The ethnographic method in the sex work arena brings into question what participation means, and whilst there are those that maintain "going native" jeopardizes the professional status of the researcher (Hart, 1998: 55), others have used complete participation as the key to the insider status. For example, Wahab (2003: 629) describes how she not only conducted observations in strip clubs but decided to engage in the sex work venue. Encouraged by her participants who insisted that to really understand the job it had to be lived, Wahab took part in a peep show as a dancer, immersing herself in the context of the culture. . . .

Like the familiar debates in qualitative social science inquiry (see Labaree, 2002), the insider–outsider dilemma is a point of negotiation, confusion and reflection for the researcher in the sex work setting. Rarely are researchers' identities clearly defined as only "information gatherers." In the spirit of transparency, researchers interested in sex work qualify their intentions and character which often means blurring the roles and boundaries that other types of research and methods have the luxury of maintaining. . . .

PLEASURES AND DANGERS OF THE RESEARCH PROCESS

One account of my fieldwork experience in the sex work setting could read as a list of uncomfortable moments, scary confrontations, mistakes that led to insults, embarrassments, treading on toes and appearing unprofessional and out of my depth. Another positive account could reflect the strong bonds and lasting friendships I built with key informants, idling time away putting the world to rights, and sharing our histories, hopes and expectations. This section will reflect on some of the contrasting experiences of dangers and pleasures when conducting research in the sex work environment, highlighting the complexity of the method and the necessity of investing oneself in the process.

The practical challenges of doing research in the field have been discussed in relation to dangerous fieldwork settings or sensitive topics of inquiry (Ferrell and Hamm, 1998; Lee, 1995; Sharpe, 2000). . . . In the sexual field, despite the advantages of collecting different types of live data when immersed in the working environment, there are inherent dangers for researchers who operate in illegal environments that are isolated. Several researchers describe how they have met with opposition from potential participants, other hustlers on the street and territorial pimps who take issue with a researcher on their patch (see O'Neill, 1996). . . . Sometimes obvious risks are expected when working with populations at the margins of society, but, as I describe later, the emotional risks of such work are often unknown when the research is designed. Other hazards in the field make sex work a tricky subject for the well-intended researcher. Researchers have been mistaken for plain clothes police (see Barnard, 1992: 145; Sharpe, 2000: 366), journalists (Sanders, 2005b), or accused of spying for rival competitors (Lever and Dolnick, 2000)—all of which add extra hurdles to achieving safety, credibility and, of course, a sample! . . .

THE EMOTIONAL TOIL OF DATA GATHERING

The emotional effort needed to research sex work is stark in both the pragmatics of the fieldwork and the efforts needed to dissect, reflect and understand the researcher's own position in a complex social activity. What Melrose

(2002) calls the "labour pains" of researching sensitive areas like prostitution are often given little attention as the researcher is expected to apply emotional labour to manage the feelings of others as well as their own responses. Although not always the case, informal conversations and taped interviews with women who work in prostitution can involve the disclosure of disturbing and unpleasant data consisting of tales of exploitation, abuse, violence, desperation, drug use and hopelessness.

Melrose, like others (Miller, 1997; O'Connell Davidson and Layder, 1994: 216–7; Sharpe, 2000: 365), documents how stories provoke feelings of anger, rage and despair both in the data collection phase and again in the analysis stage. In a current project with men who buy sex from female sex workers, such feelings of anger and contempt have been a consequence of listening to the other side of the story. In a minority of cases, as interviewees have left my office I have felt pure rage at their misogynist attitudes and belief that if they buy the services of a sex worker then they can do as they please. It is difficult to understand or accept these experiences as research but maintaining a professional attitude and response to people who incite such negative feelings is the only reason why the project has not been shelved.

The dangers of the sexual field are not only related to the physical safety of the researcher as the emotional investment in the endeavour is significant and needs to be reflected upon and managed. At times the field relations with participants can prove to be very intense. To bridge the scepticism and doubts held by potential participants the researcher knowingly or unknowingly enters into a degree of self-disclosure. . . . Participants always wanted to know why I was interested in sex work and whether I could be tempted or indeed had the guts to sell sexual services for money. Such curiosity could not be ignored and a natural process of self-disclosure and identification became an integral part of how field relations were secured. I recall this process as natural rather than manipulative because it was not a chore to engage in in-depth conversation with the participants as I shared many experiences with them. Yet although disclosure brought me closer to the women, this self-investment also opened up vulnerabilities and concerns about keeping my private life protected from the demands of the fieldwork setting and the public academic eye. At the same time, having to do some personal soul searching also made me confront my stereotypes and prejudices about sexuality and lifestyles. Not something that is generally written into the research design.

The intensity of the research does not necessarily decrease as time lapses between the fieldwork and the safety of the academic corridors. In processes of self-reflection, what was experienced cannot be fully understood until the "after" phase of the data collection, writing up and dissemination (see Roberts and Sanders, 2005). It is in the after phases that the journey can be considered as a whole, the mistakes highlighted and good practice recognized as worthy of repeating or sharing with peers. It is also in the "after" phase that there are dilemmas about whether we make our academic careers off the backs of the people who have supplied the material. Making a successful academic career through permanent positions, book contracts and promotions from the experiences of those in the sex industry brings added suspicions of exploitation. The information used to make that career is based on experiences of individuals involved in what some consider an immoral or inhumane exchange of sex for money, or an institution that exists as a prop for patriarchy and wider unequal power structures that subjugates women. . . . Collaborative research partnerships that work alongside informants, offering directorship and control to those who are normally subjected to the research process is a step towards reducing the exploitative nature of social science research. . . .

CONCLUDING COMMENTS

Despite its criticisms and dwindling application, here I have argued that there is great value in small-scale ethnographic research, especially collaborative in nature, into the sex industry that is concentrated both in time and space. Yet at every stage there are hurdles and challenges, often from within the institution as questions are posed by ethics committees of the appropriateness and feasibility of the sex industry as a worthy topic of study.

Sex work research diverges from institutional patterns and accepted paths of information gathering, transgressing expectations of the types of group that are worthy of research or will produce useful knowledge (Pyett, 1998). In addition, the nature of the sex work environment and the political issues surrounding prostitution demand that the researcher make personal investment (such as self-disclosure) into the research process. The demands of emotional labour on the researcher are complex and intense. Researchers have to confront hostile and volatile environments that need to be managed with care, making skills in negotiation, conflict management, role-playing and keeping quiet an essential part of the fieldwork toolkit.

The challenges do not stop as the researcher leaves the field. The writing up process demands considerable reflection on all aspects of the fieldwork and decisions have to be made about what to reveal and what to confine to the fieldwork diary. Continually promoting research into sex work, tirelessly applying (and re-applying) for funding and pushing to disseminate findings amongst the decision-makers is also part of the methodological challenges that face those committed to this important social issue. Pragmatics aside, to advance the theoretical arguments and knowledge regarding the nature and place of prostitution in contemporary life, research needs to be directed at wider issues relating to the politics of gender and social issues. O'Neill (2001: 187) suggests some of these wider social issues such as the feminization of poverty, violence and abuse in the home, and routes into sex work such as homelessness and leaving care are intrinsically linked to finding out more about prostitution. Researchers have the responsibility not to produce more of the same but to address the questions and areas that are often pushed to one side, constantly rejected by funding bodies and appear to be in discord with national political objectives. As Shaver (2005: 307) comments, challenges to stereotypes and the victimization of sex workers needs to be implicit in the methods that are employed to produce knowledge about these groups. If there is to be any advancement in the sociology of sex work, separate aspects of the industry should not be studied in isolation, and female sex workers should not remain the only focus of investigation.

REFERENCES

Barnard, M. 1992. "Working in the Dark: Researching Female Prostitution," in H. Roberts (ed.) *Women's Health Matters*, pp. 141–56. London: Routledge.

Cooper, K., Kilvington, J., Day, S., Ziersch, A., and Ward, H. 2001. "HIV Prevention and Sexual Health Services for Sex Workers in the UK," *Health Education Journal* 60(1): 26–34.

Ferrell, J., and Hamm, M. S. 1998. *Ethnography at the Edge: Crime, Deviance and Field Research*. Boston. MA: Northeastern University Press.

Hart, A. 1998. *Buying and Selling Power: Anthropological Reflections on Prostitution in Spain*. Oxford: Westview Press.

Hubbard, P. 1999a. *Sex and the City. Geographies of Prostitution in the Urban West*. Aldershot: Ashgate.

Hubbard, P. 1999b. "Researching Female Sex Work: Reflections on Geographical Exclusion, Critical Methodologies and 'Useful' Knowledge," *Area* 31(3): 229–37.

Labaree, R. 2002. "The Risk of 'Going Observationalist': Negotiating the Hidden Dilemmas of Being an Insider Participant Observer," *Qualitative Research* 2(1): 97–122.

Lee, R. 1995. *Dangerous Fieldwork*. London: Sage.

Lever, J., and Dolnick, D. 2000. "Clients and Call Girls: Seeking Sex and Intimacy," in R. Weitzer (ed.) *Sex for Sale*, pp. 85–100. London: Routledge.

Maher, L. 2000. *Sexed Work: Gender, Race and Resistance in a Brooklyn Drug Market*. Oxford: Oxford University Press.

Mattley, C. 1997. "Field Research with Phone Sex Workers," in M. Schwartz (ed.) *Researching Violence Against Women*, pp. 146–58. London: Sage.

Melrose, M. 2002. "Labour Pains: Some Considerations on the Difficulties of Researching Juvenile Prostitution," *International Journal of Social Research Methodology* 5(4): 333–51.

Miller, J. 1997. "Researching Violence Against Street Prostitutes," in M. Schwartz (ed.) *Researching Sexual Violence Against Women*, pp. 144–56. London: Sage.

O'Connell Davidson, J. 1998. *Prostitution, Power and Freedom*. London: Polity.

O'Connell Davidson, J., and Layder, D. 1994. *Methods, Sex and Madness*. London: Routledge.

O'Neill, M. 1996. "Researching Prostitution and Violence: Towards a Feminist Praxis," in M. Hester, L. Kelly and J. Radford (eds) *Women, Violence and Male Power*, pp. 130–47. London: Open University Press.

O'Neill, M. 2001. *Prostitution and Feminism*. London: Polity Press.

Pyett, P. 1998. "Doing it Together: Sex Workers and Researchers," *Research for Sex Work*, 1. URL (accessed June 2006): http://hcc.med.vu.nl/artikelen/pyett.htm

Roberts, J. M., and Sanders, T. 2005. "'Before, During and After': Ethnography, Reflexivity and Pragmatic Realism," *Sociological Review* 53(2): 294–313.

Sanders, T. 2005a. *Sex Work. A Risky Business*. Cullompton, UK: Willan.

Sanders, T. 2005b. "Researching the Online Sex Work Community," in C. Hine (ed.) *Virtual Methods in Social Research on the Internet*, pp. 66–79. Oxford: Berg.

Sanders, T. 2005c. "It's Just Acting: Sex Workers' Strategies for Capitalising on Sexuality," *Gender, Work and Organization* 12(4): 319–42.

Sharpe, K. 2000. "Sad, Bad And (Sometimes) Dangerous To Know: Street Corner Research With Prostitutes, Punters and the Police," in R. King and E. Wincup (eds.) *Doing Research on Crime and Justice*, pp. 362–72. Oxford: Oxford University Press.

Shaver, F. 2005. "Sex Work Research: Methodological and Ethical Challenges," *Journal of Interpersonal Violence* 20(3): 296–319.

Wahab, S. 2003. "Creating Knowledge Collaboratively with Female Sex Workers: Insights From a Qualitative Feminist and Participatory Study," *Qualitative Inquiry* 9(4): 625–42.

Challenges of Funding Sex Research

Mindy Stombler and Amanda M. Jungels

Getting funding for sex research has always been challenging. In the 1950s, Alfred Kinsey and his colleagues lost funding from the Rockefeller Foundation following publication of their controversial report on women's sexuality. More recently, the National Health and Social Life Survey (1994)—essentially a national sexual "census"—lost federal funding following opposition by Representative William Dannemeyer and Senator Jesse Helms. The researchers were forced to dramatically reduce the scope of their project after conservatives in Congress lobbied against funding sexuality research.[1] Other grant-seekers report that they find themselves in a very defensive position. According to James Wagoner, president of Advocates for Youth, "For 20 years it was about health and science, and now we have a political ideological approach. . . . Never have we experienced a climate of intimidation and censorship as we have today."[2] The cost of designing and implementing large-scale projects often necessitates outside funding, and yet few organizations outside of the federal government offer the level of funding that is necessary to conduct this kind of research [see "Large Scale Sex: Methods, Challenges, and Findings of Nationally Representative Sex Research" for more discussion about the challenges of designing large-scale sex research projects].

Before researchers are able to seek funding, they must first receive approval from the Institutional Review Board (IRB) at their home institution. IRBs are designed to maintain ethical standards and to protect research participants, but even this process has become politically fraught for sex researchers. In 2011, Janice Irvine surveyed members of the American Sociological Association's Section on Sexualities. Due to IRBs conceptualizing sex research as "sensitive," involving vulnerable populations, and inherently riskier, Irvine found that 45 percent of the sex researchers in her sample reported trouble getting their research proposals approved, hindering the progress and design of their research. Researchers responded to the obstacles in a variety of ways, including avoiding doing research on certain populations likely to face additional scrutiny from IRBs (such as sexual minorities or adolescents); compromising their research design or methodology; placing IRB restrictions above the desires of their respondents (for example, using pseudonyms for respondents because the IRB required it, despite the fact that the respondents did not wish to be anonymous); or even giving up on sexuality research entirely.[3] This type of scrutiny has not only threatened researchers' academic freedom, but has also "prohibit[ed] the production of sexual knowledge and silence[d] the voices of diverse sexualities—knowledge which might itself challenge cultural fears about sex."[4]

Even if a project receives IRB approval, sex researchers who seek funding often are subject to additional roadblocks. In 2003, there was a strong Congressional effort to block the funding of four National Institutes of Health (NIH) grants. Peer scientists had already judged these grants to be "outstanding" in an independent review process. The grants called for research on sexual risk-taking and its link to sexual arousal, the sexual habits of older men, Asian sex workers, and sexual and gender identity among American Indians. Conservative politicians argued that the government had no business funding such inappropriate topics. Efforts to block the funding were narrowly defeated by two votes in the House.[5]

Today's economic climate has made funding sex research even more tenuous. As local, state, and federal governments wrestle with reduced budgets and increasing debts, funding for many types of research have been threatened—but sexuality research is often singled out as "wasteful" and "bizarre." In 2011, The Traditional Values Coalition (TVC) called for a moratorium on grants awarded by the National Institutes of Health (NIH) and a federal investigation of the NIH's granting process because of "bizarre projects" that amounted to "institutional waste."[6] One study that was heavily criticized was characterized by the TVC as a 10-year, 10-million-dollar study to determine the average penis size of gay men; in reality, this study was conducted to understand the relationship between penis size, condom slippage/breakage, and STI infection rates—and it was not federally funded.[7]

Although some scientists will continue to apply for large government grants, others are becoming increasingly discouraged and are turning to alternative sources. Aside from the federal government, sources for funding sex research include a handful of private institutions and universities, whose resource pools are often more limited.[8] This lack of available funding reduces the scope of the sex-related research projects that do get carried out. For example, a recent extensive sex survey conducted by the CDC had to cap its sample at age 44, ignoring the sexual behaviors of the older generation that brought us the sexual liberation movement.[9] The economic stimulus package of 2009 (formally known as the American Recovery and Reinvestment Act) included additional funding for scientific research, but those projects that did not "reap economic rewards in the foreseeable future" (including social science and public health research) were criticized as being wasteful.[10]

As conservative politicians fight to reduce funding available for sex research, researchers feel pressured to focus on topics for which funding is available, such as pharmaceutical research. This trend necessarily narrows the breadth of researchable topics to those connected to potential profit making. This trajectory was advanced in 2011 when Senator Tom Coburn (a Republican from Oklahoma) singled out the National Science Foundation (NSF) and suggested the elimination of all funding for research that did not have "practical uses outside of academic circles and clear benefits to mankind and the world."[11] Psychologist Geoffrey Miller claims that his research on kissing (why couples kiss less the longer they remain involved) is valuable for society but not necessarily fundable: "kissing could help couples rejuvenate a marriage and reduce divorce rates . . . but it's less threatening and more profitable to study orgasms."[12] In fact, Mark Schwartz of the Masters and Johnson clinic claims that the survival of the study of sexual behavior is a result of the HIV/AIDS epidemic and the development of Viagra "because the pharmaceutical companies suddenly became very interested in the fact that they can make huge amounts of money off the genitals."[13] Leonore Tiefer, a sex researcher interviewed in Chapter 5, cautions sex researchers about their overreliance on pharmaceutical money, insisting it contributes to a medical model of sexuality where all sexual problems can be fixed with a pill.[14]

Following the AIDS crisis and the public's concern with teen pregnancy rates, researchers who studied sexually transmitted infections (STIs) and reproductive health had a decent chance of being funded. But today, even these researchers have their share of challenges.

Recently scientists who study HIV/AIDS and other STIs claim they have been warned by government officials to avoid the use of certain key words in their grant applications. Grants that include terms like "sex workers," "men who sleep with men," "anal sex," "needle exchange," "prostitute," "gay," "homosexual," and "transgender" are rumored to face additional scrutiny in an already fiercely competitive arena.[15] Ironically, this self-censorship of controversial terms has made it harder to assess whether funding has declined for sex research, as it is difficult to determine what researchers are actually studying when they submit disguised or reframed research proposals.[16] Even research that is clearly related to public health concerns (such as why young men do not use condoms correctly or the effect alcohol has on college students' casual sex habits) can come under fire as being inappropriate uses of federal funding.[17]

In addition to reframing how they present their research proposals to IRBs and funding sources, researchers must tackle the issue of how to present their research results to the media: issues of inaccurate, politicized, sensationalized, or misused findings are common concerns for sex researchers.[18] Presenting sensitive or controversial findings to the public is viewed as a "fundamental skill" by many researchers, especially those who fear that their results may be "misused or misinterpreted."[19] While controversy generates publicity for the researchers and the media outlets, it can also "threaten funding, result in restrictive policies, and lead to negative consequences for the individual or the field."[20] This fear of reprisal has led some researchers to avoid appearing in the media to report findings at all; in today's global media culture, local media coverage of a research controversy can quickly turn into "unwelcome" national attention.[21]

Frustrated by the increasing interference of politicians, researchers—and even federal agency directors—have been fighting back.

For example, scientists from a range of disciplines have formed the Coalition to Protect Research (CPR), an organization "committed to promoting public health through research [and promoting the idea that] sexual health and behavior research is essential to providing a scientific foundation for sound public health prevention and intervention programs."[22] Organizations like this and the Society for the Scientific Study of Sexuality (SSSS) call for politicians to respect the scientific peer review process and to actively fund sex research. Some researchers, particularly those targeted by the Congressional effort to block NIH funding in 2003, have been reinvigorated by the controversy brought on by their research, wearing it as a "badge of honor," insisting that they will continue to do sex research, even if they must engage in self-censorship to do so.[23]

NOTES

1. Senator Helms and Representative Dannemeyer were also leaders in the successful effort to de-fund the American Teenage Study, a project designed to study "patterns of adolescent sexual and contraceptive behavior and the cause of these patterns" (106). In Udry, J. Richard. 1993. "The Politics of Sex Research." *The Journal of Sex Research* 30 (2):103–110.

2. Navarro, Mireya. 2004. "Experts in Sex Field Say Conservatives Interfere with Health and Research." *The New York Times.* July 11.

3. Irvine, Janice. 2012. "Can't Ask Can't Tell: How Institutional Review Boards Keep Sex in the Closet" *Contexts* 11(2): 28–33.

4. ibid.

5. McCain, Robert Stacy. 2003. "Sex and Child Health: Critics Wonder Why NICHD Funds Studies." *The Washington Times.* September 18: A02.

6. Traditional Values Coalition (TVC). 2011. "NIH Wastes Millions on Bizarre 'Research.'" Retrieved September 28, 2011 from http://www.traditionalvalues.org/content /Press%20Releases/31645/NIH%20Wastes%20Millions

7. Moisse, Katie, and Mikaela Conley. 2011. "Study of Gay Men's Sexual Health Called Waste of Taxpayer Money; Study not Government-Funded." Retrieved on September 28, 2011 from http://abcnews.go.com/Health/MensHealth /study-gay-mens-sexual-health-called-waste-taxpayer /story?id=14125898

8. American Experience: Kinsey, Online Forum, Day 2. February 15, 2005. Retrieved December 12, 2005 from www .pbs.org/wgbh/amex/kinsey/sfeature/sf_forum_0215.html.

9. Hunter, Jennifer. 2005. "Sex Study Spurns Generation of Love." *Chicago Sun-Times.* October 5:63.

10. Radnofsky, Louise. 2010. "Science Stimulus Funds Called Wasteful." *Wall Street Journal*, August 12. Retrieved September 28, 2011 from http://online.wsj.com/article/ SB10001424052748704268004575417541178463762 .html.

11. Coburn, Tom A. 2011. "The National Science Foundation: Under the Microscope." Retrieved on September 28, 2011 from http://coburn.senate.gov/public /index.cfm?a=Files.ServeandFile_id=2dccf06d-65fe-4087 -b58d-b43ff68987fa

12. Clark, Justin. 2005. "Sex: The Big Turnoff." *Psychology Today.* Jan/Feb.

13. Clay, Rebecca. 2003. "Sex Research Faces New Obstacles." *APA Online.* Retrieved December 12, 2005 from www.apa.org/monitor/apr03/obstacles.html.

14. Tiefer, Leonore. 1995. *Sex is Not a Natural Act and Other Essays.* Boulder, CO: Westview Press.

15. Goode, Erica. 2003. "Certain Words Can Trip up AIDS Grants, Scientists Say." *The New York Times.* April 18: Section A, Column 6, National Desk: 10.

16. Kempner, Joanna. 2008. "The Chilling Effect: How Do Researchers React to Controversy?" *PLoS Medicine* 5(11): 1–8.

17. Radnofsky, Louise. 2010. "Science Stimulus Funds Called Wasteful." *Wall Street Journal*, August 12. Retrieved September 28, 2011 from http://online.wsj.com/article /SB10001424052748704268004575417541178463762 .html.

18. McBride, Kimberly R., Stephanie A. Sanders, Erick Janssen, Maria Elizabeth Grabe, Jennifer Bass, Johnny V. Sparks, Trevor R. Brown, and Julia R. Heiman. 2007. "Turning Sexual Science Into News: Sex Research and the Media" *Journal of Sex Research* 44 (4): 347–358.

19. Kempner, Joanna, Jon F. Merz, and Charles L. Bosk. 2011. "Forbidden Knowledge: Public Controversy and the Production of Nonknowledge" *Sociological Forum* 26 (3): 475–500.

20. McBride, Kimberly R., Stephanie A. Sanders, Erick Janssen, Maria Elizabeth Grabe, Jennifer Bass, Johnny V. Sparks, Trevor R. Brown, and Julia R. Heiman. 2007. "Turning Sexual Science Into News: Sex Research and the Media" *Journal of Sex Research* 44 (4): 347–358.

21. Kempner, Joanna, Jon F. Merz, and Charles L. Bosk. 2011. "Forbidden Knowledge: Public Controversy and the Production of Nonknowledge" *Sociological Forum* 26 (3): 475–500.

22. Coalition to Protect Research (CPR). Retrieved December 16, 2005 from www.cossa.org/CPR/cpr.html.

23. Kempner, Joanna. 2008. "The Chilling Effect: How Do Researchers React to Controversy?" *PLoS Medicine* 5(11): 1–8.

3

REPRESENTING SEX

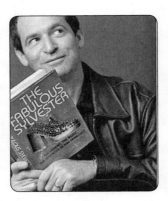

AN INTERVIEW WITH

JOSHUA GAMSON

Joshua Gamson, Ph.D., is a Professor of Sociology at University of San Francisco. His research and teaching focus on the sociology of culture, with an emphasis on contemporary Western commercial culture and mass media, social movements, and the history, theory, and sociology of sexuality. He is the author of Claims to Fame: Celebrity in Contemporary America *(California, 1994);* Freaks Talk Back: Tabloid Talk Shows and Sexual Nonconformity *(Chicago, 1998); and* The Fabulous Sylvester: The Legend, The Music, The Seventies in San Francisco *(Henry Holt, 2005).*

What led you to begin studying sexuality?

I didn't know it at the time, but studying sexuality began for me as part of what some scholars have called "identity work." I was a 23-year-old graduate student at UC Berkeley, and I'd decided it was time to figure myself out a bit better, and a big part of that seemed to be figuring out my sexuality a bit better. I knew that the

Bay Area was a great place to do that, given the history of sexual subcultures—gay ones, especially—but somehow I didn't want to just take myself out exploring. So I decided to study it, come at my personal life from the outside in, as it were. When I had a statistics paper to do, I made it about public opinion about homosexuality, for instance. When I took a graduate seminar in participant observation research, I eventually decided on a field site that would get me into San Francisco, among gay and lesbian people: the AIDS activist group ACT UP. That turned into a very rewarding research experience, and to do it I had to teach myself some of the literature on sexuality-based social movements, so it fed my head. But it also fed my identity. That work moved me into a part of the gay community that I liked, felt comfortable in, and identified with; it helped me see myself as gay, and to actually experience gayness without shame or apology. It was a case of personal identity leading to intellectual pursuit and then back to personal identity. That back and forth continues to this day.

How do people react when they find that you study sexuality?

It depends on which people are doing the reacting, I suppose. Back when I started, my more senior colleagues would generally seem mystified, as if they couldn't quite figure out what there was to study about sexuality. Some, I'm certain, didn't and still don't think it's a legitimate area of study, but I think a lot of people just didn't know how to have a conversation about studying sexuality. That's rarely the case any more, partly because over the last decade the field has become much more established and much less marginalized in sociology—and partly because sexuality has been such a significant political and public policy focal point. Younger people seem to think it's kind of cool that I study sexuality, or cool that there is such a field of study. Then there are always those who want to joke about how much fun the "research process" must be.

Which of your projects have you found most interesting? Why?

My two book projects were the most interesting to me, for sure. The book on TV talk shows, *Freaks Talk Back*, was interesting to me for a whole slew of reasons. I found it really interesting to investigate how the everyday production routines— the kinds of things talk show producers think about, talk about, worry about, and do all the time to get a show made—affected LGBT topics. Usually, when scholars and activists talk about "cultural visibility," they have only a vague sense of what kinds of institutional and organizational processes shape that visibility, and I felt like I was pushing past that vagueness. I was also really interested in the experiences of guests, and learned a lot about sexuality politics from that—in particular, the internal struggle over who best represents "gayness," which is very much a class-based divide. I became very interested in how complicated media visibility was for sexually-stigmatized and gender-nonconforming populations: How gay and lesbian respectability was shored up on the shows by demeaning or stereotyping transgender and bisexual guests; how the exposure of class and race diversity among LGBT populations only really came about through the extraordinarily exploitative, confess–accuse–pull hair kind of shows, like [*Jerry*] *Springer*. Media visibility has really changed since then, but that project tuned me in to dynamics of gay visibility I still see all around me.

My most recent book, *The Fabulous Sylvester*, was interesting in a whole other kind of way. It's a sort of combination biography (of the 1970s openly gay, sometimes crossdressing, African American disco star Sylvester) and cultural history (of San Francisco's gay subcultures, in which Sylvester lived and through which he rose to fame; and of AIDS, from which Sylvester died). So it was interesting partly because it was a different sort of project, more narrative and less analytical scholarly. It was interesting to me because it put me into contact with Sylvester's life and friends, and his story is just beautiful, and beautiful largely because his sexuality was such an integrated part of who he was—he was never closeted, and he suffered quite a bit for that, but he eventually became an international disco star by putting gay "fabulousness" to music, while refusing to be reduced to, or by, sexuality, and by never apologizing for being gay and sexual. I also loved delving into 1970s gay liberation cultures, which were so creative and novel and important, and which have been largely lost to AIDS, assimilation, and fear.

What ethical dilemmas have you faced in studying sexuality?

I haven't really experienced ethical dilemmas, frankly. I'm not studying sexual behavior, and I've never studied covert sexual populations, so I've never had concern about revealing things that might hurt the subjects. I always tell people I'm a researcher, and give them the option of not participating, or of participating without having their name used, and sometimes people take me up on that. When I'm interviewing, they always have the option of having me turn off the tape recorder. The closest I've come to an ethical dilemma is in dealing with the question of how what I write might be used by others, such as journalists or policymakers who have an anti-gay agenda—which is, of course, totally out of my control. I don't think I've ever made a decision to censor myself for fear that the wrong people would use it in a way that damages those to whom I'm loyal and allied, but I certainly am careful how I frame and phrase things.

What do you think is the most challenging thing about studying sexuality?

The most challenging thing for me is that it's a constantly moving target. Again, I don't study sexual behaviors, but instead sexual identities, movements, politics, cultures, and cultural representations. One can easily be at the end of a project and find the phenomenon entering some radically different new phase, so that one has to be ready to always rethink and revise. (Maybe that's one of the reasons I enjoyed doing the Sylvester book, since it was more historical.) Media visibility is a good example: Ten years ago, when I finished the talk show book, the issue was still that LGBT people were mainly invisible on television or restricted to narrow stereotypes;

the issues now, after *Ellen*, *Will and Grace*, *Queer as Folk*, *The L Word*, *Queer Eye*, and so on, are quite different. The talk show study, over the course of just a few years, went from being a statement about the limits and paradoxes of LGBT media visibility to being an account of a historical moment. A study of same-sex marriage laws now, to take another example, is going to face the same sort of difficulty; things are changing so rapidly in legislation and law related to sexuality. That's not an insurmountable challenge, and I'd rather study something that is active and volatile than something inert. But sexual cultures and politics don't stand still for their snapshot.

Why is it important to do sex research?

Most basically, because sex is an important part of human existence, and it's been so smothered by shame and negativity that there's still plenty that's not well understood. Although it hasn't always been the case, and I suspect won't be forever, sexuality has also become a significant basis for people's identities and self-understandings, and it affects their life chances and life paths in various ways— where they wind up living, what kinds of jobs they can and can't get. And sexuality is one of several significant bases of social inequality, and therefore is a very significant arena of politics. These are things that need to be understood, both just because more knowledge is better than less, and because sexualities research can help us figure out what needs to be changed and how to change it—the research can inform the pursuit of social justice.

If you could teach people one thing about sexuality, what would it be?

That it's both more significant and less significant than it's been made out to be: Sexuality is not just a phenomenon of nature, and not just "personal," but a phenomenon of society, and political; at the same time, at the root of all of this politics is just sex, just the fun and sometimes funny things people do with their bodies, together and alone.

REPRESENTIN' IN CYBERSPACE: SEXUAL SCRIPTS, SELF-DEFINITION, AND HIP HOP CULTURE IN BLACK AMERICAN ADOLESCENT GIRLS' HOME PAGES

CARLA E. STOKES

INTRODUCTION

Although hip hop culture has historically provided a space for disenfranchized youth of colour, including young women, to resist oppression (Rose, 1994), there is widespread criticism of sexist and misogynist sexual scripts in mainstream rap and R&B music and videos, which are extremely popular among Black American youth (MEE Productions, 2004). Concerned parents, scholars, colleges/universities, girl-serving organizations, magazines, filmmakers, rap artists, and Black women and girls have raised questions about the potential influence of derogatory sexual messages in hip hop-influenced popular culture on the sexual and psychological development of Black adolescent girls (Stokes and Gant, 2002; Cole and Guy-Sheftall, 2003; Wingood et al., 2003; MEE Productions, 2004; Pough, 2004; Weekes, 2004; Stephens and Phillips, 2005; Bullock, 2006), who are disproportionately burdened by sexually transmitted infections and HIV/AIDS (Wingood et al., 2003)—particularly in the southern region of the USA (Rangel et al., 2006). . . .

Sexual scripting theory (Simon and Gagnon, 1986) identifies three levels of sexual scripts—cultural scenarios, interpersonal scripts, and intrapsychic scripts—which provide a conceptual framework for understanding how sociocultural and individual factors shape Black girls' sexual script development. Cultural scenarios are guidelines for sexual behaviours, and exist at the level of society or culture (e.g.,

mass media, peers, family, and religious institutions) (Simon and Gagnon, 1986; Stephens and Phillips, 2005). The media are an important source of information about sexual and romantic scripts for girls as they learn to negotiate their sexuality (Brown and Stern, 2002). As girls and young women interact with others in social settings at the interpersonal script level, they draw from cultural scenarios and their own 'personal desires, fantasies, and intentions (i.e., intrapsychic scripts)' (Carpenter, 1998: 158). The process of developing a sexual identity is particularly complicated for Black American girls, because they negotiate their emerging sexuality amidst contradictory and discrepant cultural scenarios from the mainstream media, hip hop culture, and peers that may conflict with those valued by their parents, and the larger Black American culture (Stokes, 2004; Stephens and Phillips, 2005; Brown et al., 2006). This article examines the potential role of cultural-level sexual scripts in the media, hip hop culture, and youth cyberculture in shaping southern Black adolescent girls' interpersonal sexual scripts online.

From "Representin' in Cyberspace: Sexual scripts, Self-Definition, and Hip Hop Culture in Black American Adolescent Girls' Home Pages," by Carla E. Stokes. *Culture, Health & Sexuality*, Volume 9, Issue 2, 2007, pp. 170–184. Copyright © 2007 Routledge, reprinted by permission of the publisher (Taylor & Francis Ltd, http://www.tandf.co.uk/journals).

BACKGROUND

Sexual scripts in hip hop culture and Black adolescent girls' sexual development

The sexuality of Black American women and girls is widely stigmatized in the academic and popular literatures, as well as in television shows, hip hop cinema (Pough, 2004), and popular magazines. Denigrating representations of Black female sexuality have pervaded American culture and mass media since slavery (Wyatt, 1997; Collins, 2000). Stephens and Phillips (2003) argue that "controlling" images (Collins, 2000) of Black women and girls as hypersexual "Jezebels", loyal "Mammy's", emasculating "Matriarchs", materialistic "Welfare Queens" (Collins, 2000), and foul-mouthed "Sapphires" (Wyatt, 1997) provide the foundation for similar sexual scripts in contemporary hip hop culture. While some aspects of hip hop are not misogynistic, commercialized hip hop has been extensively criticized for perpetuating hypersexual and deviant representations of Black women and girls (Stokes and Gant, 2002; Stephens and Phillips, 2003; Pough, 2004; Bullock, 2006). Although some Black women artists assert agency and resist derogatory representations of Black female sexuality, young Black women are often sexually objectified and portrayed in passive roles in popular rap, R&B, dancehall songs, and music videos. In contrast, hip hop songs and videos often portray men as "pimps" and "thugs" who have more power in intimate relationships (Rose, 1994; Emerson, 2002; Neal, 2005; Pough, 2004; Stokes, 2004; Ward et al., 2005). Moreover, strip club culture is increasingly pervasive in mainstream rap and R&B music and videos that feature female exotic dancers and other sexual content (Neal, 2005; Bullock, 2006).

Misogynistic cultural scenarios in the mainstream media and commercialized hip hop are concerning from a public health standpoint because they perpetuate gender inequality and glorify risky sexual behaviour, but rarely portray healthy sexual messages or possible negative health outcomes (Brown et al., 2006). This is potentially problematic in light of recent studies that show that the mass media influences Black young people's sexual attitudes and behaviours (Wingood et al., 2003; MEE Productions, 2004; Ward et al., 2005). Wingood and colleagues (2003) found that sexually active African American adolescent girls residing in the southern region of the USA, who reported greater exposure to rap music videos at baseline, were significantly more likely than girls with less exposure to report multiple sexual partners or to have acquired a new STI over the 12-month follow-up period. However, as the authors noted, it is difficult to determine whether causal relationships exist because potential mediating factors were not examined. A recent longitudinal survey of racially and ethnically diverse American young people conducted by Martino et al. (2006) found that male and female youth who listened to music with degrading sexual content were more likely to "subsequently initiate intercourse and to progress to more advanced levels of non-coital sexual activity, even after controlling for 18 respondent characteristics that might otherwise explain these relationships" (pp. e430–e431). The limited body of existing research suggests that the media and hip hop may constrain Black girls' and young women's sexual development; however, limitations in the samples and assessment of media use hinder the validity and generalizability of the findings (Ward et al., 2005).

The large body of literature on girls' and young women's sexual and psychological development has been criticized for depicting adolescent girls in particular, as passive cultural consumers with limited control over their own identity construction (Bragg and Buckingham, 2002; Emerson, 2002; Stern, 2002); and few studies have investigated girls' ability to resist sexual media content (Brown and Stern, 2002) or the role of girls as media producers (Kearney, 2006). Conversely, qualitative research has shown that some girls resist messages from the media and dominant culture by creating their own media. Although a handful of scholars have begun to investigate the role of hip hop in the lives of Black American girls, little is known about how this group interacts with or produces media.

Adolescent girls' cyberculture and use of the Web for identity construction

The population of young people online has grown rapidly in recent years (Lenhart and Madden, 2005), and Internet use among young urban women from diverse ethnic backgrounds is widespread (Borzekowski and Rickert, 2000; Kearney, 2006). While persisting racial/economic differences in Internet access cannot be ignored, a recent survey administered to 2,000 low-income urban Black youth aged 16–20 years residing in ten cities across the USA revealed that the overwhelming majority had Internet access (MEE Productions, 2004). Girls participate in a wide range of online social activities including using email and instant messaging, participating in and moderating bulletin board discussions and chat rooms, offering help with web design (Lenhart and Madden, 2005), and hanging out in social networking sites. They also create online cultural productions by producing home pages, e-zines (electronic magazines) (Stern, 2002; Mazzarella, 2005; Kearney, 2006; Polak, 2006), and "blogs" (Bortree, 2005; Scheidt, 2006).[1] Some girls 'remix' (manipulate) online content into new artistic creations for their peers and others (Stokes, 2004; Lenhart and Madden, 2005). Approximately 22 percent of online young people aged 12–17 report having created their own home page (Lenhart and Madden, 2005). However, because a comprehensive directory does not exist, it is impossible to accurately estimate the total population of girls' home pages (Stern, 2004).

Although the creative and empowering ways girls use the Internet have become overshadowed by the moral panic surrounding girls' vulnerability online (Mazzarella, 2005), scholars have begun to explore sexuality and identity construction in girls' bulletin board postings (Smyres, 1999; Grisso and Weiss, 2005), blogs (Bortree, 2005), home pages, and websites (Takayoshi et al., 1999; Stern, 2002; Kearney, 2006; Polak, 2006). . . . Taken together, studies of bulletin boards in websites for teenage girls reveal that some girls reproduce dominant patriarchal discourses and gender stereotypes (Grisso and Weiss, 2005). . . .

Despite these intriguing findings, published research to date on girls' home pages is limited given its primary focus on White girls. The invisibility of Black girls' home pages in the empirical literature may be partially attributed to the common misperception that "girls who currently create home pages are most likely White" (Stern, 2002: 268) and have privileged access to web design skills as a result of economic privilege (Stern, 2002; Kearney, 2006). Consequently, Black girls' use of home pages to explore their sexuality has been overlooked, and deserves attention.

This paper fills a gap in the literature by investigating home pages constructed by Black adolescent girls in a youth-oriented website. . . . The main research questions were: how do Black girls use home pages to construct sexual self-definitions; what sexual scripts exist in Black girls' home pages; and how are Black girls' online sexual scripts related to dominant discourses in hip hop?

CONTEXT AND METHODS

This study is part of an ongoing investigation of Black girls' home pages that began in 2001 with a pilot study in "NevaEvaLand" (pseudonym), a social networking website with thousands of Black American adolescent members (Stokes, 2004). NevaEvaLand provides an online space for young people to "hang-out", connect with friends, and meet new people. The site provides template-based home page publishing tools, which allow girls to create personalized, searchable home pages without requiring knowledge of HTML. Girls create and modify their pages, which are connected to others via hyperlinks to friends' home pages. They receive feedback and validation from other users who can send private messages and post public comments. Some, but not all, girls in NevaEvaLand appear to create home pages in part to attract a romantic/sexual partner (Stokes, under review).

The data described in the present study were collected from December 2003 to February 2004. . . . Using domain-driven and opportunistic sampling, [I] selected home pages that contained substantive, information-rich textual narratives and references to constructs of interest (e.g., sexuality, gender-role norms, dating, hip hop, self-definition). Given the disproportionate impact of HIV/AIDS on Black women and girls in the southern states of the USA, other eligibility criteria were: being a female author between the ages of 14–17, who was "Black", "African American", or otherwise of African descent, and resided in the District of Columbia or one of seven southern states in the USA with Black Americans constituting 60 percent or more of the cumulative AIDS cases through June 2002 *and* incident AIDS cases reported from July 2001 through June 2002 (Alabama, Delaware, Georgia, Maryland, Mississippi, North Carolina, and South Carolina).[2]

Age, gender, and race/ethnicity were determined from explicit references (i.e., self-reported demographic information in the authors' profile). Because home pages are in the public domain, the University of Michigan Institutional Review Board (IRB) granted an exemption for examining these documents, without contacting the authors.

Data analysis

. . . . [I] used a protocol to guide data collection in the early stages of fieldwork, and wrote descriptive summaries of each page, including a general description of the tone, stylistic features, images, multimedia content (songs and music videos), appropriation of hip hop and youth culture, and the authors' description of her appearance. Home pages were collected until the content became redundant. The final core sample included 216 pages, which were approximately evenly distributed across states, and by ages within states, with the exception of home pages from Georgia, which were oversampled ($n = 101$) in response to the disproportionate impact of HIV and AIDS on Black women and girls residing in Georgia. Because home pages are evolving documents that are updated and deleted unpredictably, the author downloaded electronic copies of each home page to facilitate ongoing coding (Stokes, 2004).

A smaller sample of 27 Georgia pages that reflected the preliminary themes uncovered in the larger sample was selected to facilitate in-depth analyses. . . . Data were reduced into major categorical themes, and home pages were coded until new categories and relations among categories were no longer being discovered (Miles and Huberman, 1994).

. . . . During the third phase, preliminary conclusions were verified by consulting with an expert panel of 10 Black young women aged 14–18 years who resided in the Atlanta, USA area; were familiar with the Internet and/or were NevaEvaLand home page authors; and were knowledgeable about American hip hop and southern Black youth culture. In order to address regional differences in girls' vernacular and music preferences, the panellists were recruited from Atlanta-based mentoring programs for Black girls (two were recruited through snowball sampling). The demographic characteristics of the panellists were similar to the home page authors. Informed consent was obtained from parents and legal guardians of the panellists and note takers, and written assent was obtained from each girl. Each participant was given a US $15 cash incentive at the end of the meeting. IRB approval was obtained for consulting with the panellists. During the meeting, feedback was solicited on excerpts from pages that illustrated the most salient themes. The panellists confirmed the emerging themes and clarified questions about Black online youth culture, girls' home pages, songs, celebrities, geographic nuances, images, and vernacular. A pseudonym was assigned for the panellists' names and home page authors' screen names to protect their privacy. Unless otherwise indicated, the findings reported here are from the 27 home pages in the in-depth sample.

FINDINGS

Demographic characteristics of the in-depth sample

The core and in-depth sample shared similar demographic characteristics. The mean age of the in-depth sample was 15.6 years. Most (81.5%) of the girls reported that they were enrolled in high school; 14.8 percent reported that they were in junior high (3.7% did not respond). As part of setting up their profile, prospective NevaEvaLand members were asked to check one or more boxes corresponding with their "race" (options include "Black", "Asian", "Latino", "Native American", or "White"). The majority (66.7%) self-identified solely as "Black". The remainder selected "Black" and "Latino" (3.7%); "Black" and "Native American" (14.8%); "Black" and "Asian" (3.7%); or "Black", "White", and

"Native American" (11.1%). Girls were also asked to report their sexual orientation. While the majority selected "Heterosexual" (63%), the remainder selected "Bisexual" (11.1%), "None of Your Business" (3.7%), or deliberately concealed their sexual orientation (22.2%). . . . 40.7% of the girls reported that they were single. Fewer reported that they were "dating" (25.9%) or "involved" with a "partner" (33.3%). While the girls reported listening to a range of musical genres, the five most popular were rap (100%), R&B (96.3%), Caribbean/reggae (51.9%), pop (40.7%), and dance (29.6%).

Sexual self-expression and sexual scripts

Girls in NevaEvaLand constructed technologically sophisticated home pages that addressed a variety of topics. The authors widely adopted the hip hop cultural practice of "representin" (also known as "reppin")—in other words, constructing self-definitions to elevate their social status and align themselves with desirable persons, places, or things (e.g., friends, neighborhoods, clubs, clothing brands, etc.). For example, "sweetiepooh" wrote: "I stay in Atlanta and go to NevaEva High School (pseudonym). Representin' the class of "06" HOE". Girls expressed their sexuality by aligning themselves with physically attractive cartoon dolls that were dressed in revealing clothing and popular hip hop fashions.[3] Some selected images of dolls in sexy poses and sexual positions, or engaged in sexual acts. Consistent with previous research, girls' screen names were a vital part of their online identities (Stern, 2002), and appeared to be selected in part, to "represent" and/or to attract potential romantic/sexual partners (Strokes, 2004).

The in-depth analysis revealed six pervasive sexual scripts with roots in controlling images of Black female sexuality (Collins, 2000): "Freaks" (n = 9); "Virgins" (n = 3); "Down-Ass Chicks/ Bitches" (n = 4); "Pimpettes" (n = 4); and Resisters who disrupted stereotypical sexual scripts

(n = 7). With the exception of the Resisters, the names of the scripts are . . . used by the girls to describe themselves. . . . Although these sexual scripts were overlapping to some degree, they were conceptually distinctive, and provide a useful method for organizing the home pages into meaningful categories.

"A lady in the street, but a freak on the Web": The "Freak"

Consistent with sexual scripts in hip hop, one-third of the girls in the in-depth sample distanced themselves from the "good girl" script (Tolman, 2002) by portraying themselves as "Freaks"—a contemporary manifestation of the sexually insatiable "Jezebel" image (Collins, 2004).[4] The panellists described a "Freak" as a person who is sexually adventurous and "down for whatever" (willing to "do anything" with a person they are intimately involved with). "Sexeyellafemme" (age 15) wrote, "I AM A FREAK. FA SHO . . . I like to run sh!t in and out tha bed. I am wonderful in bed . . . I am down fo whateva". Acknowledging sexual double standards, the panellists emphasized that "boys can be freaks too". The panellists reported that "freaky" girls like to touch people and do "stuff" they "wouldn't do around their parents". They made an important distinction between being a "Freak" and being "freaky"— emphasizing that "virgins" can be "freaky". Reciting lyrics from the song, "Yeah!" (Usher, 2004)—"we want a lady in the street but a freak in the bed"—the panellists explained that it is considered socially acceptable for a girl to be "classy" [elegant] and a "lady" in public, but selectively freaky in private, behind closed doors, or on the Web. Moreover, the panellists distinguished "hoes" from Freaks, arguing that hoes will "do anything" and "mess around with everybody they see" (engage in sexual activity). In contrast, a Freak may be "down for whatever", but she may not *act* upon her sexual

desires. For instance, a 14-year-old girl from Mississippi, USA described herself as "Somewhat of a Freak, but Never a Hoe"—a fairly common attitude expressed by Freaks in the in-depth sample.

Four types of Freaks emerged among the home page authors: (1) hard-core Freaks who were "down for whateva"; (2) soft-core Freaks who were "kinda freaky"; (3) "closet"/"undercover" Freaks who were unwilling to publicly associate their off-line identities and reputations with their freaky home page performances; and (4) girls who gave off the impression that they were "freaky" because their pages were dominated by explicit sexual references and sexual media content. Collectively, one-third (n = 3) of the Freaks included positive references to religion, and all reported listening to a wide range of music including rap and R&B (n = 9), reggae (n = 7), dance (n = 5), pop (n = 4), Latin (n = 3), alternative (n = 2), and jazz (n = 1). In the latter category, "MiaX-Rated" (age 17) selected the sexually explicit rap song, "P-Poppin" (pussy poppin') (Ludacris, 2003), which played in the background. Moreover, she selected a background image of the rapper Trina and several pornographic images. A few of the girls posted sexually explicit imagery and pornography featuring humans and cartoon characters engaged in sexual acts. Some of the Freaks expressed sexual subjectivity and desire (Tolman, 2002) by including references to giving and receiving sexual pleasure. The panellists suggested that girls perform the Freak script in order to attract attention from prospective romantic/sexual partners in NevaEvaLand.

"My goodies stay in the jar": The Virgin

Despite the pervasiveness of sexual content in NevaEvaLand, three of the girls proudly described themselves as "Virgins". . . . The Virgins created home pages that were more polite and friendly in tone than the others (excluding the Resisters), and presented themselves as well rounded—emphasizing their intelligence, positive personality characteristics, and life goals. Collectively, the Virgins reinforced the "good girl" image that Black girls have been historically encouraged to adopt by their parents and other adults (Wyatt, 1997; Stephens and Phillips, 2003). Some of the girls selected images that supported their virginal self-representations. For instance, "EastsideMami" (age 16) programmed a scrolling marquee that moved across her home page with the text, "IM A PROUD VIRGIN BABY". Collectively, all of the Virgins listened to rap, R&B, and pop music (two also listened to jazz). With the exception of one girl who selected sexually explicit animé images, Virgins did not include content that suggested that they might be sexually experienced (e.g., sexual quizzes, sexually explicit images, etc.). Instead, in order to construct an image of respectability in a sexualized online environment, these girls warned viewers not to ask them about "freaky" matters. Virgins also informed viewers that they are not "Freaks" and do not perform certain sexual acts such as oral sex. Although none of the Virgins in the in-depth sample included violent or aggressive content in their home pages, two included religious references.

"Ain't scared to fight a ho": The Down-Ass Chick/Bitch

Four of the girls in the in-depth sample performed a sexual script from hip hop and popular culture—the "ride-or-die" "Down-Ass Chick/ Bitch", which has origins in the "controlling" images of the confrontational Sapphire and the loyal, self-sacrificing, and nurturing Mammy, who put the needs of others above her own (Collins, 2004). . . . These girls defined themselves in relation to male partners by portraying themselves as fiercely loyal girlfriends who are "down for their man" and willing to engage in destructive behaviours, including committing

or being an accomplice to crimes for his benefit. According to Duncan-Mao (2006), the Down-Ass Bitch will "hold his stash [money], hide his gun, take the weight [accept responsibility] and go to jail for him—all in the name of love" (p. 82). Pough (2004) points out that the Down-Ass Chick/Bitch lifestyle is a reality for some Black girls who have internalized the notion that it is acceptable to commit crimes for their partners. This is concerning, because Black women comprise the fastest growing prison population in the USA (Pough, 2004). The expert panellists emphasized the importance of loyalty also and reported that a Down-Ass Chick/Bitch would never snitch on her man or friends. . . .

All of the Down-Ass Chicks/Bitches selected rap songs for their home pages, and they were more likely than the other girls to report that they listened to rap and R&B music exclusively (one girl reported that she also enjoyed reggae); and none included religious references. The girls in this category resembled some female rappers in that they performed a hard-core, confrontational, and sometimes violent persona in their pages (Pough, 2004)—describing themselves as "loud", "gangsta girls", "head bussas", and "thug misses", who "ain't scared to fight a ho". Moreover, "BaDunkaDunk" (age 17) emulated female rappers who have reclaimed and redefined the word "bitch"—such as Lil' Kim and Trina. Likewise, she proudly defined herself as a "bitch" and adopted an aggressive persona directed towards other girls: "i can be the biggest and meanest B Y T C H if u F U U C K wit me in the wrong way and if u want i will be more than happy to prove it". While, the girls in this category appropriated ghetto-centric imagery and aligned themselves with rap artists/groups and others with hypermasculine and tough personas (e.g., Trillville, T.I., 50 Cent, Three 6 Mafia, Trick Daddy, etc.), some emphasized the importance of sexual pleasure, honesty, and trustworthiness. Others resisted the notion that it is acceptable for males to cheat on their partners or exert power over females (Stokes, under review).

"Ladies is pimps too": The Pimpette

Four of the girls in NevaEvaLand responded to the influence of pimp culture in hip hop, youth culture, and American culture by defining themselves as "Pimps", "Pimpettes", and "Pimpstresses" who redefined traditional gender dynamics. The origins of the Pimpette persona can be traced to several controlling images: the materialistic Gold-Digger (a contemporary manifestation of the Matriarch/Welfare Mother images), Bad Bitch, Sapphire, and Jezebel (Collins, 2004). While the Pimpette script is connected to hip hop culture and the sex trade and street economy, the public discourse and academic literature has overlooked girls who define themselves in relation to pimps. The expert panel described a Pimpette as a "female pimp" who is able to manipulate a relationship for sexual and/or economic gain while maintaining a romantic/sexual network consisting of more than one romantic/sexual partner. Describing the difference between a pimp and a "player", one panellist noted, "pimps have benefits, players don't". Even though the expert panel suggested that sexual activity was involved in "pimpin", the Pimpettes in the in-depth sample created home pages with minimal sexual content in comparison to the Freaks.

Moreover, like the Down-Ass Chicks/Bitches, the Pimpettes were more likely to listen to rap and R&B exclusively (one girl also listened to reggae, and another listened to dance), and none of the Pimpettes included religious references. The Pimpettes' home page performances reflected themes addressed by female rap artists such as Lil' Kim, Foxy Brown, Trina, and Gangsta Boo—such as being in control of their lives and romantic/sexual partners, refusing to tolerate violence from males, bragging about their sexuality, and demanding female pleasure (e.g., emphasizing that males should be sexually experienced) (Pough, 2004, Rose, 1994). In contrast to the Down-Ass Chicks/Bitches who exhibited extreme loyalty to one male partner, Pimpettes are expected to be in control of their romantic/sexual partners and emotions (e.g., "never fighting over a nigga"). To this end, several of the Pimpettes indicated that they do not tolerate abusive boys or "cheaters". Two of the Pimpettes in the in-depth sample also included violent and/or aggressive content directed toward males, similar to revenge fantasies described by some female rappers (Rose, 1994).

The Resisters

Patricia Hill Collins (2000) argues that "when self-defined by Black women ourselves, Black women's sexualities can become an important place of resistance" (p. 128).... [I] labelled seven of the girls "Resisters" because they resisted the sexual scripts performed by other girls in the in-depth sample through self-representations and counter discourses that disrupted the dominant cultural scenarios in NevaEvaLand. What distinguished the Resisters from the other girls is that they have begun the critical process of creating independent self-definitions. The Resisters were similar to the Virgins in that they rejected the Freak script and described themselves as well-rounded, personable, and "sweet", but none explicitly stated that they were "virgins". "Downsouthgagirl" (age 17) wrote: "I'm a southern gurl so I'm sweet and I have manners and all that good stuff." Moreover, the seven Resisters listened to the widest range of music including rap and R&B ($n = 7$); reggae ($n = 4$); pop ($n = 4$); dance ($n = 2$); jazz ($n = 2$); latin ($n = 2$); rock ($n = 2$); alternative ($n = 1$); and world ($n = 1$). More than half ($n = 4$) of the Resisters included positive references to religion or spirituality. . . . None of the Resisters posted sexual photographs of themselves or included violent/aggressive content.

The Resisters subverted media stereotypes about Black girls and created their own safe spaces within a homophobic online peer culture saturated with contradictory messages. In this regard, Resisters follow in the tradition of Black female performers, songwriters, and producers who challenge controlling images of Black womanhood within blues, rap, and R&B music through resistant narratives and counter discourses within the male-dominated music industry (Rose, 1994, Emerson, 2002). For instance, "SugarPlum" (age 16), described herself as "fun BUT NOT HO-ISH", and provided the following self-description:

if u looking for a fashion model
u got da wrong 1
if u looking for a girl wit DOUBLE D's (.) (.) [breasts]
U GOT DA WRONG 1
If u looking for a free ride hoe
u really got da wrong 1
so dont even read any further.

DISCUSSION

. . . . This study challenges assumptions that girls are passive consumers who are unable to engage with, interpret, or resist media messages.

The Web provides girls with a potentially anonymous space to experiment with their sexuality without the potential embarrassment or risks of face-to-face encounters. Many of the girls reproduced gender inequality and stereotypical representations of Black female sexuality in their home pages—but they also claimed space on the Web to try on identities and resist dominant sexual script discourses and sexual double standards. It can be argued that the Freaks resisted the "good girl" sexual script, while simultaneously performing the hypersexual Jezebel script. In contrast, the Virgins and Resisters subverted hypersexual scripts of Black female sexuality and resisted sexual pressure from their home page viewers. Although the Down-Ass Chicks/Bitches performed a potentially problematic identity, they resisted dominant discourses of sexuality and femininity by adopting traditionally masculine attitudes. However, they fail to express sexual subjectivity, given their focus on their partners' needs and subordination of their own identities. The Pimpettes resisted patriarchal masculinity ideologies by reversing traditional gender role expectations. Although the Resisters appeared to be the most successful in disrupting stereotypical female sexual scripts in NevaEvaLand, some of their home pages contained contradictions, and not all were able to resist problematic ideologies simultaneously. Robinson and Ward (1991) point out that there is a critical difference between "resistance for survival and resistance for liberation". The latter occurs when "Black girls and women are encouraged to acknowledge the problems of, and to demand change in, an environment that oppresses them" (p. 89). In contrast, it appears that some girls in NevaEvaLand responded to oppressive gender politics by adopting short-term survival strategies that may ultimately impair healthy development. However, it would be naïve to expect all girls to consistently challenge and resist oppression, amidst the numerous contradictory messages and struggles they face in their daily lives.

Although these findings provide valuable information about Black girls' sexual scripts, there are several methodological limitations. First, the findings should not be considered as representative of all Black American girls, or those who author home pages. Second, it is important to point out that although the sexual scripts identified here are robust, they overlap in some ways, and should not be interpreted as discrete categories. For instance, although four of the girls in the in-depth sample performed the Pimpette script exclusively, one Freak, one Down-Ass Bitch, and one Virgin included references to this script. The author also observed additional sexual scripts in NevaEvaLand that were not pervasive in the in-depth sample. Third, . . . it was not possible to determine whether any of the girls performed conflicting scripts through multiple home pages. As the panellists pointed out, girls can pretend to be anyone in cyberspace. . . . However, it should be noted that who girls are pretending to be online may provide insight into their sexual development offline. Consulting with the panellists in person was extremely beneficial because the girls were able to provide valuable insight into Black girls' home pages. Whether or not all of the girls provided truthful portrayals about themselves or were experimenting with their sexuality, their unique cultural productions provide considerable insight into the previously hidden world of Black girls' home pages and sexual lives on the Web. . . .

In sum, this study complicates the understanding of Black adolescent girls' sexuality and suggests that sexuality education programmes that ignore the role of media in the lives of Black girls may be ineffective. While efforts to encourage commercial media producers to distribute more balanced portrayals of Black women and girls are important, this study sheds light on the sophisticated ways in which Black girls have taken control of their own representations. The findings provide evidence of the need to develop multidimensional approaches to health and sexuality education to help girls construct healthy sexual self-definitions and navigate the multiple and contradictory sexual messages they encounter in their daily lives. Parents (and other relatives), schools, health care providers, girl-serving organizations, religious institutions, and mentors should work with Black girls to provide safe spaces for them to critically analyse gender politics, examine their own self-definitions and attitudes about sexuality, and develop healthy, affirming, mutually respectful, and equitable sexual identities and relationships. Such strategies might identify and consult with girls who demonstrate resistance to oppressive cultural scenarios and utilize them as peer educators. These programmes should demonstrate respect by (1) collaborating with girls; (2) building on the empowering aspects of hip hop and youth culture; and (3) recognizing girls as knowledgeable about the role of media in their lives.

This research suggests that media literacy education targeting parents, health care providers, and practitioners may be beneficial in helping concerned adults stay informed about youth culture and the empowering aspects of media. Although media literacy education is important, girl-centred media education programmes that "move beyond the protectionist approach of the media literacy movement" are also needed to critically engage girls in challenging oppression by creating their own media (Kearney, 2006: 109). One example of a girl-centred media education programme that builds upon this research is exemplified by the work of HOTGIRLS, Inc. (Helping Our Teen Girls In Real Life Situations), a non-profit in Atlanta, Georgia, USA that seeks to foster healthy sexual development in Black adolescent girls by integrating health and media education with peer leadership development and training in web design and media production. In conclusion, while much of the media attention has focused on condemning individual artists and regulating content on commercial media distribution channels (e.g., Black Entertainment Television), it is important to emphasize that media messages and girls' self-representations in home pages reflect racism, misogyny, patriarchy, and capitalism in American culture (Stokes, 2004). Thus, the most promising strategy for transforming denigrating representations of Black female sexuality is to eliminate the pervasive social inequalities that perpetuate the oppression of Black women and girls.

NOTES

1. Short for weblog, a blog is "a frequently modified website that allows updating with items that are grouped primarily by the time and/or date of posting. Entries usually appear in reverse chronological order" (Scheidt, p. 194).

2. Although U.S. states are required to report AIDS cases, HIV infection reporting is voluntary (Reif et al., 2006). Because accurate state-level HIV/AIDS data for Black adolescent girls aged 14 to 17 are not available for all U.S. states, the author used the latest state-level incident and cumulative AIDS case data available from the Henry J. Kaiser Foundation State Health Facts Online database (Kaiser Family Foundation, 2003).

3. Cartoon dolls are the virtual version of paper dolls, and are created using graphic design and paint programs (Stokes, 2004).

4. The "freak on the web" phenomenon is described in the rap song "MySpace Freak" (C-Side, 2006).

REFERENCES

Bortree, D. S. 2005. "Presentation of Self on the Web: An Ethnographic Study of Teenage Girls' Weblogs." *Education, Communication and Information*, 5: 25–39.

Borzekowski, D. L. G., and Rickert, V. I. 2000. "Urban Girls, Internet Use, and Accessing Health Information." *Journal of Pediatric and Adolescent Gynecology*, 13: 94–95.

Bragg, S., and Buckingham, D. 2002. "Young people and sexual content on television: A review of the research." Accessed 28 August 2006, available at: http://www.mediarelate.org/medrelreviewofresearch.PDF.

Brown, J. D., and Stern, S. R. 2002. "Mass media and adolescent female sexuality." In G. M. Wingood and R. J. DiClemente (eds) *Handbook of Women's Sexual and Reproductive Health* (New York: Kluwer Academic/Plenum Publishers), pp. 93–112.

Brown, J. D., Engle, K. L., Pardun, C. J., Guo, G., Kenneavy, K., and Jackson, C. 2006. Sexy media matter: Exposure to sexual content in music, movies, television, and magazines predicts Black and white adolescents' sexual behavior." *Pediatrics*, 117: 1018–1027.

Bullock, L. 2006. "'Uncut' is cut from BET's lineup." Accessed 2 August 2006, available at: http://www.Blackpressusa.com/news/Article.asp?SID=3&Title=National+News&NewsD=9946.

Carpenter, L. M. 1998. "From girls into women: Scripts for sexuality and romance in *Seventeen* magazine, 1974–1994." *The Journal of Sex Research*, 35: 158–168.

Cole, J. B., and Guy-Sheftall, B. 2003. *Gender Talk: The Struggle for Women's Equality in African American Communities* (New York: Ballantine Books).

Collins, P. H. 2000. *Black Feminist Thought: Knowledge, Consciousness, and the Politics of Empowerment* (New York: Routledge).

Collins, P. H. 2004. *Black Sexual Politics: African Americans, Gender, and the New Racism* (New York: Routledge).

C-Side (featuring Jazze Pha). 2006. MySpace Freak. Accessed 15 September 2006, available at: http://www.myspace.com/csideonline.

Duncan-Mao, A. 2006. "Lil' Kim: It Has Been Said." *XXL Magazine*, May, pp. 82–86. Accessed 4 September 2006, available at: http://xxlmag.com/online/?p=651.

Emerson, R. A. 2002. "'Where My Girls At?' Negotiating Black Womanhood in Music Videos." *Gender and Society*, 16: 115–135.

Grisso, A. D., and Weiss, D. 2005. What are gURLS talking about?" In S. R. Mazzarella (ed.) *Girl Wide Web: Girls, the Internet, and the Negotiation of Identity* (New York: Peter Lang), pp. 31–49.

Kaiser Family Foundation. 2003. State Health Facts. Accessed 11 November 2003, available at: http://www.statehealthfacts.org.

Kearney, M. C. 2006. *Girls Make Media* (New York: Routledge).

Lenhart, A., and Madden, M. 2005. Teen content creators and consumers [Washington DC: Pew Internet and Family Life Project]. Accessed 4 September 2006, available at: http://www.pewinternet.org/pdfs/PIP_Teens_Content_Creation.pdf.

Ludacris. 2003. "P-Poppin'". *Chicken-N-Beer*. Def Jam.

Martino, S. C., Collins, R., Elliott, M., Strachman, A., Kanouse, D., and Berry, S. 2006. Exposure to Degrading versus Nondegrading Music Lyrics and Sexual Behavior among Youth." *Pediatrics*, 118: 430–431.

Mazzarella, S. R. 2005. *Girl Wide Web: Girls, the Internet, and the Negotiation of Identity* (New York: Peter Lang).

MEE Productions. 2004. *This is my reality—the price of sex: An inside look at Black urban youth sexuality and the role of media* (Philadelphia, PA: MEE Productions).

Miles, M. B., and Huberman, A. M. 1994. *Qualitative Data Analysis: An Expanded Sourcebook*. Second edition (Thousand Oaks, CA: Sage Publications).

Neal, M. A. 2005. *The New Black Man* (New York: Routledge).

Polak, M. 2006. "It's a gURL thing: Community versus commodity in girl-focused netspace." In D. Buckingham and R. Willett (eds) *Digital Generations: Children, Young People, and New Media* (Mahwah, NJ: Lawrence Erlbaum), pp. 177–191.

Pough, G. D. 2004. *Check it While I Wreck It: Black Womanhood, Hip-Hop Culture, and the Public Sphere* (Boston, MA: Northeastern University Press).

Rangel, M. C., Gavin, L., Reed, C., Fowler, M. G., and Lee, L. M. 2006. "Epidemiology of HIV and AIDS among Adolescents and Young Adults in the United States." *Journal of Adolescent Health*, 39: 156–163.

Reif, S., Geonnotti, K. L. and Wherren, K. 2006. HIV Infection and AIDS in the Deep South. *American Journal of Public Health*, 96, 970–973.

Robinson, T., and Ward, J. V. 1991. "'A belief in self far greater than anyone's disbelief': Cultivating resistance among African American female adolescents." In C. Gilligan, A. G. Rogers, and D. L. Tolman (eds) *Women, Girls and Psychotherapy: Reframing Resistance* (New York: Harrington Park Press), pp. 87–103.

Rose, T. 1994. *Black Noise: Rap Music and Black Culture in Contemporary America* (Hanover, NE: University Press of New England).

Scheidt, L. A. 2006. Adolescent diary weblogs and the unseen audience." In D. Buckingham and R. Willett (eds) *Digital Generations: Children, Young People, and New Media* (Mahwah, NJ: Lawrence Erlbaum), pp. 193–210.

Simon, W., and Gagnon, J. H. 1986. Sexual Scripts: Permanence and Change. *Archives of Sexual Behavior,* 15: 97–120.

Smyres, K. M. 1999. Virtual Corporeality: Adolescent Girls and Their Bodies in Cyberspace." *Cybersociology.* Accessed 4 September 2006, available at: http://www .socio.demon.co.uk/magazine/6/smyres.html.

Stephens, D. P., and Phillips, L. D. 2003. "Freaks, Gold Diggers, Divas, and Dykes: The Sociohistorical Development of Adolescent African American Women's Sexual Scripts." *Sexuality and Culture,* 7: 2–49.

Stephens, D. P., and Phillips, L. D. 2005. "Integrating Black Feminist Thought into Conceptual Frameworks of African American Adolescent Women's Sexual Scripting Processes." *Sexualities, Evolution, and Gender,* 7: 37–55.

Stern, S. 2002. "Sexual Selves on the World Wide Web: Adolescent Girls' Home Pages as Sites for Sexual Self-Expression." In J. D. Brown, J. R. Steele, and K. Walsh-Childers (eds) *Sexual Teens, Sexual Media: Investigating Media's Influence on Adolescent Sexuality* (Mahwah, NJ: Erlbaum).

Stern, S. 2004. Expressions of Identity Online: Prominent Features and Gender Differences in Adolescents' World Wide Web Home Pages. *Journal of Broadcasting and Electronic Media,* 48: 218–243.

Stokes, C. E. 2004. "Representin' In Cyberspace: Sexuality, Hip Hop, and Self-Definition In Home Pages Constructed By Black Adolescent Girls In The HIV/AIDS Era." Unpublished Doctoral Thesis, Department of Health Behavior and Health Education, University of Michigan, Ann Arbor.

Stokes, C. E. Under review. " 'What I Like in a Guy': Ideal Partner Preferences in Internet Home Pages Constructed by Southern Black Adolescent Girls in the Hip Hop Era."

Stokes, C. E., and Gant, L. M. 2002. "Turning the Tables on the HIV/AIDS Epidemic: Hip Hop as a Tool for Reaching African-American Adolescent Girls." *African American Research Perspectives,* 8: 70–81.

Takayoshi, P., Huot, E., and Huot, M. 1999. "No Boys Allowed: The World Wide Web as a Clubhouse for Girls." *Computers and Composition,* 16: 89–106.

Tolman, D. L. 2002 *Dilemmas of Desire: Teenage Girls Talk About Sexuality* (Cambridge, MA: Harvard University Press).

Usher (featuring Lil Jon and Ludacris). 2004. "Yeah!" *Confessions.* LaFace/Arista.

Ward, L. M., Hansbrough, E., and Walker, E. 2005. "Contributions of Music Video Exposure to Black Adolescents' Gender Schemas." *Journal of Adolescent Research,* 20: 143–166.

Weekes, D. 2004. Where my girls at?: Black girls and the construction of the sexual." In A. Harris (ed.) *All About the Girl: Culture, Power, and Identity* (New York: Routledge), pp. 141–154.

Wingood, G. M., DiClemente, R. J., Bernhardt, J. M., Harrington, K., Davies, S. L., Robillard, A., and Hook, E. W. 2003. "A prospective study of exposure to rap music videos and African American female adolescents' health." *American Journal of Public Health,* 93: 437–439.

Wyatt, G. E. 1997. *Stolen Women: Reclaiming Our Sexuality, Taking Back Our Lives* (New York: J. Wiley).

GEISHA OF A DIFFERENT KIND: GAY ASIAN MEN AND THE GENDERING OF SEXUAL IDENTITY

CHONG-SUK HAN

INTRODUCTION

Shortly before midnight, bodies gyrate to ear-numbing music on a small wood-paneled dance floor on the third level of R-Place, a local gay bar. The rhythmic pump from refrigerator-sized speakers high above on rafters, urge patrons to, "get on off of your feet." As naked torsos bump and grind, scents of cigarettes and alcohol linger in the air. The already small dance floor, tucked neatly into the rear corner, is even more crowded than usual due to the presence of a small, plastic, K-Mart variety kiddie-pool occupying key, center-floor, property. Yet, as oddly out of place as such paraphernalia might be, patrons dance easily and freely around it, almost unconscious of its presence; or at least, unwilling to acknowledge the awkwardness of its mere existence. For those moving in synch to the music, and to those observing the movement of bodies from the sidelines, the small tub and the gold-painted bar that rises out of it and reaches nearly up to the ceiling, is a familiar sight. These are the props required for one of the most staple of entertainments at gay bars around the country, the wet underwear contest.

To these same patrons, the participants in the competition are also a familiar bunch, a cast of characters predictably representing that which is widely valued and desired in the gay community. Young, thin, and overwhelmingly white, the contestants mirror the images found on gay billboards and magazine covers. Deviations from the formula are met with sympathetic laughter or outright disdain. An older man, whose appearance may be frail but is nonetheless full of life, is met with hoots of encouragement. An obese man is confronted with verbal mocks. "That is so gross," I hear someone yell behind me. Making no attempt to lower his volume, the same voice yells out, "What *is* he thinking?" Whether tolerated or castigated, those deviating from the formula never "win." There isn't much room for diversity in this arena, and none seems to be encouraged with a prize.

If the visual image of the "winners" represents what is physically valued and desired in the gay community, their actions represent what is desired behaviorally. Each "performance" is a display of masculinity. Contestants flex muscles, saunter across the floor, and proudly display their manhood for the participants to see. One contestant who just finished 100 crunches—because "the guy with the best abs usually wins"—before coming on stage told me, "you never wear boxers, it doesn't show it off." Apparently, the bigger the "display," the bigger the cheers, and bigger the likelihood of winning. Here, like in many other arenas of contemporary gay life, femininity is discouraged.

Even the most cursory read through gay personal ads makes the emphasis on "masculinity" blatantly clear. "Straight acting," is a marketing gimmick. In fact, if "straight acting" is a plus for those advertising themselves, "no femmes," is an equally striking warning to potential suitors that femininity is not desired.

From "Geisha of a Different Kind" by Chong-Suk Han, *Sexuality & Culture*, Vol. 10, Issue 3, 2006. Copyright © 2006, Springer. Reprinted with kind permission from Springer Science + Business Media.

In this arena of gay life, men are to be men. "If I wanted to fuck a girl, I would find one," a young gay man told me regarding his desire for a "real" man. According to Levine, this hypermasculinization of the gay male image, thus gay male desire, can be traced to "the gay male world of the 1970s and 1980s [that] catered to and supported this hypermasculine sexual code." As a response to the stigmatized "sissies" that defined what it meant to be gay, the "gay clone" came to represent a hypermasculine image for the gay community. "[The gay clones] butched it up and acted like macho men," Levine wrote, "the manliest of men" (1998: 7). Stereotypical images of effeminate gay men still exist, to be sure. However, most of these representations seem to be found in media outlets geared toward heterosexual consumption. When found within gay media, these images seem to represent a form of camp, where gender boundaries are actively challenged for the sake of entertainment value. More importantly, not only is there a "preference" for masculinity within the gay community but also a strong anti-effeminate bias (Taywaditep, 2001).

Yet, here, in the mecca of masculinity, or at least the visual display of it, one racial group of gay men occupies a predominantly feminine space. If the performances of the white contestants are a reflection of the desire for, and expectation of, masculinity, the performances of all-too rare Asian contestants are a reflection of expected femininity. On this particular night, the lone Asian contestant stands quietly waiting among the other contestants for his turn in the tub. While waiting in line, he is noticeably shy, half hiding behind a larger, muscular white contestant. When his name is called, he blushes and shrinks further behind his human shield until the MC coaxes him onto the "stage." While being [led] into the pool, the Asian contestant continues his "performance," giggling with one hand over mouth and feigning hesitation. Where "real" men pushed their way into the pool, the Asian man is pushed into it. Yet, once in the pool, his performance becomes vividly sexual. Hips gyrate and legs fly into the air as the contestant simulates a lone sex act with the giant pole. Whereas the white contestants thrust into the pole, taking the "dominant" position of inserter, the Asian contestant pushes his ass up against it, in the submissive role of receiver.

"Damn," one of his friends yells out, "I knew *she* would tear it up!"

Another friend answers, "You know it." Despite the initial display of hesitation, despite having to be "forced" into the pool, and despite what appeared to be an overly shy demeanor, the spectators *expected* a sexualized performance. To his friends, and many watching the performance, the "unexpected" turn of events was nothing but expected.

Constructing Gender, Sexuality, and Race

Gender theorists have long argued that gender is a social construction. Butler (1990) maintains that rather than merely being constructed, gender is also performed and it is these performances that give meaning to gender and gender identities. As such, gender is not something we are born with, instinctively knowing how to behave within its confines, but a learned identity reinforced by behaviors thrust onto us by societal expectations of "appropriate" gender behavior. . . .

. . . Much like scholarship on gender, scholarship from queer theorists has also maintained that "queerness" is never just about sexual acts. . . . Gay identities—like gender identities—are formed and negotiated through a wide range of social interactions within the confines of our social positions that we occupy in society and the influences that we take from it, that defines what it means to be "queer" (Vance, 1995). Thus, "being" queer is not merely about our choice of sexual partners but is intimately tied to our sense of self that we continuously perform when we are in public in order to make sense of our sexual identities. . . .

Sexual acts, even outside of sexual identity, are also marked by domination and subordination. During intercourse, it is the penetrating partner who "possesses" the penetrated partner (Dworkin, 1987). Not surprising then, the "receiving" partner in gay intercourse is seen as the passive, submissive, "feminine" actor while the penetrating partner is seen as the active, dominant, "masculine" actor. As such, gender roles are performed and reinforced even during the intimate act of sexual intercourse.

Likewise, students of race have often pointed to the social construction of race and have documented how "race"—rather than a primordial fact—is a socially constructed illusion rooted deeply in time and place (Omi and Winant, 1994). What it means to be a member of a racial category is often contested and changed. During interactions, meanings surrounding race are constantly negotiated and re-negotiated, thereby changing what is meant by "racial" minorities all together. While much less has been written about how race is performed in public, Steele and Aronson (1998) [argue] that racial expectations are often reinforced through personal behaviors.

Yet examining the life experiences of those who are simultaneously gendered, sexed, and raced is never as simple as engaging an additive analysis. Rather, the intersections of race and sexuality form new identities separate from the individual racial and sexual identities that they represent (Nagel, 2003). More importantly for our discussion, not everyone experiences racial, sexual, and gendered categorizations in the same way. Within these categories also lie subcategories. Often a member of the subcategory also inhabits a subcategory of yet another category. Members within these multiple categories do not simply experience being "raced" along with being "gendered." Rather, people who are raced, gendered, and sexualized, experience unique societal pressures specifically because

they are raced, gendered, AND sexualized. Gay Asian men do not simply feel racial and sexual oppression but are oppressed in unique ways and experience unique identity issues precisely because they are gay, Asian, and "male."

In this paper, I examine how gay Asian men have been constructed in the Western, mostly American, imagination and how that construction has affected the development of a gay Asian male identity. It should be noted that "gay Asian men" encompasses a large group of people from different cultural, historical and social backgrounds. Cultural and historical norms regarding homosexual acts and homosexual identities are different in different parts of Asia. However, as Espiritu (1992) points out, identity formation for Asian Americans in the United States are more a reflection of common experiences they found within Western borders than the discrepant histories and cultures of their homelands. Thus, I am more interested in factors that have contributed to how gay Asian men come to make sense of themselves within "Western" borders. As such, my discussion is limited to Asian men who live within "Western" borders, particularly the United States. Within this narrative, by "Asian" men, I mean those with ancestral roots in East and Southeast Asia (including the Philippines). While West and South Asians have also been influenced by similar historic projects of racial formation discussed by Omi and Winant (1994), their "Western" experience is sufficiently different enough to warrant a different discussion (Shankar and Srikanth, 1998).

Historic Construction of Asian "Masculinity"

The West thinks of itself as masculine—big guns, big industry, big money—so the East is feminine—weak, delicate, poor . . . but good at art, and full of inscrutable wisdom—the feminine mystique. . . . I am an Oriental. And being an Oriental, I could never be completely a man.

—Song Liling in David Henry Hwang's *M. Butterfly*

According to Said, "The Orient was almost a European invention, and had been since antiquity a place of romance, exotic beings, haunting memories and landscapes, remarkable experiences" (1978: 1). But rather than a method of describing the "Orient," along purely "romantic" lines, orientalist discourse acted as a "political vision of reality whose structure promoted the difference between the familiar (Europe, the West, 'us') and the strange (the Orient, the East, 'them')" (Said, 1978: 43) that acted to promote the domination and superiority of all that was "West" against all that was "East." The orientalist project also had the consequence of homogenizing vastly different cultural groups with different views, regarding not only appropriate gender roles but homosexual acts, and placing them all under the umbrella of the "oriental."

That is, what it "means" to be Asian, from a Western perspective, is an entirely constructed image, largely based on Western "expectations" of what is normal and what is "foreign." As such, images painted about what it means to be "Asian" often focus on stereotypical, one-dimensional portrayal of Asians and Asian Americans who are nearly always presented as one in the same despite divergent histories, cultural backgrounds, and points of origins. These types of portrayals, then, present gay Asian men, and all other Asians, as being a "certain" way, a way that is distinctively different from the "West," one dimensional, and, fundamentally foreign. But more importantly, as being "inferior." By doing so, it portrays Asian and Asian Americans as being interchangeable with each other. In the Western imagination, all Asians come to be represented by the singular image of the "oriental" despite their points of origin or current locations.

Perpetuating this mirage of Western superiority, orientalist discourse took on a distinctively gendered tone. Within this narrative were the messages of the feminized Asian male body. Hinging on this masculine superiority of the West, Asian bodies, both male and female, were painted with feminine brushstrokes. . . . Even in today's media, Chen notes that "Asian men are rarely portrayed as anything other than housekeepers, waiters, or ruthless foreign businessmen" (1996: 68).

This distinction, particularly useful as a means of justifying the "masculine thrust" on the Asian continent by European colonial powers, became an easy way to maintain hierarchical relations even within Western borders.

For Asian men, the discourse of domination focused largely on the "feminine" East opposed to the "masculine" West. Historic projects that have hindered Asian American family formations and excluded Asian men from the "masculinized" labor market of the "West," have simultaneously produced an image of Asian men that has both racial and gendered implications. . . . [P]opular media portrayals further emasculated Asian and Asian American men until they, "[were] at their best, effeminate closet queens like Charlie Chan and, at their worst, [were] homosexual menaces like Fu Manchu" (Chan et al., 1991: xiii). . . .

Asian men have also been portrayed as being more "traditional" and "conservative" when it comes to sex, while being portrayed as meek asexual houseboys or as sexual deviants (Hamamoto, 1994). While the stereotypes of Asian men being sexual deviants and sexual conservatives may seem contradictory, they both serve the purpose of emasculating Asian men in a process that Eng [2001] calls "racial castration." According to Fung [1996], this desexualization of Asian men helps neutralize concerns regarding a rapidly reproducing racial class and thus eases the mainstream's fear of a growing "yellow peril," eager to dominate Western locations. If Asian men are not "true" men, capable of sexuality—thus, sexual reproduction—they become less threatening to Western minds. . . .

Even when presented as masculine "heroes" by the dominant culture, Asian men continue to be denied sexual prowess. For example, in the blockbuster movie *Romeo Must Die,* the main "hero" of the film, played by Jet Li, makes no romantic connection with the female lead. When compared to the other films in the action movie genre using the "damsel in distress" formula, the omission of a sexual relationship (implied or explicit) between the male "hero" and the female lead is striking. On a similar thread, the popularity of Jackie Chan in a string of American mainstream films has yet to land him a girl. Instead, his role seems to be limited to playing the comedic sidekick to a male lead who does get the girl (*Shanghai Noon*) or to a female lead who is not the least bit interested in him romantically (*The Tuxedo*). Also, it is important to note that the roots of their "heroic" acts are based on "ancient" and "mysterious" Eastern ways that continue to shroud Asian men under the veiled cloak of orientalism. As such, "Asian men are not able to fulfill their role as 'real men' because they are 'weak,' 'passive,' and 'eunuch-like'" (Chen, 1996: 68).

Representations of Gay Asian Men

Given the longstanding racial feminization of Asian men in western discourse, looking at same-sex sexuality for gay Asian men involves more than looking at homosexual acts *per se,* but also at the intersections of race, gender, and sexuality and the way that racial and sexual categories have been created for them (Leong, 1996). For example, in *Immigrant Acts,* Lowe (1996) points out that nineteenth- and twentieth-century immigration policies including exclusion led to the formation of a racialized and gendered Asian male subject. Lowe stresses the judicial processes that led to the demasculinization of Asian male immigrants through a legal process that led to the inability of Asian men to form heterosexual unions due to immigration

laws that barred the arrival of Asian women and anti-miscegenation laws that forbade Asian men from marrying non-Asian women. Left without potential life partners, Asian men lived in predominantly male communities, forever condemned to a life of bachelorhood. Also, limited career opportunities due largely to restrictions on Asian labor left them with little options other than traditionally "feminine" occupations such as laundry workers, cooks, and domestics. Western notions of appropriate dress also added to the feminization of Asian men whose full pants and long queues (in the example of Chinese American men) led to further feminized view of this group (Chen, 1996).

Thus, conceptions of sexual identity for gay Asian men in the United States are intimately tied to the same processes that led to Asian Americans being racialized, feminized, and marginalized by the mainstream. While heterosexual Asian men have been able to function within the growing Asian American community with various degrees of success, gay Asian men continue to be marginalized both by the dominant society and their respective Asian American communities. More importantly, the 1965 Immigration Law that favored family reunification also helped heterosexual Asian men by allowing them to bring their wives from Asia or return to Asia to find wives. Not only are gay Asian men marginalized, they are made invisible by a new process of racial formation—stressing Asian American "family" values and perpetuating the model minority image for Asian Americans—that simply denies the existence of gay Asian Americans (Leong, 1996). Mainstream discussions about Asian Americans often focus on their traditional and family values—two arenas dominated by heterosexist discourse. If Asian men are torchbearers for these values, they simply cannot be gay. At the same time, studies on sex and (homo)sexuality have largely ignored racial minorities in their discussions.

Not surprising then, gay Asian men are virtually non-existent in the gay media as well. Reading through gay publications, it is almost as if no gay Asian men exist outside of the "fantasy cruises" to the "Orient." As Cho notes:

The pain of being a gay Asian, however, is not just the pain of direct discrimination but the pain of being negated again and again by a culture that doesn't acknowledge my presence. . . . Not only did I have to deal with the question of sexual invisibility as a gay man, there was also the issue of racial invisibility (1998: 2).

When portrayed at all, they are often presented in the feminized "other" to a masculinized white male. For example, a recent ad by Servicemembers Legal Defense Network (SLDN), as a part of their "Let Them Serve" ad campaign which appeared in *The Advocate, Genre,* and other numerous gay and lesbian publications around the country, shows a gay Asian male attempting to provide comfort to what is implied to be his white male lover. In the ad, the Asian male is looking lovingly at his partner with his hands resting gently on his partner's shoulder while his partner is looking solemnly away. The caption which reads, "let him serve," is meant to convey the message that the "masculine" white male is prevented from serving bravely in the armed forces, a fact which dismays him greatly. It is the white male who is the "soldier" while the Asian male is the spouse who stands lovingly beside him during his time of need for feminine emotional support.

When gay Asian men are the objects of gay publications, such as in the magazine *Oriental Guys,* the most famous publication among what Hagland (1998) calls the "rice queen magazines," in reference to "rice queens," non-Asian gay men who prefer Asian sex partners, they are "portrayed as an exotic but ultimately pliant sexual creature whose sexuality is directed outward toward the [gay white male]." Within the context of these magazines, which are produced by white men and meant for white male consumption, descriptions of Asian men take on a noticeably orientalist tone. Hagland quotes one passage from the magazine describing a gay Asian male:

Jamie is playful and mischievous. There is a boy still playing inside. . . . Jamie is proud. He knows his heritage and his roots. . . . He is a rare blend. Tenderness and strength. Playful innocence and unexpected wisdom. . . . He exemplifies exactly what is most enticing and mysterious about all of Asia itself (1998: 278).

The description of Jamie, written by Victor Davis, illustrates how gay Asian men are viewed through the lens of gay white male desire. First, Jamie is both a child and an adult, possessing both "playful innocence and unexpected wisdom." The Asian "child" is to be dominated by white male adult but is also capable of providing the implied sexual "enticement" of the "East." The infantilization of Asian men is not new to gay publications but is a longstanding practice of orientalist discourse describing Asian men. As a "child," the feminized Asian male is not capable of achieving the maturity required of adults, much in the way that women are also not capable of achieving "adulthood" (Lim, 1994). Also, he is both tender and strong, taking on an androgynous trait. It is this exotic mysticism that is most noticeable about Asia, and by extension Asian men. Not surprisingly, knowing "his heritage and roots" is important to the white male. As one gay white man told me regarding his preference for newly immigrated men:

The [Asian guys] who were born here, or even grew up here, are too pushy and demanding. Too much like American guys. I think the guys who just got here are more polite and respectful, they have a better understanding of their culture (emphasis added).

It is not simply a phenotype that this man finds attractive but "cultural" traits that he believes some Asian men possess that others do not. It is his desire for someone who is "polite and respectful" that drives his sexual quest. As such, the attraction is not based entirely on physical traits but on an orientalized vision of what someone who "knows his heritage and his roots" is able to provide.

Gay Asian men don't fare much better in American hardcore pornography. As Fung (1996) notes, Asian men are used only as the vassals which fulfill the white males' sexual desires. Within the context of video pornography, it is the white male who is at the center of attention, who is the target of desire, and the "active" partner in sexual intercourse. Asian men, simply provide the "props" required for the white male to reach sexual climax. Ultimately, gay Asian men are nothing but, "feminized bottoms who serve white studs with their asses" (Browning, 1994: 196). In print pornography, white men are often shown full-frontal, while Asian men are shown mostly from the back (Hagland, 1998). Clearly, it is the white male cock (manhood) that is desirable as opposed to the Asian male, whose most desirable attribute is his ass (womanhood). For example, Leong quotes a letter written to *Oriental Guys* where the reader gushes:

The image of Sakoi, the handsome Thai adonis featured in this issue (no. 13, 1994) took my breath away. To me he epitomizes that tantalizing fusion of androgynous beauty and potent masculinity, that set Asian males apart. . . . The buns shot is a real prick teaser, firm rounded buns and hairless scrotum, leading one's eye to the centre of one's desire . . . (1996: 13).

To this reader, and based on the inclusion of this particular letter by the editors of the magazine, many other readers, the "centre of one's desire" when it comes to Asian men is the "buns."

Because gay Asian men are racialized and gendered, their predicted role performance involves becoming the "feminine" counterpart to the "masculine" gay white male. Much like the way that women are "rewarded" for playing the feminine role, gay Asian men are "rewarded" by the dominant gay community for performing their prescribed gender roles. Because being with a gay white man is seen by gay Asian men as being favorable to being with other men of color, they learn to behave in the ways that will allow them to be desirable to white men. Writing for the Gay Asian Pacific Support Network, Jason Chang notes:

Most of the gay Asians I knew would only date white guys, and most of us just accepted this as the norm. But as I looked more deeply into the phenomenon, I was astonished by how widespread it was, at just how huge a percentage of gay Asian men were attracted only to white men. I thought of how my gay Asian friends and I accepted dates from Caucasian men we weren't even attracted to, just so we could have a white partner (2001: 58).

Moreover, he goes on to write:

I started noticing that in gay magazines and newsweeklies, almost every personal ad placed by a "GAM" (gay Asian male) was for a "GWM" (gay white male). . . . It wasn't just that gay Asian men were mainly looking for Caucasian partners, it was also that many were strongly, viscerally opposed to ever dating another Asian (2001: 59).

Unfortunately, for gay Asian men, being with a white partner often means acting the part of the feminine, mysterious, and submissive sexual "other." A gay Vietnamese American social worker told me:

I did a small mini-experiment in a gay chat room. I posted two profiles, they were exactly the same, except on one, I put that I was Asian and on the other, I didn't put a race. I was going to say "white"—but I didn't want to lie. Well, the guys who responded to the profile without my race started with something like, "hi" or "what's up?" They guys who responded to my profile that said "Asian" were much more aggressive. They said, something like, "Do you like to be fucked?" But the most interesting thing is, the guys who didn't know I was Asian would negotiate about being a top or bottom. The guys who knew I was Asian would automatically assume I was a bottom and if I told them that I wasn't, they would stop the conversation right away.

In the context of this performance, gay Asian men are limited in their ability to question the sexual actions of the dominant white partner or to negotiate a sexual role for himself. Rather, he is expected to take on the role that is prescribed to him if he wants the "prize" of white male companionship. In fact, David Henry Hwang argues that within gay Asian/white relationships:

The Asian virtually always plays the role of the "woman"; the [white male], culturally and sexually, is the "man". . . . [Gay Asian men] would be taunted with phrases which implied they were "lesbians" if they dated other Asian men. (1986: 98)

So ingrained is the feminine gender role among gay Asian men that dating another Asian man would be akin to lesbianism, where two women enter into a mutually romantic and sexual relationship. Hagland also notes the lesbianization of intra-Asian male coupling. According to Hagland:

The intra-Asian coupling portrayed [in gay porn] is constructed largely by Caucasians for their own gratification: the Asians, whether constructed in fictional narrative or choreographed in pornographic video and film, perform for the "gaze" of the GWM much as the "lesbians" in heterosexual pornography perform in the genre of "fake lesbianism" (1998: 285).

Much like the "fake lesbians" in straight-male pornography, the sexual act is not performed for their satisfaction but for that of the voyeur. As such, the implication is that they would not "normally" be engaging in such acts but do so in order to please the white male. Likewise, when I asked one gay Asian man why he does not date other Asian men, he told me, "It would be like dating my *sister* (emphasis added)." Also, for some gay Asian men, femininity becomes a strategy for attracting "masculine" white men. Manalansan describes a Filipino cross-dresser in New York City who favors "exotic" *nom de plumes* such as "Suzy Wong" or "Nancy Kwan," who specifically targets men who are attracted to "beautiful, oriental" cross-dressers rather than "compete in the hypermasculine, gym-oriented world of mainstream gay life," (1996: 54) where nobody would give him a second look due to his "slight build." Feminization also means that gay Asian men have little control over who they date. Even in gay bars, gay Asian men seem to play the role of the "woman" waiting to be chosen. As Cho recalls about his days at a gay bar:

While white men cruised looking for their prey, most Asians stood back, lined up against the wall like beauty pageant queens waiting to be chosen. . . . With all the attention focused on white guys, I instinctively knew that as a gay Asian, I rarely had the power to choose and would always be the one chosen (1998: 3).

Again, the pursuit of white male companionship limits the opportunities for gay Asian men to choose, pursue, and conquer the sexual targets of their choice. Instead, they are led into the submissive position of waiting to be chosen and being grateful for the opportunity. . . .

DISCUSSION

In *Black Skin, White Masks*, [Frantz Fanon] describes how stereotypical images can lead to a "consciousness of the body that is solely a negating activity" for blacks (1967: 110). According to Fanon, negative stereotypes perpetuated by the dominant culture are internalized by blacks and leads to the devaluation of the black body. In the process, blacks come to favor white bodies and begin to associate all positive things with whiteness while associating all negative things with blackness. [Fanon's] work on internalized racism (1967) along with theories of internalized colonialism (Memi, 1965) also provides important insights to how the dominant discourse is internalized by subaltern groups. Thus, when gay Asian men internalize these stereotypes, they also internalized the corresponding expectations, leading them to perform them in much the way that gender is performed. In a classic case of "self-fulfilling prophecies," expectations about performances can actually lead to behavior (Berger et al., 1985; Steele and Aronson, 1998). If gay Asian men are expected to perform certain roles, and many gay Asian men expect to perform them, many gay Asian men will act in accordance with these expectations.

Sadly, many gay Asian men seem to have accepted the stereotypes presented to them by the dominant gay community. For example, in his article, "Using chopsticks to eat steak," Kent Chuang quotes a young gay Asian man as stating:

There [in Europe] we [Asians] are considered exotic. The Europeans treat us like special people, like a real woman. They buy us dinner and drinks and even drive us back to the hotel (emphasis added) (1999: 34).

Not only are they exotified by gay white men, gay Asian men also tend to exotify themselves. By doing so, gay Asian men further alienate themselves from, and marginalize themselves in, the mainstream gay community.

In addition, Asian men themselves have also bought into the gay western notion of what is desirable. Ayers explains that:

The sexually marginalized Asian man who has grown up in the West or is western in his thinking is often invisible in his own fantasies. [Their] sexual daydreams are populated by handsome Caucasian men with lean, hard Caucasian bodies (1999: 91).

Mirroring this sentiment, gay Asian men who recently appeared on a local cable access television show in Seattle aptly titled, "Rice Queens" all indicated a preference for "blonde, blue-eyed, masculine guys." Not surprising then, Phua and Kaufman (2003) found that gay Asian men were the most likely among all racial groups to indicate a preference for "only" white men in internet personal ads. While 31 percent of gay Asian men explicitly indicated "white only" in their personal ads, only 8 percent indicated "Asian only" as their preference with none explicitly preferring another race. Also, in a survey of gay Asian men in San Francisco, Choi and her colleagues (1995) found that nearly 70 percent of gay Asian men indicate a preference for white men. This high percentage is particularly telling given that within gay Asian communities, San Francisco is seen as a mecca for "sticky rice," Asian men who prefer to date other Asian men. If even in this mecca, the vast majority of Asian men prefer to date white men, anecdotal evidence suggests that the percentage is much higher in other locales. More damaging to the gay Asian population is that most of these men seem to be competing for the attention of a limited number of "rice queens" (Ayers, 1999). Other writers also note this phenomenon. Chang (2001) notes that it is this competition for a limited number of white men who prefer Asian men that leads to gay Asian men to view each other as competitors rather than compatriots. This competition hinders the formation of a unified gay Asian community and further acts to splinter those who should be seen as natural allies.

In addition, gay Asian men report feeling inadequate within the larger gay community that stresses a Eurocentric image of physical beauty (Ayers, 1999; Choi et al., 1998; [Chang,] 1999). Given these feelings of inadequacy, gay Asian men may suffer low levels of self-esteem and actively pursue the company of white men in order to feel accepted by the gay mainstream. In addition to seeking the company of white men over that of other Asian men, the obsession with white beauty leads many gay Asian men to reject all aspects of themselves as Asian. For example, Chang writes about how he tried desperately to avoid anything related to his Chinese heritage and his attempts to transform his "shamefully slim Oriental frame . . . into a more desirable western body." (1999: 33)

Sadly, when gay Asian men are deeply integrated into the dominant gay community, they are more likely to be exposed to these stereotypes and, in turn, these stereotypes are more likely to influence them. While no empirical study about gay Asian male socialization into the dominant gay community yet exists, Carrier and Magana (1992) found that for gay Mexican American men, sexual behavior was influenced by their level of socialization into the gay "white" majority and their enculturation into the Mexican community. . . . As gay Asian men begin to learn the "rules" of conduct within the gay community, they learn that they are not likely to find a white male partner unless they can provide for the orientalized fantasy. Thus, they internalize these stereotypes and learn to perform them in gay interactions.

Rather than simply affecting their self-esteem and choice of partners, the gendered racialization of gay Asian men within the gay community has larger consequences. For example, Wilson and Yoshikawa (2004) point out that social discrimination faced by gay Asian men within the gay community can lead to detrimental results in their health and well-being, particularly when it comes to HIV risk behaviors. In addition, the "feminine" role adopted by gay Asian men may lead to a higher vulnerability to same-sex domestic abuse for gay Asian men, especially for those with white partners (Poon, 2000).

According to Walters (1998), the development of healthy group and self-identities among members of oppressed groups, including the facilitation of the pressures of the dominant society with the competing demands of their own ethnic, racial, and sexual communities, can lead to psychological well-being for gays and lesbians of color. In her work, she finds that gay Native Americans who are more enculturated into Native American communities are better equipped to handle the emotional stress of being gay in a gay white community. O'Donnell et al. (2002) found a similar pattern within gay Latino men. In their study, gay Latino men who were better attached to their ethnic communities were much less likely to engage in unprotected anal intercourse than those who were not connected to their Latino communities. Clearly, the behavioral "demands" placed on gay Asian men due to their racialized and gendered position within the larger gay community, if added to a lack of enculturation into their respective Asian American communities, is likely to hinder the development of healthy group and self identities for this group.

REFERENCES

Ayers, T. 1999. China doll: The experience of being a gay Chinese Australian. In P. Jackson and G. Sullivan's (Eds.) *Multicultural queer: Australian narratives*. New York: Haworth Press, Inc.

Berger, J., Wagner, D., and Zelditch, M. 1995. Expectation states theory: Review and assessment. In *Status, rewards, and influence*. J. Berger and M. Zelditch (Eds.). San Francisco, CA: Jossey-Bass.

Browning, F. 1994. *The culture of desire: Paradox and perversity in gay lives today*. New York: Vintage Books.

Butler, J. 1990. *Gender trouble: Feminism and the subversion of identity*. New York: Routledge.

Carrier, J. M., and Magana, J. R. 1992. Use of ethnosexual data on men of Mexican origins for HIV/AIDS prevention program. *The time of AIDS*. G. Herdt and S. Lindenbaum (Eds.). London: Sage.

Chan, J., Chin, F., Inada, L., and Wong, S. (Eds.) 1991. *The big Aiiieeeee! An anthology of Chinese American and Japanese American literature*. New York: Meridian.

Chang, K. 1999. Using chopsticks to eat steak. In P. Jackson and G. Sullivan's (Eds.) *Multicultural queer: The Australian narratives*. New York: Haworth Press, Inc.

Chang, J. 2001. The truth about GAM. *aMagazine*. February/March. 58–60.

Chen, C.H. (1996). Feminization of Asian (American) men in the U.S. mass media: An analysis of The Ballad of Little Jo. *Journal of Communication Inquiry* 20(2): 57–71.

Cho, S. (1998). *Rice: Explorations into gay Asian culture and politics*. Toronto: Queer Press.

Choi, K.H., Coates, T.J., Catania, J., et al. 1995. High HIV risk among gay Asian and Pacific Islander men in San Francisco. *AIDS* 9: 306–307.

Choi, K.H., Yep, G.A., and Kumekawa, E. 1998. HIV prevention among Asian and Pacific Islander American men who have sex with men: A critical review of theoretical models and directions for future research. *AIDS Education and Prevention, 10* (Suppl A): 19–30.

Dworkin, A. (1987). *Intercourse*. New York: Free Press.

Eng, D. (2001). *Racial Castration: Managing Masculinity in Asian America*. Durham, NC: Duke University Press.

Espiritu, Y. 1992. *Asian American Pan-Ethnicity*. Philadelphia, PA: Temple University Press.

Fanon, F. 1967. *Black Skin, White Masks*. New York: Grove.

Fung, R. 1996. Looking for my penis. *Asian American sexualities*. R. Leong (Ed.). New York: Routledge.

Hagland, P.E.P. 1998. "Undressing the oriental boy": The gay Asian in the social imagination of the gay white male. *Looking queer: Body image and identity in lesbian, bisexual, gay and transgender communities*. D. Atkins (Ed.). New York: Harrington Park Press.

Hamamoto, D. 1994. *Monitored Peril: Asian Americans and the Politics of TV Representation*. Minneapolis, MN: University of Minnesota Press.

Hwang, D. 1986. M. *Butterfly*. New York: Plume Books.

Leong, R. 1996. Home bodies and the body politic. *Asian American sexualities*. R. Leong (Ed.). New York: Routledge.

Levine, M. 1998. *Gay macho: The life and death of the homosexual clone*. New York: New York University Press.

Lim, S. 1994. Gender transformations in Asian/American representations. *Gender and Culture in Literature and Film East and West: Issues of Perception and Interpretations*. N. Masavisut, G. Simson, and L. Smith (Eds.). Honolulu, HI: University of Hawaii Press.

Lowe, L. 1996. *Immigrant Acts*. Durham, NC: Duke University Press.

Manalansan, M. 1996. Searching for community: Filipino gay men in New York City. *Asian American sexualities*. R. Leong (Ed.). New York: Routledge.

Memi, A. 1965. *The colonizer and the colonized*. Boston, MA: Beacon Press.

Nagel, J. 2003. Race, ethnicity, and sexuality: *Intimate Intersections, Forbidden Frontiers*. Oxford: Oxford University Press.

O'Donnell, L., Agronick, G., Doval, A., Duran, R., MyintU, A., and Stueve, A. 2002. Ethnic and gay community attachments and sexual risk behaviors among urban Latino young men who have sex with men. *AIDS Education and Prevention, 14*(6): 457–471.

Omi, M., and Winant, H. 1994. *Racial formation in the United States*. New York: Routledge.

Phua, V., and Kaufman, G. 2003. The crossroads of race and sexuality: Date selection among men in Internet "personal" ads. *Journal of Family Issues 24*(8): 981–994.

Poon, M.K. 2000. Inter-racial same-sex abuse: The vulnerability of gay men of Asian descent in relationships with Caucasian men. *Journal of Gay and Lesbian Social Services, 11*(4): 39–67.

Said, E. 1978. *Orientalism*. New York: Vintage Books.

Shankar, L.D., and Srikanth, R. 1998. *A part, yet apart: South Asians in Asian America*. Philadelphia, PA: Temple University Press.

Steele, C., and Aronson, J. 1998. How stereotypes influence the standardized test performance of talented African American students. *The Black-White Test Score Gap*. C. Jencks and M. Philips (Eds.). Washington D.C.: Brookings Institute.

Taywaditep, K.J. 2001. Marginalization among the marginalized: gay men's anti-effeminancy attitudes. *Journal of Homosexuality 42*(1): 1–28.

Vance, C. 1995. Social construction theory and sexuality. *Constructing masculinity*. M. Bergre, B. Wallis, & S. Watson (Eds.). New York: Routledge.

Walters, K. 1998. "Negotiating conflicts in allegiances among lesbians and gays of color: Reconciling divided selves and communities," in *Foundations of social work practice*. G. Mallon (Ed.). New York: Harrington Park Press.

Wilson, P., and Yoshikawa, H. 2004. Experiences of and responses to social discrimination among Asian and Pacific Islander gay men: Their relationship to HIV risk. *AIDS Education and Prevention 16*(1): 68–83.

GAY-FOR-PAY: STRAIGHT MEN AND THE MAKING OF GAY PORNOGRAPHY

JEFFREY ESCOFFIER

Situational homosexualities emerge when heterosexually-identified individuals encounter institutional settings that permit or reward homosexual behavior. Simon and Gagnon's (Gagnon and Simon, 1973; Simon and Gagnon, 1986) theory of sexual scripts allows us to understand situational sexualities as the result of interplays among stereotyped social cues, prescribed role-playing, enabling social conditions, and the converging intra-psychic motivations of participating individuals. Both the norms that regulate sexual behavior and the enabling social conditions that elicit and permit homosexual conduct from heterosexually-oriented participants can be activated using sexual scripts that circulate throughout the culture. Cues and social roles are embedded in culturally available scenarios, while the enabling conditions are often those material circumstances (prisons, barracks, economic need, drug use, or porn studio) that limit or exclude the supply of potential heterosexual sex partners (Escoffier, 1999). In contrast to its use in the 1940s and 1950s, I distinguish situational sexuality from sexual behavior as governed by the individual's sexual identity which, over the course of his life, is constantly forged, reinforced, interrupted and reconfigured within and through culture and history.

In many cases, sexual scripts are situationally specific. The "situation," in part, emerges from the characteristics (gender, race, age) of the potential population of sex partners which constrain or normalize a sexual repertoire not normally chosen by the situated individual. Albert Reiss's classic essay "The Social Integration of Queers and Peers" explored a form of homosexual prostitution that took place between young men ("peers") who did not "define themselves either as hustlers or as homosexuals" and homosexual men ("queers") who performed fellatio upon them (Reiss 1961, p. 102). Reiss found that certain norms governed the sexual transactions that occurred between the young men and homosexuals, the most important that it be undertaken "solely as a way of making money: sexual gratification cannot be actively sought as a goal in the relationship." Another was that the transaction between them "must be limited to mouth-genital fellation. No other sexual acts are tolerated" (ibid.). Reiss also found that the young men defined someone as homosexual "not on the basis of homosexual *behavior,* but on the basis of participation in the homosexual *role,* the 'queer' role."

In this article I examine the homosexual activities of a group of men whose primary sexual identities are not gay, yet who regularly perform in gay pornographic videos. These men are widely known in the porn industry and among spectators as "gay-for-pay," the implication being that they would not engage in homosexual conduct were they not paid to do so. Of course, there are many explanations for such behavior. I will argue that this group of men exemplifies "situational homosexuality." There is no irrefutable evidence establishing these men as *really* straight or *actually* gay but

From "Gay-for-Pay: Straight Men and the Making of Gay Pornography" by Jeffrey Escoffier, *Qualitative Sociology* Vol. 26, Issue 4, 2003. Copyright © 2003, Human Sciences Press, Inc.

in denial. However, all sexual conduct in the video porn industry is to one degree or another an example of situational sexuality inasmuch as the performers are often required to engage in sexual acts for monetary compensation that they would not otherwise choose to perform and with partners for whom they feel no desire.

THE GAY PORN INDUSTRY: IDENTITY POLITICS AND MARKETS

Since the late 1960s, the pornography industry in the United States has grown rapidly. While there is little reliable information about its size or annual revenues, experts estimate that the "adult entertainment" industry—which includes "XXX" videos and DVDs, Internet porn, cable and satellite porn, peep shows, phone sex, live sex acts, sex toys, and porn magazines—takes in somewhere between eight and ten billion dollars per year. That is comparable to Hollywood's annual domestic ticket sales or the annual revenues of professional sports. Again, while there are no reliable estimates, the gay market represents a significant portion of this amount—probably from ten to twenty-five percent (Antalek, 1997a; Rich, 2001; Thomas, 2000).

Until the early 1970s male homosexual pornography was produced and distributed under "black market" conditions. The first commercial male pornographic films were probably made in the late 1960s, but they were few in number (Waugh, 1996). Only after the gay movement had gained momentum were companies formed explicitly to produce gay male pornography. The production and distribution of commercial gay pornography took off between 1970 and 1985. Initially, gay pornographic movies were made by amateur filmmakers, and to some degree, many of the films made in this period represented an expression of the filmmaker's own newly "liberated" homosexuality—this was especially true for many of the performers.

This development also reflected the liberating effect of the sexual revolution: during the same period, straight erotic films, such as I Am Curious (Yellow), Deep Throat, The Devil in Miss Jones, and Last Tango in Paris, often played in mainstream movie houses. Wakefield Poole's gay Boys in the Sand opened in 1973, followed shortly by Jerry Douglas's Back Row (1974) and, like straight erotic movies, both films played in mainstream movie houses.

After 1985, production of gay pornography entered a new period in which video technology and extensive ownership of VCRs lowered its cost and made pornography more accessible. It became inexpensive and easy to rent. The new technology also enabled pornography to be viewed privately and at home. The AIDS crisis reinforced the privatized experience, some viewers turning to video porn out of fear of engaging in homosexual activities.

Moreover, starting in the mid 1980s, the gay market developed into a lucrative and dynamic growth sector for many industries, supplying specialty consumer goods to satisfy the aesthetic, social and sexual preferences of homosexuals. The commercial development of gay male pornography also benefited greatly from the growth of the gay market and urban gay communities by supplying erotic images to a growing number of self-accepting gay men. This demand helped shape the business in a number of ways: the standards of physical attractiveness, the repertoire of sexual acts, the production values, and the narrative conventions closely reflected the prevailing attitudes of gay male consumers.

In the early days of gay commercial pornography, it was difficult to recruit performers because homosexual behavior was still highly stigmatized and production was illicit. The performers were frequently recruited by the filmmakers (who were primarily gay) from among friends, casual sexual partners and boyfriends (Douglas, 1996a). There was no pre-existing network or agents to recruit performers for gay pornographic films. . . .

Today, the gay pornography industry has a highly developed infrastructure of production companies, distribution networks and technical services, as well as agents and scouts for performers. If the first phase (1970–1985) in the development of commercial gay pornography attracted primarily gay men as performers, the second phase (post–1985) began to attract performers who did not identify as gay or homosexual. One contributing factor is that male performers were better paid in the gay pornography industry than in the straight side of the business. Given the heterosexual focus of straight pornography and the primarily male audience, the industry's female performers are better paid than most of the male performers. The prolific director Chi Chi Larue estimates the number of straight men in gay pornographic videos to be sixty percent. I suspect that this is on the high side, or it may merely reflect her selection of performers for her own work. By the mid 1980s, there was active recruiting of performers by scouts, photographers and others who work in the gay segment of the industry.

THE SPECTATOR OF GAY PORNOGRAPHY: DOCUMENTARY ILLUSION AND IDENTITY EFFECTS

Pornography probably has a more significant role in the life of gay men than it does among comparable groups of heterosexual men. Gay men often turn to gay pornography for cultural and sexual validation. As film critic Richard Dyer has noted, gay pornography contributes to the education of desire—it provides knowledge of the body and of sexual narratives, and examples of gay sexuality and of sexuality within a masculine framework. Since most gay men have become adults without having been socialized in the social and sexual codes of

their communities, pornography can contribute to that as well (Dyer, 1992).

The pleasure and sexual excitement that viewers of porn experience depend, to some degree, on the patterns of social and sexual interactions (i.e., the narratives, cues and symbols) that circulate in the larger culture (Kipnis, 1996; Loftus, 2002). The gay spectator's psychological response to the fictive world of pornography and sexual fantasy—the symbolic conditions of sexual arousal—and the everyday life of social roles, values and social structures is mediated by the ideological and social developments of the gay community; not only do psycho-social elements predominate in the organization of the pornographic materials, but both the immediate social context and wider social environment also influence the sexual response to pornography (Gagnon and Simon, 1973, pp. 260–265). Gagnon and Simon, in their analysis of pornography, show that an individual's fantasy life and his capacity for sexual arousal is significantly influenced by cultural context and historical situation. For example, in gay porn condoms are widely used (for many years they have appeared in almost all videos) for anal intercourse, in sharp contrast to their virtual absence in heterosexual pornography. Some gay men find that they are not aroused by the sexual action in "pre-condom" era movies, made before the discovery of AIDS—in this way the ideological and social context clearly influence the potential for sexual excitement.

In the case of video pornography, its effectiveness stems from its ability to satisfy the viewer's expectation that the sex is plausibly "real" in some way—a pornographic film or video is a "document" of sexual pleasure, of successful arousal and orgasm. The viewer's sexual arousal presumes the suspension of *disbelief* in pornography's fictional character. A "documentary illusion" exists in the photographic pornographic genres, which promise to enact certain sexual fantasies and certify them through the "authenticity" of *erections* (although some significance may be lost with the increased use of Viagra and other drugs) and *orgasms*. The psychological as well as the ideological power of pornography is achieved through this certification of sexual fantasy by its "documented" sexual conclusions—visibly displayed orgasms (Patton, 1988, pp. 72–77; Williams, 1989, pp. 93–119; Barthes, 1986).

Viewers' responses and reviews of porn videos often minimize the genre's ambiguous expectations between fantasy/fiction and real sex. The sexual acts portrayed must seem genuinely exciting to the performers in order to arouse the viewer (they must be realistically credible), while also representing fantasies that invoke the culture's sexual scenarios. Reviewers sometimes will stress the "realness." "Ultimately what viewers want to see," one reviewer writes, "is guys *having* sex, not actors *pretending* to have sex. A few times there were some moans and some 'Oh, yeah, fuck me!' that sounded like typical porno soundtrack, but other than that this all seemed very authentic" (Foxxe, 1999). . . .

Pornography's *identity effects* are enunciated through the genre's dominant semantic and syntactical conventions: the "standard" narrative sequence (kissing, oral sex, rimming, anal intercourse) of sexual acts, a convincingly energetic performance and, most importantly, the *erections* and visible *orgasms* that authenticate (and narratively close the scene) the embodied forms of homosexual desire. Operating within the "documentary illusion" the erections and the orgasms putatively "prove" to a gay male spectator that these "sexually desirable, masculine, and energetic performers" are *really* gay—thus affirming the gay male identity. An individual video may often deviate from these generic expectations, either through failure to provide a credible performance or by offering new or creative sexual variations.

In addition to its identity effects, gay male porn also has a somewhat paradoxical "hetero/masculinist effect," in which the generic conventions that consolidate and reinforce gay male identity coexist with frequent representations of "straight" men engaging in homosexual acts. In this way gay porn reinforces the incongruity between male homosexual desire—stigmatized, abject—and the heterosexual dominance of the masculine regime of desire. It serves to situate homosexual *desire* within masculine territory irrespective of heterosexual or gay identities (Pronger, 1990, pp. 125–176). Thus, the widespread employment of straight performers in gay pornography intensifies the contradiction between *gay male identity* and *homosexuality without identity,* conferring legitimacy on homosexual *behavior* independent of gay identity.

The creation of a market for gay pornography relies upon the cultural and economic significance of gay identities, and not—however widespread it may be among males—homosexual desire (Bronski, 1984, pp. 166–174; Burger, 1995; Harris, 1997; Chasin, 2000). Its expansion into other identity markets continues to reflect a significant trend in the gay pornography business, hence the growing number of videos targeting various demographic or sexual audiences—Latinos, black men and other gay men of color, the leather, S/M and bear subcultures, and all sorts of sexual specialties like spanking, uniforms and other fetishisms (Suggs, 1999).

The central ambivalence between *identity* and *behavior* in gay male porn frames the reactions of spectators to—along with their libidinal investments in—porn "stars" (Dyer, 1979, pp. 17–19). The gay men who buy or rent and view a video expect the sexual pleasure portrayed to be "authentic" enough to produce an orgasm. For the most part, the orgasm affirms the sexual act leading up to it and contributes to the viewer's own sexual arousal (Patton, 1988;

Williams, 1989). But if the performer isn't gay, then the potential "meaning" of the orgasm is ambiguous. It can mean that orgasm is "acted" (or dramatically fabricated in some sense—"It's really only a heterosexual orgasm!"), or it can mean that even a straight man experienced an orgasm from sex with a man—this is one of the central ambiguities of gay porn (Pronger, 1990, pp. 125–154). It potentially undermines the viewer's willingness to suspend disbelief in the fictional aspect of the porn video. Thus, while every pornographic movie made for a gay male market manifestly performs at least two tasks—to sexually stimulate its viewers and, in some way, to affirm their sexual identity—it may also perform a third and more contradictory task: to provide evidence of *homosexuality without identity* (Bech, 1997, pp. 17–84). It may do so either narratively, through the inclusion of scenes portraying straight men having credible sex with gay men, or by employing "known" heterosexual (gay-for-pay) performers to credibly represent gay male sexuality.

THE THEORY OF SEXUAL SCRIPTS

. . . Gagnon and Simon introduced a thoroughgoing conception of sexual behavior as a learned process, one that is possible not because of instinctual drives or physiological requirements, but because it is embedded in complex social scripts that are specific to particular locations in culture and history. Their approach stressed the significance of individual agency and cultural symbols in the conduct of our sexual activities. . . . No previous theorists of sexuality had interpreted sexual behavior as so completely social. They redefined sexuality from being the combined product of biological drives and social repression into an arena of creative social initiative and symbolic action. . . . In their theory they argue that individuals utilize their interactional skills, fantasy materials and cultural myths to develop "scripts" (with

cues and appropriate dialogue) as a means for organizing their sexual behavior (1973; Simon and Gagnon, 1986).

Sexual arousal and the performance of sexual acts frequently depend upon the meanings and cues of the social and cultural context. In fact, human sexual behavior is organized by structured expectations and prescribed interactions that are coded like scripts. The theory of sexual scripts as formulated by Gagnon and Simon provides a useful analytical framework for exploring the dynamics of sexual performance in pornographic production. Scripts are metaphors for the narrative and behavioral requirements for the production of everyday social life. In their theory of sexual scripting, Simon and Gagnon (1986) suggest that these "scripts," with cues and appropriate dialogue, which are constantly changing and which reflect different cultural groups, circulate in societies as generic guidelines for organizing social behavior. They distinguish three distinct levels of scripting: *cultural scenarios* provide instruction on the narrative requirements of broad social roles; *interpersonal scripts* are institutionalized patterns in everyday social interaction; and *intrapsychic scripts* are those that an individual uses in his or her internal dialogue with cultural and social behavioral expectations (ibid., pp. 98–104). For example, interpersonal scripts help individuals to organize their self-representations and those of others to initiate and engage in sexual activity, while the intrapsychic scripts organize the images and desires that elicit and sustain an individual's sexual desire. Cultural scenarios frame the interpersonal and intrapsychic scripts in the context of cultural symbols and broad social roles (such as race, gender, or class) (Goffman, 1976).

Thus the making of pornography, like other forms of sex work, relies upon the learned sexual responses of its participants—much of the sexual behavior shown in pornography is a display of situational sexuality. However, unlike other forms of sex work, gay pornography as a representational genre, which often implicitly reflects as well as affirms an *identitarian* agenda, is explicitly marketed to self-identified gay men. However, the gay male pornography industry routinely recruits men who do not identify as gay or homosexual to perform in gay videos. In addition, non-gay-identified men frequently have used their work in gay pornography to launch lucrative careers as escorts. Nevertheless, the fact that industry gossip about sexual orientations circulates constantly demonstrates how important these issues are to the industry's operation as well as to the audience's response (for examples of this kind of fan discourse see the forums at www.atkol.com). In gay pornographic videos, the ability of actors who are self-defined and otherwise behaviorally heterosexual to perform homosexual acts, maintain erections (both while penetrating or being penetrated) and have orgasms provides the opportunity to explore the construction of situational homosexuality on the gay pornography set.

One distinctive characteristic of video pornography is that it is a dramatic fabrication of sexual activity that also requires demonstrations of "authentic" sexual signs, that is, erections and orgasms. The dramatic fabrication is achieved not only by the performers enacting sexual scenes but also by elaborate editing and montage of the filmed sexual acts themselves. Usually the filming of a sexual scene requires many takes, stops and starts, and requires the performers to regain their erections. The maintenance and refreshing of erections—"wood" in the industry vernacular—is a constant preoccupation of video pornographers.

The gay pornography business, through its employment of men who are heterosexual or who do not self-consciously identify as gay, provides straight actors with social conditions that enable situationally specific sexual behavior. The pornography industry supplies (1) the social and physical space where these sexual activities can take place; it provides (2) other actors who expect to engage in sexual activities with one another; and it offers (3) narratives of sexual activities that invoke the culturally available sexual scripts that elicit and activate the filmed sexual activities. Pornographic video production is obviously a "situation" in which sexual activity can take place: it provides access to sexual experiences for its participants (Simon and Gagnon, 1986, pp. 104–107).

GAY-FOR-PAY AS A PORN CAREER: CONSTRUCTING THE PERSONA

It is common practice that when anyone enters the porn industry they adopt a stage name—a *nom de porn*—by which they will be known to viewers. This protects the performer's privacy despite what is often a very visible public presence. In addition to taking the *nom de porn,* the performer must create his "character" as a performer. This persona is a "career script" through which the performer integrates traits of personality, physical characteristics and sexual performance style.

The new "porn star" fashions himself from the cultural myths and social roles that define male sexuality or violate masculine roles, or that affirm homosexual desire or draw upon ethnic or racial beliefs. Performers must obviously also draw upon their "intrapsychic" fantasies and beliefs. Thus one performer may create his persona as the aggressive, dirty-talking "top" (the one who penetrates). In Rod Barry's case, his persona enables him to play the military man having sex in the barracks, a white trash hillbilly who fucks his cousin Seth but who won't kiss (they are "fucking cousins, not kissing cousins"), or a man who, in his first scene as a "bottom" (the one who is penetrated), "aggressively" urges on the man who tops him (Escoffier, 2000). Another performer might create his persona as an exclusive top, a man with a large penis and a man who never kisses—elements drawn from sexual scripts, from both cultural scenarios and intrapsychic fantasies or fears.

Whatever his sexual preferences, when any man seeks employment in gay pornographic video production he must justify his choice from a number of perspectives. Participation in gay pornographic video production is, to some degree, a socially stigmatized activity (especially for those who do not identify as gay), not only because it is a form of sex work and because most people believe that public sexual performance negatively affects those who participate in it, but also because homosexuality is still a stigmatized form of sexuality. Thus, every new entrant into the porn business must give himself *permission* to engage in it (Simon and Gagnon, 1986, pp. 109–110; Abbott, 2000). Men who identify as heterosexual wanting to work in the gay porn industry must overcome the standard presumption that only gay men would want to perform in gay pornographic films. Obviously, the description of these performers as "gay-for-pay" presumes that the permission they require is primarily economic. But economic permission is often entangled with other reasons, such as curiosity or latent homosexual fantasies, such as in the following example:

Um, well, I was straight before I found out about gay videos, but I was a straight person with, like, thoughts and feelings. And through my twenties, they got real strong. I almost thought I would try to have an interlude or a contact with a man. I thought about it, yeah, I was, like, one of those straight-curious types. But then I got into gay video, and I decided I can simultaneously make money and fulfill a fantasy. The money's a perfect way to justify going into the sexual world. I guess I consider myself formerly straight and now I'm sexually bi with a lifestyle of straight" (Paul Morgan, in Spencer, 1998).

Permission for some performers can come from surprisingly odd sources. One performer, who had "danced" in local Latino gay bars in Jackson Heights in New York City, gave one of the more unusual forms of permission:

Interviewer: *How did you get started in this business?*
Tiger Tyson: *I just went in and did the video Tiger's Brooklyn Tails about two years ago. It turned out very*

successful. I didn't know I was going to become this whole character.
I: *Did making films come naturally?*
TT: *It was something new, being that I'm bisexual. You could say I lost my virginity on video . . .*
I: *You haven't bottomed on film. Would you?*
TT: *No, never. I would probably turn into a little punk . . . I wouldn't feel right being on the bottom.*
I: *Do you now date guys?*
TT: *No. Actually I'm engaged. She's very supportive. . . . I met her at Magic Touch while I was dancing for gay men, and she knows all about the videos. My mother is even supportive . . . that's why I don't bother to think I'm doing something wrong. If my mother doesn't feel disgraced, I feel good about it" (Straube, 1999).*

Dancing or stripping in gay bars, as Tyson's story suggests, is a common way of entering the world of gay porn, where other dancers or agents will scout for producers of gay videos (De Marco, 2002). But many of the young straight men who enter the gay porn industry develop their permission to engage in homosexual activity in a video by using a surprisingly limited number of "scripts." One of the most common narratives that gay-for-pay performers tell of their entry into the industry is the story of responding to a modeling ad or the approach of a recruiter who misleadingly offers to set up a photo shoot that turns out to be a nude photo shoot or porn audition. Brian Estevez, who worked in the industry in the late 1980s, gives this account of his recruitment:

Brian Estevez: *They wanted to see my whole body . . . and I thought: "What the fuck is this?" . . . At that point, I began to wonder what was going on and what the deal was. I turned to the old guy and said, "You told me modeling. What is this shit?" He then told me that these guys had big companies and that they made movies. I told him I didn't want to do movies—and then he started talking money and I swear . . . I don't know . . . I guess money manipulated me . . . I didn't want to do it!*
Interviewer: *And then the next step?*
BE: *. . . and I went ahead, even though I'm very straight to this day.*

I: Now about being straight . . .

BE: . . . You know, I grew up very straight—never had any homosexual tendencies.

I: You didn't connect it in any way to sexual pleasure?

BE: I didn't get any sexual stimulation from it. Even to this day, even in a sexual act, even if I have a hard-on and everything—I still didn't connect it to "Wow, this feels good."

I: And yet you started in films as a bottom?

BE: Well, I didn't have a lot of choice.

I: I'd think a straight boy would be a bit put off—that being a top would be more logical . . . more straight.

BE: I know—and that's how I felt. I'd much rather be a top, and in my later movies I didn't bottom anymore. It's just when they manipulated me into the business, they manipulated me into being a bottom. They told me that I wasn't big enough or buff enough to play a top role, so I was labeled a bottom—a small, hot guy who gets dick up his ass. After a few times around, I said, "Fuck it—I'm not doing that anymore."

I: Was the fact that you were doing it eating away at you?

BE: [quietly] Yeah—being a top would have been easier on my ego.

I: Did you enjoy it while it was happening?

BE: No, I didn't, because suddenly, out of nowhere, I was taking these big, hot monster dicks up my ass. It wasn't pretty (Richards, 1991).

Estevez's construction of permission to perform in gay porn involves a series of disclaimers: "I'm very straight to this day," "I didn't get any sexual stimulation . . . even if I have a hard-on," and "I didn't have a lot of choice [to bottom]." Elaboration of permission and the construction of a persona often go hand-in-hand. Estevez's account illustrates this when he explains that "they manipulated me into being a bottom. They told me that I wasn't big enough or buff enough to play a top role, so I was labeled a bottom—a small, hot guy who gets dick up his ass . . . being a top would have [been] easier on my ego." Eventually, he refused to bottom, and in his later videos he only topped. However, it is clear from the permission Estevez gives himself and his ambivalence about the roles he performs in

gay pornography that his persona is fashioned from other socially prevalent sexual scripts. Particularly noteworthy is his need to disclaim the evidence of erections as signifiers of sexual pleasure in a publication for gay men.

Constructing a persona is an important step for any new entrant in the gay industry, but for the straight performers it is probably the most important step. Gay men can rely to some extent on their private sexual personalities. For the heterosexual man, constructing a persona becomes the basis for navigating the demands of directors, agents, interviewers and audience members, and provides a foundation for determining what sexual acts and roles he will perform. In part, the persona is the self-conscious construction of a "personal" sexual script that draws on the individual's intrapsychic script as well as on grand cultural scenarios. The persona is a sort of sexual resume which the actor constructs around the kind of permission that he gives himself for entering the gay pornography business, but it is also based on the image that he wishes to project of who he is as a sexual performer. The persona is what sociologist Erving Goffman has called (following certain vernacular uses) a "front": " . . . that part of the individual's performance which regularly functions . . . to define the situation for those who observe the performance" (1959, pp. 22–30). The actor's porn persona consists of a hodgepodge of beliefs about gender, sexuality, identity, acceptable sexual scripts that he may engage in, and his repertoire of acceptable sexual acts. Thus the actor's porn persona is a "situational sexual identity" that is constructed to be used within the confines of a porn career and the gay porno business. The persona is important because it enables the performer to have a self-concept that gives him permission to engage in homosexual activity and thus to sustain a credible sexual performance, to have erections and to produce orgasms.

Once the actor has his porn persona, he will use it to negotiate auditions, interviews with the press, street encounters with fans and, most importantly, performances. He will use the persona to answer questions about why he started doing gay pornography (e.g., "I'm in it for the money"), his sexual orientation, his physical assets as a sexual performer (muscles, penis size, a "fuckable" ass), those particular sex acts he will or won't do, and to limit who is cognizant of his career in gay porn, and to provide plausible excuses for any failure to turn in credible performances. Another aspect of a porn persona is whether the actor engages in professionally related activities like escorting or dancing. Usually, people in the industry—agents, directors or journalists—help new entrants develop their porn personas. Often, industry insiders inject a more palpable "marketing spin" into a new actor's persona. Insiders also supply standard terms like "top," "bottom" or "versatile" for roles involving anal intercourse, or more complex terms like "sex pig," "trade" or "straight bottom" to characterize the actors' porn performances.

When a gay-for-pay performer successfully conveys sexual pleasure, fans begin to question the performer's sexual orientation. Frequently a performer will concede that he is in fact bisexual. Describing himself as sexual is at least as common:

Interviewer: *Obviously, you think of yourself as heterosexual . . .*
Rod Barry: *[interrupting] I wouldn't say "heterosexual." I'd say "sexual."*
I: *What's the difference between being sexual and bisexual?*
RB: *I think bisexual means you're a switch-hitter, you like it both ways. Sexual is you like an orgasm and you don't care how you get it . . . (Douglas, 1998a).*

Porn personas are intentionally constructed to facilitate work in the porn industry, but they often reflect intrapsychic investments. Rod Barry's description of himself as "sexual" may be more than a justification or permission to engage in homosexual sex. Over the course of his career he has insistently characterized himself as "sexual" or even "omni-sexual" rather than gay or bisexual: "Don't call me gay. Don't call me straight. Don't call me bisexual. Just call me sexual. I can cater to anybody . . . a gay male, a transsexual, or a female," he proclaimed in another interview (Antalek, 1997b). He suggests a sexuality for himself that encompasses a wide range of "object choices" and roles (top or bottom); his image may embody an emerging style of masculine sexuality, one envisioned by Foucault: "What these signs and symbols of masculinity are for is not to go back to something that would be on the order . . . of machismo, but rather to invent oneself, to make oneself into the site of production of extraordinarily polymorphous pleasures" (Escoffier, 2000; Foucault quoted in Halperin, 1995, pp. 89–90).

Virtually every actor who makes a name for himself as a top is challenged to bottom at some point in his career. Rod Barry, a former Marine and one of the top gay-for-pay porn stars in the late 1990s, was frequently asked if he would bottom. He always replied, "Where's the bucks?" The decision to bottom is justified in many ways but, like other aspects of the persona, involves repackaging symbolic resources, social roles and culturally available sexual scripts:

I: *Was "getting fucked" a big step or just another step?*
RB: *Another step. Obviously, it's a big step, because in the industry, everybody makes a big deal out of it . . . That day was, to me, like any other day. Except for the fact that I was "getting fucked". . . . It's different from what I was doing, but it's just like any other day at the office.*
I: *Did you feel that you were playing a feminine role at that moment?*
RB: *No. No. No. And if you watch the movie, I don't think so, because I'm an aggressive top and I was also an aggressive bottom, playing the same way, like reaching around and grabbing his ass and pulling him: "Do it right!" (Douglas, 1998a)*

Barry's performance as a bottom was very favorably reviewed by fans and critics. In a review in *Manshots*, director Jerry Douglas wrote: "Either Barry is one hell of an actor or he does delight in bottoming . . . his pleasure seems downright palpable. His energetic response to the rutting, the sparkle in his eyes, his joyous grin, and his rockhard erection all confirm that he is indeed as exciting a bottom as he is a top" (Douglas, 1998c, pp. 38–39). . . .

The longer their porn careers, the more actors are under pressure to revise their personas, to expand their repertoire of sex acts, and to put themselves into new situations in order to avoid becoming too predictable, and therefore boring to their fans. An integral dynamic of the porn industry, and for many forms of sex work, is a steady pressure for "fresh meat." . . . Most porn actors are aware of this retrogressive dynamic and try to develop a career strategy for their post-porn careers. Some leave the industry and go into other careers or businesses. Some work behind the scenes in porn, while others increasingly rely on escorting or some other form of sex work—which usually just stretches out the retrogressive dynamic over a longer period. Some performers will try to hold onto their fans by expanding their sexual repertoire—they will bottom or do a gang bang picture. But this progression usually leads to lower budget productions as well. "One interesting thing about this business," director Kristen Bjorn observed, "is that the longer you are in it, the less money you are paid. Once you are an old face, and an old body, forget it. You're through as far as your popularity goes" (De Walt, 1998). . . .

WOOD AND MONEY SHOTS: SEXUAL PERFORMANCE AS WORK

. . . While porn actors, like other sex workers, may exclude certain activities from their repertoire, their sexual behavior is governed by the demands and constraints of the video production context. Heterosexual actors in gay pornography must necessarily engage in homosexual sex acts. However, in the context of video production, three other factors help to define their sexual activities. One is the constant interruption of the homosexual activities in which they engage. A second is the use of various forms of heterosexual pornography—such as straight porn magazines or hetero porn videos shown on television monitors on the sidelines—as aids in maintaining their erections and stimulating orgasm. Third is post-production and editing, which result in the illusion of an "authentic" sexual performance. The finished movie is the combined product of the credible sexual performances of the actors, the director's skill in motivating and preparing the actors to perform the sexual acts filmed, and the success of post-production editing in sustaining the credibility and coherence of the sex portrayed and minimizing any discrepancies between the actors' personas and their sexual performances.

For the straight actor in gay pornography, it is the on-set performance of homosexual acts that defines his ability to successfully manage the situationally specific sexual demands. Many of these heterosexual actors claim that their first sexual encounter with another man was on the set of a gay porn video. Thus, even before his first homosexual experience, a straight actor must choose his repertoire of sexual acts. Certainly his most significant decision is whether or not he will engage in anal intercourse as a top or as a bottom. The repertoire of sex acts is very much a part of the actor's development of his porn persona. The shaping of his persona is dependent on those sexual scripts—those that exist in the culture at large, his own intrapsychic ones or those he can imagine in his everyday life—in which he is able to invest his energy. Thus, for the straight actor, there is a continuum from the "trade" role, where the actor refuses all "gay" sex roles or reciprocity, to that of "sex pig," where he engages energetically in all aspects of sexual activities, to the "straight bottom" role, in which the straight actor engages primarily as a bottom.

The trade role is the gay porn role in which the actor "presumably" can maintain the most distance from the stigma of being labeled as homosexual but, ironically, the straight bottom is a role that allows the performer to demonstrate that he is not aroused even though he is being penetrated—QED he is not gay. The straight bottom, since he does not even need to produce an erection, requires even less of a libidinal investment than does an actor with a trade persona. However, the straight bottom role may also be adopted when an actor doesn't have the confidence or ability to maintain an erection in order to anally penetrate his co-star. One such performer, Tim Barnett, during an interview questioning his choice of roles, responded:

Interviewer: *Since you were relatively new to male-male sex . . . did you lay out any rules? . . . Was the whole menu of what you [were] going to do discussed, or was it just "You're going to bottom"?*

Tim Barnett: *I think it was more or less discussed when I came out [to Los Angeles].*

I: *The scene was filmed around what you were willing to do?*

TB: *Right. And I'm very versatile . . .*

I: *Was there ever any question . . . whether you would top or if it would be a flip-flop?*

TB: *. . . They wanted me to top Greg or do a flip-flop, and it just never came about. . . . I just don't know if I'm comfortable enough with the sex yet that I would be a top.*

I: *It's easier to be a bottom.*

TB: *It's a lot easier to be a bottom (Douglas, 1996b).*

Despite the relative "ease" of bottoming, the *1996 Adam Gay Video Directory* (Anonymous, 1996) was, nevertheless, critical of Tim Barnett's performances: "Tim is a big beefy blonde who just loves to get fucked. Unfortunately, he enjoys giving his co-stars pleasure so much he rarely has time to maintain his own erection." (Here the reviewer maintains the public

pretense of Barnett's libidinal investment, attributing his lackluster performance to his focus on giving pleasure to his co-stars.) Even gay actors, like straight actors, may have difficulties staying hard while being penetrated. That can be ignored, if they project some form of libidinal engagement. Without any erections or effective engagement a straight bottom cannot give a credible performance.

Once the actor decides on the acts he is willing to perform, the major practical issue is the enactment of a credible performance of sexual acts. As I have already mentioned, heterosexual actors often use straight porn magazines, straight videos on monitors or "fluffers" (performers who fellate the actor offcamera) to help themselves achieve erections. Tim Barnett, the straight bottom quoted above, was asked if he used the person he was playing opposite to or if he drew on his own private world to get himself aroused. The actor answered: "Both. It really depends who it is. I really like my nipples played with, and sometimes the other person will be the kind of person I'd like to have playing with my nipples. A lot of times I'll use a magazine" (Douglas, 1996a).

Another adaptation is the development of what might be called a "professional" work ethic on the porn set. Still photographer Greg Lenzman discusses one such actor:

Usually, with the gay-for-pay, there are certain things they will not do or they don't have that energy. But there are some exceptions. Rod Barry, who started off more as a straight—I think he's now moved on to a lot of stages in his video career . . . [H]e will give all for his shoots and is very supportive of other performers. He's a joy to work with on a set, and you just know you're going to have a good scene with Rod Barry. The scene with Rod bottoming for the first time was just like an evolution" (Douglas, 1998b).

Dirk Yates, the director-producer who discovered Rod Barry, concurred:

He seemed pro from the first day I met him. . . . He did twenty-nine scenes in a year. He started right off the bat.

And I believe the guy's straight—maybe I'm wrong—but I've never seen such a performer. He would never turn you down on anything" (Lawrence, 1999).

To porn video viewers, an important element is the sexual chemistry of the performers. It is unclear how often this is really the performers' chemistry or the result of editing and post-production work. How do performers who are not gay manage to project the sexual appeal needed to attract viewers? Gay-for-pay performer Rod Barry insists that "porno is all about energy" (Douglas, 1998a).

Kristen Bjorn, probably the most successful contemporary director of gay porn, has made a series of videos using predominantly performers who do not identify, in any sense, as gay or homosexual (Jamoo, 1997). While most of his actors are Latin American and European (and therefore from societies with different "sexual scripts"), they nevertheless have a large following of American gay men. Both Bjorn and his assistant director, who goes by the name of "the Bear," have discussed the desirability of using straight actors many times. In one interview, the Bear notes:

. . . Straight men usually have less of a problem getting erections for still photography as well as video. I believe that they are better prepared to come to work knowing that sexual energy must come from themselves through fantasy, memories, erotic magazines, etc. Gay men often come to work thinking that their work is going to be a realization of a sexual fantasy that they have had for a long time. When they realize that they are not in control of the sexual activity, partners, and duration, they become detached and often bored with it and one another. When a gay model is turned on to another model, it can be great to film. In many cases the models are not that excited by each other, especially after four full days of filming the same sex scene. As one model put it at the end of a scene, "That was the longest trick that I ever had!" Once a gay model has decided that he is not sexually interested in the other models, it seems most difficult to bring him into the action and get him aroused. Straight boys don't seem to be as dependent upon the excitation of the other models nor as concerned whether or not they are exciting their partners. But when a gay model perceives that he is not arousing his partner, as often happens in scenes that involve gay and straight models together, it can make him feel insecure with himself. This affects his ability to get erections and ejaculate. Straight models are not as sensitive to the stimuli that can make or break a gay model's performance (Bear, 1999).

The dynamics between gay men and straight actors is another important factor in the production of credible homosexual performances. Homophobic attitudes on the part of a straight actor often undermine the necessary "sexual chemistry." Gay actors often complain about working with straight performers. As the Bear notes, gay men are much more sensitive to the sexual chemistry between themselves and the straight actors. The identity issue frequently surfaces in gay men's assessment of working with heterosexual actors. Tommy Cruise, who explicitly identifies as a bisexual and as a bottom, comments:

One of the things I hate is working with straight guys, because if they're not attracted to me, then I don't like it. People say, "What is your favorite guy like?" It doesn't matter as long as they like me. That turns me on. If someone wants to fuck me really bad, that just turns me on—because they want me. Don't ask me why, I don't really know. That's what does it for me. It's not very enjoyable for me when I'm with a straight guy. A lot of straight guys, they don't even want me touching them. I'm like, "Why are you even in the business?" I've only worked with two straight guys who were okay—and one of them actually blew my mind. He was the strangest dude I ever saw. He was like, "Okay, time to get a hard-on." Boom, he'd get a hard-on. It's like he's standing there like a friggin' robot. "Okay, time to come." Boom, he comes. He was so on-cue, it was kind of freaky, but he was so good to work with (Douglas, 1999).

Cruise's remarks point to the importance of the straight actor's attitude towards gay men and homosexuality, in addition to his intrapsychic need for his sexual partners to find him attractive. Buddy Jones, a gay man who has performed in several Kristen Bjorn movies, found it enjoyable to work with a straight actor. He reported:

> . . . *It was a turn-on working with a straight boy . . . who was eating my ass and sucking my dick. And he was really good at that, especially the rimming. I was concerned about turning him on while he was fucking me, because I was really turned on. I thought that in his mind he was just working. But then his hard cock was up my ass and his hot cum shot all over me, and it kind of made me wonder if he was really enjoying it* (Bear, 1999).

One gay man, Eric Hanson, who performs primarily as a top, says that his favorite co-star is "straight bottom" Kurt Stefano: " . . . He has a great persona about him. I think it's the straight thing going on with him. Straight-acting guys are a total turn-on" (Adams, 1998).

By itself, the porn persona is not sufficient for the successful management of sexual performances. . . . Getting wood and producing orgasms are merely the certifying components of sexual performances in pornographic movies. Porn actors must convincingly play the roles of men engaged in sex in other ways in order to sustain a credible homosexual performance. As one porn actor after another iterates in interviews throughout the gay press and pornography magazines, making porn is hard work (no pun intended).

THE CAMERA FRAME: SEXUAL SCRIPTS AND VIDEO PRODUCTION

. . . For straight performers, the gay porn video set provides highly structured access to homosexual activity. It is a social space dense with sexual cues (Simon and Gagnon, 1986, pp. 105–107). Video production organizes the space (both physical and social) where sex will take place. But the making of pornography necessarily invokes the culture's generic sexual scenarios—the sex/gender scripts; racial, class

and ethnic stereotypes; the dynamics of domination and submission; and various reversals and transgressions of these codes. Porn video scripts utilize these cultural and symbolic resources. These culturally significant symbolic codes help mobilize the actor's private desires and fantasy life in the service of the video's sexual narrative.

The making of a porn video requires not only the performance of real sexual acts but also the simulation of a coherent sexual "narrative." Real sex acts are usually performed, but the video representation of them is more coherent than the actual sexual activity being filmed. The shooting of any sexual scene is made up of an apparently simple sex act photographed from several different perspectives. In fact, the performed act is interrupted many times to arrange shooting angles and lighting and to allow the actors to "get wood"— to regain their erections.[1] For example, the cameraman crawls under actors fucking doggie-style, then shoots them from above to show penetration of the ass, then from behind the active party to catch yet another penetration shot of the hard penis going in and out. Then the "money shots" (shots of the actors ejaculating) of all the performers in the scene have to be choreographed, often at the end of many hours of filming. The actors may need help of various kinds to help them ejaculate— heterosexual porno magazines, porn videos on monitors, or manipulation by one of their co-actors such as biting their nipples, inserting a finger in their anus, or kissing them. Thus a 15-to-20-minute sexual scene that the viewer sees is edited and patched together, with soundtrack added, from footage shot over a six or seven hour period. . . .

Ultimately, it is the director's choreography of sexual performances and the effectiveness of the editing process that give pornography its quality as an idealization of sexual performance. Whatever shortcomings commercial pornography exhibits—the repetitiveness of sexual activities, inadequate performances (flaccid erections, lackluster orgasms, bored actors) and shoddy production values—they are exacerbated by the idealization that pornography as a medium promotes. . . .

The director uses the porn actor's persona as the raw material for the sexual plot when choreographing the sexual combinations. Of course, sometimes actors can't successfully manage the persona that they want to project. For example, if a straight performer whose persona presents him as "trade" (i.e., he will not perform oral sex, allow himself to be penetrated, or kiss) can't get an erection, making him unable to penetrate the performer assigned to play bottom, then he and the director must negotiate some modification in order to have a credible sex scene. If he isn't fired and replaced, the actor with the "trade" persona may have to perform outside his persona—perform oral sex or agree to bottom— in order to get paid. In the last couple of years, Viagra has helped in achieving and maintaining erections, but there are still numerous other problems involving an actor's ability to live up to his persona and perform credible sex.

CONCLUSION

The making of gay male pornography provides an interesting example of the dynamics of situational homosexuality. Since performing in pornography is a kind of sex work, the performers' sexual conduct is a specific response to their customers' preferences and does not represent the preferred sexual responses of the performer. In other words, the sex that is performed is that for which, the customer is willing to pay (Adams, 1999, pp. 102–121).

In gay pornography, the participants have had to develop a "persona" or "front" (a *nom de porn,* sexual histories, a repertoire of sex acts) to negotiate the social demands they must contend with as sexual participants. Like any front,

it is more manageable if it is, to some degree, consistent with biographical attributes of the participant. But the persona also provides the performer with a way of invoking the potential cultural scenarios and sexual scripts that are compatible with his intrapsychic scripts (Goffman, 1959). The production process of gay pornography creates a *situation* that enables straight men to engage in homosexual sex for money. It is a highly organized commercial space that supplies sex partners, symbolic resources and other erotic stimulants, and a video production technology that can produce coherent and credible sexual narratives and images.

The *identitarian* expectations of gay spectators shape both the making of a pornographic video and their interpretations of the sexual performances. It is commonly presumed that when an actor in a pornographic video has an erection while being penetrated he must be gay. In contrast, I have argued that credible homosexual performance, whether or not it sexually arouses the performer, can take place without conscious identification as a homosexual person or even without spontaneous preference for homosexual forms of activity.

Situational homosexualities emerge when heterosexually identified individuals encounter situations that enable or reward homosexual behavior. Situational homosexuality is socially constructed sexuality. All sexual performance is fundamentally situational and does not always result in long-lasting social psychological commitment to any one form of sexual activity. It is a process that draws on both *intrapsychic scripts* and *cultural scenarios* and integrates them into the *interpersonal scripts* of everyday social life. The theory of sexual scripts presumes that sexual performance is not about discovering and pursuing one's intrapsychic desires (the presumptive core sexual self), but about defining and constructing scenarios of desire using cultural scenarios and negotiating interpersonal situations (Gagnon and Simon, 1973; Foucault, 1997). The men who work in the gay porn industry—whether gay, straight or "sexual"—must all construct scripts in order to perform. In this way they are no different from any person engaging in sexual activity—since all sexual performance is situational.

NOTES

1. This has changed to some degree since the introduction of Viagra in 1998. Regaining erections is now much quicker.

REFERENCES

Abbott, S. A. 2000. Motivations for pursuing an acting career in pornography. In R. Weitzer (Ed.), *Sex for sale: Prostitution, pornography and the sex industry* (pp. 17–34). New York: Routledge.

Adams, J. C. 1998. The Adams report, www.radvideo.com /news/adamhans.html.

Adams, M. 1999. *Hustlers, escorts, porn stars: The insider's guide to male prostitution in America.* Las Vegas: The Insider's Guide.

Anonymous. 1996. Current performers: Tim Barnett. In *1996 Adam Gay video directory* (pp. 7–8). Los Angeles: Knight Publishing.

Antalek, J. 1997a. Porn in the USA. Q *San Francisco,* October/November (http://qsfmagazine.com/9711 /index.html).

Antalek, J. 1997b. Porn in the USA: Rod Barry. Q *San Francisco,* October/November (http://qsfmagazine .com/9711/index.html).

Barthes, R. 1986. The reality effect. In R. Barthes (R. Howard [Trans.]), *The rustle of language* (pp. 141–148). New York: Hill and Wang.

Bear. 1999. Interview with Buddy Jones. *Manshots,* 11 (pp. 30–33, 80).

Bech, H. 1997. *When men meet: Homosexuality and modernity.* Chicago: University of Chicago Press.

Bronski, M. 1984. *Culture clash: The making of Gay Sensibility.* Boston: Alyson.

Burger, J. R. 1995. *One-handed histories: The eroto-politics of gay male video pornography.* Binghampton: Harrington Park Press.

Chasin, A. 2000. *Selling out: The gay and lesbian movement goes to market.* New York: St. Martin's Press.

De Marco, J. R. G. 2002. The world of gay strippers. *The Gay and Lesbian Review,* 9, March/April (pp. 12–14).

De Walt, M. 1998. The eye of Kristen Bjorn. *Blueboy,* January (pp. 52–55).

Douglas, J. 1996a. Jaguar Productions: Interview with Barry Knight and Russell Moore. *Manshots,* 8, Part 1: June (pp. 10–15); Part 2: August (pp. 10–15, 72).

Douglas, J. 1996b. Interview with Tim Barnett. *Manshots,* 8, February (pp. 30–33, 72–73).

Douglas, J. 1998a. Interview with Rod Barry. *Manshots,* 10: June (pp. 53–57, 72–73).

Douglas, J. 1998b. Behind the camera: Interview with Greg Lenzman. *Manshots,* 10: August (pp. 10–15, 81–82).

Douglas, J. 1998c. *Beach buns* (review). *Manshots,* 10: November (pp. 38–39).

Douglas, J. 1999. Interview with Tommy Cruise. *Manshots,* 11: October (pp. 66–71, 78–79).

Dyer, R. 1979. *Stars.* London: British Film Institute.

Dyer, R. 1992. Coming to terms: Gay pornography. In R. Dyer, *Only entertainment* (pp. 121–134). London: Routledge.

Escoffier, J. 1999. Non-gay identified: Towards a post-identitarian theory of homosexuality. Paper presented at the annual meeting of the Eastern Sociological Society, March 6.

Escoffier, J. 2000. Dirty white guy: Rod Barry's career from Marine to porn star. Unpublished paper.

Escoffier, J., and Spieldenner, A. 1998. Assessing HIV prevention needs for immigrant men who have sex with men (MSM) in New York City. Grand Rounds, HIV Center for Clinical and Behavioral Studies, Columbia University, School of Public Health, New York, April 30.

Foucault, M. 1997. Sex, power and the politics of identity. In M. Foucault (P. Rabinow [Ed.]), *The essential works of Michel Foucault, 1954–1984, volume I: Ethics, subjectivity and truth* (pp. 165–173). New York: The New Press.

Foxxe, A. 1999. Home bodies. *Unzipped,* August 31 (p. 40).

Gagnon, J. H., and Simon, W. 1973. *Sexual conduct: The social sources of human sexuality.* Chicago: Aldine.

Goffman, E. 1959. *The presentation of the self in everyday life.* New York: Doubleday Anchor.

Goffman, E. 1974. *Frame analysis.* New York: Harper & Row.

Goffman, E. 1976. *Gender advertisements.* New York: Harper & Row.

Halperin, D. 1995. *Saint Foucault.* Cambridge: Harvard University Press.

Harris, D. 1997. The evolution of gay pornography: Film. In D. Harris, *The rise and fall of gay culture* (pp. 111–133). New York: Hyperion.

Jamoo 1997. *The films of Kristen Bjorn.* Laguna Hills: Companion Press.

Kipnis, L. 1996. How to look at pornography. In L. Kipnis, *Bound and gagged: Pornography and the politics of fantasy in America* (pp. 161–206). New York: Grove Press.

Lawrence, D. 1999. *The Dirk Yates collection: Adam Gay video erotica.* Los Angeles: Knight Publishing.

Loftus, D. 2002. *Watching sex: How men really respond to pornography.* New York: Thunder's Mouth Press.

Patton, C. 1988. The cum shot—three takes on lesbian and gay sexuality. *OUT/LOOK,* 1: 72–77.

Pronger, B. 1990. *The arena of masculinity: Sports, homosexuality and the meaning of sex.* New York: St. Martin's Press.

Reiss, A. 1961. The social integration of queers and peers. *Social Problems,* 9: 102–120.

Rich, F. 2001. Naked capitalists. *The New York Times Magazine,* May 20, (pp. 51–56, 80–81, 92).

Richards, R. W. 1991. Interview with Brian Estevez. *Manshots,* 3: 53–58,79.

Simon, W., and Gagnon, J. 1986. Sexual scripts: Permanence and change. *Archives of Sexual Behavior,* 15: 97–119.

Spencer, W. 1998. Interview with Paul Morgan. *Manshots,* 10: December, (pp. 52–57, 72–73).

Stoller, R. J. 1991. *Porn: Myths for the twentieth century.* New Haven: Yale University Press.

Straube, T. 1999. Porn profile: Tiger Tyson. *HX,* May 14, (p. 68).

Suggs, D. 1999. The porn kings of New York. *Out,* June, (pp. 85–89).

Thomas, J. A. 2000. Gay male video pornography: Past, present and future. In R. Weitzer (Ed.), *Sex for sale: Prostitution, pornography and the sex industry* (pp. 49–66). New York: Routledge.

Waugh, T. 1996. *Hard to imagine: Gay male eroticism in photography and film, from their beginnings to Stonewall.* New York: Columbia University Press.

Williams, L. 1989. *Hard core: Power, pleasure and the "frenzy of the visible."* Berkeley: University of California Press.

What We Know about Pornography

Clive M. Davis and Naomi B. McCormick

WHAT IS PORNOGRAPHY?

The word *pornography* derives from a Greek word meaning "writing about prostitutes." Although there is no widely accepted modern definition, the common element in all definitions is that the material is sexually explicit. Controversy revolves around whether specific depictions are art or smut, good or bad, innocuous or harmful. People often label as pornographic material that violates their own moral standards and use the terms *artistic* or *erotic* for sexual materials they find acceptable.

Pornography must be distinguished from obscenity. *Obscenity* is a legal term identifying material that has been judged by the courts to have violated specific statutes pertaining to sexually explicit material. Central to these statutes is whether the material violates community standards of acceptability and whether it involves minors. Thus, many books, movies, and even advertisements that are acceptable today could have been judged obscene earlier in our history.

THE EFFECTS OF EXPOSURE TO SEXUALLY EXPLICIT MATERIAL

Since the 1960s, research has been conducted to assess the effects of exposure to sexually explicit material. Primary attention has been paid to commercially produced materials intended to generate sexual arousal and/or activity in adult audiences. Three components have been of principal interest: (a) the degree of explicitness, (b) whether the material also contains aggression, and (c) whether it depicts women in demeaning and degrading ways. . . .

Reactions

People vary in response to sexual materials: Some react negatively to all depictions, whereas others find at least some material acceptable and arousing. Materials that are liked produce more positive emotions and greater sexual arousal than those that are disliked, for both sexes. Nonetheless, sexual arousal may occur even when people are mildly offended. Men tend to respond more positively to the more hard-core and male-dominated material; women tend to react more negatively to this material.

Individuals who hold authoritarian beliefs and have conservative social and religious attitudes tend to experience more sex guilt and react more negatively to explicit materials. Even if they do experience arousal, they judge the material to be undesirable.

Hypermasculine men tend to hold more negative and sexist attitudes toward women. They also are likely to believe that women respond positively to dominant, aggressive men. These men react more positively to scenes of sexual aggression and degrading portrayals of women. Most people, both men and women, respond negatively to this type of material.

Changes in Sexual Attitudes and Sexual Behavior

Repeated exposure generally increases tolerance of explicit material and to the behaviors depicted, except for those who start out with negative attitudes. Those who are aroused by the material are likely to engage in sexual acts, such as masturbation or coitus, within a few hours of exposure. Repeated short-term exposure results in increased disinterest and satiation, but after a period of no exposure, the impact is regained.

Attitudes toward Women and Aggressive Behavior

For obvious ethical, moral, and legal reasons, researchers have not conducted experiments to determine whether exposure to material in which high levels of sexual explicitness and violence are both present leads to increased sexual violence. They have, however, looked at whether men with a history of such exposure are more likely to have committed sex crimes. Sex offenders tend to come from restrictive and punitive home environments. Compared to nonoffenders, they have had more undesirable experiences during childhood, including heightened exposure to sexual and physical abuse. Some offenders have had more exposure to explicit materials than other men, but early exposure alone does not increase the risk of becoming a sex offender.

In controlled laboratory research, individuals have been exposed to material containing (a) both aggression and explicit sex, (b) only aggression, and (c) only the sexual material. The results suggest it is exposure to aggression that triggers aggressive behavior. Exposure to sexual material alone does not increase aggression toward women. For most people, aggression and sex are incompatible. For a small percentage of men predisposed to aggression toward women, however, combining sex and aggression does stimulate arousal and aggressive responses.

The impact of exposure to sexist, demeaning material depends on the person's preexisting attitudes. Under some conditions, those predisposed to negative views become more calloused and accepting of these negative views.

IS PORNOGRAPHY HARMFUL?

The answer is complex: "It depends." For those who believe that anything fostering more permissive attitudes toward sexuality or that even viewing others engaging in sexual acts is morally wrong, then exposure to explicit sexual material is clearly unacceptable. Others, however, believe that there is nothing wrong with permissive attitudes and being stimulated by explicit materials. Indeed, materials depicting consensual activity have been used in beneficial ways by therapists and educators to reduce anxiety and to improve sexual knowledge, and by individuals and couples to enhance their sexual pleasure. . . .

Exposure to material that contains sexist or violent depictions can promote undesirable attitudes and behaviors. Increased censorship, however, will not be effective in addressing the problems, for three reasons. Firstly, censorship is most often directed toward only the most sexually explicit material, leaving the much more problematic sexist and violent content of R-rated material untouched. Secondly, censorship would not end sexual exploitation or violence. The roots of those behaviors are far deeper in the culture. Sexist, sexually explicit material is more a symptom than a cause of female subordination and sexual

violence. Finally, restrictions beyond the existing obscenity laws and protection for minors would create numerous other problems in a free, democratic society. Few sexual scientists judge the evidence as warranting additional restrictions.

RECOMMENDED READINGS

Davis, C. M., and Bauserman, R. 1993. Exposure to sexually explicit materials: An attitude change perspective. *Annual Review of Sex Research*, 4: 121–209.
Donnerstein, E. L., and Penrod, S. 1987. *The question of pornography: Research findings and policy implications.* New York: Free Press.
Fisher, W. A., and Barak, A. 1991. Pornography, erotica, and behavior: More questions than answers. *International Journal of Law and Psychiatry*, 14: 65–83.
McCormick, N. B. 1994. *Sexual salvation: Affirming women's sexual rights and pleasures.* Westport, CT: Praeger.

Source: "What Sexual Scientists Know . . . About Pornography" by Clive M. Davis and Naomi B. McCormick, *What Sexual Scientists Know* 3(1). Reprinted by permission of the Society for the Scientific Study of Sexuality.

OUT OF LINE: THE SEXY FEMMEGIMP POLITICS OF FLAUNTING IT!

LOREE ERICKSON

I'd like to tell you a story, which as it turns out, is in fact at least three related stories.

STORY ONE: A DAY LIKE ANY OTHER DAY

One day, which really could be any day, I left my house in a rather good mood. I had found a lovely patch of sunshine to sit in while I waited for the bus. Soon I was joined by another bus rider who stood about four or five feet away from me. In a minute or two another person passed by with no real difficulty, but found it necessary to grumble at me while passing that I should have "parked [my] car" (more appropriately called a wheelchair) elsewhere as I was blocking the sidewalk. I wasn't blocking anything. The person who was waiting with me was shocked that this other person had made such a rude, ableist comment. I was not surprised. Nor was I surprised by the message behind his words, which was: *You are in the way. You and "your car" are taking up too much space.* I just let it go and waited. I was relieved when the bus that arrived moments later was accessible, and was a bit surprised when the other person waiting stepped to the side to allow me on, rather than rushing/pushing past me—as many people tend to do, making the bus more difficult to navigate.

As I waited for the driver to ready the bus, the person who had been waiting with me looked at the step of the bus and then to my power wheelchair and asked if I needed help. I simply replied that the bus has a ramp. Behind this sort of well-intentioned query is the ever-present assumption that I am in need of help. I get this also when I am sitting somewhere waiting to meet a friend. People just come up to me and ask if I am okay.

As the bus pulled away, I was thinking about how back-to-back these moments were when I heard a loud shrill voice from the back of the bus, "you're *amazing*!" I froze. "The way you just whipped that little cart of yours right in that spot." I ignored it, too tired after three ableist encounters in ten minutes to offer any witty comebacks in response, and too angry to feel like educating anyone.

These three encounters are not isolated or individual experiences. Sadly, they are common and systemic. These three moments only tell us some of what disability means, how it appears, and how it is done. Disabilities, and many associated experiences, are often reduced to essentialized biomedical[1] limitations or malfunctions of certain bodies. Disability can more accurately be described as a process enacted through social relations. While the term disability appears to describe bodies and how they act/move/ inhabit/sense/ think/exist/communicate, the label carries the weight of how these bodies are deemed inferior to other bodies through illusory, arbitrary, and compulsory social and economic standards designed to enable certain ways of being over others. Disability is a complex, intersectional, cultural, and fluid constellation of experiences and constructs.

While this is my story of systemic ableism, it is not—and could not be—every story of systemic ableism. My story is reliant on my particular embodiment and cultural context, which includes, but is not limited to, physical disability, whiteness, with a high level of education. As a thirty-something-year-old, queer femmegimp who lives below the poverty line, I am marked by a unique interplay of identities. Disability never appears in isolation; it is always interrelated with a matrix of other marginalities and privileges. Systemic ableism manifests based on other marginalities (race, other experiences of disability, class, gender, and beyond).

The encounters in the story above tell something about how people make sense of my body: both the anxieties they project onto it and the simultaneous erasures they enact. These are moments among many where the relations of power reveal themselves. For example, the idea that people take up "too much space" underscores the notion that some people are worthy of occupying space and others are not—and is reminiscent of other sociohistorical practices of isolation and segregation. In *Reading and Writing Disability Differently*, Tanya Titchkosky writes, "The meaning of disability is composed of conflicts of inclusion and exclusion as this intersects with our ordinary ways of recognizing people . . . or not." (2007: 6)

STORY TWO: WHY I BECAME A PORN STAR

Disabled people are often imagined as being in the way; unimportant; in need of help; or called "inspirational" for doing ordinary things. Disabled people are imagined as less capable than or not as good as "normal" people (a problematic term as well). All of these attitudes

simultaneously bolster and create policies and practices that propagate the association of disability with undesirability. We see this in state-sponsored practices of funding and mandating institutionalization via incarceration in prisons, psychiatric wards/hospitals, group homes, and nursing homes over community based support; immigration policies using racist, capitalist, and ableist definitions of who counts as desirable citizen; in historic and contemporary eugenic ideals (affecting marginalized bodies and minds of all varieties), "lives not worth living" rhetoric and consequent denial of medical treatment to those deemed unworthy; as well as welfare and disability income programs that keep us impoverished and hungry.

The same structures that impact other areas of our lives, creating an overwhelming climate of devaluation, also regulate our sexual lives.[2] From forced and coerced sterilization to institutional surveillance that limits privacy, there are multiple systems that pathologize, control, and punish the sexual explorations and expression of disabled people. Common paternalistic assumptions hypersexualize and/or portray disabled people as hypervulnerable. This damaging ideology is used to justify segregation. Disabled people—all people—need affirming resources, sex-positive information, and ways to realize their sexual potentials. Anti-sex laws in many U.S. states criminalize certain sexual activities that may be preferred ways for some disabled people to experience pleasure and express desire.

Disabled people are also often subjected to medical and psychological gawking that objectifies, stigmatizes, and pathologizes our experiences of our bodies, including our minds (Blumberg, 1994). Many children who are born with or acquire their disabilities early on are told directly and indirectly to not expect to have a family or anyone ever romantically love them (*Willing and Able: Sex, Love and Disability*, 2003). Disabled people experience the cumulative effects of this extensive system of desexualization every day.

People have begun organizing around this site of oppression as honestly and effectively as we have for other issues of access and justice. There are many particular barriers associated with this type of organizing and it is often deprioritized. In part, this is because there has been a disconnection between sexuality and other needs. It can be argued that one should focus more on needs such as housing, adequate attendant care, employment, transportation, and the like. However, this omission of sexuality ignores how profoundly interconnected all of these aspects of our lives are. Another part of the struggle to include sexuality as an organizing goal requires us to challenge the way sex operates in Western society. We learn to associate shame with sex. We are surrounded by images that convey a very narrow definition of sex and of desirable bodies. We learn we are not supposed to talk about sex. This framing of normative desire is larger than life and does not make room for a whole range of enjoyable experiences and possibilities. When sex is thought of a bountiful playground for the relatively few who can approximate the illusory ideals of the desirable body (skinny, white, able-bodied, rich, etc.), then sex, desire, and pleasure for the rest of us remains relatively invisible. Sex and sexual expression are also often dismissed as frivolous "wants" rather than fundamental aspects of humanity. This is especially true for people with disabilities.

Felt as a personal and private emotion, shame is spun to internalize, naturalize, and individualize many of the oppressions mentioned above as well as others. As Abby Wilkerson argues, "shame is not so much a psychological state of individuals as such (even though it may shape individual subjectivity), but rather a socially based harm which oppressed groups are subject to in particular ways. . . . Shame is deployed as a 'political resourc[e] that some people use to

silence or isolate others'" (Wilkerson, 2002: 45). I would like to expand this idea to include how shame is used not only as a tool of social control to isolate us from each other, but to keep us from accessing those very parts of ourselves, our bodies, our desires, and our experiences (usually wrapped up in our differences from that illusory ideal mentioned earlier) that hold the most potential for change by offering us a different way of being in the world.

Rather than hide away, deny, and ignore those very sites of the deepest shame, we must not only embrace them and learn from them, we need to *flaunt* them.

What better way to flaunt conventions of sexuality than by making porn? Pornography is surrounded by shame. We feel shame for watching, enjoying it, making it, and buying it. The content of porn also often instills shame in us. We can feel badly for not living up to certain standards (both in terms of not fitting the mold of which bodies are seen as beautiful and in terms of not measuring up in regards to sexual prowess and skills). There is porn that demeans our identities and experiences and replicates oppressive power dynamics. Porn is complex, multifaceted—and yes—powerful. Rather than attempt to regulate and control it, which only drives it more underground and into the hands of those with privilege, we need to follow in the work of sex-positive feminists and explore the many benefits that pornography made from such alternative perspectives have to offer (Erickson, 2007).

This all may seem an unlikely beginning to porn stardom. By making queercrip porn I moved out of line and took the "queer" and "wonky" path to place new stories within reach. I took this path to open up new possibilities and imaginings.

My journey began in a progressive sex shop in San Francisco in 2000; I was looking at an issue of *On Our Backs*, a lesbian porn magazine, featuring an article on sex and disability.

I was so excited—until I opened to the article. There was *one* picture of someone in a wheelchair with someone sitting on their lap kissing them. This one picture—the only image combining sex and disability I had found up to that point in my life—was inverted, so the image was obscured and barely recognizable. I wanted to see bodies that looked and moved and felt like mine represented in the exciting, but clearly still problematic, queer sexual culture. I wanted to see something that reflected my desires! I wanted to know that desiring people like me was possible. I resolved then and there to become a porn star.

I began with a series of photos and in the summer of 2006, I made a short film called *want*. *Want* weaves together sexually explicit images with everyday moments and scenes of the ableist world. It works to get people hot *and* poses an insightful, complex, honest, and sexy image of disability and gender transgressive bodies. *Want* was clearly wanted. It won several awards, and continues to screen internationally at numerous film festivals, conferences, and workshops.

I wouldn't be making porn right now if I weren't so pissed off. I would not be making porn if I hadn't struggled for most of my life to be recognized as a sexy and sexual being, or if the world wasn't so fucked up. But making porn is one of the best things I've ever done. On a political level it allowed me to make a movie that would not only offer a moment of recognition of how sexy queercrips could be, but also a way to tell others how I wanted to be seen. Making this video allowed me to take up space and reconceptualize what is sexy.

Personally, it was an amazing experience—and not just because of all the really great sex. The three of us (my co-star, the video artist, and I) created a space of comfort, beauty, respect, and desire. To be able to share that with others is truly remarkable. That day was one of the first times in my life that I truly felt

wanted for exactly who I am. The first time was with my first lover. Unfortunately, experiences like these are rare for many people. Despite the sheer joy of the day—I must have been smiling for days afterward—it took me a while to work up the nerve to watch the video footage. I was afraid that what I might see would allow all those stories I was trying to erase to reemerge and pollute my experience of that day. While there were some bits that were hard to watch, it turned out to be not so bad—and kind of hot. I could see that I was sexy. I still feel that pull of doubt, but I am building up a whole host of stories, salacious stories, to counter the other ones.

STORY THREE: BEING A PORN STAR IS HARD WORK

Before this turns into a simple story of overcoming adversity, I would like to complicate things a bit. "Flaunting it" is not without its difficulties, but it does help to loosen up the knots a bit and free up more space for imagining. Our bodies, identities, desires, and experiences have multiple meanings, and thus, we need multiple stories. We need stories of love, lust, and other stuff. We need the success stories and the stories of pain and frustration. We also need stories about the work that stories being told about us, *without* us, do. These stories still inform our stories. We also need to look at the work that our stories do. Here are some stories that attempt to do that work.

Mainstream porn uses a series of conventions to shape the discourse of what is considered sexy. As I mentioned earlier, we can feel shame for not measuring up to these standards. Despite my politics, while editing, I found myself tempted to recreate those standards. I wanted to edit out the messy stuff, the very things that made this particular porn different. Wouldn't leaving in these sites of shame make it so that we wouldn't have to feel bad that when we don't fall seamlessly into bed with our hair splayed out perfectly on the pillow? I've seen other porns that do this; they show pauses for gloves and lube, the negotiation process: "try moving my leg here," or "I like this," or "touch me here." How powerful would it be to show that when we fell back or slipped, it didn't ruin anything? We just kept going. Then I realized that, within the constellation of power relations, I had somewhat contradictory aims. How far could I go toward a new vision of sexy and still be recognized as sexy? How far could I go away from that standard referent and not be discounted as too different or have my film written off as a fetish film? If, as Foucault contends, we can never get outside of power, then how do we create something new without reinforcing oppressive ideologies? In the end I compromised; I showed bits of both.

Despite all the recognition, there are also times of misrecognition. I find these particular moments quite revealing. They are useful not just in highlighting how difficult it can be to unlearn conceiving of only certain bodies as desirable, but also what possibilities there are for bodies to take. A perfect example of this is how people assume that my co-star and I are lesbians. I only have space to offer partial explanations here. Some of this assumption is explained by normative readings of gender which argue that a certain tone of voice implies a corresponding gender or that a dildo is a dildo, when sometimes what may appear to some as a dildo is someone's cock. Another explanation is that representations of genderqueer boy/femmegimp love are still rare, leaving many to not even realize that these experiences and identities are imaginable. I am also interested in thinking through what work it does to read the film and thus the identities and bodies portrayed in the film as lesbian. I am often either seen as straight or a lesbian, this is more complicated and interesting than I can really take up here, but both readings (straight or lesbian)

erase the desiring of gender-transgressive bodies (both his and mine). This assumption also presumes that desire occurs along heteronormative binary axes of gender and sex and sexuality. In addition, the way that disabled people are often denied agency contributes to a lack of recognition of subversively performed gender expression. Hot boy/femme lovin' action must be made unintelligible, yet again, to keep certain bodies and desires in line.

The first time I screened *want* at a festival, during the Q and A section, one of the other directors commented that "eventually your chair just faded away and you were just a hot girl getting fucked." For this viewer, this was meant as praise: the all too familiar "I was so hot he forgot I was in a wheelchair" compliment. I was not fulfilling the asexual posterchild stereotype that he views as being what disability *is*; and thus, disability and hot sexiness could not exist as simultaneously. So in his viewing he made what he considered to be the less desirable bit disappear. But, my wheelchair will not just fade away; when I am hot I am still disabled. I feel it is important to mention here that I had to win an obnoxious email argument about why my screening had to be held in an accessible theatre to make the exchange even possible. And sorry, no, you can't keep your little bubble of queer sex-positivity or the locations of said activities exactly the same and include me. The alignment of the inaccessible location of the event and his ablest views of hotness are not accidental.

Films like mine are unsettling as well as productive. What is made possible in the moments where we recognize being out of line, being crooked, being variant, as red smoking hot? This is especially true when being *in* line means hiding the parts that *don't* fall in line, so that we never feel fully recognized. As already discussed, shame is a panoptical device used to urge bodies toward assimilation and normalcy. In my life, the many ways not having the privilege of hiding certain sites of shame has been complicated and in some ways hard, but it has also opened up new possibilities and ways of being-in-the-world. In *want* I show myself as a body that is explicitly sexual and also needs intimate daily personal care. Bodies that cannot or do not hide their interdependence, needs, and leakiness as well as others do, have faced a long history of violence, discrimination, and desexualization. Being regarded as a dependent body is certainly one of the major ways that disabled bodies have been cast as undesirables. I wanted to bring these two supposedly disparate parts of me together because I am certain that disability will never be fully desirable until notions of dependency and care are reworked. I also wanted to show how adopting a non-traditional model of meeting my care needs through a collective of people has not only enabled my sexual expression, but opened up a space for so much more. The mutuality of these caring relationships contributes to new ways of being-in-the-world-with-others.

In the article "Loving You Loving Me: Tranny/Crip/Queer Love and Overcoming Shame in Relationships," Samuel Lurie states, "being desired, trusting that, reciprocating that cracks us open" (2002: n.p.). Remaining open and vulnerable is scary because of shame, past hurts (both systemic and interpersonal), and the very real chance of harm, but it is also hard because it means we have to tell new stories. We have to tell stories that contradict the omnipresent chorus that tells us that we are not good enough to be wanted. These stories can be hard to tell because they can sometimes be hard to believe, but they need to be told because in their telling, they make change possible. As Eli Clare argues:

Never are we seen, heard, believed to be the creators of our own desires, our own passions, our own sexual selves. Inside this maze, the lives of queer crips truly disappear. And I say it's time for us to reappear. Time for us to talk sex, be sex, wear sex, relish our sex, both the sex we do have and the sex we want to be having. I say it's time for some queer disability erotica, time for an anthology of crip smut, queer style. Time for us to write, film, perform, read, talk porn. I'm serious. It's time (Clare, 2002: n.p).

I screened *want* at a queer conference in Massachusetts; afterward, a young woman with a disability thanked me for my video and told me she had never had a romantic relationship. She said before that moment she had never even thought it was a possibility for her. So while my story tells many stories, there is most definitely a love story or two in there that are also stories of resistance and systemic change.

NOTES

1. The term biomedical here is used to encompass biological, psychological, intellectual and medical practices and praxis not acting as interrelated systems.

2. This is true of many experiences of marginalization. An easy comparison is made when looking at laws regarding marriage in the prohibition of interracial marriages, same-sex marriages, and so on.

REFERENCES

Blumberg, L. 1994. Public Stripping. In B. Shaw (Ed.). *The Ragged Edge: the Disability Experience from the Pages of the First Fifteen Years of The Disability Rag.* Lousiville, KY: Advocado Press. 77–81.

Clare, E. 2002. *Sex, Celebration, and Justice: A Keynote for QD2002.* Paper presented at the Queer Disability Conference, San Francisco, CA.

Erickson, Loree. 2007. Revealing Femmegimp: Sites of Shame as Sites of Resistance for People with Disabilities. *Atlantis: A Journal of Women's Studies* 32: 1.

Lurie, S. 2002. *Loving You Loving Me: Tranny/Crip/Queer Love and Overcoming Shame in Relationships.* Retrieved July 15, 2004, from www.bentvoices.org

Titchkosky, Tanya. 2007. *Reading and Writing Disability Differently: The Textured Life of Embodiment.* Toronto: University of Toronto Press.

Wilkerson, A. 2002. Disability, Sex Radicalism, and Political Agency. *NWSA Journal, 14*(3): 33–57.

Willing and Able: Sex, Love and Disability, SexTV Documentary, 2003.

THE PORNING OF AMERICA

CARMINE SARRACINO AND KEVIN M. SCOTT

How has porn changed the way we see one another and ourselves? How has it altered our personal relationships and our sexual behavior? How has it changed the social order? How has it shaped our individual identities, and our national identity? To begin to answer these questions, we need to have some understanding of the development of pornography in America.

GROWTH OF THE PORN RUNT

Nathaniel Philbrick's *In The Heart of the Sea: The Tragedy of the Whaleship Essex* (2000) tells about a surprisingly sexually active religious sect in colonial America: the Quakers living off the coast of Massachusetts on Nantucket Island. In this community, where men were at sea hunting whales for long periods of time, sometimes even years, it was an open secret that the women had learned to pleasure themselves. Their journals contain opaque references to their masturbatory activities, including code words for dildos, such as *he's at homes*. In 1979, homeowners remodeling a house in the historic district of Nantucket found a six-inch dildo made of clay.

Still, examples of what might be considered porn from seventeenth- and eighteenth-century America are rare, and consist mainly of cheaply printed pamphlets, called chapbooks, containing smutty jokes, lewd drawings, and cartoons.[1] The chapbooks were produced surreptitiously, bought for a penny or two, and passed around among males.

Unlike the Nantucket Quakers, the Puritans, the largest group of earliest settlers, kept their secret sex lives, if they had them, secret.

And yet, as we will show, the Puritans figure importantly in the construction of the American idea of pornography.

Despite the stereotype of them as austere and sexually repressed, the Puritans were quite sexually active. Recent scholars, for instance, have examined the records of births, deaths, and marriages in various colonies and discovered that quite often the date of a first child's birth was less than nine months from the time of the parents' marriage. This may well have been a result of the practice of bundling, in which prospective couples were allowed to sleep in the same bed, typically in the home of the young woman's parents, provided they were individually restrained in garments or separated by a board. Unsurprisingly, many young people found their way around these obstacles and into each other's embrace. Also, remarriage after the death of a spouse often happened quickly, without the observance of what many today would consider a proper period of mourning. One cannot help wondering whether the later marriage had originated as a liaison of some sort.[2]

But the reason we connect the Puritans with pornography has to do with their religious condemnation of sexuality as sinful and satanic, and the denial (whether hypocritical or not) of their own sensual nature, which they constantly tried to hold in check. . . .

Pornography, as it grows and strides across America over the mid-nineteenth and twentieth centuries, and then dominates American culture at the turn of the new millennium, typically has an essentially Puritan point of view on sensuality and sex. The vocabulary of the typical Internet porn site could be written by one of Nathaniel Hawthorne's *Scarlet Letter* Puritans: Sex is *sinful! Nasty! Naughty!* The only difference in this regard between the Puritans and the pornographers is that from the same starting point they go not merely in different, but in opposite, directions. Porn revels in what Puritanism rejects.

In the world of porn, sex is dirty, the women are sluts—but unlike what happens in the world of Puritanism, in porn all restraints are off. . . . The immensely popular contemporary series of porn films called *Girls Gone Wild* is a Puritan nightmare come horribly, horribly true. . . .

FROM THE CIVIL WAR TO CELEBRITY CULTURE: PORN COMES INTO ITS OWN

In all the changes wrought by the Civil War, from the earthshaking to the trivial, the oddest may be this: the War Between the States marked the beginning of the pornography industry in America.[3]

In the middle of the nineteenth century, for the first time, it became technologically possible to cheaply and quickly produce multiple prints of a photograph. And just when this happened, the Civil War separated hundreds of thousands of men and boys from their wives and sweethearts. For most of them it was their first time away from home. They were lonely and bored in camps. The words *horny* and *hooker* came into widespread usage.[4]

Photographs of all kinds were important to the soldiers. In the pockets of their frock coats they carried ambrotypes of their loved ones. They mailed home small calling cards, called *cartes de visite,* showing themselves photographed in uniform, wielding Colt revolvers

and bowie knives. And deep down in their haversacks, or under the straw mattresses of their winter quarters, they hid stereoscopic photos of seductive women. When viewed through a special holder, two side-by-side photographic images transformed into the three-dimensional form of a girl clad only in see-through gauze, or brazenly lying with her legs spread. The popular *carte de visite* had a prurient incarnation: a prostitute's nude form occupied the space normally reserved for the image of the gallant soldier.

It did not take long for some to spot a market opportunity, however illicit. Young men may have been horny before the war, but they were spread thinly across a nation of farms. Now they were amassed in camps, by the thousands and tens of thousands, away from the prying eyes at home that would certainly have prevented them from trafficking in pornography via the mail. Companies such as G. S. Hoskins and Co. and Richards & Roche in New York City sent out flyers and catalogs to the soldiers, detailing their offerings: photographs of Parisian prostitutes; condoms and dildos; even miniaturized photographs that could be concealed in jewelry such as stickpins, and that, when held close to the eye, revealed a couple engaged in a sex act.

Despite the sea of catalogs that were printed, only a handful survive. From time to time field commanders "cleaned up camp" and built bonfires with the copious material. No doubt countless more after the war fell victim to former soldiers' pangs of conscience or to the fear that a family member might happen upon them. *In The Story the Soldiers Wouldn't Tell: Sex in the Civil War,* Thomas P. Lowry reviews five catalogs, including one that ended up in the National Archives because a Capt. M. G. Tousley wrote to President Lincoln complaining of the obscene catalogs and thought to include a sample. We don't know whether Lincoln ever saw the catalog, but it is droll to imagine him, in those darkly serious days, paging through "mermaids wearing only mist and foam," and "The Temptation of St. Anthony," showing the "naked charms" of the seductresses, and "Storming the Enemy's Breastworks," in which a Northern soldier quite literally assaults the breasts of a Southern belle.

A new industry had been created, and a lot of money was changing hands. So much obscene material was passing through the mail that the Customs Act of 1842, which contained the first federal antiobscenity legislation, was strengthened in 1857. In 1865, in an attempt to check the flood of pornography triggered by the Civil War, a federal statute prohibited the use of the mail to ship obscene books and pictures. After the war, alarmed moralists led by the zealous crusader Anthony Comstock, who was truly obsessed with stamping out smut, passed the Comstock Act of 1873, making it illegal to trade in "obscene literature and articles of immoral use." As Walter Kendrick notes in *The Secret Museum: Pornography in Modern Culture,* Comstock himself, in 1874, reported seizing and destroying in a two-year period 134,000 pounds of "books of improper character" as well as 194,000 pictures and 60,300 "sundries" such as "rubber articles."

Those who today look to legislation, or to a moral crusade, as the best means to limit if not eliminate pornography, would do well to recall Comstock's relentless, but ultimately futile, efforts. Attorney General Edwin Meese and his Commission on Pornography, convened about a hundred years after Comstock's campaign (the commissions final report was issued, and almost immediately ignored, in 1986), could have saved time and energy had it recalled that earlier zealot's failure.

And zealot he certainly was. Comstock, who was not above using false names and even disguises to investigate obscene materials, pursued wrongdoers with the tenacity of a pit bull. He drove one offender, W. Haines, a surgeon

by training who became rich producing more than three hundred obscene books, to suicide.

Before Haines, an Irishman, appeared on the scene, America had only imported from Europe, but not produced, obscene books. Haines changed all that. By 1871 he was selling one hundred thousand such books a year. The night before he killed himself, Haines received a message: "Get out of the way. Comstock is after you. Damn fool won't look at money." In later years Comstock, who would blush at an indelicate photograph, boasted about the suicide, which he regarded as a victory over the forces of evil.

But neither the criminalization of obscenity in 1865 nor Comstock's obsessive crusade killed off pornography. Another war, the Great War, was not far on the horizon, and it would once again concentrate huge numbers of lonely, horny men and with photographic and printing technologies further advanced, offer them an improved, more enticing product.

Porn's birth weight had been low, and the runt was pushed into the dark alleys of American life. But there it thrived. By the end of the twentieth century, it had emerged mature and powerful—son of the European curators' Frankenstein. Widely known if not respected, it had corporate offices in New York, Chicago, and Los Angeles. Its annual earnings at the turn of the twenty-first century were estimated at $10 billion to $14 billion. . . .

From the Civil War until recent times, pornography was marginalized and stigmatized. Lately, though, it has moved from the edges to the mainstream of American culture. But more than that—and far more importantly—it has now become the dominant influence shaping our culture.

Porn spread beyond a particular segment of the population—soldiers at war—and began to enter the mainstream of American culture via early porn films variously known as blue movies, stag movies, and smokers. These were typically anonymous productions, and the participants were often, like outlaws, masked. Not only were they not like us, they were, visually, the opposite of us: we show our faces and hide our genitals; they hid their faces and showed their genitals.

Further, the individuals who appeared in these short movies (fifteen to twenty minutes long) were not "acting" in any sense. The women were usually prostitutes, photographed performing sexual acts with their johns.

But by the turn of the twenty-first century the outlaws had become entertainers, celebrities even, acting in scripted movies. Many of these porn stars were so familiar to so many Americans that a sophisticated and highly regarded exhibit of their portraits, the XXX exhibit, could be shown in a major art gallery. Rather than misfits and deviants, then, they had become, in about a hundred and fifty years, people like you and me. They had become like us and we in turn had come to imitate the way they dressed, talked, and behaved sexually. Our identities merged to such a degree that what had been marginalized and stigmatized became instead the norm.

"SHE'S GONNA LOOK JUST LIKE A PORN STAR!"

Dr. 90210 is a reality television show on the E! network featuring patients undergoing plastic surgery. A recent show was typical of the offerings.

"Heather Ann," an attractive, self-employed beautician in her twenties, was about to receive breast implants. As she was sedated in preparation, she expressed anxiety about undergoing surgery to her mother and boyfriend.

Then the cameras followed Dr. Robert Rey, a Harvard Medical School graduate, as he deftly inserted implants to enlarge Heather Ann's breasts. Camera cutaways showed the patient's mother and boyfriend fidgeting and chatting nervously throughout the procedure. Finished, Dr. Rey cleaned up and went to the waiting room. He assured Heather's mother and boyfriend that everything had gone very well, adding: "She's gonna look just like a porn star!" They beamed back at him.

Even as a joke—a lighthearted comment to break the tension—we cannot imagine anything comparable from a doctor speaking to a patient's family members much before the mid-1990s, by which time porn had been destigmatized for most Americans. Dr. Rey did not know the mother and boyfriend well, but well enough to surmise that neither was, say, a Christian fundamentalist. For the most part, only religious extremists and the elderly (who tend to think of porn in terms of its earlier, stigmatized incarnations) would now take offense at the easygoing comparison of a daughter or girlfriend with a Porn Star.

Porn stars, like celebrities in general, had become not only culturally accepted but even objects of emulation, as exemplified by popular books published in 2004 and 2005, *How to Make Love Like a Porn Star,* by Jenna Jameson, and *How to Have a XXX Sex Life,* by "the Vivid Video stars," eight performers well known in the industry—all functioning now as educators of a public eager to learn their sex secrets. So destigmatized had the term become that girls and young women playfully sported T-shirts emblazoned with the words PORN STAR.

The release of the porn film *Deep Throat* in 1972 would be a pivotal event in the cultural changes that permitted Dr. Rey his icebreaker. But the mainstreaming of porn actually began in those innocent days of the 1950s, with Hugh Hefner and *Playboy* magazine.

Before *Playboy* started publication in 1953, porn was low-rent. As we have seen, the earliest pornography in seventeenth- and eighteenth-century America consisted of ribald tales badly printed and shabbily bound. Through the nineteenth century and most of the twentieth, pornography was typically printed on cheap paper, featuring grainy photographs of prostitutes and their johns. Prostitutes were depicted as desperate women—alcoholics and drug addicts, victimized by brutal pimps. The marginalization of the women and men in the photographs was evident in the illegal, seedy-looking presentations of porn and the underground nature of the porn industry.

The communications theorist Marshall McLuhan famously said, "The medium is the message." On its simplest level this complex understanding may be applied to *Playboy's* presentation of soft-core pornography. The "message" in the medium of the cheap catalogs sold to Civil War soldiers, for instance, was: *Here are deviants, losers, engaged in sinful, taboo, illicit—but tempting! exciting! sexual behavior. Want to take a peek?* (While of course allowing the partaker to remain on the other side of the line separating darkness from light.)

Shame—the shame of poverty, of transgression, the shame of the outsider—was in a sense encoded into the early presentations of pornography. Shame inhibits identification. We don't want to see as "ourselves" those who are socially, morally, and legally stigmatized.

Heffner, however, imitated prestigious magazines such as *The Saturday Evening Post* and *The New Yorker* in the quality of paper and sophisticated formatting and graphics he used, publishing only the best writers and photographers. Most importantly, he featured seminude and nude photographs of "the girl next door"—an All-American girl who, in a typical profile, enjoyed long walks on the beach, playing the guitar, and sharing a candlelit bottle of wine with a special someone.

The principal element in the mainstreaming of porn is that it enters the world that the readers/viewers themselves inhabit or would like to inhabit. It must enter their actual or desired reality in order for them to identify with it. . . . The playmates were, in their own way, as distant from the men and women who read *Playboy* as the catalog hookers were from the farm boy soldiers marching to Gettysburg.

Through *Playboy*, however, pornography (albeit soft core) not only detached itself from the negative associations of earlier porn, but also in fact attached itself to the polar opposite of those negatives. If earlier porn inhibited individuals' readiness to identify with losers, *Playboy*, on the contrary, made them feel like the affluent, smart, informed winners they aspired to be.

Within this elevation of the social context of pornography, in 1972 *Deep Throat* took porn movies in an entirely new direction, much as *Playboy* had done for print porn. *Deep Throat* abandoned the stag movie format, and instead starred an actress, billed as Linda Lovelace, along with a supporting cast. Instead of the twenty-minute length of the traditional 8-mm stag movie, it ran about an hour and a half. And—wonder of wonders—it was actually scripted, with characters and a plot (of sorts), as well as all the sex expected of a blue movie. It was, in other words, in all its basic elements a Hollywood movie, but with the added feature of plenty of graphic sex.

To say that the movie is a cultural milestone (as has become fashionable since the release of the 2005 documentary *Inside Deep Throat*) does not exaggerate its significance. Top celebrities—the likes of Frank Sinatra, Mike Nichols, and Sammy Davis Jr.—not only admitted watching the film, but raved about it. (The documentary features such intellectual luminaries as Gore Vidal, Norman Mailer, and Camille Paglia, with cameos by the political satirist Bill Maher and Hugh Hefner.) From a financial point of view, the movie was an unprecedented blockbuster: shot for around $24 thousand, it has grossed perhaps as much as $600 million in worldwide revenues from an audience estimated at 10 million viewers. In the industry of pornography, nothing like it had ever been seen—or probably even imagined.

What explains *Deep Throat*'s acceptance and cultural assimilation? Although not billed as a porn comedy, the film adopts a goofy comic tone right from the outset. The camera follows Linda Lovelace walking along the docks in Miami, and getting into her car as credits roll and a sound track plays. For a couple of minutes the camera watches over her shoulder from the backseat as she drives (a somewhat eerie shot for those who know that the actress was involved in three serious car wrecks, the third fatal in 2002, when she was fifty-three. In fact, camera angles were carefully planned in *Deep Throat* to avoid showing a scar on her abdomen that had resulted from an earlier accident.)

When Linda arrives home, she finds her mother in the living room, legs spread over a chair, enjoying cunnilingus. Well, sort of enjoying: in addition to its silliness, a tone of ennui pervades the film. Her mother, for instance, languidly lights a cigarette, tilts up the head of her busy partner, and asks, "Mind if I smoke while you're eating?" The sound track plays "Taking a Break from the Mundane."

The structure of the film is simple, consisting of typical 8-mm sex loops, without dialogue but with musical accompaniment, interspersed with a plot based on a nutty premise: Linda learns from a Dr. Young, a psychiatrist, that the reason she cannot achieve orgasm is that her clitoris is in her throat. Concluding her gynecological examination, he announces, "No wonder you hear no bells, you have no tinkler!" During the exam, the sound track consists of a dirty version of Mickey and Sylvia's well-known "Love Is Strange."

One more example of the slapstick humor that characterizes the film: Dr. Young consoles Linda, "Having a clitoris deep down in the bottom of your throat is better than having no clitoris at all." "That's easy for you to say," she objects. "Suppose your balls were in your ear?" He is momentarily flummoxed, until a lightbulb pops on over his head: "Well, then I could hear myself coming!"

Humor, even lame humor, is disarming. From a propagandistic point of view, the makers of *Deep Throat* had stumbled onto a mass-market presentation of porn that would assist its acceptance, its normalization.

First, the opening credits announced, "Introducing Linda Lovelace As Herself." We had an actress, then, rather than the prostitute of a typical 8-mm stag movie, but she was "playing herself"—an ordinary, attractive young woman—someone we might know. Once the movie begins, the humor takes over and in effect tells us to lighten up, not to take it seriously. It's just entertainment, dizzy and raunchy, like some weird, *X-rated I Love Lucy*.

It worked. The star, Linda Lovelace, appeared in an extensive photo layout by Richard Fegley in *Playboy* in April 1973, and the next month on the cover of *Esquire* magazine dressed in a polka-dot dress modestly buttoned to the white wing collar and wearing white gloves—a send-up of the girl next door, but the girl next door nevertheless.

Hidden beneath the appearance of an ordinary young woman starring in a new kind of porn film, however, lay an altogether different reality—one representative, in fact, of "old porn." Linda Susan Boreman, "Linda Lovelace," was a former prostitute who had appeared in such 8-mm stag movies as *Dogarama* (also known as *Dog Fucker*) in 1969, and *Piss Orgy* in 1971. Her husband/manager, Chuck Traynor, had forced her—often at gunpoint, she later claimed—to perform in the stag movies and in *Deep Throat*. Add to this submerged reality the heavy use of hard drugs by Linda, her husband, and others in the movie, along with mob involvement (mainly financial, but some theaters were reportedly strong-armed into featuring *Deep Throat*), and the film seems quite far afield indeed from mainstream American culture's notions of acceptability.

Still, the crucial step had been taken: Linda Lovelace presented herself in some important ways as "one of us." She was, after all, the star of a kind of movie we recognize as legitimate: one that plays in theaters, not in the back rooms of smoky men's clubs, features attractive actors in a narrative that defused its illicit subject matter with a comic outlandishness, had a sound track and rolled credits, and was viewed and praised by well-known and respected figures. As film critic Richard Corliss pointed out in a March 29, 2005, *Time* online article, "That Old Feeling: When Porno Was Chic," even comics such as Johnny Carson and Bob Hope, cultural icons in 1972, made jokes about *Deep Throat,* conferring a kind of blessing on the film, tacitly legitimizing it and its place in the world.

The film was quickly followed by another in 1972, *Behind the Green Door.* In it, Marilyn Chambers was in fact billed as "the All-American Girl." Chambers (who would in 1975 marry Chuck Traynor, divorced from Linda Lovelace) was indeed so all-American looking that just as *Behind the Green Door* was released, Ivory Snow soap flakes put out a newly designed box featuring a photo of a mother holding her baby. The mother was none other than Marilyn Ann Briggs, otherwise known as Marilyn Chambers, the suddenly famous porn star. Procter and Gamble abashedly withdrew the box design.

Like *Deep Throat, Behind the Green Door* imitated the Hollywood movie and contained a hip sound track, an important element in getting the audience to identify with the characters in the film. Again, to paraphrase McLuhan, an audience does not so much listen to a sound track as put it on, bathe in it. A sound track of hits feels familiar and comfortable, making everything associated with it more familiar and comfortable.

These two movies from 1972 launched the porn movie industry as we know it today, catapulting its stars to celebrity status and playing to larger and larger audiences of men and women, especially through the addition of video (and later DVD) rentals and sales.

Beginning in the early 1970s, then, it became increasingly easy to acquire porn without buying it under the counter or from a shady character on a street corner. One could simply go to the neighborhood theater or, beginning in the 1980s, to a hotel or motel with in-room pay-per-view. In the 1990s, of course, porn would come right to your home through cable offerings such as Vivid, the Spice Channel, and the Playboy Channel. In these ways, the acquisition of porn has become quick and easy, a critical step in its destigmatization.

But the story of the mainstreaming of pornography, with its shaping influence on American life and culture, is more complex and subtle than simply the evolution of the pornographic movie industry. If *Deep Throat* took porn films in a totally new direction by imitating Hollywood, and by drawing on girl-next-door and all-American stereotypes, soon enough Hollywood and ordinary people would in turn begin imitating porn.

In the same year as *Deep Throat* and *Behind the Green Door,* Marlon Brando starred in Bernardo Bertolucci's *Last Tango in Paris,* which transgressed the limits of traditional Hollywood treatments of sex, even containing an infamous "butter scene" of anal penetration. But the film was controversial, and not in any sense mainstream. It was originally unrated, then later rated NC-17.

Fast-forward to the mid-1990s, however, and a Hollywood movie could now deal with explicit sex, including such taboos as anal sex. The celebrated film *Leaving Las Vegas* (1995), for instance, contained these lines delivered by the prostitute Sera (played by Elisabeth Shue) to Ben Sanderson (Nicholas Cage): "So for five hundred bucks you can do pretty much whatever you want. You can fuck my ass. You can come on my face—whatever you wanna do. Just keep it outta my hair, I just washed it."

It is impossible to imagine those lines ever finding their way into a Hollywood movie without the decades of porn films preceding it. Later in the movie, Sera is anally gang-raped, and we see her nude in the shower (an overhead shot) with blood washing down her legs and into the drain. The film was regarded as somewhat risqué, but not seriously controversial. It was rated R. In fact, Elisabeth Shue was nominated that year for an Academy Award for Best Actress for her role as Sera, and Nicholas Cage won the Oscar for Best Actor.

If Hollywood had been transformed by porn (a character like Sera could not have existed in a movie of the 1950s, 1960s, or even the 1970s), so had the audience. Only an audience in a sense made ready by the kind of porn films that *Deep Throat* pioneered would accept such language and images in a Hollywood movie.

SOFTENING THE CONTOURS

Two films from the 1970s and early 1980s— *Pretty Baby* (1978) and *Blame It on Rio* (1984)— are instructive in showing the major role that Hollywood played in normalizing pornography, thereby increasing its power to influence and eventually dominate American culture. . . .

In much the same way that Hugh Hefner glamorized soft-core pornography through the sophistication of *Playboy* as a physical artifact, [in *Pretty Baby*] Louis Malle took on a subject that had only been dealt with in the most taboo kinds of hard-core pornography— child pornography and child prostitution—and made his treatment not only acceptable but admirable. . . .

Although the film is indeed about a misfit photographer, . . . it nevertheless also plays to the prurience of the audience, which is viewing what would in other less-normalized contexts be regarded (and perhaps even prosecuted) as child pornography. But the film distances itself from child pornography by first of all being

about child prostitution, and then further distances itself because it clearly does not in any sense endorse prostitution, and in fact presents us with the pathos of a prostitute who is sexy, savvy, and also enjoys playing with her very first doll. . . .

So *Pretty Baby*, in 1978, after the era of *Deep Throat* and other Hollywood-like porn movies, could present the topic of child-as-sex-object in candid and graphic ways that, by contrast, Stanley Kubrick's *Lolita* could not dare in 1962. In Kubrick's movie, a nude scene of Sue Lyon as Lolita was so unthinkable it was never even proposed by Vladimir Nabokov, who wrote the screenplay, or Stanley Kubrick, who directed. *Lolita* and Humbert Humbert (James Mason) were not allowed even to kiss, let alone display any kind of sexuality—as later they would in the 1997 remake of *Lolita* starring Jeremy Irons and Dominique Swain.

Two years after [starring in] *Pretty Baby*, Brooke Shields was back on the screen in *The Blue Lagoon*, again nude, now as an early teen (both fictionally and in fact). Just as *Deep Throat* opened a door for other porn movies to crowd through, so *Pretty Baby* opened a farther door for the unabashed portrayal of children as sex objects, frequently partnered with adults. . . .

In 1980 Brooke Shields moved offscreen to star in ads for Calvin Klein jeans. The most famous of these showed Shields slightly bent over (presumably having just pulled on a pair of jeans) beginning to button her enticingly open blouse, with the tag line: "Nothing comes between me and my Calvins." She was now fifteen years old and a familiar sex symbol in America and overseas as well. A teenager functioning as a sex symbol had by now become, culturally speaking, accepted as normal— thanks in large part to the barrier-breaking influence of pornography (such as *Deep Throat*) on Hollywood mainstream movies.

The contours of the taboo had been sufficiently softened that, by the 1980s, children as sex objects had become culturally familiar in movies, on television, and in advertisements—with all sorts of off-shoots. For instance, beauty pageants for very little girls—five or six, and even younger—swelled into a multimillion-dollar industry of local, regional, and national competitions involving highly paid consultants and coaches, clothing designers, makeup specialists, and so on. Arguably, the winner of these pageants is the child who most successfully combines adult sexuality with childlike innocence. (The most well known of such child beauty queens, of course, is Jon Benét Ramsey, who was murdered in 1996.)

Calvin Klein's use of children as sex objects continued in the 1990s with an ad campaign featuring children in highly sexualized situations. When rumors began circulating that he was being investigated on charges of the sexual exploitation of children, he began pulling the ads in August 1995. Sexualized children, however, continued to appear in ads, movies, and on television. Consider, for instance, the Olsen twins.

Mary-Kate and Ashley Olsen have become a brand name. After the twins turned eighteen, in June 2004, they took over control of their corporation, Dualstar Entertainment Group, a company that brings in over a billion dollars a year and has made each of the twins worth a reported $137 million. The twins first gained fame as the character Michelle Tanner on the sitcom *Full House,* starting their acting careers at less than a year old. The show ran for eight years, so the country watched them grow up nearly from their birth. . . . More than any other single popular-culture figure, the twins, for over a decade, determined what tweeners could aspire to. And while Dualstar has always marketed the twins as wholesome American girls, their popularity has grown, in significant part, due to the steady porning of Mary-Kate and Ashley. Whether the marketing of the twins intentionally adopted the imagery of

porn or whether the online porn community merely appropriated the twins, they became the fuel for an online porn engine that combined pedophilia and kiddie porn with twin and sister porn. . . .

The imagery of the Olsens began to change as they entered puberty. With increasing frequency, they were photographed in clothing that was tight and revealing but still maintained, if only marginally, their persona as sweet and wholesome girls. As they moved through their teen years, these photographs steadily grew more sensual, culminating in photo shoots for *Allure* and *Rolling Stone* in the spring of 2004, before their eighteenth birthdays.

The increasing sexuality of the twins and their marketing during their teen years paralleled their increased presence online. "Olsen twins" became a phrase that, if Googled, led to cloaked porn sites. The porn community was so aware of the sexual allure of the twins that it used their names as a "Google-beater," including the words "Olsen twins" on their sites, which otherwise had no Olsen content, simply to increase hits—a strategy that assumes that a high percentage of people looking for Olsen twin information would be happy to find themselves landing on a porn site. Other porn sites, many of them dedicated to celebrity shots, have entry sites that simply list the names of the most famous female celebrities intermixed with keywords like "boobs naked nude sex hot" in order to capture web searches. "Olsen twins" is always on the list.

"Twin tracker" websites were sprinkled throughout the Internet in the years leading up to the twins' eighteenth birthdays, with reverse docks counting down to the very minute when they would be "legal." The twins were such a porn commodity that they became the subject of a porn community debate online—is it okay to Photoshop the heads of underage women onto the bodies of performing porn stars, as was common? The community was split on the issue, but the simple fact of the discussion demonstrates the unspoken assumption that the Olsen twins were fit subjects of sexual interest.

Though the porn community was undeniably fascinated with the Olsen twins, it is not clear whether the twins, or their management company, were colluding in their online porn popularity in order to heighten their mainstream popularity or profitability. Yet it is hard to imagine that their agent or manager could have been unaware of the uses to which the online porn community was putting the twins' images. *Playboy*'s "Twins and Sisters" site includes women in trademark Olsen poses, though the Olsens appear clothed. In shot after shot, the public was presented with images of the twins leaning in toward each other, faces and mouths close, as if about to kiss. Caught by paparazzi on red carpets, the twins would snap into their standard pose, Mary-Kate's arm around Ashley's hip, Ashley's arm around Mary-Kate's neck (or vice versa). It is a pose that forces their torsos tantalizingly close, and the ease with which they assumed their positions showed how well coached and practiced they were.

The porning of the Olsen twins reached its height in the *Allure* and *Rolling Stone* articles, which essentially announced their legal status—a "Hey, we'll be legitimate sex objects next month!" message. The *Rolling Stone* article, which acknowledged the latent pedophilia of their marketing campaign by headlining them as "America's Favorite Fantasy," included images of the twins draped over each other in clearly erotic poses. The cover showed them leaning toward each other, their hands pulling at clothing and touching in a way clearly evocative of twin porn.

The signature photo for the *Allure* article showed the twins—still underage—in an unabashed sexual embrace, breasts together, mouths open in porn-pose ecstasy, their hands sliding into each other's clothing. The article, which emphasized their essential youth and innocence, also discussed whether they would ever do nude scenes ("Probably not"), the suggestiveness of the photo shoot ("If everybody knew we were straddling each other . . . oy vey . . . All those dirty old men out there . . ."), and an anecdote about Mary-Kate using her finger to "slowly, firmly" remove some excess lip gloss from Ashley's lip and "slowly smear[ing] it on her own, slightly open mouth."

On one level, certainly, the twins consented to the articles in order to ease their movement into more mature careers, but the stories were also explicit acknowledgments of the porned sexualization of children. One *Rolling Stone* photo combined both messages, their youth and their sexuality, by putting them in the clothing of little girls dressing up, but with highly sexualized makeup and hairstyles, and with Ashley pulling a pearl necklace through her puckered lips—the kind of imagery dirty old men would find fascinating.

Not only are children, such as the Olsen twins, sexualized, they are also targeted as consumers of sexually charged products. *Playboy*, for example, has marketed a *Playboy* skateboard, a *Playboy* snowboard, and a pink Bunny tracksuit. The target market for such products is supposed to be eighteen- to twenty-five-year-olds, but reportedly Playmate Pink glitter cream and Bunny Pink lipstick are big hits with preteen girls.

Sexually revealing clothing, sometimes called the stripper look or slutwear, is specifically target-marketed to children as well as adults. In 2002 Abercrombie & Fitch, for example, began selling thongs in its stores catering to children, with the words EYE CANDY and WINK WINK printed on them. Thongs are also available with Simpsons and Muppets characters. . . .

In June 2005 a spokesperson for Sony Computer Entertainment announced that it "could not stop" software makers from producing and marketing pornographic discs for the

PlayStation Portable game console, most of whose users are children. Almost 3 million of these handheld consoles, which Sony introduced in March 2005, had been delivered to Japan and the United States by June of that year. Two pornographic filmmakers had discs on the market by July, and several more followed shortly after.

At the same time, July 2005, the video game industry changed the rating of the very popular Grand Theft Auto: San Andreas, from M for mature to AO, adults only. After initial denials, Take-Two Interactive Software, makers of the game, which plays not only on PCs but also on Xbox and PlayStation 2 consoles, acknowledged that scenes of pornographic sex had indeed been programmed into the game, and could be unlocked through an Internet download, called a mod (short for *modification*) in the gaming community.

By the 1980s, not only had children become thoroughly sexualized in movies, advertisements, and marketing, but something more general had begun to occur: the sexualization of just about everyone, regardless of age or status in society.

In other words, if we ask how porn has shaped us, how it has affected how we see ourselves and one another, one answer is that we are coming to see ourselves and one another in sexual terms first and foremost, regardless of age, and regardless as well of marital, professional, or social status. Like Heather Ann with her sexier breasts—*Everyone a porn star!* . . .

. . . . In the real world of America in the early years of the twenty-first century, everyone—from professional athletes to teachers to the president of the United States—is seen in sexual terms. A national online site allowing students to rate college professors, for instance, includes the possibility of adding a special symbol, a chili pepper, to the male or female professor's rating if he or she is "hot." And for those who are hot, student comments often

focus more on the professor's allure and on sexual fantasies than on his or her attributes as a teacher.

The most compelling example of such universal porning occurred during the presidency of Bill Clinton. Details of the president's sex life, which were publicly revealed during his impeachment, included an initial encounter with an intern that could have come right out of a porn script. An attractive young woman snaps the waistband of her thong at the president of the United States. Like someone playing "Mister President" in a porn film, the real-life president eagerly responds to this come-on by engaging in oral sex with the young intern in the Oval Office. In one session, she masturbates with a cigar for his titillation. In another—well, we all saw the movie.

A number of polls indicated a pattern in the responses of Americans. Young people in high school and college (who view porn as entertainment and casual sexual encounters as a norm) were mainly amused by it all. Older Americans, especially those over fifty, who still attached stigma to porn, were shocked.

By 2008, however, it had become difficult to imagine anyone being truly shocked by real-life examples of "right out of a porn movie" sex. Let's consider just the most famous of recent scandals involving older male politicians and younger—sometimes very much younger—females and males:

- In 1974 Representative Wilbur Mills (D-Ark.) was found to be having an affair with a young stripper named Fanne Foxe, aka "the Argentine Firecracker," who jumped into the Tidal Basin in Washington, D.C., when police pulled over their car.
- In 1983 the House Ethics Committee censured Representatives Dan Crane (R-Ill.) and Gerry Studds (D-Mass.) for having had sexual relationships with seventeen-year-old pages, Crane with a female, Studds with a male.

- In 1988 former senator Gary Hart's relationship with actress/model Donna Rice derailed his presidential bid.
- In 1989 Stephen Gobie, the former gay lover of Barney Frank (D-Mass.), admitted having operated a male prostitution ring out of the congressman's apartment.
- In 2001 the U.S. senator Garry Condit (D-Calif) admitted to an affair with missing and presumed dead Chandra Levy, a young woman in her twenties, ending his political career—because of his casual response to her disappearance rather than the affair.
- In 2006 Representative Mark Foley (R-Fla.) resigned from Congress when it was revealed that he had been sending "dirty e-mails" to teenage House pages.
- In 2007 Senator Larry Craig (R-Idaho) pled guilty to disorderly conduct after being caught in a police sting operation investigating lewd acts in a Minneapolis airport men's public restroom. Craig had been widely considered a "family values" conservative.

Politics was only one source of scandals involving sex between older, more powerful adults and young partners. Religion and education were two other similarly tainted institutions.

- In 1987 Jim Bakker, a televangelist reportedly bringing in a million dollars a week in donations from followers, confessed to a sexual liaison with a young woman, Jessica Hahn (who later appeared nude in *Playboy*). That scandal was followed by a spate of similar stories involving celebrity ministers caught in sexual transgressions, the most famous of which, in the following year, 1988, was Jimmy Swaggart, who wept his confession to a national audience.
- Beginning in 2002 and extending through the next few years, reports proliferated of hundreds of Catholic priests who had

molested and raped young boys and girls. Bishops who simply moved the offending priests from one diocese to another as the crimes were brought to their attention had in effect, it turned out, protected serial rapists.
- In 1996 a thirty-six-year-old schoolteacher, Mary Kay Letourneau, gained notoriety when her sexual relationship with one of her sixth-grade students, a thirteen-year-old boy, became known. Her case was soon followed by innumerable others involving male and female high school and middle school teachers having sex (and sometimes, like Letourneau, having children) with their teenage and even preteen students.

We could go on. To see just how jaded we have become by such events, try telling someone a made-up story about having just seen a news report in which a respected individual (choose anyone in the public eye) was reported having sex with someone unlikely (make it as outlandish as you want). There may be some surprise, some heads may shake in disgust, but it's a good bet that people will accept the story as true.

Our readiness to believe almost any example of sexual pairing, however outrageous, is fueled by the fact that we are exposed not only to sensational anecdotes (which though significant are usually atypical) but also to instances of sex being infused into mainstream culture everywhere we look. Let us catalog some examples of this cultural porning, just to sample the field:

- World Wrestling Federation mixed tag team matches, which receive heavy television coverage, can only be described as soft-core porn, featuring unsubtle double entendres in the pre-match challenges and taunts ("I'm gonna slam her ass!"), and scantily clad men and women in clearly sexual positions (in their male-female and female-female pairings) during the match.

- Female athletes have become increasingly sexualized, and even marketed in soft-core formats for their sexuality rather than their athletic prowess. Anna Kournikova, for example, never a top singles professional tennis player, nevertheless became a media darling, receiving more attention than better players simply because of her sex appeal and her willingness to flaunt it. In a way, she set the pattern (seminude/nude, highly suggestive calendars and posters, advertisements, appearances in movies) that other female athletes, both professional and amateur, now must follow.
- High school cheerleaders have so dramatically sexualized their routines, often bumping and grinding like strippers, that in one recent instance, a state congressman in Texas, Representative Al Edwards, proposed legislation that would put an end to "sexually suggestive" performances at high school athletic events and other extracurricular competitions.
- Dirty dancing has gotten even dirtier. At the turn of the nineteenth century, waltz partners were thought by some alarmed moralists to be mimicking sexual intercourse. Imagine what they would make of contemporary "grinding" and "freaking," popular forms of dancing in which the female bends over and presses her buttocks against the pumping groin of her partner.
- Nude calendars have become commonplace. Beginning on a large scale in the 1990s, groups of all sorts, usually connected with charities or not-for-profit organizations, began publishing such calendars as a fundraising ploy. One of the most well-known featured the Australian women's soccer team, the Matildas, in 1999. A dedicated website lists hundreds of nude calendars for sale, consisting of photos of amateur, volunteer models ranging in age from early twenties to senior citizens, raising money

for athletic teams, theatrical companies, volunteer fire fighters, and disease research. These calendars range from depictions of naked grannies holding kittens and puppies (raising money for animal shelters) to buff male rugby players, clearly conveying the message: *Everyone a porn star!*

And the list goes on. Porn chat rooms, for example, abound on the Internet. Such spaces invite ordinary people to participate in the creation of pornography, mainly in the form of "cybering," having imagined sex, in real time, with a partner or partners in the room. The participants, who often admit that they are simultaneously masturbating, describe in detail what they are "doing" with the other (or others), how they are responding, and so on. These "performances," to describe them that way, are sometimes enhanced with webcams for one or both (or all) participants to view. Further enhanced with voice, the results can be quite complex and sophisticated, even indistinguishable from the offerings of professional porn websites.

Chatropolis, a site with both free and pay options, advertises itself as one of the largest and most active chat sites on the Web, offering about 230 chat rooms, most with a maximum capacity of twenty-five people. Not all rooms are full all the time, but if, let's say, on average, half the number of possible chatters are online, that means about three thousand are in Chatropolis at any given moment. Chatters come and go throughout the day and night, however, sometimes merely changing rooms within the site, but also logging in fresh, so the total number of chatters on this one site alone in the course of a day is huge, certainly in the thousands, perhaps even the tens of thousands.

One Chatropolis room is called "Legal Today." Another, at the other end of the age spectrum, is "Perverted Old Men." Still another links the extremes of age, "Across the Generations."

Some rooms cater to phone sex, such as "Call Me." Others to sexual preferences, such as "Analopolis."

Thousands of such chat sites (free and pay, large and small) are available on the Internet. For years Yahoo, for instance, offered hundreds of rooms with cam and voice options, many exclusively pornographic—"PA Girls for Sex," for example, and many others, such as user rooms (rooms created by users) focusing on specific sex acts and fetishes, particular sexual orientations, such as bi and lesbian, and so on.[5] Even an unscientific, thumbnail approximation, then, would conservatively find millions of Americans of all ages in such chat rooms— all in this together—every day. . . .

THE AMATEURS TAKE OVER

If it is true, as we have suggested, that not only has porn become mainstream but that the mainstream has become porned, it would follow that porn produced by professionals would merge with a new kind of porn created by secretaries, bakers, nurses, auto mechanics, housewives, schoolteachers—ordinary people from the mainstream of American society who, à la Timothy Greenfield-Sanders, have come to see porn stars like themselves, and who therefore see themselves as porn stars. And indeed this is exactly what we do find.

Throughout the 1980s and 1990s, "amateur" porn movies were produced in great quantity, created by and large by professionals who employed unknown porn actors billed as amateur performers. Since the turn of the millennium, however, as digital video cameras and cell phones with video capability have enabled people to record their own sexual activities and post the results via their computer on a dedicated website, there has been a skyrocketing increase in true amateur porn. The number of such websites (such as Private Porn Movies, YourAmateurPorn, and Best Home Sex) is growing exponentially. Even websites that are not specifically for amateur porn become such sites de facto, because some members use their webcams on these sites to broadcast themselves masturbating or having partnered sex.

It may well be the case that true amateur porn is the future of porn in America. And to say this is perhaps to announce the end of porn. Because just as it is true that if everything in the world were blue there would be no word *blue,* when blue movies are everywhere, there are no more blue movies.

The final result of the porning of America, then, may well be the end of the recognition of porn as something separate from the mainstream. Pornography will have shrunk to porn and porn further shrunk away altogether, disappearing because it can no longer be distinguished from what we see everywhere around us on the Internet (on innumerable amateur sites, in chat rooms, on MySpace, Craigslist, Stickam, and so on), on cable television, in movies, magazines, advertisements, and music videos. Porn will have become our cultural wallpaper.

NOTES

1. The following books, from which we draw in this chapter, provide a detailed examination of the early history of pornography in the West: Walter Kendrick's *The Secret Museum: Pornography in Modern Culture* (New York: Viking, 1987); Isabel Tang's *Pornography: The Secret History of Civilization* (London: Channel 4 Books, 1999); and Julie Peakman's *Mighty Lewd Books: The Development of Pornography in Eighteenth-Century England* (Houndmills, Basingstoke, U.K., and New York: Palgrave Macmillan, 2003).

2. Certainly these facts have a social and historical underpinning. A Puritan couple typically observed a long betrothal, and so were in effect "married" before the formal ceremony. And life in the colonies was so tenuous, and death rates so high, that survival itself required speedy remarriage to maintain the necessary production rate of offspring. Our point here is simply that the Puritans had undeniably active sex lives.

3. The best study of prostitution and pornography in the Civil War, from which we have drawn some examples of period pornography, is Thomas P. Lowry's *The Story the*

Soldiers Wouldn't Tell: Sex in the Civil War (Mechanicsburg, Pa.: Stackpole Books, 1994). Lowry, an MD, also has some chilling descriptions of venereal diseases and their often ghastly treatments.

4. The word *hooker* has been traced to General Joseph "Fighting Joe" Hooker, who permitted prostitutes to encamp near the soldiers on the theory that it was better for soldiers to deal with boredom and release pent-up energy with prostitutes than to get drunk, fight, and gamble. Another theory on the origin of the term is that prostitutes used to fall into step with prospective clients and "hook" an arm through the arm of the male.

5. In the summer of 2005, Yahoo shut down the user rooms because of allegations that the sites were being used for child pornography. Initially, they were unclear about whether such rooms might be reopened, with some corrective modifications, but as of this writing they have not reappeared.

SEXUALITY IN A VIRTUAL WORLD

CARY GABRIEL COSTELLO

Sexual activity is one of the great pleasures of the flesh. But if sex is understood as an embodied, physical pleasure, why would so many people engage in sexual activities in a virtual world, where skin cannot touch skin? It is clear to me as a sociologist who has been conducting research in the virtual world of Second Life™ for over four years that sexuality is an important component of the virtual lives of many of my 94 interviewees—although they are aware that this doesn't make sense to some people. In the words of my interviewee Saige[1]:

I learned pretty quickly not to tell my friends who don't understand Second Life about my sex life here. They think the idea is kinky, but at the same time kind of boring and pathetic. It's "fake" to them, and tacky, like playing with a blow-up sex doll. They don't have a clue how real it is. *Rawrrr!* I've had some verrry hot sex here.

In this reading I will explore why virtual sexuality is found to be so compelling and so real by many of my interviewees.

First, a bit about Second Life. The most populous of the assortment of virtual worlds, Second Life has an official total population of about 12 million; of these, well over a million log in in a given month (Linden Lab, 2011). Basic accounts are free, so Second Life is accessible to anyone with a computer with good graphics capabilities.[2] The population of Second Life differs from the popular conception of a "gamer" demographic: the average resident is 33 years old in real life, and over 42 percent are female (KZERO Research, 2007).

Virtual worlds like Second Life are not "video games" but simply online 3D settings for social interaction in avatar form. With no goals or points to win, the motivation for becoming a "resident" of Second Life is mainly social. People spend time with friends, go shopping for clothes, visit dance clubs, play games, attend classes, create art and visit exhibits, etc.—just as in real life. Sophisticated users experience interactions in Second Life as fully real in the social sense. Residents follow rules of social interaction familiar from real life: act with courtesy, maintain an appropriate social distance when standing or sitting with other avatars, don't lie to others or cheat them (Boellstorff, 2008, Meadows, 2008). The social world bustles, and supports a substantial economy in virtual clothing, homes, toys, artwork, etc.: approximately ten million (real) U.S. dollars are spent per month by Second Life residents on virtual goods and services (Linden Lab, 2011). Since one doesn't need to eat, sleep, work, or attend to other pragmatic needs in Second Life, social life is particularly intense. Emotional bonds and sexual interactions emerge as natural aspects of this sociality.

People try out Second Life for a wide variety of reasons. Some are invited "inworld" by friends; some are gamers or the technologically facile and are curious about virtual worlds in general; some have read about a specific art circle or support group; some have learned of academic or business projects that interest them. But those who stay engaged and become what I call "sophisticated users" (those who have spent at least an average of an hour a day inworld for three months) usually do so because they become socially engaged. Some are just highly social people. "There's this stereotype of people who use Second Life as pimply-faced losers living in their parents' basements. . . . It's totally off-base. My friends and I have busy, successful real lives—we just enjoy being together in this crazy place," said Edison. But a substantial segment of experienced Second Life residents find their socializing in real life constrained. These individuals often experience social life in Second Life as very rewarding, and invest in it deeply.

One demographic that is well-represented in Second Life is people with disabilities. My interviewee Mitsuko had a seizure condition that made seeing people difficult, since she couldn't drive and lived in a rural area. "Without Second Life, I could call or email people, but I'd only really spend time together with friends every week or two. With Second Life, I get to be with friends all the time, and go out and do whatever together." Ramses had a mobility impairment, and while he got around fine in his wheelchair, he found dating problematic. "Girls here see the real me. Strong, real. Out there [in real life] they see me as weak. I don't want pity dates." Sometimes Ramses used a wheelchair in Second Life, to reflect his real life disability, but other times he said, "I don't, so people see me instead of the chair." He could come out to them as mobility impaired in real life once they had already gotten to know him.

Interviewees' barriers to a fully satisfying social life outside Second Life were often themselves social in nature. Some had actual social disabilities—Second Life has a substantial population of people with social anxiety and autism spectrum disorders who, while significantly limited in their interactions in real life, are much less limited in Second Life. "Sometimes a big crowd will bother me here, but most times I'm fine," said Logan. "Lots of my friends have no idea that I haven't been able to go to a real life club like this for ten years. Urk—my heart would be pounding, I'd panic." But for most of my interviewees with social limitations, the problems were not disabilties as much as issues of odd working hours, personality style,

social isolation, or marginalization. Epona snorted, "So I'm a pagan lesbian living in the Bible Belt and taking care of her mom. Think I go out on a lot of dates?" Pels explained:

Employment and a natural inclination towards solitude makes me less than the epitome of a swinging bachelor most of the time. Between relationships the sex life can be pretty empty and I often have generous downtime between them, due in part to needing time to get over someone or just generally wanting time alone. Second Life is a cushion of affection and good intimate times when I may not want that much social contact in real life.

Critics of Internet socializing often claim that spending a substantial amount of time online inappropriately displaces more valuable real life socializing (e.g., McPherson et al., 2006). But for my interviewees, virtual world social lives complemented or filled a gap in their non-virtual social lives, adding support and spark to their lives.

As is clear from my interviewee quotes, their virtual-world social lives often included romantic and erotic components. For many, dating in Second Life had come as a surprise. Some people enter Second Life specifically hoping to find a romantic partner, but that is not the norm. The majority of my 94 interviewees had had relationships in Second Life, not because they had entered the virtual world in search of one, but as a natural outgrowth of developing an intensive virtual social life.

You may wonder how a person goes about having sex in a virtual world. The Second Life avatar has a set of stock abilities—walking, sitting, and flying. To make one's avatar engage in other activities, one can purchase animations, or employ those others have made available on their property. There is a booming market in animations, made by Second Life residents using pose-modelling software or motion capture technology, allowing people in Second Life to do most anything: arm-wrestle, fly a kite, cook, ride piggyback, shoot with bow and arrows, cuddle, dance, kiss . . . and engage in a wide variety of sexual activities. When a couple (or, if interested, more) wish to have sex, they typically make use of an item that has been preloaded with an assortment of animations. Most popular are beds, prosaically enough, but sexual animations are also available in hot tubs, crystal grottoes, and many other exotic settings (the making of which is a multimillion dollar business (see *Eros, LLC vs. Linden Research*, 2008)). The partners mouseclick on the bed or other setting, and each clicks to agree to allow the object to animate their avatars. They may then select from the available animations, typically starting with kissing and caressing, then moving to their choice of oral, manual, and penetrative sex options, and finishing with postcoital cuddles. The partners speak to one another via vocal or typewritten chat, describing how they feel, what they want, etc., and sync the move from animation to animation to match their conversation. Due to the workings of the basic Second Life avatar functions, the partners' avatars will maintain eye contact, adding to the sense of intimacy. Sometimes the partners will "play along at home" by masturbating, and sometimes not.

A person unfamiliar with Second Life would probably imagine that the experience would only be pleasurable or satisfying for a person who was "playing along at home," but many of my interviewees vehemently disagreed. Some framed this in terms of emotional satisfaction. "Loving is loving—it's not about who had X orgasms when," said Isla. "There's nothing better than hearing her moan for me," said Chell. "Knowing she is hot for me is what means the most, not whether I'm getting off in real life." But what is fascinating is that many report the experience of virtual sex actually to be physically pleasurable even when unaccompanied by self-stimulation.

It is beyond the scope of this short reading to explain the neurological basis for sensation in a virtual body. Suffice it to say that while we typically experience sexual pleasure as taking place in our genitals, orgasm itself takes place in the brain (as is evident to anyone who has ever had an orgasmic or "wet" dream). We are equipped by the mirror neuron system to identify with prosthetics and avatars, but the ability to have sensually pleasurable and orgasmic experiences without actual genital stimulation long predates the invention of virtual worlds. Consider the experience of my interviewee Khushi:

My first experience of [orgasm without physical stimulation] was not in Second Life, it was when I was in deep meditation and had a mystical sexual experience. An orgasmic rush sort of entered me from the root chakra and rushed up into my body and suddenly I was filled with sexual energy. It was one of the best sexual experiences of my life.

Recognizing the ability to experience sexual pleasure without self-stimulation, Khushi actually preferred sexual experiences in Second Life that were not accompanied by "playing along at home." She found that "when I'm really embodied in Second Life I can have an orgasm that's often much more powerful than any orgasm I get when I physically cum." For Khushi, pure avatar-on-avatar sexuality, without enfleshed distractions, allowed her to identify fully with what she was doing in the virtual world with her partner—to feel embodied in her avatar—and was the ideal form of virtual sexuality. Not many of my interviewees discussed having "hands-off" orgasms as Khushi did, but many reported physical erotic sensation. "I love how in a well-made pose set or dance, I can totally feel it—our thighs moving against each other, his lips moving down my neck—brrrrr," purred Saige.

Identifying with their avatar bodies and feeling attracted to the avatars of their partners were central to the erotic lives of my interviewees. One reason that residents of Second Life reported finding virtual sexual encounters satisfying had to do with the fundamental pleasure they took in being in their own avatar bodies (see Cooper et al., 2007). Many studies show that residents of Second Life identify strongly with their avatars, invest a great deal of time in shaping and clothing them, and enjoy living "inside" them (Myers, 2007; Hansen, 2006; Munster, 2006; Castranova, 2005; Foster, 2005; Ben Ze'ev, 2004; Kushner, 2004; Donath, 1999; Hales, 1999; Argyle and Shields, 1996). Being able to create avatars that conformed exactly to their sense of ideal self removed many of the inhibitions that average people experience with regard to real life sexuality due to insecurities and bodily dysphoria. People are frequently embarrassed by their size, wrinkles, warts, and asymmetries. The avatar need not reflect any of these. Unsurprisingly, the typical human avatar has a Hollywood-perfect form: young, smooth, taut, and tall (Meadows, 2008). My interviewees often remarked wryly on how "well-equipped" male avatars were. Morrissey confessed,

OK, I admit it, I'm pretty well-hung here. In real life I'm pretty average. But [in Second Life] everyone's well-hung, so basically I'm average here too. None of my partners has ever complained I look unrealistic or anything. In fact, nobody's ever really said a single thing about the size of my cock, except for the time I wore a giant banana instead as a joke.

Not having to experience anxiety over perceived bodily flaws or inadequacies let people feel uninhibited sexually. It also produced a certain level of uniformity in human avatars that actually encouraged some to feel more uniquely attractive in nonconforming avatar bodies. Khushi, for example, had a very plump avatar form, and said she received many compliments and only rare negative comments about having what she termed a "plush" shape.

Attraction to a partner's body is just as important a part of virtual sexuality as it is in the world of flesh and bone. My interviewees often spoke at length about their admiration for the avatars of their lovers. Physical lust and romantic investment in the partner's body was described as not only no less a factor than it would be in real life, but actually as intensified by the fact that partners had crafted their avatars as true representations of their selves.

The idea that sexual intimacy in the virtual world was fully real was reiterated by many of my interviewees—so long as the partners had formed their avatars as authentic self-representations. Interestingly, there were two contrasting schools of thought about an "authentic" avatar form, which I have termed *ciscarnate* and *transcarnate* philosophies. (I draw here on trans gender scholarship; see Serano (2007) and Rubin (2003).) Adherents of *ciscarnate realism* hold that identity is inevitably tied to the real life body and ethical avatars should look like individuals' real-life bodies. The avatar is seen as a tool for communication between two real individuals sitting behind computer screens, and is believed ideally to be "transparent," conveying a clear picture of the real-life self. Ciscarnate lovers invested in their partners' avatar bodies as honest and true representations of their lovers' real-life forms (idealized a bit by the absence of warts, trimming of tummy, etc., which were deemed acceptable enhancements, just as getting teeth capped in real life is accepted). Ciscarnate realists accepted some idealization, but believed that certain correspondences were mandatory—most fundamentally race and sex. A person whose avatar differed along these dimensions from their real-life body was viewed as inauthentic and deceptive.

Proponents of *transcarnate reality,* on the other hand, believe that real-life body forms are arbitrary, and that enlightened avatar forms should express an individual's inner truth, which may have little relation to the real-life flesh. Avatar forms that are very unlike the real-life body in expressing an individual's sense of self are seen as enlightened rather than deceptive. Transcarnate lovers seemed to invest very deeply in their partners' avatar bodies as manifestations of the inner, true self that in real life one might never see, being distracted by arbitrary aspects of the flesh (sex, color, age, even species). Thus, transcarnate lovers felt they could touch their partners in ways impossible in real life. As Omega said, "I am certainly a fan of flesh touching flesh, but here in Second Life we can touch soul to soul."

Clearly, embodiment in an avatar removes many constraints on sexuality experienced in real life. For transcarnate realists, the paradigmatic example is trans gender embodiment, and Second Life draws many people who have not gender transitioned in real life, but do have trans gender or genderqueer identities. For these individuals, Second Life provides a sanctuary where they can safely express their experienced inner truths. Gender transition entails huge social risks in real life—but in the virtual world, changing sex can be done instantly, painlessly, and with "perfect" results. Given this ease, the proportion of individuals in Second Life who have trans gender forms is substantially higher than the proportion in real life. This ease was also the source of a lot of trans panic on the part of ciscarnate realists, who viewed trans embodiment as unethical, deceptive, and "unhealthy." Ciscarnate realists expressed anxiety and anger over the idea that they might become sexually involved with a trans gender avatar. Emerald exclaimed, "if u want a real relationship. . . . i dont want u to have the same thing in your pants that i have in mines. lies!!! . . . . deception!!! . . . . will ruin u whether in a 'virtual world' 'game' or Real Life."

Those with trans gender avatars in Second Life were well aware of the panic of the ciscarnate—or, as Omega snidely put it, the transphobic fear that "you meet a girl in a Second Life bar, and find out she's a 300 lb. plumber from Jersey named Vic, exploring his long-suppressed eye for getting the bag to match the shoes." It deterred some with trans gender avatars from becoming sexually active. Others, however, asserted a transcarnate ethics of authenticity, believing that they were displaying their true inner gender, and thus that it was in Second Life rather than in the flesh that they could have sexual interactions in which their form did not deceive their partners. "Initially, as Tylluan [a female avatar], I feared that people would be loving me under false pretenses," Tylluan explained. But as she spent more time living in her female avatar, Tylluan came to accept her female embodiment, not as a fiction, but as her inner truth. "This freed me to accept desire, and to make the leap to being sexual." Only in her avatar, in which she could express an authentic sense of self, was she sufficiently comfortable to be intimate—in real life she remained celibate.

There were other populations in Second Life that were also subject to moral outrage on the part of ciscarnate realists—especially furries, people who presented in humanoid animal forms. Identifying with an animal totem or "fursona," or simply preferring to embody as a wolfman or bunnygirl, while accepted by transcarnate realists, was seen as deluded and "sick" by ciscarnate realists. Those objecting to furry avatars seemed particularly obsessed with their sexual lives. Talia sniffed,

Sorry, not into bestiality . . . I just don't get it. They're into all this "yiffing" all the time. Do you know they have like special dog penises and things? It's pretty sick. What a waste of time. They could be having a real relationship, like I have with Jax. Instead they do their weird roleplaying, and have a lot of weird sex. I just want to tell them to grow up and stop making Second Life look bad.

Those who had furry avatars in Second Life tended to shrug at those with ciscarnate objections to their furry forms. "Actually, I'm more comfortable in my nonhuman forms because I can make them asexed and avoid getting hit on all the time," explained Ginko. Pels, who was sexually active, said he didn't have a preference for the species, human or otherwise, of his partner, and pointed out that there were plenty of women with human avatars who were attracted to his tigerishness. These transcarnate realist women appreciated the additional possibilities of his tiger body—for example, the erotic use of the tail, "tickling bits, curling around a thigh," as he put it.

Some of the constraints from which people could be liberated in Second Life were only appreciated by the transcarnate realists: the ability to embody in novel ways. But there were other constraints from which all could be liberated. For example, space and place restrictions abundant in real life due to social class (such as the ability to enjoy sexual relations on a perfect, private tropical island) or physics (such as the ability to have sex on a cloud in the sky) were removed. My interviewees enjoyed all sorts of inviting trysting-spots: treehouses, moody gothic castles, undersea mermaid grottoes, sleek spaceships, and seaside beach houses galore.

Another set of constraints from which all were freed were the sexual limitations placed upon them by lack of mobility, flexibility, or athleticism. Some of the sexual positions found in a typical sex bed are worthy of the Kama Sutra. There are no limits to stamina or strength, and erections can be maintained indefinitely. For those whose real-life sexual experiences have been fairly "vanilla" and predictable, the variety of options presented by sex bed animations add spice, and expand the sexual imagination.

The consequences of trying new things in Second Life are low. One will not choke trying oral sex, catch a sexually transmitted infection, or face an unwanted pregnancy. Furthermore, there is no real risk of rape, which adds a great deal of security and confidence. A few of my interviewees had had the experience of trying out a sex animation while exploring a store

or space and having a stranger hop into the partner position, but for those who found this unamusing, all they had to do was leave the bed or pose-set. If a person made unwelcome advances, the other party could instantly teleport out of the location. Stalking an unwilling partner is difficult in a world where everyone has the power to mute another at will, and where landowners have the ability to eject and ban an offender that is much more effective than any restraining order in real life.

The safety from negative consequences liberated many to explore aspects of sexuality they had never tried in real life. It is easy to travel to a faraway area to have a casual sexual encounter, allowing low-risk sampling of same-sex activity, multiple-partner encounters, fetish play, etc. While often lacking in the emotional intensity of sexual activity in committed relationships, casual encounters offer opportunities for exploring identity and interests that many reported finding rewarding. Forms of erotic activity initially merely sampled could become longterm interests and lead to shifts in identification and self-concept. Examples that my interviewees raised with some frequency were bisexuality, polyamory, gender transgression, and BDSM.

For females, bisexuality appeared almost normative in Second Life. For example, many sex beds include two sets of gendered animations, "Girl/Boy" and "Girl/Girl." "I started to feel like someone's maiden aunt from Peoria," snorted Fillis about her initial reluctance to snuggle with another woman. For males, sexual activity with other males is less expected, but still little stigmatized, which many generally heterosexual men thought was a good thing. Pels explained, "Second Life helped break down a bit of my, um, well not homophobia, I've never been homophobic, but let's say, increased my comfort range when it came to rubbing up on a guy in a friendly way. Overall I think that's a good thing in life in general—I'd feel terrible if

I was weird about say, being hit on by a guy, and maybe made them feel bad by my response."

Similarly, expanding one's repertoire beyond monogamy, genderconforming appearance, or "vanilla" sex bore few costs, socially or literally. Sampling BDSM is easy (no need to buy expensive equipment or learn to tie fancy knots) and there is no risk of unintended injury to self or partner when engaging in activities more serious than some simple blindfolding and spanking. More conservative Second Life residents might object, say, to a male avatar wearing a latex dress, but as Omega pointed out, "You can't get jumped." So for many, sexuality was simply more freely expressed.

Sexuality was more free in Second Life, but that should not be confused with how meaningful it was to Second Life residents. "I have learned a lot about my desires . . . a lot about my nature . . . an acceptance of those facets of myself," said Cypher. And many long-term Second Life residents had relationships that lasted for years. Second Life has a standard method of registering partnerships, so that one's partner appears on one's profile, which many take advantage of, and weddings and commitment ceremonies are common inworld (Radde-Antweiler, 2007). Further, many move relationships that begin in Second Life into real life (Holahan, 2008). A few of my interviewees were living with or married to partners they met in Second Life. "It's all one life now, real and virtual," smiled Soleil.

So: we started with the question of why so many people would be sexually involved in a virtual world where skin cannot touch skin. Social connection, self-expression, erotic pleasure and love provide the explanations—just as they do in any world. It seems we have the same interests, hopes, and capacities in any place you find us, including virtual spaces like Second Life.

NOTES

1. All avatar names have been changed to protect the privacy of the individuals in Second Life, although they follow naming conventions of the virtual world.

2. Accounts and information are available at http://secondlife.com/.

REFERENCES

Argyle, Katie, and Rob Shields. 1996. "Is There a Body on the Net?" pp. 58–69 in *Cultures of Internet: Virtual Spaces, Real Histories, Living Bodies*, edited by Rob Shields. London: Sage.

Ben Ze'ev, Aaron. 2004. *Love Online: Emotions on the Internet*. Cambridge: Cambridge University Press.

Boellstorff, Tom. 2008. *Coming of Age in Second Life: An Anthropologist Explores the Virtually Human*. Chicago: University of Chicago Press.

Castranova, Edward. 2005. *Synthetic Worlds: The Business and Culture of Online Games*. Chicago: University of Chicago Press.

Cooper, Robbie, with Julian Dibbell and Tracy Spaight. 2007. *Alter Ego: Avatars and their Creators*. London: Chris Boot.

Donath, Judith S. 1999. "Identity and Deception in the Virtual Community." pp. 25–59 in *Communities in Cyberspace*, edited by Marc A. Smith and Peter Kollock. London: Routledge.

Eros, LLC vs. Linden Research Inc. Complaint. 2008. http://media.taterunino.net/eros-vs-lri-Complaint_-_FINAL.pdf, retrieved 24 October 2011.

Foster, Thomas. 2005. *The Souls of Cyberfolk: Posthumanism as Vernacular Theory*. Minneapolis: University of Minneapolis Press.

Hales, N. Katherine. 1999. *How We Became Posthuman: Virtual Bodies in Cybernetics, Literature, and Informatics*. Chicago: University of Chicago Press.

Hansen, Mark B. N. 2006. *Bodies in Code: Interfaces with Digital Media*. New York: Routledge.

Holahan, Catherine. 2008. "So I Married an Avatar." *Bloomberg Businessweek Online* 14 February 2008, http://www.businessweek.com/technology/content/feb2008/tc20080214_131079.htm, retrieved 24 October 2011.

Kushner, David. 2004. "My Avatar, My Self." *Technology Review* 3: 50–55.

KZERO Research. 2007. "There.com vs. Second Life: Demographics." http://www.kzero.co.uk/blog/therecom-vs-second-life-demographics/, retrieved 24 October 2011.

Linden Lab. 2011. "The Second Life Economy in Q3 2011." Second Life Blog, Featured News. http://community.secondlife.com/t5/Featured-News/

The-Second-Life-Economy-in-Q3-2011/ba-p/1166705, retrieved 24 October 2011.

McPherson, Miller, Lynn Smith-Lovin, & Matthew E. Brashears. 2006. "Social Isolation in America." *American Sociological Review*, 71(3): 353–375.

Meadows, Mark Stephen. 2008. *I, Avatar: The Culture and Consequences of Having a Second Life*. Berkeley, CA: New Riders.

Munster, Anna. 2006. *Materializing New Media: Embodiment in Information Aesthetics*. New Hampshire: Dartmouth.

Myers, Jack, with Jerry Weinstein. 2007. *Virtual Worlds: Rewiring Your Emotional Future*. NY: Myers Publishing.

Radde-Antweiler, Kersten. 2007. "Cyber-Rituals in Virtual Worlds: Wedding-Online in Second Life." *Masaryk University Journal of Law and Technology* 1(2): 185–196.

Rubin, Henry. 2003. *Self-Made Men: Identity and Embodiment among Transsexual Men*. Tennessee: Vanderbilt University Press.

Serano, Julia. 2007. *Whipping Girl: A Transsexual Woman on Sexism and the Scapegoating of Femininity*. California: Seal Press.

LEARNING ABOUT SEX

AN INTERVIEW WITH

RITCH C. SAVIN-WILLIAMS

Ritch C. Savin-Williams, Ph.D., is a developmental psychology professor of Human Development and Director of the Sex & Gender Lab at Cornell University. His research centers on the psychological strength and well-being of same-sex attracted youth, biologic and self-report measures of sexual orientation, the sexual contin-uum, and the sexual development of youth. He is author of The New Gay Teenager *(Harvard University Press, 2005),* "Mom, Dad, I'm Gay": How Families Negoti-ate Coming Out *(American Psychological Association, 2001), and* ". . . And Then I Became Gay:" Young Men's Stories *(Routledge, 1998).*

What led you to begin studying sexuality?

My interest in adolescent sexual development centers on providing the most accu-rate information available on the normative developmental trajectories experienced by today's youth. I am less interested in what places youth at risk than in their coping skills, resiliency, and abilities to do well. Clearly, sexual development during adolescence has been a taboo topic for researchers, except insofar as it is a medical, public health, social, or political problem. For example, we know a lot about unsafe sex, but little about the meaning or significance of sexuality for an adolescent's enjoyment of daily life or conception of the future. We know a lot about the whats and whens of sexual intercourse but little about other sexual behaviors such as kissing and oral-genital contact. Contraception, pregnancy, sexually transmitted diseases, number of sex partners, and the linkage of vaginal-penile intercourse to clinical and social problems are common topics of sex researchers; sexual desire, pleasure, physical and emotional intimacies, the meaning of sex, what is sex, and sexual minorities are uncommon. I want to help promote the positive aspects and complexity of sexuality for adolescent development.

How do people react when you tell them you study sexuality?

Envy and a desire to tell them more; it is a great conversation topic because nearly everyone has a sexuality or has experienced it.

What ethical dilemmas have you faced in studying sexuality? Could you tell us about one particularly thorny dilemma and how you solved it?

University review boards demand parental permission for inclusion of their under-18 youth in behavioral research. Few parents want us to ask their sons and daughters about sexuality matters. One approach is to retrospectively ask over-17 youth about their sexual histories. This skirts one dilemma but compounds another—we aren't listening to the sexual lives of adolescents as they are experiencing them. So much has transpired in the sexual development of adolescents prior to age 18, especially in this cohort of youth. Second, sometimes gaining parental permission places youth at risk for parental censure or chastisement, such as when same-sex attracted youth want to talk about their lives but have not yet disclosed their sexuality to parents. Making this case to university review boards has allowed me to interview 16- and 17-year-olds—but even this resolution appears to imply that at age 16—but not before—young people become capable of making a decision to share their sexual history.

What do you think is most challenging about studying sexuality?

The most challenging aspect of my work has been convincing adult authorities to end the silence about adolescent sexuality, showing them that it is "okay" to ask youth about their sexual development. Many adults are incredibly anxious about sexuality, especially about their own child's sexuality; youth are aware of this discomfort and lack of knowledge and so decide not to talk to their parents about the fullness of their sex life. My task is to let adolescents speak for themselves; I am merely a conduit and translator, and occasionally an interpreter of their lives.

Why is sex research important? How does your work on adolescent sexuality relate to everyday life?

We know a considerable amount about many aspects of adolescents' lives. Their sexual development is the last frontier. The silence and the medicalization of their sexuality causes too many youth to feel embarrassed about their sexuality, to question their normality, and to spend far too many hours chastising themselves for "impure" thoughts and behavior. The existence of misinformation is rampant and, yet, the visibility and acceptance of sexual diversity in this generation of youth are unheralded. Among youth the silence has been lifted and most adults remain clueless. Specifically as related to sexual-minority issues, the attitude of this generation is, "What's your problem?!" During this next year I have undertaken a new project to hear the sexual lives of young men and women who are neither straight nor gay/lesbian but occupy the middle of the sexual spectrum.

Of the projects you have done over the course of your academic career, which was most interesting and why?

The most memorable and life-altering have been the intensive, in-depth interviews I have conducted with over 350 young men and women of all sexualities during the past decade. These youth willingly shared their sexual histories with honesty and insight that humbled me. Their developmental sex trajectories have been so divergent from my own that it was as if I was privy to a new experience of growing up. Their thrilling, humorous, candid, and, at times, heart-wrenching stories about growing up in the 1990s and now in the 2000s have convinced me that we must hear their stories. In particular, listening to the lives of same-sex-attracted young women were remarkably awe-inspiring and persuaded me that they constitute one of the most resilient, healthy, spirited groups of youth I have ever encountered.

If you could teach people one thing about sexuality what would it be?

Sexuality is not all you are but it is an important fabric of your life. Sex is to enjoy and add meaning to your life.

THE DEATH OF THE STORK: SEX EDUCATION BOOKS FOR CHILDREN

WENDY SIMONDS AND AMANDA M. JUNGELS

WHY NOT THE STORK?

You may say, "Isn't it easier and less embarrassing to tell them about the stork?" There are several reasons. . . . Even if he doesn't suspect anything at 3, he is surely going to find out the truth or the half-truth when he's 5 or 7 or 9. It's better not to start him off wrong and have him later decide that you're something of a liar. And if he finds out that you didn't dare tell him the truth, it puts a barrier between you, makes him uneasy. He's less likely to ask you other questions later, no matter how troubled he is (Spock and Rothenberg, 1992: 511).

"Does it feel good when a mommy and daddy make a baby?" he asked.

Joey's father answered, "It feels very nice, especially since you're able to be so close to someone you love."

"Hey," Joey said in an excited voice, "maybe sometime you two can show me how you do it."

Joey's parents smiled and laughed, but Joey knew it was a nice laugh and they weren't making fun of him.

"Joey, when a mommy and daddy make love, it's private, just something for the two of them," said Joey's father.

"Well, when can I do it? When can I make a baby?"

"When you get older, Joey," said Joey's mother. (Brooks and Perl, 1983)

This hokey conversation from *So That's How I Was Born!*, a sex education book aimed at preschoolers, exemplifies the sort of sexual honesty Spock and Rothenberg prescribe advising against the stork story. And certainly everyone believes that honesty is the best policy. But there's more than one way to be honest, and there are multiple truths about sexuality. We educate kids based on our perceptions of social reality, often without questioning norms to which we've grown accustomed. We also educate kids without knowing we're doing it—with offhand remarks or behaviors that we're not aware they notice. When we do intend to teach, we can now select from a variety of texts designed to help us. Parents may choose sex education books because doing so gets them off the hook altogether from discussing sex with their kids, or they may use the books as supplementary material. Several of these books have introductory notes to parents instructing them about instructing their kids. Sex education books for children both represent and shape cultural ideologies about children, sexuality, and procreation.

In the U.S., teaching sex to children in any form seems to induce cultural anxiety and controversy. An early sex-ed pamphlet addressed to teens by Mary Ware Dennett, *The Sex Side of Life: An Explanation for Young People* (1919), was deemed obscene under the Comstock Law in 1922, which banned sending any materials related to sexuality, contraception, or abortion through the U.S. mail (see Moore, 2007 and Solinger, 2005 for more complete historical discussions). This decision was overturned on appeal in 1930; the ruling stated: "an accurate exposition of the relevant facts of the sex side of life in decent language and in manifestly serious and disinterested spirit cannot ordinarily be regarded as obscene" (cited in Solinger, 106). Sex-ed books gained legal respectability on shaky grounds. What, after all, constitutes "accuracy"? Who decides what the "facts" are and which of them are "relevant" to children?

Authors, since this time, have continually asserted their credibility by presenting themselves as *scientific* authorities on what morally constitutes "accurate" "facts" about "sex."

In this reading, we discuss recent sex-ed books for children. In our research, we found no books about sex targeted to young children published before the late 1960s. Publishers apparently began to perceive young children as a market for this sort of didactic material as a result of a particular combination of cultural forces that together promoted resistance to authority and more openness about sexual matters in the late 1960s and early 1970s: the student movement, the feminist movement, the gay rights movement (all of which are indebted to the Civil Rights movement); hippie subculture; the so-called sexual revolution; and the human potential movement (promoting psychological growth techniques and practices). Advice books on sexuality for adults also flourished during this time (e.g., see Ehrenreich and English, 1986; Simonds, 1992), and sex education programs proliferated in U.S. public schools (Moran, 2000). The notion that children should be educated about sex before adolescence developed as cultural views of adolescents *as* sexual became accepted by educators and doctors. Thus, adolescents were in need of sexual education—especially regarding management and control. Moran describes the development of these ideas, beginning at the turn of the twentieth century (2000). Patton (1996) writes that the way in which we now conceive of adolescence is "as a time of turmoil between a period of innocence (childhood) and one of accomplished identity and safety (adulthood)" (75). So how do we present sexuality to innocents to prepare them for impending turmoil?

In order to consider this didactic medium systematically and sociologically, we examined all the androgynous (not addressed specifically to one gender) non-religious picture books about sex geared toward young children currently in print and available through Amazon.com in 2008, sex-ed books for older kids, and advice books for parents regarding talking with children about sex. In all, we surveyed fourteen books for young children, seven for adolescents, and eleven for parents. (These books are arranged by category in the bibliography.) Our sample spans 40 years; the earliest is a 1979 reprint of a 1968 book, and the most recent book was published in 2008.

These books, taken together, address a loose set of problems parents face in their presumed desire to present a variety of complex, baggage-laden topics to children in an understandable way without feeling deeply uncomfortable in the process. Talking about sexuality and child-bearing with children creates a multifaceted dilemma. Parents are, in essence, attempting to create openness about a range of topics they may feel unable to be truly open about. First there is the issue of deterrence: How can parents present sexuality without making it seem too appealing? Second, how ought adults avoid frightening children with all the ways that sexual encounters and their outcomes can be painful, even horrible? How should parents balance a desire not to frighten with the goal of offering them information that might protect them from sexual dangers and unintended consequences (sexual predators, rape, sexually transmitted diseases, teen pregnancy, abortion, not to mention heartbreak)? Fourth, how can parents deal with, acknowledge, respond to evidence of, and instruct them about their own sexuality? And fifth, how do adults teach children appropriate contexts for expressions of sexuality?

What are appropriate contexts, after all? In the rest of this essay, we look at how authors of sex-ed books for children and advice books for parents contextualize sexuality. These books reify (and occasionally resist) heteronormative, gendered, and medicalized sociosexual conventions through an examination of five general topics: procreative/sexual anatomy; procreative sex; childbirth; managing childhood sexuality; and alternatives to procreative sex. Our primary focus is on the books for young children; we supplement this discussion of these books with interpretations of the books for older children and for parents.

CHANGING BODIES

In sex books for young and older kids, authors foreground the primary discussion of procreative sex with brief anatomy lessons. They equate biological sex with gender: There are people with penises and people with vaginas, and this is what makes them boys or girls. Eventually, boys and girls grow up into men and women and make babies together utilizing these parts. Laurie Krasny Brown and Marc Brown (1997) preface their presentation of genital difference with a litany of ways in which boys and girls *may* be different (clothes, hairstyles, playing styles, emotions). After each example they write that the difference is "sometimes, but not always" evident. Harris and Emberley (2006) have a similar discussion (including that "girls play with dolls and teddy bears! And so do boys!" and "boys have very big and strong muscles. So do girls!"), but also concludes that boys and girls are "not all that different" (12–13).

Despite claims of similarity, divergent anatomy is central in these discussions of difference: "Actually the only sure way to tell boys and girls apart is by their bodies. If you're a boy, you have a penis, scrotum, and testicles. If you're a girl, you have a vulva, clitoris, and vagina" (11–12). This text appears alongside illustrations of a naked boy and girl, with labeled body parts. The cartoon girl proclaims, "Look! Our bodies are more alike than different!" Harris and Emberley (1999) include a similar picture, with the text "Most parts of our bodies . . . are the same and look quite the

same whether we are female or male. . . . The parts that are different are the parts that make each of us a female or a male" (10). Occasionally, authors omit the clitoris from their depictions of girls' bodies, as in Saltz's (2005) book *Amazing You,* or describe girls' sex organs as if they are somehow based on boys' sex organs. For example, in a description of sexual arousal in girls, Foster (2005) describes the elongation of the clitoris as an example of how, "in some ways, a female's clitoris is like a male penis" (29). In the book *Boys, Girls and Body Science,* Hickling (2002) frames her discussion of sexual development with the device of a teacher interacting with elementary-aged students; these students present their ideas about sexual development and the teacher redirects them along the "correct" path. For instance, a student asks whether "girls have balls," and the teacher responds that "girls have two ovaries inside their abdomen and they are sort of like balls" (np). Early fetal development begins with undifferentiated female internal sex organs, not male parts. So, in actuality, "balls" are like ovaries, not vice versa. Yet authors' language tends to centralizes boys' bodies, and to make girls' bodies secondary and/or deviant.

Authors do not mention the possibility of not being able to tell bodies apart easily, nor do they broach the topic of gender identity that doesn't "match" genitalia, nor do they question the bifurcated social constructs of girl and boy, man and woman. As Joey's mother says in *So That's How I Was Born!* (Brooks and Perl, 1983), "a boy's body isn't better than a girl's body and a girl's body isn't better than a boy's. They're just different from the time they're born and each is special in their own way." In this way, authors proclaim gender difference as essential (rooted in dimorphic biological sex), while also contradictorily claiming the difference doesn't matter. Perhaps introducing sex and gender ambiguity and fluidity would confuse kids. The majority of babies are born genetically dimorphous, after all, and most people appear to grow up relatively comfortable with socially constructed gender divisions. Yet in other cases, it is not the frequency of a phenomenon that determines whether authors will present it; some of these books include discussions of occurrences at least as infrequent as intersexuality or gender-bending identities (e.g., multiple births, home births, adoption), apparently without worrying about the confusion these mentions might cause. Authors seek to demystify some social practices but leave others untouched, and in so doing appear to take most cultural norms for granted.

To cite another example, the vast majority of illustrations and photographs of children and their families in these books only show racially alike families. Though the majority of those pictured are white, illustrators and photographers include children and adults interacting with each other across racial boundaries. In the original version of this chapter, written in 2001, there was only one clear depiction of an interracial family (Smith and Wheatley, 1997, 14). Harris and Emberley (1999) had a few illustrations that *might* have been interracial family groups. In 2008, only Harris and Emberley continued to include these images in their work: their book *It's Not the Stork!* for preschool-aged children depicts and discusses families in a multitude of ways, including foster, adoptive, blended, gay and lesbian, and intergenerational families (2004; 2006); one of the families depicted may be a gay, interracial family. Harris and Emberley also present interracial families in the birthing section, with women of color giving birth, accompanied by white fathers (2004, 42). In their book for older children, Harris and Emberley again depict interracial intimacy (2006, 55–56). While other authors do discuss different family forms (adoptive, foster, and intergenerational), and also present and promote multicultural interactions among people, no others depict or discuss interracial intimacy.

MAKING LOVE AND MAKING BABIES

Children do, indeed, ask their parents "Where did I come from?" or "How are babies made?" Thus, many parents find themselves working backward from baby (or pregnancy) to heterosexual sexuality. We suspect that if children initiate conversations about sexuality apart from procreation many parents don't know what to do or say, so they may end up in the procreation story because it's easier for them to deal with than sexuality on its own.

Sexual information conveyed in the books for young children tends to be vague, to reinforce heteronormativity, and to represent penile–vaginal intercourse as the only example of sexual activity in which men and women engage. Sometimes authors omit the act altogether, as in Joanna Cole's *How You Were Born* (1993) and Alastair Smith's *How Are Babies Made?* (1997):

In a woman's body are egg cells. The egg cell is round. It does not have a shell like a chicken's egg. In a man's body are sperm cells. The sperm cells have long tails and can swim. When a sperm and an egg join together, they form a special cell that can grow into a baby. (Cole, 1993, 19)

How does the baby start? A tiny sperm from the man's body has to join up with a little egg from the woman's body. (Smith, 1997, 5)

When authors do discuss penile–vaginal intercourse, they describe it as pleasurable and functional for both men and women, and portray it taking place within the context of loving relationships:

Sexual intercourse may seem gross or nice, scary or funny, weird or cool—or even unbelievable to you. But when two people care for each other, sexual intercourse is very loving. Kids are much too young to have sexual intercourse. (Harris and Emberley, 1999, 29)

When a woman and a man who love each other go to bed, they like to hug and kiss. Sometimes, if they both want to, the man puts his penis in the woman's vagina and that feels really good for both of them. Sperm come out through the man's penis. If one tiny sperm meets a tiny egg inside the woman's body, a baby is started, and the man and woman will be the baby's parents. (Gordon and Gordon, 1992)

None of the authors writing for young children describes orgasm, though clearly they present the emission of sperm as momentous. Eggs and sperm are personified in gendered ways; Lisa Jean Moore writes: "There is a preponderance of narratives describing the exceptionalness of the one sperm that gets to fertilize the egg. Other than primping and batting eyes to be attractive to the sperm, eggs typically are passive" (2007, 62). Authors depict sex cells as engaged in analogous romances to those of their producers.

The reason for sex in these books is parenthood. Brooks and Perl (1983) label the lovers "mommy" and "daddy" before the fact, thus presenting sex as predicated on this goal of future parenthood:

*One of the ways a mommy and daddy show they love one another is by hugging each other very close. In bed, they can get really close when a daddy puts his **penis** inside the special opening between a mommy's legs which is called a **vagina**. The sperm comes out of the daddy's penis and goes into the mommy's vagina, and then the sperm meets the egg and a baby starts. (Brooks and Perl, 1983).*

Andry, Schepp, and Hampton's *How Babies Are Made* (1979) and Baker's *The Birds and the Bees* (1990) are more lackluster than the others in their descriptions of procreative sex:

The sperm, which come from the father's testicles, are sent into the mother through his penis. To do this, the father and mother lie down facing each other and the father places his penis in the mother's vagina. Unlike plants and animals, when human mothers and fathers create a new baby they are sharing a very personal and special relationship. (Andry, Schepp, and Hampton, 1979)

When men and women mate, the penis becomes stiff and is inserted into the vagina, which has become larger and moist, ready to receive it. (Baker, 1990)

These authors make heterosex sound like a cross between directions for putting together a bookcase and a recipe for baking a cake. (Imagine the seductive dialogue: "Hey baby, I have some sperm I'd like to send you through my penis! May I insert it?" "Oh yeah, my vagina is large and moist, ready to receive!")

Many books present humans' procreative method after first laboriously introducing habits of other plant and animal species. This approach makes sex seem natural and scientific. "By relying on science, these children's books bolster their contents as being objective and truthful" (Moore, 2007, 51). Andry, Schepp, and Hampton (1979) interestingly sever this naturalistic connection with other living things, separating humans out by insisting on our emotional superiority ("unlike plants and animals . . ."). They want to show that sex is more than just the casual rubbing together of stamens and pistils. The experts writing for parents endorse grounding sex in satisfying long-term connection between adults. For instance, Spock and Rothenberg (1992) advise, "Parents shouldn't ever let the anatomical and physiological explanation of sex stand alone but always connect it with the idealistic, spiritual aspects" (509).

Our favorite among the books for young children is Babette Cole's *Mommy Laid an Egg OR Where Do Babies Come From?* (1993). Cole uses humor throughout the book, both in the prose and in her illustrations, which mix a cartoon family together with raucous, childlike stick-figure drawings. The book begins with the cartoon parents misinforming their children, "some babies are delivered by dinosaurs," "you can make them out of gingerbread," and "sometimes you just find them under stones." The children respond with laughter, and say "what a bunch of nonsense!" They proceed to instruct their parents about procreative sex, all the while pointing to their crude comical illustrations.

Girl: *"Mommies do have eggs. They are inside their bodies."*

Boy: *"And daddies have seeds in seed pods outside their bodies. Daddies also have a tube. The seeds come out of the pods and through the tube."*

Girl: *"The tube goes into the mommy's body through a hole. Then the seeds swim inside using their tails."* (Cole, 1993)

On the page where the boy proclaims "here are some ways . . . mommies and daddies fit together," Cole illustrates his words with child-like drawings of the mommy and daddy cavorting in a variety of imaginative positions while linked at the crotch, including holding balloons, bouncing on a big ball (labeled "space hopper"), and lying on a skateboard. These are raunchy yet clean, because they are children's drawings (and do not depict genitalia, only breasts). The language is crude in a childish way, yet the botanical allegories don't seem embarrassingly goofy, just goofy in a fun way. Sex seems fun for once—not just a pleasant sperm-delivery arrangement. Why else would the participants wear party hats? Yet, at the same time, this language of "fitting together," which recurs in several books, reinforces the notion that hetero-normative, procreative sex is natural and right.

In the six books for young children that include illustrations of sexual encounters (the other seven do not depict the act), the man is on top in three, and the man and woman are side by side in two (and, as noted, Cole shows a number of positions [1993]). The copulators are all under the covers except in Baker's drawing (which is decidedly unrevealing despite the nudity of the illustrated characters) (1990).

HAVING BABIES

The next step after procreative sex in all of these books is pregnancy and birth. After a brief discussion of the growth of the fetus and changes in the mother's body, authors tell how babies are born. They depict childbearing as wonderful,

a job to be done together by a mommy and a daddy (who cheers her on). Many authors tell the story of birth from the point of view of the baby, which is apparently the perspective with which they imagine child readers will identify. Authors do not discuss pain in childbirth, although Cole (1993) comes close, referring to contractions as "sharp twinges called labor pangs" (30). Authors portray labor as a biological (muscular) activity, as hard work that a woman does, or both. Birth is described as awesome and wonderful for the parents.

Marc Brown (Brown and Brown, 1997) and Michael Emberley (Harris and Emberley, 1999) both depict women in the lithotomy position (on their backs, with feet in stirrups) surrounded by masked and gowned people. The daddies are also decked out in medical garb, though in Emberley's drawing he doesn't wear a mask. Laura Krasny Brown (1997) writes "When a baby is ready to be born, muscles in the mother's womb begin to tighten and relax, tighten and relax, helping her push out the baby. In most births, the baby comes out the vagina, which stretches to let it pass through" (28). Similarly, the text accompanying Emberley's drawing says:

When a baby is about to be born, the muscles in the mother's uterus begin to squeeze tight. This is called "labor." "Labor" is another word for "work." A mother's muscles work very hard to push and squeeze the baby out of the uterus and into the vagina. Then the mother's muscles push and squeeze the baby's body through the vagina. The vagina stretches wide as the baby's soft, wet, and slippery body travels through it. (Harris and Emberley, 1999, 56–57)

Even though these authors' descriptions of labor and birth sound like they might have been written by midwives, they tend to depict medical management of the process as normal. Four of the eighteen authors mention alternatives to hospital birth, but none depicts it. Joanna Cole (1993) writes: "Your mother and father went to the hospital or childbirth center where you were to be born. If you were born at home, then the doctor or midwife came to your house" (31). The photographs accompanying this text show couples in more casual hospital or birth center settings than the settings depicted in the other books, but none are at home. Sol and Judith Gordon write: "Some babies are born at home. But most women like to go to the hospital for the birth of their baby" (1992). This text is accompanied by a drawing of a woman lying in the lithotomy position in a hospital, a masked woman birth attendant standing between her legs holding a screaming baby up for her (and us) to see. We are positioned behind and above the woman's head, watching the baby come out from her vantage point, but we can also see her face, and she looks happy. We rarely see a vaginal view of birth except in Cole's (1993) child drawing, which shows a baby sticking out of a round-blob mother and saying "Hello Mommy!" Harris and Emberley (2004) depict both a vaginal view of birth and a woman in the lithotomy position in the same set of illustrations (63). All other illustrations show babies mediated by medical personnel in medical settings both during and after birth.

As mentioned, authors writing for young children often seek to present labor and birth from the baby's perspective—these authors tend to present the birthing process as both fun and exciting. In *Boys, Girls and Body Science* (Hickling, 2005), Nurse Meg describes to a class of elementary students how the birthing process happens. This dialogue is accompanied by a picture of a woman in the lithotomy position who appears serene and peaceful—if not unconscious:

"But what would happen if you kept squeezing on a balloon?" asked Meg.

"It would pop," said Nicholas.

"That is exactly what happens," said Meg. "After a few hours, the water bag breaks and the water comes pouring out of the mum's vagina and makes it all wet and slippery, just like a water slide. So, the first water slide that

you ever had was the day you were born when you came slip-sliding down your mum's vagina."

All the children loved the water slide story and made swooshy noises as they waved their arms around.

Harris and Emberley (2006) use the same "balloon" analogy in a much more effective way, explaining that a pregnant woman's uterus does *not* pop because her uterus and skin are stretchy—"like a balloon." This response is an excellent example of how an analogy can be used to explain a phenomenon to a young child in a way that is correct, yet understandable to the child.

TEACHING ABOUT TOUCHING

A few of the sex books for young children explicitly address children's sexuality within the context of danger. Brown and Brown (1997) and Harris and Emberley (1999) attempt to differentiate between touching that is "okay" and "not okay"—that is, between masturbation and sexual abuse. Brown and Brown (1997) write:

Touching and rubbing your genitals to feel good is called masturbation. Some of us try this; some of us don't. However, it's best to do this private kind of touching off by yourself.

Touching others is just as important. . . . If someone doesn't want to be touched, then respect his or her wishes—don't do it! . . . Everyone needs good touches to feel loved and happy. . . . But no one has the right to touch you in a way that feels wrong or uncomfortable.

If you don't like the way someone touches you, speak up and tell him or her to stop. If that doesn't work, tell your mom or dad or another grownup. Your body belongs to you, and you should say who touches it! (16–19)

Harris and Emberley (1999) go into more detail about both masturbation and abuse, and like Brown and Brown, the discussion of masturbation leads into the issue of abuse. The Browns differentiate between self-touches that feel good, touches from others that *are* good, and those that feel wrong or are somehow dislikable. Harris (1999) makes the same points, and goes into more detail about contentiousness over masturbation: "Every family has its own thoughts and feelings about masturbation. . . . Some people and some religions think it's wrong to masturbate. But most doctors agree that masturbation is perfectly healthy and perfectly normal, and cannot hurt you or your body" (69). Doctors apparently have the last word and validating authority on the subject. This is ironic, given that well into the twentieth century, sex educators backed up denouncements of masturbation as pathological with medical authority. (See Conrad and Schneider, 1992, 180–181, on nineteenth-century conceptualizations of masturbation as disease; and Moran, 2000, 57, on lasting sex educational prohibitions.)

Harris and Emberley next define touches that are not okay: "But if any person touches any part of your body and you do not want them to, say "STOP!". . . . Sexual abuse happens when someone touches the private parts of a person's body and does NOT have the right to do that" (1999, 70). Harris and Emberley acknowledge that sexual abuse is "always wrong," that it "can hurt" or "feel gentle," and thus, that it can be "very confusing" (70). They advise, like the Browns, that children tell someone they trust if they experience sexual abuse, and reassures readers that it is "NEVER your fault" (70–71).

Kleven's book *The Right Touch* (1997) is one of the few children's books we found that discusses only sexual abuse, and no other sexual education topics. In this book, a mother tells her son the story of the attempted sexual abuse of a young girl by a neighbor. The text is accompanied by Bergsma's illustrations of "whimsical, elfin-like people" (np) that seemed too cute to us for this topic. Kleven portrays child abuse as potentially everywhere: "grown-ups, babysitters, and bigger kids" can be abusers. Child readers are urged to be self-protective at all times. The mother in the story says, "no

one has the right to touch private parts of your body without a good reason, not even Dad or me" (Kleven, 1997). How a child determines what constitutes a "good reason" is not clear. Kleven asserts that many children in bad-touch-situations-in-the-making have "warning feelings" when "things are not safe" (1997). This position suggests to readers that knowing how to recognize a sexual predator is innate and universal: so if one fails to escape danger, one is somehow to blame.

One book that describes masturbation in an overtly positive way is Bell's *Changing Bodies, Changing Lives* (1998). Bell writes that "having masturbated helps you enjoy lovemaking more," and gives descriptions of how boys and girls masturbate (1998, 83). In addition, Bell provides advice for what to do "if you don't have orgasms and want to," and addresses the pressure that many teenagers, especially girls, feel about orgasms:

It is not surprising that girls and women have orgasms less easily than boys and men do. First, there's anatomy. A boy can't miss his penis. He touches it several times a day . . . most boys discover masturbation, and it is pretty easy for them to figure out how to do it. But a girl's clitoris, and certainly her vagina, are more hidden. Also, she may be taught as a child not to touch her genitals.

Then there is sex education, or lack of it. Most girls are never taught that they have a clitoris and what it is and does. Since orgasm usually depends at least in part on a girl's clitoris getting stimulated, not knowing about your clitoris can make orgasms pretty hard to have.

Third, girls in general are brought up to be less accepting and proud of their sexuality than boys are. This is part of the double standard. A teenage boy finds that his sexual adventures are usually tolerated or even encouraged. A girl, however, is told she must be the one to say, "No!" and hold off a boy's sex drive. She rarely hears about her own sex drive. So it can be hard for her to let her sexual responses flow freely, and let go enough to have an orgasm. . . .

But for both girls and boys, feeling that you have to have orgasms to be a "liberated" person can add to the

confusions and pressures that many of us feel about sex.
Try not to let yourself feel pressured to come.

Authors writing for older kids and parents all discuss masturbation and sexual abuse in similar terms to those utilized by those writing for young children. They describe masturbation as normal and generally healthy; they describe sexual abuse as always dangerous.

Books for teens tend to combine the topic of sexual abuse with discussions of rape (Basso, 2003; Bell, 1998). Bell discusses the "sexual script" that occurs because the "man is 'supposed' to be dominant, to be sexually powerful and demanding. The woman, on the other hand, is 'supposed' to be coy and shy and passive, to lead men on but not let them get 'too far'?" (1998, 128). She argues that girls have to learn to "give straightforward messages. Boys have to learn to believe what girls are saying. It is important to say yes *only* when you mean yes; and to really mean no when you say no" (1998, 129).

Basso addresses the issue of dealing with sexual scripts, but in a slightly different, less clear manner: when "your mouth is saying one thing and your body language is saying another, your partner may become confused" (2003, 218). He lays out a table of poorly matched body language and verbal messages ("'Stop!' + Smile = He/she is just playing") and a table of well-matched body language and verbal messages ("'Stop!' + Serious or angry look on your face = I don't want you to do that") (1998, 218–219). Here, if an individual sends "mixed messages," then s/he should not be surprised if her/his partner continues to pressure her/him for sex. Unlike Bell, Basso does not discuss how "peer pressure" might devolve into a date-rape scenario. Despite the gender-neutral framing of the "information" in this table, it is clear from Basso's extended discussion of danger and risk-taking that rape victims are girls and women, and that rapists and potential rapists are boys and men.

Basso discusses date rape and stranger rape in a way that infantilizes women and reinforces heteronormative sexual scripts. His definition of rape seems only to include those cases that include physical harm, verbal threats, or limited capacity due to drugs or alcohol (2003, 233). Even though Basso argues that, "it doesn't matter what a female wears, says, or does, there is never any excuse for rape" (234), and that, "ladies, you are free to wear anything you want any way you want, and you can act any way you want" (237), he contradicts these statements, outlining several scenarios in which young women inadvertently place themselves at risk. Here is just one example:

You wear a short, tight skirt and loose blouse that shows off some cleavage. . . . Your message: I'm being fashionable and wearing something that is in style. Male interpretation: She's sexy! She wants me to see her breasts because she wants to have sex with me. (237)

Young women are advised to be careful about what they wear; to know their dancing might be interpreted as sexually provocative; and to avoid casual touches to avoid sending the wrong message to their dates. Boys are advised that they are responsible for their actions "regardless of the situation or condition" (i.e., intoxication) (239). Boys are told that, "when a female says no, she means no. Although the female may have led you on, she has every right to change her mind, and you must honor her decision" (234). Basso continues with a bizarre analogy, in which he compares committing rape to getting ticketed for speeding:

It's like driving a shiny red Corvette with a racing stripe down the side. Suddenly a police officer pulls up behind you, flashes his/her lights and gives you a speeding ticket. Is it fair to get a speeding ticket just because you're driving a shiny red Corvette? Just because a female dresses a certain way doesn't mean she should be treated a certain way based on YOUR assumptions. Of course, comparing rape to a speeding ticket is like comparing a nuclear explosion to a firecracker—rape is a devastating crime. (234).

Well, the good news is, "you can avoid the embarrass-ment of being arrested as a rapist" if you just drive your date home and behave responsibly. (240)

Basso clearly identifies with male readers. Beyond the offensive analogy, we are troubled by the message that what a boy should seek to avoid is the "embarrassment of being arrested as a rapist," rather than *being* a rapist.

In childhood, inappropriate sexual touching and sexual activity is *never* okay, no matter who does it, and no matter the context. In adolescence, the messages become mixed: inappropriate sexual touching and sexual activity is usually not all right, unless you confused your partner—then, can you blame them? Didactic presentations of boundaries become mired in a discourse of thwarted or dangerous desires for boys and provocative yet (rightfully) reluctant girls. We find Basso's gendered messages about date rape especially troubling; ultimately, he places the responsibility for control of sexual limits on young women, and implicitly blames girls when boys feel "led on." It is not possible that a girl might pressure a boy to have sex or attempt to rape him. Same-gender situations are notably absent in all these discussions.

In contrast to the warnings they issue about abusive sex, authors describe "sex play" between children as generally harmless. Westheimer and deGroat (1998) acknowledge only that this occurs among boys, writing: "Sometimes groups of boys will masturbate together. There's nothing wrong with doing this in privacy" (53). In books for parents where masturbation and sex-play are discussed, the goal seems to be allaying parents' fears of impending gayness or sexual excessiveness (non-normativity). Regarding solitary masturbation, Eyre and Eyre (1998) and Spock and Rothenberg (1992) warn against too much of this good thing. Spock and Rothenberg discuss what they call "excessive masturbation," never specifying how often is too much. They do attempt, after raising this specter, to keep parents calm:

It's important for parents to know that the fear that some-thing will happen or has happened to the genitals is one of the most common causes of excessive masturbation in young childhood. To tell such children that they'll injure themselves makes matters worse. To tell them that they're bad and that you won't love them any more gives them a new fear. (504)

Even as they introduce this behavior as abnormal, Spock and Rothenberg (1992) reassure parents that sexual exploration is natural, writing:

I think that whatever your personal beliefs or feelings, you should avoid threatening or punishing your children when they reveal their natural sexuality. . . . It's important to try to say something about how normal and universal the activity is. It's good for children to feel they can ask their parents about sex. (506)

This seemingly conflicting advice could be confusing to parents, especially those who have themselves been brought up by parents who disapproved of masturbation.

In a prescripted dialogue between a father and a son who asks "Is masturbation bad?" (meant to be helpful for parents seeking to initiate discussion with their kids) the Eyres (1998) propose replying: "Everyone at least experiments with it. But it can be a problem if it becomes a habit or happens too often" (105). The father then advises the son to "think about how beautiful and awesome it can be with the beautiful and special wife you'll have some-day. . . . If you try to do this, you won't feel like masturbating as often, and when you do, at least you'll be thinking about the best kind of sex that will happen someday with your wife" (106). The Eyres propose monogamous married sex as an anti-erotic fantasy to *curb* boys' sexual urges. With a similar weird twist, Maxwell (2008) warns that "obsessive masturbation to only one kind of stimulation" can lead to "difficulty reaching orgasm within a relationship" (58). She claims to have seen this in her practice as a clinical psychologist, but admits that, "there is no current research to support that this is the case with most men" (58). Thus, she urges parents to talk to their children (read: boys) about porn. She proclaims, "Demeaning pictures or pictures that promote dominance of one person over another, can, over time, train a person to respond only to that form of stimulation" (58–59). All authors who write about sexual urges and danger in children stress that they are natural or normal, even as they coach parents about how to best protect, contain, constrain, and train these desires in socially desirable ways.

WORDS YOU MAY HAVE HEARD

Authors of sex books for young children tend to limit discussion of sexual issues to procreative sex, and occasional mentions of masturbation and child abuse. Authors of sex books for adolescents all cover masturbation and sexual abuse, but beyond this they tend to discuss sexual diversity (anything other than penile–vaginal intercourse) in a very limited way. For instance, Westheimer and deGroat offhandedly mention anal and oral sex in her section on AIDS: "some people think they can avoid AIDS by practicing anal intercourse (putting the penis in the anus) or oral sex (putting it in the mouth). They are dead wrong" (Westheimer and deGroat, 1998: 74).

Throughout these books, authors depict loving sexual relationships between men and woman as normative. When they do discuss alternatives—gayness, lesbianism, and bisexuality (transgenderedness is discussed only by Lefkoff [2007])—they treat them with a liberal touch, yet cordon these topics off into short sections of their own. These authors advocate tolerance, but are careful to avoid endorsing or advocating nonheterosexual activities. The following are examples of discussions of "homosexuality" from two books for teens and one for adults (set up as a prescribed parental response to a child's question):

Some people prefer to have sexual experiences with persons of their own sex. They are called homosexuals. Most boys and girls have homosexual thoughts occasionally. Some even have homosexual experiences. This doesn't mean that they are homosexual. The people properly called homosexual are those who, as adults, have sexual contacts only with persons of their own sex. . . . Some people enjoy sexual relations with both sexes throughout their adult life. They are called bisexuals. Modern psychologists no longer see homosexual or bisexual behavior between consenting adults as a disorder. (Gordon and Cohen, 1992, 28)

Why Are Some People Straight and Others Gay?
Psychologists do not really know what causes a person's sexual preferences. Some believe that whether a person is straight or gay depends on experiences in early childhood. Others think homosexuality might be an inherited, or built-in preference. . . .

Is Homosexuality a Sickness?
No. People used to believe that homosexuality was a form of mental illness, but now psychiatrists say that it is not. Homosexuality is just one way people can express love.

Can Homosexuals Choose Not to Be Gay?
Homosexuals can choose not to practice homosexuality. . . . But for most gay people, it is probably not possible to choose how they feel inside and which sex they are attracted to. (Cole and Tiegreen, 1988, 75)

Is It Bad to Be a Homosexual?
We don't think so, but that's one of those questions that different people have different opinions about. Some people think that you should only have sexual relations with a person of the other sex, and that anybody who doesn't choose to do that is not doing the right thing. In this family we agree with the scientists and doctors who say that a homosexual is just different from a heterosexual, but not bad or sick or strange. Certain people who don't approve of homosexuals are sometimes very cruel to them, so many homosexuals are hurt and tend to be very private about their personal lives. That's too bad, we think, because it's very hard and sad to have to hide that you love someone. (Calderone and Ramey, 1982, 87)

Even as they attempt to advocate openmindedness, authors frame sexual nonconformity as deviant by using the clinical term *homosexual*, by discussing lesbian/bisexual/gay sexuality via questions that are pointedly negative, and by emphasizing that it was once officially pathological. By consistently presenting medicine as the arbiter of the current non-pathology of "homosexuality," authors do not question medical authority or effectively critique its past homophobia. Calderone and Ramey's discussion of homophobia, although disapproving, also presents it as a valid point of view. They describe "some people" who think that only straight sex is "the right thing." Authors denounce cruelty and violence, but do not usually explicitly denounce homophobic beliefs; often they take this stance in the name of respect for religious orthodoxy. Maxwell writes, in this vein:

I don't address issues of homosexuality in public schools because I embrace the principle that respecting diversity means respecting those parents whose religious convictions are opposed to homosexuality. . . . I also tell them [kids] that no religion has ever supported humiliating, disrespecting, or harming another human being and that the word "gay" should never be used as a put-down, not even as a "joke." (2008, 65)

Here, Maxwell grants homophobia credibility as long as it is religiously-based; she also likens being gay to being persecuted for one's religious identity, presumably to elicit empathy for victims of homophobia from religious readers. This is a fine line to be walking, indeed.

The Eyres (1998) are the only authors among our sample who are *overtly* homophobic. They discuss "homosexuality" in one paragraph (which precedes a paragraph on AIDS), saying "we shouldn't judge a person who is gay, but it can be a sad situation because it doesn't allow for the birth of children or for the kind of family that a heterosexual couple can have" (97). In contrast, a few authors do actually denounce homophobia, usually by explaining that gayness is "not a choice" (Levkoff, 2007, 89),

and then proclaiming that, anyway, discrimination is morally wrong:

There has never been a reason to treat people with disrespect. Homophobia is as bad as any other type of hatred—including racism and religious persecution. People should be judged according to their character, not who they sleep with. (Levkoff, 2007, 90)

We must teach our children tolerance so that some other child's life is not made miserable by name-calling, harassment, or violence. We must teach tolerance so our kids know that any question they have about sexual orientation is okay and that we love them for who they are. (Schwartz and Capello, 2000, 186)

Some people disapprove of gay men and lesbians. Some even hate homosexuals only because they are homosexuals. Usually these people know little or nothing about homosexuals, and their views are based on fears or misinformation, not facts. People are often afraid of things that they know little or nothing about (Harris, 2004, 18)

Even advocates of respect for sexual diversity tread with a great deal of caution, and in so doing, undercut their affirmation of gayness in children. Many of the authors writing for older kids and adults seek to reassure readers that nonheterosexual urges and experiences might well be transitory. Though the categories they introduce have the same essential ring to them as gender does in the books for young kids, authors recognize some flux on the road to a permanent sexual identity. But because authors explain that eventually sexual identity (straight, gay, lesbian, bisexual) is permanent, this changeability often comes across as an experimentation phase.

Are you homosexual? It's difficult to know. Some people don't figure out if they're gay or straight until their late teens or their twenties. Having a crush on, or even kissing or touching, someone of your own sex does not necessarily mean that you're gay. (Westheimer and deGroat, 1998, 54)

Because there are so many negative ideas in our society about being gay, young people may panic if they have any feelings or daydreams about people of their own sex. Yet most of them will not end up being gay. Naturally, a small percentage will—about five to ten percent. . . . But most will not. They are simply going through a stage of growing up. (Cole, 1988, 76)

[A] child's sex experimentation at an early or late age has no bearing on his or her sexual orientation. . . . Usually they don't think of their same-sex play as homosexual. But . . . some children end up very worried that because they want to touch a friend of the same sex, or already have, that means they're gay. It doesn't. And it's normal—all the varieties of sex play among kids are normal. (Morris, 1984, 85)

Most of the books addressed to parents offer advice about what parents should do if they think their kids aren't straight. Ratner and Chamlin (1985) pose the hypothetical question, "Will my son's love of 'dressing up' lead to homosexuality?" And they respond, "No. Many parents discourage boys from playing 'dress-up' and 'house,' but at certain ages, certainly preschool, it's appropriate. Preschoolers actively assume many different roles" (35). They imply that at a certain age, gender-bending will—and should—straighten out. Spock and Rothenberg (1992) imply this as well, saying "When parents think that their little boy is effeminate or their little girl too masculine, they may worry that the child will grow up to be a homosexual or lesbian. In fact, the majority of such children will grow up to be heterosexual" (52). However, they then recommend therapy for a boy who wants to play with girls and dolls, and who wants to wear dresses ("I would assume that something had gotten mixed up in his identification"), as well as for a girl who plays "only with boys" and is "**always** unhappy about being a girl" (52). A girl who prefers to play with boys and who "occasionally" wishes she were a boy, "but also [enjoys] playing with girls" does not concern them (52).

Levkoff is the only author among those writing to parents who discusses the social construction of gender and of sexual identity, and she endorses parental acceptance of all forms of self-expression among kids. At the same time, she presents parental emotional responses to a child's coming out as gay (there is no discussion of parental response to transgenderedness) as almost entirely unpleasant: "It can be an emotionally challenging time. . . . Most people speak of grief and mourning, as if they have lost a loved one. . . . It is natural and it will pass. What we hope is that these turbulent and complex feelings will bring you, in the end, to acceptance. But it isn't an easy road" (2007, 99).

Harris and Emberley (1999) are the only authors of books for young children who explore alternatives to heterosexuality, and they, along with Levkoff, are the only authors in our sample who explain that love and sexual behavior can be multifaceted without invoking the past pathologizing or current acceptance of medical experts: "There are lots of kinds of love—like love between a parent and child, love between friends, love between kids, love between teenagers, and love between grownups. There can be love between a female and a male, or a male and a male, or a female and a female" (Harris and Emberley, 1999, 31). They go on to explain the terms homosexual, heterosexual, gay, lesbian, bisexual and straight, and proclaim "A person's daily life—having friends, having fun, going to work, being a mom or dad, loving another person—is mostly the same whether a person is straight or gay." This text appears with an illustration of a possibly interracial gay male couple and their two kids eating dinner (32). Authors seek to promote harmony across difference by positing that difference is overshadowed by commonalities among people, regardless of sexual identity.

SO WHAT SHOULD WE TELL THE KIDS?

First let us sum up what we *do* tell the kids in the discourse of these didactic books: that the central focus of sexuality is procreative penile-vaginal intercourse; that this form of sexuality is "natural" and good; that participants should be monogamous adults; and that proper sexual expression is based in love and enacted in private. Many authors writing for older kids and adults do acknowledge other sorts of sexual behavior, but these discussions are limited and not integrated into presentations of what is clearly the main event. Nonheterosexual activities are marginalized. The books can be seen as precursors to school-based sex education programs, which increase the focus on dangers, often advocate abstinence, and are notoriously heterosexist and devoid of discussions of gendered or sexual power dynamics (e.g., see Irvine, 2004; Luker, 2007; Raymond, 1994; Watney, 1991).

When do we tell children that some sex is amazing, some is lovely, some is dull, some becomes repugnant in retrospect, and some is horrible while it's happening? When do we tell them about its potential variety and variability? When do we expose children to a peerlike level of sexual honesty in which we speak to them of the intensity of desire, the fickleness of lust, the pain of rejection? Or do we simply not venture this far into the murky depths of sexuality? Do we just let them find out whatever they'll find out by themselves from people we can only hope will not hurt them or mess up their lives? All the while, we must bear in mind that something we say to them today could be the impetus for therapy later. What truths, warnings, and recommendations do we dare to communicate? In short, our task is absurd and impossible the more we ponder it, yet most of us would agree that to say nothing would be worse than to make some kind of attempt.

So we're back where we started, with Spock and Rothenberg's (1992) admonition against the stork, in favor of the truth. There is no absolute truth about sexuality, so we have to decide what and how we want to discuss sexuality with our children. Sex education books for children and parents are generally a step in the right direction, and are certainly better than nothing, in our view. But they are not as comprehensive or critical or political as they could be.

Imagine sex education books that would present gender and genitals as socially constructed; sexuality could then more easily be conceived by young readers as taking place on a continuum rather than as written in stone. Imagine books that present sex as not only the cause of procreation but also as recreational, as indeed it is for most people engaged in it most of the time. Imagine books that present sexual activities other than penile–vaginal intercourse as satisfying and good for body and soul (or even just for body!). Imagine sex educational books that would acknowledge and contest power dynamics based on gender and sexual categories—books that would urge children to interrogate, rather than reify, these categories. Imagine the sex lives that might develop out of such an antifoundational foundation. Would you buy these books for your children?

REFERENCES

Sex Books for Young Children

Andry, Andrew, Steven Schepp, and Blake Hampton (ill.). 1979 (1968). *How Babies Are Made*. Boston: Little, Brown.

Baker, Sue. 1990. *The Birds and the Bees*. Swindon, Bologna, New York: M. Twinn.

Brooks, Robert, and Susan Perl (ill.). 1983. *So That's How I Was Born!* New York: Aladdin.

Brown, Laura Krasny, and Marc Brown. 1997. *What's the Big Secret?: Talking about Sex with Girls and Boys*. Boston: Little, Brown.

Cole, Babette. 1993. *Mommy Laid an Egg OR Where Do Babies Come From?* New York: Chronicle Books.

Cole, Joanna, and Margaret Miller (photo.). 1993 (1984). *How You Were Born*. New York: Mulberry.

Davis, Jennifer, and Laura Cornell (ill.). 1997. *Before You Were Born: A Lift-the-Flap Book*. New York: Workman.

Gordon, Sol, Judith Gordon, and Vivien Cohen (ill.). 1992 (1974). *Did the Sun Shine before You Were Born?: A Sex Education Primer*. Amherst, NY: Prometheus Books.

Harris, Robie H., and Michael Emberley (ill.) 2006. *It's Not the Stork! A Book about Boys, Girls, Babies, Bodies, Families and Friends*. Cambridge, MA: Candlewick Press.

Harris, Robie H., and Michael Emberley (ill.). 1999. *It's So Amazing!: A Book about Eggs, Sperm, Birth, Babies, and Families*. Cambridge, MA: Candlewick Press.

Hickling, Meg, and Kim La Fave (ill.) 2002. *Boys, Girls and Body Science.* Maderia Park, British Columbia, Canada: Harbour Publishing Co. Ltd.

Kleven, Sandy, LCSW, and Jody Bergsma (ill.). 1997. *The Right Touch: A Read Aloud Story to Help Prevent Child Abuse.* Bellevue, WA: Illumination Arts.

Saltz, Dr. Gail, and Lynne Cravath (ill.). 2005. *Amazing You! Getting Smart about Your Private Parts.* New York: Penguin Group USA.

Smith, Alastair, and Maria Wheatley (ill.). 1997. *How Are Babies Made?* London: Usbourne Publishing.

Sex Books for Older Children

Basso, Michael J. 1998. *The Underground Guide to Teenage Sexuality.* Minneapolis, MN: Fairview Press.

Basso, Michael J. 2003. *The Underground Guide to Teenage Sexuality, 2nd Edition.* Minneapolis, MN: Fairview Press.

Bell, Ruth. 1987. *Changing Bodies, Changing Lives.* New York: Random House.

Cole, Joanna, and Alan Tiegreen (ill.). 1988. *Asking about Sex and Growing Up: A Question-and-Answer Book for Boys and Girls.* New York: Beech Tree.

Foster, Lorri. 2005. *Let's Talk about S-E-X, 2nd Edition.* Minnetonka, MN: Book Peddlers.

Gordon, Sol, and Vivien Cohen (ill.). 1992 (1977). *Facts about Sex for Today's Youth.* Amherst, NY: Prometheus Books.

Harris, Robie H., and Michael Emberley (ill.) 2004. *It's Perfectly Normal: Changing Bodies, Growing Up, Sex and Sexual Health.* Cambridge, MA: Candlewick Press.

Westheimer, Ruth, and Diane deGroat (ill.). 1998 (1993). *Dr. Ruth Talks to Kids: Where You Came From, How Your Body Changes, and What Sex Is All About.* New York: Aladdin.

Sex Books for Parents

Berkenkamp, Lauri, and Steven C. Atkins. 2002. *Talking to Your Kids About Sex from Toddlers to Preteens: A Go Parents! Guide.* Chicago: Nomad Press.

Calderone, Mary S., and James W. Ramey. 1982. *Talking with Your Child about Sex: Questions and Answers for Children from Birth to Puberty.* New York: Random House.

Eyre, Linda, and Richard Eyre. 1998. *How to Talk to Your Child about Sex.* New York: Saint Martin's Griffin.

Levkoff, Logan. 2007. *Third Base Ain't What It Used to Be: What Your Kids are Learning About Sex Today—and How to Teach Them to Become Sexually Healthy Adults.* New York: New American Library.

Maxwell, Sharon. 2008. *The Talk: What Your Kids Need to Hear from YOU about Sex.* New York: Avery.

Morris, Lois B. 1984. *Talking Sex with Your Kids.* New York: Simon and Shuster.

Ratner, Marilyn, and Susan Chamlin. 1985. *Straight Talk: Sexuality Education for Parents and Kids 4–7.* New York: Viking.

Richardson, Justin, and Mark A. Schuster. 2003. *Everything You Never Wanted Your Kids to Know about Sex (But Were Afraid They'd Ask).* New York: Three Rivers Press.

Roffman, Deborah M. 2002. *How'd I Get in There in the First Place?: Talking to Your Young Child about Sex.* New York: Perseus Publishing.

Schwartz, Pepper, and Dominic Cappello. 2000. *Ten Talks Parents Must Have With Their Children about Sex and Character.* New York: Hyperion.

Spock, Benjamin, and Michael B. Rothenberg. 1992 (1945). *Dr. Spock's Baby and Child Care.* New York: Pocket Books.

Other Sources

Conrad, Peter and Joseph W. Schneider. 1992. *Deviance and Medicalization: From Badness to Sickness.* Philadelphia: Temple University Press.

Ehrenreich, Barbara, and Diedre English. 1986. *ReMaking Love: The Feminization of Sex.* Garden City, NY: Anchor Press/Doubleday.

Irvine, Janice. 2004. *Talk about Sex: The Battles over Sex Education in the United States.* Berkeley: University of California Press.

Luker, Kristin. 2007. *When Sex Goes to School: Warring Views on Sex and Sex Education Since the Sixties.* New York: W.W. Norton.

Moran, Jeffrey P. 2000. *Teaching Sex: The Shaping of Adolescence in the 20th Century.* Cambridge, MA: Harvard University Press.

Moore, Lisa Jean. 2007. *Sperm Counts: Overcome by Man's Most Precious Fluid.* New York: New York University Press.

Patton, Cindy. 1996. *Fatal Advice: How Safe-Sex Education Went Wrong.* Durham, NC: Duke University Press.

Raymond, Diane. 1994. "Homophobia, Identity, and the Meanings of Desire: Reflections on the Cultural Construction of Gay and Lesbian Adolescent Sexuality." In *Sexual Cultures and the Construction of Adolescent Identities,* edited by Janice M. Irvine. Philadelphia: Temple University Press.

Simonds, Wendy. 1992. *Women and Self-Help Culture: Reading between the Lines.* New Brunswick, NJ: Rutgers University Press.

Solinger, Rickie. 2005. *Pregnancy and Power: A Short History of Reproductive Politics in America.* New York: New York University Press.

Watney, Simon. 1991. "School's Out." In *Inside/Out: Lesbian Theories, Gay Theories,* edited Diana Fuss (pp. 387–401). New York: Routledge.

What Do I Say to My Children?

Sol Gordon and Judith Gordon

Sex educators Sol Gordon and Judith Gordon stress the importance of being an askable parent in their book *Raising a Child Responsibly in a Sexually Permissive World*.[1] Here are their responses to some of the most frequently asked questions:

WHEN SHOULD I TELL?

The answer is simple: It is time to tell whenever the child asks. If you are an askable parent, your children may come to you with questions about sex from the time they are two or three years old. Young children's questions are sometimes nonverbal. For example, a child may constantly follow you into the bathroom. To encourage them, you could say, "It looks like you're wondering about something—can I guess what it is?"

Some shy children might ask no questions at all, even of the most askable parents. If your child hasn't raised sexuality-oriented questions by age five, you should start the conversation. Read a book with your child. Tell him or her about a neighbor or a relative who is going to have a baby. While it's fine on occasion to make analogies to animals, do not concentrate on them in your explanations. People and animals have very different habits.

HOW EXPLICIT SHOULD I BE?

Make it a point to use the correct terminology. Avoid such childish expressions as "pee-pee" or "wee-wee." . . . [P]arents can be explicit without overstating the case or feeling compelled to describe sexual relations to a child who hasn't yet grasped much more basic ideas. It is also wiser to say at the start that a baby has its beginning in the mother's uterus, not the stomach, because a child's imagination can easily picture the fetus being mixed up with the food.

IS THERE SUCH A THING AS GIVING TOO MUCH SEX EDUCATION TOO SOON?

Parents worry a great deal about whether they can "harm" their children with "too much" information or by telling their children things that they won't understand. Let us state again that despite the protests of a few "experts," knowledge is not harmful. It does not matter if the child doesn't understand everything you say. What counts is that you are an askable parent. If the child can trust you not to be rigid or hostile in your response or to give misinformation, he or she will ask you questions and use you as a source of wisdom and guidance. . . .

WHAT ABOUT EMBARRASSING QUESTIONS IN PUBLIC?

Children have a great knack for asking the most delicate questions in the supermarket or when special guests have come to dinner. The best approach, no matter how embarrassed you are, is to tell the child that he or she has asked a very good question; if you still have your wits about you, proceed to answer it then and there. In most cases, your guests will silently applaud. If you feel you can't answer the question right away, it is very important to praise the child for asking and to state specifically when you will discuss it. In general, it is better to risk shocking a few grown-ups than to scold or put off your own child.

NOTE

1. Gordon, S., and Gordon, J. 2000. *Raising a Child Responsibly in a Sexually Permissive World*, Second Edition (pp. 43–46). Holbrook, MA: Adams Media.

Source: Raising a Child Responsibly in a Sexually Permissive World, Second Edition (Holbrook, MA: Adams Media), pp. 43–46. Reprinted with permission.

SEXUALITY EDUCATION AND DESIRE: STILL MISSING AFTER ALL THESE YEARS

MICHELLE FINE AND SARA I. MCCLELLAND

Michelle Fine's (1988) article "Sexuality, Schooling, and Adolescent Females: The Missing Discourse of Desire" was published in the *Harvard Educational Review* almost twenty years ago. In that essay, Fine questioned [how] schools taught young people about sexuality. She argued that schools, by positioning young women primarily as potential victims of male sexual aggression, seriously compromised young women and men's development of sexual subjectivities. The capacity of young women to be sexually educated—to engage, negotiate, or resist—was hobbled by schools' refusal to deliver comprehensive sexuality education. . . .

Educated as neither desiring subjects seeking pleasure nor potentially abused subjects who could fight back, young women were denied knowledge and skills, and left to their own (and others') devices in a sea of pleasures and dangers. Even before Fine's article, but especially in the two decades since, feminist scholars, educators, and activists have voiced concern about the missing discourse of female desire (see Rose, 2003; Snitow, Stansell, and Thompson, 1983; Tolman, 2002; Vance, 1993).

Today we continue to worry. Our worries, however, stretch to include the severe and unevenly distributed educational and health consequences of the federal education campaign promoting abstinence only until marriage (AOUM). This educational crusade has been unleashed through public institutions and laws advocating the virtues of abstinence, the dangers of unmarried sex, and the promised safety of heterosexual marriage.

This article focuses on sexuality education through the window of the federally funded AOUM movement. Using federal abstinence guidelines, interviews with sexuality educators, visits to abstinence-only conferences, conversations with youth in schools, and evaluations of abstinence curricula, we critically analyze the history of AOUM policies and the consequences of AOUM for distinct groups of young women living and desiring at the embodied intersections of gender, sexuality, race, ethnicity, class, and disability. . . . The sexual subjectivity of young women remains our focus in this discussion because their bodies bear the consequences of limited sexuality education and are the site where progressive educational and health policies can have significant effect.

CONTEMPORARY ANALYSIS OF SEXUALITY EDUCATION

Adolescent desires develop within the context of global and national politics, ideologies, community life, religious practices, and popular culture; in family living rooms, on the Internet and on MTV; in bedrooms, cars, and alleys (Douglas, 1966; Foucault, 1988; Phillips, 2000). We situate our analysis of adolescent sexuality education within a human rights framework, allied with struggles over reproductive rights, political economy, health care, education and prison reform, structural and personal violence (see Correa, 1994; Correa and Petchesky, 1994; Impett, Schooler, and Tolman, in press; Luttrell, 2002; Nussbaum, 2003; Petchesky, 2005; Roberts, 2002; Sen, George, and Ostlin, 2002; Sen, 1994; Tolman, Striepe, and Harmon, 2003; Zavella, 2003).

We understand further that while all young people, by virtue of age, depend on the state and develop under state regulations, the adverse consequences of state policies that curtail education and health are not equally distributed. In fact, national policies concerning sexuality fall unevenly on girls, poor and working-class youth, teens with disabilities, Black and Latino adolescents, and lesbian/gay/bisexual and transgender youth. . . .

While early seeds of the abstinence movement can be traced back to the 1981 Adolescent Family Life Act (AFLA), and followed up fifteen years later by the Personal Responsibility and Work Opportunity Reconciliation Act signed into law by President Clinton in 1996, the contemporary AOUM campaign marks a moment when social policy, ideology, and educational practice are being aligned for abstinence, for heterosexual marriage, and against critical education about power, desires, or dangers. . . .

The argument for abstinence only until marriage is beginning to assert a kind of natural cultural authority, in schools and out. . . . Dialogue is being censored in many classrooms and beyond, with serious educational and health consequence for young women—for some more than others, but indeed for us all.

THICK DESIRE

This article picks up where we left off in 1988. Almost twenty years later, for better or worse, the discourse of adolescent desire is no longer missing (Harris, 2005). It has been splashed all over MTV, thoroughly commodified by the market, and repetitively performed in popular culture. A caricature of desire itself is now displayed loudly, as it remains simultaneously silent (Burns and Torre, 2005; Harris, 2005; Tolman, 1994, 2002, 2006). . . .

Today we can "google" for information about the average young woman's age of "sexual debut," if she used a condom, got pregnant, the number of partners she had, if she aborted or gave birth, and what the baby weighed. However, we don't know if she enjoyed it, wanted it, or if she was violently coerced. Little has actually been heard from young women who desire pleasure, an education, freedom from violence, a future, intimacy, an abortion, safe and affordable child care for their babies, or health care for their mothers. There is almost nothing heard from the young women who are most often tossed aside by state, family, church, and school—those who are lesbian, gay, bisexual, queer, or questioning (LGBTQQ), immigrant and undocumented youth, and young women with disabilities. While these marginalized young people may yearn for quality education, health care, economic well being, and healthy sexual lives, day to day they attend underfunded schools, contend with high-stakes testing, endure heightened police surveillance, are seduced by military recruitment promises, and are surrounded by fundamentalist ideologies working to reconstitute their public school classrooms and penetrate courts and state legislatures (Fine, Burns, Payne, and Torre, 2004). . . .

Thus, as a friendly amendment to the 1988 essay—and with the wisdom of hindsight and living in a different global politic—we offer educators and researchers a historic revision to the missing discourse of desire. We offer instead a framework of *thick desire*, arguing that young people are entitled to a broad range of desires for meaningful intellectual, political, and social engagement, the possibility of financial independence, sexual and reproductive freedom, protection from racialized and sexualized violence, and a way to imagine living in the future tense (Appadurai, 2001, 2004; Nussbaum, 2003). We understand that young women's thick desires require a set of publicly funded enabling conditions, in which teen women have opportunities to: (a) develop intellectually, emotionally, economically, and culturally; (b) imagine themselves as sexual beings capable of pleasure and cautious about danger without carrying the undue burden of social, medical, and reproductive consequences; (c) have access to information and health-care resources; (d) be protected from structural and intimate violence and abuse; and (e) rely on a public safety net of resources to support youth, families, and community.

A framework of thick desire situates sexual well being within structural contexts that enable economic, educational, social, and psychological health. In this essay, we seek to understand how laws, public policies, and institutions today both nourish and threaten young women's sense of economic, social, and sexual possibility (Appadurai, 2004; Nussbaum, 2003). . . . By examining the changes in sex education policy over the past two decades, and the effects on distinct groups of young women, we can see that enabling conditions for thick desire ossify as *public assistance* and are replaced with *punishing morality* as neoliberalism and fundamentalism frame public educational policy. . . .

ABSTINENCE ONLY UNTIL MARRIAGE

The 1981 passage of the Adolescent Family Life Act marked the first federal law expressly funding sex education "to promote self-discipline and other prudent approaches" (Adolescent Family Life Act, 42 U.S.C. § 300z [1982 and Supp. III 1985], as cited in Kelly, 2005). In 1996, with the

Congressional passage of the Personal Responsibility and Work Opportunity Reconciliation Act, AOUM education funds gained an additional funding source through the approval of Title V of the Social Security Act. Under Title V, the U.S. Department of Health and Human Services (DHHS) allocates $50 million annually in federal funds to the states. Since 1982, when funding was first earmarked for AOUM education, over one billion dollars has been spent through federally sponsored programs (including AFLA, Title V, and CBAE; *Sexuality Information and Education Council of the U.S. [SIECUS]*, 2004c). For the 2007 budget, President Bush advocated for and was granted $204 million in AOUM funding and, according to the U.S. Office of Management and Budget (2006), the federal budget "supports increasing funding for abstinence-only education programs to $270 million by 2009."*

Virtually all of the growth in funding since 2001 has come from the Community Based Abstinence Education (CBAE) program (Santelli et al., 2006a; SIECUS, 2004c). CBAE funding is typically granted to community and local organizations, but states are eligible to apply, and many states use this funding stream to bolster their existing AOUM school programming that rely on federal Title V monies (SIECUS, 2004a). Programs funded under CBAE are explicitly restricted from providing young people information about contraception or safer sex practices—this includes organizations that

---

*Editor's note: In 2009, President Obama announced that the 2010 federal budget would eliminate funding for abstinence-only until marriage programs. In September 2011, Rep. Randall Hultgren (R-IL) initiated legislation to restore this funding through the Abstinence-Centered Education Reallocation Act. In December 2011, the Senate passed omnibus bill H.R. 2055, which includes extensive funding for comprehensive family planning and teenage pregnancy prevention programs. The bill also offers funding for abstinence-only educational measures. This bill was signed into law by President Obama on December 23, 2011.

might use nonfederal funds to do so (Santelli et al., 2006a; see SIECUS, 2004a, for description of federal AOUM funding streams).

All federally funded abstinence programming must adhere to the following series of principles . . . According to Section 510(b) of Title V of the Social Security Act (U.S. DHHS, 2003, p. 14), the term "abstinence education" means an educational or motivational program that

a. has the exclusive purpose of teaching the social, psychological, and health gains to be realized by abstaining from sexuality activity;

b. teaches abstinence from sexual activity outside marriage as the expected standard for all school-age children;

c. teaches that abstinence from sexual activity is the only certain way to avoid out-of-wedlock pregnancy, sexually transmitted diseases, and other associated health problems;

d. teaches that a mutually faithful monogamous relationship in the context of marriage is the expected standard of sexual activity;

e. teaches that sexual activity outside marriage is likely to have harmful psychological and physical effects;

f. teaches that bearing children out of wedlock is likely to have harmful consequences for the child, the child's parents, and society;

g. teaches young people how to reject sexual advances and how alcohol and drug use increase vulnerability to sexual advances;

h. teaches the importance of attaining self-sufficiency before engaging in sexual activity.

The eight central tenets of AOUM education impose a strict set of criteria on educators who are looking to educate young people about their sexuality. The . . . points are designed to discourage teenage sexual behavior and, ultimately, to reduce rates of teenage pregnancy and sexually transmitted diseases. At the same time, however, they also introduce ideological intrusions that are not merely about reducing sexual behavior, but also instruct young people

to adopt very specific normative relationships to their sexuality. There is, notably, the "expected standard" that sexual activity occurs only within the context of marriage, a move that places not only teenage sexual behavior but the sexual choices made by people of all ages and all sexual orientations outside the limits of appropriate behavior. Furthermore, the eight central tenets of AOUM suggest a direct and (im)moral route from nonmarital sex to disease and social problems. Insisting that young people be instructed that "sexual activity outside of the context of marriage is likely to have harmful psychological and physical effects" and that "bearing children out of wedlock is likely to have harmful consequences for the child, the child's parents, and society" does not lodge sexuality education in a foundation of information and support for a healthy adult sexuality. Instead, it lodges sexuality education in fear and shame, firmly burying discussions of desire and pleasure.

The promise of federal dollars often pushes the schools and communities in impoverished areas into accepting these curricular restrictions in order to fill funding gaps. Students who are most in need of education and health care—poor urban and rural students—are thereby the most likely to be mis-educated through these curricula. . . . The distribution of AOUM curricula favors communities with high levels of teen sexual activity and teen pregnancy and, importantly, imposes religious and moralizing curricula more strongly on youth who have already been sexual and who most need information about how to avoid pregnancy and sexually transmitted diseases. . . .

Marriage Legislation and Promotion

In addition to the federal monies devoted to AOUM programming, other relevant policy shifts have focused state energies and funding on encouraging men and women to marry if they have a child together. The 1996 Personal Responsibility and Work Opportunity Reconciliation Act established a financial incentive to reduce out-of-wedlock childbearing. It authorized $100 million in annual bonus payments to the five states that achieved the largest reduction in out-of-wedlock births among welfare and non-welfare teens and adults and reduced abortion rates among that population to less than the 1995 level in their state. In 2000, four new measures were created for the High-Performance Bonus, including a measure of family formation and stability. The marriage bonus is awarded to a state that can demonstrate an increase in the percent of children who reside in married couple families (Ooms, 2001). . . .

Federal policies that promote marriage . . . punish poor single mothers for not choosing to marry. This type of monetary and institutional enforcement of marriage negates their right to form intimate associations on their own terms (Mink, 2002). By targeting communities with high rates of children born outside marriage, federal marriage policies not only dictate who receives funding, but also place blame for societal woes on those individuals who are most denied enabling conditions for thick desire . . .

What Is Taught in Schools: The Chill

. . . . It is estimated that 33 percent of all public schools now offer AOUM curricula (Planned Parenthood, 2005a). Since 1988, the number of sex education teachers who teach AOUM has grown tenfold, from 2 percent to 23 percent (Santelli et al., 2006a). As abstinence funding and education spread across the nation, the net of teen activities considered in violation of abstinence regulations stretches as well. In 2006, the federal guidelines for funding AOUM education underwent substantial revisions (see U.S. DHHS, 2006). The new guidelines explicitly endorse the U.S. government's support of abstinence. However, instead of encouraging adolescents to avoid sexual intercourse, the new definition casts a much wider net of proscribed activity: "Sexual activity refers to any type of genital contact or sexual stimulation between two persons including, but not limited to sexual intercourse" (pg. 5). Apparently in responding to criticism that abstinence previously had not been adequately defined (Santelli, Ott, Lyon, Rogers, and Summers, 2006b), this updated version creeps into the territory of all things "stimulating." This broad definition of abstinence removes any possibility for sex education curricula to mention how teens might engage in non-intercourse behaviors, even in an effort to remain "technically" abstinent.

These guidelines set up an impenetrable wall between youth and adults, reducing the likelihood that conversations will occur between young people and educators, health-care practitioners, and youth workers. The loss of these conversations puts young people's health at risk. . . . Again, we can see that the costs of constricted talk are quite severe for some groups of youth. Consider, for instance, Harilyn Rousso's (2001) finding that young women with physical and sensory disabilities are far less likely than their nondisabled peers to receive any kind of sexuality education and are far less likely to talk to their mothers, friends, or teachers about sexuality and reproduction. Combine this with the finding that disabled youth are almost twice as likely to report sexual abuse as are nondisabled children, with estimates that 39 percent to 68 percent of disabled girls and 16 percent to 30 percent of disabled boys are sexually abused before the age of eighteen (Rousso, 2001). . . . With disproportionate histories of abuse and little in the way of home or peer guidance around sexuality, students with disabilities make clear the need for more information although they receive less.

The 2006 federal guidelines regarding AOUM education funding cut off any discussion of how teenagers might develop healthy sexual behaviors for present or future relations. In the name of protection, the teenage sexual body has been sent underground with little information and almost no protection.

A CLOSER LOOK AT THE AOUM CONTENT

In 2004, a systematic review of the abstinence-only curricula was commissioned by U.S. Representative Henry A. Waxman, ranking minority member of the Committee on Government Reform (2004), to evaluate the scientific and medical accuracy of thirteen of the most commonly used of these curricula. Reviewers found that two-thirds of the programs contained basic scientific errors (e.g., warnings that sweat and tears are risk factors for HIV transmission); relied on curricula that distorted information about the effectiveness of contraceptives (e.g., claims that condoms fail approximately 31 percent of the time); blurred religion and science (e.g., presenting as fact that life begins with conception); and reinforced stereotypes about girls and boys as scientific facts (see Brown, 2005).

Many curricula for AOUM programs link nonmarital sex with disease and possible death (see Kempner, 2001, for further discussion). Researchers have noted that these curricula often include scare tactics such as the video titled *No Second Chance,* in which a student asks a school nurse, "What if I want to have sex before I get married?" to which the nurse replies, "Well, I guess you'll just have to be prepared to die" (as cited in Levine, 2002). The national AOUM program Family Accountability Communicating Teen Sexuality (FACTS) instructs students that "there is no such thing as 'safe' or 'safer' premarital sex. There are always risks associated with it, even dangerous, life-threatening ones" (Fuller, McLaughlin, and Asato, 2000, as cited in Kempner, 2001). Young people are being instructed continually to believe sexual activity is dangerous to their health.

The Press for Heterosexual Marriage

In the AOUM curriculum, not only is teen sexuality always bad, but heterosexual marriage is always good. In fact, marriage is presented as the only context for safe sex. The pro-marriage language of the AOUM curricula was strengthened in 2005, when programs once designed to discourage "*premature* sexual activity" and to encourage "abstinence" were redesigned to discourage "*premarital* sexuality activity" and encourage "abstinence only until marriage" decisions (Dailard, 2005). The framework for AOUM funding demanded that abstinence curricula define marriage as "a legal union between one man and one woman as a husband and wife, and the word 'spouse' refers only to a person of the opposite sex" (U.S. DHHS, 2006). In addition, funding restrictions required that having sex within marriage be presented as the only way for teens to avoid getting STDs and related health problems. Heterosexual marriage was presented as the answer to safe sex even as same-sex marriage was fought by many of these same abstinence advocates.

In this push for heterosexual marriage, we see a telling instance where the chance to educate teens about the potential dangers inherent in early (and any) marriage gets lost. The little research that exists on teen marriage has found that young marriages often have high levels of violence. Young mothers who marry are more likely to have a second child shortly after the first than those who do not, and teenage women who marry and then divorce have worse economic outcomes than teenage mothers who never marry (Seiler, 2002). Teen marriage significantly reduces the likelihood that a woman, especially a young mother, will return to school. A study of African American teenage mothers found that 56.4 percent returned to school within six months of having a baby if they did not marry, compared to 14.9 percent of those who did marry (Seiler, 2002). In

AOUM instruction, these problems of heterosexual marriage are sidelined, the risks of contracting sexually transmitted diseases, including HIV within marriage, are ignored, and the issue of same-sex marriage is silenced.

Homophobic Violence and Harassment

For lesbian, gay, bisexual, transgender, queer, and questioning (LGBTQQ) youth, the AOUM curriculum not only fails to address their very real educational needs and concerns, but, more significantly, it colludes in the homophobic harassment already present in public school settings. More than one-third of LGBTQQ students report hearing homophobic remarks from teachers or school staff, and nearly 40 percent indicated that no one intervened when homophobic comments were made (Brown and Taverner, 2001). . . . Because the abstinence model is predicated on waiting until marriage for sexual expression, and marriage is not an option for these youth, the AOUM curricula not only denies LGBTQQ youth legitimacy, but it also asks them to hold aside (and silence) significant pieces of their identities in order to participate in the *moral* community of students (Opotow, 1990) who deserve sexuality education. This is particularly true when the conversation turns to misinformation about same-sex practices, the presumed failures of condoms, and the much repeated claim that sex inside marriage is the only form of healthy sexuality.

A QUESTION OF ACCOUNTABILITY: EDUCATIONAL AND HEALTH CONSEQUENCES

Given the fact that the aim of AOUM policies is to protect the health of young people, one would assume that this instruction would be joined by an ambitious evaluation of the health and sexual outcomes of those youth who are exposed to AOUM curricula. This has not been

the case. Instead, concern for adolescent health has been set aside and replaced with a simple evaluation focus on whether or not students endorse beliefs about abstinence and marriage. This can be seen in the guidelines produced by the U.S. DHHS. In 2005, programs that received federal AOUM funding were required to include demonstrable outcomes, such as a reduction in STDs and pregnancies among adolescents (U.S. DHHS, 2005). By 2006, the U.S. DHHS stepped away from using behavioral and health outcomes as a way of judging a program's success and replaced these with the requirement that programs demonstrate that they "create an environment within communities that supports teen decisions to postpone sexual activity until marriage" (U.S. DHHS, 2006). This shift is important as it marks a distinct lack of accountability for education and health behaviors on the part of AOUM programs.

That these programs are no longer required to improve young people's health in order to be considered successful is worrisome in light of empirical data about how abstinence education actually affects adolescent (and later, adult) sexual health. These include how long youth remain abstinent, what choices they make when they decide to have sex (including sexual behaviors and contraception use), and the long-term consequences of learning exclusively about the dangers of sexuality.

One way to measure the question of what choices young people make when they decide to engage in sexual activity is to measure STD rates after young people take "virginity pledges," an exercise that exists within some AOUM programming. Bearman and Brückner (2001) found that "pledgers" typically delayed their first heterosexual intercourse an average of eighteen months later than nonpledgers. In a follow up, however, Brückner and Bearman (2005) found that 88 percent of the middle and high school students who had sworn to abstain did, in fact, have premarital sex—and, importantly, often had unprotected sex. Pledgers were 30 percent less likely than nonpledgers to use contraception once they became sexually active, and also less likely to use condoms and seek medical testing and treatment.

Other adolescent health researchers have studied the "user-failure" rates for abstinence; in other words, the numbers of youth who promise to be abstinent until marriage, but in fact do have premarital sex. By studying teens that abstained for a period of time, Haignere and her colleagues (Haignere, Gold, and McDanel, 1999) found that abstinence education had a user-failure rate between 26 percent and 86 percent. This rate is higher than the condom user-failure rate, which is between 12 percent and 70 percent. These findings highlight the temporary quality of virginity pledges and the nonsustainability of intentions to abstain. . . . Youth who have been instructed using AOUM curricula and who have pledged to remain abstinent are becoming sexually active with no information about how to do so successfully and safely.

These young people are being educated to mistrust condoms and contraception, to feel shame about their premarital sexuality, and to remain silent about their own sexual development. By insisting that a pledge of abstinence is enough to guarantee subsequent sexual decision-making—by condemning premarital sexual activity, contraception, and condoms—educators, policymakers, and families are placing young people at risk. Even adults who want young people to remain abstinent until marriage recognize that it is unlikely they will do so. . . .

Research has repeatedly shown that students in comprehensive sexuality education classes—those that teach various strategies to reduce pregnancy and disease, and to pursue healthy sexual development—do not engage in sexual activity more often or earlier than those in AOUM classes; they do, however, use contraception and practice safer sex more consistently when they become sexually active (Kirby, 1997, 1999, 2000, 2001). Kirby (1997) found that "the weight of the evidence indicates that these abstinence programs do not delay the onset of intercourse" (p. 25). Kirby also found evidence that programs that address both abstinence and contraception resulted in better sexual health outcomes for young people. . . . [In addition,] quasi-experimental evaluation of condom distribution programs found that school-based access to condoms does not increase rates of sexual activity, but does heighten the use of condoms by students who are sexually active (Guttmacher et al., 1997). Moving educational and health resources to schools does not appear to increase sexual activity, but does contribute to a sense of sexual responsibility.

It is clear that sexuality education must serve all youth with information, support, and resources that allow young people to make informed decisions about their bodies and their sexual health. As you will see from what follows, young people desperately need and deserve far more information, sustained and safe conversations with peers and adults, and more sophisticated critical skills to negotiate the pleasures and dangers of their quite active—and often uninformed—sexual lives.

SEX IN NUMBERS

. . . . The statistics that follow tell us something about what young women are doing with their bodies, but they do not tell us about sexual subjectivities (Horne and Zimmer-Gembeck, 2006)—that is, if these activities were wanted or enjoyed by these young women. When we see high rates of STDs and pregnancy among teenage girls, *whom* do we imagine (Wyatt, 1994)? Do we imagine a girl we consider a desirous subject, a victim, or both? And what of her access to a quality high school, college, health insurance, a place to call home? Have we learned whether her school district was adequately financed with certified educators? Was she able to attend a high school that offered her a sense of cultural belonging, a chance to enquire, a strong curriculum of advanced mathematics, science, writing, and informed college counseling? Has her community received more resources devoted to policing and criminal justice than education, more military recruiters than sexuality educators? Was she taught about masturbation, LGBTQQ sexualities, abortion, pleasures, and dangers? Could she confide in anyone about her stepfather, uncle, disability-related caretaker, or mother abusing her? How many sick or dependent relatives was she caring for because the state didn't?

In the end, what do statistics on sexual behaviors tell us about the presence, absence, or subversion of enabling conditions for thick desire? More importantly, what do they obscure about a girl's access to health-care, insurance, the quality of her school, or the wide variation of sexual histories within her racial group? As we turn now to the seductive details of teen sexuality—rates, types, and consequences—we hope that the reader will ingest these numbers critically, always imagining real young women developing real bodies at vibrant intersections, affected by distant international and federal policies, local institutions, communities, complex intimate relations, and itchy, unformed, and still developing desires for a better tomorrow.

Teen Heterosexual Sex and Pregnancy

The Centers for Disease Control and Prevention (CDC) report that more than one-third of fifteen- to seventeen-year-old males (36 percent) and females (39 percent) have had vaginal intercourse; almost one-third have given oral sex (28 percent of males and 30 percent of females); and more have received oral sex (40 percent of males and 38 percent of females). Adolescent females are about twice as likely to report same-sex sexual contact as males (Mosher, Chandra, and Jones, 2005, p. 9).

International comparisons are critical because they allow us to consider what these numbers reveal about adolescent life in the United States. Teens in the United States, on average, begin having heterosexual intercourse at 17.4 years of age; the average age is 18 in France, 17.4 in Germany, and 17.7 in the Netherlands (Feijoo, 2001). Yet young women in the United States are *nine* times more likely to become pregnant than young women in the Netherlands. The U.S. teen pregnancy rate is almost twice that of Great Britain, four times that of France and Germany, and more than ten times that of Japan. . . .

Despite these international comparisons, by 2000, U.S. teen pregnancy rates had dropped to an all-time low for White, Black, and Latina women (CDC, 2005; National Campaign to Prevent Teen Pregnancy, 2005). Teen birth rates also dipped from 89.1 for every 1,000 young women in 1960 to 41.7 in 2003; 18.3 teen births per 1,000 for Asian Americans; 28.5 for Whites; 68.3 for African Americans and 83.4 for Latinas (Kaiser Family Foundation, 2004). Santelli and colleagues (2004) have suggested that the recent decline in pregnancy rates can be attributed to a combination of decreased sexual experience and increased use of contraception.

Condoms, Contraception, and Abortions

Using our 1988 benchmark to track progress, we can see that young women's risk of pregnancy has declined by 21 percent from 1991 to 2003, largely because of improvements in contraceptive use among White and Black teens. In 1991, in a sample of surveyed high school girls, 22 percent used the pill only and 35 percent condoms only. By 2003, 14 percent used the pill and 49.3 percent used condoms (Santelli, Morrow, Anderson, and Lindberg, 2006c).

What looks like good "individual" news seems a bit more complex "relationally" in our ethnographic conversations with diverse groups of high school students in the New York metropolitan area, where we got an earful about the gendered politics of negotiating condom use:

Michelle: So, for those young people who do engage in sex, do they use condoms?
Young men: Sometimes, yeah, not always.
John: Really, I like it raw.
Michelle: Do you worry about pregnancy or disease, HIV?
Kevin: Yeah, we got SuperAids in this town.
Lawrence: Nah . . . Magic Johnson's OK—if you got money you don't get AIDS, they got medicines, but for the rest of us, it will kill you in three weeks.
Michelle: Can young women carry condoms and pull them out as needed?
Marcos: No way, I wouldn't trust the girls to do that. They would stick pin holes in the condoms.
Two young women: (*appearing shocked*) Why would we do that?
Steve: To get the baby, then you think he'll stick around.
Michelle (*after viewing a bag that the teacher displayed of more than twelve forms of contraception, all to be used by/inserted into young women*): So what if there were a pill for young men. You can have an erection, ejaculation, just no sperm. Would you use it?
(*Half of the students say "yes" while the other half give other responses.*)
Young men: No way, I'm not putting anything into my body. Could kill you. Could make you sterile.
(*Two young women roll their eyes.*)

In this conversation we heard young men who were worried about HIV/AIDS but who still preferred to have sex "raw." In another setting, we heard that many "guys where I live" considered "protection is for soft n—gers." We heard young men and women agree that with access to enough money, a person could avoid dying from AIDS, like Magic Johnson, but those without money were likely to die within three weeks. In another school, the young men worried aloud that their partners may not be clean: "I make sure she carries Baby Wipes and uses them before we get involved." Young men were clear that they didn't want to insert chemicals or barriers into their bodies, as young women rolled their eyes and detailed the labors, risks, and burdens of assuming sole responsibility for protection. Across our conversations with youth, however, young men and women agreed that conversations like these were desperately needed in order to dispel the myths and layers of misinformation that are already part of how young people learn about sex. . . .

In one of the schools, our conversation turned to the question of abortion. The discomfort in the room was palpable; we could feel the strong resistance to acknowledging abortions in this low-income, predominantly African American and immigrant community.

Michelle: So, do people in this school talk about how you can get an abortion if you need or want one?
Teacher: Not so much in this community. They don't really get abortions here.
Students: We don't talk about it that much.

Most of the young people (and their educators) knew much about the pregnancies and births in their community, but not about the abortions. We sent them the local statistics to contradict the shared sense that "they don't really get abortions here." . . . It is clear that there is a silent yet highly regular process that young women are engaging in—privately, maybe with a friend or relative, perhaps with shame, perhaps with a sense of relief, but likely imagining themselves to be the only young women in their community having an abortion. . . .

If young women are expected to carry the burden of unwanted pregnancies or of abortion, why do they have to do so silently? According to the CDC report on "abortion surveillance" (Strauss et al., 2004), which reflects state-reported abortions only and does not include procedures performed by private physicians, 18 to 19 percent of all abortions are performed on teens. This is not a trivial matter that should be ignored in sexuality curricula.

SEXUALLY TRANSMITTED DISEASES

Evidence on venereal disease is also critical to a full understanding of the consequences of sexual behavior. In 2003, women age 13 to 19 accounted for half of the HIV cases in their age group. This number demonstrates the growing impact of HIV on women, and young women in particular. As a comparison, women age 20 to 24 accounted for only 37 percent of the HIV cases in their age group. Again, these numbers fall unevenly across ethnicities and most seriously affect women of color. . . . . Young people most at risk for pregnancy and sexually transmitted diseases are also more likely to experience medical indigence, rely on publicly funded health care, and report lower rates of physician contact (Fuligni and Hardway, 2004; Office of Women's Health, 1998).

The wretched combination of rising drop out/push out rates, expansion of the criminal justice system into communities of color, and uninsured health care (Nussbaum, 2003) bodes poorly for young women's sexual health and reproductive freedom. . . . With the introduction and growth of funding and programming for AOUM curriculum in schools, many of these young women are taught to just say no—with no attention to the contexts in which they live, the institutions they inhabit, or the families in which they reside. When we read these statistics on sexual outcomes, we may blame (or pity) the young women themselves, either way camouflaging their (dis)abling contexts (Geronimus and Thompson, 2004). . . . The state slips gently off the hook as the young woman stands alone, holding the consequences and the blame.

Taking Positions

Two groups have distinct reactions to the material about teen sexuality and health outcomes presented above. Both agree that young people should be healthy and free of sexual coercion and that abstinence is a reasonable choice for adolescents. Both are anxious to reduce unintended pregnancies, STD rates, and all forms of sexual coercion. Where these two groups part ways lies in how they view young people's, and especially young women's, sexuality. One group—which includes most parents and educators (Dailard, 2001; Darroch, Landry, and Singh, 2000)—is committed to providing detailed information to young people about their bodies in order to encourage young women and men to make decisions that are driven by their own experience of sexual agency, desire, and an informed consideration of sexual dangers.

In fact, a national poll undertaken by National Public Radio, the Kaiser Family Foundation, and the John F. Kennedy School of Government (2004) found that 90 percent of parents of junior and senior high school students believed it was very or somewhat important to have sexuality education as part of the school curriculum, while 7 percent of parents did not want sex education to be taught in school at all (p. 5). Sixty-seven percent of parents of junior and senior high school students stated that federal government funding "should be used to fund more comprehensive sex education programs that include information on how to obtain and use condoms and other contraceptives," instead of funding programs that have "abstaining from sexual activity" as their only purpose (p. 7). People in this group argue that healthy sex lives are developed through comprehensive sexuality education, trusting relationships with adults and peers, and sufficient emotional and medical support in the form of contraceptives, access to abortion and child care, and protection against STDs. Healthy sexual lives require serious education and ongoing conversation about how to pursue pleasure, understand consequences, and protect against violence and coercion (see Tolman, 2002, 2006).

"We need to encourage self-denial, self-restraint. They need to control their impulses" (Allen, 2005).

AOUM advocates argue that by teaching abstinence only, social problems such as teen pregnancy, STDs, or family violence will be avoided because it is the act of sex that is seen as inherently injurious—both to the teen and to the social fabric (see Santelli et al., 2006a, for discussion). If all sexual activity were to cease prior to marriage, AOUM advocates argue those problems that stem from sex (STDs, psychological problems, etc.) would also cease. AOUM advocates argue that media, readily available contraception, and poor parenting encourage teen sex and that these circumstances cause family violence, incarceration, etc. . . .

Those advocating comprehensive sexuality education maintain that AOUM education requires an unrealistic expectation of sexual behavior; enforces gender rules that inhibit development of female desire; targets Black and Latino youth and reaffirms stereotypes about race and sexual promiscuity; takes money away from other public services, such as schools and clinics; inscribes and enforces a heterosexual marriage model (bringing in the family values rhetoric through the back door); sidelines LGBTQQ teens; censors teachers; undermines school-based conversations about sexuality and health clinic resources; and, ultimately, places blame for social ills on young women who are asked to bear the brunt of all subsequent social problems if they engage in sexual activity, either because they wanted to, were forced to, or felt compelled to for reasons other than their own sexual desire. . . .

SEXUAL SURVEILLANCE: IMPLICATIONS FOR EDUCATORS

Despite the press for AOUM, many teachers and health-care practitioners continue to teach the comprehensive sexuality curriculum, always with an opt-out provision for families that choose for their child to not participate in the class (for a discussion of the history of comprehensive sex education, see Goldfarb, 2005; Kirby, Alter, and Scales, 1979). Those who persist in teaching comprehensive sexuality education, however, report experiencing a "chill" on what they can and can't teach, despite parents' desire for comprehensive sexuality education. For example, more than nine in ten teachers believe that students should be taught about contraception, but one in four are prohibited from doing so (Darroch et al., 2000). At the school level, there are policies in place that enforce these silences within the classroom; 35 percent of public school districts require that abstinence be taught as the only option

---

Editor's note: Another small but quite powerful and well-funded group sees the statistics on teen pregnancy, abortions, and STDs as evidence that sexual activity is inherently dangerous for young people. They believe that sexual health can be found only in adult, married, heterosexual relations. Against teen sexuality and for heterosexual marriage, this second group advocates for teaching sexual abstinence only until marriage. They maintain that if sexual behaviors are successfully halted—not discouraged—the dangerous aspects of sexuality will be avoided. . . . Assumptions about the need to control sexual urges undergird this line of argument. . . . Claude Allen, the former assistant to the president for domestic policy, who justified the need for AOUM education as an obligation of the state, argued that the government should actively promote self-restraint over self-destruction, and that it is the citizens' responsibility to control their own sexual impulses (Allen, 2005).

for unmarried people, and either prohibit the discussion of contraception or limit discussion to its ineffectiveness (Guttmacher Institute, 2002). There are regional differences as well: Over half of the districts in the South have an abstinence-only policy, compared with 20 percent of districts in the Northeast (Landry, Kaeser, and Richards, 1999). This chill of censorship in the classroom extends to the specifics of what is taught. For example, only 21 percent of junior high teachers reported that they taught the correct use of condoms in 2000; only 14 percent of U.S. school districts discuss abortion and sexual orientation (Kelly, 2005). Some school boards, like those in Franklin County, North Carolina, have ordered that chapters be sliced out of health books if they reveal more than what the abstinence-only state law permits (Kelly, 2005). In Lynchburg, Virginia, school board members refused to approve a high school science text until the illustration of a vagina was covered or cut out (Texas Citizens for Science, 2004).

Beyond censorship, a kind of sexual vigilantism has been unleashed by public school administrators, particularly in low-income schools and poorer communities. In 2004, the principal of a New York City middle school accused a group of thirteen- and fourteen-year-old girls of skipping school to attend a hooky party. The girls (not the boys) were suspended until they would submit to HIV, STD, and pregnancy tests, and the young women were required to turn the results over to the school (see New York Civil Liberties Union [NYCLU], 2004). In California, a high school principal called the mother of a young lesbian student to tell her about a series of "run-ins [the student had] with the principal . . . over her hugging, kissing, and holding hands with her girlfriend." The student was not only counseled to leave her school, but her privacy rights were administratively violated as the principal "outed" her to her mother (Lewin, 2005, p. A21). The Gay-Straight Alliance Network has sued a number of districts, on behalf of students' right to safety and freedom from harassment. . . .

Dissent and Resistance

Historically and today, there have been waves of resistance against the AOUM movement, launched by human rights groups, educators, feminists, lawyers, parents, youth, and healthcare providers throughout the nation and globally. Despite a relentless and well-funded assault from the Right, over the past twenty years we have seen waves of a broad-based commitment to deep and comprehensive sexuality education by youth, educators, community members, and feminist lawyers. . . .

In the spirit of democratic access to education and public health, many are arguing for comprehensive sexuality education. In response to the well-funded and chilling campaign launched at the state and federal levels, in 2005, Representative Barbara Lee (D-CA) and Senator Frank Lautenberg (D-NJ) introduced the Responsible Education about Life (REAL) Act in Congress (H.R. 2553 and S. 368). Formerly known as the Family Life Education Act, REAL would allocate $206 million federal dollars to states for medically accurate, age appropriate, comprehensive sex education in schools, including information about both abstinence and contraception (U.S. House of Representatives, 2005; U.S. Senate, 2005). This legislation spells out a few important differences that would be included in federal sexuality education requirements: for example, these curricula must "not teach or promote religion," stress "the value of abstinence while not ignoring those young people who have had or are having sexual intercourse," and insist that information "about the health benefits and side effects of all contraceptives and barrier methods" be provided to young people (Boonstra, 2002, p. 3). To date, over one hundred organizations, including the

American Medical Association, American Public Health Association, and the American Psychological Association, have come out publicly in support of this legislation (p. 2).

Moving from the national to the local level, we see communities organizing to resist the pressures and strings that come with federal funding. In Texas, scientists and educators have joined to create a website (http://www.texscience.org) where they can post informed protests against textbook censorship in their communities. The Colorado Council of Black Nurses returned $16,000 in abstinence-only funding because they believed that the dollars interfered with responsible health education (Planned Parenthood, 2005b). Due to the organization and protests of adolescent health advocates and a group of high school students, the Board of Education of the Chicago Public Schools voted in 2006 to require its schools to offer comprehensive sexual education in grades 6–12, including information about contraception (Mendell, 2006). Finally, youth and youth advocates have created a series of websites for and by young women and young men, addressing questions of pleasure, danger, sexuality, and health for young people seeking information.[1]

Finally, there are a number of comprehensive sexuality education resources available for use in and outside of school settings (Bay-Cheng, 2003; Brick and Taverner, 2003; Brown and Taverner, 2001; Mabray and LaBauve, 2002; Mackler, 1999; SIECUS, 1998, 2004b; Taverner and Montfort, 2005). Community-based organizations, the Unitarian Church, and other groups serving youth have stepped up to the challenge and offered courses, seminars, and workshops on healthy sexual development (Unitarian Universalist Association, 2006a, 2006b). Rich sex education curricula remain available through SEICUS (2004b, 2005). In the face of a massive policy onslaught, there are seeds of resistance and mobilization in every sector of the nation. . . .

CONCLUSION: THEORIZING THICK DESIRE AND FANTASIZING CRITICAL SEXUALITY RESEARCH

Thick desire places sexual activity for all people, regardless of age or gender, within a larger context of social and interpersonal structures that enable a person to engage in the political act of wanting. Wanting can be interpreted in any number of ways, but it necessarily positions a young person as feeling entitled to that which comes in the future. It includes wanting to have unhindered access to structural and institutional supports, such as education, health care, and protection from coercion. With wanting securely in place and thick desire as an organizing frame, it is possible to theorize about young women's sexual and reproductive freedoms not merely from a perspective of minimal loss, but from a perspective that sees them as entitled to desire in all of its forms; entitled to publicly funded enabling conditions across racial, ethnic, class, sexual, geographic, and disability lines. . . .

To elaborate on a vision for critical sexuality studies, we argue that youth sexuality be theorized about and studied inside a stew of desires for opportunity, community, pleasure, and protection from coercion and danger. Adolescents need good schools, health-care, and freedom from violence (structural, institutional, family, and intimate) in order to develop healthy sexual subjectivities. Given this frame, sexuality and reproductive struggles must be linked to fights for equity in school finance, civil/queer/feminist/disability rights, health care, school and prison reform, affirmative action, and access to higher education. Economic, social, and corporeal struggles must be linked through the bodies, imaginations, dreams, and demands of young women and men.

Further, comprehensive sexuality education and youth development must help young women and men navigate across the dialectics of danger and pleasure. Risk cannot be severed from pleasure. They are braided, parasitic, nested inside one another. An exclusive focus on risk not only alienates, but also distorts the complexity of human relations and sexual desire. Therefore, it is naïve to educate for pleasure without attending to risk; but more perverse to imagine that teaching only about risk will transform human behavior. . . .

Turning now to the question of sexuality education, we repeat the words of young people we met from various communities, ranging from those in extreme poverty to those more middle class. When we asked, "What do you need in the way of sexuality education?" young people were clear: "More conversations like this, where we're asked what we think, what we want to know." And yet, according to one of the speakers at the Network for Family Life Education conference in New Jersey in 2005, such pedagogical contexts are unfortunately growing extinct: "In sexuality education, talk is becoming a four-letter word" (Rodriguez, 2005). . . .

One young woman in a high school focus group explained to us, "I do not want to have sex until I am married. So I don't really need these conversations." Later in the group she spoke again, a bit less calm and detached, "But, when I am ready, where will I learn about contraception or even about what might feel good for me? Where will I learn about sexuality after high school? Will it magically happen when I marry?" Denied sexuality education, she will likely lack the knowledge, sense of entitlement and skills to find out in the future what she doesn't know but needs to. . . .

We introduced the concept of thick desire in this discussion, and we hope to make it a lens through which to conceptualize and evaluate youth-based education and social policies across public institutions. Instead of merely documenting risk and loss, we call for policies and research that recognize how macro-structures, public institutions, practices, and relationships affect "personal decisions," particularly

for those without private supports and buffers. Thick desire is offered as a framework to move us away from mourning the "missing discourse of desire" and on to demanding more publicly subsidized educational, social, legal, economic, and health care supports for young people as they develop complex social and sexual biographies in adolescence and beyond. It is a way of evaluating policies, both local and global. Thick desire is meant to be a tool to see what is missing *and* to say what needs to be in place.

In this spirit, we invite educators, youth organizers, policy analysts, community activists, YMCA directors, health clinic professionals, and youth to create a surge of information and conversation about sexuality, power, and justice. Researchers, educators, community workers, lawyers, youth, and progressive clergy can come together to demand that thick desire be the benchmark—a progressive form of accountability—for measuring the extent to which a community supports full youth development (for an example, see the Forum for Youth Investment, http://www.forumforyouth investment.org). Campaigns and research projects for healthy youth development can be launched in schools, community centers, libraries, clinics, afterschool programs, and on the Internet, in which conversations about desire, danger, power, and bodies can be reclaimed as spaces for doubt, giggles, honesty, negotiation, struggle, pleasure, pain, and information. Young people are dying for good conversation about sexuality, and are dying without it.

NOTE

1. For examples of websites, see the following: http://www .Scarleteen.com, "sex positive sex education"; http://www .sxetc.org, "a web site by teens for teens"; http://www .MySistahs.org, "by and for young women of color"; and http://gURL.com, "an online community and content site for teenage girls."

REFERENCES

Allen, C. 2005, November 3. *Untitled.* Paper presented at the conference of the Department of Health and Human Services, Strengthening Abstinence

Education Programs through Scientific Evaluation. Baltimore, MD, USA.

Appadurai, A. 2001, July. New logics of violence. *Seminar,* #503. Retrieved July 31, 2006, from http://www.india-seminar.com/2001/503/503%20 arjun%20apadurai.htm

Appadurai, A. 2004. The capacity to aspire: Culture and the terms of recognition. In V. Rao and M. Walton (Eds.), *Culture and public action* (pp. 59–84). New York: Russell Sage Foundation.

Bay-Cheng, L. 2003. The trouble of teen sex: The construction of adolescent sexuality through school-based sexuality education. *Sex Education, 3*(1): 61–74.

Bearman, P., and Brückner, H. 2001. Promising the future: Virginity pledges and the transition to first intercourse. *American Journal of Sociology, 206:* 859–912.

Boonstra, H. 2002. Legislators craft alternative vision of sex education to counter abstinence-only drive. *The Guttmacher Report on Public Policy, 5* (2): 1–3. Retrieved July 31, 2006, from http://www.guttmacher.org/pubs /tgr/05/2/gr050201.pdf

Brick, P., and Taverner, B. (2003). *Educating about abortion.* New York: Planned Parenthood.

Brown, S. 2005, September 21. *Untitled.* Letter to Commissioner Peter McWalters, Rhode Island Department of Education. Retrieved July 31, 2006, from http://www.riaclu.org/documents/sex_ed_letter.pdf

Brown, S., and Taverner, W. 2001. *Streetwise to sex-wise: Sexuality education for high risk youth.* New York: Planned Parenthood.

Brückner, H., and Bearman, P. 2005. After the promise: The STD consequences of adolescent virginity pledges. *Journal of Adolescent Health, 36:* 271–278. Retrieved July 31, 2006, from http://www.iserp.columbia.edu/people /downloads/after_the_promise.pdf

Burns, A., and Torre, M. E. 2005. Revolutionary sexualities. *Feminism and Psychology, 15*(10): 21–26.

Center for Disease Control. 2005, February 4. QuickStats: Pregnancy, birth and abortion rates for teenagers aged 15–17—United States, 1976–2003, *Morbidity and Mortality Weekly Report, 54* (4): p. 100. Retrieved July 31, 2006, from http://www.cdc.gov/mmwr/preview /mmwrhtml/mm5404a6.htm

Committee on Government Reform, Minority Staff, Special Investigations Division. 2004, December. *The content of federally-funded abstinence-only education programs.* Washington, DC: United States House of Representatives. Retrieved July 31, 2006, from http://reform.democrats.house.gov /Documents/20041201102153-50247.pdf

Correa, S. 1994. *Population and reproductive rights.* London: Zed Books.

Correa, S., and Petchesky, R. 1994. Reproductive and sexual rights: A feminist perspective. In G. Sen, A. Germain, and L. Chen (Eds.), *Population policy*

reconsidered: Health, empowerment and rights (Harvard series on population and international health (pp. 107–126). Cambridge, MA: Harvard University Press.

Dailard, C. 2001, October. Community health centers and family planning: What we know. *The Guttmacher Report on Public Policy, 4* (5). Retrieved July 31, 2006, from http://www.guttmacher.org/pubs/tgr/04/5 /gr040506.html

Dailard, C. 2005, November. Administration tightens rules for abstinence education grants. *The Guttmacher Report, 8*(4): p. 13. Retrieved July 31, 2006, from http://www .guttmacher.org/pubs/tgr/08/4/gr080413.html

Darroch, J. E., Landry, D. J., and Singh, S. 2000. Changing emphases in sexuality education in U.S. public secondary schools, 1988–1999, *Family Planning Perspectives, 32:* 204–211, 265.

Feijoo, A. N. 2001. *Adolescent sexual health in Europe and the U.S.: Why the difference?* (2nd ed.). Washington, DC: Advocates for Youth.

Fine, M. 1988. Sexuality, schooling, and adolescent females: The missing discourse of desire. *Harvard Educational Review, 58*(1): 29–51.

Fine, M., Burns, A., Payne, Y., and Torre, M. 2004. Civics lessons: The color and class of betrayal. *Teachers College Record, 106:* 2193–2223.

Foucault, M. (1988). *Politics, philosophy and culture.* London: Routledge.

Fuligni, A. J., and Hardway, C. 2004, Summer. Preparing diverse adolescents for the transition to adulthood. *Children of immigrant families, 14*(2): 99–119. Retrieved August 11, 2006, from http://www.futureofchildren.org /usr_doc/fulignihardway.pdf

Geronimus, A. T., and Thompson, J. P. 2004. To denigrate, ignore, or disrupt: The health impact of policy-induced breakdown of urban African American communities of support. *Du Bois Review, 1:* 247–279.

Goldfarb, E. 2005. What is comprehensive sexuality education really all about? Perceptions of students enrolled in an undergraduate human sexuality course. *American Journal of Sexuality Education, 1*(1): 85–100.

Guttmacher Institute. 2002. *Sexuality education. Facts in brief.* New York: Author. Retrieved July 31, 2006, from http://www.guttmacher.org/pubs/fb_sex_ed02.pdf

Guttmacher, S., Lieberman, L., Ward, D., Freudenberg, N., Radosh, A., and Des Jarlais, D., 1997, September. Condom availability in New York City public high schools: Relationships to condom use and sexual behaviors. *American Journal of Public Health, 87:* 1427–1433.

Haignere, C. S., Gold, R., and McDanel, H. J. 1999. Adolescent abstinence and condom use: Are we sure we are really teaching what is safe? *Health Education & Behavior, 26*(1): 43–54.

Harris, A 2005. Discourses of desire as governmentality: Young women, sexuality and the significance of safe spaces. *Feminism and Psychology, 15:* 39–43.

Horne, S., and Zimmer-Gembeck, M. J. 2006. The female sexual subjectivity inventory: Development and validation of a multidimensional inventory for late adolescents and emerging adults. *Psychology of Women Quarterly, 30*: 125–138.

Impett, E., Schooler, D., and Tolman, D., in press. To be seen and not heard: Femininity ideology and adolescent girls' sexual health. *Archives of Sexual Behavior.*

Kaiser Family Foundation. 2004. *Kaiser state facts.* Menlo Park, CA: Author. Retrieved June 21, 2006, from http://www.statehealthfacts.kff.org/cgi-bin/healthfacts.cgi

Kelly, K. 2005, October 17. Just don't do it. *U.S. News and World Report*, pp. 44–51.

Kempner, M. E. 2001. *Toward a sexually healthy America: Abstinence only until marriage programs that try to keep our youth "scared chaste."* New York: Sexuality Information & Education Council of the United States.

Kirby, D., Alter, J., and Scales, P. 1979. *An analysis of U.S. sex education programs and evaluation methods.* Atlanta, GA: Center for Disease Control, Bureau of Health Education.

Kirby, D. 1997. *No easy answers: Research findings on programs to reduce teen pregnancy.* Washington, D.C.: The National Campaign to Prevent Teen Pregnancy.

Kirby, D. 1999. Sexuality and sex education at home and school. *Adolescent Medicine: State of the Art Reviews, 10*: 195–209.

Kirby, D. 2000, July. *Effective approaches to reducing adolescent unprotected sex, pregnancy, and childbearing.* Washington DC: Report to the Surgeon General.

Kirby, D. 2001. *Emerging answers: Research findings on programs to reduce teen pregnancy.* Washington DC: National Campaign to Prevent Pregnancy.

Landry D. J., Kaeser, L., and Richards, C. L. 1999. Abstinence promotion and the provision of information about contraception in public school district sexuality education policies. *Family Planning Perspectives, 31*: 280–286.

Levine, J. 2002. *Harmful to minors.* Minneapolis: University of Minnesota Press.

Lewin, T. December 2, 2005. Openly gay student's lawsuit over privacy will proceed. *New York Times*, p. A21.

Luttrell, W. 2002. *Pregnant bodies, fertile minds.* New York: Routledge.

Mabray, D., and LaBauve, B. 2002. A multidimensional approach to sexual education. *Sex Education, 2*(1): 31–44.

Mackler, C. 1999, August/September. Sex ed: How do we score? *Ms. Magazine*, pp. 67–73.

Mendell, D. 2006, April 27. Sex ed to cover birth control: Abstinence will be city classes' focus. *Chicago Tribune.* Retrieved April 27, 2006, from http://www.chicagotribune.com/news/local/chicago/chi-0604270023apr27,1,2262647.story

Mink, G. 2002. From welfare to wedlock: Marriage promotion and poor mothers' inequality. *The Good Society, 11*(3): 68–73.

Mosher, W. D., Chandra, A., and Jones, J. 2005, September 15. *Sexual behavior and selected health measures: Men and women 15–44 years of age, United States, 2002. Advance Data From Vital and Health Statistics.* Atlanta: Centers for Disease Control and Prevention. Retrieved July 31, 2006, from http://www.cdc.gov/nchs/data/ad/ad362.pdf

National Campaign to Prevent Teen Pregnancy. 2005, April 13. *Declining teen birth rates contribute to improvements in child well-being in all states.* Washington, DC: Author. Retrieved March 8, 2006, from http://www.teenpregnancy.org/whycare/pdf/National_Press_Release.pdf

National Public Radio, Kaiser Family Foundation, and Harvard University. 2004, January. *Sex education in America: General public/parents survey.* Menlo Park, CA: Kaiser Family Foundation. Retrieved July 31, 2006, from http://www.npr.org/programs/morning/features/2004/jan/kaiserpoll/publicfinal.pdf

New York Civil Liberties Union. 2004. *The reproductive rights project: 2004 in review.* New York: Author. Retrieved July 31, 2006, from http://www.nyclu.org/rrp_annualreport_2004.html

Nussbaum, M. 2003. Women's education: A global challenge. *Signs: Journal of Women in Culture and Society, 29*: 325–355.

Office of Women's Health. 1998. *Women of color health data book: Adolescents to seniors.* Bethesda, MD: National Institutes of Health.

Ooms, T. 2001, May 22. *Testimony of Theodora Ooms.* House Committee on Ways and Means, Subcommittee on Human Resources. Washington, DC. Retrieved March 8, 2006, from http://www.smartmarriages.com/ooms.testimony.html

Opotow, S. 1990. Moral exclusion and injustice. *Journal of Social Issues, 46*(1): 1–20.

Petchesky, R. P. 2005. *Global prescriptions.* London: Zed Books.

Phillips, L. 2000. *Flirting with danger.* New York: New York University Press.

Planned Parenthood Federation of America, Inc. 2005a, January. *Abstinence-only "sex" education.* New York: Author. Retrieved March 8, 2006, from http://www.plannedparenthood.org/pp2/portal/medicalinfo/teensexualhealth/fact-abstinence-education.xml

Planned Parenthood Federation of America, Inc. 2005b. *The war on women: A pernicious web. A chronology of attacks on reproductive rights. Planned Parenthood report on the administration and congress.* New York: Author. Retrieved July 31, 2006, from http://www.plannedparenthood.org/pp2/portal/files/portal/medicalinfo/femalesexualhealth/report_waronwomen-chronology.pdf

Roberts, D. 2002. *Shattered bonds: The color of child welfare.* New York: Basic Books.

Rodriguez, M. 2005. *Talking to Teens*. Presented at the conference of the Network for Family Life Education. New Brunswick, NJ.

Rose, T. 2003. *Longing to tell*. New York: Farrar, Straus, Giroux.

Rousso, H. 2001. *Strong, proud sisters: Girls and young women with disabilities*. Washington, DC: Center for Women Policy Studies.

Santelli, J. S., Abma, J., Ventura, S., Lindberg, L., Morrow, B., Anderson, J.E., et al. 2004. Can changes in sexual behaviors among high school students explain the decline in teen pregnancy rates in the 1990s? *The Journal of Adolescent Health*, 35(2): 86.

Santelli, J. S, Ott, M., Lyon, M., Rogers, J., Summers, D., and Schleifer, R. 2006a. Abstinence and abstinence-only education: A review of U.S. policies and programs. *Journal of Adolescent Health*, 38: 72–81.

Santelli, J. S, Ott, M., Lyon, M., Rogers, J., and Summers, D. 2006b. Abstinence-only education policies and programs: A position paper of the society for adolescent medicine. *Journal of Adolescent Health*, 38: 83–87.

Santelli, J. S., Morrow, B., Anderson, J., and Lindberg, L. 2006c, June. Contraceptive use and pregnancy risk among U.S. high school students, 1991–2003. *Perspectives on Sexual and Reproductive Health*, 38: 106–111.

Seiler, N. 2002, April. *Is teen marriage a solution?* Washington, DC: Center for Law and Social Policy.

Sen, G. 1994. Reproduction: The feminist challenge to social policy. In G. Sen and R.C. Snow (Eds.), *Power and decision: The social control of reproduction* (pp. 5–18). Boston: Harvard School of Public Health.

Sen, G., George, A., and Ostlin, P. (Eds.) 2002. *Engendering international health: The challenge of equity*. Cambridge, MA: MIT Press.

Sexuality Information and Education Council of the U.S. (SIECUS). 1998. *Filling the gaps: hard to teach topics in sexuality education*. Washington, DC: Author. Retrieved March 8, 2006, from http://www.siecus.org/pubs/filling_the_gaps.pdf

Sexuality Information and Education Council of the U.S. (SIECUS). 2004a. *State profiles (2004): A portrait of sexuality education and abstinence-only until marriage programs in the States*. Washington, DC: Author. Retrieved July 31, 2006, from http://www.siecus.org/policy/states/

Sexuality Information and Education Council of the U.S. (SIECUS). 2004b. *National guidelines task force: Guidelines for comprehensive sexuality education* (3rd ed.). Washington, DC: Author. Retrieved March 8, 2006, from http://www.siecus.org/pubs/guidelines/guidelines.pdf

Sexuality Information and Education Council of the U.S. (SIECUS). 2004c. *Federal spending for abstinence only until marriage programs (1982–2006)*. Washington, DC: Author. Retrieved July 31, 2006, from http://www.siecus.org/policy/states/2004/federal-Graph.html

Sexuality Information and Education Council of the U.S. (SIECUS). 2005, September 26. *How medical inaccuracies, fear, and shame in federally funded abstinence only until marriage programs put our youth at risk*. Washington, DC: Author. Retrieved March 8, 2006, from http://www.siecus.org/media/press/press0114.html

Snitow, A., Stansell, C., and Thompson, S. 1983. *Powers of desire: The politics of sexuality*. New York: Monthly Review Press.

Strauss, L. T., Herndon, J., Chang, J., Parker, W. Y., Bowens, S. V., Zane, S. B., et al. 2004, November 26. Abortion surveillance—United States, 2001. *Weekly Report, 53* (SS09): 1–32. Retrieved August 4, 2006, from http://www.cdc.gov/mmwr/preview/mmwrhtml/ss5309a1.htm

Taverner, B., and Montfort, S. 2005. *Making sense of abstinence: Lessons for comprehensive sex education*. Morristown, NJ: Planned Parenthood.

Texas Citizens for Science. 2004. *Texas adopted censored, inadequate and danger health education textbooks in 2004*. Midland, TX: Author. Retrieved March 8, 2006, from http://www.texscience.org

Tolman, D. L. 1994. Doing desire: Adolescent girls' struggles for/with sexuality. *Gender and Society*, 8: 324–342.

Tolman, D. L. 2002. *Dilemmas of desire*. Cambridge, MA: Harvard University Press.

Tolman, D. L., Striepe, M., and Harmon, P. 2003. Gender matters: Constructing a model of adolescent sexual health. *The Journal of Sex Research, 40*(1): 4–12.

Tolman, D. L. 2006. In a different position: Conceptualizing female adolescent sexuality development within compulsory heterosexuality. In L. Diamond (Ed), *New directions in child and adolescent development: Positive female adolescent sexuality, 112* (pp. 71–89). San Francisco: Jossey-Bass.

Unitarian Universalist Association. 2006a. *Our whole lives: Sexuality education for grades 4–6*. Boston, MA: Author. Retrieved June 21, 2006, from http://www.uua.org/owl/4-6.html

Unitarian Universalist Association. 2006b. *Our whole lives (OWL)*. Boston: Author. Retrieved June 21, 2006, from http://www.uua.org/owl/what.html

U.S. Department of Health and Human Services. 2003. *Understanding Title V of the Social Security Act: A guide to the provisions of the federal maternal and child health block grants*. Rockville, MD: The Maternal and Child Health Bureau. Retrieved August 4, 2006, from http://www.dph.state.ct.us/BCH/Family%20Health/cyshcn/understandingtitlev.pdf

U.S. Department of Health and Human Services. 2005. *Family and youth services bureau: Administration on children, youth, and families; Community-based abstinence* education program. *Funding opportunity number HHS-2005-ACF-ACYF-AE-0099.* Rockville, MD: Author.

U.S. Department of Health and Human Services. 2006. *Family and youth services bureau: Administration on children, youth, and families; Community-based abstinence education program. Request for proposals. Funding opportunity number: HHS-2006-ACF-ACYF-AE-0099.* Rockville, MD: Author. Retrieved August 4, 2006, from http://www.acf.hhs.gov/grants/pdf/HHS-2006-ACF-ACYF-AE-0099.pdf

U.S. House of Representatives. February 10, 2005. *H.R. 2553. 109th Congress, 1st session.* Washington, DC: Author. Retrieved August 4, 2006, from http://www.advocatesforyouth.org/real_hr2553.pdf

U.S. Office of Management and Budget. August 4, 2006. *Health and human services: Enhancing the faith-based and community initiative.* Washington, DC: Author. Retrieved August 4, 2006, from http://www.whitehouse.gov/omb/budget/fy2007/hhs.html

U.S. Senate. 2005, February 10. *S. 368. 109th Congress, 1st session.* Washington, DC: Author. Retrieved August 4, 2006, from http://www.advocatesforyouth.org/real_s368.pdf

Vance, C. 1993. *Pleasure and danger: Exploring female sexuality.* New York: Harper Collins.

Wyatt, G. E. 1994. The sociocultural relevance of sex research. *American Psychologist,* 49: 748–754.

Zavella, P. 2003. Talkin' sex: Chicanas and Mexicanas theorize about silences and sexual pleasures. In G.F. Arredondo, A. Hurtado, N. Klahn, O. Najera-Ramirez, and P. Zavella (Eds.), *Chicana feminisms: A critical reader* (pp. 228–253). Chapel Hill, NC: Duke University Press.

Advancing Sexuality Education in Developing Countries: Evidence and Implications

Heather D. Boonstra

. . . .Most young people today begin to have sex at about the same age as in the past: in their middle to late teens. By their 18th birthday, more than 40 percent of women in Latin America and the Caribbean report having had sex, as do close to 60 percent in Sub-Saharan Africa. (The age at which young women in the United States typically initiate sex is similar: By age 18, about 52 percent of U.S. women have had sex.[1]) For the majority of young men, sex occurs prior to marriage; however, premarital sex has also become more common among females, at least in part because of delays in the age of marriage.

Parents and other family members, of course, have always played a critical role in the physical, emotional, and sexual development of young people. At the same time, there is increasing acceptance of the notion that, in today's world, these sources of education are insufficient and that more organized, formal approaches are called for. There is also a growing advocacy movement—including at the global level within the United Nations—for the recognition of comprehensive sexuality information and education as a basic human right.[2] Still, sexuality education of any kind is not available in many regions of the world, adolescents' knowledge of sexual and reproductive health is not detailed, and myths are common. For example, many adolescents think that a young woman cannot get pregnant the first time she has sexual intercourse or if she has sex standing up.[3] Some adolescents still report a belief that HIV can be transmitted through a mosquito bite or that a man who is HIV-positive can be cured by having sex with a virgin.

In regions and communities throughout the developing world, therefore, policymakers and youth-serving professionals are grappling with how best to address the wide-ranging needs of young people. They are weighing what is possible, considering both the political realities and context, and are taking a close look at the evidence for different approaches.

A LOOK AT THE EVIDENCE

The last few decades have seen a proliferation of curriculum-based interventions, both in and out of school. For a long time, these curricula emphasized the medical aspects of sex and reproduction, human anatomy and development. Today, although having a basic understanding of human biology and the reproductive system is still considered crucial, programs have evolved to include a broader range of topics. Two basic approaches have emerged, each supported by different perspectives on what is best for children and young people. The abstinence-only approach focuses primarily, if not exclusively, on promoting abstinence outside of marriage, on moral as well as public health grounds. The comprehensive approach, on the other hand, supports young people's ability to decide whether and when to have sex, but also recognizes that sexual debut in adolescence is normative behavior and thus seeks to prepare youth with the knowledge and skills they need for healthy sexual lives.

Abstinence-only Approaches

Over the last three decades, especially in the United States but also in parts of the developing world, much of the focus of sexuality education—at least among politicians, if not program planners—has been on trying to convince young people to delay the initiation of sex, generally until after marriage. This approach is based on the premises that sex before marriage itself is a problem because it is morally wrong and that young people can be convinced to wait, even well into their 20s. These "abstinence-only-until-marriage" programs focus primarily or exclusively on the putative benefits of abstaining from sex. They may also distort and actively denigrate the effectiveness of contraceptives and safer-sex behaviors.

This kind of education has become increasingly marginalized, as several well-designed studies conducted over the last 15 years have shown just how futile the focus on stopping young people from having sex is. For example, in 2007, investigators at the Centre for Evidence-Based Intervention at the University of Oxford conducted an international literature search for randomized or quasirandomized trials of abstinence-only programs in high-income countries.[4] (The researchers assumed that high-income settings may present optimal conditions for showing the effectiveness of abstinence-only programs.)

Despite its international focus, the search found only 13 studies that met the standards for inclusion—all conducted in the United States, and with a total sample of nearly 16,000 youth. The researchers concluded that programs that exclusively encourage abstinence are ineffective, saying "when compared with a variety of control groups, the participants in these 13 abstinence-only program trials did not report differences in risk behaviors or biological outcomes."

These findings are similar to those of another comprehensive review of sex and HIV education programs published in 2008.[5] The analysis, conducted by Douglas Kirby, reviewed 56 studies with a strong experimental or quasiexperimental design, including eight studies of abstinence programs based in the United States. (Notable among these was an evaluation—conducted by Mathematica Policy Research at a cost of nearly $8 million—of four model abstinence-only programs that were carefully selected as having the most promise.) Study results indicate that abstinence-only programs are not effective at stopping or even delaying sex. . . .

Moreover, research suggests that strategies that promote abstinence while withholding information about contraceptives can actually place young people at increased risk of pregnancy and STIs. For example, young people who take "virginity pledges" are just as likely as those who do not to have sex, but they are less likely to use condoms or other forms of contraception when they become sexually active.[6] These virginity pledges, which are a centerpiece of many abstinence-only programs, originated in the United States in the early 1990s, but have since been implemented in developing countries as well. For example, leaders of True Love Waits, probably the best known of these programs, report that nearly one million young people across Africa have signed their pledge.[7]

More Comprehensive Approaches

. . . . Some adults, parents and politicians—who may be conservative but pragmatic—believe that although sex among adolescents is troubling, it is inevitable and unavoidable, and society must accept this reality and concentrate on helping adolescents avoid the negative consequences of sex. Others go further and assert that the formation and testing of romantic attachments and the physical expression of sexual feelings are a natural and developmentally appropriate part of the transition to adulthood. Therefore, they say, young people should be approached with respect and equipped with the knowledge and skills they need to feel comfortable and confident about their sexuality.

These different motivations for comprehensive sexuality education have gradually made their way into policies and programs, which vary between countries. For example, in the United States, the focus on keeping young people safe has been translated into prevention-oriented programs. Although these programs may cover a wide range of topics—from fertility and reproduction to STIs, from relationships and communication to gender norms, culture and society—they are primarily aimed at helping adolescents minimize their risk of adverse outcomes. Northern European countries such as Sweden and the Netherlands, by contrast, embrace a more positive attitude toward adolescent sexuality, based on the premise that young people are "rights-holders," and therefore are entitled to information and education, as well as the right to express and enjoy their sexuality. These rights-based or "holistic" programs are concerned, of course, with equipping young people to avoid unintended pregnancy and STIs, but they are focused less on behavior and outcomes per se, and more on reflection and choice. The underlying assumption is that empowering young people to make considered, informed decisions about their own lives and helping them to develop the critical thinking skills and sense of self necessary to do so will result in better sexual and reproductive health in the broadest sense—including pleasure, love and sexual well-being.

It has long been recognized that those countries that have a more open and positive attitude toward sexuality have better sexual health outcomes. Cross-national comparisons show that, despite similar levels of sexual activity, adolescent pregnancy rates are consistently lower in many Western European countries than in other regions of the world.[8,9] Experts say this is because, in Western Europe, sex among adolescents is generally accepted, with little to no societal pressure to remain abstinent.[10] But with that acceptance comes strong cultural norms that emphasize that young people who are having sex should take actions to protect themselves and their partners from pregnancy and STIs. In keeping with this view, government-supported schools in many Western European countries provide—and even require—comprehensive sexuality education and offer easy access to reproductive health services.

In fact, the evidence for a positive impact on behavior from evaluations of comprehensive sexuality education programs throughout the world is strong. According to a rigorous 2008 review of the evidence of comprehensive sexuality education's impact on sexual behavior, effective programs can not only reduce misinformation, but also increase young people's skills to make informed decisions about their health.[11] Commissioned by the United Nations Educational, Scientific and Cultural Organization (UNESCO) as part of the development of the *International Technical Guidance on Sexuality Education*, the review included 87 studies from around the world with experimental or quasiexperimental designs: 29 from developing countries, 47 from the United States and 11 from other developed countries. Nearly all of the programs increased knowledge, and two-thirds had a positive impact on behavior: Many delayed sexual debut, reduced the frequency of sex and number of sexual partners, increased condom or contraceptive use, or reduced sexual risk-taking. More than one-quarter of programs improved two or more of these behaviors. And most tended to lower risky sexual behavior by, very roughly, one-fourth to one-third.

In addition, at least one study has demonstrated that comprehensive sexuality education programs are potentially cost-effective as well. In 2010, UNESCO commissioned a study of the health impact and cost-effectiveness of school-based sexuality education in Estonia.[12] Sexuality education in that country is included as a component of compulsory human studies courses for grades 5–7 and, importantly, is strongly linked to youth-friendly sexual health services in the community. According to the study, between 2001 and 2009, after the introduction of sexuality education in Estonia, there were significant improvements in adolescent sexual and reproductive health: Nearly 4,300 unintended pregnancies, 7,200 STIs and 2,000 HIV infections among adolescents aged 15–19 were averted. . . .

Finally, no study of comprehensive programs to date has found evidence that providing young people with sexual and reproductive health information and education results in increased sexual risk-taking. . . .[13]

These findings can be extremely useful in gauging the impact of various comprehensive programs on those sexual behaviors that directly affect pregnancy and sexual transmission of HIV and other STIs. But because they are so focused on behaviors, they provide little insight into how well these strategies work to achieve other desired outcomes—such as greater gender equality, critical thinking skills, a sense of confidence and belief in the future, and sexual pleasure. Measureable indictors of these kinds of outcomes have yet to be developed. . . .

Source: "Advancing sexuality education in developing countries: evidence and implications," by H. D. Boonstra. *Guttmacher Policy Review,* 2009, 14(3):18–23. Reprinted by permission of the Guttmacher Institute.

REFERENCES

1. Guttmacher Institute, special tabulations of data from the 2006–2008 National Survey of Family Growth.

2. United Nations, Report of the United Nations Special Rapporteur on the right to education, July 23, 2010. <http://www.right-to-education.org/sites/r2e.gn.apc.org/files/SR%20Education%20Report-Human%20Right%20to%20Sexual%20Education.pdf>, accessed Aug. 4, 2011.

3. Biddlecom AE et al., *Protecting the Next Generation in Sub-Saharan Africa: Learning from Adolescents to Prevent HIV and Unintended Pregnancy,* New York: Guttmacher Institute, 2007. <http://www.guttmacher.org/pubs/2007/12/12/PNG_monograph.pdf>, accessed Aug. 4, 2011.

4. Underhill K, Montgomery P and Operario D. 2007. Sexual abstinence only programmes to prevent HIV infection in high income countries: Systematic review, *BMJ,* 335(7613): 248–252.

5. Kirby D. 2003 The impact of abstinence and comprehensive sex and STD/HIV education programs on adolescent sexual behavior, *Sexuality Research & Social Policy,* 5(3): 18–27.

6. Rosenbaum J. 2009. Patient teenagers? A comparison of the sexual behavior of virginity pledgers and matched nonpledgers, *Pediatrics,* 123(1): e110–e120.

7. True Love Waits International grows worldwide. *Florida Baptist Witness,* Feb. 10, 2011, <http://www.gofbw.com/news.asp?ID=12600>, accessed July 31, 2011.

8. Santelli, J., Sandfort T and Orr M, 2008 Transnational comparisons of adolescent contraceptive use: What can we learn from these comparisons? *Archives of Pediatrics & Adolescent Medicine,* 162(1): 92–94.

9. Singh S and Darroch JE. 2000. Adolescent pregnancy and childbearing: Levels and trends in developed countries, *Family Planning Perspectives,* 32(1): 14–23, <http://www.guttmacher.org/pubs/journals/3201400.pdf>, accessed Aug. 4, 2011.

10. The Alan Guttmacher Institute (AGI). 2001. Can more progress be made? Teenage sexual and reproductive behavior in developed countries, *Executive Summary,* New York: AGI, <http://www.guttmacher.org/pubs/summaries/euroteens_summ.pdf>, accessed July 31, 2011.

11. United Nations Educational, Scientific and Cultural Organization (UNESCO). 2009. International Technical Guidance on Sexuality Education: An Evidence-Informed Approach for Schools, Teachers and Health Educators. <http://unesdoc.unesco.org/images/0018/001832/183281e.pdf>, accessed Aug. 4, 2011.

12. UNESCO. 2011. *School-Based Sexuality Education Programmes: A Cost and Cost Effectiveness Analysis in Six Countries,* <http://www.unesco.org/new/fileadmin/MULTIMEDIA/HQ/ED/pdf/CostingStudy.pdf>, accessed Aug. 4, 2011.

13. Speizer IS., Magnani RJ and Colvin CE. 2003. The effectiveness of adolescent reproductive health interventions in developing countries: A review of the evidence, *Journal of Adolescent Health,* 33(5): 324–348.

SEX, LOVE, AND AUTONOMY IN THE TEENAGE SLEEPOVER

AMY T. SCHALET

The vast majority of American parents oppose a sleepover for high school-aged teenagers, while Dutch teenagers who have steady boyfriends or girlfriends are typically allowed to spend the night with them in their rooms. This contrast is all the more striking when we consider the trends toward a liberalization of sexual behavior and attitudes that have taken place throughout Europe and the United States since the 1960s. In similar environments, both parents and kids are experiencing adolescent sex, gender, and relationships very differently. A sociological exploration of these contrasts reveals as much about the cultural differences between these two countries as it does about views on adolescent sexuality and child rearing.

ADOLESCENT SEXUALITY IN CONTEMPORARY AMERICA

Today, most adolescents in the United States, like their peers across the industrialized world, engage in intercourse—either opposite or same-sex—before leaving their teens (usually around seventeen). Initiating sex and exploring romantic relationships, often with several successive partners before setting into long-term cohabitation or marriage, are now normative parts of adolescence and young adulthood in the developed world. But in the United States, teenage sex has been fraught with cultural ambivalences, heated political struggles, and poor health outcomes, generating concern among the public, policy makers, scholars, and parents. American adolescent sexuality has been dramatized rather than normalized.

In some respects, the problems associated with adolescent sexuality in America are surprising. Certainly, age at first intercourse has dropped in the United States since the sexual revolution, but not as steeply as often assumed. In a recent survey of the adult American population, sociologist Edward Laumann and colleagues found that even in the 1950s and '60s, only a quarter of men and less than half of women were virgins at age nineteen. The majority of young men had multiple sexual partners by age 20. And while women especially were supposed to enter marriage as virgins, demographer Lawrence Finer has shown that women who came of age in the late 1950s and early '60s almost never held to that norm. Still, a 1969 Gallup poll found that two-thirds of Americans said it was wrong for "a man and women to have sex relations before marriage."

But by 1985, Gallup found that a slim majority of Americans no longer believed such relations were wrong. Analyzing shifts in public opinion following the sexual revolution, sociologists Larry Petersen and Gregory Donnenwerth showed that among Americans with a religious affiliation, only conservative Protestants who attended church frequently remained unchanged. Among all other religious groups, acceptance of pre-marital sex actually grew, although Laumann and colleagues reported a majority of the Americans continued to believe sex among *teenagers* was always wrong. Even youth agreed: six in ten fifteen- to nineteen-year-olds surveyed in

From "Sex, Love, and Autonomy in the Teenage Sleepover," by Amy Schalet. *Contexts*, Volume 9, No. 3, August 2010, pp. 17–21. Copyright © 2010, American Sociological Association. Reprinted by Permission of SAGE Publications.

the 2002 National Survey for Family Growth said sixteen-year-olds with strong feelings for one another shouldn't have sex.

Part of the opposition to adolescent sexuality is its association with unintended consequences such as pregnancy and sexually transmitted diseases. In the United States, the rate of unintended pregnancies among teenagers rose during the 1970s and '80s, dropping only in the early '90s. However, despite almost a decade and a half of impressive decreases in pregnancy and birth rates, the teen birth rate remains many times higher in the United States than it is in most European countries. In 2007, births to American teens (aged fifteen to nineteen) were eight times as high as in the Netherlands.

One would imagine the predominant public policy approach would be to improve education about, and access to, contraception. But "abstinence-only-until-marriage" programs, initiated in the early 1980s, have received generous federal funding over the past fifteen years, and were even written into the recent U.S. health reform law (which also supports comprehensive sex education). For years, schools funded under the federal "abstinence-only" policy were prohibited from educating teens about condoms and contraception and required to teach that sex outside of heterosexual marriage was damaging. A 2004 survey by NPR, the Kaiser Family Foundation, and Harvard University found that most parents actually thought that contraception and condom education should be included, but two-thirds still agreed sex education should teach that abstinence outside of marriage is "the accepted standard for school-aged children." And for most parents, abstinence means no oral sex or intimate touching.

While American parents of the post-Sexual Revolution era have wanted minors to abstain, few teens have complied. Many American teenagers have had positive and enriching sexual experiences; however, researchers have also documented intense struggles. Comparing teenage boys and girls, for example, University of Michigan sociologist Karin Martin found that puberty and first sex empowered boys but decreased self-esteem among girls. Psychologist Deborah Tolman found the girls she interviewed confronted dilemmas of desire because of a double standard that denies or stigmatizes their sexual desires, making girls fear being labeled "sluts." Analyzing the National Longitudinal Survey of Adolescent Health, researchers Kara Joyner and Richard Udry found that even without sex, first romance brings girls "down" because their relationship with their parents deteriorates.

Nor are American girls of the post-Sexual Revolution era the only ones who must navigate gender dilemmas. Sociologist Laura Carpenter found that many of the young men she interviewed in the 1990s viewed their virginity as a stigma which they sought to cast off as rapidly as possible. And in her ethnography, *Dude, You're a Fag*, C.J. Pascoe found boys are pressured by other boys to treat girls as sex objects and sometimes derided for showing affection for their girlfriends. But despite public pressures, privately boys are as emotionally invested in relationships as girls, found Peggy Giordano and her associates in a recent national study out of Toledo, Ohio. Within those relationships, however, boys are less confident.

In the 1990s, the National Longitudinal Study for Adolescent Health found that steady romantic relationships are common among American teenagers. Girls and boys typically have their first intercourse with people they are dating. But the Toledo group found that once they are sexually experienced, the majority of boys and girls also have sex in non-dating relationships, often with a friend or acquaintance. And even when they have sex in dating relationships, a quarter of American girls and almost half of boys say they are "seeing other people" (which may or may not include sexual intercourse).

TEEN SEXUALITY IN THE NETHERLANDS

In a late 1980s qualitative study with 120 parents and older teenagers, Dutch sociologist Janita Ravesloot concluded that in most families, parents accepted that sexuality "from the first kiss to the first coitus" was part of the youth phase. In middle class families, teenagers reported that parents accepted their sexual autonomy, but didn't engage in elaborate conversations with them because of lingering feelings of shame. Working-class parents were more likely to use their authority to impose norms, including that sex belonged only in steady relationships. In a few strongly religious families—Christian or Islamic—parents categorically opposed sex before marriage: here there were "no overnights with steady boy- or girlfriends at home."* But such families remain a minority. A 2003 survey by *Statistics Netherlands* found that two-thirds of Dutch fifteen- to seventeen-year-olds with steady boy- or girlfriends are allowed to spend the night with them in their bedrooms, and that boys and girls are equally likely to get permission for a sleepover.

This could hardly have been predicted in the 1950s. Then, women *and* men typically initiated intercourse in their early twenties, usually in a serious relationship (if not engagement or marriage). In the late '60s, a national survey conducted by sociologist G. A. Kooy found most respondents still rejected premarital sex when a couple was not married or planning to do so very shortly. But by the early 1980s, the same survey found that six out of ten respondents no longer objected to a girl having intercourse with a boy as long as she was in love with him. Noting the shift in attitudes since the 1950s, Kooy spoke of a "moral landslide." His colleague, sociologist Evert Ketting, even went as far as to speak of a "moral revolution."

What changed was not just a greater acceptance of sex outside of the context of heterosexual marriage. There was also serious new deliberation among the general public, health professionals, and the media about the need to adjust the moral rules governing sexual life to real behavior. As researchers for the Guttmacher Institute later noted. "One might say the entire society has experienced a course in sex education." The new moral rules cast sexuality as a part of life that should be governed by self-determination, mutual respect, frank conversation, and the prevention of unintended consequences. Notably, these new rules were applied to minors and institutionalized in Dutch health care policies that removed financial and emotional barriers to accessing contraceptives—including the requirements for a pelvic examination and parental consent.

Indeed, even as the age of first sexual intercourse was decreasing, the rate of births among Dutch teenagers dropped steeply between 1970 and 1996 to one of the lowest in the world. What distinguished the very low Dutch teenage birth rate from, for instance, that of their Swedish counterparts, was that it was accompanied by a very low teen abortion rate. Despite the AIDS crisis, by the mid-1990s, funding agencies were so confident that, in the words of demographer Joop Garssen, youth were doing "wonderfully well," they decided further study of adolescent sexual attitudes and behavior wasn't warranted.

Sex education has played a key role. Sociologists Jane Lewis and Trudie Knijn find that Dutch sex education curricula are more likely than programs elsewhere to openly discuss female sexual pleasure, masturbation, and homosexuality. The Dutch curricula also emphasize the importance of self-reliance and mutual respect in negotiating enjoyable and healthy sexual relationships during adolescence.

A 2005 survey of Dutch youth, ages twelve to twenty-five, found the majority described their first sexual experiences—broadly defined—as well-timed, within their control, and fun. About first intercourse, 86 percent of women and 93 percent of men said, "We both were equally eager to have it." This doesn't mean that gender doesn't matter. Researcher Janita Ravelsoot found that more girls than boys reported that their parents expected them to only have intercourse in relationships. Girls were also aware that they might be called sluts for having sex too soon or with too many successive partners. And although most of the 2005 respondents said they were (very) satisfied with the pleasure and contact they felt with their partner during sex, men were much more likely to usually or always orgasm during sex and less likely to report having experienced pain.

It also appears that having sex outside of the context of monogamous romantic relationships isn't as common among Dutch adolescents, especially older ones, as among their American counterparts. Again in the 2005 survey, two-thirds of male youth and 81 percent of Dutch females had their last sex in a monogamous steady relationship, usually with a partner with whom they were "very much in love." Certainly, Dutch adolescents have "non-relational" sex—indeed, one in three males and one in five females had their last vaginal or anal sex outside of a monogamous romantic relationship. That said, relational sex seems to remain the norm, especially as young people age: two-thirds of fifteen- to seventeen-year-olds, and three-quarters of those eighteen to twenty, had their last intercourse in a monogamous relationship. Among the oldest group—nineteen- to twenty-four-year-olds—almost half of gay men surveyed, six in ten straight men and lesbians, and nearly three-quarters of straight women were in long-term relationships.

EXPLAINING THE DIFFERENCES

So why do parents in two countries with similar levels of development and reproductive technologies have such different attitudes toward the sexual experiences of teenagers? Two factors immediately spring to mind. The first is religion. As the Laumann team found, Americans who do not view religion as a central force in their decision-making are much less likely to categorically condemn teenage sex. And devout Christians and Muslims in the Netherlands are more likely to exhibit attitudes towards sexuality and marriage that are similar to those of their American counterparts. That Americans are far more likely to be religiously devout than the Dutch, many of whom left their houses of worship in the 1960s and '70s, explains part of the difference between the two countries.

A second factor is economic security. Like most European countries, the Dutch government provides a range of what sociologists call "social" and what reproductive health advocates call "human" rights: the right to housing, healthcare, and a minimum income. Not only do such rights ensure access, if need be, to free contraceptive and abortion services, government supports make coming of age less perilous for both teenagers and parents. This might make the prospect of sex derailing a child's life less haunting. Ironically, the very lack of such rights and high rates of childhood poverty in the United States contributes to high rates of births among teenagers. Without adequate support systems or educational and job opportunities, young people are simply more likely to start parenthood early in life.

While they no doubt contribute, neither religion nor economics can solve the whole puzzle. Even Dutch and American families matched on these dimensions still have radically divergent views of teenage sexuality and the sleepover. After interviewing 130 white middle-class Dutch and American teenagers (mostly 10th graders) and parents, I became convinced that a fuller solution is to look at the different cultures of independence and control that characterize these two middle classes.

In responding to adolescent sexuality, American parents emphasize its dangerous and conflicted elements, describing it in terms of "raging hormones" that are difficult for young people to control and in terms of antagonistic relationships between the sexes (girls and boys pursue love and sex respectively; and girls are often the losers of the battle). Moreover, American parents see it as their obligation to encourage adolescents' separation from home before accepting their sexual activity. Viewing sex as part of a larger tug of war between separation and control, the response to the question of the sleepover, even among many otherwise socially liberal parents is, "Not under my roof!"

Dutch parents, by contrast, downplay the dangerous and difficult sides of teenage sexuality, tending to normalize it. They speak of . . . a process of becoming physically and emotionally ready for sex that they believe young people can self-regulate, provided they've been encouraged to pace themselves and prepare adequately. Rather than emphasizing gender battles, Dutch parents talk about sexuality as emerging from relationships and are strikingly silent about gender conflicts. And unlike Americans who are often skeptical about teenagers' capacities to fall in love, they assume that even those in their early teens fall in love. They permit sleepovers, even if that requires an "adjustment" period to overcome their feelings of discomfort, because they feel obliged to stay connected and accepting as sex becomes part of their children's lives.

These different approaches to adolescent sexuality are part of the different cultures of independence and control. American middle-class culture conceptualizes the self and (adult) society as inherently oppositional during adolescence. Breaking away from the family is necessary for autonomy, as is the occasional use of parental control (for instance, in the arena of sexuality), until teenagers are full adults. Dutch middle-class culture, in contrast, conceptualizes the self and society as interdependent. Based upon the assumption that young people develop autonomy in the context of ongoing relationships of interdependence, Dutch parents don't see teenage sexuality in the household as a threat to their children's autonomy or to their own authority. To the contrary, allowing teenage sexuality in the home— "domesticating" it, as it were—allows Dutch parents to exert more informal social control.

WHAT IT MEANS FOR KIDS

The acceptance of adolescent sexuality in the family creates the opportunity for Dutch girls to integrate their sexual selves with their roles as family members, even if they may be subject to a greater level of surveillance. . . . By contrast, many American girls must physically and psychically bifurcate their sexual selves and their roles as daughters. . . .

American boys receive messages ranging from blanket prohibition to open encouragement. One key message is that sex is a symbol and a threat—in the event of pregnancy—to their adult autonomy. . . . By contrast, Dutch boys, . . . like their female counterparts . . . say permission comes with a social control that encourages a relational sexuality and girlfriends their parents like. . . .

These different templates for adolescent sex, gender, and autonomy also affect boys' and girls' own navigation of the dilemmas of gender. The category "slut" appears much more salient in the interviews with American girls than Dutch girls. One reason may be that the cultural assumption that teenagers can and do fall in love lends credence to Dutch girls' claims to being in love, while the cultural skepticism about whether they can sustain the feelings and form the attachments that legitimate sexual activity put American girls on the defensive. . . .

In both countries, boys confront the belief and sometimes the reality that they are interested in sex but not relationships. But there is evidence in both countries that boys are often emotionally invested. The American boys I have interviewed tend to view themselves as unique for their romantic aspirations and describe themselves, as Jesse does, as "romantic rebels." "The most important thing to me is maintaining love between me and my girlfriend," while "most guys are pretty much in it for the sex," he says. The Dutch boys I interviewed did not perceive themselves as unusual for falling in love (or for wanting to) before having sex. Sam, for instance, believes that "everyone wants [a relationship]." He explains why: "Someone you can talk to about your feelings and such, a feeling of safety,

---

*Note, this quote and subsequent quotes from Dutch sources are the author's translations. Names have been changed to protect anonymity.

I think that everyone, the largest percentage of people wants a relationship."

CULTURE'S COST

How sexuality, love, and autonomy are perceived and negotiated in parent-child relationships and among teenagers depends on the cultural templates people have available. Normalization and dramatization each have "costs" and "benefits." On balance, however, the dramatization of adolescent sexuality makes it more difficult for parents to communicate with teenagers about sex and relationships, and more challenging for girls and boys to integrate their sexual and relational selves. The normalization of adolescent sexuality does not eradicate the tensions between parents and teenagers or the gender constructs that confine both girls and boys. But it does provide a more favorable cultural climate in which to address them.

The Experiences of Lesbian, Gay, Bisexual and Transgender Youth in American Schools

Joseph G. Kosciw, Ph.D., Emily A. Greytak, Ph.D., Mark J. Bartkiewicz, M.S., Madelyn J. Boesen, M.A., and Neal A. Palmer, M.S.

In 1999, the Gay, Lesbian & Straight Education Network (GLSEN) identified the need for national data on the experiences of lesbian, gay, bisexual, and transgender (LGBT) students and launched the first National School Climate Survey (NSCS). At the time, the school experiences of LGBT youth were under-documented and nearly absent from national studies of adolescents. For more than a decade, the biennial NSCS has documented the unique challenges

LGBT students face and identified interventions that can improve school climate. The survey explores the prevalence of anti-LGBT language and victimization, the effect that these experiences have on LGBT students' achievement and well-being, and the utility of interventions in lessening the negative effects of a hostile school climate and promoting a positive educational experience. The survey also examines demographic and community-level differences in LGBT students' experiences. The NSCS remains one of the few studies to examine the school experiences of LGBT students nationally. . . .

In our 2011 survey, we examine the experiences of LGBT students with regard to indicators of negative school climate. . . .

We also examine:

- the possible negative effects of a hostile school climate on LGBT students' academic achievement, educational aspirations, and psychological well-being; and
- whether or not students report experiences of victimization to school officials . . . and how these adults address the problem. . . .

In addition, we demonstrate the degree to which LGBT students have access to supportive resources in school, and we explore the possible benefits of these resources. . . . Given that GLSEN has more than a decade of data, we examine changes over the time on indicators of negative school climate and levels of access to LGBT-related resources in schools.

GLSEN used two methods to obtain a representative national sample of lesbian, gay, bisexual, and transgender (LGBT) youth to participate in a survey: 1) outreach through national, regional, and local organizations that provide services to or advocate on behalf of LGBT youth, and 2) targeted advertising on the social networking site Facebook. For the first method, we asked organizations to direct youth to the National School Climate Survey, which was available on GLSEN's website, through their organizations' emails, listservs, websites, and social networking sites. Additionally, a paper version of the survey was made available to local community groups/organizations with limited capacity to access the Internet. To ensure representation of transgender youth, youth of color, and youth in rural communities, we made special efforts to notify groups and

organizations that work predominantly with these populations. For the second method, we posted advertisements for the survey on Facebook, targeting all users between 13 and 18 years of age who gave some indication on their profile that they were lesbian, gay, bisexual, or transgender. The final sample consisted of a total of 8,584 students between the ages of 13 and 20. Students were from all 50 states and the District of Columbia and from 3,224 unique school districts. About two thirds of the sample (67.9%) was White, about half (49.6%) was female, and over half identified as gay or lesbian (61.3%). Students were in grades 6 to 12, with the largest numbers in grades 10 and 11.

KEY FINDINGS: HOSTILE SCHOOL CLIMATE, ABSENTEEISM, LOWERED EDUCATIONAL ASPIRATIONS AND ACHIEVEMENT, AND POORER PSYCHOLOGICAL WELL-BEING

Schools nationwide are hostile environments for a distressing number of LGBT students, the overwhelming majority of whom hear homophobic remarks and experience harassment or assault at school because of their sexual orientation or gender expression.

- 84.9% of students heard "gay" used in a negative way (e.g., "that's so gay") frequently or often at school, and 91.4% reported that they felt distressed because of this language.
- 71.3% heard other homophobic remarks (e.g., "dyke" or "faggot") frequently or often.
- 61.4% heard negative remarks about gender expression (not acting "masculine enough" or "feminine enough") frequently or often.
- 56.9% of students reported hearing homophobic remarks from their teachers or other school staff, and 56.9% of students reported

hearing negative remarks about gender expression from teachers or other school staff.

- 63.5% felt unsafe because of their sexual orientation, and 43.9% because of their gender expression.
- 81.9% were verbally harassed (e.g., called names or threatened) in the past year because of their sexual orientation, and 63.9% because of their gender expression.
- 38.3% were physically harassed (e.g., pushed or shoved) in the past year because of their sexual orientation, and 27.1% because of their gender expression.
- 18.3% were physically assaulted (e.g., punched, kicked, injured with a weapon) in the past year because of their sexual orientation, and 12.4% because of their gender expression.
- 55.2% of LGBT students experienced electronic harassment in the past year (via text messages or postings on Facebook), often known as cyberbullying.

The high incidence of harassment and assault is exacerbated by school staff who rarely, if ever, intervene on behalf of LGBT students.

- 60.4% of students who were harassed or assaulted in school did not report the incident to school staff, most often believing little to no action would be taken or the situation could become worse if reported.
- 36.7% of the students who did report an incident said that school staff did nothing in response.

Many LGBT students avoid classes or miss entire days of school rather than face a hostile school climate. An unsafe school environment denies these students their right to an education.

- 29.8% of students skipped a class at least once in the past month because they felt unsafe or uncomfortable.

- 31.8% missed at least one entire day of school in the past month because they felt unsafe or uncomfortable.
- Students who experienced higher levels of victimization because of their sexual orientation were three times as likely to have missed school in the past month than those who experienced lower levels (57.9% vs. 19.6%).
- Students who experienced higher levels of victimization because of their gender identity were more than twice as likely to have missed school in the past month than those who experienced lower levels (53.2% vs. 20.4%).

School safety affects student success. Experiencing victimization in school hinders LGBT students' academic success and educational aspirations.

- Students who were more frequently harassed because of their sexual orientation or gender expression had lower grade point averages than students who were less often harassed (2.9 vs. 3.2).
- Students who experienced higher levels of victimization in school because of their sexual orientation or gender expression were more than twice as likely to report that they did not plan to pursue any post-secondary education (e.g., college or trade school) than those who experienced lower levels (10.7% vs. 5.1%).

Experiences of harassment and assault in school are related to poorer psychological well-being for LGBT students:

- Students who experienced higher levels of victimization based on their sexual orientation or gender expression had higher levels of depression than those who reported lower levels of those types of victimization.
- Students who experienced higher levels of victimization based on their sexual orientation or gender expression had lower levels of self-esteem than those who reported lower levels of those types of victimization.

SOLUTIONS: GAY-STRAIGHT ALLIANCES, INCLUSIVE CURRICULUM, SUPPORTIVE EDUCATORS, AND COMPREHENSIVE POLICIES

Gay-Straight Alliances (GSAs) and similar student clubs can provide safe, affirming spaces and critical support for LGBT students. GSAs also contribute to creating a more welcoming school environment.

- Students with a GSA in their school heard fewer homophobic remarks, such as "faggot" or "dyke," and fewer expressions where "gay" was used in a negative way than students in schools without a GSA.
- Students with a GSA were more likely to report that school personnel intervened when hearing homophobic remarks compared to students without a GSA—19.8% vs. 12.0% said that staff intervened "most of the time" or "always."
- Students with a GSA were less likely to feel unsafe because of their sexual orientation than those without a GSA (54.9% vs. 70.6%).
- Students with a GSA experienced less victimization related to their sexual orientation and gender expression. For example, 23.0% of students with a GSA experienced higher levels of victimization based on their sexual orientation, compared to 38.5% of those without a GSA.
- Students with a GSA had a greater sense of connectedness to their school community than students without a GSA.

Yet, less than half (45.7%) of students said that their school had a GSA or similar student club.

A curriculum that includes positive representations of LGBT people, history, and events (i.e., an inclusive curriculum) can promote respect for all and improve LGBT students' school experiences.

- Students in schools with an inclusive curriculum heard fewer homophobic remarks, including negative use of the word "gay," the phrase "no homo," and homophobic epithets (e.g., "fag" or "dyke"), and fewer negative comments about someone's gender expression than those without an inclusive curriculum.
- Less than half (43.4%) of students in schools with an inclusive curriculum felt unsafe because of their sexual orientation, compared to almost two thirds (67.5%) of other students.
- Less than a fifth (17.7%) of students in schools with an inclusive curriculum had missed school in the past month compared to more than a third (34.8%) of other students.
- Students in schools with an inclusive curriculum were more likely to report that their classmates were somewhat or very accepting of LGBT people than other students (66.7% vs. 33.2%).
- Students in schools with an inclusive curriculum had a greater sense of connectedness to their school community than other students.

However, only a small percentage of students were taught positive representations about LGBT people, history, or events in their schools (16.8%). Furthermore, less than half (44.1%) of students reported that they could find information about LGBT-related issues in their school library, and only two in five (42.1%) with Internet access at school reported being able to access LGBT-related information online via school computers.

The presence of educators who are supportive of LGBT students can have a positive impact on the school experiences of these students, as well as their psychological well-being.

- About half (53.1%) of students who had many (six or more) supportive staff at their school felt unsafe in school because of their sexual orientation, compared to nearly three fourths (76.9%) of students with no supportive staff.

- Less than a quarter (21.9%) of students with many supportive staff had missed school in the past month compared to over half (51.2%) with no supportive staff.
- Students with greater numbers of supportive staff had a greater sense of being a part of their school community than other students.
- Students with many supportive staff reported higher grade point averages than other students (3.2 vs. 2.9).
- Students with a greater number of supportive staff also had higher educational aspirations—students with many supportive staff were about a third as likely to say they were not planning on attending college compared to students with no supportive educators (5.1% vs. 14.9%).

Although almost all students (95.0%) could identify at least one staff member supportive of LGBT students at their school, only about half (54.6%) could identify six or more supportive school staff.

Policies and laws that explicitly address bias-based bullying and harassment can create safer learning environments for all students by reducing the prevalence of biased behaviors. Comprehensive policies and laws—those that specifically enumerate personal characteristics including sexual orientation and gender identity/expression, among others—are most effective at combating anti-LGBT bullying and harassment.

- Six in ten (59.5%) students in schools with comprehensive policies heard homophobic remarks (e.g., "faggot" or "dyke") often or frequently, compared to almost three quarters of students in schools with generic, non-enumerated policies (73.3%) or no policy whatsoever (73.8%).

- Students in schools with comprehensive policies were more likely than students in schools with a generic policy or no policy to report that staff intervened when hearing homophobic remarks (28.3% vs. 12.2% vs. 8.8%) or negative remarks about gender expression (19.0% vs. 10.5% vs. 8.4%).

However, only 7.4% of students reported that their school had a comprehensive policy (i.e., that specifically included both sexual orientation and gender identity/expression) and only 15.6% reported that their policy included either sexual orientation or gender identity/expression.

Results from the NSCS provide evidence that students who live in states with comprehensive anti-bullying/harassment laws experience less victimization because of their sexual orientation or gender expression and are more likely to have supportive resources, including a comprehensive school policy. Yet, only 15 states plus the District of Columbia have comprehensive laws that include sexual orientation and gender identity.

CHANGES IN SCHOOL CLIMATE FOR LGBT YOUTH OVER TIME

Increases from past years in school resources may now be showing a positive effect on school climate for LGBT youth. . . . The 2011 NSCS marks the first time our findings show both decreases in negative indicators of school climate (biased remarks and victimization) and continued increases in most LGBT-related school resources and supports. Our results indicate a general trend that, while still prevalent, homophobic remarks (e.g., "dyke" or "faggot"), are on the decline. Students in 2011 reported a lower incidence of these remarks than all prior years. The percentage of students hearing these remarks frequently or often has dropped from over 80% in 2001 to about 70% in 2011.

There has also been a small but consistent decline in the frequency of expressions such as "that's so gay" since 2001. However, there has been little change over time in the incidence of hearing negative remarks about gender expression. Between 2001 to 2009, LGBT students' reports of harassment and assault remained relatively constant. In 2011, however, we saw a significant decrease in victimization based on sexual orientation. Changes in harassment and assault based on gender expression were similar to those for sexual orientation—verbal harassment was lower in 2011 than in all prior years, and physical harassment and assault were lower in 2011 than in 2009 and 2007.

We have also observed some changes in the availability of LGBT-related resources over time. In 2011, we saw small increases from previous years in the percentage of students who reported having a GSA at school. The percentage of LGBT students with a GSA in their school was statistically higher in 2011 than all previous years except for 2003. The percentage of students with access to LGBT-related Internet resources through their school computers also showed a continued increase in 2011, and the percentage of students reporting positive representations of LGBT people, history, or events in their curriculum was significantly higher in 2011 than all prior survey years except for 2003. In contrast, the percentage of students who had LGBT-related resources in their school library peaked in 2009 and decreased slightly in 2011. There have been no changes over time in the percentage of students reporting inclusion of LGBT-related content in their textbooks. There was a continued trend in 2011 of an increasing number of supportive school staff over the past decade, including a small but statistically significant increase from 2009 to 2011. Finally, in 2011, we saw a large increase in the percentage of students reporting any type of anti-bullying/harassment policy at their school. However, there was no increase in the percentage of students reporting that their school had a comprehensive policy, i.e., one that included protections based on sexual orientation and gender identity/expression.

DEMOGRAPHIC AND SCHOOL CHARACTERISTIC DIFFERENCES IN LGBT STUDENTS' EXPERIENCES

LGBT students are a diverse population, and although they may share some experiences related to school climate, their experiences may also vary by both students' personal characteristics and those of their school. In the full 2011 National School Climate Survey report, we examine differences in students' experiences based on race/ethnicity, gender, school level, school type (public, religious, private non-religious), region, and locale. Major findings regarding these differences are highlighted below.

Compared to other LGBT students, transgender students faced the most hostile school climates whereas female non-transgender students were least likely to experience anti-LGBT victimization. In addition, gender nonconforming students experienced more negative experiences at school compared to students whose gender expression adhered to traditional gender norms.

- Transgender students were most likely to feel unsafe at school, with 80.0% of transgender students reporting that they felt unsafe at school because of their gender expression.
- Female students in our survey reported lower frequencies of victimization based on sexual orientation and gender expression and were less likely to feel unsafe at school.
- Gender nonconforming students reported higher levels of victimization and feeling unsafe at school. For example, 58.7% of gender nonconforming students experienced verbal harassment in the past year because of their gender expression, compared to 29.0% of their peers.

LGBT students attending schools in the Northeast and the West reported lower frequencies of victimization and hearing homophobic remarks and had greater access to resources and support than students in the South and Midwest.

- Students in the Northeast and the West reported hearing "gay" used in a negative way less frequently than students in the South and the Midwest.
- Overall, LGBT students from schools in the Northeast and the West reported significantly lower levels of victimization than students from schools in the South and the Midwest.
- In general, students in the Northeast were most likely to report having LGBT-related resources at school, such as inclusive curricula and supportive school personnel, followed by students in the West. Students in the South were least likely to have access to these resources and supports.

LGBT students in rural areas and small towns were less safe in school than students in urban and suburban areas. They also had fewer LGBT-related resources or supports in school.

- Students in rural/small town schools reported the highest frequency of hearing anti-LGBT language at school. For example, 53.8% of rural/small town students reported hearing homophobic remarks such as "fag" or "dyke" frequently, compared to 41.4% of suburban students and 39.0% of urban students.
- Students in rural/small town schools experienced higher levels of victimization in school based on sexual orientation and gender expression.
- Students in rural/small town schools were least likely to have LGBT-related school resources or supports, particularly Gay-Straight Alliances and supportive school personnel.

On all of the indicators of school climate in the survey, middle school students fared worse than high school students and had fewer LGBT-related resources and supports.

- Students in middle school reported higher frequencies of victimization on sexual orientation and gender expression than students in high school. For example, about a third (35.5%) of middle school students experienced regular physical harassment (sometimes, often, or frequently) based on their sexual orientation, compared to less than a quarter (21.4%) of high school students.
- Although middle school students were less likely to have access to every resource and support about which we asked, the disparity between middle and high school students was greatest for Gay-Straight Alliances (6.3% for middle school students vs. 52.6% for high school students).

CONCLUSIONS AND RECOMMENDATIONS

It is clear that there is an urgent need for action to create safe and affirming schools for LGBT students. . . . Therefore, we recommend the following measures:

- Advocate for comprehensive bullying/harassment legislation at the state and federal levels that specifically enumerates sexual orientation, gender identity, and gender expression as protected categories alongside others such as race, religion, and disability;
- Adopt and implement comprehensive bullying/harassment policies that specifically enumerate sexual orientation, gender identity, and gender expression in individual schools and districts, with clear and effective systems for reporting and addressing incidents that students experience;
- Ensure that school policies and practices, such as those related to dress codes and

school dances, do not discriminate against LGBT students;

- Support student clubs, such as Gay-Straight Alliances, that provide support for LGBT students and address LGBT issues in education;
- Provide training for school staff to improve rates of intervention and increase the number of supportive teachers and other staff available to students; and
- Increase student access to appropriate and accurate information regarding LGBT people, history, and events through inclusive curricula and library and Internet resources.

Taken together, such measures can move us toward a future in which all students have the opportunity to learn and succeed in school, regardless of sexual orientation, gender identity, or gender expression.

Source: The 2011 National School Climate Survey: The Experiences of Lesbian, Gay, Bisexual and Transgender Youth in Our Nation's Schools (excerpted Executive Summary); Authors: Joseph G. Kosciw, Emily A. Greytak, Mark J. Bartkiewicz, Madelyn J. Boesen, and Neal A. Palmer. © 2012 Gay, Lesbian & Straight Education Network. Reprinted with permission.

FIGHTING TEENAGE PREGNANCY WITH MTV STARS AS EXHIBIT A

JAN HOFFMAN

MTV's [reality television shows] *16 and Pregnant,* . . . *Teen Mom* and . . . . *Teen Mom 2* . . . have received swipes for glamorizing teenage pregnancy, and conferring girls-gone-wild celebrity on their stars. But that is not how Megan Clark, who teaches family consumer sciences to high school students in a small Kansas town, regards the programs. They have become a popular element in her freshman life-skills classes, and in parenting courses for older students. "They're sucked into the drama of it," Ms. Clark said, "but they see that they don't ever want to be in that situation. I talk about abstinence first and foremost, but I listen to them, so I know they're not abstinent. So the show offers a good opportunity to teach them about condoms and birth control."

With DVDs and episode discussion guides distributed by the National Campaign to Prevent Teen and Unplanned Pregnancy, public-school health educators, church-group leaders, clinic nurses, social workers and parents are using the shows to prompt discussion about sex education, family and romantic relationships, and shattered dreams. In her classes, Ms. Clark notes how MTV's teenage mothers try to manage school, sick babies, sleep deprivation, rent, errant boyfriends, and rearview glimpses of their carefree lives. "Then I ask my students to make up a budget if they had to live on their own with a baby," she said. . . . "The biggest debates are over how the girls disrespect their own parents," she said. On [a] reunion special of *Teen Mom 2,* Dr. Drew Pinsky, hand holder to the reality-TV stars, raised that question with Jenelle and her mother, Barbara. The daughter had been video-taped shoving her mother and stealing her credit cards. Was Jenelle lovable? Dr. Pinsky asked. Teary-eyed, exhausted, Barbara replied dully, "No." Ms. Clark said that in her class she asks students: "How do you treat your own parents? If you were put in that situation, how would that affect your relationship with them?" Ms. Clark and other educators say they have never been criticized for using the shows. (The National Campaign to Prevent Teen and Unplanned Pregnancy has distributed 3,000 DVDs and guides to Boys and Girls Clubs of America chapters alone.) But she said that she didn't want to test limits by showing [the] episode, "No Easy Decision," [where] one teenager who has an infant becomes pregnant again. After much agonizing, she and her boyfriend chose abortion.

The MTV episodes, which went on the air in June 2009, show high school girls far along in unplanned pregnancies. Some are good students and pretty, popular cheerleaders; some are self-described party girls. Some come from financially comfortable, two-parent homes; others from homes riven by divorce, alcohol, and severe economic stress. Scenes can be tender, harrowing, or headshaking. Relationships among relatives, between the couples, and with the girls' erstwhile friends change throughout dewy pregnancies, tested by dirty diapers. . . . Despite the tabloid derision and paparazzi attention that are almost a necessary byproduct of reality TV shows, the impact extends far beyond their ratings triumphs. (The season finale of *Teen Mom 2* . . . drew 4.7 million viewers, and was the top-rated show that day in the 12 to 34 demographic.)

[In summer 2010], in a national telephone poll of young people ages 12 to 19 commissioned by the National Campaign, 82 percent of those who had watched *16 and Pregnant* said the shows helped them understand the challenges of pregnancy and how to avoid it. Only 15 percent said the show glamorized pregnancy. In a study with Boys and Girls Clubs of America chapters in one Southern state, the campaign learned that after watching *16 and Pregnant* with a group leader, nearly half the teenagers talked to a parent about it. As educators and parents note, it is easier to talk with a teenager about sex when the topic involves a television character. This is true, to an extent. Rachel Siegel, 13, from Miami, has watched *16 and Pregnant* with her mother. "My mom asks the same questions 50 times," Rachel said. "The shows make it easier for her to talk about having my own sex life and my own body, but it's still a little weird for me to talk to her about it."

On Tuesday nights at the Bridger Clinic, a reproductive health center in Bozeman, Montana, Cindy Ballew trains high school students to become peer educators who visit middle and high school classes to discuss pregnancy prevention and relationships. Ms. Ballew's sessions usually begin with an MTV episode. To focus her students, she asks: "What did you see that you thought was a healthy decision? What did you see that was not?" When students deplore the waywardness of the boyfriends, who almost all disappear in some fashion, Ms. Ballew responds: "We discuss why so many men can't step up. How challenging it must feel to them. I say: 'Can you imagine that maybe he's

depressed? And that's why he never works or helps with the baby?' Each episode has teachable moments." Maren Studer, 18, was one of those watching the shows in Ms. Ballew's sessions. "I learned that some teens are better at handling the challenges of pregnancy and parenting than others," Ms. Studer said. "Even though Catelynn and Tyler are the least dramatic and entertaining of the couples, I appreciate what they did by placing their baby for adoption."

Although the shows are perceived as cautionary tales for girls, Stacy Wright, of Kansas City, Missouri, watches them with her older sons, one a high school freshman, the other a junior. Referring to one episode, Mrs. Wright told them: "Here's a boy who thought the girl was taking care of the birth control and he wouldn't have to deal with it. Sorry, but you can't trust them. Drive defensively."

The United States has the highest teenage birth rate among the fully industrialized countries, although that number has slowly declined over the last 20 years. Even so, in 2009, 410,000 teenagers, ages 15 to 19, gave birth—or 1,100 a day. The economy is a major factor in the recent decline. But educators speculate that *16 and Pregnant* may be giving teenagers pause as well. "There is no question that these shows are affecting the conversation about teen pregnancy and teen motherhood," said Sarah Brown, chief executive of the National Campaign to Prevent Teen and Unplanned Pregnancy. "This generation of teens is very oriented to reality shows in general. They seek them and they believe them. These shows resonate powerfully."

In the right setting, an episode may not even need a discussion guide. When patients have an appointment with the nurse at the teenage reproductive health center in Rome, Georgia, Angela Robinson, the center's program coordinator, may show episodes in the waiting room. "The kids will tell the nurse, 'I sure don't want to be like the girl on MTV!' "

Ms. Robinson said. " 'I want something that's effective.' " A social worker, who did not want to be identified to protect her job, said that she shows the episodes to groups of violent teenagers in a West Coast juvenile detention center. Sometimes the girls are pregnant or already have babies. Often the boys are fathers. "The kids have many questions that we can answer," the social worker wrote in an e-mail. "Discussions have included child development, taking care of a newborn, how the teenagers acted in the episode. Other educational material is too outdated, too advanced for their level. The kids are highly receptive and attentive to this show."

Among professionals who work with teenagers about pregnancy prevention, the shows prompt criticism and qualified admiration. Dr. Sari Locker, a sex educator who teaches adolescent psychology at Columbia, said, "They show the hardships of teen pregnancy and raising a baby, but they don't provide more meaningful sex education that might help them prevent that pregnancy, have a positive body image and negotiate dating." [The] documentary "Let's Talk About Sex" . . . explores the contradiction for American teenagers living in a highly sexualized culture, but one with poor access to realistic sex education.

. . . At Sex::Tech, a conference on technology and sex education, the MTV shows' executive producers, Morgan J. Freeman and Dia Sokol Savage, were peppered with questions about casting, compensation and race. Most teenagers in the shows have been white. The producers said that the new season is more diverse. They would not disclose compensation for the girls, but said that reports of six figures are wildly exaggerated. Casting is challenging, they said. They look for girls who want to share their stories to caution others. But producers must also obtain agreements from prime participants, including parents, boyfriends and medical personnel. Deb Levine, the executive director of ISIS Inc., a sex health education program that sponsored the conference, said that the MTV shows impressed even veteran sex educators. "All day long, that's all everyone was talking about," she said, "how sex education has to intersect with popular culture."

SEXUAL RISK AND THE DOUBLE STANDARD FOR AFRICAN AMERICAN ADOLESCENT WOMEN

AMY M. FASULA, KIM S. MILLER, AND JEFFREY WIENER

The disproportionate rates of HIV/AIDS for Black women in the United States are staggering (CDC, 2005), and young Black women are at particularly high risk. In 2002, AIDS was the leading cause of death for Black women of ages 25–34 (Anderson and Smith, 2005), and many of these women were likely infected as adolescents or young adults. In addition, 13- to 19-year-olds have the highest proportion of AIDS cases among females (43%) (CDC, 2004). The primary mode of HIV transmission for adolescent and adult women of all race and ethnicity categories is through unprotected heterosexual contact (CDC, 2005).

These trends highlight the critical need to develop new intervention strategies that address young Black women's HIV risk in their heterosexual interactions more effectively. We need to create innovative approaches to HIV prevention that speak directly to the lived experiences of Black women in their intimate relationships with men. Furthermore, such prevention efforts need to begin early in the sexual socialization process, before sexual behaviors have begun and sexual scripts have already taken hold. In order to develop such early, socially relevant HIV interventions, we need to gain a richer understanding of Black girls' sexual socialization as it relates to heterosexual risk.

One aspect of sexual socialization relevant to sexual risk reduction is the sexual double standard (SDS). Under this social norm, males are afforded more freedom and power than females to engage in and direct heterosexual interactions, which may limit young women's ability to fully control their sexual risk reduction behaviors (Connell, 1987; Holland, Ramazanoglu, Sharpe, and Thomson, 2004; Tanenbaum, 2000; Tolman, 2002). Parents, particularly mothers, play a key role in adolescents' sexual socialization (Downie and Coates, 1999; Miller, Kotchick, Dorsey, Forehand, and Ham, 1998; Nolin and Petersen, 1992; Rosenthal and Feldman, 1999) and mother-adolescent sexual discussions have positive effects on reducing adolescent sexual risk (DiIorio, Kelley, and Hockenberry-Eaton, 1999; Fasula and Miller, 2006; Miller, Levin, Whitaker, and Xu, 1998; Whitaker, Miller, May, and Levin, 1999). Therefore, in this paper, we qualitatively explore the SDS in African American mothers' sexual messages to sons and daughters, specifically in terms of daughters' sexual risk reduction.

[Adolescents'] gender is a factor in mother-adolescent sexual discussions. Mothers are more likely to talk to daughters, are more comfortable talking with daughters (DiIorio, Hockenberry-Eaton, Maibach, Rivero, and Miller, 1996), and talk about a wider range of topics with daughters than with sons (for a review see DiIorio, Pluhar, and Belcher, 2003). The reasons mothers put more emphasis on daughters' sexual socialization may be related to their identification and comfort in talking with same-gender children about sexual topics and the increased social and physical sequelae of pregnancy and STDs for females.

Ironically, however, in mothers' attempts to protect daughters from negative sexual health outcomes they often reinforce an SDS that may limit daughters' sexual agency and risk reduction preparedness (DiIorio et al., 1999; Downie and Coates, 1999; Espiritu, 2001; Nolin and Petersen, 1992; O'Sullivan, Meyer-Bahlburg, and Watkins, 2001). For example, in a study with African American mothers and adolescents, topics discussed by mothers and fathers emphasized consequences of STDs, HIV and condom use more for sons, and normal development and abstinence more for daughters (DiIorio et al., 1999). Similarly, Levin and Robertson (2002) found that ethnic minority mothers were more accepting of sons than of daughters carrying condoms, even when mothers thought their son or daughter was sexually active. This paradoxical situation in which mothers believe daughters to be sexually active, yet do not want them to carry condoms pointedly illustrates the dangers the SDS sets up for young women.

These findings suggest that it is of critical importance to women's HIV prevention efforts to understand how the SDS specifically affects daughters' sexual risk reduction socialization . . .

In this study we examined gender differences and SDS patterns in African American mothers' messages to 15- to 17-year-old sons and daughters about sexual topics. In particular, we focused our analyses on mothers' messages related to sexual risk reduction . . .

METHODS

The data for this study were taken from a larger study, the Family Adolescent Risk Behavior and Communication Study (FARBCS). FARBCS was a cross-sectional study with Black and Hispanic mother-adolescent dyads

which examined the effects of individual, family, peer, and environmental factors on adolescent risk reduction behaviors. . . . Of these, 907 . . . mother-adolescent dyads were successfully interviewed—259 Black dyads in Montgomery and 172 in the Bronx. . . .

Mother and adolescent were interviewed separately, with the mother's interview conducted, when possible, before the adolescent interview. . . .

To create the sample for the current analyses, we started with the 431 dyads in which the adolescent self-identified as Black. To control for potential effects of mother's race, we then excluded 67 dyads in which the mother did not self-identify as Black, leaving a sample of 364 dyads. Next, to focus our analyses on the SDS, we included only dyads that reported SDS attitudes in the closed-ended data. Attitudes about adolescents having sex, having many partners, and getting pregnant/getting someone pregnant were determined by mothers' and adolescents' responses (never ok, sometimes ok, always ok) to questions such as "What do you think about male [female] teenagers your age having sex?" Adolescents were also asked about their perceptions of the mother's attitudes (e.g., "What does your mother think about male [female] teenagers your age having sex?"). If either the mother or the adolescent indicated that any behavior was more acceptable for males than for females, the dyad was included in the study analyses. Of the 364 Black dyads, 35% held at least one SDS, for a final sample of 129 dyads. . . .

RESULTS

Sample Characteristics

The majority (65%) of the mother-adolescent dyads were from Montgomery, AL. . . . Mothers were typically between 35 and 44 years of age (66%); education attainment of mothers in the sample ranged from less than a high school diploma (16%); to a college degree or above (16%); the majority were employed outside of the home either full-time (54%) or part-time (15%); and 43% were married at the time of the interview. Most mothers attended religious services at least one to two times per month (71%). Nearly all of the mothers were the biological parent of the participating adolescents (92%), and they had on average four children, including the participating adolescent. All of the dyads self-identified specifically as African American.

The age of the adolescents at the time of the interview ranged from 14 to 17 years, with a mean of 15 years. Mother-daughter dyads comprised 53% of the sample. The majority of sons (85%) reported ever engaging in intercourse, whereas the majority of mothers perceived their son (51%) not to be sexually active. For daughters, 37% reported ever engaging in intercourse although only 27% of mothers thought their daughter was sexually active.

Qualitative Results

Our analyses revealed one overarching theme and four sub-themes related to the SDS and mothers' sexual risk reduction socialization. The primary theme was the "clean" and "dirty" girl dichotomy. The sub-themes were: (1) sexual guidance for sons, conflict and controls for daughters; (2) discouraging daughters' sexual risk reduction preparedness; (3) challenges to passive condom preparation for daughters; and (4) proactive condom preparation for sons.

The Clean and Dirty Girl Dichotomy

In mothers' sexual risk reduction messages, the gender ideology of the "good" and "bad" girl dichotomy, which stigmatizes female sexual knowledge and experience, intersects with disease prevention to create the clean and dirty girl dichotomy. In discussions with sexually active

and non-sexually active sons about avoiding STDs and HIV, a consistent theme emerged of mothers categorizing women as clean and dirty, and some used disparaging terms such as "slutty" or "scaliwags" to define safe and unsafe female partners. For example, the mother of a sexually active son said, "[I told my son to use condoms] whether or not he thought that the girl was clean. . . ." And a sexually active son stated "[My mother told me that to prevent HIV] . . . use a condom if you're gonna have sex. Don't bring a slutty girl in the house. . . ." In addition to such statements, several mothers warned their sons that pretty women can also be dirty. For example, a mother of a sexually active son stated, "I told him that appearance says nothing, she can be the prettiest girl in school and infect everyone on the football team. . . ."

Although mothers of both sons and daughters warned their adolescents, "You never know" if a person is infected, none of the mothers labeled males as "good or bad," "clean or dirty" or "handsome but dirty." The ways mothers tried to protect daughters from being labeled dirty or their discomfort with their daughters' sexual development based on this aspect of the SDS ran through each of the following sub-themes.

SEXUAL GUIDANCE FOR SONS, CONFLICT AND CONTROLS FOR DAUGHTERS. Conflict and controls over sexual issues consistently recurred in the mother-daughter data, for both sexually and non-sexually active daughters. Some mothers and daughters argued about the highly charged issues of sex and pregnancy. A number of these arguments, however, occurred because daughters were not allowed to date or have a boyfriend, or they argued about talking to boys. For example, a sexually active daughter stated, "[The reoccurring arguments with my mother are] mostly about boys. She doesn't want me to have a boyfriend." Half of the daughters restricted from dating or talking to boys were already sexually active.

In contrast, it was rare for mothers and sons to report reoccurring arguments about sexual issues. Of those that did, the majority were about sex and pregnancy, rather than dating or talking with girls. In fact, the data suggested that when mothers noticed sons taking an interest in girls, rather than triggering arguments, they often used these events as the impetus for discussions to help guide their sons about sexuality. For example, a mother of a sexually active son stated, "[The sexual discussions with my son start because] a lot of girls call the house for him and I just tell him to be careful and take precautions." And a mother of a non-sexually active son stated, "[The sexual discussions with my son start] 'cause I care and I want him to know. Sometimes I overhear them telling about what girls they've gone to bed with."

DISCOURAGING DAUGHTERS' SEXUAL RISK REDUCTION PREPAREDNESS. Following this restrictive stance toward daughters' sexual guidance and preparation, some mothers overtly discouraged their daughters (but never sons) from obtaining safe sex methods. Mothers often told both sons and daughters that abstinence from sex was the only way to protect themselves from negative sexual outcomes. In nearly half of these messages to daughters, however, the mothers went one step further and told their daughters not to obtain other forms of protection, such as birth control pills or condoms. As the mother of a non-sexually active daughter stated, "[I told my daughter that] no birth control method is foolproof. I did not specify one over another. I told her that she did not need it and not to participate in the school programs where birth control is distributed. . . ." The following quote from a sexually active daughter illustrated the paradox these messages created for sexually active daughters'

prevention efforts: "[My mother said] that if I wanted to be on birth control it was for people that slept around. She says the best way to prevent pregnancy is to not have sex."

CHALLENGES TO PASSIVE CONDOM PREPARATION FOR DAUGHTERS. Some mothers did encourage their daughters to obtain, carry, and use condoms if they had sex—although these messages were more common for sons than for daughters. Some mothers' messages even ran counter to the SDS and explicitly challenged a passive female role in condom use. These messages, however, revealed a perception by mothers that there were social norms that promoted shame and passivity for female condom preparation and use. In these messages mothers told daughters "not to be ashamed to provide her own condoms," and not to depend on the man for condoms. Neither the link between condoms and shame nor messages of "don't depend on the woman for condoms" came up in the sons' data.

PROACTIVE CONDOM PREPARATION FOR SONS. Condom skills and access are important aspects of condom preparation. Mothers in this study were consistently more proactive in providing sons with these resources than either sexually active or non-sexually active daughters. In particular, mothers commonly reported that they provided their sons with condoms. A mother of a sexually active son illustrated a typical example, "I bought [my son] some [condoms], gave him permission to buy some for himself and asked his father to have a talk with him." Additionally, condoms were part of pubertal socialization and skills development for some non-sexually active sons. For example, a mother of a non-sexually active son provided him with condoms after his first wet dream. Another explained, "[My son and I have] talked about condoms. I gave him packages of them that told how to use them on the back. I told him he need to use them to ask me and I'll get them for him."

In contrast to the way condoms were encouraged, provided, and treated as part of the "facts of life" for sons, mothers of even sexually active daughters were more removed from the process of providing their daughters with condom protection. Only one mother told her daughter that she would buy her condoms when she was ready to have sex; two gave their daughters permission to obtain condoms at school; and none reported giving their daughter condoms.

DISCUSSION

The study findings illustrated how the SDS affects the content and process of mothers' sexual risk reduction socialization for sons and daughters. Mothers typically took a proactive approach with sons and a neutral or prohibitive approach with daughters regarding sexual risk reduction. Mothers used sons' sexual interest as impetus for sexual guidance. They often encouraged sons to carry and use condoms, and some provided sons with condoms. However, daughters' sexual interest often resulted in restrictions and arguments; mothers did not provide daughters with condoms, and some explicitly discouraged daughters' sexual risk reduction preparedness. Previous research on adolescent sexual development and risk help contextualize how mothers' SDS messages and this neutral or prohibitive approach to daughters' sexual risk reduction socialization may affect their ability to protect themselves from sexual risk.

Similar to previous research, the good girl and bad girl dichotomy was an overarching theme related to young women's sexuality (Fullilove, Fullilove, Haynes, and Gross, 1990; Gilmore, DeLamater, and Wagstaff, 1996; Hutchinson, 1999; Tanenbaum, 2000; Wilkins, 2004). Under this ideology, it is considered deviant, even unnatural, for girls and women to experience and express sexuality, thus girls

and women are considered good or bad based on their perceived knowledge and experience of sexuality (Eyre, Hoffman, and Millstein, 1998; Fullilove et al., 1990; Hutchinson, 1999; Tanenbaum, 2000; Wilkins, 2004). For young women undergoing their sexual development, this asexual message is likely to result in an underdeveloped sense of themselves as a sexual being (Fullilove et al., 1990; Thompson, 1995; Tolman, 2002; Tolman and Brown, 2001).

Without a strong sexual self, young women are likely to deny the possibility or the experience of sexual desire, which can create barriers to actively developing attitudes about how, when, and why they would or would not engage in sexual behaviors (Holland et al., 2004; Thompson, 1995; Tolman, 2002; Tolman and Debold, 1994). This sexual denial reduces young women's agency in their sexual decisions (Holland et al., 2004; Monahan, Miller, and Rothspan, 1997; Nolin and Petersen, 1992; Thompson, 1990; Tolman, 2002; Tolman and Debold, 1994; Whitley and Schofield, 1986).

In addition, this aspect of the SDS is deeply embedded in the heterosexual romance script in which males are supposed to pursue sex and females are supposed to resist and say no, whether they want to have sex or not (Muehlenhard, 1988; Muehlenhard and McCoy, 1991). Under this scenario women are left to act as "gatekeepers" and merely respond to men's actions rather than take an active role in their sexual encounters (Campbell, 1995; Fine, 1988; Hartley and Drew, 2001; Holland et al., 2004; Muehlenhard, 1988; Muehlenhard and McCoy, 1991; Tolman, 1996). Without strong grounding in their own sexuality, young women are likely to put the sexual decision-making power into the hands of their male partners, thereby limiting their ability to ensure safe sexual behaviors (Wingood and DiClemente, 1998).

In these data, the good girl/bad girl dichotomy was transformed by the threat of STDs and HIV into categorizing young women as clean or dirty. This transformation added another layer to the social stigma of the bad girl by defining her not only as deviant, but also dangerous and diseased. Furthermore, the theme of pretty but dirty introduced suspicion that any girl may be dirty. The challenges mothers made to this aspect of the SDS also revealed the shame associated with being deemed dirty and the passive role females are expected to take in condom preparation.

This need for young women to distance themselves from the dirty girl image can have detrimental effects on their sexual risk behaviors. The deliberate planning necessary to ensure safe sex is in direct conflict with the idea that good girls don't have sex (Hillier, Harrison, and Bowditch, 1999; Holland et al., 2004; Wight, 1992). Condoms in particular run counter to the good or clean girl image because condom use is often associated with sexual promiscuity and disease (Dahl, Darke, Gorn, and Weinberg, 2005; Loxley, 1996). The social stigma of being labeled dirty or the shame of providing condoms was apparent in the data and revealed the intense conflict that condoms present for young women. Thus, those women who see themselves as good and clean, and want to avoid being labeled as dirty by partners or others are likely to avoid planning for and using condoms (Gilmore et al., 1996; Holland et al., 2004; Tolman, 2002).

In addition to the way the SDS affects young women's sexual risk behaviors, the study findings suggested that the SDS limits the effectiveness of daughters' sexual risk reduction socialization. Most striking were the reports of mothers explicitly prohibiting daughters from obtaining condoms or birth control. This theme powerfully illustrated how the SDS can transform mothers' concern for daughters' sexual health into messages and socialization processes that can actually put daughters at risk. The findings from a recent longitudinal study highlight the potential detrimental effects of such messages for sexually active daughters. Sexually active daughters' perception that their mothers disapproved of them having sex predicted lower contraception use one year later (Sieving, Bearinger, Resnick, Pettingell, and Skay, 2007).

The theme of restrictions and arguments about dating and sexuality for daughters follows along this prohibitive approach to protecting daughters' sexual health. Instead of creating an environment for open and safe dialogue and guidance about sexuality, this approach may encourage daughters to keep their sexual experiences secret (O'Sullivan et al., 2001), thereby creating missed opportunities to promote sexual risk reduction at critical times in their transition to sexual activity. This environment of conflict, secrecy, and missed opportunities has important implications for daughters' sexual risk.

Mothers' lack of openness, comfort, and rapport in parent-adolescent sex discussions is associated with greater adolescent sexual risk behaviors (Dutra, Miller, and Forehand, 1999; Fasula and Miller, 2006; Kotchick, Dorsey, Miller, and Forehand, 1999; Whitaker et al., 1999). In addition, risk reduction messages are more effective if they are given before adolescents become sexually active (Kirby, Barth, Leland, and Fetro, 1991; Miller, Levin et al., 1998). For instance, in a study using the full FARBCS data, mothers talked to sons about condoms earlier than daughters and these condom discussions predicted adolescent condom use at first and subsequent intercourse—but only if the discussion happened prior to sexual debut (Miller, Levin et al., 1998). Furthermore, adolescents' lack of condom use at first intercourse was associated with a 20-fold decrease in the likelihood of future regular condom use (Miller, Levin et al., 1998).

Finally, even when mothers encouraged their daughters to obtain, carry, and use condoms their sexual guidance was abstract and removed. Positive attitudes and encouragement for sexual risk reduction behaviors are essential, but not sufficient to ensure condom use. Daughters still need to seek out condom skills, knowledge, and access before they can use them correctly.

Thus, under the ideology of the SDS, mothers' sexual socialization is likely to be less effective in helping their daughters learn to avoid sexual risk and more likely to deny their daughters the agency they need to prevent negative sexual outcomes. Teaching adolescents to delay sexual intercourse has a great deal of merit. However, when it is done by making them less knowledgeable about their own sexuality, promoting male privilege and female passivity, and limiting risk reduction skills and access, it does not adequately equip young women to take control of their sexual experiences. Furthermore, it can create critical missed opportunities to help daughters establish behaviors that can set the stage for a lifetime of healthy sexual behaviors.

In contrast to the neutral and prohibitive approaches for daughters, mothers' sexual risk reduction socialization for sons outlines an ideal comprehensive, proactive approach to ensuring sons' sexual health. First, mothers used "teachable moments" in their sons' sexual development to open a dialogue for relevant, information- and skill-based sexual discussions. Condoms were introduced early in their pubertal development, so that sons could develop attitudes and expectations about sexuality that included safer sex practices. And mothers reduced one of the critical steps necessary for condom use—they provided sons with direct access to condoms.

PUBLIC HEALTH IMPLICATIONS

. . . At the individual level, adolescent sexual guidance programs can provide young African American women with the knowledge and skills to identify and communicate their own sexual needs, and help them feel that it is empowering, rather than shameful, to be in command of their own sexuality. For both male and female youth, they can also illuminate and challenge SDS expectations, and encourage heterosexual scripts that emphasize open communication, mutual respect, and responsibility between partners.

At the familial level, public health initiatives can support African American families through group-level interventions where parents can come together, share their stories, and gain support from one another. Given the importance of religion in this sample, it may be particularly useful for parents to connect with other parents in their religious organizations. In such supportive environments, parents can explore their own SDS attitudes, learn about the negative implications of the SDS, and develop the confidence and tools to talk to their sons and daughters about sexuality without reinforcing the SDS. Programs should also emphasize that the SDS already puts daughters at a disadvantage for sexual risk reduction preparation. To counteract these negative effects on daughters' sexual risk reduction it is even more important that parents provide them with comprehensive, proactive sexual risk reduction socialization.

Finally, the study findings revealed that daughters in particular may receive incomplete sexual risk reduction socialization at home. Thus, community-level programs can fill critical gaps in providing young women with the information, encouragement, and resources they need to protect themselves from HIV and other negative sexual health outcomes. . . .

REFERENCES

Anderson, R. N., and Smith, B. L. 2005. Deaths: Leading causes for 2002. *National Vital Statistics Reports, 53*(17).

Campbell, C. A. 1995. Male gender roles and sexuality: Implications for women's AIDS risk prevention. *Social Science Medicine, 41*(2): 197–210.

CDC. 2004, 7/31/06. HIV/AIDS surveillance in adolescents and young adults (through 2004). Retrieved 1/11/07, 2007, from http://www.cdc.gov/hiv/topics /surveillance/ resources/slides/adolescents/index.htm

CDC. 2005. *HIV/AIDS surveillance report, 2004. Vol. 16.* Atlanta: US Department of Health and Human Services. Centers for Disease Control and Prevention.

Connell, R. W. 1987. *Gender and power: Society, the person and sexual politics.* Stanford: Stanford University Press.

Dahl, D. W., Darke, P. R., Gorn, G. J., and Weinberg, C. B. 2005. Promiscuous or confident? Attitudinal ambivalence toward condom purchase. *Journal of Applied Social Psychology, 35*(4): 869–887. doi:10.1111/j.1559 -1816.2005.tb02150.x

DiIorio, C., Hockenberry-Eaton, M., Maibach, E., Rivero, T., and Miller, K. S. 1996. The content of African American mothers' discussions with the adolescents about sex. *Journal of Family Nursing, 2*(4): 365–382.

DiIorio, C., Kelley, M., and Hockenberry-Eaton, M. 1999. Communication about sexual issues: Mothers, fathers, and friends. *Journal of Adolescent Health, 24*(3): 181–189.

DiIorio, C., Pluhar, E., and Belcher, L. 2003. Parent-child communication about sexuality: A review of the literature from 1980–2002. *Journal of HIV/AIDS Prevention & Education for Adolescents & Children, 5*(3/4): 7–32.

Downie, J., and Coates, R. 1999. The impact of gender on parent-child sexuality communication: Has anything changed? *Sexual and Marital Therapy, 14*(2): 109–121.

Dutra, R., Miller, K. S., and Forehand, R. 1999. The process and content of sexual communication with adolescents in two-parent families: Associations with sexual risk-taking behavior. *AIDS and Behavior, 3*(1): 59–66.

Espiritu, Y. L. 2001. 'We don't sleep around like white girls do': Family, culture, and gender in Filipina American lives. *Signs: Journal of Women in Culture and Society, 26*(2), 415–440. doi:10.1086/495599

Eyre, S. L., Hoffman, V., and Millstein, S. G. 1998. The gamesmanship of sex: A model based on African American adolescent accounts. *Medical Anthropology Quarterly, 12*(4): 467–489.

Fasula, A. M., and Miller, K. S. 2006. African American and Hispanic adolescents' intentions to delay first intercourse: Parental communication as a buffer for sexually active peers. *Journal of Adolescent Health, 38*(3): 193–200. doi:10.1016/j.jadohealth.2004.12.009

Fine, M. 1988. Sexuality, schooling, and adolescent females: The missing discourse of desire. *Harvard Educational Review, 58*(1): 29–53.

Fullilove, M. T., Fullilove, R. E., III, Haynes, K., and Gross, S. 1990. Black women and AIDS prevention: A view towards understanding the gender rules. *The Journal of Sex Research, 27*(1): 47–64.

Giltnore, S., DeLamater, J., and Wagstaff, D. 1996. Sexual decision making by inner city black adolescent males:

A focus group study. *Journal of Sex Research, 33*(4): 363–371.

Hartley, H., and Drew, T. 2001. Gendered messages in sex ed films: Trends and implications for female sexual problems. *Women and Therapy, 24*(1/2): 133–146. doi:10.1300/J015v24n01_16

Hillier, L., Harrison, L., and Bowditch, K. 1999. 'Neverending love' and 'blowing your load': The meanings of sex to rural youth. *Sexualities, 2*(1): 69–88.

Holland, J., Ramazanoglu, C., Sharpe, S., and Thomson, R. 2004. *The male in the head: Young people, heterosexuality and power* (second ed.). London: The Tufnell Press.

Hutchinson, J. F. 1999. The hip hop generation: African American male-female relationships in a nightclub setting. *Journal of Black Studies, 30*(1): 62–84.

Kirby, D., Barth, R., Leland, N., and Ferro, J. 1991. Reducing the risk: Impact of a new curriculum on sexual risk-taking. *Family Planning Perspectives, 23*: 253–263.

Kotchick, B. A., Dorsey, S., Miller. K. S., and Forehand, R. 1999. Adolescent sexual risk-taking behavior in single-parent ethnic minority families. *Journal of Family Psychology, 13*(1): 93–102.

Levin, M. L., and Robertson, A. A. 2002. Being prepared: Attitudes and practices related to condom carrying among minority adolescents. *Journal of HIV/AIDS Prevention & Education for Adolescents & Children, 5*(1/2): 103–121, doi:10.1300/J129v05n01_07

Loxley, W. 1996. 'Sluts' or 'sleazy little animals'? Young people's difficulties with carrying and using condoms. *Journal of Community & Applied Social Psychology, 6*(4): 293–298.

Miller, K. S., Kotchick, B. A., Dorsey, S., Forehand, R., and Ham, A. Y. 1998. Family communication about sex: What are parents saying and are their adolescents listening? *Family Planning Perspectives, 30*(5): 218–235.

Miller, K. S., Levin, M. L., Whitaker, D. J., and Xu, X. 1998. Patterns of condom use among adolescents: The impact of mother-adolescent communication. *American Journal of Public Health, 88*(10): 1542–1544.

Monahan, J. L., Miller, L. C., and Rothspan, S. 1997. Power and intimacy: On the dynamics of risky sex. *Health Communication, 9*(4): 303–321.

Muehlenhard, C. L. 1988. 'Nice women' don't say yes and 'real men' don't say no: How miscommunication and the double standard can cause sexual problems. *Women and Therapy, 7*(2–3): 95–108.

Muehlenhard, C. L., and McCoy, M. L. 1991. Double standard/double bind: The sexual double standard and women's communication about sex. *Psychology of Women Quarterly, 15*: 447–461.

Nolin, M. J., and Petersen, K. K. 1992. Gender differences in parent-child communication about sexuality. *Journal of Adolescent Research, 7*(1): 59–79.

O'Sullivan, L. F., Meyer-Bahlburg, H. F. L., and Watkins, B. X. 2001. Mother-daughter communication about sex among urban African American and Latino families. *Journal of Adolescent Research, 16*(3): 269–292.

Rosenthal, D. A., and Feldman, S. S. 1999. The importance of importance: Adolescents' perceptions of parental communication about sexuality. *Journal of Adolescence, 22*(6): 835–851.

Sieving, R., Bearinger, L., Resnick. M. D., Pettingell, S., and Skay, C. 2007. Adolescent dual method use: Relevant attitudes, normative beliefs and self-efficacy. *Journal of Adolescent Health, 40*(3): 275.e215–275.e.222. doi:10.1016/j.jadohealth.2006.10.003

Tanenbaum, L. 2000. *Slut!: Growing up female with a bad reputation.* New York: Perennial.

Thompson, S. 1990. Putting a big thing into a little hole: Teenage girls' accounts of sexual initiation. *The Journal of Sex Research, 27:* 341–361.

Thompson, S. 1995. *Going all the way: Teenage girls' tales of sex, romance, and pregnancy.* New York: Hill and Wang.

Tolman, D. L. 1996. Adolescent girls' sexuality: Debunking the myth of the urban girl. In N. Way (Ed.), *Urban girls: Resisting stereotypes, creating identities* (pp. 255–271). New York: New York University Press.

Tolman, D. L. 2002. *Dilemmas of desire: Teenage girls talk about sexuality.* Cambridge, MA: Harvard University Press.

Tolman, D. L., and Brown, L. M. 2001. Adolescent girls' voices: Resonating resistance in body and soul. In R. K.

Unger (Ed.), *Handbook of the psychology of women and gender* (pp. 133–155). New York: John Wiley and Sons, Inc.

Tolman, D. L., and Debold, E. 1994. Conflicts of body image: Female adolescents, desire, and the no-body body. In S. Wooley (Ed.), *Feminist perspectives on eating disorders* (pp. 301–317). New York: The Guilford Press.

Whitaker, D. J., Miller, K. S., May, D. C., and Levin, M. L. 1999. Teenage partners' communication about sexual risk and condom use: The importance of parent-teenager discussions. *Family Planning Perspectives, 31*(3): 117–121.

Whitley, B., and Schofield, J. W. 1986. A meta-analysis of research on adolescent contraceptive use. *Population and Environment, 8:* 173–203.

Wight, D. 1992, Impediments to safer heterosexual sex: A review of research with young people. *AIDS Care, 4*(1): 11–21.

Wilkins, A. C. 2004. Puerto Rican wannabes: Sexual spectacle and the marking of race, class, and gender boundaries. *Gender and Society, 18*(1): 103–121. doi:10.1177/0891243203259505

Wingood, G. M., and DiClemente, R. J. 1998. Partner influences and gender-related factors associated with non-condom use among young adult African American women. *American Journal of Community Psychology, 26*(1): 29–51. doi:10..1300/J013v46n02_02

PUT ME IN, COACH: SEX LESSONS FOR ADULTS

DIANA SPECHLER

A Manhattan studio apartment feels especially cramped when you're watching the couple who live there take a sex lesson. Even scrunched into the farthest corner of the love seat, I can't put more than a few inches between me and the bed, where Mike, a fitness-center manager, lies atop his girlfriend, Shannon. While I scribble furiously in my notebook ("I feel like I shouldn't be watching this") and struggle to keep my expression blank, Mike holds Shannon's face and kisses her, grinding his body against hers. He peels her tank top over her head, slips off her pants, unhooks her bra, slides her red panties down her legs, and strips to his boxer briefs. Mike has some serious abs. In fact, both he and Shannon are toned and lithe, as if they fell in love at the gym. (They did.)

Shannon and Mike (not their real names) are "warming up," in the words of their sex coach, Eric Amaranth, who kneels beside the bed, offering tips and encouragement. Watching this gorgeous couple writhe on the sheets (they seem pretty warm already), I have trouble imagining that their sex life is anything short of pornographic. So why do they need coaching? "They want to learn more," Amaranth says. "Everyone should. Some people think it's wrong to work on sex—that it should just flow naturally because of how the two people feel about each other. Come on! Sex isn't always about lovemaking. Sure, that's a form of sex, but there's also animalistic, hot fucking." I've touched on one of Amaranth's biggest pet peeves—the idea that you are who you are in bed, and that sexual prowess can't be learned. "That is such a destructive myth," he says, shaking his head. Personally, I never subscribed to that myth. Probably because I'd never heard of it. Before meeting Amaranth, it hadn't occurred to me to seek formal sex guidance (isn't that what the Internet is for?) or to reject it. But after hanging out with him a few times and tagging along to a couple of his talk sessions (tonight is the first time I've seen his clients naked), I'm intrigued.

A few minutes ago, before the clothes came off, Amaranth used a vagina-like toy called a Fleshlight to show Mike how to stimulate the G-spot with two fingers "for 100 percent coverage," and now he rolls two Magnum XLs onto a pair of vibrators—a necessary safety precaution, since he uses the same toys for all of his "guided" sessions. On the hardwood floor, toys of all shapes and sizes, three brands of lube, a prostate massager, the Fleshlight, a clear cock ring, and a silicone butt plug sit on a white towel. It's like a sexy version of your dentist's tool tray, if your dentist specialized in a different orifice.

Amaranth is straight-backed, wiry, and fastidious—shirt tucked in, dark hair cut close to his scalp, beard cropped short on his whittled jaw. You might mistake him for a religious ascetic if he weren't always saying things like, "There are things men don't know about hand jobs, like how to hold the glans with a diagonal grasp so that the coronal ridge has full contact with its surface area." (Obviously.) Mike's the one who looks like a sex pro, standing there in his underwear, tattoos scattered on his muscular torso. But the pupil just takes the vibrators from his sensei and nods thoughtfully. In addition to coaching—a two-hour session runs $240—Amaranth offers health-and-wellness tips; sex-enhancement workouts; personal shopping for toys and lingerie; and for those willing to shell out up to $7,000, a full sex-life makeover. His client list includes newlyweds, 18-year-old "beginners," premature ejaculators, couples who have young children and are desperate "to figure out how they can still have a sex life," middle-aged single ladies on the cusp of cougardom, and sexual alpha types who are hungry for Amaranth's "advanced" secrets. Then there are the Mikes and Shannons, regular people who fuck respectably without guidance but who thought a little sex coaching might be fun. "There's stuff you can only learn through lots of practice," Amaranth says. "And if you can't get solid, powerful technique down, then you'll never be a sex god."

As a young man, Amaranth started reading about sex for the same reason most guys start reading about sex: he really wanted to have some. He loved the way women looked when they were aroused. He wanted to master the art of getting women off. Nothing was going to stop him, not even his virginity. When the time came to have sex, he was going to be ready. And the more he read about sex, the more engrossed he became in the details. In college, he felt dissatisfied with his professors' myopic focus on sex therapy—all that soft stuff about feelings and emotional connection—and their dearth of knowledge about applied sex education. (By then he'd started applying his own education, having lost his virginity at 19.) So he turned to the work of Betty Dodson, pioneer of sexual liberation, queen of the vibrator, one of the original members of the "sex-positive feminist movement," and author of *Sex for One: The Joy of Selfloving*, a book about masturbation that has sold over 1 million copies internationally since its release (forgive the pun) in

1974. At 22, after corresponding with Dodson for months, Amaranth took a bus to New York from his college in Virginia and showed up on her doorstep. Hours after he offered himself as a student, they chucked that charade and hopped into the sack. So began Amaranth's apprenticeship with Dodson, and also, despite their forty-seven-year age gap, their ten-year love affair. Amaranth ignored criticisms of the relationship. So what if his old lady was, well, an old lady? Who wouldn't want to go to bed with one of the world's leading sex teachers? He holds that most people don't appreciate the full spectrum of hot. "Big breasts and a tiny waist, yeah, okay, that's hot. But so is sex done with advanced technique. When both partners really know what they're doing, that's hot." Undeniably, Betty Dodson knew what she was doing. And after ten years of banging her, so did Eric Amaranth.

Mike is kneeling on the bed in front of Shannon, tentatively wielding one of the Magnum-wrapped vibrators. Amaranth asks Shannon which kind of "pressure" she prefers, and then tells Mike to use the toy on her through a towel. "I like it better without," Shannon says, and Mike flings the towel aside. As you've probably gathered, Amaranth is passionate about the power of toys. They enhance sex, he says, because they free the body from its usual constraints. With toys, a couple isn't restricted to four hands, two mouths, and one penis that comes in one size and is sometimes out of commission. "When I have sex," Amaranth explains, pointing to a few dildos, "that's my penis and that's my penis and that's my penis." (You might think a groovy, sex-positive guy like Amaranth would dispense with the clinical language and opt for raunchier slang. And sometimes he does—when the client requests it. Otherwise he keeps it cleanish. He's also impervious to the giggly, immature reactions that the subject of sex elicits in most people. He could probably say "vagina" ten times, slowly, without laughing, while staring you in the eye.) "But what if a woman doesn't want her boyfriend to fuck her with a bunch of dildos?" I wonder. "That's okay," Amaranth says. "If she has a strong aversion, it's unethical to keep harping, but she should be interested in at least trying it out. If you have too many blocks, resentments form. And that's destructive to your sex life." As we discuss these "blocks," I offer the example of anal sex—a classic male enthusiasm that many women abhor. "What can a couple do to find common ground in the anal-sex department?" "Start with smaller things," Amaranth says. "You don't have to start with the penis. Also, he should combine the anal penetration with clitoral stimulation, because at first anal penetration alone won't create an orgasm. Later, once the sensations have been integrated, he'll be able to bring her to orgasm with just penetration."

Although perfecting anal-sex technique might sound like a dream job, being a sex coach, especially a male sex coach, has its drawbacks. Take, for example, the one-on-one sessions Amaranth does with straight women who want help masturbating. Predictably, this kind of session can become a blue-balls hatchery. Once he met a client, a businesswoman in her late thirties, in a hotel room. As Amaranth knelt on the floor at the foot of the bed, guiding her through "manual clitoral stimulation paired with G-spot vibrator stimulation" (his words for what others might call, simply, "masturbating with gusto"), she moaned, "I so want your cock inside me!" Incidents like this are not uncommon, but he says he remembers his manners every time. "Thank you for that vote of confidence," he told her, "and for the honor. But I'm just the guy giving you instructions." Every once in a while, those instructions simply aren't enough. "Do you ever have couples who just suck at sex?" I ask. "No matter how much coaching you give them?" "It can be tough for people who have severe coordination issues,"

he says. "This one woman said she couldn't make men come. We did a session where we were each holding a dildo, so I could demonstrate a technique and she could copy it. And I saw what the problem was: Her coordination was so bad, she couldn't even do the up-down, up-down motion." Fortunately, he says, the hopeless moments are a lot less common than the big, satisfying breakthroughs. "The woman will have the first G-spot orgasm of her life, and then the guy's high-fiving me. One time the couple took me out for sushi."

Forty-five minutes into the session, as Mike tests out the two vibrators, Shannon isn't just relaxed—she seems to have forgotten we're even there. In turn, I relax, too. I've been hiding behind my notebook, feeling like some Jane Goodall of the Upper West Side, but now I stop writing and just watch: A pink flush rises from Shannon's chest to her cheeks, her breathing quickens, and her back arches. She clutches Mike's thighs and digs her nails in. Amaranth reminds them that it's not "orgasm time" just yet. He wants Shannon to have a wider range of experiences first. He tells her that if she thinks she's about to come, she should force herself to take a ten-second break. Shannon complies, pushing away the vibrator. Lying spreadeagled on the bed, panting, she rakes her fingers through her sweaty hair. But just moments later, she starts squirming again. Mike resumes with the toy, and Amaranth asks him whether he can feel her vagina opening. When Mike says that he can, Amaranth offers him a larger dildo. With ten minutes left in the session, Amaranth tells Shannon that she's welcome to finish. At this point, Mike is moving a fluorescent pink dildo in and out of her while she draws small circles on her clit with an Eroscillator, a toy designed by the inventor of the first successful electric toothbrush. Shannon, having delayed her orgasm several times, explodes and pulls Mike down on top of her. They lie spent, their breathing synchronized, in a tangle of limbs. Amaranth smiles. "Cuddle time," he says.

He uses the remainder of the session to explain a few sex positions that Mike and Shannon can try later. ("We do that one all the time!" Mike says proudly when Amaranth details a tummy-down, man-on-top configuration.) As a gift, he presents Mike with a brand-new cock ring. "This isn't just something to use if your dick isn't getting hard. Even if you're 100 percent hard, this will bring you to 110 percent. You know the hardness you have when you come? With this, you'll have that hardness the whole time. Then when you come, your hardness will be at 115 percent."

Shannon pulls on a pair of yoga pants and fishes her tank top off the floor. Mike, still in just his underwear, starts tidying up the apartment, making small talk. While Amaranth washes his toys in the sink, Mike and Shannon tell me their story. They started dating a year ago. They're training for a triathlon. They don't mind sharing such a small living space; they're just happy to be together. And although they claimed to hire Amaranth out of "curiosity," they fell in love on the sly and left their marriages for each other. So doesn't it make sense that they would hire a sex coach to preserve what they know can get lost? Wouldn't it make sense for most couples?

For a culture as sex-obsessed as ours, it's a little weird that so many people just wing it. Shouldn't we all welcome Amaranth's sextopian vision? It's a world where everyone fucks at the highest level, nobody ever gets laid the same way twice, and your girlfriend can't wait to hop into bed every night—with you and all your penises.

SEXUAL BODIES

AN INTERVIEW WITH

LEONORE TIEFER

Leonore Tiefer, Ph.D., is clinical associate professor of psychiatry at the New York University School of Medicine in New York City and has a private practice in sex therapy and psychotherapy in Manhattan. Recently, Dr. Tiefer has become internationally known as the primary spokesperson for a movement that challenges the medicalization of women's sexual problems by the pharmaceutical industry (for more information, see www.newviewcampaign.org). Both the Society for the Scientific Study of Sexuality and the Association for Women in Psychology selected her for their Distinguished Scientific Career Awards in 2004.

What led you to begin studying sexuality?

I see sexuality as one of the most interesting and complex topics in all of academia. In the 1960s, I majored in psychology and in psychology grad school (UC Berkeley) I was at first attracted to the subject of learning and conditioning. But after two years of research on learning in rats I felt bored, and I became more interested in physiological psychology—the study of the biological bases of behavior. Frank Beach had a very active research group studying mating behavior in rodents and dogs, and although at that time (he changed later) he wouldn't fund women grad students to work in his lab, he allowed us to do experiments and participate in seminars. I studied hamster sexuality for my dissertation and then directed an animal lab for seven years in my first academic job. *But*, and this is a big but, I began to question the value of animal research on sexuality when the women's liberation movement (now called "second wave") hit me in the 1970s. After a sabbatical working with human sexuality issues, I decided I was really interested in sexuality, but that I wasn't suited to animal work and I doubted its ultimate significance. I re-specialized as a clinical psychologist specializing in sexuality. I also studied the new work in sexuality emerging from women's and gay and lesbian studies. Feminist politics combined with my biological and psychological background provided a well-rounded view of sexuality.

How do people react when they find that you study sexuality?

Usually they express political opinions first (about abortion or porn or sex ed), and ask personal questions about their own sexual life second. I have learned that no matter how strong the opinions, most people feel undereducated when it comes to sexuality and appreciate the opportunity to talk with an "expert." Ironically, however, my "expert" opinion is that sexuality is complicated and my answers to their questions usually involve more variables than they had anticipated.

Which of your projects have you found most interesting? Why?

I had the opportunity to participate in a monthly New York intellectual seminar on sexuality that lasted 11 years (1982–1993). Participants were journalists, writers, political activists, and a wide range of humanities professors. I was the only "official" sex expert. Members presented papers on topics ranging from gays in World War II to Picasso's sojourn in Barcelona to histories of food to "dirty" postcards. You cover a lot of ground in 11 years! The seminar always focused on how these various cultural events arose from and affected sexuality. The seminar completely changed my idea of what kind of thing sexuality was—from a biopsychological aspect of individual experience to a socially constructed ever-changing sociocultural phenomenon. This consciousness-changing occurred slowly. Standards of evidence were completely different than in my psychological training and the topics taxed my general knowledge base (World War II? Barcelona?). But when, slowly and gradually, I finally got it that sex was constructed differently within groups, generations, genders, religions, and regions, my eyes were permanently opened in a way few conventionally trained sexologists can understand.

What ethical dilemmas have you faced in studying sexuality?

I became an activist against the medicalization of sexuality after Viagra was approved in 1998. I saw corporations taking advantage of people's lack of education about sexuality to promote drugs with marginal benefits and various dangers. It made me angry to see few other sexologists resisting the financial opportunities and propaganda of the pharmaceutical industry, but I have found many allies in public health, women's health, investigative journalism, and health reform. My ethical dilemma has occurred because throughout my years of activism, I have continued my clinical private practice doing sex therapy. People come to me for help with their personal sexual problems and I have to put their concerns and perspectives first, and refrain from lecturing or moralizing about the things that are on my mind. On occasion I even recommend that someone try one of the new sex drugs because in his or her individual case they might be helpful, even though I believe that for society at large they are the very opposite. Even when I think a person's problem has been caused by all the exaggerated public relations claims about the new drugs, I don't ever say, "I told you so." That's not my role as a clinical psychologist.

What do you think is the most challenging thing about studying sexuality?

The subject is very complicated, and many professionals and academics are unwilling to read widely outside their primary field. I think to be a good sexologist you have to be somewhat well versed in psychology, physiology, sociology, anthropology, history, law, religion, media studies, and gender studies.

Why is it important to do sex research?

It's important to do good sex research, but it's a waste of time to do foolish or trivial sex research. Good quality research—qualitative research, especially—can help shed light on topics many areas of society want to be hidden in darkness. Ignorant people can be shamed, guilt-tripped, and manipulated, and they raise ignorant children. Our media-saturated world requires an informed public, and good sex research is part of the information base essential in modern culture. For example, many states in the United States now have grossly uninformed laws about the dangers of "sex offenders" and are punishing people far too harshly for minor offenses. Ambitious politicians manipulate an ignorant public. The same thing happens with sex education or new contraceptive methods. The public is easily scared into taking a repressive position because they are uninformed. Movies and TV (and drug ads) promote ecstatic sex, but the public lacks the knowledge to assess these images. Good sex research will narrow the gap.

If you could teach people one thing about sexuality, what would it be?

As the title of my book says, I believe that "Sex Is Not a Natural Act." At least in the twenty-first century it's not. Everything about sex is the result of cultural influences and totally saturated with cultural meaning. Madison Avenue has hyped the pleasures and right-wing values have hyped the dangers—and, oddly, both insist that sex is a "natural" result of evolution (or God)—and that learning, practice, reading, reflection, conversation, and research are unnecessary. I believe just the opposite.

Is there anything else you'd like to add?

Every college and university should have a Department of Sexuality Studies. At the present time it is impossible to get the kind of multidisciplinary education I think every sexologist needs. You have to do it all on your own. As a consequence, few sexologists are well trained. Such departments would employ sexuality scholars who would generate interesting new theory and research. I wish I could be in such a department.

THE G-SPOT AND OTHER MYSTERIES

ELISABETH O. BURGESS AND AMY PALDER

Is there a G-spot? One common question about female sexuality is whether there is a localized place in the vagina, often referred to as the G-spot, which causes especially pleasurable sensations when stimulated. The G-spot, or Grafenburg spot, was named for Dr. Ernst Grafenburg, a German gynecologist who first described this spot in 1950. Although Grafenburg often is credited with discovering this spot, descriptions of sensitivity in a specific area of the vagina can be found across cultures and historical periods (Sevely and Bennett, 1978; Ladas, Whipple, and Perry, 1982). Yet, contemporary sexologists disagree about the significance of the G-spot and its prevalence in the female population. Those in support of the G-spot claim that it is either a bundle of nerves, possibly representing the root of the clitoris, or a gland, or series of glands, that produces lubrication. Those who believe the G-spot is a myth argue that there is no anatomical evidence that it exists.

Over the past two decades, the G-spot has gained widespread acceptance by the mass media. Numerous articles on sexual pleasure in the popular press, self-help literature, and on the Internet describe the G-spot and provide instructions on using it for sexual pleasure (for instance, Cass, 2007; Hicks, 2006; Paget, 2004; Solot and Miller, 2007; Sundahl, Ladas, and Sprinkle, 2003; and Winks, 1998). These readings frequently cite the book *The G-spot and other recent discoveries about human sexuality* (Ladas, Whipple, and Perry, 1982) as evidence that all women have G-spots. Ladas et al. (1982) reported that the G-spot is located through deep pressure to the anterior vaginal wall. These researchers and other colleagues argue that this spongy mass, about the size of a quarter and the shape of a bean, can be found about halfway up the anterior (or belly) side of the vagina. The mass becomes more rigid or identifiable when a woman is sexually aroused (Perry and Whipple, 1981; Zaviacic, Zaviacicova, Holoman and Molcan, 1988; Zaviacic and Whipple, 1993). According to self-reports, the G-spot produces orgasms that are "more intense" and "full body" than other female orgasms (Davidson, Darling, and Conway-Welch, 1989; Ladas et al., 1982; Perry and Whipple, 1981). Ladas et al. (1982) report that in a study supervised by Perry and Whipple, a medical professional was able to locate a G-spot in each of over 400 female volunteers (p. 43). Because Ladas et al. found that all women in their study had G-spots, they explain that women who have not been able to locate their G-spots are either not sufficiently aroused or not using the proper technique to locate it.

Yet, while many women believe the G-spot exists, not all women have heard about the G-spot and many women have not found their own G-spots. A survey of over 1000 women found that although 85.3% of the women surveyed believed that a sensitive area existed in the vagina, only 65.9% reported having such an area (Davidson et al., 1989). This survey also found that angle of vaginal entry, position of vaginal intercourse, and a woman's degree of emotional involvement with her partner affected her ability to orgasm from being stimulated in this area. Because traditional sexual positions such as the "missionary position" fail to stimulate the anterior wall of the vagina, women who explore other sexual practices such as manual stimulation from a partner or vibrator may be more likely to discover a G-spot (Ladas et al., 1982).

In contrast, some researchers strongly dispute the existence of the G-spot. Alzate and colleagues (Alzate and Hoch, 1986; Alzate, 1985) argue that the walls of the vagina are sensitive to touch, but there is no specific area in the vagina that produces orgasm. These authors also argue that there is no anatomical evidence of a G-spot and critique previous research for using small clinical samples and anecdotal evidence. In a recent review of the literature on the G-spot, Hines (2001) calls it a myth and goes on to say that "the widespread acceptance of the reality of the G-spot goes well beyond available evidence" (p. 361). Other prominent sex researchers, including Masters and Johnson, do not discuss the G-spot or an especially sensitive area in the vagina but instead focus on the clitoris as the locus of female orgasms (Masters and Johnson, 1966).

Some feminist researchers also dispute the existence of the G-spot, but for different reasons. These scholars fear that the "discovery of the G-spot" and subsequent emphasis on vaginal orgasms support Freudian notions about the female orgasm and privilege heterosexual male-centered models of sexuality. These authors emphasize the clitoris as the primary location of the female orgasm and sexual empowerment for women (Ehrenreich, Hess, and Jacobs, 1987; Gerhard, 2004). Other feminist researchers believe that, because of cultural preferences about (hetero)sexual behavior, many women prefer to view the vagina as an important location of orgasmic response. These scholars recognize that orgasm is not merely a physiological response but it is also an emotional and psychological response to sexual stimuli and, as such, orgasms centered in the vagina should not be ignored (Hite, 1976; Schneider and Gould, 1987). However, if such a spot does exist, even supporters such as Ladas (2001) argue that it is harmful to think of the G-spot as the holy grail of female sexuality. In a critical review of the discourse of female orgasm, Tuana (2004)

argues that this false dichotomy of clitoral and vaginal orgasm ignores the perspective that the majority of the clitoris is internal (see also Moore and Clarke, 1995; O'Connell, Sanjeevan and Hutson, 2005). Moreover, Tuana finds that some models of female anatomy that do include the G-spot ignore the feminist argument for a perineal sponge which is located between the posterior wall of the vagina and the rectum and also can become engorged during sexual stimulation. In sum, regardless of the politics of measuring and defining female genitalia, the female body contains many potential erogenous zones. Whether individuals find stimulation of these locations pleasurable depends on the social context, the expertise of their partner, and personal preference.

Do women ejaculate? Another common debate about the sexual body is whether women ejaculate. For centuries, erotic literature and sex research has alluded to the elusive female orgasm that results in a squirt of liquid from the woman (Belzer, 1981; Sevely and Bennett, 1978). Contemporary researchers disagree as to where it comes from, what it is, and whether it is something that all women are capable of releasing.

Most often associated with G-spot stimulation, female ejaculation is the release of fluid through the urethra at the climax of an orgasm. One common concern about female ejaculation is whether the fluid is urine, a result of incontinence, or whether it is similar to male ejaculate. Self-reports indicate that this fluid is different from urine in smell, consistency and color (Davidson et al., 1989; Belzer, 1981; Taormino, 2000). Chemical analyses of female ejaculate have been less conclusive. While Goldberg et al. (1983) found the expelled fluid to be chemically similar to urine, numerous other clinical studies argue that the consistency of this fluid is significantly different from urine (Addiego, Belzer, Moger, Perry, and Whipple, 1981; Belzer, Whipple, and Moger, 1984; Wimpissinger, Stifter, Grin, and Stackl, 2007; Zaviacic, Zaviacicova, Holoman and Molcan, 1988). Additionally, a recent study concluded that women who reported experiencing female ejaculation are not more likely to experience urinary problems than women who do not report ejaculation (Cartwright, Elvy, and Cardozo, 2007). Regardless of these findings, without larger samples of ejaculate, it would be difficult to reach any definitive conclusions.

A related controversy associated with female ejaculation concerns the source of the fluid. The most common theory is that the Skene's glands, which surround the urethra, secrete fluid into the urethra that is then ejaculated upon orgasm. Researchers who support this theory argue that female ejaculate may have a different consistency, at different times, for different women. In addition, reported rates of ejaculation among women vary from 10% to over 50% (Ladas et al., 1983; Bullough, David, Whipple, Dixon, Allgeier, Rice, and Drury, 1984). Only a few women report ejaculating fluid with every orgasm. Although manipulation of the G-spot is not required to produce female ejaculation, women who experience pleasure or orgasms through stimulation of the G-spot are more likely to report experiencing ejaculation (Davidson et al., 1989). Either way, by focusing solely on chemical components of the fluid, researchers are ignoring the role this event plays in sexual satisfaction.

Female ejaculation also has become the subject of several self-help sexuality books and sexuality workshops. According to an article by Taormino (2000), female ejaculation was the subject of one of the workshops at the 2000 Michigan Womyn's Festival. After the workshop, several women participated in the "First Annual Ejaculation Contest," competing in categories such as "speed," "distance," "quantity," and "best single handed job." While reports based on non-clinical trials do not receive scientific approval, the nature of this contest helps to alter negative stigma associated with female ejaculation.

There are several important implications of this research on female ejaculation. Because female ejaculation is not a widely known phenomenon, women who experience the expulsion of fluids frequently feel shame or anxiety (Davidson et al., 1989). Many women, particularly those who are uncomfortable examining the fluid, assume that any release of fluid is urine and a sign of urinary incontinence. In some cases women may seek and receive medical treatment for urinary incontinence when this is not, in fact, the problem. If women were aware that the expulsion of fluid was a normal and healthy bodily function, they would feel free to enjoy a pleasurable event rather than perceive themselves as deviant (Cartwright, Elvy and Cardozo, 2007; Winton, 1989).

REFERENCES

Addiego, Frank, Edwin G. Belzer, Jill Comolli, William Moger, John D. Perry, and Beverly Whipple. 1981. Female Ejaculation: A Case Study. *The Journal of Sex Research,* 17, 13–21.

Alzate, Heli. 1985. Vaginal Eroticism: A Replication Study. *Archives of Sexual Behavior,* 14, 529–537.

Alzate, Heli, and Zwi Hoch. 1986. The "G-Spot" and "female Ejaculation": A Current Appraisal. *Journal of Sex and Marital Therapy,* 12, 211–220.

Belzer, Edwin G. 1981. Orgasmic Expulsions of Women: A Review and Heuristic Inquiry. *The Journal of Sex Research,* 17, 1–12.

Belzer, Edwin G, Whipple, Beverly, and William Moger. 1984. On Female Ejaculation. *The Journal of Sex Research,* 20, 403–406.

Bullough, Bonnie, Madeline David, Beverly Whipple, Joan Dixon, Elizabeth Rice Allgeier, and Kate Cosgrove Drury. 1984. Subjective Reports of Female Orgasmic Expulsion of Fluid. *Nurse Practictioner,* 9, 55–59.

Cartwright, Rufus, Susannah Elvy, and Linda Cardozo. 2007. Do Women with Female Ejaculation Have Detrusor Overactivity? *Journal of Sexual Medicine,* 4(6), 1655–1658.

Cass, Vivienne. 2007. *The Elusive Orgasm: A Woman's Guide to Why She Can't and How She Can Orgasm.* New York: Marlowe and Company.

Davidson, J. Kenneth, Carol A. Darling, and Colleen Conway-Welch. 1989. The role of the Grafenburg Spot and Female Ejaculation in the Female Orgasmic Response: An Empirical Analysis. *Journal of Sex and Marital Therapy,* 15, 102–120.

Ehrenreich, Barbara, Elizabeth Hess, and Gloria Jacobs. 1986. *Re-Making Love: The Feminization of Sex*. New York: Anchor Books.

Gerhard, Jane. 2004. The Politics of the Female Orgasm. In M. Stombler, D. M. Baunach, E. O. Burgess, D. Donnelly, and W. Simonds. (Eds.). *Sex Matters: The Sexuality and Society Reader* (pp. 213–224). Boston: Allyn and Bacon.

Hicks, Donald L. 2006. *Unleashing Her G-Spot Orgasm: A Step-by-Step Guide to Giving a Woman Ultimate Sexual Ecstasy*. Berkeley, CA: Amorato Press.

Hines, Terence M. 2001. The G-Spot: A Modern Gynecological Myth. *American Journal of Obsterics and Gynecology*, 185, 359–362.

Hite, Shere. 1976. *The Hite Report: A Nationwide Study of Female Sexuality*. New York: Dell.

Goldberg, Daniel C., Beverly Whipple, Ralph E. Fishkin, Howard Waxman, Paul J. Fink, and Martin Weisberg. 1983. The Grafenberg Spot and Female Ejaculation: A Review of Initial Hypotheses. *Journal of Sex and Marital Therapy*, 9, 27–38.

Ladas, Alice. 2001. Review of *Secrets of Sensual Lovemaking* and *The Good Vibrations Guide*. *Journal of Sex Education and Therapy*, 26, 150–151.

Ladas, Alice, Beverly Whipple, and John Perry. 1982. *The G-Spot and Other Recent Discoveries about Human Sexuality*. New York: Plenum.

Masters, W. H., and V. E. Johnson, 1966. *Human Sexual Response*. Boston: Little, Brown.

Moore, Lisa Jean and Adele E. Clarke. 1995. Clitoral Conventions and Transgressions: Graphic Representations in Anatomy Texts, c. 1900–1991. *Feminist Studies*, 21(2), 255–301.

O'Connell, H. E., K. V. Sanjeevan, and J. M. Hudson. 2005. Anatomy of the Clitoris. *The Journal of Urology*, 174, 1189–1195.

Paget, Lou. 2004. *Orgasms: How to Have Them, Give Them, and Keep Them Coming*. New York: Broadway Books.

Perry, John D., and Beverly Whipple. 1981. The Varieties of Female Orgasm and Female Ejaculation. *SIECUS Report*.

Schneider, Beth E. and Meredith Gould. 1987. Female Sexuality Looking Back into the Future. In Beth B. Hess and Myra Marx Ferree (Eds.). *Analyzing Gender: A Handbook of Social Science Research* (pp. 120–153). Newbury Park, CA: Sage.

Sevely, J. L. and J. W. Bennett, 1978. Concerning Female Ejaculation and the Female Prostate. *The Journal of Sex Research*, 14, 1–20.

Solot, Dorian, and Marshall Miller. 2007. *I Love Female Orgasm: An Extraordinary Orgasm Guide*. New York: Marlowe and Company.

Sundahl, Deborah, Alice Ladas, and Annie Sprinkle. 2003. *Female Ejaculation and the G-Spot: Not Your Mother's Orgasm Book!* Alameda, CA: Hunter House, Inc.

Taormino, Tristan. 2000. Pucker Up. *Village Voice* (September 5) 45(35), 130.

Tuana, Nancy. 2004. Coming to Understand: Orgasm and the Epistemology of Ignorance. *Hypatia*, 19(1), 194–232.

Winks, Cathy. 1998. *The Good Vibrations Guide: The G-Spot*. San Francisco: Down There Press.

Wimpissinger, Florian, Karl Stifter, Wolfgang Grin, and Walter Stackl. 2007. The Female Prostate Revisited: Perineal Ultrasound and Biochemical Studies of Female Ejaculate. *Journal of Sexual Medicine*, 4(5), 1388–1393.

Winton, Mark A. 1989. Editorical: The Social Construction of the G-Spot and Female Ejaculation. *Journal of Sex Education and Therapy*, 15, 151–162.

Zaviacic, Milan, Alexandra Zaviacicova, Igor Karol Holoman, and Jan Molcan, 1988. Female Urethral Explusions Evoked by Local Digital Stimulation of the G-Spot: Differences in the Response Patterns. *The Journal of Sex Research*, 24, 311–318.

Zaviacic, Milan, and Beverly Whipple. 1993. Update on the Female Prostate and the Phenomenon of Female Ejaculation. *Journal of Sex Research*, 30, 148–151.

Hung: A Meditation on the Measure of Black Men in America

Scott Poulson-Bryant

Allow me to introduce myself.

My name is Scott and I am a black man in America. I've never done hard time. I've never been arrested. I don't have any kids. I know I'm invisible to many, but I also know that I'm highly visible to more.

I've been told that I am a success story.

I like to think that I measure up.

I'm a suburban kid. I was educated at an Ivy League university that at the time was dubbed the "hot college" because everyone wanted to go there. I've had some success in the Manhattan media world, and don't they say that if you can make it in New York, New York, you can make it anywhere? . . . I live in NYC in the summer and Miami's South Beach in the winter, because I want to and because I can. I've had successful relationships, and I love my parents and my parents love me.

Sure, I like to think that, in the grand American rat race that is life, I measure up.

But even with a laundry list of accomplishments that makes my résumé attractive, there are still days when I go to the gym and I get out of the shower and wrap my towel close around me, because I am a black man, and for a black man I just may not—in the swinging-dick sense of the words—"measure up."

That's because, you see, I'm what people call a grower and not a show-er. In other words, my soft hanging dick is not the monster of Mapplethorpean proportions that draws looks of wonder and awe. Of course many men are growers rather than showers, but that doesn't mean I'm not still conscious of it. Partly because I'm a man—and men are concerned about those things—but also partly because I am a black man.

In other words, I should be hung like a horse. I should be the cock of the locker-room walk, singing and swinging and getting merry like every day is, for hung brothers, Christmas.

But I'm not. I guess I could spend the last few seconds of my shower doing my own fluff job, spanking little Scott into some semierect state that speaks more to the size of my actual sex-ready self. But would it be worth it? To let that towel fly free just in case I get some stares from the dudes lining the room, stepping into their own boxers and briefs and bikinis? Of course it would be worth it, because I am a black man and black men are hung like horses. I'm not. So what kind of black man am I?

But here's the thing. I don't want to measure up in the locker room. I don't want to be the stereotype. I don't want to be Mister Myth, because if I am, then I'm just a dick; the big dick in the locker room; the recipient of the real, live, guy-on-guy penis envy no one talks about; the guy white boys hate yet want to be; the brother other black dudes recognize as representative of their gender; the stone-cold stud with a dick of doom. I think of black-man dick and I think that once upon a time we were hung from trees for being, well, hung. The sexual beast, the loin-engorged predator, the big-dicked destroyer not just of pure pristine white women but also of white men's sense of themselves. That's where black men have found themselves, culturally speaking: hung. Strung up from trees; lynched to protect the demure pureness of white women; dissed to soothe the memory sin of slave-raping white masters; castrated to save the community from the sexual brutality black men trail behind them like a scent—the scent of the stereotypical boogeyman created by the fears of a nation. And I don't want anything to do with that ugly American history, the stereotypes that have been created to control me—do I?

Hell yeah, my inner ear tells me, I do. Fuck history. Let's be real here: Who doesn't want to have the biggest dick in the room?

Speaking of history, here's a flashback, my own first history lesson, if you will.

The place: Providence, Rhode Island. The time: spring 1986, my sophomore year in college.

I'm dancing at the RISD Tap Room, a smoky second-floor dive just down the hill from Brown University, a sorta rathskeller hangout for the artsy students who attend the Rhode Island School of Design and the local beer drinkers who love them. I'm dancing, like I said, a plastic cup of beer in my hand, a baseball cap on my head, wearing a cotton Oxford shirt and a pair of Levi's jeans. I'm sorta buzzed and I want a cigarette. I look around for a smoker . . .

There's one, a white girl in a plain T-shirt with a bushy crown of brown curls, nodding her head to the synthesizer beat of Depeche Mode while she sits at a bruised-up little wooden table behind me and my crew. She smiles at me and holds open the soggy red-and-white box of Marlboros sitting on the table among the cups of beer. I take a cig. She flicks her Bic. I lean in to light the smoke. Before I can pull away, she says, "You are so cute." And I say, "Thanks," and start dancing again. By the time the next record starts, she's standing next to me, dancing next to me, sustaining eye contact with a vengeance.

We dance. We talk. We laugh. Her name is Kelly and she's from Michigan and she was a student in Providence but she's dropped out to work and "experience life." She asks me at one point, apropos of, it seems to me at the time, nothing, "What size shoe do you wear?" I look down at my Nikes, wondering where that question came from, and that's what I say to her: "Where does that question come from?" She shrugs and smiles and says, "I just noticed, that's all. Then again, you are a big guy." We dance some more. And drink some more beer. And laugh some more. By the time she's grinding against me, to a song that doesn't exactly require any sort of grinding, I'm beginning to see the light. This girl wants me. She wants me bad. Here I was, dancing and drinking in the RISD Tap Room, feeling cooler than cool, a Brown sophomore in Levi's and a button-down shirt, dancing with a white girl to the guitar strains of the Cure, and she wants to bed me. Not that I went out looking for it—which, when you're a well-raised young black man like me, is what you tell yourself when a white girl comes on to you.

When you're a well-raised young black man like me the voice in your inner ear sometimes sounds like your dad, your dad who grew up in the South in the forties and fifties, who knew what it was like to live life on the front lines of the constant battle for black male respect. When you're a well-raised young black man like me, you check yourself when a white girl's dangling the come-on, and you wonder what it is about you that made her seek you out. Are you just black enough to nab a white chick? Or are you, like she says, just a cute guy who likes to dance and smoke in the Tap Room because the Tap Room is the cool place to be?

Cut to Kelly's off-campus apartment . . . there is no door to Kelly's room, just some Indian-type fabric hanging across the doorway, blowing in the slight breeze from the open window near her bed.

We're done, me and Kelly. I'm a little new to this, this meeting a strange girl and going to her spot and getting some ass. I'm also new to sex with white girls. I didn't do it in high school and the only girl I'd fooled around with at Brown was a black chick who, I'd later find out, didn't really want to be with dudes anyway. But we're done, me and Kelly, and we're lying there, twisted in the sheets, sweating, postorgasmic, passing a cigarette between us like we're in some French New Wave movie.

She turns to me, reaches down, and touches my dick. And she smiles. "That was really good," she says. And then she says, "I thought you'd be bigger than you are."

I look down at myself, turn to her, and shake my head. "So did I."

Which was true.

"Why?" I ask her.

"Because you're black," she replied. "Black guys have big penises."

I didn't know what to say to that. Inside, I felt this sudden explosion of self-doubt. Partly because I'd had a cousin who'd explained to me when I was a kid that if you have a little dick, you're not a man. I knew I didn't have a little dick, but apparently I didn't measure up to expectations, for myself and this chick at least. So this is what happens when you fool around with white girls? Later a buddy of mine, upon hearing this story, says yes, it is, telling me, "You got White-Girl-ed."

Which in his mind meant I'd been dragged home with Kelly because I was black, because she was white, and because she was experiencing a little of what Spike Lee would soon popularize as Jungle Fever.

See, White-Girl-ed meant that I hadn't been out there trolling to bed a white chick. White-Girl-ed meant that I hadn't had to go out there trolling for a white chick. I didn't have to, my buddy explained, because there were enough of them out there trolling for us, for black men, for the big black dick of their fantasies, for the big black dick they had probably been warned their whole lives against seeking out. And why was that exactly? The flip side of fantasy, the other side of desire, was the distorted fun-house-mirror image of black men as objects of fear; the myth of the black man as the big-dicked beast, always on the lookout for vulnerable white girls and eager to purloin them of their purity, had been so culturally enforced that trolling for white girls was pointless: endowed with the enduring myth of sexual aggressor, demonized by it though we may be, black men only end up being more attractive to them.

"White people believe in myths," he said. "They have to, or else they couldn't exist. Nor could we," he added, "in their eyes, at least."

This was the beginning of an education for me, an education in the twisted ways in which race and sex rage through American culture, fanning the flames that are constantly charring the walls of America, the place James Baldwin called "this burning house of ours." Sure, I'd seen *Roots*. Sure, I knew my black history, all the names and dates and events that built the totems of black pride that defined my community and myself. I'd been educated in the ways of white folks, about the hurtling

inevitability of racism rearing its ugly head, even in a world where some of my best friends were white. I'd even heard my father's words about dating white women, about the very real possibility of some white people (and some black people) taking issue with such behavior. I'd heard all that.

What I didn't have was any insight into the potential for self-discovery that occurs when all the discordant strands of lessons I'd learned were braided into one big cohesive lesson. Because it wasn't only Kelly's bold forthrightness that bothered me, her "white" way of making me feel "black" when all I was trying to be was a guy. I was also bothered by my response to what she'd said to me. For me, through all the lessons learned up to then, there had never been an intersection of race and sex before I'd lain down with the white chick in Providence. I'd risen from her bed a changed man.

"So did I." That had been my response to her statement. "So did I," as in: I agree, I thought I'd have a bigger dick, too. There was shame in that response but also a nagging question, as in: Why the shame? What had seeped into my consciousness about my emotional self that could be so affected by a quantitative judgment about my physical self? I partly knew the answer to that. The same cousin who'd told me about the lack of masculinity that came with a little dick had also once told me—when I was about thirteen—that eight and a half inches was average. And I knew I wasn't packing an eight-and-a-half-inch dick, and since I was probably about to stop growing, I never would be packing an eight-and-a-half-inch dick. I thought of myself as damaged and I was ashamed of it. Of course some of this also had to do with my thorough lack of sexual experience. I had no idea what women wanted and I had no idea whether I'd be able to satisfy them with whatever size dick I had. I'd had sex before but I was, essentially, an emotional virgin. And an idiot, truth be told, still carrying around my cousin's Guide to Sex in my teen-aged brain.

I ultimately had to figure out that my cousin's lectures to me were all about us being guys. Black guys, yes, but guys nonetheless. Now I had my experience with Kelly and my college buddy's White-Girl-ed education to add a race element to that. What was it about my "guy-ness" that was truly supposed to be defined by my "blackness"?

More sex with Kelly didn't exactly answer all the questions I suddenly had—except one: that I wasn't the first black guy she'd slept with. More sex with Kelly did, however, change both my sexual and racial relationship to her. I knew now that I was a "black" guy having sex with a "white" woman. And there was something actually liberating about that. All the cards were on the table and there was nothing political or cultural to bluff through anymore. The well-raised young black guy in me didn't behave in such a well-raised way when we got together two more times. Some-how I'd figured out that even if I didn't have the huge black penis of her fantasy I could still fuck her like I did. We were louder, rougher, tougher, blacker. We never met each other's friends. We only screwed like animals in the room with the Indian-print cloth across the door. She thought I'd be bigger and so had I. But it was enough for both of us. Because, I suppose, at the end of the day, in the sweaty, postcoital silence poked through with ciga-rette puffs, we both sort of suspected about my dick what James Baldwin had written in *Just Above My Head:* "It was more a matter of its color than its size . . . its color was its size."

Ultimately, when the sex had run its course, when I'd gone my way and she'd gone hers—sexually satisfied on her part, a little mortified on mine—my sexual education was in full swing.

The discovery that I could be affected by someone else's devotion to culturally pre-scribed mythology; that I could actually want to maintain the myth, yet tug against the very pull of it; that I would have to live up to my own expectations as well as the misplaced expecta-tions of others—this was my sexual revolu-tion. It was everything I'd gone to college for. It was the beginning of my desire to want to understand "desire," to find the place where we transcended the usual stereotypes, yet carried them around with us like stowed luggage we knew we'd have to deal with but wouldn't have to look at during the whole trip. I'd been some-body's black buck before I knew that that's what she'd wanted me to be. Yet, just like she'd expected and just like I'd wanted to, I'd turned her out—she'd certainly come back for more. I could be ashamed of one of those roles, and still live to brag about the other to my friends.

Come to find out I wasn't the only brotha who'd experienced this—definitely not there at Brown, there in Providence—aptly named, looking back. *Providence*, as defined by *The American Heritage Dictionary:* "Care or prepa-ration in advance; foresight."

My history lessons would be informed by the present-tense discussions of life with my black brothers, other young black guys like me caught up in similar circumstances, try-ing to make history while we found ourselves caught up in American history's far- and long-reaching web. We shared the eternal conflict of "measuring up"—balancing the burden of the white stereotype with the complicated desire to maintain the myth, to grow up from the Big-ger Thomas within, yet stay on speaking terms with the Dolomites we yearned to be.

THE SORCERER'S APPRENTICE: WHY CAN'T WE STOP CIRCUMCISING BOYS?

ROBERT DARBY

People have always eaten people,
What else is there to eat?
If the Juju had meant us not to eat people
He wouldn't have made us of meat.
　　　—Flanders and Swann, "The Reluctant Cannibal"

The pediatrician spent hours resuscitating and assessing the injuries of a boy who had been born unable to breathe, without a pulse, and with a broken humerus and depressed skull fracture resulting from a difficult forceps delivery. He then visited the mother, whose first question was "When can he be circumcised?" Such a sense of priorities indicates the privileged place of male circumcision in modern America and highlights the difficulties in explaining what Edward Wallerstein [(1985)] has called "the uniquely American medical enigma." Why does routine circumcision persist in the United States long after it has been abandoned in the other English-speaking countries that originally took it up? Despite critical statements from the American Academy of Pediatrics and the College of Obstetricians and Gynecologists in 1971, 1975, 1978, 1983, 1989, and 1999, the operation is still performed on well over half of all newborn boys. Today, despite strong statements against non-therapeutic circumcision of minors by the British Medical Association, the Royal Dutch Medical Association, the Royal Australasian College of Physicians and health authorities in Germany and Scandinavia, the American Academy of Pediatrics has set the seal on American exceptionalism by adopting a new (2012) policy statement that emphasizes the future benefits of circumcision while downplaying harm, human rights and bioethics. Although it does not recommend circumcision as a routine, it considers the benefits great enough to authorize parental choice in the matter and coverage by insurance programs.

The U.S. experience contrasts with that of the other countries in which routine circumcision had once been common. In Britain, the procedure was widely recommended in the 1890s, reached its peak of popularity in the 1920s (at a rate of about 35 percent), declined in the 1950s, and all but disappeared by the 1960s. In Australia, the incidence of circumcision peaked at over 80 percent in the 1950s, but it declined rapidly in the 1980s after statements by pediatric authorities. Today it stands at about 12 percent. The Canadian pattern is broadly similar, though the decline was slower until the late 1990s, when rates fell sharply. In New Zealand, the procedure was nearly universal between the wars, but fell so precipitately in the 1960s that now fewer than 2 percent of boys are circumcised—most of them Pacific islanders, done in late childhood for "traditional" cultural reasons. We thus face a classic puzzle of comparative sociology: Why did routine circumcision arise in the first place? Why only in Anglophone countries? Why did it decline and all but vanish in Britain and its dominions? Why does it survive in the United States?

From "The Sorcerer's Apprentice: Why Can't We Stop Circumcising Boys?" by Robert Darby. *Contexts*, Vol. 4, No. 2, May 2005, pp. 34–39. Copyright © 2005, American Sociological Association. Reprinted by Permission of SAGE Publications.

Nobody has firm answers to these questions. The rise of circumcision was associated with the "great fear" of masturbation and anxiety about juvenile sexuality; the misidentification of infantile phimosis (the naturally non-retractile state of the juvenile foreskin) as a congenital abnormality; the puritan moralities of the nineteenth century; dread of many incurable diseases, especially syphilis, and the rising prestige of the medical profession, particularly surgeons, leading to excessive faith in surgical approaches to disease control and prevention. Most of these features were common to all European countries, however, and the factors that provoked the particular Anglophone pattern remain obscure. The fall of circumcision in Britain was associated with other medical advances, especially the discovery of antibiotics, the decline of anxiety about masturbation, concern about complications and deaths, and the development of a more positive attitude toward sexual pleasure. In 1979, an editorial in the *British Medical Journal* attributed much of the trend to a better understanding of normal anatomical development and the consequent disappearance of fears about childhood phimosis.

The same editorial contrasted the British case with the situation in the United States, where the majority of boys were still circumcised, and many doctors defended the procedure with some vehemence. It offered no suggestions as to why the experience of the two leading Anglophone powers diverged so sharply after the 1940s, but clues may be found in the relatively low incidence of circumcision in Britain, its concentration among the upper classes, and the fact that even at the height of its popularity it was a minority practice that lasted scarcely more than two generations. In the United States, generous medical insurance policies after World War II allowed more families to take advantage of surgical procedures, and the introduction of Medicaid in the 1960s permitted even the poor to enjoy many of the same services as the rich. The practice thus came to affect the vast majority of U.S. males and to endure for more than two generations, with the result that there were soon few doctors and parents who were familiar with the normal (uncircumcised) penis and thus knew how little management it needed. In Britain, there were always doctors and relatives who had not lost touch with the way things used to be. In my research on Britain and Australia, I found that routine circumcision began as a doctor-driven innovation, became established in the medical repertoire, spread rapidly, and then declined slowly as doctors ceased to recommend it. Since parents had absorbed the advice of the generation before and many fathers had been circumcised themselves, they continued to ask for it. The fundamental reason for the circumcision of boys is a population of circumcised adults.

The American situation remains puzzling: Why has a custom initiated by our Victorian forebears prospered so mightily in the age of medical miracles? Some doctors blame parents for demanding circumcision, while parents accuse physicians of suggesting and even urging the operation, and of not warning them about risks and possible adverse effects. Critically minded doctors call for "the organized advocacy of lay groups . . . rather than the efforts of the medical profession," while others object to the interference of "outsiders" in what they insist is a strictly clinical matter. Wallerstein felt that the practice continued because "medical and popular literature abounds in serious errors of scientific judgment," with the result that the medical profession is reluctant to take a firm or united stand. Although few think there is any real value in circumcision, and many regard it as cruel and harmful, doctors seem mesmerized by the force of parental demand and social expectation. Like the sorcerer's apprentice in *Fantasia*, they watch helplessly as the waters mount, waiting for the master magician to return and restore normality.

There has been remarkably little research into this problem. Circumcision is a highly controversial subject, but most of the debate is at a fairly simplistic level (the pros and cons), not on why the practice continues. Those who defend circumcision regard it as an unproblematic hygiene precaution or at least a parent's right to choose, and often become annoyed when critics ask them to justify it. Discussion of the issue is hampered by uncertainty as to the incidence of routine circumcision, its social distribution, and the reasons parents want it or agree to have it done.

We know in a broad sense that the practice became common around the time of the First World War and reached a peak in the 1960s, but it is only since 1979 that consistent and reasonably accurate figures based on the National Hospital Discharge Survey have become available. These cover only neonatal circumcision (performed before mother and boy leave the maternity hospital) and show that the rate nationally declined from 64.5 percent in 1979 to 55.9 percent in 2008. They also show significant differences by region: in the northeast a decline from 66.2 percent to 65.3 percent; in the mid-west from 74.3 percent to 71.1 percent; in the south from 55.8 percent to 54.6 percent; and in the west from 63.9 percent to 40.5 percent. It may be seen that the reduction over this period is not impressive and that nearly all of it is in the west, but also that the figure for 1979 is lower than that given in some other sources of data. The figures are also broken down by race, showing that while circumcision used to be less common among African Americans the difference vanishes as we reach the present.

More recent preliminary figures from the Centers for Disease Control (CDC), using different data sources, report a decline from 58.4 percent in 2001 to 54.7 percent in 2010, but give no breakdown by region or social

characteristics. The same report notes the importance of financial incentives: the incidence of circumcision is 24 percentage points lower in states that do not cover circumcision through Medicaid. Race differentials are of interest because an alleged lower incidence of circumcision among African Americans has been cited by circumcision advocates as an explanation for their higher rate of HIV infection, and thus as an argument for circumcision as a control tactic. Even if there was a difference in the past it has been of declining significance since the 1960s, when the introduction of Medicaid allowed poor people (including Blacks) to access inessential medical treatments. Apart from this point, there is abundant evidence that in many places there was no difference between African-American and white circumcision incidence, and that African Americans quite often reported a higher rate. Of greater interest are the data in a study by the CDC that sought to assess the lifetime risk of HIV infection. These data showed the lifetime risk of HIV among Black men to be 6.23 percent with 73 percent circumcised, yet a lifetime risk to Hispanics of only 2.88 percent with a circumcision rate of 42 percent. This suggests either that there is no connection between circumcision and reduced susceptibility to HIV; that circumcision increases the risk of HIV; or that being Black in the United States is a greater risk factor for HIV than "lack of circumcision."

Preventive circumcision has always been an experimental and controversial surgery, never endorsed by the medical profession as a whole. Given the uncertainty of its benefits, the high risk of harm, and the significance of the organ being so dramatically altered, you might expect a few ultranervous adults would elect to have it done to themselves but not for millions to impose it on their babies. Nobody suggests that the practice continues because the inhabitants of Indiana are healthier than those of California or because Americans in general are healthier than the populations of countries such as Scandinavia or Japan, where circumcision is rare. Indeed, readily available statistics suggest the opposite. Although per capita health spending is vastly greater in the United States than anywhere else, health outcomes on such key indicators as infant mortality, life expectancy, and the incidence of Sexually Transmitted Diseases (STDs) are significantly worse in the United States than in comparably developed countries where most men retain their foreskins. Far from circumcision being a protection against STDs, as often claimed, Laumann found that circumcised men had more STDs, and the United States reports an HIV incidence six times greater than Japan. Moreover, in a recent survey of child health outcomes of countries ranked by the Organisation for Economic Cooperation and Development (OECD), the United States scored so badly that on many indicators (such as infant mortality) it was ranked near the bottom with places such as Turkey and Mexico. The OECD study of thirty countries ranked the United States 24th in overall child health and safety and 23rd in material well-being.

If American health outcomes are no better than those of non-circumcising countries, why does this "health precaution" survive on a mass scale? Robert Van Howe suggests seven lines of inquiry: (1) the foreskin is the focus of myths, misconceptions, and irrationality affecting the medical profession and public alike; (2) a lack of respect for the rights and individuality of children; (3) a contrasting exaggerated respect for the presumed sensibilities of religious minorities who practice circumcision for cultural reasons; (4) the reluctance of physicians to take a firm stand against circumcision and to refuse parental requests; (5) a bias in American medical journals, which tend to favor articles with a pro-circumcision tendency; (6) a failure to subject circumcision to the normal protocols for surgery, such as the need for informed consent, evidence of pathology, and proof of net direct benefit; and (7) strong financial incentives to perform the operation, which is generally covered by medical insurance.

To these suggestions might be added the role of the armed forces. During the two world wars, the U.S. military made a concerted effort to circumcise servicemen because it believed this would make them less susceptible to venereal disease. Military discipline forced men to submit to a procedure they would not otherwise have agreed to, and thousands of men were circumcised in their late teens and early 20s. When they returned home and became fathers, doctors began asking whether they wanted their sons circumcised. Remembering the ordeal that they or their buddies had endured from the operation as adults, many said yes, thinking it would avoid the need to do it later when the pain was thought to be worse than in infancy. With two generations circumcised, the foreskin became a rare sight, and knowledge of its sexual role and how to care for it was lost.

The importance of financial incentives has been stressed by a number of critics. In their analysis of Medicaid funding, Amber Craig and [Dan Bollinger (2006)] found that low and declining rates of circumcision correspond to regions where the procedure is not funded, notably in California, which dropped coverage in 1982. Even more striking is their finding that the higher the rebate, the higher the incidence of circumcision—vivid proof of the power of market signals. Nor do the advantages of circumcision—for doctors—end there. Despite optimistic claims that the rates of injury and death are low, there has never been an adequate assessment of long-term complications, and they are certainly more frequent than most people think. The dirty little secret in pediatric surgery is that badly performed circumcisions, causing discomfort or poor cosmetic outcomes, often necessitating repeat operations and repair jobs, are common; one attorney who specializes in medical malpractice reports that some urologists see at least one such case each week. In this way the division of professional labor ensures that the benefits of circumcision are spread far beyond the original doctors: their mistakes provide work for many colleagues and the disasters add lawyers to the equation.

Lack of unanimity and conviction among the medical profession has been stressed by Lawrence Dritsas, who attempts to deconstruct the AAP's unwillingness to make a firm recommendation and its corresponding tactic of throwing the burden of [decision-making] onto parents. He quotes an article that offered this explanation:

We are reluctant to assume the role of active advocacy (one way or the other) because . . . the decision is not usually a medical one. Rather, it is based on the parents' perceptions of hygiene, their lack of understanding of the surgical risks, or their desire to conform to the pattern established by the infant's father and their own societal structure. (Maisels et al., 1983, p. 453)

He translates this to mean that circumcision is irrational but that, contrary to the usual protocol, "parental wishes become sufficient, while medical necessity, normally a guiding rule for the surgeon's knife, takes a back seat." Dritsas contrasts this hands-off approach with the AAP's ethically based rejection of female genital mutilation (where the possibility of a health benefit is not even entertained). In its statement on informed consent the AAP says, "Providers have legal and ethical duties to their child patients to render competent medical care based on what the patient needs, not what someone else expresses. . . . The pediatrician's responsibility to his or her patient exists independently of parental desires or proxy consent." Except, it seems, when it comes to male circumcision.

Dritsas is puzzled by the contradictions in AAP policy and explains them in terms of medical culture and the apprenticeship model of professional training, which does not encourage students to question authority. "For a physician to cease performing circumcisions represents a condemnation of past practice and an admission of error," he writes, and nobody holding the power of life and death wants to be seen as doing that. The doctors are thus in much the same position as the parents themselves, whose unconsidered assumption that the baby will be circumcised is an expression of the authority of their grandparents' physicians who convinced prior generations that it was the thing to do. Dritsas criticizes the stance of the AAP as reminiscent of the response of Pontius Pilate when confronted with the problem of what to do with Jesus. In his view, what they are really saying is that, "as scientific doctors, we find ourselves unable to recommend or deny this procedure; therefore, you will decide, and we shall be your scalpels." Although these comments were made in response to the 1999 policy, the new policy is not so different that they have become inapplicable: circumcision is still "not recommended"; the choice is still thrust upon parents. This abdication of responsibility contrasts with the proactive stances of pediatric bodies in Britain, Australia, New Zealand, Canada, and Europe, which have seen it as their duty not only to discourage parents from seeking circumcision but, in the end, to refuse to perform the operation. Their view is that the appropriate person to make the decision is the one who must wear the life-long consequences.

There must be an explanation for these national differences. The medical profession is not an independent force; its members are subject to the same social pressures that shape the beliefs and condition the actions of everybody else. Several recent commentators have thus argued that circumcision should not be seen as a medical issue at all but as an expression of social norms. At a superficial level this has long been known. In the 1950s Dr. Spock urged circumcision because it would help a boy to feel "regular," and pediatricians since then have noted that "entrenched tradition of custom is probably the greatest obstacle faced by those who would decrease the number of circumcisions done in this country" [(Metcalf, Osborn and Mariani, 1983)]. But it is only recently that the sociological aspect of the question has received serious attention. In a comprehensive survey of the history of modern circumcision and the debate over its "advantages," published in 2002, Geoffrey Miller shows how late Victorian physicians succeeded in demonizing the foreskin as a source of moral and physical decay. Acting as "norm entrepreneurs" they "reconfigured the phallus," transforming the foreskin from a feature regarded as healthy, natural, and good into one feared as polluted, chaotic, and bad. The incessant quest for novel associations between the foreskin (often expressed as "lack of circumcision") and nasty diseases is a tribute to the lasting success of their enterprise.

As a legal scholar, Miller is surprised at the law's indifferent or often supportive attitude toward what one might expect it to regard as an assault, or at least a mutilation, but he points out that the law is an expression of the surrounding culture and cannot be expected to be too far ahead of prevailing norms. Even so, he considers routine circumcision in the mainstream community to be on the way out. Although still normative, it is in decline and edging toward the critical halfway mark, or "tipping point," where the incidence can be expected to fall precipitously as parents come to believe that their children will now face stigma if they are circumcised. Like foot binding in China or wife-beating in nineteenth-century Britain, a widely accepted social convention is "likely to collapse as the culture reaches a 'tipping point' and turns against the practice." Although it has high scare value, the evidence from poverty-stricken African countries that circumcision of adult men can reduce the risk of HIV transmission during unprotected heterosexual intercourse in regions of high HIV prevalence is clearly delaying this process, but is unlikely to halt it permanently.

Sarah Waldeck offers a subtle analysis of how norms contribute to a person's behavioral cost-benefit calculations, how the desire to have a child circumcised fits into this assessment, and thus why parents continue to seek it. She is particularly interested in the "stigma" supposedly attached to the uncircumcised penis in a society where most males are cut, and she considers the role of the popular media in perpetuating a stereotype of the foreskin as somehow disagreeable. She also notes that few parents have any clear reasons for wanting their sons circumcised and produce them only when challenged. The most common justifications turn out to be the supposed need to look like the father or peers and not to be teased in the proverbial locker room. If "health benefits" are mentioned at all, they enter as an afterthought or when other arguments fail. Waldeck still subjects the medical case to scientific, legal, and ethical scrutiny, and finds it inadequate to justify the removal of healthy body parts from non-consenting minors. She concludes with a discussion of how the American norm might be changed and suggests three specific strategies: requiring parents to pay for the procedure; requiring doctors who perform the operation to use effective pain control; and tightening the informed consent process. . . .

When preventive circumcision was introduced in the late nineteenth century, concepts of medical ethics, informed consent, therapeutic evidence, and the cost-benefit trade-off were rudimentary. Neither the morality nor the efficacy of the procedure was seriously debated, nor was there any study of its long-term consequences; it became established in the medical culture of Anglophone countries by virtue of the authority of its early promoters. No matter how many statistics-laden articles get published in medical journals, circumcision cannot shake off the traces of its

Victorian origins. It remains the last surviving example of the once respectable proposition that disease could be prevented by the preemptive removal of body parts, which, though healthy, are thought to be a weak link in the body's defenses. In its heyday, this medical breakthrough, described by Ann Dally as "fantasy surgery," enjoyed wide esteem and included excisions of other supposed foci or portals of infection, such as the adenoids, tonsils, teeth, appendix, and large intestine. Few doubted that if the doctor thought you or your children were better off without any of these, it was your duty to follow his orders.

Because there was no real debate about the propriety or efficacy of preemptive amputation as a disease-control strategy when it was first introduced, those who wanted to remove healthy body parts from children were able to throw the burden of proof onto their opponents. Instead of the advocates having to demonstrate that the gain outweighed the loss, it was up to the doubters to prove that the loss outweighed the gain. The consequence is that what should have been a debate about the introduction of preventive circumcision in the 1890s has turned into a debate about its abolition a century later. Miller and Waldeck are probably right to argue that circumcision will not die out until the uncut penis becomes an acceptable—perhaps the preferred—option. But the transformation of attitudes will not seem so improbable, nor is the task of affecting it so daunting, if we remember that there is no need to invent a new norm, merely to restore the sensibility that governed the Western world before the late nineteenth century. In the 1870s, when Richard Burton remarked that Christendom "practically holds circumcision in horror,"

(*Note on terminology:* In this article "circumcision" or "routine circumcision" means circumcision of normal male minors in the absence of any medical indication or valid religious requirement, on the decision of adults, and without the consent of the child.)

the observation was ceasing to be true, but it was certainly the case before Victorian doctors reconfigured the phallus and bequeathed a thorny problem to their successors.

REFERENCES

Craig, A., and D. Bollinger. 2006. "Of Waste and Want: A Nationwide Survey of Medical Funding for Medically Unnecessary Non-Therapeutic Circumcision." In *Bodily Integrity and the Politics of Circumcision*, George C. Denniston, et al. (Eds.). New York: Springer.

Dritsas, Lawrence. 2001. "Below the Belt: Doctors, Debate and the Ongoing American Discussion of Routine Neonatal Male Circumcision." *Bulletin of Science and Technology* 21: 297–311.

Laumann E. O., C. M. Masi, and E. W. Zuckerman. 1997. "Circumcision in the United States: Prevalence, prophylactic effects, and sexual practice." *Journal of the American Medical Association* 277: 1052–7.

Miller, Geoffrey. 2002. "Circumcision: Cultural-Legal Analysis." *Virginia Journal of Social Policy and the Law* 9: 497–585.

Maisels, M. J., B. Hayes, S. Conrad, and R. A. Chez. 1983. "Circumcision: The effect of information on parental decision making." *Pediatrics* 71: 453.

Metcalf, T. J., L. M. Osborn, and E. M. Mariani. 1983. "Circumcision: A Study of Current Practices." *Clinical Pediatrics* 22 (Aug): 575–9.

Organisation for Economic Cooperation and Development. *Doing Better for Children*. September 2009.

Perera, C. L., F.H.G. Bridgewater, P. Thavaneswaran, and G. J. Maddern. 2010. "Safety and efficacy of nontherapeutic male circumcision: A systematic review." *Annals of Family Medicine* 8(1): 64–72.

Policy statements on circumcision by medical organizations: www.cirp.org/library/statements/ and www.circinfo.org/doctors.html

Sansom, S. L., V. S. Prabhu, A. B. Hutchinson, Q. An, H. I. Hall, et al. 2010. Cost-effectiveness of newborn circumcision in reducing lifetime HIV risk among U.S. males. PLoS ONE 5(1): e8723.doi:10.1371/journal.pone.0008723. Comment by "Hanabi" at http://www.plosone.org/article/comments/info%3Adoi/10.1371/journal.pone.0008723.

Van Howe, Robert. 1997. "Why Does Neonatal Circumcision Persist in the United States?" In *Sexual Mutilations: A Human Tragedy*, Marylin Milos and George Denniston (Eds.). New York: Plenum.

Waldeck, Sarah. 2003. "Using Circumcision to Understand Social Norms as Multipliers." *University of Cincinnati Law Review* 72: 455–526.

Wallerstein, Edward. 1985. "Circumcision: The Uniquely American Medical Enigma." *Urologic Clinics of North America* 12: 123–32.

THE POLITICS OF ACCULTURATION: FEMALE GENITAL CUTTING

LISA WADE

Modern democracies around the globe are struggling to build functional, integrated, egalitarian nations in the face of social conflicts deemed "cultural." This crisis of culture derives, in part, from the multiplicitous and paradoxical meanings of the term. Used to describe time-honored traditions, unconscious habits, group identities (racial, ethnic, and other), the character of nation-states, religious practices, and both "high" and "folk" art, culture is both condemned as a primary obstacle to the spread of human rights and celebrated as a human right in itself (Benhabib, 2002; Cowan, Dembour, and Wilson, 2001; Merry, 2006). Indeed, the term seems to have lost any coherent meaning even as it has become increasingly politicized (Eriksen, 2001; Fraser, 1995; Turner, 1993).

As illustrated by Susan Okin's (1997) famous question, "Is multiculturalism bad for women?" the challenge of managing (so-called) cultural difference is crystalized in conflicts over women's rights. Practices like dowry murders, honor crimes, sex-selective abortion, forced or arranged marriage, and female genital cutting (FGC) are all framed as cultural problems that test the limits of cross-cultural tolerance. Culture itself is often held accountable for the perpetuation of these practices, alongside or instead of individuals, such that the well-being of girls and women seems to be incompatible with cultural preservation (Narayan, 1997). The apparent incommensurability between feminism and multiculturalism has spurred a voluminous literature in which culture has been both defended and derided. . . .

More recently, however, scholars have been interrogating the assumptions behind this discussion of Okin's question. These scholars have argued that the object driving the multiculturalism/feminism debates is not "culture," but our model of culture. While most anthropologists and sociologists of culture adopt various dynamic models (e.g., Bourdieu, 1977; Sewell, 1992; Swidler, 2001), public debates often assume a reified model, selectively applied, in which culture is characterized by timelessness, internal coherence, clear boundaries, and determinism (Benhabib, 2002; Merry, 2006; Narayan, 2000). It is this reified model that makes the answer to Okin's question appear to be "yes" by presupposing that some groups, but not others, are rigidly bound to an un-reformable (patriarchal) culture.

I contribute to this emerging literature in two ways. First, instead of looking at cultural practices and cultural groups, I focus on cultural change. I show that the reified model of culture also shapes our perception of acculturation, with serious consequences for our ability to manage the compromise and accommodation essential to multicultural democracies. Second, I interrogate how the dynamic model of culture is discursively mobilized. I show that

From "The Politics of Acculturation: Female Genital Cutting," *Social Problems*, Vol. 58, Issue 4, 2011, pp. 518–537. Copyright © 2011, The Society for the Study of Social Problems Inc. Reprinted by permission of University of California Press.

the dynamic model, just like the reified model, can be used by actors to shape perceptions of social change in troubling ways. The adoption of a dynamic model, then, does not necessarily mean that contests will be more civil, inclusive, or productive.

I make these arguments with an examination of the role that culture played in a debate over a proposal by U.S. physicians to offer a modified female genital cutting procedure to immigrants. Somali patients at Seattle, Washington's Harborview Medical Center were requesting that physicians perform genital cutting on their daughters. In Somalia, 98 percent of women undergo infibulation, a practice that involves the removal of labial tissue, trimming of the clitoris, and fusing of the anterior vulva (WHO, 2008). Wanting to attend to their patients' "cultural needs," and desiring to reduce the chance that girls would be subjected to infibulation, a group of physicians proposed to offer a procedure in the clinic: a one-centimeter incision in the clitoral foreskin. Before they could implement the plan, however, opponents to the procedure began calling and writing the hospital. Those targeted reported that the objectors were angry and sometimes threatening. Cowed by the level of controversy and the intensity of the opposition, the Medical Center revoked its support for the proposal . . .

Drawing on interviews, original documents, and newspaper coverage, I analyze how advocates and critics of the proposal used culture to defend and attack the procedure. I show that the conflict rested on whether the move from infibulation to an incision was framed as cultural change or persistence. Opponents of the proposal (hereafter: "opponents") argued that Somali interest in the incision was proof of their *in*ability to throw off the ancient patriarchal practices to which they were obedient. They critiqued Somalis for being *in*flexible and physicians for being *grossly* flexible. From the physicians' perspective, however, this was

a stunning mischaracterization. They saw the procedure as essentially symbolic; it was, literally, the *least* they could do. From their perspective, then, adoption of the alternative procedure would be a testament to Somali cultural flexibility and their own respect for cultural differences.

I argue that these dramatically different interpretations of the physicians' proposal are explained by differences in the implicit models of culture used by opponents and physicians. Physicians assumed a dynamic model of culture that attributed to Somalis an ability to adapt to (a presumably egalitarian) U.S. culture, Opponents, in contrast, applied a reified model of culture that made anything but abandonment appear to be cultural persistence. I argue, further, that both models, as mobilized by these actors, failed to capture the complexity of this difficult compromise. Because opponents used the reified model of culture, they reinforced negative stereotypes and fomented cross-cultural intolerance. They failed to recognize Somali women's autonomy, privileged Western over Somali ideas about the symbolic meaning of genital cutting, and trivialized the abandonment of infibulation. Physicians using the dynamic model of culture did not make these mistakes, granting Somali women autonomy from culture, independence from the men in their lives, and the ability to reflect thoughtfully. Physicians, however, used the dynamic model against opponents. Romanticizing acculturation to the United States, and their own ability to rather effortlessly chaperone the abandonment of infibulation and its patriarchal meanings, they felt comfortable excluding socially relevant constituencies such as feminists and anthropologists from their deliberations and, when their proposal brought opposition, they dismissed opponents' concerns as irrelevant, even ridiculous.

This incident occured in 1996, but the intervening years have brought little clarity. In 2010, the American Academy of Pediatrics published a position statement endorsing a "ritual nick." Their logic, and that of those who emerged to oppose them—which I discuss in more detail below—was essentially the same as in 1996. And, just as they did 15 years [earlier], the physicians responded to the opposition by revoking their recommendation. This case study, then, remains timely and illuminates a still active debate. . . .

REVIEW OF THE LITERATURE

The Politics of Culture

Many sociologists of culture, even when they otherwise disagree, understand culture to be a complex collective repertoire of practices and ideas (e.g., Bourdicu, 1977; Sewell, 1992; Swidler, 2001). Because its logics and imperatives are often contradictory, people's values and behaviors are not determined; instead, culture serves as a resource with which people strategically and pragmatically make sense of the world. Culture inevitably evolves as actors accept and challenge meanings, borrow from other cultures, negotiate with other individuals, and react to economic, political, and technological change. Among sociologists, Ann Swidler's (1986) "toolkit" is the most well-known metaphor for what I will call a *dynamic* model of culture.

One of the tools in this cultural toolkit is "culture" itself (hereafter sans quotations) and politics is one arena in which the idea is mobilized (Fraser, 2000). Indeed, it is now common to use culture as a basis for rights claims and resource allocation at both national and transnational levels (Cowan et al., 2001; Eriksen, 2001; Fraser, 1995; Turner, 1993). In some cases we see strategic essentialism (Spivak, 1985). Indigenous groups "orientalize" themselves (Said, 1978) to appeal to both national and international audiences and national leaders defend against "Westernization" by claiming

that it amounts to cultural imperialism (Jackson, 1995:19; see also Chanock, 2002; Cowan, 2001; Merry, 2001; Narayan, 1997; Sieder and Witchell, 2001). Western countries have made similar moves: French lawmakers, for example, resisted passing anti-sexual harassment laws with the argument that doing so required seeing France through an American cultural lens (Saguy, 2003). Individuals can also use respect for cultural difference to claim special rights based on cultural membership, such as the right of Sikhs to refrain from wearing motorcycle helmets and hardhats and the right to turn to faith-based conflict resolution instead of secular law (Cowan et al., 2001; Razack, 2007). Groups not previously identified as cultural are also tapping into pro-multiculturalism discourses. For example, some religious groups are fighting the separation of church and state by claiming that the inclusion of their beliefs in public education is consistent with multiculturalism (Davies, 1999).

Culture, however, can also be used to negatively portray group members and justify the withdrawal of rights and resources. Economically and politically powerful nation-states penalize less powerful nation-states who do not work to eradicate "harmful traditional practices" (Boyle, 2002; Merry, 2006), wars and other aggressive interventions are justified with references to backward, barbaric, and evil cultures (Abu-Lughod, 2002; Cooke, 2002; Stabile and Kumar, 2005), and cultural practices, like veiling, are banned on the premise that they are incompatible with a "neutral" public sphere (Bloul, 1994; Dustin and Phillips, 2008; Mushaben, 2005). Individuals can also demonize their own culture for individual gain. They can, for example, obtain asylum by claiming that they are persecuted members of an oppressive culture (Piot, 2007; Razack, 1995) and gain leniency in sentencing on the supposition that "their culture made them do it" (Fournier, 2002; Phillips, 2003; Volpp, 1994).

The Power of Culture: Reified and Dynamic Models

The power of culture in these arguments comes from its reification. To reify culture is to: (1) presume that cultural groups have nonambiguous boundaries and nonoverlapping memberships (Benhabib, 2002; Gupta and Ferguson, 1992; Narayan, 1997, 2000); (2) essentialize cultural content as unchanging, internally coherent, and universally embraced (Abu-Lughod, 1991; Anthias, 2002; Parekh, 1995; Rudy, 2000); and (3) attribute causal power to culture such that it is "superautonomous" relative to the autonomy of its members (Calmore, 1992:2185; see also Appadurai, 1988; Benhabib, 2002; Phillips, 2007). Widely criticized by academics, this view of culture is also called a "package picture" (Narayan, 1998, 2000), a "billiard ball conception" (Tully, 1995), an "essentialist model" (Cowan et al., 2001; Merry, 2006), and a "reductionist sociology of culture" (Benhabib, 2002). Following Nancy Fraser (2000), I call it a "reified model of culture."

A reified model is strategically useful because only a culture that is presumed to persist independent of historical change and interpenetration with other cultural groups can be argued to deserve perfect preservation or require total destruction. When the culture or cultural practice in question is celebrated, a reified model allows insiders to insist on protectionism and isolationism; only if we imagine cultures to be unchanging is change threatening to cultural survival. When a culture or cultural practice is condemned, the same model calls for intervention to force cultural group members to abandon their culture; only if we imagine culture to be totalizing is forced abandonment the route to the enhancement of human rights. In contrast, a dynamic model takes for granted that cultures change and, thus, are never perfectly authentic or entirely unredeemable. To frame a practice as cultural in this context does not mean, then, that the practice must be preserved exactly as is, nor eradicated completely for the sake of human rights.

Importantly, powerful groups often characterize themselves as culture-less or only lightly cultural (the dynamic model) at the same time that they frame others as culture-bound (the reified model). . . . Members of non-Western societies, then, are often portrayed as hopelessly backward, incapable of change and, ultimately, "imperfectible" (Lazreg, 1988:87; see also Pournier, 2002; Merry, 2006; Mohanty, 1988; Volpp, 1994, 2000).

These divergent relationships to culture attributed to Western and non-Western societies influence not just portrayals of cultural groups, but portrayals of their cultural practices, and even what practices are understood to be cultural at all. In many instances, social problems in societies deemed culture-bound are described by members of other societies as *cultural* practices related to the beliefs, values, and traditions of the entire group. In contrast, social problems in Western societies are often individualized, understood to be caused by bad people, not bad societies. Uma Narayan (1997), for example, has shown that the rationale behind "dowry murders" in India is framed in U.S. discourse as cultural and characterized as a normative national characteristic with deep historical roots. Domestic murders in the United States, however, which occur at a similar frequency, are seen as the unfortunate result of a few unusually bad men and not reflective of American culture. . . . Meanwhile, Pascale Fournier (2002), examining the use of the "cultural defense" to moderate sentencing in sexual assault cases, has found that lawyers sometimes argue that immigrants are prone to violence by virtue of their membership in a "primitive" culture; lesser sentences are justified by pointing to culture as a coperpetrator. Drawing on Narayan's observation that dowry murders are often framed as "death by culture"

(p. 103), Fournier calls the cultural defense "rape by culture" (p. 81).

In each of these cases, culture is identified as the cause of social problems, a tendency that functions primarily to condemn the culture in question, at the expense of providing an explanation for why a problematic practice persists. Foreign men rape, murder, and mutilate women, the culture frame implies, because that is "how they are." At best, to say "they do it because they do it" is tautological and, at worst, it *mis*represents cultural beliefs and practices as independent from the economic, technological, and political forces that influence their persistence, emergence, and disappearance (Narayan, 1997; Turner, 1993). . . .

Models of Culture and the Compatibility of Multicultural and Feminism

Just as the reified model gives cultural arguments their power, it is this model, especially as it is applied asymmetrically, that makes it seem as if feminism and multiculturalism are incompatible. A dynamic model of culture assumes that women in different cultural contexts can use their own cultural tools to empower themselves. This is the premise behind the insistence on the existence of feminisms. Pluralizing the term acknowledges that women's liberation may look differently for different women (e.g., Abu-Lughod, 2002; Collins, 1991; Narayan, 1997). . . .

If we believe that the culture to be integrated is *immutably* patriarchal, however, embracing [it] is equivalent to embracing patriarchy, logically leading to a denial of the agency of some women. [They] must reject [their] culture, we imagine, or embrace patriarchy. When women contest the idea that their choices are manifestations of their complicity with patriarchy, they can be dismissed as falsely conscious. Since they are believed to be incapable of liberating themselves, it is concluded that they must be liberated by members of societies to which we

ascribe gender egalitarianism and dynamism. Lightly cultural people, then, must step in to help the culture-bound. The phenomenon is succinctly described by Gayatri Spivak's (1988) phrase "white men [and women] are saving brown women from brown men" (p. 296). . . .

[This logic is] used to invalidate the opinions of women who support female genital cutting, Wairimu Ngaruiya Njambi (2004) argues that the "decision to avoid as well as to opt for female circumcision is both within the realm of cultural possibility" (p. 283; see also Ahmadu 2001). Yet, U.S. discourse about FGCs all too often portrays women who support genital cutting as patriarchal pawns, contrasting them with a supposedly liberated American woman (Wade, 2009). . . .

Okin's question as to whether multiculturalism is bad for women, then, depends very much on how the idea of culture is mobilized. Insofar as a reified model of culture is driving our national and transnational politics—and there is good evidence to suggest it is (Benhabib, 2002; Fraser, 1995; Merry, 2006; Narayan, 1997)—then societies can either be multicultural or egalitarian, but not both. Driven by this logic, states take the counterintuitive step of restricting women's rights in the interest of their own liberation. . . .

Cultural change, like practices and peoples, is subject to social construction. The perception that a culture has changed, or not, is the product of ideological and discursive projects, as well as practical and material realities. Whether something counts as cultural preservation or disruption, then, is the outcome of contests between social agents who select and fetishize certain aspects of cultural practice and specific time periods as "traditional." Describing research by Olayinka Koso-Thomas (1987), Narayan (1998) offers the example of changes in genital cutting rituals in Sierra Leone. Some Sierra Leonean proponents of the cutting insisted that continuing the practice was crucial to the survival of local culture. Koso-Thomas observed that almost all of the related ceremonial and educational practices had disappeared in response to other economic and social changes. The cutting itself, however, was fetishized as the critical link between the present and the past, while the fact that the practice of genital cutting was very different today was dismissed as unimportant. . . .

METHODS

Data used to investigate the controversy at Harborview Medical Center (hereafter: "Harborview") included newspaper coverage, material from the University of Washington archives, and interviews. . . .

The first set of interviewees was culled from . . . newspaper accounts. Using a snowball method of sampling, I identified additional individuals to interview, ultimately completing nine interviews with physicians, other hospital staff, and individuals involved with the media.[1] . . . I attempted to determine the trajectory of events, the important participants, and perceptions of various actors and their motivations. . . . When I include quotations from these interviews, I indicate the interviewee with an "Int" for "interview" and a number ranging from one to nine (e.g., Int9). Because of the small number of high-profile individuals involved in this controversy, I offer no additional details as to their identities in order to protect confidentiality. . . . I reconstituted a timeline and the facts of the controversy with the newspaper accounts, archived documents, and interviews. . . .

FINDINGS

Overview of the Controversy

Harborview Medical Center's mission is to provide culturally responsive health care. To achieve this goal, the hospital disseminates knowledge about different healing traditions through a website, EthnoMed (ethnomed.org). Aimed at the wider medical community, the site is a repository of "cultural information" about ethnic groups and their health beliefs. Harborview also modifies standards of care in ways that satisfy "cultural" as well as "medical" needs. . . .

Blending Western with non-Western medicine placed significant demands on the hospital and its employees, but they prided themselves on trying to live up to their mission. Accordingly, when a resident obstetrician/gynecologist, Leslie Miller, asked her colleagues if they could devise a productive way to respond to Somali mothers' requests for female "circumcision," the response was positive. My informant, describing their reaction, continued: "it didn't seem to be an odd and unusual thing . . . that's what we do, is we try to make sure that everybody is really comfortable . . . that's what we were so proud of doing at Harborview . . . meeting people's cultural needs" (Int6). Finding a way to fold genital cutting into Harborview's practice, then, fit nicely with the mission of the institution, which both ascribed cultural motivations to its patients and counted upon their ability to adapt to a modified Western medical approach.

On this rationale, the medical director approved a plan to hold focus groups with Somali mothers. The initiating physician, Miller, facilitated three discussions with a total of 36 women. Notes from the focus groups indicate that the mothers were amenable to a modified version of genital cutting. Because they had all undergone infibulation as girls, they were intimately familiar with the short- and long-term suffering that often accompanied the practice and they did not want their daughters to be infibulated. But neither did they want to abandon the practice entirely. An informant reported: "[T]hey were not interested in their daughters having *that* [infibulation] done to them. But at the same time they weren't interested in the daughters not having *anything* done" (Int8). The mothers explained that they desired to preserve some form of the practice as a nod to their religion and tradition, but also because they believed that it bonded their daughters to their community and marked the transition from girl to woman. Aesthetics, "purity," and the prevention of premarital sex, they claimed, were not considerations.

The notes revealed that the mothers asked that clinics offer a procedure in which a small piece of tissue would be removed as painlessly as possible. Miller explained that they would not remove tissue, but could possibly offer a small incision in the prepuce (or foreskin) of the clitoris that would draw blood. The mothers, with one exception, agreed that this would be sufficient. Similar compromises had been made in East Africa and elsewhere, so some of the mothers may have been familiar with this kind of alternative (though Somalia has been particularly isolated in this regard) (Gruenbaum, 1991; see also Abed et al., 1995; Isa, Shuib, and Othman, 1999).

The following June a committee convened to discuss whether Miller's proposal satisfied principles of medical ethics and, if so, to work out the details of its delivery. The eight-member committee included only physicians: a urologist, a plastic surgeon, and five pediatricians, one of whom was a specialist in bioethics. Defending the idea of an impermeable professional boundary, physicians saw the issue as firmly within their "scope of practice" and subject to the same privacy laws that guarantee the right to abortion in the United States. When asked if nonphysicians had been consulted, one informant insisted: "this is a matter of privacy between a patient and a family. . . . [It's not any] outsiders' business if there is consent with discussion with a patient and family. So, no . . ." (Int3). In line with this thinking, the physicians did not consult with other experts or interest groups, such as anthropologists or anti-FGC activists.

Subsequent to deliberation, the committee wrote a proposal recommending that the medical staff at the Children's Clinic offer a one centimeter incision in the prepuce (foreskin of the clitoris) under a topically applied local anesthetic. Described as a "prepotomy" ("prep" referring to the prepuce and "otomy" meaning incision), there would be no tissue removal, no need for sutures, and little or no scarring. The procedure would be performed on girls 11 and older who signed a consent form after being interviewed separately from their parents to ascertain their understanding of and desire for the procedure. It would then be performed by physicians under "direct supervision and assistance of Somali midwives," with a follow-up three days later. The clinic and the midwife would split a $40 fee. The medical director sent the recommendation to the state attorney general for review in light of the (then-pending, but soon to be passed) federal law against "female genital mutilation."

The effort to stop implementation of the proposal was led by Patricia Schroeder, Meserak Ramsey, and Mariama Barrie-Diamond. Schroeder was a U.S. Representative (D–Colorado) and the sponsor of the anti-FGM law. Ramsey and Barrie-Diamond grew up in Ethiopia and Sierra Leone, respectively, and later moved to the United States; both underwent infibulation as children. Barrie-Diamond had written about her genital cutting experience for *Essence* magazine. Ramsey had founded the U.S. arm of an organization dedicated to the eradication of FGCs, the Foundation for Women's Health Research and Development. In addition to contacting the hospital personally, all three publicized the proposal through the media, activist networks, and conferences. As a result, the hospital began receiving letters and phone calls from individuals opposed to the proposal.

My informants interpreted the outcry to be the machinations of "rabid feminists" (Int5), "zealots" (Int3), and "radicals" (Int2). Nevertheless, the opponents were ultimately successful in halting the implementation of the physicians' proposal. The attorney general concluded that the procedure would not violate the law, but told the medical director to abandon the proposal nonetheless. Still frustrated many years later, one informant behind the proposal remarked that they had made a "spectacular misjudgment of the political climate" (Int6). Reflecting the weariness of the proposal's advocates, *The Seattle Times* (1996) story about the decision to abandon the proposal was four sentences long and quoted a hospital spokesperson saying only: "we're not going to do it." How did the physicians and their opponents come to have such diametrically opposed evaluations of the proposed procedure?

The Physicians' Logic

The minutes from the committee meeting, my interviews, and the quotations from physicians included in newspaper accounts reveal physicians' rationale for endorsing the proposal. Prepotomy, they argued, was a significant departure from infibulation and, therefore, a meaningful cultural change enacted thoughtfully by a self-conscious community. Though they were proposing to cut girls' genitals, physicians and hospital staff insisted that the prepotomy was different: "No one was out to practice female genital mutilation," said one informant (Int6); while another explained, "It's not *that* you are doing a procedure down there, it's *what* you're doing down there" (Int1). When pushed in the news coverage, the hospital staff insisted that they were not proposing to perform "female genital mutilation" or "female circumcision." The medical director, for example, explained: "No one is contemplating doing those rituals most people asso-

ciate with female circumcision . . . Medical and ethical standards would prohibit any procedures that mutilate or unnecessarily remove tissue from a female's genitals" (Paulson, 1996). Similarly, the obstetrician-gynecologist who initiated the deliberations was quoted saying that the mothers were "asking for a small incision, a bloodletting . . . It's very different than what happened to them" (Paulson, 1996). And a public relations officer explained: "We are not now doing female circumcisions at Harborview, nor are we considering doing female circumcisions" (Brune, 1996). From their perspective prepotomy was not "mutilation"; the move to prepotomy, then, marked a significant and positive cultural change.

Reflecting the medical center's commitment to cultural compromise, physicians expressed mixed ideas about Somali culture. Ultimately, though, they applied a dynamic model of culture, believing that the Somalis were capable of choosing to adapt to U.S. culture without entirely abandoning their traditions. On the one hand, physicians saw culture as a powerful force in the lives of their patients. They expressed this with the language of "cultural need," a phrase that was used by four of my informants and appeared in two news articles and four of the archived correspondences. That they took cultural influence seriously is evident in their concerns that the mothers of their Somali patients would have their daughters infibulated in the absence of an alternative. Physicians remarked that the mothers threatened to take their daughters to Somalia if Harborview did not offer a procedure; others mentioned that there was a traditional practitioner in Vancouver who was known to do infibulations, and they discussed one focus group participant who said that, if the physicians did not offer a procedure, she would do it herself. Physicians believed, then, that immigrants held "traditional" or "historical" health-related beliefs that they could not be expected to abandon wholesale upon arrival in the United States.

On the other hand, physicians did not see Somalis as culture-bound. In fact, they envisioned that prepotomy would be a "bridg[e]" between infibulation and abandonment of genital cutting altogether. One informant explained:

we were dealing with a group that's not yet fully acculturated into the United States . . . you are probably more likely to make progress by working with them in a way that didn't harm their children, and then sort of allowing them to . . . recognize that this past practice was not such a good idea . . . The odds were that their daughters who would become acculturated to the United States would probably not be coming back in 20 years seeking the same sort of thing for their daughters. And so that this was seen as sort of a bridging procedure (Int1).

Instead of a blind following of tradition, physicians argued that the Somalis' desire for genital cutting was "analogous" to that of Jewish families in the U.S. who practice male circumcision (Int5):

So the male circumcision . . . is very important and everybody recognizes it as a legitimate cultural need. Female circumcision, you know, has not had that same recognition. But it certainly has the same long tradition. It's been done for thousands of years. It's been done over many different religious groups. It continues to be done, even though it's been made illegal in many countries. And so I think you have to ask, well why are people doing it? Are they doing it just because they are uneducated and, you know, don't understand this is a barbaric procedure? Or is it really meeting some need within the society (Int5)?

Comparing FGCs and male circumcision, physicians resisted the idea that Americans were culture-less and Somalis culture-bound. Instead, they drew connections between Somali and American culture. From their perspective, Somalis were not incomprehensibly "traditional," they were like Jewish Americans who also followed a tradition of medically unnecessary genital cutting because of its symbolic meaning.

Physicians and hospital staff also believed that the ritual could be modified symbolically as well as physically. One informant suggested that:

there was a possibility to transform this particular procedure into really a coming of age procedure that involved a lot of intergenerational communication, really history, health training, and education; that you could transform this into something that could be very positive for families and for their own communities (Int6).

They believed, then, that something quite good could come out of prepotomy. This sense was facilitated by their dismissal of the concern that genital cutting was a way to symbolically indoctrinate Somali girls into a gendered subservience. They saw Somali women as powerful members of their community. One informant said:

The stereotype of, you know, the submissive woman being forced to have this procedure by sort of a patriarchal society doesn't really hold up, you know, in my own personal experience with this culture. These [Somali women] are very strong, capable women who run their families with a usually pretty clear control (Int6).

Drawing on familiar feminist ideas, committee members agreed that, if anything, it would be *inequitable* to deny girls the procedure, especially given that the procedure they had in mind involved less physical alteration and risk than male circumcision. Prepotomy, committee members felt, was simply a matter of "medical equity" or equal treatment for different kinds of patients (Int9). They had already modified the standard of care for Somali boys: they were circumcising them at puberty instead of infancy, per Somali tradition. Offering a procedure to girls, too, seemed only fair.

In sum, committee members believed that the Somali community "needed" an alternative to infibulation. They felt strongly that, if they failed to offer a procedure, girls would undergo a procedure that was more extensive, painful, and dangerous than the one they could offer. In that sense, they ascribed power to culture to shape Somali choices. However, they rejected the idea that Somalis could not change and the notion that Somali women were subject to a superautonomous culture. Instead, Somali culture included traditions that were followed for complex reasons that Somalis could be reflective about, just like Americans. With the support and encouragement of physicians, they believed, Somalis would choose prepotomy and later abandon cutting altogether. Even as they saw culture as an influential force, then, their model of culture allowed for cultural evolution. This was a dynamic model. . . .

The Opponents' Logic

One of the physicians named in the newspaper coverage received phone calls and letters from opponents of the proposal. He kept and archived 25 letters and 17 postcards from an elementary school class (which I count as one "letter"); all but one objected to the proposal. These letters reveal that the resistance to the physicians' proposal centered around disagreement as to whether the move from infibulation to prepotomy was, truly, change.

The opponents' contrasting evaluation of the Somali interest in abandoning infibulation in favor of a prepotomy reflected a belief that they were essentially culture-bound. Opponents' arguments against the proposal involved a contrast between a "traditional" Somali culture and a culture-less or lightly cultural America characterized primarily by its commitment to protecting the supposedly universal rights of its citizens. For many opponents, the United States was an exemplar of social progress,

whereas Somalis were "traditional" and genital cutting was the embodiment of their cultural backwardness. Representative Schroeder's letter is illustrative of this approach, contrasting "mainstream" Western medicine with "barbari[sm]." She writes: "Quite frankly this apparent push for such a barbaric procedure by a respected, mainstream medical establishment both baffles and horrifies me." Another opponent insists, simply, "This horrible violence has no place in a civilized and democratic society . . ." (Manitoba, Canada).

Echoing Okin, some opponents explicitly placed the idea that Somalis have a right-to-culture in opposition to human rights. One, for example, argued: "even if the parents of children are authorising this operation, the rights of little girls should be considered above the so-called 'cultural rights' of ignorant parents" (West Sussex, UK). Other speakers also freely described the difference between "them" and "us" in terms of a linear notion of progress. One, who used the term "slice" (instead of the physicians' preferred "incision"), wrote:

We, as a civilized society must be vigilant in protecting the rights of all children, especially in this country. . . . The little girl's [sic] whose parents come from Somalia or wherever, are growing up American, which means equality and protection is their right (New York, NY).

This opponent contrasted America, a civilized country that protects children's rights, to Somalia, a country that does not. Similarly, Ramsey, one of the activists who spearheaded the opposition, was quoted in *The Seattle Times* (Ostrom, 1996) arguing that girls "*in this country . . . have a right to protect their bodies*" (emphasis added). Another opponent echoed her: "this is taking away their rights." Opponents' arguments against the proposal, then, characterized Somalis as irrational and ignorant carriers of old traditions. In contrast, the United States was culturally superior or, perhaps, culture-less, having evolved into a rational society organized around universal truths.

Believing the Somalis to be culture-bound, opponents evaluated the move to prepotomy as a continuation instead of an interruption of their cultural practices. While the extent of cutting and tissue removal was significant to physicians, it failed to impress opponents. They asserted that all forms of genital cutting were unacceptable, prepotomy no less than infibulation. They noted, correctly, that the prepotomy involved cutting genitals and was, thus, genital cutting. One informant explained that opponents argued that the practice was "a bad thing *in any form* and we can't do it" (Int8). Another, recalling a conversation with a particular opponent, explained that she objected to "*anybody* having *anything* to do with anything about sexual parts of a woman's body . . ." (Int5).

The letters, too, suggested that opponents felt that both infibulation and prepotomy were fairly and accurately described by the phrase "female genital mutilation." One opponent, who described the prepotomy as a "limited form of female genital mutilation," explicitly objected to any genital cutting, no matter how minimal; she headlined her letter: "STOP ANY TYPE OF FEMALE GENITAL MUTILATION" (Seattle, WAa; capitalization in the original). For this opponent, that the procedure was "limited" did not mean it was not "mutilation." Likewise, Representative Schroeder warned physicians that she entirely intended for a "ritual bloodletting" to be equivalent to infibulation under the law. She wrote: "The clear intent of the legislation the President signed was to criminalize *any* medically unnecessary procedure involving female genitalia. What Harborview appears to be considering would violate that clear intent."

In addition to objecting to the prepotomy, some opponents were concerned that offering one version of genital cutting would open the door to others. Physicians might perform increasingly extensive procedures once becom-

ing comfortable with the idea of cutting female genitals and facing an "escalation" of "demands and pressures" from immigrants (Seattle, WAb). This concern is certainly not baseless. Given that physicians perform male circumcisions and intersex and cosmetic female genital surgeries, it seems reasonable to worry that they might do to Somali teenagers what they are already doing to adult women and children of both sexes.

For opponents, prepotomy also represented the persistence of Somali cultural practice because they believed that the ritual, however minor, would allow the *symbolic* meaning of cutting to survive. Less optimistic than physicians about the possibility that the move to prepotomy would be accompanied by change in the practice's meaning, opponents argued that genital cutting was designed to teach girls their subordinate place in Somali society and, therefore, infibulation and prepotomy were symbolically identical. They explained: it "is the manifestation of society's fear of women's sexuality" (Manitoba, Canada) and is done "solely to make men feel as though they are in control of the womyn [sic] in their lives" (Ontario, Canada). The reporter for *The Seattle Times* (Ostrom, 1996) articulated this objection when, after describing the proposed procedure and discussing the medical rationale, she noted that: "None of that has placated those who say that even talking about cutting female genitals legitimizes a barbaric practice, one that disempowers women and serves to keep them out of the American mainstream." The reporter explains that opponents are uncomfortable entertaining the idea of an alternative cutting procedure on the assumption that doing so threatens to prop up foreign patriarchy in the United States. So, when physicians argued that the prepotomy was only "symbolic," opponents explained that this was *precisely* the problem. In truth, how exactly prepotomy would have been made meaningful is difficult to know.

The extent of the cutting and potential for harm was significant for physicians, then, but not for opponents who felt that the prepotomy was physically and symbolically equivalent. For them, a move to prepotomy represented a continuance of the Somali's genital cutting practice, not its end. Therefore, it was not cultural change, it was cultural persistence.

Based on the beliefs that compromise was impossible (because Somali culture was deeply traditional and resistant to change) and that adoption of the prepotomy represented continuance and not adaption, opponents concluded that the physicians were capitulating to instead of compromising with Somali culture. Criticizing physicians for being *excessively* flexible, one opponent wrote: "Are we bending over backwards to meet demands from an immigrant cultural group that we envision as not having much power in the United States?" (Seattle, WA). For opponents, then, offering a genital cutting procedure did not help Somalis adapt to American culture through compromise; rather, it was adopting (backward) Somali values wholesale. The physicians' flexibility was equivalent to becoming "barbaric" and "uncivilized."

Indeed, if prepotomy was "savage," "evil," and "an act of barbarism," then so were the physicians and their procedure (East Sussex, UK; also Hempstead, NY; New York, NY; San Jose, CAa; Washington, DC; Westhung, NY; West Sussex, UK). One opponent wrote: "Whatever your reasoning concerning cutting young girls, it is clearly wrong. Even if a child asks for this ritual, she is only speaking the words of her parents. Barbaric, uncivilized words. Just like yours" (New York, NY). For the opponents, offering a prepotomy was a misguided attempt at political correctness and a ceding of American values to an immigrant group who was "insist[ing]" upon cultural accommodation (Napa, CA; San Jose, CA).

These arguments are consistent with a reified model of culture that wraps some cultures but not others in nonpermeable packages with straightforward memberships and discrete boundaries. Their description of Somali culture as "traditional" and the unfavorable comparison with a modern, progressive United States, placed Somalis among those people [who] are assumed to bring an ancient culture unchanged through time. Attributing a profound resilience to Somali culture, they foreclosed the possibility of (true) cultural adaptation. Even if the material practice changed, they argued, the symbolic meaning of genital cutting would persist. From the opponents' point of view, then, Somalis were not compromising, they were demanding that the United States adapt to them. Likewise, physicians were not multicultural heroes modeling cross-cultural tolerance, they were culturally relativist villains who were sacrificing sacred American values by capitulating to the backward beliefs of an immigrant group.

Despite their strong language and use of a reified model, however, opponents raised important questions. We do not know how prepotomy would have been made meaningful by the Somalis. Nor could we ensure that social pressure would not make adolescent consent meaningless. And physicians do, indeed, perform more extensive procedures on infants and adult women; it is not unreasonable to be concerned that we might add adolescent girls to the list of individuals who can legally undergo genital cutting practices.

SUMMARY OF FINDINGS AND ONGOING RELEVANCE

. . . . The physicians' argument that the adoption of prepotomy signified meaningful cultural change was driven by a commitment to a dynamic model of culture. They rejected the idea that Somalis were irrationally committed to uniquely barbaric practices as well as the idea that Americans were entirely autonomous from culture. Comparing FGCs to male circumcision and emphasizing Somali women's autonomy from both men and their culture, physicians described a group of women who were negotiating issues familiar to Americans: imperfect traditions and sensitive family and community relationships. . . .

In contrast, opponents subscribed to a reified model of culture that led them to interpret the request for the modified procedure as the persistence of a genital cutting tradition. Opponents characterized Somali culture as obstinately tied to an ancient patriarchy. They observed that the change was only a move from one form of genital cutting to another and they imbued the practice with a stable, discernable, coherent meaning that would persist even in the face of changing contexts (from Somalia to Seattle) and practices (from infibulation to prepotomy). . . .

This debate is far from resolved. In 2010, the American Academy of Pediatrics (2010b) released an official statement in support of a similar procedure in clinics: a "pricking or incising the clitoral skin . . . no more of an alteration than ear piercing" (p. 1092). They supported such a procedure with the same logic articulated by the physicians in 1996. "The ritual nick," they argued:

is not physically harmful and is much less extensive than routine newborn male genital cutting . . . [and it] may build trust between hospitals and immigrant communities, save some girls from undergoing disfiguring and life-threatening procedures in their native countries, and play a role in the eventual eradication of FGC (p. 1092).

Using a now-familiar logic, Equality Now (2010) mobilized an opposition movement in response. In their "Urgent Alert," they argued that "pricking, piercing and incising of girls' genitalia are forms of female genital mutilation . . ." designed to oppress women and they recommended a letter writing campaign to pressure the AAP to retract its recommendation (p. 1).

The World Health Organization, United Nations Population Fund, United Nations Children's Fund, and United Nations Development Fund for Women also issued a joint press release condemning the AAP recommendation (WHO et al., 2010). Joining Equality Now in using the term "mutilation" instead of the physicians' "cutting," they described a nick as a violation of human rights, contesting the claim that "some forms of FGM are not harmful," and they argued that offering a "nick" may "give way to more invasive procedures" (pp. 1-2).

One month after the statement, the Academy revoked their recommendation (AAP 2010a).

CONCLUSIONS

The lessons learned from the controversy at Harborview Medical Center are consistent with the literature on debates about veiling in Western societies . . . and other practices like voluntary sex segregation, the desire to enter polygamous relationships, and arranged marriages (Ahmed, 1982; Arndt, 2000; Deveaux, 2007; Dustin and Phillips, 2008). This research has shown that a reified model of culture can harden cross-cultural antagonism, in part by making cultural tolerance seem incompatible with feminist principles, thereby justifying controlling and penalizing policies. In my case study, opponents of the prepotomy, informed by this model, reinforced negative stereotypes of Africa and rejected the possibility that the Somalis could transform genital cutting into something materially and symbolically consistent with gender equality. They also trivialized

---

Editor's note: In November 2012, the United Nations Member States approved a groundbreaking resolution calling for an end to "female genital mutilation" worldwide (United Nations, 2012).

the abandonment of infibulation, castigating physicians for pursuing a harm reduction strategy designed to protect girls from the worst kind of genital cutting. Instead, they endorsed zero tolerance, a position echoed in the federal U.S. law against "female genital mutilation" that would pass that year. Meanwhile, American culture remained uninterrogated on the assumption that it was superior, based on rational truths, or both. For the opponents, feminism was indeed incompatible with multiculturalism.

In addition to confirming the existing literature on cultural groups and practices, this case shows that a reified model can also shape perceptions of cultural *change* by disallowing the possibility of meaningful cultural adaptation altogether. If opponents could perceive the move from infibulation to prepotomy as no change at all—if they objected to both the potential symbolic meaning of the practice as well as the material outcome—then it is likely that there is nothing the Somalis could have done, short of an overt rejection of Somali culture in favor of mainstream American values, that would have been satisfying to the opponents.

This is a suggestive finding. It suggests that, for some, perceptions of a lack of autonomy from culture are not dependent on the choices a presumably culture-bound person makes. Instead, insofar as the reified model of culture drives perceptions, the fact that people are believed to be culture-bound may shape the evaluation of *all* of their choices. As a hypothetical, imagine that a Somali girl who immigrated with her parents as a child, and who was spared genital cutting, elects to undergo labiaplasty as an adult. Imagine she approaches the plastic surgeon with the same concerns that nonimmigrant American women bring: a concern that her labia are too large, too long, or asymmetrical. If the same dynamics are at play in the interpretation of her motivations as were at play in the opponents' framing of prepotomy, it is likely that some will say that she is seeking "female genital mutilation." No matter how similar "their" practices become to "ours," then, Somalis and other members of groups deemed culture-bound may face scrutiny that others do not. The same choices that nonimmigrant American women make—the choice to undergo cosmetic genital surgery, but perhaps also the choice to marry young, be a stay-at-home mother, eschew higher education, dress modestly, or attend a fundamentalist or orthodox church—may be more likely to be interpreted as a sign of internalized oppression when Somali women make them. In other words, all choices made by someone who is presumably culture-bound can be interpreted as manifestations of her lack of autonomy, and can be used to condemn her culture as well.

It remains to be seen if using this lens to analyze similar debates will reveal similar phenomenon. If a young Somali girl did not submit to any kind of genital cutting, but still chose to protect her "honor" until marriage, is she interpreted as principled or traditional? If a Muslim woman chooses not to cover her hair, but wears, instead, a cloth-covered barrette as a reference to the hijab, is she oppressed or innovative? Likewise, if an Indian woman refuses to allow her parents to arrange her marriage, but promises not to marry unless she has their approval, is this compromise or submission? Understanding how models of culture shape perceptions of cultural change may shed great light on these debates. . . .

The dynamic model of culture . . . may be used to mischaracterize cultural change in two ways. First, it may undersell cultural resilience, offering those who mobilize it an opportunity to trivialize social justice concerns and dismiss activists and scholars as irrelevant. This is the concern that Okin (1997) was articulating when she posed her question: "is multiculturalism bad for women?" Okin is taking seriously whether we are able to *ensure* that we are protecting both marginalized communities and their most vulnerable members. While the reified model of culture suggests that we cannot do both, the dynamic model can be used to suggest that her question is not worth asking.

Second, the dynamic model of culture allows one to dismiss the possibility that acculturation into American society may reinforce or even introduce the ideology and practice of women's subordination. An immigrant group can be acculturated into *new* ways of oppressing its women (Espiritu, 2000; Hondagneu-Sotelo, 1994). The physicians believed that the prepotomy would initiate acculturation to a society in which "genital mutilation" did not happen. In fact, however, adult women increasingly undergo genital alteration in U.S. clinics and hospitals: a woman can legally have collagen injected into her "g-spot" or her hymen "reconstructed"; she can have her clitoral foreskin removed (circumcision proper) or her clitoris reduced in size; she can have her labia trimmed if she thinks they are "obtrusive" or engorged with injections of fat if she thinks they are "too thin"; and she can have [the] size of her vaginal opening reduced with stitches for a tighter fit during penile-vaginal intercourse (colloquially known as a "husband's stitch" when it is performed during an episiotomy repair). These are defined by some as "enhancing" instead of "mutilating," but in some cases the effect is not dissimilar to what we include under the label "female genital mutilation" when it occurs elsewhere (Lewis and Gunning, 1998; Sheldon and Wilkinson, 1998). In other words, while the physicians saw the prepotomy as a "bridging" procedure between infibulation and the abandonment of genital cutting, it could just as easily become a bridge between American-reviled and American-endorsed genital cutting, with an already available, legal cosmetic procedure emerging as a new coming-of-age ritual for young Somali girls.

This hypothetical suggests that people drawing on the dynamic model of culture may take for granted that acculturation will conform to a set of progressive values that they believe permeate their own culture. This may lead to overly simple evaluations of the ease with which cultural change can be chaperoned and the easy dismissal of the need to engage with other constituencies. An analysis informed by the dynamic model, in other words, can be facile if it suggests that life-affirming cultural change is easy and inevitable, erasing the vision and vigilance required to establish truly functional, integrated, egalitarian nations.

NOTE

1. My university's institutional review board (IRB) did not grant me permission to interview Somali community members because of concerns that they might self-incriminate.

REFERENCES

Abed, Asali, Naif Khamaysi, Yunis Aburabia, Simha Letzer, Buteina Halihal, Mōshe Sadovsky, Benjamin Maoz, and R. Belmaker. 1995. "Ritual Female Genital Surgery among Bedouin in Israel." *Archives of Sexual Behavior* 24(5): 573–77.

Abu-Lughod, Lila. 1991. "Writing Against Culture." Pp. 137–62 in *Recapturing Anthropology: Working in the Present*, edited by R. G. Fox. Santa Fe, NM: School of American Research Press.

———. 2002, "Do Muslim Women Really Need Saving? Anthropological Reflections on Cultural Relativism and Its Others." *American Anthropologist* 104(3): 783–90.

Ahmadu, Fuambai. 2001. "Rites and Wrongs: An Insider/ Outsider Reflects on Power and Excision." Pp. 283–312 in *Female 'Circumcision' in Africa: Culture, Controversy, and Change*, edited by Bettina Shell-Duncan and Ylva Hernlund. Boulder, CO: Lynne Rienner Publishers.

Ahmed, Leila. 1982. "Western Ethnocentrism and Perceptions of the Harem." *Feminist Studies* 8(3): 521–34.

American Academy of Pediatrics (AAP) Committee on Bioethics. 2010a. "American Academy of Pediatrics withdraws Policy Statement on Female Genital Cutting." *AAP News Room*, May 27. Retrieved June 14, 2010 (www.aap.org/advocacy/releases/fgc-may27-2010 .htm).

———. 2010b. "Policy Statement on Ritual Genital Cutting of Female Minors." *Pediatrics* 125(5): 1088–93.

Anthias, Floya. 2002. "Beyond Feminism and Multi-culturalism: Locating Difference and the Politics of Location." *Women's Studies International Forum* 25(3): 275–86.

Appadurai, Arjun, 1988. "Putting Hierarchy in Its Place." *Cultural Anthropology* 3(1): 36–49.

Arndt, Susan. 2000. "African Gender Trouble and African Womanism: An Interview with Chikwenye Ogunyemi and Wanjira Muthoni." *Signs* 25(3): 709–26.

Benhabib, Seyla. 2002. *The Claims of Culture: Equality and Diversity in the Global Era.* Princeton, NJ and Oxford, UK: Princeton University Press.

Bloul, Rachel. 1994. "Victims or Offenders? 'Other' Women in French Sexual Politics." *The European Journal of Women's Studies* 3(3): 251–68.

Bourdieu, Pierre. 1977. *Outline of a Theory of Practice.* Cambridge, UK: Cambridge University Press.

Boyle, Elizabeth Heger. 2002. *Female Genital Cutting: Cultural Conflict in the Global Community.* Baltimore, MD: Johns Hopkins University Press.

Brune, Tom. 1996. "Refugees' Beliefs Don't Travel Well: Compromise Plan on Circumcision of Girls Gets Little Support." *Chicago Tribune*, October 28. Retrieved December 11, 2004 (http://articles.chicagotribune.com /1996-10-28/news/9610280094_1_somali-community -circumcision-refugees).

Calmore, John, 1992. "Critical Race Theory, Archie Shepp, and Fire Music: Securing an Authentic Intellectual Life in a Multicultural World." *Southern California Law Review,* 65: 2129–230.

Chanock, Martin. 2002. "Human Rights and Cultural Branding: Who Speaks and How." Pp. 38–67 in *Cultural Transformation and Human Rights in Africa,* edited by Abdullahi An-Na'im. London, UK and New York; Zed Books.

Collins, Patricia Hill. 1991. *Black Feminist Thought: Knowledge, Consciousness, and the Politics of Empowerment.* New York: Routledge.

Cooke, Miriam. 2002. "Saving Brown Women." *Signs* 28(1): 468–70.

Cowan, Jane, 2001. "Ambiguities of an Emancipatory Discourse: The Making of a Macedonian Minority in Greece." Pp. 152–76 in *Culture and Rights: Anthropological Perspectives,* edited by Jane Cowan, Marie-Bénédicte Dembour, and Richard Wilson. Cambridge, UK: Cambridge University Press.

Cowan, Jane, Marie-Bénédicte Dembour, and Richard Wilson, 2001. "Introduction," Pp. 1–26 in *Culture and Rights: Anthropological Perspectives,* edited by Jane Cowan, Marie-Bénédicte Dembour, and Richard Wilson. Cambridge, UK; Cambridge University Press.

Davies, Scott. 1999. "From Moral Duty to Cultural Rights: A Case Study of Political Framing in Education." *Sociology of Education* 72(1):1–21.

Deveaux, Monique. 2007. "Personal Autonomy and Cultural Tradition." Pp. 139–66 in *Sexual Justice/ Cultural Justice: Critical Perspectives in Political Theory and Practice,* edited by Barbara Arneil, Monique Deveaux, Rhita Dhamoon, and Avigail Eisenberg. London, UK and New York: Routledge.

Dustin, Moira and Anne Phillips. 2008. "Whose Agenda Is It? Abuses of Women and Abuses of 'Culture' in Britain." *Ethnicities* 8(3): 405–24.

Equality Now. 2010. "Urgent Alert (April 29): Equality Now Calls on the American Academy of Pediatrics to Retract a Portion of their Policy Statement Endorsing Type (IV) Female Genital Mutilation of Female Minors." Retrieved May 9, 2010 (www.equalitynow.org /node/584).

Eriksen, Thomas. 2001. "Between Universalism and Relativism: A Critique of the UNESCO Concept of Culture." Pp. 127–48 in *Culture and Rights: Anthropological Perspectives,* edited by Jane Cowan, Marie-Bénédicte Dembour, and Richard Wilson. Cambridge, UK: Cambridge University Press.

Espiritu, Yen Le. 2000. *Asian American Women and Men: Labor, Laws, and Love.* Walnut Creek, CA: Alta Mira Press.

Fournier, Pascale. 2002. "The Ghettoisation of Difference in Canada: 'Rape by Culture' and the Danger of a 'Cultural Defence' in Criminal Law Trials." *Manitoba Law Journal* 29: 81–119.

Fraser, Nancy, 1995. "From Redistribution to Recognition? Dilemmas of Justice in a 'Post-Socialist' Age." *New Left Review* I/212 (July/August): 67–93.

———. 2000. "Rethinking Recognition." *New Left Review* 3 (May-June): 107–20.

Gruenbaum, Ellen. 1991. "The Islamic Movement, Development and Health Education: Recent Changes in the Health of Rural Women in Central Sudan." *Social Science and Medicine* 33 (6):637–45.

Gupta, Akhil and James Ferguson. 1992. "Space, Identity, and the Politics of Difference." *Cultural Anthropology* 7(1): 6–23.

Hondagneu-Sotelo, Pierrette. 1994. *Gendered Transition: Mexican Experiences in Immigration.* Berkeley: University of California Press.

Isa, Ab. Rahman, Rashidah Shuib, and M. Shukri Othman. 1999. "The Practice of Female Circumcision among Muslims in Kelantan, Malaysia." *Reproductive Health Matters* 7(13): 137–44.

Jackson, Jean. 1995. "Culture, Genuine, and Spurious: The Politics of Indianness in the Vaupés, Colombia." *American Ethnologist* 22(1): 3–27.

Koso-Thomas, Olayinka. 1987. *The Circumcision of Women: A Strategy for Eradication.* London, UK: Zed Books.

Lazreg, Marnia. 1988. "Feminism and Difference: The Perils of Writing as a Woman on Women in Algeria." *Feminist Studies* 14(1): 81–107.

Lewis, Hope and Isabelle Gunning. 1998. "Cleaning Our Own House: 'Exotic' and Familial Human Rights Violations." *Buffalo Human Rights Law Review* 4:123–40.

Merry, Sally Engle. 2001. "Changing Rights, Changing Culture." Pp. 31–55 in *Culture and Rights: Anthropological Perspectives,* edited by Jane Cowan, Marie-Bénédicte Dembour, and Richard Wilson, Cambridge, UK: Cambridge University Press.

———. 2006. *Human Rights and Gender Violence: Translating International Law into Local Justice.* Chicago and London, UK: The University of Chicago Press.

Mohanty, Chandra. 1988. "Under Western Eyes: Feminist Scholarship and Colonial Discourses." Pp. 51–80 in *Third World Women and the Politics of Feminism,* edited by Chandra Mohanty, Ann Russo, and Lourdes Torres. Indianapolis: Indiana University Press.

Mushaben, Joyce. 2005. "More Than Just a Bad Hair Day." Pp. 182–223 In *Crossing Over: Comparing Recent Migration in the United States and Europe,* edited by Holger Henke. Lanham, MD: Lexington Books.

Narayan, Uma. 1997. *Dislocating Cultures: Identities, Traditions, and Third World Feminism.* New York: Routledge.

———. 1998. "Essence of Culture and a Sense of History: A Feminist Critique of Cultural Essentialism." *Hypatia* 13(2): 86–106.

———. 2000. "Undoing the 'Package Picture' of Cultures." *Signs* 25(4): 1083–86.

Njambi, Wairimu Ngaruiya. 2004. "Dualisms and Female Bodies in Representations of African Female Circumcision: A Feminist Critique." *Feminist Theory* 5(3): 281–303.

Okin, Susan. 1997. "Is Multiculturalism Bad for Women?" *Boston Review* 22(5): 25–8.

Ostrom, Carol. 1996. "Harborview Debates Issue of Circumcision of Muslim Girls." *The Seattle Times,* September 6, Retrieved December 11, 2004 (http://community.seattletimes.nwsource.com/archive/?date=19960913&slug=2348974).

Parekh, Bhikhu. 1995. "Cultural Pluralism and the Limits of Diversity." *Alternatives* 20(4): 431–57.

Paulson, Tom. 1996. "Harborview, Somalis Try to Compromise on Female Circumcision." *Seattle Post-Intelligencer,* September 13. Retrieved December 11, 2004 (www.highbeam.com/doc/1G1-64677311.html).

Phillips, Anne. 2003. "When Culture Means Gender: Issues of Cultural Defence in the English Courts." *Modern Law Review* 66(4): 510–31.

———. 2007. "What is 'Culture'?" Pp. 15–29 in *Sexual Justice/Cultural Justice: Critical Perspectives in Political Theory and Practice,* edited by Barbara Ameil, Monique Deveaux, Rita Dhamoon, and Avigail Eisenberg, London, UK and New York: Routledge.

Piot, Charles. 2007. "Representing Africa and the Kasinga Asylum Case." Pp. 157–66 in *Transcultural Bodies:*

Female Genital Cutting in Global Context, edited by Ylva Hernlund and Bettina Shell-Duncan. New Brunswick, NJ and London, UK: Rutgers University Press.

Razack, Sherene, 1995. "Domestic Violence as Gender Persecution: Policing the Borders of Nation, Race and Gender." *Canadian Journal of Women and the Law* 8(1): 45–88.

———. 2007. "The 'Sharla Law Debate' in Ontario: The Modernity/Premodernity Distinction in Legal Efforts to Protect Women from Culture." *Feminist Legal Studies* 15(1): 3–32.

Rudy, Kathy. 2000. "Difference and Indifference: A U.S. Feminist Response to Global Politics." *Signs* 25(4): 1051–53.

Saguy, Abigail C. 2003. *What is Sexual Harassment?: From Capitol Hill to the Sorbonne.* Berkeley: University of California Press.

Said, Edward. 1978. *Orientalism.* New York: Vintage.

Seattle Times, The. 1996. "Hospital Won't Circumcise Girls." *The Seattle Times,* December 5. Retrieved December 11, 2004 (http://community.seattletimes.nwsource.com/archive/?date=19961205&slug=2363272).

Sewell, William. 1992. "A Theory of Structure: Duality, Agency, and Transformation." *American Journal of Sociology* 98(1): 1–29.

Sheldon, Sally and Stephen Wilkinson. 1998. "Female Genital Mutilation and Cosmetic Surgery: Regulating Non-Therapeutic Body Modification." *Bioethics* 12(4): 263–85.

Sieder, Rachel and Jessica Witchell. 2001. "Advancing Indigenous Claims through the Law: Reflections on the Guatemalan Peace Process." Pp. 201–25 in *Culture and Rights: Anthropological Perspectives,* edited by Jane Cowan, Marie-Bénédicte Dembour, and Richard Wilson. Cambridge, UK: Cambridge University Press.

Spivak, Gayatri Chakravorty. 1985. "Subaltern Studies: Deconstructing Historiography." Pp. 337–38 in *Subaltern Studies IV,* edited by Ranajlt Guha. Delhi, India: Oxford University Press.

———. 1988. "Can the Subaltern Speak?" Pp. 271–313 in *Marxism and the Interpretation of Culture,* edited by C. Nelson and L. Grossberg, Chicago: University of Illinois Press.

Stabile, Carol and Deepa Kumar. 2005. "Unveiling Imperialism: Media, Gender, and the War on Afghanistan." *Media, Culture, and Society* 27(5): 765–82.

Swidler, Ann. 1986. "Culture in Action: Symbols and Strategies." *American Sociological Review* 51:273–86.

———. 2001. *Talk of Love: How Culture Matters.* Chicago: University of Chicago Press.

Tully, James. 1995. *Strange Multiplicity: Constitutionalism in an Age of Diversity.* Cambridge, UK: Cambridge University Press.

Turner, Terence. 1993. "Anthropology and Multiculturalism: What is Anthropology that Multiculturalists Should be Mindful of It?" *Cultural Anthropology* 8(4): 411–29.

United Nations. 2012. "UN Committee Approves First-ever Text Calling for End to Female Genital Mutilation." Retrieved December 19, 2012 (http://www.un.org/apps /news/story.asp?NewsID=43625&Cr=violence+against+ women&Crl=#.UNIaKKzheSo).

Volpp, Leti. 1994. "(Mis)Identifying Culture: Asian Women and the 'Cultural Defense'." *Harvard Women's Law Journal* 17: 57–80.

———. 2000. "Blaming Culture for Bad Behavior." *Yale Journal of Law and the Humanities* 12: 89–117.

Wade, Lisa. 2009. "Defining Gendered Oppression in U.S. Newspapers: The Strategic Value of 'Female Genital Mutilation.' " *Gender and Society* 23(3): 293–314.

World Health Organization (WHO). 2008. *Eliminating Female Genital Mutilation: An Interagency Statement.* Geneva, Switzerland: World Health Organization.

WHO, UNFPA, UNICEF, and UNJFEM. 2010. "Regarding the 'Policy Statement-Ritual Genital Cutting of Female Minors' from the AAP." Retrieved June 14, 2010 (www.who.int/reproductivehealth/topics/fgm /fgm_app_statement.pdf).

FIXING THE BROKEN MALE MACHINE

MEIKA LOE

The quest for manhood—the effort to achieve, demonstrate, and prove masculinity—is rooted deep in American history, starting at least with the nineteenth century's self-made man.[1] But in the early twenty-first century, when gender equity is believed to be increasingly achievable and men are no longer the sole family breadwinners, male power and control are no longer assured. Scholars specializing in masculinity studies have had much to say about male confusion in the roughly thirty years preceding Viagra. Attempts to understand and locate "masculinity in crisis" are varied and incomplete, but crucial to an understanding of the success of the Viagra phenomenon.[2] . . .

Today, a new and profitable masculine recovery movement is being generated with the aid of a pharmaceutical drug, and the male body is reemerging as a site for confidence and control. . . . Now, millions of men turn to Viagra to reclaim something they lost. . . . [T]his . . . is a silent movement, forged by individuals who may be vaguely aware of other men pursuing "recovery" of potency confidence, and "life" at the same time. But for most of the participants, the recovery process is too personal and too stigmatizing to discuss.

The silence, privacy, and relative invisibility of this movement proved difficult for a sociologist wanting to talk with Viagra consumers. Many times I asked myself, Where do those who are wanting to recover their potency "hang out," besides in doctors' offices? This question was difficult to answer and left me feeling sympathy for the men who wanted an answer to the same question. Where did men turn who wanted to talk with other men about their experiences with ED or Viagra? In the end, the communities I found that are built around the experience of erectile dysfunction and recovery were support groups and Internet chat rooms. The majority of men featured in this chapter were members of male support groups or ED-themed Internet chat rooms when they agreed to talk with me. What emerges is a discussion of bodies in need of "fixing."

MALE BODIES IN NEED OF FIXING

In the late twentieth century, masculinity scholars began to write about the connections between manhood and men's bodies. Australian social scientist R. W. Connell wrote, "True masculinity is almost always thought to proceed from men's bodies."[3] Sander Gilman's work revealed how "aesthetic surgeries" such as penile implants can help in the achievement of masculinity. And sociologist Michael Kimmel suggested that the realms of health and fitness have replaced the workplace in the late twentieth century as the next major testing ground for masculinity, where body work inevitably becomes a "relentless test."[4] But few masculinity scholars have taken a critical perspective on current theories of the body as a machine or as a surface imprinted with social symbolism.[5] Likewise, limited scholarship on male sexual bodies suggests that sexuality, particularly heterosexuality, is a proving ground for masculinity.[6]

Only recently have researchers, particularly feminist social scientists, begun to expand their inquiries to include the medicalization of male bodies.[7] Since Viagra's release, a small number of women social scientists have written about the ways in which this product promises to reinforce "phallocentrism" or, in my words, "erect the patriarchy."[8] In other words, some are concerned that a product like Viagra may hinder ongoing efforts for gender equality. Others are concerned about the new commodification of masculinity and the related proliferation of mass insecurity around manhood.[9] Additionally, medical sociologists Mamo and Fishman have written about Viagra's potential for liberatory or disciplinary effects.[10] In contrast, most male scholars who study masculinity have yet to fully take up the question of the new medicalized male body or, more specifically, the Viagra body.[11]

How have men themselves responded to this newfound medical attention? In the following pages, medical professionals and patients use the language of "trouble" and "repair" as they grapple with "deficient" body parts, the concept of manhood, and medical diagnoses. In the process, they expose as constructs that which we take for granted; they imagine their bodies as machines, and they use Viagra as a tool for fixing their broken masculinity. And finally, they discover that Viagra not only solves problems but sometimes produces them as well.[12]

A PROBLEMATIC PACKAGE

Several years after Viagra's debut, I had a fascinating conversation with a doctor and his longtime patient about sexual dysfunction. Upon hearing about my research, a man I will call Gray had volunteered to help by bringing me to talk to the only expert he knew on Viagra, his doctor.[13] Dr. Bern, an internist in private practice in his seventies, and Gray, a retired business owner in his eighties, had a fifty-year history together.[14] As we sat in Dr. Bern's office in Los Angeles, California, discussing my research project, both men tried to convince me that masculinity was intimately tied to penile functioning.

DR. BERN: You see, sexual dysfunction in males is peculiar. I'm sure if someone is a paraplegic and can't walk he would feel psychologically deprived. But beyond the great obvious lack—people who don't see or hear as well, they don't feel like they have lost their manhood, you see. I must tell you, and I'm not a psychiatrist, but I think it is far more prevalent in males than it would be in females. The fact that if women don't have sexual gratification . . . It isn't that they don't miss it, but they don't have the psychological burden that males seem to have. Maybe it's a throwback to the time when the caveman went and dragged a woman out on his shoulder.

ML: So sexuality is integral to male identity?

Gray: Absolutely! [My wife and I] talked about it for a long time—well, a couple of weeks before the [prostate] operation itself. We talked about it's possible we may not be able to have sex because the apparatuses they had out didn't necessarily work. So you could go for the rest of your life without having sex. And [the doctor] is so right. You feel part of your manhood is gone.[15]

Doctor Bern uses an evolutionary example to construct contemporary male sexuality as overt, desirous, assertive, and central to masculinity, in contrast to femininity, which is passive and nonsexual. Manhood is seen as the ability to have sexual control of and desire for women. Most importantly, though, Dr. Bern and Gray agreed that the trouble associated with erectile dysfunction involves the psychological burden of the loss of manhood. Most of my male interview subjects, both consumers and practitioners, were in agreement on this point. If the penis is in trouble, so is the man.

You probably wouldn't understand it—it's a big part of manhood. Ever since you're a little boy growing up that's a part of your masculinity. And whether it's right or wrong, and however you deal with it—that's, well, I'm dealing with it and I seem to be okay. If a man gets an erection, or the boys in the shower compare each other, that's your masculinity. A lot of men don't like to admit it. (Phil, fifty-four years old, white, heterosexual, insurance broker)[16]

[Viagra] makes my penis larger, length and width-wise, and that's inherent to the macho thing of men. With impotence, I felt like part of my manhood has been lost. (Byron, seventy years old, white, heterosexual, unknown occupation)[17]

After many of these conversations, I began to see that for men like Byron, Phil, and Gray, gender and sexuality may be difficult to separate out. Masculinity requires sexuality, and vice versa.[18] In contrast, femininity has traditionally been constructed in opposition to masculinity and, thus, sexuality.[19] What these men were telling me was that sexuality, or "erectile health," is compulsory for men, integral to achieving and maintaining manhood. (Implicit here is the requirement that heterosexual desire is compulsory for men.) Or as Australian cultural critic Annie Potts would put it, in a phallus-centered world, "Every man must pump up for phallocracy."[20]

While men may not discuss their masculinity problems openly with a doctor, the comments above and Viagra's recent block-buster success are representative of a new global concern for the "broken," or impotent, male. Some social scientists have argued that gender is "accomplished" in daily life through our interactions with others. In other words, we perform and interactively "do" masculinity or femininity through our appearance, body language, tone of voice, etc. Following this logic, the "accomplishment" of masculinity is situated, to some extent, in erectile achievement.[21] Fixing the "male machine" and ensuring erectile functioning, for the patients quoted above and countless others, is a way to ensure masculin-ity. Just as some social scientists have argued that cosmetic surgery is institutional support for women to successfully accomplish and "do" femininity,[22] Viagra can be seen as a biotechno-logical tool used to ensure masculinity by fixing the broken male machine.

THE POORLY FUNCTIONING MALE MACHINE

As Donna Haraway first argued in her ground-breaking essay the "Cyborg Manifesto," we are all "cyborgs." A cyborg is a hybrid creature composed of both organism and machine who populates a world ambiguously natural and crafted.[23] Think of Arnold Schwarzenegger in *The Terminator,* for example. Today, most medical language about the body reflects the overlap between humans and machines. Medical texts regularly describe bodies using mechanical terminology such as "functioning" and "maintenance." In her research into twentieth-century understandings of health and the body, anthropologist Emily Martin found that the human body is commonly compared to a disciplined machine. Like a machine, the body is made up of parts that can break down.[24] Similarly, Elizabeth Grosz argued that in a postmodern world, the body is treated as a mechanical structure in which components can be adjusted, altered, removed, and replaced.[25] Illness, then, refers to a broken body part. Fixing this part ensures the functioning of the machine. The metaphor of the body as a smoothly functioning machine is central to the way Viagra has been presented. In this [reading], you will see how doctors and patients use mechanical metaphors to make sense of body and gender trouble, or "broken" masculinity.

Such industrial metaphors are used regularly by Viagra spokesperson Irwin Goldstein, who is known for describing erectile functioning as "all hydraulics" and suggesting that dysfunction requires rebuilding the male machine.

Following this metaphor, common treatment protocols for erectile dysfunction center on treating the penis, the broken part, separately from the body, the machine. In the new science of sex, penile dysfunction can be measured in a variety of ways: degree of penile tumescence (rigidity), penetrability (ability to penetrate the partner), sustainability of erection, and satisfaction with performance. These measures are figured into Pfizer-distributed "sexual health" scales and questionnaires. While they may not always do so, doctors are encouraged by Pfizer sales representatives to use these resources and to center their sexual health discussions with patients around erectile performance, asking patients to rate their erections in terms of penetrability, hardness, maintenance, and satisfaction levels.

For Pfizer, the focus is on treating the dysfunctional penis. Emphasis is on "optimal" or "maximal" performance—rigidity and sustainability of the erection—which means that anything less than such performance constitutes erectile dysfunction. . . .

Likewise, in the world of science, Goldstein has written that "submaximal rigidity or submaximal capability to sustain the erection" is another way of understanding erectile dysfunction.[26] In other words, "maximal" erectile rigidity and longevity are normal and expected. This understanding of the penis as dysfunctional and fixable (even perfectible) is exemplified in the following statements by two white men in their fifties; Dr. Curt, a urologist in a medical clinic, and Chuck, a heterosexual architect.

What I do is say [to patients complaining of erectile dysfunction], "Tell me about the erections. When you were twenty years old let's say they were a ten, rock hard. Where would they be now on a scale from one to ten?" So I give them some objectible [sic] evidence that they can give me. They'll say, "Oh, now it's a two." A lot of guys say it's now a seven or eight. I say, "Can you still perform with a seven or eight?" They say, "Yeah, but it's not as

good as it was." (Dr. Curt, urologist in medical clinic)[27]

I'd say as far as functioning sexually, I'm probably at 70 percent. I just can't get hard enough to penetrate. Everything works but the erection. If I were to rate my erectile functioning prior to surgery, with now, I'd say it's at 75 percent. It will never be back to 100 percent, I know that. So I'm somewhat satisfied. And the doctors always tell me that this is a long process, and that I need to be patient about getting back to functioning. So I'm in a wait-and-see mode. (Chuck, fifty-three years old, white, heterosexual, architect)[28]

Many patients who are currently looking for treatment for erectile dysfunction inhabit the in-between, "mild ED" arena (in terms of performance rankings from one to ten) and appear to be concerned with restoring their "machine" to a "normal" level of functioning. Despite Chuck's focus on "getting back to functioning," sexual standards have changed, I believe in part as a response to Viagra, and now "normal" is often not enough.[29]

It is important to point out that while many of these discussions are focused on the penis, they may also reflect expectations about normal manhood and aging. As we have learned, to be normal sexually means being normal in terms of gender, and vice versa. Also implicit in these pursuits of "normality" is a sense of denial and rejection of bodily change and perhaps aging. Thus, Chuck may be just as focused on "getting back to" manhood and youth as he is on "getting back to" normal sexual functioning.

TROUBLE WITH NORMAL

In some cases, Viagra is used by heterosexual and homosexual men who feel that normal penile functioning is not good enough, and extra-normal functioning is now the goal. While these men claim they do not "need" Viagra, they are more satisfied with their performance when they do use it.[30] In the quotations below, Viagra consumers Will and Stanford imply that the pre-Viagra penis is slow, unpredictable, and uncertain, and, thus, problematic.

[I was] totally surprised in my ability to stay erect without effort and the ability to repeatedly snap to attention. Amazing effect. Sorta magical in a way. (Will, fifty-three years old, white, homosexual, program coordinator)[31]

I noticed that if I get titillated [after using Viagra], then the penis springs to attention. Not atypically. But more facile. It's easier. I don't know if it takes less time. It's more convincing. It's not like maybe I'll get hard and maybe I won't. It's like "Okay, here I am!" (Stanford, sixty-five years old, white, heterosexual, counselor)[32]

For Will and Stanford, the Viagra body may be preferable to the natural body because it is consistent and predictable. While rigidity is the goal, part of optimal penile performance is to appear flexible; thus, the Viagra body is, in part, a flexible body.[33] According to . . . Emily Martin, flexibility is a trait cherished and cultivated in all fields, including health.[34] In *Flexible Bodies,* Martin shows how the healthiest bodies in the postmodern era are disciplined machines that also exhibit current cultural ideals such as flexibility, fitness, and elasticity. Viagra can be used as a tool to achieve this ideal elastic body—a body that is always "on call."

Interestingly, the Viagra body is both flexible and controlled, in contrast to the cultural stereotype of men as virile and "out of control." Whereas women have historically been called upon to regulate and control male (mostly teenage) hypersexuality, men are now able to regulate, as well as empower, their bodies with the help of a pill. For Stu, the "on-call" Viagra penis will consistently respond when it is needed, whereas the "natural" body is unpredictable, and therefore unreliable.

Erections are a lot more temperamental than people are willing to admit. But we have this image of masculinity and expectations of male sexuality as being virile and always ready to go and be the conqueror.

And I think that this pill allows people to finally live out that myth (laughs). That was one of the things I had to learn early on is that I had irrational expectations of sexuality. And that men don't have big erections every time they want to, usually, and that to believe that one did was to set oneself up for disappointment. (Stu, thirty-six years old, white, homosexual, student)[35]

As Stu points out, Viagra exposes the flawed "natural" body and enables a man to achieve mythic, powerful, and controlled masculinity. By appearing "natural," the Viagra body can easily replace the problematic body in order to avoid the inevitable disappointment. In this way, the Viagra body exists somewhere between artificial and natural, and even beyond to super-natural levels.

For many, the promise of Viagra is the fact that it can deliver "optimal" results, pushing the consumer beyond his own conceptions of "normal" functioning. In this way, Viagra comes to be seen as a miracle cure because it not only "fixes" the problem but also makes it "better." Below, Viagra is described as an enhancement drug. . . .

It's pretty amazing if you can take a pill and get a better erection. Or even an erection . . . [Viagra is] the first type of medication like this, and for it to work, I mean, is it a wonder drug? Well maybe some of the antibiotics maybe, or diabetes drugs—those are wonder drugs. But in the sexual area, you could say in terms of sexual activity and all of that, yeah, it's a wonder drug. (Dr. Tobin, urologist in private practice)[36] . . .

The entire world relies on drugs simply because they work, or solve—or help—physical conditions. Why is Viagra any different if it is able to extend—excuse the pun—the full and most zestful part of being human? (Will, fifty-three years old, white, homosexual, program coordinator)[37]

As the voices above reveal, doctors and patients tend to collaborate in imagining Viagra as a magic bullet that can "extend" the realm of "normal" and push people to the next level: extranormality, or superhumanness. By pushing the boundaries of erectile function, performance, and sexuality, Viagra sets new standards and, ironically, marks countless male bodies as in need of repair. Consequently, millions of men are now convinced that their sexual and masculine performance can be improved with Viagra.

VIAGRA TO THE RESCUE?

Viagra can also come to the rescue for men who feel that they are not quite masculine enough. While culture, the media, the economy, or relationships can be a source of "male crisis," such factors are complicated to fix. However, when the problem is located solely in the individual body and treated as a physiological dysfunction, the repair can seem easier. Even clinical psychologists, who acknowledge that the trouble can be psychological, social, or relational, may join medical practitioners in seeing Viagra as a tool for regaining body function and repairing confidence and masculinity. Viagra, as a recent biotechnological innovation and medical treatment, represents progress on the path towards health and freedom.

Some consumers take Viagra hoping to restore or supplement not only "natural" physiological function but also "normal" masculinity and heterosexuality.[38] Others choose not to use Viagra, claiming that Viagra is more problem than solution in that it can produce an artificial and uncontrollable body. This section will reveal how patients and doctors grapple with medical solutions, the promise of Viagra, and the necessity of repairing broken male bodies and masculinities.

In an era of advancing sexual medicine, patients and doctors now collaborate in their judgments about successful medical solutions.[39] Both may agree that Viagra will enhance or fix gender, sexuality, and maybe even health and aging. . . .

Other doctors and consumers construct their own, sometimes counterhegemonic or contrary meanings about medicine and sexual dysfunction. This may mean reframing what is problematic and in need of treatment or redefining popular conceptions of what is "normal" and "natural." Below, I illustrate how the growing relationship between sexuality and medicine becomes accepted, and how the repair of broken sexual bodies becomes associated with quick and efficient medical solutions, to the point where such solutions are taken for granted by all involved. In the process, ideologies about what is natural versus artificial, functional versus dysfunctional, and excessive versus deficient are used to make sense of the troubled and fixable body.

Medicalization, or the increased treatment of previously nonmedical problems with medicines, is generally viewed as an inevitable feature of our contemporary lives. Medical professionals like Drs. Pellis . . . and Redding do not question what they see as the forward march of medical science. Instead, these practitioners tend to embrace this push towards new knowledge, solutions, and healthier bodies as beneficial, inevitable, and unstoppable.

It started a long time ago. Sexuality is a mind/body connection. Even Freud said it; one day there will be medical solutions to sexual problems. So he foresaw it as inevitable. (Dr. Pellis, psychiatrist in medical clinic)[40] . . .

It's true—science is getting to that point. [Doctors are] better able to help the body in ways it can't help itself. We don't know what else the medications do—just what they do do. But as with guns or anything, it is a tool, and the more medications that come out, the less the coincidence of stigma around mental health seems to occur. (Dr. Redding, psychotherapist in private practice)[41]

As science enables doctors to help "when bodies can't help themselves," medical solutions are increasingly normalized and accepted, and their professions are legitimated. Even among mental health practitioners such as Dr. Redding, quoted above, medications can be seen as "tools" to help professionals do their jobs and cut through the stigma of mental health work.

Then again, for some medical professionals who don't write prescriptions or who work outside of the current medical system, medicalization is a force to be reckoned with. Drs. Blackwood [and] Bern . . . find themselves becoming defensive as they witness their previously accepted ideas about health and treatment slowly become outmoded.

Everything is medicalized, and HMOs vote in favor of medication over therapy. I think it's a travesty. I find it very disturbing. (Dr. Blackwood, psychologist in private practice)[42]

I happen to be a therapeutic nihilist. I'm a firm believer that the less medicine you take for anything, the better off you are. That doesn't mean I won't use medication. But I don't run and jump in areas. (Dr. Bern, internist in private practice)[43]

. . . These doctors take issue with a health care system and a culture that creates and validates expanding medicine. . . . Such contrary voices appear deviant in a world that generally embraces medical science as unquestioned progress, and even as the path towards health and freedom.[44]

More often than not, medical professionals and journalists couch the discovery and availability of Viagra in the language of scientific progress. After a barrage of Pfizer promotion, media attention, "scientific" reporting on the high prevalence of erectile dysfunction, and the clear popularity of Viagra after its debut in 1998, the medical professionals I interviewed are generally convinced that ED is a "major public health concern" and that Viagra is a "magic bullet" treatment.[45] Employing discourses of scientific advancement, most medical practitioners construct Viagra as a vast improvement over previous treatments for erectile dysfunction, which are now constructed as risky, painful, expensive, time consuming, and complicated. Viagra's success comes in part from this construction as the biotechnological answer to erectile dysfunction that promises the most freedom, simplicity, and expedience, due to its convenient pill form. . . .

It has really helped a lot of people. I've seen some great successes. And it's certainly much easier to do than the other alternatives—penile injections, prostheses, all of these vacuum devices. The alternatives are all more complicated than simply popping a pill. (Dr. Loud, urologist in private practice)[46]

Viagra is really great because it is just a pill and as long as it works it's great. And you don't have to stick needles in, or use cumbersome equipment. . . . Instead of going to see a counselor and spending a lot of money and time on a problem that may not necessarily get better with psychotherapy—this way you take a pill and get better. (Dr. Cummings, urologist in medical clinic)[47]

[For . . . Drs. Loud] and Cummings, simply "popping a pill" is constructed as quick, easy, and painless—not nearly as threatening as the other options: chemicals delivered through needles, equipment hooked up to the body, or months of counseling. This sentiment is shared with consumers like Thorn and Scott, who have tried other available options for treating sexual dysfunction, such as pumps and psychological counseling.

[The vacuum pump] is difficult from a standpoint. . . . It's all the apparatuses, the preparation, and even with the constriction ring which is basically like a tourniquet, I still could not hold a firm enough erection for penetration. So it just didn't work for that effect. It's really tough because it takes all the spontaneity out of it. (Thom, fifty-three years old, white, heterosexual, engineer)[48]

Viagra is so popular in my belief because it cuts out the "middle man" as it were . . . all the psycho-sexual counseling that one would have to go through in order to get to the root of the problem. I know what my problem is without some psycho babbler telling me! It's lack of confidence in the size of my penis! (Scott, thirty-seven years old, Welsh, heterosexual, manager)[49]

Thom and Scott are among the millions of men who like Viagra for its spontaneity and ease. Medical solutions have been so successful that sometimes devices and pharmaceuticals appear to be the only options for treatment. Ricardo, a sixty-one-year-old Mexican-American consumer of Viagra, says he's tried every type of treatment and considered every gadget available, seemingly unaware that alternatives to prescription treatments exist (e.g., therapy).[50] "I've tried everything. There's a gadget for everything. . . . Don't forget, years ago we didn't have any of this. I'm really okay—I finally ended up with a pump that works. I tell everybody, 'Man, I'm back!'"[51] Ironically, with recent "advances" in medical technology, the production of seemingly straightforward and accessible treatments, the availability of medication online, and direct-to-consumer advertising, consumers are finally free to cut out the "middle man"—the therapist, doctor, or health-care practitioner—and just get what they need, quickly and easily. In fact, with the push towards health-care efficiency and insurers' reticence to cover counseling, I have been told that referrals to therapists to treat the psychological dimensions of ED have decreased substantially.[52]

Medicine continues its forward march, impacting bodies and lives in such a way as to blur the line between what is real and what is man made. This tension between "the natural" and "the artificial" is a common theme in my conversations with others about Viagra. Pfizer's most crucial selling point (after constructing a widespread need for Viagra) involves convincing consumers that Viagra not only is the easiest treatment to use but also is as close to "natural" as one can get. A 1999 Pfizer ad reads, "Achieve erections the natural way—in response to sexual stimulation." Not only is a pill simple and efficient, but Viagra enables

the body to work normally and "naturally." Following Pfizer's lead, medical professionals construct Viagra as restorative, moving men smoothly and easily from dysfunction to "normal functioning."[53]

These are distraught, angry, guilty people. . . . We're just trying to restore them to normal. Or just get them to some functioning—to relieve personal distress. (Irwin Goldstein, urologist in sexual dysfunction clinic)[54] . . .

Generally, there's a need for this stuff. Many medications inhibit sexual functioning. And people with diabetes tend to need it. Viagra seems to work quite naturally. And it's selling like crazy. (Long, chain-store pharmacist)[55]

According to those quoted above, Viagra can be understood as a medical treatment for dysfunction, which can restore and relieve distressed and deficient people and bodies. Like these medical professionals, I felt for the men I spoke with, many of whom had admitted their concerns only to their doctors (amazingly not even to their partners) and to me.[56] These men wondered if they were "normal" but suffered in silence because of the shame they associated with their bodies, and because of the lack of close friendship networks to turn to for support.[57] For these men, admitting to impotence (even to themselves) was like conceding that they were no longer young or masculine in a culture that conflates these identities with sexuality and sexual health. Thus, the project of restoring "normal functioning" cannot be divorced from the achievement of "normal masculinity." In this way, both patients and doctors construct Viagra not only as a treatment for erectile dysfunction but also as a pill that restores masculinity.

VIAGRA: A DOSE OF MASCULINITY

"Erectile performance," or achievement of an erection with the potential to penetrate and ejaculate, is central to the "accomplishment" of heterosexual masculinity, according to medical definitions of erectile functioning. By defining terms in this way, medicine is actively shaping what is permissible and ideal in terms of gender roles.[58] Male roles and expectations are clearly laid out in Pfizer's 2000 definition of erectile dysfunction; in a brochure designed for doctors ED is described as "the consistent inability of a man to achieve and/or maintain an erection sufficient for satisfactory sexual performance." We are left to assume that successful masculine performance requires a specific and successful penile performance, involving consistency, achievement, and satisfaction. Is this really the case?

In my conversations with male consumers, I asked if Viagra could be seen as a masculinity pill of sorts. Most affirmed this idea, reiterating the link among erections, potency, and masculinity. Below, it is apparent that white, heterosexual, male consumers ranging from twenty-seven to seventy-five years of age have literally bought into the idea of a masculinity pill.

ML: Is Viagra a masculinity pill?
FRED: (He laughs.) I can't argue with that. Without it you aren't much of anything.
ML: What do you mean?
FRED: If you have an impotency problem to any degree, you look for something to help it with, or you abstain completely. If they feel like this is a masculinity problem, I guess they are right. (Fred, seventy-five years old, white, heterosexual, retired Marine)[59] . . .

Viagra to me is a miracle pill! It does boost confidence as well as other things! I suppose it can be called a masculinity pill, for without an erection, I believe that my masculinity is somewhat diminished! (Scott, thirty-seven years old, Welsh, heterosexual, manager)[60] . . .

According to these men, Viagra can be seen as a treatment for lost, "diminished," troubled, or incomplete masculinity. As Fred mentioned above, impotence reveals that a man is "not much of anything." Over and over in my interviews, in the face of erectile difficulty or even

deficiency, male consumers cast themselves as incomplete, or "half a man." Taking a dose of Viagra allows men to be "whole" again. . . .

However, even for "complete" men, Viagra appears to offer an "extra boost" of masculinity. In the quotations below, both patients and practitioners describe how men use Viagra to enhance their masculinity—to construct themselves as studs and supermen. Interestingly, these medical professionals acknowledge the fact that patients may not be "sexually dysfunctional" before taking Viagra but may just be curious about having a "better" erection.

Some men, like [my] older clients, used [Viagra] just for that extra hardness. They could always get an erection, but [they would say] "I'm sixty-five and it just don't work like it used to." So they might be a little softer. So they'd use it just to harden things up. So they just felt like studs. (Dr. Pemel, sexual health practitioner in private practice)[61]

It's the superman complex. It's that "faster, shinier, bigger" sort of thing. Men feel they've gotta do/have this: the new TV, the car, and the latest products. You know by the numbers that not all the guys getting [Viagra] have erectile dysfunction. (Wilshore, pharmacist)[62]

I am not a macho type at all, but Viagra certainly has made me feel more masculine and sexy at sixty! (Pal, sixty years old, white, heterosexual, retired court administrator)[63]

Practitioners also work to perpetuate the relationship between "complete" manhood and "normal" erectile function. Erectile health equals healthy and complete masculinity to many consumers and practitioners. A man who is dysfunctional may be constructed as castrated, lacking a penis, and/or lacking manhood. For example, conference programs for the 1999 conference on "The Pharmacologic Management of Erectile Dysfunction"—underwritten by several pharmaceutical companies with Pfizer as the largest donor—showed on the outside page a profile of a man cut in half who becomes whole on the inside page where "objectives for treatment" were listed. . . .

When erectile functioning decreases, confidence and sense of masculinity tend to disappear as well, and the body reveals this loss in its posture. Below, Bob, a black heterosexual barber in his sixties, and Pemel, a white forty-something sexual health practitioner, shared with me how the image of a "shrinking" man conveys the way erectile dysfunction can visibly take its toll.[64] As I flipped through Bob's booklet, "Keys to Great Sex for Men over Fifty," I showed him the first page, which reads in large letters, "YOUR PENIS SHRINKS 19.8% AS YOU GET OLDER," part of an ad for testosterone treatment. I asked if he believed this.

Yes, that's what prompted me [to buy the treatment]. Oh yeah, you wake up in the morning and you know something is different. Reading this stuff makes you more aware of what is happening. After taking stuff, there is a difference, a change. (Bob, sixty-two years old, black, heterosexual, business owner)[65]

This whole thing psychologically, men being impotent, it's just devastating. It just affects so much. Testosterone levels. The ability to produce muscle in our bodies. I mean, men just shrink when they just don't have a strong erection. So it's interesting. Not that they become waifs, but . . . in the cases I've seen once they start to have more erections, they are more interested, hormonally things are flowing, testosterone is being produced more, and they are kind of feeling bigger and bulkier and more manly in many ways. (Dr. Pemel, sexual health practitioner in private practice)[66]

Here, the norm for males is to be big and bulky, not shrinking and diminutive. This theme of loss came up frequently in conversations with practitioners and consumers, although expressed and constructed in various ways. Many times loss of erectile function is seen as a death. Social scientist Annie Potts, in a critical commentary on "The Hard-On," reminds us that the experience of "the fallen flesh"—or the limp penis causing the body to appear desexed, soft (feminine), and powerless—is a common male horror story because it feminizes the body, rendering the person unidentifiable as a man.[67] . . .

[Other men] literally compared erectile dysfunction to death. For them, Viagra is constructed as a tool for restoring not only masculinity but also "life" itself.

Sexual dysfunction is no joke. These people have horrible lives, they may lose their relationships, and they come in a fairly desperate condition. Some say they'd rather be dead. Both men and women. And their lives are destroyed. They have nowhere to turn. They are not themselves. All of that. (Irwin Goldstein, urologist in sexual dysfunction clinic)[68]

I'm fifty-five and for some reason I just didn't seem to feel like I was alive and well like I was when I was twenty years old. And you know, I thought that shouldn't be so because that's not the way it is. I've never talked to anybody about that situation, so I told my doctor. For some reason or other I said I'd like to try something to see if I'm still alive or not. And so anyway he says, "Do you want to try this Viagra?" I say I don't like drugs or anything artificial. Maybe my time is over and that should be the end of that. But then I tried [Viagra]. (Joel, fifty-five years old, white, heterosexual, unknown occupation)[69]

. . . For most of these consumers, an active, erect penis symbolizes normal health, masculinity, and sexuality. A limp penis or absence of virility appears to symbolize death of the body as well as of manhood. To capture this [lack of interest] in life that comes with erectile failure, Pfizer has chosen the tag line "Love Life Again" to sell its product.

As we have seen, for both male consumers and (usually male) practitioners, communicating about pain, loss, and concerns associated with sexual problems can be difficult, embarrassing, and heavily laden with metaphor, myth, and shame.[70] Phrases such as "it's over" and

"I'm no longer alive," along with labels such as "shrinking," "eunuch," and "incomplete" reveal male discomfort with discussing sexuality and convey the degree of importance erectile functioning plays in men's sense of self, masculinity, and health. These men visit doctors with their complaints to investigate ways to fix their selves, their manhood, and their health. In the process, patients look to practitioners and those around them to provide a rationale for their troubles. . . .

REPAIR = TROUBLE

Not all consumers buy into the techno-fix model. Some consumers commented that although Viagra may promise bodily repair or enhancement, it can actually cause more trouble than it's worth. In this section, consumers indicate that Viagra creates problems, not solutions. For Joel and Don, Viagra is constructed as techno-trouble, rendering the male body increasingly out of control.

I don't ever want to try [Viagra] again. The thing about it is, the side effects could be very dangerous for someone a little older than I am. Because you do end up with palpitations. Your body is just not your body. So if [your functioning is] not normal, I think it's better to just let it go at that. Or make pills that are much, much weaker. But I wouldn't recommend it for anybody. (Joel, fifty-five years old, white, heterosexual, unknown occupation)[71]

I have tried it. I went a long time and the bottom line is I don't like it. It hasn't done me any good and it had a harmful side effect—heartburn and indigestion. I'm a little fearful of it. I'm a healthy guy and I don't take any maintenance medicines of any kind. My system seems to be functioning nicely. I think I'll just leave it alone. (Don, sixty-seven years old, white, heterosexual, retired fire captain)[72]

As we saw earlier, some men see Viagra as a tool to create the ideal flexible body. For other consumers, Viagra may produce a body that is overly rigid and inflexible. For them, the Viagra effect is "unnatural" and uncontrollable, and consequently undesirable for both Dusty, a homosexual student, and Stanford, a heterosexual counselor in his sixties.

Well, I also didn't like it because it was unnatural. Like you were hard and you stayed hard. And I also didn't like the fact that it guaranteed things would be sexual until you weren't hard. I didn't like the idea of being forced into being sexual. You can't do anything nonsexual when you are on it. So basically it guarantees that the entire period you are on it is going to be sexual. (Dusty, seventeen years old, white, homosexual, student)[73]

The idea that I thought was hilarious at first—that erection that won't go away—is not hilarious at all. In fact it happens and sometimes endangers one's life. (Stanford, sixty-five years old, white, heterosexual, counselor)[74]

For Stanford and Dusty, Pfizer's Viagra tag line, "Love Life Again," is inappropriate. Instead of regaining an appreciation for life, these men see Viagra as dangerous or even deadly. While priapism or death can occur in rare instances of Viagra use, and even Pfizer admits that Viagra is not for everyone, neither Stanford nor Dusty experienced real bodily danger while taking Viagra. Nonetheless, both take Viagra seriously, remaining cautious and seeming to prefer the natural way to the artificial alternative.

Rather than lose control of their bodies or experience trouble through repair, some men construct alternatives to the pharmaceutical quick-fix model, accepting their bodies as they are or just "leaving it alone." Despite overwhelming evidence that Viagra is associated with the production of normal and/or mythic masculinity, men like Ollie and Joel work hard at reconstructing masculinity as separate from "erectile health." They insist that heterosexual masculinity can be achieved without the help of Viagra or consideration of erectile potential.

Oh no, if you don't feel like a man before you take the pill, you're not a man anyways. No, you have to know where you're at. If you have a little misfunction, that's minor. But you have to be a man before you go through that. It's not a macho pill. (Joel, fifty-five years old, white, heterosexual, unknown occupation)[75]

I've talked to a lot of different men about this. Some cannot live without sex. They feel their sex makes them the man that they are. And I'm not sure how important that is to me. I'm a man anyways. It's about self-esteem. What do you think about yourself to begin with? (Ollie, sixty-four years old, black, heterosexual, printer)[76]

For many, Viagra fits perfectly in a society that is known for pushing the limits of normal. Some men are critical of American culture and Viagra's role in perpetuating the endless pursuit of the quick fix. Hancock and Miles warn of a hedonistic, money-driven, artificial world, where there is a pill for everything. For them, Viagra exists in this world as a crutch or bandaid solution to larger social problems.

We are willing to take the latest thing that is fast and painless. Also, Americans seem to think happiness is their birthright. They take Viagra to become better, happier. And supermen. All that stuff about self-worth, image, and sex life, it's what people want. . . . And maybe those guys who think they need Viagra just need to chill out and reduce stress in their lives. It's about lifestyle modification more than anything, I think. Maybe we are too lazy and it just takes too long. We want something to work fast. (Hancock, sixty-nine years old, white, heterosexual, retired teacher)[77]

I think there is a gross overuse of drugs for happiness and well-being. Feeling depressed, get a script for a mood enhancer . . . feeling tired, get a pill for energy . . . want to have better sex, get some blue magic. What about the age-proven solution of removing or reducing the problems or stress factors affecting your life and then seeing if pharmacological agents are still needed? (Miles, forty-five years old, white, heterosexual, paramedic)[78]

Here, Miles and Hancock construct society as drug-infused, producing individuals who are dependent upon pills for health and happiness. They, along with Stu and Ollie, are critical of corporate and biotechnological attempts at constructing needs, desires, and easy markets for products.

How do I express this? This is a . . . capitalist hegemony of our emotions. We live in a state of anomie, or at least we are told that we do, and we're also told what to do about it. Have you seen these commercials? I have files of "The Paxil Christmas" that I cut out of a magazine. [There is t]his young college-aged woman in a family Christmas portrait and it says, "You can go home this year and have a good time. Paxil." Paxil and Prozac and Zoloft—that's what it was. They ran these ads and marketed them to different age groups and they are telling us what the problem is—creating a problem—and they give us a solution. We all have anxieties and relationship issues, and they do this to make it look like the way to solve your relationship issue is to take Paxil. The way to deal with your crazy family is to take Paxil. That way you don't have to address the relationship issues, substantive issues. I have a big problem with that. (Stu, thirty-six years old, white, homosexual, student)[79]

I think everything we do nowadays is overblown. I just see that society is just driving us crazy, making us jump through hoops and do things we really don't need to do. So a drug for everything . . . I think they—or not they, but the way things are set up, is to make you want to do things. Even if you don't want to do it, you are driven if you pay attention to what's going on. I'm not that kind of person. I won't let you do me that way. You won't be able to drive me that way. I just don't believe in it. (Ollie, sixty-four years old, black, heterosexual, printer)[80]

These men are clearly critical of Viagra's potential to enforce social and gender ideals. They refuse to "buy into" mythic masculinity, and they see through the problematic language used to describe medical progress as well as so-called widespread public health crises. In this way some men do resist and reframe masculinity, biotechnology, and medical science in ways that make sense to them. Rather than construct their bodies as troubled, with Viagra as a technofix or magical solution, these consumers see Viagra as problematic, contributing to larger social problems. These skeptical voices, however, are easily drowned out by the overwhelming chorus of those who sing Viagra's praises.

MASCULINITY, BIOTECHNOLOGY, AND RESISTANCE

At the turn of a new century, the desire to "fix" and "erect" male sexuality and power in a male-dominated society appears to be strong. This desire is perhaps a reaction to the gains of women's liberation and sexual empowerment, and as some of the men I spoke with pointed out, we are also living in a time of self-help movements, expanding medicalization, great social change, and personal crisis. Today it is not uncommon to hear about American social problems such as "male betrayal," the "malaise among men," and the "masculinity crisis." Just as Betty Friedan warned against women "buying into" their own victimhood in the 1960s, so now it is argued that men are buying into commercially packaged manhood in many forms, including "amped-up virility" and "technologically-enhanced supermanhood."[81]

When Lewis Carroll wrote *Alice's Adventures in Wonderland* in 1865, the idea of an ingestible tonic that would answer Alice's wishes and make her "grow large" was a magical, fantastical fantasy. Today, we all inhabit this magical reality, surrounded and tempted by endless products packaged in promises of personal transformation. This is the era when the "magic bullet" for sexual energy, confidence, and masculinity comes in the form of a pill. Today, so-called lifestyle drugs of all types are available to anyone with access to the Internet and a credit card. And Americans have a newly transformed relationship with biotechnology, one that goes beyond "healing" to "transforming" and "fixing" bodies with the help of reproductive technologies, hormones, implants, surgeries, and other technological innovations.

Today, enhancement technologies are not just instruments of self-improvement or even self-transformation—they are tools for working on the soul.[82] The new player in this enhancement tale is the man who has been told he is sick. With Viagra, a highly successful masculine empowerment campaign is underway, centered around a new, late-twentieth-century tool, a magic blue pill that promises to produce and enhance male "magic wands." The doctor's tools are now turned back on the doctor himself. The male body is constructed as in need of repair, and is a new site for medical and biotechnological innovation and healing. With health and fitness as the new testing ground for masculinity, Viagra enters doctors' and patients' worlds, envisioned as cutting-edge biotechnology and used, I argue, as a cultural and material tool in the production and achievement of "true" manhood. Then again, Viagra can lead to male confidence without even being ingested. One of my informants told me that he purchased Viagra at a time of intense sexual insecurity with a partner but hasn't had a chance to use it. He is hoping that just having it around will make him a more self-confident lover. Others echoed this idea, that simply pills in the medicine cabinet was enough of an assurance.

The implications of constructing the male body as sexually potent, or as a technologically enhanced machine, can be both hurtful and helpful, as medical professionals, Viagra consumers, and their partners have discovered. Here I think of a friend's lesson about the importance of antidepressants: "You can't start a revolution if you're so depressed you can't get out of bed!" Similarly, during the course of this research, practitioners told me that their

patients would not be attentive to their partners' sexual needs or desires if they were insecure or paralyzed by their own. Thus Viagra
enabled them to be more confident and attentive to themselves as well as to their partners.
In this way, it is important to acknowledge
that prescription drug use has the potential to
enable broad social change.

Nonetheless, social historian Lynne Luciano warns,

Medicalizing impotence lures men into believing
there is a standard for erections to which they must
adhere. By quantifying the normal erection—it has
to be just hard enough to achieve penetration and last
long enough to achieve ejaculation—medicalization
forces men to conform to its specifications for
masculinity. The results are twofold: first, men,
like women, have their sexuality and desirability
linked to physical parameters; second, emotion,
sexual technique, and the role of one's partner are
rendered insignificant. By making the erection the
man, science isn't enhancing male sexuality, but
sabotaging it.[83]

Like Luciano, many social theorists have
recently expressed concern with the state of
manhood in America. Sexologist and practicing
therapist Wendy Stock points out that to focus
on male bodies as Viagra-infused, finely tuned,
flexible machines perpetuates a detached,
unemotional masculinity. She comments,
"Although a common cultural male fantasy is
to be able to function like a machine, as the
sexual equivalent of the Energizer Bunny, both
men and women may lose something if medical
interventions allow us to function without the
necessity of emotional connection. Is the ability to perform like a sexual machine desirable,
individually or on a cultural scale?"[84] Similarly,
feminist journalist and social commentator
Susan Faludi warns of a "performance culture . . . where people are encouraged to view
themselves as commodities that are marketed
and fine-tuned with chemicals, whether it's
Viagra or Prozac or Botox injections."[85]

Despite such warnings, sexual medicine
continues to expand, as experts and market-
ers find ways to understand and treat a wider
and wider range of sexual troubles for men and
women. At a major international conference
on sexual dysfunction in 2003, definitions and
treatments for "rapid ejaculation" and "delayed
ejaculation" were being discussed and final-
ized. For women, delay or absence of orgasm,
arousal, or desire is cause for medical intervention. Insurers also intervene, by setting rules
about who has access to sexual health treatments, and how many. Meanwhile, performance anxiety will only grow as the definition
of "normal" sexuality and masculinity narrows.
As sexual medicine gets more and more commonplace, what will be the ramifications for
those who don't follow medical protocol? For
those who have little interest in sexuality, or in
medical models of sexuality? Lynne Luciano
poses similar questions, with no clear answers:

What happens to a man or woman who doesn't
want to take drugs to enhance sexuality, who is
content to age without the benefit of pills and
potions? How far are we willing to go in our public discourse about how much sex is enough, and
what constitutes good sex, and how central a role
sex should play in relationships? Medical advances
and healthier lifestyles offer men hope for longer
and more potent sex lives than at any other time
in history. But expectations are likely to continue
to outpace reality. Not even Viagra can guarantee
sexual success for all men, all the time. What it
can guarantee is a continuing moral and ethical
debate.[86]

The individual stories in this [reading] add
up to what I see as a larger, disturbing story
about the pressures and requirements for being
fully male in American society, and even worldwide. Are we doing our men a service in the
Viagra era? As the doctors and patients that I
interviewed and quote in this chapter reveal,
Viagra can and is being used to enforce and
perpetuate an ideal masculinity. In this way

consumers collaborate with medical professionals and pharmaceutical companies in an attempt to understand and fix "broken" bodies. Perhaps of more interest, my data also reveal the struggle with the necessity for the Viagra-enhanced body, and what that struggle represents. As men negotiate their relationship to this product, mainstream ideas about sexuality, masculinity, and health are both reinforced and redefined in important ways. For example, some men insist that "doing" masculinity does not require sexual performance. Others are critical of a society that increasingly promotes and depends upon biotechnology for achieving health and happiness. They have their own ideas about manhood, medicalization, and biotechnology that may or may not fit with Pfizer's. In general, this chapter reveals men complicating manhood by constructing not only corporate corporealities[87] but also "various and competing masculinities" in the Viagra era.[88] As most of us do, the men I spoke with are constantly negotiating social and cultural pressures to be healthy, young, sexual, and in control.

For Pfizer, fixing the broken male machine is supposed to be a simple process with the help of Viagra. The men in this chapter suggest otherwise, pointing out that the bodily "repair" process, the man, and the culture he belongs to are all more complex than Pfizer may acknowledge.

NOTES

1. Michael Kimmel, *Manhood in America: A Cultural History* (New York: Free Press, 1996).

2. In the 1970s and 1980s, gender scholars began to complicate and problematize normative (and thus prescriptive) white, heterosexual "hegemonic masculinity." For more on hegemonic masculinity, see Robert Connell, *Masculinities* (Berkeley: University of California Press, 1995). Michael Messner, *The Politics of Masculinities: Men in Movements* (Thousand Oaks, CA: Sage Publications, 1997) argues that a singular, reductionist, unified masculinity does not reflect a society in which "at any given moment there are various and competing masculinities." Responding to feminist scholarship, early masculinities

scholars argued that patriarchy forces men to oppress themselves and other men. Such scholars inspired many inquiries into male competition, power struggles, and self-objectification. Joseph Pleck's *The Myth of Masculinity* (Cambridge: MIT Press, 1981) suggested that hegemonic masculinity and the promotion of unattainable ideals caused men to experience "sex role strain" in trying to attain the unattainable. In this way, Pleck sparked an interest in male confusion and "crisis" related to out-of-date, inflexible, contradictory, turn-of-the-century sex roles. Similarly, Lynne Segal, in *Slow Motion: Changing Masculinities* (London: Virago, 1990) warned that lived masculinity is never the seamless, undivided construction it becomes in its symbolic manifestation. She argued that in the late twentieth century, masculinity was not in crisis per se, but it was less hegemonic than before. While contemporary, increasingly visible and complicated masculinities can exist in tension with potentially outdated roles and expectations, this tension can also lead to confusion about manhood and how to "do" it.

3. Connell, *Masculinities*, 45.

4. Kimmel, *Manhood in America*, 332.

5. Connell proposes his own model, the "body-reflexive" model, in which the social relations of gender are experienced in the body and are constituted through bodily action. See Connell, *Masculinities*, 60–64.

6. See, for example, Susan Bordo, *The Male Body: A New Look at Men in Public and Private* (New York: Farrar, Straus, and Giroux, 1999); Marc Fasteau, *The Male Machine* (New York: Dell, 1975); Kimmel and Messner, *Men's Lives;* and Michael Kimmel, *Manhood in America*.

7. See, for example, Annie Potts, "The Essence of the Hard-On," in *Men and Masculinities* (3:1, 2000): 85–103. Also see Leonore Tiefer, "The Medicalization of Impotence: Normalizing Phallocentrism," *Gender and Society* (8, 1994): 363–77, and *Sex Is Not a Natural Act and Other Essays* (San Francisco: Westview Press, 1995).

8. See, for example, Potts, "The Essence of the Hard-On"; Tiefer, *Sex Is Not a Natural Act;* Lynne Luciano, *Looking Good: Male Body Image in Modern America* (New York: Hill and Wang, 2001); and Barbara L. Marshall, " 'Hard Science:' Gendered Constructions of Sexual Dysfunction in the 'Viagra Age,' " *Sexualities* (5:2, 2002):131–58. Phallocentrism refers to the phallus, a male organ that symbolizes power and control.

9. See, for example, Bordo, *The Male Body*.

10. Laura Mamo and Jennifer Fishman, "Potency in All the Right Places: Viagra as a Technology of the Gendered Body," *Body and Society* (7:4, 2001): 13–35.

11. A very limited cohort of scholars, primarily historians, has written about how white men's heterosexual bodies have been normalized and naturalized and, in rare

cases, pathologized. See Bordo, *The Male Body.* Also see Vern Burlough, "Technology for the Prevention of 'les maladies produites par la masturbation,' " *Technology and Culture* (28:4, 1987): 828–32; and Kevin Mumford, "Lost Manhood Found: Male Sexual Impotence and Victorian Culture in the United States," *Journal of the History of Sexuality* (3:1, 1992). Kevin Mumford explores how male impotence was medicalized, constructed, and cured historically. Starting from advertisements promising male virility and vigor, Mumford traces the "crisis of masculinity" along with modernization and the changing American conceptions of male sexuality and masculinity from the 1830s to the 1920s.

12. All names have been changed to protect the identity of my informants. The twenty-seven male consumers I spoke with are a self-selected group who responded to the interview requests I made through Internet postings, newspaper advertisements, practitioner referrals, senior-citizens organizations, personal contacts, and prostate cancer support- group meeting announcements. Those consumers who volunteered for an interview generally had experience with Viagra and had an interest in sharing this experience because it had affected their lives in some way (good or bad). A group of men from a post-prostate-surgery support group agreed to speak with me over the phone under conditions of anonymity and confidentiality about their experiences dealing with surgery-induced ED. Interestingly, all had tried Viagra, and none had had any "success" with it, a fact that turned several of the interviews into "ranting" sessions, which rendered visible how emotionally invested these consumers were in Viagra's promise. Of the twenty-seven male consumers I spoke with, all but two had tried Viagra, and half of these discontinued using Viagra after the initial trial because of unsatisfactory response or preference for a different product. This "take rate" is representative of the larger population of Viagra users nationally; Pfizer's research has shown that over half of those who receive a prescription for Viagra do not request a refill.

13. In addition to being the only Viagra expert known to most men, their doctors are the only person most men feel comfortable talking to about their sexual problems.

14. I also spoke with twenty-two medical practitioners. Six of the twenty-two medical professionals I spoke with are female; sixteen are male. Eight are acclaimed experts in sexual medicine, regularly publishing and delivering lectures on female sexual dysfunction.

15. Dr. Bern, interview with author, tape recording, California: August 2000.

16. Phil, phone interview, tape recording, May 2000.

17. Byron, phone interview, tape recording, May 2000.

18. In *The Male Body,* Susan Bordo explores the link between masculinity and the phallus throughout Western history from Roman phallic gods to St. Augustine's "lustful member" to John Bobbitt's detachable penis to Clinton's not-so-private parts (24–25). Bordo argues that for as long as we can remember, the phallus has embodied our cultural imagination, symbolic of power, permission, defiance, and performance. Annie Potts adds that medicine and sexology produce and perpetuate the idea that an erect penis signifies "healthy" male sexuality—a destructive form of hegemonic masculinity that "ignores the diversity of penile pleasures" (89).

19. The idea that female sexuality can only be awakened by (or responsive to) the male was popular in marriage manuals of the early twentieth century and currently exist in medical discourse about female sexual dysfunction. . . .

20. Potts, "The Essence of the Hard-On," 98. Potts argues that we need an expansive view of male sexuality that need not rely on phallic ambitions. This would require a rethinking of penis power, "a relinquishment of this organ's executive position in sex," and an "embrace of a variety of penile styles: flaccid, erect, and semiflaccid/semierect" (100).

21. For more on gender as an accomplishment, see Candace West and Don Zimmerman, "Doing Gender," *Gender and Society* (1, 1987): 125–51; and Candace West and Sarah Fenstermaker, "Doing Difference," *Gender and Society* (9:1, 1995): 8–38. Also see West and Fenstermaker, *Doing Gender: Doing Difference* (New York: Routledge, 2002).

22. See, for example, Diane Dull and Candace West, "Accounting for Cosmetic Surgery: The Accomplishment of Gender," *Social Problems* (38:1, 1991): 54–71; and Kathy Davis, *Reshaping the Female Body: The Dilemma of Cosmetic Surgery* (New York: Routledge, 1995).

23. Donna Haraway, *Simians, Cyborgs, and Women: The Reinvention of Nature* (New York: Routledge, 1991): 149.

24. See Emily Martin, *Flexible Bodies* (Boston: Beacon Press, 1994).

25. Elizabeth Grosz, *Space, Time, and Perversion: Essays on the Politics of Bodies* (New York: Routledge, 1995): 35.

26. See any of Goldstein's coauthored reports in the *International Journal of Impotence Research,* volumes 10, 11, 12, and 15.

27. Dr. Curt, interview with author, tape recording, California: August 2000.

28. Chuck, phone interview, tape recording, May 2000.

29. Differing markedly in age, health, and reason for using Viagra (and, less markedly, in race, occupation, and sexual orientation), my sample is representative of a diversity of Viagra users. Pfizer identifies its largest market as "men over forty years of age." Pfizer Pharmaceuticals, Inc., *Patient Summary of Information about Viagra,* Fact Sheet, 1999, 2000; and *Uncover Ed,* Pfizer Informational Brochure, March 2000. In my sample of male consumers, diseases, medications, and surgeries were the most

frequently cited reasons for trying Viagra. Ten of the twenty-seven male consumers I interviewed experienced erectile difficulties after undergoing prostate surgery. Others blamed erectile dysfunction on age (four), diabetes (one), heart problems (one), and medications (two). Three consumers cited psychological (self-esteem) factors as the main cause of their erectile difficulties. Perhaps of most interest is the significant number of interviewees who denied they had erectile dysfunction (seven), and instead explained that they used Viagra as an assurance or enhancement drug. Pfizer does not officially acknowledge or discuss this population of Viagra users in its promotional or training information, although these users may fall into the "mild ED" and "psychological and other factors" categories.

30. Nora Jacobson found this to be the case with breast implants in her book *Cleavage: Technology, Controversy, and the Ironies of the Man-Made Breast* (New Brunswick, NJ: Rutgers University Press, 2000). Some have suggested that gay males are a ready market for the "enhancement" uses of Viagra, including several of my gay interview subjects. But both gay and straight men in my interview pool expressed interest in the enhancement uses of Viagra.

31. Will, interview with author, tape recording, California: September 2000.

32. Stanford, interview with author, tape recording, California: August 2000.

33. Previous treatments for ED included a liquid injected directly into the penis, which would produce an erection for several hours (Caverject). Viagra is constructed as a superior treatment due to its simple delivery (as a pill) and production of a penis that will wait to become erect until the user is ready.

34. See Martin, *Flexible Bodies.*

35. Stu, interview with author, tape recording, California: October 2000.

36. Dr. Tobin, phone interview, tape recording, May 2000.

37. Will, Ibid.

38. Potts, in "The Essence of the Hard-On" (94), reminds us that the true mark of therapeutic success is restoration of "phallic manhood."

39. This idea comes from Riessman, "Women and Medicalization: A New Perspective," *Social Policy* (14:1, 1983).

40. Dr. Pellis, interview with author, tape recording, California: May 2000.

41. Dr. Redding, interview with author, tape recording, California: May 2000.

42. Dr. Blackwood, phone interview, tape recording, May 2000.

43. Dr. Bern, Ibid.

44. Peter Conrad and Joseph Schneider, *Deviance and Medicalization: From Badness to Sickness* (London: Mosby, 1980); and Riessman, "Women and Medicalization."

45. See Edward Laumann, A. Paik, and R. Rosen, "Sexual Dysfunction in the United States: Prevalence and Predictors," *JAMA* (281:6, 1999): 537–44. . . .

46. Dr. Loud, interview with author, tape recording, California: August 2000.

47. Dr. Cummings, interview with author, tape recording, California: August 2000.

48. Thom, phone interview, tape recording, May 2000.

49. Scott, e-mail interview, e-mail transcript, May 2000.

50. There is a long-standing struggle between therapists and practitioners to locate the source of erectile dysfunction and treat either physiological or psychological manifestations of the problem.

51. Ricardo, phone interview, tape recording, August 2000.

52. Barbara L. Marshall, 'Hard Science.'

53. Viagra competitor Enzyte is an over-the-counter product that offers "natural male enhancement," which seems to put Viagra in the "unnatural" (synthetic) category.

54. Irwin Goldstein, phone interview, tape recording, November 2000.

55. Long, interview with author, tape recording, California: October 2000.

56. I never expected to be a stand-in for consumers' doctors. In these cases where consumers asked for advice, I awkwardly assured them that I was not an expert on ED, but judging from my interviews with other male consumers, their experiences sounded normal. If the side effects they mentioned sounded potentially dangerous (like heart palpitations or trouble breathing), I advised them to contact their doctors as soon as possible.

57. Interestingly, several of the men I spoke with, primarily those who had undergone prostate surgery, felt more of a stigma associated with incontinence than with impotence. This is yet another area where millions of men suffer in silence.

58. See Janice Raymond, *Transsexual Empire: The Making of the She-Male* (New York: Atheneum, 1994).

59. Fred, phone interview, tape recording, August 2000.

60. Scott, Ibid.

61. Dr. Pemel, interview with author, tape recording, California: August 2000.

62. Wilshore, interview with author, tape recording, California: May 2000.

63. Pal, email interview, e-mail transcript, August 2000.

64. Bordo, in *The Male Body,* argues that in a culture where "big and bulky" represent male ideals, "shrinkage"

is feared, as evidenced in popular culture *(Seinfeld, Boogie Nights,* etc.).

65. Bob, interview with author, tape recording, California: August 2000.

66. Dr. Pemel, Ibid.

67. Potts, "The Essence of the Hard-On," 96.

68. Irwin Goldstein, Ibid.

69. Joel, interview with author, tape recording, California: October 2000.

70. Relationship experts have described this "delicate dance" that couples do when they are dealing with situations like sexual dysfunction. Without open communication between partners, the fear of "failure" can lead to avoidance and alienation, which can only exacerbate the problem.

71. Joel, Ibid.

72. Don, Ibid.

73. Dusty, interview with author, tape recording, California: August 2000.

74. Stanford, Ibid.

75. Joel, Ibid.

76. Ollie, phone interview, tape recording, May 2000.

77. Hancock, phone interview, tape recording, May 2000.

78. Miles, e-mail interview, e-mail transcript, August 2000.

79. Stu, Ibid.

80. Ollie, Ibid.

81. Quoted in Susan Faludi, *Stiffed: The Betrayal of the American Male* (New York: Morrow, 1999): 602.

82. See Carl Elliott, *Better Than Well: American Medicine Meets the American Dream* (New York: Norton, 2003): 53.

83. Luciano, *Looking Good,* 165.

84. Wendy Stock and C. Moser, "Feminist Sex Therapy in the Age of Viagra," in *New Directions in Sex Therapy: Innovations and Alternatives,* P. Kleinplatz, ed. (New York: Brunner-Routledge, 2001): 27.

85. P. J. Huffstutter and Ralph Frammolino, "Lights! Camera! Viagra! When the Show Must Go On, Sometimes a Little Chemistry Helps," *Los Angeles Times,* July 6, 2001, A1.

86. Luciano, *Looking Good,* 204.

87. I have Michael Kimmel to thank for helping me come up with this term.

88. This phrase is borrowed from Michael Messner's *Politics of Masculinities.*

IN SEARCH OF (BETTER) SEXUAL PLEASURE: FEMALE GENITAL "COSMETIC" SURGERY

VIRGINIA BRAUN

In this article, I explore the role of "sexual pleasure" in accounts of female genital "cosmetic"[1] surgery (FGCS). FGCS procedures are some of the newest to become popularized in the arsenal of surgical and other cosmetic procedures aimed at transforming the (female)[2] body in some way. My classification of genital surgery as FGCS does not include surgery for transsexual or intersex people,[3] nor is it "female genital mutilation" (FGM).[4] Procedures for (cosmetic) genital alteration include: labiaplasty/labioplasty (labia minora reductions), labia majora "augmentations" (tissue removal, fat injections), liposuction (mons pubis, labia majora), vaginal tightening (fat injections, surgical tightening), clitoral hood reductions, clitoral repositioning, G-spot "amplification" (collagen injected into the "G-spot," which swells it significantly), and hymen reconstruction (to restore the *appearance* of "virginity").

Like cosmetic surgery generally, FGCS can be seen as both *surgical* practice and *cultural* product (see Adams, 1997; Fraser, 2003) and practice (Haiken, 2000). Dubbed the "designer vagina," FGCS has received considerable media attention in recent years. Headlines range from the sensational—"I've saved my sex life" (M30)[5]—to the serious—"Designer vagina service a first for NZ" (N10). There is an apparent increase in the popularity of FGCS. . . . By some accounts, this increasing popularity is due, at least in part, to media coverage.

The material practice of FGCS, and women's participation in it, are enabled within particular sociocultural (and technological) contexts which render certain choices possible, and locate cosmetic surgery as a solution (K. Davis, 2003). The contexts of women's ongoing, widespread, and increasingly specific, body dissatisfactions (Bordo, 1997; Sullivan, 2001), ongoing negative meanings around women's genitalia (Braun and Wilkinson, 2001, 2003), and women's engagement in a wide range of body modification practices—such as hair removal (Toerien and Wilkinson, 2004)—cohere to render women's genitalia a viable site for surgical enhancement. . . .

In this article, I focus specifically on the issue of (female) sexual pleasure in accounts of FGCS. Female sexual pleasure appears as a central concern, mirroring a broader sociocultural shift towards the "eroticization of female sexuality" (Seidman, 1991: 124) with women's sexual pleasure located as central in (hetero)sex (e.g., Braun et al., 2003; Gordon, 1971) and beyond. . . . This increased attention to pleasure has also resulted in an increased attention to the body and sexual technique (Seidman, 1991), with possible concurrent increases in feelings of sexual inadequacy (Hart and Wellings, 2002). I will show that the story of FGCS is, at least in part, a story of the (legitimate) search for (better) female sexual pleasure, and argue that this functions not only to legitimate, and promote, FGCS, but also to reaffirm particular models of desirable sexual bodies and practices.

From "In Search of (Better) Sexual Pleasure: Female Genital 'Cosmetic' Surgery" by Virginia Braun, *Sexualities*, Vol. 8, No. 4, 2005, pp. 407–424. Copyright © 2005 by SAGE Publications, reprinted by Permission of SAGE Publications.

THEORIZING AND RESEARCHING FGCS

This article is part of a broader project on FGCS which analyses data drawn from two datasets: media accounts and surgeon interviews. The research is situated with a (feminist) social constructionist framework (Burr, 1995; Tiefer, 1995, 2000; White et al., 2000), which theorizes language and social representations as an integral part of the production of social (and material) realities for individuals, as well as producing possibilities for individual practices. Sexuality is thus a material, but always social, practice (Connell, 1997; Jackson and Scott, 2001). . . .

My convenience sample was located primarily through Google searches using terms like "designer vagina" and "labiaplasty", and through surgeon websites. . . . My [media] analysis in this article focuses on the [data from 31] print [magazines]. . . .

Twenty-four surgeons were contacted and invited to take part in semi-structured interviews, with 15 agreeing. . . .

FGCS AND FEMALE SEXUAL PLEASURE

Women's sex lives or their sexuality was often reported to be impeded in some way, with pre-operative genitalia:

Extract 1: Woman's Day Magazine, NZ, 2004

Amanda was utterly miserable. She no longer enjoyed sex with Russell, the husband she adored, and on those rare occasions when they made love, Amanda would insist they switch off the lights. (M30)

In this and other extracts, general pre-surgical sexual "impediments" were noted. In addition, specific causes of such sexual impediments were identified in many accounts:

Extract 2: male plastic surgeon, UK

S1: . . . In my practice it is not—quite often it's not purely cosmetic but there are functional complaints with the labia the size of the labia too . . . for example . . . it can be painful during intercourse because the labium keeps going in and out with every thrust.

Although physical pain was often discussed, the *psychological* response to genital morphology was frequently highlighted as the crux of the problem which "hampered" or "ruined" their sex life:

Extract 3: male plastic surgeon, NZ

S6: I think most . . . of the women that I've dealt with have thought that this was a real impediment to sexual enjoyment . . . not so much from their point of view as their partner's point of view . . . if they were worried about their partner not liking whatever they could see or touch or whatever then they felt tense themselves . . . and so the enjoyment of everything goes (spiralling) . . . down. . . .

Extract 4: Cosmopolitan Magazine, AUS/NZ, 1998

Sarah, a 27-year-old secretary is a case in point. Throughout puberty, she thought her vaginal lips were too long and was embarrassed by one that hung lower than the other.

"They ruined my sex life," she recalls. "I never felt confident during sex—I felt like a freak. I'd never let anyone see me naked." (M1)

Extract 5: New Woman Magazine, AUS, 2003

. . . the biggest problem was sex. I've been with my boyfriend since I was 15 but I always felt self-conscious when we made love. I'd engineer positions so that he'd always be behind me and couldn't see my vagina, and I'd never have oral sex because I couldn't bear him seeing me up close. (M20)

The psychological problems invoked to explain a (pre-surgery) sexual impediment included embarrassment, self-consciousness, lack of confidence, and shame. The inclusion of such concepts fits with Frank's (2003) observation of an "inflation of the language of pain" around medicine to include such psychological concepts. In my data, this negative psychological response to *appearance* often resulted, via other psychological responses like anxiety or self-consciousness, in an inability to "receive" oral sex from a male partner, an account which fits with women's reports of various genital anxieties, particularly around oral sex (Braun and Wilkinson, 2003; Reinholtz and Muehlenhard, 1995; Roberts et al., 1996). Women's reports of genital anxiety reflect a range of negative sociocultural representations of women's genitalia (Braun and Wilkinson, 2001), and it seems some women "live these [negative] cultural meanings in their embodiment" (Roberts et al., 1996: 119). However, my concern is not just about women's embodiment, as psychology here provides the "moral justification" (Frank, 2003) for cosmetic surgery to alleviate this distress.

While *impeded* sexual possibilities and pleasures were central in media and surgeons' accounts of why women might choose to have FGCS, *increased* sexual pleasure as an outcome of surgery was the main area in which sexual pleasure was discussed. FGCS, in a variety of forms, was represented as increasing sexual pleasure. The *aim* of sexual enhancement was often explicitly stated in the titles of magazine articles about FGCS—such as "THE G-SHOT . . . plastic surgery for your orgasm" (M22)—and in the setting up of media stories:

Extract 6: New Woman Magazine, UK, date unknown

Would you go under the knife to improve your sex life? These four women did. (M29)

Extract 7: Marie Claire Magazine, UK, 2000

What are the reasons for surgery? Firstly, to improve their sex lives. (M4)

Extract 8: Marie Claire Magazine, US, 2000

Some women are going under the knife to change the appearance of their genitals, while others are having surgery in the hopes of better orgasms. (M3)

In some, the possibility of increased sexual pleasure was initially framed with mild scepticism:

Extract 9: Cosmopolitan Magazine, AUS/NZ, 1998

Doctors [in the US] claim to be able to boost women's sexual pleasure, taking them to previously uncharted erotic heights. And their secret weapon in the quest for sexual ecstasy? The scalpel. (M1)

Extract 10: Marie Claire Magazine, UK, 2000

The sales pitch being that sexual gratification of the female is diminished if friction is lost because of a slack vagina, so this procedure tightens up your bits and helps you reach orgasm. (M4)

Extract 11: FQ Magazine, NZ, 2004

Will sex be mind-blowing once you've been trimmed or tightened? Well, the jury is still out. (M31)

Any initial scepticism in reporting the doctors' "claim" that the operations "supposedly increase sexual pleasure" (M3) was typically not reiterated in most media accounts of surgical results and patient experiences, or in surgeon accounts. Instead, overwhelmingly, increased pleasure was noted:

Extract 12: Cleo Magazine, NZ, 2001

Feedback from patients suggests their sex lives have improved enormously. (M7)

Extract 13: male urologist, AUS

S7: I've known women who are mono-orgasmic to become multiply orgasmic as a result.

All procedures, even ostensibly cosmetic ones such as labiaplasty, were frequently framed as being "successful" in terms of increased sexual pleasure:

Extract 14: Cosmopolitan Magazine, AUS/NZ, 2004

I am no longer embarrassed to be naked and my sex life has improved because I'm more confident. (M23)

Extract 15: Company Magazine, UK, 2003

I was so thrilled with my new vagina, Dan and I "tried it out" after just four weeks. What a difference—it was like my whole sex life was beginning again. Suddenly I discovered how amazing oral sex could be, because I could finally relax and be myself during sex. I didn't have to worry about my boyfriend seeing me naked. (M18)

In these extracts, improved sexual function was identified as a key outcome of "cosmetic" procedures. In Extract 15, psychological changes post-surgery allowed the woman to experience cunnilingus. Surgery reportedly expanded women's sexual repertoires. However, such reports continue to situate heterosex within the bounds of normative heterosexuality, through the suggestion that certain sexual acts (cunnilingus) can only be engaged in, and enjoyed, by either or both partners, within a very limited range of female genital aesthetics. This aesthetic is one where the labia minora do not protrude beyond the labia majora—a youthful, almost pre-pubescent aesthetic, and one often associated with, and derived from, the "unreal" vulvas displayed in heterosexual male-oriented pornography (see Adams, 1997; S. W. Davis, 2002). This was explicitly noted:

Extract 16: Shine Magazine, AUS/NZ, 2001

A lot of women bring in *Playboy,* show me pictures of vaginas and say, "I want to look like this." (M5)

The genital produced is one in which diversity is replaced with conformity to this particular aesthetic, a "cookie cutter" (I25) genital. FGCS becomes a practice of changing women's diverse bodies to fit a certain (male-oriented) aesthetic of what women's genitals *should*

look like, if they are to engage in cunnilingus (or other sexual activities). With male (hetero)sexuality continuing to be constructed as *visual* (e.g. Moghaddam and Braun, 2004), with desire based on the aesthetic, such accounts reinforce a traditional model of male sexuality, and female sexuality alongside it. FGCS effectively becomes surgery to change bodies to fit, and to enable certain sexual practices, through psychological/emotional changes enabled by bodily transformation. A pathologization of "large" labia minora has a long history, and a long association with perceived sexual "deviance" (S. Gilman, 1985; Terry, 1995). FGCS appears to offer a surgical process for subsequently passing—to oneself, as well as others—as "sexy" or just as "normal" (see K. Davis, 2003).

In these accounts, sexual pleasure occupies a status of almost unquestioned good. . . . There are "cultural expectations that each individual has a right and a duty to achieve and give maximum satisfaction in their sexual relationships" (Nicolson, 1993: 56). FGCS is framed as a viable means to achieve this. A key question to consider, however, is what (female) sexual pleasure is being offered:

Extract 17: Cosmopolitan Magazine, AUS/NZ, 1998

Four months after the operation, Kate claims to be enjoying the best sex of her life . . . "removing the excess fat has made me much more easily aroused. Now I achieve orgasm easily and often." (M1)

Extract 18: New Woman Magazine, AUS, 2003

"The G-Shot procedure is all about maximising sexual pleasure for women. By injecting a fluid made up partly of collagen we can increase the G spot to three or four times its normal size, so it's easier to stimulate.

"The effects last about four months and my patients tell me how even something as gentle as yoga is giving them orgasms!" (M20)

Extract 19: New Woman Magazine, UK, date unknown
What a result though! All I have to do is think about sex and I can feel my G-spot react. Even during my spinning class I can feel the bike seat pressing on it—and I have to pretend I'm just enjoying the workout! I've also had my first ever multiple orgasm and it was great. (M29)

The conception of "sexual pleasure" for women was typically synonymous with orgasm—or multiple-orgasm. By prioritizing orgasm over other forms of sexual pleasure, such accounts work to reaffirm an orgasm imperative (Heath, 1982; Potts, 2000). Orgasm was framed, a-contextually, as positive—the possibility of orgasm in non-sexual situations was identified not negatively (as, for instance, impeding the woman's ability to partake in exercise without fear of orgasm). . . . Typically, orgasm was framed in unequivocally positive ways:

Extract 20: Cleo Magazine, NZ, 2003
Rosemary is promised about four months of orgasmic delights . . . having heard about the G-Shot through a friend who raved about her endless climaxes, Rosemary had no hesitation in handing over US$1,850 for a dose of heightened pleasure. (M22)

Therefore, the accounts of pleasure in heterosex—and it typically *was* heterosex—presented in the data failed to offer any radical questioning of orgasm as the pinnacle of sexual pleasure and achievement (Jackson and Scott, 2001; Potts, 2000). "Better" sex typically meant orgasmic sex (or, sometimes, simply more sex), and more (and better) sex was inherently framed as good. By locating orgasm as so central to women's sexual pleasure, other ways in which sex could be more pleasurable—e.g. more fun, more intense, more relaxed, more intimate—were relegated to second place, if any, behind orgasm. This affirms what Seidman (1992: 7) has identified as a "new tyranny of orgasmic pleasure."

Although physical changes, such as an enlarged G-spot or tighter vagina, were often identified as resulting in increased pleasure, *psychological* elements were also highlighted as key in explanations for increased sexual pleasure, post-surgery:

Extract 21: male plastic surgeon, UK
S1: when you feel better about what you look like down there if you feel happier with the cosmetic aspect of . . . yourself of your genitalia then you are more relaxed in the bedroom . . . and a lot of patients report back to me that they do feel better and therefore have better sex because . . . they're less embarrassed. . . .

Extract 22: Flare Magazine, CA, 1998
What does work, according to Angela, is the boost in self-esteem that stems from feeling sexually confident. "I spent years not feeling good about myself and my sexuality," she says. "I started to retreat from my husband. I tried to avoid him sexually because every time we tried, it was disastrous."
It all gets back to the psychosexual response, says Dr Stubbs. (M26)

Extract 23: Shine Magazine, AUS/NZ, 2001
My sex life has improved so much since the operation—we have more sex now than we've ever had. I'm much more into my boyfriend and now that I'm tighter, I'm much more confident about initiating sex. Even better, my boyfriend is enjoying sex with me more, as there's much more stimulation for him, too. (M5)

In these extracts, the psychological was invoked as an essential ingredient in the production of female pleasure, and, indeed, situated as a primary reason this surgery was effective in producing increased sexual pleasure for women. . . .

Extract 23 is relatively unusual in that increased male sexual pleasure was noted. Women were the primary focus in accounts of sexual pleasure, with comparatively little discussion of male sexual pleasure. This is not surprising, as cosmetic surgery is necessarily often framed as "for oneself" rather than for others (see Fraser, 2003). Where male sexual pleasure was referred to, it was often positioned as secondary to, or less important than, female sexual pleasure. For instance, Extract 23 situates her boyfriend's increased sexual pleasure as secondary to her pleasure, as an added bonus, something that makes it "even better." . . .

Overall, the prioritizing of female sexual pleasure and general lack of discussion of male sexual pleasure work to construct FGCS as something that is in the (sexual) interests of women, rather than in the sexual interests of (heterosexual) men. Through current accounts, FGCS is effectively constructed as a liberatory action for women—it produces sexual pleasure, which is, socioculturally, almost mandatory for women—rather than a capitulation to unreasonable patriarchal demands on women's bodies. However, while FGCS offers (apparent) empowerment to individuals who have it, albeit within a limited range of options, it simultaneously reinforces oppressive social norms for women (see Gagne and McGaughey, 2002; Gillespie, 1996; Negrin, 2002).

FGCS: NORMATIVE HETEROSEXUALITY, GENERIC BODIES, AND GENERIC PLEASURES

The central role that (female) pleasure plays in accounts of FGCS is revealing in terms of contemporary discourses of (hetero)sexuality and what it could/should mean to be a woman in the West today. Women's sexual pleasure—or ability to orgasm—appears as a central concern for women, and indeed for society. The account is almost exclusively one where, sexually, women should be comfortable in their bodies and should be able to enjoy sex—and the more sex, and sexual pleasure, the better.

Women are represented as (inherently) entitled to sexual pleasure, and indeed, inherently (hetero)sexual. That *these* women are not sexually "liberated," sexually "satisfied," or, even, as sexually satisfied as other people appear to be, is, at least in part, what is "wrong" with their preoperative genitalia. In this sense, accounts of FGCS and women's sexual pleasure fit squarely within a discourse of liberal sexuality (Hollway, 1989), and even, within some feminist discourse around the importance of equality in sex (see Braun et al., 2003). It also affirms an imperative for "more and better sexual gratification" (Hart and Wellings, 2002: 899), by whatever means possible.

However, the construction of female sexual pleasure in relation to this surgery fails to challenge the bounds of normative heterosexuality. First, sexual pleasure was often (although not exclusively) framed as being derived through coitus, particularly in the case of vaginal tightening, and the sexual pleasure that is derived was typically orgasmic. In this sense, it can be seen to be (at least in part) a practice of designing bodies to fit certain sexual practices, rather than designing sexual practices to fit bodies. We then have to ask whether it is so different from the "love surgery" of the now disgraced Dr James Burt, who surgically altered women's genitalia to make them more amenable to stimulation during coitus (Adams, 1997). As Adams (1997: 64) noted, such surgeries "make women conform to traditional heterosexual values." The same criticism applies to FGCS: the sexual "freedom" that is being produced is a freedom to enjoy sex within a very limited frame of reference.

Moreover, at the same time as it constructs the legitimate female body as an orgasmic one, it reinforces this "ideal" as something not all women necessarily (easily) achieve (without surgery). So sexual pleasure, through orgasm, is simultaneously situated both as what most women can/should do and as a current impossibility for some women. The very construction of FGCS as surgery to enhance or enable orgasm fits with an ongoing construction of a woman's orgasm as difficult to achieve, in contrast to a man's inevitable one (Jackson and Scott, 2001; Moghaddam and Braun, 2004). Moreover, although couched in terms of liberation of women (to a "full" enjoyment of sex), rather than pathology, the framing of FGCS as a solution to "sub-par" sexual pleasure on the woman's part decontextualizes sex, locating any deficiency in the woman's body/mind, and offering an individualized solution. In this way, FGCS fits within a broadening medicalization of sexual behaviour (Hart and Wellings, 2002; Tiefer, 1997), which, Tiefer (1997: 112) has argued, has "only reinforced a limited script for heterosexual sexual life."

These points raise the question of the generic versus the particular. The idea of a surgical "fix" or enhancement of (lack of) sexual pleasure locates sexual pleasure at the level of the *individual* body, rather than in relation to a "fit" between bodies/people and the practices they are engaged in. In this sense, the sexual enhancement of the body is framed as generic sexual enhancement, regardless of with whom, and how, one might be having sex. This framing disregards the particularities of sex, with different partners, with different practices, for different purposes, and, indeed, in different moods, modes, and venues. Sex, sexual pleasure, and even sexual desires vary hugely according to this range of contextualizing variables. Accounts of FGCS not only fail to account for this, but actually work to promote the idea of generic sexual pleasure as possible.

The context of consumer culture provides another angle from which to examine public discourse around FGCS. Bordo's (1997: 42) analysis identifies that a consumer system "depends on our perceiving ourselves as defective and that [it] will continually find new ways to do this." Media accounts that demonstrate a

"cure" to some problem for women can be seen to also contribute to the creation of that problem in the first place. FGCS, and media coverage of it, have the potential to produce consumer anxiety (S. W. Davis, 2002). One item commented that media coverage had "taken a very unusual phenomena and concocted a new "embarrassing problem" that could get readers squinting nervously at the privates" (M28). In the case of labiaplasty, then, there is the potential that "a brand-new worry is being created" (S. W. Davis, 2002: 8). In these accounts, the appearance and sexual function of women's genitalia are rendered *legitimately* problematic and sub-optimal; this part of the body is legitimately commodified, and positioned as "upgradeable" (see Negrin, 2002). More than this, these media have the potential to construct the very nature of problems and their *solutions,* simultaneously. Both the problem of aesthetically "unappealing" genitalia and the desire for better sex have a ready worked-up solution—surgery.

While FGCS might seem relatively arcane, a form of cosmetic surgery very few women would access, and one that is unlikely to become popular, the surgeons I interviewed indicated that media coverage seems to increase demand for their services. This fits with Kathy Davis's (2003: 134) observation that media coverage of new surgical interventions "seduc[es] more individuals to place their bodies under the surgeon's knife" (see also Wolf, 1990). The history of other cosmetic procedures does nothing to dispute this concern. Indeed, as Haiken has commented in her history of cosmetic surgery, individual change can often be "easier" than social change. . . .

The appearance of FGCS raises important questions about the alteration of the body in the pursuit of pleasure, which I have only started to address. If media coverage can contribute to the nature of, and legitimate, a "new" problem for women, with a ready-made surgical solution, we need to continue to act as "cultural critics" (Bordo, 1993), and question the assumptions on which such surgery rests, and the models of sexuality, bodies, and practices it promotes.

NOTES

1. My classification of these surgeries as "cosmetic" is not necessarily the way surgeons or the women themselves would classify them. Some of these surgeries are primarily (or exclusively) done for functional reasons, and even where cosmesis is prioritized, the notion that surgery is purely cosmetic is challenged through diverse accounts of "functionality."

2. Although cosmetic surgery is increasingly popular among men, it is important to retain some sense of the gendered context in which cosmetic procedures originated and became popularized, such that women were (and continue to be) the primary consumers of cosmetic surgery (see K. Davis, 2003, for a discussion of the limitations of "equality" analyses in relation to cosmetic surgery).

3. The techniques might be the same or similar in some instances. At a more theoretical level, the practices around the construction of "normal" genitalia through FGCS are, like other genital surgeries, part of the ongoing social, and material, construction of (gendered) genital meaning and appearance. Moreover, an inappropriately "masculine" appearance/perception of their genitalia was one of the reported reasons some women desired FGCS. The constructed genitalia tend to display *more* gendered genital difference (bigger penises, tighter vaginas, smaller labia minora). So while much cosmetic surgery can be seen to produce the surgical "erasure of embodied difference" (K. Davis, 2003: 133), the one difference that is promoted, rather than erased, in FGCS is "gendered" (genital) difference.

4. A comparison between these western practices and FGM was rarely mentioned in the data, and a focus on notions of "free choice," purported low risk to health, and likely increased sexual pleasure, all rhetorically constructed FGCS as inherently *different* [from] FGM. However, Manderson and colleagues (Allotey et al., 2001; Manderson, 1999) point to contradictions between how FGM and FGCS are treated in the West (see also S.W. Davis, 2002; Essen and Johnsdotter, 2004; Sheldon and Wilkinson, 1998).

5. Quotations from data are coded by letter and number: S = surgeon; M = magazine; N = news media; I = Internet material other than "Internet magazines." Numbers were applied sequentially across each data source, starting from 1. In the surgeon extracts, material in parentheses (like this) indicates a best guess as to what was said at that point on the tape.

REFERENCES

Adams, A. 1997. "Moulding Women's Bodies: The Surgeon as Sculptor," in D. S. Wilson and C. M. Laennec (eds.) *Bodily Discursions: Gender, Representations, Technologies,* pp. 59–80. New York: State University of New York Press.

Allotey, P., Manderson, L. and Grover, S. 2001. "The Politics of Female Genital Surgery in Displaced Communities," *Critical Public Health* 11: 189–201.

Bordo, S. 1993. *Unbearable Weight: Feminism, Western Culture, and the Body.* Berkeley: University of California Press.

Bordo, S. 1997. *Twilight Zones: The Hidden Life of Cultural Images from Plato to O.J.* Berkeley: University of California Press.

Braun, V., Gavey, N. and McPhillips, K. 2003. "The 'Fair Deal'? Unpacking Accounts of Reciprocity in Heterosex," *Sexualities* 6(2): 237–61.

Braun, V. and Wilkinson, S. 2001. "Socio-cultural Representations of the Vagina," *Journal of Reproductive and Infant Psychology* 19: 17–32.

Braun, V. and Wilkinson, S. 2003. "Liability or Asset? Women Talk about the Vagina," *Psychology of Women Section Review* 5(2): 28–42.

Burr, V. 1995. *An Introduction to Social Constructionism.* London: Routledge.

Connell, R. W. 1997. "Sexual Revolution," in L. Segal (ed.) *New Sexual Agendas,* pp. 60–76. New York: New York University Press.

Davis, K. 2003. *Dubious Equalities and Embodied Differences: Cultural Studies on Cosmetic Surgery.* Lanham, MD: Rowman and Littlefield.

Davis, S. W. 2002. "Loose Lips Sink Ships," *Feminist Studies* 28: 7–35.

Essen, B. and Johnsdotter, S. 2004. "Female Genital Mutilation in the West: Traditional Circumcision versus Genital Cosmetic Surgery," *Acta Obstetricia et Gynecologica Scandinavica* 83: 611–13.

Frank, A. W. 2003. "Connecting Body Parts: Technoluxe, Surgical Shapings, and Bioethics." Paper presented at the *Vital Politics* Conference, London.

Fraser, S. 2003b. *Cosmetic Surgery, Gender and Culture.* Houndmills: Palgrave Macmillan.

Gagne, P. and McGaughey, D. 2002. "Designing Women— Cultural Hegemony and the Exercise of Power Among Women Who Have Undergone Elective Mammoplasty," *Gender and Society* 16: 814–38.

Gillespie, R. 1996. "Women, the Body and Brand Extension in Medicine: Cosmetic Surgery and the Paradox of Choice," *Women and Health* 24(4): 69–85.

Gilman, S. 1985. *Difference and Pathology: Stereotypes of Sexuality, Race and Madness.* Ithaca, NY: Cornell University Press.

Gordon, M. 1971. "From an Unfortunate Necessity to a Cult of Mutual Orgasm: Sex in American Marital

Education Literature 1830–1940," in J. M. Henslin (ed.) *Studies in the Sociology of Sex*, pp. 53–77. New York: Appleton-Century-Crofts.

Haiken, E. 1997. *Venus Envy: A History of Cosmetic Surgery*. Baltimore, MD: The Johns Hopkins University Press.

Haiken, E. 2000. "The Making of the Modern Face: Cosmetic Surgery," *Social Research* 67: 81–93.

Hart, G. and Wellings, K. 2002. "Sexual Behaviour and its Medicalisation: in Sickness and Health," *British Medical Journal* 324: 896–900.

Heath, S. 1982. *The Sexual Fix*. New York: Schocken Books.

Hollway, W. 1989. *Subjectivity and Method in Psychology: Gender, Meaning and Science*. London: Sage.

Jackson, S. and Scott, S. 2001. "Embodying Orgasm: Gendered Power Relations and Sexual Pleasure," in E. Kaschak and L. Tiefer (eds.) *A New View of Women's Sexual Problems*, pp. 99–110. New York: The Haworth Press.

Manderson, L. 1999. "Local Rites and the Body Politic: Tensions Between Cultural Diversity and Universal Rites", paper presented at the *Sexual Diversity and Human Rights: Beyond Boundaries* conference, Manchester, July.

Moghaddam, P. and Braun, V. 2004. "?'Most of us Guys are Raring to go Anytime, Anyplace, Anywhere': Male (and Female) Sexuality in *Cosmopolitan* and *Cleo*," Manuscript under submission.

Negrin, L. 2002. "Cosmetic Surgery and the Eclipse of Identity," *Body and Society* 8: 21–42.

Nicolson, P. 1993. "Public Values and Private Beliefs: Why do some Women Refer Themselves for Sex Therapy?" in J. M. Ussher and C. D. Baker (eds.) *Psychological Perspectives on Sexual Problems: New Directions in Theory and Practice*, pp. 56–76. London: Routledge.

Potts, A. 2000. "Coming, Coming, Gone: A Feminist Deconstruction of Heterosexual Orgasm," *Sexualities* 3: 55–76.

Reinholtz, R. K. and Muehlenhard, C. L. 1995. "Genital Perceptions and Sexual Activity in a College Population" *Journal of Sex Research* 32: 155–65.

Roberts, C., Kippax, S., Spongberg, M. and Crawford, J. 1996. "Going Down": Oral Sex, Imaginary Bodies and HIV," *Body and Society* 2(3): 107–24.

Seidman, S. 1991. *Romantic Longings: Love in America, 1830–1980*. New York: Routledge.

Seidman, S. 1992. *Embattled Eros: Sexual Politics and Ethics in Contemporary America*. New York: Routledge.

Sheldon, S. and Wilkinson, S. 1998. "Female Genital Mutilation and Cosmetic Surgery: Regulating Non-therapeutic Body Modification," *Bioethics* 12: 263–85.

Sullivan, D. A. 2001. *Cosmetic Surgery: The Cutting Edge of Commercial Medicine in America*. New Brunswick, NJ: Rutgers University Press.

Terry, J. 1995. "Anxious Slippages Between "Us" and "Them": A Brief History of the Scientific Search for Homosexual Bodies," in J. Terry and J. Urla (eds.) *Deviant Bodies: Critical Perspectives on Difference in Science and Popular Culture*, pp. 129–69. Bloomington: Indiana University Press.

Tiefer, L. 1995. *Sex is Not a Natural Act and Other Essays*. Boulder, CO: Westview Press.

Tiefer, L. 1997. "Medicine, Morality, and the Public Management of Sexual Matters," in L. Segal (ed.) *New Sexual Agendas*, pp. 103–12. New York: New York University Press.

Tiefer, L. 2000. "The Social Construction and Social Effects of Sex Research: The Sexological Model of Sexuality," in C. B. Travis and J. W. White (eds.) *Sexuality, Society, and Feminism*, pp. 79–107. Washington, DC: American Psychological Association.

Toerien, M. and Wilkinson, S. 2004. "Exploring the Depilation Norm: a Qualitative Questionnaire Study of Women's Body Hair Removal," *Qualitative Research in Psychology* 1: 69–92.

White, J. W., Bondurant, B. and Travis, C. B. 2000. "Social Constructions of Sexuality: Unpacking Hidden Meanings," in C. B. Travis and J. W. White (eds) *Sexuality, Society, and Feminism*, pp. 11–33. Washington, DC: American Psychological Association.

Wolf, N. 1990. *The Beauty Myth*. London: Vintage.

THE PLEASURES OF CHILDBIRTH

INA MAY GASKIN

Is childbirth always painful? Although at first thought it might seem easy to answer this straightforward question with a loud and unequivocal yes, the truth is less simple. It is true that many women who have given birth more than once answer in the affirmative. But I have given birth four times without pain or medication, so my answer is not always. There are exceptions, and from them we can gain important insights about labor and birth.

I am far from being alone in saying that birth is not always painful. In fact, under the right circumstances and with good preparation during pregnancy, labor and birth can even be pleasurable for many women. How do I know? I have worked as a midwife for over thirty years, and many of the women I have attended have told me so. I have been with them during these ecstatic experiences, virtually all of which occurred in women who took no pain-numbing medication. Just as compelling, my own body has informed me.

Let's start by looking at some of the written evidence that exists. Numerous reports of painless birth have been gathered over the last couple of centuries by missionaries, travelers, soldiers, and doctors. Ezra Stiles, an early American clergyman and educator, wrote during the period of 1755 to 1794: "I have often been told that a pregnant Squaw [sic] will turn aside and deliver herself, and take up the Infant and wash it in a Brook, and walk off" (Vogel cited in Speert, 1980, p. 1).

Judith Goldsmith, a modern-day writer, has gathered many reports from European observers of various cultures. Among them is the following account of Guyanese women of South America in 1791: "When on the march an Indian is taken with labor, she just steps aside, is delivered, wraps up the baby with the afterbirth and runs in haste after the others. At the first stream that presents itself she washes herself and the infant" (1990, p. 2). Another seemingly painless birth was that noted by a visitor to the island of Alor, near Java, who witnessed six births without seeing a mother show real signs of pain. Sweat and soft groans were noted, but each of the six women gave birth easily (2). Livingston Jones, a visitor among the Tlinget people of Alaska, remarked: "The vast majority of Tlinget women suffer very little and some not at all, when their children are born. They have been known to give birth while sleeping" (cited in Goldsmith, 1990, p. 2).

Giving birth while sleeping! How can this be? As unusual as this seems, it can and does occasionally happen. Dr. Alice Stockham describes a doctor's account of a birth that took place in 1828:

On his arrival he found the house in the utmost confusion, and was told that the child had been born before the messenger was dispatched for the doctor. From the lady herself he learned that, about half an hour previously, she had been awakened from a natural sleep by the alarm of a daughter about five years old, who slept with her. This alarm was occasioned by the little girl feeling the movements, and hearing the cries of an infant in bed. To the mother's great surprise, she had brought forth her child without any consciousness of the fact. (1890, p. 3)

Stockham's book *Tokology*, published late in the nineteenth century, quoted a world traveler

From "The Pleasures of Childbirth" by Ina May Gaskin. *Arizona Choices*, Volume 1, Number 5, December 2005/January 2006. Reprinted by permission of Ina May Gaskin.

who said, "I know of no country, no tribe, no class, where childbirth is attended with so much pain and trouble as in North America" (1890, p. 11). She believed that the reputed better performance of peasant or indigenous women in birth was largely due to their superior physical vigor from a healthy diet and regular exercise. European-American women could have healthy births, too, she argued, adding:

I attended a neighbour of mine in four different confinements. I never was able to reach her before the birth of the child, although I lived only across the street, and, according to her injunctions, always kept my shoes "laced up." She sent for me, too, at the first indication of labor. There was always one prolonged effort and the child was expelled. (1890, p. 15)

Another lady patron had two children without a particle of pain. With the first she was alone with her nurse. During the evening she remarked that she felt weary and believed that she would lie down. She had been on the bed no more than twenty minutes when she called to her nurse, saying: "How strangely I feel! I wish you would see what is the matter," when to their astonishment the child was already born. (1890, p. 3)

Even though it is possible to find an occasional reference in U.S. medical textbooks of the nineteenth and twentieth centuries to women of "civilized" cultures giving birth with little or no apparent pain, such accounts are usually the exception rather than the rule. In general, childbirth pain is viewed to be severe and intrinsic to the process of labor and birth. Even in texts written during the nineteenth century, when anesthetics and analgesics were not yet a normal feature of care giving, there is little recognition that childbirth pain can vary tremendously according to the position adopted (or required) by the mother during labor and birth.

In one of the exceptional works, *Labor among Primitive Peoples,* published in 1883, Dr. George Engelmann made a huge contribution by synthesizing knowledge drawn from obstetrics, cultural anthropology, and massage therapy. Renowned as an accomplished biologist, archaeologist, and anthropologist, he corresponded regularly with a long list of scholars and explorers who also studied the medical practices of people who still lived according to "primal" ways. His book supports the general observations about the greater ease of birthgiving among indigenous women compared with their "civilized" sisters.

To Engelmann, the short, comparatively easy labors of women who lived in cultures untouched by civilization could be explained by several factors. He noted that these women typically led active lives right up to the time they went into labor. But his correspondence with physicians who knew about indigenous ways of giving birth convinced him that it was not just exercise during pregnancy that made birth easier for indigenous women. He thought their behavior in labor was at least as important a factor. Unlike European-American women, who stayed in their beds during the last weeks and months of pregnancy and in labor, indigenous mothers moved about freely and adopted various positions, many of them upright, during the different stages of labor. There was no supposedly superior class of women in these societies to sanction practices and positions that were obstetrically fashionable, and there was no prudery, so they behaved according to instinct. Equally important, the clothing they wore during pregnancy did not hamper free movement or full expansion of the lungs. The comfortable and practical clothes of indigenous women contrasted sharply with the clothing styles of prosperous civilized women of the nineteenth century, a period when corsets with whalebone or steel stays were typically worn laced so tightly that women wearing them sometimes suffered displacement of their kidneys, liver, and other organs. Fainting was common among corset-wearers because tight lacing kept them from breathing deeply.

To his great credit, Engelmann was one of the few North American doctors who took the view that civilized women had something to learn from women who were more in tune with nature. He was very frank about his opinion that women whose connection with their instincts had not been altered by civilization were far more able to give birth without complication, protracted labor, or unbearable pain, and that physicians, as well as European-American women, had much to learn from them. "The savage mother, the Negress, the Australian or Indian, still governed by her instinct, is far in advance of the ordinary woman of our civilization," he emphasized (1883, p. xvii).

Nineteenth-century feminist philosopher and writer Elizabeth Cady Stanton regarded pregnancy as a natural state rather than an illness, and she knew from her own experience that labor and birth could be painless. Instead of accepting physicians' advice to stay in bed from the seventh or eighth months of pregnancy until a month after giving birth, she kept on with her usual work until she went into labor with each of her seven children. She felt that confinement (restriction of movement by clothes or social custom) was the cause of women's difficult labors, as well as their numerous postpartum ailments. After the birth of her fifth child, she wrote:

I never felt such sacredness in carrying a child as I have in the case of this one. She is the largest and most vigorous baby I have ever had, weighing twelve pounds. And yet my labor was short and easy. I laid down about fifteen minutes and brought forth this big girl. I sat up immediately, changed my own clothes, put on a wet bandage, and after a few hours' repose sat up again. Am I not almost a savage? For what refined, delicate, genteel, civilized woman would get well in so indecently short a time? Dear me, how much cruel bondage of mind and suffering of body poor woman will escape when she takes the liberty of being her own physician of both body and mind? (1971, p. 4)

Probably the best-known physician in the twentieth century to study the riddle of pain in childbirth (at least, in the English-speaking world) was Dr. Grantly Dick-Read. He included the story of the first pain-free birth he ever witnessed in *Childbirth without Fear* [(first published in 1944)] because it amazed him enough to change forever the way he thought about childbirth. The birth in question took place in the Whitechapel district of London around 1913. Despite the fact that the mother was laboring in the poorest of hovels, with the rain pouring in through a broken window, Dick-Read remarked on the atmosphere of "quiet kindliness" in the room. The only note of dissonance during the entire experience stemmed from his attempt to persuade the laboring woman to let him put the chloroform mask over her nose and mouth as the baby's head was being born. Dick-Read (1959) wrote:

She, however, resented the suggestion, and firmly but kindly refused to take this help. It was the first time in my short experience that I had ever been refused when offering chloroform. As I was about to leave some time later, I asked her why it was she would not use the mask. She did not answer at once, but looked from the old woman who had been assisting to the window through which was bursting the first light of dawn; then shyly she turned to me and said: "It didn't hurt. It wasn't meant to, was it, doctor?" (p. 5)

For months and years after that experience, Dick-Read thought about the woman's question and eventually came to realize that "there was no law in nature and no design that could justify the pain of childbirth" (1959, p. 39). Later experience in World War I in foreign lands gave him chances to witness many more apparently painless births. The sum of all these experiences plus his own battlefield experience of terror and loneliness led him to articulate his theory of why some women experience pain in birth while others do not. "It slowly dawned on me that it was the peacefulness of the relatively painless labor that distinguished it most clearly from the others. There was a calm, it seemed almost faith, in the normal and natural outcome of childbirth," he wrote (1959, p. 34).

Dick-Read was the first physician to write about birth as a spiritual experience and to discuss fear as a major contributing factor to pain in childbirth. He wrote that the pain of what he called "cultural childbirth" was caused by a combination of fear and muscle tension caused by ignorance of the birthing process, isolation during labor, and uncompassionate care received in hospital labor and delivery wards.

Remember the soft groans mentioned earlier, in reference to a Javanese birth that took place in the nineteenth century? It is worth noting that the only way one could write about orgasm during that period of U.S. history was to allude to soft moans or groans. By the 1970s times had changed, and a new group of people began to weigh in on the topic of painless birth: women who, in the tradition of Elizabeth Cady Stanton, had given birth themselves and had something to say about their experience. Among them were Raven Lang (1972), Jeannine Parvati Baker (1974), and myself (1975). Not only did these writers mention painless birth, they also mentioned the phenomenon of orgasm during labor or birth.

Since the appearance of these books, virtually nothing has been written on this subject. When I began hearing from young women that many were opting for elective cesarean as a way of avoiding pain during labor and birth, I began to wonder why so many writers and childbirth educators never mentioned the possibility of it. Is it so rare that they simply can't conceive of it, or do they wish to avoid raising women's expectations given that many women would still experience pain even if they knew that orgasm was a possibility? I began asking young women if they had ever heard of women having ecstatic labors and births and found that most hadn't.

Curious about how many women I could find who had orgasmic experiences in labor or birth, I decided to conduct a small survey among some close friends. Of 151 women, I found 32 who reported experiencing at least one orgasmic birth. That is 21 percent—considerably higher than I had expected. Most of the women had their babies on The Farm (the community in Tennessee where my colleagues and I have been practicing midwifery for over a quarter-century), but interestingly, some said the orgasm occurred during a hospital birth. I have included some of the women's comments below, as they perhaps shed some light on what factors are present when women have birth experiences such as these. (I have changed the women's names out of respect for their privacy.)

Julia: I had an orgasm when I had my fourth child. It happened while I was pushing. We went to the hospital after I had been "stalled" at nine centimeters for a while, attempting a home birth with some midwives who made me nervous. I no sooner got inside the door than I began having overwhelming urges to push that baby OUT!!! I orgasmed as she was being born. They just barely got me onto the delivery table in time for her birth, but I was oblivious to all that because it was feeling so good to get her out.

Margaret: I had a cosmic union orgasm, a bliss-enhanced state. In a way, this has had a permanent effect. I can still go to that place.

Vivian: Being in labor felt like work; but giving birth, the actual process of passing the baby's entire body out of my womb (which did happen quite quickly), was indescribably incredible, particularly the first time.

Marilyn: My last birth was very orgasmic in a sustained sort of way, like I was riding on waves of orgasmic bliss. I knew more what to expect, was less afraid, and tried to meet and flow with the energy rather than avoid or resist as I had the first time. The effect was probably mostly psychological in that it gave me tremendous satisfaction just to have accomplished such a difficult passage safely. I felt great for months afterward, which helped me feel positive about myself in general. This, in turn, affected how I felt about myself sexually. I also think that, for me, learning to let go and let my body take over in labor (as opposed to thinking about it with my mind all the way through!) helped me tap into a part of me I never knew before and helped me feel more willing to let go while making love.

Janelle: Giving birth was like pre- and post-orgasm by the second or third birth but did not contain the pulsation felt at climax. Being in tune with rushes [contractions], pushing, deeply relaxing in between was a very sexual and powerful experience but higher than orgasm, because orgasm can seem more self-gratifying and is short-lived. Giving birth is such a spiritual experience, so miraculous, you are very in tune with God and seeing the divinity in everyone that the sexual part is not that important. You are totally immersed in selfless love and so the blissful and sexual feelings are a byproduct, a gift of allowing your body to do what it knows how to do while your consciousness is very expanded.

Paula: I have been pondering this question for some time. I have always felt that labor and birth were like one big orgasm. The contractions were like waves of pleasure rippling through the body. I only found the final few centimeters of dilation as extremely strong and slightly less pleasurable. But I felt like labor and birth were/are a continuous orgasm. I can't say that it is like the orgasm experienced during sexual intercourse, where I find myself being engulfed and lost in the wave of orgasm. The type I experienced during labor and birth was a more all-consuming feeling that required more of my attention than that experienced during sex. However, I do feel that it is an orgasm. The birth itself is very orgasmic as the baby comes through the birth canal—extremely pleasurable and rewarding.

Maria: I had to think about this one for a few days. At first I thought "no," but there certainly were sensations in the first stage during dilation that were incredibly intense when Ted would kiss me or I would bury my face in his neck during a rush. I did not have a particularly hard time during the first stage of any of my births and remember enjoying the birthing process for the most part. The general excitement, rushes of energy, and all the touching were very pleasurable. The sensations weren't the same as an orgasm exactly, but

when the rushes would end, the total splash-out [relaxation] was very similar to how I feel after orgasm now (which I call the wet-noodle effect). For me, however, the second stage was another story. I remember not liking that part because of the intense stinging of the tissue stretching. I always thought I was weird since I liked the first stage and couldn't really get into the second stage. Anyway, it goes without saying that good energy rushes are enjoyable and, even though I don't know if my inner muscles were twitching rhythmically or not, having a baby was the greatest energy sweep ever. I think it is very probable that it is much larger than an orgasm rush, or certainly different. One other thing I think might be true—I think it is possible that I hadn't perfected the art of having superorgasms back then when I was so young and having the babies. Since then, over the years, I have become quite good at it, so I'm not sure if that lack of experience could have kept me from experiencing some of those sensations during labor and birth.

Some of the women described, instead of orgasm, a euphoria that had some similarities to the bliss they associate with sexual pleasure.

Elayne: I didn't have an orgasm, but I felt a little bit like it when I had my first baby. And that was only at the transition shortly before pushing. For a moment I felt like [I do] . . . shortly before orgasm—being high, having pain, and being afraid [of] what's coming next. And I felt all this at the same time.

Alicia: No, I can't say I would describe the experience as "orgasmic." Rather, it was "euphoric." To say it was orgasmic would describe the experience in almost a base way. Rather, it was spiritual.

Nanette: I wouldn't say I experienced orgasm either in labor or giving birth. However, I would say the sensation of out-of-controlledness (!) was comparable. My sister says that giving birth was "like" the biggest orgasm ever—but only "like" it—so it sounds like a qualitative difference. I remember you telling me that my brain had migrated to my pelvic area, which was where it was needed, and I think you were right—the births of all three children are a delightful blur that was so much just being there and experiencing it with my body and not my head.

To conclude, I'll speak from personal experience. It is easier to reach orgasm if one is not feeling violated, angry, frightened, distracted, or goal-oriented. I'm sure that it is easier when there is no one shouting at you when and how to push or counting. As I mentioned earlier, I haven't encountered any reports of orgasm in women who had received pain medication. Orgasm is more possible if one is touched in just the right way—at the right place, the right pace, the right amount of pressure, and the right time. The challenge for women and their caregivers during birth is to come up with a system of pregnancy preparation and birth care that is not inimical to orgasm during labor and birth.

REFERENCES

Baker, Jeannine Parvati. 1974. *Prenatal Yoga and Natural Birth*. Berkeley, CA: North Atlantic Books.

Dick-Read, Grantly. 1959. *Childbirth without Fear* (2nd revised edition). New York: Harper and Row.

Engelmann, George. 1883. *Labor among Primitive Peoples*. St. Louis, MO: J. M. Chambers and Co.

Gaskin, Ina May. 1977. *Spiritual Midwifery*. Summertown, TN: The Book Company.

Goldsmith, Judith. 1990. *Childbirth Wisdom from the World's Oldest Societies*. Brookline, MA: East-West Health Books.

Lang, Raven. 1972. *The Birth Book*. Palo Alto, CA: Genesis Press.

Stanton, Elizabeth Cady. 1971. *Eighty Years and More: Reminiscences of Elizabeth Cady Stanton 1815–1987*. New York: Schocken.

Speert, Harold. 1980. *Obstetrics and America: A History*. Chicago: American College of Obstetricians and Gynecologists.

Stockham, Alice. 1890. *Tokology*. Melbourne, Australia: Butler and Tanner, Frome and London.

Vogel, V. J. 1970. *American Indian Medicine*. Norman: University of Oklahoma Press.

BOUNDARY BREACHES: THE BODY, SEX AND SEXUALITY AFTER STOMA SURGERY

LENORE MANDERSON

INTRODUCTION

Intimacy and privacy constellate not only specifically around sexual acts, but also in the most general ways of the body itself. People with bodily anomalies, and their sexual partners, are particularly aware of the contradictions of the body and its exposure in intimate acts when the body and its imperfections are exposed. Absent body parts and various bodily dysfunctions complicate individuals' social and sexual lives. People with bodies that are changed dramatically and irrevocably after surgery must similarly adapt, and in doing so must re-negotiate their bodies as a sexual canvas. The difficulty of this adaptation has been highlighted in literature on the social and sexual impact of breast, gynaecological and to a lesser degree, testicular cancer, when surgery has included mastectomy, vulval excision or the removal of a testis (Schultz, Van de Wiel, Hahn, and Bouma, 1992; Andersen, 1994; Gilbar, Steiner, and Atad, 1995; Lalos and Eisemann, 1999; Anllo, 2000; Fobair et al., 2001; Lagana, McGarvey, Classen, and Koopman, 2001; Joly et al., 2002; Schultz and Van de Wiel, 2003; Gurevich, Bishop, Bower, Malka, and Nyhof-Young, 2004). But body image and sexuality are also affected by other surgery. In this paper, the surgical change is the creation of a stoma, an artificial opening on the side of the abdomen. Surgery to close or remove the urethra or anus (and/or rectum) can result from several serious conditions; following surgery, elimination and other bodily practices become highly managed acts.

Around one in 1,000 people in the developed world, depending on the country and its medical services, have a stoma. The surgery is undertaken for a number of conditions, some congenital, such as anorectal or urethral malformations, and others due to disease or other reasons for failure to function: bladder cancer, spinal cord injuries, colorectal cancer, an intestinal blockage or internal injury, inflammatory bowel disease or an intestinal abscess. Inflammatory bowel diseases such as ulcerative colitis or Crohn's disease are universally severe and incapacitating, circumscribing individuals' professional and personal lives. These have no predictable prognosis and no options for control or cure; surgery is necessary to ease the symptoms and improve quality of life. For other diseases such as cancer, stoma surgery can be life-saving.

In surgery, the bowel or bladder is diverted to empty through an opening (stoma) in the abdomen. The stoma permits the attachment of a changeable, watertight bag that fills with urine or [feces] and is emptied manually. Some people are able to dispense with the bag and instead are able to irrigate on a routine basis and wear a small stomal cap over the stoma. With ulcerative colitis, the surgery may be temporary, with an anastomosis performed later to preserve the anal sphincter and normal intestinal patterns, thereby also improving social and

From "Boundary Breaches: The Body, Sex, and Sexuality after Stoma Surgery" by Lenore Manderson, *Social Science & Medicine*, Vol. 61, No. 2, pp. 405–415. Copyright © 2005, Elsevier, with permission from Elsevier.

sexual functioning and quality of life (Bigard, 1993; Oresland et al., 1994; Damgaard, Wettergren, and Kirkegaard, 1995). Many people do not have this option, however, and must continue to use a stoma and bag, or a stoma, plug and irrigation.

An important and ongoing tension exists for people who, on an everyday basis, have to deal with their bodies as objects, caring for the stoma, preventing lesions and infections, changing bags and so on. The tension is both to establish a routine such that the stoma does not intrude in everyday life, and despite the artificial management of [feces] and/or urine, to establish an illusion of normalcy. Individuals' sense of themselves, and others' perceptions of them, are informed by presumptions of a link between the physical body and the self (Manderson, 2000), and managing a stoma impacts on self-image and sexual/social relationships (Klopp, 1990; Cohen, 1991; Gloeckner, 1991). Individuals need to separate self from substance—the subject (the "real" self) from the object (body-with-stoma). The challenge for many is to establish, or re-establish, a sense of identity unrelated to the body, so that they are recognised for "themselves," despite and apart from the barrier to this that their non-conforming body might present. Some people are able to make this first step without difficulty, and for them, the problem lies in others' difficulty in doing this. Others find it more difficult. Reluctance to discuss the nature of the surgery is influenced by cultural ideas of delicacy and aesthetics in relation to changed bodies and body functions. The particular difficulty for individuals with a colostomy or ileostomy is the link with defecation, sensory and cultural aversions to feces, and the need therefore to reconcile or manage potential and actual experiences of disgust. Miller reflects on how the idiom of disgust consistently invokes *sensory* experience: of being "too close" to the object of disgust, and

of having to smell it, see it, and touch it (Miller, 1997). Disgust is a visceral emotion; so is lust. Hence the contradictions for those who must reconcile sexuality and their stoma.

BACKGROUND

As noted, stoma surgery is conducted for a variety of chronic and acute conditions. Inflammatory bowel diseases and chronic bladder problems are particularly prevalent, and cause considerable anxiety and depression, often in combination with and exacerbated by pain and reduced energy (Sewitch et al., 2001; Smolen and Topp, 2001). The physical effects of these diseases, their unpredictability, and the importance for individuals of organizing around their bodily needs, impact on family and interpersonal relationships, work, the social environment and leisure (Cuntz, Welt, Ruppert, and Zillessen, 1999; Peake, Manderson, and Potts, 1999; Hjortswang et al., 2003; Peake and Manderson, 2003). Given the psychological, social and physical impact of such conditions, surgery is often the preferred treatment (Casellas, Lopez-Vivancos, Badia, Vilaseca, and Malagelada, 2000). For people diagnosed with cancer, stoma surgery offers remission of disease and extended life expectancy.

Post-surgery, increased control over the body (as for inflammatory bowel disease or urinary incontinence) and over disease progression (for cancer) usually offers people enhanced quality of life, less anxiety and higher self-esteem (McLeod and Baxter, 1998; Rauch, Miny, Conroy, Nyeton, and Guillemin, 2004). Adjustment to the post-surgical body is not unproblematic, however (Follick, Smith, and Turk, 1984; Sahay, Gray, and Fitch, 2000). The continued impact of cancer diagnosis arguably explains the differences in outcome among individuals following stoma surgery. Cancer survivors, in particular, must cope with a variety of physical problems and psychological difficulties associated with continuing sense of loss of control and uncertainty of prognosis (Schag, Ganz, Wing, Sim, and Lee, 1994; Little, Jordens, Paul, Montgomery, and Philipson, 1998). For example, men and women who had surgery for bladder cancer had greater difficulties than those who had had surgery for incontinence or bladder dysfunction in terms of sexual and social activities (see Nordstrom and Nyman, 1991; Nordstrom, Nyman, and Theorell, 1992). Nevertheless, all people who have had stoma surgery must learn to use a bag and care for the stoma, prevent skin inflammation and excoriation, manage accidental leakage and overcome fear of leakage, and overcome embarrassments related to sound and smell. They must also adapt to a changed body image that may have profound impact on their psychological wellbeing, and social and sexual identity (Kelly, 1992). Routine management practices impact on self-esteem, and by virtue of its location, the stoma presents explicit problems for intimacy (Weerakoon, 2001; Carlsson, Bosaeus, and Nordgren, 2003).

The relationships between abject bodies and personhood, implied in the cases of incontinence and stoma surgery, raise interesting questions in relation to mind/ body. In understanding the cognitive leaps that individuals post-surgery must make to adapt to body change, it is important—and not necessarily easy—for individuals to separate the body and mind; to insist, contra contemporary philosophical and ethical theorizing (Grosz, 1994; Kempen, 1996; Burkitt, 1998; Switankowsky, 2000), that body and mind are separate, and that while the self is embodied, personal worth cannot be determined on this basis. Individuals' relationships to their own bodies and their relationships with others, social membership and sexual identity, are informed by such suppositions—that the individual is normal, and that the self is other than the abject body. Little qualitative research has been undertaken

on bowel disease and stoma surgery that would allow us to explore these issues. Even qualitative papers focus on the experience of illness rather than its embodiment, and slide over the subjective experience of the stoma and sexuality. Little and colleagues, e.g., observe that "(w)e live with taboos—bowel movements, menstruation, sexuality—which we do not usually discuss" and note that a colostomy "brings reminders of bodily functions that we know and never discuss" (Little et al., 1998, p. 1489).

In this paper, men and women's experiences of adapting to a stoma are explored. As noted already, the presence of a stoma and taboos relating to elimination complicate the establishment and maintenance of intimate relationships. An interrogation of discomfort related to the stoma draws attention to the disease that informs individuals' attitudes to bladder and bowel dysfunction, and more generally, to diseased and disordered bodies.

METHODS

The data on which this paper is based were collected as part of a larger, ongoing study on body change, chronic disease, disability and social inclusion. Thirty-two participants responded to a research note placed in *Ostomy Australia,* a national journal provided three times a year to all Australians (26,000) who receive government-subsidized stoma supplies. Unstructured interviews were conducted with 18 of these people in three states at their choice of venue, usually their home. Because interviews were lengthy (2–5 h), several were conducted over two sessions to allow for full accounts of illness, surgery and subsequent experiences. All interviews were tape-recorded and transcribed for thematic analysis. In addition, 14 people whose area of residence made personal interviewing difficult responded to questionnaires which collected basic demographic and medical data and elicited their experiences of diagnosis, surgery, adjustment to the stoma, and its ongoing impact. In response to the open-ended questions, people often wrote extensive narratives; some wrote more than once as new ideas came to them. Some also elaborated on their responses verbally, using a cassette tape sent to them for this purpose; these tapes were transcribed and treated as interview texts for the purpose of identifying dominant themes. In this paper, interview extracts and written comments are attributed to interviewees or respondents using pseudonyms selected by them. Quotes are taken from a select number of respondents who were most articulate, but their experiences and perspectives were shared by other participants.

All participants were Australian-born or immigrants who were English-language speakers. Thirty-four percent (11) were male; 66 percent (21) female, ranging in age from 24 to 82 years at the time of the interview (mean age 45 years). At the time of first surgery, 75 percent (24) were married or living in a de facto relationship; four divorced after the stoma and three established new partnerships, and so when they participated in the research, 71 percent of respondents had partners with whom they lived. Seventy-eight percent had children (median 2, range 1–4). Consistent with the general Australian population, all had at least some secondary schooling; 50 percent had a tertiary education or post-graduate qualifications. Approximately 31 percent (10) were in professional or managerial positions, and six only were involved in full-time home duties at the time of surgery. At the time of interview or return of questionnaire this had changed dramatically, primarily because of the interval between surgery and study participation. The majority had had stoma surgery more than 5 years prior to interview with a range from 6 months to 42 years. During the study, 50 percent of participants were working at home or retired. This diversity makes generalization difficult, but as is common in qualitative studies,

the purpose of the research—and this paper—was to explore the diversity of experiences and perceptions, not to seek associations.

Data from questionnaire returns, cassettes, letters and interviews were supplemented and triangulated by articles, letters and biographic accounts published in *Ostomy Australia,* and by participation and observation of local meetings and national conferences of voluntary associations for people with stomas, and professional conferences of stoma therapists; these provided insight into the interpersonal and wider social issues that face people with stomas and provided a measure of validity and reliability to the data from interviewees and questionnaire respondents.

ADAPTING TO CHANGE

Loss of bodily control over body waste, Isaksen (1996, 2002) argues, places individual identity and human dignity at risk. Incontinence and surgery to correct this, or surgery to prevent the spread of disease, can subvert notions of adulthood, and while surgery can be liberating, it can also strip individuals of autonomy and inhibit their ability to live productive and fulfilling lives. Individuals find meaning in their corporeal as well as their social, emotional and intellectual selves. This is challenged by surgery as well as illness. Participants were clear about the advantages of surgery, including "improved quality of life" for those whose lives had previously been circumscribed because of incontinence and those for whom surgery was life saving. Others reflected that they were now able to maintain "constant, acceptable weight," felt physically healthier and stronger, had developed positive coping skills, and relative to what they had expected, were pleased with how the stoma looked.

But these advantages did not negate the disadvantages. A number spoke of their discomfort with the appearance of the stoma ("I was revolted when I saw photos showing the red lips well after I had adjusted to my surgery"). Some reported a loss of control over their weight, found "waste removal a challenge," had to manage constant bowel movements, had difficulty passing gas, had problems with noise, had excoriation around the stoma, and had slight [fecal] soiling. Others found it hard to accept the bag as permanent, were distressed by scarring, and found it extremely difficult to adjust to changed body appearance. One participant, e.g., reflected on the powerfulness of her image of a "hanging bag" and spoke at length of the difficulties: "Do people see the bag? Do I smell? Can they hear the plastic rustle?" (Lorraine). Research participants recounted that they were reassured by their physicians that "sex would not be a problem as (partners) would not be turned off by the bag." And many, but not all, people found that family and friends were supportive. When one interviewee learnt that she would have "a thing hanging off (her) stomach," she told her partner to "go, go and get a life," and "just pushed him right out of (her) life." After surgery, she withdrew almost entirely from social life and for 10 years, from her early 30s to her early 40s, she rarely went out and had no intimate relationships:

It was like going through a grieving period for about 5 years. I didn't want to know about it (the stoma) . . . I just hated myself; there is no other way of describing my feelings. I just was beside myself. It is just the fact that you have got something hanging off your stomach that is full of weight . . . this thing hanging there, that I would just like to rip it off and throw it away, you know, if I could. It is all to do with body image, isn't it? How does one overcome this? (Babaloo).

When she was 42, this participant established an intimate relationship. Her partner at the time of the interview makes jokes about the bag, and assures her that the stoma "doesn't make any difference." However, she is profoundly embarrassed by the bag and avoids him seeing her naked. Dimity similarly reported that her husband had been "absolutely wonderful and he says he doesn't even notice the bag and everything else," but she reflected that she can feel it and knows it is there, and her husband's joint role as nurse and lover disproves to her his lack of awareness. As she explained, if you can give your partner an enema and clean her up after a burst bag or an "accident," how can you ignore it? Dana recounted that her husband said that "he didn't care at all about her stoma or various related accidents. He just says, 'Okay, let's change the sheets. You go and hop in the shower and I'll wash the clothes.'" But because of her self-consciousness, she did not think she would be able to develop another sexual relationship were he not around.

Men as well as women often reported their partners were fairly matter-of-fact about spillage and leaks, but they were no less embarrassed and uncomfortable: "Well, we're really good, I'm more freaked about it than she is I think. In a way she's very good. And she says she's not into body image, which I like to believe. I have my own problems with the thing because well, I'll tell you, it's so painful for me" (Phoenix). Others were less sanguine. Gary, e.g., reflected on the difficulties he faced in adjusting to a permanent colostomy bag, and watching what he drank and ate; he spoke of his embarrassment with distended bags, smell and noise: "I feel like a baby when I have to take spare clothing bags, wipes, creams, and deodorizers when I go out." As these participants pointed out, post-surgery as well as in illness, individuals with limited bladder or bowel control to an extent are repositioned as child-like, at times needing the kind of care provided to a child and dependent in ways contradictory to constructions of adulthood and adult social relations. Incontinence and dependence on others for assistance in the event of loss of control contradicts internalized ideas of autonomous adulthood and adult sexuality. Occasional leakage, concerns about bodily appearance and self-consciousness were compounded for those whose friends or family were not supportive or who treated the individual, after surgery, as if still sick. . . .

DISGUISE AND DISCOMFORT

For many men and women who participated in this study, incontinence of the bladder or the bowel leads to feelings of depression and loneliness, as well as presenting practical dilemmas that impose a social and emotional burden—the need to manage the environment by identifying where toilets and change rooms are located, arranging for supplies if planning a lengthy trip, carry pads and/or changes of clothing, and so on (Peake et al., 1999; Fultz and Herzog, 2001; Peake and Manderson, 2003). While stoma surgery reduces the risk of accidents and so dilutes the anxiety of risk of exposure as incontinent, it does not eliminate the risk, and people with stomas continue to be mindful of their bodies. In sex, people who are incontinent must monitor their bladder and bowel, controlling their bodies while at the same time desiring to be submerged in and free from bodily consciousness. Dimity spoke of being self-conscious with her husband because of the multiple ways that her body might reveal itself: "he could feel through my skin impacted [feces] or something. Those kinds of things, I mean even if there was no smell or no sound, that he would touch my stomach." And Babaloo:

Basic things like, if you have sex, is there a risk of the stoma coming off, I mean the bag coming off, or will it hurt you? I mean internally, by losing your rectum, are you the same person internally? What effect will it have to have a penis pressing against the walls of your vagina when there is no rectum? And if you have got that vigilance there as well, and this affects sexual response . . . you are lying on the bed and half of you is on auto-pilot and the other half of you is thinking, hang on, is the bag still safe,

or, oh yuk, I can hear it go gurgle, gurgle or squish, squish?

The bag is always an intruder. Dimity reflected that many people . . . coped with "all the other bits," but they didn't cope "in the bedroom." Many were especially fearful that the bag would be noisy, smell or come off. Such exposure is a risk regardless of whether a partner (or any other) knows about the stoma. Pleasurable sex, idealized, is about being able to lose control, but people can only lose control when they are confident their bodies are in control in the first place. Like Babaloo, Dimity emphasized this when she spoke of her inability to "let go" and [lose] control for sexual pleasure, following as well as before surgery:

When we first went to bed, I was like, I used to have to hang on, I was literally clenched because of fear, like I never knew if I was going to be letting off wind or something more than that and it took me a long, long time to feel comfortable.

People are advised by counsellors and stoma therapists "to get around it and be creative." While a number of people were curious about the extent of creativity—the degree to which others might incorporate the stoma into love-making, for instance—for most people, the stoma was unsightly, to be protected and kept secret, and the bag was potentially so intrusive that creativity was unimaginable. It is not only the physical breach of the boundary—smell, sound or leak—but also the presence of the bag as a container of abject fluid and solid that strips a moment of its sensual potential. Breaches in bodily control have the potential to undermine the sexual relationship, and so in establishing sexual relations, people need to reconstruct privacy and dignity, and preserve the notion of bodily aesthetics in the process. Both men and women with stomas often had a strong sense of being sexually unattractive, even if in other respects their social life was enhanced following surgery (Bjerre, Johansen, and Steven, 1998). Those without partners when they had surgery had to disclose to potential sexual partners, and were often deeply self-conscious. Individuals found it difficult to sexualize a body that is also a defecating/urinating body, when the two images are so visibly confused, as Perdita explained:

You can actually see through (the bag), and you can see what's in it and especially when it comes to sexual relations with male/female, whoever the ostomate may be, they find it very hard to come to terms with this.

Most research participants were comfortable about having a stoma, if at all, only with their own or other children such as nieces or nephews, extending their general willingness to talk about body functions to small children to include their own abject bodies. Mia, for instance, was simply amused by her 3-year-old niece's fascination when she emptied her bag, and she was happy for the child to go with her to the toilet, "Because she's a child and she's not going to judge me. She doesn't see that as being, you know, freaky different. She says, 'Cool.' Yeah, cool different kind of thing, soy." Christine's grandchildren similarly took great interest in her stoma: "They would find me in the bathroom and would watch 'the procedure' while continuing a conversation and asking questions." The ease of men and women with stomas in this context was essentially no different to people's general comfortableness in bathing and using the toilet in front of small children. With adults, however, self-consciousness governed comportment or the etiquette of body practice. Warwick commented that although his libido had diminished due to radiation and chemotherapy, his relationship with his wife was also affected by the fact that he had a hernia and had a bag "filled with [feces]," [that was] noisy and needing to be emptied every three hours. In his words, she was not "sympathetic: she finds the bag repulsive and does not like the sight of my hernia or my

body." Further, as already noted, few women were comfortable being seen naked, with or without the bag, by their partners:

He certainly hasn't seen it (the stoma) naked or anything like that. He respects my privacy, he doesn't push the issue. He doesn't badger me to see it, or anything like that. You know, he doesn't walk in—I mean, when I'm in the shower, or—because he knows that it would make me uncomfortable and make me angry (Mia).

Many participants reflected on the importance of disguising the stoma and bag to avoid obvious confrontation. Mia, again, explains this:

It's really not a sexy thing to see, so that's probably why I don't want him to see because we—I mean, if we have a sexual relationship. With my family—I don't know. I'm sure they wouldn't think anything of it, but . . .

Is it the stoma itself that you think is not sexy, or . . . ?

It's definitely the [feces] in the bag. The stoma itself, it wouldn't worry me in the slightest. It's the fact that I shit in a bag. And I carry it around with me all the time.

Dana wore a cover around her abdomen to protect the stoma and bag, and her partner shared her view that it was better to wear it "because it's more secure"; he, as well as she, felt more comfortable because it protected against possible leakage and reduced awkward noise. Ted was divorced because his wife "couldn't handle looking at him" with his bag on. When he wanted to start another relationship, he searched for something to disguise the bag, "a cover or cummerbund or something" that would make his appearance "much more appealing to the opposite sex" than looking at the bag with its contents. In bed, Babaloo always wore a nightgown around her abdomen, and addressed at length her frustration about finding feminine and sexy underwear to cover and protect the bag; on several occasions she sent away for garments that proved to be "preposterous" and decidedly "unsexy." This was a recurrent complaint. Phoenix found the idea of a cummerbund silly:

About the only time I've ever worn a cummerbund was way back when I was doing ballroom dancing and a more ridiculous piece of equipment I've never come across. . . . Prancing into bed with a cummerbund, I just feel like a bloody Christmas present or something. You're trying to hide this thing, but what do you do, draw attention to it with a bloody cummerbund.

SEX AND SEXINESS

Values relating to bodily parts and sexual repertoires are relevant in any context, as well as in relation to physical disability, and the most rigid interpretations of these inform illiberal notions of the right to desire, to be desired and to be sexually active. Part of disgust, Miller argues, "is the very awareness of being disgusted, the consciousness of itself" (1997, p. 8). Disgust is a visceral response which, provoked by [fecal] waste, urine, associated odours and sounds, is accompanied by culturally constructed ideas of danger of contamination and defilement. However, the feeling of disgust is produced for the owner of the body, the source of that which is disgusting, by the conflation of material and symbol. This is equally so for others in contact with the producing body if not the matter itself. In a sexual relationship, therefore, both individuals—the owner of the problematic body and his or her partner—must find ways to set aside reactions of disgust, and so put [feces], farts, rumblings and smells out of mind, both by ignoring obvious embodied reminders of the stoma (such as the bag), overlooking minor intrusions, and making light of occasional crises that threaten to replace lust with disgust and sex with hygiene. The tacit and sometimes explicit recognition of this dilemma between lust and disgust influences individual comportment in sex as well as in more public moments in everyday life:

All my friends know about my stoma and I am quite comfortable talking to strangers about it. My husband won't even look directly at it, especially when I am catheterizing, not because he thinks it ugly but he disappears when I'm having a cannula sited. Our relationship hasn't altered, not our sex life. He doesn't "cringe" if he touches the bag on my tummy when we make love; it is just as if it wasn't there (Christine).

The participants in this study commonly had extensive histories of ill health, diagnoses and medical tests before surgery, followed by the abnegation of the body and associated periods of depression. In consequence, many had lengthy periods of sexual inactivity, and sometimes doubted their ability to be responsive: "I had no idea whether I would or whether I wouldn't or whether I would still have the same sensations. I think I have, probably not as quite as intense, but I don't have a big problem with that . . . if you are not testing out the muscles in the interim then if nothing else, you are starting out from a little lack of use" (Babaloo). Lynette similarly reflected on the difficulty of coping with an intimate relationship: "For the record, I just backed off. Also, I have noticed that I tend to be much quieter or sedate in larger social settings. I think it may be that I don't feel overtly confident."

Bodily surveillance, including body emissions and the appearance of the body and the bag, were for many people complicated by other health concerns, which compounded libidinal response. Dimity reflected on how constant pain, nausea, antidepressants, fear of accidents, fear of additional pain from intercourse, and tiredness probably all contributed to her not feeling sexy, and to worrying about this fact:

There is just no desire. I have virtually no sexual desire whatsoever. We have sex. We should have sex. My husband is always saying to "touch me, or kiss me, or . . ." and I just think, "Oh, I am supposed to be doing that" because I feel literally nothing, which is terrible. I am 28. You know, I should be enjoying it. That is the whole thing you know, we don't have to worry about pregnancy, or diseases. This should be a time when it is fantastic, but no . . . I mean there is no desire, no nothing there, and there hasn't been, probably for two years. I mean, any sort of chance of developing a fabulous sex life has sort of been diverted into feeling and being sick.

Mia shared this view, relating her inability to feel sexual to quite simple, material things, such as clothing:

I see girls wearing hipsters, or something like that. I'd like to wear those, or a—tight—something swingy, something like that. I mean, part of feeling sexy, I think, is feeling sexy in what you wear. And when you're wearing big baggy pants, it doesn't make you feel sexy in your own mind. So I'm really lucky in that my fiancé tells me, you know, every day that I'm beautiful and things like that.

Some partners had difficulty regaining desire or feeling erotically towards the partner with a stoma, as indicated earlier; the sight, sounds, odours and occasional contact with the stoma and/or its contents destroyed any possible desire and its exploration. Gertrude reflected on her husband:

I am thinking about sex and I don't know how I will go on that. I thought I had better heal a bit more. My husband has very low libido anyway unfortunately, but it came in handy for this present time. I knew there was always a reason for everything. But I am soon going to be through this and then the old problem of his low libido will be back. That is his problem, not mine.

Some older men and women were no longer sexually active and stoma surgery had little effect on this. Faith, for instance, over a 15-year period had cervical cancer, a hysterectomy, an appendectomy, ileostomy, a urostomy, and finally, her vagina was removed. Her husband had had major heart surgery, and as she explained it:

Well, his heart didn't allow (sex), so that was the end of it. It doesn't worry me, no. But up until I got sick and before my husband got sick, we have a good sex life. But then it's just passed, because we're both on heavy medication and that's it.

For several partners, however, the conflated roles of lovers and carers complicated intimacy. Isaksen (1996) suggests that care work is always structured by bodily taboos related to elimination, the management of incontinence, and specific body parts. Reactions of disgust or distaste are tabooed and techniques of distancing develop. He is writing of the professional distanciation of paid carers; in intimate relationships a different kind of distancing takes place. As noted earlier, some interviewees reported that their partners were able to be pragmatic, making light of noise, dismissing occasional leaks as unfortunate accidents to minimize embarrassment, and quickly running baths and changing bed clothes as the need arose. However, not all partners were able to adjust to these transposed roles as carers and lovers. Ian, for instance, cares for his wife when required, cleaning her when bags burst, bathing her and changing sheets. But this has been at the cost of a sexual relationship. His wife Sara explains his sexual withdrawal from her as over-determined because his mother also had a stoma; she feels that he oscillates between caring for her as if she were a child and as if she were his elderly mother. Neither the child nor the mother can also be his sexual partner. Gertrude's husband similarly adapted to her stoma by placing her in the position of child. Since her surgery, he has been comfortable being in the bathroom when she changes a bag, although he would never enter the bathroom previously if she were on the toilet and was never comfortable discussing bowel movements:

My husband makes me laugh because before, he was always very self-conscious about being on the toilet, and if I went in or if I left the door (of the toilet) open he would sigh and huff and all that sort of thing . . . and now he will walk in on me, just emptying my bag out and start cleaning his teeth and walk out because he will say "Well, that smell is a bit over powering at times" and I say to him "well, you wouldn't have come near me with a barge pole if I had been going to the toilet the normal way," and he went "Oh yeah," Because it is a completely different concept, he doesn't really consider that as bad as sitting on the toilet and doing a poo.

Gertrude and her husband no longer have a sexual relationship: his comfortableness about the stoma occurred as he withdrew from her sexually, and she feels that his role as carer gave him permission to do so. He has explained to her his sexual [lack of interest] otherwise—that she is "too fat" for him to find her desirable. She reflects: "The stoma has helped me to realise that it is not me, it is him, and so I just continue on my way . . ."

. . . Stomal surgery was not inevitably problematic, not all individuals had negative experiences consequently, and many were able to overcome boundary breaches. Several who had surgery following extended periods of incontinence, often with pain and infection, reported a significant improvement in their quality of life and had no regrets. Many who had a colostomy, ileostomy or urostomy following diagnosis of cancer were relieved that surgical intervention was possible and were pragmatic about their treatment choices. In addition, people were able to negotiate, and to overcome embarrassment and discomfort to varying degrees.

Although individuals hold onto specific notions of body function and boundary, therefore, social notions of boundaries are elastic, influencing the diversity of sexual repertoire (e.g., with respect to anal and oral sex), and allowing intimacy even if the boundaries overlap and body control is unpredictable. Two cases provided illustrations of this. Perdita's marriage broke down after her colostomy for colorectal cancer. She divorced; after 10 years of abstinence (pre- and post-marriage and operation), she commenced a new relationship. "I knew that there would be somebody out there who would want me one day and I would deal with the colostomy when it happened. I didn't worry about it. I couldn't afford to anyway because stress is your worst enemy when you've had cancer." Perdita told her new lover about her stoma on their way to bed. Others find a way of diversion when the materiality of the stoma and the abject body intervened in sex. Vanessa, who had an ileostomy after years of suffering from Crohn's disease, maintained that neither she nor any of her "various partners over the 20 years since the surgery" had had a difficulty with the bag. If anything, she claimed it was "a novelty which can be ignored," although she also reflected that a leaking bag could be a "pest" if a leak occurred or the bag burst in someone else's bed, as once happened when the bag "flew off" in the height of passion. She described one particular relationship she had with a war veteran who had lost both his legs, and in doing so she illustrates how humour and the inherent comedy of coupling operate to dilute the potential of shame, embarrassment and humiliation. She illustrates too how a sexual relationship of any kind requires its participants to relax the rules of etiquette and establish trust in order for intimacy to take place. In writing down her experiences for this study, she checked with him [about] his views of the relationship and reported to me in a second letter: "We made an amusing sight in bed and understood each other very well. We had a short conversation on the topic of my bag and his lack of legs! He said it has/had never worried him and he equates his legs with my bag!"

CONCLUDING REMARKS

Control of bodily functions is a passage to and precondition of conventional adulthood. Sexual negotiation and autonomy, too, is informed by constructions of adulthood. For many men and women, the sense of self as a valued adult and as a sexual being was threatened not only by the illness that led to surgery, but also by the lived experience of having a stoma. The permanent loss of continence also challenges others in relation to them, as evident in the ways that men and women narratively position partners in supporting and accommodating them after surgery, and express their concern about placing excessive demands on them. Not all couples stay together, and in some cases, as discussed, separation occurs on the initiative of the person with the stoma. In other cases, husbands and wives leave their partners, illustrating the difficulties both for the person at the centre of the bodily crisis, and for those nearest to him or her, in adjusting to dramatic, unforeseen and undesirable changes to the body. Partnership crises illustrate also how difficulties related to the stoma, and the increased need of the person with the stoma for psychological, physical and often financial support, compound other conflicts and tension. Partners who stay in the relationship but cease sexual relations reinforce for the person with the stoma fears of the loss of physical desirability. Spouses and lovers who stay and maintain sexual relations play a major role in reaffirming the adult status and desirability of their partners post-surgery.

The self-selection of participants in this study raises questions about the generalizability of findings, and the ability to which the data might be interpreted and extrapolated to other populations, particularly given that most research points simply to the positive outcomes of individuals following stoma surgery. However, research conducted to date has relied primarily on psychometric instrumentation and has not provided individuals with the freedom to explore the complex issues that they face following surgery (e.g., Northouse, Mood, Templin, Mellon, and George, 2000). In this study, individuals did include the positive aspects of having a stoma—most emphasized improved quality of life—but at the same time, they reflected on the difficulties of adjustment to the

stoma and new bodily disruptions. Given the cultural background of participants, the discussion on sexuality after stoma therapy pertains particularly to Australians, although arguably it might be extended to other contexts. It is significant, of course, that stoma surgery is most common in industrialized country settings, but taboos relating to fecal material and acts of elimination are near universal. Further research is required to understand how individuals negotiate their bodies and interact with sexual partners after stoma surgery in other cultural and social settings.

An awareness of these difficulties has implications in terms of patient care and advice. A number of authors have drawn attention to the psychological distress that affects this group of people, and consequently the importance of the care provided to assist adaptation and outcome (Sahay et al., 2000; Sewitch et al., 2001, 2002; van der Eijk et al., 2004). In Australia and the United Kingdom, a stoma therapist or stoma therapy nurse provides patients with assistance in adjusting. Concerns about health status, and specifically about the stoma, appear to depend on the disease state preceding the surgery and the ability of the patient to adapt to the changes. The data presented in this study suggest, in addition, that adaptation is not simply about professional/patient interaction, nor about interaction of the person with a stoma and his or her partner. Cultural attitudes to the body, body image and sexuality play an important role in individuals' ability to adjust to body change. Miller (1997, p. xi) maintains that "(l)ove bears a complex and possibly necessary relation to disgust" involving "a notable and non-trivial suspension of some, if not all, rules of disgust" for pleasure to be possible. As reflected in the experiences of men and women with stomas, sexual pleasure requires that various physical bodily boundaries and social inhibitions be suspended, and that the transgressions of boundaries be negotiated.

REFERENCES

Andersen, B. L. 1994. Surviving cancer. *Cancer, 74*(4): 1484–1495.

Anllo, L. M. 2000. Sexual life after breast cancer. *Journal of Sex and Marital Therapy, 26*(3); 241–248.

Bigard, M. A. 1993. Functional results of ileal pouch-anal anastomosis. *Annales De Chirurgie, 47*(10); 992–995.

Bjerre, B. D., Johansen, C., and Steven, K. 1998. Sexological problems after cystectomy: bladder substitution compared with ileal conduit diversion—a questionnaire study of male patients. *Scandinavian Journal of Urology and Nephrology, 32*(3); 187–193.

Burkitt, I. 1998. Bodies of knowledge: beyond Cartesian views of persons, selves and mind. *Journal for the Theory of Social Behaviour, 28*(1); 63–82.

Carlsson, E., Bosaeus, I., and Nordgren, S. 2003. What concerns subjects with inflammatory bowel disease and an ileostomy? *Scandinavian Journal of Gastroenterology, 38*(9): 978–984.

Casellas, F., Lopez-Vivancos, J., Badia, X., Vilaseca, J., and Malagelada, J. R. 2000. Impact of surgery for Crohn's disease on health-related quality of life. *American Journal of Gastroenterology, 95*(1): 177–182.

Cohen, A. 1991. Body image in the person with a stoma. *Journal of Enterostomal Therapy, 18;* 68–71.

Cuntz, U., Welt, J., Ruppert, E., and Zillessen, E. 1999. Inflammatory bowel disease, psychosocial handicaps, illness experience and coping. *Psychotherapie Psychosomatik Medizinische Psychologie, 49*(12): 494–500.

Damgaard, B., Wettergren, A., and Kirkegaard, P. 1995. Social and sexual function following ileal pouch-anal anastomosis. *Diseases of the Colon and Rectum, 38*(3): 286–289.

Fobair, O. H. K., Koopman, C., Classen, C., Dimiceli, S., Drooker, N., Warner, D., Davids, H. R., Loulan, J., Wallsten, D., Goffinet, D., Morrow, G., and Spiegel, D. 2001. Comparison of lesbian and heterosexual women's response to newly diagnosed breast cancer. *Psycho-Oncology, 10*(1): 40–51.

Follick, M. J., Smith, T. W., and Turk, D. C. 1984. Psychosocial adjustment following ostomy. *Health Psychology, 3*(6): 505–517.

Fultz, N. H., and Herzog, A. R. 2001. Self-reported social and emotional impact of urinary incontinence. *Journal of the American Geriatrics Society, 49*(7): 892–899.

Gilbar, O., Steiner, N., and Atad, J. 1995. Adjustment of married couples and unmarried women to gynecological cancer. *Psycho-Oncology, 4*(3): 203–211.

Gloeckner, M. 1991. Perceptions of sexuality after ostomy surgery. *Journal of Enterostomal Therapy, 18:* 36–38.

Grosz, E. 1994. *Volatile bodies: toward a corporeal feminism.* Bloomington: Indiana University Press.

Gurevich, M., Bishop, S., Bower, J., Malka, M., and Nyhof-Young, J. 2004. (Dis)embodying gender and sexuality in testicular cancer. *Social Science and Medicine, 58*(9): 1597–1607.

Hjortswang, H., Jarnerot, B., Curman, B., Sandberg-Gertzen, H., Tysk, C., Blomberg, B., Almer, S., and Strom, M. 2003. The influence of demographic and disease-related factors on health-related quality of life in patients with ulcerative colitis. *European Journal of Gastroenterology and Hepatology, 15*(9): 1011–1020.

Isaksen, L. W. 1996. Unpleasant aspects of corporeality. *Sociologisk Forskning, 33*(2–3), 71–86.

Isaksen, L. W. 2002. Toward a sociology of (gendered) disgust—images of bodily decay and the social organization of care work. *Journal of Family Issues, 23*(7): 791–811.

Joly, F., Heron, J. F., Kalusinski, L., Bottet, P., Brune, D., Allouache, N., Mace-Lesec'h, J., Couette, J. E., Peny, J., and Henry-Amar, M. 2002. Quality of life in long-term survivors of testicular cancer: a population-based case-control study. *Journal of Clinical Oncology, 20*(1), 73–80.

Kelly, M. 1992. Self, identity and radical surgery. *Sociology of Health and Illness, 14*(3): 392–415.

Kempen, H. J. G. 1996. Mind as body moving in space—bringing the body back into self-psychology. *Theory and Psychology, 6*(4): 715–731.

Klopp, A. L. 1990. Body image and self-concept among individuals with stomas. *Journal of Enterostomal Therapy, 17:* 98–105.

Lagana, L., McGarvey, E. L., Classen, and Koopman, C. 2001. Psychosexual dysfunction among gynecological cancer survivors. *Journal of Clinical Psychology in Medical Settings, 8*(2): 73–84.

Lalos, A., and Eisemann, M. 1999. Social interaction and support related to mood and locus of control in cervical and endometrial cancer patients and their spouses. *Supportive Care in Cancer, 7*(2): 75–78.

Little, M., Jordens, C. F. C., Paul, K., Montgomery, K., and Philipson, B. 1998. Liminality: a major category of the experience of cancer illness. *Social Science and Medicine, 47*(10): 1485–1494.

Manderson, L. 2000. The gendered body: negotiating social membership after breast and gynecological cancer surgery. *Psycho-Oncology, 9*(5): S20.

McLeod, R. S., and Baxter, N. N. 1998. Quality of life of patients with inflammatory bowel disease after surgery. *World Journal of Surgery, 22*(4): 375–381.

Miller, W. I. 1997. *The anatomy of disgust.* Cambridge, MA: Harvard University Press.

Nordstrom, G., Nyman, C. R., and Theorell, T. 1992. Psychosocial adjustment and general state of health in patients with ileal conduit urinary-diversion. *Scandinavian Journal of Urology and Nephrology, 26*(2): 139–147.

Nordstrom, G. M., and Nyman, C. R. 1991. Living with a urostomy—a follow-up with special regard to the peristomal- skin complications, psychosocial and sexual life. *Scandinavian Journal of Urology and Nephrology, Supplementum, 138:* 247–251.

Northouse, L. L., Mood, D., Templin, T., Mellon, S., and George, T. 2000. Couples' patterns of adjustment to colon cancer. *Social Science and Medicine, 50*(2): 271–284.

Oresland, T., Palmblad, S., Ellstrom, M., Berndtsson, I., Crona, N., and Hulten, L. 1994. Gynecological and sexual function related to anatomical changes in the female pelvis after restorative proctocolectomy. *International Journal of Colorectal Disease, 9*(2): 77–81.

Peake, S., and Manderson, L. 2003. The constraints of a normal life: the management of urinary incontinence by middle aged women. *Women and Health, 37*(3): 37–51.

Peake, S., Manderson, L., and Potts, H. 1999. Part and parcel of being a woman: female urinary incontinence and constructions of control. *Medical Anthropology Quarterly, 13*(3): 267–285.

Persson, E., Severinsson, E., and Hellstrom, A. L. 2004. Spouses' perceptions of and reactions to living with a partner who has undergone surgery for rectal cancer resulting in a stoma. *Cancer Nursing, 27*(1): 85–90.

Rauch, P., Miny, J., Conroy, T., Nyeton, L., and Guillemin, F. 2004. Quality of life among disease-free survivors of rectal cancer. *Journal of Clinical Oncology, 22*(2), 354–360.

Sahay, T. B., Gray, R. E., and Fitch, M. 2000. A qualitative study of patient perspectives on colorectal cancer. *Cancer Practice, 8*(1): 38–44.

Schag, C. A. C., Ganz, P. A., Wing, D. S., Sim, M. S., and Lee, J. J. 1994. Quality-of-life in adult survivors of lung, colon and prostate-cancer. *Quality of Life Research, 3*(2): 127–141.

Schultz, W. C. M. W., and Van de Wiel, H. B. M. 2003. Sexuality, intimacy, and gynecological cancer. *Journal of Sex and Marital Therapy, 29*(1), 121–128.

Schultz, W. C. M. W., Van de Wiel, H. B., Hahn, D. E. E., and Bouma, J. 1992. Psychosexual functioning after treatment for gynecological cancer: an integrative model, review of determinant factors and clinical guidelines. *International Journal of Gynecological Cancer, 2*(6): 281–290.

Sewitch, M. J., Abrahamowicz, M., Bitton, A., Daly, D., Wild, G. E., Cohen, A., Katz, S., Szego, P. L., and Dobkin, P. L. 2001. Psychological distress, social support, and disease activity in patients with inflammatory bowel disease. *American Journal of Gastroenterology, 96*(5): 1470–1479.

Sewitch, M. J., Abrahamowicz, M., Bitton, A., Daly, D., Wild, G. E., Cohen, A., Katz, S., Szego, P. L., and Dobkin, P. L. 2002. Psychosocial correlates of patient–physician discordance in inflammatory bowel disease. *American Journal of Gastroenterology, 97*(9), 2174–2183.

Smolen, D. M., and Topp, R. 2001. Self-care agency and quality of life among adults diagnosed with inflammatory bowel disease. *Quality of Life Research, 10*(4): 379–387.

Switankowsky, I. 2000. Dualism and its importance for medicine. *Theoretical Medicine and Bioethics, 21*(6): 567–580.

van der Eijk, I., Vlachonikolis, I. G., Munkholm, P., Nijman, J., Bernklev, T., Politi, P., Odes, S., Tsianos, E. V., Stockbrugger, R. W., and Russel, M. G. 2004. The role of quality of care in health-related quality of life in patients with IBD. *Inflammatory Bowel Diseases, 10*(4): 392–398.

Weerakoon, P. 2001. Sexuality and the patient with a stoma. *Sexuality and Disability, 19*(2): 121–129.

6

SEXUAL PRACTICES

AN INTERVIEW WITH

MICHAEL REECE

Michael Reece, Ph.D., MPH serves as Director of the Center for Sexual Health Pro-motion at Indiana University, a center that conducts research designed to advance conceptual and methodological approaches to studying sexual health and to train the next generation of sexuality and sexual health scholars. The center's work is focused on four key areas, including: a) conducting nationally representative assessments of sexual and sexual health behaviors that provide an empirical foundation for those who need population-based data to support their work in public health and medicine, b) advancing the methods used to study sexual behavior through innovative designs like technology-based daily diaries, c) developing measures for sexuality-related research that are not only valid and reliable but that are attentive to unique cultural norms and changes in the human sexual repertoire, and d) exploring the manner in which humans acquire and use products that promote sexual health and that improve sexual function and pleasure, such as vibrators, condoms, and lubricants.

What led you to begin studying sexuality?

When I was an undergraduate student, I volunteered as a peer sexuality educator at the University of Georgia. I used to conduct workshops for fraternities and sororities, mostly on the topic of sexual assault and acquaintance rape. Later, after earning my MPH degree, I led the office of HIV prevention for a state health department in the Southwestern United States. In that work, I started to believe that our public health interventions were off base; we were focused only on things like condom use, but we didn't understand that condom use doesn't occur in a vacuum, it occurs within the context of a sexual event. I became convinced that the only way to prevent public health problems like HIV, STIs, and unintended pregnancy was to better understand the nature of sexual behavior itself. I felt that we needed to understand sexual behavior at its core and that by only looking at sexuality for its potential contributions to disease we were missing something. That led me to pursue a doctoral degree and ultimately led me to Indiana University which has always been known as a leading university for studying sexuality.

How do you tell people you study sexuality and how do they react?

It depends. I don't tell everyone. . . . However, when I do tell people, what I find is that they think that it is much more mystical than it actually is. People seem to think that it must be so exciting to know lots of things about people's sexual lives. I've never had a negative reaction actually. I think . . . that people are genuinely curious about sexuality; most have never had a chance to discuss it and they are intrigued by the fact that there is research that helps them to compare their sexual lives to those of others.

What ethical dilemmas have you faced in studying sexuality?

My team is incredibly attentive to ensuring people that they can trust us when they disclose information about their sexual lives. We go to extremes to inform people about what we are going to ask, why we are asking it, and what we will be doing with it. So one important ethical issue is that you have to be sincere about keeping people's data confidential and about ensuring them that there is a really valid scientific purpose.

In an early study at Indiana University, my team studied the behaviors of men who were having sex with other men in campus bathrooms, locker rooms, and other locations. This was called "cruising" and it was incredibly taboo. One of the most popular places for men to "cruise" was in a bathroom that was right down the hall from my office. This study was conducted over ten years ago, but on a regular basis I still run into men who participated in that study when I am on campus or out in the community. We told these men at the beginning of the study that if we were to encounter them in a public place after the study that we would pretend that we did not know them. And I do that. When I see these men I don't make any gestures toward them at all. I think they are surprised that I still do this after ten years, but we had made a commitment that we would not acknowledge them unless they spoke first. So it is not just the notion of maintaining data confidentially in traditional ways like not using identifiers in datasets. Maintaining high ethical standards also requires a long-term pledge to being absolutely sincere in your commitments to participants.

Why is sex research important?

From an everyday perspective, sexuality research is very important because people are incredibly curious about who does what with whom and about how the behavior of others compares to their own. Particularly in the United States, we are rarely provided with the opportunity to have open discussions about sexuality, creating incredible challenges in people's romantic and sexual lives. So, sexuality research is vital to helping people have access to information that enables them to better understand their own sexuality.

From an academic perspective, sexuality research is also essential. Sexual behavior is perhaps the most common behavior of humans. . . . So, in terms of an academic commitment to understanding societies and behaviors, we must remain committed to sexuality research. Academic institutions should be willing to support sexuality research because it is among the most common of all denominators of our existence.

From a sexual health or public health perspective, we must understand sexual behaviors if we are going to change them. We can't understand condom use without understanding the relational, situational, and other factors that influence the decision-making process of two or more individuals during a sexual event. We just can't change behaviors that we don't understand.

Can you describe some of the findings from your recent research?

Perhaps two of our most recent studies were the National Survey of Sexual Health and Behavior (NSSHB) and the National Men's Sex Study. The NSSHB was the first nationally representative study of the sexual lives of Americans in close to two decades. It provided important data about the current nature of the sexual repertoires of both adolescents and adults indicating that our sexual lives are incredibly diverse. The results also illustrated that "sex" is more than intercourse. While intercourse remains the most common behavior, there are many sexual events that don't involve intercourse, and when it does occur, it is typically accompanied by other behaviors. This study also provided data that suggested that adolescents are among the most responsible when it comes to sexuality—with those aged 14–17 having the highest rates of condom use in the country, a trend that public health has been documenting for the past decade. We followed this study with one that was very similar but was focused on gay and bisexual men. In that study, we surveyed over 25,000 men and found that gay and bisexual men also have extremely varied sexual lives. Among the least reported behaviors was anal intercourse—which is completely contrary to what most people think constitutes gay sex. The most common behavior reported by gay and bisexual men was kissing their partner. People always ask me if I'm surprised that kissing was the most frequent behavior; I usually say that I'm not surprised by the finding but instead I'm shocked that most researchers have never collected data on kissing and that when we only ask about gay sexuality in the context of HIV (and thus mostly having asked only about condom use and anal intercourse), we get very warped understandings of their lives.

Of the projects you've done over the course of your academic career, which did you find most interesting and why?

I would say that I think our early study of men's cruising on college campuses was one of the most interesting studies that I've ever done. Cruising is incredibly taboo; at its foundation it is reliant upon anonymity and secrecy. So, I learned an incredible amount about how to do sexuality research on such topics. The men's willingness to participate in extensive interviews about this behavior still fascinates me. Also, most people who had considered this issue before had never considered the positive aspects of cruising; what do men get out of it other than sex? Participants in that study were incredibly articulate about how such behaviors helped them to better understand their own sexuality and about how it often resulted in many positive outcomes—that is just something that had never been documented.

If you could teach people one thing about sexuality what would it be?

There is no "normal" when it comes to sexual behaviors. All of us have very diverse desires and needs when it comes to sexuality and communicating with your partners about those desires and needs is critical.

THE PURSUIT OF SEXUAL PLEASURE

B. J. RYE AND GLENN J. MEANEY

Sex and sexuality are surprisingly difficult terms to define. In one sense, sex can be seen as a collection of behaviors related directly or indirectly to stimulation of the genitals; our bodies then respond to this stimulation with a reflex that is pleasurable and tension-releasing (i.e., orgasm). This . . . definition does not, however, provide much insight into the role that sexuality plays in our lives. Rather, sexuality can be thought of as an institution defined by shared social meaning that is constructed around the simple stimulation of genitals; sex, in this sense, is what we make it (e.g., DeLamater and Hyde, 1998; Foucault, 1976/1978). At the individual level, human sexuality is subjective and represents how we experience and express ourselves as sexual beings. At a cultural level, sexuality can be constructed to serve a variety of needs: sex is a means of procreation, an intimate bonding ritual, even a form of social control (Foucault, 1976/1978; Hawkes, 1996; Weeks, 1981). For some, sex is work (e.g., prostitution, "spousely duty"). For others, sex is play. . . . [T]his reading will focus on the "playful" aspect of sex. In particular, we will discuss the more physical gymnastics involved in the pursuit and attainment of *sexual pleasure*—"sex for fun." We hope to show how pleasure is a primary motivator for sexual activity and how social constructions of sexuality are built around this fundamental desire for sexual pleasure. . . .

Our perspective on sexual pleasure is constructed from a review of mainly Canadian and U.S. literature concerning sexual activity and sexual behavior. We supplement this review from our own ongoing survey of Canadian university students. . . . We . . . focus our discussion on a very North American version of the pursuit of sexual pleasure.

THE PURSUIT OF SEXUAL PLEASURE

What Is Sexual Pleasure?

Broadly defined, sexual pleasure involves the positive feelings that arise from sexual stimuli (Abramson and Pinkerton, 1995). Sexual pleasure may result from a variety of activities that involve sexual arousal, genital stimulation, and/or orgasm. . . . While it may seem self-evident, people are more likely to engage in sexual behaviors they consider pleasurable than sexual behaviors that they find less pleasurable (Browning et al., 2000; Pinkerton et al., 2003).

It is seldom overtly stated, but sexual pleasure is very important in our society. Achieving sexual arousal and orgasm is significant enough to people that manuals of sexual technique have been compiled—such as the venerable *Kama Sutra* (trans., 1994), *The Joy of Sex* (Comfort, 1972), and *Sex for Dummies* (Westheimer, 1995). There are university courses, television shows (e.g., *The Sex Files*, Colby, 2006), websites (e.g., www.sexualityandu.ca), sex stores, and shows (e.g., *The Stag Shop*, see www.stagshop.com; *The Everything to Do with Sex Show*, see www.everythingtodowithsex.com) devoted to human sexuality and the attainment of the highest level of sexual

From "The Pursuit of Sexual Pleasure" by B. J. Rye and Glenn J. Meaney, *Sexuality & Culture*, Volume 11, Issue 1, December 2007, pp. 28–51. Copyright © 2007, Springer. Reprinted by permission of the authors.

satisfaction possible. Clearly, people have a great interest in sexual pleasure. This pleasure can be pursued in many forms—and can occur in solitary and/or partnered contexts. Perhaps the simplest sexual activities are those in which an individual can engage alone, such as masturbation and sexual fantasy.

Solitary Sex

Fantasy

Sexual fantasy has the appeal of being the safest form of sexual enjoyment: One can fantasize any time, one can have total control, and there are no (direct) consequences (Doskoch, 1995). Sexual fantasy is difficult to research, especially because it is difficult to define exactly what constitutes fantasy (see Byrne and Osland, 2000). Leitenberg and Henning (1995: 470) define sexual fantasy as "almost any mental imagery that is sexually arousing or erotic to the individual." Byers and colleagues (Byers, Purdon, and Clark, 1998; Little and Byers, 2000; Renaud and Byers, 1999) prefer the term *sexual cognitions,* which may have positive or negative connotations. Sexual thoughts can take many forms, some of which may not be pleasurable to the individual. . . .

The great majority of men and women engage in sexual fantasy, either as an activity by itself (i.e., daydreaming), or in conjunction with other sexual activities, including masturbation and partnered sex. For example, when asked "how often do you think about sex?", 97 percent of men and 86 percent of women responded with a few times a month or more (Laumann et al., 1994). In terms of content, men seem more likely to have explicitly sexual fantasies (Ellis and Symons, 1990), to imagine themselves in positions of dominance (Byers, Purdon, and Clark, 1998; Hsu et al., 1994), to see themselves as the "doer," (Byers, Purdon, and Clark, 1998; Knafo and Jaffe, 1984) and to fantasize about multiple partners (Ellis and

Symons, 1990). Women tend to have more emotional and romantic fantasies and to see themselves in positions of submission (Hsu et al., 1994; McCauley and Swann, 1978). Lesbians and gay men tend to have fantasies similar to heterosexual women and men, respectively, except that they typically imagine same-sex partners (Hurlbert and Apt, 1993; Keating and Over, 1990; Masters and Johnson, 1979; Robinson and Parks, 2003). In general, people report a wide variety of content in sexual fantasy. People who have more sexual fantasies tend to have fewer sexual problems and report more sexual satisfaction than people who have fewer fantasies (Byrne and Osland, 2000; Leitenberg and Henning, 1995).

. . . Renaud and Byers (1999) found that all of their New Brunswick university student sample reported having had sexual thoughts at some time. Both men and women reported more positive than negative thoughts, with men reporting more of both positive and negative thoughts. Participants reported a wide variety of content in sexual thoughts. . . . Little and Byers (2000) [found that] . . . [p]eople often enjoyed having sexual fantasies while in public places, and people in committed relationships were not more likely to evaluate sexual thoughts as negative. Our survey of Ontario students enrolled in an introductory sexuality course (1999–2006) indicated that 63 percent of women and 78 percent of men—who have had sex—fantasize while engaging in sexual activity with a partner. Our students fantasize in greater numbers (98 percent of men; 93 percent of women) during masturbation—sexual self-stimulation.

Masturbation

Historically, masturbation has been stigmatized and associated with immorality and pathology, but it is quickly gaining respect as a common and healthy sexual activity (Coleman, 2002). A recent survey of American university students (Pinkerton et al., 2002) found that about two-thirds of the women and almost all of the men reported masturbating at least once. Both genders reported frequent masturbation in the past three months. People masturbated more if they perceived social norms in support of this behavior (Pinkerton et al., 2002). More sexually active people masturbated more often, indicating that masturbation is not a substitute for other sexual activity (also see Davis et al., 1996).

Men tend to masturbate fairly uniformly whereas women tend to have more varied masturbation techniques from woman-to-woman (see Masters and Johnson, 1966). There were no gender differences in reasons for masturbating: the majority of men and women stated that they masturbated to relieve sexual tension and the second most commonly cited reason was for physical pleasure (Laumann et al., 1994). . . . Of all sexual behaviors, masturbation seems most clearly motivated by pleasure, or at least, release of tension. . . .

Partnered Sexual Activity

A common North American sexual script suggests that we have a shared idea about the sequence of partnered sexual behaviors that proceeds from kissing and touching ("petting" above the waist) to more intensive touching ("petting" below the waist or manual stimulation of the genitals) to oral sex to genital-to-genital contact to vaginal or anal intercourse (Gagnon and Simon, 1987; Laumann et al., 1994; McKay, 2004). Of course, there are a multitude of variations on this script and many behaviors have been omitted from this generic description. In almost all cases, kissing is a starting point.

Kissing

Kissing is a very common behavior with same-sex and other-sex couples reporting that they usually kiss when they have sex (Blumstein and Schwartz, 1983). In a U.S. study of university students, most (96%) had "dry" kissed someone and a large majority (89%) reported having "French-kissed" (i.e., kissed with open mouths). Ninety-one percent (91%) of men and 95 percent of women who participated in our human sexuality student survey indicated that they were experienced French-kissers, as well. A representative study of Canadian youth found that about a third to half of seventh-grade students, approximately two-thirds of ninth-grade students, and about eight out of ten eleventh-grade students reported engaging in "deep, open-mouth" kissing (Boyce et al., 2003). It should be noted that, while kissing is generally considered an erotic activity in North American society, it is not considered erotic in all cultures (Harvey, 2005). When kissing is considered erotic, however, it is often a precursor to petting (kissing, of course, may accompany petting).

Touching

Petting is a rather odd term for sexually touching another person—usually interpreted as meaning in the genital region. This is also known as mutual masturbation or being masturbated by a partner. This is a common behavior amongst university students . . . (Browning et al., 2000; Pinkerton et al., 2003). . . . Over a third of seventh-grade students, about two-thirds of ninth-grade students, and eight out of ten eleventh-grade students indicated that they had engaged in "touching above the waist at least once." The incidence of hand-genital contact was less common—with about a quarter to a third of seventh-grade students, slightly over half of ninth-grade students, and about three-quarters of eleventh-grade students responding yes to "touching below the waist at least once" (Boyce et al., 2003). Mutual masturbation is a common sexual behavior and being masturbated by one's partner tends to be ranked as highly pleasurable relative to some other sexual behaviors (Pinkerton et al., 2003). Another form of touching is oral sex: sexual stimulation of the genitals by mouth.

Oral Sex

People frequently engage in oral sex. Recent national surveys in the United State indicated that a large majority of adult men (79–85%) have had oral sex performed on them (called fellatio) while many women (73–83%) have received oral sex (called cunnilingus) (Laumann et al., 1994; Mosher, Chandra, and Jones, 2005). About 90 percent of adults have had oral sex (Mosher et al., 2005). This has changed somewhat since the Kinsey surveys (1949, 1953) which indicated that about 60 percent of men and women had engaged in oral sex. Our survey of sexuality students indicated that between 80 percent and 85 percent of women and men had performed and received oral sex. Not surprisingly, oral sex is becoming more common among Canadian adolescents, as well (Boyce et al., 2003; McKay, 2004).

There is an emerging literature where researchers and lay people alike discuss adolescent oral sex as an activity on the rise as a "substitute" for intercourse—as this helps prevent pregnancy, reduce STIs risk, and maintain "virginity" (Barrett, 2004; McKay, 2004). Mosher and others (2005) found that just over 10 percent of teenagers (15–19 years old) have had oral sex without intercourse with about 55 percent of all teens having had oral sex.

[E]ducators and researchers consider this to be a natural increase as oral sex rates have increased for adults as well (Burnett, 2004; McKay, 2004). One of the major reasons why youth engage in oral sex is that it is fun and pleasurable (Barrett, 2004). Similarly, university students ranked receiving oral sex as the second most pleasant activity after vaginal intercourse (Pinkerton et al., 2003).

Penis-in-Vagina Intercourse

Pinkerton and others (2003) found that penis-in-vagina intercourse was rated as the most pleasurable sexual activity (as did Laumann et al., 1994). This is a behavior in which almost all adults have engaged at least once (Laumann et al., 1994; Mosher et al., 2005; Wellings et al., 1994). In terms of U.S. university students, around 80 percent have had vaginal intercourse (Browning et al., 2000; Pinkerton et al., 2003). Our sample of Canadian sexuality students had slightly fewer men indicating that they have had vaginal intercourse (75%) compared to women (79%). Most of these students (40–45%) had their first intercourse between the ages of 16–18 years; this is congruent with the representative survey of Canadian youth finding that between 40–46% of eleventh-grade students have had intercourse at least once (Boyce et al., 2003).

While there are *many* different positions for intercourse, there are four "basic" positions: man-on-top ("missionary"), woman-on-top, side-by-side, and rear entry ("doggie style"). Each position has certain "advantages." For example, the woman-on-top position is good when a man has poorer ejaculatory control, allows the woman to control sexual positioning and rhythm, and allows greater accessibility to the clitoris (a key organ to female sexual pleasure). The man-on-top is the recommended position when a couple is trying to become pregnant. Rear entry is good when a woman is pregnant or when particularly deep penile insertion is desired. . . . While vaginal intercourse is considered pleasurable by most people, a substantial minority of people also report enjoying anal sex.

Anal Sex

Anal sex can take different forms. There is penis-in anus intercourse whereby a man inserts his penis into the rectum of his partner.

As the anus has no natural lubrication, a sterile lubricant gel is recommended (e.g., Astroglide, K-Y Jelly) so as to reduce the likelihood of trauma to the anus (e.g., tearing tissue, damaging sphincters). It is recommended that the inserter wear a condom. Because anal intercourse typically involves some tearing of the tissue, there is a direct route for pathogens into the blood stream, making this a very efficient route for HIV transmission and other STIs. It is important that the penis be washed after anal intercourse and prior to any further genital contact. For example, if a man removes his penis from the anus and inserts it into the vagina, various bacteria can be transferred to the vagina.

Anilingus or "rimming" is oral stimulation of the anus. Again, because of the presence of bacteria and possibly other STI pathogens (e.g., gonorrhea, hepatitis), it is prudent to use a barrier (e.g., cut a condom up the side or use a dental dam). Some people enjoy digital stimulation of the anus by having fingers or the hand inserted in the anus during sexual arousal.

Anal intercourse is not as commonly performed as the other sexual activities discussed thus far. A representative U.S. sample found that roughly a third of adults have had anal sex (Mosher et al., 2005). . . . About one-fifth to a quarter of university students in two U.S. samples reported ever having experienced anal intercourse (Browning et al., 2000; Pinkerton et al., 2003). In our sexuality student survey, about one-fifth reported having had anal intercourse. Laumann and others asked their participants if they had experienced anal sex *in the past year* and approximately 5–10% had experienced anal sex that recently. Finally, Laumann and others posed an interesting set of questions to their participants about how "appealing" a variety of sexual behaviors were. When asked about various forms of anal sex, between 1% and 5% of people rated anal contact as "very appealing" (including stimulating a partner's

anus, having anus stimulated by a partner's finger, and anal intercourse).

Techniques of Same-Sex Couples

A substantial minority of people are lesbian, gay, or bisexual (LGB; Laumann et al., 1994). A recent representative U.S. survey found that around 8–10 percent of adults identified as LGB (Mosher et al., 2005). About 9 percent of men and 6 percent of women in our human sexuality class self-identified as LGB. One does not need to be LGB to engage in same-sex behavior; 6 percent of men and 11 percent of women indicated that they have had a same-sex sexual partner in their lifetime (Mosher et al., 2005). Laumann and others (1994) found that about 3 percent of men and women rated having a same-gendered sexual partner as "very appealing."

Same-sex couples tend to engage in similar sexual behaviors as other-sex couples including kissing, hugging, mutual masturbation, oral stimulation, and penetrative sex (Blumstein and Schwartz, 1983; Masters and Johnson, 1979). Male couples sometimes engage in interfemoral intercourse; this is where one man thrusts his penis between the thighs of the other man. Female couples may engage in tribadism whereby "two women rub their vulvae together to stimulate each other's clitoris to orgasm" (Wikimedia Foundation, 2006; also see Caster, 1993) or, there may be mons-to-thigh stimulation. Other-sex couples also engage in this non-penetrative genital-to-genital stimulation (Kinsey et al. [1953] call this apposition; "dry humping" is a more common, but less sophisticated, description).

Masters and Johnson (1979) observed and compared the sexual behaviors of same-sex couples to other-sex couples and found differences in arousal *techniques* rather than sexual behaviors. In general, the same-sex couples tended to "take their time" in comparison to opposite-sex couples. That is, Masters and Johnson characterized heterosexual couples as more "performance oriented"—oriented toward the penis-in-vagina act—in contrast to the same-sex couples, who engaged more in pleasure-seeking throughout the sexual encounter. There were no differences between heterosexual and homosexual people of the same gender in terms of masturbation techniques.

Spicy Sex

Thus far, we have discussed relatively common sexual activities. There are practices that are not necessarily common or usual but that are pleasurable for many people. . . . [I]t is important to remember that uncommon does not equal pathological. Most sexual behaviors can be placed on a continuum from healthy (e.g., having a mild or strong preference) to pathological (e.g., when the behavior/object becomes a necessity or a substitute for a human relationship; see Hyde, DeLamater, and Byers, 2006). Spicier activities may be an indication of the importance of sexual pleasure. While many of the "vanilla" techniques are quite pleasurable, they are often socially scripted, and are cheap and easy in which to engage. More "spicy" techniques may require creative thought, monetary expense, or even travel plans. The trouble that people are willing to go through for the "spicier" activities might indicate that these are primarily pleasure-seeking activities.

Sex Toys

Sex toys" are devices that people use to enhance their sexual pleasure (e.g., vibrators, dildos) and, while sex toys have been around for years (in the late 1800s, early 1900s as "medical devices"; see Maines, 1999), people have become more open about discussing sex toys perhaps because of popular media portrayals (e.g., *Sex and the City,* King, Chupack, Melfi, Bicks, Raab, et al., 2006; *The L Word,* Chaiken,

Golin, and Kennar, 2006) and books and stores devoted to sex toys (e.g., Venning and Cavanah, 2003). . . . In our survey of human sexuality students, about a third of women had experience with a "mechanical aid" compared to 8 percent of men. This is quite different from the representative survey of American adults which found less than 1 in 20 (< 5%) of men and women rated vibrator/dildo use as appealing (Laumann et al., 1994). Laumann and others found that the more educated women in their sample found vibrator/dildo use the most appealing—education may impact attitudes toward sex toy use.

Davis et al. (1996) conducted a study of women who use vibrators. . . . The results suggested that many of the women . . . found that clitoral-vibrator stimulation usually triggers an orgasm, they used their vibrators on a variety of sexual sites (clitoral, vaginal, and anal), and in a variety of ways (circular motion, up/down, or back/forth). Most (80%) of the sample used the vibrator during partnered sex—sometimes with the partner watching the woman use the vibrator while sometimes the partner held the vibrator for the woman. Women, who were lesbian and were more likely to, reported being younger when they first used a vibrator and were slightly more likely to use a vibrator with a partner than were bisexual or heterosexual women.

Sexually Explicit Material

Use of erotica—sexually explicit depictions—is also a relatively common aid in autosexual or partnered sexual activity. Erotic materials are broad-ranging and may include books, magazines, videos/DVDs, live shows (e.g., exotic dancers), telephone sex, and cybersexuality (e.g., sex in chat rooms, webcam sex). Laumann and others (1994) found that as many as one out of five men used some form of erotic materials when fantasizing/masturbating while fewer women did (as many as one in ten). These researchers asked about the appeal of "watching other people do sexual things" (which might be interpreted as erotica or, alternatively, voyeurism) and found that 5 percent of men and 1 percent of women found this activity sexually appealing. In the human sexuality student survey, a majority of men and women had favorable attitudes toward erotic materials, although there was a gender difference such that men were more favorable than women were.

Online sexual activities have increased in recent years. . . . A study of people who use the Internet indicated that 80 percent of participants used the web for sexual purposes. Of those people, about a third had engaged in "cybersex." Cybersex was defined as "when two or more people are engaging in sexual talk while online for the purposes of sexual pleasure and may or may not include masturbation" (Daneback, Cooper, and Månsson, 2005: 321). This cybersex most commonly took the form of a sexual encounter in a "chat room" with the second most popular medium being instant messenger-type programs.

Sexual Internet activities are probably on the rise because of the fact that these materials are affordable, readily available, and can be accessed anonymously (Cooper, McLoughlin, and Campbell, 2000). The Internet allows people with uncommon sexual proclivities to both find and support others with similar interests. As well, the Internet offers users the opportunity to experiment with new behaviors in a relatively safe setting, satisfy curiosity, and seek out new information. While there has been a substantial discussion of "Internet sex addiction," sexually compulsive Internet users typically already have a history of unconventional sexual practices (i.e., diagnosable paraphilias, risky sexual activity). Many people who are recreational users of online sexual material spend less than an hour per week, on average, visiting sexual websites (Cooper et al., 1999).

Sadomasochism

Sadomasochism (S&M) is a term that collectively describes a variety of sexual behaviors which may involve the administration of pain (e.g., use of clothespins/clamps, hot wax, spanking), deliberate humiliation (e.g., use of a gag, face slapping), physical restriction (e.g., handcuffs, chains), and hypermasculine activities (e.g., cockbinding, watersports, rimming) that are experienced as pleasurable by both partners (Alison, Santtila, Sandnabba, and Nordling, 2001; Sandnabba, Santtila, and Nordling, 1999). The S&M scene typically involves fetishistic elements such as leather clothing and whips, and ritualistic activity such as bondage. S&M has been characterized as fantasy-oriented and role-playing scripted behavior.

. . . [T]here is a distinct subculture of psychologically well-adjusted individuals who engage in S&M activities—many of whom belong to S&M "clubs" (Alison et al., 2001; Sandnabba et al., 1999). Partners in S&M activities described here refer to consenting S&M participants. People who have participated in research studies about the S&M subculture have been found to be well-integrated into society in general as they tend to be highly educated and earn high incomes (Alison et al., 2001; Mosher and Levitt, 1987; Sandnabba et al., 1999). Most of these people report engaging in S&M activities occasionally and in non-S&M sexual activities frequently—which indicates that the S&M activities were not part of a "diagnosable paraphilia" (Sandnabba et al., 1999). Most of the information known about S&M involves men; it is sometimes difficult to obtain adequate samples of women within the S&M subculture (Mosher and Levitt, 1987; Sandnabba et al., 1999). In a study of men, Sandnabba and colleagues (1999) found the most common S&M behaviors to include (in order): oral sex, bondage, wearing leather outfits, flagellation (e.g., whipping), anal intercourse, rimming, handcuffs, and the use of chains, dildos, and verbal humiliation; at least 70 percent of all of the men interviewed participated in each of these behaviors. The most popular role-play for heterosexual men was master/slave (for Mosher and Levitt's, 1987, sample, too) while, for gay men, the most common role-play was a "uniform scene" (e.g., police officer and arrestee).

Although we do not know how many people practice S&M, we do know that people fantasize about and/or have a sexual response to S&M activities. . . . While S&M fantasies appear to be fairly common, we do not know how many people act upon these fantasies.

Sex on Vacation

There is a phenomenon that has recently begun to be documented whereby people travel for the purpose of obtaining sex outside of their community. Much of this literature has focused on heterosexual men who travel to areas such as the Caribbean or Southeast Asia for sexual gratification. While most of these men do not view themselves as engaging prostitution services, the transactions are clearly a form of commercialized sex. Researchers and theorists in this area actually find that sex tourists of this sort tend to be racist, sexist, and believe in their own Western cultural superiority over the people in these Third World locales (O'Connell Davidson and Sánchez Taylor, 1999).

Heterosexual women are also sex tourists who "purchase" the sexual services of local men (e.g., Cabezas, 2004; Herold, Garcia, and DeMoya, 2001). In Sánchez Taylor's (2001) study of single women vacationing at resorts in the Dominican Republic and Jamaica, approximately a third had engaged in sexual relations with local men; this was significantly more new sexual contacts compared to single women vacationing in Europe. Over half of the women with "vacation" sex partners had remunerated the sex partner in some way (e.g., cash, gifts).

These women did not view themselves as being consumers of prostitution services despite the economic element to their relationship; rather, they tended to characterize these sexual behaviors as "holiday romances." However, the men tend to be in lower socioeconomic positions (e.g. "beach boys," hotel workers), often live in poverty, and earn a living through various forms of "hustling." Interviews with the men indicated that they do not conceptualize themselves as prostitutes or sex trade workers but they acknowledge that they reap financial and material benefits from entering into a series of fleeting sexual relationships with female tourists. These men even have strategies to assess which women are likely to be the most "generous" (Sánchez Taylor, 2001).

A different type of sex tourism is popular with university students who are on vacation. This involves having casual sex with a relative stranger while on spring break. By *relative stranger,* researchers mean that the individual has met the sexual partner while on vacation and typically known the sex partner for 24 hours or less. . . . Matika-Tyndale and colleagues . . . 1997; 1998) found . . . approximately 16 percent of students vacationing in Daytona Beach had engaged in sexual intercourse with a new casual partner (this excludes those traveling with their boyfriend/girlfriend). Almost half (46%) reported "fooling around in a sexual way" with a new partner; this involved sexual activity excluding intercourse. In the spring break subculture, sexual norms are more permissive than what is expected "back home" . . . (Mewhinney, Herold, and Maticka-Tyndale, 1995). Having a partner "back home" did not seem to deter vacationers from having casual sex; one-fifth to one-quarter of people who were currently in a relationship had intercourse with a casual partner while they were on vacation.

It seems that being on vacation—away from the social constraints of "home"—creates a subculture of sexual permissiveness whereby one can have sex for solely the purpose of having sex (e.g., for fun, to "let loose"). As one student characterized casual sex during spring break vacation: "It is generally expected . . . to have a great time and that includes having sex" (Mewhinney et al., 1995: 278). There are similar destinations that are known for tourist-tourist casual sex such as Ibiza and Cape d'Azur that cater to non-students populations (O'Connell Davidson and Sánchez Taylor, 1999). The fact that some will go through so much trouble for the purpose of having sex lends credence to the unspoken value we place on sexual pleasure. The pursuit of sexual pleasure can be seen clearly, not only in sex tourism, but in the multi-faceted behaviours we have chosen to call "spicy" sex.

Spicy sex encompasses a diversity of behaviors, many of which we have *not* discussed (e.g., group sex and swinging, other commercialized sex, cross-dressing, etc.). What is interesting about these diverse behaviors is that, while not popular with everyone, people who engage in these behaviors tend to find a social group who are supportive of the activities (e.g., fantasia parties for those who have an interest in sex toys, S&M clubs, online chat groups devoted to various sexual acts). It is possible that when there is a supportive social network for the "spicy" sexual behavior, people will be more comfortable with their "less common" sexual behavior (see Kutchinsky, 1976, Sandnabba et al., 1999). . . .

What Can We Conclude about Sexual Pleasure?

What is sexually pleasurable is in the eye of the beholder. "Sex" and "sexual pleasure" are very much "social constructions" in that certain attitudes, behaviors, and activities are considered taboo. Societal norms exert a great deal of social control over what is "acceptable" sexuality. In Western society dominated by Christian

values, there is a tendency to view the pursuit of sex for pleasure's sake as hedonistic; for example, a person who has casual sex tends to be viewed negatively (Parrinder, 1996). The pleasure of sex for a particular person depends not entirely on attaining orgasm but on the context and psychological state of the individuals involved (Mah and Binik, 2005). How a person has internalized the cultural messages about various aspects of sexuality will have a profound impact on the person's experience of sexual pleasure. For example, if sex is seen solely as a means of procreation—a strongly Christian perspective (Parrinder, 1996)—there may be great guilt associated with feeling pleasure if one engages in sexual behavior solely for pleasure purposes. Similarly, when sex is fundamental to the maintenance of a long-term relationship, it can become an obligatory duty (see Hawkes, 1996, . . . for a discussion). In both cases, sex can become a matter of performance-pressure and anxiety.

In the eighteenth and nineteenth centuries, sex was officially defined in terms of the social and interpersonal functions it fulfilled; there was little mention of sex as a pleasurable experience (or, if so, it was pleasurable only for men). When attention was drawn to the sexual pleasure of women (somewhat ironically, by the work of Freud), social forces constrained that pleasure to marriage. People seeking sexual pleasure outside of marriage were labeled as "deviant" (Hawkes, 1996). Our current societal views on sexual pleasure have their roots in our Victorian history of sex negativity and the subsequent need to "quell" or control a dangerous instinct (Foucault, 1976/1978; Weeks, 1981, 1986).

Current North American attitudes toward sexual pleasure run the gamut from "only for procreation" to "okay when in love or when dating" to "anything goes." While there is no consensus, sex with love or in the context of a committed relationship tends to be deemed as more acceptable and changes in attitudes toward sex tend to relate to concurrent changes in sexual behavior (Barrett et al., 2004). Views about sexuality and sexual pleasure are constantly changing (DeLamater and Hyde, 2003). Enhanced discussions about sexual pleasure will occur as our society incorporates an increasingly positive perspective on sexual pleasure into the existing sexual scripts (Gagnon and Simon, 1987). This positive view of sexual pleasure will need to be incorporated into scripts at all levels: the intrapersonal (i.e., self-acceptance of sex for personal pleasure), the interpersonal (i.e., acceptance of one's partner(s), friends, family, etc. as enjoying sex for pleasure reasons), and finally, the overarching cultural scripts (i.e., schemas for the sexuality of men, schemas for the sexuality of women, environments that reinforce rather than punish the concept of sexual pleasure for pleasure's sake).

While the social discourse surrounding sexuality will continue to evolve and to complicate the meanings attached to sexuality, the avoidance and guilt associated with sexual pleasure seems to be lessening. In fact, a new discourse appears to be arising that specifically and explicitly emphasizes the often-lost pursuit of sexual pleasure (McKay, 2004; Abramson and Pinkerton, 1995). This pursuit, in itself, can become a source of enlightenment spurred by the realization of simple, physical pleasures associated with human sexuality. The dark side of sexuality will continue to exert its influence, of course, in the specters of sexual harassment, sexual coercion, stalking, paraphilias, and related phenomenona. . . . But, an acceptance of sexual pleasure would open avenues for personal satisfaction that will, hopefully, serve as a safeguard against such negative outcomes.

REFERENCES

Abramson, P. R., and Pinkerton, S. D. 1995. *With pleasure: Thoughts on the nature of human sexuality.* New York: Oxford University Press.

Alison, L., Santtila, P., Sandnabba, N. K., and Nordling, N. 2001. Sadomasochistically oriented behavior: Diversity in practice and meaning. *Archives of Sexual Behavior,* 30(1): 1–12.

Barrett, A. 2004. Oral sex and teenagers: A sexual health educator's perspective. *Canadian Journal of Human Sexuality,* 13(3/4): 197–200.

Barrett, M., King, A., Lévy, J., Maticka-Tyndale, E., McKay, A., and Fraser, J. 2004. Canada. In R. T. Francoeur and R. J. Noonan (Eds.), *The Continuum complete international encyclopedia of sexuality* (pp. 126–181). New York: Continuum.

Blumstein, P., and Schwartz, P. 1983. *American couples.* New York: Morrow.

Boyce, W., Doherty, M., Fortin, C., and MacKinnon, D. 2003. *Canadian youth, sexual health and HIV/AIDS study.* Toronto, ON: Council of Ministers of Education.

Browning, J. R., Hatfield, E., Kessler, D., and Levine, T. 2000. Sexual motives, gender and sexual behavior. *Archives of Sexual Behavior,* 29(2): 135–153.

Byers, S., Purdon, C., and Clark, D. A. 1998. Sexual intrusive thoughts of college students. *Journal of Sex Research,* 35(4): 359–369.

Byrne, D., and Osland, J. A. 2000. Sexual fantasy and erotica / pornography: Internal and external imagery. In L. T. Szuchman and F. Muscarella (Eds.), *Psychological perspectives on human sexuality* (pp. 283–305). Toronto, ON: Wiley.

Cabezas, A. L. 2004. Between love and money: Sex, tourism, and citizenship in Cuba and the Dominican Republic. *Signs: Journal of Women in Culture and Society,* 29(4): 987–1015.

Caster, W. 1993. *The lesbian sex book.* Boston, MA: Alyson.

Chaiken, I., Golin, S., and Kennar, L. (Producers) 2006. *The L word* [Television series]. Showtime.

Coleman, E. 2002. Masturbation as a means of achieving sexual health. *Journal of Psychology and Human Sexuality,* 14(2/3): 5–16.

Colby, C. (Producer). 2006. *The sex files* [Television series]. Discovery Channel.

Comfort, A. 1972. *The joy of sex: A gourmet guide to love making.* New York: Simon & Schuster.

The complete kama sutra: The first unabridged translation of the classic Indian text (A. Danielou, Trans.). (1994). Rochester, VT: Rock Street Press.

Cooper, A., McLoughlin, I. P., and Campbell, K. M. 2000. Sexuality in cyberspace: Update for the 21st Century. *CyberPsychology & Behavior,* 3(4): 521–536.

Cooper, A., Putnam, D. E., Planchon, L. A., and Boies, S. C. 1999. Online sexual compulsivity: Getting tangled in the net. *Sexual Addiction & Compulsivity: The Journal of Treatment and Prevention,* 6(2): 79–104.

Cooper, A., Sherer, C., Boies, S.C., and Gordon, B. 1999. Sexuality on the Internet: From sexual exploration to pathological expression. *Professional Psychology: Research and Practice,* 30(2): 154–164.

Daneback, K., Cooper, A., and Mansson, S.-A. 2005. An Internet study of cybersex participants. *Archives of Sexual Behavior,* 34(3): 321–328.

The dark side of sexuality (n.d.). Retrieved April 22, 2006 from http://www.sju.ca/courses/course.php?course=408& id=29&ad=10&dir=sexuality

Davis, C. M., Blank, J., Lin, H.-Y., and Bonillas, C. 1996. Characteristics of vibrator use among women. *Journal of Sex Research,* 33(4): 313–320.

DeLamater, J. D., and Hyde, J. S. 1998. Essentialism vs. social constructionism in the study of human sexuality. *Journal of Sex Research,* 35(1): 10–18.

DeLamater, J. D., and Hyde, J. S. 2003. Sexuality. In J. J. Ponzetti, Jr. (Ed.). *International encyclopedia of marriage and family, Volume 3.* (2nd ed.) (pp. 1456–1462). New York: Macmillan/Thomson Gale.

Doskoch, P. 1995, September / October. The safest sex. *Psychology Today,* 28: *46–49.*

Ellis, B. J., and Symons, D. 1990. Sex differences in sexual fantasy: An evolutionary psychology approach. *Journal of Sex Research,* 27(4): 527–555.

Foucault, M. 1978. *The history of sexuality: Vol. 1. An introduction* of (R. Hurley, Trans.). New York: Pantheon. (Original work published 1976)

Gagnon, J. H., and Simon, W. 1987. The sexual scripting of oral genital contacts. *Archives of Sexual Behavior,* 16(1): 1–25.

Harvey, K. 2005. *The kiss in history.* Manchester: Manchester University Press.

Hawkes, G. 1996. *A sociology of sex and sexuality.* Philadelphia, PA: Open University Press.

Herold, E., Garcia, R., and DeMoya, T. 2001. Female tourists and beach boys: Romance or sex tourism? *Annals of Tourism Research,* 28(4): 978–997.

Hsu, B., Kling, A., Kessler, C., Knapke, K., Diefenbach, P., and Elias, J. E. 1994. Gender differences in sexual fantasy and behavior in a college population: A ten-year replication. *Journal of Sex and Marital Therapy,* 20(2): 103–118.

Hurlbert, D. F., and Apt, C. 1993. Female sexuality: A comparative study between women in homosexual and heterosexual relationships. *Journal of Sex and Marital Therapy,* 19(4): 315–327.

Hyde, J. S., DeLamater, J. D., and Byers, E. S. 2006. *Understanding human sexuality* (3rd ed., Canadian). Toronto, ON: McGraw-Hill Ryerson.

Keating, B. A., and Over, R. 1990. Sexual fantasies of heterosexual and homosexual men. *Archives of Sexual Behavior,* 19(5): 461–475.

King, M. P., Chupack, C., Melfi, J., Bicks, J., Raab, J., et al. (Producers). 2006. *Sex and the city* [Television series]. New York: HBO.

Kinsey, A. C., Pomeroy, W. B., and Martin, C. E. 1949. *Sexual behavior in the human male.* Philadelphia, PA: Saunders.

Kinsey, A. C., Pomeroy, W. B., Martin, C. E., and Gebhard, P. H. 1953. *Sexual behavior in the human female.* Philadelphia, PA: Saunders.

Knafo, D., and Jaffe, Y. 1984. Sexual fantasizing in males and females. *Journal of Research in Personality,* 18(4): 451–462.

Kutchinsky, B. 1976. Deviance and criminality: The case of voyeur in a peepers' paradise. *Diseases of the Nervous System,* 37(3): 145–151.

Laumann, E. O., Gagnon, J. H., Michael, R. T., and Michaels, S. 1994. *The social organization of sexuality: Sexual practices in the United States.* Chicago, IL: University of Chicago Press.

Leitenberg, H., and Henning, K. 1995. Sexual fantasy. *Psychological Bulletin,* 117(3): 469–496.

Little, C. A., and Byers, E. S. 2000. Differences between positive and negative sexual cognitions. *Canadian Journal of Human Sexuality,* 9(3): 167–179.

Mah, K., and Binik, Y. M. 2005. Are orgasms in the mind or the body? Psychosocial versus physiological correlates of orgasmic pleasure and satisfaction. *Journal of Sex and Marital Therapy,* 31(3): 187–200.

Maines, R. P. 1999. *The technology of orgasm: "Hysteria," the vibrator, and women's sexual satisfaction.* Baltimore, MD: Johns Hopkins University Press.

Masters, W. H., and Johnson, V. E. 1966. *Human sexual response.* Boston, MA: Little, Brown.

Masters, W. H., and Johnson, V. E. 1979. *Homosexuality in perspective.* Boston, MA: Little, Brown.

Maticka-Tyndale, E., and Herold, E. S. 1997. The scripting of sexual behaviour: Canadian university students on spring break in Florida. *Canadian Journal of Human Sexuality,* 6(4): 317–328.

Maticka-Tyndale, E., Herold, E. S., and Mewhinney, D. 1998. Casual sex on spring break: Intentions and behaviors of Canadian students. *Journal of Sex Research,* 35(3): 254–264.

McCauley, C., and Swann, C. P. 1978. Male-female differences in sexual fantasy. *Journal of Research in Personality,* 12(1): 76–86.

McKay, A. 2004. Oral sex among teenagers: Research, discourse, and education. *Canadian Journal of Human Sexuality,* 13(3/4): 201–203.

Mewhinney, D. M., Herold, E. S., and Maticka-Tyndale, E. 1995. Sexual scripts and risk-taking of Canadian university students on spring break in Daytona Beach, Florida. *Canadian Journal of Human Sexuality,* 4(4): 273–288.

Mosher, C., and Levitt, E. E. 1987. An exploratory-descriptive study of a sadomasochistically oriented sample. *Journal of Sex Research,* 23(3): 322–337.

Mosher, W. D., Chandra, A., and Jones, J. 2005. Sexual behavior and selected health measures: Men and women 15–44 years of age, United States, 2002. *Advance data from vital and health statistics, no. 362.* Hyattsville, MD: National Center for Health Statistics.

O'Connell Davidson, J., and Sánchez Taylor, J. 1999. Fantasy islands: Exploring the demand for sex tourism. In K. Kempadoo (Ed.), *Sun, sex, and gold: Tourism and sex work in the Caribbean* (pp. 37–54). Oxford: Rowman Littlefield.

Parrinder, G. 1996. *Sexual morality in the world religions.* Oxford: One-world.

Pinkerton, S. D., Bogart, L. M., Cecil, H., and Abramson, P. R. 2002. Factors associated with masturbation in a collegiate sample. *Journal of Psychology and Human Sexuality,* 14(2/3): 103–121.

Pinkerton, S. D., Cecil, H., Bogart, L. M., and Abramson, P. R. 2003. The pleasures of sex: An empirical investigation. *Cognition and Emotion,* 17(2): 341–353.

Renaud, C. A., and Byers, E. S. 1999. Exploring the frequency, diversity, and content of university students' positive and negative sexual cognitions. *Canadian Journal of Human Sexuality,* 8(1): 17–30.

Robinson, J. D., and Parks, C. W. 2003. Lesbian and bisexual women's sexual fantasies, psychological adjustment, and close relationship functioning. *Journal of Psychology and Human Sexuality,* 15(4): 185–203.

Sánchez Taylor, J. 2001. Dollars are a girl's best friend? Female tourists' sexual behaviour in the Carribean. *Sociology,* 35(3): 749–764.

Sandnabba, N. K., Santtila, P., and Nordling, N. 1999. Sexual behavior and social adaptation among sadomasochistically-oriented males. *Journal of Sex Research,* 36(3): 273–282.

Venning, R., and Cavanah, C. 2003. *Sex toys 101: A playfully uninhibited guide.* New York: Fireside.

Warren, W. K., and King, A. J. 1994. *Development and evaluation of an AIDS/STD/Sexuality program for Grade 9 students.* Kingston, ON: Social Program Evaluation Group, Queens University.

Weeks, J. 1981. *Sex, politics, and society.* New York: Longman.

Weeks, J. 1986. *Key Ideas: Sexuality* (P. Hamilton, Series Ed.). London: Tavistock.

Wellings, K., Field, J., Johnson, A. M., and Wadsworth, J. 1994. *Sexual behavior in Britain: The national survey of sexual attitudes and lifestyles.* London: Penguin.

Westheimer, R. K. 1995. *Sex for dummies.* Chicago: IDG Books Worldwide.

Wikimedia Foundation 2006. Tribadism. Retrieved February 26, 2006 from http://en.wikipedia.org/wiki/Tribadism

How American Teens View Sex

Madison Park

Teenagers do not fear warts and bodily havoc caused by sexually transmitted diseases. The ones who abstain from sex are more worried about the wrath of God. A report by the National Center for Health Statistics that surveyed 4,662 teenagers asked those who abstained why they had chosen not to have sex. The top reason for both males and females between the age of 15 and 19 was that sexual intercourse was "against religion or morals." They were least likely to be concerned about STDs.

The report on teenage sexual activities released [in October 2011] found that the rate of teenagers having sex has declined slightly from the last report released in 2002, but this change was not substantial. It follows an overall trend of decline in teenage sex in the last 20 years. . . . The report also found increases in male teens using condoms and females using injectable birth control, such as Depo-Provera, or contraceptive patches at the time of their first sexual intercourse.

Here are [some] of the study's findings. . . .

The birth rate of 39.1 births per 1,000 females [in 2009] is a historic low for the United States, which had teenage birth rates as high as 53 in 1988. But the report points out that the teen birth rate has fluctuated in the last two decades. The U.S. teenage birth rate remains fairly high compared with Canada, which had 14 teenage births per 1,000. Germany's rate was at 10 and Italy at 7.

[Among female[s] in the 15–19 range who've never been married, [43%] have had sexual intercourse at least once. This percentage was based on 2,284 females surveyed for the report—the largest sample ever interviewed for this type of report. "Overall, in the 20-year period from 1988 through 2006–2010, the percentage of teenaged females who were sexually experienced declined significantly (from 51 percent in 1988 to 43 percent in 2006–2010)," according to the report. Historically, black female teenagers were more likely to be sexually experienced than Latinos and whites. The rate of sexual experience was 57 percent for black teenagers in 2002, but has now dropped to 46 percent. Because of that decrease, "now we don't see a racial difference" among female teenagers, said Martinez.

[Among] males 15–19 who've never been married, [42%] have had sexual intercourse at least once. This percent was based on 2,378 males surveyed. Unlike the females, the racial differences in [males'] teenage sexual experiences are still present. "Black teenagers had significantly higher percentages sexually active (38%) compared with both Hispanic (30%) and non-Hispanic white (25%) teenagers," according to the report.

Forty-one percent [of] female teenagers . . . say they abstained because of religious or moral reasons. For males, 31 percent of them cited this reason. The second most common reason for males was that they hadn't "found the right person yet," followed by the fear of getting a girl pregnant. For females, their second most common answer was that they didn't want to get pregnant, followed by not having found the right person yet. . . .

Seventy-eight percent [of] female teenagers . . . used a contraceptive during their first sexual experience. These methods include condoms, hormonal pills, emergency contraception and patches. The most common method was condoms at 68 percent, followed by the pill at 16 percent. For male teenagers, 85 percent reported using contraception at their first intercourse, also with condoms as the most popular method. Eighty-six percent [of] female teenagers . . . used contraceptives during their most recent sexual intercourse. The most popular contraceptive remained the condom, followed by the pill and other hormonal methods. For males, 93 percent reported using contraceptives during their most recent intercourse.

GETTING, GIVING, FAKING, HAVING: ORGASM AND THE PERFORMANCE OF PLEASURE

BREANNE FAHS

The phenomenon of women's orgasms has long troubled scholars, therapists, theorists, activists, and scientists. Constructed as a symbol of sexual satisfaction by some, it has also taken on political meaning in the age of Victorian repression, during the women's liberation movement, and as the Western world moves into new frontiers of medicating women's sexual desire. Such historical shifts—from orgasm as a treatment for hysteria to a signal of patriarchal obedience, from a measure of women's liberation to a medicalized performance—reveal its importance as a cultural marker of gender politics. Orgasm unveils ideologies about the status of women, beliefs about gender and sexuality, and it serves as a concise reminder of the age-old claim that "the personal is political."

This [reading] examines orgasm—and, specifically, faking orgasm and the pressures women face to orgasm—as it relates to the cultural mandate for sexual performance. I interrogate several aspects of orgasm within partnered relationships: the construction of orgasm as a "gift" from a partner, similarities and differences in heterosexual and lesbian relationships with regard to orgasm, women's descriptions of themselves as "on stage" during sex, pressures women face to please partners, and, finally, women's justification for faking orgasm during sex. Key exploratory questions include: What are the effects of orgasm being constructed as something a partner "gives" to a woman? How do women experience themselves when performing a "fake" orgasm (and can one definitively distinguish a fake orgasm from a real one)? How do women negotiate the complexities of a partnered relationship in their performance of orgasm? What significance does orgasm have for women's sexual satisfaction? How is orgasm both personal and political?

HISTORICAL CONTEXT

. . . . A transition from orgasm as a regular and healthy part of women's sexuality to orgasm as a sign of social deviance dominated the moral anxieties of the Victorian age. Rachel Maines (1999) outlined the historical connection between orgasm and mental health: "In the Western medical tradition genital massage to orgasm by a physician or midwife was a standard treatment for hysteria, an ailment considered common and chronic in women" (p. 1). . . . Thus, if the marriage bed (i.e., penetrative vaginal intercourse) did not cure hysteria, the male doctor as a proper substitute assumed responsibility. . . . Carroll Smith-Rosenberg (1985) more clearly articulated this timeline: "Highly respected medical writers in the 1820s and 1830s had described women as naturally lusty and capable of multiple orgasms. They defined women's frigidity as pathological. By the 1860s and 1870s, however, their professional counterparts counseled husbands that frigidity was rooted in women's very nature. Women's only sexual desire, these doctors argued, was reproductive" (p. 23).

. . . .Thus, the Victorian era normalized lack of orgasm and women's distance from their sexuality. Laqueur (1990) stated, "When, in the late eighteenth century, it became a possibility that 'the majority of women are not much troubled with sexual feelings,' the presence or absence of orgasm became a biological signpost of sexual difference" (p. 4). So, as the difference between the sexes came to justify a variety of social inequalities, so too did these inequalities breed *sexual* difference (in behavior, attitude, and socialization). Women were no longer entitled to sexual pleasure. . . . Women became the symbolic representation of restraint, a carefully constructed (and politically significant) shift. Such restraint, in which women denied their sexual impulses in order to fit into polite society, also helped to define male sexual aggression, appetite, and desires. . . . During this period, . . . chastity became, for women, a symbol of status; lack of sexual desire linked womanliness with social mobility. . . .

The Victorian era, which enforced women's sexual repression and, at times, their physical confinement, also famously asserted the (medicalized, eroticized) correlation between women's bodies and mental illness. Such correlations reinscribed notions of women's sexual repression, as women's bodies were labeled as entities to be controlled and tamed. The threat of the untamed female body enshrouded such discourses. This was particularly true for hysteria which, as Gilbert and Gubar (1984) noted, came into being during the Victorian era as a "female disease" that took its name from the Greek word *hyster,* meaning "womb."[1] Doctors believed women's ailments resulted from the uterus becoming dislodged from its proper place, resulting in the womb wandering throughout the body. This "wandering womb" caused women's "hysterical" symptoms and ultimately resulted in madness (Bullough, 1999). This fact was not insignificant, as such correlations have laid the foundation for existing definitions of mental illness today. The relationship between women's reproductive systems and their mental illnesses constructed mental illness as fundamentally a woman's problem that required male control and repression.[2]

Psychoanalysis and the Rejection of Sexual Repression (Early 1900s–1970s)

By the end of the nineteenth century, "What came under scrutiny was the sexuality of children, mad men and women, and criminals; the sensuality of those who did not like the opposite sex; reveries, obsessions, petty manias, or great transports of rage" (Foucault, 1978, p. 39). Repression reigned, and women's orgasms fell into the shadows. Foucault (1978) argued that this focus on repression created a cultural obsession about sex; ironically, in the public denial of sexual interests and desires, sexuality became a dominant and pervasive force. . . .

Arising out of the context of severe repression of sexuality, the work of Sigmund Freud sought to make visible the connections between repression of sexuality and obsession with sexuality, allowing psychoanalysis to take root, both in Europe and in the United States. Suddenly, ideas about sexuality as a driving force of human behavior made sense. Like the sex research that was to follow psychoanalysis, the premise of psychoanalysis was to rebel against the repression of sexuality and to instead speak about sexuality in the public sphere. At the same time, these efforts to rebel against repression served both to free women's sexuality from the constraints of repression and to simultaneously constrain it.

Several important paradoxes appear in the way psychoanalysis shaped women's sexuality: (a) Though psychoanalysis functioned as the first "revolt" against the repressive discourses of the Victorian era, it nevertheless reinstituted these repressive discourses by portraying women as naturally passive and domestic and as having relentless "penis envy"; (b) psychoanalysis succeeded in partially bringing women's sexuality into public discourse, but it nevertheless kept women's sexuality hidden and obscure by its overemphasis on male sexuality and masculinist ideas of intercourse and penetration (consequently, women's orgasms could only occur via the vagina rather than the clitoris); (c) psychoanalysis allowed for the existence of women's sexuality (i.e., women *did* have sexual subjectivity), while simultaneously maintaining essential differences between men (as active, dominant, phallic) and women (as passive, inferior, and envious). Psychoanalysis was both repressive and antirepressive. . . .

Kinsey, Masters and Johnson, and Critiques of Psychoanalysis (1948–1975)

. . . . Psychoanalysis also further reinforced the discourse of repression while simultaneously advocating a new performance standard. Similar conflicts were also notable in the emerging research of Alfred Kinsey (1948; 1953) and Masters and Johnson (1966), as these American researchers sought to study both men's and women's sexuality from an empirical perspective. While psychoanalysis argued that both men and women were driven by unconscious sexual wishes and desires, Kinsey and Masters and Johnson sought to empirically demonstrate that mainstream Americans were engaging in a wider variety of sexual behaviors and "nontraditional" lifestyles. . . .

While this research brought sexuality into the public sphere and thereby normalized sexual variety, it also perhaps sparked new perceptions of the *normal*.[3] Women suddenly faced a shift in public perception of women as asexual and pure to a new definition of women as sexually obsessed (Freud), driven toward vaginal orgasm, and sexually active in a diverse group

of sexual behaviors (Kinsey, Pomeroy, Martin, & Gebhard, 1953; Masters & Johnson, 1966). Within this changing climate, feminists were quick to criticize many aspects of psychoanalysis but seemed more ambiguous in their assessment of the work of Kinsey and Masters and Johnson (sometimes using the work of Kinsey and Masters and Johnson to argue against Freud's assertions) (Buhle, 1998). . . .

Arguments about vaginal and clitoral orgasm in Freud's writings also inspired much feminist criticism. Freud's celebration of the vaginal orgasm (a stance that rejected earlier ideas that women should *never* orgasm) established a new performance standard for women (i.e., that vaginal orgasm is superior to clitoral orgasm). Freud asserted that puberty represented a crucial moment of sexual differentiation, because girls transferred their sexual focus from the clitoris to the vagina. Freud argued that girls must "hand over [the clitoris'] sensitivity, and at the same time its importance, to the vagina. . . . With the abandonment of clitoral masturbation a certain amount of activity is renounced. Passivity now has the upper hand" (Laqueur, 2002, p. 393). According to Freud, the clitoris, once the reigning site of sexual pleasure, must render itself inferior in the name of "mature adult sexuality.". . . (cited in Gerhard, 2000, p. 453). Importantly, if such a transfer was not complete, "[a woman] ran the risk of suffering from such psychological problems as penis envy, hostility toward men, hysteria, and neurotic discomfort" (Gerhard, p. 453).

Thus, as the Victorian era of repression and silence around sexuality gave rise to psychoanalysis and empirical sex research as "revolts" against repression, so too did the 1950s era of domesticity and passivity give rise to the women's liberation movement and the sexual revolution. These changes in climate around sexuality were, in part, nurtured by increasingly fervent criticisms of psychoanalysis, which naturalized women's passivity, anger, and hostility about women's continued subjugation in the bedroom (brought to light by the work of de Beauvoir, Friedan, Kofman, and many others), and increasing empirical evidence that despite efforts to silence public discourse about sexuality, Americans were engaging in a wide variety of sexual behaviors previously characterized as "fringe," including homosexuality, oral sex, anal sex, group sex, masturbation, and so on. Increasing distaste for repressive ideologies, as well as the spread of more information about women's actual sexual lives, contributed to the momentum leading toward sexual revolution and women's liberation.

Sexual Liberation and the Rise of Second-wave Feminism (Late 1960s–1990s)

Sexual Revolution and Women's Liberation Movement

. . . . While debates about the meaning of vaginal versus clitoral orgasm occupied much of the public discourse surrounding orgasm, particularly in light of Freud's claim that women would outgrow the clitoral orgasm as they became mature women, it is also noteworthy that women's orgasms came to stand in for liberation in its entirety—a symbol of women's improved social and cultural status. If women could embrace sexual pleasure via orgasm and reject their repressed upbringings, they had arrived at a moment when, supposedly, other inequalities would also vanish. Activism surrounding women's orgasms represented a central feature of the midcentury women's movement and the sexual revolution. It was at this point in history that women collectively fought against the legacies of repression that had so long denied women's pleasure and contained it within the mandates of propriety, decorum, modesty, and silence.

. . . . During the women's liberation movement, women lobbied publicly for orgasms—the right to have them, the right to talk about them, and the right to reject the false claim of the vaginal orgasm as superior to the clitoral orgasm (Jeffreys, 1990). For example, Anne Koedt (1973) cited the then-recent scientific work of Kinsey and colleagues (1953) and Masters and Johnson (1966)—which found that women orgasmed more frequently and easily from clitoral stimulation than vaginal stimulation—as more factual than Freud, and less attached to proper ideals of womanhood. . . . Ti-Grace Atkinson argued,

The construct of vaginal orgasm is most in vogue whenever and wherever the institution of sexual intercourse is threatened. As women become freer, more independent, more self-sufficient, their interest in (i.e., their need for) men decreases, and their desire for the construct of marriage which properly entails children (i.e., a family) decreases proportionate to the increase in their self-sufficiency. (1974, pp. 13–14)

. . . . Activism around women's orgasms during this time focused on reclaiming orgasm on women's own terms, rejecting vaginal orgasm as a symbol of maturity, and embracing other means to achieve pleasure, most notably via lesbian sexual expression.[4]

. . . . While many feminists celebrated their newfound public right to claim orgasm in their personal lives, other radical feminist groups faulted feminist claims of sexual liberation. In particular, some radical feminists argued against *both* the tyranny of the vaginal orgasm *and* the championing of clitoral orgasm. They argued that the celebration of the clitoral orgasm mandated sexual performance in troubling ways. For example, the 1970s radical feminist group based in Boston, Cell 16, argued that patriarchy placed women in the midst of an "orgasm frenzy" (Densmore, 1973, p. 110), obsessed with women's right to enjoy their bodies at the expense of a larger social critique. This argument was echoed by

Sheila Jeffreys (1990), who claimed retrospectively that sexual liberation in the 1960s and 1970s merely substituted one form of oppression for another. Instead of repressing women's sexuality and teaching women not to enjoy sex, these new norms forced women to have sex and to orgasm on demand.... Roxanne Dunbar (1969) argued that sexual liberation became equated with "the 'freedom' to 'make it' with anyone anytime" (p. 49) and that this ignored women's experiences of sex as "brutalization, rape, submission [and] someone having power over them" (p. 56). Other feminists argued that the sexual freedom campaigns of the 1960s and 1970s merely functioned to allow men to have sexual access to greater numbers of women and did not represent freedom at all. . . .

Contemporary Orgasm Research

. . . . Nearly all subsequent sex research has supported the "radical" women's movement claim that the clitoris best facilitated women's orgasms. Darling and Davidson (1987) found that, for many women, the quest for a high consistency of vaginal orgasm with a partner has become more burdensome than enjoyable. The notorious Hite Report confirmed this, saying that intercourse is not particularly suited for women's orgasms (Hite, 1976). Repeated studies have found that stimulation of the clitoris leads to the most consistent orgasms for women. Still, other research showed that many women still conceptualized intercourse as the ultimate sexual experience and believed that orgasm should be achieved through intercourse above all other sexual acts (Davidson and Moore, 1994). Cognitive pressures to orgasm during sex represent a major part of women's sexual lives (Dove and Wiederman, 2000).

Empirical research on orgasm has found conflicting reports of the frequency of women's orgasms. Reports of how often women experience orgasm vary widely and are rarely consistent across populations. Some researchers suggest that women experience orgasm in a fundamentally different way than men (Mah, 2002; Mah and Binik, 2001), most often pointing to women's increased difficulty achieving orgasm compared to men. Hunt (1974) found that 53 percent of 1,044 women surveyed reported coital orgasm "all or almost all" of the time, while Raboch and Raboch (1992) found that 52.2 percent of the 2,423 married women surveyed had experienced orgasm in the course of 70–100 percent of "coital encounters." Janus and Janus (1993) found that 56 percent of women ages 18–26, 67 percent of ages 27–38, 66 percent of ages 39–50, and 50 percent of ages 65 or over reported frequent orgasm during sex. Other studies reported the percentage of women who frequently experience orgasm at 25–30 percent (Butler, 1976; Hurlbert, Apt, and Rabehl, 1993; Wallin, 1960). Notably, measures of orgasm frequency most often rely on self-report, suggesting that frequency of actual orgasm might be lower if women do not know if they have ever *had* an orgasm.

De Bruijn (1982) found that many women with masturbatory experience still did not orgasm regularly with their partner during intercourse. Similarly conflicting reports were noted in studies assessing women's sexual dysfunction, with some research showing that women had high rates of sexual dysfunction[5] (Berman et al., 2003; Ellison, 2001; Shifren, 2008), while other research showed that women were generally not sexually dysfunctional (Walker-Hill, 2000). Importantly, very little attention has been paid to attributions of sexual dysfunction, in other words, whether a woman's sexual dysfunction is due to her own limitations or to her partners' limitations. Research on sexual dysfunction typically focuses on frequency (or lack thereof) of orgasm and/or arousal without attending to the specific causes for these dysfunctions or whether sexual dysfunction even exists at all.

Research has also yielded conflicting reports on women's feelings about orgasm and its significance in their sexual lives. Such research has shown that, at times, women tended to downplay the significance of orgasm when reporting on sexual satisfaction, while at other times, women emphasized orgasm as the most important feature of sexual satisfaction. By downplaying the significance of orgasm, women may reveal that they do not value their orgasmic pleasure, or it could reflect women's emphasis on alternative definitions of pleasure, as women may value emotional connectedness over orgasm. For example, Sprecher Barbee, and Schwartz (1995) and Pinney, Gerrard and Denney (1987) found that women linked sexual satisfaction with intimacy and close relationships, and Pazak (1998) found that emotional consistency, warmth, and time together were the most important factors (more important than orgasm) for women when determining levels of sexual satisfaction. Similarly, Haavio-Mannila and Kontula (1997) found that reciprocal feelings of love and versatile sexual techniques were most highly correlated with sexual satisfaction, while Kimes (2002) found that experiencing orgasm was much less important to women when assessing their sexual satisfaction than it was to men.

Other research, however, has found that women prioritized orgasm when assessing sexual satisfaction. This could reflect women valuing their own pleasure, or it could reflect a social norm in which orgasm becomes a benchmark of "good sex." For example, Means (2001) found that women identified orgasm as a major feature of sexual satisfaction and that single women were particularly focused on identifying orgasm and sexual arousal as key defining features of sexual satisfaction.

FAKING ORGASM

Coupled with this emphasis on orgasm as one common definition of sexual satisfaction, pressure to orgasm and faking orgasm have started to emerge in sex research. Bryan (2002) asked women about their experiences with faking orgasm and found that women faked orgasm because of concern for their partner's feelings, desire for the sex acts to end, enhancement of sexual excitement for self and partner, experience of themselves as abnormal or inexperienced, avoidance of conflict, and importance of orgasm to the relationship. Women faked orgasm most frequently during penile-vaginal intercourse without additional clitoral stimulation, less frequently during foreplay and penile-vaginal intercourse with additional clitoral stimulation, and during oral sex. She found that, on average, women faked orgasm 1 in 5 times they had sex with a partner, and that women who rarely orgasmed reported higher amounts of faking orgasm. Wiederman (1997) also directly addressed the issue of faking orgasm and found that more than one-half of women faked orgasm during sexual intercourse. Those who faked were significantly older, viewed themselves as facially more attractive, reported having had first intercourse at a younger age, reported greater numbers of lifetime sexual partners, and scored higher on measures of sexual esteem. Interestingly, this study also found that those who faked orgasm tended to have moderate to high self-esteem, high desire to please their partner, and difficulty communicating with their partner. Roberts, Kippax, Waldby, and Crawford (1995) also found that there were vast perception gaps between men and women about the occurrence of orgasm and that, while most women in their sample reported faking orgasm, few men thought they had ever been with a partner who faked orgasm. These studies strongly suggest that women internalize the need to perform as "good sexual partners" in ways that may prioritize performance over experience.

Some researchers have criticized the cultural emphasis on the performance of orgasm, calling instead for a more complicated understanding of women's sexuality. Research has shown that heterosexual women care more about achieving orgasm for their *male partners' sake* than for their own sexual enjoyment (Nicolson & Burr, 2003). . . . These researchers argued that pressures placed upon women to orgasm reflect a patriarchal interest in forcing women to "ejaculate" through moaning and vocal sounds: "Men make a mess, women make a noise" (Jackson and Scott 2001, p. 107).

CONTEMPORARY NARRATIVES OF ORGASM

The Gift Metaphor

. . . . Notably, the women I interviewed often conceived of orgasm as a kind of *gift* they received from a partner. Linguistically, the gift paradigm signifies that women constructed their partners as having the power to *provide* orgasm *to* them rather than attributing the action to themselves. For example, 33-year-old Lori said, "I feel really good about my body and our relationship when he gives me an orgasm, and I think it kind of affirms him too, like he's been able to accomplish this thing, my pleasure, I mean." Though 43-year-old Dawn mentioned some mutuality, she echoed Lori's sentiment: "A lot of sex is timing, and that means we need connection. We give each other orgasms, but actually having physical intercourse doesn't happen as often as I might want it to." Bonnie, age 51, added another statement that implied the gift metaphor, saying, "I think he likes it when I orgasm. I think it makes him feel like, 'Oh, I'm talented' or whatever."

Women also regularly referred to their partners as *giving* them orgasm or doing things *to* them rather than situating themselves as fully embodied in the actions. For example, Margaret, age 54, took a relatively passive posture about *getting* orgasm from her partner: "I don't always orgasm. I've never had an orgasm through penetrative sex. So, usually after my husband has had his orgasm, he has to masturbate me in order for me to get an

orgasm." . . . . When discussing her reasons for engaging in sex exclusively with women, Diana, age 50, talked about how men did *not* give her orgasms: "With men I had to use a vibrator to orgasm. Never once did a man give me an orgasm, either vaginally or through oral, clitorally. And, not always with women either."

. . . . This construction of the gift metaphor appeared both in heterosexual relationships and in same-sex relationships. For example, lesbian-identified Leigh, age 21, described giving her partner an orgasm:

Everybody likes orgasms but I think in most occasions I think I'd rather have my partner have an orgasm than me, because then I feel like, if I don't but that person does, I feel a sense of accomplishment with myself, but then if I do too that's like an added bonus. That's like my number one thing, to give her an orgasm, like that satisfies me when that happens to my partner.

. . . . Even women who chose not to have sex with men still retained ideas about women's (lack of) sexual agency. In other words, it appears that gender socialization from an early age—oriented toward pleasing men and "receiving" orgasm—sticks with women regardless of their sexual identity as an adult.

. . . . The gift paradigm also arose even when women discussed their own orgasms, as they distanced themselves from their bodily action. Some women, like Janet, seemed to claim that their body acted as a separate agent from their mind:

I don't always orgasm, and sometimes I think it makes my girl feel like she's not doing something right, but it's not like that. I mean, I can't help that nothing comes out, that's not my problem, you know? That's just my body, and if I orgasm I orgasm, and if I don't I don't. That's something you can't really control, like there's no button that you can just push and be like, "Orgasm now." I can't help what my body physically does, like whether I come or not.

When I asked Anita, age 46, about her feelings during orgasm, she described a similarly detached and mechanical sensation: "Sometimes he can make me orgasm, and I appreciate that. He'll just go to work on me, and I'll suddenly feel like my body gives an orgasm to him."

Interestingly, the gift paradigm almost never appeared when women discussed their male partner's orgasms, in that women did not construct themselves as "givers" of orgasm when having sex with men. More often, men *had* orgasms, rather than received them. Language of action and agency conferred upon men appeared repeatedly when discussing male orgasm, even while women ascribed responsibility for their own orgasms onto their (male) partners. For example, 54-year-old Marilyn described sex with her husband by saying, "He would always come. Well, he would have problems holding his erection, so he always came first. . . . If he would hit the right spots, it wouldn't take very long, but um, he didn't always hit the right spot." Women only claimed agency in the act of "giving" their partner an orgasm when women discussed "giving" an orgasm to another woman or "giving" an orgasm to their (separated) bodies. To *have* an orgasm is to *get* an orgasm from someone else.

The tangible ways in which women's orgasms become a commodity here are startling; women's orgasms become products that partners . . . invest labor into. . . . If the orgasm is a commodity, what does this mean for women's experiences of it? How does the model of commodification affect their consciousness? Further, if one constructs women as themselves commodities, then what is the relationship between women (commodity 1) and orgasm (commodity 2)?

Demand for Orgasm

. . . .When talking with women directly about orgasm, a prominent theme of feeling pressure to orgasm emerged, as women struggled both to *feel* pleasure and to demonstrate their pleasure to sexual partners. Often, this pressure was self-generated, as women described their partner's perceptions of pleasure as overshadowing their actual experience of that pleasure. This was well-articulated by Kate, age 25, who experienced a great deal of self-induced pressure to orgasm:

Putting pressure on myself to orgasm feels strange. For something that's supposed to happen spontaneously, supposedly, it feels like there's a lot of thought put into this and a lot of anxiety around it, like this is some kind of benchmark of not only the sex, but who this person is as a lover, or how I am as a lover, or how I am as a woman. It just is supposed to be an index of how liberated you are, how in touch with your body or yourself you are.

She went on to comment directly about orgasm as a kind of sexual performance:

I think it's always a performance to some extent, so it's just different degrees of conscious performance. . . . I don't think I've faked it that often. Maybe a handful of times. Often times I was in a situation where it *did* seem to matter to the person, that they were performing well, or that they needed some kind of encouragement or some kind of reinforcement of their own experience. As I mentioned before, sex feels sometimes to me like a service. It's like, okay, I can do that thing for you if it's this important to you.

Other women articulated similar experiences, in that internally generated pressure to orgasm overshadowed the intrinsic pleasure they felt in the context of sex. Esther, age 44, articulated this when she said,

[Pressure to orgasm] makes it even harder. There's more tension, trying to figure out the right combination or position, the right stimulation or whatever, so that adds more pressure which means mostly likely it's not going to happen . . . I think that's like a society thing, because that's what we've been taught, you know, that women are supposed to have multiple orgasms, and if I'm not doing that, then there's something seriously wrong with me.

Other women directly perceived this pressure as overtly coming *from* their partners, indicating that the commodification of women's orgasms—and the construction of women's orgasms as *something partners invest labor into*—can be directly demanded from partners, particularly in heterosexual contexts. For example, Niko, age 23, said, "From my partners, I feel a lot of pressure. I feel like if a partner really wants me to feel good, orgasm probably means more to him than myself, so if I don't have an orgasm, it's a problem. When I'm by myself, I don't feel any pressure." When asked how this made her feel, she responded that she felt *pressured*: "In a way I feel very touched, but I also want to communicate to him that it's really not the most important thing to me, but it's hard to change how people see orgasm. . . . He really wants me to have one. He really cares about me. I think it feels good emotionally to him, but I feel a lot of pressure." Jill, age 32, who described herself as completely nonorgasmic, communicated a similar sentiment of partner-induced pressure: "I have in the past felt as though my partner was trying to pressure me . . . I kind of got the impression that he was very invested in whether or not I had an orgasm and was somewhat annoyed or upset or distressed that he wasn't performing up to spec or something." Dorothy, age 19, communicated some of the hazards of being pressured into both sex *and* orgasm, saying, "I didn't even want to have sex in the first place! He'd say to me, 'I can't be done unless you're happy,' and it felt like so much pressure."

This feeling of partnered pressure appeared primarily in descriptions of heterosexual exchanges but also in the context of same-sex relationships. Bisexual women described that *both* men and women demanded the performance of orgasm, though the experience had different implications depending on the partner's gender. For example, Nora, age 23, said:

Mostly I feel like it's a partner that pressures me to orgasm. There are a lot of men, again, that really expect you to, and it's been awkward with women even sometimes too. I guess with women I feel more pressured to pleasure them in turn, and that sometimes makes me feel uncomfortable. Whereas with men, I'm never really that worried because I like them to get off, but I know one way or another they can do it and that's not a big deal. Men will ask you, "Is it great?" You"ll be like "Yeah, yeah." But usually it's more *them* that wants to get you off. I don't enjoy it when a guy wants to get me off or is like looking for something to happen. I'm like, no man, you just need to do your thing, and it'll be fine. Don't waste 15 minutes trying to do whatever you're trying to do that's not really working.

This description reveals that eroticism remained laden with commodified overtones, particularly as the pressure to *give* orgasm overlapped with the pressure to *have* orgasm.

This does not suggest that all male partners were preoccupied with women's orgasms, though most women said that their male partners felt invested in ensuring that they had at least one orgasm. Some women, however, expressed ambivalence about how much their partner cared about their orgasms, at times citing length of the relationship as the predictor of increased pressure they felt to orgasm. This may reflect a pattern where length of relationship correlated with men's interest in women's orgasm, and as such, one-night stands or new relationships involved less concern for women's orgasms. For example, 23-year-old Courtney felt that short-term sexual encounters involved less pressure to orgasm:

I would say mostly guys don't really seem to care, but I think they enjoy it, and they like you to orgasm because that makes them feel better about themselves. It's just the ones that have really cared have been the ones that have had sex with me repeatedly for a while, and they're the guys that are more attentive to like, "Did you come?" Other guys, I felt like they didn't really care, like I'm sure they'd like me to, but it's not a must have.

Carol, age 38, also felt like her male partners did not always care about her orgasm, expressing both frustration and relief about this fact: "I've slept with men who don't seem to give a shit about whether I come. That makes me a little angry, but I also feel like I don't have to bother with faking." Clearly, these statements reveal the delicate balancing act that occurs about orgasm for those women currently in relationships, as partners *not* caring can feel as troubling as partners caring in a way that *demands* orgasm.

Self-blame about Orgasm

Many sex researchers have noted the profound psychological impact of differential experiences of orgasm for men and women (Tiefer, 2004). Because men more often say that they always or almost always orgasm in the context of sex, while women report a much wider range of orgasmic expression (e.g., many women report that, despite lifelong sexual activity, they have *never* had an orgasm), this difference can promote a complicated relationship between women and their orgasms (Laumann, Paik, and Rosen, 1999). Among the women I talked to, many struggled to achieve orgasm regularly during intercourse, and nearly all women commented that they did not *always* orgasm during intercourse without clitoral stimulation. This was occasionally framed as a response to their partner's inadequacies . . . though most often it was discussed as a failure of one's own ability to orgasm. Self-blame about not experiencing enough pleasure represented a major theme in my conversations with women. For example, 51-year-old Geena articulated the tension between not meeting others' expectations and not meeting her own:

I've definitely felt pressured with a partner . . . I feel like if I didn't orgasm, the other person would think they were less, or they didn't do something well enough or right enough or good enough. That it

would be somehow their fault. I don't believe that's true, because it's really up to me to have the orgasm. It lies with me, with my body; my body ultimately decides. Sometimes everything can be right with me, but my body doesn't want to have one . . . I'm either having too much internal dialogue, or I feel like I can't get into that moment. I'm more imagining what this looks like or some external view of this, and it's like I'm actually on stage as opposed to being in the moment with somebody. If I get stuck in that, I'm not going to be able to have an orgasm with somebody.

Ruth, age 46, echoed this sentiment even more forcefully, saying that she felt self-blame for not having an orgasm: "During times where I have not been able to orgasm, I felt worthless and angry at myself, like why would my body deny itself. It didn't make sense to me. I've never had an orgasm from intercourse though. It's always just been manually." Diana added that she felt distressed by a partner's impatience with her orgasm:

When you have arousal and you're experiencing pleasure and being aroused and having an orgasm, that's letting your partner know that she's pleasuring you and that adds to her arousal and her complete experience, so yes, I feel pressure sometimes, because it helps her to feel more aroused . . . I've had a partner that gets impatient. I can feel her getting impatient . . . Ultimately, that's what you want, to please your partner. . . . I want her to have an orgasm, definitely. If she's not, and I'm feeling inadequate, maybe she doesn't desire me, and there is no arousal, so maybe a little shame too.

Women who regularly experienced orgasm also mentioned self-blame surrounding orgasm as an important issue for them. Notably, orgasm as a *form of labor* inscribed as something (male) partners *invest into women* appeared frequently during the interviews. For example, Aya, age 25, described this context of labor directly: "I feel pressure from myself to orgasm, because I just feel like there's all that energy, like *work* that's being done that doesn't go anywhere. I'm really a very efficient person, so whenever that happens, it's like a waste. He wants to know that he can bring this about for me, and I want to show him that." Fiona, age 24, expressed similar feelings of wasted labor when discussing both male and female partners:

I put pressure on myself to kind of coordinate an orgasm. For instance, if he was fingering me in my vagina and using his tongue, and/or I was using a toy, and it was just not progressing to a higher state of self-pleasure or pleasure in general, I think about how tired he's getting. I'm just kind of pressuring myself and saying that he's not interested anymore, that he's putting so much work into this. I do a lot of that kind of thinking, like thinking about how he's probably not enjoying himself rather than focusing on how good it feels to for me. I used to feel that way with lesbians too, but at least lesbians could appreciate that feeling and had probably been in that position of having someone work on them for a long time and nothing was happening. With men, it can be really strenuous.

Self-blame about this lack of validation for (male) sexual labor was also communicated in women's frustrations at their sometimes inconsistent orgasmic ability. Priya, age 23, said, "It's just sort of frustrating when you want something to happen, and it's not happening, so you try and make it happen a little bit more. It's frustrating sometimes if you're trying to orgasm, and someone's trying to help you do that, and you just can't get there." . . .

Faking Orgasm

Given the amount of self-blame that surrounds inconsistent orgasmic expression, faking orgasm also represented a common technique to avoid the blame and pressure women felt to climax. This theme of faking orgasm appeared frequently in my discussions with women, as they invested sexual labor into the sexual exchange regardless of their actual physical experiences of orgasm. Questions of authenticity arose repeatedly when discussing sexual pleasure, as

many women reported that they had successfully faked orgasm either occasionally or regularly, a finding consistent with recent research that suggests that over half of women have faked orgasm (Wiederman, 1997). Connected to discussions of performing well as a sexual partner, a majority of women reported that they had, with variable frequency, faked orgasm during sex with some of their partners in order to give the appearance that they enjoyed sex more than they actually did. Faking orgasm occurred not only in heterosexual couplings, but also in same-sex partnerships, though mention of faking orgasm in heterosexual couplings occurred far more often.

When asked about the reasons for faking orgasm, women reported that they faked for three primary reasons: first, to spare the partner's feelings; second, to end the sexual encounter and/or to encourage the partner to orgasm; third, to respond to the partner's pressure for them to orgasm. In many cases, women reported faking orgasm for all three reasons. For example, 29-year-old Mitra said:

I fake often because, you know, he's going to feel bad about himself, or he's going to feel like I haven't enjoyed myself, so I just feel like I need to have one to make him happy, or sometimes you're tired and that's the signifier to be done. . . . I feel like orgasm is what sex is for men, and they think that that's what it is for women too. So, I feel like I could never really tell him that I'm faking, because men like to think, oh no one's ever faking with me. He's a good lover. It's not like he doesn't care about his partner's sexual satisfaction, and I think that makes me all the more compelled to fake. To me, it's much better to just fake it. Everyone's ego is intact, and you can just move on.

. . . . Many heterosexual women claimed that faking orgasm allowed them to spare a partner's feelings, a theme that directly reveals the way in which cultural scripts demand attention to, and concern for, *men's* pleasure above that of *women's* pleasure. Such concern for the feelings of women's partners indicated an expectation for women to nurture and care for others (particularly men) in their lives. For example, Marilyn felt urgent about pleasing her husband: "I faked just to make him happy, and I'd just say I did to make him happy. We go back to the same thing. It was about pleasing him and keeping him happy. It was always, 'Was it as good for you as it was for me?' 'Oh yeah honey, oh yeah.' So, you know, you just make the sounds that you did when you really didn't." Women spoke, at least implicitly, about the way in which their sexual partnerships demanded that they serve as a mirror for their partner's egos. . . . Margaret [said:] "Faking orgasm is strange, a bit theatrical really, and you're doing it for your partner, not for you. I did it probably because the other person was obviously into their own orgasm and seemed to expect that you were going to join in with whatever was going on for him at the time. I didn't want him to feel inadequate."

One can interpret these statements, perhaps, as a gesture of love and affection toward partners, as orgasms symbolize a kind of unique affirmation that *both* partners typically perceive as important. For example, when asked why she faked orgasm, Janet added that she wanted her partner to feel like a competent lover: "Because I felt like if I wasn't responding in any way, she'd really feel like she wasn't doing her job, or doing what she was supposed to be doing or she might feel like she was doing something wrong you know? I wanted to make her feel all right." Esther, who said she faked orgasm 80 to 90 percent of the time, echoed these sentiments, claiming that sparing the partner's feelings mattered more than her experience:

I don't want the person I am with to feel like they're not able to do what they think they should be able to do. If they think that they're good in bed, they wanna please a women, and if I don't fake it, then there's something wrong with them, and they're not

pleasing me, so that's part of my giving. Okay, I'll let you think that's what you did, but you actually didn't.

When asked how that made her feel, she responded, "A little bit guilty because it's a lie, but at the same time I feel like I'm building their ego, helping them feel okay as a man." Such statements suggest that, while, superficially, faking orgasm may symbolize deeply internalized oppression (e.g., one's own pleasure as frankly less significant than one's partner's pleasure), faking orgasm may also represent, for women, a gesture of care, affection, love, and nurturance.

On the more practical side—and perhaps indicative of women's busy, hectic lives that often demand caretaking of others—faking orgasm also resulted from fatigue and exhaustion. Indeed, most women reported working outside the home *and* doing a majority of the housework. Women sometimes said that they faked orgasm because they were physically and psychologically drained and wanted to stop the sexual interaction and rest.

. . . . At times, this physical exhaustion was connected to emotional weariness or boredom with sex. For example, Susan said, "I've faked orgasms to get it over with. I wanted to go to sleep, or it was just kinda getting boring. It's like, all right already! Maybe this will help you. I'll scream a little bit and writhe about and then you can come, and I can go to sleep and you can go home."

Many women faked orgasm as a direct result of their partner's pressure to orgasm, revealing the way that sexual performance is at times *demanded* and *expected* both explicitly and implicitly. For example, Brynn faked in order to avoid conflict:

I have faked an orgasm in order to just be able to have that person be like, "Oh okay, finally, they climaxed" or whatever. I don't have to worry about anything, and I can just let them have their ego trip.

It just kind of got them off my back. . . . If I didn't fake an orgasm, or if I didn't fake being pleased, then it was like he's obviously not done, and he's going to just keep pounding the hell outta ya until he hears something. I faked it all the time with him.

Charlotte, age 34, also faked to avoid conflict: "I've faked it because I knew he was wanting to do it, and I didn't want to turn him away and say nah I don't feel like it, or be mean or nothing [sic]. I wasn't really all the way into it, and he would be angry if he knew that."

Sometimes, partners communicated pressure to orgasm directly and intensely, often by using emotional manipulation, as in 44-year-old Charlene's description of her ex-husband:

I've faked it because there were times where if I didn't seem to have one quick enough for him, then he would like start with the whole guilt thing, like, "You don't really love me, do you?" kind of thing. If I was honest about not coming, he would say that it was a symbol of me not loving him. . . . Once someone says you're not having an orgasm because you don't love me, it's pretty hard to have an orgasm then. I'd just fake it and that made him happy, so the pressure's gone now. So far as he's concerned, I always had one! He'd get off my back, excuse the pun!

. . . . Many women felt that their partners put a significant amount of emotional energy into their orgasms. As seen with the previous examples, the question remains open as to whether this pressure to orgasm represents a genuine indicator of generosity or affection; certainly, it seems clear that women's orgasms matter less than their *performances* of those orgasms.

Faking orgasm did not seem to correlate with women's level of sexual experience, orgasmic ability, or number of partners, though sex with men predicted faking orgasm. For example, highly experienced and highly orgasmic Nora told me, matter-of-factly, "Generally all those situations where you're coerced into it by men or give into it or are pushed into having sex, you end up faking the orgasm and faking the pleasure. No doubt about it—just because

you're like, 'Okay fine, let's just do this,' and you totally fake it. That's the easiest way to get rid of a situation sometimes." Maria, age 21, echoed this sentiment, saying, "I always faked orgasm with men, just to make it stop. I couldn't have been less interested in it, and I felt like if I didn't orgasm, they'd get angry and maybe violent."

Women who had never experienced orgasm also described frequent instances of faking orgasm. For example, Jill reprimanded herself for her lack of orgasmic ability:

I am not entirely certain that I have ever in my life had an orgasm. . . . My body does not seem to necessarily respond properly to things, so it's mostly my brain that's getting off. . . . It would be nice [to orgasm]. I would like to know what all the fuss is about . . . I exaggerate the degree of pleasure I receive from something that I either think my partner enjoys or wish to encourage as it's headed in at least the right direction.

. . . Interestingly, one woman who claimed that she had never faked an orgasm said that she may consider doing so if the need arose, indicating the degree of acceptance and complicity women have in normalizing faking orgasm as an acceptable part of life.

When asked why she would feel the need to fake it, [Lucy] responded that faking orgasm represents being a "good wife":

Just that if my husband was trying to get me off, and I wasn't able to come, especially if it happened when he was trying to put forth effort, taking his time, and doing everything right, and he's still not able to, and if I didn't have a good reason, like I was not feeling sick or something, then I would probably feel bad. More than anything I wouldn't want him to feel bad . . . I hear so many women do, and she was trying to teach us, and she was like, "You need to be good to your husband! Be good to him!"

These statements indicate the intensity of the normative pressures women (particularly heterosexual women) face to put their partner's sexual needs, satisfaction, and desires above their own.

Even women who consciously resisted this often admitted difficulty with full honesty about orgasm with their partners. Julie, age 23, described a history of faking orgasm and vowed never to again return to faking orgasm rather than communicating authentic pleasure:

I hate faking orgasm and the pressure I feel, partly because I simply *refuse* to fake it. I used to fake it sometimes and then I realized that's a horrible thing to do. In the past, particularly my male partners have been like, "Are you coming? Are you coming?" I want to say, "Yeah," because, you know, for their little egos, but I sometimes do feel pressured. Most of the time, though, I just sort of insist on orgasms with my partners. Sometimes I really want one, and it's just not happening because the stars haven't aligned!

Thus, orgasm, in its many manifestations, reflects a number of dynamics in women's relationships: perceptions that they must please (male) partners at their own expense, concern for feeling sexually normal, and avoidance of negative consequences, whether emotional, physical, psychological, or literal.

CONCLUSION

. . . . From the Victorian days to the advent of psychoanalysis, from the early empiricists to the sexual revolution, orgasm has stood in for much more than a mere physiological process. It harbors a great history of gender relations, power struggles, and political symbolism. This makes it all the more imperative to examine its meaning today, particularly as women experience this new *mandate* to orgasm as a defining feature of their status as "good sexual partners."

Part of the reason that faking orgasm, responding to pressure to orgasm, and constructing orgasm as a "gift" have such prominence in women's lives may be the way women learn to internalize ideas about orgasm as the primary reason for sex (itself a common cultural script) *and* because they constantly receive messages (from partners, from the media, from schools, from the culture at large) that women's pleasure matters less than men's pleasure. . . .

Most women experience their orgasms as somewhat scattered, fluid, inconsistent, flexible, and *highly* contingent upon the circumstances of the encounter. Again and again, women felt that their partners indicated that it was *unacceptable* for women not to orgasm during every sexual encounter. (To know whether men perceive this as true, more studies about men's subjective experiences with sex are needed). For women, the range of negativity that arose from this fact—from shame about their body's "failures," feelings of resentment toward partners for their lack of support, conflict about how to manage their need to support their partners' egos while sacrificing their own pleasure, and inability to explore different means of achieving orgasm—speaks to the conflicts and contradictions at hand when women negotiate sexual pleasure.

. . . . Not only did women discuss orgasm as something a partner *gave* to them, but they, in turn, frequently made attempts to sacrifice their own orgasmic pleasure in the name of affirming a partner's abilities or not hurting a partner's feelings. This presents a real dilemma: If women prone to faking orgasm fully disclose when they do or do not orgasm, this may emotionally wound some of their sexual partners. Is there a space where women can feel liberated enough *not* to orgasm and *not* to fake orgasm, if they choose? If women and their orgasms are constructed as *commodities,* how can women meaningfully resist the demands of those who construct them as objects? If women's orgasms symbolize (male) sexual prowess, how does this affect women's sexual consciousness? What does this dilemma reveal about sexual relationships, gender, orgasm, and power?

In moving toward a more . . . liberatory politics of orgasm, several possibilities become apparent. First, if people deconstruct and dismantle the existing definitions of pleasure and satisfaction, such that orgasm is one of *many* forms of pleasure women can experience, this opens up space to value other forms of pleasure that women enjoy. . . . People should expand definitions of pleasure such that orgasm is rendered one of many ways to enjoy the body and sexuality.

Women want to reflect back to their partners the affirmation that their partners long for; this is not itself problematic. The troubling elements here are the *terms* within which this affirmation is demanded or extracted, particularly if these terms demand performances that reproduce gender inequalities. How might women and their partners differently negotiate affirmation, sexual pleasure, and the mutual rewards of sex? Can orgasm become a *means* toward something rather than an *end* goal? If women *have* orgasms rather than *get* them as a "gift," will this facilitate a greater sense of embodiment and empowerment? Might better communication about orgasm facilitate more equitable relationships in general? Among these interview participants, highly orgasmic women not inclined to fake orgasm also were the women who had the most equitable relationships with their partners a fact that speaks to the symbiosis among sexual, interpersonal, and cultural scripts. As this [reading] shows, by examining orgasm as a literal and symbolic marker of equality and inequality, one can better explore the interplay among gender, power, sexuality, and culture. . . .

NOTES

1. "Hysteria" is currently defined by Merriam-Webster's dictionary as "a nervous disorder marked especially by defective emotional control, unmanageable fear, and outbursts of emotion." Hysteria also has many common uses, most notably "hysterical," "hysterics," and the DSM-IV-adopted "histrionic personality disorder."

2. Note that, according to the National Institute of Mental Health, women are 2–3 times more likely to be diagnosed with depression, 10 times more likely to be diagnosed with an eating disorder, 2–3 times more likely to attempt suicide, and twice as likely to receive an anxiety disorder diagnosis (APA, 1994).

3. This may have been particularly true given that the book about men (1948) was released a full five years before the book about women (1953), likely sparking interest and anxiety about normative female sexuality.

4. Notably, however, not all feminists accepted the link between advancing women's rights and deconstructing the primacy of heterosexuality in women's sexual lives; indeed, many resisted the unification of gay and lesbian rights movements with the feminist movement.

5. Ellison (2001) questioned participants about recent sexual concerns with their previous partners, and found that 34 percent reported low sexual desire or desire discrepancy, 28.5 percent reported difficulties with physical responsiveness (e.g. female arousal and orgasm, male partners' erectile difficulties, ejaculatory control), 16 percent disliked their sexual technique, 7.5 percent had difficulty finding a consistent sexual partner, and the remaining 5 percent included such difficulties as fertility issues, pregnancy concerns, STDs, women's body/health, infidelity, and shifts in sexual orientation.

REFERENCES

Atkinson, T. 1974. *Amazon odyssey: The first collection of writings by the political pioneer of the women's movement.* New York: Link Books.

Berman, L., Berman, J., Miles, M., Pollets, D., and Powell, J.A. 2003. Genital self-image as a component of sexual health: Relationship between genital self-image, female sexual function, and quality of life measures. *Journal of Sex & Marital Therapy*, 29(1): 11–21.

Bryan, T. S. 2002. Pretending to experience orgasm as a communicative act: How, when, and why some sexually experienced college women pretend to experience orgasm during various sexual behaviors. *Dissertation Abstracts International*, 63; 2049.

Buhle, M. J. 1998. *Feminism and its discontents: A century of struggle with psychoanalysis* Cambridge: Harvard University Press.

Bullough, V. L. 1999. *The wandering womb: A cultural history of outrageous beliefs about women*. Amherst: Prometheus Books.

Butler, C.A. 1976 New data about female sexual response. *Journal of Sex & Marital Therapy*, 2(1):40–46.

Darling, C. A., and Davidson, J. K. 1987. The relationship of sexual satisfaction to coital involvement: The concept of technical virginity revisited. *Deviant Behavior*, 8(1): 27–46.

Davidson, J. K., and Moore, N. B. 1994. Guilt and lack of orgasm during sexual intercourse: Myth versus reality among college women. *Journal of Sex Education and Therapy,* 20(3): 153–174.

De Bruijn, G. 1982. From masturbation to orgasm with a partner: How some women bridge the gap—and why others don't. *Journal of Sex & Marital Therapy,* 8(2): 151–167.

Densmore, D. 1973. Independence from the sexual revolution. In A. Koedt, E. Levine, and A. Rapone (Eds.), *Radical feminism* (pp. 107–118). New York: Quadrangle Books.

Dove, N. L., and Wiederman, M. W. 2000. Cognitive distraction and women's sexual functioning. *Journal of Sex & Marital Therapy,* 26(1): 67–78.

Dunbar, R. 1969. Sexual liberation: More of the same thing. *No More Fun and Games,* 3:49–56.

Ellison, C. R. 2001. A research inquiry into some American women's sexual concerns and problems. *Women & Therapy,* 24(1-2): 147–159.

Foucault, M. 1978. *The history of sexuality, Volume 1.* New York: Vintage Books.

Gerhard, J. 2000. Revisiting "The myth of the vaginal orgasm": The female orgasm in American sexual thought and second wave feminism. *Feminist Studies,* 26(2):449–476.

Gilbert, S. M., and Gubar, S. 1984. *The madwoman in the attic: The woman writer and the nineteenth-century literary imagination.* New Haven: Yale University Press.

Haavio-Mannila, E., and Kontula, O. 1997. Correlates of increased sexual satisfaction. *Archives of Sexual Behavior,* 26(4): 399–419.

Hite, S. 1976. *The Hite report: A nationwide study on female sexuality.* Oxford: Macmillan.

Hunt, M. 1974. *Sexual behavior in the 1970s.* Oxford: Playboy.

Hurlbert, D. F., and Apt, C. 1993. Female sexuality: A comparative study between women in homosexual and heterosexual relationships. *Journal of Sex & Marital Therapy,* 19(4): 315–327.

Hurlbert, D. F., Apt, C., and Rabehl, S. M. 1993. Key variables to understanding female sexual satisfaction: An examination of women in nondistressed marriages, *Journal of Sex & Marital Therapy,* 19(2): 154–165.

Jackson, S., and Scott, S. 2001. Embodying orgasm: Gendered power relations and sexual pleasure. *Women & Therapy,* 24(1-2):99–110.

Janus, S. S., and Janus, C. L. 1993. *The Janus report on sexual behavior.* New York: Wiley & Sons.

Jeffreys, S. 1990. *Anticlimax: A feminist perspective on the sexual revolution.* New York: New York University Press.

Kimes, L. A. 2002. "Was it good for you too?" An exploration of sexual satisfaction. *Dissertation Abstracts International,* 62: 4791.

Kinsey, A. C., Pomeroy, W. B., and Martin, C. E. 1948. *Sexual behavior in the human male.* Philadelphia: Saunders.

Kinsey, A. C., Pomeroy, W. B., and Martin, C. E. 1953. *Sexual behavior in the human female.* Philadelphia: Saunders.

Koedt, A. 1973. The myth of the vaginal orgasm. In A. Koedt, E. Levine, and A. Rapone (Eds.), *Radical feminism* (pp. 199–207). New York: Quadrangle Books.

Laqueur, T. 1990. *Making sex: Body and gender from the Greeks to Freud.* Cambridge: Harvard University Press.

Laqueur, T. 2002. *Solitary sex: A cultural history of masturbation.* New York: Zone Books.

Laumann, E., Paik, A., and Rosen, R. C. 1999. Sexual dysfunction in the United States. *Journal of the American Medical Association,* 281(6): 537–544.

Mah, K. 2002. Development of a multidimensional model of the psychological experience of male and female orgasm. *Dissertation Abstracts International,* 62: 5947.

Mah, K., and Binik, Y. M. 2001. The nature of human orgasm: A critical review of major trends. *Clinical Psychology Review,* 21(6): 823–856.

Maines, R. P. 1999. *The technology of orgasm: "Hysteria," the vibrator, and women's sexual satisfaction.* Baltimore: Johns Hopkins University Press.

Masters, W. H., and Johnson, V. E. 1966. *Human sexual response.* New York: Bantam Books.

Means, M. C. 2001. An integrative approach to what women really want: Sexual satisfaction. *Dissertation Abstracts International,* 61: 4417.

Nicolson, P., and Burr, J. 2003. What is "normal" about women's (hetero)sexual desire and orgasm? A report of an in-depth interview study. *Social Science & Medicine,* 57(9): 1735–1745.

Pazak, S. J. 1998. Predicting sexual satisfaction and marital satisfaction. *Dissertation Abstracts International,* 58:6244.

Pinney, E. M., Gerrard, M., and Denney, N. W. 1987. The Pinney Sexual Satisfaction Inventory. *Journal of Sex Research,* 23(2): 233–251.

Raboch, J., and Raboch, J. 1992. Infrequent orgasms in women. *Journal of Sex & Marital Therapy,* 18(2); 114–120.

Roberts, C., Kippax, S., Waldby, C., and Crawford, J. 1995. Faking it: The story of 'Ohh!' *Women's Studies International Forum,* 18(5–6): 523–532.

Shifren, J. L., Monz, B. U., Russo, P. A., Segreti, A., and Johannes, C. B. 2008. Sexual problems and distress in United States women: Prevalence and correlates. *Obstetrics & Gynecology,* 112(5):970–978.

Smith-Rosenberg, C. 1985. *Disorderly conduct: Visions of gender in Victorian America.* New York: Oxford University Press.

Sprecher, S., Barbee, A., and Schwartz, P. 1995. "Was it good for you too?" Gender differences in first sexual intercourse experiences. *Journal of Sex Research,* 32(1): 3–15.

Tiefer, L. 2004. *Sex is not a natural act and other essays.* Boulder, CO: Westview.

Walker-Hill, R. 2000. An analysis of the relationship of human sexuality knowledge, self-esteem, and body image to sexual satisfaction in college and university students. *Dissertation Abstracts International,* 60:4560.

Wallin, P. 1960. A study of orgasm as a condition of women's sexual enjoyment of intercourse. *Journal of Social Psychology,* 5(1): 191–198.

Wiederman, M. W. 1997. Pretending orgasm during sexual intercourse: Correlates in a sample of young adult women. *Journal of Sex & Marital Therapy,* 23(2): 131–139.

A SEXUAL CULTURE FOR DISABLED PEOPLE

TOBIN SIEBERS

Sexuality is not a right which must be earned or a posses-sion that must be purchased, but a state of being acces-sible to all individuals. Even those who sometimes have to fight for that access.

—*Lucy Grealy, "In the Realm of the Senses"*

The emergence in recent decades of people who define their identities based on sexual preferences and prac-tices is transforming the landscape of minor-ity politics. Sexual minorities are fighting for the rights and privileges accorded to majority populations on many legal and political fronts. The fight over gay marriage is only the most public and contentious of current struggles for full and equal rights by a sexual minority. Pro-ponents of minority sexual identity attack the neat division between the private and public spheres, the relevance of the traditional fam-ily and its institutions of marriage and child rearing, and the moral certainty that sexuality is better controlled or repressed than set free. Claims that sexuality is a major part of a per-son's identity, that sexual liberation is a good in itself, and that sexual expression is a civil right crucial to human happiness have led to new conceptions of civic life linked to sex. . . .

Disabled people have long struggled to take control of their bodies from medical authorities and to gain access to built environments and public institutions. Like [other] sexual minori-ties, . . . disabled people experience sexual repression, possess little or no sexual autonomy, and tolerate institutional and legal restrictions on their intimate conduct. Moreover, legal and institutional forces inhibit their ability to express their sexuality freely and to develop consensual relationships with sexual partners.

It would be an exaggeration to define the oppression of disabled people exclusively in the sexual context; not many people with dis-abilities consider themselves a sexual minor-ity. Nevertheless, I want to argue that disabled people do constitute a significant sexual minor-ity and that recognizing their status as sexual citizens will advance the cause of other sexually oppressed groups. "Sexuality is often," Anne Finger explains about people with disabilities, "the source of our deepest oppression; it is also often the source of our deepest pain. It's easier for us to talk about—and formulate strategies for changing—discrimination in employment, education, and housing than to talk about our exclusion from sexuality and reproduction" (9). The facets of my argument are multiple, but most of them rely on the power of disability as a critical concept to defamiliarize how we think currently about sex. First, thinking about disabled sexuality broadens the definition of sexual behavior. Second, the sexual experi-ences of disabled people expose with great clarity both the fragile separation between the private and public spheres, as well as the role played by this separation in the history of regu-lating sex. Third, co-thinking sex and disability reveals unacknowledged assumptions about the ability to have sex and how the ideology of ability determines the value of some sexual practices and ideas over others. Finally, the sex-ual history of disabled people makes it possible to theorize patterns of sexual abuse and vic-timization faced by other sexual minorities.

My argument will hinge on what I call the "sexual culture" of people with disabilities. This phrase is meant to set in motion a process of defamiliarization directed at experiences so intimate and unspoken, so familiar and yet mysterious, that few people will discuss them. These experiences are bundled under what is colloquially called a "sex life"—a term I contrast heuristically to "sexual culture." Sexual culture refers to neither gender assignation nor sexual preference, although obviously they are components of sexual being. Sexual culture references the experience of sex itself. By sexual culture, I mean to suggest two ideas about how disabled sexuality disrupts the notion of a sex life: first, sexuality assumes a larger role in the quotidian life of people with disabilities than the usual phrase "sex life" indicates; second, the idea of a sex life is ableist. Being able-bodied assumes the capacity to partition off sexuality as if it were a sector of private life: that an individual *has* sex or a sex life implies a form of private ownership based on the assumption that sexual activity occupies a particular and limited part of life determined by the measure of ability, control, or assertiveness exercised by that individual. People with disabilities do not always have this kind of sex life. On the one hand, the stigma of disability may interfere with having sex. On the other hand, the sexual activities of disabled people do not necessarily follow normative assumptions about what a sex life is. Neither fact means that people with disabilities do not exist as sexual beings. One of the chief stereotypes oppressing disabled people is the myth that they do not experience sexual feelings or that they do not have or want to have sex—in short, that they do not have a sexual culture.

Two cautions must be remarked before I undertake an extended argument about the sexual culture of disabled people. First, the distinction between sex life and sexual culture does not turn exclusively on the issue of privacy. While disabled people sometimes lack privacy for sex,

their situation is not unique. Gay, lesbian, bisexual, queer, and transgendered people also suffer from a lack of sexual privacy, and economic resources may determine whether people have sex in private or public. Crowded housing situations, for example, are as offensive to the conception of private sexual expression as health care facilities. The distinction between sex life and sexual culture relies not on privacy but on access as defined in a disability context: sexual culture increases access for disabled people not only by breaking down the barriers restricting them from sexual locations but also by bringing sexual rights to where they live. Second, the idea of sexual culture strips away what one might call the existential connotations of a sex life. Existentialism posits that identities are constructed by ourselves for ourselves, that all values are subjective, that we are responsible for our choices, and that we are condemned to be free. The notion of sexual culture relies on different presuppositions about identity. I define sexual identities as theory-laden constructions, combining both objective and subjective values, used by individuals to make choices, to test the consequences of their actions, and to explore the possibilities and responsibilities of their sexuality. Sexual culture is designed as a concept to provide a deeper, more sustained idea of how sex and identity interconnect by resisting the partitioning and privatization characteristic of a sex life. It means to liberate sex, allowing it to overflow the boundaries of secured places and to open up greater sexual access for people with disabilities.

NO WALKS ON THE BEACH

I am looking for an intelligent, literate woman for companionship and, perhaps, sexual play. I am, as you see, completely paralyzed, so there will be no walks on the beach.
                                                    —Personal ad

Sex always happens somewhere. We go to certain places to fall in love or to have sex. A sex life, perhaps to our disappointment, tends to occur in the same places—the bedroom, hotels, automobiles, health clubs, baths, and so on. Sex will not happen if we do not have access to such places or if we cannot return to them once we discover that they permit sexual activity. If sex is walking together on the beach, if it is running across a field of flowers to meet in an embrace, what is the nature of sex apart from the ability to walk or to run? If a person's wheelchair gets stuck in the sand or if low vision makes it uncomfortable to dash across a field, does it mean that this person will have little chance of having sex? Clearly, people who do not do these things or go to these places manage to have sex, but that is not exactly the point. The point is to ask how the ideology of ability determines how we think about sex.

The ideology of ability represents the able body as the baseline of humanness. Absence of ability or lesser ability, according to this ideology, marks a person as less than human. The preference for ability permeates nearly every value in human culture, including the ability to have sex. In fact, sex may be the privileged domain of ability. Sex is the action by which most people believe that ability is reproduced, by which humanity supposedly asserts its future, and ability remains the category by which sexual reproduction as such is evaluated. As a result, sex and human ability are both ideologically and inextricably linked. Mark O'Brien recounts a story about the belief that the inability to have sex robs the disabled person of human status:

We watched a movie about disability and sexuality. The movie consisted of four or five able-bodied men joking and laughing about how they once lugged their crippled friend up a flight of stairs to a whorehouse. . . . After the movie, a doctor talked about disability and sexuality. . . . I will always remember his closing line: "You may think you'll never have sex again, but remember . . . some people do become people again." (O'Brien and Kendall, 80)

The doctor is speaking loosely about sex and membership in the human community, but he employs a widespread prejudice used against those who have lost human status along with the ability to have sex. What is it about sex that bestows human status? Barbara Waxman-Fiduccia argues that disability assumes the characteristic of a sexual perversion because disabled people are thought unable to produce "quality offspring" (168–69). It is reproduction, then, that marks sexuality as a privileged index of human ability. In fact, the ideology of ability underlies the imperative to reproduce at many levels, establishing whether an individual supposedly represents a quality human being. First, sex appeal determines the opportunity to have sex. The greater a person's capacity to attract partners, the more opportunities to have sex. Second, a person must be able physically and mentally to have sex. Third, a person must be able to reproduce, to be either virile or fertile. To fail to be able to reproduce is somehow to fail as a human being. Finally, successful reproduction is thought to pass our essential abilities and qualities to our children. The predominant assumption is that what we are will be visited upon our children. If a person does not measure up to society's ideas about ability, that person's opportunities to have sex will be limited. People with disabilities share with gay men and lesbians the suspicion by majority populations that they cannot, will not, or should not contribute to the future of the human race. They will not reproduce, but if they do, the expectation is that the results will be tainted. Social stigma would have little impact on sexual behavior if it were not for the fact that ability represents the supreme measure of human choices, actions, thoughts, and values.

The concept of a sex life encapsulates many of the ways in which the ideology of ability distorts current attitudes about sexuality. At the most superficial level, a sex life is described almost always in the context of health. A sex life must be, first and foremost, a healthy sex life, and the more healthy a person is, the better the sex life is supposed to be. Whence the imperative in today's culture to "work on" one's sex life, to "improve" or "better" it, to do special exercises or adopt a particular diet for it, "to spice it up"—all for the purpose of discovering "the ultimate pleasure." These and other catchphrases attend the commodification of sex as healthy and satisfying, but the connection between a sex life and ability runs deeper than cliché. When disability is linked to sex, it becomes a clinical matter in which each disability betrays a particular limitation of sexual opportunity, growth, or feeling. The literature on sex and disability recites a litany of limitations for each category of impairment. The blind have trouble with sex because it centers supposedly on a visualization of the body as integral whole, and lacking sight, they cannot visualize what a body is (Hamilton, 239). The mobility impaired and paralyzed are apparently cut off from sources of information about sex from peers, and their sexual development remains stunted (Shuttleworth, 265–66). Because of language delays, deaf people are believed to be emotionally and sexually immature, living without the language tools needed to meet the high standards of communication required for sex (Job, 2004; 264, 266). Disabled women are said to tolerate sexism and objectification (Fine and Asch, 29-30). In general, people with disabilities are thought to suffer from distorted body images, considering themselves ugly, and they do not feel at home with typical gender roles.

Because a sex life depends on ability, any departure from sexual norms reads as a disability, disease, or defect. Moreover, the equation runs in the other direction as well: disability signifies sexual limitation, regardless of whether the physical and mental features of a given impairment affect the ability to have sex. . . . Many people in the disability community are still waiting, as Corbett Joan O'Toole explains, to hear a story in which a man or woman who chooses to be lovers with a disabled person is congratulated by family and friends for making a good choice (217). What sea change in current scientific, medical, political, and romantic attitudes would be necessary to represent disabled sexuality as a positive contribution to the future? To reconceive sexuality apart from ability, it would be necessary to imagine the sexual benefit of a given impairment, to claim and celebrate it as a sexual advantage.

PRIVATE PARTS IN PUBLIC PLACES

I was very shy before my accident. Dealing with lots of nurses doing extremely personal things to you—sometimes in front of other people—knocks off your shyness.
                                                        —*A quadriplegic*

If people with disabilities are to develop a sexual culture, they will need to access safe spaces where they may develop new erotic theories and modes of being. A major obstacle to this project is the separation between the private and public spheres and the history of this separation in regulating sexuality in general and disabled sexuality in particular. Feminists identify the private/public split as a source of gender and sexual oppression because it often reifies gender differences and disempowers women. First, men have more power than women to draw the lines between private and public life. Second, men often use this power to maintain or to increase their advantage over women, forcing them into dependency, using privacy to conceal sexual violence, and stifling any attempts by them at political protest. Because the state is reluctant to enter the private sphere, women are imprisoned there, made vulnerable to abuse by domestic partners and given the status of second-class citizens.

Disability studies support the feminist argument that the private/public split is responsible for political oppression, while deepening the perception that privacy is abandoned at a terrible cost. The experience of disabled people with the medical model has been key to this perception. The medical model thrives by sustaining an essential difference between nondisabled and disabled people, defining disability not as a flourishing of biological diversity but as an individual defect that medical professionals cure or eradicate in order to restore a person to the superior state of health required by the ideology of ability. . . .

The presence of disability exposes the fragility of the traditional separation between private and public because economic factors do not obtain for disabled people in expected ways. Medicalization opens privacy to assault, and while economic privilege may make this assault less intrusive, it does not eliminate it. A private room in a hospital, no matter how expensive, is not like a hotel room, although it is leased for a certain period. No "Do Not Disturb" sign, controlled by a patient, will ever hang on the doorknob. Doctors, nurses, aides, and janitorial staff enter and exit at will. Despite the persistent fantasy that doctors, nurses, and nurse assistants provide sexual services, hospital trysts and erotic sponge baths are not part of their job descriptions. In fact, their professionalization hinges on being able to invade privacy while divorcing that invasion from its sexual associations. It may be acceptable, Dominic Davies explains, for a male patient to get an erection when having his penis washed, but "consensual, vigorous washing is seen as forbidden" (183–84). As long as medical staff *act* professionally, they do not consider themselves responsible for sexual side effects, and yet they cross erotic boundaries constantly, with little real regard for the consequences of their actions. Patients in medical institutions do not possess the same rights as non-disabled staff. It is as if sick or disabled individuals surrender the right to privacy in exchange for medical care, even though caregivers work for them. "The difference between those of us who need attendants and those who

don't," Cheryl Marie Wade claims, "is the difference between those who know privacy and those who don't" (88).

Group homes and long-term care facilities purposefully destroy opportunities for disabled people to find sexual partners or to express their sexuality. Even though inhabitants in group homes pay rent for their rooms, the money buys no functional privacy or right to use personal space. The staff usually does not allow renters to be alone in their room with anyone of sexual interest. Renters are subjected to intense surveillance, their activities entered in the day log. In many care facilities, staff will not allow two people to sit together alone in the same room. Some facilities segregate men and women. Add to these restrictions the fact that many people with disabilities are involuntarily confined in institutions, with no hope of escape, and the enormity of their oppression becomes palpable. The intimate lives of disabled men and women, as O'Toole phrases it, are "monitored, documented and discussed by others" (220). Medical authorities make decisions about access to erotic literature, masturbation, and sexual partners.

The unequal power relations between staff and patients encourage sexual abuse. We are only beginning to gather data on the sexual abuse of people with disabilities, but initial statistics indicate that the incidence of abuse is high (Ward, 2006; 1349), perhaps two to ten times more than the experience of the nondisabled population (Kaufman et al., 2003, 8; Shakespeare, 1999, "Sexual Politics" 63). It is puzzling that paralyzed women are especially vulnerable, given that disabled women are not considered sexually attractive by mainstream society, until a closer look is given to the conditions of abuse. A woman unable to leave her bed is a woman always in bed, and conventionally a bed is a sexual site. Paralysis is also pictured easily as sexual passivity or receptiveness—an invitation to sexual predators, since the erotic imagination thrives on clichéd positions and gestures. . . .

Frequently, . . . abuse is premeditated, representing acts of discipline, payback, or sexual harassment. O'Toole reports that many disabled women experience unacceptable touching by male doctors during medical examinations; they are sometimes publicly stripped and displayed to medical students. These women recount feelings of fear, embarrassment, vulnerability, and shame; they often try to separate themselves from their bodies, pretending that nothing is happening to them.

Personal choice and autonomy are constitutive features of the private sphere, but once subjected to medicalization, individual preference and self-determination evaporate. When the right to privacy and the medical model come into conflict, a new public sphere, controlled by medical figures and supportive of their authority, appears on the horizon. This medical zone of publicness replaces for people with disabilities everything formerly considered private. It engulfs them in an invasive and discriminatory space where they are viewed exclusively as medical subjects and the most casual stranger feels empowered to touch them, to comment on their disabilities, and to offer medical advice or charity. The medical model too often makes of the world a hospital where the disabled are obliged to be perpetual patients and the nondisabled have the right to play doctor.

THE EROTICS OF DISABILITY

Because I am so sensitive to touch, so acutely aware of a breeze on my neck, a ring on my finger, the rib of a sock pressing into my ankle, when I choose to participate in sexual contact, my unusually heightened physicality works for and not against me.
—Amy Wilensky, "The Skin I'm In"

As a sexual minority, people with disabilities face many limitations on their intimate behavior and erotic feelings. But, aware of their oppression and defiant of its injustice, they have begun to explore an alternative sexual culture based on the artfulness of disability. The progress has been slow because the fight for access has usually targeted the public sphere. . . . Consequently, we know much more about the public dimension of disability than about its private dimension; we are at the beginning of a period of sexual investigation for disabled people, where information is scarce and ethnography and sharing of practices need to be pursued.

Nevertheless, there are signs that people with disabilities are claiming a sexual culture based on different conceptions of the erotic body, new sexual temporalities, and a variety of gender and sexed identities. These emerging sexual identities have at least two significant characteristics. First, they represent disability not as a defect that needs to be overcome to have sex but as a complex embodiment that enhances sexual activities and pleasure. Second, they give to sexuality a political dimension that redefines people with disabilities as sexual citizens. It is crucial to understand that sexual citizenship does not translate merely into being able to express sexuality in public—a charge always levied against sexual minorities—but into the right to break free of the unequal treatment of minority sexualities and to create new modes of access for sex. In the case of disabled people, sexual citizenship has particular stakes. Some specific agenda items include: access to information about sexuality; freedom of association in institutions and care facilities; demedicalization of disabled sexuality; addressing sexual needs and desires as part of health care; reprofessionalization of caregivers to recognize, not deny, sexuality; and privacy on demand.

While certain aspects of the body are not open to transformation, sexual desire and erotic sensation are remarkably flexible. For example, people with paralysis, who have lost feeling in traditional erogenous zones, have found ways to eroticize other parts of their body. They also develop new ways to please their partners by creating erotic environments adjustable to differently abled bodies. As feminists have made clear, normative sexuality requires a distinctive mapping of the body into limited erogenous zones (Irigaray, 1985). A parallel geography exists between the places on the body marked for sex and the places where bodies have sex. Although it is considered kinky to have sex in out of the way places, it does not usually cross one's mind to summon sexual feelings in places on the body not already demarcated by them. Andrew Vahldieck (1999) adds a particularly vivid and thoughtful account to the literature on sex after spinal cord injury about the erotics of the disabled body:

There's a bumper sticker that proclaims, "Quads Make Better Lovers" and perhaps it's true. One positive by-product of adapting to a disability is having to learn to go with the flow of experience, both mentally and physically. After severe spinal injury, one must begin again, and this includes developing alternate sense faculties. My erotic self need not be solely localized at the tip of my cock, where I've lost much sensation; I have learned that other areas of my body can be erotically sensitive and responsive. Sensation is mobile. My passion, desire and heat can be creatively restrained or refocused on more sensitive areas: ears, lips, neck, shoulders. In doing so, I can transfer sensual feeling into areas where sensation is diminished.

Just as important has been learning to free myself from a preoccupation with my own pleasure. To give myself over to my partner. To slow down, not because I'm disabled and have to, but because I want to. This has proved crucial, paradoxically, to building up my own libidinous momentum. By relaxing into a quiet, tender space while stroking and touching my lover, I can engage vicariously in her enjoyment and stimulation so intensely as to share in her—and expand upon my own—felt pleasure. How curious that pleasing women orally has never been held as a form of manly sexual expression. Speaking as a man labeled "severely disabled," this may truly be considered a high and most subtle erotic art.

Disabled sexuality not only changes the erotics of the body, Vahldieck implies, but also transforms the temporality of lovemaking. For example, in the same way that narrative temporality has a beginning, middle, and end, normative sexuality requires beginning, middle, and end points. This is especially true of penetrative sex. Penetration has a preparatory phase, a period of sustainment, and a climax—all designed to prop up the physiognomy of the penis. One gets it up, gets it in, and keeps it up for as long as possible, until one loses it. Penetrative sex figures as a race against fatigue—a performance with a beginning, middle, and end. It also smacks of the assembly or production line, where part after part is added until the product is finished. The dependence of sex on penetration, incidentally, represents one reason why people tend to partition their sex life from everyday existence. Because the temporal phases of penetrative sex are so indelible, its narrative seems relatively autonomous, and it is easy to think of it as an activity apart from all other facets of life.

Because disabled people sometimes require advanced planning to have sex, their sexual activity tends to be embedded in thinking about the day, not partitioned as a separate event. Among disabled people, the so-called sex act does not always qualify as an action or performance possessing distinct phases such as beginning, middle, and end. Moreover, the myth that sex must be spontaneous to be authentic does not always make sense for people who live with little privacy or whose sexual opportunities depend on making arrangements with personal attendants. Rather, disabled sexuality has an ebb and flow that spreads it out among other activities, and its physiognomy does not necessarily mimic conventional responses of arousal, penetration, or orgasm. "I used to get stuck, needing orgasm, needing penetration, etc.," one woman explains. "Now, my sexuality has matured. . . . For example, one of the greatest highs I get (full-body orgasms? or spiritual-like orgasms?) is from having my neck bit" (Kaufman et al., 2003, 126). Some people without bodily sensation report experiencing mental orgasms when engaged in kissing, verbal play, or sexual fantasy. Others remark that sexual pleasure grows more intense with the advent of disability, owing either to physical changes or to a greater awareness of their body: "Since I became paralyzed in both legs I have noticed that I have varying kinds of orgasms, depending upon the situation. For example, when I play with myself and rub my clit a certain way my orgasms are much more intense. Sometimes my leg will go into spasm and my crotch feels tingly" (Kaufman et al., 2003, 52).

A crucial consideration for people with disabilities is not to judge their sexuality by comparison to normative sexuality but to think expansively and experimentally about what defines sexual experience for them. Sex may have no noticeable physical signs of arousal or may not conclude with an orgasm. When touching is involved, the places being touched may not be recognizable to other people as erogenous zones, which makes sex in public possible and a lot of fun. Sex may extend beyond the limits of endurance for penetrative sex, resembling slow dancing instead of the twist. It may seem kinky by comparison to what other people are doing. According to O'Toole, disabled sex often surprises a person's community, no matter how radical. For example, in Boston in the mid-1990s, Connie Panzarino marched in a gay pride parade with a placard reading. "Trached dykes eat pussy all night without coming up for air" (O'Toole, 2000, 212). That a woman with little movement below the neck could be the active partner in sex and use her disability to enhance her partner's pleasure stunned and shocked people. "This disabled woman," O'Toole notices, "was using her disability as an advertisement for a sexual partner. She was appealing to partners

who like extended oral pleasure. She was turning her apparent severe disability into a distinct sexual advantage" (220-21). O'Toole also mentions an account given by a lesbian amputee about enhancing the pleasure of her partners: "Can I just say that my two leg stumps make fabulous sex toys. I really think my amputated body is tailor-made for lesbian sex: I can crawl on top of my lover and grind my leg into her cunt in ways that I couldn't if I had 'real' legs. Having my little stumps gives me much more freedom of motion and I can get closer, deeper into her that way. Plus, pushing myself into her and away from her and into her again, moving my hips and legs against/on her body is the closest I have come to slow-dancing in years and I love it" (215).

Disabled people may advance a different sexual geography both for the body and for the places where bodies express their sexuality. Just as disabled persons may change places on the body not usually associated with sexual feeling into erogenous zones they reorganize places inhabited by bodies as locations for sexual culture. . . . As one woman explains it, "if you are a sexually active disabled person, and comfortable with the sexual side of your life, it is remarkable how dull and unimaginative non-disabled people's sex lives appear" (Shakespeare, 2000, 163).

New formations of gender and sexed identity may be the final frontier of sexual citizenship for people with disabilities. Although present currents on the Left and Right wish to abolish identity entirely, especially identities connected with sickness and perceived weakness, gender and sexed identities make sexuality present as a mode of being not easily closeted away or partitioned into isolated temporal and spatial segments. Claiming an identity based on sexual culture thrusts one's minority status into the foreground, politicizes it, and creates the opportunity to clarify sexual needs and desires. It also resists the closeting of gender and sexuality central to Western attitudes about sex. It may be especially valuable for people with disabilities to assert sexed identities, since Western attitudes seem married to the argument that "sex is sick," giving people perceived to be "sick" extra purchase in making counterarguments.

Apart from the urgency of political resistance, it may simply be the case that different identity formations suit people with disabilities better. They often complain that conventional notions of male and female or straight and gay do not apply to them (Shakespeare, 2000, 163), and it is fairly obvious that their sexual practices depart from many of the founding myths of normative sexuality. Disabled people do not embody gender in "natural" ways because gender stereotypes do not allow it. "It's like I don't have any maleness," one disabled man complains (Shuttleworth, 2000, 272). Certain disabilities appear to offer specific gender limitations. Men with cerebral palsy cannot touch or hug their female partners in the ways to which they are accustomed (Shuttleworth, 2000, 269). Blindness changes sexual flirtation from afar between men. But another person puts a positive spin on flexible gender identity: "Why should men be dominant? Why should sex revolve around penetration? Why should sex only involve two people? Why can't disabled people be assisted to have sex by third parties?" (Shakespeare, 2000, 163). O'Toole notes that no lesbian equivalent of the missionary position exists, and that partners are not obliged to have orgasms in the same position at the same time (213). Disabled sexuality embraces a similar flexibility. The sexed identities of disabled people are of value to all sexually active people, Shakespeare claims, because they allow for a continuum of sexual practices and encourage a greater willingness to embrace diversity, experimentation, and alternative sexual techniques (1999, 58). If we are to liberate disabled sexuality and give to disabled people a sexual culture of their own, their status as a sexual minority requires the protection of citizenship rights similar to those being claimed by other sexual minorities. The challenge of sexual citizenship for people with disabilities is great because they remain one of the largest unrecognized minority populations; little awareness exists about the manner of their oppression; sex is a taboo subject for everyone and for disabled people in particular; and the unquestioned embrace in most societies of ability as an ideology denies participation in the public sphere to those not deemed quality human beings. Integral to sexual citizenship for people with disabilities is the creation of a safe space with different lines of communication about disabled sexuality; they need in effect to invent a new public sphere receptive to political protest, public discussion, erotic association, and the sharing of ideas about intimate practices and taboos, erotic techniques and restrictions, sexual innovation and mythologies.

In the clash of the culture wars, some people have argued for a monoculture where we abandon all identities except nationality, while other people argue for a multiculture where we embrace many identities—racial, ethnic, gendered, national, and sexed. The call for a disability culture in general and a sexual disability culture in particular will arouse, no doubt, the anger of the first group and garner, with luck, the support of the second. But the stakes in the emergence of a sexual culture for disabled people are greater than the dispute between these two political factions. The stakes concern questions about fundamental rights expected by all citizens in a democratic society: freedom of association and intimate companionship; authority over their own body; protection from violence, abuse, and oppression; and the right to pursue a sexual future of their own choosing. Because every citizen will become sooner or later a disabled citizen, the struggle of people with disabilities for sexual rights belongs to everyone.

REFERENCES

Davies, Dominic. 2000. "Sharing Our Stories, Empowering Our Lives: Don't Dis Me!" *Sexuality and Disability* 18.3: 179–86.

Fine, Michelle, and Adrienne Asch, eds. 1988. *Women with Disabilities: Essays in Psychology, Culture, and Politics.* Philadelphia: Temple University Press.

Finger, Anne. 1992. "Forbidden Fruit." *New Internationalist* 233: 8–10.

Grealy, Lucy. "In the Realm of the Senses." *Nerve* 25 October 2001. (http://www.nerve.com/dispatches /Grealy/RealmOfTheSenses/).

Hamilton, Toby. "Sexuality in Deaf Blind Persons." 1979. *Sexuality and Disability* 2.3: 238–46.

Irigaray, Luce. 1985. *This Sex Which Is Not One.* Trans. Catherine Porter. Ithaca: Cornell University Press.

Job, Jennifer. 2004. "Factors Involved in the Ineffective Dissemination of Sexuality Information to Individuals Who Are Deaf or Hard of Hearing." *American Annals of the Deaf* 149.3: 264-73.

Kaufman, Miriam, Cory Silverberg, and Fran Odette. 2003. *The Ultimate Guide to Sex and Disability: For All of Us Who Live with Disabilities, Chronic Pain, and Illness.* San Francisco: Cleis.

O'Brien, Mark, with Gillian Kendall. 2003. *How I Became a Human Being: A Disabled Man's Quest for Independence.* Madison: University of Wisconsin Press.

O'Toole, Corbett Joan. 2000. "The View from Below: Developing a Knowledge Base about an Unknown Population." *Sexuality and Disability* 18.3: 207–24.

Shakespeare, Tom. 2000. "Disabled Sexuality: Toward Rights and Recognition." *Sexuality and Disability* 18.3: 159–66.

———. 1999. "The Sexual Politics of Disabled Masculinity." *Sexuality and Disability* 17.1: 53–64.

Shuttleworth, Russell P. 2000. "The Search for Sexual Intimacy for Men with Cerebral Palsy." *Sexuality and Disability* 18.4: 263–82.

Vahldieck, Andrew. "Uninhibited." *Nerve.* 19 November 1999. (http://www.nerve.com/PersonalEssays/Vahldieck /uninhibited/).

Wade, Cheryl Marie. 1994. "It Ain't Exactly Sexy." *The Ragged Edge: The Disability Experience from the Pages of the First Fifteen Years of* The Disability Rag. Ed Barrett Shaw. Louisville: Advocado Press. 88–90.

Ward, Amy Paul. 2006. "Rape." *Encyclopedia of Disability.* Ed. Gary L. Albrecht. Thousand Oaks, CA: Sage. 1348–51.

Waxman-Fiduccia, Barbara Faye. 2000. "Current Issues in Sexuality and the Disability Movement." *Sexuality and Disability* 18.3: 167–74.

Wilensky, Amy. "The Skin I'm In." *Nerve.* 24 October 2001. (http://www.nerve.com/PersonalEssays/Wilensky/skin/).

What's a Leg Got to Do with It?

Donna Walton

What's a leg got to do with it? Exactly what I thought when, during a heated conversation, a female rival told me I was less than a woman because I have one leg.

Excuse me. Perhaps I missed something. How could she make such an insensitive comment about something she had no experience with? Was she some expert on disabilities or something? Was she, too, disabled? Had she— like me—fought a battle with cancer that cost her a limb? For a split second, my thoughts were paralyzed by her insensitivity. But, like a defeated fighter who returns to the ring to regain victory, I bounced back for a verbal round with Ms. Thang.

I am woman first, an amputee second and physically challenged last. And it is in that order that I set out to educate and testify to people like Ms. Thang who are unable to discern who I am—a feisty, unequivocally attractive African American woman with a gimpy gait who can strut proudly into any room and engage in intelligent conversation with folks anxious to feed off my sincere aura.

It is rather comical and equally disturbing how folks—both men and women—view me as a disabled woman, particularly when it comes to sexuality. They have so many misconceptions. Straight women, for example, want to know how I catch a man, while most men are entertained with the idea that because I have one leg sex with me must be a blast.

I have even been confronted by folks who give me the impression that they think having sex is a painful experience for me. Again, I say, What's a leg got to do with it?

For all of those who want to inquire about my sexual prowess but dare not to, or for those who are curious about how I maintain such positive self-esteem when life dealt me the proverbial "bad hand," this story is for you. But those who have a tough time dealing with reality probably should skip the next paragraph because what I am about to confess is the gospel truth.

I like sex! I am very sexual!! I even consider myself sexy, residual limb and all. You see, I was a sexual being before my leg was amputated 19 years ago. My attitude didn't change about sex. I just had to adjust to the attitudes of others.

For example, I remember a brother who I dated in high school—before my leg was amputated—then dated again five years later. The dating ended abruptly because I realized that the brother could not fathom the one-leg thing. When he and I were home alone, he was cool as long as we got hot and bothered with my prosthesis on. However, whenever I tried to take off my artificial leg for comfort purposes, he immediately panicked. He could not fathom seeing me with one leg.

I tried to put him at ease by telling him Eva's story from Toni Morrison's novel *Sula*—that "my leg just got tired and walked off one day." But this brother just could not deal. He booked.

On the other hand, my experiences with lesbians have varied; they don't all book right away, but some have booked. Not all are upfront with their feelings 'cuz women are socialized to be courteous, emotional, and indirect, sparing one's feelings. Instead, some tend to communicate their discomfort with my missing limb in more subtle ways. For example, one lesbian I dated did not want to take me out to bars, clubs and other social settings. My lop-sided gait was an embarrassment, and the fact that I use a cane garnered unwanted attention for her. Behind closed doors, she did not have any problems with it. How we would be perceived by trendy lesbians was her main concern.

Conversely, I have had positive experiences with lesbians as well. For instance, I have dated and been in love with women who have been affirming and supportive while respecting my difference. My wholeness has been shaped by all of these experiences. Without hesitation, I can now take off my prosthesis, be comfortable hopping around on one leg and the sex . . . is still a blast.

How does a woman with one leg maintain such a positive self-esteem in a society where people with disabilities are not valued? Simply by believing in myself. I know you're saying, "That sounds much too hokey." But as I said earlier, this is the gospel truth.

I was 19 years old when my leg was amputated. I was diagnosed with osteogenic sarcoma, bone cancer. During the first five years after my surgery, concentrating on other folks' perceptions of me was the least of my concerns. I was too focused on beating the odds against dying. You see, I was given only a 15 percent chance of survival—with spiritual guidance and support from my family—I had made the very difficult decision to stop taking my chemotherapy treatments. Doctors predicted that, by halting the dreadful chemotherapy, I was writing my own death certificate. However, through what I believe was divine healing, my cancer was eradicated.

Before this cancerous ordeal, I was not strong spiritually, and my faith was rocked when my leg was amputated because I thought I was to keep my leg. At the time, I could not see past the physical. After my amputation, I was preoccupied with the kinds of crippling thoughts that all the Ms. Thangs of the world are socialized to believe: that I was not going to be able to wear shorts, bathing suits or lingerie; that my womanness was somehow compromised by the loss of a limb.

If you have a disability and are in need of some fuel for your spirit, check out any novel by Toni Morrison (*Sula* is my favorite because of the one-legged grandmother, Eva) or Khalil Gibran's *The Prophet*. These resources helped me build self-esteem and deal with my reality.

Ultimately, building positive esteem is an ongoing process. To that end, I am currently producing a motivational video that will outline coping strategies for female amputees.

No matter what your disability or circumstance, you cannot give in to a defeatist attitude. When you do, your battle is lost. There is a way of fighting back. It is called self-esteem.

Believe in yourself, and you will survive—and thrive.

Source: "What's a Leg Got to Do With It?" This article originally appeared in *HealthQuest: Total Wellness for Body, Mind & Spirit*, Volume 1, Number 3, Winter 1993–94, pages 50–51. It is reprinted by permission.

THE PRIVILEGE OF PERVERSITIES: RACE, CLASS AND EDUCATION AMONG POLYAMORISTS AND KINKSTERS

ELISABETH SHEFF AND CORIE J. HAMMERS

INTRODUCTION

This article focuses on *kinksters*—people involved in "kinky" or "perverted" sexual acts and relationships frequently involving bondage/discipline, dominance/submission and/or sadism/masochism (BDSM, also referred to as sado-masochism), and *polyamorists*—people who engage in openly conducted, multiple partner, romantic and/or sexual relationships. Popular usage among polyamorists and kinksters indicates that people who identify themselves as kinky are more likely to accept and celebrate the pervert moniker, and polyamorists who do not identify themselves as kinky appear less likely to think of themselves as perverts. Conventional society, however, generally classifies as perverts people who have multiple and concurrent romantic and/or sexual relationships, engage in group sex and/or openly espouse non-monogamy. Polyamorists are thus defined as perverts by the popular imagination, even if they themselves do not identify as such.[1]

Being accused of being a pervert can have detrimental consequences such as alienation from family and friends (Barker, 2005a; Califia, 2000), harassment (Wright, 2006), loss of a job or custody of a child (Dalton, 2001; Hequembourg, 2007; Klein and Moser, 2006), physical attack (Keres, 1994), public excoriation and incarceration (Attias, 2004; White, 2006). Although everyone involved in "perverted" sex risks social censure, people unprotected by social advantages are more vulnerable to the discriminatory impacts of this sexual stigma than are those shielded by racial and/or class privileges. This insulation provides greater social latitude to engage in and redefine sexual or relational "deviance" than that available to those burdened by racism, poverty, inadequate education, limited job prospects and other forms of discrimination (Collins, 1996, 2005; Sanday, 2007; Steinbugler, 2005). . . .

Scholars are increasingly emphasising the intersections of sexuality with other elements of social stratification (Collins, 1996, 2005; Schippers, 2000; Sharma and Nath, 2005). Disability, (trans)gender, sexual orientation, age—these elements and more—influence the ways in which people choose to, or are able to, express their sexual selves. In this article, we focus on race, education and class for three reasons. First, as white, middle-class sexuality researchers, we have attempted to address the implications of the overwhelmingly white populations who participated in our research. Second, race, education and class stand out as important constants in the field, indicating their significance for analysis. Finally, researchers have identified demographic characteristics, and especially race, as important factors impacting sexuality and specifically salient to research on polyamory and BDSM (Haritaworn, Lin, and Klesse, 2006; Langdridge and Barker, 2007). For instance, Willey (2006) and

From "The Privilege of Perversities: Race, Class, and Education Among Polyamorists and Kinksters," by Corie J. Hammers and Elisabeth Sheff. *Psychology & Sexuality*, Vol. 2, No. 3, September 2011, pp. 198–223. Copyright © 2011 Routledge, reprinted by permission of the publisher (Taylor & Francis Ltd, http://www.tandf.co.uk/journals).

Noël (2006) examined poly discourse and highlighted the ways in which whiteness and class privilege are central to polyamory and those claims that seek to "naturalise" the practice of polyamory. As Willey noted, many feminist poly activists justify polyamory on the grounds that monogamy is unnatural and patriarchal because it works to quell our uncontainable sexual "drives" while being deeply implicated in female subjugation. Yet, this same 'liberationist' rhetoric has historically been used to marginalise and stigmatise the poor and the people of colour for *their* "uncontrollable" urges and *their* inability to conform to the monogamous, nuclear family (white) ideal.

. . . . It is our strong belief that in studying only those who are most accessible and visible within poly and BDSM subcultures—those overwhelmingly white and middle class—we fail as researchers to understand alternative mappings of non-monogamous desire and BDSM practices. . . . Our objectives here are multi-fold, and we document the affiliation between polyamory and BDSM; demonstrate through a meta-analysis of extant literature the ways in which research on alternative sexual communities has often (unwittingly) reinforced and (re)constituted a homogenous image of these non-conformist subcultures; support and augment this analysis with our own empirical data; and provide recommendations to improve research methods. By highlighting the race and class privileges that operate throughout these processes, we aim to foster dialogue about the ways in which we as sexuality researchers can mitigate this privilege and its potential impact on our collective research. . . .

COMMUNITY CHARACTERISTICS

Although polyamorous and kinky identities are distinct, the populations practicing them share such a variety of traits and considerable overlap in membership that they warrant joint analysis (Bauer, 2010). . . .

Neither academicians nor community members have achieved consensus on precise definitions of kinkiness or polyamory. In line with other researchers (Barker, 2005a, 2005b; Haritaworn et al., 2006; Weitzman, 2006, 2007), we define polyamory as a form of association in which people openly maintain multiple romantic, sexual and/or effective relationships. Polyamorists use the term *poly* as a noun . . . an adjective . . . , and an umbrella term that includes polyfidelity or relationships based in sexual and emotional fidelity among a group larger than a dyad.

With its emphasis on long-term, emotionally intimate relationships, polyamory differs from the form of swinging based on emotional exclusivity with one partner and sexual non-monogamy with multiple partners. Polyamory is also not adultery: the poly focuses on honesty and (ideally) full disclosure differs markedly from the attempted secrecy definitional to adultery. Both men and women have access to multiple partners in polyamorous relationships, distinguishing them from those that are polygynous or polyandrous. Polyamorists routinely debate the definition of the term, the groups it includes and who is qualified to claim it as an identity.

Kinky people, relationships and communities share many characteristics with polyamorists, with a myriad of potential additional dimensions that can make kink even more complex. Kinksters are people who identify as kinky, frequently including (but not limited to) those who participate in BDSM; have multiple sexual and/or play partners; engage in role play and/or costuming as part of their sexual behaviour; have fetishes; blend gender characteristics; and/or modify their bodies in conjunction with or to augment their sexual practices. BDSM, the primary umbrella under which many of these identities are encompassed . . . is the practice of consensual exchanges of personal power including (but not limited to) scripted "scenes" involving some combination of corporal or psychic "punishment", intense physical stimulation (often pain), role playing and/or fantasy and/or varied sexual inter-actions (Langdridge and Barker, 2007; Moser and Kleinplatz, 2006a; Weinberg and Kamel, 1995). Among kinksters, definitions of who qualifies as a sexual partner and what counts as a sex act encompass far greater variety than those considered sex acts or partners among "vanilla" (non-kinky) people. Typically, BDSM and poly communities cohere around a specific gender and sexual orientation. For instance, most public play parties are geared specifically towards gay men, lesbians or bisexual/heterosexual people. This is in part due to the origins of the BDSM subculture in the United States, which began as a gay male phenomen[on] that later diverged to include lesbian, heterosexual and bi/pansexual communities (Ridinger, 2002). These various groups tend to self-segregate by sexual orientation and gender, although the growth of virtual and physical kink community has encouraged some amalgamation as well.

Poly and kinky research respondents empha-sise negotiation, honesty, consent and personal growth as important components of successful relationships (Sheff, 2005a, 2005b, 2006, 2007, 2010; Barker and Ritchie, 2007; Weitzman, 2006, 2007). Similarly, many of them main-tain multiple relationships with varied levels of emotional and sexual intimacy. Kinkiness appears to be a broader base for an identity than polyamory, encompassing a greater range of relationships and types of practices/identi-ties. Many kinky people have multiple partner relationships but do not necessarily primar-ily identify as polyamorous—the number of people involved in their relationships is but one component among many aspects of kink identity, sexuality and relationships. For some, mostly non-kink poly people, the multiplicity of the relationships determines their status as poly. Those polys who engage in kinky sexual activities are more likely to view sexuality more broadly and numerosity as one, not necessarily the defining, element of their sexual identities.

Additionally and more importantly, for the purposes of this article, the poly and kinky populations who have participated in research primarily comprise white, well-educated, middle-class professionals. . . .

METHODS

The data for this article come from three sources: our own original research; others' stud-ies of kinksters and polyamorists; and commu-nication with other researchers online. . . .

Original Research

Sheff's longitudinal study of polyamorists has thus far produced two waves of data col-lected through participant observation, content analysis, Internet research and in-depth inter-views. The first portion of the study (*Gender, family, and sexuality: Exploring Polyamorous communities* 1996–2003) provided the base of 40 in-depth interviews with adults who iden-tified as poly, and extensive participant obser-vation data collected at a wide variety of poly events including co-ed and women's support groups, potlucks, community meetings and two national conferences. The second wave of data collection (*Polyamorous families study* 2007–present) focuses on polyamorous families with children and includes 15 previous respon-dents[2] and has expanded the sample to incor-porate an additional 41 people, for a current total sample of 81 across both studies. Race is the most homogeneous demographic charac-teristic, with 89 percent of the sample identi-fying as white. Socio-economic status is high among these respondents, with 74 percent in professional jobs. Fully 88 percent report some college education, with 67 percent attaining bachelor's degrees and 21 percent completing graduate degrees.

Sheff also conducted a study of intersecting sexual identities (*Overlapping identities study*

2005) examining the overlap between polyamorists, swingers, people with fetishes and those
who practice BDSM. Of the 64 respondents
(31 men, 27 women and 6 others),[3] 31 were
involved in BDSM, 19 in polyamory and 6
in swinging. The majority of respondents (58
or 90%) identified as white, with two African
Americans, one Filipina, two people of multiracial heritage and one who identified himself
simply as "other" also participating. Respondents were also highly educated, with all but
three respondents (95%) having completed or
currently enrolled in an undergraduate degree,
and 48 (75%) of them completing at least some
graduate school. All of the 26 respondents
who reported fetishes were also involved in
BDSM, and the two groups are so intricately
involved that distinguishing between them
did not provide any useful analysis. Swingers, however, stood out as socially distinct—if
racially, economically and educationally similar
to the other respondents. They neither identified themselves strongly with the other groups,
nor were they identified as integral to a joint
identity the way polys and kinksters identified
each other. Although there are certainly intersections between polys and swingers (and to
a lesser extent kinksters and swingers), these
focus groups indicated a much stronger affiliation between polyamorists and kinksters than
between either group and swingers.

In her ethnographic research on Canadian lesbian/queer bathhouses (*Bathhouse
culture study* 2004), Hammers also found a
largely white and well-educated population.
Approximately 80 percent of the 33 interview
respondents identified as white, with over half
attaining either undergraduate or graduate
degrees. Although highly educated, most of
these women were only marginally middle class
(Hammers, 2008). Hammers' current project,
which explores the US lesbian/queer BDSM
community (2007 to present), has found this
population, like the bathhouse subculture, to

be a relatively homogenous one. As with the
bathhouse study, data for this BDSM project
come from in-depth interviews with lesbian/
queer BDSM practitioners/attendees and participant observation data derived from attendance at a variety of public lesbian/queer/
women-only BDSM events in the United
States. A total of 40 in-depth interviews with
BDSM practitioners and self-identified kinksters have been conducted thus far. Of these,
36 individuals identify as white. Approximately
76 percent reported some university education,
with 70 percent having attained a bachelor's
degree.

Thus, a major interweaving theme that binds
our studies and informs our views on race in the
research setting, and the inadequate attention
paid to race when it comes to alternative sexual
subcultures, comes through at this juncture.
We find that these alternative sex publics—
which encompass such things as community
meetings, national conferences, bathhouse
events and public BDSM play parties—are
predominantly white. It is this whiteness, we
believe, that sexuality scholars must address.

Others' studies of kinksters and polyamorists

To find pertinent studies, we searched in Google
Scholar, as well as Sociological Abstracts and
Sociological Collection in the Galileo search
engine, using the search terms *BDSM, sadomasochism, kink, SM* and *polyamor*. To be eligible for inclusion, studies had to focus on
polyamory and/or kinkiness and contain at least
some demographic data relevant to the target
populations. Both the communities involved
in and the literature on kink and BDSM share
a core identity built on sadomasochism, so we
include them in a single category. Polyamory is
one form of non-monogamy, but other forms
of non-monogamy (polygyny, infidelity) are so
diverse as to lack a similar common foundation.

The intersection between swinging and poly-amory is complex, ambiguous and common enough to gain its own moniker of 'swolly'[4] and clearly warrants further investigation, although space constraints prohibit its inclusion in this analysis.

Communication with researchers online

Once we had amassed a list of polyamory and kink studies, we posted our bibliography to PolyResearchers, an online discussion group composed of academicians, journalists, researchers and clinicians dedicated to the discussion of research on polyamory.[5] We asked the membership to review the list to inform us if we had missed any studies. No members were able to identify any missing studies.

The Poly Researchers' list similarly granted us access to many of the researchers whose work we reviewed, allowing us to attain additional data that were not included in the published pieces. If a published piece did not include demographic data but did include an email address for correspondence, we would contact the investigator(s) and request the additional data. All 12 of the researchers we contacted for more information regarding their studies responded to us with the requested data. . . .

RESULTS OF STUDIES OF KINKSTERS AND POLYAMORISTS

The composite results from these 36 studies (20 of kinksters, 14 of polys and 2 of both) indicate a largely homogeneous universe populated with highly educated, white, middle- and upper-middle-class professionals, confirming numerous researchers' conclusions (Sheff, 2005a, 2005b; Sandnabba, Santtila, Alison, and Nordling, 2002; Spengler, 1977). These studies employed a variety of methods: six used surveys or e-interviews conducted entirely online; four "offline" studies reported relying heavily on the Internet to recruit their samples and for some supplementary data collection; 12 used interviews; one combined interviews and a questionnaire; and 14 used questionnaires distributed in person or through magazines, at organisation/club meetings or at events. Twenty-one of the studies were conducted in the United States, five in Western Europe, two in Australia and one in China. There are three unpublished masters' theses and four unpublished dissertations. Sample sizes range from a low of six (Matthews, 2006; Mosher, Levitt, and Manley, 2006) to a high of 6,997 (Brame, 2000) and span over time from Spengler's trailblazing 1977 study of male sadomasochists in Western Germany to Barker and Langdridge's 2010 volume that includes original research on polyamory. The percent of people of colour in the sample varies from a low of zero in four studies (Barker and Ritchie, 2007; Cook, 2005; Matthews, 2006; Mosher et al., 2006) to a high of 48 in Tomassilli, Golub, Bimbi, and Parson's (2009) study of lesbians and bisexual women in New York City.

Unique cases

Some studies contribute to multiple areas or provide qualitative data unsuitable for tables. Taormino's (2008) study of 126 people in "open relationships" includes data on polys and kinksters, with 62 percent identifying as polyamorous or polyfidelitous and 51 percent identifying as kinky. Of the entire sample of 126 people, 82 percent identified as white and 77 percent as middle class or above. As previously discussed, Sheff's *Overlapping identities study* of polyamorists, swingers, kinksters and those with fetishes yielded similar results.

In the sole randomly selected sample of which we are aware, Richters, de Visser, Rissel, Grulich, and Smith (2008) surveyed a representative sample of 19,307 residents of

Australia aged 16–59 years old and found that 1.8 percent of the sexually active respondents (2.2 percent of men and 1.3 percent of women) reported being involved in BDSM in the last year. Results also indicate that people involved in BDSM are more likely to have been "non-exclusive in a regular relationship (i.e., had sex with someone else besides their regular partner)" (Richters et al., 2008, p. 1663) in the last 12 months than are people with no involvement in BDSM, confirming the association between non-monogamy and BDSM. The study measured ethnicity through country of birth and language spoken at home, and only 1.3 percent of respondents spoke anything but English in their homes. Although respondents who engaged in BDSM also had higher levels of education, Richters (personal communication, 2009) cautioned that:

My impression is that we cannot be certain whether the apparent high education levels and social class of BDSM people as anecdotally reported is an artifact of self-selection for study. It may be real, which would not be surprising given that BDSM is often highly verbal and symbolic. Nonetheless, our analysis clearly showed that demographic and psychological variables were swamped by the strong differences in sexual interest and breadth of experience/repertoire.

Although this most representative sample finds virtually the same racial, ethnic, class and educational characteristics of the other studies with less-randomly selected samples, the authors note that these select demographic characteristics are overshadowed by the sample's sexual characteristics.

REASONS FOR THESE RESULTS

Although it is quite unlikely that these samples are representative of the actual range of kink and poly people, they are certainly representative of the range of people involved in mainstream poly and kink communities. . . . One plausible rationale is that poly and kinky

people hold the same kind of racist views as do others of their social ilk. Living in the United States, Australia, and/or Western Europe would make it virtually impossible for polys and kinksters to escape the pervasive racism and classism endemic in those societies and the accompanying white privilege (or lack thereof) that inflects their lives. In our experiences, poly and kink communities tend to eschew open racism and often support such liberal ideals as equality and celebration of diversity. White privilege, however, generally remains as invisible in these groups as is in more conventional society, thus becoming the dominant racial paradigm. . . .

Internet recruitment

Because the Internet serves as a primary tool for sexuality researchers to both engage and recruit target populations (Waskul, 2004), it is no surprise that numerous respondents in these kink and poly studies identify the Internet as a crucial element of their access to sexual non-conformist communities (Sheff, 2005a; Weber, 2002; Weitzman, 2006). The web has profoundly reshaped sexual minorities' communities, identities, networks and communications, and nine of the researchers cited in this article avail themselves of this expanded opportunity by examining poly and kink populations that would have previously been extremely difficult to find, or may in fact not exist, without the Internet. Although it is reasonable to recognise the Internet as an important site of community evolution, it is not sensible to rely so heavily on a single resource that will definitionally provide a limited sample.

Although the Internet has expanded sexual opportunity (for some) and created a virtual world wherein sexual minorities can find affirmation and community (Weinrich, 1997), this technological tool also reproduces (and possibly strengthens) pre-existing inequalities. Initial research indicated that the majority of Internet users were male, overwhelmingly white, middle class and well educated (Warf and Grimes, 1997), with an average income that was twice that of the national average (Kantor and Neubarth, 1996). Current research identifies lingering disparties in computer ownership (Ono and Zavodny, 2003) and use (Chakraborty and Bosman, 2005), which continue to disadvantage people of colour (Mossberger, Tolbert, and McNeal, 2008). Internet use and its impacts are complex, however, and measuring access alone is insufficient—researchers must also account for a variety of factors that shape the ways in which people use the Internet (Jackson, Ervin, Gardnera, & Schmitt, 2001; Roderick, 2008). Thus, depending on one's race and class location, the Internet can both enhance and hinder sexual opportunity and sense of belonging for members of unconventional sexual cultures, often reproducing predominately white and relatively affluent alternative sexual communities.

Protections afforded by privileges

Although they do not completely insulate people from the risks associated with deviance, race and class privileges can provide buffers to mitigate the myriad potential negative outcomes related to sexual and relational nonconformity. Like other sexual minorities, kinky and poly people have lost jobs, child custody and families' and friends' esteem. Indeed, Pallotta-Chiarolli (2006, p. 51) found that two indigenous Australian children in her study of poly families:

[. . .] kept to themselves in order to discourage any intimacy with other children that could lead to discovery and a further reason to harass them, as they were already experiencing ongoing racist harassment. They had also been warned by their parents not to let white teachers know or else they'd be taken away from their family, a theme that was all too real for this family whose own childhoods had been mostly spent in mission homes after being

removed from their families as part of Australia's racist and assimilationist policies.

Their family's experiences with racism sensitised them to the need to remain concealed to avoid further racialised persecution.

As groups comprised mainly white people with relatively high socio-economic statuses, mainstream polyamorists' and kinksters' privileges can buffer them from some of the negative impacts people risk when they eschew conventionally sanctioned roles. Respondents' levels of education and occupations indicate that they are generally skilled professionals with careers endowed with greater job security than low-skill, low-paying jobs, where employees are far more easily replaced and often subject to greater surveillance and less autonomy. Courts have repeatedly demonstrated their endorsement of conventional heterosexual families over those with sexual and/or gender nonconforming members (Klein and Moser, 2006; Polikoff, 1993). The intersections of these varied privileges bestow middle-class people with greater freedom to engage in behaviours and relationships that risk social approbation. Coupled with a relative lack of public awareness of polyamory and kinky relationships, these privileges allow some to pass as sexually or relationally conventional when they wish to do so, thus avoiding the consequences that can accompany detection. People in disadvantaged positions are often subject to levels of surveillance that make non-conformity riskier than it would be for others with greater resources. "Perversity" then becomes another luxury more readily available to those who are already members of dominant groups.

Deterrents to participation

There are a number of factors that can combine to dissuade people of colour and those of lower socio-economic status from participating in mainstream poly and kink communities. These include expense, discomfort with being a numerical minority, the potential for discrimination, communities of colours' negative assessments of sexual minorities and issues of identity.

Expense

Scarce funds can deter people with low incomes from participating in some kink and poly community events. Fetish wear, admission to public sex environments such as "dungeons" and "toys" such as floggers can be expensive, selecting-out entire categories of people with little discretionary income. This is quite problematic, because 11 of the research samples to which we refer were drawn at least in part from those attending public "play parties" and thus reflect only a portion of the population that is readily accessible—people with Internet access and the privacy to use it, who are involved in groups or organisations and/or willing and able to afford to "play" in public. . . .

Tokenism, potential discrimination and community rejection of sexual minorities

In her study of polyamorists in the Western United States, Sheff's respondents of colour cited a number of barriers to participation in poly community events. Yansa, a 29-year-old kink- and poly-identified African American health-care provider, reported acute discomfort when attending a poly pool party in the San Francisco Bay Area. She observed that:

I was not sure if they wanted me there. Like I felt like maybe I had walked in on somebody else's thing and I wasn't invited . . . . [there were] 75, 80 naked people in this huge pool and I walked in and everybody just turned and looked . . . and I realized I am the only Black person here. I was the only person in a swimming suit so that could have been another issue, too, like maybe she's lost her way, what is she doing here?

Yansa's discomfort at being the sole Black person at the party was compounded by her unawareness of the community (un)dress code. Although the setting was "clothing optional" in that people were neither compelled to nor barred from wearing clothing, the norm was universal nudity while in the swimming pool and various stages of undress to full clothing on the pool deck.

Though Yansa's initial discomfort eased as she socialised at that and other parties, she remained uneasy about the increased potential risks she faced for sexual non-conformity. She reported already feeling vulnerable at work because of her race and fearing that being a known polyamorist would mean termination. She described her employers as

[. . .] executives who went to Wharton and Harvard and were Republicans and assholes . . . very, very closed-minded. And I got the impression that they were already not comfortable with me being a person of color. To throw in the other stuff that I did may confirm their stereotypes about Black people or they may have just thought she's the weirdest shit on the planet, I don't trust her. . . . We don't want her on this job anymore, someone may find her out.

Yansa noted several reasons other African Americans had discussed with her for their lack of desire to attend poly or kink community events or identify as polyamorous or kinky. "I've heard from Black folk that they think it's a nasty white person thing to do. And they throw out the whole scenario of slavery[—]you know they raped us and they took our women and impregnated them . . . that any respectable educated cultured Black person in their right mind wouldn't even think about doing something so disgusting." She similarly reported that:

I've had Black people in the community tell me that they don't want to feel like the token Black . . . the novelty like the fat girl or the Asian girl. I don't want to feel like people are attracted to me and wanting to play with me or date me because they're trying to figure out something. Like I'm some anthropological experiment or something.

It was not only their fear of objectification and denunciation of past abuses and negative stereotypes that deterred Yansa's compatriots of colour from joining the local poly community, but their active rejection of poly or kinky subcultures as white, foreign and potentially corrupt.

Victor, a poly-identified 36-year-old African American therapist, artist and college instructor, was more optimistic. He noted that the poly community in which he socialised was "monochromatic", though he was not sure if that was because of "issues of either privilege or even cultural interest." The whiteness of the setting did not bother him, in part because he had grown up in mostly white neighbourhoods and was thus "acclimated" to white people, and in part because he felt that, "People who are interested in really relating with people and good whole truth telling are going to tend to be less racist . . . I've actually felt a lot of acceptance." Victor pointed out that his socioeconomic status gave him access to a lifestyle that others did not have the freedom to enjoy. "It's sort of privilege related . . . if you're not worrying about certain things, then you have the privilege or the space to explore alternatives. . . . The freedom to explore polyamory sort of comes from a freedom either financially or just psychologically not having to [struggle to] survive in other ways." Even so, when thinking about mainstream African American communities' possible reactions to polyamory, he noted that, "I can imagine being in a room of Black people and them going 'That sounds like crazy white folks, that's some crazy shit'."

Identity

People of colour, already labouring under stigma and racism, might be more reluctant to assume a potentially disadvantageous identity than white or ethnic majority people. Laksha, a 26-year-old African American graduate student and participant in Sheff's *Overlapping identities study* who identifies as bisexual, poly and "mostly vanilla", asserts that:

I think African Americans are much less likely to go into a BDSM setting and think, ok, these are my people, this is my family, and take on that label. It is similar to feminism, in that many African American women have feminist principles and take feminist action and even participate in what some would consider feminist activism, but do not identify with the label. White people can more readily walk into the room and identify with the people, see them as their tribe, because race does not stand out to them, so kink can become their organizing identity. But it is not that easy for African Americans; race always stands out to us in a situation like that.

The disadvantage of a stigmatised identity, coupled with the added weight of racial strain that white or ethnic majorities do not experience, as well as feelings of discomfort or lack of belonging in the setting, can contribute to people of colour's reluctance to identify with kink and poly subcultures.

That many who might appear to be poly or kinky by others' definitions do not self-identify as such has important implications for the construction of identities. Although Victor asserted that mainstream African Americans would reject an organised poly identity, he hypothesised that there were ". . . communities of color where there are multipartner relationships going on I don't know whether they would call it poly or not. Probably not. . . . I think that populations tend to self select." Undoubtedly, there are people who openly maintain non-monogamous relationships or enjoy being spanked during sex, behaviours characteristic of (respectively) poly and kinky relationships, but nonetheless do not identify with those communities.

Equally certain is the existence of people who identify as poly or kinky but do not attend meetings or join groups. Again, it could be that those who feel marginalised or different from the more "visible" members of the poly and kink community will remain outside the very organisations that purportedly represent their ilk. It is also possible that people of colour involved in unconventional sexual practices are just as active but more clandestine and maintain their own, more exclusive, list-servs, events and private sexual venues. Precisely how these more underground sexual networks and private play parties might differ from the more visible sexual subcultures requires additional research.

Finally, the (almost all-white) researchers' race could deter people of colour from participating in research on kink and polyamory. Hammers' (2008) attempts to interview women of colour who chose to participate in lesbian/queer bathhouse culture certainly testify to this issue and the power that inheres within the researcher–interviewee relationship. This power differential is particularly salient when the focus is on sex and non-normative sexual practices. Many of the women of colour Hammers approached for her bathhouse study refused to speak to her precisely because she is white. Those people of colour who chose to participate in the study often linked the lack of participation by other people of colour to the perceived potential predation and appropriation of participants' experiences by the researcher. Only a few women of colour agreed to talk to Hammers about their experiences, several of whom expressed concern about other women of colour discovering their decision to do so.

RESEARCH STRATEGIES

Past strategies

. . . . Researchers examining kinky and poly populations have dealt with issues of class and race in a variety of ways. Measuring race and class is quite complex even in a single society, and when the research is international it becomes very difficult to establish common meanings indeed. . . . Class status does not necessarily translate directly from income in a single nation, much less internationally: some have middle-class status with little disposable income, and others have money to spend but are not considered middle class. Although education and class can be strongly correlated, some poly or kinky people are highly educated but "underemployed" or work in comparatively low-paid fields of counselling and academia and thus have less disposable income than their level of education might suggest.

Alternately, Bauer (2008, p. 238) questioned the stereotype of:

BDSM people being overwhelmingly highly educated and of middle- to upper class . . . [because] my sample is rather diverse in this regard. However, some interviewees put forth the idea that high-quality BDSM is only for those whom they perceive to be highly educated, "intelligent" or "classy" individuals, thus endorsing potentially excluding class-based criteria for membership in the community.

Bauer's (2008, p. 238) respondents report that the majority of the play parties they attend were populated primarily by white people and that "the race thing is partly class stuff and it's partly because most of the play parties that I've been to have been organized by white people."

Like class, measuring race presents a myriad of complexities, and researchers took a variety of approaches to this task. Of the reviewed studies, eight ignored the category of race altogether, rendering it virtually irrelevant in its invisibility (e.g. Sandnabba, Santtila, and Nordling, 1999, 2002). The fact that race was left unproblematised indicates that the populations were most likely white. . . . Others (14) collected data on race but refrained from addressing racial issues in their analysis. This lack of discussion indicates that many of these researchers were oblivious to, or actively chose to ignore, the impacts race can have on the construction of sexual identities. Still other researchers have attempted to oversample people of colour (e.g. Sheff, 2005a, 2005b,

2006; see also Connolly, 2006; Klesse, 2007, p. 157). Sheff endeavoured to recruit as many respondents of colour as possible, interviewed all three people of colour in the Midwestern poly community and travelled to the California Bay Area with the explicit intent of increasing sample diversity. Even so, she found the demographic characteristics of the numerous mainstream poly communities in the Bay Area to closely mirror the Midwestern sample. . . .

Some researchers (E. Cook, personal communication, 2007; L. Wolf, personal communication, 2008) did not collect data on race because they perceived it as unrelated to their topic of study. Others intentionally avoided collecting data on race. G. Brame (personal communication, 2007) reported that:

I did not set out or want to study what role if any race plays in SM. In part that is because, for economic and socio-political reasons, minorities are under-represented in the Scene. BDSM communities cut across all socio-economic, political lines; but while I suspect just as many minorities engage in kinky sex, . . . they do not tend to join sexual communities in number, the way mainstream white people do, so the population is very heavily skewed towards white. . . .

L. Wolf (personal communication, 2008) . . . pointed out that, "Racial categories are not readily translatable in international research; they are just not meaningful because there is no continuity or agreed upon definitions".

The studies we review represent six different countries, and whereas most of them were conducted in the "West", one was completed in Hong Kong (Ho, 2006). Ho's study underlines the complexity of defining race, especially at an international level. As ethnic Chinese living in Hong Kong, Ho's respondents are either 0 percent people of colour or 100 percent people of colour, depending on the perspective used to judge. In their own social context, they are members of the social majority, and thus would not appropriately be considered people of colour (0%) in a numerical minority sense because the point of reference is the same racial and ethnic group. They would also evade the stigma, social pressures and disadvantages attached to being a "minority" not only numerically, but with the attendant deprivation of social privileges. In the larger discussion in literature, however, Ho's respondents could be classified as 100 percent people of colour, because they are all Chinese. In that construction, they are people of colour in relationship to the external white measure, rather than their internal measure of majority status.

This begs the question "People of color from whose perspective?" The term *people of colour* implies some neutral colourless other to which they are compared—the white perspective that underlies both mainstream poly and kink communities, as well as the research that seeks to understand them. M. Pallotta-Chiarolli (personal communication, 2008) highlighted this linguistic issue and clarified that:

In Australia, the respectful term is "indigenous Australians." Indigenous Australians find the term "people of color" offensive, as it doesn't differentiate between their experiences of colonialism, genocide, etc. and the experiences of Africans and others who are migrants and refugees.

Although in the United Kingdom some scholars use Black and Minority Ethnics to describe these populations, *people of colour* remains the standard language in the United States. We use it here not only because it is the standard scholarly rhetoric of our academic peers, but more importantly because it is the language our respondents use. Even so, the terminology is difficult and we acknowledge the problematic nature of the term. . . .

Recommended strategies

There are a number of strategies that scholars can use to deal with these research issues. First and most obviously, we must attend to them. Measuring class and race/ethnicity should be a standard research practice, on par with measuring gender. . . . Sexual value systems and the meanings attached to particular sex acts and arrangements stem from Western, white heteropatriarchal standards of sex/gender normativity. Race is never not related to one's topic of study: race confounds the study of sexuality precisely because of its continued neglect.

Learning to deal with the complexities of measuring race is key to the success of inclusive research and requires a broader discussion of race, nationally and internationally. Scholars can use journals, conferences and online forums to discuss methodological issues and establish greater international communication. On an individual methodological level, researchers can ask respondents to self-identify racially and/or ethnically. When reporting their results, scholars should explain their terms and respondents' social locations to give readers the information necessary to understand respondents' racial and ethnic identities in the context of their own cultures.

Second, scholars studying this area must continue to oversample people of colour. This becomes complex, as who is "of colour" is difficult to define. . . . This process must be accomplished with sensitivity to avoid the mistakes of previous researchers who, in the process of getting to "know and understand" certain groups, have been guilty of fetishizing "the other" (Probyn, 1993).

Third, researchers in this area must shift their recruitment strategies to include a far broader range of options rather than relying so heavily on the Internet and homogeneous snowball samples (often coordinated through email or other Internet interactions as well). Although these sampling and recruitment methods remain useful, such complete dependence on them produces skewed and monochromatic samples. . . .

Fourth, increasing the number of researchers of colour examining these groups could significantly boost participation among kinksters and polyamorists of colour. Methodological literature indicates that disadvantaged groups such as people of colour (Collins, 1996), lesbians (England, 1994) and women (Gilbert, 1994) may be more open to participate in research conducted by those perceived as members of their own underprivileged group. . . .

Fifth, it is important to understand the reasons why individuals do *not* identify with particular alternative sexual communities, despite participating in behaviours characteristic of those communities. Such an understanding will facilitate a broader examination of the full range of people having kinky sex or multiple partners and the ways in which people select the components of their identities. Furthermore, these studies can illuminate privileges that facilitate or hinder peoples' associations with particular identities, and the interlocking web of characteristics such as age, gender, race/ethnicity, ability, orientation, and experience that shape individuals' sexualities in idiosyncratic ways.

Sixth, researchers should study behaviour, as well as identity. Studies that include only people who identify as kinky or poly will miss these potential respondents whose behaviours may match the target population but whose self-identification precludes their participation in the study. This creates a double bind, because researchers must clearly define their sample populations to conduct a coherent analysis. On the one hand, relying on self-identification as a selection criteria has a long tradition in sexualities research (Berenson, 2002; Chung and Katayama, 1996; Golden, 1996; Rust, 2000) in part because it has proven problematic in the past when researchers assigned identities to behaviours and in part because it can be difficult to build a sample when investigating sexual minorities, and seeking people who self-identify and are willing to participate in research is one of the primary ways in which sexuality scholars have been able to conduct their research. On the other hand, relying on self-identification eliminates the category of persons who engage in the behaviour but do not classify it as an organising principle for self-identification, thus missing large sections of the population of practitioners (Savin-Williams, 2005; Vrangalova and Savin-Williams, 2010).

Most importantly, researchers must move beyond simple "bean counting" to an examination of how race impacts the ways in which people "do" sexuality. How does being Black and queer impact sexuality? Asian and gay affect sexual practices? Latina and poly shape identity formations? Native American and kinky affect participation in public organisations? To date, too many studies neglect to address these issues because they begin from a white frame, often fail to problematise race and thus assume a homogenous sample, all despite (potentially) statistically accounting for race.

CONCLUSION

Finally, we must consider that, on some level, there might not be anything to be *done* about the dearth of people of colour in samples of sexual minorities. It is possible that polys and kinksters of colour are less interested in being studied and potentially less desirous of engaging in public sexual interactions or becoming a member of a group founded on sexual status that might then provide contact with researchers—in effect self-selecting to abstain from community and research involvement. Clearly, attempting to recruit people of colour into research samples will provide a far richer analysis of kinky and poly relationships, groups and communities. But is the virtual absence of people of colour in these samples so passive— so completely based on exclusion? We think

not. In fact, to assume that the "we" (the almost exclusively white researchers who study alternative sexual communities) can control what "they" (people of colour who have unconventional sex lives) do is the ultimate act of hubris. Maybe "they" *elect* not to participate.

This dynamic is obviously far more complex than simple omission or self-selection. It calls into question the meanings of alternative sexualities and those who found their identities upon them. Who is authorised to determine the particular characteristics associated with any specific identity, much less function as the arbiter of those with legitimate claims to assume that identity? How people construct their identities is, to varying degrees, up to them: identity is *inherently* self-defined. To deny that choosing to or refraining from claiming a specific sexual identity is a self-directed, socially constructed, moment is to deny people of colour sexual subjectivity. . . .

Too frequently white researchers approach their studies from a white frame of reference and thus (usually unintentionally) exclude consideration of people of colour from the original research design. This initial exclusion then telescopes through the research project to shape the questions researchers ask and the populations they query. Research on poly and kinky populations remains impoverished to the degree that people of colour, as well as other social and numerical minorities such as people with disabilities and the aged, are absent from the analyses. There must be more sexuality research, particularly research that is mindful of privilege and intersections of oppression. . . .

NOTES

1. The authors do not claim the right to define others' identities, but rather use the term *pervert* to describe polyamorists both because conventional society views them as such and for theoretical coherency.

2. Because the initial study was not designed to be a longitudinal research project and the Institutional Review Board (IRB) required that [Sheff] destroy all identifying

information, [Sheff] was only able to locate those members of [her] my original sample who retained enough contact with mainstream polyamorous communities to receive the calls for participation in the follow-up study. . . . Of the 17 previous respondents [Sheff] was able to locate, 15 agreed to participate in the follow-up study. Only one of the previous respondents who consented to an interview no longer identified as polyamorous and had started seeking a monogamous relationship.

3. On the questionnaire, there was a line adjacent to the *other* category for self-identification. The responses were so varied that [Sheff] aggregated them in to a single category of *other* for ease of discussion.

4. Ken Haslam coined the term "swolly" to denote the intersection between poly and swing behaviours, identities and communities.

5. PolyResearchers is an online discussion group that facilitates research into polyamory by allowing members to share resources, research findings and seek each others' advice. . . .

REFERENCES

Attias, B. 2004. Police free gay slaves: Consent, sexuality, and the law. *Left History*, 10(1): 55–83.

Barker, M. 2005a. On tops, bottoms and ethical sluts: The place of BDSM and polyamory in lesbian and gay psychology. *Lesbian & Gay Psychology Review*, 6(2): 124–129.

Barker, M. 2005b. This is my partner, and this is my . . . partner's partner: Constructing a polyamorous identity in a monogamous world. *Journal of Constructivist Psychology*, 18: 75–88.

Barker, M., and Langdridge, D. 2010. *Understanding non-monogamies*. London: Routledge.

Barker, M., and Ritchie, A. 2007. Hot bi babes and feminist families: Polyamorous women speak out. *Lesbian & Gay Psychology Review*, 8(2): 141–151.

Bauer, R. 2008. Transgressive and transformative gendered sexual practices and white privilege: The case of the dyke/trans/BDSM communities. *Women's Studies Quarterly*, 36(3/4): 233–253.

Bauer, R. 2010. Non-monogamy in queer BDSM communities: Putting the sex back into alternative relationship practices and discourse. In M. Barker and D. Langdridge (Eds.), *Understanding non-monogamies*. London: Routledge.

Berenson, C. 2002. What's in a name? Bisexual women define their terms. *Journal of Bisexuality*, 2(2/3): 9–21.

Brame, G. 2000. *BDSM/Fetish demographic survey*. Retrieved from http://www.gloriabrame.com/therapy/bdsmsurveyresults.html

Califia, P. 2000. *Public sex: The culture of radical sex*. San Francisco, CA: Cleis Press.

Chakraborty, J., and Bosman, M. 2005. Measuring the digital divide in the United States: Race, income, and personal computer ownership. *The Professional Geographer*, 5(3): 395–410.

Chung, Y., and Katayama, M. 1996. Assessment of sexual orientation in lesbian/gay/bisexual studies, *Journal of Homosexuality*, 30(4): 49–62.

Collins, P. 1996. *Black feminist thought*. New York, NY: Routledge.

Collins, P. 2005. *Black sexual politics: African Americans, gender, and the new racism*. New York, NY: Routledge.

Connolly, P. 2006. Psychological functioning of bondage/domination/sado-masochism (BDSM) practitioners. *Journal of Psychology & Human Sexuality*, 18(1): 79–120.

Cook, E. 2005. *Commitment in polyamorous relationships* (Unpublished Master of Arts in Liberal Studies (Psychology)). Regis University, Denver, CO. Retrieved from http://www.aphroweb.net/papers/thesis/chapter-4.htm

Dalton, S. 2001. Protecting our parent-child relationships: Understanding the strengths and weaknesses of second-parent adoption. In M. Bernstein and R. Reimann (Eds.), *Queer families, queer politics: Challenging culture and the state* (pp. 201–220). New York, NY: Columbia University Press.

England, K. 1994. Getting personal: Reflexivity, positionality, and feminist research. *The Professional Geographer*, 46(1): 80–89.

Gilbert, M. 1994. The politics of location: Doing feminist research at "home". *The Professional Geographer*, 46(1): 90–96.

Golden, C. 1996. What's in a name? Sexual self-identification among women. In R. Savin-Williams and K. Cohen (Eds.), *The lives of lesbians, gays, and bisexuals: Children to adults* (pp. 229–249). Fort Worth, TX: Harcourt Brace.

Hammers, C. 2008. Making space for an agentic sexuality?: The examination of a lesbian/queer bathhouse. *Sexualities*, 11(5): 547–572.

Hammers, C. 2004. Queer exclusions and corporeal silences: The promises and limitations of queer in public sexual spaces. In S. Hines and T. Sanger (Eds.), *Transgender Identities: Towards a social analysis of gender diversity*. London: Routledge.

Haritaworn, J., Lin, C., and Klesso, C. 2006. Poly/logue: A critical introduction to polyamory. *Sexualities*, 9(5): 515–529.

Hequembourg, A. 2007. *Lesbian motherhood: Stories of becoming*. New York, NY: Routledge.

Ho, P. 2006. The (charmed) circle game: Reflections on sexual hierarchy through multiple sexual relationships. *Sexualities*, 9(5): 547–564.

Jackson, L., Ervin, K., Gardnera, P., and Schmitt, N. 2001. The racial digital divide: Motivational, affective, and cognitive correlates of internet use. *Journal of Applied Social Psychology*, 31(10): 2019–2046.

Kantor, A., and Neubarth, M. 1996. Off the charts: The internet. *Internet World*, 7(12): 44–51.

Keres, J. 1994. Violence against S/M women within the Lesbian community: A nationwide survey. *Female trouble*. National Coalition for Sexual Freedom. Retrieved from http://www.ncsfreedom.org/index.php?option=com _keyword&id=214

Klein, M., and Moser, C. 2006. SM (sadomasochistic) interests in a child custody proceeding. *Journal of Homosexuality*, 50: 233–242.

Klesse, C. 2007. *The specter of promiscuity: Gay male and bisexual non-monogamies and polyamories*. London: Ashgate Publishers.

Langdridge, D., and Barker, M. 2007. Situating sadomasochism. In L. Darren and B. Meg (Eds.), *Safe, sane and consensual*. New York, NY: Palgrave MacMillan.

Matthews, M. 2006. *Lesbians who engage in public bondage, discipline, domination, submission, and sadomasochism (BDSM)*. Ann Arbor, MI: ProQuest Company.

Moser, C., and Kleinplatz, P. 2006a. Introduction: The state of our knowledge on SM. *Journal of Homosexuality*, 50: 2–3.

Moser, C., and Kleinplatz, P. 2006b. *Sadomasochism: Powerful pleasures*. New York, NY: Routledge.

Mosher, C., Levitt, H., and Manley, E. 2006. Layers of leather. *Journal of Homosexuality*, 51(3): 93–123.

Mossberger, K., Tolbert, J., and McNeal, R. 2008. *Digital citizenship: The Internet, society, and participation*. Cambridge, MA: MIT Press.

Noel, M. 2006. Progressive polyamory: Considering issues of diversity. *Sexualities*, 9(5): 602–620.

Ono, H., and Zavodny, M. 2003. Race, Internet Usage and E-Commerce. *The Review of Black Political Economy*, 30(Winter): 7–22.

Pallotta-Chiarolli, M. 2006. Polyparents having children, raising children, schooling children. *Lesbian & Gay Psychology Review*, 7(1): 48–53.

Polikoff, N. 1993. We will get what we ask for: Why legalizing gay and lesbian marriage will not dismantle the legal structure of gender in every marriage. *Virginia Law Review*, 79(7): 1535–1550.

Probyn, E. 1993. *Sexing the self: Gendered positions in cultural studies*. New York, NY: Routledge.

Richters, J., de Visser, R., Rissel, C., Grulich, A., and Smith, A. 2008. Demographic and psychosocial features of participants in bondage and discipline, 'sadomasochism', or dominance and submission (BDSM): Data from a national survey. *The Journal of Sexual Medicine*, 5(7): 1660–1668.

Ridinger, R. 2002. Things visible and invisible. The leather archives and museum. *Journal of Homosexuality*, 43, 1–9.

Roderick, G. 2008. The stylisation of internet life?: Predictors of internet leisure patterns using digital

inequality and status group perspectives. *Sociological Research Online*, 13: 5.

Rust, P.C. 2000. Bisexuality: A contemporary paradox for women. *Journal of Social Issues*, 56: 205–221.

Sanday, P. 2007. *Fraternity gang rape: Sex, brotherhood and privilege on campus*. New York, NY: NYU Press.

Sandnabba, N., Santtila, P., Alison, L., and Nordling, N. 2002. Demographics, sexual behaviour, family background and abuse experiences of practitioners of sadomasochistic sex: A review of recent research. *Sexual and Relationship Therapy*, 17(1): 39–55.

Sandnabba, N., Santtila, P., and Nordling, N. 1999. Sexual behavior and social adaptation among sadomasochistically oriented males. *The Journal of Sex Research*, 36(3): 273.

Savin-Williams, R. 2005. *The new gay teenager*. Cambridge, MA: Harvard University Press.

Schippers, M. 2000. The social organization of sexuality and gender in alternative hard rock: An analysis of intersectionality. *Gender and Society*, 14(6): 747–764.

Sharma, J., and Nath, D. 2005. Through the prism of intersectionality: Same sex sexualities in India. In G. Misra & R. Chandiramani (Eds), *Sexuality, gender, and rights: Exploring theory and practice in South and Southeast Asia*. New Delhi: Sage.

Sheff, E. 2005a. *Gender, family, and sexuality: Exploring polyamorous community* (Ph.D. dissertation). University of Colorado at Boulder, Colorado.

Sheff, E. 2005b. Polyamorous women, sexual subjectivity, and power. *Journal of Contemporary Ethnography*, 34(3): 251–283.

Sheff, E. 2006. Poly-hegemonic masculinities. *Sexualities*, 9(5): 621–642.

Sheff, E. 2007. The reluctant polyamorist: Auto-ethnographic research in a sexualized setting. In M. Stombler, D. Baunach, E. Burgess. D. Donnelly, and W. Simonds (Eds.), *Sex matters: The sexuality and society reader*, 2nd ed. (pp. 111–118). New York: Pearson, Allyn, and Bacon.

Sheff, E. 2010. Strategies in polyamorous parenting. In M. Barker and D. Langdridge (Eds.), *Understanding non-monogamies* (pp. 169–181). London: Routledge.

Spengler, A. 1977. Manifest sadomasochism of males: Results of an empirical study. *Archives of Sexual Behavior*, 6(6): 441–456.

Steinbugler, A. 2005. Visibility as privilege and danger: Heterosexual and same-sex interracial intimacy in the 21st century. *Sexualities*, 8(4): 425–443.

Taormino, T. 2008. *Opening up: A guide to creating and sustaining open relationships*. San Francisco, CA: Cleis Press.

Tomassilli, J., Golub, S., Bimbi, D., and Parsons, J. 2009. Behind closed doors: An exploration of kinky sexual behaviors in urban lesbian and bisexual women. *The Journal of Sex Research*, 46(5): 438–445.

Vrangalova, Z., and Savin-Williams, R. 2010. Correlates of same-sex sexuality in heterosexually identified young adults. *The Journal of Sex Research*, 47(1): 92–102.

Warf, B., and Grimes, J. 1997. Counterhegemonic discourses and the internet. *Geographical Review*, 87(2): 259–274.

Waskul, D. (Ed.), 2004. *Net.seXXX: Readings on sex, pornography, and the Internet.* New York, NY: Peter Lang.

Weber, A. 2002. Survey results: Who are we? And other interesting impressions. *Loving More Magazine*, 30:4.

Weinberg, T., and Kamel, G. 1995. S&M: An introduction to the study of sadomasochism. In T. Weinberg (Ed.), *S&M: Studies in dominance & submission.* New York, NY: Prometheus Books.

Weinrich, J.D. 1997. Strange bedfellows: Homosexuality, gay liberation and the internet. *Journal of Sex Education and Therapy*, 22(1): 58–66.

Weitzman, G. 2006. Therapy with clients who are bisexual and polyamorous. *Journal of Bisexuality*, 6(1/2): 137–164.

Weitzman, G. 2007. Counseling bisexuals in polyamorous relationships. In B. Firestein (Ed.), *Becoming visible: Counseling bisexuals across the lifespan* (pp. 312–335). New York, NY: Columbia University Press.

White, C. 2006. The spanner trials and changing laws on sadomasochism in the UK. In P. Kleinplatz and C. Moser (Eds.), *Sadomasochism: Powerful pleasures.* New York, NY: Hayworth Press.

Willey. A. 2006. Christian nations, polygamic races, and women's rights: Toward a genealogy of non/monogamy and whiteness. *Sexualities*, 9(5): 530–546.

Wright, S. 2006. Discrimination of SM-identified individuals. *Journal of Homosexuality*, 50(2): 217–231.

THERE'S MORE TO LIFE THAN SEX? DIFFERENCE AND COMMONALITY WITHIN THE ASEXUAL COMMUNITY

MARK CARRIGAN

In 2001 the American college student David Jay, exasperated by the lack of awareness he found concerning asexuality, created the Asexuality Visibility and Education Network (AVEN). It started as a small page on his university account but has since grown rapidly, acting as a catalyst for a burgeoning and increasingly self-conscious asexual community which, as well as its active online message board, now includes a varied offline social life and an increasingly visible campaigning presence. AVEN members throughout the world produce pamphlets, lead workshops, arrange local meetings and speak to the media (Brotto et al., 2010). Partly as a result of these efforts, asexuality has recently begun to attract the attention of the popular media. Articles such as Westphal (2004), Cox (2008) and Bootle (2009), as well as a recent BBC documentary tied to the latter piece, have helped introduce asexuality to a wider audience. Yet as Scherrer (2008) notes there remains a striking shortage of academic literature exploring asexuality.

This has begun to change recently with the international attention that Bogaert (2004) brought to asexuality. In this article Bogaert engages in a secondary analysis of a large pre-existing dataset to investigate demographic characteristics associated with asexuality. This dataset included a question about sexual attraction, which offered the response of "I have never felt sexually attracted to anyone at all" which Bogaert takes to be indicative of asexuality (Bogaert, 2004: 281). Through operationalizing asexuality this way, Bogaert found that 1.05 percent of the respondents were asexual and, on this basis, developed an account of demographic predictors of asexuality. Bogaert (2006) attends to the conceptual questions implicit in his earlier article and argues for the utility of treating asexuality as a distinct sexual orientation. He also makes a case against the reduction of asexuality to clinical pathology. However both articles rest on a problematic definition which, though brought into explicit focus, remains uncorrected in the later work. While Bogaert (2004) makes an interesting case as to demographic predictors of a lack of sexual desire, this suggests little about factors associated with taking on an asexual identity because, as he recognizes himself, the categories are not co-extensive. Also this definition itself is variously stated as exhibiting "little or no sexual attraction to males or females", "having no sexual attraction for either sex" and "having no attraction for males or females" (Bogaert, 2004: 279–281). The data presented in the present article suggest that "attraction" is far from synonymous. Furthermore defining asexuals as experiencing no sexual attraction, rather than low, excludes a sizable number of those who self-identify as asexual. . . .

Prause and Graham's (2007) was the first research project to explicitly recruit self-identified asexuals. It involved a small qualitative study as a preliminary to a larger online survey study, which included both sexual and asexual respondents. The survey study was primarily focused on exploring the differential characteristics which obtain between sexual and asexual individuals and, as such, falls within the same etiological framework as Bogaert (2004, 2006). However Prause and Graham (2007: 353) suggest that "given the rich data derived from these interviews about self-identified asexuals, future qualitative studies might be warranted. Similarly Brotto et al. (2010) report on another mixed-methods study of asexuality. . . .

Scherrer (2008) represents a commendable example of the use of such methods, conducting open-ended online surveys investigating the identities and lived experience of self-defined asexuals recruited through the AVEN website. While Prause and Graham (2007) and Brotto et al. (2010) only approached the issue of identity tangentially, Scherrer (2008) does so explicitly and this concern frames the analytic focus of her article. She collects data concerning the meaning that the sexual holds for self-identified asexuals, their self-understanding as to the ontological basis of their identity, the role which romance plays in the formation of this identity and the intersections between this identity and other minority sexual identifications. . . .

Scherrer argues that "inquiry into asexual identity is important as those researchers who have explored asexuality have primarily approached it as either a behaviour (lack of sexual acts) or a desire (lack of desire for sexual acts)" (Scherrer, 2008: 622). This focus flows from their concern for etiology rather than subjective insight; in other words, causal explanation rather than hermeneutic understanding. However, as Scherrer (2008) suggests, identification as asexual cannot be divorced from either the subjective meanings which that identification holds for individuals nor the processes of intersubjective negotiation through which such meanings emerged. Tacit confirmation of this claim can also be found in Prause and Graham's conclusion (2008) that distinguishing between the sexual and the non-

sexual is a crucial part of coming to an asexual identity. Therefore even an explicitly etiological inquiry must attend to the subjective dimensions of asexual experience. . . .

The identities and lived experience of self-identified asexuals are the specific focus of the present article because . . . a diverse range of experiences fall under the popular AVEN (2009) definition of an asexual as "someone who does not experience sexual attraction". A recognition and understanding of this diversity, as well as the commonalities which facilitate it, is a necessary starting point for research that attempts to understand and/or explain asexuality and asexuals. To this end I conducted a mixed-methods qualitative study of self-identified asexuals utilizing semi-structured interviews and online questionaires, as well as an analysis of asexual forums, websites and blogs. . . .

This article presents the initial results of this study, relating particularly to the diversity within the asexual community and the underlying commonalities which facilitate that diversity. In doing so it aims to elucidate personal and communal aspects of asexual experience which, as well as being sociologically interesting in their own right, illustrate the subjective dimensions to the causal processes which etiologically focused researchers investigate. . . .

METHODS

My initial interest in asexuality arose through two friends who identified as asexual. It was through conversations with them, as I attempted to understand some initially very unfamiliar ideas, that I began to plan this research. These informal conversations, which continued throughout the research process, helped me acquire a basic familiarity with the language and ideas prevalent within the asexual community. It also allowed them to offer assessments of my emerging interpretations (Ezzy, 2002: 68).

The research itself was mixed-methods, combining semi-structured interviews with an open-ended online questionnaire and a thematic analysis of a variety of asexual forums, websites and blogs. . . . In total I conducted eight interviews. . . . A total of 174 people responded to the questionnaire and, of these, 130 completed it in full. . . . I have anonymized all distinguishing names and details from the interviews. Where names are given, these are pseudonyms for interviews. Where names are not given, these are questionnaire respondents.

ASEXUAL IDENTITY AND EXPERIENCE

The front page of the AVEN website (2009) defines an asexual as "someone who does not experience sexual attraction" and due to the popularity of the AVEN website this definition has been highly influential. While many identify under this definition, it is also widely seen as an umbrella term and, as such, is not taken to be an exhaustive description of the attitudes and orientations prevalent amongst asexuals. The umbrella term acts as a common point of identification rather than constituting a shared identity per se. While it undoubtedly represents a commonality in the self-understanding of many asexuals, it also conceals a significant degree of heterogeneity as to the personal reasons that individuals have for defining as asexual. In this section I will present and explain the diverse range of identifications that constitute this heterogeneity. Here is a small selection of the answers given by questionnaire respondents when asked why they identify as asexual:

I'm 25 years old and I've never had a crush on or any sexual attraction to anybody and I honestly get confused when people say they're "horny" because I have no idea how that feels. I'm not denying there's still a chance that I may be "a late bloomer" or just "haven't found the right person for me yet", but constantly defining this aspect of myself in terms of

"maybe someday" just felt like I was kidding myself. As far as I'm concerned, an asexual is simply someone who doesn't feel the desire to actually have sex, and for me, it fits.

I am simply uninterested in having sex, not repulsed, and if my partner insisted on having sex I would oblige willingly. It's just not the emotional connection for me that it seems to be for most other people.

I define as asexual because it explains how I can find males attractive without wanting to have sex with them, as well how that lack of sexual desire for males does not translate to wanting to have sex with females.

I am not at all interested in sex. It doesn't disgust me or bother me . . . it just doesn't register.

I identify as asexual because I do not get the urge to have sex. If I do have sex, I only like it for the first minute or so, and then I am satisfied and would like to stop. Basically, sex is not necessary in my life and I could live without it. There are other things I would rather do. Being an asexual doesn't mean that one can't be attracted to people. I'm attracted to both males and females but mostly in terms of emotional or intellectual attraction.

I find the idea of sex utterly disgusting. I honestly think I would vomit if I ever had sex.

A variety of reasons lead individuals to identify as asexual and before we can begin to understand them it is important to gain some acquaintance with the terms that asexuals use to describe themselves. As Chasin (2009) observes "within the asexual community, there is a clear and creative generation of new words and discourses, which asexual people use to explain and shape their experiences, relationships and identities." . . . Many are conversational terms among asexuals but others, such as "sex-averse" and "a-fluid", are more rarely encountered. . . .

A central distinction is made between romance and sex, which may be counter-intuitive from the perspective of a mainstream sexual culture that regards the latter as the culmination of the former. As Scherrer (2008: 636) puts it, "asexual identities make explicit a romantic dimension of asexuality as distinct from an asexual identity based on lack of sexual attraction." Many asexuals feel attraction but without any sexual component to it, instead regarding it as romantic and/or emotional. Others feel attraction that is distinctly aesthetic. As one questionnaire respondent wrote,

I've never understood how beauty relates to sex. I can love and be intensely passionate about people, however. When I say somebody is beautiful, I mean it in the sense that a picture is beautiful, or an animal, or a child. It has nothing whatsoever to do with sex though, and doesn't relate to sex in my mind.

Within this group of romantic asexuals, orientation varies: heteroromantics only feel romantic attraction to the opposite sex, homoromantics to the same sex, biromantics to both sexes and panromantics without reference to sex or gender.[1] Some romantic asexuals actively seek relationships because, as Brotto et al. (2010) suggest, "the closeness, companionship, intellectual and emotional connection that comes from romantic relationships" is personally desirable. Others are simply open to the possibility, given their experience of romantic attraction, without actively seeking it or assigning it any priority in their lives. Aromantic asexuals experience no romantic attraction and have no desire to pursue romantic relationships. In some cases this may be a matter of simple lack of interest and a prioritization of the platonic, as in the case of one respondent who, when explaining their lack of interest in ideas of romance, wrote "I vastly prefer to maintain close friendships. I would rather have a romantic relationship than only have loose friendships, however." Similarly Scherrer (2008) found that "self-identified aromantic asexual individuals tend to describe their ideal relationships as primarily friendship-like." In other cases though, romance may be actively and viscerally rejected, as exemplified by the respondent who wrote of their "*disgust*" at ideas of romance and annoyance at the priority commonly ascribed to them within people's lives.

With regards to sex, attitudes also vary. Those who are sex-positive[2] endorse sex as positive and healthy, sometimes with a concomitant intellectual and/or cultural interest in it, without experiencing sexual desire or seeking to engage in it themselves. Those who are sex-neutral are simply uninterested in sex: as one typical respondent put it, "I don't find it disgusting, just not something I care to experience." However some may be willing to have sex in certain contexts. For instance Paul, a 22-year-old asexual, told me of his willingness to have sex within the context of a committed relationship:

Assuming I was in a committed relationship with a sexual person—not an asexual but someone who is sexual—I would be doing it largely to appease them and to give them what they want. But not in a begrudging way. Doing something for them, not just doing it because they want it and also because of the symbolic unity thing.

In some cases, as with Paul, this willingness had been enacted in the context of an actual relationship whereas for others it was simply an openness to the possibility. As well as pleasing a partner, for some people it may be a source of intimacy and confirmation without being enjoyed in a way that is, per se, sexual. This qualifies the findings of Brotto et al. (2010) that asexuals who have sex do not find it brings them closer to their partners, although for others it may simply be a "chore" which is a term that came up at numerous points in the interviews and questionnaires. However for those who are sex-averse or anti-sex, the idea of sex, let alone the actual practice of it, is deeply problematic. Here too there is variety, as some are rendered mildly uncomfortable by sex ("I don't really like it, because it feels a bit weird and unnatural to me, and genitalia aren't exactly beautiful"), others find themselves slightly revolted by it ("I find the whole idea of sexual contact slightly repulsive") and then there are those for whom it is disgusting and deeply distressing. Although for those who are anti-sex these feelings are a generalized response to sex, for others, those who are sex-averse, the feelings relate to themselves and not to others:

I believe I differ from many other repulsed (as opposed to indifferent) asexuals in that it is purely the idea of *myself* having sex that I find disgusting. The idea of others doing it does not bother me in the slightest, apart from finding depictions of female sexuality a little uncomfortable as it reminds me of myself.

However not everyone fits under the strict definition supplied by the umbrella term. Demisexuals experience sexual attraction as a consequence of romantic attraction but not independently of it. When they are emotionally connected to a person sexual attraction may ensue but only directed toward that person. Grey-a is a catch-all term which refers to those who fall in the perceived grey area between sexual and asexual. For instance one questionnaire respondent described himself as physically though not sexually attracted to other men; he did not desire sex but was able to take physical pleasure in it. A-fluid was a term used by Jess, a 21-year-old asexual, which described her own asexuality in terms of a more general fluidity held to apply to sexuality as a whole. While Jess was the only participant to use the term a-fluid it was striking that the theme of sexual fluidity emerged in a number of the questionnaires and interviews.

IDENTITY AND COMMUNITY

. . . . One of the most curious features of the asexual community is that it has simultaneously facilitated the articulation of individual difference and the solidification of a communal

identity. In this section I will explore the commonalities found within asexual experience with a view to understanding the genesis of the earlier discussed diversity and gaining insight into the common trajectory through which individuals come to identify as asexual. . . . The following is the story told by a questionnaire respondent of how they came to identify as asexual:

The year I was sixteen (and for some time after) I spent a lot of time in the company of a few people who were very sexual and it was through their near-constant talk of sex that I was finally convinced that sexual attraction was real. I had heard that something would happen to make you want to have sex with another person, but I had never experienced it myself. In fact, I did not really believe that a person could have physical feelings "down there" that they identified as sexual feelings, despite having learned what erections etc. were in my health class. I thought everyone was like me, until my classmates and friends begin to talk about sex. Then I realized that I was not like them, and for a while I thought I must be immature . . . except that in every other way they seemed so much *less* mature than I. I thought there might be something wrong with me, except that I am otherwise in perfect health. Then, one night while I was surfing the Internet, I came across an embarrassingly girly website which included, as one of its pages, a "definitions" page. I suppose the point was that sheltered girls with Internet access could look up all the words they were afraid to ask their parents about and get solid, medical definitions. The first word on the list was "asexual" and it caught my interest, because I had never heard it before. I clicked on the link which read the same thing AVEN does, "Asexual: a person who does not experience sexual attraction" and it was like coming home. I knew immediately that this was me and that I wasn't alone.

Although the specific biographical details vary greatly with different individuals, many of the elements of the foregoing story are typical of asexual experience: adolescent experience gives rise to a sense of difference from a peer group, provoking self-questioning and the assumption of pathology (i.e., "I thought there might be something wrong with me") before self-clarification is attained through the acquisition of a communal identity. In the case of this story a sense of difference emerged for the individual relatively late. While she had been exposed to sex education it had left her with an attitude of disbelief; given that nothing in her own experience had confirmed what she was told about sexual feelings it led her to regard the notion as fictitious. When she saw incontrovertibly that her peer group experienced such feelings, it left her suddenly aware of how she differed from those around her. Perhaps she was simply immature? Or was there something wrong with her? Neither of these self-explanations were sustainable so it was only when she became acquainted with the notion of asexuality that she was able to achieve self-clarification, as the acquisition of a communal identity brought the self-questioning process to an end. As noted, the details of the story are biographically specific but the elements (individual difference, self-questioning, assumed pathology, self-clarification and communal identity) typify asexual experience more widely.

My results indicate that a sense of individual difference was a crucial biographical factor in the lives of the majority of participants and this reflects the findings of Brotto et al. (2010) in their in-depth telephone interviews. However the point at which individuals start to develop a sense of individual difference varies, as does what they consider constitutes that difference. . . .

As well as coming to some awareness of this difference, inevitably under their own descriptions, it must constitute something to be explained before it sparks self-questioning. For instance Eve, a 20-year-old asexual, came to an awareness during her school years of the apparent interest in sex that her peers showed but assumed it was merely a pretence at adulthood. As she put it to me, "I've never attempted

to be one of the cool kids. So I thought they were getting peer pressure that I wasn't privy to because I wasn't one of the cool kids. I wasn't in those conversations". So during her school years this sense of difference never sparked self-questioning because it was explained away as merely *apparent*. It was not the case that her peer group were sexual and she was not but rather that her peer group wanted to act "cool" and, since she differed in this respect, that was the cause of the apparent difference. So a nascent sense of asexual difference (i.e., an awareness of not experiencing sexual attraction while being surrounded by those who do experience it) was subsumed under a prior and independent sense of being different, in respect of not being one of the "cool kids." It was not until she had left school that she began to believe that in fact the behaviour of her peer group was, at least in part, genuine and that, unlike her, they did have a desire for sex. This in turn prompted self-questioning which, in conjunction with an article she had read at an earlier age (Westphal, 2004), led her to begin identifying as asexual. In contrast to Eve, many participants recounted how an apparent sense of difference failed to develop into an active concern because of an awareness of temporality. As in the case of James, a 35-year-old asexual, describing how he felt as a young undergraduate, when he was planning on travelling the world prior to undertaking doctoral studies,

I assumed that I would find someone one day but I'm not ready for that at the moment and it's far more convenient not to be tied down with a girlfriend at the moment. Particularly planning to do a PhD and then go overseas and get some overseas experience. It's convenient not to have a girlfriend and have to drag someone halfway around the world.

James's immediate concerns, his PhD and his impending travels, acted to displace any sense of difference he felt; while his peer group may have been concerned with sex and relationships, his immediate involvements occupied him, leading to the assumption that at some point a concern for sex and relationships would organically emerge within his life. This sort of temporal displacement can be engendered by the attitude of others, as in the (rather typical) cases of the respondent whose friends tried to convince him "that my asexuality was just a phase, and that someday I would find 'the right person', whatever that means" or the respondent who described how "some people have thought that I'm a late bloomer and that I just haven't found the right person yet." These are pernicious ideas for someone trying to come to a sustainable understanding of their apparent difference, as the recurring thought that it might all just be a "phase" (i.e., a quirk of their present state rather than a significant and enduring feature of them) precludes the sort of self-questioning which might allow self-clarification. It also illustrates how the demand of others for explanation (e.g., "why aren't you interested in dating and sex?") is intimately intertwined with self-questioning (e.g., "why aren't I like everyone else?"). . . .

When self-questioning begins to take place, the individual attempts to make sense of their apparent difference by forming explanations of it. In a very important sense this process is, at least tacitly, a theoretical one; the individual tries out different hypotheses in the search for one that "fits" (a term which came up repeatedly in the questionnaires) and facilitates self-clarification. Depending on their placement within society, individuals have access to differing material and cultural resources and this conditions the potential explanations available to them. Perhaps the most readily available explanations are those that make sense of individual difference in terms of an assumed pathology. Prause and Graham (2007) found that 56.2 percent of their asexual participants understood asexuality to involve some form of pathology. My own data suggests that this

finding is misleading when considered in terms of biographical trajectory; it underrepresents the assumption of pathology at an early stage of self-questioning but overrepresents it among those who have come to an asexual identity. Identity acquisition is a temporal process, which takes place within changing social and cultural contexts and, as such, personal factors associated with it must be understood in reflexive and biographical terms.

This capacity for reflexivity can be seen in the way that pathologizing explanations are considered but rejected, as the individual comes to other, more affirming, self-understandings. Even so, when the theory in question is a personal one, ensuing from a highly individualized process of self-questioning, it still lacks the affective force that a communal identity can provide. For instance David, an asexual man in his 30s, explained to me how he reasoned that there must be others like himself who, as he saw it, stood as an opposite to bisexuals (attraction to either gender rather than both) but that "it was always a slight drag on my psyche, that there's no else like me so I'm not sort of 'normal' as such". It was only when he later came across an article in a newspaper that this "drag" ended as his theory was confirmed through discovery of the asexual community. There are, however, cases where the individual pursues a pathologizing sequence of explanations at great personal cost. For instance witness the experience recounted by one respondent,

I came to identify as asexual this way: I have never understood the desire to engage in the acts that define sex, from kissing on down the list. . . . This issue haunted me for years until finally, when I was engaged to be married, I knew that I couldn't walk down the aisle until I solved what we called the sex issue. So I went into therapy. I explored every corner and crevice of my childhood. After psychological reasons were ruled out, I took hormone tests to see if my body was functioning properly. When the tests came back as "normal", I still lobbied to be prescribed low-levels of testosterone. I got the prescription and took testosterone to jump-start my sex drive. The testosterone didn't work, so I switched to progesterone after a few months. I lamented the feeling that I was somehow "broken", that I was somehow "less of a person". I continued to look for psychological reasons in therapy. I continued to engage in sexual activities even though I'd rather take the LSATs or swim the Pacific than be naked with another human. After over a year of hormone therapy, after exclusive sex therapy with my partner, after the kind of lament and struggle that so many of the kids I mentor experience when they're struggling with their sexuality, my relationship ended. I continued in therapy, and I continued to wonder why I was broken. It was another six months before I finally identified myself as asexual, and coming out to myself and the world was one of the most liberating experiences I've ever encountered . . . I'm comfortable with it. I'm relieved by it. . . . It makes all the sense that nothing made before and I'm glad to not spend countless hours worrying about why I am broken anymore. I'm happy, and I'm proud of my asexuality.

While the possibility of identifying as asexual was foreclosed, this respondent was led through successive attempts to explain her apparent pathology; none were sustainable but equally none served to question the underlying assumption that the absence of sexual desire represented an unwelcome abnormality. The fact no underlying problem was found through the various forms of therapy she undertook only seemed to make the problem more elusive, rather than problematizing the assumption of pathology itself. As she put it later in the questionnaire, "I only ever had sex because I thought I was *supposed* to, not because I *wanted* to".

This "sexual assumption", which sees sex as a culmination of and perquisite for human flourishing, was encountered by a majority of participants. This ubiquitous affirmation of sex, its perceived normalcy and centrality to a healthy life, can preclude self-acceptance as a culturally

available option for asexuals because of the concomitant repudiation of asexuality as pathological. While this assumption would not necessarily command universal assent when considered reflectively, the pervasiveness of the assumption becomes apparent when considering the experience of asexuals, as do some of the pernicious consequences of it. It invites attempts to negotiate understandings of human flourishing which do not hinge on sexual expression and sexual fulfilment, and the steady growth of the asexual community demonstrates, inter alia, the success of these attempts. For instance the aforementioned respondent eventually came across AVEN and, as we saw, her lack of sexual desire became a source of pride and affirmation rather than worry and pain. The discovery of an asexual community can have a profound effect on the self-understanding of the individual, as exemplified by the typical experience of another respondent,

In a period where I was more actively trying to figure things out, I found the asexual community. Not experiencing sexual attraction made sense to me as a way of explaining this difference I couldn't understand. More than this, I felt that I could relate to the experiences of other asexuals. This was very important to me because it counteracted the message that people like me don't exist. Now I identify as asexual as a matter of solidarity with other asexuals.

The acquisition of a communal identity serves to ward off pathology and ambiguity, as an individual sense of difference gives way to the sense of a shared communal trait. As another respondent put it, "it validates my non-interest and allows me to remember that it doesn't make me broken". In this way it facilitates a self-clarification and self-acceptance, which was previously lacking, leading the individual from an individualized questioning process to participation in a shared community. However it is crucial to note that a minority of participants did achieve self-clarification independently of the community and, when this was the case, the community held little for them beyond, for instance, a potential source of asexual partners. . . . For this group an absence of sexual desire has been relatively unproblematic and they see it as a minor difference, with the consequence that they do not identify strongly with the community. . . .

So while there was a prevalent trajectory among participants (individual difference, self-questioning, assumed pathology, self-clarification and communal identity) it should not be taken as an exhaustive account of the experience of being asexual. Rather it represents certain core aspects in the experience of those who share common subjective attitudes and orientations within socio-cultural contexts which, while diverging in many ways, share a generic repudiation of asexuality.

CONCLUSION

This article has presented the preliminary findings of my research, as pertaining to the differences and commonalities within the asexual community, with the intent of offering a hermeneutically grounded starting point for further inquiry into the area. While the AVEN (2009) definition of an asexual as "someone who does not experience sexual attraction" commands widespread assent, it also conceals a great degree of diversity. A range of attitudes and orientations toward sex and romance can be found within the asexual community, as well as an evolving vocabulary within which to articulate these differences. This diversity stands in contrast to the common experiences and needs which bring people to the asexual community, as different individuals in different circumstances nonetheless share common core experiences as they confront socio-cultural contexts which affirm sex and repudiate asexuality. In fact these common-

alities facilitate the aforementioned diversity, as similar experiences lead people to the online and offline forums where discussion and debate allows the asexual vocabulary to expand, thus articulating individual difference while simultaneously entrenching participation in the community. . . .

However further questions remain which are beyond the scope of the data collected. It seems plausible to suggest that there have been individuals who have not experienced sexual attraction long before the relatively recent emergence of a socioculturally available asexual identification. If this is so then how have structural and cultural changes facilitated the emergence of asexual identities? How might the emergence of the asexual community, as a corporate agent, generate further structural and cultural change? I would tentatively suggest that the emergence of asexuality has its roots in what Weeks (2007: 3) calls the "long, convoluted, messy, unfinished but profound revolution" taking place in our intimate lives and that, furthermore, it represents a continued outgrowth of this still unfinished process. The individualization of sexual choice has, it seems, led to the problematization of sexual desire itself and it is only through understanding the potential trajectory of this process that we might begin to sketch out the consequences it could hold for society, culture and intimate life.

NOTES

1. Although this could be construed as similar to biromanticism, in actuality it rests on a crucial distinction: the object of one's romantic attraction may *happen* to be of either sex or gender but this is incidental to the attraction. Sex or gender are not experienced as being relevant to romantic attraction.

2. It should be noted that although this is a term used online, only one survey respondent (describing herself as "very sex-positive") and no interviewees explicitly used it to describe themselves. As a term it also has political connotations, pertaining to the "sex-positive movement", which many asexuals who are positive about sex would distance themselves from.

REFERENCES

AVEN. 2009. Asexuality Visibility and Education Network homepage. URL (accessed 6 July 2009): http://www.asexuality.org/home/

Bogaert AF. 2004. Asexuality: Its prevalence and associated factors in a national probability sample. *Journal of Sex Research* 41(3): 279–287.

Bogaert AF. 2006. Toward a conceptual understanding of asexuality. *Review of General Psychology* 10(3): 241–250.

Bootle O. 2009. No sex please: An asexual life. *The Independent*, March 17 URL (accessed 12 June 2009): http://www.independent.co.uk/life-style/health-and-families/features/no-sex-please-an-asexual-life-1646347.html.

Brotto LA, Knudson G, Inskip J, Rhodes K and Erskine Y. 2010. Asexuality: A mixed methods approach. *Archives of Sexual Behavior* 39(3): 599–618.

Chasin CJ. 2009. *Amoeba in Their Habitat. The Asexual Community: An Ecological and Discursive Perspective*, URL (accessed 30 March 2010): http://www.asexualexplorations.net/home/documents/Amoeba_Chasin_2009.pdf.

Cox P. 2008. First person: We're married, we just don't have sex. *The Guardian*, September 8 URL (accessed 12 June 2009): http://www.guardian.co.uk/lifeandstyle/2008/sep/08/relationships.healthandwellbeing.

Ezzy D. 2002. *Qualitative Analysis: Practice and Innovation*. London: Routledge.

Prause N and Graham CA. 2007. Asexuality: Classification and Clarification. *Archives of Sexual Behaviour* 36(3): 341–355.

Scherrer K. 2008. Asexual identity: Negotiating identity, negotiating desire. *Sexualities* 11: 621–641.

Weeks J. 2007. *The World We Have Won*. Oxford: Routledge.

Westphal SP. 2004. Feature: Glad to be asexual. *New Scientist Magazine*, October 14 URL (accessed 12 June 2009): http://www.newscientist.com/article/dn6533-feature-glad-to-be-asexual.html.

Grandma does *WHAT!?*: Talking with Older Adults about Sex

Christina Barmon, Alexis A. Bender, and Elisabeth O. Burgess

When we teach about sexuality and aging, the overarching sentiment we get from students of all ages is that they don't want to know about their parents' or grandparents' sex lives. They joke that they know they must have had sex at least as many times as they have children, but they don't want to know any details or talk to them about it. Even those of us who consider ourselves open-minded in regard to sex don't necessarily want to talk to our parents or grandparents about their fantasies or kinks. In pop culture, with the recent exception of the cougar or MILF[1,] sex is the domain of the young and conventionally attractive. Many younger people mistakenly assume that older people do not want sex and are so undesirable and unattractive that nobody would want to have sex with them; they wouldn't even want sex with each other. Contrary to these sentiments, older adults do want and have sex. Hopefully, we can start to think about parents and grandparents in a very different way, and maybe begin to communicate more effectively with them.

Although the frequency of sexual activity does decline with increasing age, even more so for women than for men (Waite et al., 2009), this decline cannot simply be attributed to age. Many older adults are still interested in sex and engage in a wide variety of behaviors. In the largest nationally representative study on sexuality and aging to date, Waite et al. (2009) found that 84 percent of men and 62 percent of women between the ages of 57 and 64 years old reported having penile-vaginal sex with a partner in the past year. That number declined to 38 percent of men and 17 percent of women in the 75–85 year-old age group. While fewer older adults are sexually active, those who are having penile-vaginal sex tend to have it once or twice a week. This trend remains fairly constant, declining only at the oldest ages (Waite et al., 2009).

While penile-vaginal intercourse decreases with age, other forms of sexual activity, such as mutual masturbation, oral sex, and masturbation, tend to remain stable over the life course (Bretschneider and McCoy, 1988; Lindau et al., 2007). Waite et al. (2009) found a decline in masturbation and oral sex with age. However, they attribute this to cohort differences rather than to age differences. They found that while more than half of older adults between the ages of 57 and 64 reported engaging in oral sex, this reduces to 28 percent of men and 36 percent of women between the ages of 75 and 85. The trends were similar for masturbation. This sharp difference between those two age groups most likely represents cohort differences between those who were teenagers in the 1940s and those who came of age during the sexual revolution.

While there is evidence of a decrease in sexual activity with chronological age, the largest predictors of decline in sexual activity among older adults include lack of available partners, health status, and the mental and physical health of one's partner (Gott and Hinchliff, 2003; Lindau et al. 2007). A lack of interest in sexual activity is much more dependent on life circumstances than age. In fact, a life course perspective on sexuality suggests that people most likely have similar fantasies, interests, and desires toward the end of their lives as they did in earlier years (Burgess, 2004). In other words, if someone places a higher or lower priority on sex at a younger age, this probably remains constant with age. Similarly, if someone is kinky at a younger age, they will most likely retain their kinkiness as they get older. At all ages, opportunity structure and physical functioning influence our sexual experiences.

It is not just our students who shy away from talking to older adults about sex. Preliminary findings from our research in assisted living facilities show that caregivers and family members also have a difficult time with this topic (Burgess et al., 2011). As life expectancy increases and a larger percentage of our population is over 65 years old, we are more likely to interact with older adults in our families, workplaces, and communities. Family members, health professionals, social workers, direct care workers, assisted living and nursing home staff members should be aware of older adults' needs for privacy, autonomy, access to information regarding sexual health, and the ability to make their own decisions. Furthermore, institutional policies should reflect those needs and provide training as necessary.

We propose that communication about sexuality and older adults requires the same straightforward approach as with any age group. Sex education and access to protection must be part of the conversation. For example, due to physiological changes as we age, sexual pleasure, functioning, and desire may shift (Burgess, 2004). Sex education can introduce new sexual techniques, positions, and aids to enhance sexual pleasure to accommodate physiological changes that begin in middle age. Additionally, many older adults do not think that they are vulnerable to sexually transmitted infections (STIs). There is a dearth of nationally representative data on STIs, but scholars have found that the population of older adults with HIV/AIDS is growing (Lindau et al., 2007, and Fritsch, 2005, in this volume). Lifelong sex education would provide aging individuals with the tools to make healthy decisions about sexual activity. Finally, when some older adults face limitations due to cognitive impairment, families and caregivers should openly confront ethical issues, such as the ability to consent to sex. All of these subjects require efforts to achieve comfort communicating about sex across age groups. We will, no doubt, all learn something from the conversation.

NOTE

[1] The term "MILF" (Mom I'd Like to Fuck) is a pop culture slang term popularized by the movie *American Pie* and primarily associated with teenage boys who are lusting after a friend's mom they think is hot (Taormino, 2007). The term "cougar" is a derogatory slang term used to describe a middle-aged woman who is perceived as predatory and is involved in or interested in relationships with younger men.

REFERENCES

Bretschneider, Judy G. and Norma L. McCoy. 1988. "Sexual Interest and Behavior in Healthy 80–102-Year-Olds." *Archives of Sexual Behavior.* 17(2): 109–129.

Burgess, Elisabeth O. 2004. "Sexuality in Midlife and Later Life couples." Pp. 437–454 in *The Handbook of Sexuality in Close Relationships*, edited by John H. Harvey, Amy Wenzel and Susan Sprecher. Mahwah: Lawrence Erlbaum Associates Inc.

Burgess, Elisabeth O, Alexis A. Bender, Christina E. Barmon, and Marik Xavier-Brier. 2011. "Not My Mother:" Challenges of Intergenerational Communication about Sex and Intimacy in Assisted Living. Presentation at Gerontological Society of America Annual Meetings, November 2011, Boston, MA.

Fritsch, Teresa. 2005. "HIV/AIDS and the Older Adult: An Exploratory Study of Age-Related Differences in Access to Medical and Social Services." *The Journal of Applied Gerontology.* 24: 35–54.

Gott, Merryn and Sharron Hinchliff. 2003. "How Important is Sex in Later Life? The Views of Older People." *Social Science & Medicine.* 56: 1617–1628.

Lindau, Stacy T., Philip L. Schumm, Edward O. Laumann, Wendy Levinson, Colm A. O'Muircheartaigh, and Linda J. Waite. 2007. "A Study of Sexuality and Health Among Older Adults in the United States." *New England Journal of Medicine.* 357: 762–774.

Taormino, Tristan. 2007. "The Rise of MILFs and Mommies in Sexual-Fantasy Material." *The Village Voice*, October 30. Retrieved January 26, 2012 from http://www.villagevoice.com/2007- 10-30/columns/the-rise-of-milfs-and-mommies-in-sexual-fantasy-material/.

Waite, Linda J., Edward O. Laumann, Aniruddha Das, and L. Philip Schumm. 2009. "Sexuality: Measures of Partnerships, Practices, Attitudes, and Problems in the National Social Life, Health, and Aging Study." *The Journals of Gerontology Series B: Psychological Sciences and Social.* 64: 56–66

"RECLAIMING RAUNCH"? SPATIALIZING QUEER IDENTITIES AT TORONTO WOMEN'S BATHHOUSE EVENTS

CATHERINE JEAN NASH AND ALISON BAIN

INTRODUCTION

It's a Thursday evening at a private party at Club Toronto on Mutual Street just south of Toronto's gay village. Beneath a rainbow awning outside a converted Victorian redbrick house, a queue of women stretches along the sidewalk. At 8:45 p.m. the queue begins to move forward. Volunteer security guards in yellow shirts and headsets check I.D. before letting women purchase tickets that gain them entrance into a women-only bathhouse event called the Pussy Palace.

Behind a heavy black door, buzzed open for each patron, a volunteer sits on a stool and hands out a clean, white towel to each guest. Music pulsates loudly from a turntable set up beside a fake fireplace in a red painted lobby. Lesbian porn plays on a widescreen TV beside the entrance to a faux-Grecian outdoor pool. On the pool deck, women, in different stages of dress and undress and some in different stages of transition from female to male and male to female, claim plastic desk chairs and sunbeds while others play in the pool. A cupid game is set up on the wall of the lifeguard station. Women line up to have numbers playfully written on their bodies. These women will check back later to see if anyone has left a message for them.

Another exit off of the pool deck leads to a hot tub. In the steamy red glow of a glassed changing room, women [peel] off clothes and step into the bubbling water. A notice on the wall of the changing room lists where different Pussy Palace services can be found: temple priestess and portraits, 333; g-spot room, 444; dancers, outside room 222; massage, 3rd floor;

cupid game, 2nd floor; dungeon space, 4th floor, breast play, 3rd floor, top of stairs; food, 2nd floor; and sling room, 222.

On the second floor, under the bright lights of a chandelier, two leather-backed armchairs are set up for lap dancing. Volunteer dancers sift through discarded lingerie strewn on the floor and pull on their outfits of choice before each dance. To their left is the locker room. In here, women, who have brought outfits to change into, swap street clothes for combinations of leather, rubber, lace, mesh and cotton. Further along the corridor, a deaf volunteer sells cold water and pop, and oversees a table of finger food. A wide, wooden-banistered staircase leads up. With each new floor the lighting is dimmer and the hallways narrower. There are mirrors everywhere; reflections distort, disorient and startle.

Most of the doors on the third floor are closed. The musky scent of essential oils wafts from beneath a door that has a sign-up sheet for sexual counselling with a "temple priestess." Around the corner, a room is set up for erotic massage. The rest of this floor contains a labyrinth of small rooms. Those rooms not yet in use have clear plastic waste disposal bags draped over their door handles. A sliver of light beneath doors suggests occupancy; and the occasional gasp or moan of pleasure confirms it. Other doors are wide open, the

From "'Reclaiming Raunch'? Spatializing Queer Identities at Toronto Women's Bathhouse Events" by Catherine Jean Nash and Alison Bain, *Social & Cultural Geography*, Volume 8, Issue 1, 2007, pp. 47–58. Copyright © 2007 Routledge, reprinted by permission of the publisher (Taylor & Francis Group, http://www.tandf.co.uk/journals).

turquoise plastic mattress covers of the single beds exposed and piles of crumpled linen and screwed-up toilet paper on the floor.

Up the final flight of stairs to the fourth floor, the air is close. There is hardly room to squeeze by the door marked "g-spot" where a young woman in a white bikini with soft pink rabbit ears ushers patrons in. Further along the corridor, the floor of the sadomasochism room is sticky underfoot. A black vinyl-covered straight-backed bench provides seating. Two women dressed in black leather wield whips and direct scenes that use the floor-to-ceiling chains. Out the back door of this attic dungeon the fire escape descends again to the pool deck below.

Pussy Palace events, like the one described above, began in the fall of 1998 and have been held on an irregular basis once or twice a year since then. The inaugural Pussy Palace, Canada's first women-only bathhouse event, was attended by over 350 women. The organizers of the Pussy Palace event interpret their high attendance figures as indicative of an untapped desire in Toronto's queer women's community for spaces supportive of uninhibited, casual and playful sexual encounters. These women's bathhouse events are a new form of women's sexualized social space that, as of yet, has gone unexamined in scholarly literature.

In North American gay male culture, the bathhouse is more than just a building, a space or an "event." It can be interpreted as a sexual sanctuary, a safe haven, a second home to some, a hiding place to others. For over a century, bathhouses have functioned in North American cities as places for men to engage in same-sex activity. . . .

The bathhouse holds a highly regarded place in historical socio-political lexicons depicting the distinctive gay male culture of Western cities, yet it is no longer exclusive to gay men (Dangerous Bedfellows, 1996; Hocquenghem, 1978; Hodges and Hutter, 1974; Jeyasingham, 2002; Leap, 1991). Women, as our Toronto case study demonstrates, are developing a bathhouse culture of their own.

For the Toronto Women's Bathhouse Committee (TWBC), the Pussy Palace events are expressly political projects, designed to contest preconceived ideas about women's gendered and sexualized selves—"reclaiming raunch," as one of the organizers put it, for women and their sexual expression. More specifically, the TWBC takes issue with what they regard as the deleterious impact of a particularly inflexible and restrictive version of lesbian feminist ideologies on the ability of women, and lesbians in particular, to experience the full range of sexual and gender expression. Accordingly, the committee seeks to undo the perceived "damage" wrought by these ideologies through the "queering" of spaces—that is, through the establishment of locations that provide the opportunity to experience alternative sexual practices and behaviours. In so doing, the TWBC has grappled with challenging questions about: what "queering" spaces actually means in policy and practice; the politics and power relations inherent in sexualized space; and the contested nature of body, gender, and sexual identity formation and interaction.

In this [reading], we examine both the possibilities and the problems evoked in the TWBC's creation of a particular form of "queer" sexualized space. We argue that the process of "queering space," is neither a neutral nor an uncontested process. This is especially the case given that the TWBC deploys a particular definition of "queer" that paradoxically opens up a space of liberating sexual possibility but also disciplines gendered and sexualized identities. This paradox of simultaneous liberation and constraint, in turn, raises broader questions about the political and social implications of queer politics and practices which needs more critical and self-conscious reflection. This [reading[, . . . critically examin[es] queer identities and spaces. . . .

Our research project is informed by the current geographical work on the production of gendered and sexualized urban spaces. Feminist geographers, in particular, have argued for a spatialized understanding of the constitution of social identities (gender, sexuality, "race," age, ability) and hierarchical social relations (e.g. Duncan, 1996; McDowell, 1999). . . . [S]pace and identity are linked in the fluid constitution of sexualized and gendered selves (Bell and Valentine, 1995; Bouthillette, 1997; Lauria and Knopp, 1985; Rothenberg, 1995; Valentine, 1993a, 1993b, 1995). Our consideration of the constitution of women-only bathhouse space is attentive to the ways in which sexuality and gender are constituted (un)intentionally within that space. . . .

[B]athhouse events represent an attempt to reformulate space so as to provide for the opportunity to experience alternative behaviours and practices through which new identities, in this case queer identities, can come into being. . . .

[T]he TWBC seeks to create a space that fosters behaviors that challenge not only the heteronormative prohibitions on women's gendered and sexual expression but also long-standing lesbian feminist proscriptions on lesbians' sexual and gendered expressions of identity. . . .

While it is clear that the TWBC is striving to create a queer space . . . . when women transgress gay male space and appropriate gay male sexual norms to produce queer space, they . . . . challenge essentialist lesbian subjectivities and sexual practices, and disrupt fixed understandings of gendered and sexualized selves. . . .

QUEER BEGINNINGS: THE PUSSY PALACE

. . . . In the spring of 1998, the owner of "Come As You Are," a women's sex shop who had attended a women's bathhouse event in Seattle, met with friends . . . to discuss the possibility of organizing a similar event. . . . [T]he . . . non-profit Toronto Women's Bathhouse Committee (TWBC) was born with a mandate to address what the original organizers saw as the serious lack of institutional spaces for women to develop a "sexual imagination, literature, techniques, art or knowledge" (Dhanani and Fong, 1998: 211). Committee members approached several Toronto bathhouse owners to use their facilities for women-only events. Only one institution, Club Toronto, agreed. . . .

BEHIND THE SCENES OF QUEER EROTICISM: FEMINISM IN PRACTICE

The TWBC positions their agenda firmly within a feminist framework and regards their endeavours as politically transformative for women. Their main goal has been to challenge what they regard as the debilitating effects of what they term "1980s lesbian feminist politics" as well as what they regard as wider mainstream prohibitions against women's sexual expression. In formulating an alternative sexual and gendered identity the TWBC uses the label "queer," and draws on particular conceptualisations of class and gay male sexual experience to describe the sexual behaviours or practices they seek to encourage. Accordingly, the committee seeks to challenge a perceived gendered code of sexual passivity among women by "queering" women's sexualities and genders through a particular spatial strategy; the bathhouse event.

Defining Queer Sexuality: Lesbian Feminism, Gay Men and Class

. . . . [The TWBG's] . . . self-appointed mandate is to open up the possibility for non-monogamous and casual sexual practice in order to break down the constraints imposed in an earlier historical era. . . . TWBC uncritically positions gay male casual sexual activities (e.g., public cruising and bathhouse sex) as the standard of sexual freedom to which women should aspire. This includes the ability to have multiple partners and to practise sadomasochism and alternative sexual practices previously eschewed by lesbian feminists as wrong or personally damaging.

The TWBC also argues that because women have not had the sexual freedom to explore their sensual worlds, they have not developed "the same institutions as gay men have for anonymous sex" including spaces such as the bathhouses and the cultural cues and practices facilitating sexual activity in other public spaces (Dhanani and Fong, 1998: 21). One of the goals of the TWBC is to create an institutional basis that encourages women to engage in more casual sexual expression not only in the bathhouse events but in public spaces such as parks and bars as well as private house parties and clubs. Having the opportunity to actually use gay male bathhouse space, designed specifically for the experience of casual sex, was seen as central to the TWBC's goal of creating alternative practices and institutional spaces.

In formulating an alternative view of what lesbian sexuality should encompass, the TWBC has embraced a stereotypical view of working-class sexuality as coarse, common, vulgar, lustful and uninhibited—attributes deemed appropriately "raunchy". Staging the bathhouse events at what was described as a "grungter" club used by older "street boys" and a more working-class clientele, was deliberate in terms of celebrating working-class sexuality. With a "hamster cage" odour, sticky floors, peeling paint and a rundown appearance, Club Toronto was understood to communicate a particular queer sexual identity. . . .

Defining Queer "Women": The Politics of Transgenderism

The TWBC embraces spatial "queerness" by billing the Pussy Palace as a queer women's event and a queer women's space. Accordingly, within the queer space of the bathhouse, the TWBC encourages people to explore, experiment or play with gender, and to challenge the rigidity of gender categories, stereotypes, norms and expectations. The TWBC does not take a bio-determinist view of gender nor does it assume that women are biologically female. Instead, the TWBC has broadly positioned the category "woman" in a gender continuum that includes biological females, as well as transgendered people who are non-operative, pre-operative or post-operative.[1] As such, it does not expect people's gendered self-presentation (the ways in which they act, dress or live) necessarily to correspond directly with behaviours habitually associated with the genitalia they possess (Armstrong, 2004). The inclusion of male-to-female (MTF) and female-to-male IFTM) transsexuals originally, however, elicited much debate. The central conundrum being that the body could no longer be regarded as fixed, yet it became unclear how to delimit the boundaries of "woman" for the purposes of admitting gender-ambiguous persons into a women-only space. Much anxiety centered on how maleness might be expressed in a sexualized space where semi-naked people identify as women yet may possess male genitalia. In the end, an invitation to transgendered women was nonetheless included in the advertisement for the first Pussy Palace event. A founding organizer sketched out some of the dilemmas and the goodwill involved in discussing transgendered women:

We had to have discussions about what the policy on trans-women was. What are we doing? And what does trans-woman mean? Those were interesting discussions. In the end, we just went: 'trans-women were welcome'. We didn't know what that was going to mean. We didn't necessarily know how we were going to deal with those reactions. We just knew that that was the right thing to do. (Julia, 5 December 2003)

Yet, then and now, TWBC members hold different ideas about transgendered women. As a committee they did not completely work through what it might mean to invite people into a space that while queer, was also politically marked as belonging to women.[2]

At the first bathhouse, several transgendered women reported transphobic experiences whereby spaces emptied upon their arrival and direct and indirect comments were made: "So, like, are you the token fag?"; "Are you an honorary woman for the night? A friend of the committee?"; "He must work here"; "Don't you know that this is a women's bathhouse?"; "Is *that* a man?" (Saleh, 1999: 7). Reactions centred on recognizing biological markers of maleness in what is billed as a women's space. Paradoxically, there seemed to be a greater appreciation of masculinity in FTM transgendered bodies as "dyke boys" and butches than in MTF bodies. As a member of the security team explained: "'A lot of the women that are there have more trouble with folks that are transitioning from male to female than the reverse because I think that there's this idea that the female to male is almost on a continuum of masculinity in a female body" (Joss, 1 April 2004)[3]. Interestingly, in the queer women's community, where transitioning is increasingly common, FTMs are more highly regarded as sexual partners than MTFs, not only for the reason that Joss suggests, but also because attraction to an FTM can operate through a reconfiguration of the butch–femme binary. As Hemmings (2002) explains, many FTMs learn to express their sexual desire as butches in lesbian communities, and they are therefore more easily welcomed.

Eventually, word of transphobic experiences filtered back to the TWBC, inspiring diversification of the committee through recruitment of a MTF with strong ties to the trans-community and an ability to act as a consultant on transgender issues. Upon joining the committee, she undertook a survey of the trans-community's impressions of the Pussy Palace. The survey results demonstrated the need for a more overt statement of the inclusiveness of the bathhouse events and inspired the development of a transgender policy circulated to participants prior to an event and posted on the Pussy Palace website:

Transsexual/transgendered women and trans-men are welcome at the Pussy Palace, as are all women in our community, and as such they must be treated with respect by other participants at the Pussy Palace. If you are uncomfortable with their presence or cannot guarantee you will treat them with respect, it is better if you don't attend. . . . This is non-negotiable. Anyone harassing women who are trans will be asked to leave.[4]

Initially, however, the policy did not embrace trans-men. It was only when a FTM who had attended events while transitioning confronted committee members about the policy's non-inclusiveness that the wording was changed. . . . [T]he committee concluded that: "Trans-men have always been a part of our community. We're not going to start excluding them now. End of discussion" (Carolyn, 5 May 2004). Given the prevalence of butchness and "female masculinity" more generally, the committee determined that FTMs and MTFs, in whatever stage of transition, should be welcomed. While some lesbian women were (and are) concerned about the masculinization of lesbian culture, others argue that "because there's a lot of women that are transitioning to become something other than a woman, it's unavoidable— you have to spread your mind open to the idea of men in your community and women that associate with them aren't as huge of a demon" (Jan, 5 June 2004).

Despite developing a trans-friendly policy and creating spaces designed to encompass alternative sexual practices, the TWBC cannot control desire:

You know, they can't make people hit on each other and they can't make sure that everybody's having a great time, but they can create the space where that's a possibility. And it takes some damn fucking brave trans-women to show up in that space and to use it as their own, and to really politicize women. And that's what's happened. (Joss, 1 April 2004)

For queer space to generate the queer identities envisioned by the TWBC, desire must be multi-directional and multi-faceted. Yet desire in the Pussy Palace remains conditioned by more traditional constructions of gendered and sexualized identities. It is the traditional "butch–femme" binary expressed in biologically female bodies that is most commonly displayed in the "queer" spaces of the "women's" bathhouse. There are FTMs and MTFs present, but they do not represent the majority of participants, nor do they occupy the most central and visible spaces. Ironically perhaps, one can question how "transgressive" a space may actually be when it does little to break down the classical binary categories of gender. In the present case, the women's bathhouse events seem to simply reassert an understanding of gender as the various performances of the traditional masculine and feminine and does little to undermine or support alternative understandings that are radically undermining or subversive.

CONCLUSIONS

With each reincarnation of the Pussy Palace, the Toronto Women's Bathhouse Committee attempts to constitute what they define as a "queer" women's bathhouse culture that challenges a lesbian feminist de-sexualization of lesbianism, and that facilitates and embraces "other" bodies and genders. The TWBC sees itself as embracing an "erotic-positive" (Kinsman, 1996) "pro-sex feminism" (Califia, 2003) that emphasizes: the value of pleasure; the importance of a woman's right to control her own body; the expansion of choice and consent in people's erotic lives; and the acceptance of contradictions within communities and individuals. For the TWBC, a pro-sex feminism

attempts to foster an inclusive atmosphere where lesbians, gay men, transgendered people, sex workers and other sexual minorities share a common "queer" space. . . .

While queer may ostensibly be about the rejection of categories, identities and subject positions, the practice or enactment of queer at the bathhouse seems to be about the creation of more and equal opportunities to act out various formulations of classic masculinity and femininity rather than the dismantling of these constructs all together (Jeffreys, 2003).

The bathhouse events also raise difficult questions about the constitution and availability of material and symbolic spaces where lesbian identities and ways of being can be expressed. . . . [T]he advent of a queer politics has resulted in loss of lesbian space, both geographically and intellectually. Lillian Faderman (1997: 226) notes, for example, that queer women "now seem to have given up entirely a *conceptual* space for themselves as lesbians in adopting the term and the concept 'queer'" (emphasis added). Further, there is a case to be made that so-called "queer dykes," through their privileging of gay male culture and their dismissal of lesbian feminism, have contributed to the accelerated loss of material lesbian social and cultural spaces as well with the closure of women's bookstores, coffee houses, bars and clubs (Case, 1997; Jeffreys, 2003). . . .

The experience at the TWBC events demonstrates that while queer spaces are often presented as progressive, inclusive and tolerant, these same spaces may be exclusionary or limiting despite efforts at openness. The way in which the TWBC puts "queer" into a spatialized practice demonstrates how queering space is a process through which identities and spaces are disciplined, bounded and defined. The TWBC utilizes a definition of 'queer' that draws on gay male sexual practices, involves a specific understanding of working-class sexuality and allows for the inclusion of transgendered bodies. In so doing, the TWBC creates a space in which certain expressions of gendered and sexualized identities are valorized and others are discounted. In particular, certain forms of female masculinity are celebrated and the identity of "lesbianness" because of its association with monogamy, domesticity and emotion is rejected. . . . While the goal of queering of space is laudable in its celebration of difference, its vague current usage by the TWBC imposes its own sets of marginalizations that flatten out identities that have made many lives meaningful.

NOTES

1. The term "transgender" is shorthand for people who live outside of normative sex/gender relations (Namaste, 2000).

2. For example, the name of the event, Pussy Palace, is not necessarily trans-inclusive as not all trans-people have genital surgery and possess a "pussy."

3. Several authors have written about the erasure of femmes and femme-phobia within lesbian culture and history (Harris and Crocker, 1997, Rugg, 1947).

4. <www.pussypalacetoronto.com> (accessed 24 August 2004).

REFERENCES

Armstrong, J. 2004. The body within: the body without. *Globe & Mail* 12 June: R4.

Bell, D. and Valentine, G. (eds) 1995. *Mapping Desire: Geographies of Sexualities*. London and New York: Routledge.

Bouthillette, A.-M. 1991. Vancouver's lesbians. In Ingram, G. B., Bouthillette, A.-M. and Retter, Y. (eds) *Queers in Space: Communities/Public Places/Sites of Resistance*. Seattle, WA: Bay Press, pp. 213–232.

Califia, P. 2003. *Sex Changes: Transgender Politics* (second edition). San Francisco: Cleis Press.

Cote, S.-E. 1997. Toward a butch-feminist retro-future. In Heller, D. (ed.) *Cross Purposes: Lesbian Feminists and the Limits of Alliance*. Bloomington: Indiana University Press, pp. 205–220.

Dangerous Bedfellows 1996. *Policing Public Sex*. Boston: South End Press.

Dhanani, Z. and Fong, T. 1998. Wet & Wild, Xtra! 10 Sep.; 21.

Duncan, N. 1996. *BodySpace: Destabilizing Geographies of Gender and Sexuality*. London and New York: Routledge.

Erderman, L. 1947. Afterword. In Heller. H. (ed.) *Cross-purposes: Lesbians, Feminists and the Limits of Alliance*. Bloomington: Indiana University Press, pp. 221–229.

Hemmings, C. 2002. *Bisexual Spaces: A Geography of Sexuality and Gender*. London and New York: Routledge.

Hoequenghem, G. 1978. *Homosexual Desire*. London: Alyson and Busboy.

Hodges, A. and Hutter, U. 1974. With downcast gays: aspects of homosexual self oppression. In Gross, L. and Woods. J. D. (eds) *The Columbia Reader on Lesbian and Gay Men in Media, Society and Politics*. New York: Columbia University Press, pp. 551–561.

Jeffreys, S. 2001. *Unpacking Queer Politics*. Cambridge: Polity Press.

Jayasingham, D. 2002. Ladies' and "gentleman": location, gender and public sex. In Francis, K. E. and Chedgzoy, M. P. (eds) *Queer Place: Sexuality and Belonging in British and European Contexts*. Burlington. VT: Ashgate, pp. 79–88.

Kingsman, G. 1996. *Regulation of Desire: Sexuality in Canada*, second edition. Montreal: Black Rose Books.

Lauria, M. and Knopp, L. 1985. Towards an analysis of the role of gay communities in the urban renaissance. *Urban Geography* 6: 152–169.

Leap, W. (ed.) 1999. *Public Sex/Gay Space*. New York: Columbia Press.

McDowell, L. 1999. *Gender. Place and Identity*. Minneapolis: University of Minnesota Press.

Rothenburg, T. 1995. And she told two friends: lesbians creating urban social space. In Bell, D. and Valentine, C. (eds) *Mapping Desire: Geographies of Sexualities*. London and New York: Routledge, pp. 166–181.

Saleh, T. 1999. Transfixed in (lesbian) paradise. *WillyBoy* 7: 5–9.

Valentine, G. 1993a. (Hetero)Sexing space: lesbians perceptions and experiences of everyday places. *Environment and Planning D: Society and Space* 11: 395–413.

Valentine, G. 1993b. Negotiating and managing multiple sexual identities: lesbian time-space. *Transactions of the Institute of British Geographers* 18: 237–248.

Valentine, G. 1995. Queer country: rural lesbian and gay lives. *Journal of Rural Studies* 11: 113–122.

VISIBILITY AS PRIVILEGE AND DANGER: HETEROSEXUAL AND SAME-SEX INTERRACIAL INTIMACY

AMY C. STEINBUGLER

INTRODUCTION

In "Thinking Sex," a pivotal essay from the 1984 volume, *Pleasure and Danger,* Gayle Rubin argues that sexuality is organized into systems of power that reward some individuals and activities while suppressing others. Describing this "sex hierarchy" as privileging particular types of sexual behavior and corresponding lifestyles, Rubin differentiates "good, normal, natural" sexuality which is heterosexual, monogamous, procreative, same-generation, vanilla, in private, and so on, from "bad, abnormal, damned" sexuality that includes homosexual, unmarried, promiscuous, non-procreative, casual, cross-generational, or sadomasochistic sex. Rubin (1984) argues that those who practice "good sexuality" are rewarded with respectability, legality, and mobility, while those who practice "abnormal sexuality" suffer disreputability, criminality and restricted mobility. Yet Rubin omits a dimension that in the United States has long structured perceptions of sexual conduct—interracial sexuality. Interracial sexual relations, especially between African Americans and Whites, have been restricted and criminalized in the United States, while monoracial . . . heterosexuality is legally, politically and socially sanctioned.[1] . . .

[N]ot only [is] Rubin's omission . . . significant, but . . . her failure to include race as central to her theoretical frame has profound implications for the way we conceptualize sexuality. Ignoring racial difference in intimate relations, Rubin neglects the fundamental manner in which racial hierarchies have structured and regulated sexual behaviors and identities.[2] . . .

While it is notable that in 1984 Rubin overlooked interraciality in theorizing sexual hierarchy, more striking perhaps is that 20 years later a systematic empirical analysis of interracial sexuality has not been undertaken. Intersections of race and sexuality have been meticulously theorized . . . and interraciality has been examined from postcolonial and historical perspectives . . . yet sexuality scholars have not produced sustained empirical research examining heterosexual and queer interraciality.[3] . . .

In the United States the racial–sexual boundaries that have historically been most strictly and violently upheld are those between African Americans and Whites. During 300 years of chattel slavery a pernicious double standard existed regarding interracial sexual relations. Slave owners, by virtue of their racial, political, and economic power were able to take sexual license with enslaved women, and cloak these violations in silence and denial (Davis, 1983; James, 1996; Collins, 2000). To evade culpability for this abuse, Whites constructed African American women as overly sensual, lustful and rapacious, possessing such excessive sexuality that even the most strong-willed, reasonable White man eventually succumbed. In contrast, Black men might be murdered and castrated

From "Visibility as Privilege and Danger: Heterosexual and Same-Sex Interracial Intimacy in the 21st Century," by Amy C. Steinbugler. *Sexualities,* Vol. 8, No. 4, October 2005, pp. 425–443. Copyright © 2005, SAGE Publications. Reprinted by Permission of SAGE Publications.

for even the slightest suspicion of intimacy with a White woman. The myth of the Black rapist was used to justify the lynching of thousands of Black men in the late nineteenth and early twentieth centuries (Wells, 1997 [1892]). . . .

Visibility as a Form of Heterosexual Privilege

Within a heterosexual paradigm, presumptions of heterosexuality infuse the social world. Heterosexuality prescribes what is proper intimacy (Rich, 1980), who is a proper citizen (Evans, 1993; Richardson, 2000), and what is a proper family (Donovan et al., 1999; Weeks et al., 2001). . . . Paradoxically, the naturalization of heterosexuality ensures its simultaneous visibility and invisibility in social identities and social spaces—heterosexuality is "invisibly visible" (Brickell, 2000). As a normative category, heterosexuality is invisible as such, yet heterosexual intimacy is overtly visible in social spaces. . . .

Cohen argues that multiple identities—including race, gender, and class—limit the entitlement and status individuals receive from "obeying a heterosexual imperative" (1997: 442). Carbado (2000: 117) suggests a list of 44 heterosexual privileges[4] acknowledging the safety of being visibly heterosexual in public spaces in a U.S. context. He asserts that an important element of heterosexual privilege is that a man and a woman can comfortably express affection in any social setting, even a gay one, without wondering whether kissing or holding hands will render them vulnerable to violence. Carbado highlights the ease through which heterosexual couples may navigate social spaces, assuming that they will be recognized as a couple and that no violence will stem from this recognition. His list demonstrates that visibility may be one of the most fundamental heterosexual privileges. Yet for Carbado, the hypothetical heterosexual couple, while not necessarily White, is implicitly monoracial.

Research suggests that Carbado's list of privileges may not hold true for heterosexual interracial couples (Rosenblatt et al., 1995; Dalmage, 2000; Childs, 2005; Hildebrandt, 2002).

Same-Sex Intimacy: "Up from Invisibility"?

While research on heterosexuality casts visibility as an unspoken privilege, sexuality scholars proclaim a rise in visibility among gays and lesbians in the United States (Dow, 2001; Battles and Hilton-Morrow, 2002; Shugart, 2003). . . . [S]cholars of media and culture turn a critical eye to the influx of gays and lesbians into mainstream culture, announcing an "era of visibility" (Walters, 2001: xvi). Elements of this "explosion of gay visibility" include news coverage of gay-related issues, gay sport stars and rock stars, gay TV characters, gay cartoon characters, gay entrepreneurs, gay days at theme parks, a gay MasterCard and even a gay beer, Triangle Brew (Walters, 2001). Yet media representations of gays and lesbians continue to reflect a particular gay demographic—mostly White, mostly male, mostly middle, upper-middle class (Gross, 2001: 4), and implicitly monoracial.

Simultaneously, media scholars admit a significant disjunction between lived experiences and cultural representation. . . . Because heterosexuals have been established as a *socially* inscribed class and gays and lesbians as a *sexually* inscribed class, queer sexuality is relegated to private realms and out of the public eye (Richardson, 1996).[5] "When gay people engage in behaviors allowed for heterosexuals (such as holding hands and kissing), they make public what society has prescribed should be private. They are accused of flaunting their sexuality and thereby are perceived as deserving or even asking for retribution, harassment or assault" (Herek, 1992: 95). . . .

[Scholars] argue that for "non-heterosexuals," "the simple pleasures of everyday life" are constrained by knowledge of a persistent stigma about non-heterosexuality (Weeks et al., 2001: 184). The result is a constant need to "self-monitor," continually assessing the amount of risk they will take to keep safe on the streets and in their homes (2001). Using interview data from the same project, Donovan et al. suggest that even as non-heterosexuals live in constant vigilance, they also experience a lack of recognition and validation for their relationships. These respondents express a desire for fuller citizenship as a way of protecting, affirming and removing the stigma from their lives (1999: 699). Indeed, risks associated with visibility and frustrations associated with invisibility are simultaneous experiences in the lives of same-sex couples. . . .

Interracial Intimacy: In/visibility and Racial Difference

. . . When examining the relationship between visibility and sexuality, . . . scholars have continued to assume sexual relationships are monoracial. The problems with such an assumption are threefold. First, presuming monoraciality ignores the rapidly increasing number of interracial relationships in the United States.[6] Second, analyzing interracial sexual relationships allows us to see how racial difference may disrupt heterosexual privileges and further marginalize lesbians and gay men. Lastly, the violent history associated with interracial sexuality in the United States may create a difficult social environment that both heterosexual and same-sex interracial couples must navigate.

Given that the United States has been persistently haunted by the specter of interracial sexuality, little is known about how these couples experience visibility or invisibility in public spaces. Assumptions of monoraciality dominate literature on heterosexuality while relationships between White and Black men or White and Black women remain desperately undertheorized. How does this history of violence surrounding interracial heterosexual-

ity in the United States mediate the everyday visibility of interracial couples? How do queer interracial couples navigate social spaces dominated by presumptions of heterosexuality and monoraciality? . . .

RESEARCH METHODOLOGY

Data for this analysis comes from 16 interviews conducted with a nonrandom sample of eight Black/White interracial couples in Philadelphia and New York City in 2004. [F]our were heterosexual and four were same-sex couples. Of the heterosexual couples, two involved a Black man and a White woman and two involved a Black woman and a White man. Of the same-sex couples, two couples were gay and two were lesbian. This research focuses only on Black/White couples. . . .

Heterosexual Interraciality: Seen and Unseen Moments of Dislocation

A recurring experience in the narratives of interracial couples is their *visual dislocation* in public settings, e.g., while waiting in line at a food counter or a restaurant. If they are not holding hands or being physically affectionate, in a crowd of people they are assumed by the quick glances of strangers to be unrelated. Almost every couple I spoke to—regardless of sexuality—had one of these stories to tell. The significance of these instances to the couples themselves varied from indifference to annoyance and anger. For instance, Vera, a 33-year-old White woman, who has a 12-year-old White daughter, Becky, from a previous marriage and a 6-month-old daughter, Kaya, with her Black husband, Kalvin, relays her frustration at not being recognized as a family.

We'll be next to each other [in line] and the clerk will say, "Can I help you, sir?" or something like that. Just assuming we are not together, even though we all may be standing there together and it may be all four of us standing there together. The people just assume that you're not with this person because he is not White.

On some occasions, these disconnections provoked ire. Warren, a 28-year-old White man, voiced his resentment at the persistent inability of strangers to see himself and his Black wife Nakia as together, while allowing that he may possess heightened sensitivity.

WARREN For instance [we're] waiting in line for a deli and she pays and they're like, "Can I help you?" I'm like, "I'm with her. Don't you get that?" Why would I stand so close to her? People look at you, like you're not [together]. It happens all the time.

ACS How do you feel when that happens?

WARREN Well, it pisses me off. I mean small things . . . a small thing like that pisses me off. I don't understand the ignorance, but maybe I would react the same way. Because you never know who is with who or what. So maybe I'm the one that is oversensitive.

In a society in which both living and social spaces are racially segregated[7] the infrequency of interracial intimacy may render these strangers' oversights understandable or seemingly unremarkable. Persons in monoracial relationships may sometimes experience such misunderstandings. Yet the persistent and cumulative nature of these small events in the everyday lives of interracial couples is meaningful to these respondents. While these instances may not convey outright hostility or aggression, . . . they do affirm the marginal or outsider status of interracial intimacy, underscoring the normative status of mono-racial intimacy and the invisibility of closeness across racial lines.

MOMENTS OF VISIBILITY

Though heterosexual interracial couples feel invisible in particular situations, in others they endure prolonged stares or comments. The sexual–racial configuration of the couple—a White woman with a Black man versus a Black woman with a White man—had a lot to do with

when and how they felt conspicuous in public settings. When I asked Kalvin, a 30-year-old Black man married to Vera, a White woman, whether they get noticed as an interracial couple, he dryly explains strangers' stares.

I think they are more starstuck because I am an incredibly handsome man and my wife is remarkably beautiful. That's the way I look at things. You have to kind of hypnotize yourself to believe why those people are staring at you.

Kalvin's reference to hypnosis reflects the constancy of the looks and stares he and Vera receive when they are out to eat, at the mall, or at a baseball game. I ask him *who* tends to stare.

I think, in my opinion the Black race is more vocal. The Black women are upset because this White woman came and took one of their men, one of their good brothers. . . . You'll see the dirty looks from some of the Black women, who are sitting in a group of Black women *(mimics their sighs)*. You'll see them stare you up and down, and I'll grab my wife and kiss her or something. I'll give them a show if they want. It doesn't matter to me.

Kalvin's comments reveal that he is quite used to the disapproval he encounters from Black women and is not threatened by it. Similarly, Scott, a 32-year-old Black man, interprets the reactions he gets from Black women as "disapproval" or "dismissal," though he attempts to shrug them off. His White partner, Tamara, who is 30, has a more difficult time with the hostility she perceives.

I feel very threatened by Black women because I feel like they're looking at me like I've taken one of their men.

As Tamara continues, it appears that she does not fear physical retaliation but feels both concerned and frustrated by the sexual and racial politics that surround her relationship with Scott.

In addition to the displeasure they saw in the faces and comments of Black women, heterosexual couples consisting of a Black man and a White woman experienced more serious and physically aggressive threats from White men, and in one instance, a White woman. Both couples had experienced verbal confrontations involving racial slurs and threats of violence. Scott described an experience he had while dating a White woman in Greece three years before he met Tamara. While walking with his then-girlfriend through the crowded streets of a little town at 9 o'clock on a warm night in August, he was attacked by five "neo-Nazi skinheads." The attackers chased him through the streets and eventually beat him nearly to death with railroad ties. Though Scott prides himself on not living in fear of another attack, he remains vigilant and hyperaware in public settings. Incidents of physical violence were uncommon among my respondents, but most couples had a few frightening stories they carried with them.

Black women in relationships with White men received a different manner of attention and their experiences of visual dislocation appeared more typical. Moments of heightened visibility were less common, but they did occur. Warren, a 28-year-old White man, explains that when he is out with his wife, Nakia, a 29-year-old Black woman, the most common reaction they get is from Black men.

Warren [We had] problems as an interracial couple. . . . We would get a lot of troubled comments from a lot of Black men.
ACS What would they be likely to say?
WARREN They'd be like, "Whoa, sister what are you doing with this guy?" I mean it was never—on occasion once or twice was it Black women. At least not outspoken it wasn't White people. The most outspoken was Black men who did not like the fact that you could—a White man could have one of their Black sisters. They definitely did not like that. It wouldn't be a problem for a Black man, if a brother has a White woman. That's cool. The other way it doesn't work.

Warren was able to recall a few instances where he and Nakia had been antagonized by Black men, but those altercations never resulted in physical threats. . . .

The experiences of these interracial couples suggests a more nuanced connection between race, sexuality, and visibility. Interraciality serves to disrupt the workings of heterosexual privilege in two ways. First, couples report numerous experiences of visual dislocation, moments where they are rendered visibly separate from each other by strangers who do not recognize interracial intimacy. Second, when their intimacy is acknowledged by others—often precipitated by physical displays of affection—it is sometimes met with hostility or aggression. In addition, the extent to which these couples are "seen" differently by Blacks and Whites illustrates the relevance of race to the operation of heterosexual visibility.

SAME-SEX PARTNERS: INVISIBLE INTIMACY?

Like the heterosexuals I spoke to, gay and lesbian couples also discussed being in line together in a deli or grocery store and being approached for assistance separately by the counter clerk or cashier. Yet these couples also experienced a much deeper, more acute sense of visual dislocation in public places.

Both gay and lesbian couples explain that unless they are holding hands or being physically demonstrative, strangers often will not recognize their partnership. When I asked Thad, a 46-year-old White man, whose Black partner of seven years is 28, whether he thinks people recognize him and Lucas as a couple, he pauses and takes a deep breath. "You know, I don't really think about that a lot. But if I do think about it, I would assume, no. I would think that they wouldn't. I would think they would look at us and go 'What are those guys doing together?'" Leslie, a 37-year-old White woman who's been with her Black partner, Sylvia, for seven years, explains what she sees as people's inability to recognize interracial intimacy in almost any form.

I think, it's really sad, but I think that people think it's so unusual for people of different races to have any kind of intimate relationship, even a friendship, that people don't consider it, you know. And like that's why depending on where we are I feel like Sylvia's work friend, that people are like, "Oh, who's this random White woman that's with you?" Like it doesn't occur to people that we could be close—even if we weren't lovers—that we could be important to each other in that way that you might want to say hello to both of us.

For Leslie this lack of recognition is most troubling when it comes from men who approach Sylvia when the two of them are walking on the street.

A lot of times I feel invisible and particularly with men who will walk—if we're together—they'll walk straight up to her on the street and start talking to her without even making any eye contact or looking at me in any way. So I feel like when men pick her out like I'm invisible completely. Which is really gross, it's a gross feeling.

Francine, a 23-year-old Black woman, also experiences forward gestures by men when she's with her 22-year-old White partner, Kap. But unlike the story Leslie related, these advances are made while Francine and Kap are walking down a street holding hands.

Kap and I were talking about this last night, or a couple nights ago, about why we think people don't recognize us as a couple . . . or why men hit on me when she's with me. And so she was like, "You know what? They wouldn't do that if I were a Black man." And I was like "You're right . . . and if you were a Black dyke, they would probably still hit on me, but not as much." But because of who she is they do hit on me. . . . I'm talking about Black men hitting on me, because that's usually who hits on me. Um, so, I guess that's like the way that they interact with us differently because we're interracial—the fact that they don't read us as a couple or that they don't respect that even if they do read us as a couple.

Francine's continual experience of being approached by men in front of her White female partner exemplifies the ways that queer interracial relationships become invisible in certain public spaces. Her assertion that men would not approach her if Kap were a Black man reflects her sense that monoracial heterosexuality is seen as legitimate. Her suggestion that if Kap were a Black lesbian, she might still be "hit on," but "not as much" shows that even when queer intimacy is acknowledged, it is often disrespected.

Sylvia, a Black lesbian, reports that this disrespect sometimes comes in the form of insults hurled by passersby. Describing an experience she and her White partner, Leslie, had in their old New York neighborhood that was both racially mixed and had a sizable lesbian population, she explains:

There was one night we were going out and we were holding hands, two blocks from our house maybe. . . . and this family—what looked like a family, a woman and maybe three or four kids, who'd I say were all under the age of ten, Black family, I don't know where they were from—they were coming towards us and as they passed us one of the boys in the back screamed out "Dyke!". . . . And the mother's just walking and, like, keeps [walking] her family around the block.

In sum, lesbian and gay interracial couples in this study possess a much stronger sense than heterosexual respondents that their relationship is "invisible" to others in non-queer spaces. These couples violate both U.S. conventions of monoraciality and of heterosexuality and many Americans are not conditioned to recognize romantic intimacy outside of these conventions. Yet when their connection is recognized, it comes with the risk of verbal abuse. . . .

MANAGING VISIBILITY

For both the heterosexual and same-sex interracial couples I interviewed, tensions surround visibility. Feeling as if they are visually dissociated from each other in public places can be a taxing and tedious experience. Yet for many there is danger in being perceived as sexual partners. Apparent from respondents' narratives is that couples anticipate hostile reactions in particular public contexts, and often self-police or regulate their behavior so as not to draw unwelcome attention.

Almost every gay or lesbian respondent expressed feelings of cautious restraint in spaces they did not perceive to be queer or accepting of non-heterosexual identities. Many relayed an increased sense of comfort and safety, and a greater inclination to be physically affectionate in queer spaces, whether it be a bar or club, or a gay area or neighborhood. . . .

We can consider the constant self-awareness and self-regulation in which most queer interracial couples, and some heterosexual couples engage as a process of "working" one's identity (Carbado and Gulati, 2000). This work takes the form of deciding when it is safe to show physical affection and what forms of affection will be permissible. Interracial couples often do significant amounts of identity work as proactive defense.

Importantly, this self-monitoring suggests visibility and invisibility are not states of being but ongoing processes in which queer interracial couples often (and heterosexual interracial couples sometimes) engage. . . . While—depending upon the skin tone and appearance of each partner—their racial difference may be apparent, without physical contact like handholding or hugging, their sexual intimacy may be invisible. Johnson has argued that in public same-sex couples are often expected to "pass" as heterosexual friends instead of same-sex lovers, "a performance of heterosexuality that is particularly oppressive for gays and lesbians since it involves self-policing and self-regulating the most 'innocent' forms of sexual affection" (2002: 328). . . . Because many queer interracial couples are unable to perform monoraciality in

public spaces, there may be even greater pressure to pass as heterosexual friends. To simultaneously transgress norms of heterosexuality and monoraciality is to violate the basic tenets of the U.S. heterosexual paradigm.

BECOMING AND UNBECOMING INTERRACIAL: THE SOCIAL GEOGRAPHY OF VISIBILITY

Across categories of sexuality, gender and race, respondents emphasized the importance of locality—street block, neighborhood, borough, city, geographic region or even nation—in their perceptions of visibility and recognition. When I ask Warren, a 28-year-old White man, about his experiences with his Black wife Nakia in New York City, his response reflects an attunement to the social landscapes of individual neighborhoods.[8]

Yeah I think 80 percent of the city we feel comfortable in, especially Manhattan, even all the way to Washington Heights, which is Harlem. There are certain parts where you might feel a bit more uncomfortable. I think a place like this is just perfect. . . . It's kind of what you would look for because people are nice, people are open. You're just a regular old couple, there is no interracial in the couple, you're just a couple and people look at you like that. It's not like, 'Oh they're different. That's interesting.' . . . What I'm saying is that you just kind of blend in and you're just a couple. I think maybe if we go to Harlem and go to 105th [street] and walk around hand in hand, we're not just a couple; we're suddenly becoming an interracial couple. We can go to certain parts in Brooklyn that are either predominantly White or Jewish Orthodox, or predominately Black, you suddenly become this interracial couple again. It's because the environment changes, not because you change.

. . . [H]is own neighborhood . . . includes enough other interracial couples that he does not feel particularly conspicuous walking hand in hand with Nakia. In other neighborhoods, however, that are predominantly Black or predominantly

White; they "become" an interracial couple. Thus his sense of his own visibility as part of an interracial couple is intricately tied to the social geography of his city.

While Warren describes the social terrain of a single metropolitan area, Mabel, a 43-year-old Black woman, who has been with her husband, Hank, for 13 years, described to me her heightened awareness of her visibility when she is away from Philadelphia with her family. Every summer she and Hank take their three children to his family's cottage on Cape Cod for two months. She describes being more "attuned" in Cape Cod because "there are hardly any African Americans."

For queer couples, the sexual environment of social landscapes was particularly important. As discussed earlier, gay and lesbian respondents felt less compelled to manage their visibility in queer spaces. Racial difference, however, does not disappear within queer spaces and must be negotiated by interracial partners. For couples that desire and can find racially diverse queer spaces, this experience can be positive. When I asked Sylvia, a 29-year-old Black lesbian, how it felt to be an interracial couple in a queer space, she explained:

There are ways . . . it's totally normal and in some ways more normal to be an interracial queer couple. . . . I don't know but I think like in some ways when you feel outside of your community it's easier to connect with someone.

In New York City Sylvia and Leslie are able to go to queer spaces that are racially mixed. Diverse racial atmospheres are important in order for each of them to feel comfortable. For couples in Philadelphia, gay and lesbian spaces are often racially segregated and diversity can be elusive.[9]

For Francine, a queer Black woman, being in a "people of color queer space" is extremely important for her, but it's not something she feels she needs to share with her partner, Kap.

Like Black dyke bars in Philly. They are not spaces for White people. There are no White people in those spaces. So first of all it would be like totally inappropriate for me to bring her. And then second of all, I wouldn't. I wouldn't feel comfortable because, like it would just be so random if I brought a White person into the space. And also, it's really important to me to have um, people of color of spaces that are like for people of color where I can go and be a person of color without my White girlfriend. And she's really appreciative of that . . . So I think it's important to make that distinction though cause you know saying "queer spaces" isn't really, I know I've said it a hundred times, isn't an adequate description. Especially in Philadelphia, because the queer worlds are very segregated.

Francine spends most of her social life in queer spaces, some of which are Black and some of which are White. While those spaces often allow her and her partner, Kap, to feel "safe" and "recognized," their racial dynamics can make her feel hypervisible as part of an interracial relationship.

CONCLUSION

. . . [B]y implicitly constructing same-sex couples as monoracial, scholars fail to consider the extent to which heterosexuality and White supremacy together saturate public spaces to render queer interraciality profoundly invisible. By analyzing interracial narratives of visibility and invisibility, I have offered a critique of the monoracial bias of sexuality research. I conclude with three important points. . . .

While heterosexual interraciality may be privileged relative to queer interraciality, heterosexual respondents in this study shared numerous experiences of invisibility as well as experiences of heightened visibility in which they had been verbally or physically threatened because the race of their sexual partner did not conform to norms of heterosexual monoraciality. That White supremacy in the United States proscribes legitimate sexual behavior even among heterosexuals underscores the extent to which heterosexuals are a *sexually* as well as socially inscribed class. . . . While moments of visual dislocation frustrate both heterosexual and queer interracial couples, recognition of sexual intimacy can invoke the possibility of verbal or physical violence. At times interracial couples must therefore "manage" their visibility (Lasser and Tharinger, 2003) by "passing" as heterosexual friends (Johnson, 2002). Conditioned to anticipate possible hostility in public spaces, queer respondents engaged in this identity work more frequently than did heterosexual respondents. . . . I argue that locality is intricately tied to issues of visibility and invisibility. . . . [R]acial dynamics inhere to sexual landscapes, structuring permissible sexual behaviors and identities. Public spaces are not simply heterosexual or queer; they are imbued with assumptions about proper racial intimacy. . . . [T]he nexus of racial difference and sexual intimacy is not only a productive site for examining visibility, but crucial terrain from which to theorize intersectionality, privilege, and marginalization.

NOTES

1. As Rubin (1984) points out, the only adult sexual behavior legal in every state is the placement of the penis in the vagina in wedlock. At the time Rubin wrote her essay, this had only been true for 17 years, since *Loving v. Virginia* legalized interracial marriage across the United States in 1967.

2. Special thanks to France Winddance Twine for emphasizing the necessity of such a critique.

3. Two notable exceptions to this point are Ruth Frankenberg's (1993) *White Women, Race Matters* and Stefanie K. Dunning's (2009) *Queer in Black and White: Interraciality, Same-Sex Desire, and Contemporary African American Culture*.

4. Carbado's list can be seen as in conversation with Peggy McIntosh's work on White privilege (1988).

5. There is debate abound this point. Boykin (1996) suggests that "Heterosexual orientation has become so ingrained in our social custom, so destigmatized of our fears about sex, that we often fail to make any connection between heterosexuality and sex." Carbado (2000) argues

that the socially constructed normalcy of heterosexuality is not the result of a "desexualization" but rather the sexualization of heterosexuality as normative and natural.

6. According to Lofquist et al.'s analysis of the 2010 U. S. Census, 6.9 percent of heterosexual married couples are interracial. A much smaller percentage of all heterosexual married couples (less than 1 percent) are Black/White (See U.S. Census Bureau, 2012, Appendix Table 1). The percentage of interracial gay and lesbian couples is 14.1 percent and 11.4 percent, respectively. Only 2 percent of gay couples and 1.7 percent of lesbian couples are Black/White pairs (see U.S. Census Bureau, 2003, "Hispanic Origin and Race of Female Unmarried Partner Households," and "Hispanic Origin and Race of Male Unmarried-Partner Households.")

7. With a dissimilarity index for African Americans of 64.7, New York City, where Warren and Nakia live, is among the most racially segregated cities in the nation (Glaeser and Vigdor, 2012). The index of dissimilarity for African Americans in Philadelphia in 2010 is 62.6 (ibid).

8. According to the 2010 U.S. Census, New York City is 33 percent White, 23 percent Black, 13 percent Asian, and 29 percent Hispanic (of any race).

9. There is no official index with which to measure the racial segregation of queer spaces. According to the 2010 U.S. Census, the racial composition of Philadelphia is 37 percent White, 42 percent Black, 6 percent Asian and 12 percent Hispanic (of any race).

REFERENCES

Battles, K. and Hilton-Morrow, W. 2002. "Gay Characters in Conventional Spaces: *Will and Grace* and the Situational Comedy Genre," *Critical Studies in Media Communication* 19(1): 87–105.

Boykin, K. 1996. *One More River to Cross: Black and Gay in America*. New York: Doubleday.

Brickell, C. 2000. "Heroes and Invaders: Gay and Lesbian Pride Parades and the Public/Private Distinction in New Zealand Media Accounts," *Gender, Place and Culture* 7(2): 163–78.

Carbado, D. 2000. "Straight Out of the Closet," *Berkeley Women's Law Journal* 15: 76–124.

Carbado, D. and Gulati, M. 2000. "Working Identity," in *Cornell Law Review*. 85: 1259–1308.

Childs, E. C. 2005. *Navigating Interracial Borders: Black-White Couples and Their Social Worlds*. New Brunswick: Rutgers University Press.

Cohen, C. J. 1997. "Punks, Bulldaggers and Welfare Queens: The Radical Potential of Queer Politics?" *GLQ* 3: 437–65.

Collins, P. H. 2000. *Black Feminist Thought: Knowledge, Consciousness and the Politics of Empowerment*. London: Routledge.

Dalmage, H. M. 2000. *Tripping on the Color Line: Black–White Multiracial Families in a Racially Divided World*. New Brunswick, NJ: Rutgers University Press.

Davis, A. Y. 1983. *Women, Race and Class*. New York: Vintage Books.

Donovan, C., Heaphy, B., and Weeks J. 1999. "Citizenship and Same-Sex Relationships," *Journal of Social Policy* 28(4): 689–709.

Dow, B. J. 2001. "*Ellen*, Television, and the Politics of Gay and Lesbian Visibility," *Critical Studies in Media Communication* 18(2): 123–40.

Dunning, S. K. 2009. *Queer in Black and White: Interraciality, Same Sex Desire, and Contemporary African American Culture*. Bloomington: Indiana University Press.

Evans, D. T. 1993. *Sexual Citizenship: The Material Construction of Sexualities*. London: Routledge.

Frankenberg, R. 1993. *White Women, Race Matters: The Social Construction of Whiteness*. Minneapolis: University of Minnesota Press.

Glaeser E., and J. Vigdor. 2012. "The End of the Segregated Century: Racial Separation in America's Neighborhoods 1890–2010." Civic Report No. 66, Center for State and Local Leadership at the Manhattan Institute.

Gross, L. 2001. *Up from Invisibility: Lesbians, Gay Men and the Media in America*. New York: Columbia University Press.

Herek, G. M. 1992. "The Social Context of Hate Crimes: Notes on Cultural Heterosexism," in G. M. Herek and K. T. Berrill (eds.) *Hate Crimes: Confronting Violence Against Lesbians and Gay Men*. London: Sage.

Hildebrandt, M. D. 2002. "The Construction of Racial Intermarriage: A Comparison of the Effects of Gender, Race, Class and Black Ethnicity in the Daily Lives of Black/White Couples," unpublished dissertation: Columbia University.

James, J. 1996. *Resisting State Violence: Radicalism, Gender and Race in U.S. Culture*. Minneapolis: University of Minnesota Press.

Johnson, C. 2002. "Heteronormative Citizenship and the Politics of Passing," *Sexualities* 5(3): 317–36.

Lasser, J. and Tharinger, D. 2003. "Visibility Management in School and Beyond: A Qualitative Study of Gay, Lesbian and Bisexual Youth," *Journal of Adolescence* 26: 233–44.

Lofquist D., Lugalia, T., O'Connell, M., and Feliz, S. 2012. Households and Families: 2010. Washington D.C.: U.S. Census Bureau, U.S. Department of Commerce, C2010BR-14.

McIntosh, P. 1988. "White Privilege and Male Privilege: A Personal Account of Coming to see Correspondences through work in Women's Studies," Working Paper 189: Wellesley College Center for Research on Women.

Rich, A. 1980. "Compulsory Heterosexuality and Lesbian Existence," *Signs: Journal of Women in Culture and Society* 5(4): 631–60.

Richardson, D. 1996. "Heterosexuality and Social Theory," in D. Richardson (ed.) *Theorising Heterosexuality*. Philadelphia, PA: Open University Press.

Richardson, D. 2000. *Rethinking Sexuality*. London: Sage.

Rosenblatt, P. C., Karis, T. A., and Powell, R. D. 1995. *Multiracial Couples: Black and White Voices*. New York: Sage.

Rubin, G. 1984. "Thinking Sex: Notes for a Radical Theory of the Politics of Sexuality," in C. Vance (ed.) *Pleasure and Danger: Exploring Female Sexuality*. London: Routledge.

Shugart, H. A. 2003. "Reinventing Privilege: The New (Gay) Man in Contemporary Popular Media," *Critical Studies in Media Communication* 20(1): 67–91.

U.S. Census Bureau. 2012. Appendix Table 1. Interracial/Interethnic Married Couple Households: 2010. *Households and Families. C2010BR-14*. Washington, D.C. http://www.census.gov/population/www/cen2010/briefs/tables/appendix.pdf

U.S. Census Bureau. 2003. Table 3, Hispanic Origin and Race of Male Unmarried-Partner Households for the United States: 2000. March 13.

U.S. Census Bureau. 2003. Table 4, Hispanic Origin and Race of Female Unmarried-Partner Households for the United States: 2000. March 13.

U.S. Census Bureau. 2003. "Children's Living Arrangements and Characteristics: March 2002," *Annual Demographic Supplement to the March 2002 Current Population Survey, Current Population Reports, Series P20–547*.

Walters, S. D. 2001. *All the Rage: The Story of Gay Visibility in America*. Chicago: University of Chicago Press.

Weeks, J., Heaphy, B., and Donovan C. 2001. *Same Sex Intimacies: Families of Choice and Other Life Experiments*. London: Routledge.

Wells, I. B. 1997 [1892]. "Southern Horrors: Lynch Law in all its Phases," in J. J. Royster (ed.) *Southern Horrors and Other Writings: The Anti-Lynching Campaign of Ida B. Wells, 1892–1900*. Boston: Bedford Books.

BECOMING A PRACTITIONER: THE BIOPOLITICS OF BDSM

MARGOT WEISS

BDSM is a project, a practice of developing oneself as a skilled practitioner, of learning how to be a practitioner (see Weiss, 2006). Becoming a practitioner takes work on the self: finding the community, attending events, learning techniques and skills, and educating oneself. These practices are forged in relation to the community norms and rules, but—as Foucault emphasizes—it is not a question of complying with the rules, but of transforming oneself through one's own interpretation of the rules. As he argues, the proper use of pleasure, one's self-mastery in relation to pleasure, produces a "solid and stable state of rule of the self over the self" ([1984] 1990, 69; see also 91–92). This rule is less a strict rule of conduct and more about individualizing, moderating, and elaborating conduct, subjecting the self to his own moral mastery. Foucault's understanding of self-mastery in relation to the rules of pleasure is useful here, as SM practitioners also learn to elaborate codes of conduct, to subject themselves to a kind of self-mastery that is supplementary to, rather than in strict compliance with, social and community norms. As Foucault argues, in time, these practices of the self "evolved into procedures, practiced and taught. It thus came to constitute a social practice, giving rise to relationships between individuals, to exchanges and communications, and at times even to institutions" ([1984] 1988, 45). . . . The rules, worked on as part of the labor of becoming an SM practitioner, also produce this particular SM community and the circuits and exchanges it endorses.

Working at BDSM play is also work on the self: it produces and consolidates subjectivities and communities. It is deeply class-inflected, relying not only on the income and time to attend courses and conferences, but also on shared forms of community recognition—education, expertise, and mastery—that are most available to professional-class practitioners. This exclusivity, however, is displaced and obscured in community discourse; these forms of recognition are hegemonic precisely because they construct an ideal, class-restricted community member (the professional practitioner with sufficient means and proper education) toward which other, nonaffluent practitioners aspire. Universalizing ideologies, therefore, normalize such careful work on oneself and one's pleasures. Bailey, a white, heterosexual bottom in her mid-forties, explains that she got into the scene after joining a local SM e-mail list: "I found out about munches [group meals]. I started showing up, and from there I just networked the hell out of it. So I've been active in the public community in the Bay Area going on six years now. Two years ago I did six national events. Last year I probably did four . . . [although this seems like a lot], more-educated people, more-knowledgeable people, more-affluent people tend to be at the national conventions. And I'm like, 'Well, I want to learn more. That's why I'm going.'" Thinking of the rules in this way focuses attention on self-mastery and knowledge as an active practice of modulation, testing, analysis, and self-cultivation.

This form of self-mastery . . . is articulated especially strongly around the rules, especially rules—like Safe, Sane, and Consensual—that require practitioners to forge their own practices of safety. Safe, Sane, and Consensual (SSC) is the mantra of SM in the United States today. Coined in 1983 by David Stein, as part of the statement of purpose of GMSMA (Gay Male S/M Activists), the slogan was popularized across the country and is now widely endorsed by BDSM organizations.[1] . . . Stein notes that the slogan was originally understood to distinguish "defensible" SM, practiced on "willing partners for mutual satisfaction," from "harmful, antisocial, predatory behavior," "the coercive abuse of unwilling victims." Beyond being a motto, however, Safe, Sane, and Consensual has become critical to the social organization of SM; it is the primary way practitioners distinguish between good, safe, acceptable SM and bad, unsafe, unacceptable practice. To ensure that the community of practitioners corresponds to SSC rules, several practices have become standardized; the two largest, most institutionalized are negotiation and using safewords.

Although it is likely that old guard scenes involved some sort of negotiation, today, all BDSM scenes are supposed to involve fairly formal negotiation.[2] Like the infamous Antioch College rules that required explicit and specific verbal consent for every sexual act, negotiation ensures that there will be informed consent throughout the play, and that each player's desires and fantasies will be responded to in the course of the scene.[3] Unlike the Antioch rules, negotiation is supposed to be done before the play, thus requiring anticipatory foresight. During negotiation, one should divulge any emotional, physical, or sexual information that may be important (for example, one should tell one's partner about the child abuse that may crop up and force the scene to end abruptly, or how one's carpal tunnel syndrome might impact bondage, or that the word *slut* is acceptable, but *whore* is not). One should also explain the kinds of SM play one particularly likes. Finally, one should describe one's limits; the most common limit is "dead people, kids, and shit," although there are many other limits.

SM guidebooks explain how to negotiate with a partner in excruciating detail; Wiseman's *SM 101*, one of the most popular, has a ten-page "long form" for negotiation that lists sixteen categories with spaces so that practitioners can fill in the blanks with their own desires, limits, and protocols. The categories include people involved; place; how long the scene will last; emotional and physical limits; presence and kind of sex and safe-sex procedures; presence and kind of bondage and pain; what, if any, marks can be left; and safewords (Wiseman, 1998, 58–62). Many people rely on verbal negotiation, but many others use these highly formalized checklist negotiation forms to plan a scene.

Similarly, the use of safewords—words like *red* or *safeword* or *pineapple* that are unlikely to come up during a scene—was introduced in the 1970s and has now become a crucial part of contemporary SM. Wiseman recommends having two safewords, "one for 'lighten up' and one for 'stop completely.'" He adds, "I also strongly recommend using the 'two squeezes' technique. If the players will use a gag or a hood, they *must* agree upon non-verbal 'safe signals'" (1998, 62; italics in original).[4] Semipublic play parties almost always have a house safeword, usually *safeword* or *red*. Viewed as a last resort, safewords function as an out for when the scene has gone too far—when it has exceeded the boundaries of either player. Thus, like negotiation, safewords have become an institutionalized procedure of safety.

Many practitioners find this level of planning and negotiation ridiculous. Lady Hilary, for example, explained that "rules now are for safety." "Not that safety's not important, but . . . none of the rules enhance the dynamic. 'Oh, let's over-process how we're going to play. So you want to be spanked five times—okay, fine, but six I can't do.' And then I have to do this, so that's how some people negotiate a scene. It's now lost the tension." Pam, a white, bisexual slave in her fifties, described coming out into the scene in her twenties, when "it wasn't a bunch of negotiation." "I found who he [gesturing to Vince] was as a person and his character and everything else and that was enough to serve him." With the new players, she explained, you sit down and negotiate "an hour and a half for a twenty-minutes scene." "And I'm just like . . . 'you're boring the shit out of me.' " Pam is in service to her master Vince, a white, gay man in his mid-forties; they play without safewords or negotiation because, as she explains, "he knows just where I am at every moment, and plus if something does happen that he's not aware of, I can just say it. I don't have to go 'beige' or 'yellow' or 'green' or whatever the hell they're all doing." Vince agrees: "I think that we can think about sex or we can have sex. And so my question and my process has always been 'Is this someone that I can connect with? Can I sense you? Can I feel you?' . . . If that's possible, then I don't really need to negotiate because all I really need to do is pay attention."

Here, practitioners' concern that the more mechanical exercise of negotiation destroys the heart of modern BDSM parallels the mainstream press's response to the Antioch rules. Like the excessive zeal of mandatory bicycle helmet laws, the rules were seen as political correctness gone awry. These critics of both safewords and negotiation argue that by codifying very specific ways of doing SM, the intense connection that SM can create between partners is destroyed, that excessive negotiation will diminish interpersonal intimacy. Taking sex, a practice that is supposed to be spontaneous and magical, and delineating and codifying it

seems counterproductive to many. Indeed, this is one of the most common vanilla responses to SM that I hear: how can a scene that is negotiated ahead of time be hot, believable, or fun?

There are two related ways to approach this question. The first is to note the pleasure that inheres in the rules. So, for example, in a front-page news story in the *New York Times* on the Antioch rules, Jane Gross reported that students liked the policy. They thought that talking about sex was erotic, that it was more about setting up "ground rules" than a rigid checklist, and that the policy effectively addressed rape (1993). In this case, negotiation is a practice that carries with it some unintended pleasures: the pleasures of describing one's desires in detail, for example, a pleasure (bound to safety) that many people—especially women who have sex with men—emphasized when contrasting SM sex with vanilla sex. . . . The second approach, which I follow here, is to note that community pressure to be safe, sane, and consensual does not ask practitioners to blindly follow the rules, but rather to negotiate their own relationship to these rules, to define safety and risk for themselves. This work creates a relationship between individual subjects and social norms, a relationship in which one's enactment, disavowal, or disregard of the rules is a form of self-subjugation and self-mastery in accordance with professional-class standards. This provides one way to read SSC SM and the rules as technique, allowing us to see the community debates about the rules and their pleasures as themselves part of the construction of SM practitioners.

For example, many of the BDSM practitioners with whom I spoke agreed that Safe, Sane, and Consensual was a simplistic slogan, but they had varying opinions about its value. Most thought that SSC was a good policy, but that it couldn't really be followed to the letter. Many also felt that it was, as Teramis puts it, "an easy sound bite for newbies to digest . . .

a good tone to strike for the masses," or "created as outreach or propaganda, and I think it's best in that role," in Anton's words. Others liked it for its usefulness in conveying to medical professionals, psychologists, or the police the difference between BDSM and abuse, rape, torture, or violence—as well as between BDSM practitioners and psychopaths.

A few unconditionally liked the phrase. For example, Monique Alexandra—a Latina, bisexual bottom/submissive/masochist in her mid-thirties—thought that the use of negotiation and safewords in the community made her feel comfortable and, more important, safe: "I want things that are exciting, but I want to know I decided to have that done, and that at any point I can say whatever the codeword is and it will stop. . . . Safety is very important to me; I would not play with anyone who has the attitude 'I won't negotiate because it's boring.'" For some, the emphasis on safety reduced the fear that people coming in to the scene may experience, but it didn't make BDSM any less erotic. As Mustang explains: "Safe doesn't mean you're driving around in your Suburban . . . Some of these people are pretty far out on the edge . . . It's people doing things safely and yet still getting what they need." For him, community resources, experts on things like "rope or whipping or electricity," and medical doctors and lawyers who are "kink aware," are all aspects of community development "not available ten years ago."[5] This development means that there is "community support to say, 'here's what edge play is, here's what it means, here's the things you need to do, here's what you can't do, and here are the risks you're taking when you do it,' so there's informed consent." "I think that's a wonderful thing . . . It's what saved me."

Yet many people pointed out that there was no way to be truly safe, sane, or even consensual. For example, Chris told me that "we need some way of distinguishing this [SM] from abuse." "[But] my opinion is also that we've picked the wrong three words. I can't think of any activity . . . that I would wholeheartedly call safe . . . [and] the definition of sanity is actually a legal issue." He continued, half joking: "Now if it were something like informed, consensual, and involving a level of risk that was comparable to, say, everything that everybody on the planet does, I'd be all for that." For this reason, many prefer RACK (risk-aware consensual kink), a term coined by Gary Switch of TES in the late 1990s.[6] Teramis argues: "You can't define for somebody what's safe for them. You can't define if what somebody's doing is sane for them. [What matters is] that I'm aware of the risks, I'm informed, I've given consent, and it's making me happy."

Practice—being "informed," learning the risks, being educated—leads here to less safe, sane, and consensual SM, but this is not surprising. Rather, it is through these community practices of education, classes, orientations, and the like that practitioners take responsibility for their own practices of safety, that they map out their own relationship to the rules. So, for example, Domina and Hayden told me that they play without limits or safewords, as do Jezzie and Anton. Jezzie explained that she initially needed SSC to feel comfortable in the scene, but then she "kind of outgrew it." "Safe, well, what if I knowledgeably want to do something risky? Sane, what the hell does that mean? I mean, I'm in the mental health profession!" For her, SSC is "like training wheels." Once one is a part of this community, having learned social norms through educational structures, one should "outgrow" or cultivate one's own rules.

This is why many, like Annalee—a white, bisexual genderqueer/pervert/voyeur in her early thirties—insisted on their own definition of the terms. Annalee explains: "I'm a fan of consensual sex, however you each consent with your partner. You can each consent like, 'okay, I consent to having you push my boundaries until I say *red*,' which might not be somebody else's definition of safe, sane, and consensual, which would be like, 'we will agree on ten acts to be performed in this order.' I'm not a fan of the 'ten acts in this order.' I just think it's too much to remember . . . If I'm playing with friends, or partners, we know each other well enough that we can push these limits and [do] whatever the hell we feel like doing. There's a lot of safety built into it, and that's how I define safe, sane, and consensual." All of these debates point to the ways practitioners work with and customize the rules and definitions of safe, sane, consensual, and negotiated. The rules provide a social structure, a scaffolding, within which people cultivate their own ways of being practitioners with—and against—the rules.

RISK AND SOCIAL PRIVILEGE

In a speech critiquing the SSC mantra of contemporary BDSM, Alison Moore argues that "when we invent these sorts of simplistic slogans to differentiate our behavior from nonconsensual violence, what we end up with is often a set of definitions that do not reflect anyone's way of doing SM." She continues: "For me the whole beauty of SM play is that it doesn't always make sense, that it does take us outside our 'safety-zone,' that it is frightening; it taps into the purest essence of sex which is ultimately chaotic, chthonic, exhilarating, exuberant, a dizzying abyss, an electrifying scream . . . There is no political slogan to describe this."[7] Moore neatly summarizes the desire that many people have: to have sex that is unsafe. SM sex is already edgy sex, in that it is—to the general public, at least—forbidden, dark, and prohibited. It is also risky, although generally no more physically risky than football, rock climbing, or other sports. Maintaining this allure of the clandestine, outlaw, or dangerous is important to practitioners, and

this is one reason they remain ambivalent about the rules, as well as the cultural mainstreaming of SM fashion and, to some degree, practice.

At the same time, practitioners are quick to rely on precisely the binaries established by SSC to assert that SM is not what stein referred to as "harmful, antisocial, predatory behavior," and what many would call simple, sociopathic sadism. The rules, then, solicit a complex technology: they create a social context within which SM practice is understandable—as sexual and as desirable—and they also demand that individual practitioners chart their own relationship to that edge between safety and risk, control and the "abyss."

Here, risk must be understood as productive and desirable, not merely aversive. This is, in part, a critique of the "risk society" thesis of Anthony Giddens and Ulrich Beck, which—in the words of Merryn Ekberg—suggests that societies like the United States are characterized by a "collective consciousness of anxiety, insecurity, uncertainty and ambivalence" that produces "an ethos of risk avoidance" (2007, 346, 344). As Ekberg puts it in a review essay, these understandings posit the risk society "in contrast to primary, industrial modernity, which was characterized by the safety, security, predictability and permanence of inherited traditions, such as class location, gender roles, marriage, family, lifetime employment and secure retirement." The risk society, however, "is characterized by a dislocation, disintegration and disorientation associated with the vicissitudes of detraditionalization" (346).

Although many scholars agree that risk, anxiety, and security are key discourses in the contemporary United States, this universalizing meta-theory has come under attack in recent years (Zaloom, 2004; see also T. Baker and Simon, 2002; Mythen, 2007). First, as Ekberg notes, "communities have not disappeared [due to social dislocation], rather they have reformed around risk and safety . . . risk is now the collective bond holding communities together as imaginary risk communities" (2007, 346). Second, imagining a "collective consciousness" of risk aversion "negates the possibility of a risk-seeking culture" (362). The desirability of risk—its pleasure and benefits—is part of this ethos and combines with the community- and subject-producing aspects of risk. . . .

Building and mastering BDSM skills produce new subjects in relation to an evaluative community. The community evaluates one's education, trustworthiness, experience, and skill. So, for example, Bailey explained to me that a DM at a party once stopped her friend: "One of the things he's very good at and he teaches is Japanese rope bondage, in particular suspension bondage. And . . . the last two years in a row they stopped the scene before he [had finished the] suspension because they didn't think he was safe. And if there's anyone I would trust to do that, it would be him. He knows his stuff." Here trust is based on knowledge and skill, in terms of one's public persona. Waldemar, a white, bisexual mostly top in his early thirties, explains that he has no problem making play dates: "I'm well known, and people trust me and they like what I do." Francesca, a white, bisexual, pain slut bottom in her late forties, explains that if she were playing with a friend, she "could probably take a lot more stressful [forms of play]." "It's a matter of trust, how much do I trust this person? And trust is based on knowledge for me."

Concepts of risk also entail "edgework," or "the personal exploration of the limits of both the context and the individual's ability to control it" (Celsi, Rose, and Leigh, 1993, 16). Here, as Richard Celsi, Randall Rose, and Thomas Leigh note, in an essay exploring the motivations of skydivers, "many high-risk performers learn to like working at the edge of their abilities, 'to push the envelope'" (16). Skydivers

want "thrills," but also "high-risk performers seek controllable risk contexts where their abilities can be challenged" so that they can "attain mastery, self-efficacy, and flow" (16). Of course, the edge is not a fixed limit; it changes based on ability, knowledge, experience, and confidence level. Hence risk is not to be avoided but managed; not a static relationship, but a boundary of self-improvement and skill.

In SM, edgework might be productively discussed in terms of edge play, a category of play that is physically or psychologically risky or dangerous (see also Henkin and Holiday, 1996, 66). Examples of edge play include suspension bondage, electricity, cutting, piercing, branding, enemas, water sports, scat, breath play, knife play, blood play, gun play, terror play, intense humiliation, race and cultural trauma play, singletails, and fire play—all kinds of play in which the risk of physical or emotional damage are fairly high. Patrick Califia adds to this list mind games, consensual nonconsent, abduction and kidnapping, catheters and sounds, and scarification (2002, 193–215). The management of risk is central to the classification of edge play. Some of these play forms are edge play because they risk unintentional physical harm, such as falling during suspension bondage. Some risk long-term bodily damage, death (for example, heart stoppage with electricity play and suffocation during breath play), disease, or psychological trauma. Yet these definitions are not stable; familiarity changes what counts as risky SM. For example, many participants think play piercing is no longer edge play because so many people do it, and the techniques have become standardized. Single-tail whips, too, became trendy during my fieldwork, and there were many classes on how to throw or crack them correctly; this made the use of singletails at semipublic parties much less edgy. Breath play, on the other hand, is widely prohibited, at least for now.

The desirability of managed risk, in edge play, is an opportunity to fashion oneself as a person with skills and knowledge in relation to SM as a risk community. This is why many people told me that they do breath play, but not *that kind* of breath play. Domina, for example, told me: "I don't do much in the way of breath play. I might put a gas mask on somebody and put my hand over the intake, but I don't believe in breath play because you can kill people doing it."[8] Anthony described a scene in which a woman was encased in Saran Wrap: the top wrapped it around her body, over the top of her head, and finally across her face. The top then "ripped it off [from the roll] and walked away and left her there flopping and struggling for breath, and then finally when the thing [Saran Wrap] started sucking way in [to her mouth], he pops his finger in it." Anthony has adapted this scene for himself, using a latex mask that he rips off just in time. But then, he tells me, "in reality I'm only holding her nose for maybe twenty or thirty seconds; it's not really that long at all. It's not really breath play." For Anthony, the scene had what he termed "symbolic value," but it wasn't "really all that edgy." "I do some knife play, but I don't really slice anybody up. I'll cut a couple layers of epidermis and then blood will pool up on the cut." These practitioners, by claiming that their play isn't *really* dangerous, are actively redefining their practices as manageable—SSC—risk.

Other practitioners enjoy imaginatively violating community standards. There are community jokes and T-shirts that say "unsafe, insane, nonconsensual," an homage to the outlaw quality of SM play. In our interview, Vince explained that he and Pam "play with the edges, we play with that monster." Pam clarified the point: "It's kind of like running a marathon or climbing a mountain, it's like 'Can I do it? Where are my edges? Where do I stop? Where do I start?' . . . If you always stay in your safety zone, how do you know what you can do?" SM play, for these practitioners, *should* be unsafe, a place where boundaries and limits can be pushed outside of a personal safety zone.

Yet these practitioners also forge an ethical relationship with the self based on techniques, self-mastery, and community norms or rules. Sybil—a white, bisexual dominant/mistress in her mid-fifties—told me: "This whole thing about 'edge play' is a joke. Edge play is not heavy, it's what's heavy to you. So edge play is . . . blood and heavy whipping . . . to some people, [but] that's not all there is to edge play. If you have a phobia of needles, that's edge play. If you're freaked out because you're a woman and I don't want you to wear pink lingerie, that's edge play. Whatever makes you nervous and you don't want to go there, I want to go there 'cause that's where the exchange of power comes from." Sybil's comments show how community rules incite individual or personal responses: the self-cultivation of practice. The point here is not that breath play or edge play is strictly prohibited, thus inciting the desire to do it. Rather, self-mastery as a practitioner requires the production and subsequent personal refinement of community rules.

As Liz Day notes, all the authors in the SM essay collection *Leatherfolk* (Thompson, 1991) claim that SM is transgressive (of nature, culture, materiality, and discourse) because it is "outlaw" (Day, 1994, 243). These essayists, like the practitioners who argue that SM is (or should be, or used to be) outlaw, read the limitations imposed by community rules as a coercive form of disciplinary power, forcing practitioners to choose between replication (obeying SM community rules) or transgression (operating outside of, or in violation of, these rules). Rather, these community debates about edge play, risk, and safety produce knowledges that, in turn, encourage practitioners to position themselves in relation to these rules and thus this ethical community. In edge play, then, pleasure comes from defining and marking the boundaries and limits of what can be done; in policing and enforcing these boundaries in the community and in one's own play; and in mastering the rules—the knowledge, skills, and techniques of self-improvement—that make being a practitioner possible.

Here, risk is not aversive, nor does it stand outside of or serve as an escape from the demands or "constraints of modern social routines" imagined as boring, banal, or routinized (Zaloom, 2004, 365). Although these practitioners—like high-risk hobbyists such as rock climbers and skydivers—imagine their practice as a break from the "real world" that is simultaneously closer to their authentic selves, the management of risk is actually a way of aligning their play selves with "real life." Indeed, imagining a risk community as a break from the real world is . . . a way of bracketing off SM play as a priori "safe" and "fantasy." This bracketing works as an alibi to screen off SM as safe precisely when it is most productive—of selves, communities, and social inequalities.

In this way, rather than a general ethos or collective consciousness, risk functions to produce differentiated subjects. As Bruce Braun writes, white, middle-class people "constitute themselves as middle-class and white precisely through the externalization of as many risks as possible . . . and through barricading themselves from many others . . . hence, if you are white and middle-class, 'risk' is something you take on voluntarily, not something you are subject to" (2003, 199). Therefore, he argues, adventure-sport advertisements both construct the "proper" risk-taking subject and naturalize racialized and classed hierarchies (199; see also Simon, 2002). Representations of risk and ability do not passively reflect but rather justify social inequality. In SM, the ability—or desire—to take on a socially constructed risk is one way in which the community is produced as white and middle class, and, cyclically, con-

tinues to appeal to—and produce—these same practitioners. . . .

NOTES

1. David Stein's essay "Safe, Sane, Consensual" was presented in a workshop at the Leather Leadership Conference in Washington, D.C., in April 2000 and is archived at the Leather Leadership Conference website: http://www.leatherleadership.org. An updated version was published in 2002 as "Safe, Sane, Consensual: The Making of a Shibboleth" in *VASM Scene 20* (September/October).

2. This is not to say that all people negotiate; for example, most people in 24/7 (full-time) or M/s relationships do not use safewords or negotiate with each other, although they may use safewords, limits, and negotiation when they play with others. Many people also cease using safewords and negotiation when they know their partner well. For example, Bailey, who is usually a bottom, told me that she decided to top her partner: "It was awesome because I knew him long enough that I knew he didn't want to negotiate. He just wanted it to happen. I wouldn't normally do that with people if I didn't know them really well, but that's the cool part about really knowing your partner. You can make judgment calls like that."

3. The Antioch rules were created in 1992 in response to the crisis of consent in legal and social definitions of rape, especially date rape (see Soble, 1997). Anton reminded me of this link when he said he thought that SSC "has sort of infected the community with . . . this sort of safety-first mentality that I don't agree with at all . . . There are some people who I think take [it] too far. You have to go through a rigorous checklist before you do anything—you know, this sort of . . . what is that college, the university that put those rules for dating in place where you had to ask people before you could—'May I touch your breast?'" "Antioch?" I asked, and he replied "Antioch, yeah, these sort of Antioch rules for BDSM."

4. "Two squeezes" is a way for a top to check in on a bottom. The top squeezes the bottom's arm or leg twice; if all is well, the bottom gives two squeezes in return. A "safe signal" or "drop safe" is a non-verbal safeword, such as an object that the bottom can drop on the floor.

5. Mustang is referring to an online community service managed by Race Bannon called "Kink Aware Professionals," a list of kink-friendly doctors, therapists, and lawyers across the United States.

6. Gary Switch's essay, "Origin of RACK; RACK vs. SSC," was originally posted on the Eulenspiegel Society's (TES) e-mail list in the late 1990s. An archived version of the post can be found at http://www.leathernroses.com /generalbdsm/garyswitchrack.htm.

7. Alison Moore's speech, "Out of the Safety Zone: Codes of Conduct and Identity in SM Communities," was presented at the Bob Buckley memorial discussion for Sydney Leather Pride Week, April 25, 2002. It is currently archived at: http://tngc.org/tngc/NC_safetyzone.html.

8. This is similar to what Califia advises in his section on breath play: "Avoid any activity that may injure or kill someone . . . on the other hand, it's very common for a top to briefly cut off the bottom's air with the palm of their hand. I think this can intensify excitement in a low-risk fashion. So please don't call the S/M police if you see this being done" (2002, 203).

REFERENCES

Baker, Tom, and Jonathan Simon, eds. 2002. *Embracing Risk: The Changing Culture of Insurance and Responsibility.* Chicago: University of Chicago Press.

Braun, Bruce. 2003. "'On the Raggedy Edge of Risk': Articulations of Race and Nature after Biology." In *Race, Nature, and the Politics of Difference,* Donald S. Moore, Anand Pandian, and Jake Kosek (Eds.), 175–203. Durham: Duke University Press.

Califia, Patrick. 2002. *Sensuous Magic: A Guide to S/M for Adventurous Couples.* Pittsburgh: Cleis.

Celsi, Richard L., Randall L. Rose, Thomas W. Leigh. 1993. "An Exploration of High-Risk Leisure Consumption through Skydiving." *Journal of Consumer Research* 20 (1): 1–23.

Day, Liz. 1994. "'Transgression': The 'Safe Word' in S/M Discourses." *Mattoid* 48:241–53.

Ekberg, Merryn. 2007. "The Parameters of the Risk Society: A Review and Exploration." *Current Sociology* 55 (3): 343–66.

Foucault, Michel. (1984) 1988. *The Care of the Self.* Vol. 3. *The History of Sexuality.* Translated by Robert Hurley. New York: Vintage.

Gross, Jane. 1993. "Combating Rape on Campus in a Class on Sexual Consent." *New York Times,* September 25.

Henkin, William A., and Sybil Holiday. 1996. *Consensual Sadomasochism: How to Talk about It and How to Do It Safely.* San Francisco: Daedalus.

Mythen, Gabe. 2007. "Reappraising the Risk Society Thesis: Telescopic Sight or Myopic Vision?" *Current Sociology* 55 (6): 793–813.

Simon, Jonathan. 2002. "Taking Risks: Extreme Sports and the Embrace of Risk in Advanced Liberal Societies." In *Embracing Risk: The Changing Culture of Insurance and Responsibility,* Tom Baker and Jonathan Simon (Eds), 177–208. Chicago: University of Chicago Press.

Soble, Alan. 1997. "Antioch's 'Sexual Offense Policy': A Philosophical Exploration." *Journal of Social Philosophy* 28 (1): 22–36.

Thompson, Mark, ed. 1991. *Leatherfolk: Radical Sex, People, Politics, and Practice.* Boston: Alyson.

Weiss, Margot. 2006. "Working at Play: BDSM Sexuality in the San Francisco Bay Area." *Anthropologica* 48 (2): 229–45.

Wiseman, Jay. 1998. *SM 101: A Realistic Introduction.* San Francisco: Greenery.

Zaloom, Caitlin. 2004. "The Productive Life of Risk." *Cultural Anthropology* 19 (3): 365–91.

7

SEXUAL DISEASE

AN INTERVIEW WITH

HÉCTOR CARRILLO

Héctor Carrillo, Ph.D., is Associate Professor of Sociology and Gender Studies at Northwestern University, where he is also a member of the Governing Board of the Latina and Latino Studies Program. Carrillo is broadly interested in the social scientific study of sexual cultures and sexual identities, as well as their practical implications for people's behaviors and health. Carrillo is the author of the award-winning book The Night Is Young: Sexuality in Mexico in the Time of AIDS *(University of Chicago Press, 2002). He currently conducts research on the intersections among sexuality, migration, and health. In particular, he has recently completed a study of sexuality and HIV prevention among Mexican gay and bisexual male immigrants. He is also conducting ongoing research on the cultural meanings of adult male circumcision as an HIV prevention strategy among Mexican migrants, and on the identities of heterosexually identified men who are sexually attracted to men. At Northwestern, he teaches courses on the social, cultural, and policy-related aspects of sexuality.*

What led you to begin studying sexuality?

In the late 1980s, I became a staff member at the San Francisco AIDS Foundation, where I was put in charge of creating the Spanish AIDS Hotline for Northern California. This was one of the first services of its kind in the nation. As I began to work on this project, I realized that research on the sexual cultures of Latino/a populations was scarce. The little that was known about Latino/a sexualities often reflected a somewhat stereotypical sense of cultural difference between Latinos and non-Latinos. In the literature that existed at the time, Latinos/as were frequently portrayed as Catholic and traditional, and Latino/a sexualities were assumed to always reflect the values of machismo. I felt that to design more effective HIV prevention programs we needed a more nuanced understanding of Latino/a sexual cultures—one that took into account how Latino/a sexualities were changing and that also considered a range of experiences within Latino/a communities. I decided to obtain a doctoral degree in public health at the University of California, Berkeley, and eventually to become a sexuality researcher.

How do you tell people you study sexuality and how do they react?

My experience is that people generally feel that we need to know more about this topic. People often refer to the fact that sexuality is an issue about which they learned very little in school or while growing up, and they express the view that more sex education is needed. But of course there is no consensus about what shape such education should take. There are also people who, upon learning about the kind of research that I do, do not ask me any further questions. Their silence makes me wonder if the topic does not interest them, whether they find it somewhat awkward or embarrassing, whether they see sexuality as a private matter that should not be publicly discussed, or whether they feel (because of conservative values) that sexuality should not be researched.

What do you think is most challenging about studying sexuality?

People often think that sexuality, because it can be such a socially charged topic, is a difficult topic to research. However, precisely because sexuality is often a taboo subject, many people want to discuss it and are willing to share their personal stories in the context of sexuality research projects. What is perhaps more challenging is the broader politics of research and the way in which sexuality research is sometimes used within the so-called culture wars. Conservative social actors who would prefer that our society not learn more about sexuality or sexual diversity see nothing valuable in funding sexuality studies; they thus often strongly oppose any efforts to conduct sexuality research.

Why is sexuality research important? Why is it important to do research on sexual health?

Sex and sexuality occupy an important place in people's lives. They can be an essential source of intimacy and pleasure, and they are powerfully linked to our human sense of connection. However, sexual contact can also result in the transmission of sexually related diseases, and the intimacy associated with sexual interaction can imply a strong emotional component that can result in some emotional vulnerabilities. It is therefore crucial for people to learn how to maximize the positive aspects of their sexualities while minimizing the possible negative ones. That requires that we know more, based on solid research, about sex and sexuality, about our sexual cultures, about our sexual desires, and more generally about how a diversity of people live their sexual lives. More broadly, sexuality also reflects many aspects of how society is organized and vice versa, and thus I find that studying sexuality from a sociological perspective is crucial to understanding our society more generally.

Can you describe some of the findings from your recent research?

My research on Mexican sexualities has revealed that, contrary to what is commonly assumed, there is considerable social change in Mexico in relation to sexuality and sexual cultures. This became evident in my research in Guadalajara, Mexico during the 1990s, and more recently in the research that I have conducted with Mexican immigrants in California. By focusing on migration, my current research is also showing what happens to Mexican sexualities when they are "on the move." In fact, my study of Mexican gay and bisexual male immigrants has confirmed that for some immigrants, their sexuality and their desire to migrate are tightly linked, as part of a phenomenon that I call "sexual migration"—international migration that is primarily (or at least partially) motivated by sexuality. My research has also revealed that immigrants' sexualities shift some upon arrival in the United States as a result of cross-cultural interaction and participation in new sexual contexts. In this sense, my research further confirms what social scientists have been saying now for decades: that the social context considerably influences how people interpret their sexualities, a conclusion that questions the idea that sexuality reflects purely individual desires. This has also become evident in my research with heterosexually identified men who have sex with men, which is generating new knowledge about how these men, within the social contexts of the United States, make sense of their heterosexual identities and sexual behaviors with men—that is, why they see no contradiction between the two. Instead of being in denial about their sexual desires, as is commonly assumed, these men indeed have developed elaborate logics for why their heterosexual identities accurately describe them. And those logics reflect cultural expectations about men and masculinity.

If you could teach people one thing about sexuality what would it be?

A central message in my classes is that sexuality provides an interesting and helpful window to understand society and how society works. But I also emphasize that studying sexuality from a sociological perspective is helpful for us to realize that our sexualities are socially shaped and reflect not only our individual desires but also the sexual cultures and expectations to which we have been exposed over the course of our lives.

SECONDARY PREVENTION OF SEXUALLY TRANSMITTED INFECTIONS: TREATING THE COUPLE AND COMMUNITY

ADAM SONFIELD

. . . . INFECTIONS AND THEIR CONSEQUENCES

There are more than two dozen infections that are today recognized as being transmitted largely or exclusively through sexual contact. U.S. public health authorities, by and large, focus on a limited set of these STIs, according to such factors as how common and contagious they are, how easily they are to detect and treat, and how much impact they may have on the public health.

For a variety of reasons, including because the most common STIs are often or usually asymptomatic, estimates of the incidence (new cases) and prevalence (total existing cases) of most STIs are difficult to make. The most recent national data, now a decade old, estimated that 19 million new STI cases occur each year, half of them among 15–24-year-olds, and that 65 million Americans overall have at least one viral STI, most commonly genital herpes.

Despite their ubiquity, STIs far less commonly have any major, lasting impact on individuals' health. HPV is the clearest example, with several million HPV infections among Americans each year leading to 4,000 cervical cancer deaths. Pap tests are so effective, in fact, that current federal guidelines recommend testing at three-year intervals, rather than what has been the long-time standard of testing every year.

At the other end of the STI spectrum is HIV. AIDS is, despite considerable medical advances, still considered to be ultimately fatal, but early treatment with antiretroviral drugs and other medical and lifestyle interventions (such as quitting smoking and improving diet) can greatly delay the onset of the disease. And with ongoing, high-quality care, HIV-positive Americans can live long lives with minimal symptoms. Current federal guidelines, consequently, recommend routine HIV screening for all Americans, regardless of perceived risk.

Syphilis, too, is important to catch early, because if untreated for years, the infection can ultimately cause irreversible damage to the nervous system and heart, possibly leading to blindness, insanity, paralysis and death. Because of the severity of the disease and the then-high prevalence of the infection, the discovery that penicillin can cure syphilis completely was a major public health advance in the 1940s, and the U.S. government has since attempted to eliminate the infection in this country.

Somewhere in the middle of this spectrum are chlamydia and gonorrhea. Routine screening for chlamydia among women younger than 26 is widely recommended by the government and medical associations, and is considered a cost-effective, but underutilized, form of preventive health care by the U.S. Preventive Services Task Force because of its ability to reduce rates of pelvic inflammatory disease (PID). Estimates of how often chlamydia (or other infections, including gonorrhea) lead to

From "For some sexually transmitted infections, secondary prevention may be primary," by Adam Sonfield. *Guttmacher Policy Review*, 2009, 12(2):2–7. Reprinted by permission of the Guttmacher Institute.

PID, and of how often PID leads to infertility or other serious complications, vary widely, in large part because it would be unethical to allow an infection to progress untreated. (Indeed, today's ethical standards were developed largely in response to the infamous Tuskegee study, which did exactly that for black men infected with syphills.) Roughly, it appears that 10–40 percent of untreated chlamydia cases will lead to PID and that perhaps 20 percent of women with PID will develop infertility. This progress typically occurs over a matter of years, however, and antibiotic treatment will eliminate the infection and stop the progression of PID.

Despite the various screening guidelines, only four in 10 young women are tested for chlamydia, although that rate has risen by two-thirds in just seven years. Similarly, in 2006, only 40 percent of Americans 18–64 had been tested for HIV (excluding blood donations), and 10 percent in the prior 12 months. Pap tests are considerably more common, but 17 percent of American women aged 18–64 in 2005 had not been tested in the past three years.

TREATING THE COUPLE

Screening and treating a woman or man also provides benefits to that patient's partner. Numerous studies have found that people who know that they have HIV or another serious STI are more likely than those without such knowledge to talk with their partners about risk and protection and are less likely to engage in high-risk behavior. And treatment of infected men and women can directly protect their partners against infection—something that is true not only for curable, bacterial infections, but also for many viral infections that can only be suppressed. Recent studies have shown that common drugs to treat and suppress herpes can reduce transmission by half. The findings are even stronger for HIV, with the risk of trans-mission so low among HIV-positive individuals without detectable viral loads that some experts have begun to argue that condom use may not always be necessary for discordant couples (where one partner is HIV-positive and the other, HIV-negative).

At the same time, screening and treatment of a patient's partner is also crucial for that original patient to break the cycle of reinfection that is seen commonly among patients with curable infections such as chlamydia and gonorrhea. The need to break this cycle has long been recognized by health care providers, and they have responded in part by making rescreening three months after treatment the standard of care. But going further, by getting the partner to come in for testing and treatment, can be difficult, particularly when the partner is asymptomatic.

Distributing home-based testing kits—at health centers, schools, workplaces, shelters or via the Internet—is one potential tactic to address this problem, as are educational and communication-skills-training efforts to help patients convince their partners to come in for testing and treatment. The tactic that has generated by far the most interest in recent years is expedited partner therapy (EPT), in which the original patient's health care provider will provide a supply of or prescription for antibiotics to the partner without an actual diagnosis for the partner. This tactic works best with infections like chlamydia and gonorrhea, where effective single-dose therapies are available to minimize the chance of improper or incomplete treatment. It is not considered appropriate for syphilis, in contrast, because single-does treatment is not available and because of the frequency of allergies to penicillin, the standard treatment for that infection.

EPT has received public endorsements over the past several years by the Centers for Disease Control and Prevention (CDC), the American Medical Association and the American

Academy of Pediatrics, following several CDC-sponsored studies that found it led to substantial reductions in recurrent infections and, at the same time, saved scarce public health resources. Several studies indicate that even before those endorsements, it was widely, if quietly, practiced by providers across the country. However, the CDC has also highlighted a long list of implementation issues, including the possible presence of other STIs, missed opportunities for counseling, difficulties in obtaining funding or insurance coverage and legal liability concerns stemming from EPT's sometimes uncertain legal status, including whether a provider may treat or write a prescription for someone they have not directly evaluated.

TREATING THE COMMUNITY

The public health response to STIs has traditionally recognized that even treating the couple is not enough. By and large, people's sexual activity typically occurs within a relatively closed network, and epidemiologists have found that the behaviors—especially, having concurrent multiple partners—of even a small fraction of the members of a network can have profound ripple effects. The real-life evidence of these network effects can be seen in the disproportionately high STI rates among men who have sex with men (MSM) and among African Americans. The incidence of HIV and syphilis, for example, are significantly concentrated among MSM, and the rates of many STIs are several times higher among black women and men than among their white counterparts. . . . In both cases, there is a range of reasons for the disparities, including lack of access to health care and persistent discrimination. But the spread of STIs within these communities is fundamentally fueled by the facts that sexual networks among MSM and among African Americans are largely closed, and that a substantial minority of both communities practice high-risk behaviors.

Part of the traditional policy response to this problem has been to promote sex education to change peoples' behavior regarding multiple partners and condom use, and vaccination for those infections (currently, HPV and Hepatitis B) where that option is available. These efforts have had many well-documented successes and will continue to be central to addressing STIs going forward.

Yet, STI testing and treatment have also long been a central component of public health efforts to reduce STI rates in a community. The tactic of tracing, notifying and treating the partners of infected patients, for example, was central to the U.S. campaign against gonorrhea, which reduced the prevalence of that infection by three-quarters between the mid-1970s and the mid-1990s. . . . Today, facing limited resources to carry out such a labor-intensive activity, the CDC recommends that public health authorities focus their partner services efforts on syphilis and HIV, and limit their use for other STIs to high-risk cases. In fact, EPT for chlamydia and gonorrhea is in many ways a response to the limited resources available for comprehensive partner services, which include counseling, testing, treatment and referral services and link people with a broader set of health and social services. CDC guidelines emphasize that partner services should be client-centered, confidential, voluntary, nonjudgmental, culturally appropriate and free. These ideals, however, pose serious challenges, including the potential to spark physical or emotional abuse and legal obligations related to mandatory reporting and the duty to warn against imminent danger.

Ultimately, partner services and related community-based efforts to promote STI testing and treatment can and have had a substantial impact on STI rates. Part of that success is by identifying and exploiting the same social and sexual networks that help spread STIs in the first place. By identifying the people who are the "hubs" of a network, these efforts can educate them about their STI status and the risks of their behavior, cure or suppress the infection itself and efficiently identify large numbers of other at-risk members of the network. All of this can have major, positive ripple effects in curbing the spread of STIs within that network.

Moreover, by linking high-risk members of a community with other key government and non-profit services—to reduce substance abuse, prevent violence, provide job training, and improve nutrition and living conditions—treating STIs can also help to address the broader problems in a community. This approach dovetails with an increasing recognition among public health experts that to effectively address STIs in the community, we need to "treat" the community itself. In this "reproductive justice" perspective, STIs are a symptom of broader community problems, from a lack of jobs and housing to high rates of crime and imprisonment to poor health care access and infrastructure. A 2008 study by University of Washington researchers, for example, found a clear link between these types of negative contextual factors and the likelihood of having a current or recent STI. Many other studies have demonstrated links between high-risk sexual behavior and other high-risk behavior, such as drug use and violence, indicating that they have common root causes.

POLICY AND POLITICS

Advocates, public health experts and policymakers have all been working to turn the promise of secondary prevention into a reality. Leading the way at the federal level is the CDC's Division of STD Prevention. Its current five-year strategic plan, adopted in October 2008, includes overarching strategic goals that emphasize preventing and reducing disparities in four potential types of STI-related harm: infertility, cancers, adverse pregnancy

outcomes and increased susceptibility to HIV transmission. (The latter two dangers may stem from a wide variety of STIs, some of which—like herpes and trichomoniasis—are otherwise notable mostly as irritants and as sources of psychological distress.)

Screening and treatment for chlamydia—which can be tied to three of those four potential harms—has been an object of particular focus for the CDC and other public health authorities, as well as nonprofit groups like the American Social Health Association (ASHA). For example, in 2008 the CDC helped launch the National Chlamydia Coalition as a way of bringing together provider and consumer groups to increase knowledge of and support for efforts to increase chlamydia screening and treatment. ASHA and other members of the coalition have also pushed to expand programs that provide free or subsidized screening and treatment at safety-net health centers, such as the CDC's antichlamydia Infertility Prevention Program. Fred Wyand, media and communications manager with ASHA, notes that "a key part in breaking the cycle of infection with chlamydia is for all partners to be treated, but this presupposes that individuals (and their health care providers) know their status to begin with. That so many chlamydia infections are asymptomatic underlines the importance of testing, and the need for adherence to screening guidelines."

On a related front, the CDC has worked over the past several years to eliminate the legal confusion surrounding EPT for chlamydia and gonorrhea, partnering with researchers at Georgetown and Johns Hopkins Universities to analyze state laws and with the American Bar Association to convince states to clarify and change those laws when necessary. This effort has paid dividends, with nine states adopting new policies since 2006 to allow and encourage EPT, including a high-profile law passed by New York in 2008.

State-level advocates for EPT report that strong support from health care provider associations, local health departments and front-line clinicians has been crucial to gaining legislative support even in conservative areas, such as upstate New York and states like North Dakota and Utah, both of which passed new laws in 2009. High prevalence rates for chlamydia and gonorrhea have also turned heads: According to John Peller, director of government relations at the AIDS Foundation of Chicago, legislation to legalize EPT in Illinois has been boosted by the fact that Chicago's Cook County is "number one in the nation in gonorrhea rates and number two in chlamydia"— which has provided ammunition for the broad coalition of medical and public health groups supporting the bill that, by mid-May 2009, had passed both houses and appeared likely to become law.

Public health authorities and clinicians in states that have legalized EPT expect it to be a helpful new tool in their toolbox, particularly when partner tracing for many clients is impractical and local health departments are short staffed. A January 2009 article in the *Baltimore Sun* highlighted the potential of this tool, reporting that a pilot program at two city clinics authorized by the state in 2007 is paying off, with a 41 percent decline in three-month reinfection rates for gonorrhea and chlamydia clients. It is too soon to evaluate the impact of legislation enacted in Minnesota in 2008, but the state's department of health has had impressive turnout for its training and outreach sessions, according to Sarah Stoesz, president and CEO of Planned Parenthood Minnesota, North Dakota, South Dakota. EPT is now the standard of care at the organization's Minnesota health centers.

Nevertheless, no one tactic will be a silver bullet in stemming the STI epidemics. Some experts have promoted steps such as expanded coverage of STI screening in private insurance plans and the promotion of home testing kits for various STIs, to remove barriers related to access, embarassment and confidentiality. Stoesz, for one, emphasizes the critical need for additional funding for outreach, education and treatment. EPT itself is inexpensive, so it is not adding to clinicians' funding problems, but it will take some time for EPT to actually save public dollars by reducing the community's STI rates. "It's easy to pass EPT when there's no need for a budget behind it," she observes, asserting that securing additional state dollars to fight STIs is far more difficult, particularly in the current fiscal environment.

Culture-war politics also continue to be a barrier. During the debate early in 2009 over the economic stimulus package, congressional Republicans took issue with $400 million proposed by Senate Democrats for infectious disease screening and prevention, focusing their ire on the portion of that funding that would have gone toward STI-related efforts. Advocates argued to no avail that the CDC's STD budget had declined by 15 percent since 2002, that the funds would help fight an urgent public health priority and that the funds would create health care jobs and shore up state budgets.

Beyond the ever-present need for funding, advocates describe a need to treat the broader problems in the community. Hard-hit communities in cities like Minneapolis, Chicago, Baltimore and New York appear to have reached a tipping point because STIs are so widespread. Reversing that trend is possible, but it is considerably more difficult to find and treat infected men and women than it is for STIs to spread. What is needed, says the AIDS Foundation's Peller, is to change the environment: "So many factors contribute to STIs, starting with the lack of access to health care in the community."

VENEREAL DISEASE: SIN VERSUS SCIENCE

ELIZABETH FEE

Ways of perceiving and understanding disease are historically constructed. Our social, political, religious, and moral conceptions influence our perceptions of disease, just as do different scientific and medical theories. Indeed, these different elements often cannot be easily separated, as scientists and physicians bring their own cultural ideas to bear in the construction of scientific theories. Because these cultural ideas may be widely shared, their presence within medical and scientific theory may not be readily apparent. Often, such cultural conceptions are more obvious when reviewing medical and scientific theories of the past than they are in contemporary medical practice.[1]

Just as cultural conceptions of disease may be embodied in the framing of scientific theories, so these theories also influence popular perceptions of disease. At times such scientific theories may reinforce, or contradict, other cultural conceptions, such as religious and moral ideas or racial stereotypes.

In the case of the venereal diseases, it is clear that our attitudes embody a fundamental cultural ambivalence: are venereal diseases to be studied and treated from a purely biomedical point of view—are they infectious diseases like any others—or are they to be treated as social, moral, or spiritual afflictions?[2] As the name implies, venereal diseases are inevitably associated with sexuality—and therefore our perceptions of these diseases tend to be entangled with our ideas about the social meanings and moral evaluation of sexual behaviors. In the case of syphilis, a major killer in the first half of the twentieth century, health officials could decide that the true "cause" of syphilis was the microorganism *Treponema pallidum,* or they could define the "underlying cause" as "promiscuous sexual behavior." Each claim focuses on a different part of social reality, and each carries different messages of responsibility and blame. Each is part of a different language in which the disease may be described and defined. The first suggests the primacy of the medical clinic for treating disease; the second, the primacy of moral exhortation.

Throughout the twentieth century struggles have been waged over the meaning and definition of the venereal diseases. At times these diseases have been blanketed in silence, as though they belonged to a "private" realm, not open to public discussion. Wars, however, have tended to make venereal diseases visible, to bring them out of the private sphere and into the center of public policy discussions; this has highlighted the struggles over their proper definition and treatment. In World War I, for example, the American Social Hygiene Association consistently equated venereal disease with immorality, vice, and prostitution.[3] Its members thus tried to close down brothels and taverns, to arrest prostitutes, and to advocate continence and sexual abstinence for the soldiers. The Commission on Training Camp Activities tried to suppress vice and liquor and also to organize "good, clean fun": sports

From "Sin vs. Science: Venereal Disease in Baltimore in the Twentieth Century" by Elizabeth Fee (1988), *Journal of the History of Medicine and Allied Sciences,* Vol. 43, No. 2, 1988, pp. 141–164. Copyright © 1988, Oxford University Press. Reprinted by permission of Oxford University Press, Inc.

events, theatrical entertainments and educational programs.[4] The Army, however, quietly issued prophylactic kits to the soldiers and made early treatment after possible exposure compulsory. Any soldier who failed to get treatment could face trial and imprisonment for neglect of duty. . . .

When dealing with major disease problems, we often try to find some social group to "blame" for the infection. During the war, educational materials clearly presented the fighting men as the innocent victims of disease; prostitutes were the guilty spreaders of infection. Indeed, prostitutes were often presented as implicitly working for the enemy against patriotic American soldiers.[5] In many communities prostitutes would be the focus, and often the victims and scapegoats, of the new attention to venereal infections. Prostitutes—the women responsible for the defilement of the heroic American soldier—would be regularly rounded up, arrested, and jailed in the campaign against vice.

The end of the war, however, brought a waning of interest in venereal disease and a return to "normal life," freed of the restrictions and regulations of military necessity. The energetic public discussion of venereal disease again lapsed into a public silence. Prostitutes and their customers were again permitted to operate without much official harassment; health departments quietly collected statistics on venereal disease but avoided publicity on the subject.[6]

This essay will examine the subsequent history of venereal disease, and especially syphilis, by focusing on a major industrial city, Baltimore, to see how the struggle between the moral and biomedical views of disease was played out in the context of city politics in the 1930s and 1940s. Although syphilis is no longer a significant public health problem, this account should be useful in helping us to reflect on the . . . problem of AIDS (acquired immune deficiency syndrome) today.

TREATMENT FOR VENERAL DISEASE: THE PUBLIC HEALTH CLINICS

In Baltimore in the 1920s a great social silence surrounded the problem of syphilis. Since venereal diseases carried such negative social stigma, only a small proportion of cases were ever reported. Deaths from syphilis were often attributed to other causes as physicians endeavored to save patients and their families from possible embarrassment. A social conspiracy of silence resulted: patients did not talk about their diseases, physicians did not report them, the health department did not publicize them, and the newspapers never mentioned them. The diseases were thus largely invisible. Most hospitals and some physicians refused to treat patients with venereal diseases; some physicians specialized in these diseases and made a great deal of money from private patients.[7] Many patients, however, could not afford private medical care.

In the aftermath of the war, the city health department began quietly to treat venereal diseases in its public clinics. The first such clinic, opened in 1922, had 13,000 patient visits in its first year of operation. The clinic population grew so fast that the city soon opened a second clinic, and then a third. These patients, brought to the public clinics through poverty, were recorded in health department files as venereal disease cases. Like all the diseases of the poor, these cases attracted little public attention.

The venereal disease problem in Baltimore was, however, made publicly visible by a survey conducted by the United States Public Health Service in 1931.[8] The survey defined syphilis as a major problem in Baltimore, and as a problem of the black population. The reported "colored" rate was 22 per 1,000 males and 10 per 1,000 women; this contrasted with a reported white rate of 4 per 1,000 men and 1.3 per 1,000 women. Of course, whites were more likely to be seeing private physicians and thus less likely to have their disease reported to the health department. Syphilis, originally perceived as a disease of vice and prostitution, was now a black disease. . . .

THE DEPRESSION: RESTRICTING TREATMENT

During the Depression public clinics became more crowded than ever, with over 84,000 visits in 1932 alone. The city health department, already burdened with tight budgets and increasing health problems of every kind, complained that the hospitals in town were dumping poor patients on the city clinics.[9] . . .

In 1933 the problem of overcrowding became so acute that the city health department decided to treat only patients at the infectious stage of syphilis. They discontinued treatment to any patients who had received sufficient drugs to render them noninfectious to others, even though they had not been cured.[10] . . .

VENEREAL DISEASE AND RACISM

In the 1930s as today, health statistics were gathered by race but not by income. The statistics on venereal diseases confirmed the definition of syphilis as predominantly a black or "colored" problem. In fact almost all infectious diseases were far more prevalent among blacks than whites, reflecting the effects of poverty, poor housing, and overcrowding. . . .

While [Ferdinand] Reinhard [the head of the bureau of venereal diseases] described the black venereal disease problem as an effect of economics and social conditions, most whites saw venereal diseases simply as a question of sexual morality. Blacks were popularly perceived as highly sexual, uninhibited, and promiscuous. . . . White doctors saw blacks

as "diseased, debilitated, and debauched," the victims of their own uncontrolled or uncontrollable sexual instincts and impulses.[11] . . . [H]ealth officials were certainly convinced that the main issue was sexual behavior, and they were equally convinced that it was the sexual behavior of the black population that had to be changed.

Since the problem was clearly understood as one of sexual behavior, the city health department began an energetic public education project aimed at changing sexual attitudes— by persuasion or by fear. In 1934 the department directed a new program on sex hygiene at the black population. They gave talks at the Colored Vocational School and the Frederick Douglass High School, and organized exhibits for Negro Health Week and for the National Association of Teachers in Colored Schools. They distributed nearly 14,000 pamphlets on venereal diseases. A "social hygiene motion picture" with the discouraging title *Damaged Lives* played in twenty-three theaters, thus reaching over 65,000 people, one-tenth of Baltimore's adult population.[12]

The main aim of this health propaganda was to stress the dangers of sexual promiscuity, but it also emphasized the need for early detection and treatment of disease. . . . Pamphlets distributed by the Social Hygiene Association and the city health department continued to urge chastity before marriage and sexual fidelity within marriage as the proper solutions to syphilis.

In 1935 syphilis was by far the most prevalent of the communicable diseases occurring in the city, with 5,754 reported cases; the next most prevalent disease was chickenpox—not a disease considered of much importance—with 3,816 reported cases.[13] . . . The facilities for actually treating syphilis were still completely inadequate.

Syphilis deaths were now running at between 110 and 150 per year. As Reinhard complained,

"Any other group of diseases scattered throughout the community to this extent would be considered to have taken on epidemic proportions and would be cause for alarm on the part of health authorities.[14] . . .

Reinhard continued for several years to struggle against the partial treatment plan and to advocate extended clinic facilities, sufficient for all syphilis patients, and staffed with black physicians, nurses, and social workers. It seemed, at the time, to be a one-man campaign. Most physicians approved of the fact that the health department was not offering treatment, the proper domain of fee-for-service medicine. Particularly during the depression years, when many physicians found it difficult to make a living on patient fees, the medical profession was antagonistic to efforts by public health officers to offer free treatments to any patients, whatever their illness.

SYPHILIS AS EVERYONE'S DISEASE: A NATIONAL CAMPAIGN

In 1936 Reinhard's "one-man campaign" against syphilis in Baltimore suddenly became part of a major national effort. Thomas Parran, Surgeon General of the United States Public Health Service, now lent the full weight of his authority to a campaign against venereal diseases. A forceful and dynamic man, Parran decided to break through the wall of silence and make the public confront the magnitude of the problem. To do this, he redefined syphilis as a diseases that struck "innocent" victims: the educated, respectable, white population. . . . Parran called syphilis "the great American Disease" and declared: "we might virtually stamp out this disease were we not hampered by the widespread belief that nice people don't talk about syphilis, that nice people don't have syphills, and that nice people shouldn't do anything about those who *do* have syphilis."[15] Parran's point was that nice people *did* have syphilis;

he never tired of pointing out that respectable physicians, innocent children, and heads of industry were among those infected.[16] . . .

Parran declared that half the victims of syphilis were "innocently infected": "Many cases come from such casual contacts as the use of [a] recently soiled drinking cup, a pipe or cigarette; in receiving services from diseased nursemaids, barber or beauty shop operators, etc., and in giving services such as those of a dentist, doctor or nurse to a diseased person."[17] Syphilis was just another contagious disease, although a highly threatening and dangerous one. The point was to find syphilis cases and to treat them; the state should be obliged to provide treatment, said Parran, and the patient should be obliged to endure it. Syphilis would be the next great plague to go—as soon as the public broke with the old-fashioned and prescientific notion that syphilis was "the wages of sin." . . .

[W]hile the city health department was consolidating the new biomedical approach to syphilis, it was suddenly challenged with a resurgent moral crusade against vice and prostitution, led by none other than the redoubtable J. Edgar Hoover.

MEDICAL TREATMENT OR CRUSADE AGAINST VICE?

"Captives Taken in Weekend Drive Against City's White Slave Traffic," declared the headlines of the Baltimore *Sun* on May 17, 1937.[18] . . . The raids generated great excitement and controversy, magnified when local prostitutes implicated a number of high level police officers and at least one state senator in Baltimore's "white slave trade."[19] The local newspapers took delight in reporting the activities of this organized racket, playing up Baltimore as a notorious center of vice and iniquity. . . .

State Senator Raymond E. Kennedy now implied that the city health department, like the police department, was implicitly involved in condoning vice. He demanded that all prostitutes being treated in city clinics be immediately incarcerated. Parran was called to appear as a witness before a Grand Jury investigation. On his arrival in Baltimore, however, Parran managed to turn this into a public relations coup for the health department. He announced a state survey of venereal diseases, suggested that Baltimore follow the successful Swedish model of disease control, including the provision of free drugs, and he declared to enthusiastic mass meetings that Maryland would take the lead in the fight against "social diseases."[20] . . .

Thanks to citywide publicity and political pressure on Mayor Jackson, [the health commissioner, Huntington] Williams was able to expand his budget and open the Druid Hill Health Center for black patients in west Baltimore—the first time that adequate public health facilities had been available in this area of the city.[21]

The city health department now tackled the problem of syphilis in industry. At the time, industrial workers were being fired (or never hired in the first place) if they were found to have positive blood tests for syphilis. Employers fired infected workers on the grounds that they were more likely to be involved in industrial accidents, and thus would increase the costs of workmen's compensation and insurance premiums. The health department started to provide free laboratory blood tests for industrial workers; the test results were kept confidential and those infected were referred for appropriate therapy. The health department followed individual workers to make sure they were receiving treatment but, at least in theory, no worker who accepted treatment could be fired. The fact that no guarantees were offered workers refusing therapy meant, however, that syphilis treatment was essentially made compulsory for industrial workers participating in the plan.[22] . . .

THE IMPACT OF WAR

In the late 1930s there were considerable grounds for optimism that the campaign against the venereal diseases was beginning to show results. The more open public health attitude toward syphilis as a problem of diseases rather than of morality seemed to be successful. . . . The numbers of reported cases of syphilis were decreasing each year, despite increased screening efforts and more effective reporting mechanisms. In 1938, 8,236 new cases were reported; in 1939, 7,509; and in 1940, only 6,213. . . . These records of syphilis incidence and prevalence may have been quite unreliable from an epidemiological point of view, but this was the first time that syphilis rates had even seemed to be declining; it was a natural conclusion that health department efforts were finally showing demonstrable results.

In the midst of this optimism, however, came the prospect of war and, with it, the fear that war mobilization and an influx of 60,000 soldiers would upset all previous gain.[23] In 1941, with the institution of selective service examinations, reported venereal disease rates began to climb. In Baltimore that year, 1.7 percent of the white enlistees had positive blood tests for syphilis, as had 24 percent of the black recruits.[24] Baltimore City won the dubious distinction of having the second highest syphilis rate in the country, second only to Washington, D.C. Baltimore's rate was 101.3 cases per 1,000 men examined, more than twice the national rate.[25] In an effort to justify these statistics, the city health department blamed the situation on the nonwhite population: the relatively high proportion of blacks to whites "explained" why Baltimore had the second highest venereal disease rate among the country's largest cities.[26] . . .

Such justifications were hardly likely to be sufficient for a country at war. With the war mobilization had come renewed national attention to protecting the health and fighting efficiency of the soldiers. As during World War I, the first concern was with the control or suppression of prostitution in the vicinity of army camps and with "social hygiene" rather than treatment programs. The May Act passed by Congress made prostitution a federal offense in the vicinity of military camps. . . .

[T]he Baltimore police seemed determined to prove their dedication to the attack on prostitution. By early 1943 they claimed to have closed most of Baltimore's brothels and to have driven prostitutes from the streets.[27] Police Commissioner Stanton demanded statewide legislation to allow police officers to arrest prostitutes and force them to submit to medical examination and, if infected, medical treatment.[28]

Dr. Nels A. Nelson, head of the state venereal disease control program, declared that these arrests of prostitutes and compulsory medical examinations were completely ineffective: only a few prostitutes could be arrested at any one time, and as soon as they were treated and released, they would immediately return to the streets to become reinfected and to continue to spread infection until their next arrest. The only real control of venereal disease, concluded Nelson, depended on the complete "repression of sexual promiscuity."[29] Meanwhile, the reported cases of syphilis were rapidly increasing. In 1942 the selective service records showed that almost 3 percent of the white draftees and over 32 percent of the black soldiers had syphilis.[30] . . . Between 1940 and 1942 new cases of syphilis had almost doubled, from 6,213 to 11,293, and gonorrhea rates were also climbing. . . .

Nelson of the state health department had . . . abandoned the fight against prostitution. He was busily distributing free drugs for syphilis control to private physicians, while he publicly declared the city venereal disease clinics "little more than drug pumping stations in dirty, unattractive quarters."[31] Nelson told the press he was tired of hearing the VD rate discussed as though it were only a Negro problem: "Negroes are plagued by venereal diseases because of their economic and social position."[32] . . .

The Army was also under attack for failing to organize an effective VD program.[33] Its programs and policies were plagued by contradictions; publicly, it advocated chastity, while privately, it provided prophylactics for the men. . . . The Army finally adopted a pragmatic approach and attempted to reduce the sources of infection as much as possible. The pragmatic approach lacked the fervor of a purity crusade, but tried to steer some middle course between laissez-faire attitudes and moral absolutism.

In Baltimore the new acting directors of the city's venereal disease program, Ralph Sikes and Alexander Novey, shared this pragmatic position. . . . Under their leadership health officers cooperated with the armed services in distributing prophylactic kits throughout the city: in police stations, fire houses, transportation terminals, hospitals, and clinic.[34] Implicitly, the VD control officers had thus accepted the idea that this was a campaign *against* disease, rather than a campaign *for* sexual morality; they concentrated on a fairly mechanical (if effective) approach to prevention while leaving the struggle around prostitution to social hygiene reformers, the police, and the courts.

SEX EDUCATION DURING THE WAR

During the war the city health department and a research group at the Johns Hopkins School of Hygiene and Public Health undertook a daring task—to teach "sex hygiene" in the public schools. They gave talks to groups of high school students (separated by sex), showed plaster models of male and female reproductive systems, and gave simple explanations of "menstruation, conception, pregnancy, nocturnal emissions and masturbation, but omitting intercourse and childbirth."[35] . . .

Having been assured that sex was both exciting and dangerous, students were then given a brief description of male reproductive physiology, ending with a caution against masturbation. Masturbation was not dangerous, students were told, merely unnecessary and possibly habit-forming. . . . A brief description of the female reproductive system was followed by a discussion of morals and ethics, warning of the need for judgment, but avoiding specific advice. . . . Students were urged to discuss their questions with parents and teachers and to read a social hygiene pamphlet on "Growing Up in the World Today."[36]

The third part of the presentation, on venereal diseases, emphasized the dangers of sex. Intimacy brought the germs of syphilis: sexual intercourse was the most threatening, but even kisses could carry disease. The best strategy was to avoid any possible contact with these sexual germs:

They can be caught only from an infected person and therefore, we should avoid intimate contact with an infected person. But we cannot tell by looking at a person whether he or she, is infected or not; the answer is to avoid intimate contact with all persons except in marriage. This is the only sure way of avoiding these diseases.[37]

At least for these high school students, the link between sexual morality and venereal disease was clear: sexual intimacy led to syphilis and was therefore to be avoided except in marriage. Why marital sex should be "safe" was never explained, nor was congenital syphilis ever mentioned.

AFTER THE WAR: THE NEW PENICILLIN THERAPY

By the end of World War II, the problem of syphilis was beginning to recede, both in public consciousness and in statistical measures. Part

of this was the normal relaxation in the immediate aftermath of war, the return to home and family, the desire for stability, and a reluctance to confront social and sexual problems or to dwell on their existence. Even more important, however, was the success of the new drug, penicillin: at last, venereal diseases could, it seemed, be quickly and effectively treated. Many felt it was only a matter of time before the venereal diseases were finally eliminated with the aid of modern medicine's "miracle cures."

By 1940 the new "miracle drug" penicillin had been discovered and purified: in 1943 it was first used against syphilis, but it was not yet generally available; supplies were still strictly rationed.[38] Soon, it would completely transform the old methods of treating venereal diseases. On December 31, 1944, the Baltimore City Hospitals opened the first Rapid Treatment Center for treating syphilis with penicillin. Penicillin doses for syphilis were given over eight days; since supplies of the drug were then very limited, only cases judged to be highly infectious were sent for "an eight-day cure, or what is for the present considered to be a cure."[39] From all initial reports the new experimental treatment was remarkably effective.

On June 20, 1945, Mayor Theodore R. McKeldin approved a new city ordinance making treatment for venereal diseases compulsory for the first time. Those suspected of having syphilis or gonorrhea were required to take penicillin therapy at the Rapid Treatment Center.[40] Those refusing treatment could be quarantined and isolated in the Baltimore City hospitals. . . .

The ordinance was, however, rarely invoked. Most patients were eager to go to the Rapid Treatment Center when diagnosed. In 1946 nearly 2,000 people with infectious syphilis received treatment; most were reported as completely cured. (Before penicillin, only an estimated 25 percent of patients completed the lengthy treatments considered necessary for a full cure.[41]) In 1947 the Baltimore *Sun* reviewed the city's experience with the new ordinance:

On the basis of this experience (over the last 16 months), it is clear that the protection of the public against persons carrying the disease and refusing to be treated more than outweighs the sacrifice of individual rights by so small a number. . . . Under the circumstances, the enactment of a permanent ordinance seems fully justified.[42]

The state health department in 1947 announced that "for the first time in history any resident of Maryland who contracts syphilis can obtain treatment resulting in prompt and almost certain cure."[43]

CONCLUSION: THE END OF THE STRUGGLE?

The biomedical approach to venereal diseases had apparently been stunningly successful. Diseases that only ten years before had been described as the most serious of all the infectious diseases had now been tamed by chemotherapy with a simple, safe, and effective cure. Diseases that twenty years previously had been guilty secrets, virtually unmentionable in the public press and quietly ignored by health departments, were now glorious examples of the triumph of modem medicine in overcoming ancient plagues. The ideological struggle between those who had seen the fight against venereal disease as a battle for sexual morality and those who had seen it as simply another form of bacteriological warfare was now over. The social hygiene reformers had to concede defeat to the public health officers, epidemiologists, and laboratory researchers. Or did they?

In 1947 the Maryland State Department of Health, announcing the success of the rapid treatment program, concluded its press bulletin with the warning:"To decrease the number of repeat patients and prevent venereal diseases it will be necessary to reduce sexual promiscuity. If fear of disease is a less powerful restraining factor the problem must be attacked more strongly through moral training and suppression of prostitution."[44] . . .

Even those most committed to the bacteriological view of disease seemed uneasy about the decoupling of venereal disease from sin and promiscuity: How would sexual morality be controlled if not by the fear of disease? Would "rampant promiscuity" defeat the best efforts of medical treatment?

A brief review of health statistics in the years since the discovery of penicillin suggests that syphilis has, in the main, been effectively controlled. New cases of syphilis are reported each year, and doubtless others go unreported, but the rates are relatively low. In 1986 a total of 373 cases of primary, secondary, and early latent cases were reported in Baltimore; in 1987, a total of 364 cases. Although these cases are of continuing concern to health department officials, at least from the perspective of the 1930s and 1940s, the miracle of control really has occurred. . . .

As we have since discovered, the fear and underlying ambivalence toward sexuality were only lying dormant. Public concern, horror, and fear about AIDS have recently reignited the older social hygiene movement in a new form. The once prevalent description of the black population as sexually promiscuous, sexually threatening, and a reservoir of disease has now been applied to the gay male population. AIDS is popularly seen as "caused" by gay promiscuity and, even more broadly, as a punishment for unconventional or unapproved sexual behavior, rather than simply as the result of infection by a microorganism. Venereal disease is again perceived as the "wages of sin," or, as the Reverend Jerry Falwell says: "A man reaps what he sows. If he sows seed in the field of his lower nature, he will reap from it a harvest of corruption." . . .

Both the biomedical and moral perspectives on venereal disease highlight specific aspects of a complex social reality. Venereal diseases, like all other diseases, are experienced and reproduced in a social context. We may separate the biological and social aspects for analysis, but any complete understanding of a disease problem must involve both, as interrelated parts of a single social reality.

Social and cultural ideas offer a variety of ways in which diseases can be perceived and interpreted. The germ theory provides an explanation of disease that largely—but not completely—isolates it from this social context, robbing it of some of its social (and in this case, moral) meaning. But the purely "scientific" interpretation is never wholly victorious, for social and cultural meanings of disease reassert themselves in the interstices of science and prove their power whenever the biomedical sciences fail to completely cure or solve the problem. Only when a disease condition is completely abolished do social and cultural meanings cease to be relevant to the experience and perception of human illness.

NOTES

1. For a fascinating analysis of the history of cultural and scientific conceptions of syphilis, see Ludwig Fleck, *Genesis and Development of a Scientific Fact* (1935, rpt., Chicago: 1979).

2. For an excellent recent history of the controversies around venereal diseases in the United States, see Allan Brandt, *No Magic Bullet: A Social History of Venereal Diseases in the United States Since 1880* (New York: 1985).

3. National Academy of Sciences, *Scientific and Technical Societies of the United States and Canada,* 8th ed. (Washington, D.C.: 1968), 62.

4. Edward H. Beardsley, "Allied Against Sin: American and British Responses to Venereal Disease in World War I," *Medical History* 20 (1976): 194.

5. As one widely reprinted article, said to have reached eight million readers, described 'The Enemy at Home': "The name of this invisible enemy is Venereal Disease— and there you have in two words the epitome of all that is unclean, malignant and menacing. . . . Gonorrhea and syphilis are 'camp followers' where prostitution and alcohol are permitted. They form almost as great an enemy behind the lines as do the Huns in front." "V.D.: The Enemy at Home," as cited by William H. Zinsser, "Social Hygiene and the War: Fighting Venereal Disease a Public Trust," *Social Hygiene* 4 (1918): 519–20.

6. In 1920 William Travis Howard, a member of the city health department, complained: "The Baltimore health department has never inaugurated a single administrative measure directed at the control of the venereal diseases . . . the Baltimore health department has contented itself with receiving such reports as were made and with lending its power, when called upon, to force a few recalcitrant patients to appear at the venereal disease clinic established by the United States Government." Howard, *Public Health Administration and the Natural History of Disease in Baltimore, Maryland: 1797–1920* (Washington, D.C.:1924): 154–55.

7. Baltimore City Health Department, Annual Report (1930).

8. Taliaferro Clark and Lida Usilton, "Survey of the Venereal Diseases in the City of Baltimore, Baltimore County, and the Four Contiguous Counties," *Venereal Disease Information* 12 (Washington, D.C.:20 October 1931): 437–56.

9. Baltimore City Health Department, Annual Report (1932), 62.

10. Baltimore City Health Department, Annual Report (1933), 93.

11. James H. Jones, *Bad Blood. The Tuskegee Syphilis Experiment* (New York: 981), 16–29.

12. Baltimore City Health Department, Annual Report (1934), 107.

13. Baltimore City Health Department, Annual Report (1935), 115.

14. Ferdinand O. Reinhard, "The Venereal Disease Problem in the Colored Population of Baltimore City," *American Journal of Syphilis and Neurology* 19 (1935): 183–95.

15. Thomas Parran, "Why Don't We Stamp Out Syphilis?" *Reader's Digest* (July 1936), reprinted in Baltimore *Health News* (August 1936): 3.

16. E.g. Parran, *Shadow on the Land: Syphilis* (New York: 1937). 207, 230.

17. Parran, "Why Don't We Stamp Out Syphilis?" *Reader's Digest,* 65–73.

18. "G-Men's Haul in Vice Raids Totals 47," Baltimore *Sun,* 17 May 1937.

19. "Vice Witness Names Police Lieutenant," Baltimore *Sun,* 18 May 1937; "Vice Arrests May Total 100; Bierman Named," *Sunday Sun,* 19 May 1937.

20. "Starts to Survey Venereal Disease," Baltimore *Sun,* 29 July 1937; "Venereal Disease Fight is Planned," Baltimore *Sun,* 22 August 1937; "Fight Opens Here on Social Disease," Baltimore *Sun,* 25 August 1937; "Syphilis Control Unit Begins Work," Baltimore *Sun,* 21 October 1937;

"Over 2,000 Attend Talks on Syphilis," *Baltimore Sun*, 26 October 1937.

21. Baltimore City Health Department, Annual Reports (1938), 159; (1939), 159.

22. Baltimore City Health Department, Annual Report (1938); 16; "21 Employers Asked in Drive on Syphilis," *Baltimore Sun*, 27 March 1938; "Syphilis Control is Under Way Here," *Baltimore Sun*, 22 May 1938; W. M. P., "We Join the Anti-Syphilis Crusade," *The Kalends* (June 1938), reprinted in *Baltimore Health News* 15 (July 1938): 53–54; Baltimore City Health Department, "Syphilis in Industry" (Baltimore: n.d.).

23. Baltimore City Health Department, Annual Report (1940), 149–51.

24. Baltimore City Health Department, Annual Report (1941), 139.

25. "City Shown Second in Syphilis Survey," *Baltimore Sun*, 22 October 1941.

26. "High Syphilis Rate Laid to Race Ratio," *Baltimore Sun*, 26 October 1941.

27. "Says Vice Control Has Improved Here," *Baltimore Sun*, 27 January 1943.

28. "State Law Held Needed in War on Vice," *Baltimore Sun*, 28 January 1943.

29. "Stanton Idea for Examination of Prostitutes Is Denounced," *Baltimore Sun*, 29 January 1943.

30. "Venereal Picture Dark: Dr. Huntington Williams Says No Improvement Is Expected for Some Time," *Baltimore Sun*, 21 January 1943.

31. "Clinics Here Under Fire," *Baltimore Sun*, 30 March 1943.

32. "Venereal Disease Rate High in State," *Baltimore Sun*, 15 June 1943.

33. Parran and Vonderlehr, *Plain Words About Venereal Disease*, especially 96–120.

34. Baltimore City Health Department, Annual Report (1943), 148.

35. C. Howe Eller, "A Sex Education Project and Serologic Survey in a Baltimore High School," *Baltimore Health News* 21 (November 1944): 83.

36. Emily V. Clapp, *Growing Up in the World Today* (Boston: n.d.).

37. *Ibid.*, 14.

38. For the development of penicillin therapy, see Harry F. Dowling, *Fighting Infection: Conquests of the Twentieth Century* (Cambridge: 1977): 125–57.

39. Baltimore City Health Department, Annual Report (1945), 29.

40. Baltimore City Health Department, Annual Report (1945), 145–46; "Venereal Law Made Specific," *Baltimore Sun*, 26 August 1945.

41. "End of VD—Cure Center Seen as Calamity," *Evening Sun*, 12 June 1946.

42. "A Temporary Power Made Permanent," *Baltimore Sun*, 9 January 1947.

43. "Rapid Treatment," Press Bulletin No. 1043, Maryland State Department of Health, (27 January 1947) Enoch Pratt Library, Maryland Room, Baltimore.

44. *Ibid.*

The Unexplored Story of HIV and Aging

George P. Schmid, Brian G. Williams, Jesus Maria Garcia-Calleja, Chris Miller, Emily Segar, Monica Southworth, David Tonyan, Jocelyn Wacloff, and James Scott

As people in developing and industrialized countries increasingly live longer, healthier lives, why do the scant data that exist suggest a surprisingly high prevalence and incidence of HIV among individuals 50 years of age and over ("older individuals")?

Older individuals are rarely included in Demographic Health Surveys (DHS). In the last five years, only 13 of 30 surveys included older males and none included older females. The National Health and Nutrition Examination Survey in the United States of America

(US) does not collect data from people older than 49. There is a dearth of prevalence data; what about incidence?

Incidence could be determined via case reporting, serologic incidence assays or modelling. Developing countries have limited case-reporting systems, but industrialized countries do better. In the US, case reporting from 2003 to 2006 shows the proportion of older HIV-positive individuals has climbed from 20 percent to 25 percent and numbers of cases have risen in all 5-years age bands from 45 years to 65 years and older;[1] using serology, 11 percent of 2006 incident cases are in older individuals.[2] In WHO's European Region, 8 percent of reported cases in 2005 are older.[3] Similar data from the developing world are unavailable, and modelled incidence data are not publicly available.

We have calculated prevalence by age, using UNAIDS' estimated numbers of cases of HIV and United Nations population estimates, by country. One finds a consistent pattern that prevalence in older individuals is one-quarter to one-third that of the 15–49-year age group. We have debated with our colleagues whether these findings are surprising. Most of us think "yes".

This is particularly so because prevalences for this age group are deceptively low. There is little appreciation that the older the individual, the faster the progression from HIV infection to AIDS.[1,4,5] The effect is considerable, linear and remains after adjusting for all-cause mortality.[4,5] For example, there is a life expectancy of more than 13 years in people infected at age 5–14. This declines to 4 years in those infected at age 65 or older.[5] Waning immunity with age may be the reason. Since incidence is indirectly related to duration of disease, prevalence in those aged 50 and above should be approximately doubled to be compared with those in the 15–24 year age group. While long-available anti-retroviral therapy (ART) could increase prevalence among older individuals in industrialized countries, this is not true of the developing world, where ART was introduced later.

Is the epidemiology of HIV in older individuals of purely academic interest? No, because understanding risk factors leads to interventions. Intriguingly, the Alpha Network in Africa has shown that in many sites, secondary peaks of HIV incidence appear at older ages.[6] Why might older individuals be becoming infected? We can only conjecture. In a systematic literature search, we found only one, limited, epidemiological study exploring HIV acquisition in older individuals, from urban US.

Sexual activity of older individuals in the developing world is barely researched. Many older individuals everywhere are sexually active, although interest in sex and frequency of vaginal intercourse decline with age.[7] Since 1998, erectile-dysfunction drugs have been extending the sex life of many older individuals and, at the same time, may be extending the HIV epidemic into older age groups. Many studies show that older individuals are less likely than their younger counterparts to practise safer sex. While erectile dysfunction is common and erectile-dysfunction drugs are widely distributed in developing countries,[8] no study has been done of their possible impact on the HIV epidemic, although their use in industrialized countries has been associated with risky sexual practices.[9] Whether HIV-positive men should be prescribed these drugs has been debated.[10]

If sex is the main cause of HIV infection in older individuals and many older individuals are not having penetrative intercourse, then the risk of acquiring HIV per sexual act in these individuals must be high. We can only speculate what the reasons may be. The thinning of vaginal mucosa with age may play a role; for both sexes, the prevalence of antibodies against herpes simplex virus 2 increases with age,[11] indicating continual risky sexual behaviour and enhanced risk of HIV transmission.

While sexual activity is the most likely mode of transmission, research is required to establish the relative contribution of different risk factors and modes of transmission.

One consistent finding is the failure to consider HIV as a cause of illness in older individuals. These individuals have a shorter time from diagnosis to onset of AIDS,[1] reflecting both age-related faster progression to AIDS and doctors' failure to consider HIV as a diagnosis. Screening is less common for older adults, who are assumed not to be at risk.

HIV prevalence and incidence in the over-50-year-olds seem surprisingly high and the risk factors are totally unexplored. Understanding the epidemiology of HIV infection in older individuals can lead to interventions to make these years safer and more enjoyable.

Source: "The unexplored story of HIV and ageing" by George P. Schmid, et al.: *Bulletin of the World Health Organization* 2009; 87:162–162. doi: 10.2471/BLT.09.064030. © World Health Organization 2009. All rights reserved. The World Health Organization has granted the publisher permission to reproduce this article.

REFERENCES

Available at: http://www.who.int/bulletin/volumes/87/3/09-064030/en/index.html

NOTES

1. Centers for Disease Control and Prevention. *HIV/AIDS surveillance report 2006, vol. 18.* Atlanta, GA: Department of Health and Human Services, Centers for Disease Control and Prevention; 2008. pp. 1–55.

2. Hall Hl, Song R, Rhodes P, Prejean J, An Q, Lee LM, et. al., Estimation of HIV incidence in the United States. *JAMA* 300:520-9. PMID:18677024 doi:10.1001/jama.300.5.520

3. European Centre for Disease Prevention and Control/WHO Regional Office for Europe, *HIV/AIDS surveillance in Europe 2007.* Stockholm: European Centre for Disease Prevention and Control; 2008.

4. Babiker AG, Peto T, Porter K, Walker AS, and Darbyshire JH. Age as a determinant of survival in HIV infection. *J Clin Epidemiol* 2001;54:S16–21. PMID:11750205 dol:10.1016/S0895-4356(01)00456-5

5. Collaborative Group on AIDS Incubation and HIV Survival. Time from HIV-1 seroconversion to AIDS and death before widespread use of highly-active anti-retroviral therapy. A collaborative analysis. *Lancet* 2000;355:1131–7. PMID:10791375 doi:10.1016/S0140-6736(00)02061-4

6. Zaba B, Todd J, Biraro S, et al. Diverse age patterns of HIV incidence rates in Africa. Proceedings of the XVII International AIDS Conference, Mexico City, 2008.

7. Lindau ST, Schumm LP, Laumann EO, Levinson W, O'Muircheartaigh CA, and Waite LJ. A study of sexuality and health among older adults in the United States. *N Engl J Med* 2007;357:762–74. PMID:17715410 doi:10.1056/NEJMoa067423

8. Khalaf IM, Levinson IP. Editorial. Erectile dysfunction in the Africa/Middle East Region: Epidemiology and experience with sildenafil citrate (Viagra). *Int J Impot Res* 2003;15:S1–2. PMID:12825101 doi:10.1038/sj.ijir.3900967

9. Pantalone DW, Bimbi DS, and Parsons JT. Motivations for the recreational use of erectile enhancing medications in urban gay and bisexual men. *Sex Transm Infect* 2008;84:458–62. PMID: 19028947 doi:10.1136/sti.2008.031476

10. Sadeghi-Nejad H, Watson R, Irwin R, Nokes K, Gern A, and Price D. Erectile dysfunction in the HIV-positive male: A review of medical, legal and ethical considerations in the age of oral pharmacotherapy. *Int J Impot Res* 2000;12 Suppl 3;S49–53, PMID:11002402 doi: 10.1038/sj.ljir.3900562

11. Smith JS, and Robinson NJ. Age-specific prevalence of infection with herpes simplex virus types 2 and 1: a global review. *J Infect Dis* 2002;186 Supp 1;S3–28. PMID:12353183 doi: 10.1086/343739

DAMAGED GOODS: WOMEN MANAGING THE STIGMA OF STDS

ADINA NACK

The HIV/AIDS epidemic has garnered the attention of researchers from a variety of academic disciplines. In contrast, the study of other sexually transmitted diseases (STDs) has attracted limited interest outside of epidemiology and public health. In the United States, an estimated three out of four sexually active adults have human papillomavirus infections (HPV—the virus that can cause genital warts); one out of five have genital herpes infections (Ackerman, 1998; Centers for Disease Control and Prevention [CDC], 1998a). In contrast, the nationwide rate of HIV infection is approximately 1 out of 300 (CDC, 1998b). Current sociological research on the interrelationships between sexual health, stigma, and the self has focused overwhelmingly on HIV/AIDS (Sandstrom, 1990; Siegel and Krauss, 1991; Weitz, 1989). . . .

This article focuses on how the sexual self-concept is transformed when the experience of living with a chronic STD casts a shadow of disease on the health and desirability of a woman's body, as well as on her perceived possibilities for future sexual experiences. The term *sexual self* means something fundamentally different from *gender identity* or *sexual identity*. Invoking the term *sexual self* is meant to conjure up the innately intimate parts of individuals' self-concepts that encompass how they think of themselves with regards to their experienced and imagined sensuality. Components of a sexual self may include the following: level of sexual experience, emotional memories of sexual pleasure (or lack thereof), perception of one's body as desirable, and perception of one's sexual body parts as healthy. . . .

To understand the individual-level experience of living with a chronic STD, it is important to take into account how these infections are symbolically constructed in American culture. The meanings that Americans give to being infected with an STD are intersubjectively formed during interactions. Individuals' experiences of health, illness, and medical care "are connected to the particular historically located social arrangements and the cultural values of any society" (Conrad and Kern, 1994:5). Present American social values reflect the longstanding connections between sexual health and morality: Interactions with medical practitioners and lay people are the conduit through which the stigma of STDs is reinforced (Brandt, 1987). Pryce (1998) pointed to a critical gap—the "missing" sociology of sexual disease—and asserted that this application of sociology should focus on the social construction of the body as central in the medical and social iconography of STDs.

In answer to Pryce's (1998) challenge, this research . . . sociologically analyz[es] the impact of genital herpes and HPV on women's sexual selves. This study adds to this research area by examining sexual self-transformation, starting from the point of how individuals' sexual selves are transformed by the lived experiences of being diagnosed and treated for chronic STDs. Beginning from a premise that

From "Damaged Goods: Women Managine the Stigma of STDs" by Adina Nack, *Deviant Behavior*, Vol. 21, Issue 2, 2000, pp. 95–121. Copyright © 2000 Routledge, reprinted by permission of the publisher (Taylor & Francis Ltd, http://www.tandf.co.uk/journals).

the majority of people grow up feeling sexually invincible, a variety of traumas have the capacity to disrupt a positive sexual self-concept (e.g., molestation, rape, and illness). Social-interactional traumas also transmit messages that can damage sexual selves: Some physical bodies are undesirable; some sexual preferences are unacceptable; some levels of sexual experience are immoral.

SETTING AND METHOD

The motivation for this study stems from my personal experience with STDs. My "complete membership role" (Adler and Adler, 1987) stems from legitimacy and acceptance by other women with STDs as a member of this unorganized and stigmatized group. At 20, sexual health became the center of my world when I was diagnosed with mild cervical dysplasia, the result of an HPV infection. I began an informal self-education process that helped me manage the stress of my treatments. My commitment to managing my sexual health status would become the foundation for this research project and provide me with the personal insights needed to connect with others facing STDs and the clinical knowledge necessary to be a sexual health researcher.

As a campus sexual health educator, I began to question what sexual health services were not provided. Seeing that women and men were being diagnosed and treated for STDs without receiving follow-up education and counseling, I developed a women-only support group for individuals dealing with STDs. Because of the topic's sensitive nature, I chose a gender-segregated approach to the support group and, ultimately, to the research. . . .

Unfortunately, only one woman used the support group. Initially disheartened, I began to question why people flocked to other support groups that were based on shared stigma (e.g., eating disorders and alcoholism) but failed to use this sexual health support group. Even persons living with HIV and AIDS used support groups to collectively manage their stigma. . . .

To investigate the failure of this support group, I conducted a survey among patients using a local women's health care clinic. During a month chosen at random, clinic staff gave each patient who came in for an appointment an anonymous survey about a new service being offered: a women's sexual health support group. In all, 279 completed surveys were collected. . . . Owing to the population from which the sample was drawn, generalizability is restricted to the population of women who receive women's health care services from this clinic. . . .

I performed a multiple regression analysis on the data, the results of which supported the hypothesis that a person who has been diagnosed with an STD is less likely to be interested in a sexual health support group. . . . One of the most revealing findings was that only 23.3 percent of the women were definitely interested ("yes") in a sexual health support group. . . .

I interpreted this finding to reflect that the stigma of having an STD is so severe that the perceived cost of disclosing this sexual health status to strangers outweighs the possible benefits. Because there has yet to be a moral entrepreneurial campaign to destigmatize STDs in our society, the norm remains secrecy (Brandt, 1987). . . .

On the basis of these findings, I determined that in-depth interviews were my best chance for obtaining valid data. I constructed my research methods to reflect a reciprocal intention: As the women gave their stories to me, I would offer my support and resources as a sexual health educator. . . .

My first hurdle was to achieve approval from the campus Human Research Committee. . . . Because of the confidential nature of individuals' STD diagnoses, I was not allowed to directly recruit participants. Rather, they had to approach me, usually after hearing about my research project from other participants or women's health care practitioners with whom I had consulted. . . . I used snowball sampling to generate interviews.

I conducted 28 conversational, unstructured interviews with consensual participants, who ranged in age from 19 to 56. . . . I conducted the interviews in participants' preferred locations: their homes, my home, or other private settings. The interviews lasted from 1 to 2 hours and were tape recorded with the participants' permission. When appropriate, I concluded the interview with offers to provide sexual health information and resources, either in the form of health education materials or referrals to resources.

I then analyzed the data according to the principles of grounded theory (Glaser and Strauss, 1967). . . . With each interview, I started to cluster participants' experiences around particular stages to check the validity of my initial model. The six stages of sexual self-transformation [that emerged from the interviews] in chronological order, are as follows: sexual invincibility, STD suspicion, diagnostic crisis, damaged goods, healing/treatment, and integration. . . .

STIGMA AND THE SEXUAL SELF

For all but 1 of the 28 women, their STD diagnoses radically altered the way that they saw themselves as sexual beings. Facing both a daunting medical and social reality, the women used different strategies to manage their new stigma. Each stigma management strategy had ramifications for the transformation of their sexual selves.

Stigma Nonacceptance

Goffman (1963) proposed that individuals at risk for a deviant stigma are either "the discredited" or "the discreditable." The discrediteds'

stigma was known to others either because the individuals revealed the deviance or because the deviance was not concealable. In contrast, the discreditable were able to hide their deviant stigma. Goffman found that the majority of discreditables were "passing" as nondeviants by avoiding "stigma symbols," anything that would link them to their deviance, and by using "disidentifiers," props or actions that would lead others to believe they had a nondeviant status. Goffman (1963) also noted that individuals bearing deviant stigma might eventually resort to "covering," one form of which he defined as telling deceptive stories. To remain discreditable in their everyday lives, 19 of the women used the individual stigma management strategies of passing and/or covering. In contrast, 9 women revealed their health status to select friends and family members soon after receiving their diagnoses.

Passing

The deviant stigma of women with STDs was essentially concealable, though revealed to the necessary inner circle of health care and health insurance providers. For the majority, passing was an effective means of hiding stigma from others, sometimes even from themselves.

Hillary, a 22-year-old White college senior, recalled the justifications she had used to distance herself from the reality of her HPV infection and to facilitate passing strategies.

At the time, I was in denial about it. I told myself that that wasn't what it was because my sister had had a similar thing happen, the dysplasia. So, I just kind of told myself that it was hereditary. That was kinda funny because I asked the nurse that called if it could be hereditary, and she said "No, this is completely sexually transmitted"—I really didn't accept it until a few months after my cryosurgery.

Similarly, Gloria, a Chicana graduate student . . . was not concerned about a previous case of gonorrhea she had cured with antibiotics or her chronic HPV "because the warts went away." Out of sight, out of her sex life: "I never told anybody about them because I figured they had gone away, and they weren't coming back. Even after I had another outbreak, I was still very promiscuous. It still hadn't registered that I needed to always have the guy use a condom."

When the women had temporarily convinced themselves that they did not have a contagious infection, it was common to conceal the health risk with partners because the women themselves did not perceive the risk as real. Kayla, a . . . White college senior, felt justified in passing as healthy with partners who used condoms, even though she knew that condoms could break. Cleo, a White 31-year-old . . . , had sex with a partner after being diagnosed with HPV.

So at the time I had sex with him, yes, I knew but, no, I hadn't been treated yet. That gets into the whole "I never told him," and I didn't. Part of me thought I should, and part of me thought that having an STD didn't fit with my self-concept so much that I just couldn't disclose.

Francine, a White 43-year-old professional . . . , had never intended to pass as healthy, but she did not get diagnosed with herpes until after beginning a sexual relationship with her second husband.

I think there was all the guilt: What if I bring this on you? So, I felt guilt in bringing this into the relationship. Because he had not been anywhere near as sexually active as I had. . . .

Similarly, Tasha, a White graduate student, found out that she might have inadvertently passed as healthy when her partner was diagnosed with chlamydia. "I freaked out—I was like, 'Oh my God! I gave you chlamydia. I am so sorry! I am so sorry!' I felt really horrible, and I felt really awful." . . . Even if the passing is done unintentionally, it still brings guilt to the passer.

The women also tried to disidentify themselves from sexual disease in their attempts to pass as being sexually healthy. Rather than actively using a verbal or symbolic prop or action that would distance them from the stigma, the women took a passive approach. Some gave nonverbal agreement to putdowns of other women who were known to have STDs. For example, Hillary recalled such an interaction.

It's funny being around people that don't know that I have an STD and how they make a comment like "That girl, she's such a slut. She's a walking STD." And how that makes me feel when I'm confronted with that, and having them have no idea that they could be talking about me.

Others kept silent about their status and tried to maintain the social status of being sexually healthy and morally pure. . . . Putting up the facade of sexual purity, these women distanced themselves from any suspicion of sexual disease.

Covering

When passing became too difficult, some women resorted to covering to deflect family and friends from the truth. Cleo summed up the rationale by comparing her behavior to what she had learned growing up with an alcoholic father. " . . . I learned that's what you do. Like you don't tell people those things that you consider shameful, and then, if confronted, you know, you lie."

Hillary talked to her parents about her HPV surgery, but never as treatment for an STD. She portrayed her moderate, cervical dysplasia as a precancerous scare, unrelated to sex. . . . When Tasha's sister helped her get a prescription for pubic lice, she actually provided the cover story for her embarrassed younger sister. "She totally took control, and made a personal inquiry: 'So, how did you get this? From a toilet seat?' And, I was like, 'a toilet seat,' and she believed me." . . . For Anne, a 28-year-old . . . graduate student, a painful herpes outbreak almost outed her on a walk with a friend. She was so physically uncomfortable that she was actually waddling. Noticing her strange behavior, her friend asked what was wrong. Anne told her that it was a hemorrhoid; that was only a partial truth because herpes was the primary cause of her pain. As Anne put it, telling her about the hemorrhoid "was embarrassing enough!"

Deception and Guilt

The women who chose to deny, pass as normal, and use disidentifiers or cover stories shared more than the shame of having an STD—they had also told lies. With lying came guilt. Anne, who had used the hemorrhoid cover story, eventually felt extremely guilty. Her desire to conceal the truth was in conflict with her commitment to being an honest person. . . . Deborah, a 32-year-old White professional . . . , only disclosed to her first sexual partner after she had been diagnosed with HPV; she passed as healthy with all other partners. Deborah reflected, "I think my choices not to disclose have hurt my sense of integrity." However, her guilt was resolved during her last gynecological exam when the nurse practitioner confirmed that after years of "clean" pap smear results Deborah was not being "medically unethical" by not disclosing to her partners. In other words, her immune system had probably dealt with the HPV in such a way that she might never have another outbreak or transmit the infection to sexual partners.

When Cleo passed as healthy with a sexual partner, she started "feeling a little guilty about not having told." However, the consequences of passing as healthy were very severe for Cleo:

No. I never disclosed it to any future partner. Then, one day, I was having sex with Josh, my current husband, before we were married, and we had been together for a few months, maybe, and I'm like looking at his penis, and I said, "Oh, my goodness! You have a wart on your penis! Ahhh!" All of a sudden, it comes back to me.

Cleo's decision to pass left her with both the guilt of deceiving and infecting her husband.

Surprisingly, those women who had unintentionally passed as being sexually healthy (i.e., they had no knowledge of their STD status at the time) expressed a similar level of guilt as those who had been purposefully deceitful. Violet, a middle-class, White 36-year-old, had inadvertently passed as healthy with her current partner. Even after she had preventively disclosed to him, she still had to deal with the guilt over possibly infecting him.

It hurt so bad that morning when he was basically furious at me thinking I was the one he had gotten those red bumps from. It was the hour from hell! I felt really majorly dirty and stigmatized. I felt like "God, I've done the best I can: If this is really caused by the HPV I have, then I feel terrible."

When using passing and covering techniques, the women strove to keep their stigma from tainting social interactions. They feared . . . rejection from their social circles of friends, family, and, most important, sexual partners. For most of the women, guilt surpassed fear and became the trigger to disclose. Those who had been deceitful in passing or covering had to assuage their guilt: Their options were either to remain in nonacceptance, disclose, or transfer their guilt to somebody else.

Stigma Deflection

As the women struggled to manage their individual stigma of being sexually diseased, real and imaginary social interactions became the conduit for the contagious label of damaged goods. Now that the unthinkable had happened to them, the women began to think of their past and present partners as infected, contagious, and potentially dangerous to themselves or other women. The combination of transferring stigma and assigning blame to others allowed the women to deflect the STD stigma away from themselves.

Stigma Transference

. . . Stigma is neither an emotion nor an impulse; rather, it is a formal concept that captures a relationship of devaluation (Goffman, 1963). Although the participants attributed their devalued relationship with sexual health ideals to real and imaginary others, they were not controlling unacceptable feelings. Rather, stigma transference manifests as a clear expression of anger and fear, and the women did not connect this strategy to a reduction in their levels of anxiety; in fact, several discussed it in relation to increased anxiety.

Cleo remembered checking her partner's penis for warts after her doctor told her that she could detect them by visual inspection. It became a habit for Kayla to check her partner for any visible symptoms of an STD. Gloria was more careful about checking future partners and asking if they had anything. Tasha explained, "I just felt like I was with someone who was dirty." In all four cases, the women were only sure of their own STD infections, yet in their minds these partners had become diseased.

Transference of stigma to a partner became more powerful when the woman felt betrayed by her partner. When Hillary spoke of the "whole trust issue" with her ex-partner, she firmly believed he had lied to her about his sexual health status and that he would lie to others. Even though she had neither told him about her diagnosis nor had proof of him being infected, she fully transferred her stigma to him. . . .

Kayla also transferred the stigma of sexual disease to an ex-partner, never confronting him about whether he had tested positive for STDs. The auxiliary trait of promiscuity colored her view of him: "I don't know how sexually promiscuous he was, but I'm sure he had had a lot of partners." Robin, a 21-year-old White undergraduate, went so far as to tell her ex-partner that he needed to see a doctor and "do something about it." He doubted her ability to pinpoint contracting genital warts from him and called her a slut. Robin believed that he was the one with the reputation for promiscuity and decided to trash him by telling her two friends who hung out with him. Robin hoped to spoil his sexual reputation and scare off his future partners. In the transference of stigma, the women ascribed the same auxiliary traits onto others that others had previously ascribed to them. . . .

In all cases, it was logical to assume that past and current sexual partners may also have been infected. However, the stigma of being sexually diseased had far-reaching consequences in the women's imaginations. The traumatic impact on their sexual selves led most to infer that future, as yet unknown partners were also sexually diseased. . . . They had already been damaged by at least one partner. Therefore, they expected that future partners, ones who had not yet come into their lives, held the threat of also being damaged goods.

For Hillary, romantic relationships held no appeal anymore. She had heard of others who also had STDs but stayed in non-acceptance and never changed their lifestyle of having casual, unprotected sex:

I just didn't want to have anything to do with it. A lot of it was not trusting people. When we broke up, I decided that I was not having sex. Initially, it was because I wanted to get an HIV test. Then, I came to kind of a turning point in my life and realized that I didn't want to do the one-night-stand thing anymore. It just wasn't worth it. It wasn't fun.

At this stage in her sexual self-transformation, Hillary imagined the world of possible partners having been polluted with contagion.

Anne's lesbian friends [told her] . . . future partners should be suspected of being dangerous. . . . Anne recalled [one] friend's reaction. "Those rotten men! You should just leave them alone. It's clear that you should be with women, and it's safer and better that way. Women don't do this kind of thing to each other." Her friends' guidance was an overt attempt to encourage Anne to believe that only potential male partners bore the stigma.

Instead of going by gender, Gloria, a self-identified Chicana, made a distinction based on ethnicity as a predictor of sexual health status:

Now, if it was a White man, I made 'em wear a condom because I got it from a White man, and so I assumed that there had to be something with their culture—they were more promiscuous. But, one thing I do know culturally and with the times is that Chicano men were more likely to have a single partner.

These women felt justified in their newfound attitudes about sexual partners. What was only supposed to happen to "bad" women had happened to them. Overall, these women transitioned from blaming their own naivete to blaming someone else for not being more cautious or more honest.

Blame

The women's uses of stigma transference techniques were attempts to alleviate their emotional burdens. First, the finger of shame and guilt pointed inward, toward the women's core sexual selves. Their sexual selves became tainted, dirty, damaged. In turn, they directed the stigma outward to both real and fictional others. Blaming others was a way for all of the women to alleviate some of the internal pressure and turn the anger outward. This emotional component of the damaged goods stage externalized the pain of their stigma.

Francine recalled how she and her first husband dealt with the issue of genital warts. . . . Francine's husband had likely contracted geni-

tal warts from his wild fraternity parties: "We really thought of it as, that woman who did the trains [serial sexual intercourse]. It was still a girl's fault kind of thing." By externalizing the blame to the promiscuous women at fraternity parties, Francine exonerated not only herself but also her husband. . . .

For Violet, it was impossible to neatly deflect the blame away from both herself and her partner.

I remember at the time just thinking, "Oh man! He gave it to me!" While he was thinking, "God, [Violet]! You gave this to me!" So, we kind of just did a truce in our minds. Like, OK, we don't know who gave it—just as likely both ways. So, let's just get treated. We just kind of dropped it.

Clearly, the impulse to place blame was strong even when there was no easy target.

Often, the easiest targets were men who exhibited the auxiliary traits of promiscuity and deception. Tasha wasn't sure which ex-partner had transmitted the STD. However, she rationalized blaming a particular guy. "He turned out to be kind of a huge liar, lied to me a lot about different stuff. And, so I blamed him. All the other guys were, like, really nice people, really trustworthy." Likewise, when I asked Violet from whom she believed she had contracted chlamydia, she replied, "Dunno, it could've been from one guy, because that guy had slept with some unsavory women, so therefore he was unsavory." . . .

The actual guilt or innocence of these blame targets was secondary. What mattered to the women was that they could hold someone else responsible.

Stigma Acceptance

Eventually, every woman in the study stopped denying and deflecting the truth of her sexual health status by disclosing to loved ones. The women disclosed for either preventive or therapeutic reasons. That is, they were either motivated to reveal their STD status to prevent harm to themselves or others or to gain the emotional support of confidants.

Preventive and Therapeutic Disclosures

The decision to make a preventive disclosure was linked to whether the STD could be cured. Kayla explained,

Chlamydia went away, and I mean it was really bad to have that, but I mean it's not something that you have to tell people later 'cause you know, in case it comes back. Genital warts, you never know.

Kayla knew that her parents would find out about the HPV infection because of insurance connections. Before her cryosurgery, Kayla decided to tell her mom about her condition.

. . . [I]t was kind of hard at first. But, she wasn't upset with me. Main thing, she was disappointed, but I think she blamed my boyfriend more than she blamed me.

. . . Preventive disclosures to sexual partners, past and present, were a more problematic situation. The women were choosing to put themselves in a position where they could face blame, disgust, and rejection. For those reasons, the women put off preventive disclosures to partners as long as possible. For example, Anne made it clear that she would not have disclosed her herpes to a female sexual partner had they not been about to have sex. After "agonizing weeks and weeks and weeks before trying to figure out how to tell," Diana, a 45-year-old African American professional, finally shared her HPV and herpes status before her current relationship became sexual. Unfortunately, her boyfriend had a negative reaction: "He certainly didn't want to touch me anywhere near my genitals." . . .

For Summer, a 20-year-old Native American administrative assistant, and Gloria, their preventive disclosures were actually a relief to their sexual partners. Summer decided to disclose her genital warts to a new boyfriend after they had been "getting hot n' heavy." Lying in bed together, she said, "I need to tell you something." After she disclosed, he lay there, staring at the ceiling for a couple of minutes before deeply exhaling, "I thought you were going to tell me you had AIDS." Similarly, one of Gloria's partners sighed in relief when she revealed that she had herpes; he thought she was going to say she was HIV positive.

Many of the therapeutic disclosures were done to family members. The women wanted the support of those who had known them the longest. . . . Tasha disclosed to her mother right after she was diagnosed with chlamydia.

My family died—"Guess what, mom, I got chlamydia." She's like, "Chlamydia? How did you find out you got chlamydia?" I'm like, "Well, my boyfriend got an eye infection." [laughter] "How'd he get it in his eye?" [laughter] So, it was the biggest joke in the family for the longest time!

. . . The women often unburdened their feelings of shame and guilt onto their close friends. Cleo shared her feelings with her roommate: "I told her that I was feeling weird about having had sex with this second guy, knowing that I had an STD." Kayla's therapeutic disclosure was reciprocal with her best friend. "At that time, she was also going through a similar situation with her boyfriend, so I felt okay finally to talk about it." . . . In Anne's case, her therapeutic disclosure to a friend was twofold: both to seek support and to apologize for initially having used the hemorrhoid cover story. Anne explained to her friend that she had felt too uncomfortable to tell the truth. . . .

Consequences of Disclosure

With both therapeutic and preventive disclosure, the women experienced some feelings of relief in being honest with loved ones. However, they still carried the intense shame of being sexually diseased women. The resulting emotion was anxiety over how their confidants would react: rejection, disgust, or betrayal. Francine was extremely anxious about disclosing to her husband. "That was really tough on us because I had to go home and tell Damon that I had this outbreak of herpes . . . I was really fearful— I didn't think that he would think I had recently had sex with somebody else—but, I was still really afraid of what it would do to our relationship." . . .

Overall, disclosing intensified the anxiety of having their secret leaked to others in whom they would never have chosen to confide. In addition, each disclosure brought with it the possibility of rejection and ridicule from the people whose opinions they valued most. For Gloria, disclosing was the right thing to do but had painful consequences when her partner's condom slipped off in the middle of sexual intercourse.

I told him it doesn't feel right. "You'd better check." And, so he checked, and he just jumped off me and screamed, "Oh fuck!" And, I just thought, oh no, here we go. He just freaked and went to the bathroom and washed his penis with soap. I just felt so dirty.

The risk paid off for Summer, whose boyfriend asserted, "I don't ever want to be *that guy*—the one who shuns people and treats them differently." He borrowed sexual health education materials and spent over an hour asking her questions about various STDs. Even in this best-case scenario, the sexual intimacy in this relationship became problematized (e.g., having to research modes of STD transmission and safe-sex techniques). Disclosures were the interactional component of self-acceptance. The women became fully grounded in their new reality when they realized that the significant people in their lives were now viewing them through the discolored lenses of sexual disease.

CONCLUSION

The women with STDs went through an emotionally difficult process, testing out stigma management strategies, trying to control the impact of STDs on both their self-concepts and on their relationships with others. . . .

Ironically, most of the women first tried to deny this deviant health status—one that was virtually secret through the protection of doctor-patient confidentiality laws. Although many used passing and covering techniques that relied on deceiving others, self-deception was impossible to maintain. The medical truth began to penetrate their sexual self-conceptions as soon as they fabricated their first lie. To strategize a successful ruse, it was necessary to know the scope of what they were trying to hide.

When guilt caught up with them, making it hard to pass as healthy, their goal shifted to stigma deflection. . . . However, this only delayed the inevitable—a deviant sexual self that penetrated the women's prior conceptions of their sexual selves.

After mentally transferring their stigma to real and imaginary others, all of the women finally accepted their tainted sexual health status through the reflexive dynamics of disclosure. . . . The women's sexual selves moved along a deviant career path by means of the interactive dynamics of their stigma management strategies.

. . . As the women made choices on which stigma management strategies to use, they grappled with the ramifications of internalizing this new label. Choosing passing and covering techniques meant they could remain in non-acceptance and put off stigma internalization. When they deflected the stigma onto others by means of stigma transference, the women glimpsed the severity of an STD stigma as reflected in the presumed sexual selves of real and imaginary others. Finally, the women's disclosures confirmed the new story of their tainted sexual selves.

. . . Unlike the stigma of HIV/AIDS—which carries the threat of life-changing illness, death, and contagion beyond the scope of sexual behaviors—the STD stigma lends itself to compartmentalization. The women were able to hide their shame, guilt, and fear (of further health complications, of contaminating others, of rejection, etc.) in the sexual part of their self-concept. They recognized that this part of their self-concept did not have to affect their entire identity. . . . If the impact of the STDs on their sex lives ever became too emotionally painful, the women could always decide to distance themselves from this role: choosing temporary or permanent celibacy. . . .

A narrative model of the self proposes that personal myths create the self and become "the stories we live by" (McAdams, 1996:266). I propose that we seek to understand the significance of the stories we choose not to live by. Personal STD "stories" are rarely told in American mass culture. McAdams, (1996:22) proposed that "carrying on affairs in secret"—maintaining a discreditable stigma—is a way to keep stigmatizing stories from occupying center stage in people's personal myth. However, these data suggest that individuals manage identity transformations, especially transformations into deviant identities, by constructing and sharing self-narratives through disclosure interactions. Although the women do not maintain secrecy, they do keep their STD stories from center stage. . . .

REFERENCES

Ackerman, Sandra J. 1998. "HPV: Who's Got It and Why They Don't Know." *HPV News* 8(2):1; 5–6.

Adler, Patricia A. and Peter Adler. 1987. *Membership Roles in Field Research.* Newbury Park, CA: Sage.

Brandt, Allan M. 1987. *No magic bullet: A social history of venereal disease in the United States since 1880.* New York: Oxford University Press.

Centers for Disease Control and Prevention. 1998a. "Genital Herpes." *National Center for HIV, STD & TB Prevention.* Retrieved from the World Wide Web February 4, 1998: URL.

———.1998b. "HIV/AIDS Surveillance Report." *National Center for HIV, STD & TB Prevention.* Retrieved from the World Wide Web February 4, 1998: URL.

Conrad, Peter, and Rochelle Kern, eds. 1994. *The Sociology of Health & Illness: Critical Perspectives.* 4th ed. New York: St. Martin's Press.

Glaser, Barney G. and Anselm L. Strauss. 1967. *The Discovery of Grounded Theory: Strategies for Qualitative Research.* Chicago: Aldine.

Goffman, Erving. 1963. *Stigma.* Englewood Cliffs, N.J.: Prentice Hall.

McAdams, Dan P. 1996. *The stories we live by: Personal myths and the making of the self.* New York: Guilford Press.

Pryce, Anthony. 1998. "Theorizing the Pox: A Missing Sociology of VD." Presented to the International Sociological Association.

Sandstrom, Kent L. 1990. "Confronting Deadly Disease: the Drama of Identity Construction among Gay Men with AIDS." *Journal of Contemporary Ethnography,* 19(3):271–94.

Siegel, Karolynn and Beatrice J. Krauss. 1991. "Living with HIV Infection: Adaptive Tasks of Seropositive Gay Men." *Journal of Health and Social Behavior* 32(1):17–32.

Weitz, Rose. 1989. "Uncertainty and the Lives of Persons with AIDS." *Journal of Health and Social Behavior* 30(3):270–81.

HPV Vaccines: Kids and Controversy

Evelina Sterling and Wendy Simonds

Genital human papillomavirus (usually called HPV) is the most common sexually transmitted infection. HPV can be contracted through genital contact or oral, anal, or vaginal penetrative sexual activity. Its prevalence can be explained, in part, by the fact that most people infected with HPV are unaware of their infection, as there are often no symptoms. In 90 percent of HPV cases, a healthy immune system will keep the virus in check, preventing any problems. For the other 10 percent, HPV causes genital warts, cervical cancer, or other less common (but also serious) cancers that affect the vulva, vagina, penis, anus, tongue, throat or tonsils. New research suggests that HPV also may be linked to cardiovascular disease. While most people are exposed to HPV at some point in their lives, it is impossible to predict whether or not an individual is at risk for developing any of these long-term and possibly life-threatening complications (CDC, 2011b).

In 2006, the FDA approved Gardasil, the first vaccine designed to prevent two types of HPV known to be associated with 70 percent of all cervical cancers, as well as two other HPV types associated with genital warts. (There are more than 40 different types of HPV.) The introduction of Gardasil was highly controversial, especially because its manufacturer, Merck & Co., actively lobbied states for mandates that would require the vaccine for all girls in order to attend school (Boston Women's Health Book Collective, 2011). Because the vaccine was found to be less effective if administered after exposure to HPV, mandates were proposed to target girls as young as nine in order to reach them before their first sexual experience. (Once someone has HPV—and most sexually active individuals do, regardless of sexual orientation or number of partners, the HPV vaccine is ineffective). At this writing, 41 states have introduced legislation concerning HPV vaccines, but only Texas (which was later revoked), Virginia, and the District of Columbia have enacted HPV vaccine mandates. Both Virginia and the District of Columbia allow parents to opt out easily (Gostin, 2011).

There is no doubt that cancer is serious. Cervical cancer, for example, is the eighth most common cancer among women in the United States and the second leading cancer killer of women worldwide. Over 12,000 women are diagnosed with cervical cancer in the United States each year, and about 4,000 American women die from it annually (CDC, 2011a). But should the HPV vaccine be mandatory for all girls and young women in order to prevent cancer? And should we also mandate the vaccine for all boys to prevent their associated cancers? The short answer: It's complicated. Most mandated childhood vaccines are for diseases that spread easily from person to person during regular daily contact; not for sexually transmitted diseases.

Across the political spectrum, a range of groups are voicing concerns about vaccine mandates. Religious and moral conservatives are adamantly opposed to mandating HPV vaccination. Strong proponents of abstinence-only sex education believe that lowering the risk of STIs promotes sex outside marriage. Health education experts also question the mandate, but for different reasons. Separating HPV prevention from comprehensive health education aimed at teaching adolescents to protect their sexual well-being could prove problematic. Some argue that having the vaccine could give kids a false sense of security about being protected against STIs in general, and lead to lowered concern with safer sex practices. Other critics feel parents should be encouraged to talk with their health care providers openly and honestly about what is right for their particular family, without any government intervention or industry influence.

Causing more concern, Gardasil was introduced to the public much more quickly than other previous vaccines and with limited research. Participants in clinical trials of Gardasil were primarily older girls and adult women, so there is still much to be learned about the most effective dosage and the long-term effects for younger girls, especially pre-teens, as well as boys and men. Although millions of young girls have been vaccinated against HPV using Gardasil and Cervarix (a newer HPV vaccine distributed by GlaxoSmithKline) within the past several years, the safety profiles of these drugs are just starting to become available. HPV vaccines are said to be as safe as or safer than other commonly used vaccines, but no vaccine is without risk. Common side effects reported with the HPV vaccines include fainting, pain, swelling at the injection site, headaches, nausea, and fever. According to the CDC (2011c), out of 35 million doses of Gardasil given in the United States, they received 18,727 reports of adverse events; 92 percent of these reports were non-serious. In total, there were reports of 68 deaths, but none, according to the CDC (2011c), were directly attributable to the vaccine.

Another distinguishing feature of the HPV vaccine is that it was initially recommended only for girls. Men are less likely to get HPV-related cancers. Roughly 80 percent of HPV-associated cancers affect women, and 20 percent affect men. There is neither a test to detect HPV in men nor one to detect early signs of HPV-associated (anal, penile, and throat) cancers in men. Yet males are as susceptible to HPV as females and are equally involved in transmitting the virus to others. Although the FDA and CDC both recommend the HPV vaccine for boys and young men between the ages of 9 and 26, boys have not been specifically included in any proposed mandates. Originally, much of the debate about whether or not boys should be vaccinated against HPV has focused solely on cost-effectiveness (Bixler, 2011). More recently, the CDC's recommendations for boys emphasize cancer prevention and overall immunity development in the population.

With a vaccination mandate, some adolescents who don't want—or whose parents don't want them to have—the vaccine would be pressured to have it anyway, but access to the vaccine for those with limited means would be greatly increased (as states would contribute substantially to vaccine program funding). Without a mandate, some adolescents would be prevented from getting the vaccine due to lack of parental consent, lack of access, and/or lack of financial resources.

Eliminating HPV and associated cancers requires addressing health disparities. Because the HPV vaccine must be administered in three separate doses over a period of six months to be effective, it is unclear how a successful vaccine campaign aimed at preventing cervical cancer would be administered among individuals without access to regular health care or other prevention services. The HPV vaccine is also expensive; the current cost for the whole series is $400. Those individuals who are least likely to be able to afford or access HPV vaccines on their own are also at highest risk for developing cancer due to limited access to health care. Most women, for example, who die of cervical cancer never had regular Pap tests, had false negative results, or did not receive proper follow-up (Boston Women's Health Book Collective, 2011: 616). Large differences exist in the rates of cervical cancer among women from different racial and ethnic groups. In the United States, rates of cervical cancer are 45 percent higher among Black women and 65 percent higher among Hispanic women than among White women. Death rates from cervical cancer are twice as high for Black women and 42 percent higher for Hispanic women than they are for White women (CDC 2011d). At the global level, disparities can be seen even more sharply: approximately 80 percent of all cervical cancers occur in developing countries without access to Pap tests (Cervical Cancer Action, 2011).

Programs designed to promote sexual health should take specific needs of various sexual communities into account. Many people falsely believe that the risk of HPV and other sexually transmitted infections is relatively low among women who have sex with women. Even many health care providers incorrectly assume that these women do not need to be screened, tested, or educated about HPV and other STIs. Scientific agencies also neglect people who identify as transgender or intersexed in their discussions of HPV and vaccinations. Because anyone is at risk of contracting HPV if they have sexual contact with an infected person, everyone should have access to information and services regarding HPV prevention.

Informed consent is another complex topic associated with vaccinating young boys and girls for HPV. How much involvement should minors, themselves, have in the decision-making process concerning whether or not to be vaccinated against HPV? Can 9-year-old children be part of informed health care decision-making, or should we depend solely on parents or government to decide what is right for young people's sexual health? Adolescents are able to learn about their health options and make decisions about birth control and abortion services (though these rights are constrained in many states by parental notification requirements for abortion and decreased access for poor and rural residents).

The contexts in which people (of all ages) make decisions about sexual experiences must be taken into account. Mandates that focus only on girls are paternalistic and suggest that girls' behavior ought to be brought under control.

Casper and Carpenter (2008) expand on the complexities of sexuality and sexual health among young girls neglected by the public and professional conversations on the vaccine:

On balance, the HPV vaccine controversy has reinforced prevailing understandings of women as responsible for controlling sexual activity and reproduction—and as sexually innocent and endangered. Yet a significant threat to young women—unwanted sex and abuse—is surprisingly absent from current debates; moral conservatives seem not to have recognized the need to protect "presexual" girls from assailant-transmitted HPV (p. 896).

Indeed, discussions of the HPV vaccine and the surrounding controversy in public health and medical literature do not consider the gendered power dynamics that impact heterosexual adolescent (or adult) experiences.

Regardless of the arguments either supporting or opposing the vaccine, all experts agree that HPV vaccines are not 100 percent effective in preventing HPV or its complications. In fact, 30 percent of cervical cancers are caused by HPV strains not covered by the vaccine. Thus, current cancer prevention strategies must continue. It is critical that all women have access to regular health screenings and Pap tests. Early screening is still the most effective method for preventing and identifying cancer. When found early, cervical cancer is one of the most successfully treated cancers, with a 92-percent survival rate (CDC, 2011, 2011d). Additionally, the HPV vaccine does not eliminate the need for safer sex practices. Education and barrier methods of protection (such as condoms and latex dams) remain necessary to prevent HPV, other STIs, and unintended pregnancies.

REFERENCES

Bixler, Jennifer. 2011. "CDC Committee Recommends Boys Receive HPV Vaccine." *CNN Health.* http://www.cnn.com/2011/10/25/health/hpv-vaccine/

Boston Women's Health Book Collective. 2011. "HPV Vaccines." *Our Bodies, Ourselves*. New York, New York: Touchstone, pp. 616–617.

Casper, Monica J., and Laura M. Carpenter. 2008. "Sex, Drugs, and Politics: The HPV Vaccine for Cervical Cancer." *Sociology of Health & Illness*, 30, pp. 886–899.

Centers for Disease Control and Prevention. 2011a. "Cervical Cancer Statistics." http://www.cdc.gov/cancer/cervical/statistics/.

Centers for Disease Control and Prevention. 2011b. "Genital HPV Infection—Fact Sheet." http://www.cdc.gov/std/hpv/stdfact-hpv.htm.

Centers for Disease Control and Prevention. 2011c. "Reports of Health Concerns Following HPV Vaccination." http://www.cdc.gov/vaccinesafety/vaccines/hpv/gardasil.html

Centers for Disease Control and Prevention. 2011d. "Cervical Cancer Rates by Race and Ethnicity." http://www.cdc.gov/features/dscervicalcancer/

Cervical Cancer Action. 2011. "Why Now? About Cervical Cancer." http://www.cervicalcanceraction.org/whynow/about.php

Gostin, Lawrence O. 2011. "Commentary: Mandatory HPV Vaccination and Political Debate." *JAMA*, October 6. http://jama.amaassn.org/content/early/2011/09/28/jama.2011.1525.full

CONDOM USE AND MEANING IN RURAL MALAWI

IDDO TAVORY AND ANN SWIDLER

The introduction of condoms has successfully reduced AIDS prevalence in some high-risk communities around the globe (Dowsett, 1999; Epstein, 1996; Green, 2003), but the situation in sub-Saharan Africa is far less encouraging (Hearst and Chen, 2004; Shelton, 2006). When used consistently, condoms are about 80 to 90 percent effective in preventing heterosexual transmission of HIV (Hearst and Chen, 2004; Weller and Davis, 2003). As Hearst and Chen (2004) note, however, condom use in sub-Saharan Africa is low and inconsistent, especially in "regular" relationships.[1] Sociologists and anthropologists have tried to understand resistance to condom use in terms of beliefs and attitudes (Bledsoe, 1990; Chimbiri, 2007; Johnson-Hanks, 2006; Kaler, 2004; Kalipeni, 1999; McPhail and Campbell, 2001; Obbo, 1995; Smith, 2000, 2004a), and many situate choices about sexual behavior in a larger context of social meanings (Beisel, 1990, 1997; Gagnon, 2004; Laqueur, 1990; Schalet, 2000). This article contributes to the general sociology of culture, as well as the broader issue of condom use for protection against HIV in sub-Saharan Africa. . . .

Here we explore a problem of meaning that has very clear consequences for action—whether people use a condom in a particular sexual interaction. We examine the meanings of condom use from a semiotic perspective, showing how semiotic codes allow individuals to actively and creatively negotiate the ways their own behavior is understood by others (see Derné, 1994). We also explore how semiotic codes determine the meanings of a particular action (in this case using a condom) and thus how they constrain behavior. Using data from more than 600 diaries that record rural Malawians' everyday conversations, we chart three semiotic axes that create possible meanings of condom use: the sensuality or "sweetness" of sex, the question of trust and love, and the assessment of AIDS risk as measured against the perceived dangers of condom use. These axes delineate the semiotic space in which people understand condom use in their sexual relations.

A semiotic perspective provides an explanation for an otherwise striking anomaly: even as awareness of HIV infection has become nearly universal in sub-Saharan Africa and attitudes toward condom use have changed (Thomsen et al., 2003), the use of condoms in "love" relationships—marriages, but also some short-term partnerships—remains miniscule (Chimbiri, 2007; Varga, 2000). Without a semiotic perspective on culture, this gap between attitudes and behavior with respect to condom use remains opaque. Cultural constraints on condom use are real. They do not derive from stubborn cultural beliefs that refuse to acknowledge the dangers of AIDS, rather, they derive from semiotic codes. These codes shape the meanings of condom use for actors' identities (Johnson-Hanks 2002; Smith, 2000); they shape the signals that people send about themselves and their sexual partners, and most important, they shape what the use of a condom says about the character of a sexual relationship.

From "Condom Semiotics: Meaning and Condom Use in Rural Malawi," by Iddo Tavory and Ann Swidler. *American Sociological Review*, Vol. 74, No. 2, April 2009, pp. 171–189. Copyright © 2009, American Sociological Association. Reprinted by permission of SAGE Publications.

We define "semiotic axis" as a dimension that delineates one array of possible meanings—for example, from risky and dangerous to protective and safe—within which condom use is understood. A focus on the semiotic aspects of meaning implies a focus on signs "organized around key oppositions and equations" that are "aligned with a cluster of symbolic attributes" (Silverman, 1983:36). Any cultural object, such as a condom, has multiple possible connections to other cultural meanings. The possible metaphors and meanings may be contradictory or competing, but this multiplicity of meanings allows creative interpretation and renegotiation of an object's significance (Sewell, 1992). . . .

SETTING AND METHOD

Situated in southeast Africa, Malawi is a small, densely populated country of 118,484 square kilometers with a population of about 13 million (Government of Malawi, 2007). The country is divided into three regions (northern, central, and southern) and 27 districts. It is home to many ethnic groups, the largest of which are the Chewa, Tumbuka, Lomwe, Tonga, and Yao. The AIDS rate is extremely high; approximately 12 percent (Government of Malawi, 2004; UNAIDS, 2006) of Malawi's adult population is HIV positive. AIDS is now the leading cause of death for people ages 15 to 49 (Doctor, 2002).

This study was conducted as part of the Malawi Diffusion and Ideational Change Project (MDICP), the core of which is a longitudinal survey exploring the role of social networks in shaping AIDS and fertility-related attitudes and behavior. Semistructured interviews with sub-samples of respondents supplement this project (Watkins et al., 2003). The survey began in 1998, with subsequent waves in 2001, 2004, and 2006. The MDICP study was conducted in three rural research sites: Mchinji in the central region, Rumphi in the north, and Balaka in the south. The initial 1998 sample consists of approximately 1,500 ever-married women and their husbands. This sample was interviewed again in 2001, 2004, and 2006, with the new husbands of widowed or divorced women added to the sample. In 2004, a younger sample of 1,500 men and women ages 15 to 24 (married and unmarried) was added to the survey.[2]

Our analysis is based on more than 600 journals written by local assistants. The MDICP researchers found it difficult to discover through surveys how people actually talk to one another about condoms and AIDS. They thus asked a few local assistants, who had worked as part-time interviewers for the survey project,[3] to keep journals of conversations about AIDS that they overheard or participated in during their daily lives.[4] The project paid journalists $30 for an 80-page school notebook, each about 7,500 words and typically covering several different conversations with multiple participants. The project hired 22 journalists (nine women, 13 men) between 1999 and 2006: three journalists (two men, one woman) contributed, on average, more than 30 journals a year (13 contributed more than five journals per year; the other six wrote less frequently). All journalists are high school graduates with no additional education, young (20s or early 30s), and rely on subsistence agriculture supplemented by casual labor or small-scale retail (as well as intermittent MDICP activities). The journalists were given no training except instructions to listen, to remember what was said as close to word-for-word as possible, and to write. Nor did the researchers define what they meant by "conversations about AIDS." As a result, the content of the journals reflects the journalists' assumptions about what is relevant to AIDS. The journalists recorded conversations in local languages but wrote the journals in English (entries were often hastily written, so the grammar is sometimes poor and words are omitted). . . .

These journals, collected between 1999 and 2006, produced more than 5,000 single-spaced pages, recording everything from public scandals in the marketplace and chief-court proceedings to casual conversations on local minibuses and at bars. Although there are few journalists, they capture a large population. Each journalist had a small number of friends, relatives, and neighbors who all knew each other and interacted fairly frequently. The journalists also interacted with or overheard a more heterogeneous group of strangers and acquaintances, providing a diversity of conversational settings and participants. We changed all names, and we cite journal excerpts using the journalist's pseudonym and the date of the journal. . . .

To supplement the diaries, we asked two local interviewers to conduct 20 interviews with men (N = 10) and women (N = 10) between the ages of 15 and 35. Interviewers selected a convenience sample fitting the age and gender criteria from people sitting in the market, washing clothes at the borehole, walking along the roads, and doing the other tedious and time-consuming chores that structure daily life in rural Malawi. Approximately 80 percent of those invited to participate agreed to an interview. The interviews were semistructured; the interviewer recorded and then translated and transcribed them. The interviewers asked both men and women whether they use condoms, and if not, why; whether their friends use condoms (and why or why not); and their general views on condom use. They also asked for examples of specific situations in which the respondents or their friends had accepted or rejected condom use. Male interviewers spoke to men; a woman interviewed women. . . . To get stories and opinions of both villagers and townspeople, interviewers conducted half of the interviews in the towns of Liwonde and Balaka and in the Ulongwe trading center; they conducted the other ten interviews in villages. The interviews were conducted in chiYao or chiChewa, the two most commonly spoken languages in the district.

Finally, we use data from the 1998, 2001, and 2004 MDICP survey waves to assess the degree of condom acceptance in marriage and to trace changes in condom acceptability over time. The journals come from the same districts and many of the same villages covered by the survey. They thus represent roughly the same population. The journals provide important insights into the persistent resistance to condoms that was revealed in the survey data.

"One Does Not Eat Sweets in a Wrapper": The Axis of Sensuality

Sensuality is the first semiotic axis that structures the meanings of condom use. The most common metaphor for the sexual act in Malawi, as well as in other parts of south and southeast Africa, is that of "sweetness.". . . This metaphor refers to semen and the contact with sexual fluids during sex, as well as the pleasure of the sexual act more generally. It is mostly men that talk about the sweetness of sex, but some women use this metaphor too. These conversations vary from the occasional remark that sex is "very sweet," to elaborate descriptions of how men and women feel sweetness while having intercourse. As the following excerpt shows the sensation of sweetness is important in some people's decisions not to use condoms:

Dili said, "I have said already, I believe, that I can't and I don't even think of using the condom when I am having sex because I don't see the importance [the point] of using [a condom] because when having sex I mean to feel sweet. Her real sweetness, not that I should be having sex with a condom. It's better to continue with masturbation than acting like you are having sex with a woman while you are sexing yourself and the rubber!" (Simon 6/13/2002)

This language of sweetness is closely tied to men's, as well as some women's, unwillingness to use a condom. Many diaries record people in both local languages saying, "It is the same as eating sweets in the wrappers" (see also Preston-Whyte, 1999). In other words, they believe that one cannot experience sexual pleasure when using a condom.

Condom manufacturers in Malawi also use the sweetness metaphor. One new, popular local brand of condoms is actually called *Manyuchi* (honey). This name connotes sweetness, and the condoms are chocolate-scented and tinted, using local understandings of the sweetness of sex to increase the condom's appeal. This language sometimes becomes a resource for the negotiation of condom use. One journalist reported overhearing a story of a man using the name "Manyuchi" to trick a woman into having "sweet" sex, even though she had demanded he use a condom:

Then he was going to the lady after having made a hole in the tip of the condom when the lady was absent. They were having sex [as usual, with a condom] usually while the lady took it for granted that this is safe sex. So one of the days the lady got surprised. Then she asked the man, "I feel like you are releasing sperms and I am feeling sweet." Then the man said that "oh! Don't you know that these latest Manyuchi condoms are sweet, that is why they are called Manyuchi." (Achea 7/01/2005)

The axis of sweetness describes not only sexual interactions, but also men and women who are conceived as sexually competent and desirable. This might seem deceptively similar to the English use of sweetness to refer to sexual partnership. However, while in English "sweetheart" refers to a loved partner, the language of sweetness in Malawi provides a criterion for evaluating sex itself. For example, in one diary, a wife finds out that her husband has another partner, instigating a fight between the wife and the lover in which the lover mocks the wife using the language of sweetness:

You are also a stupid woman. Your husband is fed up with you, you are no longer sweet. This is why he has come and proposed me. I did not propose to him but he was the one who came alone proposing to me and

I am sure that he can't leave me, he is satisfied of me. (Simon 6/25/2003)

The metaphors of sexuality and sensuality in Malawi seem similar to those used in American English to describe the trade-off between sensual pleasure and the benefits of condoms. There is an important structural difference between Malawian and Western semiotics of sensuality, however, that helps explain Malawians' reluctance to use condoms. For rural Malawians, sweetness refers not only to the sexual act in general, but specifically to the release of semen.[5] Contact with semen and vaginal fluids is the essence of sexual pleasure itself. So the use of condoms does not just dull sexual sensation, it eliminates its essential element. A local physiological understanding lies behind the Malawian understanding of sexual pleasure.

Different cultures use metaphors of both heat and taste to describe sex, as Emanatian (1995) shows in the case of the Chagga in Tanzania. Emanatian claims that although there is cross-cultural similarity between the African and English metaphors for sexual pleasure, English speakers tend to use metaphors of heat, force, and friction, rather than taste. These metaphors can be traced back to Renaissance England, where Shakespeare's comedies played with the idea of friction generating "heat" to make sexual unions fruitful (Greenblatt, 1986). In the African context, however, there seems to be a different ethnophysiology at play. Both men and women view the release of semen as the height of sexual sweetness. The sweetness of the semen is also related to fertility,[6] as shown in the following diary excerpt:

Some people were laughing at her husband, saying that his wife has revealed that he is a useless man in terms of sex. He does not produce live sperm. He is not sweet. He is barren. He causes his wife to suffer from *chammimba* [abdominal pain caused by either a recent birth or a long time without bearing children] because of his dead sperm. (Alice 10/29/2004)

. . . . In the West, where individuals focus on friction and movement leading to orgasm, the disadvantage of condoms is that they reduce sexual sensation (Crosby et al., 2005). In Malawi, the understanding of sweetness has very different implications. If sexual pleasure depends on the release of semen into the woman, condom use becomes much more problematic than in cultures where sensuality is tied to the friction and build-up leading to orgasm. While condoms only diminish the sensuality of friction in the Western context, they completely obliterate sensuality in the Malawian context by preventing both men and women from experiencing "the sweet."

Cancer, Sores, and AIDS: Risk, Danger, and the Condom

As elsewhere, Malawians see condoms as a way to protect against sexually transmitted infections and avoid unwanted pregnancies. Knowledge and fear of AIDS is nearly universal, with AIDS sometimes referred to in Malawi as *Mulili,* a plague of biblical proportions.[7] The calculation of risk seems clear, particularly because both government and nongovernmental organizations promote condoms as an obvious way to avoid risk. In our journals, however, and in Africa more generally, many believe that condoms pose a health risk. Stories of the pernicious effects of condoms are frequent topics of conversation and circulate among neighbors and kin.[8]

Using the MDICP journals, Kaler (2004) shows how, in Malawi, condoms are sometimes thought to be part of a Western or government plot to reduce population numbers. She argues that condoms are seen as a malevolent threat coming from above and are resisted from below. In a similar vein, Varga (1997) and Preston-Whyte (1999) describe a "condom conundrum" in South Africa: a weighing of the advantages of condom use against the value of fertility (see also Smith [2004b] for Nigeria). Although Malawians discuss these issues too, the journals suggest that condoms' possible health risks are a more pressing concern. The following excerpt shows the worry over condoms' health risks as well as a grim assessment of the alternatives:

Robert said "No, it brings cancer, both you and a wife/woman because of the liquid oil found inside the *Chisango* (condom) so cancer is like AIDS has no medicine. So it's better to be doing plain [having sex without a condom]. I can't use. And Sarah always tells me that *Chisango* brings vaginal sores and she says when used most of the times [it] brings diseases and one becomes barren. . . . Yes, the government is so clever, after seeing that the population is so high that they have introduced condoms with the aim of lessening the population, for everyone using it catches cancer dying and those using plain [i.e., not using a condom] dying as well. No escape." (Simon 2/28/2001)

In this excerpt, the "cleverness" of the government is seen as an attempt to kill off the population using condoms. There is also a valiant attempt to balance risks and benefits, but with the bleak conclusion that there is "no escape" because condoms kill but "going plain" leads to AIDS, which kills as well.

In the past few years, people have spoken less about condoms as a population control "plot," but they still do not see condoms as safe. Malawians often use medical language to describe the dangers and risks of condom use. They discuss condoms leading to "sores" and "cancer," as well as the possibility of a condom tearing and "sticking to the womb," causing infertility or death. Malawians may disagree about the gravity of the diseases caused by condom use, but most take the perils of condom use for granted:

He said that the oil found in the condoms the way he heard, said are the oils which really destroys man's fertility and as the result he develops genital sores and these genital sores if not treated early one can die of them. A lot of people refused [rejected] this statement and said that the one who was saying that to him was completely cheating [misleading him]. He said that of course he heard that the oils found in the condoms causes the genital sores as well as vagina sores but not that one can die of that. We all agreed and concluded that oil found in the condoms really develops genital sores in the penis of the man and vaginal sores in the parts of women/girls. (Simon 1/04/2003)

Malawians must weigh the risk of AIDS against the perceived risks of condom use, including the idea that condom use can cause diseases that lead to AIDS:[9]

The condoms cause some disease especially to men who put them on. They cause some sores on the penis's skin and some wounds on the foreskin. She continued by saying that she doesn't see about the importance of using the condoms because they cause other diseases and it sometimes happens that one uses the condoms and she is safe from AIDS but she [is] found sick from another disease and goes to the hospital especially the private ones, where she is injected using the unsterilized needle which the Doctor had used for injecting someone who had AIDS. In so doing she also gets AIDS. (Alice 10/25/2002)

This excerpt shows that public health information disseminated about AIDS can itself discourage condom use. Learning that unsterilized needles and transfusions can transmit AIDS is an educational success from the point of view of AIDS programs. However, when Malawians combine this information with other stories they hear about condoms, such as condoms leading to diseases and "sores," some come to believe that condoms may indirectly increase their chances of contracting AIDS.[10] On the other hand, sometimes such weighing of risks makes people more willing to use condoms:

She also said that the use of condoms are very good . . . It is better to suffer from sores than die of AIDS. If you use the condom and have sores, you can go to the hospital to explain and you can be helped by the Doctors . . . (Alice 10/25/2002)

These conflicting assessments of condom risk mean that the semiotic coding of condom use is ambiguous. In the West, a refusal to use condoms invokes a distinction between those who are rational and responsible and those who are reckless and irresponsible. For Malawians, however, the semiotics of condom use with respect to risk and danger are much less straight forward. . . .

The Inversions of Trust and Love

. . . . Almost all the interviewees and the people recorded by the journalists agreed that condoms are needed when a sexual partner cannot be fully trusted. For example, one might use a condom when a partner has additional sexual partners or leads a "promiscuous" lifestyle:

I: With whom do you use these condoms?
R: I use it to sexual partners. . . .
I: To which sexual partners?
R: To whom I don't know exactly how she moves. (Interview with a 23-year-old married man)

Although some men say they would never use a condom, our data, as well as previous studies (e.g., Varga, 2000), show that many men and women consider it reasonable to use condoms with untrustworthy partners. Indeed, many studies show that men are increasingly willing to use condoms with "non-regular partners," such as bar-girls and prostitutes (Preston-Whyte, 1999). Women also believe that condoms may be appropriate with men who are "movious" (i.e., men who sleep with many women).

The problem confronting Malawians, however, is how to define the other side of this semiotic opposition. Outside of the suspect categories, who is trustworthy? One possibility is to rely on a partner's social characteristics to determine if the person is "safe." For example, if the partner is a member of one's religious congregation and does not leave the village, or is young and presumably sexually inexperienced, one might see condoms as unnecessary. Indeed, the journals record many discussions about safe sex that revolve around a folk sociology of who is a "safe partner." Many men consider young schoolgirls to be "ideal" safe partners due to their limited sexual experience. The safety of this social category, however, is open to debate:

One day I met a man in a minibus, and when we were passing Mwemba High School there was a group of girls on the roadway at this school. The man said to me, "You see those school girls, they are on the road to be entertaining men with sex, most of the people have sex with school girls plain (without using condoms) because they think that they are young and safe. In doing that these school girls can be a major cause of the rapid spread of AIDS, because they are used to unprotected sex." He concluded by saying that it is better to avoid them in order to be safe. (Diston 9/08/1999)

The categorization of groups according to this folk epidemiology is open to debate, with people using slightly different categories and contesting the common wisdom with their own analyses. Many journals report conversations in which schoolgirls are viewed as unsafe, and men voice a series of grievances, tinged perhaps with erotic fantasy, about schoolgirls' supposedly loose morals and sexual dangers.

It is the association of condoms with unsafe partners, however, that operates semiotically to discourage condom use. The request to use a condom implies either that one does not trust one's partner, or that the requesting partner cannot be trusted (Sobo, 1995):

Women who live in the villages don't like having sexual intercourse with a condom and if they discover that you have put on they push you backwards and they tell to leave doing sexual intercourse with them because they say that you suspect themselves of having maybe HIV/AIDS or any other sexually transmitted disease that's why you have put on a condom. (Chunga 4/04/2003)

Proposing to use a condom with a spouse or steady partner signals through action that one of the partners is unsafe. This does not mean that condom use necessarily signals mistrust, but if a partner wants to use one, issues of trust must be brought to the surface, rather than remaining comfortably unspoken. In the following interview excerpt, a single young man explains that he always uses condoms. When asked what his partners think about this, he said:

R. I do tell them openly of using condoms and some partners tend to wonder and ask, . . . "What have you suspected in my body or what have you suspected yourself?" My answer is just to say, according to how dangerous the world is nowadays, there is need to protect your life and mine too and if the girl or partner is understanding she understands and three-quarters of the partners whom I have been sleeping with don't get surprised because they know that the world is dangerous.

So far, the implications of condom use seem straightforward: to use a condom is to place yourself or your partner in the unsafe category. However, questions of trust and risk do not capture the complexity Malawians face. Indeed, many Malawians are reluctant to use a condom with a loved partner or spouse even if they suspect the partner is HIV positive, a suspicion that surely relegates the partner to the unsafe category. Why, even when risk is great, do Malawians find the semiotics of intimate attachment in conflict with attempts to protect themselves against AIDS?

In surveys of attitudes, opposition to using condoms in marriage is still high, but it is declining fairly dramatically. MDICP survey respondents were asked about condom use with a spouse, first to protect against HIV/AIDS in general, and then more specifically, if they suspect or know that their partner has HIV/AIDS. . . . While majorities of men and women still consider condom use with a spouse unacceptable, from 1998 to 2004 the proportion of women who consider it unacceptable fell steadily (from 85 percent in 1998 to 58 percent in 2004). Similar changes also occurred among men, although they have been more modest. In 2004, the MDICP added a new cohort of young men and women ages 15 to 24. This new cohort shows a higher acceptance of condom use (42.8 percent for women and 29.3 percent for men) than do the original panel study participants. It is thus unlikely that the change in attitudes results from an aging effect; rather, it is a notable educational success (Kalipeni, 1999).

Even more striking is the absence of changes in behavior. Another survey (Government of Malawi, 1992, 2000, 2004) asked Malawian women whether they use a condom with their spouse. These numbers are miniscule, with 1.6 percent of women using condoms with their spouse in 1992 and 2000, and 1.8 percent in 2004 (a statistically insignificant change). This pattern of responses is interesting because in the 2004 and 2006 MDICP survey waves, 12.5 and 12.2 percent of married women, respectively, reported having a medium to strong suspicion that their spouse is currently HIV positive.[11]

Understanding the semiotic significance of condom use in defining a relationship provides a key to the discrepancies between changing attitudes about condom use within marriage, the stable rates of spouses' reported suspicions, and the tiny proportion of people who are actually willing to use condoms. This is not a matter of changing one's assessment of a partner's risk, but of employing the condom as a semiotic vehicle for establishing or affirming the status of a relationship. . . .

Suggesting the use of a condom relegates a relationship to an inferior status.

. . . . Many relationships described in the interviews go through phases: the partners use condoms at first, only to stop later (without taking an HIV test) when the relationship becomes more serious and involves love. The following diary entry shows this pattern:

Issac was not short of words as he further elaborated that people have [a] poor mindset about condoms. He said if you are in love you at first use condoms but later you change to show your love. This latter leads to spread of HIV/AIDS since you know not if one of you is HIV positive or negative. (Chihana 9/13/2005)

Malawians consider this shift—from condom use in the beginning of a relationship to "plain" sex when the relationship has solidified—not only in symbolic terms but also as a sensual reality.[12] As with the sweetness of sex, a set of bodily metaphors govern how Malawians show emotion and interpret physical experiences. Reporting a conversation in which he asked a friend about love, a journalist recorded that "love is blood." Several journalists and interviewees used the metaphor of "flesh to flesh," in which full physical contact, with co-mingling bodily fluids, embodies the status of a relationship. Using a condom not only connotes distrust or lack of love, but it actually feels like a loveless interaction (Holland et al., 1991; Ingham, Woodcock, and Stenner, 1991). When asked if he would use a condom with his wife, one man said:

The aim is to have your bloods mix, showing each other that you love each other indeed. So if there is no mixture of blood between you two, then even the wife comes to know really that you don't love her. The way I see it, my partner can divorce me right away, the day I say I am using. (Diston 6/13/2002)

With respect to condom use, the semiotic logic of love operates as an inversion of the logic of trust. In the logic of trust, the decision to use a condom rests on an assessment of a potential partner's attributes. In contrast, in the semiotic logic of love, being in a love relationship precludes using a condom even if one knows or strongly suspects that a partner poses a high risk of HIV. In the progression from an initial sexual relationship to a love relationship the logic of trust is inverted. . . .

In the initial assessment of trust, the other is categorized on a dimension of safeness and risk, and the enacted self is the calculating and knowing agent. However, when a relationship becomes a love relation, the self is simultaneously transformed: any attempt to calculate and categorize the other must be suspended; the calculating self is no longer coded as rational and safe, but as heartless and nonloving. To sustain a relationship, one must overcome the caution dictating condom use.

NAVIGATING THE SEMIOTIC SPACE OF CONDOM USE

So far, we have focused on each semiotic dimension separately. Yet in action, these axes are intertwined as people navigate the different dimensions.

. . . . The different axes are not only additive. Rather, people can switch semiotic possibilities within one interaction. This switching is often strategic; for example, when one partner wants to persuade the other to use, or not use, a condom. Even then, the semiotic possibilities provide the materials out of which people construct an interaction and its meanings.

An extended vignette from a diary written by Simon on July 8th and 10th, 2001, illustrates how different semiotic axes are intertwined: the diary tells the story of the beginning of a relationship between the diarist's friend, Richard, and a new sexual partner, Grace. After buying fish for Grace, with money borrowed from the diarist, Richard brags that she agreed to meet him the following day. Richard boasts that he never uses a condom, but particularly in this case, it would be out of the question. "I can't even take condoms," he said, "then it will mean I wasn't serious for her. For I want her to be my real girlfriend." Even before the relationship begins, Richard is anticipating the relational meaning of condom use for Grace.

Two days later, the diarist asked Richard about his meeting with Grace. Boasting, Richard said, "that Grace kept the appointment and indeed he had sex with Grace and said Grace is a nice girl, not one who is so dry, she was totally willing to have sex." Not having a place of his own, and with Grace being in high school, they decided to go the school, having sex in a classroom "without even laying a cloth." Before they began, Richard said, "Grace, I am going to have sex with you with a condom." Grace refused to use a condom, saying "that she can't feel anything, and if it is so it could have been better if she could not come and meet with him."

Grace invoked sensuality to pressure Richard not to use a condom. Not giving up quite yet, Richard told her he proposed using a condom for her sake, so that she would not get pregnant and have to drop out of school. . . . Grace told him that "she had just finished her monthly period yesterday, so how can she become pregnant?" She also said that "she knows biology and said that she is sure she can't be impregnated. And she said it's better if I didn't use a condom." In the face of such opposition, Richard changed his tone. "I was just cheating you," he said, "I can't have sex with you using a condom, you are so beautiful and I need to feel real sweetness, you can't eat a sweet while it's wrapped in its plastic paper, you can't feel sweet." Bantering after intercourse, and perhaps trying to scare him a little, Grace "stood up and said 'You have made me pregnant.' And I said 'How? You said you can't?!' and she said 'I was cheating you, I just wanted you to impregnate me and marry me.' And I said, 'I will, since you are beautiful.'"

This seemingly frivolous exchange did not preclude broaching the subject of AIDS. Yet Richard and Grace strategically used the risk of AIDS as part of their flirtatious banter. Richard said, "I even told the girl [Grace], saying that 'Look, if it is AIDS, even the radio says one can only get it through what we have done and the result is dying. So if you have AIDS you have given it to me and if I have it I have also given it to you. So it's better that our love should not end.' And we promised that if everything goes well we are meeting today as well."

Richard admitted that "indeed, friend, if Grace has AIDS, she has given it to me, I couldn't resist her attractions." As a good friend, the diarist then offered Richard reassurance in the form of his own folk sociology, saying, "She doesn't have [AIDS], she is so young for that." Richard agreed because of her age and "moreover, her body is fat and healthy. Had it been she had AIDS I would have noticed that her body had become thin, but she is fat. So we are meeting any day, even tomorrow . . . for I feel married."

This vignette exemplifies the ways in which the semiotic space of condom use both constrains and enables moments of humor and romance. The symbolism of sexual sweetness, fertility, AIDS, and, above all, condom use semiotically define the anticipation, the actual encounter, and the retrospective understanding of the new relationship. Even before the first encounter, Richard offered his unwillingness to use a condom as a sign both of his masculinity and his desire to have Grace as a "real girlfriend." Within the interaction (or at least in describing it after the fact), shifting among the different semiotic axes of condom use allowed the couple to playfully heighten the seriousness of the relationship. By invoking the risk of AIDS, Richard enhanced the intimacy signaled by not using a condom, cementing his connection to Grace, with whom he "feel[s] married." As Richard described it, the semiotics of condom use constituted the meanings and meaningfulness of the encounter.

DISCUSSION

. . . . Sweetness, risk, trust, and love are all modes of signification that shape subjects' decisions and interactions. To understand variations in Malawians' willingness to use condoms, one must first understand how these social semiotics frame everyday decisions.

Current understandings of condoms are not natural or immutable. Over the course of the AIDS epidemic, different meanings have gained prominence in different places and times. Issues such as masculinity, religious prohibitions, and distrust of government were central to the understanding of condoms in the late 1990s but are less important today. Our interviews suggest that for some younger Malawians, using condoms even with regular partners is becoming acceptable, perhaps as a marker of rational modernity (Johnson-Hanks, 2002). A new semiotic strategy seems to be emerging in which using a condom every time with every partner avoids the association of condoms with particular sorts of partners or relationships. . . .

While there is a growing sophistication in talk of discourses and practices—rather than simply "culture," "beliefs," and "norms"— when confronted with a phenomenon like the continuing resistance to condom use in Africa, culture analysts tend either to assume that Africans hold a set of "irrational" beliefs that, once corrected, will produce different behavior or, in an all too similar inversion, to explain this resistance simplistically as part of local "culture." We argue that semiotic framings define the meanings of particular actions (Swidler, 2001). By paying attention to these different semiotic axes, we can see why people do not necessarily act differently in light of new information, and why changes, when they do come, may take unexpected directions. . . .

Viewed semiotically, most cultural expressions and actions are pragmatic, not because they are directed toward material ends, but because they enact definitions of self, others, and relationships. We join scholars like Jennifer Johnson-Hanks, Steve Derne, and Elise Sobo in emphasizing how semiotic codes constrain people by making certain practices markers of valued identities. At the risk of contracting AIDS, a man may reject condoms to assert a claim to masculinity, or to communicate and enact bodily that a relationship is serious. Semiotic codes are powerful because they shape the ways we read the behavior of others (and, reciprocally, the ways we know others will read our own behavior). A woman who knows that condoms are appropriate for bar-girls and sex workers may refuse condoms, even if she fears AIDS and wishes to protect her health. She enacts unsafe sex to signal that she is not associated with an unsafe social category or to assert the primacy of her claim on her partner.

Semiotic constraint operates most powerfully at the level of relationships. Even when people believe that condom use is appropriate, or even a matter of life and death, the statement it makes about the relationship frequently trumps all other meanings. As long as condoms signal mistrust, fear, and a relationship that is not serious and will not lead to marriage, then using a condom will threaten or destroy a relationship. Data on married women's attitudes suggest that even as women find it more acceptable, in the abstract, for married people to use condoms if they suspect their spouses might be HIV positive, almost none are willing to make that statement in their own relationships, despite the very real dangers they face.

. . . . Although sociologists usually do not make policy recommendations, our semiotic approach suggests some new directions. Public health interventions in general should consider both accurate health information and semiotic framing. In Malawi, promoting condoms to prevent HIV and associating condoms with untrustworthy partners may backfire. Alternative strategies might frame condom use as a way to show love to a trusted partner; education campaigns might tackle local concerns about the dangers of condom use; and, as local entrepreneurs did with the *Manyuchi* condom, publicity might locate condom use squarely within the domain of "the sweet." Rethinking condom promotion would allow Malawians to position condom use in interactionally permissible ways—where the decision to use a condom could denote care rather than frivolity, love rather than promiscuity.

NOTES

1. Cost and availability may limit condom use, especially in very poor countries like Malawi. In our interviews and the diaries, however, cost was never mentioned as a reason for not using condoms. In Malawi, *Chisango* condoms are heavily subsidized and widely available (Kalipeni and Mbugua, 2005), costing two *kwacha* each (about 1.4 cents), inexpensive even by Malawian standards.

2. Further details about the MDICP and the data from the surveys are available at: http://www.malawi.pop.upenn.edu.

3. MDICP recruited interviewers by posting notices in local trading centers near the rural survey sites, asking high school graduates to come the next morning to fill out an application. Often as many as 200 people applied for the 40 or so positions at each site. Successful candidates had to be fluent in the local language and proficient in English, which is required in Malawi's public schools. . . . Interviewing for the MDICP lasted only about two months; it did not provide regular employment.

4. For a fuller discussion of the journals as a methodological tool and a form of social inquiry, see Watkins and Swidler (2008). . . .

5. In both chiChewa and chiYao, the same word (*umuna* and *ubenga*, respectively) refers to both sperm and semen.

6. Swidler and Watkins (2007) note the ties of unequal interdependence that make fertility and "wealth in people" critically important in African societies.

7. In the Malawi *Demographic and Health Survey* (Government of Malawi, 2004), 99.5 percent of men and 98.6 percent of women sampled knew of AIDS.

8. For related phenomena in other parts of Africa, see Johnson-Hanks (2002, 2006); Rutenberg and Watkins (1997); Watkins, Rutenberg, and Green (1995); and Watkins, Rutenberg, and Wilkinson (1997).

9. The frequency with which Malawians mention "sores" associated with condom use may indicate a high prevalence of lesions from sexually transmitted infections (STIs). When the MDICP tested for STIs in 2004, however, prevalence was low. Gonorrhea prevalence was 5.4 percent for women and .3 percent for men; chlamydia was .5 percent for women and .1 percent for men; and trichomoniasis was 2.4 percent for women (N=1,303 men and 1,497 women).

10. These findings raise another question about whether scientific information allows agents to master problems in their everyday world. Malawians are bombarded with scientific information about AIDS transmission, but this welter of different explanations and dangers might complicate and confuse their everyday actions (Houston and Hovorka, 2007).

11. The 2006 MDICP survey asked married women to use a number of beans (from 1 to 10) to assess the accuracy of different assertions presented by interviewers. Of the married women, 12.2 percent placed five or more beans in response to the assertion that "your spouse is infected with HIV/AIDS now." In the 2004 MDICP survey, 12.5 percent of married women answered "Medium" or "High" to the question: "In your opinion, what is the likelihood (chance) that your husband is infected with HIV/AIDS now?"

12. The connection between perceived love in a sexual relationship and condom use is seen in the United States as well. Sobo (1995) shows how disadvantaged African American women in Cleveland avoid using condoms to signal that a relationship is serious; condom use, on the other hand, signifies promiscuity. In Africa, it is likely that condom promotion and education has generated some of the association between condom use and lack of trust. Promotion messages often differentiate between "regular" and "nonregular" partners and emphasize the role of condoms for protecting against dangerous, high risk, and unhealthy partners (Chimbiri, 2007).

REFERENCES

Beisel, Nicola. 1990. "Class, Culture, and Campaigns against Vice in Three American Cities, 1872–1892." *American Sociological Review* 55(1):44–62.

———. 1997. *Imperiled Innocents: Anthony Comstock and Family Reproduction in Victorian America.* Princeton, NJ: Princeton University Press.

Bledsoe, Caroline. 1990. "The Politics of AIDS, Condoms, and Heterosexual Relations in Africa: Recent Evidence from the Local Print Media." Pp. 197–223 in *Births and Power: Social Change and the Politics of Reproduction,* edited by W. P. Handwerker. Boulder, CO: Westview Press.

Chimbiri, Agnes. 2007. "The Condom is an 'Intruder' in Marriage: Evidence from Rural Malawi." *Social Science and Medicine* 64(5):1102–15.

Crosby, Richard, William L. Yarber, Stephanie A. Sanders, and Cynthia A. Graham. 2005. "Condom Discomfort and Associated Problems with Their Use among University Students." *Journal of American College Health* 54(3):143–47.

Derné, Steve. 1994. "Cultural Conceptions of Human Motivation and Their Significance for Culture Theory." Pp. 267–87 in *The Sociology of Culture,* edited by D. Crane. Cambridge, MA: Blackwell.

Doctor, Henry V. 2002. "Effects of HIV/AIDS on Children in Sub-Saharan Africa: Evidence from Malawi." Paper presented at the 4th Annual Conference on HIV/AIDS and the African Child: Health Challenges, Educational Possibilities. April, Athens, OH.

Dowsett, Gary W. 1999. "Understanding Cultures of Sexuality: Lessons Learned from HIV/AIDS Education and Behaviour Change among Gay Men in Australia." Pp. 223–31 in *Resistances to Behavioural Change to Reduce HIV/AIDS Infection in Predominantly Heterosexual Epidemics in Third World Countries,* edited by J. C. Caldwell et al. Canberra, Australia: Australian National University.

Emanatian, Michele. 1995. "Metaphor and the Expression of Emotion: The Value of Cross Cultural Perspectives." *Metaphor and Symbolic Activity* 10(3):163–82.

Epstein, Steven. 1996. *Impure Science: AIDS, Activism, and the Politics of Knowledge.* Berkeley, CA: University of California Press

Gagnon, John H. 2004. *An Interpretation of Desire: Essays in the Study of Sexuality.* Chicago, IL: The University of Chicago Press.

Government of Malawi. 1992. *Malawi Demographic and Health Survey.* Zomba, Malawi: Government Printer.

———. 2000. *Malawi Demographic and Health Survey.* Zomba, Malawi: Government Printer.

———. 2004. *Malawi Demographic and Health Survey.* Zomba, Malawi: Government Printer.

———. 2007. Government of Malawi Web Page (http://www.malawi.gov.mw/).

Green, Edward C. 2003. *Rethinking AIDS Prevention: Learning from Successes in Developing Countries.* Westport, CT: Praeger.

Greenblatt, Stephen. 1986. "Fiction and Friction: Reconstructing Individualism, Autonomy, Individuality, and the Self." Pp. 30–52 in *Reconstructing Individualism: Autonomy, Individuality, and the Self in Western Thought,* edited by T. C. Heller, M. Sosna, and D. E. Wellbery. Stanford, CA: Stanford University Press.

Hearst, Norman and Sanny Chen. 2004. "Condoms for AIDS Prevention in the Developing World: Is It Working?" *Studies in Family Planning* 35(1):39–47.

Holland, Janet, Caroline Ramazanoglu, Sue Scott, Sue Sharpe, and Rachel Thomson. 1991. "Between Embarrassment and Trust: Young Women and the

Diversity of Condom Use." Pp. 127–48 in *AIDS: Responses. Interventions and Care,* edited by P. Aggelton, P. Davies, and G. Hart. London, UK: Falmer Press.

Houston, Vanessa and Alice Hovorka. 2007. "HIV/AIDS Messages in Malawi and their Implications for Effective Responses." *African Journal of AIDS Research* 6(3):205–14.

Ingham, Roger, Alison Woodcock, and Karen Stenner. 1991. "Getting to Know You . . . Young People's Knowledge of their Partners at First Intercourse." *Journal of Community and Applied Social Psychology* 1:117–32.

Johnson-Hanks, Jennifer. 2002. "On the Modernity of Traditional Contraception: Time and the Social Context of Fertility." *Population and Development Review* 28(2):229–49.

———. 2006. *Uncertain Honor: Modern Motherhood in an African Crisis.* Chicago, IL: University of Chicago Press.

Kaler, Amy. 2003. " 'My Girlfriends Could Fill a Yanu-Yanu Bus': Rural Malawian Men's Claims about their own Serostatus." *Demographic Research,* Special Collection 1:349–72.

———. 2004. "The Moral Lens of Population Control: Condoms and Controversies in Southern Malawi." *Studies in Family Planning* 35(2):105–15.

Kalipeni, Ezekiel. 1999. "AIDS and Condom Promotion in Malawi: A Critical Review." *African Rural and Urban Studies* 3(2):61–90.

Kalipeni, Ezekiel and Njeri Mbugna. 2005. "A Review of Preventative Efforts in the Fight against HIV and AIDS in Africa." *Norwegian Journal of Geography* 59:26–36.

Laqueur, Thomas W. 1990. *Making Sex: Body and Gender from the Greeks to Freud.* Cambridge, MA: Harvard University Press

McPhail, Catherine, and Catherine Campbell. 2001. " 'I Think Condoms Are Good but, Aai, I Hate Those Things': Condom Use among Adolescents and Young People in Southern African Township." *Social Science and Medicine* 52:1613–27.

Obbo, Christine. 1995. "Gender, Age, and Class: Discourses on HIV Transmission and Control in Uganda." Pp. 79–95 in *Culture and Sexual Risk: Anthropological Perspectives on AIDS,* edited by H. ten Brummelhuis and G. Herdt. Amsterdam: Gordon and Breach Publishers.

Preston-Whyte, Eleanor. 1999. "Reproductive Health and the Condom Dilemma: Identifying Situational Barriers to HIV Protection in South Africa." Pp. 139–55 in *Resistances to Behavioural Change to Reduce HIV/AIDS Infection in Predominantly Heterosexual Epidemics in Third World Countries,* edited by J. C. Caldwell et al., Canberra, Australia: The Australian National University

Rutenberg, Naomi and Susan C. Watkins. 1997. "The Buzz Outside the Clinics: Conversations and Contraception in Nyanza Province, Kenya." *Studies in Family Planning* 28(4):290–307.

Schalet, Amy T. 2000. "Raging Hormones, Regulated Love: Adolescent Sexuality and the Constitution of the Modern Individual in the United States of America and the Netherlands." *Body and Society* 6(1):75–105.

Sewell, William H., Jr. 1992. "A Theory of Structure: Duality, Agency, and Transformation." *American Journal of Sociology* 98(1):1–29.

Shelton, James D. 2006. "Confessions of a Condom Lover." *Lancet* 368:1947–49.

Silverman, Kaja. 1983. *The Subject of Semiotics.* New York: Oxford University Press.

Smith, Daniel J. 2000. " 'These Girls Today Na WarO': Premarital Sexuality and Modern Identity in Southeastern Nigeria." *Africa Today* 37(3–4):98–120.

———. 2004a. "Youth, Sin and Sex in Nigeria: Christianity and HIV/AIDS-Related Beliefs and Behaviour among Rural–Urban Migrants." *Culture, Health & Sexuality* 6(5):425–37.

———. 2004b. "Premarital Sex, Procreation, and HIV Risk in Nigeria." *Studies in Family Planning* 35(4):223–35.

Sobo, Elisa J. 1995. *Choosing Unsafe Sex: AIDS-Risk Denial among Disadvantaged Women.* Philadelphia, PA: University of Pennsylvania Press.

Swidler, Ann. 2001. *Talk of Love: How Culture Matters.* Chicago, IL: University of Chicago Press.

Swidler, Ann and Susan C. Watkins. 2007. "Ties of Dependence: AIDS and Transactional Sex in Rural Malawi." *Studies in Family Planning* 38(3):147–62.

Thomsen, Sarah C., Michael Stalker, Cathy Toroitich-Ruto, Baker Magwa Ndugga, and Peter Mwarogo. 2003. "Fifty Ways to Leave Your Rubber: How Men in Mombasa Rationalize Unsafe Sex." Presented at the Population Association of America meeting, May 1–3, Minneapolis, MN.

UNAIDS (Joint United Nations Programme on HIV/AIDS). 2007. *AIDS Epidemic Update: December 2007.*

Varga, Christine A. 1997. "The Condom Conundrum: Barriers to Condom Use among Commercial Sex Workers in Durban, South Africa." *African Journal of Reproductive Health* 1(1):74–88.

———. 2000. "Condom Dilemmas: Dynamics of Protected Sex in High Risk Groups in South Africa." Pp. 39–62 in *Towards the Containment of the AIDS Epidemic: Social and Behavioural Research,* edited by J. C. Caldwell et al. Health Transition Centre, National Centre for Epidemiology and Population Health, The Australian National University, Canberra.

Watkins, Susan C., Naomi Rutenberg, and David Wilkinson. 1997. "Orderly Theories, Disorderly Women." Pp. 213–45 in *The Continuing Demographic Transition,* edited by G. W. Jones, R. M. Douglas, J. C. Caldwell, and R. M. D'Souza. Oxford, UK: Clarendon Press.

Watkins, Susan C. and Ann Swidler. 2008. "Conversational Journals as a Method for Studying Culture in Action." CCPR Working Paper CCPR-030-06. *California Center for Population Research On-Line Working Paper Series.* University of California, Los Angeles (http://www.ccpr.ucla.edu).

Watkins, Susan C., Eliya M. Zulu, Hans-Peter Kohler, and Jere R. Behrman. 2003. "Introduction To: Social Interactions and HIV/AIDS in Rural Africa." *Demographic Research,* Special Collection 1:2–30.

Weller, Susan C. and Karen R. Davis. 2002. "Condom Effectiveness in Reducing Heterosexual HIV Transmission." *Cochrane Database System Review* 1:CD003255.

Prophylactic Circumcision: Applying Recent Research Results to the United States

Mindy Stombler[1]

Since peaking in the late 1960s, male circumcision rates have been on the decline in the United States.[2] While circumcision used to be recommended by childcare experts such as Dr. Spock, by the late 1990s, the American Academy of Pediatrics (and, in the 1970s, even Dr. Spock) no longer advocated routine circumcision.[3] In fact, anti-circumcision activism has recently reached new heights in California with a 2011 ballot measure that, although removed from the ballot by a San Francisco judge, would have banned non-therapeutic circumcision of minors in San Francisco[4] based on the proposition that it is medically unnecessary and a violation of the rights of the child.[5]

Yet research results from large-scale studies in Africa (South Africa, Kenya, Uganda) have demonstrated a "prophylactic" or preventative effect of adult male circumcision (AMC) in areas with widespread HIV infection. Studies have found that AMC reduces men's risk of infection from HIV-positive women by 51–60 percent.[6] Based on these results, the World Health Organization recognized AMC as an additional method of protection from HIV infection for adult men who have sex with infected women in regions of high heterosexual HIV prevalence[7] and in 2012 the

American Academy of Pediatrics revised their policy statement on infant male circumcision, suggesting the health benefits of circumcision outweigh the risks. They did not, however, recommend routine infant male circumcision.[8]

As the incidence of male circumcision falls, and activism against circumcision rises in the United States, what are the implications of this new research? To begin, it is important to note that while circumcision does seem to reduce the risk of HIV infection through unprotected intercourse with an infected female partner, it is by no means as effective as using a condom. Unlike in the African countries studied, Americans (especially young adults)[9] use condoms more regularly and have greater access to condoms.[10] Medical researchers in Poland, for example, worry that a focus on prophylactic AMC will give men a "false sense of security" which would push them away from more reliable condom use, increasing the risk of their own infection and that of their female sexual partners. AMC does not appear to reduce women's risk of infection when they have heterosexual sex with HIV-positive men, and studies in Rwanda indicated that AMC *increased* women's likelihood of infection. More research needs to be conducted in this area.[11] The large-scale studies conducted in

Africa indicate that AMC reduces infection risk for men who are having heterosexual sex with HIV-infected women, only, and does not reduce risk for men who are having sex with HIV-infected men. In the United States the predominant sexual mode of HIV transmission is among men who have anal sex with other men. Thus, the impact of AMC in reducing HIV prevalence would be greatly reduced in United States.[12]

AMC advocates often point to the moist environment under the foreskin of the penis as potentially harboring bacteria that can create an environment more conducive to infection. Yet researchers have not found solid evidence to support this assertion.[13] Even if it were found to be accurate, the economic position of the United States generally affords access to clean water and hygiene opportunities. The use of clean water to cleanse the penis (by pulling back the foreskin) dramatically reduces infection risks.[14] Access to clean water, hygiene opportunities, and general health care cannot be taken for granted in many parts of sub-Saharan Africa. Thus, results from research in these areas are not directly applicable to the U.S. context. Beyond issues of applicability, not all public health researchers are confident with the level of accuracy of results of the African studies,[15,16] and other studies published recently offer contradictory findings.[17]

Even if circumcision did significantly reduce the risk of HIV infection, we must also consider the risks of surgery, the significance of the foreskin for sexual function, the ethics of surgically removing normal body parts, and the importance of individual choice and informed consent, particularly as education and other methods of prevention are more effective. Would we feel comfortable applying the logic of prophylactic circumcision to women if we learned that removing the clitoral hood or labial tissue could reduce their risk of HIV infection?

In the United States, the CDC is considering the clinical trial results from Africa and developing public health recommendations. They state that while individual men may choose circumcision as an additional infection prevention measure, they need to be aware that it:

1) does carry risks and costs that must be considered in addition to potential benefits;
2) has only proven effective in reducing the risk of infection through insertive vaginal sex;
3) confers only partial protection and should be considered only in conjunction with other proven prevention measures (abstinence, mutual monogamy, reduced number of sex partners, and correct and consistent condom use)."[18]

Even in the African countries where the research has taken place, medical experts still argue that AMC "should not be promoted for itself, but as a package of interventions that include, besides AMC, condoms and female empowerment."[19]

NOTES

1. Thanks to Robert Darby for editorial advice.

2. Darby, Robert. 2005. "The sorcerer's apprentice: Why can't we stop circumcising boys?" *Contexts* 4 (2): 34–9.

3. Gollaher, David L. 2000. *Circumcision: A History of the World's Most Controversial Surgery.* New York: Basic Books.

4. Park, Madison. 2011. "San Francisco judge removes circumcision ban from ballot." Retrieved December 10, 2011 from http://www.cnn.com/2011/HEALTH/07/28/circumcision.ban.voting/index.html.

5. Jaslow, Ryan. 2011. "No circumcision in San Francisco? Jews, Muslims, sue to stop proposed ban." Retrieved December 10, 2011 from http://www.cbsnews.com/8301-504763_162-20073729-10391704.html

6. Centers for Disease Control (CDC). 2008. Male Circumcision and Risk for HIV Transmission and Other Health Conditions: Implications for the United States. 2008. *The Cochrane Review* (2009), however, claimed risk reduction ranged from 38–66%. See Siegfried N, Muller M, Deeks JJ, Volmink J. 2009. "Male circumcision for prevention of heterosexual acquisition of HIV in men (*Cochrane Review*)." *The Cochrane Database of Systematic Reviews* Issue 2, April 15. Chichester (UK): John Wiley.

7. Rogowska-Szadkowska, D. 2010. "Letter to the Editor: Is adult male circumcision a viable public health strategy for HIV prevention outside sub-Saharan Africa?" *AIDS Patient Care and STDS* 24(12): 751–2.

8. American Academy of Pediatrics. August 27, 2012. "Technical Report: Male Circumcision." *PEDIATRICS* 130(3): e756–85.

9. Reece, Michael, Herbenick, Debby, Schick, Vanessa, Sanders, Stephanie A., Dodge, Brian, and J. Dennis Fortenberry. 2010. "Condom Use Rates in a National Probability Sample of Males and Females Ages 14 to 94 in the United States." *Journal of Sexual Medicine* 7 (s5): 266–276.

10. Bryden, David. 2011. "Condom gap 'quite disturbing' according to PEPFAR." *Science Speaks: HIV & TB News*. Retrieved December 10, 2011 from http://sciencespeaksblog.org/2011/02/02/condom-gap-quite-disturbing-according-to-pepfar/.

11. Rogowska-Szadkowska, D. 2010. "Letter to the Editor: Is adult male circumcision a viable public health strategy for HIV prevention outside sub-Saharan Africa?" *AIDS Patient Care and STDS* 24(12): 751–2.

12. Centers for Disease Control (CDC). 2008. "Male Circumcision and Risk for HIV Transmission and Other Health Conditions: Implications for the United States." 2008.

13. Cold, C.J. and J.R. Taylor. 1999. "The prepuce." *British Journal of Urology* 83(1): 34–44.

14. Rogowska-Szadkowska, D. 2010. "Letter to the Editor: Is adult male circumcision a viable public health strategy for HIV prevention outside sub-Saharan Africa?" *AIDS Patient Care and STDS* 24(12): 751–2.

15. Boyle, Gregory J and George Hill. 2011. "Sub-Saharan African randomized clinical trials into male circumcision and HIV transmission: Methodological, ethical and legal concerns." *Journal of Law and Medicine* Issue 19: 316–334.

16. Darby, Robert and Robert Van Howe. 2011. "Not a surgical vaccine: There is no case for boosting infant male circumcision to combat heterosexual transmission of HIV in Australia." *Australian and New Zealand Journal of Public Health* 35 (5): 459–65.

17. Rodriquez-Diaz, Carlos E., Clatts, Michael C., Jovet-Toledo, Gerardo G., Vargas-Molina, Ricardo L., Goldsmat, Lloyd A., and Hermes García. 2012. "More than Foreskin: Circumcision Status, History of HIV/STI, and Sexual Risk in a Clinic-Based Sample of Men in Puerto Rico." *Journal of Sexual Medicine* 9 (11): 2933–2937.

18. Centers for Disease Control (CDC). 2008. P. 5 in "Male Circumcision and Risk for HIV Transmission and Other Health Conditions: Implications for the United States." 2008.

19. Rogowska-Szadkowska, D. 2010. P. 752 in "Letter to the Editor: Is adult male circumcision a viable public health strategy for HIV prevention outside sub-Saharan Africa?" *AIDS Patient Care and STDs* 24(12): 751–2.

8

SOCIAL CONTROL OF SEXUALITY

AN INTERVIEW WITH

AMIN GHAZIANI

Amin Ghaziani, Ph.D., is assistant professor of sociology at the University of British Columbia. He received his Ph.D. from Northwestern, after which he earned a postdoctoral fellowship with the Princeton Society of Fellows. His research considers political dissent among LGBT activists, the changing meanings of sexuality in today's "post-gay" era, and most recently, the in-migration of straights into gay neighborhoods. His 2008 award-winning book, The Dividends of Dissent: How Conflict and Culture Work in Lesbian and Gay Marches on Washington, *examines the effects of infighting in national LGBT demonstrations (University of Chicago Press).*

What led you to begin studying sexuality?

The summer after my junior year in college in 1997, I signed up for a San Francisco Field Studies Program with Northwestern University's School of Education and Social Policy. NU offered an internship-based practicum as a way to apply analytical frameworks from an advanced research methods course to a worksite. I worked with Positive Resource Center (PRC), the first organization in the country dedicated to helping people living with HIV/AIDS return to work. Where once people were getting sick, leaving work, and embracing inevitable death, advances in antiretroviral medical technologies in the mid-1990s enabled them to renew their lease on life. Many of these people desired to go back to work. I worked with an incredible organization that was doing just that.

That summer changed my life. It ended with me writing a 20-page report for my class. PRC used my policy recommendations to restructure many of their programs, and then–Mayor Willie Brown even acknowledged them. I had been a progressive activist during my undergraduate years, but that summer taught me that I could also use my intellect to create social change. I knew then that I wanted to go to graduate school to study sexuality.

Of the projects you have done over the course of your academic career, which was most interesting and why?

After spending my first two years of undergraduate study at the University of Michigan in Ann Arbor, I felt intellectually restless and overwhelmed by the large student body. So I transferred to Northwestern—which was indeed rigorous and stimulating in the classroom—but my new campus felt politically apathetic and rife with nonreflexive privilege.

I had to shake things up. Drawing on progressive organizing skills that I had learned in Ann Arbor, I organized a Queer Kiss-In event on April Fool's Day. My idea was to have queer students meet in a central campus area and, at noon when many classes let out, to make out. Straight people often take for granted basic acts of intimacy and affection. Queer couples that hold hands or kiss in public risk hate speech and even violence.

A week prior to my event I did what any undergraduate student organizer would do: I taped fliers throughout the campus. I quickly discovered that the groundskeepers selectively removed my fliers. In response, the day before the Kiss-In, I purchased fabulous fuchsia paint for "The Rock," a large boulder at the center of campus where it is customary for students to paint messages and advertisements of social events. When I arrived at the site around three in the morning, a group of sorority women were already there painting the rock to advertise a party. They had also pitched a tent next to the rock to guard it so no one else painted over it. And so there I was with this gorgeous paint and an occupied rock! Bleary-eyed, I looked down on the ground in a sleepy haze—and that's when the proverbial "a-ha" moment struck. All over the ground were chalked messages and taped fliers. If chalk and tape were permissible, then why not paint? A fervent fury awoke within me, and I pained "QUEER POWER" across the entire plaza area.

The NU administration responded by threatening me with possible arrest for defacing private property because of the high cost of removing the graffiti, and I retaliated by defining their threat as a breach of my First Amendment rights. As fate would have it, I was taking a course entitled "Problems and Principles in the

First Amendment." I used what I learned in that class to write op-ed pieces for local papers and to give public radio interviews. Talk about knowledge in action! After much legal and political deliberation, the university compromised. In exchange for not pursuing a lawsuit, NU allowed me to revise their policy on the allowable "medium of expression" to advertise student activities.

What ethical dilemmas have you faced in studying sexuality?

I once did a research project on club drugs, risky sex practices, and sexually transmitted infections among self-identified gay and bisexual men who attended circuit parties. These are weekend-long dance events at which sexual activity and drug use are generally prevalent among several thousand revelers. As you might expect, my co-author Tom Cook and I had some trouble with the Institutional Review Board. How do you ethically conduct an ethnographic study of drug use in a club context where you want party-goers to accept you into the fold of their friends—and where you are observing potentially illegal behavior of both drug use and sex?

We managed this problem in four ways. First, we secured a Certificate of Confidentiality from the National Institute on Drug Abuse that protected us from subpoena. Second, circuit parties attract an older demographic; you have to be at least 21 to get in the door. This resolved issues of interacting with minors. Third, when I engaged in participant observation, I deemed it necessary to appear as a partier and did not explicitly reveal my professional role. This enhanced the authenticity of my observations. And finally, because I was not going to take drugs like the majority of the attendees, I instead brought aspirin tablets with me into the party which mimicked the appearance of ecstasy. Because much of the community interacts within smaller groups of friends who ritualistically consume drugs, there was a real issue of credibility that I had to confront if I was not a part of the ingesting group. In any case, the study was a big success. We published it in a medical journal, and it was picked up by more than forty international media outlets.

How do people react when you tell them you study sexuality?

The reactions are as varied as the diversity inherent in all human beings, of course, but one particular episode stands out in my mind. I struggled during my first round on the academic job market. As I sought to make sense of my unfavorable situation, one of my advisors shared with me a shocking assessment from a colleague who taught at a sociology department where I had applied for tenure-track position. "What is his dissertation about?" asked the colleague in a private telephone conversation with my advisor, who proceeded to explain my topic of infighting in LGBT Marches on Washington. "*And* he's gay?" the colleague retorted. Although puzzled by the question, my advisor nonetheless replied, "Yes. So what?" Then the curtains were lifted: "Well, that's the problem: he's narcissistic."

I choose to remember this offensive and homophobic remark as an isolated incident, rather than how sociologists in general react when I tell them what I study. But it still stung. It taught me that bias operates at all levels, even among highly educated people. To be gay and to care about gay issues is somehow narcissistic. The personal is always political, yes, but sexuality penetrates into our imagination in unique ways.

Why is sex research important? How does your work on LGBT social movements relate to everyday life?

Sex research is important for so many reasons, but I'll just share the first two that come to my mind. One of society's favorite myths about gay people is that we're all alike. Social psychologists call this the "out-group homogeneity effect," a majority-group perception that minority group members are fairly similar to one another. Sex research enables us to debunk this pervasive bias about LGBTQ individuals. From a personal perspective, part of what makes studying sexuality right now so exciting is that we're living with a generation of scholars who have pioneered the writing of our history. Unlike other minority groups, queer people have a comparatively weaker sense of our own heritage and history. Sex research is important because we still have much about queer lives that needs to be collectively remembered and preserved. There are many more stories to tell.

If you could teach people one thing about sexuality what would it be?

The world appears and feels so much more effervescent when passion and pleasure accompany the pursuit of your craft. It's important to love what you do. Studying sexuality offers opportunities for intense intellectual stimulation and unbridled pleasures in the process of doing it.

THE SOCIAL CONTROL OF ADULT–CHILD SEX

JEFFERY S. MULLIS AND DAWN M. BAUNACH

In a New Jersey suburb, July 29, 1994, 7-year-old Megan Kanka was raped and strangled to death by Jesse Timmendequas, a 33-year-old twice-convicted sex offender who lived across the street from the Kanka residence. When questioned by police the next day, Timmendequas confessed and led them to a nearby park to show where he had hidden the body. The victim's mother told reporters that if she had known a sex offender lived nearby, her daughter would still be alive.

Three years later a jury found Timmendequas guilty and recommended the death penalty. In the three-year period between the crime and the sentencing, Megan Kanka's parents led a nationwide movement calling for local authorities to notify residents whenever a sex offender moves into the community. Their efforts were highly successful: today, every state in the United States has adopted some version of community notification—also known as "Megan's Law." Similar procedures designed to monitor the whereabouts of sex offenders, such as the requirement that offenders register their current addresses with local police, have also been implemented in Canada, England, Wales, and Australia (Lieb, Quinsey, and Berliner, 1998; Plotnikoff and Woolfson, 2000; Hinds and Daly, 2001).

These and other recent developments in the handling of sex crimes against children are the impetus behind the present reading. Our main goals are, first, to place these developments in historical and cross-cultural perspective and, second, to identify underlying commonalities in the wide range of responses to adult–child sex in modern society.[1] Such responses can be understood as *social control;* that is, they are part of a larger process by which deviant behav-

ior is defined and counteracted and conformity is encouraged. Social control is ubiquitous in human groups, and it manifests itself in a complex variety of ways. Whenever people express any kind of disapproval over the actions of others—whether they do so informally or formally, individually or collectively, peacefully or violently—social control is present. People may even respond to their own actions with disapproval, a phenomenon known as "social control of the self" (Black, 1993: 65). Social scientists study social control in order to better understand all its manifestations and effects. In this reading we use the theory of social control developed by Donald Black (1976, 1993) to classify responses to adult–child sex into four different categories of control—penal, therapeutic, compensatory, and preventive—each one a distinctive method of handling all manner of deviant behavior.

Unlike prior research on the regulation of sex crimes, we are not concerned here with whether the social response is disproportionately severe relative to the actual incidence of such crimes, nor do we focus on the functions of social control for maintaining moral boundaries in society. Excellent work has already been done along these lines. For example, Sutherland (1950) argues that the widespread passage of sexual psychopath laws between 1937 and 1949 was based on unfounded fears generated by the news media. And Jenkins (1998) shows how past "moral panics" over the welfare of children were defensive reactions against large-scale social changes such as those occurring in gender roles and sexual mores during the twentieth century. Although we recognize that the social construction of social problems is a process not always commensurate with objective conditions and that moral panics serve important functions for group solidarity, we set these issues aside and concentrate instead on simply describing and classifying variation in the social control of adult–child sex.[2] Although our purpose is mainly descriptive and classificatory, we also present some explanations of the observed variation. Finally, we examine the unintended consequences of the notification laws enacted in the wake of Megan Kanka's tragic death.

MODERN AND PREMODERN VIEWS

From the standpoint of contemporary Western norms, *child molester* is one of the most stigmatizing labels that can be applied to a person. Disgust and outrage are evoked in almost everyone at the mere contemplation of such people (Finkelhor, 1984; Holmes, 1991; Pryor, 1996). Even in prisons—within a society of sinners, so to speak—other inmates single out the child molester as particularly depraved and deserving of punishment (e.g., see Siewers 1994).[3]

The wrath reserved for child molesters is a product of our cultural construction of childhood. We will return to this subject shortly; for now we note that despite the popularized views of Sigmund Freud, who saw even infants as highly sexual beings, and despite the wealth of research that documents the existence of childhood sexuality,[4] children are commonly seen as innocently devoid of sexual motivation. This image, by extension, casts sex offenders of children as exploitive, corruptive, and blameworthy. Modern law codifies this image by portraying children as mentally incapable of consenting to sexual relations and as guiltless in criminal procedures. Thus predisposed with these cultural directives, jurors find it difficult to be impartial in deciding the facts of child sexual assault cases: "[T]hat the defendant is charged with sexual assault against a child will cause the juror to consider the defendant probably guilty, or, at the very least, the bur-

den will be placed on that defendant to prove his or her innocence" (Vidmar 1997: 6). Defendants themselves will sometimes report feeling guilty, angry, and shocked by their own actions, as indicated in the following statements from four convicted offenders (all male):[5]

I realized that it was wrong. Normal people don't do these things. (O'Brien, 1986: 46)

When I look into myself [I feel] anger, hatred for myself, sorrow, and hurt. . . . I feel disgustingly dirty, and wonder what makes me feel that I have the right to live after what I've caused. (Ingersoll and Patton, 1990: 71)

I thought, oh God, all kinds of things. Like "God, what have I done?" . . . Before [the molestation] happened this was something I would read about. And the first thing that would come to my mind was, "They ought to take that sucker out and cut his nuts off and kill him. He doesn't deserve a trial." And that's the way I felt. Then it happened to me and that's what I thought about myself. I ought to be taken out and shot. . . . But that didn't stop me from doing it. (Pryor, 1996: 166)

When I touched her the first time on her behind . . . almost every time I touched her, I said, "This isn't right." I knew it wasn't right. . . . After the first episode . . . I got mad. I picked a chair up and tossed it across the room. (Pryor, 1996: 167)

Whether these men are sincere or merely providing the socially desirable response is unknown. The more relevant point is that they echo in their sentiments the larger societal reaction—as if they realize their acts are indefensible and therefore require appropriate self-condemnation. It is interesting to note that not all sex offenders against children are similarly self-condemning. Indeed, some are adamantly unrepentant and deny that anything is wrong with the behavior. This contrary view is most clearly expressed by the handful of organizations, such as the North American Man/Boy Love Association and the René Guyon Society, dedicated to justifying and normalizing adult–child sex. The slogan of the latter organization is "Sex by year eight or else it's too late" (De Young, 1988: 584).

Such views are, of course, extremely disreputable and rare. Even so, the negative reaction that currently prevails is far from a cross-cultural universal. Excluding cases of father-daughter and mother-son incest (prohibitions against which are found in almost all known societies), the world-historical evidence contains numerous examples of adult–child sex as part of normal cultural life; these examples include both same-sex and opposite-sex behaviors involving sexually mature and immature or maturing persons. But nowhere is adult–child sex the predominant form of sexual interaction, and in those times and places where it is accepted it tends to be, like all sexual behavior, highly regulated. Perhaps the best-known example is the ancient Greek system of *pederasty* ("love of boys"), in which sexual relationships between upper-class men and boys were embedded in an educational context designed to further the younger males' social and emotional development. The sexual component of these mentor–student relationships was socially accepted, but only under certain conditions. For example, the man was expected to always be the dominant partner (penetrator) and the boy the submissive partner (penetrated) in anal and intercrural (between the thighs) sex. In addition, the boy was not supposed to actually enjoy the sexual interaction because it was considered improper for a future Athenian leader to desire taking a submissive role in any dealings with other males (Dover, 1978; Halperin, 1990). The boy also needed to be pubescent, for grown men who pursued sex with prepubescent boys were potentially subject to harsh legal punishment (Tannahill, 1992). The onset of puberty thus appears to have been an important boundary dividing the acceptable from the unacceptable in adult–child sex among Grecian males. This "puberty standard" extended to upper class Grecian girls as

well, as evidenced by their average age at marriage being between 14 and 18 and usually to a male around age 30 (Blundell, 1995).

Beyond Ancient Greece, sexual contact between adults and children has served developmental goals elsewhere, such as the South Pacific, where ethnographers in the twentieth century documented adult–child sex rituals in several island societies. For instance, the Sambian tribe, located in the eastern mountains of Papua New Guinea, believed as late as the 1970s that the fellated semen of an older male "masculinizes" a prepubescent boy, allowing the boy to mature into a fierce warrior. Thus, around age 7, boys would begin a prolonged rite-of-passage characterized by frequent oral-sexual contacts with older, sexually mature males. Again, a reversal of dominant/ submissive roles here was forbidden, and fully mature men were expected to live a heterosexual existence (Herdt, 1984).

On Kolepom, an island located on the south coast of Irian Jaya/West Papua, a prepubescent girl of the Kiman Papuan would engage in sexual intercourse with multiple men as part of an elaborate semen-centered ritual. The semen produced by the intercourse would be collected in a banana leaf and rubbed on the girl's future husband, himself either prepubescent or pubescent. The cultural meaning of this custom was two-fold: intercourse with several older men was intended to test the girl's suitability for marriage, and the rubbing of the semen helped facilitate the boy's entrance into manhood (Serpenti, 1984).

On the Polynesian island of Mangaia, boys and girls both would be initiated into adulthood through explicit instruction and practical experience in how to sexually satisfy the opposite sex. A pubescent boy, for example, would first be instructed by an older man on such techniques as cunnilingus and how to achieve simultaneous mutual orgasm with a female partner. This formal instruction would be followed by a practical application in which the boy would have sex with a mature, sexually experienced woman. Of particular importance here was teaching the boy how to delay ejaculation. Emphasis was placed on the female orgasm, which was seen as a pleasurable end unto itself for Mangaian males. Failure to induce orgasm in a future female partner might also result in a loss of social status for men, as the news would spread through gossip. Consequently, for men (and presumably for women, too), the ideal ratio of female-to-male orgasms was at least two to one (Marshall, 1971).

In addition to historical and ethnographic accounts, age of consent laws are another source of information on attitudes toward adult–child sex. The legal age of sexual consent is the minimum age at which a person is considered, by the particular government in question, to be capable of consenting to sexual activity. Although minimum age statutes may apply to both male and female children, such laws have tended to be written with specific reference to females only, reflecting the historical view of females as property in need of special protection (Oberman, 1994) and also suggesting a greater tolerance of young male sexuality.

Following English common law, most jurisdictions in colonial America considered a 10-year-old girl to be old enough to give valid consent to sexual intercourse. If the girl was younger than 10, the act was defined as felony rape or carnal abuse (Jenkins, 1998). A notable exception to the common law tradition was Delaware, which, curiously, set its age of consent at 7. Prepubescent ages such as these remained on the books in most U.S. states until the late 1800s, at which time a popular "social purity" movement began to pressure state legislatures and Congress to raise minimum ages. The moral justification for changing the laws was to prevent men from corrupting young girls and luring them into a life of prostitution, decried by purity activists as a major urban problem of the day. From 1886 to 1895, in response to the purity movement's campaign, the age of sexual consent was raised to between 14 and 18 years in the majority of states (Pivar, 1973; D'Emilio and Freedman, 1997).

At present, the age of sexual consent is 16 to 18 throughout most of the United States. Worldwide, whenever legislation specifies a minimum age, it is typically at least 14. Throughout contemporary Europe, for example, it tends to range from 14 to 16, although in a handful of European locales it is still as low as 12 (e.g., Malta, Spain, Vatican City) (Graupner, 2000).[6] During the same time span that the legal age for sex has risen, the average age at puberty has fallen (see Jenkins, 1998: 24), creating a category of people we might call *sexually mature legal minors*—youth in their mid-adolescent years caught in a limbo of hormonal urges and legal constraints.[7]

Why is adult–child sex taboo in the modern world? Why was it a culturally actionable option in earlier times and other places but not here and now? A number of factors have given shape to the current taboo, some more directly than others. Here we briefly sketch the influence of three historical developments: the spread of Christian thought, the "invention" and lengthening of childhood, and the advent of compulsory schooling. First and oldest among these is the spread of Christianity—now the leading religion of the Western world. Early Christian tenets strictly forbade all non-procreative sex, a view that can still be found among many Christian moralists and one that clearly prohibits sexual intercourse with prepubescents at the same time that it prohibits masturbation and homosexuality. Christianity also has long emphasized the innocent and vulnerable nature of children and the need to protect them from "the harsh and sinful world" (see Conrad and Schneider, 1992: 146). This view of childhood as an innocent, precious stage of life began to gain wider favor through the 1700s in Western Europe and the 1800s in the United States. Children increasingly became seen as "fragile creatures of God" (Ariès, 1962: 133) who have special needs of their own, and parents increasingly became concerned with attending to those needs by applying appropriate childrearing practices, more benevolent and nurturing in style. Some scholars (e.g., Ariès, 1962; Stone, 1977) claim this general period of history marks a dramatic turning point in family life—the "invention" of childhood—the implication being that children prior to the Enlightenment were not recognized as fundamentally different from adults. This was certainly true in several key respects. For example, both adults and children were expected to make economic contributions to the family—most children in poorer families were put to work as early as age six. However, it is likely that there was more underlying continuity than dramatic change in attitudes toward and treatment of the very young in particular (Pollock, 1983). For present purposes, the most important change from the eighteenth century onward is the gradual lengthening of that period of life referred to as "growing up," so that these ideas about the preciousness of childhood began to be applicable over a wider age range. Put differently, children remained *childlike*—relatively innocent and free from adult obligations—for a longer period of time than in earlier eras. We see this in the notion of the "teenager," which by the mid-1900s had become entrenched in popular thought and custom as a distinct age category characterized by continued development and dependency. A facilitating factor behind the lengthening of childhood was the expansion of laws requiring formal schooling during the late nineteenth and early twentieth centuries. Compulsory education from ages 6 to 16 helped solidify the separation of children from adults by creating a distinct role for children outside of the home economy and the paid labor market. Compulsory education also acted latently as an additional constraint on sexuality: Students were not supposed to have

families of their own because of the heavy burden this would place on both the student and the educational system (Killias, 1991).

These historical changes provide a normative backdrop against which the social purity agenda and other child-saving reforms become possible. To a greater degree than in centuries past, children and adults have come to live under separate social expectations, governmentally mandated and divinely ordained, with children as protected and adults as protector. Because adult–child sex, embodied by the child molester, defiles the sanctity of childhood, the child molestor has become "the most evil social type in our society" (Davis, 1983: 110–111). How do we respond to this evil?

VARIETIES OF SOCIAL CONTROL

Human societies have developed a diverse repertoire of responses to deviant behavior. Adult–child sex provokes a number of these responses. For example, it is prosecuted in criminal courts as statutory rape and treated in psychiatric hospitals as pedophilia. Drawing on Black's theoretical framework, we classify these and other examples according to the general method of social control they illustrate, whether penal, therapeutic, compensatory, or preventive. These represent different strategies for defining and handling deviant behavior. They are not necessarily mutually exclusive strategies, however. Some of the specific examples described next combine the different methods of control in ways that make our classification somewhat arbitrary. In such cases our decision to classify in one category and not another is based on the primary type of social control in evidence.

Penal Control

In the application of penal control, the deviant is defined as an offender and punishment is seen as the logical response (Black, 1976).

The criminal justice system exemplifies the formal (i.e., governmental) variety of this type of social control. From the standpoint of criminal law, sexual contact between adults and minors may be prosecuted under any number of different sex offenses, including statutory rape, sexual assault, crimes against nature, defilement of a minor, carnal knowledge of a child, and indecent liberties with a child. In modern society it is the adult who is held accountable for these offenses. The minor is not charged with any crime and is in fact perceived as the victim of criminal wrongdoing, but the extent of perceived victimization will vary directly with situational characteristics such as the age difference between those involved and whether the act is mutually consensual versus coerced. Mutual consent, however, can have complex effects, sometimes absolving the older party of wrongdoing and sometimes resulting in a form of collective liability where both old and young are punished. For example, consider the following:

A priest by the name of Johann Arbogast Gauch, who for ten years (1735–1744), while serving as village parson in the former principality of Fürstenberg (Germany), had sexual relations with a number of boys and a few girls. The sexual acts were restricted to masturbation and, with the girls, displaying of the genitals. Some of the children were willing participants; many seem to have resisted at first but were compelled to give in. It seems that the whole village had been well aware of what had been going on, but for a long time nobody interfered. After ten years, i.e., after a change on the throne of Fürstenberg, however, Gauch was finally prosecuted and sentenced to death. The children were kept in a subterranean prison for several months and the boys, as accessories to the crimes, were beaten and whipped. The oldest of the boys barely escaped death sentences. The girls only received ecclesiastical penalty for unchaste behavior. Since the sexual activities in which they had been involved were heterosexual, they were thus not considered as being too serious. (Killias, 1991: 42)

Imprisonment and torture of the younger parties and capital punishment of the adult are evidenced in this example from eighteenth-century Germany. Today, in the United States, life imprisonment of the adult, without the possibility of parole, is the most severe formal punishment meted out for child sexual abuse.[8] But if murder is also committed, as in the case of Megan Kanka mentioned at the outset of this reading, then capital punishment may be imposed with the sexual act and the age of the victim regarded as aggravating circumstances justifying the harsher penalty.

In contrast to imprisonment and other officially authorized actions, ordinary citizens have been known to apply their own brand of punishment to child molesters. These informal measures vary from covert acts apparently perpetrated by lone individuals to more organized and collective responses, and they have become more common in the wake of community notification laws. For example, the home of a convicted child molester was burned to the ground after his name and address were released to the public (van Biema, 1993). In another case, a convicted molester's car was firebombed within days of the community being notified of his release (Chiang, Gaura, and Lee, 1997). In yet another case, five gunshots were fired at the home of a known molester, injuring no one but narrowly missing a woman in an upstairs room (Hajela, 1999). In one community, 100 neighbors of a known molester protested outside his apartment building and collected signatures in a campaign to persuade his landlord to evict him (DelVecchio, 1997). In some instances the actions of neighbors have forced molesters to move to a new location in the community or to move out of town altogether (see Anderson, 1997).

It may seem incongruous to classify these informal and sometimes criminally violent acts together with official governmental sanctions. In particular, how can crimes such as arson and assault with a deadly weapon be equated with legitimate legal responses such as arrest and imprisonment? Although these acts would seem to be diametrically opposed—the difference between lawful and unlawful—Black's theory of social control leads us to consider the characteristics they share in common:

Far from being an intentional violation of a prohibition, much crime is moralistic and involves the pursuit of justice. . . . To the degree that it defines or responds to the conduct of someone else—the victim—as deviant, crime is social control. . . . This implies that many crimes belong to the same family as gossip, ridicule, vengeance, . . . and law itself. . . . In other words, for certain theoretical purposes we might usefully ignore the fact that crime is criminal at all. (Black 1993: 27, 41–42)

Paradoxically, then, the molester might be both the perpetrator of crime and the victim of crime, depending on whether public officials or private citizens are acting against him. In either case, penal social control is present.

Therapeutic Control

One of the most significant trends in the social control of deviance is the increasing use of a therapeutic model to understand behaviors that might otherwise be seen as immoral or criminal, a trend referred to as the *medicalization of deviance* (Conrad and Schneider, 1992). Therapeutic social control entails viewing the deviant as a patient, sick and in need of help (Black, 1976). The impulse behind therapy is not to punish but to treat and ideally cure the deviant, thereby restoring normalcy to the mind or body. Psychiatric treatment exemplifies this type of social control. In psychiatry and related mental health fields, sexual contact between an adult and a child (whether real or imagined contact) indicates a potential mental disorder in the adult, namely pedophilia, defined clinically as "recurrent, intense, sexually arousing fantasies, sexual urges or behaviors" involving a pre-pubescent child, in which the individual with the disorder is at least 16 years old and five years older than the child (American Psychiatric Association, 1994: 527–528). Pedophilia is distinguished from ephebophilia, which refers to an adult's sexual attraction to pubescent children or young teenagers. Ephebophilia is not widely recognized in professional therapeutic doctrine as a mental disorder. This may reflect the well-documented preference among human and other primate males for sexually mature younger partners (Ames and Houston, 1990; Okami, 1990), making ephebophilia perhaps more readily comprehensible as a biocultural norm than as a psychiatric problem.

The therapeutic control of pedophilia includes such techniques as social skills training, victim role-taking, aversion therapy, orgasmic reconditioning, surgical castration, libido-reducing drugs, and a host of other behavioral, cognitive, and pharmacological treatments (Howitt, 1995; Stone, Winslade, and Klugman, 2000). The sheer variety underscores the psychiatric belief that there is no single cause of pedophilia and that no single treatment is effective for all cases. Courts frequently order or provide such treatments as part of the criminal sentence, a practice that illustrates institutional cooperation between the criminal justice and mental health care systems in the control of deviant behavior (see Szasz, 1963). This cooperation is further illustrated by U.S. Supreme Court rulings that allow states to confine "sexual predators" for psychiatric treatment *after* they have served their prison sentences (Greenhouse 2002).[9]

Of the different treatments for pedophilia, the most controversial are surgical castration and so-called *chemical castration*. Both reduce the level of testosterone in the body, which in turn reduces sexual desire. The controversy revolves around the ethics and efficacy of castration, some claiming it is simply barbaric (especially the surgical variety) and others questioning the validity of the theory that pedophilia is in fact caused by sexual desire. In surgical castration the testes are removed, permanently reducing testosterone. Chemical castration yields a temporary reduction in testosterone via the injection of antiandrogen drugs such as Depo-Provera. Historically, castration has served both penal and therapeutic ends. It has been used throughout history as punishment for sex crimes such as rape and adultery but is intended in modern society as a medical deterrent to sexual deviance. The first European country to legalize surgical castration was Denmark in 1929, followed by Germany, Iceland, Sweden, and other countries (Heim and Hursch, 1979). A growing number of U.S. states authorize both surgical and chemical castration as a condition of parole for convicted child molesters. Because neither form has been shown to unambiguously reduce recidivism, some critics have speculated that therapists and lawmakers who advocate castration are actually seeking punishment by medical means (see Heim and Hursch, 1979; Stone et al., 2000).

Compensatory Control

In compensatory social control, the deviant is defined as a debtor who has failed to fulfill an obligation. Payment is the solution (Black, 1976), though punishment may be a byproduct. Compensatory control is seen most clearly and familiarly in civil lawsuits, in which offenders are asked to pay damages to remedy the wrongs they allegedly committed. It is also seen in lesser-known victim-compensation programs, in which the government provides payment to victims, a provision partly based on social welfare ideology and partly on the argument that the government is liable because it has failed to prevent crime (Henderson, 1985; Greer, 1994). Although both civil lawsuits and governmental funds are options available to victims of sex crimes, we focus here on lawsuits only, specifically, lawsuits against the Roman Catholic Church.

In recent years the Catholic Church has been embroiled in public scandal over pedo-philic priests, who might be more aptly termed "ephebophilic priests" because most of their known sexual activities have involved adolescents (Jenkins, 1998; Ripley, 2002). Reliable statistics are lacking on the total number of lawsuits and amount of paid compensation, but a national survey of Catholic dioceses suggests that, since the early 1960s, over 850 priests in the United States have been accused of child sexual abuse, and an estimated one billion dollars has been paid to the accusers in court-ordered and out-of-court settlements (Cooperman and Sun, 2002). Approximately 40 percent of the accused priests were removed from their ministerial positions. Only 6 percent of these were actually defrocked (removed from the priesthood altogether) (Cooperman and Sun, 2002). The Church apparently failed to promptly remove all the priests that were known to be abusers, thus enabling them to become repeat offenders:

At the same time that Church officials denied that clergy engaged in sexual activities with children, they privately assured complainants that the "problem" would be investigated and resolved immediately. In actuality, the Church began to transfer perpetrators either to active ministry in other parishes or to church-affiliated treatment centers. The international scope of the Catholic Church allowed the official hierarchy to relocate offending individuals to distant geographical locations. For Church officials, such moves [temporarily] solved the problem. (Krebs, 1998: 19, citation omitted)

However, the accumulating claims of abuse and the accompanying media scrutiny eventually forced the Church to take additional steps—the drafting of a zero-tolerance policy, "Charter for the Protection of Children and Young People." This is a truly remarkable title considering that the protection being referenced is *protection from priests*, in other words, from the Church itself.

Despite the number of civil claims against wayward priests, very few criminal charges have been brought to date (Pfeiffer and Cullen, 2002).

Why? In some cases the statute of limitations has expired, while other cases may prove to be unfounded. But, in general, the high number of civil claims and the low number of criminal charges reflects the social structure of these cases: When the accused ranks relatively high in social status, as priests do as individuals and the Catholic Church does as an organization, then compensatory control becomes more likely and penal control becomes less likely (see Black, 1993: 53–55).

Preventive Control

In preventive social control deviants are defined in terms of past transgressions and the likelihood of future offending. Prevention might be attempted by placing deviants under closer surveillance or by restricting their freedom of movement, and by potential victims taking steps to reduce their vulnerability (see Black, 1993: 8; Horwitz, 1990). Corresponding examples in the preventive control of adult–child sex are registration and notification systems, electronic monitoring devices that alert authorities when the target has ventured beyond permitted boundaries, and the informal method of avoidance, curtailing interaction with the deviant. Next we describe registration and notification as implemented in the United States. We then address the unanticipated consequences of notification.

Beginning in the mid-1990s, all fifty states became federally required to maintain sex offender registries. On release into the community, offenders are ordered to provide local law enforcement with such data as their home address, photograph, criminal history, fingerprint identification, social security number, place of employment, vehicle registration, and DNA profile. The purpose is to maintain a record of the whereabouts and characteristics of offenders. If a sex crime occurs in the vicinity of a known offender, the police have an immediate suspect. Thus the lag between the commission of the crime and apprehension/arrest is potentially shortened (Finn, 1997). Updated registries are needed for states to fulfill a second federal requirement of the 1990s, community notification (or Megan's Law), signed in 1996. Although roughly half of the fifty states had implemented notification systems before 1996, the federal version of Megan's Law required the remaining states to do so. All now have. States achieve notification in several ways, ranging from active to passive. For example, officers may distribute fliers with the offender's photo, address, and criminal history, or a centralized database may be made available to the public via the Internet (Adams, 1999). In some jurisdictions, the offender may be required to notify neighbors personally, going door-to-door. Judges have also required offenders to place warning signs in their yards and bumper stickers on their cars. As Jenkins notes, such procedures have seldom been seen in Anglo-American law, "at least not since the days when thieves, adulterers, and blasphemers were branded or otherwise mutilated in order that they be identifiable by their crimes" (1998: 199).

Consequences of Community Notification

Notification transforms a "discreditable" neighbor into a "discredited" one (Goffman, 1963; Pryor, 1996), the secret stigma now publicly known. As a result, the neighborhood at large is placed in a heightened state of uneasy awareness:

[W]hat few facts residents already had about their new neighbor—his chattiness, his bike rides, reports of his playing with children with water balloons—took on sinister implications after the police alert. (DelVecchio, 1997)

As mentioned previously, the results of notification include vandalism, assault, protest demonstrations, and subsequent migration or banishment of the offender, none of which notification was intended to produce. Notification is premised on the "parents' right to know." The information is intended to be used as part of an avoidance-prevention strategy, with parents warning their children not to go near the offender's home or walk alone in the neighborhood. Vigilantism was an unintended consequence, but states are now fully aware of its possibility. In fact, many Internet-based registries now specifically warn citizens against using the information to commit a crime. The criminal actions of notified citizens may encourage child molesters to "go underground," not registering with local law agencies, thus thwarting notification. This in turn may allow them to continue molesting, only now with greater anonymity. In this sense, notification potentially creates the crime it is designed to control.

But how common are these informal responses? Are they in fact driving large numbers of child molesters underground? Even if uncommon, it plausibly takes only a few well-publicized incidents to get the attention of numerous molesters, who may read or watch the story with great interest and then choose to act upon it by moving, not registering, and so on. We investigated these issues by conducting a Lexis-Nexis search of incidents reported in newspapers nationwide during the years 1994 to 2001. The results are presented in Figure 43.1, which shows the nature and extent of informal responses occurring before and after the federal notification statute.[10] As shown in Figure 43.1, the number of incidents increased from 1994 through 1999. This increase very likely reflects (a) the enactment of notification, as those states without it began to comply with the federal statute, and (b) the novelty of notification (i.e., people initially responded with greater outrage on learning that a pedophile lived nearby). Over time, however, as people across the country became accustomed to the laws (and perhaps resigned to their neighbors), outrage diminished, as suggested by the decrease in events from 1998 through 2001.

Perhaps the most striking finding in Figure 44.1 is the seemingly low number of incidents—115 in all—surely far fewer incidents than there were notifications in this time period. The low number, however, is consistent with the findings of other studies. For example, surveys of law enforcement specialists who routinely work with sex offenders find that name calling, verbal threats, graffiti, protest demonstrations, and minor vandalism sometimes do occur, but not nearly as frequently as expected (see Finn, 1997: 13–14 for an overview of these studies). In our data, the most common type of incident is what we call "miscellaneous protest," a category consisting mainly of scattered complaints to the police, landlords, and employers. There were forty-eight such incidents described in newspaper articles from 1994 through 2001. The second most common type of event is the comparatively organized protest demonstration (or picket), most of which occurred in front of offenders' homes. Overall, there were thirty-one pickets from 1994 through 2001. Also included in this second category are three instances of petitioning in 1996 through 1997 and two instances of petitioning in 2000 through 2001, in which individuals collected signatures supporting the ousting of offenders from their homes or jobs. We grouped these with picketing because of a tendency for petitioning and picketing to occur together. The third most common type of event is property damage, including firebombed cars, threats spray-painted on cars and lawns, homes set ablaze, and bricks and eggs thrown at homes. There were twenty-one instances of property damage. The least common event is actual physical violence inflicted on offenders. There were only ten such incidents reported in newspapers from 1994 through 2001. Two of these incidents were cases of mistaken identity in which residents beat the wrong man. In three of the ten cases the molester inflicted the violence on himself by committing suicide shortly after

FIGURE 43.1   What Happens When Sex Offenders Become Neighbors? Tracking the Consequences of Community Awareness, 1994–2001

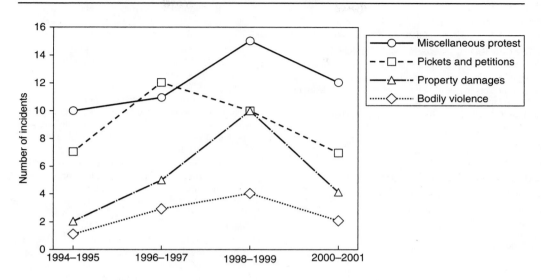

notification was made to the neighborhood. Finally, not shown in Figure 44.1 is the number of offenders evicted or otherwise compelled to relocate as a result of community actions. Overall, there were thirty-nine reported relocations, and these tended to occur during the height of the other activity, becoming less frequent from 1998 onward.

SUMMARY AND CONCLUSION

A wide range of social control is directed toward adult–child sex in modern society: imprisonment, hospitalization, castration, drug treatment, civil litigation, surveillance, assault, banishment, and even suicide, a type of self-applied social control. Extreme deviance brings forth the extremes in social control. We have sought to place these modern responses to adult–child sex in a world-historical context. Ancient Greece was examined in this regard, together with South Pacific examples and the changing legal age of sexual consent. Further, we have attempted to identify

Blackian commonalities among the different responses, focusing on penal, therapeutic, compensatory, and preventive social control.

Regarding the consequences of community notification, we anticipate a continued drop in confrontational and violent social control, at least until the next moral panic over child sexual abuse. Then it seems reasonable to expect an increase in violence against child molesters. Community notification laws, unlike many other laws, appear to be a written rule that actually has some consequence for the way people behave, for better or worse.

NOTES

1. In the scientific literature and the news media alike, adult–child sex is often referred to as *child sexual abuse, child molestation,* and *pedophilia. Pedophilia* denotes a psychiatric disorder found in some, but not all, sex offenders of children (Freund, Watson, and Dickey, 1991). Depending on the context, we use each of these alternative terms, but for general sociological purposes we prefer the more neutral term *adult–child sex* because contemporary evaluative notions of abuse, molestation, and disorder do not always fit the empirical record of this behavior. For discussion of the normative character of research on

adult–child sex and how it impedes a scientific understanding of the subject, see Ames and Houston (1990), Okami (1990), and Rind, Tromovitch, and Bauserman (2000).

2. Unless otherwise indicated, what follows is intended to apply to both incestuous and nonincestuous adult–child sex.

3. The early French sociologist Emile Durkheim suggests that even within a perfect "society of saints," certain acts inevitably will be defined as deviant, albeit to the average person the acts in question would probably be considered trifling ([1895] 1938: 68–69). Likewise, even within a society of sinners (such as a prison), there exists a moral ranking of acts from bad to worse. The fact that child molestation is considered one of the more loathsome crimes within the prison subculture—where tolerance levels for deviance are comparatively high—indicates the gravity of the stigma attached to the act in ordinary society.

4. Most college textbooks on human sexuality provide overviews of this research, and most rightly caution against equating early childhood sexuality with adult sexuality. The pleasure-seeking behavior of young children is not the same thing, subjectively at least, as the learned eroticism experienced later in life (e.g., see Rathus, Nevid, and Fichner-Rathnus, 2000: 386–392; Kelly, 2001: 163–166).

5. Almost all convicted child molesters are male. Female offenders may be more prevalent, however, than the gender profile of the convicted would suggest. For example, compared to other offending scenarios, when an adult female sexually engages an underage male the event may be less likely construed as an unwelcome advance and hence less likely to be reported to the police. It can even become a source of pride and status for the boy (see Pryor, 1996: 36–37). If it is reported, others will consider it less serious than cases involving male offenders, with arrest, prosecution, and conviction being comparatively unlikely. In one case, a father remarked that his son "should consider himself lucky to have had a sexual experience with an older woman" (Holmes, 1991: 34).

6. In the Philippines and in Thailand, where the child sex industry thrives, the ages of sexual consent are 12 and 15, respectively, except in cases of prostitution, whereupon it is raised to 18 in both countries in an attempt to curtail the exploitation of children (Graupner, 2000).

7. This term has an analogue in the healthcare context, where the *mature minor doctrine* enables older adolescents to bypass parental consent and make their own decisions regarding medical treatment. The term *minor* in this doctrine refers to those under the age of full majority rather than those specifically under the age of sexual consent.

8. On sentencing outcomes and rates of incarceration, see Cheit and Goldschmidt (1997).

9. In the most recent ruling, *Kansas v. Crane* (decided January 22, 2002), the Supreme Court specified that post-prison confinement is appropriate if offenders have a mental disorder that undermines their self-control.

10. We read newspaper articles with an eye toward counting the number of separate informal incidents resulting from notification. Newspapers tend to report more violent or organized incidents, hence minor insults and harassments are undoubtedly underrepresented. Considering the enormous media attention paid to the Kanka case and to notification legislation generally, when more visible events did occur (e.g., picketing), the news media probably were keen to report them (see Best and Horiuchi, 1985 for a similar point regarding their newspaper analysis of Halloween sadism). Overall, from the period of January 1994 through December 2001, there were 1,401 articles generated by our inclusive keyword searches. The articles were generated from the Lexis-Nexis database of 219 different newspaper sources, including major city, regional, and national newspapers, and Associated Press and state/local wire reports. During the period observed, 128 separate incidents involving 85 different molesters were reported in these sources. Figure 44.1 presents a subset of these cases (n = 115) classified according to the type of incident. The vast majority of incidents were directed at child molesters even though notification applies to other kinds of sex offenders too. Some incidents received coverage in multiple papers and on multiple days; these were counted only once. In addition, some offenders were targets in multiple incidents; these were counted as separate events. The complete details of the analysis are available on request.

REFERENCES

Adams, Devon B. 1999. *Summary of State Sex Offender Registry Dissemination Procedures.* Washington, D.C.: Department of Justice, Bureau of Justice Statistics.

American Psychiatric Association. 1994. *Diagnostic and Statistical Manual of Mental Disorders* (4th edition). Washington, D.C.: American Psychiatric Association.

Ames, M. Ashley, and David A. Houston. 1990. "Legal, Social, and Biological Definitions of Pedophilia." *Archives of Sexual Behavior* 19: 333–342.

Anderson, Nick. 1997. "Convicted Molester Will Find New Home." *Los Angeles Times,* March 13, p. B1.

Ariès, Philippe. 1962. *Centuries of Childhood: A Social History of Family Life.* New York: Vintage Books.

Best, Joel, and Gerald T. Horiuchi. 1985. "The Razor Blade in the Apple: The Social Construction of Urban Legends." *Social Problems* 32: 488–499.

Black, Donald. 1976. *The Behavior of Law.* New York: Academic Press.

———. 1993. *The Social Structure of Right and Wrong.* San Diego, CA: Academic Press.

Blundell, Sue. 1995. *Women in Ancient Greece.* Cambridge, MA: Harvard University Press.

Cheit, Ross E., and Erica B. Goldschmidt. 1997. "Child Molesters in the Criminal Justice System." *New England Journal of Criminal and Civil Commitment* 23: 267–301.

Chiang, Harriet, Maria Alicia Gaura, and Henry K. Lee. 1997. "Disclosure of Molesters Brings Fear of Vigilantism." *San Francisco Chronicle,* July 12, p. A1.

Conrad, Peter, and Joseph W. Schneider. 1992. *Deviance and Medicalization: From Badness to Sickness.* Philadelphia: Temple University Press.

Cooperman, Alan, and Lena H. Sun. 2002. "Crisis in the Church: Survey Finds 218 Priests Have Been Removed This Year." *Boston Globe,* June 9, p. A34.

Davis, Murray S. 1983. *Smut: Erotic Reality/Obscene Ideology.* Chicago: University of Chicago Press.

De Young, Mary. 1988. "The Indignant Page: Techniques of Neutralization in the Publications of Pedophile Organizations." *Child Abuse and Neglect* 12: 583–591.

DelVecchio, Rick. 1997. "Residents Want Molester Out of Santa Rosa." *San Francisco Chronicle,* July 7, p. A13.

D'Emilio, John, and Estelle B. Freedman. 1997. *Intimate Matters: A History of Sexuality in America* (2nd edition). Chicago: University of Chicago Press.

Dover, K. J. 1978. *Greek Homosexuality.* Cambridge, MA: Harvard University Press.

Durkheim, Emile. [1895] 1938. *The Rules of Sociological Method.* New York: Free Press.

Finkelhor, David. 1984. *Child Sexual Abuse: New Theory and Research.* New York: Free Press.

Finn, Peter. 1997. *Sex Offender Community Notification.* Washington, D.C.: Department of Justice, Office of Justice Programs.

Freund, Kurt, Robin Watson, and Robert Dickey. 1991. "Sex Offenses against Female Children Perpetrated by Men Who Are Not Pedophiles." *Journal of Sex Research* 28: 409–423.

Goffman, Erving. 1963. *Stigma: Notes on the Management of Spoiled Identity.* Englewood Cliffs, NJ: Prentice-Hall.

Graupner, Helmut. 2000. "Sexual Consent: The Criminal Law in Europe and Overseas." *Archives of Sexual Behavior* 29: 415–461.

Greenhouse, Linda. 2002. "Court Sets Limit on Detaining Sex Offenders after Prison." *New York Times,* January 23, p. A1.

Greer, Desmond S. 1994. "A Transatlantic Perspective on the Compensation of Crime Victims in the United States." *Journal of Criminal Law and Criminology* 85: 333–401.

Hajela, Deepti. 1999. "Linden Man Gets 10-Year Terms in Vigilante Shooting." *The Record,* February 20, p. A3.

Halperin, David M. 1990. "Why Is Diotima a Woman? Platonic Eros and the Figuration of Gender." In *Before Sexuality: The Construction of Erotic Experience in the Ancient Greek World,* edited by David M. Halperin, John J. Winkler, and Froma I. Zeitlin (pp. 257–308). Princeton, NJ: Princeton University Press.

Heim, Nikolaus, and Carolyn J. Hursch. 1979. "Castration for Sex Offenders: A Review and Critique of Recent European Literature." *Archives of Sexual Behavior* 8: 281–304.

Henderson, Lynne. N. 1985. "The Wrongs of Victim's Rights." *Stanford Law Review* 37: 937–1021.

Herdt, Gilbert H. 1984. "Semen Transactions in Sambian Culture." In *Ritualized Homosexuality in Melanesia,* edited by Gilbert H. Herdt (pp. 167–210). Berkeley: University of California Press.

Hinds, Lyn, and Kathleen Daly. 2001. "The War on Sex Offenders: Community Notification in Perspective." *Australian and New Zealand Journal of Criminology* 34: 256–276.

Holmes, Ronald M. 1991. *Sex Crimes.* Thousand Oaks, CA: Sage.

Horwitz, Allan V. 1990. *The Logic of Social Control.* New York: Plenum Press.

Howitt, Dennis. 1995. *Paedophiles and Sexual Offences against Children.* New York: Wiley.

Ingersoll, Sandra L., and Susan O. Patton. 1990. *Treating Perpetrators of Sexual Abuse.* Lexington, MA: Lexington Books.

Jenkins, Philip. 1998. *Moral Panic: Changing Concepts of the Child Molester in Modern America.* New Haven, CT: Yale University Press.

Kelly, Gary F. 2001. *Sexuality Today* (7th edition). New York: McGraw-Hill.

Killias, Martin. 1991. "The Historic Origins of Penal Statutes Concerning Sexual Activities Involving Children and Adolescents." *Journal of Homosexuality* 20: 41–46.

Krebs, Theresa. 1998. "Church Structures That Facilitate Pedophilia among Roman Catholic Clergy." In *Wolves within the Fold: Religious Leadership and Abuses of Power,* edited by Anson Shupe (pp. 15–32). New Brunswick, NJ: Rutgers University Press.

Lieb, Roxanne, Vernon Quinsey, and Lucy Berliner. 1998. "Sexual Predators and Social Policy." In Michael Tonry (ed.) *Crime and Justice: A Review of Research,* 23: 43–114.

Marshall, Donald S. 1971. "Sexual Aspects of the Life Cycle." In *Human Sexual Behavior: Variations in the Ethnographic Spectrum,* edited by Donald S. Marshall and Robert C. Suggs (pp. 103–162). New York: Basic Books.

Oberman, Michelle. 1994. "Turning Girls into Women: Reevaluating Modern Statutory Rape Law." *Journal of Criminal Law and Criminology* 85: 15–79.

O'Brien, Shirley J. 1986. *Why They Did It: Stories of Eight Convicted Child Molesters.* Springfield, IL: Thomas Books.

Okami, Paul. 1990. "Sociopolitical Biases in the Contemporary Scientific Literature on Adult Human Sexual Behavior with Children and Adolescents." In *Pedophilia: Biosocial Dimensions,* edited by J. R. Feierman (pp. 91–121). New York: Springer-Verlag.

Pivar, David J. 1973. *Purity Crusade: Sexual Morality and Social Control, 1868–1900.* Westport, CT: Greenwood Press.

Pfeiffer, Sacha, and Kevin Cullen. 2002. "Crisis in the Church: D. A. Seeks to Lift Time Limit on Rape Cases." *Boston Globe,* June 27, p. A23.

Plotnikoff, Joyce, and Richard Woolfson. 2000. *Where Are They Now: An Evaluation of Sex Offender Registration in England and Wales.* Police Research Series, Paper 126: Crown.

Pollock, Linda. 1983. *Forgotten Children: Parent–Child Relations from 1500–1900.* Cambridge: Cambridge University Press, 1983.

Pryor, Douglas W. 1996. *Unspeakable Acts: Why Men Sexually Abuse Children.* New York: New York University Press.

Rathus, Spencer A., Jeffrey S. Nevid, and Lois Fichner-Rathus. 2000. *Human Sexuality in a World of Diversity* (4th edition). Boston: Allyn and Bacon.

Rind, Bruce, Philip Tromovitch, and Robert Bauserman. 2000. "Condemnation of a Scientific Article: A Chronology and Refutation of the Attacks and a Discussion of Threats to the Integrity of Science." *Sexuality and Culture* 4: 1–62.

Ripley, Amanda. 2002. "Inside the Church's Closet." *Time,* May 20, p. 60.

Serpenti, Laurent. 1984. "The Ritual Meaning of Homosexuality and Pedophilia among the Kiman-Papuans of South Irian Jaya." In *Ritualized Homosexuality in Melanesia,* edited by Gilbert H. Herdt (pp. 292–317). Berkeley: University of California Press.

Siewers, Alf. 1994. "Prisoners Also Judge and Jury; Heinous Crimes Can Make Some Inmates a Special Target." *Chicago Sun-Times,* November 29, p. 7.

Stone, Lawrence. 1977. *The Family, Sex, and Marriage in England, 1500–1800.* New York: Harper and Row.

Stone, T. Howard, William J. Winslade, and Craig M. Klugman. 2000. "Sex Offenders, Sentencing Laws, and Pharmaceutical Treatment: A Prescription for Failure." *Behavioral Sciences and the Law* 18: 83–110.

Sutherland, Edwin H. 1950. "The Diffusion of Sexual Psychopath Laws." *American Journal of Sociology* 56: 142–148.

Szasz, Thomas. 1963. *Law, Liberty, and Psychiatry.* New York: Macmillan.

Tannahill, Reay. 1992. *Sex in History.* New York: Scarborough House.

van Biema, David. 1993. "Burn Thy Neighbor." *Time,* July 26, p. 58.

Vidmar, Neil. 1997. "General Prejudice and the Presumption of Guilt in Sex Abuse Trials." *Law and Human Behavior* 21: 5–25.

Too Young to Consent?

Elizabeth Cavalier and Elisabeth O. Burgess

In contemporary U.S. society, most sexual activity is between two people of similar ages. Approximately 74 percent of the first male sexual partners of adolescent females are the same age or one to three years older and only 8 percent of teen females have first partners six or more years older (Abma, Martinez, Mosher, and Dawson, 2004). But the legal and cultural significance of age difference is variable over the life course. The fifteen-year gap between a 55-year-old man and his 40-year-old wife is less significant than the three-year age difference between a 18- and 15-year-old having sex under the bleachers at their high school. In some states, that 18-year-old could be arrested for statutory rape, even if both parties agree the sex was consensual. Change the scenario, and now the 18-year-old is engaging in sex acts with a 10-year-old. Most people in the United States would agree that 10 is too young to consent to sex. So, where do we draw the line? Who gets to decide and why? How are these moral values legislated and prosecuted?

England developed the first known laws proscribing an age limit of 12 for consent to sexual activity in 1275. By 1576, the age limit was codified at 10 years old, and sex between individuals above and below the age of consent became a felony. Colonial America adopted these laws defining ages of consent ranging from age 10 to 12 (Cocca, 2004). Traditionally, these laws were enacted to protect the virginity of [white] girls and, in fact, were only enforced if the victim was a white female who was a virgin prior to the sexual act in question. These crimes were prosecuted as property crimes against the girl's household—premarital virginity was treated as a valuable commodity.

Since Colonial times, laws about age of consent[1] have become more complicated, the age of consent has steadily risen, and the statutes have expanded to include both female and male victims. Regulations around adolescent sexual activity in modern history have generally been couched in three different, and sometimes overlapping, areas of social concern. The first is a concern about potentially coercive sex. The second is a morality-based concern about sex between unmarried sexual partners. The third is an economically based argument, which posits that adolescent sex leads to out-of-wedlock births that pose a drain on society via the welfare system (Cocca, 2004). Depending on specific social conditions, laws around age of consent have been more or less rigidly enforced. Since the 1970s, the United States has seen a steady tightening of control around issues of adolescent sex and age of consent.

Currently, the majority of U.S. states (33 and the District of Columbia) and Canada use 16 as the age of consent. Six states have 17 as the age of consent, and another 11 have 18 as the legal age of consent. However, in the United States, the laws vary widely and can be based on a number of factors. While 12 states have a single age of consent and individuals cannot consent to sex under any circumstances below this age, other states use a more complex formula (Lewin Group, 2004). These state laws are a combination of four factors: the age of consent, the minimum age of victim (the age below which an individual cannot consent to sex under any circumstances), the age differential between victim and perpetra-

tor (the maximum difference in age between a victim and defendant where an individual can legally consent, assuming the victim is above the minimum age), and the minimum age of the defendant in order to prosecute (the age below which an individual cannot be prosecuted if the victim is above the minimum age) (Lewin Group, 2004)[2]. All of these laws focus on sexual intercourse—the laws about sexual contact (including oral and anal sex) are more complicated and unevenly enforced. Such variety in laws and enforcement creates a problem whereby sexual activity between consenting adolescents and young adults may be legal in one state, a misdemeanor in another, and a felony in a third state. In addition to legal disparities across states, enforcement differs based on the sex of the victim and defendant, the race of the victim and defendant, and the type of sexual activity in question (i.e., oral and anal sex rather than intercourse or heterosexual sex rather than homosexual sex).

Public perception and media coverage of age of consent cases do not coincide with actual rates of crime, particularly concerning the sex of perpetrators and victims. The National Incidents Based Reporting System (NIBRS) reports that 95 percent of victims in statutory rape cases are female and 99 percent of offenders of female victims are male (Troup-Leasure and Snyder, 2005). Yet popular press reports emphasize female perpetrators (often teachers) with younger male victims, such as the case of Mary Kay LeTourneau, who had two children with a student she began a sexual relationship with when she was a married 34-year-old and the student was 12 (Cavanaugh, 2007). Despite representing less than 5 percent of the cases of statutory rape and significantly less of the prosecutions (Cocca, 2004), female perpetrator/male victim statutory rape cases are sensationalized on the news and talk shows. This media coverage perpetuates the myth that there is an epidemic of older women preying on younger adolescent boys. The language that is used in coverage of these crimes glorifies and glamorizes the incidents and incites a culture of sexual panic that further reinforces norms of appropriate sexual partners and behaviors (Cavanagh, 2007). The disproportionate coverage of male victims is especially ironic considering that statutory rape laws were originally enacted to protect young girls. It was not until the early 1990s that the language of statutory rape laws was changed to include gender-neutral language allowing for the potential for male victims (Cocca, 2004). From the 1960s to the 1990s, public debate around legal and social policies about statutory rape often centered around rhetoric about protecting young girls from predatory older men. Adolescents, girls in particular, were seen as not having the legal capacity or emotional maturity to consent to sexual activity. Yet during the same time period, the juvenile justice system was also undergoing a profound shift, seeing a steady decline in treating defendants, primarily males, as juveniles and instead prosecuting them as adults, particularly for violent crimes (Schaffner, 2005). This sexual double standard illustrates a peculiar dichotomy whereby girls are treated as innocent, virginal children without the ability to be autonomous decision-makers about their sexual lives, while boys are treated as adults with the intellectual capacity to commit a crime and be held legally culpable.

Race of the victim and perpetrator is the second area where there are significant disparities in enforcement of statutory rape laws. Similar to other crimes, men of color, particularly African American men, are more likely to be arrested and prosecuted and disproportionately sentenced (Criminal Justice Policy Foundation, 2005). The case of Marcus Dixon, a black 18-year-old male who had consensual sex with a white girl who was three months shy of her 16th birthday, received national coverage and illustrated a major problem with existing laws. Although he was acquitted of rape, battery, assault, and false imprisonment, he was convicted of statutory rape, and because of the girl's age, aggravated child molestation. He was sentenced to 10 years in prison, but his sentence was overturned and he was released a year later after public outcry about the case (Melby, 2006). Likewise, the case of Genarlow Wilson, a 17-year-old black male who had consensual oral sex with a 15-year-old female, drew international attention when he was convicted of aggravated child molestation and sentenced to 10 years in prison. He served over two years before his conviction was overturned by the Georgia State Supreme Court. In a letter to the state Attorney General, former president Jimmy Carter wrote, "the racial dimension of the case is likewise hard to ignore and perhaps unfortunately has had an impact on the final outcome of the case" (Jarvie and Fausset, 2007). Disproportionate prosecuting and sentencing of black men for statutory rape reflects remnants of historical racism predicated on white fears about black men having sex with white women.

The Genarlow Wilson case also illustrates a third area of differential enforcement of consent laws based on types of sexual behavior. Had he been convicted of sexual intercourse with the 15-year-old, rather than oral sex, a child molestation charge would not have applied. More often, the differential enforcement of laws based on behavior involves disparities between heterosexual and homosexual sexual activity. Matthew Limon was released from prison in 2005 after serving almost six years in prison for consensual gay sex when he had just turned 18 and his partner was 14, nearly 15. He was convicted of criminal sodomy because Kansas' "Romeo and Juliet" law, which reduced penalties for consensual sex between two teenagers, only applied to heterosexual sex. He was sentenced to 17 years in prison, but would have only been sentenced to 15 months had his partner been female. The case went all the way to the U.S. Supreme Court which overturned the conviction, but by that time Limon had served nearly six years in prison (Melby, 2006). In many states, the statutory rape laws do not apply to married partners. This marital exemption can include total immunity to prosecution for statutory rape or a reduction in sentencing for married partners. As a result, those who do not have access to marriage—gay couples or adolescents without parental consent for marriage—are more likely to face criminal prosecution for sexual activity.

Age of consent and statutory rape laws are not designed to catch and punish persistent child sexual offenders; states have separate legislation that prohibits child molestation and pedophilia. Statutory rape laws, with their uneven and often discriminatory enforcement, have primarily served to criminalize adolescent sexual exploration. NIBRS (2005) reports that three out of 10 reported cases of statutory rape regarding juveniles involve people who considered themselves "boyfriend/girlfriend," and six out of 10 involve people who considered each other "acquaintances or friends" (Troup-Leasure and Snyder, 2005). The legislation, punishments, and moral panic around age of consent do not prevent adolescents from having sex, but they deny their sexual agency and limit their sexual partners (Cavanagh, 2007; Hunt, 2009). The Centers for Disease Control and Prevention (CDC) (2008) report that by 9th grade 27.4 percent of girls have engaged in sexual intercourse, and by 12th grade that percentage increases to 66.2 percent. For boys, 38.1 percent have engaged in sexual intercourse by 9th grade, but the percentage increases to 62.8 percent by 12th grade. The CDC also reports that over half (52.6%) of high school seniors have been sexually active in the past three months. Adolescents are having sex—the threat of criminal prosecution for sexual exploration adds unnecessary fear and anxiety over

something that even adults disagree (as evidenced by the wide disparity across states in age of consent laws). In the end, an arbitrary age limit on age of consent has often served to punish adolescent sexual exploration. Perhaps, we should instead focus our attention on defining and enforcing laws that address coercive sexual behavior.

NOTES

1. Age of consent laws traditionally define the age below which you are too young to consent to sexual behavior. These laws may also stipulate exceptions to the law. Statutory rape laws (or related statutory offenses) define the criminal punishment for those who engage in sexual behavior that violates age of consent laws.

2. A list of the state-by-state laws about age of consent can be found at http://www.lewin.com/content/publications/3068.pdf. The lowest minimum age of victim in the United States is 10, in South Dakota, and the highest age is 18, in California, Idaho, and Wisconsin. Most states have between 14 and 16 years of age as the age below which individuals cannot consent to sex for any reason.

REFERENCES

Abma, J.C., Martines, G.M, Mosher, W.D., and Dawson, B.S. 2004. Teenagers in the United States: Sexual Activity, Contraceptive Use, and Childbearing, 2003. National Center for Health Statistics. *Vital Health Stat 23 (24).*

Cavanagh, Shelia L. 2007. *Sexing the Teacher: School Sex Scandals and Queer Pedagogies.* Vancouver: University of British Columbia Press.

Centers for Disease Control and Prevention. 2008. Youth Risk Behavior Surveillance System—United States, 2007. *MMWR, 57 (SS-4).*

"Criminal Justice Policy Foundation: Sentencing Policy." 2005. Criminal Justice Policy Foundation. Retrieved January 13, 2009. (http://www.cjpf.org/sentencing/racialdisparity.html).

Cocca, Carolyn. 2004. *Jailbait: The Politics of Statutory Rape Laws in the United States.* Albany: State University of New York Press.

Hines, D.A. and Finkelhor, D. 2007. Statutory Sex Crime Relationships between Juveniles and Adults: A Review of Social Scientific Research. *Aggression and Violent Behavior, 12*: 300–314.

Hunt, Kalev. 2009. Saving the Children: (Queer) Youth Sexuality and Age of Consent in Canada. *Sexuality Research & Social Policy, 6 (3)*: 15–33.

Jarvie, J. and Fausset, Richard. 2007. "After Teen Sex Reading, He's Free." *Los Angeles Times*, October 27, pp. A9.

Lewin Group. 2004. Statutory Rape: A Guide to State Laws and Reporting Requirements. Retrieved January 13, 2009 (http://www.lewin.com/content /publications/3068.pdf).

Melby, Todd. 2006. "When Teens Get Arrested for Voluntary Sex: Laws Designed to Punish Adult Offenders Sometimes Trap Kids." *Contemporary Sexuality* 40 (2): 1–6.

Schaffner, Laurie. 2005. "Capacity, Consent, and the Construction of Adulthood." Pp. 189–205 in *Regulating Sex: The Politics of Intimacy and Identity*, edited by Elizabeth Bernstein and Laurie Schaffner. New York: Routledge.

Troup-Leasure, Karyl and Howard N. Snyder. 2005. "Statutory Rape Known to Law Enforcement." Juvenile Justice Bulletin No. NJC 208803. Washington D.C.: Office of Juvenile Justice & Delinquency Prevention. Retrieved on January 13, 2009. (http://www.ncjrs.gov /pdffiles1/ojjdp/208803.pdf).

SICK SEX

ELROI J. WINDSOR

What is sick sex? In other words, what aspects of sexuality qualify as mentally "unhealthy"? If a man has problems getting erections, or if a woman has never had an orgasm, are they dysfunctional? Do they have psychological problems? What about people who fantasize about raping or being raped? Or those who enjoy being handcuffed or tying up their partners during sex? Are they sick individuals? How about if a person has the most amazing, mind-blowing orgasms when "yiffing" (i.e., having sex) in an elaborately designed wolf fursuit?[1] Is that person certifiably insane? Among all these people, who has some kind of mental disorder? Some of these examples are common occurrences; others may strike you as more peculiar. All of these different scenarios, however, challenge the parameters of what counts as "normal" sexuality. Although humans report a wide range of fulfilling sexual fantasies and behaviors,[2] psychomedical institutions classify some of these sexual fantasies, urges, and behaviors as mental disorders.

The *Diagnostic and Statistical Manual of Mental Disorders* (DSM) is the official guidebook for mental health professionals who practice in the United States. This massive text of diagnoses is published by the prestigious American Psychiatric Association (APA). The most recent edition of the DSM is the fifth edition, published in 2013.[3] The DSM currently devotes two sections in the manual to sexual issues.[4] Here, sexual behaviors ranging from premature ejaculation to pedophilia receive official classification as disordered. But categorizations of sexual "dysfunctions" and "disorders" are rife with controversy.

DEFINING "SICK" SEX: SEXUAL DYSFUNCTION AND PARAPHILIAS

The process of classifying human behavior as evidence of mental illness has a long and troubled history. For example, the DSM grew from 132 pages in its original 1952 version to nearly 1,000 pages in the current version,[5] and between the third and fourth editions, the number of classifications of disorders rose from 180 to 297.[6] These dramatic increases have provoked skepticism regarding the validity of the categorization process: Are Americans becoming increasingly mentally ill? Are psychomedical professionals perfecting their craft? Are clinicians creating more categorizations to aid insurance reimbursement for treatments, including costly pharmaceutical interventions? Classifying human conditions as mental disorders is a subjective process[7] often fraught with political tension.[8] The diagnoses in the DSM are not even easily transferable across cultures, illustrating their socially constructed nature.[9,10] Yet as a diagnostic tool, the DSM has incredible power.[11] A mental illness label carries tremendous stigma which can result in employment discrimination, loss of voting rights and custody privileges, forced sterilization and institutionalization, and, ironically, inadequate healthcare.[12] Worse, psychiatric labeling has been unevenly leveled against already disadvantaged groups, including women and racial minorities,[13] and diagnoses have been used to legitimize the political oppression of sexual Minorities.[14]

Given this history of psychiatric labeling, what do we know about "abnormal" sexuality today? The DSM-5 lists two types of mental disorders related to sexuality: sexual dysfunctions and paraphilias.[15] Sexual dysfunctions "are characterized by disturbance in sexual desire and in the psychophysiological changes that characterize the sexual response cycle and cause marked distress and interpersonal difficulty."[16] The DSM lists nine specific sexual dysfunctions that can be grouped into four main types related to desire, arousal, orgasm, and pain. Disorders of sexual desire include "hypoactive sexual desire disorder" (low or no sexual fantasies or desires) and "sexual aversion disorder" (aversion and avoidance of genital sexual activity). Disorders of sexual arousal include "female sexual arousal disorder" and "male erectile disorder." For these disorders, women whose vaginas do not become lubricated upon arousal or maintain lubrication throughout sex can be labeled with sexual dysfunction. Men whose penises do not become or stay erect during sexual activity can be diagnosed. The disorders related to orgasm are "female orgasmic disorder" and "male orgasmic disorder." For both women and men, the diagnosis refers to a delayed or lack of orgasm during sexual activity. Men may also be diagnosed with "premature ejaculation" if they ejaculate sooner than desired or after minimal stimulation. Disorders related to sexual pain include "dyspareunia," which means genital pain during sex, and is diagnosable in women and men. In addition, "vaginismus" refers to involuntary vaginal muscle spasms that interfere with intercourse. For all of these diagnoses to be made, medical and substance-induced conditions must be ruled out. People who experience these issues must also feel significant distress about them. The DSM advises clinicians to use discretion in diagnosing so that a person's age, culture, and life circumstances are taken into account.[17]

Whereas classifications of sexual dysfunctions refer to issues that infringe upon the normative sexual response cycle or sexual intercourse, the classification of paraphilias relates to "unusual" sexualities.[18] "Paraphilias are characterized by recurrent, intense sexual urges, fantasies, or behaviors that involve unusual objects, activities, or situations."[19] The eight specific paraphilias named in the DSM relate to sexualities involving nonhuman objects, nonconsensual partners and children, and suffering or humiliation. The paraphilia "fetishism" is reserved for people who enjoy inanimate objects (such as high-heeled shoes) in their sexual behaviors, and "transvestic fetishism" is used for heterosexual males who find erotic pleasure in cross-dressing. Paraphilias related to nonconsensual sexual interactions include "exhibitionism" (exposing genitals to an unsuspecting stranger, commonly known as "flashing"), "voyeurism" (watching an unsuspecting person who is undressing or having sex, where observers are known as "peeping toms"), and "frotteurism" (sexually touching or rubbing against a nonconsenting person, which often occurs in crowded locations like trains or concert halls). Other paraphilias include "sexual sadism" (when an individual enjoys causing another person to suffer), and "sexual masochism" (when an individual enjoys suffering or humiliation). "Pedophilia" describes a person who is at least 16 years old having sexual feelings or behaviors involving a child who is usually under 14 years old. Pedophilia is the only paraphilia that does not include a criterion of causing distress before a diagnosis is made; acting on the urge is sufficient for a diagnosis of pedophilia.[20]

The DSM categorizations of specific sexual dysfunctions and paraphilias outline precisely which sexual behaviors and fantasies qualify as disordered, "abnormal" sexuality. However, these taxonomies of disorder raise important questions about the boundaries between "normal" and "abnormal" sexual practices.

IS SICK SEX SICK?

Several issues mar the sexual pathology classifications in the DSM. One major problem is that some sexual disorders are unable to be diagnosed in all types of people. In addition, the DSM's criteria for "dysfunctional" and "unusual" are subjective and informed by sociocultural norms. The DSM is also inconsistent in how it considers issues of consent in diagnosing. The DSM's qualification of requiring distress prior to some diagnoses also presents challenges. Finally, diagnostic criteria lead to gender and sexual inequalities in treatment.

Demographic Differences in Diagnosing

One major problem with sexual disorder classifications is immediately apparent and relates to *who* is diagnosable. Two paraphilias restrict diagnoses to specific groups of people. Although most people diagnosed with paraphilias are men,[21] only "transvestic fetishism" requires that the person diagnosed is male. This male must also be heterosexual. By definition, gay and bisexual men, as well as women of all sexualities, are ineligible to receive the transvestic fetishism diagnosis.[22] This specification reflects sociocultural gender norms. Men are taught to adhere to narrow standards of hegemonic masculinity or risk being ostracized from normative society.[23] In contrast, women are afforded more flexibility in gender and sexual expression.[24] If a woman sleeps in her boyfriend's underwear, for example, she can usually do so without having her gender or sexuality called into question. But can you imagine the same scenario involving a man who wears his girlfriend's silk panties to bed? The designation of transvestic fetishism for heterosexual males reifies restrictive masculinity norms for straight men while implying that gender-bending among women and gay and bisexual men is to be expected.

Another demographic specification involves age. For a person to receive the diagnosis of "pedophilia," they must be at least 16 years old and at least five years older than their sexual object choice.[25] Clinically speaking, a 15-year-old

who has sex with a child who is four years of age is not a diagnosable pedophile.[26] The DSM also states that people with pedophilia sexually objectify youth who are "generally age 13 years or younger."[27] A 75-year-old man who has sex with a 14-year-old teen is not diagnosable as a pedophile according to these guidelines. These rigid age parameters delineate disordered conduct. The DSM's clinical criteria clash with codes established by legal authorities.[28] In the United States, the legal age at which a person can consent to sex ranges from 16 to 18.[29] Thus, the aforementioned 75-year-old man may be criminally liable for his conduct, but intact psychologically, according to the DSM. These different classifications create an ideological chasm between psychomedical and legal professionals concerning "unacceptable" behavior.

Subjective Classifications of Pathology

Another major problem with sexual disorder classifications is the cultural relevancy that distinguishes between "normal" and "abnormal" sexualities. What counts as "unusual" sex? Regarding fetishism, some inanimate objects are more acceptably "sexy" than others. High-heeled boots, lacy lingerie, feathers, candles, and rose petals are often integrated into dominant narratives of "sexy" encounters. Surely many people find one of these inanimate objects central to their enjoyment of a sexual encounter. Their popularity in televised media and romance novels confirms for these people that attaching erotic meaning to these objects is not at all weird. And what about people who fetishize body parts? Technically not inanimate because they are attached to a person, large breasts and "apple-bottom booties" can be central objects of sexual attention for some people. Some people worship these body parts, lavishing bountiful attention on them during sex. Do they meet diagnostic criteria for fetishism? What if they desire these body parts exclusively during the sex act, such as through "titty fuck-ing" or anal sex? According to the definition in the DSM, these people are not clinical fetishists.

As a paraphilia, fetishism depends on socially constructed standards of "acceptable" sexual objects. Some of the inanimate objects used during sex become props that mark the normative sex scene. But other inanimate objects—flip flops, thermal underwear, yarn, book lights, and maple leaves—are not read-ily coded as "sexy" and so may provoke dis-tress in individuals who find them arousing. Similarly, some body parts are more acceptably "fetishized" than others. If someone described himself as "an ass man," few people would bat an eye. But if he admitted to being "an elbow man," his disclosure would probably evoke sus-picion. Ultimately, "fetishism" as a paraphilia illustrates the social construction of appro-priate sexualities. Some inanimate objects, and some body parts, are more acceptable to include in the trappings of sex than others.

The DSM reinforces additional boundar-ies of appropriate sex in its inclusion of sexual sadism and masochism as paraphilias regard-less of whether sadomasochist fantasies or behaviors cause a person distress. This para-philic classification stands in sharp contrast to established "kink" communities of people who openly engage in bondage, discipline, domina-tion, submission, sadism, and masochism, or "BDSM." Practitioners of BDSM often stress the central tenets of their practices as safe, sane, and consensual.[30] They adamantly object to classifying erotic pain and suffering as inher-ently pathological. They point out that pain is acceptable, even expected, in other parts of life that many people find enjoyable, such as boxing, long distance running, and ballet. The inclusion of sadism and masochism in the DSM implicitly states that sex is not an accept-able context for pain and suffering.[31] But what about people who like handcuffs and spanking during sex? How intense and how often does

pain have to be included in a sex act for it to become pathological? When does "rough" sex become "sick" sex? Acts of suffering and humil-iation are also viewed as acceptable in some contexts, such as in fraternity hazing and Cath-olic confessionals. Is it so strange that some people enjoy these things during sex? If all par-ties involved in the act consent to it, what's the harm? These questions challenge the inclusion of sadism and masochism in the DSM.

The Inconsistent Criterion of Consent

On the topic of consent, the DSM is noticeably silent on a sexual issue that plagues Ameri-can life—rape. Sexual violence is widespread throughout the United States, affecting one in 15 adults in their lifetimes.[32] People who sexu-ally assault others do not have their consent. Yet "rapism" is not listed [in] the DSM. Forcing someone to perform sexually is not considered a pathological fantasy, urge, or behavior. His-torically, the DSM has excluded coerced sex from its list of mental disorders due to fears of misusing the diagnosis as a backdoor legal strategy that would aid criminal offenders.[33,34] But this omission is remarkable, given that the DSM does include other nonconsensual and criminal acts: voyeurism, exhibitionism, frot-teurism, and pedophilia. Pedophiles do not receive shorter prison sentences due to having a diagnosable mental illness. Worry over poten-tial unintended legal consequences of psychiat-ric labeling seems unwarranted and arbitrarily applied. Once again, psychiatry as a science is at odds with the legal system.

Challenges in Assessing Distress

Another problem with the DSM is that it advises clinicians to diagnose depending on the distressed person's life situation. At first blush, this recom-mendation appears fair. If a person is not both-ered by a lack of sexual desire, for example, why burden him with a diagnosis? And if someone is only bothered by her inability to orgasm because her partner has shamed her, then surely the issue is not *her* problem, right? The challenge with this qualification is that it relies on clinicians' subjective assessments. Clinicians may impose their own sexual standards and expectations during assessments. For example, a general practitioner may feel disturbed by a man's persistent lack of sexual desire, whereas a certified sex therapist will have more comprehensive sexuality-specific training and experience that would not necessarily pathologize this client's behavior. Reliable diagnosing is challenging, even for psychotherapists using the same diagnostic criteria.[35]

Inequalities in Treatment

Finally, it is important to understand the gender and sexual inequalities that the DSM inspires. Diagnostic labeling is not the ultimate objective of mental healthcare; it is a means for treatment. The treatments for sexual dysfunction highlight "blindspots of medical discourse"[36] that rely on sociocultural norms about gender and sexuality. For example, in describing the physiological changes associated with sexual excitement, the DSM states that the "major changes" for males are limited to "penile tumescence and erection."[37] For females, it describes only "vasocongestion in the pelvis, vaginal lubrication and expansion, and swelling of the external genitalia."[38] Indicators of physiological sexual excitement found in the anus, rectum, nipples, or clitoris are noticeably absent from these descriptions. These omissions underscore a heterosexual standard that is further reinforced by the DSM's sexual pain disorders, which are diagnosable when the genital pain is associated with "sexual intercourse" and is "most commonly experienced during coitus"[39] The framing of "dysfunctional" sex implies that normal sex involves "penetrative intercourse within a heterosexual relationship."[40] This heteronormative scope excludes countless other pleasurable acts and limits the ways people enjoy sex. It also privileges heterosexual sexual standards, ignoring the sexual identity and preferences of the person seeking help. These standards then inform the ways therapists recommend treatments for their clients.

One specific inequality in treatment relates to gender. Women are diagnosed with sexual dysfunction more often than men—estimates range "from 10 percent to 52 percent of men and 25 percent to 63 percent of women."[41] Treatments for sexual dysfunction often do not differentiate between women and men's sexual responses. For example, Viagra has been prescribed as an off-label treatment for women with low arousal responses,[42] even though women's sexual arousal involves parts of the body that Viagra does not affect. Prescribing Viagra to women, then, suggests that healthcare providers view this drug as a cure-all treatment. Other treatments for sexual dysfunction are designed to help women accommodate men sexually, such as vaginal-tightening "rejuvenation" surgery or labiaplasty.[43] Where are therapies that focus on clitoral sensation, women's apex for orgasm? Phallocentric medical approaches privilege men's sexual pleasure,[44] ignoring the role of the clitoris in women's erotic response. These treatment trends also challenge whether higher rates of sexual dysfunction among women can be attributed to cultural gender and sexuality norms, rather than to some innate problem in women's sexuality.

In addition, women are not the only gender targeted by normative medical gazes. Treatments for sexual dysfunction also reify hegemonic masculinity standards. The widespread use of Viagra to treat men reinforces imperatives that a man should be able to get it up and keep it up, regardless of his desire for sex. Men's sexuality, then, becomes manageable by external medication.[45] His sexuality is reduced to the penis, discounting evidence that men can experience pleasure in other parts of their bodies, such as through anally stimulating the prostate, or "p-spot."[46] The medicalization of men's sexuality reinforces masculinity standards and avoids a whole-body approach to understanding sexuality.[47] These critiques of the classifications in the DSM are not exhaustive. But they present some challenges to the ways psychomedical institutions construct boundaries between "normal" and "abnormal" sex.

Prognosis

Although the DSM specifies a range of pathologized sexual fantasies, urges, and behaviors, it never actually describes what counts as *healthy* sexuality.[48] But based on the characteristics identified as dysfunctional, we can deduce what healthy sex entails. A person who has a healthy psychosexual disposition should have an active desire for sex. When an opportunity presents itself, healthy individuals should want to be sexual. Upon arousal, women's vaginas should become lubricated and men's penises should become erect. Throughout sex, women should stay wet and men should stay hard. Both should have an orgasm during sex, not too late and, for men, not too soon. During sex, people should not feel pain in their genitals, and women's vaginas should not spasm uncontrollably so as to interfere with penetration. Ruling out paraphilic traits, healthy sex does not require using strange inanimate objects. Straight guys should not want to crossdress. No one should expose their genitals to unwilling parties, nor should they creep around to look at people being sexual without their knowledge. No one should rub against unwilling parties, either. Healthy sex should be age-appropriate and should never involve youth. Healthy sex should not involve pain or suffering. So, based on these standards, how many people have healthy sex 100 percent of the time? To return to the first paragraph of this article, this classification system means that the man who had erection problems and the woman who never had an orgasm would be sick. So would the

people who enjoyed bondage. But the people fantasizing about rape and yiffing are not. These specific cases are used to illustrate the arbitrary ways the DSM creates boundaries between sexual "health" and "pathology;" they are not an endorsement of a need for continued or more expansive pathologizing.

Ultimately, the problems with DSM diagnoses illustrate how distinguishing between "sick" and "healthy" is tricky. Categorizations of "disorder" are informed by sociocultural norms. They are partial to political and historical trends. The evolution of "sick" sexuality illustrates how meanings of sexual pathology change over time, such as the landmark transformation brought by the removal of homosexuality from the DSM in 1973.[49] Sexual disorders are social constructions. So are the sexual preferences currently delineated in the DSM truly pathological, or are they part of normal human variation? Some clinicians are highly critical of the classification system: "Non-clinical studies of individuals with unusual sexual interests demonstrate that these individuals are indistinguishable from those with 'normophilic' (i.e., conventional) sexual interests."[50] Unusual sexual fantasies commonly enter the imaginations of all people,[51] and research shows that non-offenders have just as "deviant" fantasies as sex offenders.[52] Even the gold standard of sexual normativity—heterosexuality—could be shown to seem pathological based on the DSM's classification system. For example, given the high rate of sexual dysfunction among heterosexuals—distress and impairment related to types of sexual practices, frequency of sexual activity, as well as sexual insecurity and violence that interfere with social relationships—this sexuality meets the same flawed diagnostic criteria already in use in the DSM.[53] This assertion appears ludicrous, but it epitomizes a central problem with the DSM. "Sick" sex may be more of a subjective designation.

So, will the current list of disorders stand the test of time? Discussions about removing, revising, and adding diagnoses to the DSM-5 preceded its publication, and some of the sexual pathology classifications are being contested.[54] These debates are important because they transcend mere theoretical or intellectual exercises. The classifications in the DSM raise important questions about how psychomedical institutions manage sexuality. Furthermore, the social control of sexuality can have serious personal and political effects.[55] People can feel intense shame and disgust based on how professionals categorize them. Their sexual relationships can be strained and unfulfilling. And when classification systems regulate "appropriate" behavior, people with diagnosable sexual conditions can experience great loss. They can lose their jobs, their children, and their freedom. They can feel condemned morally and spiritually. In short, people can be made to feel sick. The state of "sick" sex is in flux. With the release of the DSM-5, new diagnostic criteria now mark new parameters of mental illness. This text has changed the mental health statuses of countless people simply through its publication. Take stock of your sexual repertoire now that the DSM-5 is here. Is your sex sick?

NOTES

1. Explanations for these activities can be found within the "furry" community. Details on the meaning of "yiff" can be read here: http://en.wikifur.com/wiki/Yiff, and a description of fursuits can be found here: http://en.wikifur.com/wiki/Fursuit.

2. Rye, B. J. and Glenn J. Meaney. 2007. "The Pursuit of Sexual Pleasure." *Sexuality and Culture* 11:28–51. Also in Chapter 6 of this book.

3. American Psychiatric Association. 2013 "DSM-5." Retrieved August 2, 2013 (http://www.psychiatry.org/dsm5).

4. The DSM-5 has a section titled "Gender Dysphoria," which includes issues faced by people whose bodies are not aligned with their internal gender identities. However, I do not discuss these classifications here, as they relate to gender and gender identity, and not sexuality. Note that "gender dysphoria" classification remains controversial. Visit www.gidreform.org for information.

5. Lev, Arlene Istar. 2004. *Transgender Emergence: Therapeutic Guidelines for Working with Gender-Variant People and Their Families.* Binghamton, NY: The Haworth Press. Current page number retrieved August 2, 2013

(http://www.amazon.com/Diagnostic-Statistical-Manual-Disorders-Edition/dp/0890425558).

6. Shorter, Edward. 1997. *A History of Psychiatry: From the Era of the Asylum to the Age of Prozac.* New York: John Wiley and Sons.

7. Rosenhan, David L. 1973. "On Being Sane in Insane Places." *Science* 179:250–8.

8. Spiegel, Alix. 2005. "The Dictionary of Disorder: How One Man Revolutionized Psychiatry." *The New Yorker*, January 3, pp. 56–63.

9. Andary, Lena, Yvonne Stolk, and Steven Klimidis. 2003. *Assessing Mental Health across Cultures.* Bowen Hills, QLD: Australian Academic Press Pty. Ltd. For several examples of culture-specific diagnostic guides, see the Cuban Glossary of Psychiatry, the Latin American Guide for Psychiatric Diagnosis, and the World Health Organization's International Classification of Diseases.

10. Cooksey, Elizabeth C. and Phil Brown. 1998. "Spinning on its Axes: DSM and the Social Construction of Psychiatric Diagnosis." *International Journal of Health Services* 28(3):525–54.

11. Conrad, Peter. 2007. *The Medicalization of Society: On the Transformation of Human Conditions into Treatable Disorders.* Baltimore, MD: Johns Hopkins University Press.

12. Hinshaw, Stephen P. 2009. *The Mark of Shame: Stigma of Mental Illness and an Agenda for Change.* New York: Oxford University Press.

13. Ali, Alisha. 2004. "The Intersection of Racism and Sexism in Psychiatric Diagnosis. Pp. 71–5 in *Bias in Psychiatric Diagnosis*, edited by Paula J. Caplan and Lisa Cosgrove. New York: Rowman and Littlefield Publishers.

14. Moser, Charles and Peggy J. Kleinplatz. 2005. "DSM-IV-TR and the Paraphilias: An Argument for Removal." *Journal of Psychology and Human Sexuality* 17(3/4): 91–109.

15. Editor's Note: This article was completed prior to the publiciation of the DSM-5. Although minor updates have been made, some remaining details refer to content from the previous edition, the DSM-IV-TR, and could not be edited at press time. Note that most of the issues raised in this article remain relevant to the current DSM-5 publication. For an overview of changes made in the DSM-5, see "Highlights of Changes from DSM-IV-TR to DSM-5" at http://www.psychiatry.org/File%20Library/Practice/DSM/DSM-5/Changes-from-DSM-IV-TR-to-DSM-5.pdf.

16. American Psychiatric Association. 2000. *Diagnostic and Statistical Manual of Mental Disorders, Fourth Edition, Text Revision* (DSM-IV-TR). Arlington, VA: American Psychiatric Association. 535.

17. Ibid.

18. Ibid, 535.

19. Ibid.

20. Ibid.

21. Kennedy, Harry. 2001. "Do Men Need Special Services?" *Advances in Psychiatric Treatment* 7:93–9. Retrieved January 18, 2012 (http://apt.rcpsych.org /content/7/2/93.full.pdf).

22. Ibid, supra 16.

23. Kivel, Paul. 1999. *Boys Will Be Men: Raising Our Sons for Courage, Caring, and Community*. Gabriola Island, B.C., Canada: New Society Publishers.

24. For example, see Rupp and Taylor's "Straight Girls Kissing" in Chapter 1 of this book.

25. Ibid, supra 16.

26. Legal classifications of sexual misconduct, however, are another matter. For details, see Mullis and Baunach's "The Social Control of Adult–Child Sex" in Chapter 8 of this book.

27. Ibid, supra 16, 571.

28. Moser, Charles. 2009. "When Is an Unusual Sexual Interest a Mental Disorder?" *Archives of Sexual Behavior* 38:323–5.

29. Glosser, Asaph, Karen Gardiner, and Mike Fishman. 2004. "Statutory Rape: A Guide to State Laws and Reporting Requirement." Retrieved January 19, 2012 (http: //aspe.hhs.gov/hsp/08/SR/StateLaws/). For a discussion of age of consent laws, see Cavalier and Burgess's "Too Young to Consent?" in Chapter 8 of this book.

30. Wright, Susan. 2006. "Discrimination of SM-Identified Individuals." *Journal of Homosexuality* 50(2-3):217–31.

31. Kleinplatz, Peggy J. and Charles Moser. 2005. "Is SM Pathological?" *Lesbian & Gay Psychology Review* 6(3):255–60.

32. Basile, Kathleen C., Jieru Chen, Michele C. Black, Linda E. Saltzman. 2007. "Prevalence and Characteristics of Sexual Violence Victimization among U.S. Adults, 2001–2003." *Violence and Victims* 22(4):437–48.

33. Frances, Allen, Shoba Sreenivasan, and Linda E. Weinberger. 2008. "Defining Mental Disorder When It Really Counts: DSM-IV-TR and SVP/SDP Statutes." *Journal of the American Academy of Psychiatry and the Law Online* 36(3):375–84. Retrieved January 26, 2012 (http: //www.jaapl.org/content/36/3/375.full).

34. Frances, Allen J. 2011. "DSM 5 Rejects Coercive Paraphilia." DSM5 in Distress, Psychology Today, May 26. Retrieved January 26, 2012 (http://www.psychologytoday .com/blog/dsm5 indistress/201105/dsm-5-rejects-coercive -paraphilia).

35. Spiegel, Alix. 2005. "The Dictionary of Disorder: How One Man Revolutionized Psychiatry." *The New Yorker*, January 3, pp. 56–63.

36. Mollenhauer, Whitney F. 2011. "Female Sexual Dysfunction: History, Critiques, and New Directions."

Thinking Gender Papers, UCLA Center for the Study of Women. Retrieved January 18, 2012 (http://escholarship .org/uc/item/8jh824nc), 3.

37. Ibid, supra 16. 536.

38. Ibid, supra 16. 536.

39. Ibid, supra 16. 554.

40. Ibid, supra 38. 6.

41. Heiman, Julia R. 2002. "Sexual Dysfunction: Overview of Prevalence, Etiological Factors, and Treatments." *Journal of Sex Research* 39(1):73–8, 73.

42. Hartley, Heather. 2006. "The 'Pinking' of Viagra Culture: Drug Industry Efforts to Create and Repackage Sex Drugs for Women." *Sexualities* 9(3):363–378.

43. Braun, Virginia. 2005. "In Search of (Better) Sexual Pleasure: Female Genital 'Cosmetic' Surgery." *Sexualities* 8(4):407–24. Also in Reading 28 of this book.

44. Drew, Jennifer. 2003. "The Myth of Female Sexual Dysfunction and Its Medicalization." *Sexualities, Evolution, and Gender* 5(2):89–96.

45. Marshall, Barbara L. 2002. "'Hard Science': Gendered Constructions of Sexual Dysfunction in the 'Viagra Age'." *Sexualities* 5(2):131–58.

46. Silverberg, Cory. 2011. "How to Find and Stimulate the Prostate." Retrieved January 26, 2012 (http://sexuality .about.com/od/analplay/ht/htprostate.htm).

47. Loe, Meika. 2004. *The Rise of Viagra: How the Little Blue Pill Changed Sex in America*. New York: New York University Press. Excerpted in Reading 27 of this book.

48. Ibid, supra 15.

49. Cooper, Rachel. 2004. "What is Wrong with the DSM?" *History of Psychiatry* 15(1):5–25.

50. Ibid, supra 15.

51. Renaud, Cheryl A. and E. Sandra Byers. 1999. "Exploring the Frequency, Diversity and Content of University Students' Positive and Negative Sexual Cognitions." *The Canadian Journal of Human Sexuality* 8(1)17–30.

52. Langevin, Ron, Reuben A. Lang, and Suzanne Curnoe. 1998. "The Prevalence of Sex Offenders with Deviant Fantasies." *Journal of Interpersonal Violence* 13(3):315–27.

53. Moser, Charles and Peggy J. Kleinplatz. 2005. "Does Heterosexuality Belong in the DSM?" *Lesbian & Gay Psychology Review* 6(3):261–7.

54. Gever, John. 2010. "Big Changes for the Psychiatrist's 'Bible'." ABC News. Retrieved January 18, 2012 (http://abcnews.go.com/Health/MindMoodNews /psychiatrist-biblerevisions-diagnostic-statistical-manual -mentaldisorders/ story?id=9795049&singlePage=true# .TxcQCYHQd_A).

55. Ibid, supra 56.

BIRTHRIGHT: A HISTORY OF PLANNED PARENTHOOD

JILL LEPORE

The Planned Parenthood health center in Brooklyn occupies ten thousand square feet on the sixth floor of an office building across the street from a courthouse. After you get off the elevator, you have to go through a metal detector. A guard behind bulletproof glass inspects your bags. The day I was there, in June, the waiting room was full; the line at the registration desk was ten deep. A bowl on the counter was filled with condoms, giveaways. A sign on the wall explained Plan B, the morning-after pill. In the waiting room, a couple of dozen women sat in rows of blue plastic chairs, texting. A few wandered over to a display of glossy brochures and picked up "Am I Ready to Have Sex?" or "Birth Control and GYN Care: For FREE. For REAL."

Aside from its proximity to the site of the United States' first birth-control clinic—opened in Brooklyn in 1916—the place is a typical Planned Parenthood clinic. Last year, seventeen thousand patients received medical care here. Two-thirds were insured by Medicaid, or paid reduced rates, or received free treatment. They were tested for S.T.I.s and U.T.I.s; they were prescribed birth-control pills and antibiotics; they were fitted for diaphragms and I.U.D.s and cervical caps; they learned how to check their breasts for lumps. They had pregnancy tests and Pap smears and abortions. . . .

Nellie Santiago-Rivera has been the director of the Brooklyn health center for the past eleven years. The corkboard behind her desk is covered with family photographs. When she was a teenager growing up in the Bronx, a friend brought her to the Planned Parenthood clinic at 149th Street to get contraception. "Birth control is not something we talked about in my family," she told me. Her parents were born in Puerto Rico. "We believed, 'You light the candle, and you pray.' " A report published in 1965, when Santiago-Rivera was a girl, found that 94 percent of women who died in New York City from illegal abortions were either black or Puerto Rican.

The Brooklyn health center is one of four clinics run by Planned Parenthood of New York City, an affiliate of the national organization. There's one in Manhattan, one in the Bronx, and one in Staten Island. There are 82 Planned Parenthood affiliates nationwide, operating nearly eight hundred clinics. Planned Parenthood says that one in five women in the United States has been treated at a Planned Parenthood clinic. Critics of Planned Parenthood, who are engaged in a sustained attack on the organization, say that most of those women are going to those clinics to have abortions, paid for, in violation of the Hyde Amendment, with taxpayer money.

"This started the day after the [2010] midterms," Cecile Richards said when we met in July. Richards, the daughter of the former Texas governor Ann Richards, has been the president of Planned Parenthood since 2006. She's long-boned and fair-haired and glamorous, and she is in the eye of a perfect political storm. "What happened at the elections had nothing to do with abortion or birth control or Planned Parenthood," she said. "It had to do with the economy." But the election reshaped both Congress and state legislatures, and her theory is that "when those guys can't figure out what to do about jobs, and they can't, their first target is women."

The campaign against Planned Parenthood has been unrelenting. . . . "We would wake up and, every day, it would be about something else," Richards said. "Some days it was about abortion. Some days it was about race. Some days it was about me. Some days it was about kids."

The fury over Planned Parenthood is two political passions—opposition to abortion and opposition to government programs for the poor—acting as one. . . . Margaret Sanger opened that first clinic in Brooklyn four years before the passage of what was called, at the time, the Susan B. Anthony Amendment: "The right of citizens of the United States to vote shall not be denied or abridged by the United States or by any State on account of sex." Women had only just got the right to vote when the Equal Rights Amendment, written by Alice Paul, was introduced to Congress: "Men and women shall have equal rights throughout the United States." Revisions were introduced in every session from 1923 to 1971. In 1972, the E.R.A. passed and went to the states for ratification. Its eventual defeat was accomplished by conservatives led by Phyllis Schlafly, who opposed the women's rights movement and supported a human-life amendment. . . .

The first birth-control clinic in the United States opened on October 16, 1916, on Amboy Street in Brooklyn. There were two rooms, and three employees: Ethel Byrne, a nurse; Fania Mindell, a receptionist who was fluent in Yiddish; and Byrne's sister, Margaret Sanger, a thirty-seven-year-old nurse and mother. Sanger and her sister came from a family of eleven children, one of whom Sanger helped deliver when she was eight years old. When Sanger began nursing poor immigrant women living in tenements on New York's Lower East Side, she found that they were desperate for information about how to avoid pregnancy. These "doomed women implored me to reveal the 'secret' rich people had," Sanger

wrote in her autobiography. (A study conducted in New York at the time found that 41 percent of women who received medical care through clinics operated by the city's department of health had never used contraception and, of those, more than half had had at least one abortion; they averaged almost two apiece.)

Between 1912 and 1913, Sanger wrote a twelve-part series for *The Call*, the socialist daily, titled "What Every Girl Should Know." Because any discussion of venereal matters violated the Comstock law, Sanger's final essay, "Some Consequences of Ignorance and Silence," was banned on the ground of obscenity. By way of protest, *The Call* ran, in place of the essay, an announcement: "'What Every Girl Should Know'—NOTHING!'"

Sanger wasn't the only person to hand out literature about contraception—Emma Goldman once spent fifteen days in the Queens County jail for doing the same thing—but she was the first to make it a movement. In 1914, Sanger began publishing *The Woman Rebel,* an eight-page feminist monthly, in which she coined the term "birth control." Six of its seven issues were declared obscene, and were suppressed. Indicted, Sanger fled the country. When she returned, in 1915, the charges against her were dropped. One of her three children, a five-year-old daughter, had just died of pneumonia, and the prosecution decided that bringing a grieving mother to trial for distributing information about birth control would only aid her cause. Determined to have her day in court, Sanger rented a storefront from a landlord named Rabinowitz, who lowered the rent when she told him what she was going to use the space for. She wrote a letter informing the Brooklyn District Attorney of her plan. Then she posted handbills in English, Italian, and Yiddish:

MOTHERS!
Can you afford to have a large family?
Do you want any more children?
If not, why do you have them?

*DO NOT KILL, DO NOT TAKE LIFE, BUT
PREVENT*
*Safe, Harmless Information can be obtained of trained
nurses at 46 AMBOY STREET.*

On the day the clinic opened, Jewish and Italian women pushing prams and with toddlers in tow lined up down the street, Sanger recalled, "some shawled, some hatless, their red hands clasping the cold, chapped, smaller ones of their children." They paid ten cents to register. Then Sanger or Byrne met with seven or eight at once to show them how to use pessaries.

Nine days later, an undercover policewoman came, posing as a mother of two who couldn't afford any more children. Mindell sold her a copy of "What Every Girl Should Know." Byrne discussed contraception with her. The next day, the police arrived, arrested Sanger, confiscated an examination table, and shut down the clinic.

Mindell and Byrne were also arrested. Mindell was convicted on obscenity charges; her conviction was eventually overturned. Byrne and Sanger were charged with violating a section of the New York State Penal Code, under which it was illegal to distribute "any recipe, drug, or medicine for the prevention of conception." (The fear was that contraception would promote promiscuity.) Byrne's lawyer argued that the penal code was unconstitutional because it infringed on a woman's right to the "pursuit of happiness." She was found guilty. Sentenced to thirty days, she went on a hunger strike and nearly died. An editorial in the New York *Tribune* begged the governor to issue a pardon, threatening him with the judgment of history: "It will be hard to make the youth of 1967 believe that in 1917 a woman was imprisoned for doing what Mrs. Byrne did."

At Sanger's trial, during which the judge waved a cervical cap from the bench, Sanger hoped to argue that the law preventing the distribution of contraception was unconstitutional: exposing women, against their will, to the danger of dying in childbirth violated a woman's right to life. But the judge ruled that no woman had "the right to copulate with a feeling of security that there will be no resulting conception." In other words, if a woman wasn't willing to die in childbirth, she shouldn't have sex. Sanger went to Queens County Penitentiary. She was sentenced to thirty days.

From the start, the birth-control movement has been as much about fighting legal and political battles as it has been about staffing clinics, because, in a country without national health care, making contraception available to poor women has required legal reform. When Sanger appealed her conviction, the judge ruled that doctors could prescribe contraception, which is what made it possible, subsequently, for Sanger to open more clinics. In 1921, Sanger founded the American Birth Control League. She received stacks of letters. "I have Ben married 4 years the 25 december and I have all Redy given Birth to 3 children and all 3 of my children ar Boys and I am all most Broken down and am only 24 years old," a Kentucky woman wrote in 1922. "mrs sanger I do want you to write me an Return mail what to do to keep from Bring these Little one to this awfel world." Mailing her that information would have broken the law. In 1926, Sanger and her colleagues went to Washington and met with sixty senators, twenty congressmen, and seventeen members of the Judiciary Committee. (Mary Ware Dennett, of the Voluntary Parenthood League, had pointed out, when she lobbied the New York State Legislature in 1924, that the very men who refused to change the law had wives who broke it: congressional families had an average of 2.7 children.) They didn't make much headway. Senator James Reed, of Missouri, told the lobbyists that "Birth Control is chipping away the very foundation of our civilization," that "women should have many children and that poverty is no handicap but rather an asset." Henry Ashurst, a senator from Arizona, said that he "had not been raised to discuss this matter with women." . . .

During the Depression, when more and more people were interested in having fewer children, Gallup polls found that three out of four Americans supported the legalization of contraception. In 1931, a committee of the Federal Council of Churches of Christ, chaired by Reinhold Niebuhr, issued a report endorsing contraception, arguing that, by separating sex from reproduction, it promoted marital love. In 1936, a federal appellate court heard *U.S. v. One Package of Japanese Pessaries*—a test case engineered by Sanger—and removed contraception from the category of obscenity. Not long after that, the American Birth Control League merged with Sanger's Birth Control Clinical Research Bureau to become the Birth Control Federation of America. Sanger, however, did not have much of a role in the new organization, whose leaders deemed the words "birth control" too radical; in 1942, despite Sanger's strenuous objection, the organization became the Planned Parenthood Federation of America.

During the Second World War, Planned Parenthood touted controlling family size as part of the war effort. Birth control continued to gain religious support. In 1946, more than 3,200 Jewish and Protestant clergy signed a resolution in support of Planned Parenthood. In the 1950s, the organization was run primarily by men interested in population control. Barry Goldwater was an active supporter of Planned Parenthood, and his wife served on the board in Phoenix. In 1956, Sanger, who had retired, wrote to a former national director, "If I told or wrote you that the name Planned Parenthood would be the end of the movement, it was and has proven true. The movement was then a fighting, forward, no fooling movement, battling for the freedom of the poorest parents and for women's biological freedom and development. The P.P.F. has left all this behind." Sanger was bitter, but she was right. Birth control, as the historian David Kennedy

once argued, was a liberal reform often turned to conservative ends.

Planned Parenthood began to wrestle with the subject of abortion in 1955, at the urging of Mary Steichen Calderone, a public-health physician who served as its medical director. (It was during Calderone's tenure that Planned Parenthood clinics began to administer Pap smears.) Abortion had been legal until 1821, when Connecticut became the first state to make abortion after quickening—at about four months—a crime. By the middle of the twentieth century, with limited exceptions, abortion had become illegal in most states. It was, nevertheless, widely practiced. "If there was even a communicable disease that affected that many people in this country, we would do something about it," Calderone said. She organized a conference and conducted a study. In an article published in 1960, she remarked on the difference between a legal abortion and an illegal one: three hundred dollars and knowing the right person.

Calderone left Planned Parenthood in 1964 to found the Sex Information and Education Council of the United States. She wanted to teach people how to talk about sex, because, as she once said, "People don't have much of a vocabulary. Or a concept of anything, except fucking." Alan F. Guttmacher, the chief of obstetrics at Mount Sinai Hospital and a clinical professor of obstetrics and gynecology at Columbia, had become the president of Planned Parenthood in 1962. Guttmacher had three priorities: improving Planned Parenthood's relationship with the black community, securing federal support for family-planning programs for the poor, and liberalizing abortion law.

The Birth Control Federation of America had established a National Negro Advisory Council and a Division of Negro Service: black doctors and public-health officials who wanted to reduce black maternal-death and infant-mortality rates through child spacing. Guttmacher hoped to strengthen these alliances, build new ones, and counter the accusation that the organization was racist. In 1962, the director of the Planned Parenthood clinic in Harlem (over whose opening, three decades earlier, W. E. B. DuBois had presided) met with Malcolm X. Malcolm X said that he thought it would be better if the organization called its service "family planning instead of birth control." (The meeting notes, sent to Guttmacher, read, "His reason for this was that people, particularly Negroes, would be more willing to plan than to be controlled.") In 1966, Martin Luther King, Jr., who, as a young minister, had joined a Planned Parenthood committee, was given the Margaret Sanger Award. In his acceptance speech, he drew parallels between the birth-control and civil-rights movements—"There is a striking kinship between our movement and Margaret Sanger's early efforts"—and celebrated Sanger for having "launched a movement which is obeying a higher law to preserve human life under humane conditions." In 1967, after a leader of the Pittsburgh branch of the N.A.A.C.P. said that Planned Parenthood was holding down the black birth rate, the assistant executive director of the national organization clarified that the N.A.A.C.P. supported family planning. In 1968, a clinic in Cleveland was set on fire.

Before the mid-1960s, birth control had largely been privately funded; clinics affiliated with Planned Parenthood ran on donations, grants, and fees for service. "I cannot imagine anything more emphatically a subject that is not a proper political or governmental activity or function or responsibility," Dwight Eisenhower said in 1959. "That's not our business." But by 1965, as concerns about overpopulation, worldwide, began to dominate policy debates, Eisenhower had reversed his position on family planning, serving with Harry Truman as co-chairman of a Planned Parenthood committee.

Meanwhile, the last legal obstacles to contraception were overcome. After Estelle Griswold, the executive director of Planned Parenthood of Connecticut, opened a birth-control clinic in New Haven, she was arrested and fined under the provisions of a Connecticut statute banning the use of contraceptives; in 1965, the Supreme Court declared that ban unconstitutional. The next year, Guttmacher testified before Congress, "We really have the opportunity now to extend free choice in family planning to all Americans, regardless of social status, and to demonstrate to the rest of the world how it can be done. It's time we get on with the job."

In 1968, Paul Ehrlich's "Population Bomb" was published, the Pope issued "Humanae Vitae," reiterating the Church's prohibition on both abortion and contraception, and Lyndon Johnson appointed a Committee on Population and Family Planning. The next year, Richard Nixon pushed Congress to increase federal funding for family planning. In the House, Representative George H. W. Bush, of Texas, said, "We need to make family planning a household word. We need to take the sensationalism out of the topic so it can no longer be used by militants who have no knowledge of the voluntary nature of the program, but rather are using it as a political stepping stone." In 1969, Nixon told Congress, "No American woman should be denied access to family planning assistance because of her economic condition." The following year, he signed Title X into law. . . .

[In 1967], Alan Guttmacher edited a book called *The Case for Legalized Abortion Now*. As a young intern in the 1920s, Guttmacher had watched a woman die of a botched abortion, and had never forgotten it. At Mount Sinai, he performed abortions until the hospital told him to stop. Laws liberalizing abortion in the 1960s and early 1970s were urged by doctors and lawyers and supported by clergy. Between 1967 and

1970, some restrictions on abortions were lifted by legislators in Alaska, Arkansas, California, Delaware, Georgia, Hawaii, Kansas, Maryland, New Mexico, New York, North Carolina, Oregon, South Carolina, Virginia, and Washington. Governor Ronald Reagan signed the California law. By 1970, the Clergy Consultation Service on Abortion, established to help women find doctors who could conduct abortions safely, was offering services in 26 states.

Women were not much involved in any of this agitation. Betty Friedan endorsed the liberalization of abortion laws at a meeting of the National Organization for Women in 1967, but women's-rights activists really began to join this effort only in 1969, the year the abortion-rights group NARAL was founded, at a conference in Chicago during which Friedan declared, "There is no freedom, no equality, no full human dignity and personhood possible for women until we assert and demand the control over our own bodies, over our own reproductive process." . . .

Most people, when they get to this chapter in American history, throw up their hands. No matter what you think of the [Roe V. Wade] ruling, what followed was awful. An early portent: ten months after Roe, Guttmacher described having shown up at Brigham and Women's Hospital, in Boston, to give a lecture, only to be confronted by a protester wearing a surgeon's gown spattered with red paint, crying "Murderer." Guttmacher wrote in the Reader's Digest that "those who oppose and those who favor legalization of abortion share a common goal—the elimination of all abortion," through better, safer, cheaper contraception, because, as he saw it, "each abortion bespeaks medical or social failure." This earned him plenty of hate mail. He died not long afterward. . . .

In 1969, in "The Emerging Republican Majority," the Nixon strategist Kevin Phillips offered a blueprint for crushing the Democrats' New Deal coalition by recruiting Southerners and Catholics to the G.O.P. At the time, prominent Democrats, including Edward Kennedy, were vocally opposed to abortion. Nixon's advisers urged him to reconsider his position on abortion and family planning. In 1970, the year Nixon signed Title X, the Department of Defense adopted a policy that doctors on military bases could in some instances perform abortions. In 1971, Patrick Buchanan wrote a memo recommending that the President reverse that policy, as part of a strategy to insure that George McGovern (the candidate Nixon wanted to run against) would defeat Edmund Muskie for the Democratic nomination. Observing that abortion was "a rising issue and a gut issue with Catholics," Buchanan wrote, "If the President should publicly take his stand against abortion, as offensive to his own moral principles . . . then we can force Muskie to make the choice between his tens of millions of Catholic supporters and his liberal friends at the New York Times and the Washington Post." A week later, in a statement to the Department of Defense, Nixon borrowed the language of the Catholic Church to speak of his "personal belief in the sanctity of human life—including the life of the yet unborn." . . .

Abortion wasn't a partisan issue until Republicans made it one. In June of 1972, a Gallup poll reported that 68 percent of Republicans and 59 percent of Democrats agreed that "the decision to have an abortion should be made solely by a woman and her physician." Fifty-six percent of Catholics thought so, too. Blackmun clipped the Washington Post story reporting this survey and put it in his Roe case file.

Nixon was reelected in November of 1972. Eight days after the Supreme Court issued its ruling on Roe, in January of 1973, a right-to-life amendment was introduced to Congress. "This poses real strategy problems," a former president of Planned Parenthood said in an interview, "because to the degree that any of us fight to keep that out of the Constitution, it brands

Planned Parenthood as pro-abortion." Gerald Ford's wife and his Vice-President, Nelson Rockefeller, supported abortion rights. In 1976, the year Congress passed the Hyde Amendment, Ann Richards ran for office for the first time, and Cecile Richards was a student at Brown. She got her birth control at Planned Parenthood in Providence.

In the late 1970s, the Republican strategists Richard Viguerie and Paul Weyrich, both of whom were Catholic, recruited Jerry Falwell into a coalition designed to bring together economic and social conservatives around a "pro-family" agenda, one that targeted gay rights, sexual freedom, women's liberation, the E.R.A., child care, and sex education. Weyrich said that abortion ought to be "the keystone of their organizing strategy, since this was the issue that could divide the Democratic Party." Falwell founded the Moral Majority in 1979; Paul Brown, the founder of the American Life League, scoffed in 1982, "Jerry Falwell couldn't spell 'abortion' five years ago." . . .

Meanwhile, opposition to abortion grew violent. In 1985, pro-life protesters picketed at 80 percent of clinics that provided abortions. Linda Gordon, in her history of the birth-control movement, reckoned the toll between 1977 and 2001: "3 doctors, 2 clinic employees, 1 clinic escort, and 1 security guard were murdered. There were also 17 attempted murders, 41 bombings, 165 arson attacks, 82 attempted bombings or arson attacks, and 372 clinic invasions."

In 1983, Planned Parenthood added to its legal department a new arm, headed by Roger Evans, to handle a growing body of litigation. Evans has served as counsel for most of the major reproductive-rights cases of the past quarter century, including *Planned Parenthood*

v. Casey. "People opposed to abortion have spent decades trying to make it more and more difficult for women to get to an abortion by placing hurdles in their path," he says. "And I think they have learned that that is a largely ineffective approach; it's more like torture." But it did have an effect: fewer and fewer places were willing to provide abortions, which made Planned Parenthood, in many parts of the country, the last abortion provider left standing. Today, more than a quarter of all abortions conducted in the United States take place in clinics affiliated with Planned Parenthood. . . .

Here is where we are. Republicans established the very federal family-planning programs that Republican members of Congress and the G.O.P.'s Presidential candidates are . . . pledging so vigorously to dismantle. Republicans made abortion a partisan issue—contorted the G.O.P. to mold itself around this issue—but Democrats allowed their party to be defined by it. And, as long as Planned Parenthood hitches itself to the Democratic Party, and it's hard to see what choice it has, its fortunes will rise and fall—its clinic doors will open and shut—with the power of the Party. Much of the left, reduced to a state of timidity in the terrible, violent wake of *Roe*, has stopped talking about rights, poverty, decency, equality, sex, and even history, thereby ceding talk of those things to the right. Planned Parenthood, a health-care provider, has good reason to talk about women's health. But, even outside this struggle, "health" has become the proxy for a liberal set of values about our common humanity. And it is entirely insufficient.

Meanwhile, however divided the electorate may or may not be over abortion, as long as Planned Parenthood is the target, the G.O.P. stands only to gain by keeping up the attack. . . .

From Contraception to Abortion: A Moral Continuum

Wendy Simonds

I've spent over two decades doing sociological research on procreative matters: I've focused mostly on investigating ways in which women seek to prevent procreation. These methods include abortion (both surgical and medical—with mifepristone, commonly known as RU-486), and emergency contraception (higher dosages of the same drugs in birth control pills, which, when taken within seventy-two hours of unprotected heterosex, can be 80 percent effective at preventing a pregnancy) (Simonds and Ellertson, 2004; Simonds et al., 1998; Simonds, 1996; Simonds, 1991; Ellertson et al., 1999). I've become fascinated by the ways in which health care workers and the women they serve think and speak about abortion and contraception as a moral issue, within a politicized climate in which anti-abortionists and pro-choice activists do rhetorical battle over women's rights and fetal status.

Each side refutes the other's language: anti-abortionists call themselves "pro-life," and refer to their enemies as "pro-abortion," whereas those who support abortion rights counter with "pro-choice," and refer to their opponents as "anti-choice," or more simply, as "antis." Each side seeks to ally itself with what the general public defines as *truly* moral, offering judgments about what the opposing value system threatens. Pro-choice activists proclaim the endangerment of individual rights, especially those of women. Anti-abortionists predict the destruction of the patriarchal heterosexual family unit by selfish (or sadly misguided) aborting women and evil profit-mongering doctors and clinic workers—all of whom they label "baby killers" (see. e.g., Ginsburg's 1989

and Luker's 1984 ethnographies of activists on both sides of the issue).

Carole Joffe writes that early anti-abortionist rhetoric in the United States in the late nineteenth century included the views that "abortion represents a threat to male authority and the 'traditional role' of women; abortion is a symbol of uncontrolled female sexuality and an 'unnatural' act. Above all, the aborting woman is selfish and self-indulgent" (1995: 29). In 1871, the AMA Committee on Criminal Abortion wrote of "the" aborting woman: "She becomes unmindful of the course marked out for her by Providence. . . . She yields to the pleasures—but shrinks from the pains and responsibilities of maternity" (Joffe, 1995: 29). Today, with the popularization of sonography, and high-tech enhanced medical photography techniques (like Lennart Nilsson's film, *The Miracle of Life*), embryonic and fetal images have become ubiquitous; anti-abortionists take advantage of this technology in their quest to personify the fetus. This relatively recent fetal fetish means that women are increasingly absent from quite a lot of anti-abortion visual rhetoric (see, e.g., Petchesky, 1987), and their absence may well go unnoticed the more accustomed people become to this manner of seeing fetuses.

Pro-choice rhetoric and representations, in contrast, are distinctly woman-centered. Legal framing of the issue is more neutral: defining the right to abortion as a right to privacy, though sexual privacy remains *another* deeply contested issue in our culture. Pro-choice rhetoric draws on both liberalism and capitalism: As Barbara Katz Rothman (1989) points out, women are portrayed as individual self-owners entitled to control over our bodies. If I "own" my body, it is mine; anything within it counts as my property, thus abortion becomes an exercise in unarguably justifiable individualism. This rhetoric sidesteps an overt discussion of sexuality, but viewing sexuality through this lens clearly means seeing women as free choosers of what they want.

Pro-choice rhetoric includes endorsements of motherhood as a *chosen* activity; the decision to abort serves as testimony to how seriously women take motherhood. As Elizabeth Karlin writes, "I am an abortion practitioner because of my utmost respect for motherhood, which I refuse to believe is punishment for a screw. I do what I do because I am convinced that being a mother is the hardest job there is" (1998: 287).

In years spent talking with health care workers and their clients, I've found that a particular moral continuum emerges that shows how anti-abortionist views of sex as shameful and women as frivolous shape aspects of the pro-choice view, too. This moral continuum is particular to our time: Bear in mind that it is only recently (the late twentieth century) that contraception has not shared the same stigma as abortion, and that abortion was not considered a moral issue until the mid-1800s. On "our" current moral continuum, late abortion is the worst, and responsible heterosex is the best. (*No sex* is another matter altogether: the anti-abortionists' ultimate moral category for unmarried women, seen as unrealistic or nonsensical by pro-choice activists.) Women who have heterosex should be "responsible"—this means, basically, that they should use contraception. So an unanticipated pregnancy that happens because a condom breaks is morally superior to an unanticipated pregnancy that occurs without any contraception; using contraception during actual sex is better than using emergency contraception the next day or the day after that; having an abortion in the first trimester is better than having one later on; and so forth. Yet at least one dominant cultural script for sex endorses being carried away (especially for women wooed by men) and another discourages women from planning for sexual encounters, because to do so indicates slutty intent (according to the script, to be prepared equates being "loose").

Poll data show that many people buy the moral dilemma approach promulgated by anti-abortionists. According to various polls, public support for first-trimester abortion is strongest (ranging between 60 and 70%). "Americans are closely divided between those calling themselves 'pro-choice' and . . . 'pro-life; now 49 percent and 45 percent, respectively. . . . It is the first time since 2008 that the 'pro-choice' position has had the numerical advantage," in Gallup polling, writes Lydia Saad (2011). Poll data show that support for limits on legal abortion has grown since the 1989 *Webster* decision gave states the right to impose various limitations on abortion (Goldberg, 1999; pollingreport.com, 2011; gallup.com, 2011). Currently, the most popular restrictions favored by Americans, according to recent poll data, are parental consent restrictions, mandatory "information" sessions (with varying content about risks and fetal development), and waiting periods (Gallup.com, 2011). A large majority supports abortion when a pregnant woman's life is endangered by the pregnancy, when her pregnancy resulted from rape or incest, or when the fetus is "defective." Support wanes (ranges from less than half to one quarter of those polled) if a woman "cannot afford any more children"; if she "does not want to marry the man"; and if the "pregnancy would interfere with [her] work or education." These poll data indicate the power of cultural attitudes about sexually active women as untrustworthy and immoral. Anti-abortionists perpetuate these attitudes in their legal assaults on abortion rights. 2011 saw an unprecedented number of restrictions introduced and enacted around the United States (Guttmacher.org, 2011). Restrictions, of course, are most onerous for young women and poor women. The *Gonzales v. Carhart* 2007 Supreme Court decision made a particular late-term abortion procedure illegal. The procedure, called "intact dilation and extraction" by doctors and "partial-birth abortion" by anti-abortionists, accounted for fewer than 1 percent of all abortions in the U.S.

In sum, depending on societal attitudes about women's sexuality, the freedom to use contraception and abortion may be conceptualized as dangerous and immoral or as an essential aspect of individual liberty. Both the legal and moral future of abortion—and other methods of limiting procreation—remain at stake.

REFERENCES

Ellertson, Charlotte, Wendy Simonds, Kimberly Springer, and Beverly Winikoff. 1999. "Providing Mifepristone-Misoprostol Medical Abortion: The View from the Clinic." *Journal of the American Women's Medical Association* 54 (Spring): 91–96, 102.

Gallup.com. 2011.

Ginsburg, Faye D. 1989. *Contested Lives: The Abortion Debate in an American Community.* Berkeley: University of California Press.

Goldberg, Carey, with Janet Elder. 1998. "Public Still Backs Abortion, But Wants Limits, Poll Says." *New York Times* (January 16): A1, A16.

Guttmacher.org.com. 2011. "States Enact Record Number of Abortion Restrictions in First Half of 2011." (July 13): http://www.guttmacher.org/media /inthenews/2011/07/13/index.html.

Joffe, Carole. 1995. *Doctors of Conscience: The Struggle to Provide Abortion before and after Roe v. Wade.* Boston: Beacon.

Karlin, Elizabeth. 1998. "'We Called it Kindness': Establishing a Feminist Abortion Practice." In *Abortion Wars: A Half Century of Struggle, 1950–2000.* Rickie Solinger, ed. Berkeley: University of California Press.

Luker, Kristin. 1984. *Abortion and the Politics of Motherhood.* Berkeley: University of California Press.

Petchesky. Rosalind Pollack. 1987. "Fetal Images: The Power of Visual Culture in the Politics of Reproduction." *Feminist Studies,* v.13, no. 2 (Summer): 263–292.

Pollingreport.com. Accessed in January, 2011. http://www .pollingreport.com/abortion.htm.

Rothman, Barbara Katz. 1989. *Recreating Motherhood: Ideology and Technology in a Patriarchal Society.* New York: W.W. Norton.

Saad, Lydia. 2011. "Americans Still Split Along 'Pro-Choice,' 'Pro-Life' Lines." Gallup.com (May 23). http://www.gallup.com/poll/147734/americans-split -along-pro-choice-pro-life-lines.aspx

Simonds, Wendy. 1996. *Abortion at Work: Ideology and Practice in a Feminist Clinic.* New Brunswick, NJ: Rutgers University Press.

———"At an impasse: Inside an Abortion Clinic." In *Current Research on Occupations and Professions* 6, Helena Z. Lopata and Judith Levy, eds. Greenwich, CT: JAI Press, 1991: 99–116.

Simonds, Wendy, and Charlotte Ellertson. 2004. "Emergency Contraception and Morality: Reflections of Health Care Workers and Clients." *Social Science & Medicine* 58: 1285–1297.

Simonds, Wendy, Charlotte Ellertson, Kimberly Springer, and Beverly Winikoff. 1998. "Abortion, Revised: . Participants in the U.S. Clinical Trials Evaluate Mifepristone." *Social Science & Medicine* 46: 1313–1323.

Choice or Coercion?: Abortion and Black Women

Zakiya Luna

Abortion is a controversial subject that is debated every national election year and at many points in between. While contentious, abortion is a common procedure; some sources suggest that one-third of U.S. women will receive one in their lifetime (Guttmacher Institute, 2011). Conflicts in the "abortion wars" are polarized between "pro-choice" and "pro-life" activists, groups holding increasingly dissimilar beliefs that make finding a middle ground difficult (Ginsburg, 1998; Luker, 1985; Munson, 2008; Tribe, 1992).[1] One recent "skirmish" between these activists is over the "Endangered Species" anti-abortion billboard campaign of 2010.

Social scientists analyze the debate over campaigns such as these because we have long recognized that attitudes and activism around abortion are useful sites through which to analyze larger social anxieties about gender, sexuality, and morality (Ginsburg, 1998; Luker, 1985). The visible groups on both sides of the abortion debate emphasize gender, sexuality, and morality concerns, but because racial minorities are not represented as having a stake in this debate, race remains largely undiscussed. Yet, Black and Hispanic women are more likely than White women to obtain an abortion (Guttmacher Institute, 2011), and historically, there have been African American groups both in support (Nelson, 2003) and in opposition to abortion rights (Prisock, 2003).

THE ORGANIZATIONS IN OPPOSITION

The pro-life Radiance Foundation (Radiance) was founded in Atlanta in 2009. Its director, Catharine Davis, had been active in pro-life politics for decades before the billboard campaign. National Right to Life is a major organization in the anti-abortion effort, and Georgia Right to Life (GRTL) is a state affiliate. GRTL hired Davis, an African American woman, in 2009 to assist with its minority outreach program. Radiance identifies as an "educational life-affirming organization" aiming to "educate audiences about pressing societal issues and how they impact the understanding of God-given Purpose." Its mission states: "We motivate people to positively affect their families, their schools and their communities. Our combination of powerfully designed media content, thorough research and personal experiences, is

unmatched and connects with people cross-culturally and cross-generationally" (Radiance, "Our Vision and Mission").

The pro-choice SisterSong Women of Color Reproductive Justice Collective (SisterSong) was founded in Atlanta in 1997. This national coalition of 80 organizations aims to "amplify and strengthen the collective voices of Indigenous women and women of color to ensure reproductive justice through securing human rights" (SisterSong, "Our Story"). Reproductive justice goes beyond abortion rights advocacy and includes "the right to have children, not have children, and to parent the children we have in safe and healthy environments" (SisterSong, "Our Story"). Loretta Ross, an African American woman, serves as the National Coordinator and has been active in the women's movement for decades. The collective coordinated the response that included various reproductive justice organizations such as SPARK Reproductive Justice Now (SPARK), a Southern reproductive justice organization, and allied organizations.

THE CONTROVERSIAL CAMPAIGN AND RESPONSE

The controversy began when Radiance placed 80 billboards throughout Atlanta in February 2010. The billboard image featured the face of an African American child under the text "Black Children are an Endangered Species." At the bottom of the billboard was a website for Radiance's campaign, Too Many Aborted (TMA). The TMA site listed the mission of the campaign: "We strongly encourage adoption and provide connections to local resources. Through speaking events and media campaigns, we expose the distortion and destruction of Planned Parenthood and its abortion advocates" (TMA, "Our Vision and Mission").

While Radiance opposed abortion generally, the TMA campaign focused on one abortion provider specifically: Planned Parenthood

Federation of America (Planned Parenthood). Radiance claimed that Black children were endangered because Planned Parenthood coerced Black women to obtain abortions. Ninety-year-old Planned Parenthood has been dogged by charges of racism for decades due to its founder, Margaret Sanger, having allied with supporters of the Eugenics movement, a movement dedicated to the practice of selective encouragement and discouragement of some populations (Planned Parenthood, 2004; Roberts, 1998). While present-day Planned Parenthood leaders explicitly state that the organization does not support eugenics, its founder's beliefs leave the health care provider vulnerable to suspicion.

In response to the billboards, SisterSong and the coalition it later headed, Trust Black Women (TBW), wanted to shift attention away from a specific abortion provider to a more general emphasis on Black women's reproductive experiences. They disagreed that Black women were targets of abortion providers. They insisted that not only should women have the right to control their bodies, but that Black women should not be blamed for their reproductive choices (Trust Black Women, 2010).

Radiance understood its activities as part of its mission "to eliminate the destruction of Life by focusing on solutions that empower women, men and children (born and unborn)" (TMA, "Our Vision and Mission"). SisterSong countered, explaining that "[t]he mere association between the born and unborn with endangered animals provides a disempowering and dehumanizing message to the Black community, which is completely unacceptable" (SisterSong, "SisterSong Collective Opposes HB 1155"). The controversy gained both local and national media attention. SisterSong and SPARK hosted a press conference at the Georgia state capitol. Their representatives, and other coalition partners such as Planned Parenthood, local residents, and legislators, denounced the billboards as racist and sexist.

Radiance took a typical pro-life stance, identifying abortion as the cause of many social ills:

Since the legalization of *Roe v. Wade*, the black community has been hit hardest with its aftermath. Urban decay has been accelerated due to rampant sexual irresponsibility, increasing single-parent poverty, fatherlessness that exceeds 70 percent, and the continuing deterioration of stable (two-parent) black families. Abortion hasn't mitigated ANY of these factors. All of these societal conditions (as evidenced in U.S. Census Bureau and CDC reports) have all risen in direct correlation with increased prominence of Birth Control policies and legalized abortion (TMA, "The Truth in Black and White").

On the surface, sexuality plays a role in this objection to abortion as Radiance argued that abortion encourages "rampant sexual irresponsibility." However, Radiance's objection has a particularly racialized tone to it by linking abortion to "urban decay."

Early on, SPARK suggested that the billboards were a direct attack on the bodies and sexuality of Black women: "The goals of these billboards are to shame, demonize and blame black women, their bodies, sexualities, and capacity to make informed decisions about their bodies" (SPARK newsletter, Feb. 11, 2010). Reproductive justice supporters like SisterSong and SPARK were taking a different approach to opposing anti-abortion activity. In their view, Black women chose to have abortions without any coercion by providers. Black women's reproductive choices were instead constrained by lack of access to health care, proper sexuality education, jobs that provided wages on which to support a family if desired, and other effects of institutional racism.

EXPANDING DEBATE INTO THE LEGISLATIVE ARENA

GRTL, Radiance's sponsor in developing the Endangered Species billboards, gained a sponsor for Georgia House Bill 1155, the Prenatal Non

Discrimination Act (PreNDA). PreNDA would have prohibited women from being coerced into having an abortion due to the race or sex of the fetus. Critics such as SisterSong argued that this was a roundabout way to prohibit abortion. The legislation was eventually defeated.

The debate then expanded geographically, as Radiance's billboard campaign extended to different states through its partnerships with local pro-life organizations. Similar billboards were erected in other cities by pro-life organizations not associated with Radiance. For example, Spanish-language billboards with the same message of "endangerment" were erected in California. They too gained public attention, although Radiance's initial billboards were given the most media attention. In December 2011, Representative Trent Franks (R–Arizona) proposed a federal anti-abortion bill similar to the Georgia bill, named the Susan B. Anthony and Frederick Douglass Prenatal Nondiscrimination Act. Various civil rights organizations and their supporters objected to the use of these two figures in the name of anti-abortion activism. The Act progressed to Committee markup in February 2012, died in May 2012, and as of the writing of this piece, was reintroduced in February 2013.

CONCLUSION

This controversy highlights how abortion is a topic that crystallizes concerns about gender, sexuality, *and* race. Pro-life activists argued that sexual freedom was creating conditions that increased the instability of Black families by promoting permissive sexual activity. Further, this activity resulted in pregnancies that abortion providers would profit from terminating, hence their supposed targeting of Black women. Reproductive justice activists argued that this anti-abortion campaign was not about supporting Black women and their children but instead restricting all women's reproductive options. In their view, to support Black women would mean

to support legislation that expanded health care or improved education for their children. The campaign also raised questions of how reproductive justice advocates could best support abortion rights while remaining focused on addressing a wide range of reproductive issues, a question that will continue to be raised. Readers may wonder if abortion is a simple matter of choice; if analysis of gender, race, and sexuality can ever be separated from each other; and if the sides of the abortion war we see commonly represented in the media (pro-life and pro-choice) are missing important perspectives. The expansion of this billboard campaign, responses by pro-choice organizations, and legislation proposed at state and federal levels suggest that the race-inflected aspect of abortion controversy will continue to command attention and perhaps require us all to think differently about what is at stake in the abortion war.

NOTE

1. I use the labels the larger movements choose for themselves. It would be more accurate to refer to SisterSong as "pro-reproductive justice," but I use the term "pro-choice" for simplicity. As described shortly, reproductive justice focuses on more than abortion rights, which is typically what people associate with the phrase "pro-choice" (see Luna, 2011, Nelson, 2003, Silliman et al., 2004).

REFERENCES

Ginsburg, Faye D. 1998. *Contested Lives : The Abortion Debate in an American Community*. Berkeley: University of California Press.

Guttmacher Institute. 2011. "Facts on Induced Abortion in the United States." http://www.guttmacher.org/pubs/fb_induced_abortion.html

Luker, Kristin. 1985. *Abortion and the Politics of Motherhood*. Berkeley: University of California Press.

Luna, Zakiya. 2011. "'The Phrase of the Day': Examining Contexts and Co-optation of Reproductive Justice Activism in the Women's Movement," *Research in Social Movements, Conflicts and Change*, Volume 32. Ashgate.

Munson, Ziad W. 2008. *The Making of Pro-life Activists: How Social Movement Mobilization Works*. Chicago: University of Chicago Press.

Nelson, Jennifer. 2003. *Women of Color and the Reproductive Rights Movement*. New York University Press.

Planned Parenthood Federation of America. 2004. "Opposition Claims About Margaret Sanger" http://www.plannedparenthood.org/files/PPFA /OppositionClaimsAboutMargaretSanger. pdf Last accessed February 1, 2012.

Prisock, Louis. 2003. "If You Love Children, Say So": The African American Anti-Abortion Movement," *The Public Eye*, 17 (3), http://www.publiceye.org/magazine/v17n3 /v17n3.pdf

Roberts, Dorothy. 1998. *Killing the Black Body: Race, Reproduction and the Meaning of Liberty*, New York: Vintage Books.

Silliman, Jael, Marlene Gerber Fried, Loretta Ross, and Elena Gutiérrrez. 2004. *Undivided Rights: Women of Color Organizing for Reproductive Justice*, Boston, MA: South End Press.

SisterSong.http://www.sistersong.net. Last accessed February 1, 2012.

Too Many Aborted. http://www.toomanyaborted.com/. Last accessed February 1, 2012.

The Radiance Foundation. http://www. theradiancefoundation.org. Last accessed February 2, 2012.

Tribe, Laurence H. 1992. *Abortion: The Clash of Absolutes*. New York : W.W. Norton & Company.

Trust Black Women. "Our Story" http://www .trustblackwomen.org/about-trust-blackwomen/our-story. Last accessed February 1, 2012.

DECONSTRUCTING "DOWN LOW" DISCOURSE: THE POLITICS OF SEXUALITY, GENDER, RACE, AIDS, AND ANXIETY

LAYLI PHILLIPS

Few issues generate more controversy in the Black community today than "the down low," also known as "the DL." On the undocumented and unconfirmed premise that the DL is linked to—"responsible for"—statistically egregious rates of HIV/AIDS among Black heterosexual women in the United States, DL discourse has become a neo-racist weapon of mass destruction that functions by engendering anxiety among and around Black people and Black sexuality. . . .

In this paper, which is less about statistics and more about framing the debate, I seek to move the DL discourse from sensationalism to sense, out of the arena of spectacle, hype, and mass hysteria and into the realm of reason and reconciliation. Contrary to prevailing notions, DL discourse actually harbors liberatory potential. By the end of this paper, after debunking a few persistent myths about the DL, I hope to have elucidated several liberatory implications of the DL phenomenon, thus allowing researchers, cultural critics, concerned members of the general public, and even people on the DL to approach the phenomenon and the issues it raises productively and humanely.

DEFINING THE DOWN LOW

The DL is a slippery concept. I offer the following "core" definition, culled from a variety of sources, scholarly, non-scholarly, and anecdotal: The DL refers to Black men who secretly have sex with other men while maintaining heterosexual relationships with women and presenting themselves as masculine rather than effeminate. Thus, the key components of the DL as it currently functions are: a) Blackness, b) sex with men, c) secrecy, d) the appearance of heterosexuality, and e) masculinity. Despite this "core" definition, the DL has taken on additional nuances of meaning, some of them contradictory, even in the popular sphere. For instance, the DL can mean secretive sex with other men even in the absence of an apparent heterosexual relationship. This could apply, for instance, to a man who is gay but either isn't ready or isn't planning to "come out." It can also mean a masculine Black gay man who only desires sex with other masculine Black gay men and who tends to keep quiet about his homosexuality, particularly in mainstream Black community contexts. Thus, DL terminology is used and can apply even when not all aspects of the core definition are invoked simultaneously. . . .

[This] forces us to ask several questions. First, can self-identification alone put someone in the DL category? Second, can someone be socially ascribed to the down-low category, even if they don't identify with the label themselves? Third, can someone be classified as DL merely by virtue of having sex with men but not looking gay or by not being public about being gay? Fourth, can women or White people be considered DL?

From "Deconstructing 'Down Low' Discourse: The Politics of Sexuality, Gender, Race, AIDS, and Anxiety," by Layli Phillips. *Journal of African American Studies*, Vol. 9, Issue 2, Fall 2005, pp. 3–15. Copyright © 2005, Transaction Publishers. With kind permission from Springer Science+Business Media.

What about people of color who aren't Black? Fifth, can a person who openly identifies as gay be classified as DL by virtue of having secret sex or relationships with a person not of their same gender? In other words, what is the "right" way to define the DL? More importantly, what are the larger implications—interpersonal, political, economic, or medical—of the various definitions we might choose? . . .

. . . In today's cultural climate—in the contemporary popular imagination—the DL is linked, rightly or wrongly, with at least three troubling phenomena: a) the spread of HIV/AIDS and, in particular, the egregiously high rates of HIV/AIDS infection among Black heterosexual women relative to other groups; b) the rift in Black male-female relationships and, by association, low rates of marriage and high rates of divorce within the Black community (which are in turn associated with single-parenthood, welfare, and the putative Black drain on public coffers); and c) Black homophobia, whether in terms of increased levels of homophobia by Black people or towards Black people. In order to ascertain the validity of the putative association between the DL and these various issues, as well as to devise appropriate solutions to the problems, the DL must be demystified, deconstructed, and reframed. . . .

TEN BASIC FACTS

. . . I will approach the phenomenon of the down low from the vantage point of ten basic facts. These ten basic facts, some more controversial than others, will serve as the organizing structure for the remainder of this [reading] . . .

Fact 1: The "Down Low" Is Not New

Despite the popular notion that the down low didn't become "a thing" until the 1990s (Denizet-Lewis, 2003), virtually all writers who address the down low phenomenon openly acknowledge that the down low has existed for a long time in the Black community (Boykin, 2005; Constantine-Sims, 2000; De Leon, 2005; Sternberg, 2001; Villarosa, 2001; but see also Julien, 1989; Neihart, 2003; Nugent, 2002; Schwarz, 2003). Not only has the DL existed for a long time, it is not limited to the U.S. context (Manago, 1998; Murray and Roscoe, 1998). Considering that the DL is not new requires us to also consider two related facts: that the DL isn't just a Black thing and the DL doesn't just pertain to men. . . .

Fact 2: The "Down Low" Isn't Just Black

Two factors account for how the DL came to be associated with Black men who secretly have sex with men during the 1990s: First, DL terminology emerged from Black popular culture. The term "down low" appears in numerous R & B and rap songs about infidelity in relationships (Boykin, 2005). Originally, "down low" infidelity was associated with heterosexual relationships; only later did it begin to connote homosexual sex among men. Second, when demographers and public health officials began to note that rates of new HIV/AIDS infection in the U.S. were proportionally highest among heterosexual African American women, they sought an explanatory theory. "Bridge theory," namely, the theory that bisexual Black men in relationships with unsuspecting women were responsible, was born (Denizet-Lewis, 2003; Villarosa, 2001, 2004). This theory converged with the emerging concept of "the down low," coming to mean masculine Black men who secretly have sex with other men while maintaining heterosexual relationships or a heterosexual image. . . .

The consolidation of this new, highly specific "down low" concept served to overshadow other pertinent facts about secretive homosexual sex among men who present themselves as heterosexual [such that the practice] also occurs widely among White men (De Leon, 2005; Sternberg, 2001; Villarosa, 2001). Boykin (2005) details several high-profile cases of White politicians, such as Governor James McGreevey of New Jersey, Congressman Michael Huffington of California, and Congressman Edward Schrock of Virginia, and business/entertainment leaders, such as music mogul David Geffen, actor Rock Hudson, comedian Peter Allen, and pop star Elton John, to prove this point. All of these men were married or linked to women at a time when their homosexuality was discovered or disclosed. Many even actively opposed or disavowed homosexuality, whether their own or others'. . . .

Fact 3: The "Down Low" Isn't Just Men

Women, too, engage in "down low" behavior. Many news stories and other anecdotal accounts document women who secretly engage in sex with other women while maintaining a feminine, heterosexual appearance (Banks, 2004; Gates, 2004). It is easy to speculate about why women who engage in such behavior have not routinely been included under the DL umbrella. First, rates of new HIV/AIDS infection among Black men have not been such to precipitate a "bridge theory" implicating bisexual Black women. The assumptions are that the virus causing HIV/AIDS passes more easily from males to females than vice versa in heterosexual sex and that Black men have more sexual partners (are more "promiscuous") than Black women. Thus, women are less likely to be viewed as "causing" HIV/AIDS in men. The persistent stereotype that HIV/AIDS is a "gay disease" contributes to this impression. In addition, remnants of the "culture of respectability" particular to Black women (Hammonds, 1994), contribute to Black women's silence around their own sexual desires and relationships, obscuring the amount and type of sex that Black women actually have. . . .

Second, two forms of sexism come into play. The first type is related to the fact that, while sex between men is generally reviled in mainstream society, sex between women is considered titil-lating if the women look feminine or straight. This pseudo-"lesbian" sex is a mainstay of the pornography industry and a staple of heterosexual male fantasies in U.S. culture. Thus, it is less subject to critique. As the adult entertainment industry continues to merge with mainstream entertainment interests, such as popular music, music videos, and movies, the likelihood of serious interest or research at the level of the state diminishes unless a clear link to compromised public health in valued community members is suspected. The second type of sexism accounts for less attention paid to the lives, behaviors, and experiences of women in general. This tendency to dismiss, ignore, or overlook women's lives pervades research, scholarship, journalism, and a host of other representational domains. . . .

Fact 4: The "Down Low" Discourse Actually Aids and Abets the Spread of HIV/AIDS

The "down low" discourse as it currently exists actually aids and abets the spread of HIV/AIDS by standing as a scapegoat for the HIV/AIDS phenomenon, allowing sexually active people who don't use protection to abdicate their personal responsibility. While no one can question the link between unprotected sex and the transmission of the virus that causes HIV/AIDS at this point in time, we have reason to question the "bridge theory" (Boykin, 2005; Johnson, 2005; Villarosa, 2004). The popular version of bridge theory allows the assertion that bisexual Black men *cause* HIV/AIDS in Black heterosexual women, when, in actuality, HIV/AIDS in Black heterosexual women is caused by the entrance of the HIV/AIDS virus into their bodies when no barriers are present. Bridge theory emphasizes sexual orientation over the failure to use barriers (condoms, dental dams, finger cots, etc.)—an action accessible to virtually all—allowing those who wish to have barrier-free sex with partners of unknown serostatus in the age of HIV/AIDS to imagine that their activity is risk-free if they know their partner's sexual orientation. Such an assumption is false and dangerous, albeit more comfortable than the thought of "safer" sex to many. . . .

Admittedly, sexism makes women more vulnerable to unprotected heterosexual sex than men (De Leon, 2005). In heterosexual relationships, men are likely to be physically stronger and older than their female sexual partners and, as a result, be able to exercise forms and amounts of power to which the women have less access. For instance, many adolescent women who contract HIV/AIDS caught the virus from an older man. In some cases, women are barred from using protection during sex by men who will abuse them if they protest. Many women rely on the men in their lives for material sustenance and thus are disempowered from contesting the wishes of the men who support them financially. Factors such as these cannot be downplayed. Yet, the discourse around the causality of HIV/AIDS can and must be corrected. Unprotected sex permits the spread of HIV/AIDS, not sexual orientation. . . .

Fact 5: The "Down Low" Discourse Feeds a Neo-racist Agenda

We must ask what end the "down low" discourse serves if not HIV/AIDS prevention. There is compelling evidence that the "down low" discourse feeds a neo-racist agenda. It does so in three ways: By keeping Black women and men at odds (a "divide and conquer" strategy), keeping Black people in the position of spectacle (subordination to the entertainment arena), and reinscribing long-standing stereotypes about hypersexuality and animalism (dehumanization).

The fact that the "down low" discourse has reignited animosities between Black women and men is evident in numerous articles (e.g., . . . Villarosa, 2004) and books (e.g., Browder, 2005), not to mention Internet bulletin boards and TV and radio programs. DL

discourse had caused some Black women to fear Black men, treat Black men suspiciously, or choose celibacy over sex with Black men. Anecdotal reports and mass media accounts suggest that many Black women—and some Black men—are angry about men on the DL. Men on the DL become scapegoats for the putative crisis in Black male-female relationships as well as for the AIDS crisis. . . .

The mass media have constructed an image of the DL man that evokes and synthesizes pre-existing tropes of the "endangered species," the "homosexual clown," and "the Black predator." The endangered species notion is called up when straight and gay commentators attempt to determine whether the DL man is "really straight" or "really gay." . . . If DL men are determined to be "gay," they then support the "endangered species" theory. . . .

The homosexual clown image is a modern-day twist on the comical Zip Coon or Black buffoon image (Riggs, 1991). Television shows from *The Flip Wilson Show* in the 1970s to *In Living Color* in the 1990s have represented the effeminate, putatively homosexual Black man as a laughing stock of the Black community, to be consumed by Black and White audiences alike. For Black audiences, the homosexual clown image reinforces (through difference) normative Black masculinity, while for White audiences, the homosexual clown reinforces notions of Black incompetence and inferiority (in this case, with regard to "appropriate" gender norms). . . .

The "Black predator" is evoked when DL men are linked with the spread of HIV/AIDS. DL men are portrayed as callous at best, nefarious as worst, as they slip in and out of presumably unprotected sexual liaisons with both women and men. It is assumed that the "DL predator" is spreading HIV/AIDS because he doesn't care enough about the woman in his life to protect her or because he feels spite about having contracted the virus himself. . . .

Hypersexuality and animalism are already associated with Black men (and women) in modern Western society. The DL discourse invokes hypersexuality by suggesting that DL men "just can't get enough" sex from women or men alone—they must have sex with both. Animalism is invoked merely by virtue of the linkage between DL men and Black sexuality, already considered to be more frequent/plentiful (promiscuous) and "freaky" than that of Whites. . . .

Fact 6: The "Down Low" Discourse Obscures the Link between Poverty and HIV/AIDS

The "down low" discourse, as a sensationalized racial discourse, obscures the more important yet less sexy link between HIV/AIDS and poverty—the biggest taboo subject in America. The reality is, the number one "social address" factor associated with HIV/AIDS infection in the world is poverty. Poor people contract HIV/AIDS at far greater rates than people who are economically privileged. Poverty is correlated with a host of other factors, from race, to needle-sharing, to lack of access to barriers for safer sex, to lack of access to appropriate medical care, even prevention and intervention. Thus, the "down low" discourse is a diversion from this important yet politically controversial fact. . . .

Fact 7: The "Down Low" Discourse Contributes to Homophobia in the Black Community

. . . Historically, the U.S. Black community has maintained a "don't ask, don't tell" posture with regard to homosexuality. Homosexual community members, while noticed, were often written off as "funny" or "just that way." Only when community members claimed a gay or lesbian identity did homosexuality become an object of scorn, derision, and ostracism. Thus, in certain respects, a "down-low" value system, with its emphasis on discretion/secrecy, has been the acknowledged norm within the Black community. . . .

Today, the perceived stakes of homosexuality and bisexuality are far greater to the mainstream Black community. HIV/AIDS, if it manifests, causes death of community members and adds the stigma of a fatal, sexually transmitted disease associated with homosexuality to the lingering stigma of race. At a time when the culture of "Black macho" is at an all-time high due to high-tech, neo-racist assaults on Black men (such as the prison-industrial complex, the increasingly disenfranchising educational and economic systems, and dehumanizing mass media imagery), the threat of perceived association with anything non-masculine—in this case, homosexuality, which is equated with effeminacy—is dire. This leads to massive anxieties around the DL phenomenon, resulting in virulent and violent forms of Black homophobia. . . .

An interesting extension of this relationship between DL discourse and Black homophobia is its negative impact on the traditionally harmonious relationship between Black gay men and Black heterosexual women (Micheal Robinson, personal communication, April 2004). . . . DL discourse has increased Black women's suspicion of Black gay men across the board, lessening the complementary amity between Black gay men and Black straight women and increasing homophobia.

Fact 8: The "Down Low" Suggests That There's a Lot More to Sexual Identity Than We Acknowledge

. . . DL men are assumed—or wished—to be "straight" or "gay." The category "bisexual" is not legitimated. On the one hand, to legitimate bisexuality would blur the clean lines that link masculinity with male heterosexuality and effeminacy with male homosexuality in the popular imagination. On another hand, the legitimation of bisexuality would also raise the issue of non-monogamous lifestyle choices and value systems that could supplant or compete with uncritically enforced norms of monogamy.

A larger issue is that the DL phenomenon suggests the possibility of sexual orientation or gender categories that have yet to be labeled or named. In our current system, these ways of being in the world are not even afforded possibility. Historically, other cultures have had names and labels for combinations of sex, gender, gender role, and sexual orientation, that don't exist or are not named in our culture (e.g., Roscoe, 2000; Williams, 1992). . . .

Fact 9: The "Down Low" Demonstrates That Sexuality and Gender Have Yet To Be Decoupled in the Popular Imagination

In the U.S. popular imagination, sex, gender, gender role, and sexual orientation fall together in neat, scripted packages. Package 1 is biologically male, a man, masculine, and heterosexual; Package 2 is biologically female, a woman, feminine, and heterosexual. These packages constitute the historical cultural ideal, but, in this day and age, they are not the only recognized constellations of characteristics. Package 3 is biologically male, a man, effeminate, and gay; Package 4 is biologically female, a woman, masculine, and lesbian. Beyond this, however, the popular imagination loses focus. What happens when people form packages that don't fall into one of these four core categories? DL men, like many other sex and gender outlaws, defy and challenge the existing packages; indeed, they create new packages. . . .

Fact 10: The "Down Low" Discourse Is an Opportunity to Re-examine and Re-frame Issues Related to Sexual Freedom and Choice

DL men force the public to consider a number of inherently controversial propositions: First, why should monosexuality (attraction to only one sex) be privileged over bisexuality (attraction to both/all genders)? Second, why should monogamous forms of relationship be privileged over polyamorous forms? Third, how relevant is sexual orientation to the transmission of the virus that causes HIV/AIDS? Fourth, what happens when people who are "straight" find themselves attracted to members of their own gender? Conversely, what happens when people who are "gay" find themselves attracted to members of another gender? Ultimately, why is sexual orientation even important in relationships where two people are genuinely attracted to each other? Fifth, in what ways are sexual orientation and gender "raced"? Stated differently, in what ways are ethnically situated "versions" of sexual orientation and gender identity or gender role incommensurate with one another, and what are the implications of this? Sixth, what are the limits of self-identification? Conversely, what are the limits of social ascription? Ultimately, whose decision is identity? Finally, what is society's responsibility with regard to the promotion of an environment that promotes and protects freedom and choice with regard to sexuality and gender? Insofar as the "down low" could compel us to address these questions squarely and with integrity, it contains liberatory potential.

Granted, the fact that deception and secrecy are associated with DL behavior is problematic. Dishonesty is not liberatory. The fact is, people have a tendency to hide what is socially unacceptable. Perhaps the DL provides us with a fresh opportunity to examine how we tend to oppress that which is different and how such cavalier oppression leads to undesirable consequences on a broad scale. In an ideal world, choices about sex, gender, gender role identity, and sexual orientation would be free and unconstrained by social convention, social scripts, social pressure, or social opinion. Additionally, disciplinary pressures created by the "isms"—racism, sexism, heterosexism/

homophobia, classism, and the like—would be non-existent. Furthermore, in an ideal world, every person would have enough information about all prospective partners to make nothing but informed decisions about potential relationships. It would become routine and unproblematic for people to disclose their preferred sex, gender, gender role identity, sexual orientation, serostatus, sexual health status, and sexual risk behaviors to prospective partners, as well as to take responsibility for their own consciously assumed sexual risk-taking. In sum, the barriers that prevent us from this ideal world should be our focus—not the "down low." . . .

REFERENCES

Banks, A. 2004. Semantics and sellouts: The low down on the down low [Electronic version]. Retrieved May 30, 2005, from http://www.geocities.com/ambwww/dlbs.htm.

Boykin, K. 2005. *Beyond the down low: Sex, lies, and denial in Black America*. New York: Carroll & Graf.

Browder, B. S. 2005. *On the up and up: A survival guide for women living with men on the down low*. New York: Dafina Books.

Constantine-Simms, D. 2000. *The greatest taboo: Homosexuality in Black communities*. Los Angeles: Alyson.

De Leon, C. 2005, May 11. It ain't all about the down low [Electronic version]. *AlterNet*. Retrieved May 13, 2005, from http://www.alternet.org/module/printversion/21962.

Denizet-Lewis, B. 2003, April 3. Double lives on the down low. *New York Times Magazine*, pp. 28–33, 48, 52–53.

Gates, S. 2004, September 28. Unexpected lesbians: The down low double life [Electronic version]. *The Hilltop*. Retrieved May 30, 2005, from http://www.thehilltoponline.com/2004/09/28/Lifestyle/Unexpected.Lesbians.The.Down.Low.Double.Life-733365.shtml.

Hammonds, E. 1994. Black (w)holes and the geometry of Black female sexuality. *Differences*, 6(2–3); 126–145.

Johnson, J. B. 2005, May 1. Secret gay encounters of black men could be raising women's infection rate [Electronic version]. *San Francisco Chronicle*, p. A1. Retrieved May 10, 2005, from http://web.lexis-nexis.com/universe/.

Julien, I. (Dir.) 1989. *Looking for Langston* [Motion picture]. United Kingdom: Water Bearer.

Manago, C. 1998, July 16. Stepping out in love, spirit and unification: An historic debate on homosexuality in the Black community [Electronic version]. *Afrikan .net Newsboard*. Retrieved May 10, 2005, from http://afrikan.i-dentity.com/wwwboard/messages/1245.html.

Murray, S. O., and Roscoe, W. (Eds.) 1998. *Boy-wives and female husbands: Studies of African homosexualities*. New York: St. Martin's Press.

Neihart, B. 2003. *Rough amusements: The true story of A'lelia Walker, patroness of the Harlem Renaissance's down-low culture*. New York: Bloomsbury.

Nugent, B. 2002. *Gay rebel of the Harlem Renaissance: Selections from the work of Richard Bruce Nugent*. Durham, NC: Duke University Press.

Riggs, M. 1991. Black macho revisited: Reflections of a SNAP queen. In E. Hemphill (Ed.), *Brother to Brother. New writings by Black gay men*. Boston: Alyson.

Roscoe, W. 2000. *Changing ones: Third and fourth genders in Native North America*. New York: Palgrave Macmillan.

Schwarz, A. B. C. 2003. *Gay voices of the Harlem Renaissance*. Bloomington: Indiana University Press.

Sternberg, S. 2001, March 15. Black men living on the down low: The danger of living 'down low' Black men who hide their bisexuality can put women at risk [Electronic version]. *USA Today*. Retrieved May 10, 2005, from http://usastuff.20m.com/.

Sternberg, S. 2001, March 15. The danger of living "down low"; Black men who hide their bisexuality can put women at risk [Electronic version]. *USA Today*. p. D1. Retrieved May 10, 2005, from http://www.thebody.com/cdc/news_updates_archive/mar15_01/bisexuality.html.

Villarosa, L. 2001, April 3. AIDS education is aimed 'down low' [Electronic version]. *New York Times*, p. F5. Retrieved May 10, 2005, from http://web.lexis-nexis.com/universe/.

Villarosa, L. 2004, April 5. AIDS fears grow for Black women [Electronic version]. *New York Times*, p. AI. Retrieved May 10, 2005, from http://web.lexis-nexis.com/universe/.

Williams, W. L. 1992. *The spirit and the flesh: Sexual diversity in American Indian culture*. Boston: Beacon.

GAY PAKISTANIS, STILL IN SHADOWS, SEEK ACCEPTANCE

MEGHAN DAVIDSON LADLY

The group meets irregularly in a simple building among a row of shops here [Lahore, Pakistan] that close in the evening. Drapes cover the windows. Sometimes members watch movies or read poetry. Occasionally, they give a party, dance and drink and let off steam. The group is invitation only, by word of mouth. Members communicate through an e-mail list and are careful not to jeopardize the location of their meetings. One room is reserved for "crisis situations," when someone may need a place to hide, most often from [his or] her own family. This is their safe space—a support group for lesbian, gay, bisexual and transgender Pakistanis. "The gay scene here is very hush-hush," said Ali, a member who did not want his full name used. "I wish it was a bit more open, but you make do with what you have."

That is slowly changing as a relative handful of younger gays and lesbians, many educated in the West, seek to foster more acceptance of their sexuality and to carve out an identity, even in a climate of religious conservatism. Homosexual acts remain illegal in Pakistan, based on laws constructed by the British during colonial rule. No civil rights legislation exists to protect gays and lesbians from discrimination. But the reality is far more complex, more akin to "don't ask, don't tell" than a state-sponsored witch hunt. For a long time, the state's willful blindness has provided space enough for gays and lesbians. They socialize, organize, date and even live together as couples, though discreetly. One journalist, in his early 40s, has been living as a gay man in Pakistan for almost two decades. "It's very easy being gay here, to be honest," he said, though he and several others interviewed did not want their names used for fear of the social and legal repercussions. "You can live without being hassled about it," he said, "as long as you are not wearing a pink tutu and running down the street carrying a rainbow flag."

The reason is that while the notion of homosexuality may be taboo, homosocial, and even homosexual, behavior is common enough. Pakistani society is sharply segregated on gender lines, with taboos about extramarital sex that make it almost harder to conduct a secret heterosexual romance than a homosexual one. Displays of affection between men in public, like hugging and holding hands, are common. "A guy can be with a guy anytime, anywhere, and no one will raise an eyebrow," the journalist said. For many in his and previous generations, he said, same-sex attraction was not necessarily an issue because it did not involve questions of identity. Many Pakistani men who have sex with men do not think of themselves as gay. Some do it regularly, when they need a break from their wives, they say, and some for money.

But all the examples of homosexual relations—in Sufi poetry, Urdu literature or discreet sexual conduct—occur within the private sphere, said Hina Jilani, a human rights lawyer and activist for women's and minority rights. Homoeroticism can be expressed but not named. "The biggest hurdle," Ms. Jilani said, "is finding the proper context in which to bring this issue out into the open." That is what the gay and lesbian support group in Lahore is slowly seeking to do, even if it still meets in what amounts to near secrecy. The driving force behind the group comes from two women, ages 30 and 33. They are keenly aware of the oddity that two women, partners no less, have become architects of the modern gay scene in Lahore; if gay and bisexual men barely register in the collective societal consciousness of Pakistan, their female counterparts are even less visible. "The organizing came from my personal experience of extreme isolation, the sense of being alone and different," the 30-year-old said. She decided that she needed to find others like her in Pakistan. Eight people, mostly the couple's friends, attended the first meeting in January 2009.

Two months later, the two women formed an activist group they call O. They asked for its full name not to be published because it is registered as a nongovernmental organization with the government, with its true purpose concealed because of the laws against homosexual acts. O conducts research into lesbian, gay, bisexual and transgender issues, provides legal advice and has helped remove people from difficult family situations, and in one case a foreign-operated prostitution ring. The group has made a conscious decision to focus its efforts on the dynamic of family and building social acceptance and awareness rather than directly tackling legal discrimination. Their current fight is not to overturn Article 377 of the Pakistan Penal Code, on "Unnatural Offenses," but to influence parents' deciding whether or not to shun their gay child. They see this approach as ultimately more productive. "If you talk about space in Pakistan in terms of milestones that happen in the other parts of the world like pride parades or legal reform or whatever, that's not going to happen for a long time," the 33-year-old organizer, who identifies as bisexual, said. "Families making space—

that's what's important to us right now." Both women say their families have accepted them, though it was a process.

There are distinct class differences at work here, particularly when it comes to self-definition. Most of those actively involved in fostering the gay and lesbian community in Pakistan, even if they have not been educated abroad, are usually college graduates and are familiar with the evolution of Western thought concerning sexuality. Mostly city dwellers, they come from families whose parents can afford to send their children to school. Those who identify themselves as gay here are usually middle and upper middle class, the 33-year-old woman said. "You will get lower middle class or working-class women refusing to call themselves lesbian because that to them is an insult, so they'll say 'woman loving woman.'" While the journalist lives relatively openly as a gay man, and says his immediate family accepts it, he understands that older gays have separated sexuality from identity, and he also recognizes that this approach is changing. Still, he sees the potential for serious conflict for younger Pakistanis who are growing up with a more westernized sense of sexual identity. "They've got all the access to content coming from a Western space, but they don't have the outlets for expression that exist over there," he said. "Inevitably they will feel a much greater sense of frustration and express it in ways that my generation wouldn't have."

That clash of ideologies was evident last year on June 26, when the American Embassy in Islamabad held its first lesbian, gay, bisexual and transgender pride celebration. The display of support for gay rights prompted a backlash, setting off demonstrations in Karachi and Lahore, and protesters clashing with the police outside the diplomatic enclave in Islamabad. This year, the embassy said, it held a similar event but did not issue a news release about it. "It is the policy of the United States government to support and promote equal rights for all human beings," an embassy spokeswoman, Rian Harris, said by e-mail when asked about the backlash. "We are committed to standing up for these values around the world, including here in Pakistan." Well intended as it may have been, the event was seen by many in Pakistan's gay community as detrimental to their cause. The 33-year-old activist strongly believes it was a mistake. "The damage that the U.S. pride event has done is colossal," she said, "just in terms of creating an atmosphere of fear that was not there before. The public eye is not what we need right now."

Despite the hostile climate, both the support group and O continue their work. O is currently researching violence against lesbian, bisexual and transgender Pakistanis. "In a way, we are just role models for each other," the 30-year-old said. When she was growing up, she said, she did not know anyone who was gay and she could not imagine such a life. "For me the whole activism is to create that space in which we can imagine a future for ourselves, and not even imagine but live that future," she said. "And we are living it. I'm living my own impossibility."

HOOKING UP: SEX IN GUYLAND

MICHAEL KIMMEL

know it's different at other schools," Troy patiently tried to explain to me. "I mean, at other schools, people date. You know, a guy asks a girl out, and they go out to a movie or something. You know, like dating? But here at Cornell, nobody dates. We go out in groups to local bars. We go to parties. And then after we're good and drunk, we hook up. Everyone just hooks up."

"Does that mean you have sex?" I ask

"Hmm," he says, with a half-smile on his face. "Maybe, maybe not. That's sort of the beauty of it, you know? Nobody can really be sure."

My conversation with Troy echoes an overwhelming majority of conversations I have had with young people all across the country. Whether among college students or recent grads living in major metropolitan areas, "hooking up" defines the current form of social and sexual relationships among young adults. The only point Troy is wrong about is his assumption that traditional dating is going on anywhere else. Dating, at least in college, seems to be gone for good.

Instead, the sexual marketplace is organized around groups of same-sex friends who go out together to meet appropriate sexual partners in a casual setting like a bar or a party. Two people run into each other, seemingly at random, and after a few drinks they decide to go back to one or the other's room or apartment, where some sexual interaction occurs. There is no expectation of a further relationship. Hookups can morph into something else: either friends with benefits or a dating relationship. But that requires some additional, and complex, negotiation.

Many adults find this promiscuity hard to grasp. What is this hooking up culture all about? What does it mean exactly? What's the *point* of all that sex? Is it even fun? For the past two years, I've been involved in a study to find out. The Online College Social Life Survey was developed initially by Paula England, a sociology professor at Stanford, and has now been administered to about 7,000 college students at nine campuses—large and small, public and private, elite and nonelite—including Stanford, Arizona, Indiana, Radford, UC Santa Barbara, SUNY Stony Brook, Ithaca College, and Evergreen State. We asked participants about their sexual behaviors, their experiences of various sexual activities, orgasm, drinking behavior, and their romantic relationships. We asked both women and men, gay and straight—but mostly straight. All were between 18 and 24. I've also consulted with other researchers at other schools, and compared our data with theirs. And I've looked at data from several large, nationally representative studies of sexual behavior among young people.

Some of what's going on won't come as that much of a shock; after all, young adulthood since the sixties has been a time of relative sexual freedom and well-documented experimentation. What may be surprising, though, is how many young people accept that hooking up—recreational sex with no strings attached—is the best and most prevalent arrangement available to them. Once, sexual promiscuity co-existed with traditional forms of dating, and young people could maneuver between the two on their way toward serious and committed romantic relationships. Now, hooking up is pretty much all there is; relationships begin and end with sex. Hooking up has become the alpha and omega of young adult romance.

And though hooking up might seem utterly mutual—after all, just who are all those guys hooking up *with*?—what appears on the surface to be mutual turns out to be anything but. Despite enormous changes in the sexual attitudes of young people, the gender politics of campus sex don't seem to have changed very much at all. Sex in Guyland is just that—guys' sex. Women are welcome to act upon their sexual desires, but guys run the scene. Women who decide not to join the party can look forward to going to sleep early and alone tonight—and every night. And women who do join the party run the risk of encountering the same old double standard that no amount of feminist progress seems able to eradicate fully. Though women may accommodate themselves to men's desires—indeed, some feel they have to accommodate themselves to them—the men's rules rule. What this means is that many young women are biding their time, waiting for the guys to grow up and start acting like men.

Yet the hooking-up culture so dominates campus life that many older guys report having a difficult time making a transition to serious adult relationships. They all say that eventually they expect to get married and have families, but they have no road map for getting from drunken sloppy "Did we or didn't we?" sex to mature adult relationships. It turns out that choosing quantity over quality teaches them nothing about long-term commitment. Nor is it meant to. The pursuit of conquests is more about guys proving something to other guys than it is about the women involved. . . .

HOOKING UP

In recent years, scholarly researchers and intrepid journalists have bravely waded in to demarcate the term "hooking up," map its boundaries, and explain its strange terrain. But the definitions are vague and contradictory. One research group refers to it as ". . . a sexual encounter which may or may not include sexual intercourse, usually occurring on only one occasion between two people who are strangers or brief acquaintances." Another study maintains that hooking up ". . . occurs when two people who are casual acquaintances or who have just met that evening at a bar or party agree to engage in some forms of sexual behavior for which there will likely be no future commitment."[1]

Our collaborative research project, The Online College Social Life Survey, found that hooking up covers a multitude of behaviors, including kissing and nongenital touching (34 percent), oral sex, but not intercourse (15 percent), manual stimulation of the genitals (19 percent), and intercourse (35–40 percent). It can mean "going all the way." Or it can mean "everything but." By their senior year, we found that students had averaged nearly seven hookups during their collegiate careers. About one-fourth (24 percent) say they have never hooked up, while slightly more than that (28 percent) have hooked up ten times or more.[2]

As a verb, "to hook up" means to engage in any type of sexual activity with someone you are not in a relationship with. As a noun, a "hookup" can either refer to the sexual encounter or to the person with whom you hook up. Hooking up is used to describe casual sexual encounters on a continuum from "one-night stands" (a hookup that takes place once and once only with someone who may or may not be a stranger) to "sex buddies" (acquaintances who meet regularly for sex but rarely if ever associate otherwise), to "friends with benefits" (friends who do not care to become romantic partners, but may include sex among the activities they enjoy together).

Part of what makes the hookup culture so difficult to define and describe is the simple fact that young men and women experience it in very different ways. They may be playing the same game, but they're often on opposing teams, playing by a different set of rules, and they define "winning," and even "scoring," in totally different ways. Sameness doesn't necessarily mean equality. . . .

DELIBERATE VAGUENESS

The phrase "hooking up" itself is deliberately vague, which is why any attempt to define it concretely will inevitably fall short. In fact, it is its very vagueness and ambiguity that characterize it.[3] . . .

. . . Yet that vagueness serves men and women in very different ways. When a guy says he "hooked up" with someone, he may or may not have had sex with her, but he is certainly hoping that his friends think he has. A woman, on the other hand, is more likely to hope they think she hasn't.

In a sense, hooking up retains certain features of older dating patterns: male domination, female compliance, and double standards. Though hooking up may seem to be mutually desired by both guys and girls, our research indicates that guys initiate sexual behavior most of the time (less than a third of respondents said this was mutual). Hookups are twice as likely to take place in his room as in hers. And, most important, hooking up enhances his reputation whereas it damages hers. Guys who hook up a lot are seen by their peers as studs; women who hook up a lot are seen as sluts who "give it up. . . ."

The vagueness of the term itself—hooking up—turns out to be a way to protect the reputation of the woman while enhancing that of the man. In addition to that conceptual vagueness after the fact, hookups are also characterized by a certain vagueness before and even during the fact as well. Most hookups share three elements: the appearance of spontaneity, the nearly inevitable use of alcohol, and the absence of any expectation of a relationship.

PLANNED SPONTANEITY

In order for hookups to work, they have to appear to be spontaneous. And they do—at least to the guys. One guy told me it's "a sort of one-time, spur-of-the-moment thing. Hookups generally are very unplanned." . . .

Yet such spontaneity is nonetheless carefully planned. Guys have elaborate rituals for what has become known as "the girl hunt."[4] There are "pregame" rituals, such as drinking before you go out to bars, since consuming alcohol, a requirement, is also expensive on a limited budget, so it's more cost-effective to begin the buzz before you set out.

There are defined roles for the guys looking to hook up, like the "wing man," the reliable accomplice and confidant. "The wing man is the guy who takes one for the team," says Jake, a sophomore at Notre Dame. "If there are, like, two girls and you're trying to hook up with one of them, your wing man chats up the other one—even if she's, like, awful—so you can have a shot at the one you want. Definitely a trooper."

When guys claim that the hookup is spontaneous, they are referring not to whether the hookup will take place, but with whom they will hook up. Women have a different view of spontaneity. Since they know that hooking up is what the guys want, the girls can't be "spontaneous" about it. They have to think—whether or not, with whom, under what conditions—and plan accordingly, remembering a change of clothes, birth control, and the like. They have to decide how much they can drink, how much they can flirt, and how to avoid any potentially embarrassing or even threatening situations. The guys lounge in comfort of the illusion of alcohol-induced spontaneity; the women are several steps ahead of them. . . .

Yet the illusion of spontaneity remains important for both guys and girls. It's a way of distancing yourself from your own sexual agency, a way of pretending that sex just happens, all by itself. It helps young people to maintain a certain invulnerability around the whole thing. It's not cool to want something too much. It's better to appear less interested—that way no one will know the extent of your disappointment if your plans don't come to fruition.

THE INEVITABILITY OF ALCOHOL

Drinking works in much the same way. Virtually all hooking up is lubricated with copious amounts of alcohol—more alcohol than sex, to tell the truth. "A notable feature of hookups is that they almost always occur when both participants are drinking or drunk," says one study.[5] In our study, men averaged nearly five drinks on their most recent hookup, women nearly three drinks. . . .

To say that alcohol clouds one's judgment would be an understatement. Drinking is *supposed* to cloud your judgment. Drinking gives the drinker "beer goggles," which typically expand one's notion of other people's sexual attractiveness. "After like four drinks a person looks a little bit better," explains Samantha, a 21-year-old senior at the University of Virginia. "After six or seven that person looks a lot better than they did. And, well, after ten, that person is the hottest person you've ever seen!" Or, as Jeff puts it, "Everybody looks more attractive when you're drunk."

But intentionally clouding judgment is only part of the story. The other part is to cloud *other people's* judgment. If you were drunk, you don't have to take responsibility for what happens. For guys, this means that if they get shot down they can chalk it up to drunkenness. The same holds true for their sexual performance if they do get lucky enough to go home with someone. In fact, drunkenness provides a convenient excuse for all sorts of potential sexual disasters, from rejection to premature ejaculation to general ineptitude born of inexperience. . . .

While both sexes might get to enjoy the lack of responsibility alcohol implies, this turns out to be especially important for the women, who still have their reputations to protect. Being wasted is generally accepted as an excuse. "What did I do last night?" you can legitimately ask your girlfriends. And then everyone laughs. It's still better to be a drunk than a slut. . . .

THE ABSENCE OF EXPECTATIONS

One of the key defining features of hooking up is that it's strictly a "no strings attached" endeavor. Young people in college—and this seems to hold true for both women and men—seems generally wary of committed or monogamous relationships. The focus is always on what it costs, rather than what it might provide. And if you consider that half of young adults come from divorced households, their cynicism is neither surprising nor unfounded. "I don't know if I even know any happily married couples," one young woman says. "Most of my friends' parents are divorced, and the ones who aren't are miserable. Where's the appeal in *that*?"

Hooking up is seen as being a lot easier than having a relationship. Students constantly say that having a relationship, actually dating, takes a lot of time, and "like, who has time to date?" asks Greg, a junior at the College of Wooster in Ohio. "I mean, we're all really busy, and we have school, and classes, and jobs, and friends, and all. But, you know," he says with a bit of a wink, "a guy has needs, you know what I mean? Why date if you can just hook up?" . . .

Guys may hook up because they get exactly what they want and don't have to get caught by messy things like emotions. "A lot of guys get into relationships just so they get steady [expletive]," another teen tells journalist Benoit Denizet-Lewis. "But now that it's easy to get sex outside of relationships, guys don't need relationships."[6] "That's all I really want is to hook up," says Justin, a junior at Duke. "I don't want to be all like boyfriend and girlfriend—that would, uh, significantly reduce my chances of hooking up, you know?"

Yet the absence of expectations that supposedly characterizes the hookup seem not to be as true for women. And this is not a simple case of "women want love, men want sex." Rather, it's a case of women being able and willing to acknowledge that there is a lot of ground between anonymous drunken sex and long-term commitment. They might not want to get married, but a phone call the next day might still be nice.

Young women today are more comfortable with their sexuality than any generation in history. There are certainly women who prefer hooking up to relationships. Women also hook up to avoid emotional entanglements that would distract them from their studies, professional ambitions, friendship networks, and other commitments. Or they hook up because they don't think they're ready for a commitment and they just want to hang out and have fun. Yet many also do it because it's the only game in town. If they want to have sexual relationships with men—and by all appearances they certainly do—then this is the field on which they must play. Some women may want more, some may not, but since more is not available either way, they take what they can get. . . .

And for the women who do want relationships, hooking up seems to be the only way to find the sort of relationships they say they want. They hope that it will lead somewhere else. . . .

RACE AND HOOKING UP

Hooking up may be a guy thing, but it is also a *white* guy thing. Of course there are exceptions, but minority students are not hooking up at the same rates as white students. This is partly because minority students on largely white campuses often feel that everything they do is seen not in terms of themselves as individuals but representative of their minority group. "There are so few blacks on campus," says Rashawn Ray, a sociologist at Indiana and part of our research team. "If one guy starts acting like a dog, well, word will get around so fast that he'll never get another date." . . .

"I know we don't do what the white kids do," said one black male student at Middlebury College in Vermont. "That's right, you don't," said his female companion. "And I don't either. If I even thought about it, my girls would hold me back." Said another black student at Ohio State, "if I started hooking up, I mean, not like with some random white girl, but like with my sisters, Oh, God, my friends would be saying I'm, like, 'acting white.'"

As a result, minority students are likely to conform to more conventional dating scripts, especially within their own communities. Our survey found that blacks and Latinos are somewhat less likely to engage in hooking up, and Asian students are *far* less likely to do so.[7]

HOOKING UP AND RELATIONSHIPS: "THE TALK"

In general, women tend to be more ambivalent about hookup culture; some report feeling sexy and desirable, others feel it's cheap and rarely leads anywhere. But when it comes to forming an actual relationship, the tilt is almost entirely toward the women. They are the ones who must negotiate whether the hooking up will proceed to a deeper level of intimacy. On many campuses, women are the ones who typically initiate the "Define the Relationship" conversation—the "DTR," or, more simply, "The Talk." "Are we a couple or not?" she asks.

Some women don't even bother to ask. "I didn't want to bring it up and just be, like, 'so where do we stand?' because I know guys don't like that question," says one women to sociologist Kathleen Bogle. Another tells her it's the women who want the relationship and the guys who make the final decision. "It always comes down to that," says Ann, a junior at Wright State University. . . .

But why are guys so relationship-phobic? Virtually every guy I spoke with said that he wanted to get married someday, and that he hoped he would be happy. Just not now and probably not until his early thirties. Their relationship phobias are less related to fears of romantic entanglements from which they would have trouble extricating themselves, and more to do with the purposes of hooking up in the first place. Hooking up, for guys, is less a relationship path than it is for women. In fact, it serves an entirely different purpose.

SEX AS MALE BONDING

In some ways hooking up represents the sexual component of young men's more general aversion to adulthood. They don't want girlfriends or serious relationships, in part, because they don't feel themselves ready (they're probably not) and also, in part, because they see relationships as "too much work." Instead they want the benefits of adult relationships, which for them seem to be exclusively sexual, with none of the responsibility that goes along with adult sexuality—the emotional connection, caring, mutuality, and sometimes even the common human decency that mature sexual relationships demand. Simply put, hooking up *is* the form of relationship guys want with girls.

Yet it's a bit more complicated than simple pleasure-seeking on the part of guys, because as it turns out pleasure isn't the first item on the hookup agenda. In fact, pleasure barely appears on the list at all. If sex were the goal, a guy would have a much better chance of having more (and better) sex if he had a steady girlfriend. Instead, guys hook up to prove something to other guys. The actual experience of sex pales in comparison to the experience of talking about sex. . . .

Hooking up may have less to do with guys' relationships with women and more to do with guys' relationships with other guys. "It's like the girls you hook up with, they're, like, a way of showing off to other guys," says Jeff, a proud member of a fraternity at the University of Northern Iowa. "I mean, you tell your friends you hooked up with Melissa, and they're like, 'whoa, dude, you are one stud.' So, I'm into Melissa because my guy friends think she is so hot, and now they think more of me because of it. It's totally a guy thing." . . .

Jeff's comments echo those I heard from guys all across the country. Hooking up is not for whatever pleasures one might derive from drunken sex on a given weekend. Hooking up is a way that guys communicate with other guys—it's about homosociality. It's a way that guys compete with each other, establish a pecking order of cool studliness, and attempt to move up in their rankings. . . .

Of course, the awesome insecurity that underlies such juvenile blustering remains unacknowledged, which is interesting since that insecurity is the driving force behind so much of sex in Guyland. The vast majority of college-aged guys are relatively inexperienced sexually. Most of them have had some sex, but not as much as they'd like, and nowhere near as much as they think everyone else has had. Perhaps they've received oral sex, less likely they've performed it, and if they have had intercourse at all it is generally only a handful of times with one partner, two if they're lucky. . . .

Yet most guys think that they are alone in their inexperience. They think that other guys are having a lot of sex, all the time, with a huge number of women. And they suspect, but would have no way of knowing, that other guys are a lot better at it than they are. Seen in this light, the hookup culture, at least for guys, is more than a desperate bid simply to keep up. It's a way to keep up, and keep quiet about it—while being rather noisy at the same time.

HOOKING UP VS. GOOD SEX

. . . With all this hooking up, friends with benefits, and booty calls, guys should feel they have it made. But there is a creeping anxiety that continually haunts guy's sexual activities, particularly these almost-men. They worry that perhaps they're not doing it enough, or well enough, or they're not big enough, or hard enough. Though the *evidence* suggests that men are in the driver's seat when it comes to sex, they *feel* that women have all the power, especially the power to say no.

And these days, those women have a new "power"—the power to compare. Many of the guys I spoke with became suddenly uneasy when the topic of women's sexual expectations came up. They shifted uncomfortably in their seats, looked down at the floor, or stared into their soft drink as if it were an oracle. . . .

I asked guys all across the country what they think is the percentage of guys on their campus who had sex on any given weekend. The average answer I heard was about 80 percent. That is, they believed that four out of every five guys on campus had sex last weekend. Actually, 80 percent is the percentage of senior men who have *ever* had vaginal intercourse in our college survey. The actual percentage on any given weekend is closer to 5 to 10 percent. This gives one an idea of how pervasive the hooking-up culture is, how distorted the vision of young men by that culture is, and the sorts of pressures a guy might feel as Thursday afternoon hints at the looming weekend. How can he feel like a man if he's close to the only one not getting laid? And if so many women are available, sexually promiscuous, and hooking up as randomly as the men are, what's wrong with him if he's the only one who's unsuccessful?

As it turns out, guys' insecurity is not altogether unfounded. Most hookups are not great sex. In our survey, in their most recent hookups, regardless of what actually took place, only 19 percent of the women reported having an orgasm, as compared to 44 percent of the men. When women received cunnilingus, only about a quarter experienced an orgasm, though the men who reported they had performed cunnilingus on their partner reported that she had an orgasm almost 60 percent of the time.

This orgasm gap extends to intercourse as well. Women report an orgasm 34 percent of the time; the men report that the women had an orgasm 58 percent of the time. (The women, not surprisingly, are far better able to tell if the men had orgasms, and reporting rates are virtually identical.)

Many women, it turns out, fake orgasm—and most do so "to make that person feel good, to make them feel like they've done their job." But some women said that they faked it "just really to end it," because they're, "like, bored with it."[8] . . .

HOOKING UP AND GENDER POLITICS

Hooking up seems disadvantageous to women in so many ways, and not only because the sex isn't so great. In fact the disincentives appear so numerous that one eventually might wonder why women bother. The hookup culture appears to present a kind of lose–lose situation. If they don't participate, they risk social isolation—not to mention that they also forego sex itself, as well as any emotional connection they may be able to squeeze out of the occasion. If they do participate, they face the potentially greater risk of "loss of value," and there's a good chance that they won't even have any fun. . . .

Since the 1990s, abstinence campaigns have been encouraging young people to take a "virginity pledge" and to refrain from heterosexual intercourse until marriage (the campaigns assume that gay and lesbian students do not exist). Abstinence-based sex education is pretty much the *only* sex education on offer in the majority of American high schools. And many parents see abstinence as the best advice they can offer their children about how to reduce their risk for sexually transmitted disease, unwanted pregnancy, or sexual assault.

At first glance, such campaigns appear to be somewhat successful. One study found that the total percentage of high-school students who say they've had heterosexual sex had dropped from more than 50 percent in 1991 to slightly more than 45 percent in 2001. . . . Whatever decline in abortion rates may have occurred is due largely to the restrictions on its availability, not a curtailment of sexual behavior. Nor do abstinence campaigns offset the other messages teenagers hear. Sociologist Peter Bearman analyzed data from over 90,000 students, and found that taking a virginity pledge does lead an average heterosexual teenager to delay his or her first sexual experience, but only by about eighteen months. And the pledges were only effective for students up to age 17. By the time they are 20 years old, over 90 percent of both boys and girls are sexually active.[9] Another campus-based survey found that of the 16 percent who had taken virginity pledges, 61 percent of them had broken their pledge before graduating. Pledgers were also less likely to use condoms, although they were just as likely to practice oral sex as nonpledgers.[10]

What's more, because abstinence-based programs are often used instead of actual sex education, few people really know exactly what "counts" in keeping your pledge. In one recent survey of 1,100 college freshmen, 61 percent believed you are still abstinent if you have participated in mutual masturbation; 37 percent if you have had oral sex; and 24 percent if you have had anal sex. On the other hand, 24 percent believed that kissing with tongues broke their abstinence pledge.[11] In the survey by Angela Lipsitz and her colleagues, the majority of those who said they "kept" their vows had experienced oral sex.[12]

At first glance, abstinence might be seen as the antithesis of the Guy Code, since promising not to have sex would negate the drive to score that is central to the Code. But abstinence actually sits easily within the Guy Code. Abstinence pledges put all the responsibility on the girls to police sexual activity—and to bear all the consequences and responsibilities if something goes wrong. Abstinence pledges also make it a lot easier for guys to maintain the good girl/bad girl, Madonna/whore dichotomy that has kept the sexual double standard in place for decades. "Does having sex with, like, a ho, actually violate your abstinence pledge?" one first-year student asked me recently. "I mean, I definitely respect the nice girls, and I am abstinent with them."

Even those who advocate prudence rather than abstinence nonetheless seem to focus all their attention on the women. If a woman ever intends to marry, and most do, hooking up is exactly the wrong way to go, say several recent commentators on the issue. . . .

Such advice ignores the pleasure-seeking behaviors and intentions of both women *and* men, and assumes that women are naturally chaste and virginal, were it not for those rapacious men. Such an image is obviously insulting to men, since it imagines them as no better than predators. And it is also probably insulting to women, who have shown themselves fully capable of seeking and enjoying sex in ways that their mothers—and certainly those grandmothers!—could never have imagined.[13] Both women and men are pleasure-seeking creatures, especially on campus, and it lets guys entirely off the hook if the focus of all the advice is only the women. . . .

Focusing all one's moralizing attention on young women only perpetuates that inequality, rather than challenges it.

HOOKING UP: THE NEW NORM

. . . It is certainly not true that all the women are hooking up in order to develop relationships, nor are all guys hooking up in the hopes of avoiding precisely the relationships that the women are seeking. Most actually want relationships. But, most say, not quite yet.

Today's college students will get married—eventually. It'll be about eight years later than their mothers and fathers did. And they'll do that by choice, because before marriage they want to establish careers, enjoy relationships, and develop autonomy. The contemporary culture of courtship is not their parents' culture of courtship, but it is no less a "culture" and no less legitimate because of that.

The students I interviewed in depth following our quantitative survey were convincing on this score. Hooking up, in their minds, is not an alternative to relationships—it's the new pathway to forming relationships. Even if only a small percentage of hookups result in relationships, most relationships do begin with a hookup. For some hooking up is most definitely in the service of a relationship—just not this particular one. . . .

POSTGRADUATE SEX IN GUYLAND

Playing the field takes a somewhat different shape after graduation. Though young people still go to bars or parties in groups, and some still drink a lot, fewer are slinking off to empty rooms to hook up. On the whole, post–college-aged people are returning to more traditional dating patterns. Bogle followed recent graduates of two colleges, and found that women and men exchange phone numbers or email addresses, and some time in the next few days they will contact each other and arrange to go to dinner or something more conventionally social. It turns out that hooking up in college has added a new act in an old drama, but it is hardly a new play. . . .

NOTES

1. Tracy A. Lambert. May 2003. "Pluralistic Ignorance and Hooking Up" in *Journal of Sex Research*, 40(2):129.

2. Our numbers seem to square with other surveys, or, perhaps, run a bit to the conservative side, since we have a large sample of colleges in our pool, and virtually all other surveys were done only at the researcher's university.

3. See, for example, Andrea Lavinthal and Jessica Rozler. 2005. *The Hook up Handbook: A Single Girl's Guide to Living It Up.* New York: Simon Spotlight. p. 3.

4. See, for example, David Grazian. "The Girl Hunt: Urban Nightlife and the Performance of Masculinity as Collective Activity" in *Symbolic Interaction* 30(2); 2007.

5. Norval Glenn and Elizabeth Marquardt. 2001. *Hooking Up, Hanging Out, and Hoping for Mr. Right: College Women on Dating and Mating Today.* New York: Institute for American Values, p. 15.

6. Laura Sessions Stepp. 2007. *Unhooked: How Young Women Pursue Sex, Delay Love and Lose at Both.* New York: Riverhead. p. 115.

7. The median number of hookups for white males, junior and seniors, was six (three for white women). The median for black and Latino males was four, and for Asians it was zero.

8. Paula England, Emily Fitzgibbons Shafer, and Alison Fogarty. 2007. "Hooking Up and Forming Romantic Relationships on Today's College Campuses" in *The Gendered Society Reader* (Third Edition), edited by Amy Aronson and Michael Kimmel. New York: Oxford University Press, manuscript, p. 7.

9. See Peter Bearman and Hannah Bruckner. January 2001. "Promising the Future: Virginity Pledges and First Intercourse" in *American Journal of Sociology*, 106(4): 859–912.

10. Angela Lipsitz, Paul D.Bishop, and Christine Robinson. August 2003. "Virginity Pledges: Who Takes Them and How Well Do They Work?" Presentation at the Annual Convention of the American Psychological Association, August 2003.

11. See Bearman and Bruckner, 2001, and Lipsitz, Bishop and Robinson, 2003.

12. Lipsitz et al., 2003.

13. For examples of this, see Laura Sessions Stepp, *Unhooked*; and Norval Glenn and Elizabeth Marquardt, *Hooking Up, Hanging Out, and Hoping for Mr. Right.*

Bullies Use Sexual Taunts to Hurt Teen Girls

Stephanie Pappas

In a sobering echo of earlier teen suicides, a 10-year-old Illinois girl took her life Nov. 11 [2011] after allegedly experiencing two years of bullying at school. And although Ashlynn Conner was just in fifth grade, her mother says her peers taunted her by calling her a slut.

As nonsensical as the word seems applied to a child, it's a common refrain for young teen and tween bullies, according to psychologist Maureen McHugh of Indiana University of Pennsylvania, who studies bullying, sexual harassment, and especially "slut-bashing," the practice of peers labeling other peers as dirty and promiscuous, oftentimes in the absence of any sexual activity at all on the part of the victim.

"Their peers know what kinds of words to use to hurt them," McHugh told [me], adding that sexuality becomes an Achilles heel in the beginning of adolescence.

"Their sexuality is emerging," McHugh said. "It's a kind of vulnerability."

SEX AND BULLYING

Not all bullying is tied to sexuality, but a number of studies find that sexual and gender-based taunts are extremely common during the teen years. Students who are gay are bullied three times as much as heterosexual kids, research finds. According to a 2010 study published in the *Journal of Adolescent Health*, 44 percent of gay male students and 40 percent of lesbians said they'd experienced bullying in the past

year, compared with 26 percent of heterosexual boys and 15 percent of heterosexual girls. . . .

. . . A study released this month by the American Association of University Women found that among 2,000 middle- and high-school students surveyed in a nationally representative study, 48 percent had been sexually harassed in the 2010–2011 school year. About 56 percent of girls had been sexually harassed, as had 40 percent of boys. Most of the students, 87 percent, said the harassment had a negative effect on them, with 37 percent of girls and 25 percent of boys saying it made them not want to go to school.

SLUT-BASHING AND DOUBLE STANDARDS

. . . Middle-school girls and young teens come under enormous pressure both to flaunt their sexuality and to keep it in bounds, McHugh said. As girls experiment with makeup and sexualized fashion, their peers police them, sometimes brutally.

"There is pressure to adopt a girly identity," McHugh said. "And there's monitoring of people wearing too much makeup or dressing too provocatively, so it's a weird fine line."

To McHugh, the fact that the "s"-word can hurt is evidence that the sexual double standard, in which guys who have sex get kudos and girls who have sex get shamed, is alive and well, albeit wrapped in a perplexing array of mixed messages.

"If they don't act sexual at all, they might be rejected, but when they act sexual, they get blasted," McHugh said. "And it's not just at that age, but in high school, and even in college."

Often, McHugh said, girls labeled "sluts" aren't even sexually active—bullies simply use the word because they know it works.

"Both boys and girls participate and use the term 'slut' as a way of criticizing people they don't like or who they're mad at," she said.

It's no secret that bullying of any sort is bad for the mental health of victims. Cyberbullying, for example, has been linked with both physical problems such as headaches and psychological problems such as emotional difficulties. And bully-ridden schools tend to be plagued by low test scores, according to an August 2011 study.

"It is serious, and not only in terms of something as devastating as suicide, but also people not doing their best in school to live up to their potential," McHugh said. "They don't apply themselves, or they skip school because they can't bear to be there. [Bullying] has a huge number of consequences for a lot of people."

Source: "Bullies Use Sexual Taunts to Hurt Teen Girls," by Stephanie Pappas, *LiveScience*, November 29, 2011, http://www.livescience.com/17211-teen-bullies-sexual-taunts.html. Reprinted by permission of Tech Media Network.

OUT IN THE COUNTRY

MARY L. GRAY

The Highland Pride Alliance (HPA), a community-based social support group for [rural eastern Kentucky] area lesbian, gay, bisexual, and transgender (LGBT) people and their straight allies, usually met at a member's house or in the basement of a local public county library. Only a few members had homes with the space and welcoming families to accommodate the six to ten regular attendees. No one could host this particular week and another community group had booked the library's meeting room. So, the HPA gathered at Dolly's House, the Christian bookstore across the county line.

Recently, the owner had decided to put some green plastic lawn chairs around carafes of flavored coffee in the store's entryway and call it a café. Dolly's House quickly became a popular youth hangout. Take a few steps past the coffee and you were in the bookstore—a room with several racks of greeting cards, books on tape, and "ready-to-order personalized Bibles." Because this was one of the Wednesday evenings when Dolly's owner closed up early to attend church, the members of the HPA shuffled their meeting to the Gas-n'-Go farther down the highway that cut through the deep river valley they routinely traversed. It was the only place open after 9 P.M. on this stretch of road where the closest town was a mile off the highway exit and had less than 3,000 people. . . .

This time, Shaun, HPA's co-chair and my main contact, was the first of his friends to arrive at the donut shop attached to the Gas-n'-Go. Shaun called to let me know that the meeting had moved and invited me to join them at the new rendezvous point. The talk of next month's HPA Halloween fundraiser turned to casual gossip and chatter regarding this evening's after-meeting plans. They could go back to Tim's place and watch some movies. That was quickly rejected. They spent hours at Tim's last night watching the then recently released (U.S. version of) *Queer as Folk* First Season collection on DVD. Other possibilities were bandied and then dismissed as "too boring" or "too far away." Joe tossed out the idea of heading over to neighboring Springhaven—20 minutes due south—to do some drag at the Wal-Mart. He was dying to try out the fake eyelashes he had bought at the Dollar Tree last weekend. The group's collective uproar of affirming whoops and laughter drew the eyes of two bleached-blond-haired women in their mid-twenties listlessly tending to the donut display case and coffee hot plates. Shaun met their tentative smiles with a large grin and a small princess-atop-a-float wave. Turning back to the group, he giggled and said softly, "Now, settle it down, y'all."

This would not be the group's first foray to the Wal-Mart Supercenter located in the county seat, population just more than 10,000. Within a few months of the Supercenter's grand opening, the HPA had reappropriated Wal-Mart, turning it into a regular gathering spot for their post-meeting social activities. At one point, the HPA website even featured photos snapped of members posing in their most memorable outfits amid Wal-Mart's aisles. The HPA had turned Wal-Mart into a meeting space, drag revue, and shopping excursion all rolled into one.

That these boisterous LGBT-identifying rural young people and their allies move among house parties, public libraries, Christian bookstores, gas stations, Wal-Mart, and websites may seem surprising. I will admit, it surprised me. I had assumed they met exclusively in friends' houses to avoid trouble or hostility from locals. But as I would learn again and again, the everyday lives of rural youth I met complicate simple dichotomies of rural and urban experience or private versus public experiences of queer visibility. I hope that by detailing the work of responding to the expectations a politics of LGBT visibility poses, particularly in an era saturated by gay visibility in the media and via the Internet, I can show that, for the people who live in them, rural communities are more than backdrops or landscapes to late-modern queer subjectivities. If, as feminist geographer Doreen Massey argues, "the social is inexorably also spatial" (Massey 1994, 265), we cannot examine the social relations of power that produce the meaning of LGBT identities without a careful consideration of how locations, rural locales in this case, matter to those relations.[1] . . .

These young people live in communities that lack the human, social, and financial capital to maintain the gay neighborhoods, bookstores, and coffeehouses found in urban settings such as the Castro in San Francisco, New York City's Christopher Street, Chicago's Boystown, or Dupont Circle in Washington, D.C. Nearly all of them live in "dry counties" where alcohol cannot even be sold let alone served in a gay bar. These youth can (and regularly do) travel to gay enclaves in Louisville, Lexington, and Nashville. But they cannot produce in their rural daily lives the sustained infrastructure of visibility that defines urban LGBT communities. Instead, they travel to each other's houses and caravan roundtrip to a larger city with a gay bar or gay-affirming church several hours away. In other words, much as historian John Howard found in his history of queer community for-

mation in rural Mississippi of the 1940s–1980s, rural queer and questioning youth make up for their lack of local numbers and gay-owned spaces by using a strategy of circulation rather than congregation (Howard 1999, 78).[2]

IMAGINING RURAL QUEERNESS

. . . Even historical accounts of the recent rural past paint private house parties as the primary location of queer possibility and community—if any community is imagined possible at all.[3] Drawing on popular documentaries screened at LGBT film festivals in the first few years of the twenty-first century, historian John Howard argues that rural LGBT lives are marked not by violence or isolation, but by "mundane, everyday trade-offs" such as "fewer public displays of affection, a greater feeling of rootedness, less pride in outness, more of a sense of safety" (Howard 2006, 101–102). As Howard notes, hate crimes directed at LGBT people are more often perpetrated by groups of men who use the safety of their numbers to single out victims living in dense urban areas (Howard, 2006, 101–102). Although LGBT-related hate crimes are not nationally recorded and systematically tracked, studies of rural crime patterns suggest that violence directed at queer difference in rural spaces (an issue I will return to at the end of this chapter) is different from, though statistically no greater than, the violence cities exact.[4] Contrary to popular representations and presumptions drawn from historical accounts, today's rural youth do not (arguably cannot) privately suffer an endemic estrangement or isolation from queer subjectivities. The trickle of denigrating national press accounts of "the homosexual lifestyle" that began in the mid-1960s presaged a veritable flood of gay visibility.[5] Rural youth in the United States have unprecedented access to national media markets. These markets saturate them in a politics of LGBT visibility that demands public recognition. Seeking acknowledgment as lesbian, gay, bisexual, or transgender means grappling with these demands no matter where one lives. Rural youth must respond to the call for LGBT visibility that structures their feelings of authenticity amid vastly underfunded, rural public spaces that prioritize allegiance to familiarity and solidarity over public claims to difference of any kind. . . .

Dragging It Up at Wal-Mart

A bright, neon archway flickering "always low prices, always food center"—hovers above the entrance to the Springhaven, Kentucky, Wal-Mart Supercenter. The blue-trimmed, one-story building starts at stoplight 14 and spans an eroding stretch of state highway that bisects the town. On this Sunday evening, young men and women hold hands and roam through the aisles. Aside from a few young Latino families, most customers are white and speak with the low, slow drawl of Southern accents.

The Supercenter has nearly 100 aisles, from a full grocery on one end to pet supplies and beauty products on the other. Rows of fabric bolts spill out of their display bins. A range of household appliances, an electronic wedding registry kiosk, floor rugs, and an extensive work-boot collection crowd the West Entrance. Monitors above the aisles blare advertisements from the DisneyHealth Network produced for Wal-Mart hawking products in between snippets of music videos. University of Kentucky logo-wear easily fills a 9-foot-by-12-foot space. There's an eatery to the right of the automated superstore double doors. Smokers fill the red and white tables, savoring their last cigarette drags before entering the smoke-free discount merchandiser that has been in this strip mall for 18 months.

The Springhaven Wal-Mart is the only business open 24 hours within an 80-mile radius. I found out about the popularity of this Wal-Mart when I asked Clay, a local teen, what he and his friends did for fun. "Most gay people around the county, we all go to Hardee's or the new Backyard Burgers." He added casually, "And then most people all haul up together in big carloads, put on some drag, runway walk the Super Wal-Mart in Springhaven and walk around for about five hours with people almost having heart attacks and conniption fits cause we're running around. . . . We take pictures of us all, post them to the website, and have fun with our little getaway from living in rural Kentucky."

When I asked other area youth about their experiences at Wal-Mart, they confirmed that performing drag in the superstore's aisles was a rite of passage for those entering the local gay scene. Joe recalled his initiation this way: "The first time I was with them, we all put on these furry jackets and we was walking through the aisles. That was fun. Me and all my friends, we all gather up several cars all the time, and now we go once or twice a month. We all just huddle up together and run up there." With the exception of a few young people working night shifts at factories or fast-food chains, Highland Pride Alliance members attended drag nights at Wal-Mart as regularly as they attended the group's more formal organizational meetings.

When asked to describe why they chose Wal-Mart, most of the young people couldn't remember, nor did they understand my surprise. To them, the Wal-Mart Supercenter seemed an obvious place to hang out. As Shaun put it, "Why wouldn't we go there?! It's the best place to find stuff to do drag. They've got all the wigs and makeup and tight clothes and stuff." Then he added, "Besides, no matter how much we bug people doing what we're doing, we're still customers too. And we have friends who work there who won't let nothing happen to us if they see any trouble start." Contrary to the anonymity Wal-Mart and other so-called big box stores might provide in the suburbs of metropolitan areas, HPA members do not experience this space as anonymous. It is their own backyard after all, and there are few options this close to where they live.

Beyond the makeshift runways and basic drag gear found in Wal-Mart's aisles, the mega-chain's national guidelines that situate its customers as "guests" also facilitate youth doing drag in its stores. As long as these young people are still readable as consumer citizens, the logic of capital cannot bar them from this queer twist on the public square. Plus, Wal-Mart's (then recent) instatement of domestic-partner benefits for employees signaled that Wal-Mart was, as Clay put it, "a tolerant place where they could expect to be accepted." Unlike their public school experiences, which were described by many as a "living hell," Wal-Mart stood out as a safe public space where they would be protected.

Part of Something Bigger

Gay rights organizations dot the rural landscape. One finds chapters of nationally organized non-profits, like PFLAG and the Gay, Lesbian and Straight Education Network. . . . One also finds statewide and regionally based groups, such as the Kentucky Fairness Alliance (KFA) and the Highland Pride Alliance. Each organization draws capital investments from donors and then circulates resources in time, training, and visibility to local residents—including youth in this study—interested in connecting to a broader community of organizers.

Rural youth seeking terrain for their queer-identity work can find fertile ground in not-for-profit organizations. . . . As one 17-year-old gay-identifying man put it, "Going to PFLAG or KFA's Lobby Days in [the State Capitol in] Frankfort and meetings and stuff like that makes me feel like I've got a whole big gay extended family out there . . . like I'm part of something bigger even when nothing's really happening in my own town." For many youth

this means taking advantage of a ready-made structure that includes things like banners, e-mail addresses, listings on national websites and directories, and an imagined network of like-minded allies and friends.

Locally grown groups with overlapping membership in these offshoots and branches of national or regional organizations are equally important. The Highland Pride Alliance, for example, has existed for nearly a decade.[6] Most members are white, gay or nonidentifying and range in age from late teens to forty-something men. All of them come from four surrounding counties. Some members found out about the group from someone they met while hanging out (or cruising) at the local state park. Others were clued in by the group's reputation or, increasingly, the group's website.

When I met Shaun, he was the driving force behind the group. When he joined the HPA two years earlier, it consisted mostly of local white men interested in quiet social gatherings. Period. They met at each other's homes and did their best to keep out of the public eye. But Shaun was 17 and stinging from harassment in public high school. He wasn't about to "go back to meeting secretly." "What was the point?" he said. In his town of 2,100, everyone knew he was gay. If they didn't know it from the common gossip of the schoolyard, they heard it from a popular Baptist minister who was once a close friend of Shaun's. . . .

Shaun instigated many of HPA's activities, such as meetings at the public library, involvement in rallies supporting a distant rural high school's efforts to form a Gay-Straight Alliance, and plans to bring the first "Meals on Wheels" service for people with AIDS to the region with support from AIDS Volunteers of Lexington. Shaun saw the building up of the HPA and its relationships to statewide groups as vital to creating opportunities for all local LGBT people. . . .

Bashing at the Wal-Mart

What follows is an account of drag gone awry in Springhaven. HPA members noted that turning the aisles of a regional Wal-Mart Supercenter into a boundary public for drag performance was fun and, to them, safe. They felt their status as "guests" could shield them from any direct harassment. They also presumed that friends who worked at Wal-Mart would intervene and protect them by asserting their positions as the default authority of this milieu. But there was also a sense of belonging that permeated their temporary occupations of these privatized zones. "This is my hometown," Clay commented. "I know a lot of the folks coming in and out of the store already. . . . I know who to steer clear of." . . .

"Maybe they thought my lipstick was too loud," Shaun giggled. "I mean really, why should they care? I wasn't hurting anyone." A month earlier, a dozen or more HPA members and their friends—ranging from 16-year-old Chris to Phillip, who had just celebrated his twenty-third birthday—sashayed through the Wal-Mart like they had on so many nights before. Typically, HPA drag nights elicited no more than occasional stares, but this time things were different.

After trying on a tight girl's T-shirt glittered with the words "Star Gazer" across the chest, Shaun walked out of the men's fitting room to find himself face-to-face with a boy from his old high school. Sneering, the boy growled, "What are you doing in the wrong dressing room, faggot?" Shaun pushed past the boy, as he had so many times before in the school hallways, rolling his eyes and clicking his tongue, "Tisst! Whaaat . . . evverr!" while nervously scanning the aisle for his friend, Clay, whom he found in the makeup section "trying on 'Shades of Passion' for the umpteenth time." Shaun and Clay gathered up as many HPA folks as they could find and headed for the checkout counter. They assumed one of their friends was working her usual shift but were informed by the young man staffing her register that she had unexpectedly taken the night off.

Shaun and Clay's voices filled with frustration and exhaustion as they recalled what happened next. "He was just a big ol' redneck with nothing better to do than give us a hard time, that's all," Clay said. Shaun added, "It wasn't anything that wouldn't or didn't happen at school . . . difference was, I thought my friend was working that night . . . she would've put him in his place." Instead, the 17-year-old boy followed the HPA youth out to the parking lot and yelled every epithet he could conjure. An older man exiting the store told the harasser to settle down, but the young man paid no attention. No one from the store intervened. Shaun yelled, "We're not hurting no one!" and then saw two more of his old high school nemeses approaching. Rather than continue the exchange, Shaun and his friends sauntered to their cars and piled in to them for the drive home.

The next day, Shaun took down the photos of HPA's Wal-Mart drag extravaganzas, as well as pictures of equally fabulous outings to the town square, from the group's website. When I asked him why he no longer wanted the photos of his friends in their tight minis and platinum wigs on the HPA homepage, he paused and said, "I just don't know if it's safe to have those up there. Someone we don't know could see them. . . . I guess I don't want anyone getting bashed because some narrow-minded homophobe from out of town saw a picture of us up there and thought we had taken things too far."

Some could read the HPA member's initial feelings of entitlement to their surroundings as an implicit assertion of their racial privilege as white young men. They anticipate moving through their surroundings without the scrutinizing that might, say, be cast on the one Latino youth who was new to the HPA.

Members of the HPA see their harassment as a response to the ways they trouble expectations and norms of their male privilege. They categorically liken it to the chiding young women receive for walking through the stores: "I know I've seen girls given a hard way because they don't dress all proper and they might be having fun, being loud. If someone's mad at me, it's because I'm being too girly—that's what being gay means to them anyways . . . that I'm being a girl." The notion of homosexuality as gender inversion persists in these communities much as it does in popular culture despite generations of gay and lesbian organizing to distance itself from the intersectionality of sexuality and gender.[7] Publicly disrupting normative gender expectations arguably remains as, if not more, contentious than homoerotic desires.

HPA youth threaten an unspoken agreement to "live and let live" when they visibly assert themselves as readable gay subjects. But they seem to break tentative, unspoken rules of occupying the boundaries of public spaces when they visibly stray too far afield from their status as familiar gay locals and become ambiguous queer objects that undo expectations of what it means to be a young man in the community. Their tentative feelings of safety are rattled more by how they challenge gender norms than by the implicitness of their sexual identities.

The mixed-class backgrounds of these youth, which range from white collar to working poor, also complicate access to a presumed privilege. The youth felt dragging it up at the Wal-Mart was more of a right than a risk. But several youth were aware that their status as "gay" would be compromised if they actually admitted to shopping for clothes at Wal-Mart, even though it's what they could afford. As Dale, a 21-year-old from Eastern Kentucky, put it, shopping at Wal-Mart is "just not gay enough." He is a student at a small Christian college. He is on financial aid and works part-

time to help support his mother and younger sister. He can only afford to buy clothes at Wal-Mart. "Sometimes it's such a burden to be gay nowadays," he lamented:

. . . because you're expected to know everything. They [his straight-identifying college friends] come to you. Well, you're gay, what do you think about this outfit? I'm, like, "I'm not that kind of gay! I may sound like I'm that kind of gay." I'm, like, "Look at me! I'm wearing Wal-Mart clothes! My entire outfit comes from Wal-Mart! Everything! I did not spend 40 bucks on this entire thing, and you're asking me about fashion!" They're, like, "But you're gay!" I'm, like, "So?! I'm a badly dressed gay man. I admit it. I embrace it. Leave me alone. Let me do my clearance aisles at Wal-Mart."

. . . Not being able to afford the consumptive markers of gay identity left Dale and his working-class peers shaken in their sense of self-identity. Alongside vicious verbal attacks lobbed in store parking lots or in school classrooms, LGBT visibility's commodification and its demanding consumer pressures posed considerable challenges to the queer-identity work of working poor kids like Dale. . . .

NEW MEDIA LANDSCAPES

. . . It is tempting to assume that the Internet and other digital media offer something entirely new to rural queer and questioning youth. But the experiences of rural youth indicate a different direction for such analyses. For these young people, new media were imagined as both a supplement to local queer-identity work and an integrated part of this local occupation. Youth didn't use new media as hideouts from the real world. . . .

As discussed earlier, Shaun quickly took down photos chronicling HPA's drag excursions after what members referred to as "the bashing at Wal-Mart." He was sad and reluctant to remove the pictures at first. Shaun was proud that he had not only taken the snapshots but also learned how to crop the images and post them to the HPA website. But after the HPA received hate e-mail through the website's interactive guestbook a few days after the heated exchange in the Wal-Mart parking lot, he thought it needed to be done.

As the person responsible for sifting through e-mail coming in from the website, Shaun bore the brunt of these comments. One was the ALL CAPS standard, "I HATE FAGGOTS. KISS MY STRAIGHT ASS." The other told the HPA that they "were welcome to have their sexuality but it was disrespectful to hang all over each other and put pictures up on the website of this" (referring to photos on the HPA website of the group dragging it up at the Springhaven Wal-Mart and around the town square a different weekend). The e-mail went on to say "they should have some respect for the county."

Although there was no need for more than one person to monitor the HPA account, Shaun wished someone else would have read the e-mails first. "It just made me so mad and sad all over again! . . . I know these people are probably the same ones we ran into—and that means it's my fault that we're getting these hate mails." Both e-mail messages referenced Rust Falls—Shaun's hometown—building his suspicion that they were likely connected to the young men from high school he confronted that night. The irony is perhaps that the author/s of these e-mails saw the HPA website as reflective of their community and a kind of public that needs monitoring. The e-mails also suggest there is room for the HPA's sexuality, indicating the quiet, if begrudging, acceptance Shaun and his friends felt in their communities. . . .

CONCLUSION

Media coverage of the 1993 New Year's Eve murder of Brandon Teena, a young female-to-male transperson, in rural Nebraska and the even greater swell of reporting and public out-

rage that followed the 1998 killing of a young gay man named Matthew Shepard in Wyoming emphasized the brutality of their deaths against a backdrop of the rural communities in which they were killed.[8] As Judith Halberstam observes, "The varied responses to the tragic murders of these two young white, rural queers have much to tell us about selective memorialization and political activism, space and sexual identity, and the mobilization of trauma" (Halberstam 2005, 17). There is much to unpack regarding the different treatments and degrees of culpability placed on these young people's bodies, most notably the relative political silence in 1993 around Brandon Teena's rape and murder compared to national vigils and outcries for gay-inclusive hate crime reforms that immediately followed Shepard's brutal murder. However, in both cases, news and film narratives placed Brandon and Matthew as young queers in the wrong place at the wrong time. Small-town, working-poor America was put on trial as horrific scenes of intolerance.[9] . . .

Ethnographic studies of queerness in rural communities suggest that cities and rural areas are differently (incomparably perhaps) intolerant toward queer difference. Shaun and other HPA members are constant reminders to their fellow rural residents that structures of familiarity are vulnerable as much from locals as from strangers. Rural communities manage the perceived threats of difference in myriad ways. They may attempt to excise queer difference, as in the case of threats of violence to HPA members outside Wal-Mart . . . or the bombardment of the HPA website with hate e-mail. Alternatively, community members might make appeals to the local status of their queerly different neighbors in an effort to maintain the fragile structures that organize the mythos of familiarity in rural life.

Lest I seem to offer a rosy picture of the oppression of queer difference in rural areas, let me reiterate: the examples of harassment explored above reflect the realities of violence in rural communities. But this violence is notably most often experienced as intimate, exacted by those these youth presume they know rather than the random acts of property destruction or "stranger danger" that pervades the psyches of most queer urban dwellers bashed outside populous city nightclubs.[10] The one critical advantage Shaun saw to the distinct quality of violence that permeates his community was that, as he put it, "I know who I need to avoid. I've been working to steer clear of those people all my life." Years later, Shaun underscored this point in a conversation with me about media representations of gay people living in rural places and, specifically, the movie *Brokeback Mountain*.

Shaun felt a certain dissonance watching Hollywood depictions of foreboding rural communities and their hapless queer inhabitants. He found Ang Lee's Academy Award–winning 2005 film about rural Wyoming cowboy lovers (Jack and Ennis) in particular "just ridiculous." When I asked him why, he seemed exasperated that he had to explain what seemed so obvious to him. "It just didn't make any sense! People in small towns don't go around killing people who have lived there all their lives [referring to the plotline that connects Ennis' fear of living with Jack to childhood memories of the brutal murder of male lovers in his hometown and, later, Jack's murder by a faceless mob]." Shaun then added, "Jack and Ennis could have lived together quietly . . . anyone who lives in a small town knows about couples or relatives like that. You know how to avoid trouble if you've lived in a place long enough." Ultimately, it was *Brokeback Mountain's* representation of isolation and unpredictable mob violence lurking around the bend that seemed most at odds with Shaun's own sense of conditional safety traveling around the boundaries of his community. It wasn't that violence couldn't happen. Indeed,

Shaun had experienced persistent verbal and sometimes physical harassment through much of his high school years at the hands of longtime, childhood friends. But for Shaun, it seemed unfathomable that such extreme violence would be exacted by a mob of people you considered neighbors. Violence inflicted by loved ones was a much more familiar scenario but, through its familiarity, seemed easier to predict and circumvent. Violence wrought by strangers in rural communities would not go unnoticed or unchecked and therefore seemed more out of place.

In the end, Shaun decided to remove HPA's photos of drag at the Wal-Mart not because he feared retribution from local "troublemakers." In fact, much like the folk belief that the most vehement homophobes are queers in disguise, Shaun assumed anyone he knew "making hay was probably gay." His greater concern was that strangers might happen to find the photos and zero in on the HPA as an easy target. . . .

. . . The study of how rural youth put new media technologies to use illustrates that what counts as public and private is evolving and shifting. In looking at this disruption, we also see the politicization of what is relegated to the realm of the public sphere and what is considered the domain of private matters. When sexualities and gender identities are framed as matters of privacy, we are prone to overlook the realities of how people use public spaces for the expressions of their private selves. Publics are vital to our experiences of the private. Rural places send up the realities of this intermixture because there is so little public infrastructure to work with, so little raw material with which to parse out the private from the public. . . .

Youth have very different access to publics and therefore relationships to privacy. Queer youth do make space for themselves. Doing so is a necessary part of their identity work as they attempt to meet the expectations of the politics of visibility that demand public recognition. This work can and does happen in surprising places in rural communities. The above examples illustrate how rural youth who identify as lesbian, gay, bisexual, and transgender or question sexual and gender norms craft a tentative yet often vibrant sense of visibility. . . . Their move . . . is a complicated response to an overall lack of public spaces in rural communities that cannot be flattened into a more personal, psychological need or desire to "be closeted" or to some imagined sense that rural communities are inherently more hostile to queer identities. Yes, they accomplish this through the use of websites and other new media technologies, but they also commandeer publics available to them. Websites, Wal-Mart, punk music, listservs, public library meeting rooms, and church skate parks are the resources available to them. They make do. They get by. . . .

NOTES

1. Doreen Massey, *Space, Place, and Gender* (Minneapolis, MN:University of Minnesota Press, 1994.

2. John Howard, "Of Closets and other Rural Voids," *GLQ: A Journal of Gay and Lesbian Studies* 13 no.1 (2006).

3. James T. Sears, *Rebels, Rubyfruit, and Rhinestones: Queering Space in the Stonewall South* (New Brunswick, NJ: Rutgers University Press, 2001); Will Fellows, *Farm Boys: Lives of Gay Men from the Rural Midwest* (Madison: University of Wisconsin Press, 1996); and for an important exception and complication, see John Howard, *Men Like That: A Southern Queer History* (Chicago: University of Chicago Press, 1999).

4. On rural crime rates that report that "intimate violence"—between relatives and longtime acquaintances—is more consistent with rates of random violence in urban centers whereas rural communities report far less crime around property, see the work of Cynthia Barnett and F. Carson Mencken, "Social Disorganization Theory and the Contextual Nature of Crime in Nonmetropolitan Counties," *Rural Sociology* 67, no.3 (2002): 372–93; and Matthew R. Lee, Michael O.Maume, and Graham C. Ousey, "Social Isolation and Lethal Violence across the Metro/Nonmetro Divide: The Effects of Socioeconomic Disadvantage and Poverty Concentration on Homicide," *Rural Sociology* 68, no. 1 (2003): 107–31.

5. See Larry P. Gross,*Up from Invisibility: Lesbians, Gay Men, and the Media in America*, Between Men—Between Women (New York: Columbia University Press, 2001),

233; Suzanna Danuta Walters, *All the Rage: The Story of Gay Visibility in America* (Chicago: University of Chicago Press, 2001); Katherine Sender, "Sex Sells: Sex, Class, and Taste in Commercial Gay and Lesbian Media," *GLQ: A Journal of Gay and Lesbian Studies* 9, no.3 (2003): 331–65; and Katherine Sender, *Business, Not Politics: The Making of the Gay Market*, Between Men—Between Women (New York: Columbia University Press, 2004). See also Martin Meeker, *Contacts Desired: Gay and Lesbian Communications and Community, 1940s–1970s* (Chicago: University of Chicago Press, 2006).

6. There is a rich scholarly literature in anthropology and sociology that examines peer networks and their role in the social construction and expansion of gay and lesbian "communities." For example, see Murray on the meaning of "community" and his convincing argument that if "community" is a sociologically viable category, gays and lesbians typify it through their collective action, shared sense of territoriality, and reliance on friends as a primary group. In Stephen O. Murray, *American Gay*, Worlds of Desire (Chicago: University of Chicago Press, 1996), 182–214. On friendship networks and their role as fundamental units of support, see David Woolwine, "Community in Gay Male Experience and Moral Discourse." *Journal of Homosexuality* 38, no. 4 (2000): 5–37.

7. See Susan Stryker on the history of this effort by early and contemporary gay- and lesbian-rights organizing in San Francisco, in particular in "Transgender History, Homonormativity, and Disciplinarity," *Radical History Review* 100 (Winter 2008): 150. See also David Valentine's recent critique of gay and lesbian social-service organizations that maintain a policing among categories of gay, lesbian, bi, and trans, often denying clients' sense of the interconnectedness of their gender and sexual modalities. In David Valentine, *Imagining Transgender: An Ethnography of a Category* (Durham, NC: Duke University Press, 2007).

8. In fact, the U.S. House of Representatives voted to pass legislation called the Matthew Shepard Act to expand existing federal hate-crime laws authorizing the Department of Justice to investigate and prosecute bias-motivated crimes based on the victim's actual or perceived sexual orientation, gender, gender identity, or disability. Current law only includes race, color, religion or national origin; eliminates the restrictions currently in place that limit federal involvement to cases in which a victim of a bias-motivated crime was attacked because he/she was engaged in a specified federally protected activity such as voting, serving on a jury or attending school; and adds "gender" and "gender identity" to the Hate Crimes Statistics Act to keep national statistics on LGBT-related hate crimes. For more on the discussion of hate crimes, see Judith Butler, *Excitable Speech: Contemporary Scenes of Politics* (New York: Routledge,

1997); for reading on hate crimes and their relationship to the Shepard murder, see Beth Loffreda, *Losing Matt Shepard: Life and Politics in the Aftermath of Anti-Gay Murder* (New York: Columbia University Press, 2000).

9. See Lisa Henderson, "The Class Character of *Boys Don't Cry*," *Screen* 42, no. 3 (2001): 299–303; and Judith

Halberstam, *In a Queer Time and Place: Transgender Bodies, Subcultural Lives*, Sexual Cultures (New York: New York University Press, 2005): 22–46.

10. Again, see the work of Barnett and Mencken, "Social Disorganization," 372–93; and Lee, Maume, and Ousey, "Social Isolation and Lethal Violence," 107–31.

LGBTQ Politics in America: An Abbreviated History

Chet Meeks and Marik Xavier-Brier

The lesbian, gay, bisexual, transgender, queer (LGBTQ) community has been the target of systematic, institutionalized forms of regulation in American society since at least the middle of the twentieth century. This means that LGBTQ people are not merely discriminated against by particular individuals, but that a social norm making heterosexuality superior is embedded in and informs the logics of all of America's core social institutions: the state, the criminal justice system, the media, education, and the family. American social institutions have worked to make any sexuality deviating from the heterosexual norm criminal and deviant. When a group of individuals is systematically regulated in such a way, they sometimes organize to create social changes in the areas of law, public opinion, or social policy. Sometimes they try to revolutionize how we think of and practice sex itself. This is what we mean by "sexual politics," and here we offer an abbreviated history of LGBTQ politics in America.

The first rumblings of LGBTQ resistance could be felt in the 1950s. Harry Hay and Rudi Gernreich organized a group called the Mattachine Society, which primarily focused on the interests of gay men. At almost the same time, Del Martin and Phyllis Lyon organized the Daughters of Bilitis, which primarily focused on the needs of lesbians. Some other groups were ONE and The Society for Individual Rights. These early groups called themselves "homophile" organizations. They emerged in response to the state-sponsored harassment and criminalization of homosexuality in America. America in the 1950s was a place where homosexuality, like communism, had come to be associated with evil and moral bankruptcy. Homophile organizations were fledgling groups, and only ever partially visible in the mainstream public sphere. They spoke through heterosexual proxies, like tolerant doctors or lawyers, in order to make their case about a given issue. Homophile groups had some successes, though. For example ONE sued the American postal service in 1958 for refusing to mail their monthly magazine. But in reality, a strong, vocal, and truly organized LGBTQ politics did not really get underway until the late 1960s.

On June 28, 1969, a brawl broke out between New York City police officers and some drag queens at a Greenwich Village bar called the Stonewall Inn. The Stonewall riots marked the beginning of a new era in LGBTQ politics. From the spirit of rebellion at Stonewall, two

LGBTQ organizations were born: The Gay Liberation Front (GLF) and The Gay Activist Alliance (GAA). Although these organizations are no longer around, the spirit and worldview that animated their respective political actions remain very much present in contemporary forms of LGBTQ struggle.

The GLF was organized by Martha Shelley, Craig Rodwell, and Jim Fourrat three weeks after the Stonewall riots. As their name suggests, the GLF espoused a liberationist worldview. According to liberationists, America is a society that systematically demonizes, criminalizes, and ghettoizes all forms of sexual and gender expression that do not conform to a very narrow standard of heterosexual "normality." Struggle and resistance, in a world like this, cannot be limited to demanding civil rights, reform, or tolerance. Rather, revolution—sexual revolution in particular—is the only viable option. Borrowing an idea from feminism, liberationists argued that "the personal is political," and they believed that only by transforming sexuality could the broader social fabric be revolutionized. They encouraged their members to experiment with new forms of "liberated" sexuality and social relationships— like non-monogamy and communal living. Liberationists, moreover, viewed the plight of LGBTQ people as indelibly linked to the problems faced by Black Americans, "third world" people and refugees, victims of American and European military aggression, and members of the working class. They struggled alongside the Black Panthers and critics of the Vietnam War, demanding justice for all oppressed people.

Although the GAA emerged at nearly the same time and in the same political climate as the GLF, they possessed a worldview that was very different from that of the liberationists. They did not believe that the plight faced by lesbians and gay men was necessarily linked to other forms of oppression, like race or class status. Neither did they believe that American society was systematically anti-queer, in the way suggested by liberationists. Rather, they believed that, at its core, America was a tolerant and just society, one that had successfully integrated a large number of minority groups. American institutions, they argued, are copious and open to change. The problem was that this tolerance had not yet been extended to lesbians, gay men, transgender people, and bisexuals.

Sexual revolution was not the answer, according to the GAA. They were not liberationists, but assimilationists. They believed that tolerance and respect for LGBTQ people had to be won through the slow, incremental reform of existing institutions. Assimilationists believe rights are granted through respectability and espouse ideas of "we're just like you" to the heterosexual community. They believe that, just as Black Americans and women had fought to gain civil rights reforms in the 1960s and 1970s, lesbians and gay men must fight to be recognized as respectable Americans. They fought to pass civil rights ordinances in cities like New York. Unlike the liberationists, they focused much less on the sexual lives of activists themselves, and they eschewed attempts to connect lesbian and gay justice to the struggles of other groups.

Although the GLF and the GAA have long since disbanded, the worldviews that animated their activism are very much alive. The liberationist worldview was reborn in the radical sexual politics of the 1980s and 1990s, in groups like Act-Up and Queer Nation. The Reagan Administration of the 1980s had completely ignored the growing AIDS epidemic, largely because gay men were the most visible victims of the disease. Also, large pharmaceutical companies were making the drugs used to treat AIDS symptoms so expensive that only the very wealthy could afford them. Against this stifling climate, Act-Up shouted "Silence equals Death," and against the growing stigmatization of gay and queer people due to AIDS, Queer

Nation shouted "We're Here, We're Queer, Get Used to It!" Like their assimilationist counterparts, Act-Up and Queer Nation linked notions of social revolution to self-transformation. Yet they believed that nothing would ever truly change until queer people had put an end to "straight tyranny," which has become known as heteronormativity. Heteronormativity sets heterosexuality as normative. It establishes same-sex relationships as bad or deviant and restricts gender identity, gender roles, and sexuality. Heteronormative culture is one that fosters a climate of discrimination against LGBTQ people in all social institutions.

While the GAA no longer exists, their goal of assimilation remains central to many of the most visible contemporary LGBTQ organizations. Coming to power largely in the 1990s, the Human Rights Campaign (HRC), the Lambda Legal Defense and Education Fund (Lambda), and the Gay and Lesbian Alliance Against Defamation (GLAAD) all borrow from the worldview of the GAA. The Human Rights Campaign has become an extremely successful lobbying organization in Washington, DC. It has over one million members and supporters, and the organization lobbies Congress continually for Federal hate crimes legislation and other legal reforms to make LGBTQ people safe and equal citizens. Both the HRC and Lambda have been making inroads in the fight toward lesbian and gay equality in the arena of marriage. In 1993, Lambda was the first organization to successfully take a marriage lawsuit to a state Supreme Court in the famous *Baehr v. Lewin* case in Hawaii. In response, a few years later, Congress passed the Defense of Marriage Act (DOMA), defining marriage as limited to one man and one woman with no state having to recognize a same-sex marriage that another state did. Since then, there have been dozens of court cases fighting to repeal DOMA. Starting in 2004, Massachusetts became the first state to

recognize same-sex marriage, and as of 2013, thirteen states and the District of Columbia recognize and grant marriage licenses to same-sex couples. In July 2013, the U.S. Supreme Court struck down part of DOMA. However, while headway has been made toward marriage equality, there are still seven states that prohibit marriage via statutory bans and 29 via amendments to their state constitutions. In terms of the media, GLAAD was declared by *Entertainment Weekly* to be one of the most successful media organizations in the country. GLAAD came into existence in an era when LGBTQ people were only vilified on television and in the media, when they were represented at all. Today, the GLAAD awards (given for fair, accurate, and positive portrayals of LGBTQ people) are coveted by many of Hollywood's most elite actors, actresses, directors, and producers. Mainstream LGBTQ organizations have also been successful in overturning the long standing "Don't Ask, Don't Tell" policy of the U.S. military in 2010, so now gays and lesbians can serve openly in the military. Many believe that this will start a ripple effect for other gay-rights issues, as many states continue to debate issues on same-sex marriage and other rights for gay partners such as hospital visitation, adoption, and health benefits.

Counter to the goals of assimilation, LGBTQ people who take a more liberationist stance have recently been arguing that assimilationists are colluding with the structures of heteronormativity; these liberationists use the term "homonormativity" to describe gays and lesbians that focus on monogamy, procreation, and traditional gender identity. Liberationists speak out against mainstream politics and seek to destabilize social institutions, power structures, and the gender binary. This split inevitably establishes a hierarchy within the gay community that is centered on the level of subscription to a mainstream presentation and values. We see that today, even while there are still debates about how the LGBTQ community believes they should be granted rights (whether through assimilationist or liberationist methods), ultimately both groups are striving for the same outcome, the end of discrimination and prejudice that keeps LGBTQ people second-class citizens.

A lot has changed in American society since the 1950s and 1960s, when the postal service refused to carry LGBTQ publications, when cities like New York still had laws requiring that everyone wear at least "three articles of gender appropriate clothing," and when police would frequently raid bars like the Stonewall Inn in order to harass their patrons. We live in the world where we see more gay characters on television, more "out" gay members in government, and court cases overturning unconstitutional laws. LGBTQ inequality nonetheless persists, as does heteronormativity, even if in more subtle forms. LGBTQ people still face violence in their everyday lives, and second-class status in most areas of social policy. In 2011, according to the Federal Bureau of Investigation, law enforcement agencies reported 1,572 hate-crime offenses based on sexual orientation. And anti-discriminatory policies such as the Employment Non-Discrimination Act (ENDA) remain unpassed and stuck in congressional committees. Currently, only 17 states and the District of Columbia have policies protecting employees from discrimination on the basis of sexual orientation and gender identity and only an additional four states have laws prohibiting discrimination based on sexual orientation. It will be up to tomorrow's LGBTQ political organizations to tackle these problems—but in doing so, they will likely borrow from the tactics and worldviews of their historical predecessors.

"HOW COULD YOU DO THIS TO ME?": HOW LESBIAN, BISEXUAL, AND QUEER LATINAS NEGOTIATE SEXUAL IDENTITY WITH THEIR FAMILIES

KATIE ACOSTA

Latina/o studies scholars have explored the role of sexuality in Latina/o familial relationships (Espin, 1997; Hurtado, 2003; Gonzalez-Lopez, 2005; Zavella, 2003). Yet this work has predominantly focused on familial tensions regarding heterosexual sexuality and virginity. In this [reading], I explore the unique tensions that sexual nonconformity creates in Latina families by exploring the complex relationships that lesbian, bisexual, and queer (LBQ) Latinas have with their families of origin. I describe how disclosure and nondisclosure of one's sexual identity changes these women's relationships with their families. The questions driving this article are: What strategies do first- and second-generation Latinas use when negotiating sexual nonconformity with their families? How do age, economic autonomy, and geographic location affect these relationships? How do these women minimize the risk of rejection from families?

I propose that sexually nonconforming Latinas' relationships with family cannot be placed into simple categories of acceptance or rejection. I offer three distinct interaction strategies that study participants report engaging in with their families of origin: (1) erasure of nonconformity, (2) sexual silencing, and (3) avoidance after disclosure. *Erasure of nonconformity* occurs when the respondent discloses her lesbian, bisexual, or queer identity to her family and they in turn try to erase it by using control and manipulation tactics. *Sexual silencing* is a strategy used by respondents who chose not to disclose their sexuality and instead are complicit with their family members in pretending

their relationships with women are platonic friendships. Even though there is no disclosure with the silencing strategy, respondents believe everyone is silently aware of their same-sex relationships. Last, the *avoidance after disclosure* strategy occurs when the respondents do disclose their lesbian, bisexual, or queer identity to family members and then become complicit with them in rendering the disclosure unheard. With this strategy, families and participants choose to separate the sexual nonconformity completely from family life. This strategy is different from the silencing strategy because it involves direct communication about the sexual nonconformity followed by a clear rejection. This strategy is also distinct from the erasure strategy because with avoidance, the respondents and their families are complicit in separating the lesbian, bisexual, or queer self from family life whereas with the erasure strategy the participants do not have that choice. . . .

FAMILISM AND NEGOTIATING SEXUALITY IN *LA FAMILIA*

Scholars have established that familism, a concept that emphasizes loyalty, solidarity, and interdependence with family, is very important for Mexican populations and vital to their survival as immigrants in the United States (Baca-Zinn, 1982). Familism has been recognized as a core value for other Latino groups as well (Vega, 1995). However, Latinos are not monolithically familistic in their values, and familism is not unique to Latina/o populations. The values of familism may vary greatly according to class, generation in the United States, and immigrant status. . . .

The values of familism are (1) familial support, the belief that one must support family in their time of need; (2) familial interconnectedness, the belief that family must remain physically and emotionally close when possible; (3) familial honor, the belief that the individual is responsible for preserving the family name; and (4) subjugation of self for family, the belief that an individual must respect family rules (Lugo-Steidel and Contrerars, 2003). *La familia*, however, does not just consist of a mother, father, and children but very often includes aunts and uncles, grandparents, compadres/coparents, and padrinos/godparents (Suarez-Orozeo, 2002). *La familia*, then, is crucial in shaping experience. When it comes to sexuality, the role of *la familia* is particularly vital. The family has the ability to control and shape Latinas' sexual or romantic relationships, and mothers in particular are the enforcers of sexual morality and heterosexuality (Gonzalez-Lopez, 2005).

Latinas sometimes grow up experiencing silence regarding sexuality, changes in their bodies, and same-sex attractions (Carillo, 2002; Zavella, 2003). What messages they do receive are heteronormative in nature, emphasizing virginity, purity, and saving oneself for marriage (Espin, 1997; Hurtado, 2003). In a study of Puerto Rican and Dominican families, Diane Mckee and Allison Karasz (2006) found that while both mothers and daughters valued two-way open communication regarding sex, sexuality, and nurturing *confianza*, both were apprehensive about participating in these conversations (Mckee and Karasz, 2006). Their hesitancy to initiate these conversations resulted in sexual silencing. Among some Latina groups,

sexual silences are combined with messages of empowerment through education and independence from men (Ayala, 2006). Still, while some Latinas are encouraged to empower themselves and not become distracted by the needs of men, the silences around relationships with women prevail. Socially acceptable intimacy among Latinas can include sharing *consejos* or advice and care work and physical displays of affection. Yet while these intimate female bonds are encouraged, lesbianism is still stigmatized (Espin, 1997; Zavella, 1997). . . .

THEORETICAL FRAMEWORK

This article utilizes a dramaturgical perspective to analyze lesbian, bisexual, and queer Latinas' social interactions with their families. Erving Goffman notes that in our everyday lives we present ourselves to others based on our internalized understandings of cultural values and social expectations in order to gain acceptance from others. In this way, we manage the impressions of ourselves that we give off to others and behave as performers of a role. Others, however, are also engaging in this performance by going along with our presentations and by managing their own impressions (Goffman, 1959). The interactional strategies that lesbian, bisexual, and queer Latinas engage in with their families demonstrate this process in action. . . .

METHODS

The data for this study consist of in-depth interviews and participant observations that were carried out between 2006 and 2008. There were forty formal interviews conducted in addition to numerous informal conversations that I engaged in at LGBTQ events as part of the participant-observation process. The interviews were conducted in Massachusetts, Connecticut, New York, and New Jersey, and the participant observation took place primarily in

New York City. As of 2000, New York, New Jersey, and Massachusetts were among ten states with the largest Latin American immigrant populations. Massachusetts, Connecticut, New York, and New Jersey are also among the ten U.S. states with the largest Caribbean population (Migration Policy Institute, n.d.). The high concentration of immigrants of Latin American or Caribbean descent in this region made it an appropriate area to conduct this research.

All formal interviewees self-identified as lesbian, bisexual, or queer Latinas, were at least 18 years of age, and lived in the geographic northeast. Participants ranged in age from 19 to 54. Eighteen of the participants were first-generation Latinas, and 22 were second-generation Latinas. . . . The study consisted of 11 Puerto Ricans, seven Dominicans, six Mexicans or Chicanas, six Peruvians, three Colombians, three Nicaraguans, two Cubans, one Guatemalan, and one Ecuadorian. Their class backgrounds varied greatly. The second-generation Latinas were predominantly raised working-class although many are currently middle-class due to achievements in higher education. In contrast, the first-generation Latinas were predominantly raised middle- to upper-class in their countries of origin. Half of these women suffered downward social mobility after migrating to the United States; the other half were mostly Puerto Rican migrants whose class level either elevated or remained the same after migration. . . . Thirty of the study participants identified as lesbian, three as queer, and seven as bisexual. . . .

ANALYSES

When I asked the interviewees to tell me about their relationships with their families of origin, they often shared with me their struggles with their mothers. Consistent with previous findings, study participants' mothers were overwhelmingly the major enforcers of sexual morality and heterosexuality in their lives (Gonzalez-Lopez, 2005). Study participants report having received more resistance and nonacceptance from their mothers than from any other member in their families. The participants report their mothers reacting to their disclosure with questions like "how could you do this to me?" or "I raised you better than that." The participants believe their mothers saw their sexual nonconformity as a reflection on their parenting and as an outcome to their failure to effectively teach normative sexuality. None of the forty study participants were disowned by family members for their sexual nonconformity. Families were often not accepting of Latinas' same-sex relationships and/or sexual orientations, but they did not rebuke these women entirely. Nonetheless, familial reactions caused guilt in the study participants and led them to engage in the invisible work of appeasing these relationships.

Erasing Nonconformity

The erasure strategy was commonly used by families as a way of rejecting their daughters without disowning them. Erasure of nonconformity predominantly occurred between very young study participants (women between the ages of 19 and 25) and those who were economically dependent on their families. The participants' young age and financial dependency made them most susceptible to the erasure strategy. Families engaging in the erasure strategy gain leverage against their loved ones because of their lack of autonomy as well as because of their respect for family values. The erasure strategy is premised on hypermanipulation and control, and families engaging in this strategy attempt to force their daughters out of dating other women. When Mariela was 16 years old, someone caught her kissing her girlfriend Alisa. Her mother confronted her, and thereafter their relationship was greatly compromised. Her experience represents the kind of familial rejection that was common with the erasure strategy. Mariela is a second-generation Colombian. She described her situation in the following ways:

So my mom approached me about it and said "oh what is this all about? How dare you? How could you do this to me? Haven't I taught you better? I told you she [Alisa] was a bad influence on you." My mom said this is going to *end right now.* She was in such a shock that all she did was yell and beat me up. But I tried to tell her this is something I chose to do. It's not because I felt influenced by anybody. But she didn't believe me. One of [the] things my mom didn't do is tell my dad. She would never tell him because she thinks he'd commit suicide if he ever found out. So she made me promise her that night that I would never tell him either.

Several years after this altercation with her mother, Mariela has kept her promise to not come out to her father. By saying that her father would commit suicide if he knew about her lesbianism, Mariela's mother is manipulating her daughter's emotions and heightening her control over her on the basis of the secret they share. Mariela's behaviors inside and outside the home are premised on the fact that she promised to keep her lesbian self a secret from her father. Latinas' subjugated position in patriarchal societies has compromised their ability to negotiate sexual nonconformity with family members. Their value on *"no faltar el respeto"* or to not be disrespectful makes them susceptible to hypercontrol as the women in their families enforce patriarchy. . . .

The study participants who engaged in erasure strategies with their parents overwhelmingly report feeling the burden of having to fulfill their parent's dreams. They bear the burden of accomplishing not only their goals but also the goals that their parents could not accomplish on account of a lack of opportunities. They overwhelmingly report taking pride in having always been "good girls" who excelled in school and carried their family's hopes and dreams proudly. Coming out to their families as women who love other women often means shattering the dreams their families had for them in order to pursue their own desires. . . .

Families engaging in erasure strategies often defer to religion as a way of rationalizing their rejection. This was the case even for families that were not otherwise very religious. In some ways, for families that are uncomfortable with their daughter's choices, religion becomes a shield that protects them from the things that make them uneasy. Kayla, a second-generation Puerto Rican who identifies as a lesbian, met her first female partner while attending college. When Kayla told her mother that she was in a relationship with another woman, her mother immediately pointed her in the direction of the church. Kayla recounts this experience below.

My mother said you need to go speak to a priest. The next day I went and found where the priest lives on campus. Father John answered the door. And I started crying right there in the doorway. He sits me down in this little area that they have right by the door and asks. "What's the matter?" And I said, "I just told my mom that I'm in a relationship with a woman. I told her that I'm gay." And then he said something that set me free. He said, "You know what, there's nothing wrong with giving your love to another human being, and that's all that you are doing. " I asked specifically, "Am I going to be kicked out of the church?" He's like no, no. I said, "Can I tell my mom that?" He said "yes."

Kayla's parents sent her to see a priest because they wanted her to confess her "sin." She went to this church full of anxiety and half expecting to be rejected yet again. Instead, Father John gave her the ammunition she needed to take down her parents' protective shield. By telling her that she was still welcome in the church and that she was not committing a sin, Father John gave Kayla what she needed to confront her parents. In her eyes, they could no longer use religion as an excuse to not accept her.

Respondents whose families engaged in erasure strategies often had self-esteem issues. For these women more so than for any other Latinas in this study, erasure created insecurities, vulnerability, and sometimes internal self-hate. These women were more likely than those in any other group to be manipulated by family members because of their age and financial dependency. Furthermore, they were ill-equipped to handle a world without familial support.

Silencing Strategies

Not all the study participants' families engaged in erasure strategies. Some participants engaged in silencing strategies with their families. Among the migrant Latinas, it was common for participants to never have had candid conversations with their parents about their sexual nonconformity. Nor have their parents ever confronted them about it. Rather, both the study participants and their families have taken to silencing this aspect of their lives altogether.

The study participants and their families have found protection in strategies of sexual silence. Sexual silence is a way for families to tacitly accept sexual nonconformity without ever directly acknowledging it. This strategy has also been referred to as *"un secreto a voz"* or an open secret (Zavella, 1997). It allows individuals to meet the expectations of normalcy because no one acknowledges or verbalizes the transgressions. Study participants rationalize sexual silencing strategies as their way of remaining respectful of their families. These relationships resemble a tacit agreement in which the families do not meddle in their daughters' personal lives and in return the daughters conduct themselves respectfully

and discreetly. Scholars have found that among Latino gay men and men who have sex with men (MSM). *"De eso no se habla"* is a tacit agreement that allows individuals to engage in same-sex behavior outside of the home and away from their families and in return their families turn a blind eye on these activities (Carillo, 2002; Lumsden, 1996). However, the dynamic taking place between these Latina women who love women and their kin is slightly different. This is not something that occurs away from the home but something that occurs in the home when no one is looking. The families do not pressure their daughters to have relationships with men, to get married, or to have children, and the daughters lead everyone to believe that their female lovers are just *"amigas"* or friends who sleep over on the weekends.

Angelica lived in her parents' home until she immigrated to the United States from the Dominican Republic in her thirties. She had several lovers while living with her parents. She describes the agreement in her home in the following ways.

They always preferred to think that I was a very studious girl, than to see the reality, which was that I didn't have a boyfriend. That the few people that I brought home were women. What they have always seen in me is female friendships. And they have met my partners without knowing they are my partners. Because the ones that I've had stable relationships with have come to my house. They've met my parents and have established relationships with them. But I've never actually come out and said I'm gay. The partner that I have now, I've been with her for five years. When I lived in Santo Domingo and she lived here [in the United States], she would come on vacation and she would stay in my house. If [my family] didn't see it, it's because they didn't want to see it.

Here, Angelica describes the avoidance strategy she engages in with her family. The difference between this type of sexual silencing and *de eso no se habla* is that Angelica's parents always knew her partners. They developed relationships with these partners and welcomed them into their home as their daughter's "*amigas*" or friends. For them, then, sexual silence is not about keeping same-sex intimacy outside the home but about engaging in such relationships under the guise of platonic friendship. . . .

. . . The utility of sexual silencing strategies is that they allow families to avoid shame in their communities. So long as lesbian, bisexual, and queer Latinas do not openly display their sexual transgression, the families are allowed to save face with the community. For this reason, these families continuously ignore Latinas' intimacy with "*amigas*" and their lack of interest in men. Family members and study participants are complicit in maintaining sexual silence because it allows them to preserve their familial bond and deflect the tumultuous complications that can come with disclosure. Participants engaging in silencing strategies were fortified by the belief that their families did accept them even if only tacitly, which is something that Latinas engaging in erasure strategies or avoidance strategies did not get. . . .

Sometimes silencing strategies were not just about pretending that participants' lovers were just amigas. In an effort to minimize rejection, sometimes participants took silencing strategies even further by pretending that they were in relationships with men. Some of the sexually nonconforming women who engaged in silencing strategies with their families pretend to have relationships with gay male friends in order to help keep up the ruse. . . .

The Latinas who held this type of agreement with their families report not wanting to bring them shame. They internalized the importance of maintaining familial honor by being discreet about their transgressions. They were greatly concerned with how their parents would be treated in the community as well as by other family members if the sexual silence was broken. In the event that disclosure did happen, mothers tried to hide this information from other family members and friends. In these instances, however, families sometimes shift from maintaining sexual silence to the avoidance after disclosure strategy.

Avoidance after Disclosure

The third arrangement that study participants reported engaging in with their families is avoidance after disclosure. This strategy can occur when participants disclose or are forced to disclose their sexual nonconformity to families but later choose with their families to render the disclosure unheard altogether. With avoidance after disclosure, it is no longer okay for Latinas to bring *amigas* home. By verbalizing the sexual transgression, new guidelines must be established whereby what Latinas do must remain unknown or out of sight. This is because after verbalization, acceptance is no longer possible.

Study participants and their families can maintain seemingly ordinary relationships by not ever acknowledging their romantic dealings with women and pretending the disclosure never occurred. Diana is a young graduate student at a prestigious university. A second-generation Dominican, she was raised by a single mother in New York City. She lives on her college campus during the school year and comes home to her mother in the summer. When Diana's mother learned she was dating women, she panicked. She entered a state of denial and tried to find a therapist to "cure" her daughter. She convinced herself that her daughter's dealings with women were part of a phase. Since this time, Diana and her mother have found a way to maintain their relationship by never discussing her queer existence. Diana describes this avoidance strategy: "It was tense for a long time. She didn't know who I was. She didn't know who she was dealing with. But we're really, really close so we got back into the swing of things and kind of, you know, we didn't talk about it, didn't really mention it. We are pretending like nothing really exists when it comes to that [the disclosure of her queer identity]." Diana's arrangement with her mother allows her to maintain two separate lives. She has the life that she shares with her lovers and LGBTQ friends and another life that she shares with her family of origin. Because her relationship with her family is contingent upon everyone pretending the disclosure never happened, these two worlds do not coexist or overlap as they do with families utilizing the silencing strategies.

Sometimes, for participants, the separation of these two worlds is maintained through geography. Maritza immigrated to the United States because her mother discovered that Lourdes, a woman she accepted in her home as her daughter's *amiga*, was in fact her lover. Once her mother learned this information, the relationship between Maritza and her family became poisonous. Immigrating to the United States became a way for Maritza to create distance between them, and over time the family came to engage in avoidance after disclosure. This separation allows Maritza and her family to maintain their bond in a way that may not have been possible in Peru.

Like all the other strategies, avoidance after disclosure comes at a price. The erasure, silence, or avoidance of Latinas' lesbian, bisexual, or queer selves can often result in their isolation. These Latinas were often raised to keep their problems within the family and to only share their struggles with their parents and siblings and not with friends or psychologists. Given this, when family members render their same-sex relationships unheard or try to erase or silence them, Latinas can be left with no one to turn to in grappling with the difficulties of their same-sex relationships. . . .

This experience speaks to how vulnerable these Latinas can be when their families are not fully accepting of their sexual nonconformity. It often leaves these women with no one to turn to in the event of physical or emotional abuse. . . .

Despite the fact that family members try to erase, silence, or avoid an important part of their selves, these women have not given up on their kin. On the contrary, they have rationalized their family's hurtful reactions and healed their own wounds in their efforts to forgive their families. In many ways, they continue to subject themselves to familial abuse because they have such a strong sense that family is central to their happiness. . . . The study participants were not judgmental of their families for rejecting them, and they did not turn away from their families even when their families gave them reason to do so. Instead, they have found ways to remain hopeful that their families would eventually move toward acceptance.

DISCUSSION AND CONCLUSIONS

This article highlights the interactional strategies LBQ Latinas engaged in with family members at first disclosure, but this is just a small segment of their relationships. These options do not exhaust the possibilities, nor are they static interactions. Participants' relationships with their families often changed over time. Sometimes they became healthier as the respondents and their family members had more time to change their outlooks and embrace their fears. . . .

The strategies that study participants engaged in cannot be reduced to a narrative of remaining in the closet. One cannot simply look at the closet as something that you are either in or out of. These women negotiate very complex arrangements with their families and lovers. As Decena notes, the closet is a coproduction. The family is just as complicit as the individual in maintaining the strategies described in this article. Arguably, those who had never disclosed and used a silencing strategy were the most successful in combining their sexual lives with their family lives. Those who had engaged in verbal disclosures were less able to combine these two aspects of the self. Therefore, the Western notion of "coming out of the closet" did not really exist for these participants in the way that we presume it does for non-Latinos. . . .

REFERENCES

Ayala, Jennifer. 2006. "Confianza, Consejos, and Contradictions: Gender and Sexuality Lessons between Latina Adolescent Daughters and Mothers." In *Latina Girls: Voices of Adolescent Strength in the United States.* Jill Denner and Bianca Guzman, (eds), 29–43. New York: New York University Press.

Baca-Zinn, Maxine. 1982. "Familism among Chicanos: A Theoretical Review." *Humboldt Journal of Social Relations* 10 (1): 224–38.

———.1998. "Race and the Family Values Debate." In *Challenges for Work and Family in the 21st Century*, Danna Vannoy and Paula Dube. (eds) 49–62. Piscataway, NJ: Aldine Transaction.

Carillo, Héctor. 2002. *The Night is Young: Sexuality in Mexico in the Time of AIDS.* Chicago: University of Chicago Press.

Espin, Oliva. 1997. *Latina Realities: Essays on Healing, Migration, and Sexuality.* Boulder. CO: Westview.

Goffman. Erving. 1959. *The Presentation of Self in Everyday Life.* New York: Anchor.

Gonzalez-Lopez, Gloria. 2005. *Erotic Journeys: Mexican Immigrants and Their Sex Lives.* Berkeley: University of California Press.

Hurtado, Aida. 2003. *Voicing Chicana Feminism: Young Women Speak Out on Sexuality and Identity.* New York: New York University Press.

Lugo-Steidel, Angel, and Josefina Contrerars. 2003. "A New Familism Scale for Use with Latino Populations." *Hispanic Journal of Behavioral Sciences* 25 (3): 312–30.

Lumsden, Ian. 1996. *Machos, Maricones, and Gays: Cuba and Homosexuality.* Philadelphia: Temple University Press.

Mckee, Diane, and Allison Karasz. 2006. "You Have to Give Her that Confidence: Conversations about Sex in Mother-Daughter Dyads." *Journal of Adolescent Research* 21(2): 158–84.

Migration Policy Institute. http://www.migrationpolicy.org (accessed August 3, 2009).

Suarez-Orozco, Carola. 2002. "Commentary." In *Latinos Remaking America,* Marcelo Suarez-Orozco and Mariela Paez (eds) 302–305. Berkeley: University of California Press.

Vega, William. 1995. "The Study of Latino Families: A Point of Departure." In *Understanding Latino Families: Scholarship, Policy, and Practice.* edited by Ruth Zambrana. 3–17. Thousand Oaks, CA: Sage.

Weston, Kath, 1991. *Families We Choose: Lesbians, Gays. Kinship.* New York: Columbia University Press.

Zavella, Patricia. 1997. "Playing with Fire: The Gendered Construction of Chicana/Mexicana Sexuality." In *The Gender/Sexuality Reader: Culture, History, Political Economy,* Roger Lancaster and Micaela di Leonardo, (eds) 392–410. New York: Routledge.

———.2003. "Talkin' Sex: Chicanas and Mexicans Theorize about Silences and Sexual Pleasures." In *Chicana Feminisms: A Critical Reader,* Gabriela Arredondo, Aida Hurtado, Norma Klahn, Olga Najera-Ramirez, and Patricia Zavella, (eds) 228–53. Durham. NC: Duke University Press.

PFLAG: Parents, Families, and Friends of Lesbians and Gays

K. L. Broad and Maura Ryan

PFLAG (Parents, Families and Friends of Lesbians and Gays) is the oldest and largest organization made up of heterosexual allies who support LGBT (Lesbians, Gay, Bisexual, Transgender) people. In 1972 Jeanne Manford marched with her son in New York City's Gay Pride Day Parade holding a sign that read, "Parents of Gays Unite in Support of our Children." During her day out, many gays and lesbians with unsupportive parents asked her to speak with their parents to convince them to be as understanding as she was. In 1973 she formed a support group, holding their first meeting in a church with 20 attendees. By 1982 PFLAG became a national organization. Today, they are a nonprofit organization with over 200,000 members, and they have 350 affiliated chapters across the United States and abroad (pflag.org).

The organization provides support for parents, family members, and friends of LGBT people. They also help LGBT people sort out how to interact with and come out to their friends and families. In addition, PFLAG educates people about issues related to sexual orientation, gender identity, and LBGT rights. They are an organization that has a central focus of providing emotional support for heterosexual family members struggling with the sexual orientation of their gay or bisexual loved ones (or the gender identity of their transgender loved ones); they simultaneously see themselves as an advocacy organization that works to ensure the equal rights of LGBT people. In short, PFLAG has a three-fold mission statement of support, education, and advocacy (Broad, 2002).

Parents in this organization often experience a shift in identity; drawing on coming out narratives in LGBT communities about the importance of identity, they begin to identify as heterosexual allies and as proud parents of LGBT people (Broad, 2002). PFLAG offers the emotional promise that parents might experience a shift in their emotional reaction to LGBT children, a move that allows them to shift beyond the grief and negative feelings of homophobia to restore their love and support for their offspring (Broad, 2011). Part of that process is one of moving from being involved primarily in the support group function of PFLAG to a step into advocacy. In so doing, PFLAG parent-advocates carefully strive to be bridges between the heterosexual community and the LGBT community. A key way they do so is by talking as parents and advocating on behalf of LGBT people in parenting terms (Broad, 2002).

Currently, some of PFLAG's top priorities are marriage equality for same-sex couples, equal adoption opportunities for same-sex couples, safe schools for LGBT youth, fostering work cultures that are LGBT-positive, and an end to discrimination in hiring, promotion, and firing (pflag.org). As well, PFLAG opposes "reparative therapy," therapy meant to change the sexual orientation of gay and bisexual people to heterosexual-only, because efforts to change someone's attraction reflect strong cultural biases against same-sex orientation (pflag.org). They have also developed the "Straight for Equality" campaign which asks heterosexual allies to: (1) "come out" by making a pledge that they believe in equality; (2) "communicate" by telling one's story of ally-ship publicly; (3) "join in" by educating one's self about LGBT issues and organizing for policy changes (pflag.org).

Some have argued that PFLAG is a raced and classed organization, providing a script for how affluent white parents react to the coming out of their affluent white children (Kadi, 1999). Others might conclude that their political agenda seeks to normalize LGBT people. For instance, Fields (2001) argues that the way heterosexual parents talk about their children depends upon dominant ideas about gender, sexuality, and families; in short, they reaffirm heteronormativity by relying on the authority of their heterosexual parent identities. PFLAG seeks to fit LGBT people into existing societal structures, rather than allowing them to exist as people outside the mainstream who have a unique culture (Goldstein, 2002). Broad (2011) similarly notes that it is a troubling position for PFLAG, as a pro-LGBT organization, to embrace the idea of grieving the loss of heterosexuality as core to its mission since this can be understood as grieving the loss of privilege and reasserting heterosexuality as the ideal. However, Broad notes that PFLAG's full message is important to keep in mind, for PFLAG is advocating that parents move out of this misinformed grief and instead embrace LGBT acceptance, advocacy, and activism. Broad's research of PFLAG as an advocacy group asserts that "PFLAG is striving to challenge a heteronormative complacent legitimation of grief and instead is sending a message that while the feelings may be real, grief is a troubling place to stay (personally) and problematic (politically)" (Broad, 2011: 412). Combined, the varied research on

PFLAG suggests that balancing the mission of being a support group and an advocacy group, as well as negotiating the position of being a heterosexual and pro-LGBT organization, is complicated. Thus, it may reproduce and reify dominant arrangements even as it seeks to challenge them.

In a social and political climate that has been defined over the last thirty years by a struggle over traditional family values, PFLAG has a unique role. PFLAG directly positions itself as opposing the political organizing done by right-wing anti-gay organizations. In response to anti-gay religious groups making the claim that they are defending traditional family values, PFLAG parents claim that they are the group that actually defends "real family values" by embracing their LGBT children and celebrating gender and sexual diversity (Broad et al., 2004: 510). PFLAG's central message is that families come in all forms and all families—families with LGBT children and LGBT people who build families—are valuable.

REFERENCES

Broad, K. L. 2002. Social Movement Selves, *Sociological Perspectives*, 45(3): 317–336.

———. 2011. Coming Out for Parents, Families, and Friends of Lesbians and Gays: From Support Group Grieving to Love Advocacy, *Sexualities*, 14(4): 339–415.

Broad, K. L., S. Crawley, and L. Foley. 2004. Doing 'Real Family Values': The Interpretative Practice of Families in the GLBT Movement, *The Sociological Quarterly*, 45(3): 509–517.

Fields, J. 2001. Normal Queers: Straight Parents Respond to Their Children's 'Coming Out,' *Symbolic Interaction*, 24(2):165–187.

Goldstein, R. 2002. *The Attack Queers: Liberal Society and the Gay Right*. NY: Verso.

Kadi, J. 1999. *Thinking Class: Sketches from a Cultural Worker*. MA: South End Press.

PFLAG. (Date of retrieval: 17 December 2011). *About Us*. PFLAG. www.pflag.org

9

SEXUAL VIOLENCE

AN INTERVIEW WITH

LYNN CHANCER

Lynn Chancer, Ph.D., is Professor of Sociology at Hunter College and the Graduate Center of the City University of New York. She is the author of four books: Sado-masochism in Everyday Life: Dynamics of Power and Powerlessness *(Rutgers University Press, 1992);* Reconcilable Differences: Confronting Beauty, Pornography and the Future of Feminism *(University of California Press, 1998);* High-Profile Crimes: When Legal Cases Become Social Causes *(University of Chicago Press, 2006); and* Gender, Race and Class: An Overview *(Blackwell, 2006). She has also written numerous articles on gender and sexuality, crime, law and deviance, sociology of culture and social theory.*

What led you to study sexuality?

The first thought that comes to mind is that, as a feminist for as long as I remember being able to think, I have taken seriously the now complicated and much misunderstood notion of "the personal as political." Something I love about feminist theory is that the usual boundaries between the social and the psychological, between rationality and feelings, and between the body and our minds, dissolve if and when one thinks/feels through a feminist framework. Thus, for a long time, I have thought not about why sociologists would, but why wouldn't we study sexuality?

But a second and more academic answer is that my first book, *Sadomasochism in Everyday Life: Dynamics of Power and Powerlessness,* was literally provoked and inspired by sexuality debates going on in the American feminist movement. Barnard College has a yearly "Feminist and Scholar" conference and, in the early 1980s, a debate over sadomasochism made that particular event controversial. The issue was that a feminist participant at the conference submitted a photo of a woman with her legs spread eagled and a razor between them for publication in the conference brochure. The administration refused, leading to intense debate among feminists about whether or not one could even be a feminist if excited by and practicing "sexual" sadomasochism, i.e., "S&M" sex. Some feminists said that to openly practice S&M was to collude with dominance and subordination (and with patriarchal societies). Others, including women in SAMOIS (a lesbian feminist S&M group), interpreted "feminist" as meaning expanded sexual freedoms. Moreover, women who were turned on by S&M sex argued S&M was not an oppressive power relationship; it was consensual and *part* of sexual freedom. From this, I started to develop arguments that became the basis of the book *Sadomasochism in Everyday Life.* The book attempted to carefully differentiate between consensual S&M sex as part of sexual freedom and coercive S&M that is obviously problematic.

Have you done any research in the area of sexual violence?

Yes. My interest in gender and crime began when I studied the New Bedford, Massachusetts rape case of 1983, a horrible case in which a woman was gang-raped on a pool table in a bar full of men, with no one calling the police. The case became the basis of the movie *The Accused* and I wrote a *Gender & Society* article to understand why many women, not just men, were active in protests against the convictions of men in that case, just one year after that shocking rape occurred. I have also done research on high-profile crimes involving rape.

How do people react to your studying sexuality?

After *Sadomasochism in Everyday Life* was published and I finally had the satisfaction of holding a copy in my hands, I recall looking at the book while riding the New York City subway and realizing that people were definitely staring at me! Only the title is on the cover—no pictures of any sort—and yet I know the title is and was provocative. I've also thought, when giving talks on the subject, that people half-expect me to come out wearing a leather skirt and carrying whips and chains—this even though an important goal of the book was to show that sadomasochistic dynamics go beyond the sphere of sexuality. I found that sadomasochistic dynamics are present in dominance/subordinate relationships at work, within racist interactions, and in gendered dynamics not necessarily involving sexuality at all.

Another memorable reaction occurred after I wrote an essay called "Prostitution and Feminist Theory." I began this piece with a hypothetical example: Since male scholars regularly undertake participant observation studies which bring them respect on "deviant" subject matters like drug use or gangs, what would happen to a female/feminist scholar who decided to conduct a sociological participant observation study of sex work? Would she, I asked, be able to find a job—or would the marginalized status of sex work malign the reception of that female/feminist sociologist's research? A professor asked me to give a talk on the paper. She took me out to a nice lunch and, at the end of the meal, turned and whispered to me, "You must have actually done participant observation on this subject, didn't you? Why else would you have written that paper?" I was amazed that this professor assumed that no one would write about sex work unless they actually did it themselves. I was struck that she saw sex work as both a negative "deviant" and an "exoticized" kind of research. After I published this piece, many young scholars—all women—around the country contacted me because they had done some kind of sex work and had been fearful to write about it explicitly. What I am delighted about, though, is that over ten years after writing that essay, I think studying sex work has become far more ordinary, far more established and much less deviant.

Why is studying sexuality important?

The study of sexuality (and sexualities) strikes me as very important for scholars in general, and sociologists in particular, to study because it is so very basic to human interaction and happiness. How could sociologists *not* study connections and intimacies, especially basic ones in sexuality, that meld minds and bodies and are found around the world, across different classes, races, ethnicities, nations and other social boundaries?

In the history of American social science, sexuality as an empirical subject has often been researched as though in isolation from the rest of social life: one studies sexual practices and behaviors but does not necessarily place them in larger cultural, social, political and economic contexts. Thus, it strikes me that there is much work still to be done not on sex in a narrow sense, but in terms of how sexuality—sexual freedom, sexual repression, sexual intimacy (or lack thereof)—affects other aspects of day-to-day life.

Of the projects you've done over the course of your career, which was most interesting? Why?

I'm glad to say that I've found every project I've done interesting. In retrospect I think *Sadomasochism in Everyday Life* was both interesting and important because, in it, I developed a theory that could be applied to sexuality as well as to a host of other dominance/subordinate relationships. I also particularly enjoyed writing a chapter on beauty and looks-ism, as I called it, for the book *Reconcilable Differences*. In this piece I argued that conventional looks are overrated in understanding attraction, and that dynamism and energy—and a composite of culturally constructed images—help to explain people's interest in one another more than conventional looks *per se*.

If you could teach people one thing about sexuality what would it be?

I think it would be to look beyond apparency, beyond the given, and not to take anything about sexuality for granted. Sexuality deserves to be studied, but in a way that respects its immense complexity and its huge role in social, cultural, and personal life.

"I WASN'T RAPED, BUT · · · ": REVISITING DEFINITIONAL PROBLEMS IN SEXUAL VICTIMIZATION

NICOLA GAVEY

When a woman says she wasn't raped but describes an experience of forced, unwanted sexual intercourse, what are we to think? Was she "really" raped, despite disowning that label for her experience? Or does her refusal of the label suggest that her interpretation of the experience as other than rape makes it so? And what does it say about our culture(s) that there can be so much ambiguity over the differential diagnosis of rape versus sex? How should we conceptualize and judge the myriad coercive sexual acts that lie somewhere between rape and consensual sex? Finally, is being the object of violence or coercion always the same thing [as] being the *victim* of such violence or coercion?

In this chapter I begin to explore some of the convoluted layers of issues in which such questions are embedded. . . . In thinking through and around these questions, I find I can't settle comfortably into a straightforward, unitary position from which to craft an argument. . . . I have concluded . . . that there are indeed murky issues at the interface between (hetero) sex and sexual victimization. Even at the most basic level, I want to talk about and against rape and sexual victimization (as though these are straightforward terms) at the same time as I destabilize these categories, in the belief that this is an important part of the same fight at a different level.

I trace some of the changes in research on rape and sexual victimization over the past two decades and consider some of the implications of the new feminist social science approach. In particular, I consider three points that raise the need to revisit current conventions for conceptualizing sexual victimization. These points concern the concept of the unacknowledged rape victim, the loose distinction between rape and attempted rape, and the use of the term *sexual victimization* to refer to a broad range of arguably normative coercive heterosexual practices. . . .

A STARTING POINT

In the title of this [reading], I refer back to Martha Burt and Rhoda Estep's 1981 paper "Who Is a Victim? Definitional Problems in Sexual Victimization." In their . . . article, Burt and Estep mapped the nascent influence of 1970s feminism on a redefinition and reconceptualization of sexual assault. They endorsed the more inclusive definition of sexual assault that was emerging from feminism at the time, drawing attention to the similarity between rape and other coercive sexual practices. Moreover, they argued strongly for the benefits for all women who have been sexually assaulted to claim the victim role. Although aware of what they called the "negative social value" and the "obligations" of the victim role, they proposed that the benefits would include "the right to claim assistance, sympathy, temporary relief from other role responsibilities, legal recourse, and other similar advantages." (p. 16).

. . . [Using] the language of victimization was imposed as a way of making sense of and opposing the moral injustice of women's oppression in the forms of violence and harassment.

THE "NEW" FEMINIST RESEARCH ON SEXUAL VICTIMIZATION

Since 1981, . . . both feminist activism and feminist social science have been instrumental in promoting a major rethinking of rape—and sexual victimization in many western societies. . . . In a very short time we moved from a climate in which rape was widely regarded as rare to one in which rape is regarded as a widespread social problem. . . .

[F]eminist empirical research was specifically designed to overcome the limitations of previous estimates of rape prevalence (which relied on reports of rape to the police or reports in national crime surveys). . . . This work introduced an important methodological point of departure from any previous attempts to measure the scope of rape. Women were asked not whether they had been raped[1] but rather whether they had had any experiences that matched behavioral descriptions of rape. For example, they were asked whether they had ever had sexual intercourse when they didn't want to because a man threatened or used some degree of physical force to make them do so (e.g., Koss et al., 1987). Moreover, this question was one among many such specific questions that women would be asked about a range of coercive sexual experiences. Such methodological refinements were designed to be sensitive to women's reluctance to report rape. They were seemingly successful, and the body of research produced shocking new data showing widespread rape and sexual victimization.

At the same time, two other important changes to the picture of rape emerged from this research. First, Diana Russell (1982; 1984)—and later, others—showed that women were far more likely to be raped by husbands, lovers, boyfriends, and dates than by strangers. Not only were the cultural blinkers that had enabled this to be regarded as "just sex" lifted, but it was found that such rapes were far more common than the stereotypical rape by a stranger. Second, . . . while rape [was] the extreme act, it [was] regarded as being on a continuum with more subtle forms of coercion, from an unwanted kiss to unwanted sexual intercourse submitted to as a result of continual verbal pressure. . . .

[These changes] have two important effects: (1) They construe experiences that would have previously fallen within the realm of sex as forms of sexual *victimization;* and 2) they implicitly invite a critical examination of the whole realm of normal heterosexual practice. . . .

Against a backdrop where rape was considered to be rare—and where complaints of rape were commonly regarded to be lies, distortions of normal sex, harmless, or provoked by the victim—the call to broaden the definition of sexual assault and victimization has been an important feminist move. Similarly, the way in which we have elaborated on the understanding of rape as a form of *victimization* has arguably contributed to more widespread concern about rape as a serious social problem. These moves [were] one part of increased focus during the 1980s on many forms of victimization, and of widespread social concern for understanding their extent and dynamics and for ameliorating and preventing their harm.

"VICTIMIZATION" IN CRISIS

[By] the late 1990s, the concept of victimization [was] arguably in crisis. Joel Best (1997) opened a . . . *Society* commentary with the unfavorable verdict that "victimization has become fashionable" (p. 9). As Richard Feldstein (1997) . . .

observed, the term *victim* . . . has been targeted for critique by neoconservatives in the United States. . . . As part of more general conservative campaigns against research and services relating to victimization, there has been critical dispute over the new feminist research on rape—especially that on "date rape." It has been claimed that the issue has been exaggerated or that it has no validity as a concept (e.g., Gilbert, 1994; Paglia, 1992; Roiphe, 1993; see also Denfeld, 1995; Sommers, 1994; Newbold, 1996). . . .

ARE VICTIMS CREATED BY A VICTIMIZATION FRAMEWORK?

There are many ways to victimize people. One way is to convince them that they are victims.

—*(Hwang, 1997, p.41)*

One strand of public concern at the moment is the fear that talk about victimization is needlessly creating victims. Moreover, critics of the movement against date rape have implied that it violates "assumptions of women's basic competence, free will, and strength of character" (Roiphe, 1993, p. 69; see also Paglia, 1992). . . .

There are various ways in which the language of sexual victimization can have material cultural effects. . . . For example, it may reinforce and perpetuate images of women as weak, passive, and asexual and images of men as sexually driven, unstoppable, and potentially dangerous. These gendered ways of being may be further enhanced by the exacerbation of women's fears about rape through media reportage and through warnings about violent sexual attacks that emphasize women's vulnerability to rape over their potential for resistance. . . . A rapist's moral infringement prescribes an experience of victimization for the rape *victim* . . . [and a] particular psychological outcome is preconfigured by calling the violence "victimization."

. . . [H]ow valid is the sort of seductive public warning in Karen Hwang's point? Are victims really created out of thin air? When feminists and other social critics name certain practices as victimization, they are drawing attention to the relationships of power that systematically privilege the experiences of some groups of people over those of others. Is the hysterical anxiety behind the suggestion that talking about victimization creates victimization a sort of head-in-the-sand approach to unpleasant social conditions—a naive hope that if a phenomenon is not seen and not heard, then it does not exist? . . . [C]ommentators such as Katie Roiphe suggest that "prior to the discourse of date rape, the experience itself did not occur, or at least not with such traumatizing after-effects as we now associate with rape" (p. 16). . . .

In light of the backlash crisis of representation of victimization . . . , it is perhaps time to revisit Martha Burt and Rhoda Estep's (1981) contention that it is in a woman's best interests to be perceived as a victim when she has experienced sexual coercion or violence. It is difficult to know how to evaluate this claim, and our attempts may benefit from some empirical analysis of women's accounts of their experiences of coercion, abuse, and violence. Few would deny that what we refer to as rape, sexual assault, sexual coercion, and sexual abuse can be victimizing. That is, they can be horrific events that traumatize women[2] and produce victims. Moreover, abusive and coercive practices can produce victims in more subtle and less horrific ways, through undermining a woman's confidence and eroding her agency over time. In the fight against rape, public feminist rhetoric has tended to privilege one of the many contradictory broader cultural meanings of rape—that is, its power to cause severe and irrevocable psychological harm to the victim. Those of us drawn to activism against rape often have firsthand knowledge of the effects of rape on friends, family members, women we have worked with, or ourselves. The potential trauma and devastating harm of rape, silenced and hidden for so many years, has now come to be almost automatically signified by the term *rape* (although not without exceptions). . . .

UNACKNOWLEDGED RAPE VICTIMS

As discussed earlier, the new research on rape has tended not to rely on asking women whether or not they have ever experienced "rape." Some studies have included this direct question along with the more specific behavioral questions about forced, unwanted sex. It has been found that only around 30 to 50 percent of women who affirm they have had an experience that meets a narrow definition of rape identify that they have experienced "rape" (e.g., Koss, 1988; Gavey, 1991a; 1991b). . . . [T]his research paradigm has . . . categorize[d] women as victims of rape if they report having had an experience consistent with the predetermined behavioral description that researchers define as rape when the questionnaires or structured interview data are analyzed. If these women do not report that they have experienced "rape" (when asked directly), then they are considered "unacknowledged" rape victims by the researchers (e.g., Koss, 1985). . . .

[S]ocial critics have targeted this feature of the feminist empirical work on rape prevalence as a major weakness of the whole body of research.[3] Neil Gilbert (1994), for example, cites as a problem of Koss's rape prevalence estimates that "almost three-quarters of the students whom Koss defined as victims of rape did not think they had been raped" (p. 23). . . . Ironically, this methodological approach is totally consistent with the positivist conventions of social and behavioral psychology . . . , where it is considered good research practice to use operational definitions for specifying precise categories of behavior that can be reliably measured. . . . For instance, it would be considered valid to classify a person as "depressed" if he or she answered a range of questions on a depression inventory in the predicted ways, even if the individual did not affirm the statement "I am depressed."

Let us consider an example of the sort of experience that could be described as an unacknowledged rape. One woman I interviewed described an experience, which occurred when she was nineteen, of waking to find her thirty-year-old male apartment mate in her bed, "groping" her (Gavey, 1990; 1992). She had no prior sexual or romantic relationship with this man, but on this night he got into her bed while she was asleep and had intercourse with her, with no apparent consideration of her lack of interest. She explained:

Ann: . . . it all happened quite quickly really, but I remember thinking quite clearly, "Well if I don't— If I try and get out of the bed, perhaps if I run away or something . . . he might rape me [pause] so I had better just . . ."

Nicola: If you try and run away you mean?

Ann: If I tried it, if I'd resisted, then he might rape me, you know. So he did anyway, sort of thing, really, when you think about it, when I look back.

This man was rough and left her bleeding. Later, she was frightened, "confused," "nervous within the house," and hypervigilant about making sure she was never asleep before he'd gone to bed. . . . Nevertheless, Ann did not conceptualize this event as rape at the time.

Technically, this encounter may not count as rape in a narrow legal sense, because it is unclear how explicitly Ann communicated her nonconsent. Most feminist analyses, however, would point out the restraints on her being able to do this, such as being only just awake and fearing that her resistance might lead to worse treatment. Feminists would also highlight the absence of reasonable grounds for this man assuming consent (e.g., Pineau, 1989). That is . . . it [is not] reasonable for a man to assume that a woman approached when she is asleep in her own bed by a man with whom she had no prior sexual or romantic relationship would be consenting to sex, in the absence of some active communication of this consent. Consequently, many feminists would describe this incident as rape or, at the very least, sexual assault. Clearly, in spite of Ann's resistance to the identity of rape victim, the experience had a negative psychological impact on her. It is impossible to know how, if at all, the effects would have been different had she viewed what happened as rape. There is some indication in her account that to have had an experience she would have called "rape" would have been worse—"if I'd resisted, then he might rape me." Indeed, it would have been a different experience and one that may have more powerfully signaled her lack of control and her vulnerability. Psychologically, she perhaps maintained more control (a meager but significant amount) and risked losing less by choosing not to "run away or something" than if she had resisted as hard as she could and been raped anyway.

During our interview several years after this incident, Ann moved toward retrospectively understanding it as rape—after explaining that she did not resist because "he might rape me," she said "So he did anyway, sort of thing . . . when I look back." . . . I . . . struggled with the validity and ethics of labeling Ann a "rape victim" at the time when she did not choose this label herself. However, . . . ambiguity . . . arises in talking about Ann's experience and how to make sense of it in the research context. . . . If this woman's experience is not considered to be rape or some form of sexual assault very close to rape (by her *or* by the man involved *or* by police, judges, and juries *or* by researchers and social theorists), then what is it? Sex? If it can be accepted as just part of the realm of sex, then it redirects a critical spotlight onto heterosexuality itself.

It is worth noting that although Ann "resisted" seeing herself as a rape victim, this did not enable her to resist the assault physically. This illuminates how it would be misleading to assume that *not* being positioned in an overt discourse of rape or victimization somehow protects a woman from sexual assault. In a situation such as that Ann faced, the mark of gender difference imposed on what is a physical contest of sorts already incites certain responses, such as immobility and fear, that aid a rapist in his attack. . . . [T]his suggests that [we need] . . . ways of understanding heterosex that don't leave room for ambiguity over a woman's entitlement to refuse unwanted sex.

A FEMINIST RESPONSE—THE METHODOLOGY

With critical reflection on the research strategy of classifying some women as unacknowledged rape victims, what do we want to say in response to the critics but also as part of ongoing . . . research practice? There is probably no straightforward answer, but I think it is important that we approach it as an open question rather than with formulaic answers. Why do so many women who have bad experiences consistent with a legal definition of rape label resist the label of "rape victim" (e.g., Koss, 1985)? And how should feminist research respond to these women's rejection of the "rape" label? These questions raise complicated issues that are at the heart of feminist theory about research practice. If we see our role as giving women voice, then it may not be legitimate to "put words in their mouths," to describe experiences as rape that women themselves do not describe in that way. However, feminist research increasingly seeks to go beyond giving women voice and reporting on women's experiences, to offer analyses and critiques that help make sense of women's experiences as they are shaped and constrained by power relations in social contexts. When women's voices don't always tell "our story," it can be troubling to know how to proceed. (See also Fine, 1992; Kitzinger and Wilkinson, 1997.)

Evaluated in this light, the feminist empirical research on rape prevalence occupies an interesting position. In its use of traditional methods to produce conventional data dressed in the language of science rather than that of feminist politics, this research has been an important part of wider feminist action. This action has had some important successes—most notably, changes to rape laws, in many English-speaking countries and in portions of the United States, to recognize rape within marriage as a crime. Widespread publicity about date rape has also led to rape prevention programs on many university campuses. Despite the limited effectiveness of these changes so far (for instance, convictions for wife rape are extremely rare), this body of research has nevertheless had a subversive and transformative role in the changing representations of rape. It has generated a profound shift in the meaning of rape, to the extent that it is no longer impossible to think of a man raping his wife or a sporting hero raping a woman he dated (although this possibility is still more likely to be readily accepted if the man is black). . . .

RESEARCH AND COMPLEXITY

. . . [R]esearch . . . has yielded the findings discussed above at a cost. It has forced closure on definitions of various forms of victimization and classified women's experiences into ready-made categories of victims. This style of methodology necessitates disregard for nuanced and possibly contradictory meanings. Moreover, researchers seem to find it reasonably unproblematic that answers to such basic questions as whether or not a particular experience counts as "rape" are constructed through the research process. The resulting certainty that can be projected about the extent and nature of rape and sexual victimization may eventu-

ally undermine the authority of the findings, when it is found that the reductive and universalizing features of this style of research don't "speak to" the experience of all women whom it ostensibly represents. Not only are decisions about who is and who is not a rape victim not always straightforward, but the partiality of new truths about the effects of rape is sometimes overlooked.

In some instances, women's reactions may be contradictory and not consistent with either dominant traditional or dominant feminist constructions of rape. One woman participating in my research (Gavey, 1990) described a situation with her boyfriend, whereby she said she wanted to say to him, "The very first time we had sex you raped me." However, she didn't always view the forced sex as rape, and she continued her relationship with this man for more than two years. She detailed a complex set of contradictory, ambivalent, and changing reactions to this and other coercive sexual experiences in the relationship. She also discussed how the usual feminist analyses of rape, such as those she later encountered at a rape crisis center, were not entirely helpful. Her reactions were not consistent with what she was hearing about how women respond to rape—because she loved the man who raped her, remembered some of their sex as "wonderful," and so on—she went through a stage of feeling that she must be a "sick" and "masochistic" person. . . .

Feminist accounts of rape need to be able to take account of such women's experiences without, in effect, dismissing them as the result of false consciousness. Carefully listening to and theorizing such ambivalent and confusing experiences may illuminate the complex relationship between heterosexuality and rape. Moreover, it may produce feminist analyses of rape that are sympathetic to all women who are raped, no matter how they experience it.

Although there may be short-term political costs, embracing a more complex and less certain position on the ways in which rape can and does affect women may ultimately be an effective political strategy. By this I mean that psychologists, therapists, and activists should continue to work on understanding, helping, and speaking about the trauma of rape but at the same time be open to accepting, for example, that not all women are traumatized by rape. . . . The notion that it may be possible to experience rape and suffer no lasting devastating psychological effects is less often articulated than is the discourse of harm. But this "finding" about the effects of rape begs the question of whether such research, which once again must compress and order experience into finite categories, is adequate to perceive more subtle, idiosyncratic, and unpredictable psychological effects of rape. . . .

IS ATTEMPTED RAPE SOMETIMES VERY DIFFERENT FROM COMPLETED RAPE?

While some experiences of sexual coercion (and presumably most, if not all, experiences of sexual coercion that fit a narrow definition of rape) are surely victimizing, some possibly are not. Is it possible that our framework for conceptualizing *all* instances of sexual assault, and many instances of unwanted sex, as victimization actually helps constitute some of these experiences as victimizing, when they might otherwise have had effects that were less disabling? Although this question shares the anxiety typical of the backlash positions, it is an important question for feminists. In particular, are experiences of attempted rape and attempted sexual assault *sometimes* very different from actual experiences of rape and sexual assault?

I can think of a personal experience, when I was sixteen, that was probably attempted rape. This episode involved being tricked into

stopping at an older male co-worker's place on the way to a party after we had finished work past midnight on New Year's Eve. I was thrown onto a bed that was just across from the front door of the flat, and he proceeded to jump on top of me and attempt to remove my pants. He was a relatively small man, and I was relatively physically strong from sports, and I remember having to struggle as hard as I could to prevent him [from] removing my pants, with the intention (it seemed to me at the time) of having intercourse with me. (This point also reminds me how it is difficult to judge when a man's actions become "attempted rape" when a man and woman are acquainted and, at some stretch of the imagination, a mutual sexual encounter could be appropriate.) Despite the fact that both of us had been drinking alcohol with other workers at the restaurant where we worked before we left, I was never in any doubt as to my lack of sexual interest in this man—at all, let alone on this occasion. I was not ambivalent in my communication with him and told him clearly, verbally, that I did not want to have sex with him, and I resisted him physically as hard as I could. Yet he seemed to have one goal on his mind, which was unchanged by my refusal. I think it was my relative physical strength that enabled me to resist him vigorously and successfully, to the point that he possibly decided not to keep trying.

Ten years later, when I was working at a sexual abuse counseling agency, the subcultural milieu encouraged me to think back on and identify this experience as attempted rape and to wonder about its negative effects on me. While this was not a totally new way of interpreting this experience, it did sediment it with more certainty. And it did induce me to scrutinize my past to look for psychological effects of this experience. I recall that I was subsequently worried about this man's "interest" in me and arranged for my mother to pick me up from work on some of the following nights.

I also recall that being able to successfully prevent a forceful attempt at unwanted sex left me feeling strong, determined, and invulnerable. Although I can't remember enough of the detail of what followed to be sure there were not also subtle negative effects on my identity and sexuality, it strikes me that such experiences of attempted rape that is successfully repelled are extremely different from experiences of completed rape, in terms of their effect on women. In my case, I did not feel like a victim. I despised his actions, but I did not feel I had been harmed. To the contrary, the effects of his attempt had probably been as empowering as they were disempowering. Was what happened "victimization"? Or is there a better way of describing it that recognizes and celebrates the power of this kind of physical resistance, of fighting back . . . ?

. . .[A]t the time I was imagining the possibility of identifying as an attempted rape victim, it seemed important to join together with women who had been sexually victimized by men, in part to make a political show of solidarity in the face of oppressive acts of male sexuality. However, I never really felt like I properly "belonged," in the sense that I didn't share the legacy of pain that some of the women around me had suffered. Moreover, it backed me into a speaking position that did not fully represent my recollected experience. That adopting an identity as an attempted rape victim would have silenced my different kind of story, which included traces of empowerment, seemed (and still seems) a relatively trivial concern in relation to the political and interpersonal importance of standing alongside women who *had* been harmed. However, perhaps there is more at stake here than some notion of making room for the "authenticity" of experiences like my own. Perhaps there is some political advantage in being able to tell lots of different stories about diverse experiences of sexual violence. In making room for a respectful plurality, we may be able to acknowledge the oppressiveness and potential pain of rape at the same time as igniting discourses that disrupt the possibilities of rape. . . .

Clearly, not all attempted rapes are the same. Some experiences will involve violent and terrifying attacks, where a woman may literally fear for her life. However, the use of behavioral descriptions in surveys to measure the extent of sexual victimization does not distinguish these discrepant possibilities.

EMPHASIZING WOMEN'S STRENGTH

. . . [T]he normative practices of therapy for rape and sexual abuse victims may inadvertently help reinforce some of the effects of victimization through their concern with trauma, recovery, and healing. Again, a particular kind of psychological subject is assumed by such therapy approaches, and arguably, this "recovering" subject is always already constituted as lacking and in need of "betterment."

. . . Sharon Marcus (1992) considers how particular constructions of rape affect the very possibility of rape . . . Marcus argues that in order to resist rape culture, we need to deny a necessary conflation between the act of rape and irrevocable harm. Marcus's feminist approach to rape is radically different from the approach of Susan Brownmiller's (1975) classic feminist analysis of rape. Marcus (1992) considers that "such a view takes violence as a self-explanatory first cause and endows it with an invulnerable and terrifying facticity which stymies our ability to challenge and demystify rape" (p. 387). She, in contrast, argues that:

in its efforts to convey the horror and iniquity of rape, such a view often concurs with masculinist culture in its designation of rape as a fate worse than, or tantamount to, death; the apocalyptic tone which it adopts and the metaphysical status which it assigns to rape implies that rape can only be feared or legally repaired, not fought. (p. 387)

Marcus instead argues for the need to "envision strategies which will enable women to sabotage men's power to rape, which will empower women to take the ability to rape completely out of men's hands" (p. 388). It is sometimes difficult to understand exactly how this sort of transformation could take place, but Marcus's . . . argument is at least suggestive that it may be possible to conceptualize rape differently, in a way that somehow renders it less powerful without trivializing it.

I suggest that a small step in this sort of transformative direction would be the opening up of all sorts of narratives of resistance—by making room for stories about how potential rape was successfully fought, about how some women who are raped do not experience overwhelming psychological despair, and so on. As I suggested earlier, the potential cost of this strategy is that it may do violence to the experience of women who are victimized and traumatized by rape. Sensitivity to this possibility is necessary so that stories of particular kinds of resistance don't come to be privileged in ways that contribute once again to a silencing of women's experiences of victimization.

Apart from concern about the . . . effects of the language of victimization, there are other questions that should be on the minds of feminists. . . . [W]e may need to observe critically the effects of backlash discourse around "victimization." In the ensuing battle over the meaning of victimization, we may need to question which sorts of tactics are most likely to be effective in the political fight against rape. For instance, will the . . . strategy of simply speaking a victim-advocacy position more loudly be sufficient, or will we need to . . . contest the very terms of the debate? . . . [Moreover,] I suggest that an unwanted kiss or touch doesn't always make a *victim,* and the effect of this rhetorical excess in the context of backlash activity may be to weaken the whole struggle against rape by acquaintances, dates,

husbands, and so on. . . . [We must recognize that we live in] a culture of heterosexuality in which power is allowed to infuse sex in different ways for women and men—ways that consistently foreground men's rather than women's rights and desires. . . .

Another problem with the way the framework of victimization is used is that it may implicitly require us to establish psychological harm in order to take a moral stand against violence and against heterosexual practice that is offensive or disrespectful without necessarily being violent (in the usual sense). That is, the injustice of sexual coercion and sexual violence may become too closely tied with the "proof" of psychological damage. . . .

SUPPLEMENTING THE LANGUAGE OF VICTIMIZATION

The new feminist research has come a long way, since Burt and Estep's article (1981), in describing the widespread problem of sexual victimization. But has it both gone too far and not gone far enough? Positivist methodologies have required us to iron out complexity, ambivalence, and contradiction. Public expectations of science have reinforced this drive for certainty in the form of concrete, definitive "findings." But when we peep behind the positivist mask, all sorts of discomforting questions arise: Are all instances of sexual coercion always victimizing? Do they always cause harm? For instance, in the arena of attempted sexual assaults, are women sometimes warriors, fighters, heroes? What are the effects of using these different kinds of language? Are the more subtle forms of sexual coercion, argued to be contiguous with rape by some feminists, best conceptualized on a continuum of sexual victimization? Or are there other ways of critiquing heterosexual practice, which routinely privileges men's sexual interests over women's? Or should both strategies be adopted simultaneously?

In case I've overstated my concerns about the language of victimization, I emphasize that I am not arguing for an abandonment of the victimization framework. Rather, I am suggesting that we need to question whether it is always appropriate or wise to talk about all the different forms and occasions of sexual coercion, sexual assault, sexual abuse, and sexual violence as *victimization*. Making connections between everyday sexual practices (such as sexual pressure in a marriage) and sexual violence has been important for highlighting the role of normative culture in sustaining problems such as rape. However, we have not always maintained a distinction between the theorization of, say, a continuum of sexual victimization and the implications for how we then understand men's and women's actions and experiences at the more normative end of the continuum. Using the language of victimization to discuss this territory of the continuum may be theoretically valid yet at the same time (wrongly?) give the impression that we believe every act that falls along the continuum is an act of "victimization," that it makes "victims." I don't think I want to insist every time a woman experiences some unwanted sexual contact, it is an experience of victimization. But far from dismissing such experiences, it seems to me the challenge is to find different ways of critiquing the ways in which our culture(s) can tolerate all sorts of injustices, inequalities, and plain unfairness in the name of normative heterosexuality.

I close this [reading] in a mood of uncertainty. I worry that my questions could lead to unnecessary and undermining problems for the feminist analyses of rape and sexual coercion that I value. Yet I raise these points in a desire to help strengthen and sharpen our critique of victimizing forms of sexual coercion, in ways that help prevent victimization and ameliorate the effects of potentially victimizing acts for individual women. If we don't ask these questions about the victimization framework, I sense we may risk leaving a fertile gap for backlash discourse to take hold. At the same time, this kind of move should create spaces for developing supplementary ways to critique both normative and violent forms of heterosexual practice—without losing sight of the possibility for both rape and more normative forms of sexual coercion to be victimizing. That is, it may enable us to issue new and more varied moral arguments against the cultural acceptance of a form of heterosexual practice in which it can be hard to tell the difference between "just sex" and rape.

NOTES

1. In some of Koss's studies women were asked this direct question in addition to many more of the specific behavioral questions.

2. Of course, men are also raped and sexually abused, but not usually by women. As I am writing largely about the rape and sexual coercion of women in heterosexual relationships, I refer to those who rape as men and those who are raped as women.

3. Another common criticism of this work centers on the ambiguity of questions about unwanted sexual intercourse and unwanted attempts that occurred "because a man gave you alcohol or drugs." Due to the ambiguity of the question, the validity of scoring affirmative responses as "rape" has been questioned. Discussion of this problem with the research is beyond the scope of this chapter.

REFERENCES

Best, J. May/June 1997. Victimization and the victim industry. *Society*, 9–17.

Brownmiller, S. 1975. *Against our will: Men, women and rape*. Harmondsworth: Penguin.

Burt, M. R., and Estep, R. E. 1981. Who is a victim? Definitional problems in sexual victimization. *Victimology: An International Journal* 6, 15–28.

Denfeld, R. 1995. *The new Victorians: A young woman's challenge to the old feminist order*. New York: Warner Books.

Feldstein, R. 1997. *Political correctness: A response from the cultural left*. Minneapolis: University of Minnesota Press.

Fine, M. 1992. *Disruptive voices: The possibilities of feminist research*. Ann Arbor: University of Michigan Press.

Gavey, N. 1990. Rape and sexual coercion within heterosexual relationships: An intersection of psychological, feminist, and postmodern inquiries. Unpublished doctoral thesis, University of Auckland.

———. 1991a. Sexual victimization prevalence among Auckland university students: How much and who does it? *New Zealand Journal of Psychology* 20: 63–70.

———. 1991b. Sexual victimization prevalence among New Zealand university students. *Journal of Consulting and Clinical Psychology* 59: 464–466.

———. 1992. Technologies and effects of heterosexual coercion. *Feminism and Psychology* 2: 325–351.

Gilbert, N. 1994. Miscounting social ills. *Society* 31 (3): 18–26.

Hwang, K. 1997. Excerpt from *The Humanist,* July/August 1997. Cited in Talking stick. *Utne Reader,* (84): 41.

Kitzinger, C., and Wilkinson, S. 1997. Validating women's experience? Dilemmas in feminist research. *Feminism and Psychology* 7: 566–574.

Koss, M. P. 1985. The hidden rape victim: Personality, attitudinal, and situational characteristics. *Psychology of Women Quarterly* 9: 193–212.

———. 1988. Hidden rape: Sexual aggression and victimization in a national sample of students in higher education. In A. W. Burgess (ed.), *Rape and sexual assault,* Vol. 2 (pp. 3–25). New York and London: Garland.

Koss, M. P., Gidycz, C. A., and Wisniewski, N. 1987. The scope of rape: Incidence and prevalence of sexual aggression and victimization in a national sample of higher education students. *Journal of Consulting and Clinical Psychology* 55: 162–170.

Marcus, S. 1992. Fighting bodies, fighting words: A theory and politics of rape prevention. In J. Butler and J. W. Scott (eds.), *Feminists theorize the political* (pp. 385–403). New York: Routledge.

Newbold, G. 1996. Commentary on Professor Mary Koss's keynote address: Redefining rape. In J. Broadmore, C. Shand, and T. Warburton (eds.), *The proceedings of 'Rape: Ten years' progress? An interdisciplinary conference,* Wellington, New Zealand, 27–30 March 1996 (pp. 144–146). Doctors for Sexual Abuse Care.

Paglia, C. 1992. *Sex, art, and American culture.* New York: Vintage Books.

Pineau, L. 1989. Date rape: A feminist analysis. *Law and Philosophy* 8: 217–243.

———. 1996. A response to my critics. In L. Francis (ed.), *Date rape: Feminism, philosophy, and the law* (pp. 63–107). University Park, PA: Pennsylvania State University Press.

Roiphe, K. 1993. *The morning after: Sex, fear, and feminism.* London: Hamish Hamilton.

Russell, D. E. H. 1982. *Rape in marriage.* New York: Macmillan.

———. 1984. *Sexual exploitation: Rape, child sexual abuse, and workplace harassment.* Beverly Hills: Sage.

Sommers, C. H. 1994. *Who stole feminism? How women have betrayed women.* New York: Simon & Schuster.

Changing the Definition of Rape

Megan M. Tesene

On December 14, 2011, the Director of the Federal Bureau of Investigation (FBI), Robert Mueller, approved a request to change the definition of rape in the Bureau's Uniform Crime Reporting Program (UCR). The change comes after ten years of advocacy from women's rights groups and activists who sought to change the FBI's outdated definition of rape, which defined rape as the "carnal knowledge of a female forcibly against her will" since 1929.[1] As noted by the FBI, law enforcement agencies, and women's rights groups, the former defini-tion was incredibly narrow, excluding male rape victims, oral and anal rapes, and those rapes that do not clearly include the use of force.

An additional criticism was that the older definition created inconsistencies between local, state, and federal crime reporting due to most local and state agencies implementing broader definitions of rape when prosecuting rapists. As women's rights groups explain, the discrepancy led thousands of rapes to go unaccounted for when crimes were reported to the UCR.[2] Because academics, legislators, and public officials rely on these statistics to create laws and set policies, having accurate statistics is of vital importance.[3] Furthermore, the UCR's statistics are used to determine how much funding is made available to programs and organizations that seek to prevent and treat sexual assault. Without accurate statistics, fewer resources are made available to those programs.

According to Director Mueller's statement to the Senate Judiciary Committee, the Bureau will move forward with implementing a broader definition that will include those crimes that constitute as rape, but were previously unaccounted for due to the outdated definition.[4] While the new definition will provide the FBI with a more comprehensive and accurate accounting of rape, it will not change criminal codes that govern the prosecution of sexual assaults.[5] Beginning in the spring of 2012,[6] the UCR will use the new definition, which defines rape as "Penetration, no matter how slight, of the vagina or anus with any body part or object, or oral penetration by a sex organ of another person, without the consent of the victim."[7] Over the next few years, local and state agencies will also make the change to ensure that reporting remains consistent across each level of law enforcement. After ten years of activism and over 160,000 emails to the FBI, women's rights advocates have applauded the change, asserting that more crimes will be reported, leading to appropriate resource allocation in the fight against sexual assault.[8]

NOTES

1. Terkel, Amanda. 2011. "FBI Director Robert Mueller: Agency Will Update Definition of Rape." *The Huffington Post.* December 15, 2011. Retrieved: December 29, 2011. http://www.huffingtonpost.com/2011/12/15/rape-definition-fbi-robert-mueller_n_1151764.html

2. Terkel, Amanda. 2011.

3. *Los Angeles Times.* 2011. "A Broader Definition of Rape." *The Los Angeles Times,* Editorial. December 22, 2011. Retrieved: December 30, 2011. http://articles.latimes.com/2011/dec/22/opinion/la-ed-rape-20111222

4. Federal Bureau of Investigation. 2011. "Rape Definition Changed." Federal Bureau of Investigation. December 30, 2011. Retrieved: December 31, 2011. http://www.fbi.gov/?came_from=http%3a//www.fbi.gov/news/podcasts/thisweek/rape-definition-changed/view

5. Savage, Charlie. 2012. "U.S. to Expand Its Definition of Rape in Statistics." *The New York Times.* January 6, 2012. Retrieved January 9, 2012. http://www.nytimes.com/2012/01/07/us/politics/federal-crime-statistics-to-expand-rape-definition.html?emc=etal

6. Terkel, Amanda. 2011.

7. Federal Bureau of Investigation. 2011. "Revised Rape Definition Approved." Federal Bureau of Investigation. December 2011. Retrieved: December 30, 2011. http://www.fbi.gov/about-us/cjis/advisory-policy-board

8. Women's Law Project. 2011. "Women's Law Project Applauds FBI Director Mueller for Acting on Recommendation to Change Rape Definition. Women's Law Project. December 15, 2011. Retrieved: December 30, 2011. http://www.womenslawproject.org/press/PR_FBI_Mueller_ChangesRapeDef.pdf

All That Sheltering Emptiness

Mattilda Bernstein Sycamore

I always liked hotel lobbies, the chandeliers and so much ceiling I'd yawn like I was oblivious really I was trying not to go in the wrong direction. If I made a mistake then the key was to act like it was the funniest thing, oh I'm so relaxed! I developed fantasies about what the receptionist did and did not know, fantasies that might involve mischief if our eyes met in a certain way—I wanted something like understanding, I'm not sure I would have called it that.

This particular hotel was the Hyatt or one of those chains, right on Central Park and the lobby wasn't on the ground level—more exclusive that way, the place was fancier than I'd expected. The mirrors sparkled and everything looked freshly-designed—camel, auburn, amber—a little different from the standard beige. I imagined the views were spectacular since the hotel was right on Central Park but tricks always have their curtains drawn, they don't want anyone to see anything not even the trees. This guy had the features of someone very popular in the '80s, swept-back hair and still a walled muscularity, disdain in his eyes he wanted to give me a massage, sure. He rubbed the hotel lotion into my back, something awful and floral-scented—strong hands I always needed a massage.

Of course then he was grinding on top of me, dick teasing my asshole—this was no surprise. Then his dick slid in, so easy and dangerous this was also familiar. I allowed a few thrusts so I could relax, then I said oh I need you to put on a condom. I was thinking about the lotion, what good would the condom do with lotion—maybe I should get a washcloth. His dick remained in my ass, so different when it slides in smoothly like foreplay instead of that desperation, push push push. I started to push myself upright, he was heavy on top of me, still thrusting as I struggled to get onto my knees I'll admit it was hot then he slammed me down on the bed. Oh. This is what's happening: his weight on my back he's holding me down I'm not sure I can get him off me.

I thought about screaming but what would that do—hotel security, they have ways of dealing with situations but nothing that would help me. Maybe no one would arrive at all, bruises or blood and more rage directed my way. At least I wasn't in pain, my asshole was relaxed I was still hard he was fucking me faster I didn't want him to come in my ass, that was the important thing. Come on my face, I said—pull out and come on my face, I want your come on my face I want to eat your come. I wasn't sure if he was listening but then he did pull out and I rolled onto my back, he straddled me with shit on his dick in my face, jerking fast and moaning I could feel his come in between my chin and neck I closed my eyes.

The bathroom was always where I'd go to breathe; in the shower I was shaking, soft towel, just hurry up I need cocktails. Studying myself in the mirror before opening the door, do my eyes look okay? Back to the trick, he had his clothes on he wasn't smiling or frowning I wondered how often he did this. He handed me $250 in three crisp bills, I smiled and said thanks, I was glad for the money I wanted to think it was worth it.

Back into the elevator, it opened automatically at the lobby so the staff could pretend not to stare in, then downstairs to the ground level past those spotless mirrors, glass doors and then I was outside. Walking fast through the wind like everything and nothing mattered I wanted safety; I hailed a cab.

If I say that cocktails cleared my head, then you know that all my analysis failed me: I didn't tell anyone, I felt stupid; I thought it was my fault. Yes, there was force; no, he didn't pull out when I asked him to—but otherwise how was this trick different from every other guy who just slid it in? Every guy who assumed that if his dick was near my asshole and I was enjoying that gentle tease, the security of arousal—then forget about words, my consent had arrived.

New York is a lonely place, it was a lonely place for me eight years ago. I felt stupid because I couldn't use language to help—I was nervous that my friends would think I was someone to worry about. I thought maybe this was a trauma to push aside, with bigger issues in the picture, from a childhood of my father splitting me open to the overwhelm of the everyday. If consent was already assumed in the public sexual cultures where I searched for beauty amid the ruthlessness of objectification without appreciation, then what about the rooms where I swallowed cock for cash? I didn't want to call it rape because it felt so commonplace. Except for the shaking afterwards, desperation mixed with a determination to escape.

RAPE MYTHS

KATIE M. EDWARDS, JESSICA A. TURCHIK, CHRISTINA M. DARDIS, NICOLE REYNOLDS, AND CHRISTINE A. GIDYCZ

INTRODUCTION

Sexual violence is an endemic problem in U.S. society . . . as evidenced by the fact that 18–25 percent of U.S. women report experiencing either an attempted or completed rape in their lifetimes (Fisher et al., 2000; Tjaden and Thoennes, 2000). Research suggests that numerous factors are related to rape proclivity and the occurence of sexual aggression, one of which is the acceptance and perpetuation of rape myths (Desai et al., 2008; Lonsway and Fitzgerald, 1994; Loh et al., 2005). In the 1970s, sociologists (e.g., Schwendinger and Schwendinger, 1974) and feminists (e.g., Brownmiller, 1975) introduced the concept of rape myths in order to explain a set of largely false cultural beliefs that were thought to underlie sexual aggression perpetrated against women. Rape myths, which include elements of victim blame, perpetrator absolution, and minimization or rationalization of sexual violence, perpetuate sexual violence against women (Payne et al., 1994). Indeed, research has documented that men's engagement in sexual violence is predicted by rape myth acceptance (Desai et al., 2008; Loh et al., 2005).

Due to the increasing accumulation of rape myth research over the past 30 years across a variety of disciplines, the purpose of this [reading] is to provide an overview of the historical origins of rape myths, document the current manifestations of these myths in U.S. society, and summarize the current body of research literature. Consistent with Brownmiller's (1975) groundbreaking feminist analysis of rape, we assert that sexual violence is perpetuated by a patriarchal system where men hold higher status and have greater power than women. We aim to demonstrate how rape ideologies emanate from this patriarchal system and are present at various levels of society. We assert that, given patriarchy's marginalization of women and their experiences, rape myths serve to legitimize sexual violence against women. Using this feminist approach, we review the current body of rape myth literature and argue that rape myths, despite their falsehood, are endorsed by a substantial segment of the population and permeate legal, media, and religious institutions. Concluding this [reading], we discuss . . . how existing data could be used to aid in eradicating rape myths at both the individual and institutional levels. . . .

EVIDENCE FOR THE EXISTENCE OF RAPE MYTHS

Research using various scales to measure rape myths document that between 25 percent and 35 percent of respondents (both male and female) agree with the majority of these rape myths (Lonsway and Fitzgerald 1994), and that men are more likely than women to endorse rape myths (Suarez and Gadalla 2010). When utilizing open-ended questions asking

From "Rape Myths: History, Individual and Institutional-Level Presence, and Implications for Change," by Katie M. Edwards, Jessica A. Turchik, Christina M. Dardis, Nicole Reynolds, Christine A. Gidycz. *Sex Roles*, Volume 65, Issue 11-12, December 2011, pp. 761–768, 770–773. Copyright © 2011, Springer Science+Business Media. With kind permission from Springer Science+Business Media.

participants to list their personal beliefs about rape victims, Buddie and Miller (2001) found that 66 percent of their college sample (comprised of women and men) endorsed some combination of rape myths. Although the majority of rape myth research has been conducted with college students, studies with non-college samples generally find similar rates of rape myth endorsement (Basile, 2002; Field, 1978). Additionally, although there are some researchers who have suggested that some rape myth rates may be decreasing over time (Edward and McLeod, 1999), the methodological differences across studies make it difficult to compare endorsement rates of these beliefs across time. Further, results from a study by Hinck and Thomas (1999) suggest that college women and students who attend rape education or rape awareness workshops are less likely to endorse rape myths than college men and students who do not attend such programs, which suggests that increases in rape education programming could lead to decreased rates of rape myth acceptance. Paradoxically, however, rape education may result less in a decreased acceptance of rape myths than in an increased reluctance to acknowledge them as a result of a newfound awareness that sexual aggression is socially unacceptable. . . .

Rape myths are also present within legal, religious, and media institutions. For example, Gylys and McNamara (1996) found that 43 percent of prosecuting attorneys sampled from a Midwestern state demonstrated a moderate to high level of rape myth acceptance. . . . Also, research demonstrates that rape myths affect police officer's interactions with victims of rape, such that police officers were less likely to believe victims whose characteristics were not consistent with a stereotypical rape victim (e.g., are not virgins, had a prior relationship with the suspect; Page, 2008). Although there is minimal empirical research on rape myths within religions institutions, preliminary research suggests that some rape myths are endorsed by a substantial number of clergy (Sheldon and Parent, 2002); there is a larger body of non-empirical, theoretical literature on religions institutions and rape myths (e.g., Fortune, 2005). Rape myths are also prevalent in the media and directly affect consumers' attitudes towards rape. For example, results from a content analysis of prime-time television dramas found that 42 percent of storylines depicted a women "wanting" to be raped, 38 percent depicted a victim lying about rape, and 46 percent featured women "asking" to be raped (e.g., by being scantily dressed; Brinson, 1992). . . . Thus, rape myths not only influence societal attitudes towards rape victims, but influence important decisions related to legal cases and how information is reported to the public.

REVIEW OF SPECIFIC RAPE MYTHS
Husbands Cannot Rape Their Wives

Research with college students suggests that 9 percent of men and 5 percent of women believe that a husband's use of physical force to have sex with his wife does not constitute rape, and in the same sample 31 percent of men and 19 percent of women indicated that a husband having sex without his wife's consent does not constitute rape (Kirkwood and Cecil, 2001). Moreover, in a national telephone survey, Basile (2002) found that only 15 percent of the sample believed that boyfriends and husbands could rape their partners. Although little research has assessed if certain groups of individuals are more likely to endorse the marital rape myth, preliminary research suggests that men (compared to women) endorse higher rates of this particular myth (Ewoldt et al., 2000). . . . Despite these beliefs, research shows that 10–14 percent of all women are raped by their husbands in their lifetime and this rises to 40–50 percent among battered women (Martin et al., 2007). Research also documents that there are numerous deleterious physical and psychological consequences to marital rape (Bennice and Resick, 2003).

In modern European and American history, husbands who raped their wives have been exempt from legal punishment (Russell, 1990). The marital rape exemption is most commonly traced back to Sir Matthew Hale (an English Chief Justice) and eighteenth-century common law (Martin et al., 2007). Hale stated that "the husband cannot be guilty of a rape committed by himself upon his lawful wife, for by their mutual matrimonial consent and contract the wife hath given up herself in this kind unto her husband, which she cannot retract" (1736, as cited in Martin et al., 2007, p. 331). This statement, the Hale doctrine, was formally recognized in the United States in 1857 under the *Commonwealth v. Fogarty* decision. Subsequently, in the *Frazier v. State of Texas* (1905) case, the court decided that the "law would not permit a woman to retract her consent to marital relations after once assuming them" (Barshis, 1983, p. 384). This set a precedent that would not be legally changed for nearly a century.

The U.S. Women's Movement in the 1970s brought national attention to marital rape. These efforts led in 1975 to South Dakota becoming the first state to make marital rape a crime and, in 1978, John Rideout being the first individual charged with marital rape (Russell, 1990). In 1979, during *Commonwealth v. Chretien*, the United States witnessed its first marital rape conviction (Bennice and Risck, 2003), and in the past 30 years all states have developed laws forbidding marital rape (Martin et al., 2007). However, 31 states plus Washington D.C. have partial or qualified exemptions to their sexual assault laws, such that marital rape is prosecutable only if the spouses are living apart, legally separated, or divorced, if physical force is used, or if the wife cannot consent due to mental impairment or incapacitation (National Center for the Prosecution of Violence Against Women, 2009).

In addition to legal institutions, some religious institutions have contributed to the myth that husbands cannot rape their wives. For instance, some people use Biblical verses such as Ephesians 5:22, "Wives, submit to your own husbands, as to the Lord," or 1 Corinthians 7:4 "The wife does not have authority over her own body, but the husband does" (New King James Version), to justify sexually aggressive behaviors (Fortune, 2005). Subsequent Biblical scripture instructs husbands to submit to their wives and suggests that wives have control over their husbands' bodies as well. However, given the patriarchal structures of many religious institutions, it is most often the right of the husband to his wife's body that is emphasized. . . . In an investigation of clergy's attitudes toward rape, clergy were given fictional marital rape scenarios and were asked whether or not the incident is rape and how much husband and wife were each to blame for the incident. . . . (Sheldon and Parent, 2002). Although 61 percent of clergy identified that the "wife did something she did not want to", 24 percent of clergy endorsed ideas that the women did not use adequate forms of self-defense (e.g., resistance, escape), and 11 percent agreed that the wife "needs to know the proper marital role," (e.g., be submissive, sexually competent). Thus, legal exemptions and religious doctrines support the notion that marital rape is not as serious as other types of sexual violence, that men, still today, possess a degree of ownership over their wives' bodies, and that marriage is equated with unconditional sexual consent.

With regard to the media, one way this institution perpetuates rape myths is by the exclusion of some stories and the focus on others. For instance, rape coverage in the news media concentrates heavily on stranger rape cases (compared to primetime episodic series, Cuklanz,

2000), even though marital rape is much more common than stranger rape (Martin et al., 2007; Russell, 1990). Although Cuklanz (2000) concluded that primetime representations of rape changed between 1976 and 1990, such that there are fewer depictions of stranger rapes and more sympathy for victims, this is not the case for marital rape depictions. Generally the rapes depicted on primetime series are those prepretrated by acquaintances or dates. Given that experimental research suggests that media portrayals of rape cases directly affects consumers' attitudes about rape (Franiuk et al. 2008a, b), it is probable that the exclusion of marital rape depictions in the media obscures the problem from the public, allowing individuals to believe that this does not happen or is not a significant problem. . . .

Women Enjoy Rape

Studies with college students suggest that 1–4 percent of female participants believe that women secretly desire to be raped (Carmody and Washington, 2001; Johnson et al., 1997), whereas 15–16 percent of men believe this myth (Edwards et al., 2010; Johnson et al., 1997). Additionally, approximately 11 percent of college men report that they believe women exaggerate how much rape affects them (Edwards et al., 2010). However, research clearly demonstrates that rape often leads to numerous deleterious physical, pyschological, and social consequences (Centers for Disease Control, 2004). . . .

The belief that rape must occur forcibly and against her will was cited by Blackstone in eighteenth-century England (Schulhofer, 1998). English law required that the victim resisted her attacker "earnestly" or "to the utmost," a perspective that carried over to the United States (Schulhofer, 1998). Although such resistance has been removed from some states' laws, evidence of physical force is often still required above and beyond verbal threats or coercion (Bryden, 2000). Due to this requirement, the absence of vaginal injury is often used as evidence against women, as it is then assumed that if she was able to self-lubricate, she must have enjoyed the forced sex act (Lees, 1996). An English law created by the 1975 case of *Director of Public Prosecutions v. Morgan* stated that a man's honest belief that a woman had consented was enough to negate his liability for rape. Though this law was repealed in 2003 by the Sexual Offense Act, "token resistance," the attitudinal belief that women mean "yes" when they say "no" to sexual advances from men (Muehlenhard and Hollabaugh, 1988), is still present in society. Indeed, men's belief in token resistance can be used as justification for not stopping sexual activity despite a woman's protests. Recent studies have found a link between men's belief in token resistance, acceptance of rape myths (Garcia, 1998), and sexual perpetration (Loh et al., 2005; Masser et al., 2006). . . .

Beliefs that women desire forced sex have been incorporated for centuries into "mainstream cultural work in art, religion, law, literature, philosophy, psychology, films, and so forth" (Dworkin 1981, p. 166). The popular eighteenth-century tales penned by sexual sadist Marquis de Sade not only celebrate the raping of women, but Sade advocated that women can and should accept rape and can choose to enjoy the experience (Dworkin, 1981). Also popular in the eighteenth-century print media were depictions of women secretly desiring sexual intercourse despite their stated refusal: "A woman's dual role as temptress and regulator [as demonstrated in song and print media] meant that her stated 'no' might still mean 'yes' to sexual overtures" (Block, 2006; p. 39). The idea that women enjoy rape was present in academic literature even into the twentieth century. . . . In present times, the most visible perpetrator of the myth that women enjoy rape is arguably the pornography industry and other sexually explicit forms of media.

Dworkin's (1981) groundbreaking book asserted that pornography portrays sexual violence as something that is desired and enjoyed by women, and that pornography fosters rape myths and leads to violence against women, all in an effort to preserve patriarchal power. In fact, recent empirical research supports Dworkin's theory; a recent meta-analysis found a direct significant and positive relationship between use of pornography (especially violent pornography) and attitudes supporting violence toward women (r = 24; Hald et al., 2010). Self-reported exposure to such materials has also been directly and positively related to rape myth acceptance. . . . Further, a meta-analysis of experimental studies found that exposure to pornography depicting nonviolent sexual activity as well as media depictions of violent sexual activity lead to increases in aggressive behaviors, with depictions of violent sexual activity leading to greater increases in behavioral aggression than nonviolent sexual activity (Allen et al., 1995). Thus, pornography itself is not the sole causative factor for aggressive tendencies or rape myth acceptance, but serves to bring these beliefs to the surface and reinforce such already held misogynistic beliefs.

It is not only pornography that elicits negative beliefs about women; a recent meta-analysis found that the use of degrading images (such as displaying pin-ups and advertisements of scantily clad women) was positively related to endorsing rape myths, with a moderate effect size (.72; Saurez and Gadalla, 2010). . . . Another media form, romance novels, which represent 40 percent of the mass paperback sales in the United States (Salmon and Symons, 2003), often include rape of the principle female character. In a historical review of romance novels, Thurston (1987) found that in 54 percent of the novels, the female lead was

raped. Mayerson and Taylor (1987) found that college women who read these stories reported higher rape myth acceptance. . . . In sum, it appears that a substantial number of individuals either believe that woman ask to be raped or can be primed to endorse such a belief in experimental studies. Although research clearly demonstrates that media is riddled with rape myths, there are very few studies that assess the direct role that media has on attitudes, and more importantly, behaviors. Thus, it should be noted that much of what we know about the role of media, and other institutions, in perpetuating the belief that women desire to be raped is limited and warrants empirical inquiry using rigorous methodological designs.

Women Ask to be Raped

"Women ask to be raped" is an umbrella under which more specific ideas, such as "she was walking at night by herself," "she is promiscuous," and "she was asking to be raped in that outfit," can be categorized (Allison and Wrightsman, 1993; Carmody and Washington, 2001). Carmody and Washington (2001) reported that approximately 21 percent of college women endorsed the myth that women are asking for trouble if they wear sexy or provocative clothing. Moreover, Johnson et al. (1997) found that 27 percent of college men and 10 percent of women endorsed the myth that "women provoke rape." A British Amnesty International poll conducted in 2005 found that 22 percent of those surveyed thought that a woman was partially or totally responsible for rape if she had many sexual partners, and 26 percent thought her partially or totally responsible for rape if she was wearing sexy or revealing clothing (Walklate, 2008). . . .

Block (2006) argued that the burgeoning emphasis in eighteenth-century America on women's ability to make autonomous decisions about their relationships with men coincided with the view that women were even more culpable than in the past for sexual behaviors, including rape. This belief played out in eighteenth-century legal proceedings, such that rape cases were more likely to be dismissed than in previous centuries . . . Accordingly, "women alleging rape were expected to act and portray themselves as *unequivocal victims* [i.e., Caucasian, middle- or upper-class, pious, submissive] if their allegations were to have any credibility" (Stevenson, 2000, p. 345). Although more subtle today, Stevenson asserted that the notion of the unequivocal victim has persisted into modern times and contributes to the current belief that women lie about being raped, especially in legal institutions. For example, research shows that jury members' attitudes toward rape (i.e., women are responsible for preventing rape, women bring rape upon themselves) were found to be the single best predictor of their decisions in rape case verdicts (Field and Bienen, 1980). . . . Additionally, in cases in which consent is less clearly delineated, such as when drugs or alcohol are implicated, mock jurors have stated that they would like more information on whether the woman was generally the type to act in a promiscuous manner (Finch and Munro, 2005). . . .

Additionally, although rape shield laws were designed to prevent bias against the victim's character, such laws are limited to sexual history and not other factors (e.g., drug or alcohol use), and information about victim behaviors are often found to be admissible to explain the circumstances that lead up to rape (Bryden and Lengnick, 1997). . . .

Cahill [2000] . . . asserted that women are expected to monitor, police, restrict, and even hinder their movements in an attempt to ensure the safety of their bodies. This underscores the widespread belief that women are responsible for preventing bodily violations and that women who are sexually victimized are culpable.

Some aspects of religiosity and religious institutions may perpetuate the belief that women are culpable for rape. In a study conducted at a Christian liberal arts college, men higher in religiosity (measured by amount of prayer and importance of religion) compared to less religious men were more likely to believe that women who are promiscuous or who dress in a provocative manner deserve to be raped (Freymeyer, 1997). Biblical scripture supports this notion. For example, *Genesis* 34 tells the story of a woman named Dinah who goes out alone to meet a woman in town, but is abducted and raped by the local prince. The general theological interpretation of the meaning of this story is that Dinah is culpable for this rape by going out alone without a companion. Theological interpretations have even implied that by going out alone she must have desired to be seen by the local men, and thus her rape was "inevitable" (Parry, 2002). . . .

Media coverage of rape cases can also contribute to victim blame by insinuating that the victim is at fault for being in a dangerous area or that promiscuous women deserve to be raped for acting inappropriately (Caringella-MacDonald, 1998). Howitt (1998) argued that media stories are often constructed from a viewpoint that is more favorable to the perpetrator (e.g., by focusing on the perpetrator's version of events) rather than the victim, and that acquittals were more likely to make the front page of a newspaper than rape convictions. . . .

Women Lie About Being Raped

Although there is great debate about the prevalence of unfounded accusations of rape (Marshall and Alison, 2006), most researchers suggest that false rape allegations are highly infrequent (Patton and Snyder-Yuly, 2007). In fact, an international report that reviewed studies and law enforcement estimates reported that approximately 2–8 percent of reported sexual assaults are believed to be false (Lonsway et al., 2007). Nevertheless, Burt (1980) found that 50 percent of community men and women believe that women lie about being raped, but more recently, Kahlor and Morrison (2007) documented in their sample of college women that participants on average believed that 19 percent of rape accusations were false. Among college men, recent data showed that 22 percent agreed that "women lie about rape to get back at men," and 13 percent agreed that "a lot of women lead men on and then cry rape" (Edwards et al., 2010). Thus, prevalence of this myth may have decreased over time, but methodological differences as well as possible changes in willingness to disclose make this hard to determine. . . .

The legal system is an institution that has a long history of perpetuating the belief that women lie about being raped (Ask, 2010; MacKinnon, 1982, 1987). The seventeenth-century judge Sir Matthew Hale asserted that rape is "an accusation easily to be made, hard to be proved, and harder to be defended by the party accused, tho' never so innocent" (Hale, 1736, p. 635). This statement would become known as the "Hale Warning" and was often read in courtrooms during rape cases up until the late twentieth century, casting suspicion on the testimonies of women who reported being raped (Ferguson, 1987). In modern court proceedings, similar language can still be heard. Matosian (1993) argued that the language used by defense attorneys in cross-examining the victim, as well as their manner of defining and identifying rape serves to recast the act as consensual or to paint victims as liars. A 1993 report prepared by the Senate Judiciary Committee found that less than one half of rape cases are convicted, 21 percent of convicted rapists are never sentenced to prison time, and 24 percent of convicted rapists receive time in local jails for less than 11 months (The Response to Rape: Detours on the Road to Equal Justice). . . .

The media is another institution that perpetuates the rape myth that women lie about being raped. Experimental research has found that the framing of rape in news stories directly affects consumers' attitudes about rape, such that after reading stories which contain rape myths, college men and women were more likely to blame the victim (Franiuk et al., 2008a). Such findings indicate that the news media's biased focus on the perpetrator's account (Howitt, 1998), victim blame, and the idea that women lie about being raped (Gavey and Gow, 2001) could have an even more pernicious effect on consumer attitudes. Also, the media seem to focus on the minority of rape cases where DNA evidence has proved that the woman made a false accusation or where acquittals were made ("All charges dropped in Duke case," 2007). Such a tendency to recall highly publicized situations and deem them as more common than they actually are is related to the social psychology principle known as the availability heuristic. According to the availability heuristic, individuals estimate the likelihood or frequency of an event based on how easily an example can be brought to mind (Tversky and Kahneman, 1973). . . .

Directions for Individual and Institutional Change

There have been burgeoning efforts to create and empirically validate the efficacy of sexual assault risk reduction and prevention programming for women and men, respectively. One component of these programs is to debunk prevailing rape myths. This is generally done by presenting the myth (e.g., women lie about being raped) and then presenting facts/research evidence (e.g., 2–8 percent of reported sexual assaults are false). The majority of sexual violence prevention programs occur with college-age individuals (Gidycz et al., 2011); however, it has also been suggested that prevention programming should begin early in life and continue throughout the life course. Also, given that younger people may endorse more overall rape myths (Ferro et al., 2008), interventions may be particularly effective if they occur prior to the time when adolescents begin dating.

Efforts must extend beyond intervening at the individual level. Specifically, it is important that intervention target institutions and the unique role that they play in perpetuating rape myths. For example, Hyman et al. (2000) pointed out that "because many of the roots of devaluing women are based on religions and cultural beliefs, church and community leaders [are] considered to be in an ideal position to provide support as well as to change social norms regarding violence" (p. 289). A reframing of religious perspectives could be useful in eradicating rape myths from religious institutions (Keener, 1996). For instance, Keener uses the Bible to support his argument that victims of rape are not responsible for their assault and retain their "moral virginity", while Turell and Thomas (2001) discuss specific ways that counselors can reframe passages in the Bible to aid Judeo-Christian sexual assault victims within a feminist framework.

Among those working within the field of media, it is the social responsibility of those reporting on rape to do so in a way that is factual and devoid of rape myths. Although salacious reports and storylines (e.g., stranger rapes, the lying "victim") may be more likely to attract viewers or sell papers, it behooves those within the field of media to promote the message to the public that these are more uncommon and that rapes most commonly occur under different circumstances (e.g., acquaintance, rarity of lying about rape). Further, journalists should be educated with regard to the fallaciousness of rape myths and the inappropriateness of

attributing equal blame to the perpetrator and victim in a rape trial story in order to achieve "fair and balanced" news reporting. Within the legal institution, the allowance of certain information in cases that promotes rape myths (e.g., discussing a victim's sexual history) needs to be eliminated. Finally, it is important to provide education to attorneys, judges, and other legal professionals on the impact of rape myths in legal decisions.

. . . Given that rape ideologies exist as a part of broader patriarchal power structures, discourses on sex and gender, masculinity and femininity, sexuality and heterosexuality, sexism and racism, and other systems of social oppression must be addressed through similar individual and institutional-level approaches (Gravey, 2005). Rectifying conceptual and methodological issues as well as continued basic research on various aspects of rape myths and related systems of oppression and individual-based discrimination will likely inform interventions efforts at individual, institutional, and societal levels.

REFERENCES

All charges dropped in Duke case (2007, April 12). *New York Times*. Retrieved from http://www.nytimes.com/2007/04/12/us/12duke.html

Allen, M., D'Alessio, D., and Brezgel, K. 1995. A meta-analysis summarizing the effects of pornography II: Aggression after exposure. *Human Communication Research*, 22: 258–283. doi:10.1111/j.1468-2958.1995.tb00368.x.

Allison, J. A., and Wrightsman, L. S. 1993. *Rape, the misunderstood crime*, Thousand Oaks: Sage. doi:10.1111/1467-9450.00310.

Ask, K. 2010. A survey of police officers' and prosecutors' beliefs about crime victim behaviors. *Journal of Interpersonal Violence*, 25: 1132–1149. doi:10.1177/0886260509340535.

Barshis, V. G. 1983. The question of marital rape. *Women's Studies International Forum*, 6: 383–393. doi:10.1016/0277-5395(83)90031-6.

Basile, K. C. 2002. Attitudes toward wife rape: Effects of social background and victim status. *Violence and Victims*, 17: 341–354. doi:10.1891/vivi.17.3.341.33659.

Bennice, J. A., and Resick, A. 2003. Marital rape: History, research, and practice. *Trauma, Violence, & Abuse*, 4: 228–246. doi:10.1177/1524838003004003003.

Blackstone, W. 1765. *Commentaries on the law of England.* Oxford: Calarendon Press.

Block, S. 2002. Rape without women: Print culture and the politicization of rape, 1765–1815. *The Journal of American History,* 89: 849–868, doi:10.2307/3092343.

Block, S. 2006. *Rape and sexual power in early America.* Chapel Hill University of North Carolina Press.

Brinson, S. L. 1992. The use and opposition of rape myths in prime-time television dramas. *Sex Roles,* 27: 359–375. doi:10.1007/BF00289945.

Brownmiller, S. 1975. *Against our will: Men, Women, and rape.* New York: Penguin Books.

Bryden, D. P. 2000. Redefining rape. *Buffalo Criminal Law Review,* 3(2): 317–479. doi: 10.1525/nclr.2000.3.2.317.

Bryden, D. P. and Lengnick, S. 1997. Rape in the criminal justice system. *Journal of Criminal Law and Criminology,* 87: 1194–1384. doi:10.2307/1144018.

Buddie, A. M., and Miller, G. 2001. Beyond rape myths: A more complex view of perceptions of rape victims. *Sex Roles,* 45: 139–160. doi:10.1023/A:1013575209803.

Burt, M. R., 1980. Cultural myths and supports for rape. *Journal of Personality and Social Psychology,* 38: 217–230. doi:10.1037/0022-3514-38.2.217.

Cahill, A. 2000: Foucault, rape, and the construction of the feminine body. *Hypatia,* 15: 43–63. doi: 10.1111/j. 1527-2001. 2000.tb01079.x.

Caringella-MacDonald, S. 1998. Parallels and pitfalls: The aftermath of legal reform for sexual assault, marital rape, and domestic violence victims. *Journal of Interpersonal Violence,* 3: 174–189, doi:10.1177/088626088003002004.

Carmody, D. C., and Washington, L. M. 2001. Rape myth acceptance among college women: The impact of race and prior victimization. *Journal of Interpersonal Violence,* 16: 424–436. doi:10.1177/088626001016005003.

Centers for Disease Control 2004. *Sexual violence facts.* Retrieved from http://www.edc.gov/ncipc/factsheets/svfacts.htm

Cuklanz, L. M. 2000. *Rape on prime time: Television, masculinity, and sexual violence.* Philadelphia: University of Pennsylvania Press.

Desai, A. D., Edwards, K. M., and Gidycz, C. A. 2008, November. Testing an integrative model of sexual aggression in college men. In A. C. Aosved (Chair), *Sexual violence perpetration: Individual and contextual factors.* Symposium conducted at the annual meeting of the Association for Behavioral and Cognitive Therapies, Orlando, FL.

Dworkin, A. 1981. *Pornography: Men possessing women.* New York: Penguin Books.

Edward, K. E., and McLeod, M. D. 1999. The reality and myth of rape: Implications for the criminal justice system. *Expert Evidence,* 7: 37–58. doi:10.1.023/A:1008917714094.

Edwards, K. M., Gidyz, C. A., and Desai, A. D. 2010. [Rape myths]. Unpublished raw data.

Ewoldt, C. A., Monson, C. M., and Langhinrichsen-Rohling, J. 2000. Attributions about rape in a continuum of dissolving marital relationships, *Journal of Interpersonal Violence,* 15: 1175–1182. doi:10.1177/088626000015011004.

Ferguson, F. 1987. Rape and the rise of the novel. *Representations,* 20: 88–112. doi:10.1525/rep.1987.20.1.99p0185u.

Ferro, C., Cermele, J., and Saltzman, A. 2008. Current perceptions of marital rape: Some good and note-so-good news. *Journal of Interpersonal Violence,* 23: 764–779. doi:10.1177/0886260507313947.

Feild, H. S., 1978. Attitudes toward rape: A comparative analysis of police, rapists, crisis counselors, and citizens. Journal of Personality and Social Psychology. 36: 136–179. doi:10.1037/0022-3514.36.2.156.

Feild, H. S., and Bienen, L. B. 1980. *Jurors and rape.* Lexington: D. C. Health.

Finch, E., and Munro, V. E. 2005. Juror stereotypes and blame attribution in rape cases involving intoxicants. *British Journal of Criminology,* 45: 25–38. doi:10.1093/bjc/azh055.

Fisher, B. S., Cullen, F. T., and Turner M. G. 2000. *The sexual victimization of college women.* Retrieved from www.ncjrs.org/txtfiles1/nij/182369.txt

Forcible and statutory rape: An exploration of the operation and objectives of the consent standard 1952. *The Yale Law Journal,* 62: 55–83.

Fortune, M. M. 2005. *Sexual violence: The sin revised.* Cleveland: Pilgrim Press.

Franiuk, R., Seefelt, J. L., Cepress, S. L., and Vandello, J. A. 2008a. Prevalence and effects of rape myths in print journalism: The Kobe Bryant case. *Violence Against Women.* 14: 287–309. doi:10.1177/1077801207313971.

Franiuk, R., Seefelt, J. L., and Vandello. J. A. 2008b. Prevalence of rape myths in headlines and their effects on attitudes toward rape. *Sex Roles,* 58: 790–801. doi:10.1007/s11199-007-9372-4.

Freymeyer, R. H. 1997. Rape myths and religiosity. *Sociological Spectrum.* 17: 473–489. doi:10.1080/027321 73.1997.9982179.

Garcia, L. T. 1998. Perceptions of resistance to unwanted sexual advances. *Journal of Psychology & Human Sexuality,* 10: 43–52. doi:10.1300/0056v10n01_03.

Gavey, N. 2005. *Just sex? The cultural scaffolding of rape.* New York: Routledge.

Gavey, N., and Gow, V. 2001. 'Cry wolf', cried the wolf: Constructing the issue of false rape allegations in New Zealand media texts. *Feminism & Psychology,* 11: 341–360. doi:10.1177/0959353501011003006.

Gidycz, C. A., Orchowski, L. M., and Edwards, K. M. 2011. Sexual violence: Primary prevention. In J. White,

M. Koss, A. Kazdin (Eds.), *Violence against women and children (Vol 2): Navigating solutions* (pp. 159–179). Washington, DC: American Psychological Association.

Gylys, J. A., and McNamara, R. 1996. Acceptance of rape myths among prosecuting attorneys. *Psychological Reports.* 79: 15–18.

Hald, G. M., Malamuth, N. M., and Yuen, C. 2010. Pornography and attitudes supporting violence against women: Revisiting the relationship in nonexperimental studies. *Aggressive Behavior,* 36: 14–20. doi:10.1002/ab.20328.

Hale, M. 1736. *Historia placitorum cornae: The history of the pleas of the crown.* London: Gyles, Woodword, and Davis.

Hinck, S. S., and Thomas, R. W. 1999. Rape myth acceptance in college students: How far have we come? *Sex Roles,* 40: 815–832. doi:10.1023/A:1018816920168.

Howitt, D. 1998. *Crime, the media, and the law.* New York: John Wiley & Sons.

Hyman, I., Guruge, S., Stewart, D. E., Ahmad, F. 2000. Primary prevention of violence against women. *Women's Health Issues,* 10: 288–293. doi:10.1016/S1049-3867(00)00066-9.

Johnson, B. E., Kuck, D. L., and Schander, P. R. 1997. Rape myth acceptance and sociodemographic characteristics: A multidimensional analysis. *Sex Roles,* 36: 693–707. doi:10.1023/A:1025671021697.

Kahlor, L., and Morrison, D. 2007. Television viewing and rape myth acceptance among college women. *Sex Roles,* 56: 729–739. doi:10.1007/s11199-007-9232-2.

Keener, C. 1996. Some biblical reflections on justice, rape and an insensitive society. In C. Kroeger and J. Beck (Eds.), *Women, abuse, and the Bible: How scripture can be used to hurt or to heal* (pp. 117–130). Grand Rapids: Baker Books.

Kirkwood, M. K., and Cecil, D. K. 2001. Marital rape: A student assessment of rape laws and marital exemption. *Violence Against Women,* 7: 1234–1253. doi:10.1177/1077801201007011003.

Lees, S. 1996. *Carnal knowledge: Rape on trial.* London: Women's Press.

Loh, C., Gidyez, C. A., Lobo, T. R., and Luthra, R. 2005. A prospective analysis of sexual assault perpetration: Risk factors related to perpetrator characteristics. *Journal of Interpersonal Violence,* 20: 1325–1348. doi:10.1177/0886260505278528.

Lonsway, K. A., and Fitzgerald, L. R. 1994. Rape myths: In review. *Psychology of Women Quarterly,* 18: 133–164. doi:10.1111/j.1471-6402.1994.tb00448.x.

Lonsway, K., Archambault, J., and Lisak, D. 2007. False reports: Moving beyond the issue to successfully investigate and prosecute non-stranger sexual assault. *National Center for the Prosecution of Violence Against Women.* Retrieved from http://www.ndaa.org/publications/newsletters/the_voice_vol_3_no_1_2009.pdf

MacKinnon, C. 1982. Feminism, Marxism, method, and the state: An agenda for theory. *Signs,* 7: 515–544. doi:10.1086/493898.

MacKinnon, C. 1987. *Feminism unmodified: Discourses on life and law.* Boston: Harvard University Press.

Marshall, B. C., and Alison, L. J. 2006. Structural behavioural analysis as a basis for discriminating between genuine and simulated rape allegations. *Journal of Investigating Psychology and Offender Profiling,* 3: 21–34. doi:10.1002/jip.42.

Martin, E. K., Taft, C. T., and Resick, P. A. 2007. A review of marital rape. *Aggression and Violent Behavior,* 12: 329–347. doi:10.1016/j.avb.2006.10.003.

Masser, B., Viki, G. T., and Power, C. 2006. Hostile sexism and rape proclivity amongst men. *Sex Roles.* 54: 565–574. doi:10.1007/s11199-006-9022-2.

Matosian, G. M. 1993. *Reproducing rape: Domination through talk in the courtroom.* Chicago: University of Chicago Press.

Mayerson, S. E., and Taylor, D. A. 1987. The effects of rape myth pornography on women's attitudes and the mediating roles of sex role stereotyping. *Sex Roles,* 17: 321–338. doi:10.1007/BF00288456.

Muehlenhard, C. L., and Hollabaugh, C. 1988. Do women sometimes say no when they mean yes? The prevalence and correlates of women's token resistance to sex. *Journal of Personality and Social Psychology,* 54: 872–879. doi:10.1037/0022-3514.54.5.872.

National Center for the Prosecution of Violence Against Women. 2009. *Summary of Spousal Rape Laws.* Retrieved from http://www.wcsap.org/pdf/Spousal%20Rape%20Statutes%202009.pdf

Page, A. D. 2008. Judging women and defining crime: Police officers' attitudes toward women and rape. *Sociological Spectrum,* 28: 389–411. doi:10.1080/02732170802053621.

Parry, R. 2002. Feminist hermeneutics and evangelical concerns: The rape of Dinah as a case study. *Tyndale Bulletin,* 53: 1–28. Retrieved from http://98.131.162.170/tynbul/library/TynBull_2002_53_1_01_PerryFeministHermeneutics.pdf

Patton, T. O., and Snyder-Yuly, J. 2007. Any four Black men will do: Rape, race, and the ultimate scapegoat. *Journal of Black Studies.* 37: 859–895. doi:10.1177/0021934706296025.

Payne, D., Lonsway, K., and Fitzgerald, F. 1994. Rape myth acceptance: Exploration of its structure and its measurement using the Illinois Rape Myth Awareness Scale. *Journal of Research in Personality,* 33: 27–68. doi:10.1006/jrpe.1998.2238.

Russell, D. 1990. *Rape in marriage.* Bloomington: Indiana University Press.

Salmon, C., and Symons, D. 2003. *Warrior lovers: Erotic fiction, evolution and female sexuality.* New Haven: Yale University Press.

Schulhofer, S. J. 1998. *Unwanted sex: The culture of intimidation and the failure of law.* Harvard University Press.

Schwendinger, J. R., and Schwendinger, H. 1974. Rape myths: In legal, theoretical, and everyday practice. *Crime and Social Justice,* 1: 18–26.

Senate Judiciary Committee 1993. *The response to rape: Detours on the road to equal justice.* Paper prepared by the majority staff of the Senate Judiciary Committee.

Sheldon, J. P., and Parent, S. L. 2002. Clergy's attitudes and attributions of blame toward female rape victims. *Violence Against Women,* 8: 233–256. doi:10.1177/10778010222183026.

Stevenson, K. 2000. Unequivocal victims: The historical roots of the mystification of the female complainant in rape cases. *Feminist Legal Studies,* 8: 343–366. doi:10.1023/A:1009270302602.

Suarez, E. B., and Gadalla, T. 2010, January. *Stop blaming the victim: A meta-analysis on rape myths.* Paper presented at the Annual Meeting of the Society for Social Work and Research, Tampa, FL.

Thurston, C. 1987. *The romance revolution: Erotic novels for women and the quest for a new sexual identity.* Chicago: University of Illinois Press.

Tjaden, P., and Thoennes, N. 2000. Prevalence and consequences of male-to-female and female-to-male intimate partner violence as measured by the National Violence Against Women Survey. *Violence Against Women,* 6: 142–161. doi:10.1177/10778010022181769.

Turell, S. C., and Thomas, C. 2001. Where was God? Utilizing spirituality with Christian survivors of sexual abuse. *Women and Therapy,* 24: 133–147.

Tversky, A., and Kahneman, D. 1973. Availability: A heuristic for judging frequency and probability. *Cognitive Psychology,* 5: 207–232. doi:10.1016/0010 -0285(73)90033-9.

Walklate, S. 2008. What is to be done about violence against women? Gender, violence, cosmopolitanism and the law. *The British Journal of Criminology,* 48: 39–54. doi:10.1093/bjc/azm050.

THE FANTASY OF ACCEPTABLE "NON-CONSENT"

STACEY MAY FOWLES

Because I'm a feminist who enjoys domination, bondage and pain in the bedroom, it should be pretty obvious why I often remain mute and, well, pretty closeted about my sexuality. While it's easy for me to write an impassioned diatribe on the vital importance of "conventional" women's pleasure, or to talk publicly and explicitly about sexual desire in general, I often shy away from conversations about my personal sexual choices. Despite the fact that I've been on a long, intentional path to finally feel empowered by, and open about, my decision to be a sexual submissive, the reception I receive regarding this decision is not always all that warm.

BDSM (for my purposes, bondage, discipline, dominance and submission, sadism and masochism) makes a lot of people uncomfortable, and the concept of female submission makes feminists really uncomfortable. I can certainly understand why, but I also believe that safe, sane and consensual BDSM exists as a polar opposite of a reality in which women constantly face the threat of sexual violence.

As someone who works in the feminist media and who advocates against violence against women and for rape survivors' rights, I never really felt I was allowed to participate in the fantasy of my own violation. There is a guilt and shame in having the luxury to decide to act on this desire—to consent to this kind of "nonconsent." It seems to suggest you haven't known true sexual violence, cannot truly understand how traumatic it can be, if you're willing to incorporate a fictional version of it into your "play." But this simply isn't true: A 2007 study conducted in Australia revealed that rates of sexual abuse and coercion were similar between BDSM practitioners and other Australians. The study concluded that BDSM is simply a sexual interest or subculture attractive to a minority, not defined by a pathological symptom of past abuse.

But when you throw a little rape, bondage or humiliation fantasy into the mix, a whole set of ideological problems arises. The idea of a woman consenting to be violated via play not only is difficult terrain to negotiate politically, but also is rarely discussed beyond BDSM practitioners themselves. Sexually submissive feminists already have a hard enough time finding a voice in the discourse, and their desire to be demeaned is often left out of the conversation. Because of this, the opportunity to articulate the political ramifications of rape fantasy happens rarely, if at all.

You can blame this silence on the fact that BDSM is generally poorly—often cartoonishly—represented. Cinematic depictions are generally hastily drawn caricatures, pushing participants onto the fringes and increasing the stigma that surrounds their personal and professional choices. While mainstream film and television occasionally offer up an empowered, vaguely fleshed-out and somewhat sympathetic professional female dom (think Lady Heather from *CSI*), those women who are sexually submissive by choice seem to be invisible. It wouldn't be a stretch to say that they are left out of the picture because, quite simply, they scare

From "The Fantasy of Acceptable 'Non-Consent'," by Stacey May Fowles. *Yes Means Yes!: Visions of Female Sexual Power and a World Without Rape*, pp. 117–125. Copyright © 2008 Jaclyn Friedman, Jessica Valenti. Reprinted by permission of Seal Press, a member of the Perseus Books Group.

us. Feminist pornographic depictions of women being dominated for pleasure are often those involving other women—that's a safe explicit image, because the idea of a male inflicting pain on a consenting woman is just too hard for many people to stomach. For many viewers it hits too close to home—the idea of a female submissive's consensual exchange of her authority to make decisions (temporarily or long-term) for a dominant's agreement to make decisions for her just doesn't sit well with the feminist community.

It's important to point out that, however you attempt to excuse it, this inability to accept BDSM into the feminist dialogue is really just a form of kinkophobia, a widely accepted prejudice against the practice of power-exchange sex. Patrick Califia, writer and advocate of BDSM pornography and practice, wisely states that "internalized kinkophobia is the unique sense of shame that many, if not most, sadomasochists feel about their participation in a deviant society." This hatred of self can be particularly strong among feminist submissives, when an entire community that they identify with either dismisses their desires or pegs them as unwitting victims.

It's taken me many years of unlearning mainstream power dynamics to understand and accept my own desire for fictional, fetishized ones. Despite this deliberate journey of self-discovery and the accompanying (and perhaps contradictory) feelings of being in total control, it's pretty evident that the feminist movement at large is not really ready to admit that women who like to be hit, choked, tied up and humiliated are empowered. Personally, the more I submitted sexually, the more I was able to be autonomous in my external life, the more I was able to achieve equality in my sexual and romantic partnerships, and the more genuine I felt as a human being. Regardless, I always felt that by claiming submissive status I was being highlighted as part of a social dynamic that sought to violate all women. Sadly, claims of sexual emancipation do not translate into acceptance for sub-

missives—the best a submissive can hope for is to be labeled and condescended to as a damaged victim choosing submission as a way of healing from or processing past trauma and abuse.

Whether or not it's difficult to accept that the desire to be demeaned is not a product of a society that seeks to objectify women, I would argue that, regardless of appearance, by its very nature BDSM is constantly about consent. Of course, its language and rules differ significantly from vanilla sexual scenes, but the very existence of a safe word is the ultimate in preventing violation—it suggests that at any moment, regardless of expectations or interpretations on the part of either party, the act can and will end. Ignoring the safe word is a clear act of violation that is not up for any debate. Because of this, BDSM sex, even with all its violent connotations, can be much "safer" than non–safe-word sex. While not very romantic in the traditional sense, the rules are clear—at any moment a woman (or man) can say no, regardless of the script she (or he) is using.

The safe, sane, and consensual BDSM landscape is made up of stringent rules and safe practices designed to protect the feelings of everyone involved and to ensure constant, enthusiastic consent. The culture could not exist if this were not the case; a submissive participates in power exchange because a safe psychological space is offered up to do so. That space creates an opportunity for a display of endurance, a relief from responsibility, and feelings of affection and security. Before any "scene" begins, the rules are made clear and the limitations agreed upon.

Finding a partner or dom to play with is the ultimate achievement in trust, and giving someone the power to hurt you for pleasure is both liberating and powerful. The more I embrace submissive sexuality, the more I come to learn that, despite all appearances to the contrary, consensual, respectful SM relationships generally dismantle the very tropes that rape culture is founded on.

A dom/sub dynamic doesn't appear to promote equality, but for most serious practitioners, the trust and respect that exist in power exchange actually transcend a mainstream "woman as object" or rape mentality. For BDSM to exist safely, it has to be founded on a constant proclamation of enthusiastic consent, which mainstream sexuality has systematically dismantled.

This, of course, doesn't mean that BDSM culture is without blame or responsibility. Despite the obvious fact that domination and submission (and everything that comes with them) are in the realm of elaborate fantasy, it is interesting to examine how those lifestyle choices and depictions (both mainstream and countercultural) influence an overall rape culture that seeks to demean and demoralize women. While consensual, informed BDSM is contrary to rape culture, more mainstream (or nonfetish) pornography that even vaguely simulates rape (of the "take it, bitch" and "you know you like it" variety) is quite the opposite. When those desires specific to BDSM are appropriated, watered down and corrupted, the complex rules that the counterculture is founded on are completely disposed of.

Herein lies the problem—with the advent and proliferation of Internet pornography, the fantasy of rape, torture and bondage becomes an issue of access. No longer reserved for an informed, invested viewer who carefully sought it out after a trip to a fetish bookstore, BDSM is represented in every porn portal on the Internet. The average computer user can have instant access to a full catalog of BDSM practices, ranging from light, soft-core spanking to hard-core torture, in a matter of seconds. This kind of constant, unrestrained availability trains viewers who don't have a BDSM cultural awareness, investment or education to believe that what women want is to be coerced and, in some cases, forced into acts they don't consent to. Over the years, various interpretations of the genre have made it into straight porn, without any suggestion of artifice—women on leashes, in handcuffs, gagged, tied up and told to "like it" are all commonplace imagery in contemporary pornography. . . .

The appropriation of BDSM imagery is problematic because while community members understand that it is important to be sensitive to the needs, boundaries and rules of players in order for a scene to function fairly and enjoyably, mainstream porn is primarily about getting off as quickly as possible. Add to that a disgraceful lack of sexual education (both in safety and in pleasure) across the country and a general belief perpetuated by the media that women are sex objects to be consumed, and you have a rape culture that started by borrowing from BDSM's images without reading its rules.

This reality raises some interesting questions for safe, sane and consensual BDSM practitioners. If, as someone who identifies as a sexual submissive, you like to fantasize about being raped, are you now complicit in this pervasive rape culture? Are you not only complicit, but also key in perpetuating the acceptability of violence, regardless of how private and personal your desire is? From another perspective—are you actually a victim? Is your fantasy merely a product of a culture that coerces you into believing that kind of violence is acceptable or even desirable?

Alternatively, is your desire (however bastardized and appropriated) still your own—your fantasy of "nonconsent" yours to choose and act out in a consenting environment? A personal choice when feminist ideology emphasizes choice above all else?

And finally, and perhaps most important, with all of its limitations, safe words, time limits and explicitly negotiated understandings of what is allowed—is the consensual SM relationship actually the ultimate in trust and collaborative "performance," its rules and artifice the very antithesis of rape?

Paradoxically, sexual submission and rape fantasy can only be acceptable in a culture that doesn't condone them. On a simplistic level, a fetish is only a fetish when it falls outside the realm of the real, and, as I mentioned, the reason why some feminists fear or loathe the BDSM scene is that it is all too familiar. When a woman is subjected to (or enjoying, depending on who is viewing and participating) torture, humiliation and pain, many feminists see the 6 o'clock news, not a pleasurable fantasy, regardless of context. Even someone who identifies as a sexual submissive, someone like me, can understand why it's difficult to view these scenes objectively. Many fantasies are taboo for precisely that reason—it's close to impossible to step beyond the notion that a man interested in domination is akin to a rapist, or that if a woman submits she is a helpless victim of rape culture. But consenting BDSM practitioners would argue that their community at large responsibly enacts desires without harm, celebrating female desire and (as is so fundamental in dismantling rape culture) making (her) pleasure central.

As a community, feminists need to truly examine whether or not it's condescending to say to a woman who chooses the fantasy of rape that she is a victim of a culture that seeks to demean, humiliate and violate women, whether or not it's acceptable to accuse her of being misguided, misinformed, or even mentally ill.

The reality is that when two people consent to fabricate a scene of nonconsent in the privacy of their own erotic lives, they are not consenting to perpetuate the violation of women everywhere. The true problem lies in mainstream pornography's appropriation of fetish tropes— while BDSM practitioners are generally serious about and invested in the ideological beliefs behind their lifestyle choices, the average mainstream porn user doesn't usually take the time to understand the finer points of dominance and submission (or consent and safety) before he casually witnesses a violation scene in a mainstream pornographic film or image.

While early black-and-white fantasy films of Bettie Page being kidnapped and tied up by a group of insatiable femmes are generally viewed as light, harmless, erotic fun, that kind of imagery, when injected into mainstream pornography (and even Hollywood), can have epic cultural ramifications. Sadly, gratuitous depictions of violence against women on the big screen have effectively taken the taboo-play element out of fetish imagery. Bombarded with an onslaught of violent images in which a woman is the victim, viewers fail to see where fantasy and fetish end and reality begins.

BDSM pornography is so excruciatingly aware of its own ability to perpetuate the idea that women yearn to be violated that it actually fights against that myth. At the end of almost every authentic BDSM photo set, you'll see a single appended photo of the participants, smiling and happy, assuring us that what we've seen is theater acted out by consenting adults, proving that fetish porn often exists as a careful, aware construct that constantly references itself as such.

The reality is that the activities and pornographic imagery of BDSM culture are problematic only because we have reached a point where a woman's desire is completely demeaned and dismissed. If women's pleasure were paramount, this argument (and the feminist fear of sexual submission) wouldn't exist. When women are consistently depicted as victims of both violence and culture, it's difficult to see any other possibilities. Feminists have a responsibility not only to fight and speak out against the mainstream appropriation of BDSM, but also to support BDSM practitioners who endorse safe, sane and consensual practice.

When the mainstream appropriation of BDSM model is successfully critiqued, dismantled and corrected, a woman can then feel safe to desire to be demeaned, bound, gagged and "forced" into sex by her lover. In turn, feminists would feel safe accepting that desire, because it would be clear consensual submission. Because "she was asking for it" would finally be true.

SEXUAL ASSAULT ON CAMPUS: A MULTILEVEL, INTEGRATIVE APPROACH TO PARTY RAPE

ELIZABETH A. ARMSTRONG, LAURA HAMILTON, AND BRIAN SWEENEY

A 1997 National Institute of Justice study estimated that between one-fifth and one-quarter of women are the victims of completed or attempted rape while in college (Fisher, Cullen, and Turner, 2000).[1] College women "are at greater risk for rape and other forms of sexual assault than women in the general population or in a comparable age group" (Fisher et al., 2000:iii).[2] At least half and perhaps as many as three-quarters of the sexual assaults that occur on college campuses involve alcohol consumption on the part of the victim, the perpetrator, or both (Abbey et al., 1996; Sampson, 2002). The tight link between alcohol and sexual assault suggests that many sexual assaults that occur on college campuses are "party rapes."[3] A recent report by the U.S. Department of Justice defines party rape as a distinct form of rape, one that "occurs at an off-campus house or on- or off-campus fraternity and involves . . . plying a woman with alcohol or targeting an intoxicated woman" (Sampson, 2002:6).[4] While party rape is classified as a form of acquaintance rape, it is not uncommon for the woman to have had no prior interaction with the assailant, that is, for the assailant to be an in-network stranger (Abbey et al., 1996).

Colleges and universities have been aware of the problem of sexual assault for at least 20 years, directing resources toward prevention and providing services to students who have been sexually assaulted. Programming has included education of various kinds, support for *Take Back the Night* events, distribution of rape whistles, development and staffing of hotlines, training of police and administrators, and other efforts. Rates of sexual assault, however, have not declined over the last five decades (Adams-Curtis and Forbes, 2004:95; Bachar and Koss, 2001; Marine, 2004; Sampson, 2002:1).

Why do colleges and universities remain dangerous places for women in spite of active efforts to prevent sexual assault? While some argue that "we know what the problems are and we know how to change them" (Adams-Curtis and Forbes, 2004:115), it is our contention that we do not have a complete explanation of the problem. To address this issue we use data from a study of college life at a large midwestern university and draw on theoretical developments in the sociology of gender (Connell, 1987, 1995; Lorber, 1994; Martin, 2004; Risman, 1998, 2004). Continued high rates of sexual assault can be viewed as a case of the reproduction of gender inequality—a phenomenon of central concern in gender theory.

We demonstrate that sexual assault is a predictable outcome of a synergistic intersection of both gendered and seemingly gender neutral processes operating at individual, organizational, and interactional levels. The concentration of homogenous students with expectations of partying fosters the development of sexualized peer cultures organized around status. Residential arrangements intensify students' desires to party in male-controlled fraternities. Cultural expectations that partygoers drink heavily and trust party-mates become problematic when combined with expectations that women be nice and defer to men. Fulfilling the role of the partier produces vulnerability on the part of women, which some men exploit to extract non-consensual sex. The party scene also produces fun, generating student investment in it. Rather than criticizing the party scene or men's behavior, students blame victims. . . .

APPROACHES TO COLLEGE SEXUAL ASSAULT

Explanations of high rates of sexual assault on college campuses fall into three broad categories. The first tradition, a psychological approach that we label the "individual determinants" approach, views college sexual assault as primarily a consequence of perpetrator or victim characteristics such as gender role attitudes, personality, family background, or sexual history (Flezzani and Benshoff, 2003; Forbes and Adams-Curtis, 2001; Rapaport and Burkhart, 1984). While "situational variables" are considered, the focus is on individual characteristics (Adams-Curtis and Forbes, 2004; Malamuth, Heavey, and Linz, 1993). . . .

The second perspective, the "rape culture" approach, grew out of second wave feminism (Brownmiller, 1975; Buchward, Fletcher, and Roth, 1993; Lottes, 1997; Russell, 1975; Schwartz and DeKeseredy, 1997). In this perspective, sexual assault is seen as a consequence of widespread belief in "rape myths," or ideas about the nature of men, women, sexuality, and consent that create an environment conducive to rape. . . .

A third approach moves beyond rape culture by identifying particular contexts—fraternities and bars—as sexually dangerous (Humphrey and Kahn, 2000; Martin and Hummer, 1989; Sanday, 1990, 1996; Stombler, 1994). Ayres Boswell and Joan Spade (1996) suggest that sexual assault is supported not only by "a generic culture surrounding and promoting rape," but also by characteristics of the "specific settings" in which men and women interact (p. 133). Mindy Stombler and Patricia Yancey Martin (1994) illustrate that gender inequality is institutionalized on campus by "formal structure" that supports and intensifies an already "high-pressure heterosexual peer group" (p. 180). This perspective grounds sexual assault in organizations that provide opportunities and resources.

We extend this third approach by linking it to recent theoretical scholarship in the sociology of gender. Martin (2004), Barbara Risman (1998; 2004), Judith Lorber (1994) and others argue that gender is not only embedded in individual selves, but also in cultural rules, social interaction, and organizational arrangements. This integrative perspective identifies mechanisms at each level that contribute to the reproduction of gender inequality (Risman, 2004). Socialization processes influence gendered selves, while cultural expectations reproduce gender inequality in interaction. At the institutional level, organizational practices, rules, resource distributions, and ideologies reproduce gender inequality. Applying this integrative perspective enabled us to identify gendered processes at individual, interactional, and organizational levels that contribute to college sexual assault. . . .

METHOD

Data are from group and individual interviews, ethnographic observation, and publicly available information collected at a large midwestern research university. Located in a small city, the school has strong academic and sports programs, a large Greek system, and is sought after by students seeking a quintessential college experience. . . .

. . . The bulk of the data presented in this paper were collected as part of ethnographic observation during the 2004–05 academic year in a residence hall identified by students and residence hall staff as a "party dorm." While little partying actually occurs in the hall, many students view this residence hall as one of several places to live in order to participate in the party scene on campus. This made it a good place to study the social worlds of students at high risk of sexual assault—women attending fraternity parties in their first year of college. . . .

With at least one-third of first-year students on campus residing in "party dorms" and one-quarter of all undergraduates belonging to fraternities or sororities, this social world is the most visible on campus. As the most visible scene on campus, it also attracts students living in other residence halls and those not in the Greek system. Dense pre-college ties among the many in-state students, class and race homogeneity, and a small city location also contribute to the dominance of this scene. Of course, not all . . . participate in the party scene. To participate, one must typically be heterosexual, at least middle class, white, American-born, unmarried, childless, traditional college age, politically and socially mainstream, and interested in drinking. Over three-quarters of the women . . . we observed fit this description.

There were no non-white students among the first and second year students on the floor we studied. This is a result of the homogeneity of this campus and racial segregation in social and residential life. African Americans (who make up 3 to 5% of undergraduates) generally live in living-learning communities in other residence halls and typically do not participate in the white Greek party scene. We argue that the party scene's homogeneity contributes to sexual risk for white women. . . .

We conducted 16 group interviews (involving 24 men and 63 women) in spring 2004. These individuals had varying relationships to the white Greek party scene on campus. Groups included residents of an alternative residence hall, lesbian, gay, and bisexual students, feminists, re-entry students, academically-focused students, fundamentalist Christians, and sorority women. . . .

We also incorporated publicly available information about the university from informal interviews with student affairs professionals and from teaching (by all authors) courses on gender, sexuality, and introductory sociology. Classroom data were collected through discussion, student writings, e-mail correspondence, and a survey that included questions about experiences of sexual assault.

Unless stated otherwise, all descriptions and interview quotations are from ethnographic observation or interviews. Passages in quotation marks are direct quotations from interviews or field notes. Study participants served as informants about venues where we could not observe (such as fraternity parties).

EXPLAINING PARTY RAPE

We show how gendered selves, organizational arrangements, and interactional expectations contribute to sexual assault. We also detail the contributions of processes at each level that are not explicitly gendered. We focus on each level in turn, while attending to the ways in which processes at all levels depend upon and reenforce others. We show that fun is produced along with sexual assault, leading students to resist criticism of the party scene.

Selves and Peer Culture in the Transition from High School to College . . .

Non-Gendered Characteristics Motivate Participation in Party Scenes

Without individuals available for partying, the party scene would not exist. All the women on our floor were single and childless, as are the vast majority of undergraduates at this university; many, being upper-middle class, had few responsibilities other than their schoolwork. Abundant leisure time, however, is not enough to fuel the party scene. Media, siblings, peers, and parents all serve as sources of anticipatory socialization (Merton, 1957). Both partiers and non-partiers agreed that one was "supposed" to party in college. This orientation was reflected in the popularity of a poster titled "What I Really Learned in School" that pictured mixed drinks with names associated with academic disciplines. As one focus group participant explained:

You see these images of college that you're supposed to go out and have fun and drink, drink lots, party and meet guys. [You are] supposed to hook up with guys, and both men and women try to live up to that. I think a lot of it is girls want to be accepted into their groups and guys want to be accepted into their groups.

Partying is seen as a way to feel a part of college life. Many of the women we observed participated in middle and high school peer cultures organized around status, belonging, and popularity (Eder, 1985; Eder, Evans, and Parker, 1995; Milner, 2004). Assuming that college would be similar, they told us that they wanted to fit in, be popular, and have friends. Even on move-in day, they were supposed to already have friends. When we asked one of the outsiders, Ruth, about her first impression of her roommate, she replied that she found her:

Extremely intimidating. Bethany already knew hundreds of people here. Her cell phone was going off from day one, like all the time. And I was too shy to ask anyone to go to dinner with me or lunch with me or anything. I ate while I did homework.

Bethany complained to the RA on move-in day that she did not want to be roommates with Ruth because she was weird. A group of women on the floor—including Bethany,

but not Ruth—began partying together and formed a tight friendship group. Ruth noted: "There is a group on the side of the hall that goes to dinner together, parties together, my roommate included. I have never hung out with them once . . . And, yeah, it kind of sucks." Bethany moved out of the room at the end of the semester, leaving Ruth isolated.

Peer Culture as Gendered and Sexualized

Partying was also the primary way to meet men on campus.[5] The floor was locked to non-residents, and even men living in the same residence hall had to be escorted on the floor. The women found it difficult to get to know men in their classes, which were mostly mass lectures. They explained to us that people "don't talk" in class. Some complained they lacked casual friendly contact with men, particularly compared to the mixed-gender friendship groups they reported experiencing in high school.

Meeting men at parties was important to most of the women on our floor. The women found men's sexual interest at parties to be a source of self-esteem and status.[6] They enjoyed dancing and kissing at parties, explaining to us that it proved men "liked" them. This attention was not automatic, but required the skillful deployment of physical and cultural assets (Stombler and Padavic, 1997; Swidler, 2001). Most of the party-oriented women on the floor arrived with appropriate gender presentations and the money and know-how to preserve and refine them. While some more closely resembled the "ideal" college party girl (white, even features, thin but busty, tan, long straight hair, skillfully made-up, and well-dressed in the latest youth styles), most worked hard to attain this presentation. They regularly straightened their hair, tanned, exercised, dieted, and purchased new clothes.

Women found that achieving high erotic status in the party scene required looking "hot" but not "slutty," a difficult and ongoing challenge (West and Zimmerman, 1987). Mastering these distinctions allowed them to establish themselves as "classy" in contrast to other women (Handler, 1995; Stombler, 1994). Although women judged other women's appearance, men were the most important audience. A "hot" outfit could earn attention from desirable men in the party scene. A failed outfit, as some of our women learned, could earn scorn from men. One woman reported showing up to a party dressed in a knee length skirt and blouse only to find that she needed to show more skin. A male guest sarcastically told her "nice outfit," accompanied by a thumbs-up gesture.

The psychological benefits of admiration from men in the party scene were such that women in relationships sometimes felt deprived. One woman with a serious boyfriend noted that she dressed more conservatively at parties because of him, but this meant she was not "going to get any of the attention." She lamented that no one was "going to waste their time with me" and that, "this is taking away from my confidence." Like most women who came to college with boyfriends, she soon broke up with him.

Men also sought proof of their erotic appeal. As a woman complained, "Every man I have met here has wanted to have sex with me!" Another interviewee reported that: "this guy that I was talking to for like ten/fifteen minutes says, 'Could you, um, come to the bathroom with me and jerk me off?' And I'm like, 'What!' I'm like, 'Okay, like, I've known you for like, fifteen minutes, but no.'" The women found that men were more interested than they were in having sex. These clashes in sexual expectations are not surprising: men derived status from securing sex (from high-status women), while women derived status from getting attention (from high-status men). These agendas are both complementary and adversarial: men give attention to women en route to getting sex, and women are unlikely to become interested in sex without getting attention first.

University and Greek Rules, Resources, and Procedures

Simply by congregating similar individuals, universities make possible heterosexual peer cultures. The university, the Greek system, and other related organizations structure student life through rules, distribution of resources, and procedures (Risman, 2004).

Sexual danger is an unintended consequence of many university practices intended to be gender neutral. The clustering of homogeneous students intensifies the dynamics of student peer cultures and heightens motivations to party. Characteristics of residence halls and how they are regulated push student partying into bars, off-campus residences, and fraternities. While factors that increase the risk of party rape are present in varying degrees in all party venues (Boswell and Spade, 1996), we focus on fraternity parties because they were the typical party venue for the women we observed and have been identified as particularly unsafe (see also Martin and Hummer, 1989; Sanday, 1990). Fraternities offer the most reliable and private source of alcohol for first-year students excluded from bars and house parties because of age and social networks.

University Practices as Push Factors

The university has latitude in how it enforces state drinking laws. Enforcement is particularly rigorous in residence halls. We observed RAs and police officers (including gun-carrying peer police) patrolling the halls for alcohol violations.... As a consequence, students engaged in only minimal, clandestine alcohol consumption in their rooms. In comparison, alcohol flows freely at fraternities.

The lack of comfortable public space for informal socializing in the residence hall also serves as a push factor. A large central bathroom divided our floor. A sterile lounge was rarely used for socializing. There was no cafeteria, only a convenience store and a snack bar in a cavernous room furnished with big-screen televisions. Residence life sponsored alternatives to the party scene such as "movie night" and special dinners, but these typically occurred early in the evening. Students defined the few activities sponsored during party hours (e.g., a midnight trip to WalMart) as uncool.

Intensifying Peer Dynamics

The residence halls near athletic facilities and Greek houses are known by students to house affluent, party-oriented students. White, upper-middle class, first-year students who plan to rush request these residence halls, while others avoid them. One of our residents explained that "everyone knows what [the residence hall] is like and people are dying to get in here. People just think it's a total party or something." . . .

The homogeneity of the floor intensified social anxiety, heightening the importance of partying for making friends. Early in the year, the anxiety was palpable on weekend nights as women assessed their social options by asking where people were going, when, and with whom. One exhausted floor resident told us she felt that she "needed to" go out to protect her position in a friendship group. At the beginning of the semester, "going out" on weekends was virtually compulsory. By 11 p.m. the floor was nearly deserted.

Male Control of Fraternity Parties

The campus Greek system cannot operate without university consent. The university lists Greek organizations as student clubs, devotes professional staff to Greek-oriented programming, and disbands fraternities that violate university policy. Nonetheless, the university lacks full authority over fraternities; Greek houses are privately owned and chapters answer to national organizations and the Interfraternity Council (IFC) (i.e., a body governing the more than 20 predominantly white fraternities).

Fraternities control every aspect of parties at their houses: themes, music, transportation, admission, access to alcohol, and movement of guests. Party themes usually require women to wear scant, sexy clothing and place women in subordinate positions to men. During our observation period, women attended parties such as "Pimps and Hos," "Victoria's Secret," and "Playboy Mansion"—the last of which required fraternity members to escort two scantily clad dates. Other recent themes included: "CEO/ Secretary Ho," "School Teacher/Sexy Student," and "Golf Pro/ Tennis Ho."

Some fraternities require pledges to transport first-year students, primarily women, from the residence halls to the fraternity houses. From about 9 to 11 p.m. on weekend nights early in the year, the drive in front of the residence hall resembled a rowdy taxi-stand, as dressed-to-impress women waited to be carpooled to parties in expensive late-model vehicles. By allowing party-oriented first-year women to cluster in particular residence halls, the university made them easy to find. One fraternity member told us this practice was referred to as "dorm-storming."

Transportation home was an uncertainty. Women sometimes called cabs, caught the "drunk bus," or trudged home in stilettos. Two women indignantly described a situation where fraternity men "wouldn't give us a ride home." The women said, "Well, let us call a cab." The men discouraged them from calling the cab and eventually found a designated driver. The women described the men as "just dicks" and as "rude."

Fraternities police the door of their parties, allowing in desirable guests (first-year women) and turning away others (unaffiliated men). . . .

Fraternities are constrained . . . by the necessity of attracting women to their parties. Fraternities with reputations for sexual disrespect have more success recruiting women to parties early in the year. One visit was enough for some of the women. A roommate duo told of a house they "liked at first" until they discovered that the men there were "really not nice."

The Production of Fun and Sexual Assault in Interaction

Peer culture and organizational arrangements set up risky partying conditions, but do not explain *how* student interactions at parties generate sexual assault. At the interactional level we see the mechanisms through which sexual assault is produced. As interactions necessarily involve individuals with particular characteristics and occur in specific organizational settings, all three levels meet when interactions take place. Here, gendered and gender neutral expectations and routines are intricately woven together to create party rape. Party rape is the result of fun situations that shift—either gradually or quite suddenly—into coercive situations. . . .

College partying involves predictable activities in a predictable order (e.g., getting ready, pre-gaming,[7] getting to the party, getting drunk, flirtation or sexual interaction, getting home, and sharing stories). It is characterized by "shared assumptions about what constitutes good or adequate participation" . . . A fun partier throws him or herself into the event, drinks, displays an upbeat mood, and evokes revelry in others. Partiers are expected to like and trust party-mates. Norms of civil interaction curtail displays of unhappiness or tension among partygoers. . . . Drinking assists people in transitioning from everyday life to a state of euphoria.

Cultural expectations of partying are gendered. Women are supposed to wear revealing outfits, while men typically are not. As guests, women cede control of turf, transportation, and liquor. Women are also expected to be grateful for men's hospitality, and as others have noted, to generally be "nice" in ways that men are not (Gilligan, 1982; Martin, 2003; Phillips, 2000; Stombler and Martin, 1994; Tolman, 2002). The pressure to be deferential and gracious may be intensified by men's older age and fraternity membership.[8] The quandary for women, however, is that fulfilling the gendered role of partier makes them vulnerable to sexual assault.

Women's vulnerability produces sexual assault only if men exploit it. Too many men are willing to do so. Many college men attend parties looking for casual sex. A student in one of our classes explained that "guys are willing to do damn near anything to get a piece of ass." A male student wrote the following description of parties at his (non-fraternity) house:

Girls are continually fed drinks of alcohol. It's mainly to party but my roomies are also aware of the inhibition-lowering effects. I've seen an old roomie block doors when girls want to leave his room; and other times I've driven women home who can't remember much of an evening yet sex did occur. Rarely if ever has a night of drinking for my roommate ended without sex. I know it isn't necessarily and assuredly sexual assault, but with the amount of liquor in the house I question the amount of consent a lot.

Another student—after deactivating—wrote about a fraternity brother "telling us all at the chapter meeting about how he took this girl home and she was obviously too drunk to function and he took her inside and had sex with her." Getting women drunk, blocking doors, and controlling transportation are common ways men try to prevent women from leaving sexual situations. Rape culture beliefs, such as the belief that men are "naturally" sexually aggressive, normalize these coercive strategies. Assigning women the role of sexual "gatekeeper" relieves men from responsibility for obtaining authentic consent, and enables them to view sex obtained by undermining women's ability to resist it as "consensual" (e.g., by getting women so drunk that they pass out).[9]

In a focus group with her sorority sisters, a junior sorority woman provided an example of a partying situation that devolved into a likely sexual assault.

Anna: It kind of happened to me freshman year. I'm not positive about what happened, that's the worst part about it. I drank too much at a frat one night, I blacked out and I woke up the next morning with nothing on in their cold dorms, so I don't really know what happened and the guy wasn't in the bed anymore, I don't even think I could tell you who the hell he was, no I couldn't.

Sarah: Did you go to the hospital?

Anna: No, I didn't know what happened. I was scared and wanted to get the hell out of there. I didn't know who it was, so how am I supposed to go to the hospital and say someone might've raped me? It could have been any one of the hundred guys that lived in the house.

Sarah: It happens to so many people, it would shock you. Three of my best friends in the whole world, people that you like would think it would never happen to, it happened to. It's just so hard because you don't know how to deal with it because you don't want to turn in a frat because all hundred of those brothers . . .

Anna: I was also thinking like, you know, I just got to school, I don't want to start off on a bad note with anyone, and now it happened so long ago, it's just one of those things that I kind of have to live with.

This woman's confusion demonstrates the usefulness of alcohol as a weapon: her intoxication undermined her ability to resist sex, her clarity about what happened, and her feelings of entitlement to report it (Adams-Curtis and Forbes, 2004; Martin and Hummer, 1989). . . .

Amanda, a woman on our hall, provides insight into how men take advantage of women's niceness, gender deference, and unequal control of party resources. Amanda reported meeting a "cute" older guy, Mike, also a student, at a local student bar. She explained that, "At the bar we were kind of making out a little bit and I told him just cause I'm sitting here making out doesn't mean that I want to go home with you, you know?" After Amanda found herself stranded by friends with no cell phone or cab fare, Mike promised that a sober friend of his would drive her home. Once they got in the car Mike's friend refused to take her home and instead dropped her at Mike's place. Amanda's concerns were heightened by the driver's disrespect. "He was like, so are you into ménage à trois?" Amanda reported staying awake all night. She woke Mike early in the morning to take her home. Despite her ordeal, she argued that Mike was "a really nice guy" and exchanged telephone numbers with him.

These men took advantage of Amanda's unwillingness to make a scene. Amanda was one of the most assertive women on our floor. Indeed, her refusal to participate fully in the culture of feminine niceness led her to suffer in the social hierarchy of the floor and on campus. It is unlikely that other women we observed could have been more assertive in this situation. That she was nice to her captor in the morning suggests how much she wanted him to like her and what she was willing to tolerate in order to keep his interest.[10]

. . . [M]en can control party resources and work together to constrain women's behavior while partying in bars and at house parties. What distinguishes fraternity parties is that male dominance of partying there is organized, resourced, and implicitly endorsed by the university. Other party venues are also organized in ways that advantage men.

We heard many stories of negative experiences in the party scene, including at least one account of a sexual assault in every focus group that included heterosexual women. Most women who partied complained about men's efforts to control their movements or pressure them to drink. Two of the women on our floor were sexually assaulted at a fraternity party in the first week of school—one was raped. Later in the semester, another woman on the floor was raped by a friend. A fourth woman on the floor suspects she was drugged; she became disoriented at a fraternity party and was very ill for the next week.

Party rape is accomplished without the use of guns, knives, or fists. It is carried out through the combination of low level forms of coercion—a lot of liquor and persuasion, manipulation of situations so that women cannot leave, and sometimes force (e.g., by blocking a door, or using body weight to make it difficult for a woman to get up). These forms of coercion are made more effective by organizational arrangements that provide men with control over how partying happens and by expectations that women let loose and trust their party-mates. This systematic and effective method of extracting non-consensual sex is largely invisible, which makes it difficult for victims to convince anyone—even themselves—that a crime occurred. Men engage in this behavior with little risk of consequences.

Student Responses and the Resiliency of the Party Scene

The frequency of women's negative experiences in the party scene poses a problem for those students most invested in it. Finding fault with the party scene potentially threatens meaningful identities and lifestyles. The vast majority of heterosexual encounters at parties are fun and consensual. Partying provides a chance to meet new people, experience and display belonging, and to enhance social position. Women on our floor told us that they loved to flirt and be admired, and they displayed pictures on walls, doors, and websites commemorating their fun nights out.

The most common way that students—both women and men—account for the harm that befalls women in the party scene is by blaming victims. By attributing bad experiences to women's "mistakes," students avoid criticizing the party scene or men's behavior within it. Such victim-blaming also allows women to feel that they can control what happens to them. . . . When discussing the sexual assault of a friend, a floor resident explained that:

She somehow got like sexually assaulted . . . by one of our friends' old roommates. All I know is that kid was like bad news to start off with. So, I feel sorry for her but it wasn't much of a surprise for us. He's a shady character.

Another floor resident relayed a sympathetic account of a woman raped at knife point by a stranger in the bushes, but later dismissed party rape as nothing to worry about " 'cause I'm not stupid when I'm drunk." Even a feminist focus group participant explained that her friend who was raped "made every single mistake and almost all of them had to with alcohol. . . . She got ridiculed when she came out and said she was raped." These women contrast "true victims" who are deserving of support with "stupid" women who forfeit sympathy (Phillips, 2000). Not only is this response devoid of empathy for other women, but it also leads women to blame themselves when they are victimized (Phillips, 2000).

Sexual assault prevention strategies can perpetuate victim-blaming. Instructing women to watch their drinks, stay with friends, and limit alcohol consumption implies that it is women's responsibility to avoid "mistakes" and their fault if they fail. Emphasis on the precautions women should take—particularly if not accompanied by education about how men should change their behavior—may also suggest that it is natural for men to drug women and take advantage of them. . . .

Victim-blaming also serves as a way for women to construct a sense of status within campus erotic hierarchies. As discussed earlier, women and men acquire erotic status based on how "hot" they are perceived to be. Another aspect of erotic status concerns the amount of sexual respect one receives from men (see Holland and Eisenhart, 1990:101). Women can tell themselves that they are safe from sexual assault not only because they are savvy, but because men will recognize that they, unlike other women, are worthy of sexual respect. For example, a focus group of senior women explained that at a small fraternity gathering their friend Amy came out of the bathroom. She was crying and said that a guy "had her by her neck, holding her up, feeling her up from her crotch up to her neck and saying that I should rape you, you are a fucking whore." The woman's friends were appalled, saying, "no one deserves that." On other hand, they explained that: "Amy flaunts herself. She is a whore so, I mean . . ." They implied that if one is a whore, one gets treated like one. [11]

Men accord women varying levels of sexual respect, with lower status women seen as "fair game" (Holland and Eisenhart, 1990; Phillips, 2000). On campus the youngest and most anonymous women are most vulnerable. High-status women (i.e., girlfriends of fraternity members) may be less likely victims of party rape.[12] Sorority women explained that fraternities discourage members from approaching the girlfriends (and ex-girlfriends) of other men in the house. Partiers on our floor learned that it was safer to party with men they knew as boyfriends, friends, or brothers of friends. . . .

Opting Out

While many students find the party scene fun, others are more ambivalent. Some attend a few fraternity parties to feel like they have participated in this college tradition. Others opt out of it altogether. On our floor, 44 out of the 51 first-year students (almost 90%) participated in the party scene. Those on the floor who opted out worried about sexual safety and the consequences of engaging in illegal behavior. For example, an interviewee who did not drink was appalled by the fraternity party transport system. She explained that:

All those girls would stand out there and just like, no joke, get into these big black Suburbans driven by frat guys, wearing like seriously no clothes, piled on top of each other. This could be some kidnapper taking you all away to the woods and chopping you up and leaving you there. How dumb can you be?

. . . Her position was unpopular. She, like others who did not party, was an outsider on the floor. Partiers came home loudly in the middle of the night, threw up in the bathrooms, and rollerbladed around the floor. Socially, the others simply did not exist. A few of our "misfits" successfully created social lives outside the floor. The most assertive of the "misfits" figured out the dynamics of the floor in the first weeks and transferred to other residence halls.

However, most students on our floor lacked the identities or network connections necessary for entry into alternative worlds. Life on a large university campus can be overwhelming for first-year students. Those who most needed an alternative to the social world of the party dorm were often ill-equipped to actively seek it out. They either integrated themselves into partying or found themselves alone in their rooms, microwaving frozen dinners and watching television. . . .

DISCUSSION AND IMPLICATIONS

We have demonstrated that processes at individual, organizational, and interactional levels contribute to high rates of sexual assault.[13] Some individual level characteristics that shape the likelihood of a sexually dangerous party scene developing are not explicitly gendered. Party rape occurs at high rates in places that cluster young, single, party-oriented people concerned about social status. Traditional beliefs about sexuality also make it more likely that one will participate in the party scene and increase danger within the scene. This university contributes to sexual danger by allowing these individuals to cluster.

However, congregating people is not enough, as parties cannot be produced without resources (e.g., alcohol and a viable venue) that are difficult for underage students to obtain. University policies that are explicitly gender-neutral—such as the policing of alcohol use in residence halls—have gendered consequences. This policy encourages first-year students to turn to fraternities to party. Only fraternities, not sororities, are allowed to have parties, and men structure parties in ways that control the appearance, movement, and behavior of female guests. Men also control the distribution of alcohol and use its scarcity to engineer social interactions. The enforcement of alcohol policy by both university and Greek organizations transforms alcohol from a mere beverage into an unequally distributed social resource.

Individual characteristics and institutional practices provide the actors and contexts in which interactional processes occur. We have to turn to the interactional level, however, to understand *how* sexual assault is generated. Gender neutral expectations to "have fun," lose control, and trust one's party-mates become problematic when combined with gendered interactional expectations. Women are expected to be "nice" and to defer to men in interaction. This expectation is intensified by men's position as hosts and women's as grateful guests. The heterosexual script, which directs men to pursue sex and women to play the role of gatekeeper, further disadvantages women, particularly when virtually *all* men's methods of extracting sex are defined as legitimate.

The mechanisms identified should help explain intra-campus, cross-campus, and over time variation in the prevalence of sexual assault. . . . We would expect to see lower rates of sexual assault on campuses characterized by more aesthetically appealing public space, lower alcohol use, and the absence of a gender-adversarial party scene. Campuses with more racial diversity and more racial integration would also be expected to have lower rates of sexual assault because of the dilution of upper-middle class white peer groups. . . .

This perspective may also help explain why white college women are at higher risk of sexual assault than other racial groups. Existing research suggests that African American college social scenes are more gender egalitarian (Stombler and Padavic, 1997). African American fraternities typically do not have houses, depriving men of a party resource. The missions, goals, and recruitment practices of African American fraternities and sororities discourage joining for exclusively social reasons (Berkowitz and Padavic, 1999), and rates of alcohol consumption are lower among African American students (Journal of Blacks in Higher Education, 2000; Weschsler and Kuo, 2003). The role of party rape in the lives of white college women is substantiated by recent research that found that "white women were more likely [than non-white women] to have experienced rape while intoxicated and less likely to experience other rape" (Mohler-Kuo et al., 2004:41). . . .

Our analysis also provides a framework for analyzing the sources of sexual risk in non-university partying situations. Situations where men have a home turf advantage, know each other better than the women present know each other, see the women as anonymous, and control desired resources (such as alcohol or drugs) are likely to be particularly dangerous. Social pressures to "have fun," prove one's social competency, or adhere to traditional gender expectations are also predicted to increase rates of sexual assault within a social scene.

This research has implications for policy. The interdependence of levels means that it is difficult to enact change at one level when the other levels remain unchanged. Programs to combat sexual assault currently focus primarily or even exclusively on education (Bachar and Koss, 2001; Leaning, 2003). But as Ann Swidler (2001) argued, culture develops in response to institutional arrangements. Without change in institutional arrangements, efforts to change cultural beliefs are undermined by the cultural commonsense generated by encounters with institutions. Efforts to educate about sexual assault will not succeed if the university continues to support organizational arrangements that facilitate and even legitimate men's coercive sexual strategies. Thus, our research implies that efforts to combat sexual assault on campus should target all levels, constituencies, and processes simultaneously. Efforts to educate both men and women should indeed be intensified, but they should be reinforced by changes in the social organization of student life.

Researchers focused on problem drinking on campus have found that reduction efforts focused on the social environment are successful (Berkowitz, 2003:21). Student body diversity has been found to decrease binge drinking on campus (Weschsler and Kuo, 2003); it might also reduce rates of sexual assault. Existing student heterogeneity can be exploited by eliminating self-selection into age-segregated, white, upper-middle class, heterosexual enclaves and by working to make residence halls more appealing to upper-division students. Building more aesthetically appealing housing might allow students to interact outside of alcohol-fueled party scenes. Less expensive plans might involve creating more living-learning communities, coffee shops, and other student-run community spaces.

While heavy alcohol use is associated with sexual assault, not all efforts to regulate student alcohol use contribute to sexual safety. Punitive approaches sometimes heighten the symbolic significance of drinking, lead students to drink more hard liquor, and push alcohol consumption to more private and thus more dangerous spaces. Regulation inconsistently applied—e.g., heavy policing of residence halls and light policing of fraternities—increases the power of those who can secure alcohol and host parties. More consistent regulation could decrease the value of alcohol as a commodity by equalizing access to it.

Sexual assault education should shift in emphasis from educating women on preventative measures to educating both men and women about the coercive behavior of men and the sources of victim-blaming. Mohler-Kuo and associates (2004) suggest, and we endorse, a focus on the role of alcohol in sexual assault. Education should begin before students arrive on campus and continue throughout college. It may also be most effective if high-status peers are involved in disseminating knowledge and experience to younger college students.

Change requires resources and cooperation among many people. Efforts to combat sexual assault are constrained by other organizational imperatives. Student investment in the party scene makes it difficult to enlist the support of even those most harmed by the state of affairs. Student and alumni loyalty to partying (and the Greek system) mean that challenges to the party scene could potentially cost universities tuition dollars and alumni donations. Universities must contend with Greek organizations and bars, as well as the challenges of internal coordination. Fighting sexual assault on all levels is critical, though, because it is unacceptable for higher education institutions to be sites where women are predictably sexually victimized.

NOTES

1. Other studies have found similar rates of college sexual assault (Abbey et al., 1996; Adams-Curtis and Forbes, 2004; Copenhaver and Grauerholz, 1991; DeKeseredy and Kelly, 1993; Fisher et al., 1998; Humphrey and White, 2000; Koss, 1988; Koss, Gidycz, and Wisniewski, 1987;

Mills and Granoff, 1992; Muehlenhard and Linton, 1987; Tjaden and Thoennes, 2000; Ward et al., 1991).

2. While assaults within gender and by women occur, the vast majority involve men assaulting women.

3. Other forms of acquaintance rape include date rape, rape in a non-party/non-date situation, and rape by a former or current intimate (Sampson, 2002).

4. On party rape as a distinct type of sexual assault, see also Ward and associates (1991). Ehrhart and Sandler (1987) use the term to refer to group rape. We use the term to refer to one-on-one assaults. We encountered no reports of group sexual assault.

5. This is consistent with Boswell and Spade's (1996) finding that women participate in dangerous party scenes because of a lack of "other means to initiate contact with men on campus" (p. 145).

6. See also Stombler and Martin (1994). Holland and Eisenhart (1990) discuss a "culture of romance" in which women derive status from boyfriends. Among the first-year women we observed, status revolved more around getting male attention than male commitment. Focus group interviews with junior and senior sorority women suggest that acquiring high-status fraternity men as boyfriends occurs after women are integrated into Greek life.

7. Pre-gaming involved the clandestine consumption of alcohol—often hard liquor—before arriving at the party.

8. Stombler and Martin (1994:156) found that fraternity men demanded "niceness" from women with whom they partied. They selected "little sisters" on the basis of physical beauty and "charm, friendliness, and outgoingness."

9. In ongoing research on college men and sexuality, Sweeney (2004) and Rosow and Ray (2006) have found wide variation in beliefs about acceptable ways to obtain sex even among men who belong to the same fraternities. Rosow and Ray found that fraternity men in the most elite houses view sex with intoxicated women as low status and claim to avoid it.

10. Holland and Eisenhart (1990) and Stombler (1994) found that male attention is of such high value to some women that they are willing to suffer indignities to receive it.

11. Schwalbe and associates (2000) suggest that there are several psychological mechanisms that explain this behavior. *Trading power for patronage* occurs when a subordinate group accepts their status in exchange for compensatory benefits from the dominant group. *Defensive othering* is a process by which some members of a subordinated group seek to maintain status by deflecting stigma to others. Maneuvering to protect or improve individual position within hierarchical classification systems is common; however, these responses support the subordination that makes them necessary.

12. While "knowing" one's male party-mates may offer some protection, this protection is not comprehensive. Sorority women, who typically have the closest ties with fraternity men, experience more sexual assault than other college women (Mohler-Kuo et al., 2004). Not only do sorority women typically spend more time in high-risk social situations than other women, but arriving at a high-status position on campus may require one to begin their college social career as one of the anonymous young women who are frequently victimized.

13. Our recommendations echo and extend those of Boswell and Spade (1996:145) and Stombler and Martin (1994:180).

REFERENCES

Abbey, Antonia, Lisa Thomson Ross, Donna McDuffie, and Pam McAuslan. 1996. "Alcohol and Dating Risk Factors for Sexual Assault among College Women." *Psychology of Women Quarterly* 20: 147–69.

Adams-Curtis, Leah and Gordon Forbes. 2004. "College Women's Experiences of Sexual Coercion: A Review of Cultural, Perpetrator, Victim, and Situational Variables." *Trauma, Violence, and Abuse: A Review Journal* 5: 91–122.

Bachar, Karen and Mary Koss. 2001. "From Prevalence to Prevention: Closing the Gap between What We Know about Rape and What We Do." Pp. 117–42 in *Sourcebook on Violence against Women*, edited by C. Renzetti, J. Edleson, and R. K. Bergen. Thousand Oaks, CA: Sage.

Berkowitz, Alan. 2003. "How Should We Talk about Student Drinking—And What Should We Do about It?" *About Campus* May/June: 16–22.

Berkowitz, Alexandra and Irene Padavic. 1999. "Getting a Man or Getting Ahead: A Comparison of White and Black Sororities." *Journal of Contemporary Ethnography* 27: 530–57.

Boswell, A. Ayres and Joan Z. Spade. 1996. "Fraternities and Collegiate Rape Culture: Why Are Some Fraternities More Dangerous Places for Women?" *Gender & Society* 10: 133–47.

Brownmiller, Susan. 1975. *Against Our Will: Men, Women, and Rape.* New York: Bantam Books.

Buchward, Emilie, Pamela Fletcher, and Martha Roth, eds. 1993. *Transforming a Rape Culture.* Minneapolis, MN: Milkweed Editions.

Connell, R. W. 1987. *Gender and Power.* Palo Alto, CA: Stanford University Press.

———. 1995. *Masculinities.* Berkeley, CA: University of California Press.

Copenhaver, Stacey and Elizabeth Grauerholz. 1991. "Sexual Victimization among Sorority Women: Exploring the Link between Sexual Violence and Institutional Practices." *Sex Roles* 24: 31–41.

DeKeseredy, Walter and Katharine Kelly. 1993. "The Incidence and Prevalence of Women Abuse in Canadian University and College Dating Relationships." *Canadian Journal of Sociology* 18: 137–59.

Eder, Donna. 1985. "The Cycle of Popularity: Interpersonal Relations among Female Adolescents." *Sociology of Education* 58: 154–65.

Eder, Donna, Catherine Evans, and Stephen Parker. 1995. *School Talk: Gender and Adolescent Culture.* New Brunswick, NJ: Rutgers University Press.

Ehrhart, Julie and Bernice Sandler. 1987. "Party Rape." *Response* 9: 205.

Fisher, Bonnie, Francis Cullen, and Michael Turner. 2000. "The Sexual Victimization of College Women." Washington, DC: National Institute of Justice and the Bureau of Justice Statistics.

Fisher, Bonnie, John Sloan, Francis Cullen, and Lu Chun-meng. 1998. "Crime in the Ivory Tower: The Level and Sources of Student Victimization." *Criminology* 36: 671–710.

Flezzani, James and James Benshoff. 2003. "Understanding Sexual Aggression in Male College Students: The Role of Self-Monitoring and Pluralistic Ignorance." *Journal of College Counseling* 6: 69–79.

Forbes, Gordon and Leah Adams-Curtis. 2001. "Experiences with Sexual Coercion in College Males and Females: Role of Family Conflict, Sexist Attitudes, Acceptance of Rape Myths, Self-Esteem, and the Big-Five Personality Factors." *Journal of Interpersonal Violence* 16: 865–89.

Gilligan, Carol. 1982. *In a Different Voice: Psychological Theory and Women's Development.* Cambridge, MA: Harvard University Press.

Handler, Lisa. 1995. "In the Fraternal Sisterhood: Sororities as Gender Strategy." *Gender & Society* 9: 236–55.

Holland, Dorothy and Margaret Eisenhart. 1990. *Educated in Romance: Women, Achievement, and College Culture.* Chicago: University of Chicago Press.

Humphrey, John and Jacquelyn White. 2000. "Women's Vulnerability to Sexual Assault from Adolescence to Young Adulthood." *Journal of Adolescent Health* 27: 419–24.

Humphrey, Stephen and Arnold Kahn. 2000. "Fraternities, Athletic Teams, and Rape: Importance of Identification with A Risky Group." *Journal of Interpersonal Violence* 15: 1313–22.

Journal of Blacks in Higher Education. 2000. "News and Views: Alcohol Abuse Remains High on College Campus, But Black Students Drink to Excess Far Less Often Than Whites." *The Journal of Blacks in Higher Education.* 28: 19–20.

Koss, Mary. 1988. "Hidden Rape: Incidence and Prevalence of Sexual Aggression and Victimization in a National Sample of Students in Higher Education."

pp. 4–25 in *Rape and Sexual Assault,* edited by Ann W. Burgess. New York: Garland.

Koss, Mary, Christine Gidycz, and Nadine Wisniewski. 1987. "The Scope of Rape: Incidence and Prevalence of Sexual Aggression and Victimization in a National Sample of Higher Education Students." *Journal of Counseling and Clinical Psychology* 55: 162–70.

Leaning, Jennifer. April 2003. "Committee to Address Sexual Assault at Harvard: Public Report." Cambridge, MA: Harvard University.

Lorber, Judith. 1994. *Paradoxes of Gender.* New Haven, CT: Yale University Press.

Lottes, Ilsa L. 1997. "Sexual Coercion among University Students: A Comparison of the United States and Sweden." *Journal of Sex Research* 34: 67–76.

Malamuth, Neil, Christopher Heavey, and Daniel Linz. 1993. "Predicting Men's Antisocial Behavior against Women: The Interaction Model of Sexual Aggression." pp. 63–98 in *Sexual Aggression: Issues in Etiology, Assessment, and Treatment,* edited by G. N. Hall, R. Hirschman, J. Graham, and M. Zaragoza. Washington, D.C.: Taylor and Francis.

Marine, Susan. 2004. "Waking Up from the Nightmare of Rape." *The Chronicle of Higher Education.* November 26, p. B5.

Martin, Karin. 2003. "Giving Birth Like a Girl." *Gender & Society.* 17: 54–72.

Martin, Patricia Yancey. 2004. "Gender as a Social Institution." *Social Forces* 82: 1249–73.

Martin, Patricia Yancey and Robert A. Hummer. 1989. "Fraternities and Rape on Campus." *Gender & Society* 3: 457–73.

Merton, Robert. 1957. *Social Theory and Social Structure.* New York: Free Press.

Mills, Crystal and Barbara Granoff. 1992. "Date and Acquaintance Rape among a Sample of College Students." *Social Work* 37: 504–09.

Milner, Murray. 2004. *Freaks, Geeks, and Cool Kids: American Teenagers, Schools, and the Culture of Consumption.* New York: Routledge.

Mohler-Kuo, Meichun, George W. Dowdall, Mary P. Koss, and Henry Weschler. 2004. "Correlates of Rape While Intoxicated in a National Sample of College Women." *Journal of Studies on Alcohol* 65: 37–45.

Muehlenhard, Charlene and Melaney Linton. 1987. "Date Rape and Sexual Aggression: Incidence and Risk Factors." *Journal of Counseling Psychology* 34: 186–96.

Phillips, Lynn. 2000. *Flirting with Danger: Young Women's Reflections on Sexuality and Domination.* New York: New York University.

Rapaport, Karen and Barry Burkhart. 1984. "Personality and Attitudinal Characteristics of Sexually Coercive College Males." *Journal of Abnormal Psychology* 93: 216–21.

Risman, Barbara. 1998. *Gender Vertigo: American Families in Transition.* New Haven, CT: Yale University Press.

———. 2004. "Gender as a Social Structure: Theory Wrestling with Activism." *Gender & Society* 18: 429–50.

Rosow, Jason and Rashawn Ray. 2006. "Getting Off and Showing Off: The Romantic and Sexual Lives of High-Status Black and White Status Men." Department of Sociology, Indiana University, Bloomington, IN. Unpublished manuscript.

Russell, Diana. 1975. *The Politics of Rape*. New York: Stein and Day.

Sampson, Rana. 2002. "Acquaintance Rape of College Students." Problem-Oriented Guides for Police Series, No.17. Washington, DC: U.S. Department of Justice, Office of Community Oriented Policing Services.

Sanday, Peggy. 1990. *Fraternity Gang Rape: Sex, Brotherhood, and Privilege on Campus*. New York: New York University Press.

———. 1996. "Rape-Prone versus Rape-Free Campus Cultures." *Violence against Women* 2: 191–208.

Schwalbe, Michael, Sandra Godwin, Daphne Holden, Douglas Schrock, Shealy Thompson, and Michele Wolkomir. 2000. "Generic Processes in the Reproduction of Inequality: An Interactionist Analysis." *Social Forces* 79: 419–52.

Schwartz, Martin and Walter DeKeseredy. 1997. *Sexual Assault on the College Campus: The Role of Male Peer Support*. Thousand Oaks, CA: Sage Publications.

Stombler, Mindy. 1994. " 'Buddies' or 'Slutties': The Collective Reputation of Fraternity Little Sisters." *Gender & Society* 8: 297–323.

Stombler, Mindy and Patricia Yancey Martin. 1994. "Bringing Women In, Keeping Women Down: Fraternity 'Little Sister' Organizations." *Journal of Contemporary Ethnography* 23: 150–84.

Stombler, Mindy and Irene Padavic. 1997. "Sister Acts: Resisting Men's Domination in Black and White Fraternity Little Sister Programs." *Social Problems* 44: 257–75.

Sweeney, Brian. 2004. "Good Guy on Campus: Gender, Peer Groups, and Sexuality among College Men." Presented at the American Sociological Association Annual Meetings, August 17, Philadelphia, PA.

Swidler, Ann. 2001. *Talk of Love: How Culture Matters*. Chicago: University of Chicago Press.

Tjaden, Patricia and Nancy Thoennes. 2000. "Full Report of the Prevalence, Incidence, and Consequences of Violence against Women: Findings from the National Violence against Women Survey." Washington, DC: National Institute of Justice.

Tolman, Deborah. 2002. *Dilemmas of Desire: Teenage Girls Talk about Sexuality*. Cambridge, MA: Harvard University Press.

Ward, Sally, Kathy Chapman, Ellen Cohn, Susan White, and Kirk Williams. 1991. "Acquaintance Rape and the College Social Scene." *Family Relations* 40: 65–71.

Weschsler, Henry and Meichun Kuo. 2003. "Watering Down the Drinks: The Moderating Effect of College Demographics on Alcohol Use of High-Risk Groups." *American Journal of Public Health*. 93: 1929–33.

West, Candace and Don Zimmerman. 1987. "Doing Gender." *Gender & Society* 1: 125–51.

Linking Sexual Aggression and Fraternities

Mindy Stombler and Marni A. Brown

"It was her first fraternity party. The beer flowed freely and she had much more to drink than she had planned. It was hot and crowded and the party spread out all over the house, so that when three men asked her to go upstairs, she went with them. They took her into a bedroom, locked the door and began to undress her. Groggy with alcohol, her feeble protests were ignored as the three men raped her. When they finished, they put her in the hallway, naked, locking her clothes in the bedroom."[1]

This scenario is more typical than you might think, regularly repeated on college and university campuses across the country. Why do fraternity membership and sexual aggression seem to be related? Researchers have explored these connections, using qualitative studies of predominantly white fraternities,[2] and have come up with some interesting findings.[3] They describe a fraternity context in which the structure, culture, and the nature of rushing and pledging often encourage sexual aggressiveness and even gang rapes. Researchers also suspect that fraternity men's narrow conceptualizations of masculinity, comprising "competition, athleticism, dominance, winning, conflict, wealth, material possessions, willingness to drink alcohol, and sexual prowess vis-à-vis women," play a major role in sexual aggression. Alcohol and drugs, combined with intense pressure to have sex with women, create a "party rape" culture in which these substances are used as "weapons against sexual reluctance."[4] The ultimate goal is to "work out a yes"[5] with available young women (who often lack power to escape the situation because of social pressure, brute force, and/or their own alcohol or drug use). Researchers also point to the consumption of pornography that degrades women as contributing to an atmosphere more accepting of sexual violence. Pornography is often celebrated in fraternity culture. While rapes are prevalent, generally, on college campuses, the numbers rise disproportionately when fraternity members and fraternity houses are taken into consideration.[6]

However, not all fraternities and their members buy into this culture or engage in sexual exploitation or assault.[7] Much depends on their traditions, guiding ideologies, relative level of prestige, and interpersonal dynamics. In addition, some fraternity men have tried to change fraternity culture by attending rape prevention programs and rethinking what it means to be a man. Universities and colleges have also begun to crack down on sexual offenses, and to require that fraternities be educated on sexual assault and familiar with the laws in their particular areas. In the process, fraternities are changing the ways in which they treat women and are revising traditional fraternity versions of masculinity.

NOTES

1. Sanday, Peggy Reeves. 1990. *Fraternity Gang Rape: Sex, Brotherhood, and Privilege on Campus.* New York: New York University Press, p. 3.

2. Researchers have not yet produced in-depth analyses of predominantly black fraternities and rape behaviors.

3. Martin, Patricia Yancey, and Robert A. Hummer. 1989. "Fraternities and Rape on Campus." *Gender & Society* 3(4): 457–473.; Sanday; Stombler, Mindy. 1994. " 'Buddies' or 'Slutties': The Collective Sexual Reputation of Fraternity Little Sisters." *Gender & Society* 8(3): 297–323.

4. Bleeker, E. T., and K. S. Murnen. 2005. "Fraternity Membership, the Display of Degrading Sexual Images of Women, and Rape Myth Acceptance." *Sex Roles 53(7/8):* 487–493; Carr, J. L., and K. M. VanDuesen. 2004. "Risk Factors for Male Aggression on College Campuses." *Journal of Family Violence 19*(5) 279–289; Martin and Hummer 1989, 460, 464.

5. Koss, Mary P., and Hobart H. Cleveland III. 1996. "Athletic Participation, Fraternity Membership, and Date Rape." *Violence Against Women 2*(2): 180–190; Martin and Hummer 1989, 464; Sanday 1990.

6. Carr and Van Duesen 2004; Bleeker and Murnen 2005.

7. Humphrey, Stephen E., and Arnold S. Kahn. 2000. "Fraternities, Athletic Teams, and Rape: Importance of Identification with a Risky Group." *Journal of Interpersonal Violence 15*(2): 1313–1322.

EFFECTS OF RAPE ON MEN: A DESCRIPTIVE ANALYSIS

JAYNE WALKER, JOHN ARCHER, AND MICHELLE DAVIES

INTRODUCTION

The occurrence of male rape outside of institutionalized settings, such as prisons, is an issue that has been neglected by society and the research literature (Stermac, Sheridan, Davidson, & Dunn, 1996). It is estimated that the help and support for male victims of rape is more than 20 years behind that of female victims (Rogers, 1998). . . . [A]lthough the reporting of male sexual assault is increasing year by year, recorded sexual offences against men are much lower than those recorded against women. In 2002, 4,096 indecent assaults and 852 rapes were recorded against men [in the U.K.] compared with 24,811 indecent assaults and 11,441 rapes recorded against women.[1] However, official figures are grossly misleading when evidence from victimization surveys are considered. Stermac et al. (1996) found that 7.2 percent of men in a general household sample of the U.S. population had experienced some form of sexual assault. Some research (e.g., Mezey and King, 1989) has found that gay and bisexual men are more likely to report sexual assault by other men than heterosexual men. Hickson et al. (1994) found that 27.6 percent of a sample of 930 British gay and bisexual men had experienced some form of sexual assault. In 45 percent of these cases, the assault committed was anal rape.

Few male rapes appear in police files or other official records. Very few male rape victims report their assault to the police because they think that they will experience negative treatment, be disbelieved, or blamed for their assault (e.g., Hodge and Cantor, 1998; King and Woolett, 1997; Mezey and King, 1989).

Further, fear of negative reactions . . . prevents men in many cases from seeking medical attention after rape. Frazier (1993) studied 74 male and 1380 female rape victims reporting to a United States hospital emergency department within three days of being raped. The men had more severe physical injuries and were significantly more likely to have been sexually assaulted by more than one perpetrator than the women were. Frazier suggested that men might only report rape to medical services under extreme circumstances, such as gang rape. In some cases, male victims approach medical services for help with physical injuries while concealing the sexual context of their assault (Kaufman, Divasto, Jackson, Voorhees, and Christy, 1980). This means that many male rape victims do not receive testing for sexually transmitted diseases that they may have contracted during their rape. . . .

Previous research has suggested that gay and bisexual men are more at risk of rape than heterosexual men for two reasons (Davies, 2002). The first is that they are at risk of being raped by dates or while in relationships with men. Hickson et al. (1994) found that current or ex-sexual partners were responsible for 65 percent of the assaults in their study of gay and bisexual men. Likewise, women who spend more time with men are more likely to be sexually assaulted than those who do not (Tewksbury and Mustaine, 2001). The second reason that gay and bisexual men are more at risk is through homophobic sexual assaults; for

From "Effects of Rape on Men: A Descriptive Analysis" by Jayne Walker, John Archer, and Michelle Davies, *Archives of Sexual Behavior*, Vol. 34, Issue 1, 2005, pp. 69–80. Copyright © 2005, Springer Science + Business Media.

example, Comstock (1989) found that 10 percent of anti-gay attacks involved sexual assault.

Most . . . research on effects of post-rape trauma has focused on female victims, using either the characteristics of the victim (e.g., the victim's age) or the assault (e.g. the severity of the assault) as correlates of trauma and recovery (Frazier and Schauben, 1994). Frazier (1993) found some differences in the ways that male and female victims coped immediately after the rape. In Frazier's study, male victims reported significantly more hostility, anger, and depression than females did. Frazier concluded that men were more likely to react with anger immediately after rape because anger is a "masculine" way to deal with trauma. However, many male victims reacted with a "controlled" style of coping exemplified by subdued acceptance, minimization of the assault, or denial (Kaufman et al., 1980; Walker, 1993). Kaufman et al. suggested that a controlled reaction reflects one aspect of male socialization, to be emotionally inexpressive to aversive situations. Furthermore, Rogers (1998) suggested that this type of coping strategy renders male victims prone to long-term psychological problems as it makes help-seeking less likely, and denial undermines men coming to terms with their rape.

After rape, most victims experience an increased sense of vulnerability. Some victims become overly concerned with taking safety precautions (Mezey and King, 1989) or change their lives drastically to avoid the possibility of rape happening again. In addition, victims may change the perceptions they have of themselves after rape. They may feel ashamed or blame themselves for their assault. In order to regain their sense of controllability of the world, they may think that they were raped because something they did caused the rape or they were raped because of the type of person they are. Although making sense of the event can be constructive, self-blame can be detrimental to the victim's recovery (Frazier and Schauben, 1994). Self-blaming also affects how people respond to the victim. For example, those who blame themselves are perceived as less well-adjusted and more responsible for the rape than those who do not (Thornton et al., 1988). . . .

. . . [S]ome negative attributions occur in males above and beyond those expected of victims generally. Many male victims become confused about their sexual orientation (e.g., Mezey and King, 1989). . . . Lockwood (1980) showed that some of the stress associated with male rape within prison related to the victim's horror of appearing gay or not masculine. For heterosexual victims, the rape may be their first experience of homosexual contact. They may question the extent to which they may have "contributed" to the assault, making attributions such as, "I must be gay" for "letting" the assault occur. McMullen (1990) suggested that it is not unusual for heterosexual victims to seek out homosexual contact after rape or, in contrast, manifest irrational loathing or hatred of all gay men (because they assumed the perpetrator(s) to be homosexual). Walker (1993) reported that 80 percent of the heterosexual victims in her study reported experiencing long-term crises over their sexual orientation. One victim stated:

Since the assault I have trouble relating to my wife. I have found myself in homosexual relationships that disgust me afterwards . . . it is almost as if I am punishing myself for letting the assault happen in the first place. (p. 26)

Gay male victims may also experience problems with their sexual orientation. When behavior that is formerly associated with consensual sexual activity becomes associated with violence, gay men can experience difficulty in defining their sexuality in a positive way. They might, for example, experience internalized homophobia or interpret the assault as "punishment" for their sexuality (Garnets, Herek, and

Levy, 1990). As in the case of female victims, male victims may perceive consensual sex after rape as "dirty" or they may lose trust in their partners or in men in general. Walker (1993), for example, reported that all of the gay men in her study experienced long-term problems with their sexuality. One victim stated: "Before the assault I was proud to be a homosexual; however, now I feel 'neutered.' I feel sex is dirty and disgusting and I have a real problem with my sexual orientation" (p. 27).

Sexual dysfunction is common in male rape victims, as in females (e.g., Mezey and King, 1989) and can continue for years after the assault. This may cause problems in existing relationships, with partners of the victim having to come to terms with the realities of living with a rape victim. . . . [S]exual problems ranged from complete inactivity to promiscuity or . . . problems with the sexual act, such as fear of "re-creating" the assault either as a victim or perpetrator.

Some male victims perceive a loss of masculinity directly, feeling less of a man. In others, it results in destructive or violent behavior towards others. Anger, revenge fantasies towards the perpetrator(s), or at society in general for being insensitive to him as a male victim are common (Anderson, 1982; Myers, 1989; Walker, 1993). . . .

. . . The aim of the current research was to provide a detailed descriptive analysis of the nature and effects of rape on a non-clinical sample of men who had been anally raped as adults (over the age of 16 years). Men were recruited from a variety of sources, mainly from press advertisements from around the United Kingdom. . . .

METHOD
Participants

. . . A total of 52 responses were received and 73 percent returned questionnaires. . . . [two] responses were received from [patients recruited in genitourinary departments] making the total sample 40.

At the time of the study, respondents had a mean age of 34 years (range, 19–75 years). At the time of the assault, most victims (70%) were between 16 and 25 years of age. . . . The mean age at the time of the assault was 24 years, and the mean time between the assault and participation in the study was 10 years. All respondents reported that they were white and of British nationality. . . .

The majority of respondents were employed at the time of the study: 3 percent as unskilled workers, 15 percent as semi-skilled workers, 12 percent as skilled workers, and 28 percent in professional occupations; 35 percent of respondents were unemployed at the time of the study.

Of the 40 respondents, 21 (53%) . . . identified as gay, 4 (10%) as bisexual, 13 (32%) as heterosexual, and 2 (5%) as asexual. Sixty percent of respondents were not in a relationship at the time of the study; however, 17 percent reported that they were in a heterosexual relationship and 23 percent in a homosexual relationship at the time of the study. Regarding their past experiences of sexual abuse, six (15%) reported to have been raped on more than one occasion, and three (7.5%) to have experienced childhood sexual abuse as well as rape as an adult. . . .

RESULTS
Characteristics and Nature of the Assault

. . . Victims were asked to indicate several characteristics of the assaults. . . . Table 55.1 details [these]. . . .

Location of Assaults

The highest proportion of assaults took place in the perpetrator's home. In one instance, the perpetrator had offered to put the victim up for the night. The victim was awoken in the early

TABLE 55.1 Assault Characteristics

CHARACTERISTIC	N	%
Victim's age at time of assault		
16–25	28	70.0
26–30	4	10.0
31–40	5	13.0
41–50	2	5.0
Over 50	1	2.0
Location of assault		
Victim's home	8	20.0
Perpetrator's home	18	45.0
Vehicle	2	5.0
Street	4	10.0
Other	8	20.0
Use of Violence		
No force	4	10.0
Physical force	21	52.5
Violent force	11	27.5
Weapon used	4	10.0
Number of Perpetrators		
One	25	62.5
Two	10	25.0
Three or more	5	12.5
Victim-perpetrator relationship		
Male family member	4	10.0
Brief acquaintance	8	20.0
Well established acquaintance	7	17.5
Lover or ex-lover	6	15.0
Person in position of trust	5	12.5
Stranger	10	25.0
Sexual acts performed during assault		
Anal penetration	40	100.0
Anal and oral penetration of victim	22	55.0
Victim masturbated	20	50.0
Victim penetrated by object(s)	6	15.0
Sadomasochistic practices	7	17.5
Victim forced to penetrate perpetrator(s)	17	42.5
Forced to masturbate perpetrator(s)	4	10.0
Forced to watch sexual assault on another person	1	2.5

hours of the morning being assaulted by the perpetrator. Assaults were also carried out in the victim's home or in a vehicle. For example, one victim was given a lift by the perpetrator. During the course of the ride, the perpetrator offered a sum of money to have sex with the victim. When he refused, the perpetrator produced a knife and made the victim get in to the back seat of the car where he was both orally and anally raped.

The remaining assaults were carried out in the street, public toilets, in the workplace, a party, and, in one case, a health club. In the last instance, five men whom the victim did not know came in to the sauna where the victim was relaxing and took turns to anally rape him. The victim was also forced to perform oral sex on all of the perpetrators.

Level of Coercion

Some form of coercion was reported in most cases. Physical force (e.g., kicking, punching, and slapping) was used in more than half the cases. Four also involved the use of a weapon (e.g., knife, baseball bat, and in one case, a gun). In addition, the threat of HIV infection was used against six of the victims. The majority of the victims experienced physical injuries during the assault, including anal lacerations and bleeding, bruises, broken bones, knife wounds, and burns. Only 14 of the victims sought medical treatment for their injuries and, and only a minority (five) disclosed the sexual nature of the assault during medical treatment (see also below). In seven cases, a non-sexual crime was also committed at the time of the rape (e.g., kidnapping, robbery, and criminal damage). In one of the most violent cases, the victim was attacked with a knife, his body was badly cut and then a noose was put around his neck. His rapists stripped him down to his underpants, poured petrol over his genital area and then set fire to him. He was later anally raped several times by the gang of men and left for dead. In another particularly violent case, the victim was anally raped by three men he met at a party. In between each assault the victim was held down and the assailants took turns to burn him with a cigarette lighter. The victim was so severely injured he was hospitalised for one month, spending several days in intensive care.

Type and Number of Perpetrators

Someone known to the victim (e.g., acquaintance, lover, or family member) was responsible for most of the assaults, although strangers carried out a significant number (25%). In most cases (62.5%), one perpetrator raped the victim, although in 25 percent there were two perpetrators. Three or more perpetrators were involved in the assault in 12.5 percent of cases.

Type of Assaults Committed

In addition to being anally raped, 55 percent of victims had also experienced oral penetration by one or more of the perpetrators. In half of the cases, the victim had been masturbated by the perpetrator(s), and, in four cases forced to masturbate the perpetrator(s). In six cases, objects had been used to penetrate the victim.

Victims' Perceptions during the Assault

Victims were asked to recall certain details of the assault . . . Table 55.2 shows victims' perceptions of the assault and of the perpetrators.

Perceived Characteristics of Perpetrators

The majority of victims (92.5%) recalled the perpetrator(s) being white. Only three perpetrators were nonwhite. Most victims knew or perceived the perpetrator(s) to be gay (42.5%) or bisexual (12.5%). A total of 22.5 percent believed the perpetrator(s) to be heterosexual, and the remaining 22.5 percent said that they did not know the perpetrator's sexual orientation.

TABLE 55.2   Victims' Perceptions of the Assault

CHARACTERISTIC	N	%
Perpetrator Ethnicity		
White	37	92.5
Black	1	2.5
Moroccan	2	5.0
Perceived sexual orientation of perpetrator		
Heterosexual	9	22.5
Homosexual	17	42.5
Bisexual	5	12.5
Unknown	9	22.5
Victim responses during assault		
Frozen fear, helplessness, submission	35	87.0
Able to fight back	11	27.0
Fear for life	26	65.0
Remarks made by perpetrator(s) during assault		
Said nothing or not remembered	13	32.5
Threats if tell anyone	2	5.0
Victim asked if enjoying it	10	25.0
Taunts and insults from onlookers	9	22.5
Pretence of love or consensual sex	7	17.5
Homophobic comments	2	5.0
Instructions on what sexual acts to perform	3	7.5
Perpetrator(s) claimed to have raped other men	1	2.5

Note: The total N does not equal 40 in some categories due to some men reporting more than one response to the question.

Remarks during the Assault

Victims were asked whether the perpetrator(s) made remarks during the assault. A quarter of the men were asked whether they were enjoying the rape. For example, one man was told: "Be a good boy and you will enjoy it." In some cases, attackers told the victim how much they were enjoying the experience, as this man explained:

One said how physically attractive I was and told me how many orgasms he had and how much he enjoyed it. Another talked to me while anally penetrating me and masturbating me about how he and his partner did this and similar awful things to men . . .

It was also common for perpetrators to verbally abuse the victim during the rape, using misogynistic (e.g., slut, bitch, whore) or anti-gay language (e.g., "you filthy queer"). This man explained how his attacker intimidated him . . .

He called me a bitch and a cunt—then called me filthy for sucking his penis—which he had forced me to do. He repeatedly said I wanted it.

Another man was subjected to homophobic comments during the assault. The attackers told him that:

I was a filthy queer and that I deserved all I got and he knew I was secretly enjoying it. To each other they shouted out encouragement and egged each other on to do more brutal things to me.

In other instances, the perpetrator(s) tried to act as if the assault was a consensual activity. . . .

He told me how much he loved me and that I could never leave him.

Responses to the Assault

When asked what their responses were at the time of the assault, the majority of victims said that they reacted with frozen fear, helplessness or submission. However, 27 percent said that they were able to put up a fight at some point during the assault. A total of 65 percent said that they feared for their lives. When asked their responses in the hours and days after the assault, the majority (78%) said that they reacted in a "controlled" style (e.g., calm, composed or subdued). A total of 72 percent also reported that the sense of helplessness and loss of control during the assault was worse than the sexual aspects of the encounter.

Disclosure of the Assault to Other People

The men were asked to identify the first person to whom they disclosed their assault. The majority (60%) stated that it was someone they knew, including friends (54%), partners (29%), and family members (17%). Of the remaining 40 percent, 11 (27.5%) said that it was a professional, such as a work colleague, health care professionals, social workers, therapist or the police (only five men ever reported their assault to the police; see below). The remaining five (12.5%) said that they had never told anyone until they participated in this study.

The length of time that passed before victims disclosed their assault ranged from a few hours to 20 years. In many instances, there was a long time between the assault and disclosure. . . . When asked about reactions that they received from the people to whom they disclosed, many reported positive reactions, such as offers of help and support. Others reported lack of support, such as insensitive remarks, or homophobic victim-blaming. . . .

Reporting to the Police

Only five men ever reported their assault to the police. Of those who did report, only one man said that the police were responsive and helpful. The other four found the police to be unsympathetic, disinterested, and homophobic. They felt that their complaint was not taken seriously and all four regretted their decision to tell the police. Only one perpetrator was subsequently convicted (and sentenced to 10 years imprisonment). However, having gone through a court case, this victim was distressed at the way he was treated in court. He stated that he was made to feel that he . . . was the assailant, and that his ordeal in court probably had a worse effect on him than the rape itself. In the other four cases, the police did not press charges.

Medical and Psychological Treatment

Medical services were utilized by 14 (35%) of the men. However, of these, only five reported the sexual context of the assault, the others only disclosing their physical injuries. . . . All of these men reported that the attitudes of the medical staff were helpful, understanding, and supportive.

Over half (58%) of the men sought psychological treatment at some point after the assault. However, in most cases help was not sought until long after the assault occurred. . . . Issues dealt with included sexuality, anger, guilt and shame, and relationship problems. All of the men who sought treatment reported that it was beneficial to some degree. In general, the most helpful aspects of the treatments included being told that it was not their fault, having someone to talk to, and someone to listen and express care and concern. However, even though the men said that the attitudes of therapists were helpful and supportive, they also felt that the professionals lacked the expertise to deal with male sexual assault issues. In addition to psychological treatment, 11 men were prescribed medication, such as anti-depressants, sleeping tablets, or anti-psychotic drugs.

Other Issues Concerning Reporting

The men were asked what advice they would offer to the police and other professionals dealing with male rape victims. The most common responses were to offer the same support to male as to female victims, such as to listen to and believe the victim, and to offer more publicity that men can become victims of rape. . . . [T]he men felt that professionals should be more empathic to men, and that work should be done to eliminate homophobia within professional services. When asked what support

services they would like to see available, the men said that services such as male rape crisis centres, and support groups in all major towns, 24-hour helplines, more easily available therapy services, and the police specially trained to deal with male rape victims.

When asked why they had participated in the study, responses focused on promoting informed publicity about male rape. For example, men said that they responded to the advertisement to try to help professionals understand male rape and what victims experience, to bring male rape to the attention of the public, to help future victims, and to establish support for male victims. . . .

Long-Term Effects of the Assault

All of the men experienced long-term negative psychological and behavioral effects after the assault. Table 55.3 shows the range of effects that the men reported. The following victim reports highlight some of the specific reactions to the assaults.

Depression, Anxiety, and Anger

Almost all the men reported depression in the weeks and months following their assaults. This man stated that in the six years after his rape he suffered from periods of severe depression:

I have felt like I have been living in a void since the assault. I suffer panic attacks, mood swings, total depression, but the medical profession have given up on me and said I am too damaged to help. I feel I have no future.

Some form of anxiety was felt by almost all the men after the assault. In some cases, anxiety focused on their interactions with men. As the following man stated:

I am extremely anxious around straight men, especially in social situations. What often can be genuine friendliness on their part can put me on edge and I think they are going to make a move on me.

TABLE 55.3 Long-Term Effects of the Assault

REACTION	N	%
Depression	39	97.5
Fantasies about revenge and retaliation	38	95.0
Flashbacks of the assault	37	92.5
Feelings of anxiety	37	92.5
Loss of self respect/damaged self image	36	90.0
Increased sense of vulnerability	36	90.0
Emotional distancing from others	34	85.0
Fear of being alone with men	33	82.5
Guilt and self-blame, e.g., for not being able to prevent the assault	33	82.5
Increased anger and irritability	32	80.0
Low self-esteem	31	77.5
Intrusive thoughts about the assault	30	75.0
Withdrawal from family and friends	29	72.5
Impaired task performance	28	70.0
Long-term crisis with sexual identity	28	70.0
Damaged masculine identity	27	68.0
Increased use of tobacco	27	67.5
Abuse of alcohol	25	62.5
Increased security consciousness	23	57.5
Suicide ideation	22	55.0
Abuse of drugs	21	52.5
Self-harming behaviors	20	50.0
Suicide attempts	19	47.5
Eating disorders, e.g., bulimia, anorexia	11	27.5

Another common response to the assaults was anger. This man was still struggling to deal with feelings of anger and revenge fantasies:

In an attempt to deal with my anger, I am attending anger management classes and I also see a psychiatrist. My need for revenge is so strong that it is as damaging as the rape itself. My anger has led me to be a psychological abuser and a bully.

Almost all the men reported that they had fantasized about gaining revenge or retaliation against the perpetrator(s). Some fantasized about killing them. . . .

Confusion about Sexuality and Masculinity

A total of 70 percent of the men reported experiencing long-term crises with their sexual orientation and 68 percent with their sense of masculinity after the assault. This man stated that since he felt that he was capable of handling confrontational situations, being raped was a shock both to his self-image and masculinity:

The sense of powerlessness I experienced during the assault totally surprised me. I thought I was pretty good at handling potentially violent situations as I worked in a night shelter for men. However, I never imagined I could be so vulnerable and become a victim. It was a big shock to my male ego.

The following man similarly wrote of the shock and long-term effects on his self-image and masculinity:

The assault was a threat to my male pride and dignity. It was a shock to find that a so-called "strong man" could become a helpless victim of sexual assault at the hands of another man. My sense of who I was (ex-army) was destroyed for about 10 years.

Another man equated his perceived loss of masculinity with his inability to prevent his assault. He also stated that negative reactions from others reinforced this view:

For a long time after the assault, I felt a failure as a man for not being able to protect myself. Other people's attitudes reinforced my feelings of inadequacy, so to compensate for my feelings I became aggressive and a bully.

Changes in Sexual Behavior

Several men reported changes in their sexual behavior after the assault. Some became promiscuous, while others refused to have sexual relations with either men or women for a considerable time after the assault. Sexual problems included erectile failure and lack of libido. One described his sexual experience after his assault as one of promiscuity and sexual compulsion:

Before the assault I was straight; however, since the assault I have begun to engage in voluntary homosexual activity. This causes me a great deal of distress as I feel I am not really homosexual but I cannot stop myself having sex with men. I feel as if having sex with men I am punishing myself for letting the assault happen in the first place.

Unlike this man, since his assault the following had not engaged in sexual relations with anyone:

Since the assault I believe I no longer have a sexual orientation. I no longer want a sexual relationship with a man or a woman. I feel sex is a horrible act and just an excuse for an individual to experience self-satisfaction.

Some of the men also expressed confusion and disgust about their sexual responses during the assault. Several of the men reported getting erections and ejaculating during the assault. These men reported that prior to the assault they had equated sexual responses with pleasure; however, after experiencing sexual responses during sexual assault, they felt that, although they were disgusted at the thought of the assault, they must have enjoyed it really because they responded sexually. This (heterosexual) man stated:

If I really thought that the sexual acts I was subjected to during the assault were so degrading and perverse, why did I ejaculate? For a long time I thought I must have really enjoyed it, therefore, I must have homosexual tendencies. I was confused for a very long time.

Loss and Grief Reactions

Almost all of the men reported feeling a loss of self-respect or self-worth after the assault. Some of the men equated losses to their self-image or their feelings of powerlessness as grief. For example, this man wrote:

I don't care about myself anymore, if someone could assault me in such a way [he was anally and orally raped] how can I be worth anything? The pain I feel is like grieving over the death of a loved one . . . now a big chunk of me is missing.

Another similarly stated:

The loss of dignity can be quite overwhelming. The very essence of one's character and being has been invaded and treated as worthless, just there for the taking.

Guilt and Self-Blame

Over 80 percent of the men reported that they experienced profound feelings of guilt and self-blame following the assault. Commonly, these feelings focused on failure to prevent the assault or inability to fight back. Some of the men blamed themselves for willingly putting themselves in a situation where they were vulnerable to assault. For example, this man stated:

For me, the worst part of the assault was I put myself at his hands. I willingly went to his house; hence, I put myself in a vulnerable position. So the blame will always be on my shoulders and the guilt will never go away.

Suicide Ideation and Self-Harm

Many of the men reported partaking in self-destructive behaviors as a consequence of the assault, such as self-harming, suicide ideation or attempts, or abuse of alcohol, drugs, tobacco or food. . . . This man stated:

I dream of killing myself to forget what happened.

Another man reported that his attempt at suicide was at the location where the assault took place (a public toilet):

In an attempt at killing myself, I drove my car into a wall next to the toilets where the assault took place.

Another reported that since the assault he has had both alcohol and eating problems, as well as experiencing mood swings and problems interacting with others:

Since the assault I have developed bulimia and an alcohol problem. I avoid physical contact with people and I have become withdrawn and moody.

Another stated that he self-harms and has severe mood swings in an attempt to cope with his problems with sex and relationship difficulties following his assault:

I have a distaste for sex and sexual acts hence I no longer have a full relationship. This has led me to self-harm, have violent outbursts and severe mood swings.

Resolution

The men were asked how much they felt they had recovered from the assault. Only one man recorded his recovery as complete; 18 (45%), however, said that they had "mostly" recovered. Thirteen (32.5%) described their recovery as "somewhat complete," and 8 (20%) said that they had not recovered at all.

DISCUSSION

This study provided a descriptive analysis of the experiences of 40 British male rape victims. . . .

The demographic characteristics of the men were consistent with previous research. . . . that has found that gay and bisexual men are more likely to report sexual assault by other men than are heterosexual men (e.g., Mezey and King, 1989). Previous research has [also] found that gay and bisexual men are more at risk of rape than heterosexual men are, because they are at risk of sexual assault by dating men, and because they are more likely to find themselves victims of anti-gay violence (Davies, 2002). The use of anti-gay language by some perpetrators in the current study denoted the homophobic context of some of these rapes. . . .

The majority of the men were young, between the age of 16 and 25 (mean age, 24) at the time of assault. . . . The figures in this study are consistent with other studies (e.g.,

Mezey and King, 1989; Stermac et al., 1996), and with routine activity theory, in that young men are more likely to put themselves in situations where sexual assault may occur than older men are (Tewsbury and Mustaine, 2001). It is possible that young men are more likely to report sexual assaults, but are no more at risk than older men. Further research is needed to investigate this possibility.

All of the men in this study were white and of British nationality. It is not clear whether this was because white men are more likely to be sexually assaulted than non-whites, because men of ethnic minorities are not as likely to report it as white men are, or because the recruitment method was inadvertently discouraging to ethnic minorities. . . .

The majority of assaults took place indoors, namely in the perpetrator's or the victim's home, and someone the victims knew carried out most assaults. This is consistent with research on female rape victims. The locations in which assaults took place are also consistent with routine activity theory. The circumstances of the male rapes described in this study are inconsistent with people's perceptions of what is considered the "stereotypic rape" (Krahé, 2000). Most people view rape as a crime that takes place outdoors, as a violent assault between two strangers (Krahe, 2000). . . . [T]he majority of the assaults involve[d] some form of violence. Physical force (e.g., kicking, punching, and slapping) was used in more than half the cases. The majority of the victims experienced physical injuries during the assault, including anal lacerations and bleeding, bruises, broken bones, knife wounds, and burns. Frazier (1993) suggested that men were more likely to report rape if they had been seriously injured. Thus, the relatively high number of violent assaults could be a result of reporting bias. . . . In a considerable minority, more than one perpetrator carried out the assault. This is consistent with Frazier's research in which it was found that male victims were more likely to have been assaulted by more than one man than females were.

When asked what their responses were at the time of the assault, the majority of victims said that they reacted with frozen fear, helplessness, or submission; however, just over a quarter of the men said that they were able to put up at fight at some point during the assault. . . . [M]en (like women) react to extreme personal threat with frozen helplessness. The belief that men should be able to fight back during sexual assault contributes to secondary victimization (Williams, 1984). . . . As the majority of male rape victims cannot fight back, self-blame for not being able to do so may contribute to the victim failing to seek help from the police, medical sources or friends and family.

Socialization can also explain the gender difference reported in initial reactions to rape. The majority of female victims are said to display an emotional "expressive" reaction to rape (Burgess and Holstrom, 1974); however, a "controlled" reaction was reported by the majority of men in this study . . . It reflects a gender role expectation that it is unmanly for men to express negative emotion even in the face of physical and emotional trauma. . . . [T]he reluctance of male victims to tell anyone about the assault, coupled with the lack of counseling and support for male victims, could explain . . . [why] many male victims suffer deep and long-lasting psychological and behavioral effects. Although each victim has a different set of long-term consequences, common reactions reported include emotional disruption manifested by depression and increased anger. There is also disturbed cognitive functioning taking the form of flashbacks to, or preoccupation with, memories of the assault and increased thoughts of suicide. Psychologically, the victims reported feeling devalued with regard to their identity and self-esteem, and they experienced a disruption in social relations due to feelings of emotional distancing. Victims also reported long-term crises with their sexual orientation, with sexual dysfunction, and suicide attempts.

How representative this sample is of all male rape victims is difficult to determine because the present research is based on victims who responded to media advertising. However, it does offer a valuable insight into the experiences of male rape victims of non-clinical origin, which to date has been missing from the research literature. Future studies might extend the current work to investigate differences between men who have been anally raped, as in the present study, compared with those sexually assaulted in other ways, such as oral rape. Future studies might also investigate the effects of repeat sexual victimization in men, such as those repeatedly sexually victimized in the course of relationship violence, and the effects of sexual violence compared with physical abuse.

NOTES

1. At the end of 2003, the legal categorization of sexual offences in the United Kingdom was subject to major change. The Sexual Offences Act 2003 includes nonconsensual oral as well as anal and vaginal penile penetration as rape. The offence of indecent assault is no longer in statute and has been replaced by two offences: assault by penetration and sexual assault. Assault by penetration includes non-consensual sexual penetration by any object other than the penis while sexual assault covers every other non-consensual sexual act. Because the data for this study were collected before the changes in law, our definition of rape includes non-consensual anal penetration only.

REFERENCES

Anderson, C. L. 1982. Males as sexual assault victims: Multiple levels of trauma. *Journal of Homosexuality, 7:* 145–162.

Burgess, A. W., and Holmstrom, L. L. 1974. Rape trauma syndrome. *American Journal of Psychiatry, 131:* 981–986.

Comstock, G. D. 1989. Victims of anti-gay/lesbian violence. *Journal of Interpersonal Violence, 4:* 101–106.

Davies, M. 2002. Male sexual assault victims: A selective review of the literature and implications for support services. *Aggressive and Violent Behavior, 7:* 203–214.

Frazier, P. A. 1993. A comparative study of male and female rape victims seen at a hospital-based rape crisis program. *Journal of Interpersonal Violence, 8:* 64–76.

Frazier, P. A., and Schauben, L. 1994. Causal attributions and recovery from rape and other stressful life events. *Journal of Social and Clinical Psychology, 13:* 1–14.

Garnets, L., Herek, G., and Levy, B. 1990.Violence and victimization of lesbians and gay men: Mental health consequences. *Journal of Interpersonal Violence, 5:* 366–383.

Hickson, F. C. I., Davies, P. M., Hunt, A. J., Weatherburn, P., McManus, T. J., and Coxon, A. P. M. 1994. Gay men as victims of non-consensual sex. *Archives of Sexual Behavior, 23:* 281–294.

Hodge, S., and Cantor, D. 1998. Victims and perpetrators of male sexual assault. *Journal of Interpersonal Violence, 13:* 222–239.

Kaufman, A., Divasto, P., Jackson, R., Voorhees, H., and Christy, J. 1980. Male rape victims: Non-institutionalized assault. *American Journal of Psychiatry, 137:* 221–223.

King, M., and Woolett, E. 1997. Sexually assaulted males: 115 men consulting a counselling service. *Archives of Sexual Behavior, 26:* 579–583.

Krahé, B. 2000. Sexual scripts and heterosexual aggression. In T. Eckes and H. M. Trautner (Eds.), *The developmental social psychology of gender* (pp. 273–292). Hillsdale, NJ: Erlbaum.

Lockwood, D. 1980. *Prison sexual violence.* New York: Elsevier.

McMullen, R. J. 1990. *Male rape: Breaking the silence on the last taboo.* London: GMP Publishers Ltd.

Mezey, G., and King, M. 1989. The effects of sexual assault on men. *Psychological Medicine, 19:* 205–209.

Myers, M. F. 1989. Men sexually assaulted as adults and sexually abused as boys. *Archives of Sexual Behavior, 18:* 205–209.

Rogers, P. 1998. Call for research into male rape. *Mental Health Practice, 1:* 34.

Stermac, L., Sheridan, P. M., Davidson, A., and Dunn, S. 1996. Sexual assault of adult males. *Journal of Interpersonal Violence, 11:* 52–64.

Tewksbury, R., and Mustaine, E. E. 2001. Life-style factors associated with the sexual assault of men: A routine activity theory analysis. *Journal of Men's Studies, 9:* 153–182.

Thornton, B., Ryckman, R., Kirchner, G., Jacobs, J., Laczor, L., and Kuehnel, R. 1988. Reactions to self-attributed victim responsibility: A comparative analysis of rape crisis counsellors and lay observers. *Journal of Applied Social Psychology, 18:* 409–422.

Walker, J. L. 1993. *Male rape: The hidden crime.* Unpublished honors thesis, University of Wolverhampton, UK.

Williams, J. E. 1984. Secondary victimization: Confronting public attitudes about rape. *Victimology, 9:* 66–81.

Women Raping Men

Denise Donnelly and Mindy Stombler

Around 1.4 percent of men (or 1 in 71) have experienced a rape or attempted rape at some point in their lives.[1] Men perpetrate most of the sexual violence against other men, but women do rape men as well. While perpetrating men are more likely to penetrate their male victims, perpetrating women are more likely to force men to penetrate them.[2]

In their article entitled "Sexual Molestation of Men by Women," P. M. Sarrel and W. H. Masters recount this story of a 27-year-old male, 178-pound truck driver, who was held captive for more than 24 hours. When he was

released, he did not tell others about his experience, fearing ridicule. He experienced erectile dysfunction following the rape:

[Sam] had been drinking and left a bar with a woman companion he had not known previously. They went to a motel where he was given another drink and shortly thereafter fell asleep. He awoke to find himself naked, tied hand and foot to a bedstead, gagged, and blindfolded. As he listened to voices in the room, it was evident that several women were present. When the women realized that he was awake, he was told to "have sex with all of them." He thinks that during his period of captivity four different women used him sexually, some of them a number of times. Initially he was manipulated to erection and mounted. After a very brief period of coitus, he ejaculated. He was immediately restimulated to erection and the performance was repeated . . . it became increasingly difficult for him to maintain an erection. When he couldn't function well, he was threatened with castration and felt a knife held to his scrotum. He was terrified that he would be cut and did have some brief improvement in erectile quality.[3]

Because Americans continue to internalize Victorian notions of gendered sexuality, where men are depicted as having strong sexual impulses and always interested in sex, they tend to assume that men are unable to be raped or sexually coerced. Even when women are depicted as sexual predators in popular culture, it is often in a favorable light, as a fantasy come true. Yet despite our cultural attitudes, women can and do rape men. And while legal definitions of rape only used to recognize women as victims, the U.S. government recently updated its definition of rape to include woman-on-man rape (see "Changing the Definition of Rape" earlier in this chapter).

The scenario above describes women using physical force and a weapon to coerce their male victim. However there are many kinds of scenarios where women rape men. For example, some women may drug men and sexually assault them during their incapacitated state by fondling them to erection or penetrating them (such as using their fingers or an object to penetrate them anally without consent or with the man too inebriated to give consent). Women may also coerce men to penetrate them by threatening them or blackmailing them. Men may become erect despite not wishing to have sex with a particular woman. Being physiologically aroused is not necessarily the same as being emotionally "turned on." Fear may produce erections. Even ejaculation is not always voluntary, as it is a spinal level reflex. Men can ejaculate without being turned on and without being erect.

The stigma men experience when raped by women acts as a deterrent to reporting the crime. Male victims may feel as if their masculinity has been impugned. We hope that as definitions of rape catch up to offending behaviors, that as a society we can begin to address this type of sexual violence.

NOTES

1. This figure does not include men in prison.

2. Black, M.C., Basile, K.C., Breiding, M.J., Smith, S.G., Walters, M.L., Merrick, M.T., Chen, J., and Stevens, M.R. 2011. "The National Intimate Partner and Sexual Violence Survey (NISVS): 2010 Summary Report." Atlanta, GA: National Center for Injury Prevention and Control, Centers for Disease Control and Prevention.

3. Sarrel, P. M., and W. H. Masters. 1982. "Sexual Molestation of Men by Women." *Archives of Sexual Behavior,* 11(2): 117–181.

RAPE AND WAR: FIGHTING MEN AND COMFORT WOMEN

JOANE NAGEL

Sexuality has always been an important, though often disregarded, aspect of all militaries and military operations. Throughout history women have been among "camp followers" providing services such as laundry, nursing, companionship, and sex to soldiers on military missions during peace and war.[1] Sometimes these women have been wives, relatives, or girlfriends, but always among their ranks have been prostitutes as well. Women who have had sex with servicemen around the world, however, have not always been volunteers. Throughout history local women have been involuntarily "drafted" in the sexual service of militaries as rape victims and sexual slaves.[2]

Rape in war is at its core an ethnosexual phenomenon. Whether a war is fought across national borders or inside state boundaries, the military front is typically an ethnosexual frontier. Differences in nationality, race, or ethnicity separate the combatants and identify the targets of aggression in military operations. Whether violence in war is from combat or sexual attack, and whether it is guns or bodies that are used as weapons, those who are physically or sexually assaulted almost always are different in some ethnic way. . . .

Sexual exploitation and abuse are important weapons of war, and rape is perhaps the most common component of war's sexual arsenal. Susan Brownmiller documents the routine practice of rape, especially gang rape, in war.[3] Moving or occupying armies use the rape of "enemy" women and girls as both a carrot and a stick: raping local women is a spoil of war for the troops to enjoy, and rape is also a technique of terror and warfare designed to dominate and humiliate enemy men by sexually conquering their women. Rape in war, as in many other ethnosexual settings, is best understood as a transaction between men, where women are the currency used in the exchange. Sexually taking an enemy's women amounts to gaining territory and psychological advantage. In countries around the world, rape often is defined as a polluting action, a way to soil the victim, her kin, and her nation physically and symbolically. Sexual warfare can extend beyond the moment of violation in situations where victims are reputationally smeared, physically mutilated, or when pregnancies or births result from sexual assaults. For instance, the widespread rape of mainly Muslim and some Croatian women by Serbian men in Bosnia in the early 1990s was partly intended to impregnate the women so that they would bear Serbian babies, "little Chetniks."[4] In order to guarantee that these rape victims could not obtain abortions, the Serbs set up concentration camps where pregnant women were imprisoned until they gave birth.[5]

Probably the best-known instance of rape in war is the so-called Rape of Nanking that occurred during the Japanese invasion of China in the winter and spring of 1938–1939,

From "Rape and War: Fighting Men and Comfort Women" in *Race, Ethnicity, and Sexuality: Intimate Interactions, Forbidden Frontiers* by Joane Nagel (181–187), © Oxford University Press, Inc. 2003. By permission of Oxford University Press.

when Japanese soldiers raped an estimated eighty thousand Chinese women and girls.[6] A less well-known instance of Japanese wartime sexual exploits was the sexual enslavement of thousands of mainly Asian women by the Japanese Imperial Army during World War II. Sexual slavery in war is a variation on the theme of wartime rape. Slavery extends the tactic of rape as a short-term strategy of a military mission into a permanent feature of military operations. The Japanese military established camps of so-called military comfort women (*Jugun Ianfu*) in Japan and other countries where Japanese troops were stationed. While there were some mainly lower-class Japanese women forced into sexual slavery, most of the estimated 200,000 women enslaved by the Japanese army were ethnic or national. Others were brought from Korea, China, Taiwan, Indonesia, Malaysia, and the Philippines to sexually service the troops.[7] Kazuko Watanabe reports that in such settings a woman's worth as a sexual commodity was based on her class and her ethnicity:

The Japanese Imperial Army divided comfort women into a hierarchical order according to class, race, and nationality. . . . Korean and most other Asian women were assigned to lower-class soldiers. Japanese and European women went to high-ranking officers. Most of the European women were Dutch [often of mixed ancestry] who were imprisoned in a prisoner of war camp in the Netherlands East Indies.[8]

Soldiers' rankings of and preferences for women of particular races and nationalities enslaved in rape camps were not unique to the Japanese military.[9] Japan was not the only country that established large-scale organized operations of forced sexual servitude during World War II. The Nazis used concentration camps in Germany and other occupied countries for more than industrial and war-related labor, their program of genocide against the Jews, and the mass deportation and killing of Roma (gypsies) and other "non-Aryan"

peoples. Sexual labor was also demanded of women internees, and both men and women prisoners were used for sexual experimentation by Nazi scientists and physicians. German concentration camps were sites of forced prostitution and sexual assault, and as was the case with Japan, not all women in the German camps were treated as "equal" when it came to sexual abuse. A woman's age, youth, and physical appearance made her more or less likely to be the target of Nazi sexual aggression.[10] And, as in so many areas of social life, even (especially) in wartime concentration camps, ethnicity mattered. There were official prohibitions against German soldiers having sex with Jewish women, though these rules often were not enforced. Many Jewish women survivors reported extensive sadistic sexual torture, as well as rape, and these assaults often were accompanied by a barrage of racial and anti-Semitic verbal abuse.[11]

The Allies also were involved in sexual violence and exploitation during World War II. Some was in the form of mass rapes, such as those committed against German women by the Soviet army.[12] In other cases, sexual abuse and exploitation resulted when military personnel capitalized on the vulnerability of women who faced economic hardship, malnourishment, or starvation because of the war's disruption of local economies and food production. Many women in occupied or liberated countries found sexual liaisons or prostitution preferable to the grim alternatives available for themselves and their dependent families. U.S. troops also committed rapes during the war and the occupation that followed. In her examination of U.S. Army records, Brownmiller found 947 rape *convictions,* not simply charges or trials of American soldiers in Army general courts-martial during the period from January 1942 to July 1947.[13]

Wartime rape did not stop at the end of World War II, nor did its ethnosexual character change after 1945. The practice of rape in war extended into major and minor conflicts during the second half of the twentieth century—in civil wars, wars of independence, and military invasions, interventions, and operations in countries and regions around the world including Bangladesh, Vietnam, Iraq, Kuwait, Bosnia, Croatia, Serbia, Rwanda, Liberia, Kashmir, and Sierra Leone.[14] The logic of rape in war is always the same: rapes are committed across ethnosexual boundaries, and rape is used by both sides for the familiar time-honored reasons—to reward the troops, to terrorize and humiliate the enemy, and as a means of creating solidarity and protection through mutual guilt among small groups of soldiers. Ethnic loyalty and ethnic loathing join hands in rape in war.

In the post-Soviet era East European nationalist conflicts, the use of rape as a weapon of war has begun to move from the shadows more fully into view. For instance, during the 1990s warfare occurred along a number of ethnic and national borders in the former Yugoslavia—between Croats and Serbs, Christians and Muslims, and against Roma, among others. The most notorious of these ethnic conflicts was in Bosnia; the conflict's notoriety stemmed in part from its sexual character, especially the mass rape of Bosnian Muslim women by Orthodox Christian Serbian men. Many of these men and women were former neighbors. Muslims and Christians had lived side by side in the city of Sarajevo and elsewhere in Bosnia for decades and many had intermarried. That peace was shattered in 1992 when "ethnic cleansing" began.

Ethnic cleansing, or the removal of one ethnic group from a territory claimed by another, followed a common pattern across the region. Groups of armed Serbian men (sometimes uniformed troops and sometimes "irregulars" who were not officially in the military and not in uniform) roamed Bosnian towns and villages in groups, opportunistically looting and pillaging houses and businesses, raping and killing mainly unarmed Muslims they encountered along the way. Survivors reported that the Serbs came through the same towns several times in waves. During the first wave, typically, some of the Muslim men were killed and the rest were rounded up to be killed later or to be interned in concentration camps. Muslim women, children, and the elderly were left behind. It was during the next waves of Serbs passing through the towns that they raped local non-Serbian girls and women.

Munevra was a forty-eight-year-old widow with three sons ranging in age from fourteen to twenty-four, ages that made them targets for the Serbs to kill or deport to concentration camps. She kept the young men hidden in the cellar as small groups of armed Serbian men repeatedly came through the town. In the spring of 1992, two men came to her house and sexually assaulted her. . . .

I was afraid my sons would hear me. I was dying of fear 'cause of my sons. They're decent people. . . . Then this man touched my breasts. He pulled up my blouse and took out my breasts. . . . He said, "For a woman your age your breasts aren't bad." Then they brought me to the other room. . . . I begged him and cried, and I crossed my legs. Then he took out his thing, you know, and he did it and sprayed it on me. When he was done the other one came and did the same thing. . . . When they left, my sons came out and . . . they asked me what happened: "What'd they do to you?" I said, "Nothing." I couldn't tell them about it. . . . I'd rather die than have them find out about it.[15]

Women's and families' shame about such incidents were part of the process of victimization and violations.[16] Munevra's experience occurred relatively early in the nationalist conflict; far worse sexual violations were in store for women as the war escalated.

The scene in Serbian so-called rape camps was a longer, more brutal nightmare for Muslim and other non-Serbian women and girls.

Twenty-six-year-old Ifeta was arrested by Serbian soldiers, most of whom she knew, and taken to a women's camp in Doboj:

Three drunken [Serbian army] soldiers . . . dragged her into a classroom . . . here she was raped by all three men "at the same time," says Ifeta, pointing to her mouth and backside. "And while they were doing it they said I was going to have a baby by them". . . . After that the rapes were a part of Ifeta's daily life. . . . It was always a gang rape, they always cursed and humiliated her during it, and the rapists very frequently forced her to have oral sex with them.[17]

Another camp internee, Kadira, described the weeks she spent at Doboj:

"They pushed bottle necks into our sex, they even stuck shattered, broken bottles into some women. . . . Guns too. And then you don't know if he's going to fire, you're scared to death". . . . Once she was forced to urinate on the Koran. Another time she and a group of women had to dance naked for the Serbian guards and sing Serbian songs. . . . She has forgotten how many times she was raped.[18]

The same pattern of sexual terror, torture, and rape used by the Serbs in their campaigns of ethnic cleansing and warfare in Bosnia was repeated in Kosovo, Yugoslavia, in 1998–1999. Once again groups of Serbian men—police, soldiers, irregulars—swept through villages invading homes and raping Kosovar Albanian (mainly Muslim) female occupants, sexually attacking Kosovar Albanian women refugees fleeing combat zones, and sexually assaulting Kosovar Albanian women who were being held hostage or detained. The Kosovo conflict ended when NATO troops entered Kosovo in June 1999.[19]

In spring 2000, the UN convened the *International Criminal Tribunal for the Former Yugoslavia* in The Hague, Netherlands, to investigate and prosecute those ordering mass killing and mass rape in the various ethnic conflicts in the former Yugoslavia.[20] This investigation raised the issue of whether rape and sexual slavery are "crimes against humanity." Enloe argues that this question reflects a new awareness and public airing of what has been a long hidden history of sexual assault, torture, and exploitation of women during war:

[T]he rapes in Bosnia have been documented by women's organizations . . . [that] have helped create an international political network of feminists who are making news of the Bosnian women's victimization not to institutionalize women as victims, not to incite men to more carnage, but to explain anew how war makers rely on peculiar ideas about masculinity. . . . [F]eminist reporters are using news of wartime sexual assaults by male soldiers to rethink the very meanings of both sovereignty and national identity. . . . If they succeed, the construction of the entire international political arena will be significantly less vulnerable to patriarchy.[21]

As the reports of human rights hearings and organizations document every year, it is not only enemy women who are the targets of sexual abuse and torture in war. I have not seen reported the establishment of rape camps with men as sexual slaves, however, men often are assaulted sexually as part of intimidation, torture, and combat in international conflicts and wars, as well as in military or paramilitary operations against internal political or ethnic insurgents. For instance, in Bosnia, there were numerous reports of cases in which Muslim and Croatian men were castrated or forced to castrate one another:

In villages, towns, cities, the countryside, and concentration camps, male and female adults and children are raped as part of more extensive torture. Many of the atrocities committed are centered on the genitalia. . . . [T]estimonies of castrations enforced on Bosnian-Herzegovinian and Croatian prisoners, and in particular of orders under threat of death that they castrate each other with various instruments and at times with their teeth, are widely available, as the [United Nations] Bassiouni Report makes clear.[22]

Men also can be vulnerable to sexualized warfare in more indirect ways. In her critique of Japan's patriarchal Confucianist view of all women and racist treatment of non-Japanese men and women, Kazuko Watanabe also identifies a danger for men. She argues that in many countries men are trapped in masculinist roles, and forced to act out patriarchal and sexual scripts that commodify and endanger them as well as the women they victimize:

Men's bodies and sexualities are also victims of militarist and consumerist capitalist societies. Men are, supposedly, unable to control their sexual impulses and are in need of prostitutes. [In World War II] Male soldiers were dehumanized to make them good fighters then stimulated by sexual desire that was fulfilled by comfort women. . . . Both the soldiers who were forced to die for the emperor on the battlefields and today's businessmen who die for their companies from karoshi (overwork) have often been rewarded with prostitutes.[23]

Watanabe's analysis suggests that although they are perpetrators of the rape and sexual abuse of both women and other men in times of war, men pay a psychological, social, and physical price for their complicity in patriarchal masculinist systems of sexual and ethnosexual violence. For instance, many soldiers display varying degrees of post-traumatic stress or "shell shock" following combat. Michael Kimmel reports that during World War I officers and doctors tended to view such disorders as "failures to conform to gender demands":

Most psychiatric treatments for shell shock involved treating the disease as the result of insufficient manliness. T. J. Calhoun, assistant surgeon with the Army of the Potomac, argued that if the soldier could not be "laughed out of it by his comrades" or by "appeals to his manhood," then a good dose of battle was the best "curative."[24]

Although modern-day soldiers suffering from post-traumatic stress are viewed with more sympathy than their historical counterparts, many, including those working in the health care industry, still view soldiers exhibiting symptoms arising from combat and military operations with some suspicion, as malingerers, frauds, or weaklings.[25]

ADDENDUM

High rates of post-traumatic stress disorder (PTSD), including suicide, among male and female soldiers in the early twenty-first-century U.S. wars in Iraq and Afghanistan led the U.S. military to try to understand the causes and treat the consequences of PTSD for an estimated one-fifth of U.S. troops.[26] Sexuality plays a role in PTSD for both men and women. Military sexual assault or "military sexual trauma" (MST) among U.S. troops was revealed to be a major cause of PTSD in the U.S. armed forces. The U.S. Department of Veterans Affairs found that 1 in 5 women and 1 in 100 men treated for PTSD at veterans hospitals reported being victims of MST.[27] From 2007–2010, the Department of Defense (2010) received over 11,000 reports of military sexual assaults.[28] A 2010 U.S. Air Force survey found that 18.9 percent of women and 2.1 percent of men reported experiencing some form of sexual assault while in the Air Force. Civilian studies of military sexual assault report much higher rates; some find as high as one-quarter of service women are sexually assaulted during their military service with many more reporting sexual harassment.[29]

Military sexual assault is only one of several faces of "sex and war" unveiled during the U.S. wars in Iraq and Afghanistan when the percent of women in the U.S. Armed Forces rose to 15 percent (from 1 percent in 1970). The increased presence of women in the U.S. military did not undermine the military's masculinist culture and mission. Studies of the two wars found that the military capitalized on its new feminine resources and developed new strategies for incorporating femininity and women's presence into its mission.[30] In the Iraq war, women soldiers were deployed not only as supply clerks, cooks, mechanics, nurses, doctors, and pilots, they also were enlisted in a variety of gender and sexual roles above and beyond the call of duty—as wives and lovers of service personnel, as targets of sexual harassment and assault, as weapons of war, and as symbols for enactments of masculine bravery. The infamous pictures of prisoner abuse in Iraq's Abu Ghraib prison prominently featured servicewomen as instruments of torture (holding leashes around the necks of Iraqi men, posing behind piles of naked male prisoners, placing their underwear on prisoners' heads). Service women also provided convenient opportunities to display male soldiers' and the military's bravery and gallantry. The staged rescue of Private Jessica Lynch from an Iraqi hospital early in the war was the subject of much media attention and multiple books and films which publicized another role for servicewomen: the damsel in distress saved by heroic men in arms.

NOTES

1. See for instance, Butler, *Daughters of Joy, Sisters of Misery.*

2. For a recent overview see Barstow, *War's Dirty Secret.*

3. Brownmiller, *Against Our Will.*

4. Allen, *Rape Warfare,* 96.

5. Ibid., 96.

6. See Iris Chang, *The Rape of Nanking: The Forgotten Holocaust of World War II* (New York: Basic Books, 1997); James Yin and Shi Young, *The Rape of Nanking: An Undeniable History in Photographs* (Chicago: Innovative Publishing Group, 1997).

7. Japan has yet to make satisfactory restitution to Korean and Filipina "comfort women" who were sexually enslaved during World War II, and some former victims have come forward to demand a public apology and accounting for their treatment; see Seth Mydans, "Inside a Wartime Brothel: The Avenger's Story," *New York Times,* November 12, 1996:A3; Maria Rosa Henson, *Comfort Woman: A Filipina's Story of Prostitution and Slavery under the Japanese Military* (Lanham, MD: Rowman and Littlefield Publishers, 1999); Sangmie Choi Schellstede, *Comfort Women Speak: Testimony by Sex Slaves of the Japanese Military* (New York: Holmes and Meier, 2000); for discussions of Japan's system of brothels, see George L. Hicks, *The Comfort Women: Japan's Brutal Regime of Enforced Prostitution in the Second World War* (New York: W.W. Norton, 1995); Keith Howard,

True Stories of the Korean Comfort Women (London: Cassell, 1995); Sayoko Yoneda, "Sexual and Racial Discrimination: A Historical Inquiry into the Japanese Military's 'Comfort' Women System of Enforced Prostitution," in *Nation, Empire, Colony: Historicizing Gender and Race,* ed. Ruth Roach Pierson and Nupur Chaudhuri (Bloomington: Indiana University Press, 1989), 237–50; for a discussion of restitution in general and specifically as it relates to the women enslaved by Japan during World War II, see Elazar Barkan, *The Guilt of Nations: Restitution and Negotiating Historical Injustices* (New York: W.W. Norton, 2000), especially chapter 3.

8. Watanabe, "Trafficking in Women's Bodies," 503–504.

9. Both sexual and nonsexual labor were also demanded of women enslaved by the Japanese (ibid., 503); the Japanese also used rape as an instrument of terror and domination, most infamous is the "rape of Nanking" in which thousands of women were raped and killed; see Brownmiller, *Against Our Will,* 53-60.

10. Brownmiller, *Against Our Will,* 61-62.

11. For firsthand accounts of women's treatment in the camps, see Sarah Nomberg-Przytyk, *Tales from a Grotesque Land* (Chapel Hill: University of North Carolina Press, 1985), 14–20; Livia E. Bitton Jackson, *Elli: Coming of Age in the Holocaust* (New York: Times Books, 1980) 59–61; Cecile Klein, *Sentenced To Live* (New York: Holocaust Library, 1988), 73–77; Lore Shelley, *Auschwitz: The Nazi Civilization* (Lanham, MD: University Press of America, 1992).

12. See Cornelius Ryan, *The Last Battle* (New York: Simon and Schuster, 1966); Barstow, *War's Dirty Secret.*

13. Brownmiller, *Against Our Will,* 76–77; these 947 convictions are only part of a much greater universe of sexual assault by U.S. troops for several reasons: most rape is not reported and when it is, convictions are relatively rare even today, much less back in the 1940s during a state of war and/or military occupation; further, these were *convictions* where the soldier was found guilty, and did not include what could only have been a much larger number of charges filed and trials conducted; further still, these records were only for convictions of Army and Air Force personnel, and did not include data on the U.S. Navy or Marine Corps; finally, these records did not include information on charges, trials, or convictions for lesser sexual crimes than rape, such as sodomy or assault with the intent to commit rape or sodomy.

14. See Americas Watch and the Women's Rights Project, *Untold Terror: Violence against Women in Peru's Armed Conflict* (New York: Americas Watch, 1992); Asia Watch and Physicians for Human Rights, *Rape in Kashmir: A Crime of War* (New York: Asia Watch, 1993); Ximena Bunster, "Surviving beyond Fear: Women and Torture in

Latin America," in *Women and Change in Latin America,* ed. June Nash and Helen Safa (South Hadley, MA: Bergin & Garvey, 1986), 297–325; Samir al-Khalil, *Republic of Fear: The Politics of Modern Iraq* (Berkeley: University of California Press, 1989).

15. Stiglmayer, "The Rapes in Bosnia-Herzegovina," 101.

16. See Elizabeth Bumiller, 'Deny Rape or Be Hated: Kosovo Victims' Choice," *New York Times,* June 22, 1999:1; Peter Finn, "Signs of Rape Sear Kosovo; Families' Shame Could Hinder Investigation," *Washington Post,* June 27, 1999:1.

17. Stiglmayer, "The Rapes in Bosnia-Herzegovina," 117-18.

18. Ibid., 118–19.

19. Human Rights Watch reports that although both sides committed sexual assault during the conflict, rates of rape by Serbian men far outnumbered instances of sexual abuse by Kosovar Albanian men during the conflict; see Human Rights Watch Report, "Kosovo: Rape as a Weapon of 'Ethnic Cleansing' " (March 21, 2000); my thanks to Hsui-hua Shen, Department of Sociology, University of Kansas, for bringing this report to my attention.

20. For early reports on the hearings and judgments of that tribunal, see Marlise Simons, "Bosnian Serb Trial Opens: First on Wartime Sex Crimes," *New York Times,* March 21, 2000:3; John-Thor Dahlburg, "Bosnian Witness Says She Endured Series of Rapes; Courts: Victim No. 50 Testifies in The Hague," *Los Angeles Times,* March 30, 2000:1; Chris Bird, "UN Tribunal Told of Bosnian Rape Camp Horrors," *Guardian,* April 21, 2000:1; Roger Thurow, "A Bosnian Rape Victim Suffers from Scars that Do Not Fade," *Wall Street Journal,* July 17, 2000:18.

21. Cynthia Enloe, "Afterword: Have the Bosnian Rapes Opened a New Era of Feminist Consciousness?" in *Mass Rape,* 219–30; progress continues to be made, slowly, in the shift toward defining rape as a human rights violation and in the prosecution of those responsible for the sexual assaults in the former Yugoslavia: on June 29, 2001, the Serbian government turned over former Yugoslavian president Slobodan Milosevic to the United Nations war crimes tribunal in The Hague, Netherlands; Marlise Simons with Carlotta Gall, "Milosevic Is Given to U.N. for Trial in War-Crime Case," *New York Times,* June 29, 2001:1; it is important to note that at about the same time the rapes and killings were happening in Yugoslavia and Bosnia, millions of men, women, and children were being raped, mutilated, and murdered in Rwanda; while Western governments dithered and delayed responding to both the Yugoslavian and Rwandan massacres and atrocities, and while an international tribunal was established in 1994 to prosecute Rwandans for their war crimes, the issue of rape as a war crime came to the fore in Yugoslavia, but not in the much larger-scale Rwandan case; perhaps it required reports of the mass rapes and sexual enslavement of white women, albeit Muslim white women, for the "civilized" world to take notice of ethnosexual violence in war.

22. Allen, *Rape Warfare,* 78; the "Bassiouni Report" is the result of an October 1992 decision by the Secretary-General of the United Nations to appoint a commission of experts "to examine and analyze information gathered with a view to providing the Secretary-General with its conclusions on the evidence of grave breaches of the Geneva Conventions and other violations of international humanitarian law committed in the territory of the former Yugoslavia" (ibid., 43).

23. Watanabe, "Trafficking in Women's Bodies," 506–507.

24. Kimmel, *Manhood in America,* 133–34.

25. Ibid.

26. In a 2008 study the Rand Corporation found that 14 percent of the 1.64 million service members deployed in Operation Iraqi Freedom and Operation Enduring Freedom in Afghanistan were positively screened for PTSD and one-third of service members suffered from PTSD, major depression, or traumatic brain injury (Tanielian and Jaycox, 2008:7 att http://www.rand.org/content/dam/rand/pubs/monographs/2008/RAND_MG720.sum.pdf accessed January 8, 2012). Seal et al. (2009) reported that 40 percent of Iraq and Afghanistan veterans receiving health care from VA hospitals between 2002 and 2008 were diagnosed with one or more mental disorders, including 22 percent diagnosed with PTSD (at http://www.rand.org/content/dam/rand/pubs/monographs/2008/RAND_MG720.sum.pdf accessed January 8, 2012).

27. Military Sexual Trauma (MST) is "psychological trauma, which in the judgment of a VA mental health professional, resulted from a physical assault of a sexual nature, battery of a sexual nature, or sexual harassment which occurred while the Veteran was serving on active duty or active duty for training" (at http://www.ptsd.va.gov/public/pages/military-sexual-trauma-general.asp accessed January 8, 2012).

28. This is a conservative estimate since it involves official reports to the DOD; in random sample surveys servicewomen and military academy cadets report much higher rates of sexual harassment and assault. The U.S. Army has instituted the SHARP program (Sexual Harassment/Assault Response & Prevention) to address these high levels of MST, but its effectiveness has not been established; see http://www.sexualassault.army.mil/index.cfm. Despite recurrent exposés, investigations, and prevention programs, the problem persists; for instance, the DOD found a 63 percent increase in sexual assaults at U.S. military academies between 2010 abd 2011

(at http://www.military.com/news/article/dod-reported
-sexual-assaults-up-at-service-academies.html accessed
January 8, 2012).

29. For an overview see *New York Times* series, "Women
at Arms: A Trust Betrayed," especially the article,
"A Peril in War Zones: Sexual Abuse by Fellow GIs"
(at http://www.nytimes.com/2009/12/28/us/28women
.html?ref=womenatarms accessed January 8, 2012) and
Corbett (2007).

30. Kampfner (2003); Eisenstein (2007); Greenberg and
Dratel (2005); Karpinski (2006); Feitz and Nagel (2008);
Nagel and Feitz (2007); Massad (2004).

REFERENCES

Corbett, Sara. 2007. "The Women's War." *New York Times
Magazine* (March 18).

Eisenstein, Zillah. 2007. *Sexual Decoys Gender, Race and
War in Imperial Democracy.* New York: Zed Books.

Feitz, Lindsey, and Joane Nagel 2007. "The Militarization
of Gender and Sexuality in the Iraq War," pp. 201–25
in *Women in the Military and in Armed Conflict*, ed. C.H.
Carreiras & G. Kümmel, VS Verlag.

Greenberg, Karen J., and Joshua L. Dratel. 2005. *The
Torture Papers: The Road to Abu Ghraib.* New York:
Cambridge University Press.

Kampfner, John. 2003. "Saving Private Lynch Story
'Flawed'." *BBC News* (5/15). http://news.bbc.co.uk/2
/hi/programmes/correspondent/3028585.stm (accessed
7/19/05).

Karpinski, Janis. 2006. *One Woman's Army : The
Commanding General of Abu Ghraib Tells Her Story.*
New York: Miramax Books.

Massad, Joseph. 2004. "Imperial Mementos." *Al-Ahram
Weekly* (May 20–26, No. 691):1.

Nagel, Joane, and Lindsey Feitz 2007. "Deploying Race,
Gender, Class, and Sexuality in the Iraq War." *Race,
Gender & Class* 14(3/4):28–47.

Seal, Karen, Thomas J. Metzler, Kristian S. Gima, Daniel
Bertenthal, Shira Maguen, and Charles R. Marmar.
2009. "Trends and Risk Factors for Mental Health
Diagnoses Among Iraq and Afghanistan Veterans
Using Department of Veterans Affairs Health Care,
2002–2008." *American Journal of Public Health* (99,
9):1651–1658.

Tanielian, Terri, and Lisa H. Jaycox. 2008. *Invisible
Wounds of War: Psychological and Cognitive Injuries,
Their Consequences, and Services to Assist Recovery.* Santa
Monica, CA: Rand Corporation.

U.S. Department of Defense. 2011. Department of
Defense Annual Report on Sexual Assault in the
Military, FY2010 at http://www.sapr.mil/media/pdf
/reports/DoD_Fiscal_Year_2010_Annual_Report_on
_Sexual_Assault_in_the_Military.pdf accessed
January 8, 2012.

10

COMMERCIAL SEX

AN INTERVIEW WITH

JACQUELINE BOLES

Jacqueline Boles, Ph.D., is a professor emeritus of sociology at Georgia State University in Atlanta, Georgia. Her research interests include sex work and sex workers, prostitution and HIV transmission, and deviant behavior. Dr. Boles is the author of over 40 articles and book chapters.

How did you get involved in the study of sexuality?

My dissertation advisor said, "Why don't you study strippers?" He knew my husband and I had been in show business and that I knew people familiar with the business. I thought, "Why not?" The great fan dancer, Sally Rand, was in town. I interviewed her and then began interviewing strippers in Atlanta clubs. About a year after I finished my dissertation, the police asked me to find out why so many prostitutes were coming to Atlanta. A colleague and I started interviewing prostitutes in the vice squad office, hooking bars, massage parlors, and on the street. That's how it all got started.

Which of your projects have you found most interesting?

In 1987, Kirk Elifson and I received a grant from the CDC to investigate HIV risk factors among male prostitutes (hustlers). We interviewed and drew blood from over 300 male prostitutes. We found that hustlers self-identified as heterosexual, homosexual, and bisexual. A hustler's self-identification was a strong predictor of HIV seropositivity. For example, heterosexual-identified hustlers refused to engage in anal receptive sex, which is a major risk factor for contracting HIV. Consequently, heterosexual-identified sex workers had the lowest rate of HIV seropositivity.

What have you found most challenging about studying sexuality?

A person can be HIV seropositive for ten years without exhibiting any symptoms. When we began our research, we needed to look at the sexual history of the hustlers over a 10-year period. How do you ask these men to account for all their sex acts over ten years? We needed to know how many partners they had, the sex of the partners, what kinds of sex acts were performed, and whether a condom was used. We faced a similar problem with drug use. Intravenous drug use is a risk factor for HIV, so we needed a history. We had to develop a workable strategy for getting accurate histories, and this took a great deal of experimentation and pre-testing of our instruments.

What have you learned from your years of research?

Too bad that sexual behavior in humans is not instinctive. If it were, we would all behave similarly, and life would be less complicated. Unfortunately, behaving sexually (or not) is associated with a number of problems: low self-esteem, jealousy and rage, sexually transmitted diseases, psychosocial adjustment issues, etc. We cannot help solve these problems unless we understand sexual behavior: what people do and how they feel about what they do. Simply asserting that a behavior is "wrong" or "immoral" will not prevent the behavior from occurring.

Have you encountered any ethical dilemmas in your research? How did you resolve these?

In our hustler study, we guaranteed the anonymity of all our study participants. They were given a patient identification number that they could use to receive their HIV serostatus from the health department. Even though we knew their serostatus, we were not allowed to inform them. Many times we knew that an HIV-positive hustler was living with an HIV-negative lover. We could not warn the uninfected person; all we could do was stress to lovers that they "get their test results." When we started our study, we did not want anything we did to have a negative impact on our study participants. We declined interviews with the media so that our results would not be sensationalized. The sex workers we studied were constantly harassed by police, and we did not want to do anything that would increase that harassment.

How do people react when they find that you are a sex researcher?

A few years ago, I was asked to substitute for a well-known prostitute/activist on a panel. After the program ended, a woman (who had come late and did not know that I was not a sex worker) came up to me and gushed, "I always wanted to meet one; now I can say I have finally met a woman of the night." I did not have the heart to disappoint her! Most people are curious about the people I have met and interviewed. They enjoy hearing about the strip clubs, massage parlors, hooking bars, and other disreputable places I frequent. I try to humanize sex workers by sharing favorite stories.

If you could teach people one thing about sex, what would it be?

I may be swimming against the current, but I would like to suggest that we are asking sex to carry too big a burden. "Good sex will make me happy; if I'm not successful sexually, then I'm a failure; there's nothing worse than a sexual loser." Sex is designed to give pleasure, but so are swimming in a clear lagoon, viewing Monet's garden, eating an ice-cream cone, and cuddling one's child. Good sex (whatever that means) is but one component of a life well lived.

SEX WORK FOR THE MIDDLE CLASSES

ELIZABETH BERNSTEIN

By the end of the 1990s in postindustrial cities such as San Francisco, a burgeoning Internet economy was in full swing, and media stories abounded which suggested that technology was pushing contemporary culture towards new frontiers of sexual tolerance by eliminating the biggest obstacles to the buying and selling of sexual services: shame and ignorance. Commentators highlighted the ease and efficiency of the new technologies and the ways in which online sexual commerce had shifted the boundaries of social space, blurring the differences between underworld figures and "respectable citizens" (Droganes, 2000; *Economist,* 2000; Prial, 1999).

Less frequently commented upon were the broader cultural underpinnings of new forms of technologized sexual exchange. Nor was there much discussion of the socioeconomic transformations that linked seemingly disparate cultural phenomena together. What were the underlying connections between the new "respectability" of sexual commerce and the new classes of individuals who were participating in commercial sexual transactions? What was the relationship between the overwhelmingly white, native-born and class-privileged women (and men) who were finding their way into sex work and more generalized patterns of economic restructuring? How did the emergence of new communications technologies transform the meaning and experience of sexual commerce for sex workers and their customers?

My discussion in this essay derives from ethnographic fieldwork carried out in five U.S. and European postindustrial cities between 1994 and 2002, a period of rapid technological growth and expansion.[1] Fieldwork consisted of on-site observations and informal interviews with participants in a variety of erotic work spaces and at sex workers' support groups; 15 in-depth, face-to-face interviews of 2–6 hours in length and an immersion in sex workers' own writings and documentary films (Bernstein, 2007). In this article, I focus on the experiences of sex workers who exemplify the ways that middle-class sex work has been facilitated by—and itself facilitates—new technologies of sexual exchange.

ECONOMIC CONCERNS IN SEXUAL LABOUR

In postindustrial cities of the West, sex workers who are white and middle class have sometimes been hard pressed to defend themselves against critics who maintain that they are atypical and unfit spokeswomen for the majority of women engaged in sexual labour, whose "choice of profession" is made under far greater constraints. Although middle-class sex workers may not be speaking for the majority when they seek to reframe sexual labour in terms of a respectable and esteem-worthy profession (Leigh, 2004; Nagle, 1997), some of the most sociologically interesting questions go unasked and unanswered if we limit ourselves to the non-majoritarian critique. Why are middle-class women doing sex work? Can sex work be a middle-class profession? Most crucially, if sexual labour is regarded as, at best, an unfortunate but understandable choice for women with few real alternatives, how are we to explain its apparently increasing appeal to individuals with combined racial, class, and educational advantages?[2]

The research that I conducted during the Internet boom years of the late 1990s suggests that economic considerations, in fact, remain highly relevant to middle-class sex workers' erotic and professional decision-making. . . . Even during the peak years of the Internet economy, well-paid, part-time work—especially for women of these "creative classes"—was, more often than not, difficult to come by. Despite the huge expansion of jobs in postindustrial dot-com economies, patterns of gendered inequality within the high technology sector meant that even white, college-educated women were likely to be excluded from the highest-paying positions.

Compared to men with similar forms of educational capital and class provenance, middle-class women in postindustrial economies are much more likely to find themselves working in the lowest-paid quarters of the temporary help industry, in the service and hospitality sectors, or in other poorly remunerated part-time jobs (McCall, 2001; Milkman and Dwyer, 2002; Sassen, 2002). Jenny Scholten and Nicki Blaze (2000) have written about their experiences living in San Francisco during the dot-com boom years and supporting their nascent writing careers by working as strippers, coining the term "digital cleavage" to refer to a gender-specific version of the more frequently remarked upon "digital divide" (the class-based gap in access to high technology). . . .

Given the gendered disparities of postindustrial economic life, the relatively high pay of the sex industry (compared to other service sector jobs) provides a compelling reason for some women from middle-class backgrounds to engage in sexual labour. Girl-X's narrative

of her decision to become a phone sex worker, which appeared in a special Sex Industry issue of the alternative parenting magazine *Hip Mama*, exemplifies one common route of passage into the Bay Area sex industry in the late 1990s:

> I had gotten bored with my day job, which was—and still is—unworthy of mention . . . The idea [of doing phone sex] excited me . . . I would no longer be subject to the indignities that came along with my previous jobs in the service industry, slinging espresso, records, books, or trendy clothes. I could barricade myself in my cave-like studio apartment all day and all night if I wanted, leaving only for special occasions, like the appearance of a Japanese noise band at one of those divey punk clubs. (Girl-X, 1997: 20)

Where Girl-X exemplifies the transition from low-end service work into sexual labour, Zoey's account of trying to support a middle-class lifestyle on $17.75 an hour (despite holding bachelor's and master's degrees) exemplifies another. Zoey was a 30-year-old former social worker who was working as an erotic masseuse when I met her. During a conversation over tea in her apartment, she described her transition into sexual labour this way:

> A year out of school I was very burnt out on the low pay, and really wanted to make more money . . . My boyfriend at the time had a good friend who had been doing sensual massage for many years and had found it tremendously lucrative . . . And so, I thought, oh, this would be a great ground for me to, you know, skip over years of torturous low pay [laughter] and actually then, to practice things that were truly dear to my heart. . . .

Sex Work and Distinction

Economic factors also served to shape middle-class sex workers' choices in other ways, ways which were not directly related to the pursuit of material sustenance in a high-tech economy but which pertained more generally to members' class-specific cultural dispositions. In

Distinction, Pierre Bourdieu's analysis of the material and social underpinnings of taste, he describes "the new petite bourgeoisie" as composed of individuals with two primary class trajectories—on the one hand "those who have not obtained from the educational system the qualifications that would have enabled them to claim the established positions their original social position promised them"—women like Anna, a sex worker I met from an affluent suburb in Colorado, who had just completed her BA but had yet to pursue an advanced degree—and on the other hand, 'those who have not obtained from their qualifications all they felt entitled to'—women like Zoey or Elise, who were dismayed that their educational credentials had not lifted them to greater heights (Bourdieu, 1984: 357). . . .

Middle-class sex workers' frequent embrace of an ethic of sexual experimentation and freedom must thus be seen not only in ideological terms, but as a particular strategy of class differentiation as well. Not incidentally, many of the middle-class sex workers that I interviewed were unpartnered and without children, and the majority described themselves as non-monogamous, bisexual, and experimental. Some sex workers even espoused an ideology of sexual fluidity that (along with the necessary economic capital) enabled them to serve as both sellers and occasional *buyers* of sexual services. In contrast to the old petit-bourgeois values of upwardly mobile asceticism and restraint (which served to distinguish this class from the working class, whose ethos rejects "pretense" and striving), the new petite bourgeoisie regards fun, pleasure, and freedom as ethical ideals worthy of strenuous pursuit. The embrace of these ideals serves as a means for members of the new petite bourgeoisie to distinguish themselves from the old petite bourgeoisie, an invisible boundary separating classes of individuals who might seem, at first glance, to exist in close proximity.

ORGANIZING THE EXCHANGE FOR AUTHENTICITY

Middle-class sex workers' sense of distinction vis-à-vis their work could also be found in the types of work situation that they favored. As researchers Melissa Ditmore and Juhu Thukral (2005) have observed, the goal for most indoor sex workers (of whatever class background) who remain in the business is usually to be able to work independently. A common trajectory is to enter the industry working for someone else and to gradually build up one's own clientele. While professional autonomy was indeed desirable for the middle-class sex workers that I spoke with, there were other organizational criteria that were important to them as well. During whatever period of time that they might spend engaged in brothel-based work with third-party management, they were inclined to remove themselves from locales that seemed to foster a purely instrumentalist relationship to the labour. . . .

I worked at a place once in a sort of gourmet neighbourhood in Berkeley—alternative but ritzy . . . But even though they acted like we were a co-op—they expected us to do all of the cleaning and answering the phones, and required us to do the laundry during our shifts, stuff that a madam would normally do—all they did was come in and collect the money . . . They also made us come to staff meetings in addition to our regular schedule. These meetings were unpaid, a waste of our time . . . I finally left when I got a chance to open my own place in the City. (Amanda, 38). . . .

THE ROLE OF NEW TECHNOLOGIES

Despite the broader structural trend which situates women of most social classes on the wrong side of the "digital cleavage," the Internet has reshaped predominant patterns of sexual commerce in ways that many middle-class sex workers have been able to benefit from. As various commentators have noted, the Internet has enabled sexual commerce to thrive not only by increasing clients' access to information but also by facilitating community and camaraderie amongst individuals who might otherwise be perceived (and perceive themselves) as engaging in discreditable activity (Lane, 2000; Sharp and Earle, 2003).[3] For women who are able to bring technological skill and experience to sex work, it is increasingly possible to work without third-party management, to conduct one's business with minimal interference from the criminal justice system, and to reap greater profits by honing one's sales pitch to a more elite and more specialized clientele (Sanders, 2005a).

During our interview, Amanda was quite explicit about the ways that the new technologies had revolutionized her practice. She recounted how, after her brief stint working in a Berkeley brothel in which she was consistently "passed up" by the predominantly working-class clientele 'in favor of younger, bustier, blonde women," she decided to give sex work another try when a friend suggested to her that she could advertise on the Internet and work out of her own space:

Now, I only advertise on the Internet. It insures me a reliable pool of well-educated, professional men with predictable manners and predictable ways of talking. When they make appointments, they keep them. My ad attracts a lot of first timers. I seem "safe," like someone they would already know, since it's clear that I have the same kind of background as they do and I seem easy to talk to. White educated women like me have a lot of appeal to professional white men. . . .

PROFESSIONALIZING SEXUAL LABOUR

As Bourdieu observes, one way that members of the new petite bourgeosie have found to embrace a sense of social distinction is via the adoption of "reconversion strategies," in which cultural capital is employed to "professionalize" marginal spaces within the labour market and to invest them with a sense of personal meaning and ethical value (1984: 368). At the meetings of sex worker activists that I attended in San Francisco, members made efforts to professionalize their trade through activities such as the demonstration of "penetration alternatives," discussions of novel and tested safe-sex techniques, and presentations of statistical studies documenting the incidence of HIV in body fluids. Meetings were also a common place for members to make referrals to one another and to circulate written materials such as "dirty trick" lists (featuring the names and phone numbers of clients who were suspected of being dangerous); legal, investment, and tax advice; and safer sex guidelines. . . .

For the middle-class sex worker I spoke with, the performance of sex work often implied a distinctive skill set that could be elaborated through education and training. Many spoke explicitly about their deliberate pursuit of special skills as a means of enhancing both their experience of doing sex work and their earning power. The forms of training that they pursued ranged from massage certification to yogic breathwork (useful, one woman explained, with clients who were interested in tantric sex) to sexual surrogacy courses to the self-conscious embellishment of skills left over from prior careers. Zoey, for example, who had completed graduate school and an internship in social work, considered her earlier training as a therapist to be vital to her current work as an erotic masseuse:

The model that I have always chosen in doing this work has actually been a psychotherapy model . . . As a therapist, in order to continue working with repetitively traumatized children, I had to be doing a ton of behind-the-scenes work so I could hold my ground and have something to give them of value . . . Because of my training as a therapist I knew, intimately, how to do that; so, I brought that to sex work too. . . .

In addition to the acquisition of skills and training, the strategic deployment of educational and cultural capital came into play for middle-class sex workers in other ways. Lisa got her job at a Sausalito massage parlour when she "faked a French accent and answered an ad for a European blonde." Sybil, like other women, described screening her clients closely, and could restrict her practice to powerful businessmen once she knew "how to ask the right questions." Whereas on the streets, many women describe their previous private-sphere heterosexual relations as constituting sufficient technical preparation to engage in sex work (Bernstein, 2007; Høigård and Finstad, 1992; Maher, 1997), for middle-class women, cultural capital, work experience and special training often constitute vital components of sexual labour.

"BOUNDED AUTHENTICITY" AND THE SINGLE SELF

Ironically, it is precisely amongst the middle-class women and men, who are the most strident purveyors of the normalizing term "sex work," that sexual labour is most likely to implicate one's "private" erotic and emotional life. Those who have fought hardest for the social and political recognition of prostitution as "work" (as opposed to a uniquely degrading violation of self) are also those for whom the paid sexual encounter is likely to include emotionally engaged conversation as well as a diversity of sexual activities (bodily caresses, genital touching, cunnilingus and even occasional mouth-to-mouth kisses, rather than simply intercourse or fellatio), requires a larger investment of time with each client (typically at least an hour, as opposed to 15 minutes for streetwalkers), and is more likely to take place within the confines of one's own home (see also Lever and Dolnick,

2000). Since middle-class sex workers generally charge by the hour rather than for specified acts, their sexual labour is diffuse and expansive, rather than delimited and expedient.

During the era of industrial capitalism in which the institution of modern prostitution in the West was consolidated, what was typically sold and bought in the prostitution encounter was an expedient and emotionally contained exchange of cash for sexual release (Corbin, 1990; Rosen, 1982; Walkowitz, 1980). Although more intimate encounters still occurred, the expansion of the brothel system during this period led to the emergence of a new paradigm of efficiently Taylorized, commercialized sex. In contrast to this, within the postindustrial paradigm of (new) middle-class sex work that I have been describing, what is bought and sold frequently incorporates a great deal more emotional, as well as physical labour within the commercial context. . . .

In my own research, evidence of middle-class sex workers' efforts to manufacture authenticity resided in their descriptions of trying to simulate—or even produce—genuine desire, pleasure and erotic interest for their clients. Whereas in some cases this involved mere "surface acting" (as with Amanda, in the next extract) it could also involve the emotional and physical labour of manufacturing *authentic* (if fleeting) libidinal and emotional ties with clients, endowing them with a sense of desirability, esteem or even love. In contrast to the "counterfeit intimacy" that some sociological researchers have presumed to occur in the commercial sexual encounter (Foote, 1954; Ronai and Ellis, 1989; Sanders, 2005b), many sex workers' depictions of their work exemplified the calling forth of genuine feeling that Arlie Hochschild (2003) has termed "deep acting" and that Wendy Chapkis (1997) has described as the "emotional labour" of sex. Hochschild distinguishes between the practices of "surface acting" and "deep acting" in emotional life

(2003: 92–3), noting that middle-class jobs typically call for "an appreciation of display rules, feeling rules," while working-class jobs "more often call for the individual's external behaviour and the products of it" (2003: 102).

When I first started out, I enjoyed the sex. I'd go to work and "have sex." Now, I don't have that association as much. But my clients seem to think that being a nice guy means being a good lover. They do things to me that they should do with a girlfriend. Like they ask me what I'm into, and apologize for coming too soon! So I need to play along. They apparently have no idea that the best client is the one that comes immediately. (Amanda). . . .

In addition to satisfying their clients' desires for bounded authenticity, many sex workers placed a premium upon ensuring that the labour felt meaningful to *themselves*. Through the recent development of blogging, a growing number of middle-class women have taken to writing about their experiences doing sex work and the satisfactions and disappointments that they have encountered. . . . [One] woman spoke to me about creating meaning and authenticity for herself in sex work by offering her clients only the kinds of erotic experiences that she herself enjoyed giving: "I don't go into those sessions teaching my clients how to pleasure me like a lover, but I *do* teach them how to pleasure me by receiving the service that I offer." For these sex workers, emotional authenticity is incorporated explicitly into the economic contract, challenging the view that commodification and intimacy constitute "hostile worlds," which has often prevailed in sociological discussions of the subject (Zelizer, 2005). . . .

CONCLUSION

The contingent of postindustrial, middle-class sex workers that I have been describing call into question a number of common presuppositions about what is necessarily entailed by the commercial sexual encounter and the likely impact of such transactions upon the body and psyche of the sex worker. These sex workers bring a constellation of subjective meanings and embodied practices to commercial sexual exchange that would not have been possible at earlier historical junctures. . . .

I have argued that the meanings with which they have endowed their labour are connected to new and historically specific conditions of possibility. These conditions include a technologically driven, postindustrial economy that has rapidly driven up the cost of living in desirable urban centers, while at the same time creating a highly stratified occupational sector (one with a limited number of time-intensive, highly paid, and hard-to-acquire professional positions, but with poorly paid temporary and part-time "junk" jobs that exist in ample quantities). These economic developments are intricately connected to some of the ways that increasing numbers of young, urban middle-class people are restructuring their intimate lives—either by delaying marriage and childbearing until these are more economically viable options, or by defying the expectations of heterosexual monogamy entirely. . . .

NOTES

1. A fuller elaboration of some of these themes is presented in Elizabeth Bernstein, *Temporarily Yours* (2007).

2. See a recent article in *The Independent*, which notes that some 40,000 university students in France (or nearly 2%) admitted to funding their studies through the sex trade (Duval Smith, 2006).

3. When I did a count of web-based advertisements in San Francisco in 2001, there were approximately 3,000. By 2005, there were some 5,000 advertisements on one popular website alone—one crude indication of the expanding scope of online sexual commerce in the city.

REFERENCES

Bernstein, Elizabeth. 2007. *Temporarily Yours: Intimacy, Authenticity, and the Commerce of Sex.* Chicago, IL: University of Chicago Press.

Bourdieu, Pierre. 1984. *Distinction: A Social Critique of the Judgement of Taste* (trans. Richard Nice). Cambridge, MA: Harvard University Press.

Chapkis, Wendy. 1997. *Live Sex Acts: Women Performing Erotic Labor.* New York: Routledge.

Corbin, Alain. 1990. *Women for Hire: Prostitution and Sexuality in France After 1860.* Cambridge: MA: Harvard University Press.

Ditmore, Melissa and Thukral, Juhu. 2005. *Behind Closed Doors: an Analysis of Indoor Sex Work in New York City.* New York: Urban Justice Center.

Droganes, Constance. 2000. "Toronto the Naughty," *National Post* 22 January.

Duval Smith, Alex. 2006. "40,000 French Students Join Sex Trade to Fund Degrees," The *Independent* 31 October (EUROPE): 20.

Economist. 2000. "Sex, News, and Statistics: Where Entertainment on the Web Scores," *The Economist Online,* URL (accessed 19 October 2000): www.economist.com

Girl-X 1997. "Will Moan for Rent Money," *Hip Mama: The Parenting Zine,* Special Issue on the Sex Industry (13): 20–4.

Hochschild, Arlie Russell. 2003. *The Commericalization of Intimate Life: Notes from Home and Work.* Berkeley: University of California Press.

Høigård, Cecilie and Finstad, Liv. 1992. *Backstreets: Prostitution, Money, and Love.* University Park: Pennsylvania State University Press.

Lane, Frederick. 2000. *Obscene Profits: The Entrepreneurs of Pornography in the Cyber Age.* New York: Routledge.

Leigh, Carol. 2004. *Unrepentant Whore: Collected Works of Scarlot Harlot.* San Francisco: Last Gasp.

Lever, Janet and Dolnick, Deanne. 2000. "Clients and Call Girls: Seeking Sex and Intimacy," in Ronald Weitzer (ed.) *Sex for Sale: Prostitution, Pornography, and the Sex Industry,* pp. 85–103. New York: Routledge.

McCall, Leslie. 2001. *Complex Inequality: Gender, Class, and Race in the New Economy.* New York: Routledge.

Maher, Lisa. 1997. *Sexed Work: Gender, Race and Resistance in a Brooklyn Drug Market.* Oxford: Oxford University Press.

Milkman, Ruth and Dwyer, Rachel E. 2002. *Growing Apart: the "New Economy" and Job Polarization in California, 1992–2000,* URL (accessed 22 February 2003): http://repositories.cdlib.org/ile/scl2002/Milkman Dwyer

Nagle, Jill. 1997. *Whores and Other Feminists.* New York: Routledge.

Prial, Dunstan. 1999. "IPO Outlook: 'Adult' Web Sites Profit, Though Few are Likely to Offer Shares," *The Wall Street Journal* 8 March: B10.

Ronai, Carol Rambo and Ellis, Carolyn. 1989. "Turn-ons for Money: Interactional Strategies of the Table Dancer," *Journal of Contemporary Ethnography* 18(3): 271–98.

Rosen, Ruth. 1982. *The Lost Sisterhood: Prostitution in America, 1900–1918.* Baltimore, MD: Johns Hopkins University Press.

Sanders, Teela. 2005a. *Sex Work: a Risky Business.* Devon: Willan Publishing.

Sanders, Teela. 2005b. " 'It's Just Acting': Sex Workers' Strategies for Capitalizing on Sexuality," *Gender, Work, and Organization* 12(4): 319–42.

Sassen, Saskia. 2002. "Global Cities and Survival Circuits," in Barbara Ehrenreich and Arlie Russell Hochschild (eds) *Global Woman: Nannies, Maids, and Sex Workers in the New Economy,* pp. 254–75. New York: Metropolitan Books.

Sharp, Keith and Earle, Sarah. 2003. "Cyberpunters and Cyberwhores: Prostitution on the Internet," in Yvonne Jewkes (ed.) *Dot.cons: Crime, Deviance, and Identity on the Internet,* pp. 36–52. Devon: Willan Publishing.

Walkowitz, Judith R. 1980. *Prostitution and Victorian Society: Women, Class, and the State.* Cambridge: Cambridge University Press.

Zelizer, Viviana. 2005. *The Purchase of Intimacy.* Princeton, NJ: Princeton University Press.

Strip Clubs and Their Regulars

Katherine Frank

Sexual services and products have long been a part of the U.S. entertainment and leisure industries. In a 1997 article for *U.S. News & World Report,* Eric Schlosser reported that in the prior year Americans spent "more than $8 billion on hard-core videos, peep shows, live sex acts, adult cable programming, sexual devices, computer porn, and sex magazines."

The number of major strip clubs catering to heterosexually identified men nearly doubled between 1987 and 1992, and an estimate for late 1998 puts the number of clubs at around 3,000 with annual revenues ranging from $500,000 to more than $5 million.

While some men dislike strip clubs or find them boring, there is a significant population of heterosexual American males who are willing to spend their money on the kind of public, voyeuristic (although interactive) fantasy available in a no-contact strip club. Despite popular beliefs to the contrary, strippers are generally not selling sex to their customers in this type of club—although they are selling sexualized and gendered services. Rather than fulfilling a biological need for sexual release, as some pop sociobiological accounts suggest, or serving a masculine need for domination, strip clubs provide a kind of intermediate space (not work and not home, although related to both) in which men can experience their bodies and identities in particular pleasurable ways. . . .

Strip clubs are stratified in terms of luxury, status, and other distinguishing features. Whereas strip clubs were once primarily located in "red light" areas of towns and cities associated with crime and prostitution, the upscale clubs are now often quite visible and work to develop reputations for safety, comfort, and classiness. Drawing on cultural markers of status—such as luxury liquors, fine dining, valet parking, and private conference rooms—upscale clubs advertise themselves as places for businessmen to entertain clients or for middle class professionals to visit after work. Dancers may be advertised as refined, well-educated women. Sophisticated sound and lighting equipment, multiple stages, large video screens, and multi-million dollar construction budgets make many contemporary strip clubs into high-tech entertainment centers. This is not to say that smaller or "seedier" clubs have disappeared. The clubs in any locale, however,

are categorized through their relationships to one another and this system of relationships helps inform both the leisure experiences of the customers and the work experiences of the dancers.

The proliferation and upscaling of strip clubs during the 1980s needs to be situated in late capitalist consumer culture as well as within a variety of social changes and developments. In many ways it makes sense that strip clubs should multiply during the last several decades, along with the panic about AIDS and fears about the dissolution of "the family." The process of upscaling in strip clubs, with a promise of "clean" and respectable interactions, alleviated fears about contamination and disease. The fact that sexual activity is not generally expected or offered in strip clubs also fit well with a growing emphasis on monogamy and marriage for heterosexuals after the sexual experimentation (and ensuing disillusionment for many) of the 1970s. There are other social changes which may be influencing this rapid increase in strip clubs as well: women's increased presence in the workforce, continuing backlashes against feminism, ongoing marketing efforts to sexualize and masculinize particular forms of consumption ("sports, beer, and women," for example), changing patterns of mobility which influence dating practices and intimate relationships, and increased travel for businessmen and more anonymous opportunities to purchase commodified sexualized services, to name just a few.

Despite their prevalence and popularity, strip clubs are still often the subject of intense public scrutiny. Local ordinances have been drafted across the nation to harass, limit or eradicate strip clubs—often citing "adverse secondary effects" such as increased crime and decreased property values in neighborhoods that house such venues as justifications for these legislative actions. Many such ordinances seem to be based on conjectures about just what the men (and women) are up to when they set foot in a strip club. There is endless speculation about drug use, prostitution, and crime—by customers, lawmakers, and people who have never even entered a strip club. . . . While these activities surface at times, in often scandalous ways—as they do in many industries—I came away from my research with a belief that most of the customers were in search of something completely different through their interactions.

Media and scholarly attention to the customers of strip clubs has been far less pervasive than that focused on the dancers or the clubs themselves. But what is it, exactly, that the customers are seeking in these venues? After all, without enough men willing to open their wallets each night the industry would cease to exist. As a cultural anthropologist dedicated to participant observation—that is, becoming immersed in the community you study—I selected five strip clubs in one city, sought employment as an entertainer, and interviewed the regular male customers of those clubs. For regulars, visits to strip clubs are a significant sexualized and leisure practice; these are not men who have wandered into a club once or twice or visit only for special occasions like bachelor parties. The majority of the regulars were men middle-aged or older with enough disposable income and free time that they could engage in this relatively private and often expensive leisure practice. I also interviewed dancers, club managers and other club employees, advertisers, and men who preferred other forms of adult entertainment.

Most of the regular customers claimed that they knew where to get sex if they wanted it, and that they chose no-contact strip clubs (or clubs that offered table-dancing rather than lap dancing) precisely because they knew that sex would not be part of the experience. While watching the dancers perform on the stages was certainly appealing, many of the regulars were also interested in the conversations that they could have with dancers. Unlike burlesque performers of years past, contemporary exotic dancers "perform" not just onstage but individually for the customers as they circulate amongst the crowd selling table-dances. Dancers are thus also selling their personalities, their attentions, and conversation to the customers. Some of the regulars returned repeatedly to see a particular dancer; others enjoyed briefer interactions with a number of dancers. Either way, talk was one of the important services being provided and conversations would focus on work, family, politics, sports, sexual fantasies, or any number of other topics.

Whether visiting a small neighborhood bar or a large, flashy gentleman's club, the customers repeatedly told me that they visited strip clubs to relax. Part of the allure of strip clubs for their patrons lies in part in their representation as somewhere out of the ordinary, somewhere proscribed and perhaps a bit "dangerous"—yet as a safe space of play and fantasy where the pressures, expectations and responsibilities of work and home can be left behind.

In many ways, then, strip clubs were seen as relaxing because they provided a respite from women's demands or expectations in other spheres, as well as the possibility (not always actualized) of avoiding competition with other men for women's attention. Strip clubs also offered the customers an opportunity for both personal and sexual acceptance from women, a chance to talk about their sexual desires without reproach or to fantasize that they were attractive enough to gain the interest of a dancer regardless of whether or not they paid her. Some customers wanted an ego boost. As one man said: "It's just absolutely an ego trip because you go in there, and if you're a warthog, bald, and got a pot belly, some good looking girl's gonna come up and go, 'Hey, do you want me to dance for you?' Seducing women is something all men wish they were better at . . . this seems like you're doing it, and it's easy!"

Strip clubs were also relaxing because they provided a safe space in which to be both married or committed and interacting with women in a sexualized setting, and the services offered fit well with these particular men's desires to remain sexually monogamous. Customers are also not expected to perform sexually or to provide any pleasure to the dancer (beyond paying her for her time), and this was also seen as relaxing by many of the men. . . .

However, because they provided a space in which many everyday expectations are inverted (by featuring public nudity, for example), the clubs were still seen as "taboo," as dangerous and exciting, by the regulars as well as safe and predictable. Many of the interviewees discussed their experiences in the language of "variety," "travel," "fun," "escape" and "adventure" and described themselves as "hunters" or "explorers" despite the fact that their experiences in the clubs were highly regulated by local ordinances, club rules, and club employees. Some customers enjoyed the fact that their visits to strip clubs took them to marginal areas of the city. Further, visits to the clubs often were unacceptable to the married regulars' more "conservative" wives or partners. Significantly, then, strip clubs are also dangerous enough to be alluring, a bit "less civilized" and rowdier than the places these middle-class customers would ordinarily enter. This balance between safety and excitement was very important, for if strip clubs lose their edge for a particular customer, or conversely, become too transgressive, he may lose interest and seek a different form of entertainment.

Understanding the motivations of the men who frequent no-contact strip clubs can help quell some of the fears that tend to drive oppressive regulation. There are indeed problems with strip clubs as they currently exist, often rooted in material inequalities between different classes of laborers, in the poor working conditions found in many clubs, in the stigma that surrounds sex work, and in double standards for men's and women's sexualities, for example. However, eradicating or more tightly regulating strip clubs does little to combat these problems, which are related to the organization of labor in late capitalism, to systemic inequalities and prejudices, and to the stigmatization and fear that still surrounds issues of sex and sexuality in the United States.

Source: "Strip Clubs and Their Regulars" by Katherine Frank, *American Sexuality Magazine*, Vol. 1, No. 4, 2003. Copyright 2003, National Sexuality Resource Center. Reprinted by permission of the author.

OVERCOME: THE MONEY SHOT IN PORNOGRAPHY AND PROSTITUTION

LISA JEAN MOORE

For a few years in the early 1990s, I worked on a national sex information switchboard. Much to my surprise, a majority of the callers were men, and their two most common questions were "What is the normal penis size?" and "Where is the clitoris?" Trained to provide anonymous, nonjudgmental, and accurate information to callers, I would respond that most penises, when erect, were between 5 and 7 inches. I would receive immediate thanks for this information, and as they hung up I remember thinking their relief was palpable. Their penises, presumably, were "okay."

As for the clitoris question, I instructed callers to place their hands in a praying position, bend their knuckles slightly and imagine this as the vagina. If the area between the thumbs was the vagina opening, the clitoris was roughly located in the place above the tips of their thumbs, in the triangular area. This answer was not as successful as the first. Many callers fumbled with or even dropped the phone while trying to follow my instructions. Some callers were clearly confused by the model itself, asking, "So it's a hole?" or "But what does the vagina really look like?" Furthermore, I was increasingly alarmed by the steady stream of female callers who asked for instructions on how to find their own clitorises or, somewhat paradoxically, wanted suggestions on how to experience orgasms exclusively through vaginal penetration. "Is there something wrong with me?" they inquired when discussing their dissatisfaction with penis-vagina penetration, often explaining that they had never experienced an orgasm during sex. Clearly, there is something baffling and mysterious about the clitoris. Even though size doesn't matter, location and purpose do. Where is it? What does it do? These callers rarely hung up with the same sense of relief as the first set of callers. The former found answers; the latter continued to question.

I use these examples to illustrate the conventional wisdom on male and female anatomy and sexual responses. In contrast to women, and whether or not each man experiences it to be true, conventional wisdom holds that men's sexuality is fairly simple. It isn't difficult to make men come, and it isn't difficult to know whether or not they have come. The phenomenon of men faking orgasm, though possible, doesn't often get discussed. Semen is, of course, the reason for this; it is thought to be the irrefutable evidence.

Although male callers rarely asked about their semen, in our training, we were instructed to provide them with these facts. Spermatogenesis, or the production of the sperm cell, takes approximately 72 days. Both Cowper's and Littre's glands, which are located in the genital area, contribute secretions in the processes of ejaculation. The prostate also adds fructose and liquefying enzymes.[1] When a man comes, a range of 2–10 milliliters of fluid is produced through his ejaculation at about 10 miles per hour. Between 200 and 500 million sperm cells are contained in most ejaculates, the equivalent of about 5–15 calories. It is estimated that a man ejaculates 5,000 times in his lifetime.[2]

Theoretically any man could repopulate the United States with just a few ejaculates (and the participation of 290 million women or less if multiple births occur).

GROWING UP: FROM INNOCENCE TO DEBAUCHERY

. . . Ejaculation is taken as external proof that a man has experienced an orgasm, despite evidence that men can ejaculate without orgasm, technically known as anorgasmic ejaculation.[3] The physical presence of the ejaculate, the seminal fluid, is a material reality that confirms men's pleasure.[4] Most pornographic entertainment reinforces this belief, as ejaculation, or the "money shot" in porn parlance, is the raison d'être of sexual encounters? The money shot signals the end of the male sexual act—cue the drum roll, he has come. Cindy Patton, an activist and scholar of human sexuality, points out that in Western culture male sexual fulfillment is "synonymous with orgasm" and that the male orgasm is "an essential and essentialist punctuation of the sexual narrative. No orgasm, no sexual pleasure. No cum shot, no narrative closure."[5] In other words, the cum shot is the period at the end of the sentence. Case closed. Alternatively, with the rare exception of anorgasmic ejaculation, both the female anatomy and orgasm are more complex, even elusive— for both men and women. That being the case, in pornography the sex act itself is centered around the male penis and orgasm. Only when that happens does conventional wisdom tell us that sex has occurred.[6]

There is an entire lexicon for the release of semen from the body; terms like ejaculation, premature ejaculation, nocturnal emissions, wet dreams, and shooting your wad are just a few. With such a wide variety of ways to describe ejaculates and the act of ejaculating, it would seem that many men are preoccupied with ejaculation, and especially measurements

of it. From the record books to website legends, claims about the feats of men and their ejaculations abound. For example, the world record for number of male orgasms is 16 in one hour. According to several unsubstantiated reports on websites, the greatest distance of an ejaculate is 18 feet 9 inches, which was achieved by Horst Schultz, who apparently also holds the record for the greatest height of ejaculate (12 feet 4 inches).

Not all ejaculates are created equal. Each time ejaculation occurs, semen contains varying proportions of ingredients. These variations are affected by diet, age, how the ejaculation was achieved (through masturbation or partner sexual stimulation, whether anal, oral, or vaginal), level of arousal, physical fitness, and number of ejaculations in the past 72 hours. The age of first conscious ejaculation, known as "oigarche," is generally between 10 and 15 years old. Nocturnal emissions, or wet dreams that are generally erotic or sexual, are accompanied by the release or ejaculation of semen. Roughly 50 percent of boys between the ages of 10 and 20 experience wet dreams, possibly as a way for the reproductive system to get rid of excess semen, although most agree that semen is reabsorbed back into the body.

But sometimes men are not physiologically in control of when and how their semen emerges. Premature ejaculation, recently renamed "rapid ejaculation" . . . is increasingly considered a medically diagnosable condition for men under 40. It is defined as ejaculation prior to the desires of both sexual partners. Although rapid ejaculation may be underreported, the National Health and Social Life Survey suggests that its prevalence is roughly 30 percent. Sex therapy, antidepressants, and lidocaine cream or related topical anesthetic agents have all demonstrated success at treating rapid ejaculation.

Regardless of the quantity of semen or the quality of its delivery during ejaculation, in the world of sex entertainment the release of semen signifies the successful conclusion of the sex act. The appearance of semen is the proof of sexual fulfillment, so the more the more better, right? It turns out that the equation is not so simple when we consider the layered meanings of sperm and semen across the worlds of pornography, prostitution, and popular culture.

FETISHIZING SEMEN

Members of the specifically heterosexual[7] sex entertainment industry, sex workers and pornographic filmmakers in particular, contribute to our understanding of sperm in important ways. From ideas about what constitutes sex or sex acts to what is considered sexy, to how men and their penises can perform, the sex industry—even if covertly—has greatly influenced popular notions of sex. Pornographic filmmakers specialize in representing a variety of techniques to animate ejaculation and semen, thereby fetishizing it. Within sex entertainment settings, semen is worshiped as a magical substance of both supernatural arousal and erotic achievement. It is depicted in films and printed media as a substance that has extraordinary power over humans. The male actors seem repeatedly shocked by the force, volume, and desirability of their semen, while the female actors can't control themselves in the presence of this semen and must slather it all over their bodies, even drink it down as if dying of thirst. Different cultures vary the themes of seminal ejaculate in their pornography. For example, in the late 1990s, *bukkake,* a style of pornography that was popularized in Japan, depicts multiple men ejaculating on a woman or group of women.[8] The use of ejaculation is part of a humiliation ritual and generally does not involve any of the female characters experiencing orgasm.

So although semen is presented as the end product of a sexual experience, it is also an object manipulated by the directors, cameras, lighting, scripts, and actors to elicit arousal. The camera lens focuses on the glory of seminal expression and encourages the viewer to witness the money shot as the reward of spectatorship. . . .

But semen does not exist in a vacuum; rather, it is a bodily fluid that is deeply implicated in history and epidemiology. At least for the past 30 years, unprotected seminal ejaculation brings to mind disease transmission—including HIV, hepatitis B and C, and sexually transmitted diseases (STDs). Being such a dangerous vector of infection, semen has become increasingly seen as grotesque—something feared and unwanted. Unprotected seminal ejaculation during vaginal or anal sex is not the only dangerous practice; semen ejaculated into the mouth, eyes, and nose can transmit herpes, chlamydia, syphilis, and gonorrhea.

As a result of these risks, exposure to semen is evermore regulated within the sex entertainment industry. California's Division of Occupational Safety and Health (CAL-OSHA) oversees and regulates workers in the adult film industry; most porn films are produced in southern California. The agency provides adult film workers with safety guidelines and employment protection from work practices that might expose them to blood and "other potentially infectious material (OPIM)."[9] According to CAL-OSHA's website, "semen and vaginal fluid are always considered OPIM." The website also provides examples of "engineering and work practice controls" used in the adult film industry. . . .

In the sex entertainment industry, some film studios demand regular HIV tests. Adult Industry Medical Health Care Foundation (AIM), a nonprofit health-care foundation concerned with sex worker mental and physical health, provides on-site testing services for performers and encourages the responsible sharing of test results between working partners.

Yet there have been HIV transmission cases within the pornography industry. As reporter Ann Regentin explains:

In 1986, John Holmes contracted the virus and continued to work without telling anyone until 1988, when he died of AIDS. In 1998, a rash of HIV cases seemed to point to Marc Wallice, who tested positive for the virus and had been caught working with faked HIV test results. In 1999, Tony Montana tested positive and immediately stopped working. As far as anyone knows, he did not infect anyone else.[10]

On April 12, 2004, porn star Darren James, who contracted the virus while shooting in Brazil, infected others through work, leading to a brief shutdown of production within the San Fernando Valley. Clearly, there are occupational risks to working in the porn industry, but these can be mitigated through precautions and regulations. Within the sex entertainment industry, then, this bodily fluid straddles the line between being supremely erotic and a lethal weapon.

Each sex worker must develop methods, practices, and professional expertise to avoid exposure to potential diseases or lethal toxins. Furthermore, fertile female sex workers must also try to limit their risk of pregnancy, an occupational hazard of frequent contact with semen. As one of my informants related to me, sex work includes aspects of "hazardous waste material" management. There are different risks associated with exposure to semen by sex workers in the porn industry. Reviewing a working partner's HIV tests is one industry standard. With the advantage of not performing sex in real time, actors and actresses in the porn industry are able to manipulate some exposure to seminal ejaculation. For example, a porn star can appear to swallow ejaculate without actually doing so. During an interview, Raylene, a porn star, stated, "I don't swallow that often because I really don't like the taste. I mean I have, but I don't really like it."[11] . . .

THE MONEY SHOT

Some recent mainstream films use semen in a different way: as props for gags or as symbols of alienation. The actual appearance of sperm in mainstream films is a relatively new phenomenon and perhaps can be seen, in some ways, as an extension of the increasingly graphic and "realistic" images of the body that are so commonplace today, especially in television crime and medical dramas. Here severed limbs, burnt bodies, and gaping wounds are regularly featured, but we often even "go inside" the body to see the actual source of the disease, parasite, or infected organ.

Given the intensely graphic nature of such shows, and given that sperm has long been readily seen and featured in pornographic films, it is perhaps not surprising that the once-taboo substance now makes its appearance in mainstream movies. In the film *Magnolia,* for example, protagonist Frank Mackey (played by Tom Cruise), is a motivational speaker for a seminar series, "Seduce and Destroy," which includes a session entitled "How to turn your 'friend' into your sperm receptacle," encouraging insecure men to use their sperm as a means of conquering and depositing waste into the female body. Taking this a step further, films like *There's Something About Mary* and *The Squid and the Whale* use sperm as, in the former, hair gel and, in the latter, a means for acting out adolescent angst. Such material would once have been considered obscene but is now enough of a novelty in mainstream film that it is capable of grabbing the audience's attention and eliciting somewhat shocked laughs. . . .

Such treatment of semen is a far cry from its standard depiction in pornographic films. Far from providing comedic relief, semen . . . often has a starring and very important role to play in these features . . . the man's ejaculation is the raison d'être for these films. The money shot, where a man ejaculates on screen, is the compulsory display of semen in most pornographic films and a number of pornographic magazines as well. Ejaculation, the release of seminal fluid often with astounding force, authenticates the pornographic film in that the sexual desire, the arousal, and the performance are seemingly based on "real" desire. As a male friend quipped to me during a more explosive money shot, "Now you can't fake that." The cum shot is typically defined where a man ejaculates onto a woman, usually onto her face (referred to as a facial) or sometimes onto her sex organs. To be classified as a money shot, the semen must be clearly visible. The "money" refers to the money the actor receives as payout for making the film, which sometimes includes a bonus for the act of ejaculation. . . .

When seminal ejaculation is the denouement of a film, there is a presumption about those watching the film. As Patton states, "Even though not everyone in this culture has a penis, the cinematic conventions which position the viewer as the person coming are fairly seamless, and it is quite easy to imagine that this is your penis, regardless of your anatomical configuration."[12] In the porn film, we are each beckoned to identify with that penis and to experience the rush of relief as ejaculate spews forth. Furthermore, Patton has argued that after the wild abandon of pornographic sex, seminal ejaculation enables the man to be responsible for the restoration of sexual order.[13] The stylized repetition of money shots is alluring in that it signals release of control, pleasure, achievement, and success.

It is not clear at what historical moment the money shot emerged as a cinematic convention, but Patton suggests that it has at least existed in the United States since the 1930s as "handmade gay male pornographic drawings from the interwar years."[14] The male orgasm demonstrated through ejaculation indicates the completion of a sex act, the scene, the movie, the book, and the encounter. It instructs the audience that the activity is over and has been successful. As an industry standard of pornographic films, the money shot was fairly commonplace after World War II.[15] . . .

GIRLS GONE WILD FOR SPERM

There is a new niche market of seminal ejaculate films that expand on the glorification of men's ejaculate. Unlike other pornographic genres, these movies focus on semen as the central theme of the narrative and the action, not solely the denouement. Titles such as *Semen Demons, Desperately Seeking Semen, The Cum Cocktail, We Swallow, Sperm Overdose* (volumes 1–6), *Sperm Dreams, Sperm Burpers* (volumes 1–5), *A Splash of Sperm,* and *Feeding Frenzy* (volumes 1–3) venture beyond the money shot toward eroticizing seminal ingestion. The contents of the promotional descriptions of the videos, as well as the videos themselves, depict a variety of women drinking and bathing in semen from diverse male partners. Women appear to be insatiable and competitive about their desire for ingesting the semen as they rush to get to the ejaculating penis, the full shot glass, or residual ejaculate on a sheet. What does it mean to see women completely overcome with their desire to drink semen? To smear it all over their bodies? What does this say about male desire and masculinity? Here is a sampling of promotional descriptions of a few films:[16]

Promo for the movie Semen Shots 2

There's nothing that a pretty girl likes more at the end of a sexual encounter than to drink her lover's cum out of a shot glass. That's the premise behind this developing series, anyway. Delilah Strong entertains five young men and takes two cocks in her pussy before swigging multiple shots of their hot spunk. Jasmyn Taliana whimpers a lot before downing her two shots. Mason Storm enjoys a bit of anal before laughing her way through two fingers of warm sperm. Rio Mariah takes a double penetration and then squeezes the contents of her pussy and ass into a glass for savoring. Monica Sweetheart looks pretty in a sheer nightie with sparkly flowers during her anal and still looks cute while tossing back some of Brian Pumper's love cocktail. . . .

Promo for Wad Gobblers, Volume 13

This video begins with an amazing wild montage of twelve or fourteen chicks all taking it in the face with gobs of splashing semen, a dozen or more beauties being blasted with emissions so powerful it shoots up their nostrils. Their tongues snake out to lap up every drop and the overflow bubbles like lava out of their mouths.

These descriptions of money shots use sensational linguistic cues to entice the reader to purchase or rent these videos. It is obvious that seminal ejaculation is the main attraction in each video, the star of the show. Women's bodies are the surfaces for seminal display or the containers to ingest semen. Using the props of shot glasses and cocktail accessories, women literally become drunk on semen, often losing control in the presence of such powerful and intoxicating fluids.

Ironically, this genre of pornography is being produced against a cultural backdrop in which semen is directly associated with risk. Warnings about HIV/AIDS and STDs are plastered on bus stops, broadcast through public service announcements on radio and television, and echoed in health-care interactions. We are told to avoid semen to lessen our risk of pregnancy, disease, and death. Some industries, such as health care and forensics, have worked to imbue the raw material of semen with risk. Similarly, fertility enterprises and spouse or partner surveillance companies market their services by both reminding us of the risk of seminal ejaculate and claiming to mitigate that risk for us.

But the constant messages about risk and danger from seminal ejaculate have likely affected men's own relationship to their semen, as well as amplified a sense of it as forbidden. These pornographic videos then capitalize on recovering and eroticizing the raw material

of semen as safe, natural, organic, whole. The commodification of semen in these videos relies on a specific form of consumption in the narrative arc. Taking the action a moment beyond the money shot, the triumph of these videos is actually the expression of reverence for semen as it is placed either in a shot glass or on a woman's face, buttocks, or breasts. The absence of, or disregard for, risk is also a saleable dimension of these videos. They sell the image of sperm as not embodying risk or, even if risky, then certainly worth that risk. In these films, these female actors are depicted as willing to debase themselves, put themselves at risk, and even become sick in order to please their men. . . .

[T]he taste of semen [is not necessarily] as delicious as the videos portray. Some have compared the scent of semen to bleach, household cleanser, or swimming pool water. The taste has been described as salty and bitter, which may explain why Semenex, a patented, all-natural powder drink has been created to sweeten semen. Semenex, with an advertised price of $54.95 for a 30-serving container, relies on testimonials similar to this one: "Tasty! I've never really had a problem with semen, except when it gets really bitter, but this product really makes drinking a man down a treat!" so says, Jenni from Mesa, Arizona. As an online ad in *Maxim* magazine claims, "Semenex is where to go for delicious sperm guaranteed. Finally, an answer to the 'I don't like the taste' argument."[17] Interviewed as part of the 2005 documentary *Inside Deep Throat* about the infamous porn movie, Helen Gurley Brown, *Cosmopolitan* editor in chief and author of the 1962 best seller *Sex and the Single Girl,* extols the benefits of semen, saying, "Women have known for years that ejaculate is good for the skin because it is full of babies . . . it's full of protein. Just rub it all over your face, and skin and chest."

While semen may get mixed reviews from actual women, in the world of pornographic films semen is no longer something that is gross, yucky, smells bad, or brings disease—rather, it is something delicious, desired, and needed. Perhaps only the bold fantasy of a world dominated by men, and their need for sexual pleasure, could provide the scenario where women actually fight with each other for the pleasure of guzzling down ounces of semen. . . .

Within the sex industries of prostitution and pornography, sperm maintains contradictory meanings. It is referred to as a dangerous, if not lethal, weapon and, alternatively, as the crowning achievement of human interaction. For sex workers who perform sex acts with actual people (as opposed to pornography film actors), seminal ejaculation is a hazardous waste material to be managed and avoided for fear of pregnancy or disease. Sex workers do not have the benefit of reviewing their partners' HIV test results before a scene. Nor are there multiple takes to "get it right." And since many male clients are socialized by pornographic videos that do not depict safe sex, many sex workers find that, while they must use latex devices to protect themselves, at the same time they must eroticize their safe sex practices or risk failing to perform the job they are being paid for.

"DEALING WITH THE JIZZ": STORIES FROM SEX WORKERS

Most sex workers handle men as if they are dangerous; they can be violent, deceiving, and vectors of disease. Despite this belief about men, most sex workers will take on the risk of intimate physical contact as long as the men have the money to pay for it. This, of course, assumes that men can afford an average $200 an hour sexual experience. In an ironic twist, sex workers and sperm banks have an inverse relationship with regard to sperm and money. Men pay sex workers for their services, which includes managing their potentially dangerous semen, while people pay sperm banks to store or purchase certifiably healthy semen. Semen

banks pay donors between $40 and $60 per ejaculate. Each ejaculate can be divided up into between two and three vials, which cost roughly $150 each. So one ejaculate divided into two samples is $(150 \times 2) - 60 = 240 profit per ejaculate. This is $40 more than the typical sex worker makes.

The analysis that follows is based on interviews conducted over a five-year period (1991–1996) with well-paid, in-call, consenting sex workers. Sex workers occasionally reject clients who use heavy drugs or alcohol, are on the bad trick list, or simply give them the creeps. A bad trick list circulates within communities of sex workers and has the names and descriptions of previously delinquent or violent male clients. Perhaps through personal stigma and immersion in an AIDS/HIV culture, sex workers view all bodily products as having degrees of toxicity. In the pursuit of self-preservation and profit, semen is treated as a carrier of pathogens, germs, and sperm that may debilitate, kill, or impregnate the worker. All sex workers interviewed about their safer sex practices stated they always use a condom for each act of vaginal and anal intercourse. Here are some of their comments about men and their sperm:

I personally do not want to have any contact with fluids that come out of a man's dick. So like today I saw somebody who had a little pre-ejaculate on his belly and what I do is I take a piece of tissue and I wipe it off, then I take another piece of tissue and I apply nonoxynol nine. (Bonny, 54; 20-year professional dominant) . . .

My party line is rubbers for fucking and rubbers for sucking. I have always been strict about it. (Hadley, 55; 25-year veteran stripper, prostitute, professional dominant) . . .

Men and their semen are viewed here as universally dangerous, distrustful, and dirty. Semen is something that must be managed. No matter how it is represented, as good or bad, or somewhere in between, at the time of its ejaculation, semen has to be dealt with. As Quincy, a 45-year-old sex worker who has been in the industry since her late 20s states,

The guys want me to really like their cum. I think many of them would like to see me roll around in it and drink it and basically bathe in it. Maybe like they see on the movies they watch. But, I can't really do that. So I just sort of pretend. There would be something nice about being able to wallow in body fluids but I am not even going to go there.

As discussed, this desire to "wallow in body fluids" is promoted in almost all pornographic videos, but it is only risk-free for the jizzee, not the jizzed upon. Quincy empathizes with her clients about semen, telling them, "I really love sperm and I wish I could swallow it. But we can pretend and I bet you will not even notice the difference." In her sex work career and as a practitioner of latex devices, Quincy claims that men do not know the difference between safer sex and unprotected sex when things are done by a professional. She claims when safer sex is seamlessly accomplished, her male clientele (and perhaps men in general) accept its use: "So it's like a Pavlovian trick to get people more comfortable with and more turned on to the possibility of safe sex. The snap of the glove or smell of condoms means something fun is going to happen."

Sex workers create safety standards for dealing with semen. They use male and female condoms, gloves, and finger cots (small latex coverings for individual fingers), as actual physical barriers that inhibit the semen from making contact with exposed body surfaces. Safer sex, as a collection of symbols, practices, and technological innovations, both protects sex workers from contamination and assures the client of standard operating procedures that reduce their own exposure to the "hazardous waste material" of previous clients. As Michelle, a 38-year-old petite blonde, states, "When my clients get a little strange about my safer sex stuff, I will say, 'Well, this might bug you a little

bit, but I promise to keep you safe' and then I will smile all sweet."

In addition to manipulations for safety purposes, sex workers have crafted techniques to make semen perform more predictably, to make this recalcitrant substance more workable. Sex workers train their clients in techniques for semen control and manipulation. For example, many sex workers instruct their clients on how to put on a condom. They can instruct men in how to maintain erections and delay ejaculation through practicing sex acts and talking about their bodies. By bringing an erect man close to orgasm and then delaying the ejaculation, sex workers talk about building a man's endurance and self-control during sex acts. They work with their clients, talking to them and coaxing them to understand their own bodies and sexual responses. Several of the women I interviewed have developed symbolic rituals of performance to promote pleasurable semen control. They place a variety of male condoms in special places on a night table or at an altar with candles and incense, "To honor the act they know will be coming soon," as Olivia put it. Most sex workers opened up male condoms during our interviews to demonstrate different techniques for placing condoms on imaginary penises using their mouth and hands, coaching men through the safer sex requirements with statements like, "Now comes the fun part," and, "I can't wait. Can you?"

When I was interviewing Michelle at her apartment, she invited me to look at an album of erotic photographs of herself in full makeup and dressed in lingerie. "This is how I look when my clients come over," she explained as we explored the ironies of attempting to be sexy and available while assiduously managing men's ejaculate. Michelle knows that in her work she cannot use the universal precautions of the health-care industry to protect herself. Rather, she must maintain her sexy, available, and pleasurable image while ensuring her survival:

I mean going to see my dentist becomes—I feel like a hazardous waste material myself. First he had some new goggles, well then he got a shield, you know, and next I expect him to come in just like—you know, a space suit next time. It's so funny. But that's what we're having to do. See the medical profession has the luxury of looking like they're in this space suit. I can't look like I'm in a space suit. I have got to look like I'm being very intimate and everything, and yet really I am trying to have my own little space suit going on here.

Ana, a 38-year-old petite, brunette sex worker, explained one of the ways she flatters men while retrieving used condoms:

It's funny because I started doing this thing with the condoms. When I take them off the guy, before I throw them away or flush them down the toilet, I show them to the guy. . . . I mean most guys because a couple of my guys might be out the door before I get a chance. But when I show them to the guy, I say something like, "Wow you must really like me a lot" or "I have never seen this much before." Lots of guys seem to really like that when you tell them that they have a lot [of semen]. They kind of get off on it.

This verbal acknowledgement and visual display of seminal volume echoes the penis size concerns explored at the beginning of this [reading]. Ana is exploiting a man's concern with size, density, and volume as a way to praise men and continue the pleasurable (safer) sexual experience. If seminal ejaculate were not contained in a condom, how else might a man know how virile he apparently is?

In spite of the acknowledged risks, sex workers are handling semen and managing men. In many instances, sex workers innovate containment strategies to limit exposure to semen while also making men feel good about their semen and their expressions of masculinity. Through the use of flattery, men are encouraged to believe they measure up or exceed other men's performances and bodies. Sex workers' (like Ana's) use of male condoms enables them to capture semen. In this context, semen is used to compliment a man on his potency. By empathizing with men about the "good old days," sex workers can enforce rules about seminal exposure, while making men feel that their semen is not hazardous. Sex workers' expertise at using latex devices enables them to make men feel taken care of, while assuring their own safety from exposure.

THE ESSENCE OF (EVERY)MAN

With the proliferation of movies and videos that glorify the money shot, the sex entertainment industry provides an avenue for men to be spectators in the celebration of unprocessed, carnal, natural semen. Unlike other industries that manage semen, such as scientific laboratories, fertility clinics, and forensics enterprises, male bodily products do not need to be technologically enhanced or scientifically manipulated to be useful or understood. Unlike the workers in these industries, porn stars do not use universal precautions of covering their bodies with latex gloves, goggles, and face masks when handling semen. In real life, most sex workers, particularly the successful ones, are not entirely cloaked in thin layers of plastic, rigidly carrying out state-regulated mandates for handling body fluids. Sex workers, in films and real life, are either very minimally dressed or naked and do not shrink away from intimate contact with seminal fluid.

As other industries that manage sperm have established, not all men are created equal. For example, a majority of men who attempt to donate sperm are rejected from sperm banks. And even outside of the fertility clinics, there are multiple reminders that most men produce semen that is gross, diseased, genetically inferior, incompetent, lazy, and unwanted. To some extent, then, the pornography industry produces images that address the needs and desires of these men. That is, since men are socialized to believe that their semen is undesirable and even disgusting to women, and possibly perceived as a health hazard, it is a relief to see representations of their semen as cherished. The raw material of male desire, seminal fluid, is produced directly from the source, and it is wanted and desperately desired in its purest form.

In these videos, there is still power associated with the man's characteristics, but power and social desirability is also assigned to the color, amount, and image of the semen itself—and the woman's positive reaction to it. No one is running to the bathroom to spit out the ejaculate, and everyone swallows with a smile. Semen, in these videos, is not abstracted into a characterization—it is not anthropomorphized—yet it is still desirable. Furthermore, the fairly recently established niche genres that focus on the consumption of semen depict women who can't get enough. They have no fear and no disgust for the substance in its natural state. No technological manipulation of semen is necessary.

While this process of appreciating everyman's sperm may seem liberating, it is still occurring within systems of male domination. The forces of hegemonic masculinity act to subjugate some men to the control of other men deemed more worthy, esteemed, or powerful. These fantasies about seminal consumption sell subjugated men the belief that they are the epitome of traditionally masculine power when they may rank quite low. While some men may opt out of a traditionally masculine set of behaviors and work to redefine masculinity, other men will literally buy into the images and tropes of pornography. Those men who are still participating in and consenting to a process that de-values them become perfect consumers of films that bolster the story of male dominance. This means that, even though these men may not directly benefit from hierarchal relations of masculine power, they will support films that depict male domination because they identify with the male protagonist. Porn becomes one of the many opiates of the wimpy men who cannot take a stand against the ultimate nonconsensual subordination of others because they themselves are so subordinated. In this way, hegemonic masculinity maintains its dominance by providing commodities that work to placate those oppressed by activities that are in reality disempowering.

My analysis of semen as represented, consumed, and manipulated within industrial and commercial sex markets further establishes sperm's elasticity of meaning. While individual men may be aware of their social worth as subordinate to other men, commercial sex work is one arena in which men can retain hope that their seminal ejaculate, their essence of manhood, is enjoyed, powerful, and spectacular.

NOTES

1. Vivien Marx, *The Semen Book* (London: Free Association, 2001).

2. Caroline Aldred, *Divine Sex: The Art of Tantric and Taoist Arts of Conscious Loving* (San Francisco: HarperCollins, 1996).

3. For recent scientific explorations of ejaculatory disorders, see David J. Ralph and Kevan Wylie, "Ejaculatory Disorders and Sexual Function," *British Journal of Urology* 95:9 (2005): 1181–1186.

4. Kalyani Premkumar, *The Massage Connection: Anatomy and Physiology.* (Philadelphia: Lippincott, Williamson and Wilkins, 2004: 436).

5. Cindy Patton, "Hegemony and Orgasm: Or the Instability of Heterosexual Pornography," *Screen* 30:4 (1989): 1–34.

6. For example, Laura M. Carpenter, *Virginity Lost: An Intimate Portrait of First Sexual Experiences* (New York: New York University Press, 2005).

7. Due to methodological constraints, this chapter primarily relies on heterosexually produced pornography and heterosexually oriented sex workers. That is not to say that viewers or participants in these industries are heterosexual, but it is to bracket the data as produced primarily for a presumed heterosexual audience. Clearly, gay porn or porn featuring men who have sex with men would be a robust site for research about semen and the eroticization of ejaculation.

8. Pamela Paul, *Pornified: How Pornography Is Transforming Our Lives, Our Relationships and Our Families* (New York: Holt, 2005).

9. *Vital Information for Workers and Employers in the Adult Film Industry,* CAL-OSHA, 2003, available at http://www.dir.ca.gov/dosh/adultfilmindustry.html (accessed October 14, 2006).

10. Ann Regentin, *What We're Really Watching,* May 26, 2004, available at http://www.cleansheets.com/articles/regentin_05.26.04.shtml (accessed October 14, 2006).

11. Interview with Raylene by Max Gunner, "Seven Inches of Pleasure," *Popsmear Online Magazine,* available at http://www.popsmear.com/lovemaking/seveninches/15.0/index.html (accessed October 14, 2006).

12. Patton, "Hegemony and Orgasm," 105.

13. Cindy Patton, "The Cum Shot: Three Takes on Lesbian and Gay Studies," *Out/Look* 1:3 (1988): 72–76.

14. Ibid., 106.

15. For a history of pornography in the United States, see Joseph Slade, *Pornography in America: A Reference Handbook* (Santa Barbara, Calif.: ABC-CLIO, 2000). As Slade states on page 323: "After the war, the cum shot, the penis ejaculating out of the vagina, became nearly universal."

16. These are a collection of descriptions taken from *Reviews,* 2004, available at www.avn.com (accessed October 14, 2006).

17. *Come Again, and Again . . . ,* available at http://www.semenex.com/maximwebguide4th.jpg (accessed October 14, 2006).

NOT FOR SALE: STOPPING SEX TRAFFICKING IN THE UNITED STATES AND WORLDWIDE

NADIA SHAPKINA

SEX TRAFFICKING: A LOCAL/GLOBAL PROBLEM

Sex trafficking is a criminal activity that involves the sale and exploitation of human beings, often women and children, in the sex trade. Many Americans believe sex trafficking is primarily a "foreign" problem, not a domestic one. However, there are many cases of sex trafficking and commercial sexual exploitation of women and children in industrialized countries, including the United States. When traffickers sell and exploit victims within national borders, this is known as domestic sex trafficking. When a national border crossing is involved, this is referred to as international trafficking. Let us consider two cases representing domestic and international trafficking.

Case 1. Domestic Sex Trafficking: Jill's Story

Jill was 14 years old when she ran away from home with a few dollars and some clothes. For her, home was not a safe place—she experienced physical, psychological, and sexual abuse there, and she had no plans of returning. Life on the streets was tough. Jill had to sleep outside, steal food, and count on only occasional access to running water. Then, she met Bruce. He was the first adult who listened to Jill. He praised her and seemed like he wanted to help. He promised to get her a job in entertainment. Under the pretense of an audition for a job, Bruce took her to a house where she was confined in a locked room. Bruce used different strategies (e.g., anger, flattery, intimidation, etc.) and methods of coercion (e.g., physical punishment) to manipulate Jill to accept the fact that she was his sex slave who had to "know her place;" he required Jill to sign a "contract" stating that she was his slave. After Bruce took Jill from Cincinnati to Los Angeles, he forced her to provide sexual services for his clients and friends. Jill was finally freed after the police arrested Bruce. Even though her life became safe after that, she struggled with many post-traumatic stress symptoms such as nightmares, flashbacks, fear, and depression. Since then, Jill has been involved in anti-trafficking activism; she cofounded a nonprofit organization that helps women escape the violent experience of the sex trade.[1]

Case 2. International Sex Trafficking: Nina's Story

When a young Russian woman, Nina, responded to a job advertisement for a position as a maid, she did not expect the job to be in Israel. However, it appeared to be a great job—working for a wealthy household in Tel Aviv with free room and board and $300 per month in salary. All travel expenses paid. This was a lucrative opportunity compared to her job as a saleswoman at a local market that paid about $20 per month. The position in Tel Aviv would help her alleviate the large debt that she and her two minor siblings had accumulated. Nina, her brother, and younger sister did not have a fairytale childhood. Their parents lost jobs in the economic downturn that followed the collapse of the former Soviet Union. Both parents developed alcohol addictions and regularly sold their children's belongings to buy vodka. When Nina turned eighteen, she took her siblings to a nearby city, found herself a job and a room to rent, and started a new life. A temporary job in Israel seemed like a good option to stay afloat financially until Nina's brother and sister became old enough to seek employment. What Nina did not know was that the job advertisement was fraudulent; it was a trafficking recruitment strategy to lure women to work in the Israeli sex trade. She agreed to apply for a passport to travel abroad and received a lump sum of money to pay off her family's debt. She and her recruiter, a middle-aged Russian man, travelled to Egypt, where foreign visitor entry requires only a $20 visa purchased at the airport. From there, Nina and four other women were taken illegally by other men (smugglers) to Israel, where they were delivered to a Tel Aviv night club. Nina was separated from the other women and locked in a dark room for a long time. The club owner told her that she was his property until she paid back the expenses he incurred delivering her to Israel. She was forced to have sex with club clients almost every day for several months, until she was able to run away. Police officers who met her on the streets of Tel Aviv detained her in a deportation facility for a while; eventually, she was allowed to travel back to Russia. After her return, Nina sought support from a nonprofit organization in Russia that helped her find a job in a convenience store, rent an apartment, and reunite with her siblings.[2]

Both cases fit the definition of human trafficking provided by the United Nations Protocol to Prevent, Suppress and Punish Trafficking in Persons:

Trafficking in persons includes the recruitment, transportation, transfer, harboring, or receipt of persons by threat or use of force or other forms of coercion, deception, abuse of power or of a position of vulnerability or of the giving or receiving of payments or benefits to achieve the consent of a person having control over another person for the purpose of exploitation.[3]

The experiences and circumstances of trafficked women can vary significantly. However, most victims, like Jill and Nina, find themselves sold into the sex trade due to economic, family, housing, and employment problems. Economic deprivation, together with insufficient social safety nets, leads to situations where victims have to rely on dubious offers of work or help. Global inequality results in limited economic opportunities for many women in developing countries, who often have to rely on migration to provide for themselves and their families. In some areas of the world, governments promote out-migration as a strategy to raise state revenues through remittances.[4] This labor migration is often unregulated or under-regulated by the state, sometimes leading to significant human rights abuses.

Different forms of gender inequality and discrimination "push" women to migrate in search of employment and better lives, while, at the same time, certain gendered industries (e.g., sex trade, garment sweatshops, domestic work, etc.) "pull" them in as the demand for their "cheap labor" increases. Racial, ethnic, caste-based, and religious discrimination further disadvantage groups of girls and women.

Technology (e.g., the Internet, cell phones, cheap transportation, etc.) facilitates the growth of the sex trade industry and changes its nature. For example, sex traffickers use chat rooms and social media to advertise sexual services by trafficked victims. Craigslist.com has recently closed its sex advertisements section in light of allegations of pimps using the website to advertise sexual services of children. The closure, however, did not eliminate the advertisements completely but displaced them to other sections of Craigslist and other websites. Buyers of sexual services use the Internet to browse for offers. For example, Kansas City cyber crime task force officers have arrested several men for attempting to buy sexual services of children, including a naval recruiter who paid for sex with an 11-year-old girl.[5] In this undercover operation, police officers placed fake online advertisements, targeting customers of trafficked children. In an international case, two Swedish nationals have been jailed for life for sex trafficking and sexual exploitation of minors in the Philippines.[6] Together with several Filipino traffickers (who received 20-year sentences), they operated a cybersex ring in which trafficked women and underage girls performed acts of a sexual nature in front of cameras for Internet customers located throughout the world. Technology is a factor that affects the changing sex trade industry and can sometimes facilitate sex trafficking practices.

Sex tourism has emerged as a subsector of the sex trade that brings customers to tourist sites for the purposes of buying sexual services. Sex trafficking is not uncommon in the sex tourist sector of the industry. Finally, war and civic conflict are important structural factors in human trafficking; the breakdown of governance and disruption of normal life increase trafficking and smuggling.

Regardless of the form that it takes, one thing is clear: even though the extent of profitability from sex trafficking varies across different criminal organizations, the total profit generated in the world economy from sex trafficking is staggering. Sex trafficking is often compared with arms trafficking and drug trafficking in terms of profitability. However, whereas drugs can be sold to the consumer only once, humans (and sex) can be continuously resold, making it an extremely profitable criminal activity. Siddharth Kara estimates the annual world-level profit from sex trafficking is about $35 billion.[7] This profitability helps explain why sex trafficking is such a widespread problem.

Characteristics of victims in confirmed cases of sex trafficking[9]

DEMOGRAPHIC CHARACTERISTICS	NUMBER OF SEX TRAFFICKING VICTIMS (% OF SEX TRAFFICKING VICTIMS)	
Female	432	(94%)
Male	27	(6%)
	459	(100%)
Age, 17 or younger	248	(54%)
Age, 18–34	188	(40%)
Age, 35 or older	12	(3%)
Age, unidentified	12	(3%)
	460	(100%)
Race, Caucasian	102	(22%)
Race, African American	161	(35%)
Hispanic/Latino origin	95	(21%)
Asian	17	(4%)
Other/unidentified race/ethnicity	84	(18%)
	459	(100%)
U.S. Citizenship, permanent residency	351	(77%)
Undocumented alien	64	(14%)
Qualified alien	1	(0.2%)
Unidentified citizenship	41	(9%)
	457	(100%)
Total number of identified victims	460	

HOW WIDESPREAD IS THE PROBLEM?

Because trafficking involves highly mobile and "invisible" groups of people, the number of trafficking victims is very difficult to estimate. However, there are some data available regarding the magnitude of the problem. The Bureau of Justice Statistics (BJS) at the U.S. Department of Justice collects information about all open and confirmed cases of trafficking in the United States. According to BJS data, there were 2,515 human trafficking incidents opened for investigation between January 2008 and June 2010.[8] Of this total, 82 percent (2,065 cases) were sex trafficking incidents. (The remaining 18 percent were cases of labor trafficking.) The table on the previous page demonstrates that sex trafficking victims identified in the United States are primarily women (94%), youth (54%), and racial and ethnic minorities (78%). Statistics on cases of international human trafficking collected by the International Organization for Migration (IOM) between 1999 and 2009 show 13,809 trafficking victims worldwide receiving assistance through IOM.[10] Sixty-eight percent were victims of sex trafficking. Official statistical data only document a small portion of the illegal economy of sex trafficking. Siddharth Kara estimates that the number of sex trafficking victims worldwide is between 500,000 and 600,000.[11]

THE PROCESS OF SEX TRAFFICKING: RECRUITMENT, TRANSPORTATION, AND EXPLOITATION

The organization of trafficking as a business operation can range from a very small group to a sophisticated multi-national network. The trafficking recruiter can be a physical person or an organization (employment agency, dancing show, etc.) that advertises well-paid employment, typically abroad. The most commonly advertised jobs are in domestic service, child and elder care, and the entertainment industry. Traffickers use different strategies to recruit women and girls. A common strategy is to recruit through acquaintanceship networks. Another is to seduce the women into a seemingly romantic relationship. For example, Marius Nejloveanu from Romania relied on a "Casanova" tactic— he used to profess his love to the women he trafficked to Spain and the United Kingdom and then brutally forced them into selling sex.

Nejloveanu ran a family-based sex trafficking ring with his father.[12] Both of them have been found guilty of sex trafficking by a British court.

Trafficking often involves transportation. Women may travel to destinations alone or accompanied by traffickers/recruiters; they may cross borders legally or illegally. The process of transporting women to a foreign country puts them in an extremely dependent position and makes them vulnerable to the control of traffickers. The women typically do not speak the local languages, their documents are taken away, and they are told that they have violated local laws.

The sex trade is concentrated in global cities, tourist zones, bars, clubs, and around military bases where there are relatively large concentrations of capital. Sex trafficking can happen in any of the settings where the sex trade usually takes place: massage parlors, street prostitution, hotel rooms, strip clubs, truck stops, or brothels. Physical coercion and psychological manipulation are central mechanisms of control in sex trafficking; they are the essential tools of profit-making. Traffickers, pimps, and guards often use violence and isolation to control women. They may separate them from potential allies, lock them up, or sell them to another bar or club to break friendships and solidarities. Other forms of control include threats to the women's relatives (children, parents, siblings, and others). Traffickers almost always appropriate women's documents and belongings to prevent them from running away.

STATE REGULATION OF THE SEX TRADE

Regulation of the sex trade differs across countries, and this is an important factor in considering protection of trafficking victims. There are four main types of sex trade regulation: Prohibitionism, Regulationism, Abolitionism, and Neo-abolitionism. I discuss the intended and unintended consequences of the different systems and identify examples of countries utilizing these systems.

Prohibitionism is a system of regulation that treats the sex trade as a crime that undermines society's morals and ethics. The state punishes all participants of the transaction—buyers ("johns"), sellers (prostitutes), and facilitators (pimps, brothel owners). Punishment can consist of a fine, citation, and/or imprisonment. This criminalizing or prohibitionist approach to prostitutes can have negative implications for sex trafficking identification—if prostitutes are treated as criminals, this can increase their fear of being imprisoned, and prevent them from reporting sex trafficking and other abuses they might experience. China, Russia, and most of the United States (except Nevada) utilize prohibitionist strategies.

Regulationism assumes that the state does not treat the sex trade as morally wrong. Prostitution is considered a practice that has to be regulated by the federal or local government. This approach results in the licensing of brothels and individual sex workers, zoning areas where the sale of sex may take place, and tax collection. Proponents of regulationism argue that the governmental control and licensing of the businesses can make the sex trade safer for both sex workers and customers. Opponents argue that the state becomes the main pimp of the industry as it collects revenues from the sex trade. Another major critique of regulationism is that this system often results in a split sex trade market, with a regulated sector for licensed sex workers and an unregulated sector where, typically, migrants work (those who cannot get legal licenses) and where sex trafficking flourishes. Examples of countries that regulate sex trade include Germany, the Netherlands, Switzerland, Austria, Turkey, and Nevada in the United States.

Abolitionism prioritizes eliminating exploitation of prostitutes by others, e.g., by pimps. Abolitionist countries punish the act of procurement (convincing or enticing someone to exchange sex for money, living on the profits from prostituting someone). Organized and controlled forms of prostitution (brothel organization, etc.) and the coercion and involvement of minors are criminalized. The sale and purchase of sex by individuals goes largely unregulated (is tolerated by authorities). Italy, Spain, and the United Kingdom are countries with abolitionist approaches to the sex trade.

Neo-abolitionism punishes procurers and clients, but not the people who sell sex. Pimps are criminalized; customers are fined; but people who sell sexual services are not considered guilty of any criminal activity because they engage in sex work to survive. (This is also known as the "decriminalization of prostitutes" approach.) Sellers are considered to be the economically and socially weaker party in the transaction. The government provides support to people who want to exit prostitution. This neo-abolitionist approach is used in Sweden and makes it easier to report sex trafficking and other abuses in the sex trade because of a lack of fear of being punished for selling sex. However, the criminalization of customers leads to the displacement of the sex trade to neighboring countries (for example, Swedish johns are known to buy sexual services in Denmark, Estonia, etc.).

These approaches to sex trade regulation affect anti-trafficking efforts because they create different contexts in which the law enforcement officers and service providers identify and assist trafficking victims. The identification of sex trafficking victims is one of the most challenging aspects of anti-trafficking work because of the many negative stereotypes about people who sell sex. In many cultures, prostitutes are often blamed for different social problems and treated as villains (especially, in prohibitionist countries). This stereotype prevents law enforcement, policy makers, judges, and other public figures from recognizing that the men and women who earn their living in the sex trade can be coerced and exploited. Traffickers often use these negative stereotypes to discourage sex trafficking victims from seeking help from police. Law enforcement practices could be improved if agents were trained to withhold negative judgment and to simply investigate cases to determine whether the crime of sex trafficking took place.

Decriminalization of sex workers is a growing initiative in many countries. Even though regulationist and neo/abolitionists often have contrasting views on the sex trade regulation, they agree that people selling sexual services in the sex trade should not be punished. They should not be afraid of being arrested or jailed when they need to report abuse and exploitation.

ANTI-TRAFFICKING LEGISLATION

International legislation defines slavery-like practices as violations of human rights. Article four of the Universal Declaration of Human Rights states that "no one shall be held in slavery or servitude; slavery and the slave trade shall be prohibited in all their forms."[13] The United Nations has also adopted a special set of minimal anti-trafficking measures that member states have to introduce when they sign and ratify the U.N. Convention Against Transnational Organized Crime and its supplementing Protocol to Prevent, Suppress and Punish Trafficking in Persons (also known as the Palermo Protocol, 2000).[14] The protocol establishes provisions in three interrelated areas: *prevention* of trafficking, *protection* of victims, and *prosecution* of traffickers. The United States has signed (December 13, 2000) and ratified (November 3, 2005) the Convention against Transnational Organized Crime. In addition, the United States has passed a series of national legal acts aimed at combating all forms of human trafficking, including sex trafficking.

The *Trafficking Victims Protection Act* (2000) has made sex trafficking a crime with severe punishment. The act also authorized the creation of the Office to Monitor and Combat Trafficking (TIP Office) within the Department of State. One of the tasks of the TIP Office is to monitor the human trafficking problem on an international level. The TIP Office issues an annual report on the state of anti-trafficking efforts in different countries of the world. Within the United States, the Trafficking Victims Protection Act has provided important tools to protect trafficking victims. It has established that victims are eligible for the Federal Victims Protection Program and created a special visa program (T visa) that allows trafficking victims to stay in the United States if they collaborate with the investigation and prosecution of traffickers.

In addition, certain states have issued their own state-level laws aimed at minimizing sex trafficking and protecting the victims. For example, New York legislators have pioneered decriminalization of minors involved in the sex trade in the 2008 Safe Harbour for Exploited Children Act.[15] This legislation recognizes that children who provide sexual services are not criminals, but victims. The Act includes provisions for such children to receive protection and specialized services. Currently, several other states are considering adopting similar legislation.

ANTI-TRAFFICKING ORGANIZATIONS

There are many governmental and non-governmental organizations involved in the fight against human trafficking; several focus specifically on sex trafficking.

The *Coalition against Trafficking of Women* (CATW) is an international non-governmental organization (NGO) that runs programs and campaigns against sexual exploitation in different regions of the world (www.catwinternational .org). CATW is well-known for its position on prostitution as a form of violence against women; it opposes violations of women's human rights in the contexts of prostitution, sex trafficking, sex tourism, pornography, and the international matchmaking industry. CATW staff members and volunteers conduct research, formulate policy recommendations, educate the public, collaborate with governments, and generate resources to provide assistance to women who find themselves in the sex trade.

The Global Alliance Against Traffic in Women (GAATW) is an international NGO that provides support to trafficking victims in different countries (www.gaatw.org). GAATW's position on prostitution differs from CATW. GAATW emphasizes that, from the point of view of people who find themselves selling sex, prostitution is a form of economic survival, typically a choice made between few alternatives. GAATW supports the decriminalization of prostitution because this would decrease the stigma of prostitution. The organization also supports the criminalization of sex trafficking and violence in the sex trade.

ECPAT International (End Child Prostitution, Child Pornography & Trafficking of Children for Sexual Purposes) is an international policy and advocacy NGO network that focuses specifically on the problem of commercial sexual exploitation of children (www.ecpat .net). Their member organizations provide trainings, evaluate policies, conduct research, and promote legal reform.

In the United States, there are several governmental agencies involved in anti-trafficking efforts (including sex trafficking). The Department of State (particularly, the TIP Office) coordinates American participation in anti-trafficking programs abroad. The Federal Bureau of Investigation, together with other local, state, and federal law enforcement agen-

cies, conducts investigations of human trafficking cases. The Department of Health and Human Services is in charge of providing trafficking victims with letters of certification and delivering support services (administered through nonprofit subcontractors).

Many nonprofit organizations and coalitions in the United States focus on the prevention of trafficking and the protection of victims. Located in Washington, D.C. and Newark, New Jersey, *Polaris Project* is one of the major anti-trafficking NGOs in the United States (www.polarisproject.org). Among its multiple programs, it operates the National Human Trafficking Resource Center that offers a 24/7 national toll-free hotline (1-888-3737-888) that receives crisis calls and tips about human trafficking cases.

CONCLUSION

Sex trafficking is a complex local/global social problem caused by economic, social, and political factors. Criminal groups use new means of communication and modes of transportation to make profit from selling women and girls as sexual commodities. Many governments, international organizations, nonprofits, and activists have stepped up to prevent this practice and protect the victims. However, growing social inequality, persistent gender inequality, and the highly mobile and hidden nature of sex trafficking makes it hard to eliminate this crime. Sustained international cooperation, political will, and partnerships between governments and civil society actors are essential in the fight against this modern day slavery.

NOTES

1. Jill Leighton's story is described in detail in: Sage, Jesse, and Liora Kasten (eds.). 2008. *Enslaved: True Stories of Modern Day Slavery.* Palgrave Macmillan.

2. Nina's case is described in more detail in: Shapkina, Nadezda, "Operation Help: Counteracting Sex Trafficking of Women from Russia and Ukraine" (2008). *Sociology*

Dissertations. Paper 35. http://digitalarchive.gsu.edu/sociology diss/35

3. UN Protocol to Prevent, Suppress and Punish Trafficking in Persons http://www2.ohchr.org/english/law/protocoltraffic.htm

4. Remittances are monies that labor migrants send back home. Certain countries (e.g., the Philippines) benefit significantly from out-migration as families, communities, and governmental revenue are supported by remittances.

5. Naval Recruiter Accused Of Child Sex Trafficking. 2009. http://www.kmbc.com/news/18901510/detail.html

6. Two Swedes Jailed for Life over Philippine Cybersex Den. 2011. http://www.bbc.co.uk/news/world-asia-pacific-13356721

7. Kara, Siddharth. 2009. *Sex Trafficking. Inside the Business of Modern Slavery.* Columbia University Press.

8. Banks, Duren, and Tracey Kyckelhahn. 2011. Characteristics of Suspected Human Trafficking Incidents, 2008–2010. http://bis.oip.usdoj.gov/index.cfm?ty=pbdetail&iid=2372

9. Ibid.

10. http://www.iom.int/iahia/page748.html Trafficking statistics can be requested by emailing AVRCTMMS@iom.int or cts-db@iom.int.

11. Kara, Siddharth. 2009. *Sex Trafficking. Inside the Business of Modern Slavery.* Columbia University Press. P. 17.

12. Wald, Jonathan. *Sex slavery: A family business.* March 4, 2001. http://thecnnfreedomproiect.blogs.cnn.com/2011/03/04/sex-slavery-a-family-business/

13. Universal Declaration of Human Rights. www.un.org/en/documents/udhr/index.shtml

14. Protocol to Prevent, Suppress and Punish Trafficking in Persons, Especially Women and Children, supplementing the United Nations Convention against Transnational Organized Crime http://www.unciin.org/Documents/Conventions/dcatoc/final_documents_2/convention_%20traff_eng.pdf

15. Title 8-A: Safe Harbour for Exploited Children Act. 2008. http://www.niin.org/uploads/digital_library/3175.pdf

MARKETING SEX: U.S. LEGAL BROTHELS AND LATE CAPITALIST CONSUMPTION

BARBARA G. BRENTS AND KATHRYN HAUSBECK

Selling sex is business. In addition to all else it may be, it is also situated in the specific forms of production and consumption at particular locales and time periods. The economic and cultural context in which sex is sold has changed significantly. Since the Second World War, a globally integrated economic system has developed, whose engine has changed from production to consumption, making service the core industrial sector (Harvey, 1989; Jameson, 1991). These forces have driven the development of new commodities, new forms of labour and new forms of consumption.[1] Most recently, travel and tourism have become the world's largest industries, employing 11 percent of all workers world wide, and producing 10 percent of the world's gross domestic product (Wonders and Michalowski, 2001: 549). Simultaneously, the non-tourist service industry has become increasingly 'touristic'—that is, rather than selling services with specific outcomes, services sell experience, spectacle, fantasy, adventure, escapism and personal interactions (Urry, 2002).

These economic changes have had profound effects on cultural practices, especially intimacy, sex and sexuality. Late capitalist mass consumption has encouraged, according to some studies, a pornographication of culture, more liberal and egalitarian sexual attitudes, and an acceptance of fleeting, temporary relationships (Bauman, 2003; Giddens, 1992; Hawkes, 1996; McNair, 2002). Studies also demonstrate an increasing commodification of intimacy and a heightened sexualization of work (Adkins, 2002; Zelizer, 2005). An important empirical question emerges: In this context, how has the sex industry changed? . . .

SHIFTING SEXUAL SERVICES: TOURIST AND TOURISTIC INDUSTRIES

We also choose to situate the sex industry in a larger context of tourism and touristic services (Wonders and Michalowski, 2001). A growing global tourist economy has spurred a growth in sex industry businesses.[2] . . . The media have made much of an apparent growth in size and respectability of the sex industries (*Economist*, 1998). The *Economist* notes "a handful of well run, imaginative businesses" are increasingly profitable, upscale, and exploiting market niches. Where this kind of growth has occurred, it has been executed in part through the use of the same marketing tactics as businesses in other tourist and touristic industries; for instance, marketing to wider audiences via upscaling, expanding services, market specialization, and expanding markets (Frank, 2002: 25). For example, the seedy, dark, secluded sex shops and strip joints of the past are being replaced by large, glitzy, and upscale adult stores and gentlemen's clubs, many with upscale restaurants. In Antwerp, in Belgium, a new upscale, chic "super brothel" has opened decorated by superstar architects and designers (Castle, 2006).

Some of these businesses are also adopting mainstream business organizational forms such as corporate structures and diversified holdings. Some legal sex industry businesses are partnering with multinational corporations, such as adult video distribution partnerships with General Motors, America Online/Time Warner, AT&T, Marriott, Hilton, Hyatt and Westin. In the US, while small private firms still dominate the legal sex industry, there is a trend toward larger national and international corporate chains. Adult businesses are even opening mainstream business enterprises such as the Vivid nightclub at the Venetian, a Las Vegas casino resort, where holographic images of adult film stars are projected onto the dance floor.

This mainstreaming has not occurred in all sectors of the adult sex industry. Just as in the non-sex industry workforce, there is labour market segmentation with primary (higher wages, more stable) and secondary (lower paying, less stable) labour markets. . . . In the secondary labour markets the pay is likely to be lower and labour conditions worse. There is deep stratification among workers in the global sex industry. The nature of the product sold is evolving, too.

Along with the growth of tourism in mainstream sectors, there has been a trend toward more touristic services. Traditionally, service work has sold emotion as much as a specific service. Research on service-providers such as restaurant servers, airline hostesses, and various salespeople has shown that managers and workers have rationalized the service product by applying assembly line principles. This "McDonaldization" of services relies on rationalized work processes, centralized work places, controlled environments, interactive scripts, standardized employment contracts and highly predictable production/consumption rituals to increase efficiency and profit and standardize emotional

services (Hochschild, 1983; Leidner, 1993; Ritzer and Liska, 1997). However, as the service industry has become more touristic, these rationalized outcome-oriented approaches have given way to decentralized, do-it-yourself workers compelled to sell uniqueness, variety and individuality. In essence, the product in these tourist/touristic leisure services becomes more an individualized, interactive experience with less rationalized and scripted outcomes (Beck, 1992; Holyfield, 1999; Sharpe, 2005). . . .

In this article, we . . . examine these changing structures and practices by looking at sex-industry organization and marketing at one local site of consumption, Nevada's legal brothels. In doing so, we emphasize that local sites may respond to global processes in different ways. We choose the legal brothels in Nevada as our site for several reasons. First, brothels sell sexual contact, sex acts, and sexual release rather than sexualized fantasies or non-contact services. . . . Prostitution remains among the most stigmatized segments of the sex industry, and research in this field has frequently conceptualized this business as deviant and fundamentally different from other service industries. Thus, brothels are exceedingly interesting place[s] to examine changes in how sex acts become touristic products. Second, while the informal economy has been dramatically affected by globalization and the growth of late capitalist tourist economies and culture, we choose to focus on legal businesses. Legal businesses are potentially more stable and more embedded in institutionalized business systems than independent prostitutes.

We are feminist sociologists who live in Las Vegas. Our research stems from a larger project on the social organization of Nevada brothels involving nearly 10 years of ethnographies, observations, formal and informal interviews with workers, managers, owners and policymakers, participation in public debates, and analysis of historical and contemporary documents, websites, media stories, and newspaper articles.[3] . . . In particular we look at changes in business forms and marketing strategies.

SHIFTING CONSUMPTION AND NEVADA BROTHELS

Nevada's sex industry exists within the context of a state whose primary source of income is tourism. Las Vegas draws more than 38 million tourists annually to more than 133,000 hotel rooms (Las Vegas Convention and Visitors Authority, 2006). . . .

The marketing of sexuality has been central to Las Vegas' growth as a global tourist resort. Despite marketing itself implicitly as a place where sexual fantasies may come true, with slogans such as "what happens here stays here," and unlike many Asian or European resort centers, prostitution itself is not explicitly marketed. . . . And as the casinos have become larger, more corporate, and answer to stockholders from around the globe, it has become important to them to look legitimate. In the large resort centers of Las Vegas and Reno, then, where prostitution of any kind is illegal, the resort industry works hard to prevent its visible forms.

Yet there are estimates that up to 3,500 illegal prostitutes work in Las Vegas' underground economy at any given time (Hausbeck et al., 2006). Illegal independent prostitutes evade casino security and discreetly work the bars and/or advertise via alternative weekly newspapers or the Internet. There are highly informal and discreet systems at a few hotels where concierges independently retain lists of preferred upscale prostitutes who can be made quickly available to the wealthiest guests. There are also thriving legal outcall entertainment businesses operating call centers that dispatch nude dancers to hotel rooms for an agency fee, and dancers may provide sexual services illegally for tips. Despite concerted

efforts by the resort industry to control public spaces around the resorts and eliminate these outcall businesses, outcall agencies advertise heavily through billboards, stands containing flyers and through individuals leafletting tourists on the sidewalks. Street prostitution is the most heavily surveilled, and police and the resort industry are vigilant in keeping obviously working-class prostitutes away from highly visible resort areas. There are also a few businesses operating legally as Asian massage parlors, where the predominantly Asian women provide "happy endings" illegally. Thus, sex tourism in the resort zones is an informal industry. While scantily clothed cocktail waitresses, partially nude shows, and sexy nightclubs lure tourists to resorts with the illusion of sexuality, the sale of sex acts is discouraged to the extent that it takes tourists away from time gambling or shopping in the casinos.

Nevada's legal brothel industry . . . helps to maintain the illusion of a sexual playground, yet the casino industry works hard to officially distance itself from the brothels both physically and politically. Brothels are a minimum of one hour's drive from any of the major resort areas and cannot market themselves as international sex tourist destinations because it is illegal to advertise. Compared to the money spent on illegal prostitution in Las Vegas and Reno, and compared to legal brothels in Amsterdam's highly concentrated urban red-light district, or even Australia's legal brothels, Nevada's brothel industry is small and geographically dispersed.

At most, 500 women work legally at any time in the entire state. While there are licenses for about 36 brothels, only about 25 to 30 are currently operating. There are 8 to 10 large brothels, housing 15 to 50 workers each, clustered about an hour's drive from Las Vegas and Reno. The rest are along the 850 miles of relatively remote stretches of desert highway linking Las Vegas to Reno, or connecting San Francisco, California, to Salt Lake City, Utah, a route that passes through Nevada. The smallest legal brothels house from 1 to 5 workers, and these tend to be several hours' drive from major resort centers. The midsize brothels are just outside of the smaller towns of Winnemucca, Carlin, Elko, Wells and Ely, with 5 to 12 workers in each. Brothels are legal in only 10 of Nevada's 17 counties. . . .

[I]t is doubtful that, without the tourist industry, the brothels would have remained legal here while the rest of the USA outlawed prostitution. Prostitution has been a part of the state's economic development since mining and railroads populated the state in the early 1900s. Mining booms and busts kept the population of the state under 80,000 until large federal dam projects around Las Vegas brought workers in the 1930s. By 1940, the state's population began climbing to 110,000 and gambling and quick divorces drove an increase in tourism. During the 1940s, some well-known writers moved to Virginia City, a gold rush town outside of Reno. From there they filled the pages of the *Saturday Evening Post, Ladies Home Journal, Gentlemen's Quarterly, the New Yorker, Gourmet* and *Town and Country Life* with articles that created our current myths about the wild and woolly west, and its legendary "soiled dove" prostitutes (Taylor, 1998). Nevada's small towns drew on these images to bolster sagging mining economies and build profitable tourism.

In the years after the Second World War, the growing urban casino industry distanced itself from prostitution as casinos struggled to gain legitimacy. Efforts to outlaw brothels by casino owners and local officials in the 1970s met with strong resistance from rural county governments, resulting in a law which technically legalized them outside of Las Vegas (Brents and Hausbeck, 2001; Hausbeck and Brents, 2000). Throughout the 1980s and early 1990s, casinos occasionally worked to shut down the rural brothels. As Las Vegas population growth pushed the state's population to nearly 2 million in 2000, the political clout of the urban casino industry has grown. But they have been unable and perhaps increasingly unwilling to close the brothels. Lately, visible players such as the mayor of Las Vegas and the owners of the Hard Rock Casino have publicly expressed desires to open brothels in Las Vegas itself.

BROTHEL BUSINESS PRACTICES: RATIONALIZED PAST TO TOURISTIC PRESENT

. . . To understand recent changes in the brothels we must first understand past organizational and marketing trends. Rural brothels historically had two major customer bases, the temporary and mobile male labour force (from the mining, construction and ranching industries) and male tourists, and they have primarily marketed themselves to the former. Since it is illegal for brothels to advertise, the primary mechanism for learning about the brothels, especially prior to the Internet, has been word of mouth and independently published book-length guides to the brothels. These methods have worked well for local temporary workers, and for regular customers.

Most brothels have provided sexual gratification in McDonaldized contexts where the provision of sex acts is highly rationalized through line-ups (where women literally form a line to allow a customer to choose among all women at once), timers (to mark the beginning and end of a timed "party"), and often a "get it in, get off and get out" mindset among workers (Hausbeck and Brents, 2002). Brothels rationalize the negotiation process and closely monitor monetary exchanges (Brents and Hausbeck, 2005). Despite the existence of bars in many brothels, most owners discourage men from hanging out without purchasing sex. Some smaller rural brothels market themselves as a sexual home away from home for nomadic working men, a marketing strategy that is not directed at tourists or is itself touristic. The few services offered in addition to sex acts include what they call the "comforts of home" (free coffee, a shower, living-room-like atmosphere, and other homey amenities). These are designed mostly to get men in the door, and those who partake in these services without purchasing sex are typically frowned upon (Hausbeck and Brents, 2000). Those brothels that do market to tourists market their "old west" experience, with western-sounding names like The Old Bridge Ranch, Kit Kat Guest Ranch, Donna's Ranch, or the Stardust Ranch.

Most of the brothels, especially those located inside the city limits of small towns, are so nondistinct that they are hardly recognizable as brothels. Low key, under-the-radar marketing is part owner choice, and part legal necessity. While the rural economy became dependent on the licensing fees, taxes, work-card fees, and secondary income, the towns have only come to accept and normalize the brothels by also embracing the notion that the sexuality is hidden and not to be encountered as one goes about daily business. Many brothel owners live in fear that any increased visibility could motivate a community backlash, or inspire local politicians to legislate them out of existence.

In the past several years, however, some larger brothels located close to tourist cities have shifted notably in marketing strategies. They are trying to appeal to broader audiences, using more mainstream business forms and selling individualized touristic experiences instead of McDonaldized standardization. They are relying on the Internet and other forms of creative marketing to get around advertising restrictions. Several of the larger brothels have invested in renovating their facilities, moving away from western or homey interiors to more upscale, stylish, and even elegant aesthetics. The Sagebrush Ranch near Reno, for example,

recently added a mahogany bar with granite countertops and red overhead lights. Themed fantasy rooms are increasingly commonplace, and even the smaller brothels are adding hot tub rooms, dungeon rooms, bachelor party rooms and other specialty spaces. Several brothels are expanding their services by adding souvenir shops, larger bars, restaurants, coffee shops and small strip clubs. While most brothels remain oriented to male customers, some are welcoming couples.

While these changes are happening in many brothels, we want to focus on two that best exemplify the shift toward touristic brothel marketing: the Resort at Sheri's Ranch, owned by Resort Entertainment Company, a corporation, and the Moonlite Bunny Ranch, owned by individual entrepreneur Dennis Hof.

THE RESORT AT SHERI'S RANCH

Sheri's Ranch began around 1982 as a small trailer home with a few wings later added for more rooms. In January 2001, Sheri's was purchased by new corporate owners who immediately began a $7 million renovation, expanded the services offered, integrated it with a hotel, and altered marketing strategies to attract more and different customers. The name was changed to The Resort and Spa at Sheri's Ranch, and the atmosphere became more elegant. They built free-standing fantasy bungalows with themes such as a Roman bacchanal, the Middle Ages, an African safari and the 1960s, and they provided new amenities for workers including a pool, a gym, facial room, full beauty salon and computer room. According to a newspaper article, the main goal in redoing Sheri's was to "draw the mainstream attention that the Nevada brothel industry has always avoided . . . [the new owner] wants the brothels to be seen as just another business in the community" (Abowitz, 2001). Sheri's has accomplished this in several ways. First, their doors are always unlocked, and one opens directly to a new $500,000 sports bar. . . .

Second, the business welcomes anyone of any gender. Unlike other brothels, where two women entering may be a novel and unusual event, here senior citizens, families and groups of friends eating and drinking, with no pressure to consume any of the services sold by the attached brothel, are commonplace. Sheri's also markets itself to swingers, organizations of couples who exchange partners for sex, receiving recommendations at various swingers' websites.

Third, Sheri's is marketing to mainstream audiences in other ways. They offer brothel tours to groups as diverse as Elderhostel and the Red Hat Society (organizations for retired citizens), university classes, and Asian tourists on outings from Las Vegas.

Fourth, the corporation is opening mainstream businesses in and near the brothel, as well as two strip clubs in Las Vegas. Sheri's added a separate 10-room, non-brothel resort hotel with a heated pool and waterfall, volleyball court, spa and a golf course. The non-brothel resort hotel markets itself to semi-adventurous couples who want to spend the night "at a brothel" without necessarily purchasing any sexual services. Inside the brothel, the décor in a hot tub party room was provided by Budweiser, a large US beer producer, allowing them to claim "sponsorship" of the room. Budweiser has helped sponsor other brothel parties and public concerts.

Fifth, the nature of the sales interaction is less McDonaldized. Working women will line up when a customer wants to purchase sex, but a customer can bypass the line-up; managers say up to 50 per cent of business is through interactions with customers by women working the bar. The setting encourages a more open, "party" atmosphere and a more individualized, less rationalized interaction. Unlike most brothels in Nevada, workers negotiate with customers a price for activities rather than charging for time spent—a significant shift in the nature of the product sold in Nevada brothels, allowing for a much more individualized and less rationalized interaction than before.

THE MOONLITE BUNNY RANCH

Up until the mid 1990s, the Moonlite Bunny Ranch was a mid-sized brothel with fewer than a dozen or so women working, located just outside of Reno and Carson City, the state capital. In the last few years, the owner, Dennis Hof, began getting adult video stars to work at his brothel, and now he markets the Moonlite Bunny Ranch as a sexualized fantasy land where you can sleep with your dream porn star. With renovations, additions, and several new business practices, it has become a large, modern, luxury brothel.

The Moonlite Bunny Ranch is not only embracing more mainstream business organization but is also more explicitly touristic in selling personalized, interactive experience and spectacle in its marketing and workplace organization. First, to the great consternation of the rest of the industry, Hof has a flamboyant and visible media style. He and several of the working women have appeared regularly on Howard Stern, various TV talk shows, a number of radio shows, and Hof has an ongoing series, *Cathouse*, on the popular cable channel HBO. He works hard to be very high profile and sees himself as bringing a message to the public that legalized prostitution is good and here to stay. Hof told us, "I'm singlehandedly trying to sanitize this vice," he said, "I'm on a mission." And as he told one reporter, "A high-profile approach brings higher-quality girls and better-quality customers" (Tanner, 2006).

Second, Hof explicitly markets his brothel as a sexualized touristic destination, or, in his words, a "singles bar, except the odds are real good." Hof markets voyeuristic transgression by making sure to tell interviewers that "Every-body comes here—every rock star, athlete and a few politicians that you'd love to know about but I can't tell you" (Cosby, 2005). Hof argues that he is able to get more money from custom-ers by approaching the "product" customers are buying as more of an experience rather than a sex act, maintaining that the customer "doesn't want to go to the room unless he feels close to you, or feels like you're friends, or there's some inner personal action going on there, okay?"

Third, like Sheri's, Hof still has women line up for customers entering the brothel but also encourages client–worker interactions in the bar area, and non-McDonaldized, personal-ized exchanges. As Violet from the Moonlite Bunny Ranch says,

part of my day is spent working the bar and just kinda hanging out talking to people. I don't get picked out of a line up a whole lot, so I have to work the bar if I want to make any money. And a lot of people will just go with me because they like my personality.

Fourth, his choice to employ porn stars is also designed to develop the fantasy experi-ence. Customers are likely to spend $5,000 to $10,000 to have an experience with, for example, the most photographed *Playboy* Play-mate in the world. "I know a guy that drove halfway across the United States to lose his virginity to [adult film star] Sunset Thomas because she was his favorite." Hof explains,

I don't want that mentality of "come in, get it up, get off, get the fuck out." Moonlight has a mentality that the girls believe they're worth the money . . . When you can look somebody in the eye with conviction and say, "great, you know, I understand oral sex, I am the best at it, and it's gonna be five hundred [dollars]," perception is reality. If you can build a perception that you're the best sexual partner in the world, and the experience that I'm gonna have with you is gonna be the ultimate experience, well, then it is.

Fifth, Hof tells us that he has expanded his relationships with the casino industry in Reno

as casinos need to distance themselves from illegal prostitution,

The casino business is kind of between a rock and hard place. They're not privately owned anymore. They're all corporate entities. They have stockholders to answer to. They can't supply prostitution, but they love to send the guys to me because it solves both things. It gets the guy laid, and it keeps the casino from having any problems.

Finally, Hof, like Sheri's owners, also hopes to appeal to women who want to buy sex.

Women are a new market. It's a new emerging market, if you will, and women are just now to the point where they, they consider spending money for something like that . . . It's interesting to watch, so, uh, we don't flaunt it, but we do it. And I like that because I think it is good business.

CONCLUSIONS

. . . . The largest of Nevada's brothels with the capital to do so are beginning to adopt mar-keting strategies that are more like mainstream businesses. They are up-scaling, expanding services, clientele and markets and using busi-ness forms similar to mainstream businesses, including corporate forms and diversification, as they try to integrate into the tourist econ-omy. The nature of the product sold involves less of a McDonaldized rationalization of outcome-oriented sexual gratification than in the past, and is aimed more at providing individ-ualized, interactive, touristic experiences. . . .

What some researchers have documented in other parts of the global sex industry, we are witnessing in Nevada brothels. There is a slow but noticeable convergence between some legal brothels and mainstream tourist and touristic businesses.

This is likely to make significant impacts on the industry. As some adult sex businesses become structurally integrated with "legiti-mate" businesses, their economic and political power are likely to increase. Las Vegas' gaming industry went through a similar mainstreaming process as they went from control by organized crime to corporate structures (Moehring, 2000). While the legal brothels are still highly stigmatized businesses, this kind of mainstreaming has already made it harder for local governments to close or increase sanctions against profitable businesses. Working conditions are also likely to improve somewhat, at least approximating other service industry jobs, in sectors that become more structurally similar to mainstream businesses. This is largely because these more upscale, touristic businesses are increasingly competing with mainstream service industries for skilled workers. . . .

Research on the sex industries can tell us much about the effects of the economic infrastructure of mass consumption and the values and attitudes of consumer culture. Employing a framework grounded in economic and cultural shifts promises to add much to analyses of sex work. It historicizes our understandings, situates changes in the economic contexts and the cultural meaning of sex in which sex work occurs, and invites examination of the social construction and material conditions of gender, sex and sexuality. . . . Only within these broader contexts of economic and cultural, political and legal change can we effectively assess the potentially empowering, exploitative, humane or inhumane elements of labour in late capitalist tourist and service industries, including sex work.

NOTES

1. In this article we use the term "late capitalism" to refer to general economic and cultural trends, based on the works of Agger (1989), Bell (1976), Jameson (1991), Lash and Urry (1994), and Mandel (1975).

2. This growth in the sex industry includes legal and illegal enterprises, formal and informal. The sex industry includes all businesses that sell explicit sexual fantasies, sexual products, sexual services and/or sexual contact, for profit. It includes prostitution, pornography, strip dancing, phone sex, Internet sex, adult video industries and a host of other sexual services.

3. We conducted research in 13 Nevada brothels, interviewing prostitutes, management and owners between 1996 and 2002. Much of our information on changes in the brothels comes from further interviews conducted between 2002 and 2006.

REFERENCES

Abowitz, Richard. 2001. "Cathouse Dreams: A Day in the Life of a Ranch—Nevada Style," *Las Vegas Weekly* 31 May: 29–34.

Adkins, Lisa. 2002. *Revisions: Gender and Sexuality in Late Modernity*. Buckingham, UK and Philadelphia, PA: Open University Press.

Agger, Ben. 1989. *Fast Capitalism: A Critical Theory of Significance*. Urbana: University of Illinois Press.

Bauman, Zygmunt. 2003. *Liquid Love: On the Frailty of Human Bonds*. Malden, MA: Blackwell.

Beck, Ulrich. 1992. *Risk Society: Towards a New Modernity*. London and Newbury Park, CA: Sage.

Bell, Daniel. 1976. *The Cultural Contradictions of Capitalism*. New York: Basic Books.

Brents, Barbara G., and Hausbeck, Kathryn. 2001. "State Sanctioned Sex: Negotiating Informal and Formal Regulatory Practices in Nevada Brothels," *Sociological Perspectives* 44(3): 307–32.

Brents, Barbara G., and Hausbeck, Kathryn. 2005. "Violence and Legalized Brothel Prostitution in Nevada: Examining Safety, Risk, and Prostitution Policy," *Journal of Interpersonal Violence* 20(3): 270–95.

Castle, Stephen. 2006. "Passports and Panic Buttons in the Brothel of the Future," *The Independent* 23 September.

Cosby, Rita. 2005. "Bunny Ranch," in MSNBC (ed.) *Rita Cosby Live and Direct*. MSNBC. URL (accessed 10 October 2006): http://video.msn.com/v/us/msnbc.htm?g= d174f457-7af1-46a6-8cff-172a7c381b3f &f=00%20

Economist. 1998. "Giving the Customer What He Wants," *The Economist* 14 February: 21–3. URL (accessed 26 October 2006): http://www.economist.com/background/displaystory.cfm?story_id=113208.

Frank, Katherine. 2002. *G-Strings and Sympathy: Strip Club Regulars and Male Desire*. Durham, NC. Duke University Press.

Giddens, Anthony. 1992. *The Transformation of Intimacy: Sexuality, Love, and Eroticism in Modern Societies*. Stanford, CA: Stanford University Press.

Harvey, David. 1989. *The Condition of Postmodernity: An Enquiry into the Origins of Cultural Change*. Oxford, UK and Cambridge, MA: Blackwell.

Hausbeck, Kathryn, and Brents, Barbara G. 2000. "Inside Nevada's Brothel Industry," in R. Weitzer (ed.) *Sex for Sale*, pp. 217–38. New York: Routledge.

Hausbeck, Kathryn and Brents, Barbara G. 2002. "McDonaldization of the Sex Industries? The Business of Sex," in G. Ritzer (ed.) *McDonaldization: The Reader*. Thousand Oaks, CA: Pine Forge Press.

Hausbeck, Kathryn, Brents, Barbara G. and Jackson, Crystal. 2006. "Sex Industry and Sex Workers in Nevada," in D. Shalin (ed.) *Social Health of Nevada: Leading Indicators and Quality of Life.* University of Nevada, Las Vegas: Center for Democratic Culture Publications. URL (accessed June 2007): http://www.unlv.edu/centers/cdclv/mission/index2.html [click *Leading Indicators*].

Hawkes, Gail. 1996. *A Sociology of Sex and Sexuality.* Philadelphia, PA: Open University Press.

Hochschild, Arlie Russell. 1983. *The Managed Heart: Commercialization of Human Feeling.* Berkeley: University of California Press.

Holyfield, L. 1999. "Manufacturing Adventure: The Buying and Selling of Emotions," *Journal of Contemporary Ethnography* 28(1): 3–32.

Jameson, Fredric. 1991. *Postmodernism, or, the Cultural Logic of Late Capitalism.* Durham, NC: Duke University Press.

Lash, Scott, and Urry, John. 1994. *Economies of Signs and Space.* London and Thousand Oaks, CA: Sage.

Las Vegas Convention and Visitors Authority. 2006. *Visitor Statistics.* Las Vegas: Las Vegas Convention and Visitors Authority. URL (accessed 13 October 2006): http://www.lvcva.com/press/statistics-facts/visitor-stats.jsp

Leidner, Robin. 1993. *Fast Food, Fast Talk: Service Work and the Routinization of Everyday Life.* Berkeley: University of California Press.

Mandel, Ernest. 1975. *Late Capitalism.* London: Humanities Press.

McNair, Brian. 2002. *Striptease Culture: Sex, Media and the Democratization of Desire.* London and New York: Routledge.

Ritzer, George and Liska, Allen. 1997. "'McDisneyization' and 'Post Tourism': Complementary Perspectives on Contemporary Tourism," in C. Rojek and J. Urry (eds) *Touring Cultures: Transformations of Travel and Theory,* pp. 96–112. London and New York: Routledge.

Sharpe, Eric. 2005. "'Going Above and Beyond': The Emotional Labor of Adventure Guides", *Journal of Leisure Research* 37(1): 29–50.

Tanner, Adam. 2006. "Nevada's Legal Brothels Given Timid Embrace," *Washington Post* 12 March: A8.

Taylor, Andria Daley. 1998. "Girls on the Golden West," in R.M. James and C. Elizabeth Raymond (eds) *Comstock Women: The Making of a Mining Community,* pp. 265–82. Reno: University of Nevada Press.

Urry, John. 2002. *The Tourist Gaze.* London and Thousand Oaks, CA: Sage.

Wonders, Nancy A., and Michalowski, Raymond. 2001. "Bodies, Borders, and Sex Tourism in a Globalized World: A Tale of Two Cities—Amsterdam and Havana," *Social Problems* 48(4): 545–71.

Zelizer, Viviana A. Rotman. 2005. *The Purchase of Intimacy.* Princeton, NJ: Princeton University Press.

Legalized Prostitution

Patty Kelly

. . . Depending on whose statistics you choose to believe, more than one in every ten American adult males have paid for sex at some point in their lives. What's more, in 2005, about 84,000 people were arrested across the nation for prostitution-related offenses.

In other words, it's not terribly uncommon. It's a part of our culture, and it's not going away any time soon. . . .

Recently, I spent a year working at a legal, state-regulated brothel in Mexico, a nation in which commercial sex is common, visible and, in one-third of the states, legal. I was not working as a prostitute but as an anthropologist, to study and analyze the place of commercial sex in the modern world. I spent my days and nights in close contact with the women who sold sexual services, with their clients and with government bureaucrats who ran the brothel.

Here's what I learned: Most of the workers made some rational choice to be there, sometimes after a divorce, a bad breakup or an economic crisis, acute or chronic. Of the 140 women who worked at the Galactic Zone, as the brothel was called, only five had a pimp (and in each of those cases, they insisted the man was their boyfriend).

The women made their own hours, set their own rates and decided for themselves what sex acts they would perform. Some were happy with the job. (As Gabriela once told me: "You should have seen me before I started working here. I was so depressed.") Others would've preferred to be doing other work, though the employment available to these women in Mexico (servants, factory workers) pays far less for longer hours.

At the Galactic Zone, good-looking clients were appreciated and sometimes resulted in boyfriends; the cheap, miserly and miserable ones were avoided, if possible.

To be sure, the brothel had its dangers: Sexually transmitted diseases and violence were occasionally a part of the picture. But overall, it was safer than the streets, due in part to police protection and condom distribution by government authorities.

Legalizing and regulating prostitution has its own problems—it stigmatizes sex workers (mostly by requiring them to register with the authorities), subjects them to mandatory medical testing that is not always effective, and gives clients and workers a false sense of security (with respect to sexual health and otherwise).

But criminalization is worse. Sweden's 1998 criminalization of commercial sex—a measure titled "The Protection of Women"—appears not to protect them at all. A 2004 report by the Swedish Ministry of Justice and the police found that after it went into effect, prostitution, of course, continued. Meanwhile, prices for sexual services dropped, clients were fewer but more often violent, more wanted to pay for sex and not use a condom—and sex workers had less time to assess the mental state of their clients because of the fear of getting caught.

New Zealand's 2003 Prostitution Reform Act is perhaps the most progressive response to the complex issue of prostitution. The act not only decriminalizes the practice but seeks to "safeguard the human rights of sex workers and protects them from exploitation, promotes the welfare and occupational health and safety of sex workers, is conducive to public health, [and] prohibits the use in prostitution of persons under 18 years of age."

Furthermore, clients, sex workers and brothel owners bear equal responsibility for minimizing the risks of STD transmission. In 2005, a client was convicted of violating the act by slipping his condom off during sex.

And this brings me to clients. I have met hundreds of men who have paid for sex. Some seek any kind of sex; others want certain kinds of sex; a few look for comfort and conversation.

Saying that all sex workers are victims and all clients are demons is the easy way out. Perhaps it's time to face this fact like adults (or at least like Mexico)—with a little less moralizing and a good deal more honesty. . . .

Source: "Legalize Prostitution" by Patty Kelly, *Los Angeles Times*, March 13, 2008. Reprinted by permission of the author.

SEX MATTERS: FUTURE VISIONS FOR A SEX-POSITIVE SOCIETY

ELROI J. WINDSOR AND ELISABETH O. BURGESS[1]

The title of this book, *Sex Matters,* is a double entendre. First, the book presents issues related to sex, the matters of sex, for readers to consider. Each chapter addresses the numerous contexts for understanding sexuality in contemporary society. We hope that these diverse topics have offered readers a greater appreciation for studies of sexuality. By applying a sociological lens to sex matters, readers can begin to understand the complex ways that social factors shape human sexuality. In addition to relaying these issues about sex, the book's title compels readers to take sex more seriously. We believe that sex *matters.* Sex and sexuality are meaningful subjects that require attention, both scholarly and personal. Our epilogue explores why sex matters and how we talk about the matters of sex. By deconstructing examples of how sexuality has become especially significant in recent times, we set the stage for an alternative perspective. In the end, we identify the potential for productive change by envisioning a more sex-positive society.

Americans live in a sex-saturated society. Few would refute this claim. But the visibility of sexual imagery does not speak to the meanings and messages they illustrate. When we examine what sex topics actually enter the public discourse and how social structures manage these topics, it is evident that this saturation promotes a narrow framework of acceptable sexuality. We illustrate that the information about sexuality available to the general public does not represent quality information or diverse perspectives.

Controversies continue to shape the public discourse of sex. When people's private matters become fodder for public consumption, sex becomes sensationalized. But the *public,* in the form of numerous social institutions, has always constructed and controlled our notions of appropriate sexuality. It is only when these instances challenge dominant ideology, that sex scandals become the top stories on talk shows and news media. By recounting some of these stories, we illustrate how controversies continue to regulate American sexuality. Consider how the following hot topics—which reflect some themes within this book—construct certain sexualities as remarkable.

SHOWCASING SPECTACULAR SEXUALITY

Scientists and social analysts enjoy debating the origins of sexual identity,[2] but marginalized categories of sexuality have recently enjoyed increased visibility in media. For decades, television has propagated heterosexual romance through game shows and reality television, such as *The Newlywed Game, Love Connection,* and *The Bachelor.* Today, television showcases more than these heteronormative fairytales. In 2007, MTV launched a new kind of dating show in *A Shot at Love with Tila Tequila.* Lesbian women and straight men competed for the attention of Tila, the bisexual bachelorette.[3] This show debuted as the number one cable show in its time slot among 18–34 year olds. The season finale attracted 6.2 million viewers, making it the highest-rated MTV show in two years.[4] MTV continued to promote the concept in a second season, *A Shot at Love 2 with Tila Tequila,*[5] and *A Double Shot at Love,* with bisexual identical twins.[6] In 2008, MTV aired *Transamerican Love Story* on its sister network Logo, "the channel for Gay America."[7] This series was the first dating show in the United States where men competed to win the heart of an openly transgender woman, Calpernia Addams.[8] Shows like these broadcast non-normative sexuality to mass audiences, expanding the televised scope of love and lust on reality TV.

None of this niche "reality" programming caused as much of a stir, however, as reports about "the pregnant man." In April 2008, Thomas Beatie, a female-to-male transgender man, wrote about his process of becoming pregnant.[9] As the first transman to publicly discuss his pregnancy, his experiences garnered incredible media attention, including an appearance on *The Oprah Winfrey Show*. His story shocked and confused many people.[10] Although Beatie was assigned a female sex at birth, he passes as a man in his daily interactions and became legally male after medically transitioning with testosterone and chest surgery. He has not had genital surgery, but hormones have developed his body so that he is able to have intercourse with his wife.[11] These details of Beatie's life raised many questions about gender and sex. His account introduced novel conversations to national audiences. Since then, media outlets continue to lavish attention on the latest transgender celebrity, Chaz Bono, as details about his gender, body, and sexuality inspire social commentary.[12]

These media examples delivered new ideas about categorizing sexuality to mainstream audiences. At first blush, the promotion of diverse identities and practices seems progressive. The media appear willing to feature marginalized groups, and some audiences appear to have thrilled at the dating exploits of sexual nonconformists. A closer analysis of these representations, however, exposes their underlying adherence to traditional sexual norms. These stories send strong messages about when, where, and by whom sex and gender norms can

be challenged. For example, even as *A Shot at Love* featured a Vietnamese-American bisexual bachelorette, the leading lady eventually chose a man in the first season's finale, reportedly under pressure from the show's producers.[13] And Thomas Beatty's pregnancy provoked angry challenges to the authenticity of his gender identity and his decision to carry a baby as a man. Like tabloid television talk shows of the 1980s and 90s,[14] these portrayals of non-heteronormative pairings serve both to challenge and reify what is normative. The transgressions featured in these stories become a spectacle to be consumed. Non-normative narratives become fascinating. What makes them so exciting to viewers is their queerness, their strangeness, which cannot exist without the notion of normality. By sensationalizing non-normative representations, the media assuage viewers' fears about their own normalcy. The public can examine these complex scenarios with great interest, while ignoring their own potentially complicated sexualities. The media reify normative practices by allowing them to be taken for granted.

POLICING APPROPRIATE SEXUALITY

Other controversial issues related to sexuality concern norms about appropriate sexual partnering. Same-sex marriage has been breaking news for over a decade. By July 2013, thirteen states plus the District of Columbia enabled same-sex couples to obtain marriage licenses. Seven additional states legally recognize same-sex relationships in other ways.[15] President Barack Obama now openly supports marriage equality and the U.S. Supreme Court has struck down part of the Defense of Marriage Act.[16] Although the recent U.S. Supreme Court ruling expands the rights for same-sex married couples at the federal level, couples living in the twenty-nine states that still ban same-sex marriage are out of luck. Although the American

Civil Liberties Union (ACLU) and other advocates have filed lawsuits in several of these states to overturn these bands, it will be years before these legal issues are resolved.[17] The controversy over marriage is a clear example of both social construction and social control. While American government inches toward granting marital rights to same-sex couples, the meanings of marriage change. In other words, marriage is under social construction—the agreed-upon meanings are in flux. As a longstanding social institution, marriage bears much symbolic and legal importance. The current effort to extend marital rights and responsibilities beyond heterosexual couples is not new, and marriage is not the stable foundation that conservative commentators tout.[18] Different social forces stake claims in the battle over same-sex marriage. Religious groups, government agencies, political organizations, and grassroots social movements struggle for power in shaping the marriage agenda. With each legislative move, and subsequent outcry or celebration, the process of social control becomes more transparent.

By regulating marriage, social institutions enforce the socially constructed norms concerning the legitimacy of sexual relationships. These meaning-making processes about "appropriate sexuality" socially control sexuality and contribute to a hostile sociocultural climate for LGBTQ people. Despite the popularity of media campaigns like the It Gets Better Project, which promises more rewarding life experiences upon reaching adulthood,[19] most LGBTQ youth encounter homophobic bullying at school,[20] and suicide among LGBTQ youth has been linked with unsupportive social environments.[21] The process of redefining marriage illustrates not simply how social construction and social control function, but also the social justice and human rights stakes in these debates.

Meanwhile, countless public figures who enjoyed the privileges of legal heterosexual marriage faced short-lived scrutiny for their sexual improprieties. Consider the scorn leveled at golf legend Tiger Woods[22] and CIA Director General David Petraeus[23] after reports about extramarital affairs surfaced. The ever-present examples of corrupted heterosexual marriages have become rather mundane, scandalizing the American people for fleeting intervals before retiring from collective consciousness. In some cases, scandalized politicians, such as Eliot Spitzer and Anthony Weiner, even seek to return to public office after some time away from public scrutiny.[24, 25] Sexual blunders of heterosexual men who vow monogamy certainly tarnish the institution of marriage. Yet defenders of "traditional" marriage direct their most earnest and well-funded activism to battling "gay" marriage. Conservative advocacy groups appear less worried about the pervasiveness of infidelity, divorce, and exhibitionism among committed straight men. Even when straight men resort to sexual abuse and violence—exemplified in charges against retired football coach Jerry Sandusky[26] and accused "Craigslist Killer" Philip Markoff[27]—they are treated as isolated incidents. Heterosexual privilege means that straight men can systematically trespass against the foundational values of contemporary marriage without calling heterosexuality itself into question. For religious and political conservatives, chronic bad behavior among straight men is not a great threat to the moral fabric of society, but two men who want to marry are.

Sex scandals about politicians and celebrities are nothing new. Normative notions of sexuality emphasize monogamy, heterosexuality, romance, and privacy. Sexual contact outside of committed relationships challenges traditional images of sexuality. Exposés of fringe sexual practices alert sexually normative Americans about the sexual deviancy of others. Scandals also encourage non-normative Americans to conceal their behaviors. Consequently, these accounts reify sexual norms. Even as the American public revels in learning juicy tidbits about sex, these salacious details are always informed by the systematic practices of social control.

WHY SEX MATTERS

Sex scandals exemplify how American society manages sexuality. People who violate sexual norms may become ridiculed social pariahs, or may endure only temporary censure. They can lose their families, careers, and freedoms for their sexual transgressions. By sensationalizing sexual transgressions as shocking and appalling, the public discourse of sex constructs and maintains a narrow framework of normative sexuality. This discourse positions certain sexualities or sexual practices as deviant anomalies worthy of intense public scrutiny. Simultaneously, the discourse renders other forms of sexuality unremarkable and mundane. It prevents normative sexualities from being examined and questioned. Consequently, normative sexualities become stabilized and difficult to dislodge. As the discourse castigates many forms of "deviant" sex, it curiously ignores the intricacies of "normal" sex.

The passion and furor that propels sex scandals demonstrate that sex does indeed matter—to many different people, in many different ways. Through the narratives of controversy, people realize the importance of adhering to sexual norms. And although controversy sends us clear messages about what *not* to do, Americans still struggle with defining healthy sexuality. The public discourse constructs healthy sex as free of disease and dysfunction. Beyond that limited scope, it is notably silent.

TOWARD A SEX-POSITIVE SOCIETY

As sexuality scholars, we believe that dominant sexual attitudes of Americans suffer from an overly negative outlook. Positive messages about sex are few and far between; they are typically found within sexual minority communities such as those centered on swinging, BDSM, and polyamory.[28] To conclude this book, we want to present readers with new ways of thinking about sexuality. We want to promote sex as important for individuals and our larger society. To achieve these goals, we describe what it means to be sex-positive.

Sex-positivity asserts, at its core, that people benefit from holding positive attitudes about sexuality. It is not a simple assertion that sex is good,[29] nor does it mean that sex should pervade every part of life. Despite the proliferation of sex in American media, this abundance of messages about sex is not the same as being sex-positive.[30] A positive sexuality can help us become more physically, emotionally, and psychologically healthy. To be sex-positive is to recognize that sex can be enriching. It is to affirm that sex matters.

CELEBRATING SEXUAL DIVERSITY

An important tenet of a sex-positive ideology is appreciation for sexual diversity. Sex-positivity rejects the notion that there is such a thing as "normal" sex.[31] People experience pleasure in numerous ways. Our bodies provide us with unique sensations worthy of exploration, and we each have our own boundaries. Sexual enjoyment is different for everyone. Sex-positivity recognizes that sexual norms are socially controlled by constraining sexual agendas. Without this restrictive management, people might have fuller sex lives. The ideology of sex-positivity recognizes that the public discourse on sex is oppressive. Social inequalities based on gender, race, sexual identity, class, size, age, and ability affect how people relate to each other in sexual relationships (as in all relationships). Our sexualities intersect with these oppressions, and sex is a site where erotic power converges.[32] Embracing sex-positivity means practicing mutually rewarding and respectful relationships.

Sex-positivity also strives to represent sexuality in diverse ways. In the media, people encounter limited depictions of sexuality that lack variety. Instead of censoring sex from media, sex-positive approaches advocate creating more varied representations of sexuality.[33] People also have the right to choose to engage with or abstain from these representations without persecution. Similarly, sex-positivity acknowledges that sexually explicit material is important for some people.[34] Commercial sex can be entertaining and empowering for both producers and consumers.[35] The economies of pornography, strip clubs, and prostitution can be restructured in ways that do not exploit workers. Sex work could be more sex-positive if it included the fair pay, benefits, security, and safety features characteristic of more conventional forms of employment.

CONSENTING TO SEX

Consent is another core feature of sex-positivity. This ideology stresses the importance of sex as consensual and voluntary, not coerced or required.[36] In practicing sex-positive sex, people need to understand and respect each other's boundaries, and recognize that feelings can change in any given situation. Sex can be intoxicating without using inebriating substances. In addition to affecting performance and satisfaction, alcohol and drugs can confuse our limits.[37]

It is also important to consider legal "age of consent" issues. It is difficult to assign a numerical value to the ability to consent to sex. It is also hard to define sexually appropriate behavior for youth of all ages. While many youth are sexually and emotionally immature, so are some adults. In the current climate of sex-negativity—which includes sexual violence against children—we must find ways to ensure that children are not exploited. Protecting children, however, can also restrict their sexual agency.[38] Respecting young people's developing sexualities means equipping them with knowledge about their bodies, helping them establish personal boundaries, and empowering them to decide when and how to become sexually active.[39]

Issues of consent become more complicated for people with limited cognitive abilities. A sex-positive approach acknowledges the rights of all people to sexual agency[40] and to sexual education.[41] It also appreciates that people with cognitive disabilities, particularly young women, face a high risk of victimization. Additionally, stereotypes about persons with cognitive disabilities or dementia may cause others to label them as problems in need of management, such as through sterilization or institutionalization.[42] Moreover, for some older adults, the onset or progression of dementia may lead to changes in sexual behavior, including misinterpreting the actions of others.[43] Overall, a sex-positive approach values the sexual agency of all individuals, regardless of age or cognitive ability, and strives to create a society where sex is always consensual and voluntary.

PROMOTING SEXUAL HEALTH

Practicing sex-positivity begins with oneself. By exploring our own bodies, we can understand our likes and dislikes. Masturbation is a healthy part of sexuality. It can be an effective way to explore our sexualities so that we can have more satisfying sex with our partners.[44] Through partnering, we can further practice sex-positivity by finding people to share in our sexual desires. Partnering can enhance our sexual growth. For some people, sex is best in monogamous relationships. For others, polyamory is ideal. A sex-positive approach to sexual exploration respects the partnering choices people make, including an acceptance of asexuality as a legitimate choice for some people.[45]

Promoting sexual health is crucial in a sex-positive society. Regardless of health status, a sex-positive approach to partnering aims to reduce both risks of transmitting sexually transmitted infections (STIs) and the stigma associated with having them. Sexual health care needs to be more comprehensive. Treating sexual "dysfunction" should extend beyond prescriptions for assorted pharmaceutical drugs. Sex therapies should move beyond focusing on rote genital performance, understanding that sex is about emotions, attraction, and desire. In managing sexual health, people need access to comprehensive, nonjudgmental healthcare. Sexual health includes safe, affordable access to contraceptive and procreative choices. Sex-positivity maintains that sexuality information and assistance should be accessible to everyone, including people who live in institutions or who require care from attendants.[46]

EDUCATING THE PEOPLE

Education is an important means to a sex-positive society. Sex education is appropriate at all levels of life because learning about sex is a lifelong process.[47] Information about sex and sexuality should be age-appropriate, accessible, and comprehensive. Sex-positive sex education does not limit discussion to sexual risk and reproduction. Instead, it emphasizes the benefits of healthy, consensual sex. To become sex-positive, people need to learn about bodies. Education should include details about sexual anatomy and non-genital erogenous zones. It should focus on strategies for staying sexually healthy—mentally and physically. Sex-positive sex education affirms that good sex is not just about skill, but also a result of open communication about desires and limits.

Educating about sex is a big responsibility. Social institutions already manage information about sex, and people learn about sex from numerous individuals, like peers and family members. A sex-positive approach to education recognizes that multiple agents can effectively deliver healthy information about sex. Some excellent resources already exist online[48] and in innovative text messaging systems designed to educate young people.[49] Ultimately, sex-positive sex education supports individuals in learning about and exploring their sexualities in ways that enrich their own personal and spiritual values.[50]

Furthermore, quality research on sexuality is essential to sex-positive sex education. We believe that before we can accurately teach about sexuality, we must be able to understand and critique sexuality from multiple perspectives. Unfortunately, contemporary sexualities research is often marginalized, published in specialty journals or dismissed by academics. A sex-positive model of sexualities research recognizes not only that sexuality applies to many disciplines—including sociology, anthropology, psychology, medicine, art, history, and religious studies—but also that research on sexualities may be interdisciplinary and not easily regimented into narrow academic boxes. Sex research on diverse sexualities from multiple perspectives must be valued and promoted by academic departments and funding agents.[51] In addition, researchers need to become versed in conveying their findings to media.[52] Effective sex research informs effective sex education.

* * * * *

In writing this epilogue, we aspired to provide readers with new ways of thinking about sexuality. As we have shown, the meanings and implications of sex and sexuality are hotly contested in American society. Sex remains a source of controversy and scandal. We believe that this discourse has the potential to change, not through censoring sensational sex stories, but by producing more varied perspectives. President Obama's lift of the global gag rule on abortion[53] and the repeal of the military's "Don't Ask, Don't Tell" policy[54] are examples of expanding discourses of sexuality. Ultimately, we advocate using a sex-positive approach to sexuality. This ideology involves multiple micro- and macro-level contributions to help foster sexual liberation. Although our discussion of sex-positivity is not exhaustive, we hope that this concluding section allowed readers to seriously consider the role of sex in society. Some people will undoubtedly reject this philosophy, and we respect their right to do so. Our assertion that *sex matters* allows for different viewpoints. But for us, it is impossible to idly accept the sexual status quo. We need change in the sociology of sexuality. Ultimately, our presumption that *sex matters* begs some kind of action. What does "sex matters" mean to you?

NOTES

1. The authors would like to thank Mindy Stombler, Wendy Simonds, Dawn Baunach, and Amy Palder for their helpful comments in constructing this article.

2. Gross, Larry, and James D. Woods. 1999. "Causes and Cures: The Etiology Debate." pp. 185–9 in *The Columbia Reader on Lesbian and Gay Men in Media, Society, and Politics*, edited by L. Gross and J.D. Woods. New York: Columbia University Press.

3. MTV. "A Shot at Love with Tila Tequila." Retrieved January 23, 2012 (http://www.mtv.com/shows/tila_tequila /season_1/series.jhtml).

4. James, Susan Donaldson. 2008. "'A Shot at Love' Explores (and Exploits) Bisexuality." *ABC News*, January 5. Retrieved January 23, 2012 (http://a.abcnews.com /Entertainment/WinterConcert/story?id=4088351&page =1#.Tx238oHQd_A).

5. MTV. 2008. "A Shot at Love 2 with Tila Tequila." Retrieved January 23, 2012 (http://www.mtv.com/shows /tila_tequila/season_2/series.jhtml).

6. MTV. 2009. "A Double Shot at Love." Retrieved January 23, 2012 (http://www.mtv.com/shows/a_double_shot_at _love/series.jhtml).

7. Logo Online. "Frequently Asked Questions: What is Logo?" Retrieved January 23, 2012 (http://www.logotv.com /about/faq.jhtml).

8. Logo Online. "Transamerican Love Story." Retrieved January 9, 2009 (http://www.logoonline.com/shows/dyn /transamerican_love_story/series.jhtml). Colin. 2007.

"Logo's New Reality Show: Transamerican Love Story." Retrieved January 23, 2012 (http://www.newnownext .com/?p=2481).

9. Beatie, Thomas. 2008. "Labor of Love: Is Society Ready for This Pregnant Husband?" *The Advocate*, April 8. Retrieved January 23, 2012 (http://www.advocate.com /article.aspx?id=22217).

10. Trebay, Guy. 2008. "He's Pregnant. You're Speechless." *The New York Times*, June 22. Retrieved January 11, 2009 (http://www.nytimes.com/2008/06/22/fashion/22pregnant .html?pagewanted=1&_r=1).

11. Oprah.com. 2008. "First TV Interview: The Pregnant Man." *The Oprah Winfrey Show*, April 3. Retrieved January 23, 2012 (http://www.oprah.com/oprahshow /First-TV-Interview-The-Pregnant-Man) and (http://www .oprah.com/showinfo/First-TV-Interview-The-Pregnant -Man_1).

12. For examples, see: Hedegaard, Erik. 2012. "Chaz Bono: I'm Saving to Buy a Penis." Retrieved January 17, 2012 (http://www.rollingstone.com/movies/news/chaz -bono-im-saving-to-buy-a-penis-20120105); Grossberg, Josh. 2011. "Chaz Bono Ends Engagement, Splits With Fiancée Jennifer Elia." Retrieved January 17, 2012 (http://www.eonline.com/news/chaz_bono_ends _engagement_splits_with/281731).

13. Cherry Grrl. 2009. Retrieved January 23, 2012 (http://cherrygrrl.com/interview-out-proud-and-on-a -mission-tila-tequila/).

14. Gamson, Joshua. 1998. *Freaks Talk Back: Tabloid Talk Shows and Sexual Nonconformity*. Chicago, IL: University of Chicago Press.

15. Human Rights Campaign. 2013. "Marriage Center." Washington, D.C.: HRC. Retrieved July 15, 2013 (http: //www.hrc.org/campaigns/marriage-center).

16. Liptak, Adam. 2013. "Supreme Court Bolsters Gay Marriage With Two Major Rulings." *The New York Times*. Retrieved July 15, 2013 (http://www.nytimes.com /2013/06/27/us/politics/supreme-court-gay-marriage.html).

17. Gabriel, Trip. 2013. "ACLU sues Pennsylvania over ban on gay marriage." *The New York Times*. Retrieved July 15, 2013 (http://www.nytimes.com/2013/07/10/us/aclu-lawsuit -aims-to-overturn-pennsylvanias-ban-on-gay-marriage.html).

18. Chauncey, George. 2005. *Why Marriage? The History Shaping Today's Debate*. New York: Basic Books.

19. It Gets Better Project. 2011. "What Is the It Gets Better Project?" Retrieved January 16, 2011 (http ://www .itgetsbetter.org/pages/about-it-gets-better-proj ect/).

20. Kosciw, Joseph G., Emily A. Greytak, Elizabeth M. Diaz, and Mark J. Bartkiewicz. 2010. "The 2009 National School Climate Survey: The Experiences of Lesbian, Gay, Bisexual and Transgender Youth in Our Nation's Schools."

GLSEN. New York. Retrieved January 16, 2012 (http://www.glsen.org/binary-data/GLSEN _ATTACHMENTS/file/000/001/1675-2.pdf).

21. Hatzenbuehler, Mark L. 2011. "The Social Environment and Suicide Attempts in Lesbian, Gay, and Bisexual Youth." *Pediatrics* 127(5):896–903.

22. Goldman, Russell. 2009. "Tiger Woods Mistress List Rises to 11." *ABC News*. Retrieved January 17, 2012 (http://abcnews.go.com/Entertainment/tiger -woods-mistresses-now-11-tabs/story?id=9289650# .TxXDWIHQd_A).

23. Barrett, D., Gorman, S., and J. E. Barnes. 2012. "CIA chief resigns over affair." *The Wall Street Journal*. Retrieved July 17, 2013 (http://online.wsj.com/article/SB1000142412 7887324073504578109252422213868.html).

24. Ball, Molly. 2013. "The Spitzer myth: Sex scandals are not political poison." *The Atlantic*. Retrieved July 17, 2013 (http://www.theatlantic.com/politics/archive/2013/07 /the-spitzer-myth-scandals-are-not-political-poison /277632).

25. Preston, Jennifer. 2011. "Weiner Confirms He Sent Private Messages to Girl, 17." *The New York Times*. Retrieved January 17, 2012 (http://www.nytimes .com/2011/06/11/nyregion/weiner-says-he-sent-private -messages-to-girl-17.html?scp=5&sq=Weiner %20twitter&st=cse).

26. Viera, Mark. 2011. "Sandusky Arrested on Charges Involving Two New Accusers." *The New York Times*, December 7. Retrieved January 17, 2012 (http://www.nytimes.com/2011/12/08/sports/ncaafootball /sandusky-arrested-on-new-sexual-abuse-charges.html).

27. Goodnough, Abby. 2009. "Details Released About 'Craigslist' Suspect." *The New York Times*. Retrieved January 17, 2012 (http://www.nytimes.com/2009/04/22/us /22boston.html).

28. Society for Human Sexuality. 2007. "A New Look at Sex." Retrieved January 23, 2012 (http://www.sexuality.org /book/index.pdf).

29. Glickman, Charlie. 2000. "The Language of Sex Positivity." *Electronic Journal of Human Sexuality* 3, July 6. Retrieved January 23, 2012 (http://www.ejhs.org/volume3 /sexpositive.htm).

30. Moore, Thomas. 1997. "Sex (American Style)." *Mother Jones* 22 (5):56–64.

31. Ibid, supra 28.

32. Collins, Patricia Hill. 2000. *Black Feminist Thought: Knowledge, Consciousness, and the Politics of Empowerment*. New York and London: Routledge; Lorde, Audre. 1978 (1984). "Uses of the Erotic: The Erotic as Power." pp. 53–9 in *Sister Outsider: Essays and Speeches by Audre Lorde*.

33. Office of the Surgeon General. 2001. *The Surgeon General's Call to Action to Promote Sexual Health and Responsible Sexual Behavior*. Rockville, MD: Office of the Surgeon General.

34. 2005. "Mission, Goals, and History: Basic Sexual Rights." *The Institute for Advanced Study of Human Sexuality*. Retrieved January 23, 2012 (http://www.iashs.edu/rights .html).

35. Frank, Katherine. 2002. "Stripping, Starving, and the Politics of Ambiguous Pleasure." pp. 171–206 in *Jane Sexes It Up: True Confessions of Feminist Desire*, edited by Merri Lisa Johnson. New York and London: Four Walls Eight Windows; Hartley, Nina. 1987. "Confessions of a Feminist Porno Star." pp. 142–4 in *Sex Work: Writings by Women in the Sex Industry*, edited by Frédérique Delacoste and Priscilla Alexander. Pittsburgh, PA: Cleis Press.

36. Ibid, supra 27.

37. Ibid.

38. Egan, R. Danielle and Gail L. Hawkes. 2008. "Imperiled and Perilous: Exploring the History of Childhood Sexuality." *Journal of Historical Sociology* 21(4):355–67.

39. Melby, Todd. 2001. "Childhood Sexuality." *Contemporary Sexuality* 35(12):1–5.

40. Wilkerson, Abby L. 2002. "Disability, Sex Radicalism, and Political Agency." *NWSA Journal* 14 (3):33–57.

41. Rurangirwa, Jacqueline, Kim Van Naarden Braun, Diana Schendel, and Marshalyn Yeargin-Allsopp. 2006. "Healthy Behaviors and Lifestyles in Young Adults with a History of Developmental Disabilities." *Research in Developmental Disabilities* 27 (4):381–99.

42. Ibid, supra 39.

43. LoboPrabhu, Sheila, Victor Molinari, Kimberly Arlinghaus, Ellen Barr, and James Lomax. 2005. "Spouses of Patients with Dementia: How Do They Stay Together. 'Till Death Do Us Part?'" *Journal of Gerontological Social Work* 44 (3/4):161–74; Tabak, Nili and Ronit Shemesh-Kigli. 2006. "Sexuality and Alzheimer's Disease: Can the Two Go Together?" *Nursing Forum* 41 (4):158–66.

44. Ibid, supra 27.

45. Petchesky, Rosalind Pollack. 1999 (2001). "Sexual Rights: Inventing a Concept, Mapping an International Practice." pp. 118–39 in *Sexual Identities, Queer Politics*, edited by Mark Blasius. Princeton, NJ: Princeton University Press.

46. Ibid, supra 33.

47. Ibid, supra 32.

48. For examples of sex-positive websites for youth, see: http://www.sexetc.org/, http://www.amplifyyourvoice.org/,

http://www.plannedparenthood.org/info-for-teens/, and http://goaskalice.columbia.edu/. Retrieved January 23, 2012.

49. Hoffman, Jan. 2011. "Sex Education Gets Directly to Youths, Via Text." *The New York Times,* December 30. Retrieved January 23, 2012 (http://www.nytimes .com/2011/12/31/us/sex-education-for-teenagers-online -and-in-texts.html).

50. SIECUS. "Position Statements: Sexuality Education." Retrieved January 23, 2012 (http://www.siecus.org/index .cfm?fuseaction=page.viewPage&PageID=494& varuniqueuserid=63126375175#sexuality%20education).

51. Ibid, supra 32.

52. McBride, Kimberly R., Stephanie A. Sanders, Erick Janssen, Maria Elizabeth Grabe, Jennifer Bass, Johnny V. Sparks, Trevor R. Brown, and Julia R. Heiman. 2007. "Turning Sexual Science into News: Sex Research and the Media." *Journal of Sex Research* 44 (4):347–58.

53. Meckler, Laura. 2009. "Obama Intends to Lift Family-Planning 'Gag Rule.'" *The Wall Street Journal,* January 23. Retrieved January 23, 2012 (http://online.wsj.com/article /SB123267481436808735.html).

54. *The New York Times.* 2011. "Don't Ask, Don't Tell." Retrieved January 19, 2012 (http://topics.nytimes.com/top /reference/timestopics/subjects/d/dont_ask_dont_tell/index .html).

NAME INDEX

SUBJECT INDEX